Survival Communications
in Massachusetts

John E. Parnell, KK4HWK

ISBN 978-1-62512-042-7

Cover design by:
Lynda Colón
FREELANCE GRAPHIC DESIGN &
MARKETING COMMUNICATIONS
www.hirelynda.webs.com

Titles available in this series:

Survival Communications in Alabama
Survival Communications in Alaska
Survival Communications in Arizona
Survival Communications in Arkansas
Survival Communications in California
Survival Communications in Colorado
Survival Communications in Connecticut
Survival Communications in Delaware
Survival Communications in Florida
Survival Communications in Georgia
Survival Communications in Hawaii
Survival Communications in Idaho
Survival Communications in Illinois
Survival Communications in Indiana
Survival Communications in Iowa
Survival Communications in Kansas
Survival Communications in Kentucky
Survival Communications in Louisiana
Survival Communications in Maine
Survival Communications in Maryland
Survival Communications in Massachusetts
Survival Communications in Michigan
Survival Communications in Minnesota
Survival Communications in Mississippi
Survival Communications in Missouri

Survival Communications in Montana
Survival Communications in Nebraska
Survival Communications in Nevada
Survival Communications in New Hampshire
Survival Communications in New Jersey
Survival Communications in New Mexico
Survival Communications in New York
Survival Communications in North Carolina
Survival Communications in North Dakota
Survival Communications in Ohio
Survival Communications in Oklahoma
Survival Communications in Oregon
Survival Communications in Pennsylvania
Survival Communications in Rhode Island
Survival Communications in South Carolina
Survival Communications in South Dakota
Survival Communications in Tennessee
Survival Communications in Texas
Survival Communications in Utah
Survival Communications in Vermont
Survival Communications in Virginia
Survival Communications in Washington
Survival Communications in West Virginia
Survival Communications in Wisconsin
Survival Communications in Wyoming

The above titles are available from your favorite online or brick-and-mortar bookstore or directly from the publisher at Tutor Turtle Press LLC, 1027 S. Pendleton St. – Suite B-10, Easley, SC 29642.

TABLE OF CONTENTS

Appendix A – Massachusetts Ham Radio Clubs

ARRL Affiliated Amateur and Ham Radio Clubs – By City

Appendix B – Massachusetts Ham Licensees by City

Survival Communications in Massachusetts

Perhaps you have prepared for WTSHTF or TEOTWAWKI with respect to food, water, self-defense and shelter. But what about communication?

Whenever there is a disaster (hurricane, earthquake, economic collapse, nuclear war, EMF, solar eruption, etc.), the normal means of communication that we're all reliant upon (cell phone, land line phone, the Internet, etc.) will probably be, at best, sporadic and at worst, non-existent.

As this author sees it, short of smoke signals and mirrors, there are three options for two-way communication in "trying times": (1) GMRS or FRS radios; (2) CB radios; and (3) ham or amateur radio. Let's consider each of these options to come up with the most acceptable one.

GMRS (General Mobile Radio Service) / FRS (Family Radio Service)

GMRS (General Mobile Radio Service) / FRS (Family Radio Service) radios work optimally over short distances where there is minimal interference. Originally designed to be used as pagers, particularly inside a building or other such confined area, these radios are low-cost and convenient to carry. Unfortunately their small size and light weight comes with a trade-off – short range and short battery life. These radios are supposed to be able to communicate for up to 25-30 miles. Right. That's on level terrain, without buildings or trees getting in the way. While battery life technology is constantly improving, you will need spare batteries to keep communicating or someway of recharging the ones in the radio. In this author's opinion, GMRS/FRS radios are not first choice when concerned with medium or long range communication.

CB (Citizens Band)

CB (Citizens Band) radios operate in a frequency range originally reserved for ham or amateur radio operation. Because of the overwhelming number of people wishing quick, low-cost, regulation-free communication, the FCC (Federal Communication Commission) split off a portion of the frequency spectrum and allowed anyone to purchase a CB radio and start communicating. No test. No license. Just personal/business communication. Today, CB radios are readily available in such outlets as eBay and Craigslist. This author has seen them at yard/garage/tag sales and at flea markets.

CB radios come in a variety of "flavors." Fixed units, sometimes referred to as base units are intended for home use. For the most part, they derive their power from the utility company. In the event of loss of electricity, most base units can also be connected to a 12-volt battery, like that in your car/truck. If you choose to obtain a fixed unit, make sure you know how to connect the unit to the battery – ahead of time. Trying to figure this out when you're under extra stress is not a good situation.

A second type of CB radio is designed to be mobile, that is, installed in your car/truck. It gets its power from the vehicle's battery. You can either attach an antenna permanently to the vehicle or have a removable, magnetic type antenna.

The third type of CB radio is designed for handheld use. They are small and light. Most weigh less than a pound and operate on batteries. Yes, using batteries in a CB poses the same limitations as those by the GMRS/FRS radios, but have the added advantage that most handheld units come with a cigarette lighter adapter. Comes in handy when you are on the move and wish to be able to communicate both from a vehicle and also when you have to abandon it.

While they have a greater range than GMRS/FRS radios, CB radios are, legally, limited to operate on 40 channels, with a power rating of four (4) watts or less. Yes, it is possible to alter CB radios to get around these limitations, but not legally,

Ham/Amateur Radio

Ham/Amateur radio is very appealing. With a ham radio, you are not limited to less than 50 miles, but can communicate with anyone in the world (who also has access to a ham radio, of course).

Standardized Amateur Radio Prepper Communications Plan

In the event of a nationwide catastrophic disaster, the nationwide network of Amateur Radio licensed preppers will need a set of standardized meeting frequencies to share information and coordinate activities between various prepper groups. This Standardized Amateur Radio Communications Plan establishes a set of frequencies on the 80 meter, 40 meter, 20 meter, and 2 meter Amateur Radio bands for use during these types of catastrophic disasters.

Routine nets will not be held on all of these frequencies, but preppers are encouraged to use them when coordinating with other preppers on a routine basis. Routine nets may be conducted by The American Preparedness Radio Net (TAPRN) on these or other frequencies as they see fit. However, TAPRN will promote the use of these standardized frequencies by all Amateur Radio licensed preppers during times of catastrophic disaster. The promotion of this Standardized Amateur Radio Communications Plan is encouraged by all means within the prepper community, including via Amateur Radio, Twitter, Facebook, and various blogs.

Standardized Frequencies and Modes
80 Meters – 3.818 MHz LSB (TAPRN Net: Sundays at 9 PM ET) 40 Meters – 7.242 MHz LSB 40 Meters Morse Code / Digital – 7.073 MHz USB (TAPRN: Sundays at 7:30 PM ET on CONTESTIA 4/250) 20 Meters – 14.242 MHz USB 2 Meters – 146.420 MHz FM

Nets and Network Etiquette

In times of nationwide catastrophic disaster, the ability of any one prepper to initiate and sustain themselves as a net control may be limited by the availability of power and other resource shortages. However, all licensed preppers are encouraged to maintain a listening watch on these frequencies as often as possible during a catastrophic disaster. Preppers may routinely announce themselves in the following manner:

• This is [Your Callsign Phonetically] in [Your State], maintaining a listening watch on [Standard Frequency] for any preppers on frequency seeking information or looking to provide information. Please call [Your Callsign Phonetically]. Preppers exchanging information that may require follow up should agree upon a designated time to return to the frequency and provide further information. If other stations are utilizing the frequency at the designated time you return, maintain watch and proceed with your communications when those stations are finished. If your communications are urgent and the stations on frequency are not passing information of a critical nature, interrupt with the word "Break" and request use of the frequency.

For More Information

Catastrophe Network: http://www.catastrophenetwork.org or @CatastropheNet on Twitter The American Preparedness Radio Network: http://www.taprn.com or @TAPRN on Twitter

© 2011 Catastrophe Network, Please Distribute Freely

In order to use a ham radio, legally, one must be licensed to do so by the FCC (other countries have analogous governmental bodies to regulate ham radio). To obtain a license is quite easy – take a test and pay your license fee. There are currently three classes of license – Technician, General, and Amateur Extra. With each of these licenses come specific abilities.

Technician class is the beginning level. The exam consists of 35 multiple choice questions randomly drawn from a pool of 395 questions. The question pool is readily available online for free downloading (http://www.ncvec.org/downloads/Revised%20Element%202.Pdf) or in such publications at *Ham Radio License Manual Revised 2nd Edition* (ISBN 978-0-87259-097-7). The current Technician pool of questions is to be used from July 1, 2010 to June 30, 2014. Be sure the question pool you are studying from is current. You will need to score at least 26 correct to pass. (Do not worry, Morse Code is no longer on the test, although many ham operators use it anyway.) You do not need to take a formal class in order to qualify to take the exam. You can learn the material on your own. Most people spend 10-15 hours studying and then successfully take the exam. The cost of taking the exam is under $20. The exam is given in MANY locations throughout the US. Usually the exam is given by area ham clubs. You do not have to belong to the club to take the exam. Check Appendix A for a listing of clubs in Massachusetts.

Topics for the Technician License in Amateur Radio

The Technician license exam covers such topics as basic regulations, operating practices, and electronic theory, with a focus on VHF and UHF applications. Below is the syllabus for the Technician Class.

Subelement T1 – FCC Rules, descriptions and definitions for the amateur radio service, operator and station license responsibilities

[6 Exam Questions – 6 Groups]

T1A – Amateur Radio services; purpose of the amateur service, amateur-satellite service, operator/primary station license grant, where FCC rules are codified, basis and purpose of FCC rules, meanings of basic terms used in FCC rules

T1B – Authorized frequencies; frequency allocations, ITU regions, emission type, restricted sub-bands, spectrum sharing, transmissions near band edges

T1C – Operator classes and station call signs; operator classes, sequential, special event, and vanity call sign systems, international communications, reciprocal operation, station license licensee, places where the amateur service is regulated by the FCC, name and address on ULS, license term, renewal, grace period

T1D – Authorized and prohibited transmissions

T1E – Control operator and control types; control operator required, eligibility, designation of control operator, privileges and duties, control point, local, automatic and remote control, location of control operator

T1F – Station identification and operation standards; special operations for repeaters and auxiliary stations, third party communications, club stations, station security, FCC inspection

---

Subelement T2 – Operating Procedures

[3 Exam Questions – 3 Groups]

T2A – Station operation; choosing an operating frequency, calling another station, test transmissions, use of minimum power, frequency use, band plans

T2B – VHF/UHF operating practices; SSB phone, FM repeater, simplex, frequency offsets, splits and shifts, CTCSS, DTMF, tone squelch, carrier squelch, phonetics

T2C – Public service; emergency and non-emergency operations, message traffic handling

---

Subelement T3 – Radio wave characteristics, radio and electromagnetic properties, propagation modes

[3 Exam Questions – 3 Groups]

T3A – Radio wave characteristics; how a radio signal travels; distinctions of HF, VHF and UHF; fading, multipath; wavelength vs. penetration; antenna orientation

T3B – Radio and electromagnetic wave properties; the electromagnetic spectrum, wavelength vs. frequency, velocity of electromagnetic waves

T3C – Propagation modes; line of sight, sporadic E, meteor, aurora scatter, tropospheric ducting, F layer skip, radio horizon

Subelement T4 - Amateur radio practices and station setup

[2 Exam Questions – 2 Groups]

T4A – Station setup; microphone, speaker, headphones, filters, power source, connecting a computer, RF grounding

T4B – Operating controls; tuning, use of filters, squelch, AGC, repeater offset, memory channels

Subelement T5 – Electrical principles, math for electronics, electronic principles, Ohm's Law

[4 Exam Questions – 4 Groups]

T5A – Electrical principles; current and voltage, conductors and insulators, alternating and direct current

T5B – Math for electronics; decibels, electronic units and the metric system

T5C – Electronic principles; capacitance, inductance, current flow in circuits, alternating current, definition of RF, power calculations

T5D – Ohm's Law

Subelement T6 – Electrical components, semiconductors, circuit diagrams, component functions

[4 Exam Groups – 4 Questions]

T6A – Electrical components; fixed and variable resistors, capacitors, and inductors; fuses, switches, batteries

T6B – Semiconductors; basic principles of diodes and transistors

T6C – Circuit diagrams; schematic symbols

T6D – Component functions

Subelement T7 – Station equipment, common transmitter and receiver problems, antenna measurements and troubleshooting, basic repair and testing

[4 Exam Questions – 4 Groups]

T7A – Station radios; receivers, transmitters, transceivers

T7B – Common transmitter and receiver problems; symptoms of overload and overdrive, distortion, interference, over and under modulation, RF feedback, off frequency signals; fading and noise; problems with digital communications interfaces

T7C – Antenna measurements and troubleshooting; measuring SWR, dummy loads, feedline failure modes

T7D – Basic repair and testing; soldering, use of a voltmeter, ammeter, and ohmmeter

Subelement T8 – Modulation modes, amateur satellite operation, operating activities, non-voice communications

[4 Exam Questions – 4 Groups]

T8A – Modulation modes; bandwidth of various signals

T8B – Amateur satellite operation; Doppler shift, basic orbits, operating protocols

T8C – Operating activities; radio direction finding, radio control, contests, special event stations, basic linking over Internet

T8D – Non-voice communications; image data, digital modes, CW, packet, PSK31

Subelement T9 – Antennas, feedlines

[2 Exam Groups – 2 Questions]

T9A – Antennas; vertical and horizontal, concept of gain, common portable and mobile antennas, relationships between antenna length and frequency

T9B – Feedlines; types, losses vs. frequency, SWR concepts, matching, weather protection, connectors

Subelement T0 – AC power circuits, antenna installation, RF hazards

[3 Exam Questions – 3 Groups]

T0A – AC power circuits; hazardous voltages, fuses and circuit breakers, grounding, lightning protection, battery safety, electrical code compliance

T0B – Antenna installation; tower safety, overhead power lines

T0C – RF hazards; radiation exposure, proximity to antennas, recognized safe power levels, exposure to others

Once your name and call sign are available in the FCC database, you have the privilege of operating on all VHF (2 m) and UHF (70 cm) frequencies above 30 megahertz (MHz) and HF frequencies 80, 40, and 15 meter, and on the 10 meter band using Morse code (CW), voice, and digital mode. For a Technician license in Massachusetts, your call sign will consist of a two-letter prefix beginning with K or W, the number one (1), and a three-letter suffix. The single digit number in the call sign is determined according to which area of the US you obtain your first license. Even though you may move to another state, you keep this number in your call sign. This is also true should you upgrade to a higher license and get a new call sign. The numeral portion of your call sign stays the same.

Call Sign Numbers

Below is a chart showing the various numbers and the state(s) in which you would obtain the number.

Call Sign Number	State(s)
0	CO, IA, KS, MN, MO, NE, ND, SD
1	CT, ME, MA, NH, RI, VT
2	NJ, NY
3	DE, DC, MD, PA
4	AL, FL, GA, KY, NC, SC, TN, VA
5	AR, LA, MS, NM, OK, TX
6	CA
7	AZ, ID, MT, NV, OR, WA, UT, WY
8	MI, OH, WV
9	IL, IN, WI

Residents of Alaska may have any of the following call sign prefixes assigned to them: AL0-7, KL0-7, NL0-7, or WL0-7. Likewise, residents of Hawaii may have the prefix AH6-7, KH6-7, NH6-7, or WH6-7 assigned.

Once you obtain your Technician license, do not stop there. Go and get your General license.

General is the second of three ham license classes. Like the Technician license, to get a General license, you merely have to take a 35-question multiple choice exam and pay your license fee. Passing is still at least 26 correct answers and the fee is the same (less than $20). Again the question pool is available for free online (http://www.ncvec.org/page.php?id=358). It is also available in such print publications as *The ARRL General Class License Manual 7th Edition* (ISBN 978-0-87259-811-9). The current General pool of questions is to be used from July 1, 2011 to June 30, 2015. Be sure the question pool you are using is current. Being a bit more comprehensive than the Technician license, the General license usually requires 15-20 hours of study to learn the material. Check Appendix A for a listing of clubs in Massachusetts where you might take your exam. Once your name and NEW call sign is listed in the FCC database, you're good to go. For a General license in Massachusetts, your call sign will consist of a one-letter prefix beginning with K, N or W, the number one (1), and a three-letter suffix.

Topics for the General License in Amateur Radio

The General license exam covers regulations, operating practices and electronic theory. Below is the syllabus for the General Class.

Subelement G1 – Commission's Rules
(5 Exam Questions – 5 Groups)
G1A – General Class control operator frequency privileges; primary and secondary allocations
G1B – Antenna structure limitations; good engineering and good amateur practice, beacon operation; restricted operation; retransmitting radio signals
G1C – Transmitter power regulations; data emission standards
G1D – Volunteer Examiners and Volunteer Examiner Coordinators; temporary identification
G1E – Control categories; repeater regulations; harmful interference; third party rules; ITU regions

Subelement G2 – Operating procedures
(5 Exam Questions – 5 Groups)
G2A – Phone operating procedures; USB/LSB utilization conventions; procedural signals; breaking into a OSO in progress; VOX operation
G2B – Operating courtesy; band plans, emergencies, including drills and emergency communications

G2C – CW operating procedures and procedural signals; Q signals and common abbreviations; full break in

G2D – Amateur Auxiliary; minimizing interference; HF operations

G2E – Digital operating; procedures, procedural signals and common abbreviations

Subelement G3 – Radio wave propagation

(3 Exam Questions – 3 Groups)

G3A – Sunspots and solar radiation; ionospheric disturbances; propagation forecasting and indices

G3B – Maximum Usable Frequency; Lowest Usable Frequency; propagation

G3C – Ionospheric layers; critical angle and frequency; HF scatter; Near Vertical Incidence Sky waves

Subelement G4 – Amateur radio practices

(5 Exam Questions – 5 Groups)

G4A – Station Operation and setup

G4B – Test and monitoring equipment; two-tone test

G4C – Interference with consumer electronics; grounding; DSP

G4D – Speech processors; S meters; sideband operation near band edges

G4E – HF mobile radio installations; emergency and battery powered operation

Subelement G5 – Electrical principles

(3 Exam Questions – 3 Groups)

G5A – Reactance; inductance; capacitance; impedance; impedance matching

G5B – The Decibel; current and voltage dividers; electrical power calculations; sine wave root-mean-square (RMS) values; PEP calculations

G5C – Resistors; capacitors and inductors in series and parallel; transformers

Subelement G6 – Circuit components

(3 Exam Questions – 3 Groups)

G6A – Resistors; capacitors; inductors

G6B – Rectifiers; solid state diodes and transistors; vacuum tubes; batteries

G6C – Analog and digital integrated circuits (ICs); microprocessors; memory; I/O devices; microwave ICs (MMICs); display devices

Subelement G7 – Practical circuits

(3 Exam Questions – 3 Groups)

G7A – Power supplies; schematic symbols

G7B – Digital circuits; amplifiers and oscillators

G7C – Receivers and transmitters; filters, oscillators

Subelement G8 – Signals and emissions

(2 Exam Questions – 2 Groups)

G8A – Carriers and modulation; AM; FM; single and double sideband; modulation envelope; overmodulation

G8B – Frequency mixing; multiplication; HF data communications; bandwidths of various modes; deviation

Subelement G9 – Antennas and feed lines

(4 Exam Questions – 4 Groups)

G9A – Antenna feed lines; characteristic impedance and attenuation; SWR calculation, measurement and effects; matching networks

G9B – Basic antennas

G9C – Directional antennas

G9D – Specialized antennas

Subelement G0 – Electrical and RF safety

(2 Exam Questions – 2 Groups)

G0A – RF safety principles, rules and guidelines; routine station elevation

G0B – Safety in the ham shack; electrical shock and treatment, safety grounding, fusing, interlocks, wiring, antenna and tower safety

With a General license, you can use all VHF and UHF frequencies and most of the HF frequencies. You would have access to the 160, 30, 17, 12, and 10 meter bands and access to major parts of the 80, 40, 20, and 15 meter bands. Of course, this is in addition to all bands available to Technician license holders.

Amateur Extra is the third of three ham license classes. Like the Technician and General classes, you merely have to pass a test and pay your fee to get your Amateur Extra license. This class of license is more comprehensive than the lower license classes. The exam is longer – 50 questions – and the minimum passing score is higher – 37. However, once you get your Amateur Extra license, all ham frequencies, VHF, UHF and HF are available for your enjoyment. The Extra exam covers regulations, specialized operating practices, advanced electronics theory, and radio equipment design.

Like for the other license classes, the question pool for the Amateur Extra license is available online for downloading (http://www.ncvec.org/downloads/REVISED%202012-2016%20Extra%20Class%20Pool.doc). It is also available in print form in such publications as *The ARRL Extra Class License Manual Revised 9th Edition* (ISBN 978-0-87259-887-4). If you are downloading the question pool from the above web address, the address is for the pool valid from July 1, 20012 until June 30, 2016.

Topics for the Extra License in Amateur Radio (July 1, 2012 to June 30, 2016)

Below is the syllabus for the Amateur Extra Class for July 1, 2012 to June 30, 2016. (If you are going to take the Amateur Extra exam prior to July 1, 2012, use the above syllabus.)

Subelement E1 – Commission's Rules

[6 Exam Questions – 6 Groups]

E1A – Operating Standards: frequency privileges; emission standards; automatic message forwarding; frequency sharing; stations aboard ships or aircraft

E1B – Station restrictions and special operations: restrictions on station location; general operating restrictions, spurious emissions, control operator reimbursement; antenna structure restrictions; RACES operations

E1C – Station control: definitions and restrictions pertaining to local, automatic and remote control operation; control operator responsibilities for remote and automatically controlled stations

E1D – Amateur Satellite service: definitions and purpose; license requirements for space stations; available frequencies and bands; telecommand and telemetry operations; restrictions, and special provisions; notification requirements

E1E – Volunteer examiner program: definitions, qualifications, preparation and administration of exams; accreditation; question pools; documentation requirements

E1F – Miscellaneous rules: external RF power amplifiers; national quiet zone; business communications; compensated communications; spread spectrum; auxiliary stations; reciprocal operating privileges; IARP and CEPT licenses; third party communications with foreign countries; special temporary authority

---

Subelement E2 – Operating procedures

[5 Exam Questions – 5 Groups]

E2A – Amateur radio in space: amateur satellites; orbital mechanics; frequencies and modes; satellite hardware; satellite operations

E2B – Television practices: fast scan television standards and techniques; slow scan television standards and techniques

E2C – Operating methods: contest and DX operating; spread-spectrum transmissions; selecting an operating frequency

E2D – Operating methods: VHF and UHF digital modes; APRS

E2E – Operating methods: operating HF digital modes; error correction

---

Subelement E3 – Radio wave propagation

[3 Exam Questions – 3 Groups]

E3A – Propagation and technique, Earth-Moon-Earth communications; meteor scatter

E3B – Propagation and technique, trans-equatorial; long path; gray-line; multi-path propagation

E3C – Propagation and technique, Aurora propagation; selective fading; radio-path horizon; take-off angle over flat or sloping terrain; effects of ground on propagation; less common propagation modes

Subelement E4 – Amateur practices

[5 Exam Questions – 5 Groups]

E4A – Test equipment: analog and digital instruments; spectrum and network analyzers, antenna analyzers; oscilloscopes; testing transistors; RF measurements

E4B – Measurement technique and limitations: instrument accuracy and performance limitations; probes; techniques to minimize errors; measurement of "Q"; instrument calibration

E4C – Receiver performance characteristics, phase noise, capture effect, noise floor, image rejection, MDS, signal-to-noise-ratio; selectivity

E4D – Receiver performance characteristics, blocking dynamic range, intermodulation and cross-modulation interference; 3rd order intercept; desensitization; preselection

E4E – Noise suppression: system noise; electrical appliance noise; line noise; locating noise sources; DSP noise reduction; noise blankers

Subelement E5 – Electrical principles

[4 Exam Questions – 4 Groups]

E5A – Resonance and Q: characteristics of resonant circuits: series and parallel resonance; Q; half-power bandwidth; phase relationships in reactive circuits

E5B – Time constants and phase relationships: RLC time constants: definition; time constants in RL and RC circuits; phase angle between voltage and current; phase angles of series and parallel circuits

E5C – Impedance plots and coordinate systems: plotting impedances in polar coordinates; rectangular coordinates

E5D – AC and RF energy in real circuits: skin effect; electrostatic and electromagnetic fields; reactive power; power factor; coordinate systems

Subelement E6 – Circuit components

[6 Exam Questions – 6 Groups]

E6A – Semiconductor materials and devices: semiconductor materials germanium, silicon, P-type, N-type; transistor types: NPN, PNP, junction, field-effect transistors: enhancement mode; depletion mode; MOS; CMOS; N-channel; P-channel

E6B – Semiconductor diodes

E6C – Integrated circuits: TTL digital integrated circuits; CMOS digital integrated circuits; gates

E6D – Optical devices and toroids: cathode-ray tube devices; charge-coupled devices (CCDs); liquid crystal displays (LCDs); toroids: permeability, core material, selecting, winding

E6E – Piezoelectric crystals and MMICs: quartz crystals; crystal oscillators and filters; monolithic amplifiers

E6F – Optical components and power systems: photoconductive principles and effects, photovoltaic systems, optical couplers, optical sensors, and optoisolators

Subelement E7 – Practical circuits

[8 Exam Questions – 8 Groups]

E7A – Digital circuits: digital circuit principles and logic circuits: classes of logic elements; positive and negative logic; frequency dividers; truth tables

E7B – Amplifiers: Class of operation; vacuum tube and solid-state circuits; distortion and intermodulation; spurious and parasitic suppression; microwave amplifiers

E7C – Filters and matching networks: filters and impedance matching networks: types of networks; types of filters; filter applications; filter characteristics; impedance matching; DSP filtering

E7D – Power supplies and voltage regulators

E7E – Modulation and demodulation: reactance, phase and balanced modulators; detectors; mixer stages; DSP modulation and demodulation; software defined radio systems

E7F – Frequency markers and counters: frequency divider circuits; frequency marker generators; frequency counters

E7G – Active filters and op-amps: active audio filters; characteristics; basic circuit design; operational amplifiers

E7H – Oscillators and signal sources: types of oscillators; synthesizers and phase-locked loops; direct digital synthesizers

Subelement E8 – Signals and emissions

[4 Exam Questions – 4 Groups]

E8A – AC waveforms: sine, square, sawtooth and irregular waveforms; AC measurements; average and PEP of RF signals; pulse and digital signal waveforms

E8B – Modulation and demodulation: modulation methods; modulation index and deviation ratio; pulse modulation; frequency and time division multiplexing

E8C – Digital signals: digital communications modes; CW; information rate vs. bandwidth; spread-spectrum communications; modulation methods

E8D – Waves, measurements, and RF grounding: peak-to-peak values, polarization; RF grounding

Subelement E9 – Antennas and transmission lines

[8 Exam Questions – 8 Groups]

E9A – Isotropic and gain antennas: definition; used as a standard for comparison; radiation pattern; basic antenna parameters: radiation resistance and reactance, gain, beamwidth, efficiency

E9B – Antenna patterns: E and H plane patterns; gain as a function of pattern; antenna design; Yagi antennas

E9C – Wire and phased vertical antennas: beverage antennas; terminated and resonant rhombic antennas; elevation above real ground; ground effects as related to polarization; take-off angles

E9D – Directional antennas: gain; satellite antennas; antenna beamwidth; losses; SWR bandwidth; antenna efficiency; shortened and mobile antennas; grounding

E9E – Matching: matching antennas to feed lines; power dividers

E9F – Transmission lines: characteristics of open and shorted feed lines: 1/8 wavelength; 1/4 wavelength; 1/2 wavelength; feed lines: coax versus open-wire; velocity factor;

electrical length; transformation characteristics of line terminated in impedance not equal to characteristic impedance

E9G – The Smith chart

E9H – Effective radiated power; system gains and losses; radio direction finding antennas

---

Subelement E0 – Safety

[1 exam question – 1 group]

E0A – Safety: amateur radio safety practices; RF radiation hazards; hazardous materials

---

Once your new call sign is listed in the FCC database, you are good to go. For an Amateur Extra license in Massachusetts, your call sign will consist of a prefix of K, N or W, the number one (1), and a two-letter suffix, or a two-letter prefix beginning with A, N, K or W, the number one (1), and a one-letter suffix, or a two-letter prefix beginning with A, the number one (1), and a two-letter suffix.

Ham radio equipment can be expensive or you can do it "on the cheap." The cost will run from a couple hundred dollars to well in the thousands, depending on what you have available. eBay, and Craigslist are good places to start looking. Most ham clubs do some sort of hamfest annually wherein club members or others are willing to part with older equipment. See Appendix A for a list of clubs in Massachusetts.

Another excellent source of equipment, as well as advice on setting the equipment up and how to use it properly, is current ham operators. In Appendix B, the author has listed all the FCC licensed ham operators in Massachusetts, listed by city, and then sorted by street and house number on the street. Who knows, maybe someone who lives close to you is a ham operator. Be a good neighbor, stop by and have a chat with him/her.

Like CB radios, ham radios come in three formats – base, mobile, and handheld. They can use the electric company for power, or operate off a car battery. In the opinion of this author, in spite of the slightly higher cost of the equipment and having to take a test to legally use the equipment, ham radio is the way to go when concerned about communication during times of crisis.

Canadian Call Sign Prefixes

Because of our proximity to Canada, many times ham contact is made with our northern neighbors. Below is a chart showing the origin of Canadian call sign prefixes.

Call Sign Prefix	Provence or Territory
CY0	Sable Island
CY9	St. Paul Island
VA1, VE1	New Brunswick, Nova Scotia
VA2, VE2	Quebec
VA3, VE3	Ontario
VA4, VE4	Manitoba
VA5, VE5	Saskatchewan

VA6, VE6	Alberta
VA7, VE7	British Columbia
VE8	North West Territories
VE9	New Brunswick
VO1	Newfoundland
VO2	Labrador
VY0	Nunavut
VY1	Yukon
VY2	Prince Edward Island

Common Radio Bands in the United States

Certain radio bands are more popular with ham radio enthusiasts than others. Below is a chart showing these bands and when they are most popular.

	Band (meter)	Frequency (MHz)	Use
HF	160	1.8 – 2.0	Night
	80	3.5 – 4.0	Night and Local Day
	40	7.0 – 7.3	Night and Local Day
	30	10.1 – 10.15	CW and Digital
	20	14.0 – 14.350	World Wide Day and Night
	17	18.068 – 18.168	World Wide Day and Night
	15	21.0 – 21.450	Primarily Daytime
	12	24.890 – 24.990	Primarily Daytime
	10	28.0 – 29.70	Daytime during Sunspot highs
VHF	6	50 – 54	Local to World Wide
	2	144 – 148	Local to Medium Distance
UHF	70 cm	430 – 440	Local

Common Amateur Radio Bands in Canada

160 Meter Band - Maximum bandwidth 6 kHz
1.800 - 1.820 MHz - CW
1.820 - 1.830 MHz - Digital Modes
1 830 - 1.840 MHz - DX Window
1.840 - 2.000 MHz - SSB and other wide band modes

80 Meter Band - Maximum bandwidth 6 kHz
3.500 - 3.580 MHz - CW
3.580 - 3.620 MHz - Digital Modes
3.620 - 3.635 MHz - Packet/Digital Secondary
3.635 - 3.725 MHz - CW
3.725 - 3.790 MHz - SSB and other side band modes*
3.790 - 3.800 MHz - SSB DX Window
3.800 - 4.000 MHz - SSB and other wide band modes

40 Meter Band - Maximum bandwidth 6 kHz

7.000 - 7.035 MHz - CW
7.035 - 7.050 MHz - Digital Modes
7.040 - 7.050 MHz - International packet
7.050 - 7.100 MHz - SSB
7.100 - 7.120 MHz - Packet within Region 2
7.120 - 7.150 MHz - CW
7.150 - 7.300 MHz - SSB and other wide band modes

30 Meter Band - Maximum bandwidth 1 kHz

10.100 - 10.130 MHz - CW only
10.130 - 10.140 MHz - Digital Modes
10.140 - 10.150 MHz - Packet

20 Meter Band - Maximum bandwidth 6 kHz

14.000 - 14.070 MHz - CW only
14.070 - 14.095 MHz - Digital Mode
14.095 - 14.099 MHz - Packet
14.100 MHz - Beacons
14.101 - 14.112 MHz - CW, SSB, packet shared
14.112 - 14.350 MHz - SSB
14.225 - 14.235 MHz - SSTV

17 Meter Band - Maximum bandwidth 6 kHz

18.068 - 18.100 MHz - CW
18.100 - 18.105 MHz - Digital Modes
18.105 - 18.110 MHz - Packet
18.110 - 18.168 MHz - SSB and other wide band modes

15 Meter Band - maximum bandwidth 6 kHz

21.000 - 21.070 MHz - CW
21.070 - 21.090 MHz - Digital Modes
21.090 - 21.125 MHz - Packet
21.100 - 21.150 MHz - CW and SSB
21.150 - 21.335 MHz - SSB and other wide band modes
21.335 - 21.345 MHz - SSTV
21.345 - 21.450 MHz - SSB and other wide band modes

12 Meter Band - Maximum bandwidth 6 kHz

24.890 - 24.930 MHz - CW
24.920 - 24.925 MHz - Digital Modes
24.925 - 24.930 MHz - Packet
24.930 - 24.990 MHz - SSB and other wide band modes

10 Meter Band - Maximum band width 20 kHz

28.000 - 28.200 MHz - CW
28.070 - 28.120 MHz - Digital Modes
28.120 - 28.190 MHz - Packet
28.190 - 28.200 MHz - Beacons
28.200 - 29.300 MHz - SSB and other wide band modes
29.300 - 29.510 MHz - Satellite
29.510 - 29.700 MHz - SSB, FM and repeaters

160 Meters (1.8-2.0 MHz)

1.800 - 2.000 CW
1.800 - 1.810 Digital Modes
1.810 CW QRP
1.843-2.000 SSB, SSTV and other wideband modes
1.910 SSB QRP
1.995 - 2.000 Experimental
1.999 - 2.000 Beacons

80 Meters (3.5-4.0 MHz)

3.590 RTTY/Data DX
3.570-3.600 RTTY/Data
3.790-3.800 DX window
3.845 SSTV
3.885 AM calling frequency

40 Meters (7.0-7.3 MHz)

7.040 RTTY/Data DX
7.080-7.125 RTTY/Data
7.171 SSTV
7.290 AM calling frequency

30 Meters (10.1-10.15 MHz)

10.130-10.140 RTTY
10.140-10.150 Packet

20 Meters (14.0-14.35 MHz)

14.070-14.095 RTTY
14.095-14.0995 Packet
14.100 NCDXF Beacons
14.1005-14.112 Packet
14.230 SSTV
14.286 AM calling frequency

17 Meters (18.068-18.168 MHz)

18.100-18.105 RTTY

18.105-18.110 Packet

15 Meters (21.0-21.45 MHz)

21.070-21.110 RTTY/Data
21.340 SSTV

12 Meters (24.89-24.99 MHz)

24.920-24.925 RTTY
24.925-24.930 Packet

10 Meters (28-29.7 MHz)

28.000-28.070 CW
28.070-28.150 RTTY
28.150-28.190 CW
28.200-28.300 Beacons
28.300-29.300 Phone
28.680 SSTV
29.000-29.200 AM
29.300-29.510 Satellite Downlinks
29.520-29.590 Repeater Inputs
29.600 FM Simplex
29.610-29.700 Repeater Outputs

6 Meters (50-54 MHz)

50.0-50.1 CW, beacons
50.060-50.080 beacon subband
50.1-50.3 SSB, CW
50.10-50.125 DX window
50.125 SSB calling
50.3-50.6 All modes
50.6-50.8 Nonvoice communications
50.62 Digital (packet) calling
50.8-51.0 Radio remote control (20-kHz channels)
51.0-51.1 Pacific DX window
51.12-51.48 Repeater inputs (19 channels)
51.12-51.18 Digital repeater inputs
51.5-51.6 Simplex (six channels)
51.62-51.98 Repeater outputs (19 channels)
51.62-51.68 Digital repeater outputs
52.0-52.48 Repeater inputs (except as noted; 23 channels)
52.02, 52.04 FM simplex
52.2 TEST PAIR (input)
52.5-52.98 Repeater output (except as noted; 23 channels)
52.525 Primary FM simplex
52.54 Secondary FM simplex
52.7 TEST PAIR (output)

53.0-53.48 Repeater inputs (except as noted; 19 channels)
53.0 Remote base FM simplex
53.02 Simplex
53.1, 53.2, 53.3, 53.4 Radio remote control
53.5-53.98 Repeater outputs (except as noted; 19 channels)
53.5, 53.6, 53.7, 53.8 Radio remote control
53.52, 53.9 Simplex

2 Meters (144-148 MHz)

144.00-144.05 EME (CW)
144.05-144.10 General CW and weak signals
144.10-144.20 EME and weak-signal SSB
144.200 National calling frequency
144.200-144.275 General SSB operation
144.275-144.300 Propagation beacons
144.30-144.50 New OSCAR subband
144.50-144.60 Linear translator inputs
144.60-144.90 FM repeater inputs
144.90-145.10 Weak signal and FM simplex (145.01,03,05,07,09 are widely used for packet)
145.10-145.20 Linear translator outputs
145.20-145.50 FM repeater outputs
145.50-145.80 Miscellaneous and experimental modes
145.80-146.00 OSCAR subband
146.01-146.37 Repeater inputs
146.40-146.58 Simplex
146.52 National Simplex Calling Frequency
146.61-146.97 Repeater outputs
147.00-147.39 Repeater outputs
147.42-147.57 Simplex
147.60-147.99 Repeater inputs

1.25 Meters (222-225 MHz)

222.0-222.150 Weak-signal modes
222.0-222.025 EME
222.05-222.06 Propagation beacons
222.1 SSB & CW calling frequency
222.10-222.15 Weak-signal CW & SSB
222.15-222.25 Local coordinator's option; weak signal, ACSB, repeater inputs, control
222.25-223.38 FM repeater inputs only
223.40-223.52 FM simplex
223.52-223.64 Digital, packet
223.64-223.70 Links, control
223.71-223.85 Local coordinator's option; FM simplex, packet, repeater outputs
223.85-224.98 Repeater outputs only

70 Centimeters (420-450 MHz)

420.00-426.00 ATV repeater or simplex with 421.25 MHz video carrier control links and experimental

426.00-432.00 ATV simplex with 427.250-MHz video carrier frequency

432.00-432.07 EME (Earth-Moon-Earth)

432.07-432.10 Weak-signal CW

432.10 70-cm calling frequency

432.10-432.30 Mixed-mode and weak-signal work

432.30-432.40 Propagation beacons

432.40-433.00 Mixed-mode and weak-signal work

433.00-435.00 Auxiliary/repeater links

435.00-438.00 Satellite only (internationally)

438.00-444.00 ATV repeater input with 439.250-MHz video carrier frequency and repeater links

442.00-445.00 Repeater inputs and outputs (local option)

445.00-447.00 Shared by auxiliary and control links, repeaters and simplex (local option)

446.00 National simplex frequency

447.00-450.00 Repeater inputs and outputs (local option)

33 Centimeters (902-928 MHz)

902.0-903.0 Narrow-bandwidth, weak-signal communications

902.0-902.8 SSTV, FAX, ACSSB, experimental

902.1 Weak-signal calling frequency

902.8-903.0 Reserved for EME, CW expansion

903.1 Alternate calling frequency

903.0-906.0 Digital communications

906-909 FM repeater inputs

909-915 ATV

915-918 Digital communications

918-921 FM repeater outputs

921-927 ATV

927-928 FM simplex and links

23 Centimeters (1240-1300 MHz)

1240-1246 ATV #1

1246-1248 Narrow-bandwidth FM point-to-point links and digital, duplex with 1258-1260.

1248-1258 Digital Communications

1252-1258 ATV #2

1258-1260 Narrow-bandwidth FM point-to-point links digital, duplexed with 1246-1252

1260-1270 Satellite uplinks, reference WARC '79

1260-1270 Wide-bandwidth experimental, simplex ATV

1270-1276 Repeater inputs, FM and linear, paired with 1282-1288, 239 pairs every 25 kHz, e.g. 1270.025, .050, etc.

1271-1283 Non-coordinated test pair

1276-1282 ATV #3

1282-1288 Repeater outputs, paired with 1270-1276

1288-1294 Wide-bandwidth experimental, simplex ATV
1294-1295 Narrow-bandwidth FM simplex services, 25-kHz channels
1294.5 National FM simplex calling frequency
1295-1297 Narrow bandwidth weak-signal communications (no FM)
1295.0-1295.8 SSTV, FAX, ACSSB, experimental
1295.8-1296.0 Reserved for EME, CW expansion
1296.00-1296.05 EME-exclusive
1296.07-1296.08 CW beacons
1296.1 CW, SSB calling frequency
1296.4-1296.6 Crossband linear translator input
1296.6-1296.8 Crossband linear translator output
1296.8-1297.0 Experimental beacons (exclusive)
1297-1300 Digital Communications

2300-2310 and 2390-2450 MHz

2300.0-2303.0 High-rate data
2303.0-2303.5 Packet
2303.5-2303.8 TTY packet
2303.9-2303.9 Packet, TTY, CW, EME
2303.9-2304.1 CW, EME
2304.1 Calling frequency
2304.1-2304.2 CW, EME, SSB
2304.2-2304.3 SSB, SSTV, FAX, Packet AM, Amtor
2304.30-2304.32 Propagation beacon network
2304.32-2304.40 General propagation beacons
2304.4-2304.5 SSB, SSTV, ACSSB, FAX, Packet AM, Amtor experimental
2304.5-2304.7 Crossband linear translator input
2304.7-2304.9 Crossband linear translator output
2304.9-2305.0 Experimental beacons
2305.0-2305.2 FM simplex (25 kHz spacing)
2305.20 FM simplex calling frequency
2305.2-2306.0 FM simplex (25 kHz spacing)
2306.0-2309.0 FM Repeaters (25 kHz) input
2309.0-2310.0 Control and auxiliary links
2390.0-2396.0 Fast-scan TV
2396.0-2399.0 High-rate data
2399.0-2399.5 Packet
2399.5-2400.0 Control and auxiliary links
2400.0-2403.0 Satellite
2403.0-2408.0 Satellite high-rate data
2408.0-2410.0 Satellite
2410.0-2413.0 FM repeaters (25 kHz) output
2413.0-2418.0 High-rate data
2418.0-2430.0 Fast-scan TV
2430.0-2433.0 Satellite
2433.0-2438.0 Satellite high-rate data

2438.0-2450.0 WB FM, FSTV, FMTV, SS experimental

3300-3500 MHz
3456.3-3456.4 Propagation beacons

5650-5925 MHz
5760.3-5760.4 Propagation beacons

10.00-10.50 GHz
10.368 Narrow band calling frequency 10.3683-10.3684 Propagation beacons
10.3640 Calling frequency

Now that you have your license (you do, don't you?), and your equipment, you are ready to go live. Below is a suggested start.

1) Assuming you have the HT set up to the appropriate frequency, and offset, press the mic button on the HT and say, "KK4HWX listening." Replace the KK4HWX with your own call sign, the one assigned to you by the FCC (it's the law). If no one responds to your call, you may wish to try again. Hopefully someone will respond to your call.

2) Once you get a response, it will be in the form of something like, "KK4HWX this is ??1??? in Eastport returning. My name is Florence. Back to you. ??1???" then a tone. Let us examine the response more closely. She first acknowledged your call sign (KK4HWX), then identified hers (??1???). From the 1 in her call sign, you know that she first got her license in Region 1, meaning she got it while a resident of CT, ME, MA, NH, RI, or VT. She then told you where she's transmitting from (Eastport). The term "returning" means that she is returning your call. Her name is Florence. The phrase, "Back to you" indicates that she is turning over the conversation to you. She then repeats her call sign. The tone indicates to you that it is okay to proceed with your response. BTW if she had used the term "Over" instead of "Back to you," it would mean the same thing, just fewer words.

3) At this point, press the mic button and continue with the conversation. You should restate your call sign often during the conversation (perhaps every 10 minutes or less and whenever you begin transmitting). Don't forget to say, "Over" or "Back to you" whenever you are giving Florence control of the conversation again.

4) When you are ready to stop the conversation, you should say goodbye or use the phrase "73", meaning "best wishes." Your conversation would end something like, "??1??? 73, this is KK4HWX clear and monitoring." The "clear and monitoring" indicates that you are going to continue to monitor the frequency. If you are not going to continue monitoring, you may wish to end the conversation with Florence with, "clear and QRT" instead. The QRT means that you are stopping transmissions.

Call Sign Phonics

Because of different accents of various people, sometimes it is difficult to understand call sign letters when spoken. For this reason, most ham operators verbalize their call sign using phonics. Below is a table listing the accepted phonics for letters and numbers.

A = ALFA
B = BRAVO
C = CHARLIE
D = DELTA
E = ECHO
F = FOXTROT
G = GOLF
H = HOTEL
I = INDIA
J = JULIETT
K = KILO
L = LIMA
M = MIKE
N = NOVEMBER
O = OSCAR
P = PAPA (PA-PA')
Q = QUEBEC (KAY-BEK')
R = ROMEO

S = SIERRA
T = TANGO
U = UNIFORM
V = VICTOR
W = WHISKEY
X = X-RAY
Y = YANKEE
Z = ZULU (ZED)
1 = ONE
2 = TWO
3 = THREE (TREE)
4 = FOUR
5 = FIVE (FIFE)
6 = SIX
7 = SEVEN
8 = EIGHT
9 = NINE (NINER)
0 = ZERO

The words in parentheses are the pronunciation or the alternate pronunciations for the words or numbers, but you will hear both used. With the letter Z, (ZED) is by far the most commonly used. With the number 9, NINER is the most common and easiest to understand ON THE AIR.

If you wish to use Morse code (CW) instead of voice communication, the "conversation" would follow the same steps, with a few modifications. To type out each word would require a lot of typing and translating. If you are like this author, more means more, i.e., more typing means more typos are likely. To help with this situation, CW enthusiasts have developed a language all their own – they use abbreviations for common phrases. Below is a chart showing some of these abbreviations.

Abbreviation	Use
AR	Over
de	From or "this is"
ES	And
GM	Good Morning
K	Go
KN	Go only
NM	Name

QTH	Location
RPT	Report
R	Roger
SK	Clear
tnx	Thanks
UR	Your, you are
73	Best Wishes

Morse Code and Amateur Radio

If you wish to use CW, but are concerned about accuracy, you might consider purchasing a Morse code translator. This is an electronic device that you place in front of your speakers. It takes the CW sounds and translates them into English and displays the transmission on an LCD display. For the reverse, you can pick up a CW keyboard. With the keyboard, you type in your message and it converts the text to Morse code. The translator does not need to be attached to your ham equipment, whereas the keyboard would.

For your convenience, below is a table showing the Morse code signals and their meaning.

Character	Code
A	· —
B	— · · ·
C	— · — ·
D	— · ·
E	·
F	· · — ·
G	— — ·
H	· · · ·
I	· ·
J	· — — —
K	— · —
L	· — · ·
M	— —
N	— ·
O	— — —
P	· — — ·
Q	— — · —
R	· — ·
S	· · ·
T	—
U	· · —
V	· · · —
W	· — —

X	— · · —
Y	— · — —
Z	— — · ·
0	— — — — —
1	· — — — —
2	· · — — —
3	· · · — —
4	· · · · —
5	· · · · ·
6	— · · · ·
7	— — · · ·
8	— — — · ·
9	— — — — ·
Ampersand [&], Wait	· — · · ·
Apostrophe [']	· — — — — ·
At sign [@]	· — — · — ·
Colon [:]	— — — · · ·
Comma [,]	— — · · — —
Dollar sign [$]	· · · — · · —
Double dash [=]	— · · · —
Exclamation mark [!]	— · — · — —
Hyphen, Minus [-]	— · · · · —
Parenthesis closed [)]	— · — — · —
Parenthesis open [(]	— · — — ·
Period [.]	· — · — · —
Plus [+]	· — · — ·
Question mark [?]	· · — — · ·
Quotation mark ["]	· — · · — ·
Semicolon [;]	— · — · — ·
Slash [/], Fraction bar	— · · — ·
Underscore [_]	· · — — · —

An advantage of using Morse Code is that when broadcasting CW, you are using reduced power, thereby saving your battery. Your battery is used only while actually transmitting or receiving.

International Call Sign Prefixes

As was stated earlier, all ham radio call signs begin with letters (or numbers) taken from blocks assigned to each country of the world by the *ITU - International Telecommunications Union,* a body controlled by the United Nations. The following chart indicates which call sign series are allocated to which countries.

Call Sign Series	Allocated to
AAA-ALZ	United States of America

AMA-AOZ	Spain
APA-ASZ	Pakistan (Islamic Republic of)
ATA-AWZ	India (Republic of)
AXA-AXZ	Australia
AYA-AZZ	Argentine Republic
A2A-A2Z	Botswana (Republic of)
A3A-A3Z	Tonga (Kingdom of)
A4A-A4Z	Oman (Sultanate of)
A5A-A5Z	Bhutan (Kingdom of)
A6A-A6Z	United Arab Emirates
A7A-A7Z	Qatar (State of)
A8A-A8Z	Liberia (Republic of)
A9A-A9Z	Bahrain (State of)
BAA-BZZ	China (People's Republic of)
CAA-CEZ	Chile
CFA-CKZ	Canada
CLA-CMZ	Cuba
CNA-CNZ	Morocco (Kingdom of)
COA-COZ	Cuba
CPA-CPZ	Bolivia (Republic of)
CQA-CUZ	Portugal
CVA-CXZ	Uruguay (Eastern Republic of)
CYA-CZZ	Canada
C2A-C2Z	Nauru (Republic of)
C3A-C3Z	Andorra (Principality of)
C4A-C4Z	Cyprus (Republic of)
C5A-C5Z	Gambia (Republic of the)
C6A-C6Z	Bahamas (Commonwealth of the)
C7A-C7Z	World Meteorological Organization
C8A-C9Z	Mozambique (Republic of)
DAA-DRZ	Germany (Federal Republic of)
DSA-DTZ	Korea (Republic of)
DUA-DZZ	Philippines (Republic of the)
D2A-D3Z	Angola (Republic of)
D4A-D4Z	Cape Verde (Republic of)
D5A-D5Z	Liberia (Republic of)
D6A-D6Z	Comoros (Islamic Federal Republic of the)
D7A-D9Z	Korea (Republic of)
EAA-EHZ	Spain
EIA-EJZ	Ireland
EKA-EKZ	Armenia (Republic of)
ELA-ELZ	Liberia (Republic of)
EMA-EOZ	Ukraine
EPA-EQZ	Iran (Islamic Republic of)
ERA-ERZ	Moldova (Republic of)

ESA-ESZ	Estonia (Republic of)
ETA-ETZ	Ethiopia (Federal Democratic Republic of)
EUA-EWZ	Belarus (Republic of)
EXA-EXZ	Kyrgyz Republic
EYA-EYZ	Tajikistan (Republic of)
EZA-EZZ	Turkmenistan
E2A-E2Z	Thailand
E3A-E3Z	Eritrea
E4A-E4Z	Palestinian Authority
E5A-E5Z	New Zealand - Cook Islands (WRC-07)
E7A-E7Z	Bosnia and Herzegovina (Republic of) (WRC-07)
FAA-FZZ	France
GAA-GZZ	United Kingdom of Great Britain and Northern Ireland
HAA-HAZ	Hungary (Republic of)
HBA-HBZ	Switzerland (Confederation of)
HCA-HDZ	Ecuador
HEA-HEZ	Switzerland (Confederation of)
HFA-HFZ	Poland (Republic of)
HGA-HGZ	Hungary (Republic of)
HHA-HHZ	Haiti (Republic of)
HIA-HIZ	Dominican Republic
HJA-HKZ	Colombia (Republic of)
HLA-HLZ	Korea (Republic of)
HMA-HMZ	Democratic People's Republic of Korea
HNA-HNZ	Iraq (Republic of)
HOA-HPZ	Panama (Republic of)
HQA-HRZ	Honduras (Republic of)
HSA-HSZ	Thailand
HTA-HTZ	Nicaragua
HUA-HUZ	El Salvador (Republic of)
HVA-HVZ	Vatican City State
HWA-HYZ	France
HZA-HZZ	Saudi Arabia (Kingdom of)
H2A-H2Z	Cyprus (Republic of)
H3A-H3Z	Panama (Republic of)
H4A-H4Z	Solomon Islands
H6A-H7Z	Nicaragua
H8A-H9Z	Panama (Republic of)
IAA-IZZ	Italy
JAA-JSZ	Japan
JTA-JVZ	Mongolia
JWA-JXZ	Norway
JYA-JYZ	Jordan (Hashemite Kingdom of)
JZA-JZZ	Indonesia (Republic of)
J2A-J2Z	Djibouti (Republic of)

J3A-J3Z	Grenada
J4A-J4Z	Greece
J5A-J5Z	Guinea-Bissau (Republic of)
J6A-J6Z	Saint Lucia
J7A-J7Z	Dominica (Commonwealth of)
J8A-J8Z	Saint Vincent and the Grenadines
KAA-KZZ	**United States of America**
LAA-LNZ	Norway
LOA-LWZ	Argentine Republic
LXA-LXZ	Luxembourg
LYA-LYZ	Lithuania (Republic of)
LZA-LZZ	Bulgaria (Republic of)
L2A-L9Z	Argentine Republic
MAA-MZZ	United Kingdom of Great Britain and Northern Ireland
NAA-NZZ	**United States of America**
OAA-OCZ	Peru
ODA-ODZ	Lebanon
OEA-OEZ	Austria
OFA-OJZ	Finland
OKA-OLZ	Czech Republic
OMA-OMZ	Slovak Republic
ONA-OTZ	Belgium
OUA-OZZ	Denmark
PAA-PIZ	Netherlands (Kingdom of the)
PJA-PJZ	Netherlands (Kingdom of the) - Netherlands Antilles
PKA-POZ	Indonesia (Republic of)
PPA-PYZ	Brazil (Federative Republic of)
PZA-PZZ	Suriname (Republic of)
P2A-P2Z	Papua New Guinea
P3A-P3Z	Cyprus (Republic of)
P4A-P4Z	Netherlands (Kingdom of the) - Aruba
P5A-P9Z	Democratic People's Republic of Korea
RAA-RZZ	Russian Federation
SAA-SMZ	Sweden
SNA-SRZ	Poland (Republic of)
SSA-SSM	Egypt (Arab Republic of)
SSN-STZ	Sudan (Republic of the)
SUA-SUZ	Egypt (Arab Republic of)
SVA-SZZ	Greece
S2A-S3Z	Bangladesh (People's Republic of)
S5A-S5Z	Slovenia (Republic of)
S6A-S6Z	Singapore (Republic of)
S7A-S7Z	Seychelles (Republic of)
S8A-S8Z	South Africa (Republic of)
S9A-S9Z	Sao Tome and Principe (Democratic Republic of)

TAA-TCZ	Turkey
TDA-TDZ	Guatemala (Republic of)
TEA-TEZ	Costa Rica
TFA-TFZ	Iceland
TGA-TGZ	Guatemala (Republic of)
THA-THZ	France
TIA-TIZ	Costa Rica
TJA-TJZ	Cameroon (Republic of)
TKA-TKZ	France
TLA-TLZ	Central African Republic
TMA-TMZ	France
TNA-TNZ	Congo (Republic of the)
TOA-TQZ	France
TRA-TRZ	Gabonese Republic
TSA-TSZ	Tunisia
TTA-TTZ	Chad (Republic of)
TUA-TUZ	Côte d'Ivoire (Republic of)
TVA-TXZ	France
TYA-TYZ	Benin (Republic of)
TZA-TZZ	Mali (Republic of)
T2A-T2Z	Tuvalu
T3A-T3Z	Kiribati (Republic of)
T4A-T4Z	Cuba
T5A-T5Z	Somali Democratic Republic
T6A-T6Z	Afghanistan (Islamic State of)
T7A-T7Z	San Marino (Republic of)
T8A-T8Z	Palau (Republic of)
UAA-UIZ	Russian Federation
UJA-UMZ	Uzbekistan (Republic of)
UNA-UQZ	Kazakhstan (Republic of)
URA-UZZ	Ukraine
VAA-VGZ	Canada
VHA-VNZ	Australia
VOA-VOZ	Canada
VPA-VQZ	United Kingdom of Great Britain and Northern Ireland
VRA-VRZ	China (People's Republic of) - Hong Kong
VSA-VSZ	United Kingdom of Great Britain and Northern Ireland
VTA-VWZ	India (Republic of)
VXA-VYZ	Canada
VZA-VZZ	Australia
V2A-V2Z	Antigua and Barbuda
V3A-V3Z	Belize
V4A-V4Z	Saint Kitts and Nevis
V5A-V5Z	Namibia (Republic of)
V6A-V6Z	Micronesia (Federated States of)

V7A-V7Z	Marshall Islands (Republic of the)
V8A-V8Z	Brunei Darussalam
WAA-WZZ	**United States of America**
XAA-XIZ	Mexico
XJA-XOZ	Canada
XPA-XPZ	Denmark
XQA-XRZ	Chile
XSA-XSZ	China (People's Republic of)
XTA-XTZ	Burkina Faso
XUA-XUZ	Cambodia (Kingdom of)
XVA-XVZ	Viet Nam (Socialist Republic of)
XWA-XWZ	Lao People's Democratic Republic
XXA-XXZ	China (People's Republic of) - Macao (WRC-07)
XYA-XZZ	Myanmar (Union of)
YAA-YAZ	Afghanistan (Islamic State of)
YBA-YHZ	Indonesia (Republic of)
YIA-YIZ	Iraq (Republic of)
YJA-YJZ	Vanuatu (Republic of)
YKA-YKZ	Syrian Arab Republic
YLA-YLZ	Latvia (Republic of)
YMA-YMZ	Turkey
YNA-YNZ	Nicaragua
YOA-YRZ	Romania
YSA-YSZ	El Salvador (Republic of)
YTA-YUZ	Serbia (Republic of) (WRC-07)
YVA-YYZ	Venezuela (Republic of)
Y2A-Y9Z	Germany (Federal Republic of)
ZAA-ZAZ	Albania (Republic of)
ZBA-ZJZ	United Kingdom of Great Britain and Northern Ireland
ZKA-ZMZ	New Zealand
ZNA-ZOZ	United Kingdom of Great Britain and Northern Ireland
ZPA-ZPZ	Paraguay (Republic of)
ZQA-ZQZ	United Kingdom of Great Britain and Northern Ireland
ZRA-ZUZ	South Africa (Republic of)
ZVA-ZZZ	Brazil (Federative Republic of)
Z2A-Z2Z	Zimbabwe (Republic of)
Z3A-Z3Z	The Former Yugoslav Republic of Macedonia
2AA-2ZZ	United Kingdom of Great Britain and Northern Ireland
3AA-3AZ	Monaco (Principality of)
3BA-3BZ	Mauritius (Republic of)
3CA-3CZ	Equatorial Guinea (Republic of)
3DA-3DM	Swaziland (Kingdom of)
3DN-3DZ	Fiji (Republic of)
3EA-3FZ	Panama (Republic of)
3GA-3GZ	Chile

3HA-3UZ	China (People's Republic of)
3VA-3VZ	Tunisia
3WA-3WZ	Viet Nam (Socialist Republic of)
3XA-3XZ	Guinea (Republic of)
3YA-3YZ	Norway
3ZA-3ZZ	Poland (Republic of)
4AA-4CZ	Mexico
4DA-4IZ	Philippines (Republic of the)
4JA-4KZ	Azerbaijani Republic
4LA-4LZ	Georgia (Republic of)
4MA-4MZ	Venezuela (Republic of)
4OA-4OZ	Montenegro (Republic of) (WRC-07)
4PA-4SZ	Sri Lanka (Democratic Socialist Republic of)
4TA-4TZ	Peru
4UA-4UZ	United Nations
4VA-4VZ	Haiti (Republic of)
4WA-4WZ	Democratic Republic of Timor-Leste (WRC-03)
4XA-4XZ	Israel (State of)
4YA-4YZ	International Civil Aviation Organization
4ZA-4ZZ	Israel (State of)
5AA-5AZ	Libya (Socialist People's Libyan Arab Jamahiriya)
5BA-5BZ	Cyprus (Republic of)
5CA-5GZ	Morocco (Kingdom of)
5HA-5IZ	Tanzania (United Republic of)
5JA-5KZ	Colombia (Republic of)
5LA-5MZ	Liberia (Republic of)
5NA-5OZ	Nigeria (Federal Republic of)
5PA-5QZ	Denmark
5RA-5SZ	Madagascar (Republic of)
5TA-5TZ	Mauritania (Islamic Republic of)
5UA-5UZ	Niger (Republic of the)
5VA-5VZ	Togolese Republic
5WA-5WZ	Samoa (Independent State of)
5XA-5XZ	Uganda (Republic of)
5YA-5ZZ	Kenya (Republic of)
6AA-6BZ	Egypt (Arab Republic of)
6CA-6CZ	Syrian Arab Republic
6DA-6JZ	Mexico
6KA-6NZ	Korea (Republic of)
6OA-6OZ	Somali Democratic Republic
6PA-6SZ	Pakistan (Islamic Republic of)
6TA-6UZ	Sudan (Republic of the)
6VA-6WZ	Senegal (Republic of)
6XA-6XZ	Madagascar (Republic of)
6YA-6YZ	Jamaica

6ZA-6ZZ	Liberia (Republic of)
7AA-7IZ	Indonesia (Republic of)
7JA-7NZ	Japan
7OA-7OZ	Yemen (Republic of)
7PA-7PZ	Lesotho (Kingdom of)
7QA-7QZ	Malawi
7RA-7RZ	Algeria (People's Democratic Republic of)
7SA-7SZ	Sweden
7TA-7YZ	Algeria (People's Democratic Republic of)
7ZA-7ZZ	Saudi Arabia (Kingdom of)
8AA-8IZ	Indonesia (Republic of)
8JA-8NZ	Japan
8OA-8OZ	Botswana (Republic of)
8PA-8PZ	Barbados
8QA-8QZ	Maldives (Republic of)
8RA-8RZ	Guyana
8SA-8SZ	Sweden
8TA-8YZ	India (Republic of)
8ZA-8ZZ	Saudi Arabia (Kingdom of)
9AA-9AZ	Croatia (Republic of)
9BA-9DZ	Iran (Islamic Republic of)
9EA-9FZ	Ethiopia (Federal Democratic Republic of)
9GA-9GZ	Ghana
9HA-9HZ	Malta
9IA-9JZ	Zambia (Republic of)
9KA-9KZ	Kuwait (State of)
9LA-9LZ	Sierra Leone
9MA-9MZ	Malaysia
9NA-9NZ	Nepal
9OA-9TZ	Democratic Republic of the Congo
9UA-9UZ	Burundi (Republic of)
9VA-9VZ	Singapore (Republic of)
9WA-9WZ	Malaysia
9XA-9XZ	Rwandese Republic
9YA-9ZZ	Trinidad and Tobago

Third-Party Communications and Amateur Radio

If all of this information about ham radios is somewhat intimidating, do not despair. "You" can still use ham radios for communications without being a licensed operator. Yes, you do have to have a ham license in order to legally transmit by ham equipment (or be under the direct supervision of someone else who is licensed), but there is an alternative – third-party communication.

Third-party communications occur when a licensed operator sends either written or verbal messages on behalf of unlicensed persons or organizations. There are two "controls" on third-party communication.

First, the communication must be noncommercial and of a personal nature. Asking a ham operator to contact another ham operator located in an area just hit by tornados and, because of being without power, phones do not work in Grandma Sally's city so you can check up on her, is okay. Asking a ham to send a message out that you have an old Chevy for sale would not be okay.

Second, the message must be going to a permitted area. Transmitting from a US location to another US location is okay, but transmitting from the US to another country may not. Because third-party communications bypass a country's normal telephone and postal systems, many foreign governments forbid such communications. In order to transmit from one country to another, the other country must have signed a third-party agreement with the US. What follows is a list of those countries that do have third-party a communications agreement with the US.

V2	Antigua / Barbuda
LU	Argentina
VK	Australia
V3	Belize
CP	Bolivia
T9	Bosnia-Herzegovina
PY	Brazil
VE	Canada
CE	Chile
HK	Colombia
D6	Comoros (Federal Islamic Republic of)
TI	Costa Rica
CO	Cuba
HI	Dominican Republic
J7	Dominica
HC	Ecuador
YS	El Salvador
C5	Gambia, The
9G	Ghana
J3	Grenada
TG	Guatemala
8R	Guyana
HH	Haiti
HR	Honduras
4X	Israel
6Y	Jamaica
JY	Jordan

EL	Liberia
V7	Marshall Islands
XE	Mexico
V6	Micronesia, Federated States of
YN	Nicaragua
HP	Panama
ZP	Paraguay
OA	Peru
DU	Philippines
VR6	Pitcairn Island
V4	St. Christopher / Nevis
J6	St. Lucia
J8	St. Vincent and the Grenadines
9L	Sierra Leone
ZS	South Africa
3DA	Swaziland
9Y	Trinidad / Tobago
TA	Turkey
GB	United Kingdom
CX	Uruguay
YV	Venezuela
4U1ITUITU	Geneva
4U1VICVIC	Vienna

Remember, before TSHTF, keep your pantry well stocked, your powder dry, and your batteries fully charged. 73

APPENDIX A

American Radio Relay League

Affiliated Amateur Radio Clubs in

Massachusetts

ARRL Special Service Club   **Hampden County Radio Association**
City   Agawam, MA
Call Sign   W1NY
Section   WMA
Links   www.hcra.org.

ARRL Affiliated Club   **BSA Venture Crew 510**
City   Agawam, MA
Call Sign   NE1C
Section   WMA
Links   www.hcra.org

ARRL Special Service Club   **Yankee Clipper Contest Club**
City   Andover, MA
Call Sign   AJ1I
Section   EMA
Links   www.yccc.org

ARRL Affiliated Club   **PHILIPS Amateur Radio Club**
City   Andover, MA
Call Sign   W1HP
Section   EMA
Links   www.qsl.net/w1hp

ARRL Affiliated Club   **Mohawk Amateur Radio Club**
City   Athol, MA
Call Sign   N1WW
Section   WMA
Links   www.mohawkarc.org

ARRL Affiliated Club   **Mohawk Contest Club**
City   Barre, MA
Call Sign   WW1DX
Section   WMA

ARRL Affiliated Club   **Mitre Bedford Amateur Radio Club**
City   Bedford, MA
Call Sign   W1ON
Section   EMA

ARRL Affiliated Club   **Boston Amateur Radio Club**
City   Boston, MA
Call Sign   W1BOS
Section   EMA
Links   www.barc.org/

ARRL Affiliated Club	**Massasoit Amateur Radio Association Inc.**
City	Bridgewater, MA
Call Sign	W1MV
Section	EMA
Links	www.w1mv.org

ARRL Affiliated Club	**Clay Center Amateur Radio Club**
City	Brookline, MA
Call Sign	W1CLA
Section	EMA

ARRL Affiliated Club	**Quannapowitt Radio Association**
City	Burlington, MA
Call Sign	W1EKT
Section	EMA
Links	www.w1ekt.org

ARRL Affiliated Club	**Genesis Amateur Radio Society Inc.**
City	Buzzards Bay, MA
Call Sign	N1ZIZ
Section	EMA
Links	www.genesisars.org/

ARRL Affiliated Club	**Radio Society Harvard Wireless**
City	Cambridge, MA
Call Sign	W1AF
Section	EMA
Links	w1af.harvard.edu/, www.hcs.harvard.edu/~w1af

ARRL Affiliated Club	**MIT**
City	Cambridge, MA
Call Sign	W1MX
Section	EMA
Links	web.mit.edu/w1mx/

ARRL Affiliated Club	**Southeastern MA Amateur Radio Association, Inc.**
City	Dartmouth, MA
Call Sign	W1AEC
Section	EMA
Links	www.semara.org

ARRL Affiliated Club	**Mystic Valley Amateur Radio Group**
City	Dorchester, MA
Call Sign	N1MV
Section	EMA
Links	qsl.net/mvarg

ARRL Affiliated Club	**Bristol County Repeater Association**
City	Fall River, MA
Call Sign	W1ACT
Section	EMA
Links	http://www.qsl.net/bcra

ARRL Affiliated Club	**Raymond J. Levesque Memorial Amateur Radio Club**
City	Fall River, MA
Call Sign	K1ZZN
Section	EMA

ARRL Affiliated Club	**Framingham Amateur Radio Association**
City	Framingham, MA
Call Sign	W1FY
Section	EMA
Links	www.fara.org

ARRL Special Service Club	**Cape Ann Amateur Radio Association**
City	Gloucester, MA
Call Sign	W1GLO
Section	EMA
Links	caara.net

ARRL Affiliated Club	**Franklin County Amateur Radio Club, Inc.**
City	Greenfield, MA
Call Sign	KB1BSS
Section	WMA
Links	www.fcarc.org

ARRL Affiliated Club	**Pentucket Radio Association**
City	Groveland, MA
Call Sign	K1KKM
Section	EMA
Links	pra625.org

ARRL Affiliated Club	**Montachusett Amateur Radio Association**
City	Leominster, MA
Call Sign	W1GZ
Section	WMA
Links	www.w1gz.org

ARRL Affiliated Club	**Algonquin Amateur Radio Club**
City	Marlborough, MA
Call Sign	N1EM
Section	EMA
Links	www.n1em.org

ARRL Affiliated Club	**Sturdy Memorial Hospital Amateur Radio Club**
City	Norton, MA
Call Sign	W1SMH
Section	EMA
Links	www.w1smh.com

ARRL Affiliated Club	**Norwood Amateur Radio Club**
City	Norwood, MA
Call Sign	K1JMR
Section	EMA
Links	www.norwood-arc.org

ARRL Affiliated Club	**Billerica Amateur Radio Society**
City	Nutting Lake, MA
Call Sign	W1HH
Section	EMA
Links	www.w1hh.org

ARRL Affiliated Club	**North Shore Radio Association**
City	Peabody, MA
Call Sign	NS1RA
Section	EMA
Links	www.nsradio.org

ARRL Affiliated Club	**Brooksby Radio Amateur Group**
City	Peabody, MA
Call Sign	W1BBV
Section	EMA

ARRL Special Service Club	**Nashoba Valley Amateur Radio Club**
City	Pepperell, MA
Call Sign	N1NC
Section	EMA
Links	www.n1nc.org/

ARRL Affiliated Club	**Northern Berkshire Amateur Radio Club**
City	Pittsfield, MA
Call Sign	K1FFK
Section	WMA
Links	www.nobarc.org

ARRL Affiliated Club	**Women Radio Operators of New England**
City	Plymouth, MA
Section	EMA
Links	www.qsl.net/wrone/

ARRL Affiliated Club	**North East Weak Signal Group**
City	Shirley, MA
Call Sign	W1RJA
Section	EMA
Links	www.newsvhf.com

ARRL Special Service Club	**Barnstable Amateur Radio Club**
City	South Dennis, MA
Call Sign	K1PBO
Section	EMA
Links	www.barnstablearc.org

ARRL Affiliated Club	**Mount Tom Amateur Repeater Association**
City	Springfield, MA
Call Sign	W1TOM
Section	WMA
Links	www.mtara.org/

ARRL Affiliated Club	**Minuteman Repeater Association**
City	Stow, MA
Call Sign	W1MRA
Section	EMA
Links	www.mmra.org/

ARRL Affiliated Club	**Pilgrim Amateur Wireless Association**
City	Taunton, MA
Call Sign	KA1GG
Section	EMA

ARRL Affiliated Club	**Taunton Area Communications Group**
City	Taunton, MA
Call Sign	KC1TAC
Section	EMA
Links	www.freewebs.com/kc1tac

ARRL Affiliated Club	**Norfolk County Radio Association**
City	Walpole, MA
Call Sign	W1AGR
Section	EMA

ARRL Affiliated Club	**Waltham Amateur Radio Association**
City	Waltham, MA
Call Sign	W1MHL
Section	EMA
Links	www.wara64.org

ARRL Affiliated Club	**Quaboag Valley Amateur Radio Club**
City	Warren, MA
Call Sign	K1QVR
Section	WMA

ARRL Affiliated Club	**Wellesley Amateur Radio Society**
City	Wellesley, MA
Call Sign	W1TKZ
Section	EMA
Links	wars.krl.com/

ARRL Affiliated Club	**Pilgrim ARC**
City	Wellfleet, MA
Call Sign	WA1YFV
Section	EMA
Links	pilgrimarc.org

ARRL Special Service Club	**Falmouth Amateur Radio Association Inc.**
City	West Falmouth, MA
Call Sign	K1RK
Section	EMA
Links	www.falara.org

ARRL Special Service Club	**Part of Westford MA - WB1GOF**
City	Westford, MA
Call Sign	WB1GOF
Links	www.wb1gof.org

ARRL Affiliated Club	**Whitman Amateur Radio Club, Inc.**
City	Whitman, MA
Call Sign	WA1NPO
Section	EMA
Links	www.wa1npo.org

ARRL Affiliated Club	**Worcester Polytechnic Institute WRL**
City	Worcester, MA
Call Sign	W1YK
Section	WMA
Links	www.wpi.edu/~wpiwa

ARRL Affiliated Club	**Central Massachusetts Amateur Radio Association Inc.**
City	Worcester, MA
Call Sign	W1BIM
Section	WMA
Links	www.cmara.org/

APPENDIX B

Amateur Radio License Holders

in

Massachusetts
(by City)

Call Sign: N1CHX
Roland J Turcotte
207 Bedford St
Abington MA 02351

Call Sign: KA1LEE
Mary Beth Talbot
913 Brockton Ave
Abington MA
023512113

Call Sign: N1CYZ
George D Minnehan
152 Central St
Abington MA 02351

Call Sign: KA1IME
Homer W May
28 Clark St
Abington MA 02351

Call Sign: KA1BLW
Robert L Philpot
94 Coleman St
Abington MA 02351

Call Sign: WA1GDJ
Gilbert M Follett
40 Davis St
Abington MA 02351

Call Sign: W1GMF
Gilbert M Follett
40 Davis St
Abington MA 02351

Call Sign: N1FZP
Robert M Mims Jr
371 Diane Circle
Abington MA 02351

Call Sign: KB1ODU
Raymond L Bolduc
69 Doris Dr
Abington MA 02351

Call Sign: KA1YQQ
William J Gage
60 Dunbar St
Abington MA 02351

Call Sign: KB1DKN
John W Young
23 Granite St
Abington MA 02351

Call Sign: W1HA
Walter A Johnson
169 Green St
Abington MA 02351

Call Sign: KB1IUB
William H O Hara Iii
192 Groveland St
Abington MA 02351

Call Sign: KB1IXJ
William H O Hara Jr
192 Groveland St
Abington MA 02351

Call Sign: WA1NYC
William H O Hara Jr
192 Groveland St
Abington MA 02351

Call Sign: KB1LEH
William H O Hara Iii
192 Groveland St
Abington MA 02351

Call Sign: AB1DT
William H O Hara Iii
192 Groveland St
Abington MA 02351

Call Sign: N1EY
William H O Hara Iii
192 Groveland St
Abington MA 02351

Call Sign: N1SOM
Jeffrey D Tracy
720 Hancock St
Abington MA 02351

Call Sign: N1SON
William M Tracy
720 Hancock St
Abington MA 02351

Call Sign: WA1YZH
David C Gurney
976 Hancock St
Abington MA 02351

Call Sign: KB1WVK
Joseph L Hutchinson
664 Hancock St
Abington MA 02351

Call Sign: N1EBM
Ryan M Murray
79 Jean Carol Rd
Abington MA 02351

Call Sign: N1FEE
Joseph A Diloreto
91 Jean Carol Rd
Abington MA 02351

Call Sign: KB1LKO
Mitch L Feldhandler
8 Kingswood Dr Sd
Abington MA 02351

Call Sign: WA1GMH
Frederick W Reader
35 Mc Kinley Dr
Abington MA 02351

Call Sign: N1YNS
John M Davidson
125 Mt Laurel Ln
Abington MA 02351

Call Sign: WA1ZBG
Peter D Matthew
175 Myers Ave
Abington MA 02351

Call Sign: KB1GVA
Anthony M Bacon
500 North Quincy St
Abington MA 02351

Call Sign: AD1Z
William L Clemons
1140 Plymouth St
Abington MA 02351

Call Sign: KC1EU
Joseph E O'Rourke
90 Priscilla Alden Rd
Abington MA 02351

Call Sign: W1CO
Joseph E Orourke
90 Priscilla Alden Rd

Abington MA 02351

Call Sign: KB1HQG
Joshua A Del Viscovo
356 Randolph St
Abington MA 02351

Call Sign: KB1KVL
Kenneth J Kavaljian
405 Randolph St
Abington MA 02351

Call Sign: KB1GDV
Christopher J Grazioso
301 Regency Ln
Abington MA 02351

Call Sign: KB1UTL
Christopher J Grazioso
301 Regency Ln
Abington MA 02351

Call Sign: WA1FVL
David A Belcher
220 Shaw Ave
Abington MA 02351

Call Sign: KB1HJN
Michael E Harris
54 Summer St
Abington MA 02351

Call Sign: KA1DZA
Robert D Pratt
239 Walnut St
Abington MA 02351

Call Sign: WA1OHX
Paul E Murphy
52 Washington St
Abington MA 02351

Call Sign: K1USN
K1usn Radio Club
123 Wyman Rd
Abington MA 02351

Call Sign: K1RV
Harold L Pugh Jr
123 Wyman Rd
Abington MA 02351

Call Sign: W1BSA

Boy Scouts Of
America Radio Club
123 Wyman Rd
Abington MA 02351

FCC Amateur Radio Licenses in Accord

Call Sign: WA1ORD
Stephen Pearl
Accord MA 02018

FCC Amateur Radio Licenses in Acton

Call Sign: KC1TD
Patrick Taber
14 Abel Jones Pl
Acton MA 01720

Call Sign: KF4KI
John B Nitzke
550 Acorn Park Dr
Acton MA 017204144

Call Sign: N2UZU
Michael J Bayer
26 Agawam Rd
Acton MA 01720

Call Sign: N1LBS
John C Dolan Jr
7 Alcott St
Acton MA 01720

Call Sign: KA1WNV
Marianne A Farrington
1 Algonquin Rd
Acton MA 01720

Call Sign: N1TVE
Timothy J Ryan
2 Arborwood Rd
Acton MA 01720

Call Sign: K1OCU
Juergen H Nordhausen
92 Arlington St
Acton MA 01720

Call Sign: N1IBZ
Jan W Grondstra
284 Arlington St
Acton MA 01720

Call Sign: W1QW
Stacy L Angle
111 Audubon Drive
Acton MA 017204258

Call Sign: AJ1Y
Joseph E Rogers
10 B Henley Rd
Acton MA 01720

Call Sign: KB1ICF
Gail L Sawyer
14 B Strawberry Hill
Rd
Acton MA 01720

Call Sign: WA1YFH
Donald J Perlstein
225 Bankside Hollow
Acton MA 01718

Call Sign: N1WUL
George L Johnston
12 Billings St
Acton MA 017202702

Call Sign: K1WMW
John D Killian
20 Birch Ridge Rd
Acton MA 01720

Call Sign: KA1AVW
Roy J Trafton
25 Birch Ridge Rd
Acton MA 01720

Call Sign: KB1HYQ
Harold Hyman
19 Black Horse Dr
Acton MA 01720

Call Sign: W1IZQ
Harold Hyman
19 Black Horse Dr
Acton MA 01720

Call Sign: KB1IUH
Satoshi Imamura
Black Horse Dr
Acton MA 01720

Call Sign: AB1BU
Satoshi Imamura

Black Horse Dr
Acton MA 01720

Call Sign: N1VQ
Satoshi Imamura
Black Horse Dr
Acton MA 01720

Call Sign: WB9BWB
Joel S Emer
20 Blackhorse Dr
Acton MA 01720

Call Sign: KB1RLR
James R Becker Jr
20 Brewster Lane
Acton MA 01720

Call Sign: AC1S
Thomas A Albertin
3 Broadview Rd
Acton MA 01720

Call Sign: N1FCR
James C Topali
16 C Strawberry Hill
Rd -30
Acton MA 017205748

Call Sign: KB1CIX
Steven J Feinstein
7 Captain Browns Ln
Acton MA 01720

Call Sign: KA1MGY
Donald N Williams
40 Central St
Acton MA 01720

Call Sign: W1BBQ
Donald N Williams
40 Central St
Acton MA 01720

Call Sign: W1QMN
Robert F Guba
376 Central St
Acton MA 017202306

Call Sign: N1GCC
James W Bricker Jr
76 Charter Rd
Acton MA 01720

Call Sign: N1EEL
Harvey H Roscoe
6 Chery Ridge Rd
Acton MA 01720

Call Sign: KC2JEI
Ralph A Stearns
12 Conant St
Acton MA 01720

Call Sign: KA1UXR
Jurgen R Brommelhoff
7 Coolidge Dr
Acton MA 01720

Call Sign: N1AVS
Alan R Day
5 Country Club Rd
Acton MA 01720

Call Sign: N1RXV
Robert W Schmeichel
Jr
23 Davis Rd Apt B16
Acton MA 01720

Call Sign: N1VLT
Larry M Zook
23 Davis Rd C11
Acton MA 01720

Call Sign: WA2CDS
Andrew J Eisenberg
13 Deacon Hunt Dr
Acton MA 01720

Call Sign: K2ZFM
David S Bodner
10 Devon Drive
Acton MA 01720

Call Sign: W2HZF
Robert K Benson
10 Devon Drive Apt
301
Acton MA 017205868

Call Sign: WZ2F
Jeffrey T Kemp
1 Drummer Rd Apt A5
Acton MA 01720

Call Sign: K1EHE
Jack B Flanagan

32 Duggan Rd
Acton MA 01720

Call Sign: N1GZD
REBECCA Harvey
7 Duston Lane
Acton MA 01720

Call Sign: K0HNL
Daniel E Busse
18 Evergreen Rd
Acton MA 01720

Call Sign: W1YQS
William B Graves
3 Fairway Rd
Acton MA 01720

Call Sign: KB1VOL
Geoffrey M Kerr
12 Faulkner Hill Rd
Acton MA 01720

Call Sign: W1DMB
Ralph E Abbott
26 Fort Pond Rd
Acton MA 01720

Call Sign: W1VGF
Warren P Moland
7 Foster St
Acton MA 01720

Call Sign: WA2PAE
Nelson R Gomm
14 Gioconda Ave
Acton MA 01720

Call Sign: WA1FGK
Lloyd F Simon
14 Grashopper Ln
Acton MA 01720

Call Sign: KB1USL
Charles A Atherton
Great Rd Apt 18
Acton MA 01720

Call Sign: W1ADL
Charles A Atherton
Great Rd Apt 18
Acton MA 01720

Call Sign: WA1SNG

Ian Macfarlane
407 Great Rd Unit 3
Acton MA 01720

Call Sign: N1OGV
William D Heimbach
14 Grist Mill Rd
Acton MA 01720

Call Sign: WA1RGG
Leslie C Kramer
22 Grist Mill Rd
Acton MA 01720

Call Sign: KB1MLZ
James C Salem
22 Half Moon Hill
Acton MA 01720

Call Sign: WW1JS
James C Salem
22 Half Moon Hill
Acton MA 01720

Call Sign: KA1JGW
Kenneth S Komisarek
33 Harris St Apt 24
Acton MA 01720

Call Sign: KB1TUU
James C Rand
23 Hartland Way
Acton MA 01720

Call Sign: N1HXG
Joseph W Gross
5 Hawthorne St
Acton MA 01720

Call Sign: W1ZHW
David E Matson
6 Hawthorne St
Acton MA 01720

Call Sign: W1UC
Richard E Wright
7 Hennessey Dr
Acton MA 017203612

Call Sign: W1LMZ
David W Berglind
29 Heritage
Acton MA 01720

Call Sign: N1NCO
John L Atkins
33 High St
Acton MA 01720

Call Sign: KB1ICH
Charles D Aaronson
111 Hosmer St
Acton MA 01720

Call Sign: KB1HJZ
Christopher F Porth
7 Iris Ct Apt B
Acton MA 01720

Call Sign: KC8SAJ
Benjamin E Marshall
3 Iris Ct Apt L
Acton MA 01720

Call Sign: KB1WCC
Mitchell E Wills
24 Joseph Reed Ln
Acton MA 01720

Call Sign: KA1UXY
Heidi J Schmelzer
3 Kelley Rd
Acton MA 01720

Call Sign: N1HCE
Peter J Wojtkiewicz
11 Lillian Rd
Acton MA 01720

Call Sign: KB1FPF
Christopher J Whitley
6 Lothrop Rd
Acton MA 01720

Call Sign: W2IIP
Richard L Brewer
29 Lothrop Rd
Acton MA 01720

Call Sign: W1QLT
John T Conover
203 Main St
Acton MA 01720

Call Sign: KB1UUZ
Lawton D Read
402 Main St
Acton MA 01720

Call Sign: KG1M
Lawton D Read
402 Main St
Acton MA 017203842

Call Sign: AG1V
Richard P Wilson Sr
505 Main St
Acton MA 01720

Call Sign: N1LYL
Philip L Sullivan
935 Main St
Acton MA 01720

Call Sign: KB1ICI
Edward F Reilly
272 Main St Unit B-8
Acton MA 01720

Call Sign: KA1MEO
John Kranak
6 Marian Rd
Acton MA 01720

Call Sign: K1HRY
Richard C Evans
31 Martin St
Acton MA 01720

Call Sign: N1HPN
Jan M Holmer
217 Meadows Edge
Acton MA 01718

Call Sign: WA1MCR
Gary P Budiansky
10 Mohawk Dr
Acton MA 01720

Call Sign: W1FDK
Donald C Null
26 Mohawk Drive
Acton MA 01720

Call Sign: KB1KLB
Krzysztof E
Kamieniecki
13 Mohegan Rd
Acton MA 01720

Call Sign: KA1RYL
Peter C Hess

31 Nagog Hill Rd
Acton MA 01720

Call Sign: W1YLV
Carlyle J Sletten
106 Nagog Hill Rd
Acton MA 01720

Call Sign: N1KUC
Thomas B Mc Connon
217 Nagog Hill Rd
Acton MA 01720

Call Sign: N1KGX
William S Yerazunis
24 Nash Rd
Acton MA 01720

Call Sign: WA1FKG
John J Lorenz
59 Nashoba Rd
Acton MA 01720

Call Sign: W1FKG
John J Lorenz
59 Nashoba Rd
Acton MA 01720

Call Sign: KA1UXU
Edna L Hryniewich
176 Newtown Rd
Acton MA 01720

Call Sign: N1OGU
Susan L Balkus
130 Nonset Path
Acton MA 01720

Call Sign: WA1QKQ
Peter A Balkus
130 Nonset Path
Acton MA 01720

Call Sign: N1NCM
Christopher L
Williams
7 Northbriar Rd
Acton MA 01720

Call Sign: N1BYT
Daniel Wissell
7 Notre Dame Rd
Acton MA 01720

Call Sign: K1EIU
Alexander P Aderer
23 Nylander Way
Acton MA 01720

Call Sign: KC5PSC
Michael G Pilman
378 Old Beaverbrook
Rd
Acton MA 01718

Call Sign: AB1BL
Bryon S Andersen
614 Old Stone Brook
Acton MA 01718

Call Sign: KB1ILI
George S Harlem
33 Old Village Rd
Acton MA 017204619

Call Sign: W1EBI
George S Harlem
33 Old Village Rd
Acton MA 017204619

Call Sign: KA1GCP
Gregg G Fleming
3 Olde Barn Way
Acton MA 01720

Call Sign: K4JMT
Leonard M Schwab
3 Olde Lantern Rd
Acton MA 017202011

Call Sign: KB1HQN
Eric S Hilfer
16 Orchard Dr
Acton MA 01720

Call Sign: KA1GNG
Robert S Wood
49 Parker St
Acton MA 01720

Call Sign: WB2FIX
Steven B Bloom
665 Pheasant Hill
Acton MA 01718

Call Sign: NM1G
Francis X Rudenauer
8 Phlox Ln

Acton MA 01720

Call Sign: KB1LM
Thomas Stylianos Jr
71 Piper Rd
Acton MA 01720

Call Sign: KG1Y
Michael Reinhold
Pope Rd
Acton MA 01720

Call Sign: W1RY
Raymond P Bintliff
2 Powder Horn Ln
Acton MA 01720

Call Sign: KB1NXM
Andrew D Ingraham
6 Puritan Rd
Acton MA 01720

Call Sign: KB1USH
Albert S Johnston
51 Quaboag Rd
Acton MA 01720

Call Sign: AB1NZ
Albert S Johnston
51 Quaboag Rd
Acton MA 01720

Call Sign: N1OFX
Robert W Jack
8 Quail Run
Acton MA 01720

Call Sign: W1JEH
James E Heller
8 Robert Rd
Acton MA 01720

Call Sign: KB1LSB
Joseph G Schatz
12 Robert Rd
Acton MA 01720

Call Sign: W1JGS
Joseph G Schatz
12 Robert Rd
Acton MA 01720

Call Sign: WB2QNL
Gim P Hom

14 Robert Rd
Acton MA 01720

Call Sign: KB1QQX
James E Heller
8 Roberts Rd
Acton MA 01720

Call Sign: KB1SZV
TODD J Mcfarlin
4 Robinwood Rd
Acton MA 017204428

Call Sign: KB1TMF
TODD J Mcfarlin
4 Robinwood Rd
Acton MA 017204428

Call Sign: N9PTF
Jayachandra P Reddy
6 Samantha Way
Acton MA 01720

Call Sign: WA3KZT
Kenneth W Hoadley
6 Samuel Parlin Dr
Acton MA 017203207

Call Sign: KB1RIC
William M Burke Jr
285 School St
Acton MA 01720

Call Sign: W1WMB
William M Burke Jr
285 School St
Acton MA 01720

Call Sign: N1EEK
Veronica Hald
80 Seminole Rd
Acton MA 01720

Call Sign: N1EEM
Mark Hald Iii
80 Seminole Rd
Acton MA 01720

Call Sign: KB1TYP
James M Huebner
7 Seneca Rd
Acton MA 01720

Call Sign: WA2JNN

James V Luciani
9 Shady Ln
Acton MA 01720

Call Sign: WA0WBJ
William G Ames
43 Stoneymeade Way
Acton MA 017205676

Call Sign: KA1UXS
Denis C Girondel
20 Summer St
Acton MA 01720

Call Sign: N1QPR
William C Northup
148 Summer St
Acton MA 01720

Call Sign: N1VJE
Shelley K Northup
148 Summer St
Acton MA 01720

Call Sign: KB1JNU
Acton
Communications Team
148 Summer St
Acton MA 01720

Call Sign: K1UUM
James F Babish
4 Tenney Cir
Acton MA 01720

Call Sign: WA1EMG
Gregory E Niemyski
2 Till Dr
Acton MA 01720

Call Sign: W1FCG
Bruce M Green
4 Trask Rd
Acton MA 01720

Call Sign: WB9MFD
Thomas C Hotaling
12 Tuttle Dr
Acton MA 01720

Call Sign: K1MFD
Thomas C Hotaling
12 Tuttle Dr
Acton MA 01720

Call Sign: W1TBG
Christopher J Whitley
Twenty Silver Hill Rd
Acton MA 01720

Call Sign: KA1WVR
Leigh J Grundy
Wampus Ave
Acton MA 01720

Call Sign: W1EVT
Clement Moritz
32 Wetherbee St
Acton MA 01720

Call Sign: KA1SJI
Selma R Garber
3 Wilson Ln
Acton MA 01720

Call Sign: KB1FBZ
Arolyn M Conwill
56 Windsor Ave
Acton MA 01720

Call Sign: N2MW
Michael F Conwill
56 Windsor Ave
Acton MA 01720

Call Sign: N1LBR
John D Abernethy
110 Windsor Ave
Acton MA 01720

Call Sign: KB1HDN
John P Mcgovern
6 Winter St
Acton MA 017202112

Call Sign: W1JMC
John P Mcgovern
6 Winter St
Acton MA 017202112

Call Sign: KD1RO
Donald R Spencer
9 Winter St
Acton MA 01720

Call Sign: W1OSL
Carlton J Walker Jr
25 Wood Lane

Acton MA 01720

Call Sign: KB1DRF
Lewis R Burgin
80 Wood Ln
Acton MA 01720

Call Sign: N1OFY
Philippos A Bottos
48 Woodbury Ln
Acton MA 01720

Call Sign: KE1HW
Kim A Peeling
Acton MA 01720

Call Sign: N1EAV
George A Affannato
Acton MA 01720

Call Sign: W1FRG
John A Cafaro
Acton MA 01720

FCC Amateur Radio Licenses in Acughnet

Call Sign: KB1PCW
Jerry F Sounik
17 Elaine Way
Acughnet MA 02743

Call Sign: N1MWC
Daniel C Augusto
18 Ansel White Dr
Acushnet MA 02743

Call Sign: N1GLN
Antone L Pauline
22 Ashley Ln
Acushnet MA 02743

Call Sign: N1XKD
Peter J Lagasse
10 Blain St
Acushnet MA
027432106

Call Sign: KA1TQO
Jerry Lizotte
22 Burt St
Acushnet MA 02743

Call Sign: KB1KGG

Arlene M Arruda
47 Burt St
Acushnet MA 02743

Call Sign: KB1EVX
Raymond A Arruda
47 Burt St
Acushnet MA
027431939

Call Sign: W1AZU
Raymond O Forand
9 Cushing Ln
Acushnet MA 02743

Call Sign: N1JFS
Jerry F Sounik
17 Elaine Way
Acushnet MA 02743

Call Sign: K1LBD
Alfred Huntington
28 Frank St
Acushnet MA 02743

Call Sign: KA1AMC
Edward J Demers
35 Frank St
Acushnet MA 02743

Call Sign: KA1DMZ
Robert J Ferreira
18 Gabriel Farm Drive
Acushnet MA 02743

Call Sign: K1DMZ
Robert J Ferreira
18 Gabriel Farm Drive
Acushnet MA 02743

Call Sign: KB1UGA
Christian T Silva
254 Hamlin St
Acushnet MA 02743

Call Sign: W1CQB
Christian T Silva
254 Hamlin St
Acushnet MA 02743

Call Sign: N1MSU
Paul E Gifford
12 Henrietta Dr
Acushnet MA 02743

Call Sign: KB1OHX
Paul A Payette
12 Henry Dr
Acushnet MA 02743

Call Sign: W1EZY
Paul A Payette
12 Henry Dr
Acushnet MA 02743

Call Sign: N1WQI
Steven P Dansereau
7 Holly Ave
Acushnet MA 02743

Call Sign: KA1WOB
Lucien A Chretien
19 Kendrick St
Acushnet MA
027431815

Call Sign: KA1FAV
Glenn H Sturgeon Jr
9 Lague St
Acushnet MA 02743

Call Sign: K1GHS
Glenn H Sturgeon Jr
9 Lague St
Acushnet MA
027431817

Call Sign: N1XXS
Gilbert T Martins
66 Laura Keene Ave
Acushnet MA 02743

Call Sign: N1HCW
Robert A Methia
14 Lisa Ave
Acushnet MA 02743

Call Sign: KC1XW
Raymond N Martin
5 Lynn Ellen Dr
Acushnet MA 02743

Call Sign: WA1CCM
Wayne C Kingsley
549 Main St
Acushnet MA
027431587

Call Sign: N1QMU
William K Hargreaves
10 Mallory St
Acushnet MA 02743

Call Sign: KB1LFZ
Joann L Martel
10 Mallory St
Acushnet MA 02743

Call Sign: N1YLQ
Michael P Leger
64 Nestles Lane
Acushnet MA 02745

Call Sign: KB1LJG
Joseph A Cote
143 Nestles Ln
Acushnet MA 02743

Call Sign: N1OFD
Gerard A Bergeron
38 Nye Ave
Acushnet MA 02743

Call Sign: W1AFD
Gerard A Bergeron
38 Nye Ave
Acushnet MA 02743

Call Sign: KB1VXF
Jeffrey A Gaipo
10 Nyes Ln
Acushnet MA 02743

Call Sign: N1IVR
Richard G Reeves
60 Pageotte St
Acushnet MA 02743

Call Sign: WA1KDD
Thomas D Carr
241 Peckham Rd
Acushnet MA
027431735

Call Sign: KA1SJD
James A La Rose
54 Pembroke Ave
Acushnet MA
027432354

Call Sign: KB1WQQ
Robert M Souza

6 Pershing Ave
Acushnet MA 02743

Call Sign: KB1OZI
Daniel Rodrigues
19 Reservation Rd
Acushnet MA 02743

Call Sign: N1WNI
Joaquim Simoes
6 Rosemeadow Ct
Acushnet MA 02743

Call Sign: N1XVP
Denatilde Simoes
6 Rosemeadow Ct
Acushnet MA 02743

Call Sign: K1ERZ
New Bedford
Vocational Hs Arc
33 Siamese Ave
Acushnet MA 02743

Call Sign: KA1QCO
Linda Enos
33 Siamese Ave
Acushnet MA 02743

Call Sign: WM1S
Michael W Enos
33 Siamese Ave
Acushnet MA 02743

Call Sign: N1XRS
Antone D Duarte Jr
14 Thomas St
Acushnet MA 02743

Call Sign: KB1IAU
Acushnet Emergency
Management Agency
14 Thomas St
Acushnet MA 02743

Call Sign: WA1EMA
Acushnet Emergency
Management Agency
14 Thomas St
Acushnet MA 02743

Call Sign: W1SMA
South Coast Ma
Amateur Radio Group

14 Thomas St
Acushnet MA 02743

Call Sign: W1EKW
Maryan J Midurski
22 Village Ave
Acushnet MA 02743

Call Sign: WA1GDU
Frank D Wydra
55 Wamsutta Ave
Acushnet MA 02743

Call Sign: W1DBX
Lawrence Lygren
11 Wilbur Ave
Acushnet MA 02743

Call Sign: KB1VKV
Thomas H Orlowski
93 Wing Rd
Acushnet MA 02743

**FCC Amateur Radio
Licenses in Adams**

Call Sign: KB1OAI
Kyle D Richardson
B East Rd
Adams MA 01220

Call Sign: WA1ZUO
Sharon Ann Chittenden
93 B Grove St
Adams MA 01220

Call Sign: KB1FRG
Kathryn M Mcdonald
45 Bellevue Ave
Adams MA 01220

Call Sign: KA1TFT
Erik D Scholz
112 Burlingame Hill
Adams MA 01220

Call Sign: KB1JOC
David W Ansley
23 Columbia St Apt 1
Adams MA 01220

Call Sign: WA1TYM
William J Rennie
114 Commercial St

Adams MA 01220

Call Sign: WA1UDJ
Nancy J Rennie
114 Commercial St
Adams MA 01220

Call Sign: KC1EB
Paul H Howcroft Jr
62 E Orchard Ter
Adams MA 01220

Call Sign: N1GXF
John R Cowie Jr
18 East St
Adams MA 012202304

Call Sign: N1CQW
Michael P Guerino
20 Forest Park Ave
Adams MA 01220

Call Sign: WA1NQK
Richard C Belanger
55 Highland Ave
Adams MA 01220

Call Sign: KB1FTC
Lawrence P Wilson
61 Howland Ave
Adams MA 01220

Call Sign: KB1FXW
Cinda K Wilson
61 Howland Ave
Adams MA 01220

Call Sign: N1ISB
Donald L Horton
106 Howland Ave Apt
37
Adams MA 01220

Call Sign: AE4CS
David Allen
7 Hoxie Brook Rd
Adams MA 01220

Call Sign: KA1RQO
John C Bassi
8 Lincoln St
Adams MA 01220

Call Sign: WB1ETA

Beverly A Brothers
31 North Summer St
Adams MA 012201568

Call Sign: K1SAV
Alan C Vigiard
15 Pearl St
Adams MA 01220

Call Sign: W1AVU
David W Scholz
Plainfield Stage
Adams MA 01220

Call Sign: N1OBL
Anthony C Mercauto
5 Sayles St
Adams MA 01220

Call Sign: KB1CXW
Scott B Krzanik
13 Simon Ave
Adams MA 01220

Call Sign: N1IUK
Leroy D Schaffrick Sr
790 Stafford Hill
Adams MA 01220

Call Sign: K1JVM
Richard E Frost
8 Walling Rd
Adams MA 01220

Call Sign: N1XWS
Cory M Adelt
5 Walnut St
Adams MA 01220

Call Sign: N1WGT
Kevin V Wood
3 Weber St
Adams MA 01220

Call Sign: KA1MED
Barry A Gazaille
8 West St
Adams MA 01220

Call Sign: WB1EPX
Craig A O Neill
5 Wilfred Ave
Adams MA 01220

Call Sign: KB1DBQ
Wilfred J Gazaille
37 Willow St
Adams MA 01220

Call Sign: KA1OLJ
Russell F Morey
Adams MA 01220

**FCC Amateur Radio
Licenses in Agawam**

Call Sign: KA1ABW
James S Wojnarowicz
24 Blair's Hill Rd
Agawam MA 01001

Call Sign: NE1C
Bsa Venture Crew 510
C/O HCRA
Agawam MA 01001

Call Sign: N1MNE
Edward J Mc Govern
Castle Hills Rd
Agawam MA 01001

Call Sign: KA1LXR
Raymond E Alheim
23 Charles St
Agawam MA 01001

Call Sign: N1KXO
Ronald N Rodier
7 Conifer Dr
Agawam MA 01001

Call Sign: W1ESL
William C Hall
50 Corey Colonial
Agawam MA 01001

Call Sign: KC1TH
Kurt J Dahdah
40 Corey St
Agawam MA 01001

Call Sign: KB1WQG
Paul J Nicosia
29 Dover St
Agawam MA 01001

Call Sign: KB1VPV
Thomas A Walker

177 Edgewater Rd
Agawam MA 01001

Call Sign: KB1OPV
Bill C Scagliarini
84 Federal Ave
Agawam MA 01001

Call Sign: KB1PQX
Suzanne Lacombe
48 Harvey Johnson Dr
Agawam MA 01001

Call Sign: KB1MIH
Jeffrey M Akley
34 Harvey Johnson Dr
Agawam MA
010012126

Call Sign: KB1NWH
Carroll E Lacombe
48 Harvey Johnson
Drive
Agawam MA 01001

Call Sign: KJ1R
Spiro Magoulas
31 Jade Lane
Agawam MA 01001

Call Sign: KB1USX
Francis P Magagnoli
1270 Main St
Agawam MA 01001

Call Sign: W1KK
Arthur Zavarella
1702 Main St
Agawam MA
010012513

Call Sign: N1MOK
Randall E Cushing
9 Mallard Cir
Agawam MA 01001

Call Sign: KB1VPM
David V Scarpa
91 Mill St
Agawam MA 01001

Call Sign: N1MFL
David V Scarpa
91 Mill St

Agawam MA 01001

Call Sign: KB1MKH
Lori J Mahaffey
429 Mill St
Agawam MA 01001

Call Sign: KD1RZ
Gary R Fontana
66 Plantation Dr
Agawam MA 01001

Call Sign: N1QFV
Vicki M Fontana
66 Plantation Dr
Agawam MA 01001

Call Sign: WB9TQU
Steven J Seals
90 Plantation Dr
Agawam MA 01001

Call Sign: AB1HG
Steven J Seals
90 Plantation Dr
Agawam MA 01001

Call Sign: N1LQG
Edward F Belanger
36 Poinsetta St
Agawam MA 01001

Call Sign: N1MOE
Steven J Lapointe
36 Raymond Cir
Agawam MA 01001

Call Sign: KB1IZH
Samuel R Lafleche
153 Regency Park
Rive
Agawam MA 01001

Call Sign: N2PRA
Joseph W Schaedler
17 Riverview Ave
Agawam MA
010012517

Call Sign: N1JJF
Charles F Daley
11 Riviera Dr
Agawam MA 01001

Call Sign: K1WNR
Robert E Camerlin
22 Silver St
Agawam MA
010012428

Call Sign: KB1FSU
Erik P Jensen
755 Suffield St
Agawam MA 01001

Call Sign: KB1FVL
Andrew P Jensen
755 Suffield St
Agawam MA 01001

Call Sign: NA1X
Joseph M Giannetti
1065 Suffield St
Agawam MA
010012997

Call Sign: AC1T
John A Balboni
188 Walnut St
Agawam MA 01001

Call Sign: KA1URP
Ryan D Bassette
224 Walnut St
Agawam MA 01001

Call Sign: W1NY
Hampden County
Radio Assn Inc
Agawam MA 01001

Call Sign: KB1HEH
Bsa Venture Crew 510
Agawam MA 01001

FCC Amateur Radio Licenses in Ahleboro

Call Sign: N1HIW
Thaddeus M Figlock
199 S Main St 2nd
Floor Front
Ahleboro MA 02703

FCC Amateur Radio Licenses in Alford

Call Sign: KA2AVR

Paul Tepper
131 West Rd
Alford MA 01266

Call Sign: KB1BS
Bruce B Schreiber
281 West Rd
Alford MA 01126

FCC Amateur Radio Licenses in Allston

Call Sign: N1OGQ
Rudolph T Bikkal
86 Brainard Rd 16
Allston MA 02134

Call Sign: KG4EGZ
Vernon A Brewer Iii
244 Brighton Ave Apt
405
Allston MA 02134

Call Sign: KB1FVC
Arthur F Laurie
459 Cambridge St
Allston MA
021342023

Call Sign: KB1VWX
Jimmy C Chau
102 Chester St Apt 1
Allston MA 02134

Call Sign: N1NWT
Bashir S Galadanci
1305 Commonwealth
Ave 16
Allston MA 02134

Call Sign: KA1MGW
Robert W Lomasney
275 Everett St
Allston MA 02134

Call Sign: KB1JEZ
Yevgeniy Y Dorfman
144 Franklin St
Allston MA 02134

Call Sign: KG6OIR
Nickolai B Zeldovich
155 Franklin St
Allston MA 02134

Call Sign: KF4PEF
Matthew D Kendall
99 Glenville Ave Apt
#3
Allston MA 02134

Call Sign: KB1VGO
Ismet B Altunkaynak
61 Gordon St
Allston MA 02136

Call Sign: N1TMF
Paul V Carter
11 Gorham St Apt#1
Allston MA 02134

Call Sign: WA1MYZ
Kevin L Quinlan
9 Griggs Pl
Allston MA 02134

Call Sign: N1OSF
Michael A Yocum
23 Long Ave 3
Allston MA 02134

Call Sign: KA1SLW
Jacques M Johnson
58 Royal St Apt 3
Allston MA 02136

FCC Amateur Radio Licenses in Amesbury

Call Sign: KB1VGD
David G Irvine
17 Ash St
Amesbury MA 01913

Call Sign: W1WKA
David G Irvine
17 Ash St
Amesbury MA 01913

Call Sign: WA1BLC
Robert R Anderson
14 Atlantic View
Amesbury MA 01913

Call Sign: N1COT
Alan R Thornton
1 Back River Rd
Amesbury MA 01913

Call Sign: N1JJM
Richard J Abbott
52 Bartletts Reach
Amesbury MA 01913

Call Sign: KB1OKO
Patrick T Prochilo
10 Boardman St
Amesbury MA 01913

Call Sign: N2BOX
Patrick T Prochilo
10 Boardman St
Amesbury MA 01913

Call Sign: W1QUY
Eprem Torosian
15 Boie Ave
Amesbury MA 01913

Call Sign: W1DYH
William R Droese
4 Carver St
Amesbury MA 01913

Call Sign: KB1KEM
Dudley J Nguyen
11 Clarks Rd
Amesbury MA 01913

Call Sign: N1BZV
William E Baker
16 Glen Devin
Amesbury MA 01913

Call Sign: KB1MTH
David W Mcbeth
22 Glen Devin
Amesbury MA 01913

Call Sign: KB1MIB
Paul D Hestand
154 Haverhill Rd
Amesbury MA 01913

Call Sign: N1CSG
Richard C Hammond
2 Heritage Vale
Amesbury MA 01913

Call Sign: N1ZYJ
Charles E Mellor
45 Highland St

Amesbury MA 01913

Call Sign: N1WHR
Phillip R Winders
9 Horton Sreet
Amesbury MA 01913

Call Sign: N1WHH
Daphne J Winders
9 Horton St
Amesbury MA 01913

Call Sign: N1KFQ
Richard E Bowen
8 Kimball Rd
Amesbury MA 01913

Call Sign: N1SRG
James E Gage
163 Kimball Rd
Amesbury MA 01913

Call Sign: N1DPK
Douglas S Mc Bride
177 Kimball Rd
Amesbury MA 01913

Call Sign: KB1WEV
Matthew S Mcbride
177 Kimball Rd
Amesbury MA 01913

Call Sign: N1UVV
Everett H Swenson
17 Lafayette St Ext
Amesbury MA
019133814

Call Sign: KB1LX
Mark P Obremski
279 Lions Mouth Rd
Amesbury MA 01913

Call Sign: KB1TRP
Donald Swenson
4 Lonvale Ln 103
Amesbury MA 01913

Call Sign: N1UVV
Donald Swenson
4 Lonvale Ln 103
Amesbury MA 01913

Call Sign: K1ETE

Howard A Dalton
473 Main St
Amesbury MA 01913

Call Sign: KA1OMB
HOLLY E Pouliot
8 Newton Rd
Amesbury MA 01913

Call Sign: KB1JJA
Linda A Noon
9 Newton Rd
Amesbury MA 01913

Call Sign: KA1QZE
George N Roy
14 Old County Rd
Amesbury MA 01913

Call Sign: KA1UDA
Melina A Roy
14 Old County Rd
Amesbury MA 01913

Call Sign: KB1TAA
Timothy R Henricks
35 Pamela Lane
Amesbury MA 01913

Call Sign: W1RYJ
Esther A Routhier
13 Pickard St
Amesbury MA 01913

Call Sign: N1VAO
Samuel J Dunning
22 Pow Wow Villa
Amesbury MA 01913

Call Sign: AC1R
James H Corliss
55 Powow St
Amesbury MA 01913

Call Sign: W1YYB
Nicholas Frank
6 Rondeau St
Amesbury MA
019133203

Call Sign: KB1UEB
Erik A Gates
11 Senee Ct
Amesbury MA 01913

Call Sign: N1MLT
Stephen Valliere Jr
17 Senee Ct
Amesbury MA 01913

Call Sign: N1UTC
Peter J Palmquist
64 W Greenwood St
Amesbury MA 01913

Call Sign: N1AQG
Joseph M H Forest
30 Warren Ave
Amesbury MA 01913

Call Sign: WA1VUS
Robert V Woitunski
12 West Winkley St
Amesbury MA 01913

Call Sign: N1VGO
Eugene N Hamel
6 Westminster St
Amesbury MA 01913

Call Sign: KB1AIG
William J Smith
82 Whitehall Rd
Amesbury MA 01913

Call Sign: AB1PR
Eric S Snyder
16 Woodwell Circle
Amesbury MA 01913

Call Sign: KA1UCZ
Richard A Cook Jr
Amesbury MA 01913

Call Sign: WZ1L
William G Poulin
Amesbury MA 01913

FCC Amateur Radio Licenses in Amherst

Call Sign: KC1KO
Donald B George Jr
135 Alpine Dr
Amherst MA 01002

Call Sign: N1KPK
Joseph Lerner

36 Amity Pl
Amherst MA 01002

Call Sign: KA1RFN
Neil J Mc Ewan
280 Amity St
Amherst MA 01002

Call Sign: KJ1U
Maurice E Shelby Jr
172 Aubinwood Rd
Amherst MA 01002

Call Sign: N1UCP
Michael W Gilbert
38 Autumn Lane
Amherst MA 01002

Call Sign: W1RRW
Glen A Guernsey
16 Autumn Ln
Amherst MA 01002

Call Sign: WB1CXK
Linwood G Buczala
200 Bay Rd
Amherst MA 01002

Call Sign: KB0MMU
Andy H Muldowney
505 Bay Rd
Amherst MA 01002

Call Sign: K1PQU
Richard J Vincent
1200 Bay Rd
Amherst MA 01002

Call Sign: KA1BAQ
Thomas C Mc Bride
1269 Bay Rd
Amherst MA 01002

Call Sign: WB2BYW
James B Mead
16 Berkshire Ter
Amherst MA 01002

Call Sign: KB1VPL
Gabor Lukacs
94 Beston St
Amherst MA 01002

Call Sign: WA1OBY

Univ Of Hartford
Amateur Radio Club
73 Blackberry Ln
Amherst MA 01002

Call Sign: WA3EEC
Ladimer S Nagurney
73 Blackberry Ln
Amherst MA 01002

Call Sign: KB1NOA
Janice S Peterman
70 Blossom Lane
Amherst MA
010023004

Call Sign: KA1QVU
Robert Winternitz
20 Bridlepath Rd
Amherst MA 01002

Call Sign: N0YSO
Miles X Liu
Brittany Manor Drive
Amherst MA 01002

Call Sign: W1GZL
Van Court M Hare Jr
1 Chadwick Ct
Amherst MA 01002

Call Sign: N1DGX
Emlen H Jones
43 Cherry Ln
Amherst MA 01002

Call Sign: N1NSN
Benjamin C Jones
43 Cherry Ln
Amherst MA 01002

Call Sign: WB1ATZ
Lawrence A Babb
52 Cherry Ln
Amherst MA 01002

Call Sign: KB1HAW
Richard E O Donnell
2 Coach Ln
Amherst MA 01002

Call Sign: AB1AJ
Richard E O Donnell
2 Coach Ln

Amherst MA 01002

Call Sign: W1AMD
Aaron M Dulles
87 Columbia Dr
Amherst MA 01002

Call Sign: KB1QXL
Timothy D Van Cleef
91 Cottage St
Amherst MA 01002

Call Sign: N1LUW
Carl C Stecker
10 Dana St
Amherst MA 01002

Call Sign: N1GJH
Regiwell A Francis
807 E Brown Bldg
Univ Of Mass
Amherst MA 01003

Call Sign: N1XFM
Mark D Droy
275 E Hadley Rd
Amherst MA 01002

Call Sign: KB2VZW
Jamieson M Cobleigh
265 E Pleasant St
Amherst MA 01002

Call Sign: W1YE
Joseph F Masteika
819 E Pleasant St
Amherst MA 01002

Call Sign: W1FWO
Robert H Gonter
888 E Pleasant St
Amherst MA 01002

Call Sign: W1RWR
Ralph H White Jr
985 East Pleasant St
Amherst MA 01002

Call Sign: KA1IUT
Natalie E R Drake
10 Eaton Court
Amherst MA 01002

Call Sign: WB1AOV

Frank R Hugus
140 Fearing St
Amherst MA 01002

Call Sign: N1JSP
George W Spiro
20 Hartman Rd
Amherst MA 01002

Call Sign: KB1LLW
Jeffrey A Spiro
20 Hartman Rd
Amherst MA 01002

Call Sign: WD8NLP
David D Sporny
200 Heatherstone Rd
Amherst MA 01002

Call Sign: KB1ALW
Walter J Weaver Jr
44 Jenks St
Amherst MA 01002

Call Sign: WB2IOO
Donald E Kroodsma
36 Kettle Pond Rd
Amherst MA 01002

Call Sign: WB2UHV
Melissa I Kroodsma
36 Kettle Pond Rd
Amherst MA 01002

Call Sign: N1MVL
Anupam D Barde
39 Kingman Rd
Amherst MA 01002

Call Sign: W1PF
Thomas E Kopec
96 Larkspur Dr
Amherst MA 01002

Call Sign: KB1GRA
Lauren L Kopec
96 Larkspur Dr
Amherst MA 01002

Call Sign: WB1BVY
Lauren L Kopec
96 Larkspur Dr
Amherst MA 01002

Call Sign: N1AXD
Myron D Smith
22 Lessey St Apt 118
Amherst MA
010022132

Call Sign: N1QLR
Gerard M Gardner
64 Logtown Rd
Amherst MA 01002

Call Sign: KB1RQW
Samuel J Gardner
64 Logtown Rd
Amherst MA 01002

Call Sign: KA1ZNF
Moses B Garbin
311 Long Plain Rd Rfd
3
Amherst MA 01002

Call Sign: KB1WAL
Michael F Kotarba Iii
69 Longmeadow Dr
Amherst MA 01002

Call Sign: KB1MBP
Sarah S Cogswell
702 Main St - Apt 2w
Amherst MA 01002

Call Sign: K1REX
Stephen R Merriman
56 Mount Holyoke
Drive
Amherst MA 01002

Call Sign: KB1VYC
Timo Friedrich
164 N East St
Amherst MA 01002

Call Sign: N1NFW
William M Harlow
58 N East St B2-A5
Amherst MA 01002

Call Sign: N1VPP
Keith J Anderson
364 Northampton Rd
Apt C
Amherst MA 01002

Call Sign: KB1WAN
Janet C Gillis
320 Potwine Ln
Amherst MA 01002

Call Sign: K1KKP
Alan Des Parrish
120 Pulpit Hill Rd #28
Amherst MA 01002

Call Sign: N1TBJ
Josua Hornick
120 Pulpit Hill Rd 24
Amherst MA
010024006

Call Sign: W1GLN
Eric S Einhorn
11 Red Fox Ln
Amherst MA 01002

Call Sign: WA1UTT
Amherst Regional Hs
Amtr Rd Assn
Rfd 3
Amherst MA 01002

Call Sign: K1TLV
Cecil E Scott
24 Riverside Park Apts
Amherst MA 01002

Call Sign: KB1NTY
Rockwell B Schrock
42 Rolling Green
Drive
Amherst MA 01002

Call Sign: N1HCC
Stanley A Eastaugh
1141 S East St
Amherst MA 01002

Call Sign: N1CVQ
Aaron A Hayden
1491 S East St
Amherst MA 01002

Call Sign: N1IJE
Paul J Bazanchuk
6 Sacco Dr
Amherst MA 01002

Call Sign: WA1MPY

Paul J Bazanchuk
6 Sacco Dr
Amherst MA 01002

Call Sign: AB1NY
Adrian Klieber
53 Salem St
Amherst MA 01002

Call Sign: KD5SJP
Patrick V Taylor
40 Sheerman Lane
Amherst MA 01002

Call Sign: K1SND
Anthony E Conklin Jr
11 Sherry Cir
Amherst MA 01002

Call Sign: KD1YD
Joseph M Boucher
17 Shumway St
Amherst MA 01002

Call Sign: KB1XX
John D Sarna
122 Spring St
Amherst MA 01002

Call Sign: KB1DUX
Theodore A Roco
10 Squire Ln
Amherst MA 01002

Call Sign: KA1WIV
Cheryl H Sesser
623 Station Rd
Amherst MA 01002

Call Sign: KB1NXQ
Daniel W Jaynes
140 Sunset Ave
Amherst MA 01002

Call Sign: W1TDD
David T Edsall
156 Sunset Ave
Amherst MA
010022020

Call Sign: KA1JTX
Matthew M Eichenlaub
21 Tamarack Dr
Amherst MA 01002

Call Sign: WA1FVP
Raymond S Frenkel
37 Tamarack Drive
Amherst MA
010022620

Call Sign: KB1DVV
Howard E Singer
26 Teaberry Ln
Amherst MA 01002

Call Sign: W1JUM
John F Jewett
130 University Dr Apt
110
Amherst MA
010022282

Call Sign: W8BFO
Howard J Wellman
39 Valley View Cir
Amherst MA 01002

Call Sign: N1OBF
Shashi D Buluswar
23 Webster Ct
Amherst MA 01002

Call Sign: KB1PVE
Western Mass Contest
Club
1184 West St
Amherst MA 01002

Call Sign: KS1Y
Western Mass Contest
Club
1184 West St
Amherst MA 01002

Call Sign: W4COW
Wesley C Randles
44 Western Lane
Amherst MA 01002

Call Sign: W4GXZ
Blanche L Randles
44 Western Lane
Amherst MA 01002

Call Sign: N1AVB
Donald L Maddox
37 Wildwood Ln

Amherst MA 01002

Call Sign: K1GY
Donald L Maddox
37 Wildwood Ln
Amherst MA 01002

Call Sign: KB1F
David R Beauvais
Amherst MA 01004

Call Sign: KB1DCB
Rithy Vong
Amherst MA 01004

Call Sign: N1JN
Jonathan H Welch
Amherst MA
010040472

Call Sign: W1JRA
Amherst College Amat
Rad Clb
Amherst MA
010040472

Call Sign: KB1HWI
Marc D Liberatore
Amherst MA
010040604

Call Sign: KB1WBS
David D Sporny
Amherst MA 01004

FCC Amateur Radio Licenses in Andover

Call Sign: KA1TZI
Fernando A Gonzalez
Sr
Andover MA 01810

Call Sign: W1FBU
Edwin E Bogusz
4 Abbot Bridge Dr
Andover MA 01810

Call Sign: K1CSO
Frederick C Eastman
103 Abbot St
Andover MA
018104835

Call Sign: K1RNK
John J Mc Clintock
80 Andover St
Andover MA 01810

Call Sign: N1JIU
Francis A Magoon
211 Andover St
Andover MA 01810

Call Sign: KA2SEF
Ronald Lasser
1 Apple Blossom Rd
Andover MA
018105401

Call Sign: N1OKE
Kurt E Guggenberger
7 Argyle St Apt 8
Andover MA 01810

Call Sign: N1WWJ
Lee J Britton
47 Balmoral St
Andover MA 01810

Call Sign: KB1VUR
Manuel J Gutierrez
37 Bannister Rd
Andover MA 01810

Call Sign: W1IQ
Allan L Kaminsky
9 Bartlet St #354
Andover MA 01810

Call Sign: K1ZCR
Harold W Tyning Jr
221 Beach St
Andover MA 01810

Call Sign: KB1VJP
Kimberlee E Nighelli
164 Beacon St
Andover MA 01810

Call Sign: W1MXC
Donald J Poulin
15 Beech Cir
Andover MA 01810

Call Sign: WA1INK
Sharon A Poulin
15 Beech Cir

Andover MA 01810

Call Sign: WA1ZNG
Alice A Poulin
15 Beech Cir
Andover MA 01810

Call Sign: KG1W
Peter D Marton
3 Belle Isle Way
Andover MA 01810

Call Sign: KA1NXH
Michael D Solt
10 Binney St
Andover MA 01810

Call Sign: KA1ULN
Arnetha Q Haynes
Box 569
Andover MA 01810

Call Sign: WA1NRT
Richard E Maltzman
18 Bradlee
Andover MA 01810

Call Sign: KC7BLB
Kirk C Liponis
8 Bradlee Rd
Andover MA 01810

Call Sign: N1OZR
Mark F TRUE
3 Bradley Rd
Andover MA 01810

Call Sign: N1MBQ
John E Trombly
12 Brady Lp
Andover MA 01810

Call Sign: KB1JLK
Michael L Connell
8 Bridle Path Rd
Andover MA 01810

Call Sign: KA1RMB
Jeremy H Kahan
65 Brown St
Andover MA 01810

Call Sign: KB1JX
Daniel P Trainor

700 Bulfinch Drive
Andover MA 01810

Call Sign: N1CFX
James P Logan
16 Burnham Rd
Andover MA 01810

Call Sign: KB1RCQ
Douglas W Ramsdell
16 Burton Farm Dr
Andover MA 01810

Call Sign: KB1VZQ
Joseph Gifun
9 Castle Heights Rd
Andover MA 01810

Call Sign: N1LOW
Karen F Angell
96 Central St
Andover MA 01810

Call Sign: KA1YGF
Adam W C Smith
4 Chadwick Cir
Andover MA 01810

Call Sign: AI7H
Allan L Kaminsky
191 Chandler Rd
Andover MA 01810

Call Sign: N1ORH
Lawrence J Bruce
254 Chandler Rd
Andover MA 01810

Call Sign: N1BEB
Jerome F Witt
20 Chatham Rd
Andover MA 01810

Call Sign: KA1TRO
Raymond C Marble
11 Chester St
Andover MA
018105815

Call Sign: K1DJC
Warren J Rosen
23 Chester St
Andover MA 01810

Call Sign: N1RTL
William A Mc Carthy
46 Chestnut St
Andover MA 01810

Call Sign: W2FPB
Ronald W Knepper
45 Clark Rd
Andover MA 01810

Call Sign: W1JG
John G Mc Davitt
Colonial Dr 11
Andover MA 01810

Call Sign: KB1ANR
Joan M Terry
Colonial Dr Apt 2
Andover MA 01810

Call Sign: N1SFU
Thomas P Alexander
5 Colonial Dr Unit A5-
8
Andover MA 01810

Call Sign: AA1TV
Gen Sato
Corporate Dr
Andover MA
018102447

Call Sign: N1PRW
Alexander R Svirsky
12 Crescent Dr 2
Andover MA 01810

Call Sign: KD1VV
Robert E Snyder
7 Crestwood Dr
Andover MA 01810

Call Sign: WI1G
Richard E Snyder
7 Crestwood Dr
Andover MA 01810

Call Sign: WA1MBO
James D Jamison
59 Dascomb Rd
Andover MA 01810

Call Sign: WA1YLC
Joseph C Ippolito

79 Elm St
Andover MA 01810

Call Sign: N1UQG
Jonathan T Taylor
4 Elysian Dr
Andover MA 01810

Call Sign: WI1B
Kenneth C Veznaian
6 Elysian Dr
Andover MA 01810

Call Sign: N1BTD
John M Mc Coy Jr
Evergreen Ln
Andover MA 01810

Call Sign: AB1KP
Richard S Gawlik
4 Exeter Way
Andover MA 01810

Call Sign: KA1DRA
Keith E Olsen
4 Farrwood Dr
Andover MA 01810

Call Sign: KB1KRH
John W Irza
10 Garfield Lane East
Andover MA 01810

Call Sign: AI1H
Francis J Witt
41 Glenwood Rd
Andover MA
018106250

Call Sign: N1DIS ·
Barbara A Witt
41 Glenwood Rd
Andover MA
018106250

Call Sign: KA1FAA
Ralph H Jannini
16 Hansom Rd
Andover MA 01810

Call Sign: K1SAY
William F King
71 Harold Parker Rd

Andover MA
018105201

Call Sign: N1PHJ
Eric P De Lacoste
68 Haverhill St
Andover MA 01810

Call Sign: N1SGA
Kenneth E Cooper
17 Hemlock Rd
Andover MA 01810

Call Sign: N1YYY
Abigail G Cooper
17 Hemlock Rd
Andover MA 01810

Call Sign: N1SJD
Gerard E Dallal
54 High Plain Rd
Andover MA 01810

Call Sign: W1HL
James H Fisk
362 High Plain Rd
Andover MA 01810

Call Sign: KA1NFW
Warren F Kearn
394 High Plain Rd
Andover MA 01810

Call Sign: K1OA
Scott A Ginsburg
421 High Plain Rd
Andover MA 01810

Call Sign: KB1HDH
Rebecca A Ginsburg
421 High Plain Rd
Andover MA 01810

Call Sign: W1MQN
Harold T Cookson
124 High St
Andover MA 01810

Call Sign: N1EVI
Timothy W Barash
8 Highvale Ln
Andover MA 01810

Call Sign: N1SWF

Craig T Burton
195 Holt Rd
Andover MA 01810

Call Sign: K1LRM
Carl L Brooks
8 Howell Dr
Andover MA
018103615

Call Sign: NV1W
James B Evans Jr
10 Ivy Ln
Andover MA
018105018

Call Sign: N1JDC
Joseph Gonda
12 Ivy Ln
Andover MA 01810

Call Sign: N1OQV
James R Hadad Ii
26 Jenkins Rd
Andover MA 01810

Call Sign: N1BLM
Ronald P Rappel
8 Lancaster Place
Andover MA 01810

Call Sign: W1RPR
Ronald P Rappel
8 Lancaster Place
Andover MA 01810

Call Sign: N1ZAE
Nancy R Caverly
11 Linda Rd
Andover MA 01810

Call Sign: AB1HE
Wilfred J Baxter Jr
47 Lovejoy Rd
Andover MA 01810

Call Sign: N1KKH
Hamilton L Clower
459 Lowell St
Andover MA 01810

Call Sign: N1MYS
Linda A Clower
459 Lowell St

Andover MA 01810

Call Sign: W1BG
Penn H Clower
459 Lowell St
Andover MA 01810

Call Sign: K1PCK
James M Moran
166 Lowell St
Andover MA 01810

Call Sign: WA1SYH
Benjamin P Kellman
125 Main St
Andover MA 01810

Call Sign: KB1KDM
Christopher R Oriel
Maple Ave
Andover MA 01810

Call Sign: K1OQQ
Arthur L Bauer Jr
14 Martingale Ln
Andover MA 01810

Call Sign: WA1DCI
Clyde H Brunquell
7 Millstone Cir
Andover MA 01810

Call Sign: W1HP
Philips Amateur Radio
Club
3000 Minuteman Rd
Attn Tony Brock
Fisher Ms-090
Andover MA 01810

Call Sign: KD1FV
James S Plummer
259 N Main St
Andover MA 01810

Call Sign: N1LJJ
Gabriella Plummer
259 N Main St
Andover MA 01810

Call Sign: N1YHV
Ronald Boulanger
101 N St
Andover MA 01810

Call Sign: KB1HYK
Arun S Gorur
4 Nob Hill Circle
Andover MA 01810

Call Sign: WA1RSV
Roger J Wilmarth
10 Nollet Dr
Andover MA 01810

Call Sign: KB1BTT
Brian W Karfunkel
22 Orchard Cr
Andover MA 01812

Call Sign: KB1CD
Nicola A Calandrello
5 Oriole Dr
Andover MA 01810

Call Sign: W1HNS
Kenneth E Pratt
56 Osgood St
Andover MA 01810

Call Sign: K1ZL
The Zl Specials
P O Box 4242
Andover MA
018100814

Call Sign: W1FOC
New England Foc
P O Box 4242
Andover MA
018100814

Call Sign: WA1G
Clarendon Hill Arc
P O Box 4242
Andover MA 01810

Call Sign: KB1DNT
Laura R Simpson
4 Peach Tree Path
Andover MA 01810

Call Sign: WA1VHD
Harold A Simpson
4 Peach Tree Path
Andover MA 01810

Call Sign: N2LDC

Jeff R Feigin
1 Phaeton Cir
Andover MA 01810

Call Sign: N1OKC
John P Cogliano
4 Phaeton Cir
Andover MA 01810

Call Sign: W1SW
Phillips Academy
Radio Club
Phillips Academy
Andover MA 01810

Call Sign: KD1DX
Peter R Holloway
5 Phoenix Pl
Andover MA 01810

Call Sign: KA1VDI
Donna H Bissett
84 Poor St
Andover MA 01810

Call Sign: N1GCG
Stephen T Bissett
84 Poor St
Andover MA 01810

Call Sign: N1TWE
Bruce A Beckwith
6 Rachel Rd
Andover MA 01810

Call Sign: W1VBD
John G Morgan
22 Railroad St Apt 103
Andover MA 01810

Call Sign: KA1FIB
Robert H Comstock
8 Random Ln
Andover MA 01810

Call Sign: KA1OOY
Peter P Rubenstein
6 Rennie Dr
Andover MA 01810

Call Sign: N1RIR
Christopher J Messineo
168 River Rd Apt 336
Andover MA 01810

Call Sign: W1TYJ
James A Mac Millan
28 River St
Andover MA 01810

Call Sign: KC1HR
Peter T Anderson
42 River St
Andover MA
018105908

Call Sign: K1USH
Edward Cole
43 River St
Andover MA
018105907

Call Sign: N1HFR
Gregg E Johnson
52 River St
Andover MA 01810

Call Sign: KB1PED
Gary C Barnaby Jr
100 River St
Andover MA 01810

Call Sign: KB1KZP
Howard M Burns
9 Rogers Brook W
Andover MA 01810

Call Sign: KD6PNT
Jennifer R Meldrum
287 S Main St
Andover MA 01810

Call Sign: WB1H
David R Meldrum
287 S Main St
Andover MA 01810

Call Sign: KB1ETF
Todd A Matton
383 S Main St
Andover MA 01810

Call Sign: KB1CEG
Danielle E Huntley
507 S Main St
Andover MA 01810

Call Sign: WB1EIP

Michael L Gikow
41 Sagamore Dr
Andover MA
018105105

Call Sign: N1BNS
Richard J Buba
358 Salem St
Andover MA 01810

Call Sign: KB1TMJ
Michael Flanagan
13 Sevilla Rd
Andover MA 01810

Call Sign: KB1FPT
Robert M Snyder
432 South Main St
Andover MA 01810

Call Sign: K1YUB
Paul D Graveline
9 Stirling St
Andover MA 01810

Call Sign: KA2CXL
Jeffrey H Saunders
2 Stouffer Cir
Andover MA 01810

Call Sign: K1CPW
Selwyn N Blake
186 Summer
Andover MA 01810

Call Sign: N1BEG
A Reed Valleau
166 Summer St
Andover MA 01810

Call Sign: KB1REC
Brian Hunter
30 Sunset Rock Rd
Andover MA 01810

Call Sign: KB1RED
Lynne A Langlois
30 Sunset Rock Rd
Andover MA 01810

Call Sign: W1WMH
John H Atchison Jr
8 Sutherland St

Andover MA
018101411

Call Sign: N1RSZ
Allen D Mackey
1 Sutton Way
Andover MA 01810

Call Sign: N1SJC
Jon S Aronson
9 Teaberry Ln
Andover MA 01810

Call Sign: KA1RMC
S David Kahan
24 Theodore Ave
Andover MA 01810

Call Sign: WA5LJC
Gerald A Reine
5 Tobey Ln
Andover MA 01810

Call Sign: W1ZB
Gerald A Reine
5 Tobey Ln
Andover MA 01810

Call Sign: WA1HGJ
Bruce A Littlefield
4 Twin Brook Cir
Andover MA 01810

Call Sign: KF1U
Edward W Gent
12 Vine St
Andover MA 01810

Call Sign: WB1AOP
Marc S Davidson
41 W Parish Dr
Andover MA 01810

Call Sign: W1LN
Marc S Davidson
41 W Parish Dr
Andover MA 01810

Call Sign: KD1NQ
Jeffrey L Hall
40 Walnut Ave
Andover MA 01810

Call Sign: W2MET

Michael E Thompson
2 Warwick Circle
Andover MA
018102573

Call Sign: K1KP
George A Brock Fisher
15 Webster St
Andover MA 01810

Call Sign: N1XJA
Michelle C Brock
Fisher
15 Webster St
Andover MA 01810

Call Sign: KB1NOW
Taylor M Brock-Fisher
15 Webster St
Andover MA 01810

Call Sign: KB1TNH
Alexander P Davidson
41 West Parish Dr
Andover MA
018103338

Call Sign: W1AND
Alexander P Davidson
41 West Parish Dr
Andover MA
018103338

Call Sign: W1WI
Eugene J Mc Hale
30 Wild Rose Dr
Andover MA
018104620

Call Sign: N1CGH
Stephen P Anderson
25 Wild Rose Drive
Andover MA 01810

Call Sign: W1CUO
Edwin Goonyep
2 Willard Cir
Andover MA 01810

Call Sign: WA1ZES
Judith A Goonyep
2 Willard Cir
Andover MA 01810

Call Sign: N1RTR
Gary R Streeter
35 William St
Andover MA 01810

Call Sign: AA1GU
Carl G Hayssen Iii
6 Winchester Dr
Andover MA
018103279

Call Sign: W1VFT
Andre A Croteau
67 Woburn St
Andover MA 01810

Call Sign: N3NJG
Timothy J Mc Govern
16 Woodhaven Drive
Andover MA 01810

Call Sign: K1AJ
Bruce T Marshall
Andover MA
018100814

Call Sign: N1VV
Clarendon Hill Arc
Andover MA
018100814

Call Sign: KB1SXF
Robert L Savard
Andover MA 01810

FCC Amateur Radio Licenses in Arlington

Call Sign: KB1OZT
Filippo M Nardin
47 Alton St
Arlington MA 02474

Call Sign: N1HIL
Bruno F Vasil Jr
19 Amherst St
Arlington MA
024743408

Call Sign: KB1BMU
Christopher M Hass
26 Amherst St
Arlington MA 02474

Call Sign: KB1UDP
Andrew C Freeman
65 Amsden St
Arlington MA 02474

Call Sign: N1LKW
David E Cummings
387 Appleton St
Arlington MA 02174

Call Sign: W1MLK
Harold P Hatch
61 Bartlett Ave
Arlington MA 02174

Call Sign: KB1CJE
Joanne N Safar
79 Bartlett Ave #1
Arlington MA
024766453

Call Sign: KA1ETM
Kenneth E Gilmore
33 Beacon St
Arlington MA 02174

Call Sign: N1GRY
Merritt C Brown
10 Belknap St
Arlington MA 02174

Call Sign: W1OHV
Ralph J Cowie Jr
22 Beverly Rd
Arlington MA 02174

Call Sign: KO1I
Charles D Martin
20 Brand St
Arlington MA 02474

Call Sign: KB1DQY
Robert L Rucinski
2 Brattle Dr Apt 3
Arlington MA 02474

Call Sign: N1IBG
Jill A Smith
12 Brattle St
Arlington MA 02174

Call Sign: N1CKO
Frank W Smith
117 Brattle St

Arlington MA
021742122

Call Sign: N1VQH
Peter H Jurgensen
159 Brattle St
Arlington MA 02174

Call Sign: N1ZOA
Mariza C Jurgensen
159 Brattle St
Arlington MA 02174

Call Sign: KB1QXZ
Peter H Jurgensen
159 Brattle St
Arlington MA 02474

Call Sign: KB1QYI
Tomas C Jurgensen
159 Brattle St
Arlington MA 02474

Call Sign: KB2JUL
Chad F Jones
132 Broadway Apt 1
Arlington MA 02474

Call Sign: KB1KEV
Shawn F O Leary
24 Browning Rd
Arlington MA 02476

Call Sign: KB1MSS
Robert Rizzo
40 Browning Rd
Arlington MA 02476

Call Sign: KA1GZD
Anthony J Aftuck
177 Cedar Ave
Arlington MA 02174

Call Sign: KA1RKX
Joachim Landefeld
154 Charlton St
Arlington MA 02174

Call Sign: KF4RIU
John W Councill Iv
57 Churchill Ave 2
Arlington MA 02476

Call Sign: KB1CKU

Dai Matsuoka
3 Colonial Village Dr
Apt 5
Arlington MA 02174

Call Sign: WA1DVR
Robert J Kalustian
38 Columbia Rd
Arlington MA 02474

Call Sign: W1QUN
Valentine T Chisholm
51 Cutter Hill Rd
Arlington MA 02174

Call Sign: N1ODH
Josh M Huber
29 Daniels St
Arlington MA 02476

Call Sign: WA1KBH
Wayne H Hagman
4 Davis Ave
Arlington MA
024741202

Call Sign: KB1GRR
Andrew P Mcmakin
12 Draper Ave
Arlington MA 02474

Call Sign: N1NJV
Kathleen Leitermann
5 Edith St
Arlington MA 02474

Call Sign: WB9CKG
Richard E Leitermann
5 Edith St
Arlington MA 02474

Call Sign: KA1SDS
Ralph M Hebb
78 Egerton Rd
Arlington MA 02174

Call Sign: KB1ANW
Thomas H Dunn Jr
46 Eustis St
Arlington MA 02174

Call Sign: N1XKY
John R Manganello
47 Everett St Unit #2

Arlington MA 02474

Call Sign: KA1QZK
Joice Himawan
Bennett
28 Fairmont St
Arlington MA 02174

Call Sign: N1WDG
Margaret R Maes
28 Fairmont St
Arlington MA 02174

Call Sign: W1XXX
Steven P Bonadio
58 Fairmont St #1
Arlington MA
024748718

Call Sign: KA1KIU
Thomas F Crosby Jr
21 Farrington St
Arlington MA 02174

Call Sign: N1JK
James E Kuhn
41 Fisher Rd
Arlington MA 02174

Call Sign: KE1EU
Christopher R
Matthews
175 Forest St
Arlington MA 02174

Call Sign: N1CID
Vincent A Natale Jr
215 Forest St
Arlington MA
021748906

Call Sign: KC1OB
Robert H Bailey
28 Glen Ave
Arlington MA 02174

Call Sign: N1QID
Gregory J Carven
73 Gloucester St
Arlington MA 02476

Call Sign: WA1NSE
Gerald J Sussman
147 Gloucester St

Arlington MA 02476

Call Sign: KB1TOZ
David P Murphy
19 Golden Ave
Arlington MA
024767029

Call Sign: KB1UBO
Charles B Murphy
19 Golden Ave
Arlington MA 02476

Call Sign: WM1I
Mark H Levine
16 Gray St
Arlington MA
024766463

Call Sign: KB6KJV
Paul R Beninger
218 Gray St
Arlington MA 02476

Call Sign: WA1BPH
Martin J Thrope
348 Gray St
Arlington MA 02174

Call Sign: AA1CD
Jason R Hobbs
75 Grove St Apt #4
Arlington MA 02476

Call Sign: AB1EF
Brian L Faull
30 Hamilton Rd #302
Arlington MA 02474

Call Sign: KB1JXQ
Brian L Faull
20 Hamilton Rd Apt
201
Arlington MA 02424

Call Sign: W1ZFI
Robert Gildea
18 Hamilton Rd Apt
207
Arlington MA
024748265

Call Sign: W1OIO
Charles T Mighill

34 Hamilton Rd Unit
405
Arlington MA 02174

Call Sign: N1YDE
Peter L Greis
36 Harvard St 2
Arlington MA 02124

Call Sign: N5TJU
Hiroshi C Bowman
30 Harvard St Apt 1
Arlington MA 02476

Call Sign: KB1IIY
Morag S Fulton
30 Harvard St First
Floor
Arlington MA 02476

Call Sign: W1QMT
James P Maimonis
16 Hathaway Cir
Arlington MA 02476

Call Sign: N1AVP
Jean G D Agostino
77 Hodge Rd
Arlington MA 02174

Call Sign: W1LVF
Michael A Brown
28 Iroquois Rd
Arlington MA 02174

Call Sign: KB1SFW
Alexander I Wilkinson
12 Irving St
Arlington MA 02476

Call Sign: KB1SFX
Yuri A Ivanov
12 Irving St
Arlington MA 02476

Call Sign: W1UIM
George S Gordon Jr
22 Irving St
Arlington MA
024766406

Call Sign: KB1SZR
DAVID Desroches
12 Jean Rd

Arlington MA 02474

Call Sign: N1XET
David L Setser
26 Joyce Rd
Arlington MA
024742913

Call Sign: KA1NAP
David Krikorian
47 Lake St
Arlington MA 02474

Call Sign: N1PHL
Mark D Halliday
122 Lake St
Arlington MA 02474

Call Sign: WA1HYV
Brian R Lomasky
86 Lancaster Rd
Arlington MA 02174

Call Sign: AC0MB
Bryan A Babcock
77 Lancaster Rd #2
Arlington MA 02476

Call Sign: AB1LD
Michael M Burns
70 Lansdowne Rd
Arlington MA 02474

Call Sign: KB1AMV
John J Galvin
5 Locke St
Arlington MA 02174

Call Sign: KD1PF
Stephen P Baker
26 Lombard Rd
Arlington MA 02476

Call Sign: WA1SJA
Ronald B Hellman
31 Longfellar Rd
Arlington MA 02174

Call Sign: KB1HIR
Sal Tuccitto
162 Lowell St
Arlington MA 02474

Call Sign: KB1LKQ

Robert R Althoff
70 Madison Ave
Arlington MA 02474

Call Sign: W1XG
James C Edgerton
128 Madison Ave
Arlington MA 02474

Call Sign: N1QD
Joseph A Harris
Magnolia St
Arlington MA 02474

Call Sign: K1DZL
Robert E Kirmes
18 Margaret St
Arlington MA 02174

Call Sign: W1JBD
Joseph H Dykens
43 Margaret St
Arlington MA 02174

Call Sign: N7FYO
Erik H Beck
7 Martin St
Arlington MA
024742811

Call Sign: KB1NAU
Kwan Hyun Cho
438 Mass Ave -419
Arlington MA 02474

Call Sign: WA1HLK
Reino F Heino Sr
155 Mass Ave Apt 6
Arlington MA
024748618

Call Sign: KA1ULW
Timothy S Mc Gavin
223 Massachusetts Ave
Arlington MA 02174

Call Sign: KB1WTX
Brett Graham
1357 Massachusetts
Ave
Arlington MA 02476

Call Sign: N1PZU
Philip K Schoenheiter

385 Massachusetts Ave
Apt 22
Arlington MA 02174

Call Sign: WB1ARY
Eric R Feigenson
215 Massachusetts Ave
Apt 27
Arlington MA 02174

Call Sign: WA2EYC
Ron M Hoffmann
975 Massachusetts Ave
Unit 105
Arlington MA
021744544

Call Sign: KB1REE
Vidyashankar
Viswanathan
93 Melrose St
Arlington MA 02474

Call Sign: WB1FOH
Jennifer R Melcher
4 Menotomy Rocks Dr
Arlington MA 02476

Call Sign: N1GCT
Michael R Dibella
29 Morningside Dr
Arlington MA 02174

Call Sign: N1ENY
Joseph M Powers
201 Mountain Ave
Arlington MA 02174

Call Sign: N1OGL
Christine M Moore
298 Mystic St
Arlington MA 02174

Call Sign: KB1TDM
Jon Jaggi
385 Mystic St
Arlington MA 02474

Call Sign: KB1DUV
Matthew B Wormser
47 Mystic St 8e
Arlington MA 02474

Call Sign: KB1MZO

James J Nishina
151 Mystic St Apt 43
Arlington MA 02474

Call Sign: KA1RIA
Gerald J Lahaie
166 Mystic Vlly Pky
Arlington MA 02174

Call Sign: AJ1C
Robert P Pinckney
101 Newport
Arlington MA
021747801

Call Sign: N1XUL
Karen E Walrath
159 Newport St
Arlington MA 02174

Call Sign: WA2KOM
Jeffrey I Schiller
159 Newport St
Arlington MA
024767833

Call Sign: KA1BUF
John F Connors
161 Newport St
Arlington MA
024767833

Call Sign: W1KNP
Horatio W Lamson Jr
72 Oakland Ave
Arlington MA 02174

Call Sign: KD1KJ
Richard G Von
Blucher
67 Old Mystic St
Arlington MA
021741005

Call Sign: KA1KHF
Robert W Cutter
68 Overlook Rd
Arlington MA 02174

Call Sign: KB1NHY
Robert E Taylor
85 Oxford St
Arlington MA 02474

Call Sign: N1SSR
Alia K Atlas
10 Palmer St
Arlington MA 02174

Call Sign: N1FKY
Roy J Watson Jr
16 Pamela Dr
Arlington MA 02174

Call Sign: KA2RVO
James L Austin
175 Park Ave
Arlington MA 02476

Call Sign: KB1JLH
Philip D Levine
88 Park Ave 103
Arlington MA 02476

Call Sign: KB1UGS
Michael E Goralski
51 Park St Unit 1r
Arlington MA 02474

Call Sign: WA1FHM
James H Hagelston
84 Paul Revere Rd
Arlington MA 02174

Call Sign: KB1JZF
William J Sullivan
7 Pelham Terr
Arlington MA 02476

Call Sign: KB1TSN
Camon A Brensinger
7 Piedmont St
Arlington MA 02476

Call Sign: KB1QZA
Brian T White
21 Piedmont St
Arlington MA 02476

Call Sign: KC1GA
Frederick L Johnston
Jr
14 Pine St
Arlington MA
024742835

Call Sign: N1JLB
Elsa Chen

60 Pleasant St 323
Arlington MA 02174

Call Sign: N1JWK
James F Roberts
60 Pleasant St Apt 323
Arlington MA
021746520

Call Sign: N1DIB
M William Mc Tighe
27 Prospect Ave
Arlington MA 02174

Call Sign: N7NJQ
Thomas G Goodsell
88 Rawson Rd
Arlington MA 02474

Call Sign: KA1RHR
John J Coates
165 Renfrew St
Arlington MA 02174

Call Sign: N1PUX
Louis F Rossetti
235 Ridge St
Arlington MA 02174

Call Sign: KA1LTS
Lyle M Hazel
96 Ronald Rd
Arlington MA 02174

Call Sign: AB1HH
James B Riley
42 Russell Place
Arlington MA
024744801

Call Sign: N1WDI
Alexander M Fraser
23 Sheraton Park
Arlington MA 02174

Call Sign: KB1KMQ
Everett M Fraser
23 Sheraton Park
Arlington MA 02474

Call Sign: KA1MRF
Elaine M Sacco
24 Sheraton Pk
Arlington MA 02174

Call Sign: N1SUT
Scott K Steinhorst
17 Silk St
Arlington MA 02174

Call Sign: WB1FYB
Beverlee B Broxton
2 Smith St
Arlington MA 02174

Call Sign: WB1FYC
V Bonnie Broxton
2 Smith St
Arlington MA 02174

Call Sign: KA1VR
Robert O Sills
64 Spy Pond Ln
Arlington MA 02474

Call Sign: WC1U
Paul H Williams
7 Stowecroft Rd
Arlington MA 02474

Call Sign: N1IWQ
Ralph L Oberlander
78 Stowecroft Rd
Arlington MA 02174

Call Sign: W1VGY
Richard S Bird
107 Summer St
Arlington MA 02174

Call Sign: N1FHN
William E Sommerfeld
185 Summer St
Arlington MA 02174

Call Sign: KB1PRL
Manuel A Balderas
174 Summer St 14
Arlington MA 02474

Call Sign: N1KFY
John R Mattioli Jr
65 Sunnyside Ave
Arlington MA 02474

Call Sign: N1LYQ
Kenneth E Domino
15 Sunset Rd

Arlington MA
024742610

Call Sign: KC8PTK
Phillip E Nevius
10 Swan Pl Apartment A
Arlington MA 02476

Call Sign: KC9EYC
Eric R Tollefson
10 Swan St Apt 1
Arlington MA 02476

Call Sign: KD1VY
Michael E Creech
105 Sylvia St
Arlington MA 02174

Call Sign: KB1URF
James Peterson
24 Tanager St
Arlington MA 02476

Call Sign: KC0VX
Jack R Porter Ii
11 Thorndike St
Arlington MA 02174

Call Sign: N1QCU
Richard N Tabler
24 Thorndike St
Arlington MA 02174

Call Sign: N1DLS
David L Setser
36 Twin Circle Drive
Arlington MA
024742126

Call Sign: KA1WAM
Stephen M Williams
58 Varnum St
Arlington MA 02174

Call Sign: KB1HHC
Jeffrey D Murray
14 Victoria Rd
Arlington MA 02474

Call Sign: W9TOX
Karl S Menger
24 Wall St
Arlington MA 02174

Call Sign: N1BHX
David W Mac Carn
9 Walnut Ter
Arlington MA 02174

Call Sign: KB1INB
Ian C Maccarn
9 Walnut Terrace
Arlington MA 02476

Call Sign: KB1WHU
Timothy L Sack
Warren St
Arlington MA 02474

Call Sign: KB1CYR
Mohanakrishna Pakkurti
148 Webster St
Arlington MA 02174

Call Sign: AH6NU
Paolo A Beltrani
25 Wellington St Unit 2
Arlington MA 02476

Call Sign: KE1MC
Paolo A Beltrani
25 Wellington St Unit 2
Arlington MA 02476

Call Sign: W1MCG
Edward Patacchiola
3 West St
Arlington MA 02174

Call Sign: KB1DEJ
Nicholas C Caruso
11 Westmoreland Ave
Arlington MA
024742712

Call Sign: KB1WWO
William J Martins
11 White St
Arlington MA 02474

Call Sign: KD1GO
Clarence S Le Drew
28 Wildwood Ave
Arlington MA 02174

Call Sign: KB1AVW
Popsi Narasimhan
61 Williams St
Arlington MA 02476

Call Sign: N1PMZ
Gordon D Weekly
24 Windermere Ave
Arlington MA 02174

Call Sign: N1IBW
William G Stevens
18 Winthrop Rd
Arlington MA
024742933

Call Sign: KB1JSU
George W Stevens
18 Winthrop Rd
Arlington MA 02474

Call Sign: WA1BWO
George W Stevens
18 Winthrop Rd
Arlington MA 02474

Call Sign: N1TC
William G Stevens
18 Winthrop Rd
Arlington MA
024742933

Call Sign: WB1CAJ
Denis Williams
155 Wollaston Ave
Arlington MA 02174

Call Sign: W1CBI
David G Oland
139 Woodside Ln
Arlington MA 02474

Call Sign: KB1DHO
Laura M Feeney
Arlington MA 02474

Call Sign: KB1TZP
Andrew P Anselmo
Arlington MA 02476

Call Sign: KB1VWY
Roberto L Araujo
Arlington MA 02474

Call Sign: N1OSG
Andrew W Bartlett
27 Bow St
Arlington Heights MA
024742714

**FCC Amateur Radio
Licenses in
Ashburnham**

Call Sign: W1JQF
Joseph L Leblanc
388 Blueberry Rd 10
Ashburnham MA
01430

Call Sign: N1FDV
Ellen A De Felippi
242 Bragg Hill Rd Rr 2
Ashburnham MA
014308000

Call Sign: KB1JDR
Walter A Carrington
100 Byfield Rd
Ashburnham MA
01430

Call Sign: K1CMF
Walter A Carrington
100 Byfield Rd
Ashburnham MA
01430

Call Sign: N8TTV
Mark W Baker
176 Cashman Hill Rd
Ashburnham MA
01430

Call Sign: KB1QLH
Bruce M Laitinen
197 Cashman Hill Rd
Ashburnham MA
01430

Call Sign: KA1LDC
Frederick C Bragdon
29 Central St

Ashburnham MA
01430

Call Sign: KB1GNQ
Michael F Miglorino
14 Corey Hill Rd
Ashburnham MA
01430

Call Sign: KB1MIG
Michael F Miglorino
14 Corey Hill Rd
Ashburnham MA
01430

Call Sign: W1MIG
Michael F Miglorino
14 Corey Hill Rd
Ashburnham MA
01430

Call Sign: K1OKR
Albert G Neal
12 Fairview Ave
Ashburnham MA
01430

Call Sign: WA1HLS
William J Nolan Sr
29 Fitchburg Rd
Ashburnham MA
01430

Call Sign: N1NMG
Harold R Long
41 Gibson Rd
Ashburnham MA
01430

Call Sign: WA1DXR
Paul G Norman
52 Gibson Rd
Ashburnham MA
01430

Call Sign: KB1UHY
Brian S O'hern
72 Hastings Rd
Ashburnham MA
01430

Call Sign: KB1VDP
Jean L Camerer
28 Hosley Rd

Ashburnham MA
01430

Call Sign: K1AVM
Jean L Camerer
28 Hosley Rd
Ashburnham MA
01430

Call Sign: KB1DRB
Victor H Leblanc
8 Lake Rd
Ashburnham MA
014301209

Call Sign: K1BXS
Ruth H Yuoska
14 Mill St
Ashburnham MA
01430

Call Sign: N1NND
Matt J Harden
2 Noel Dr
Ashburnham MA
01430

Call Sign: N1NON
Peter J Harden
2 Noel Dr
Ashburnham MA
01430

Call Sign: KB1SNF
James L Fleck
6 Penacook Dr
Ashburnham MA
01430

Call Sign: K1VNV
James L Fleck
6 Penacook Dr
Ashburnham MA
01430

Call Sign: KD1WQ
Howard V Gallagher
51 Platts Rd
Ashburnham MA
01430

Call Sign: K1IEX
Gertrude L Kenyon
98 Platts Rd

Ashburnham MA
01430

Call Sign: KB1JXI
Russell G Weeks
152 Russell Hill Rd
Ashburnham MA
01430

Call Sign: N1DBC
Scott R Gardner
180 Russell Hill Rd
Ashburnham MA
01430

Call Sign: W0BMS
Brian M Sullivan
25 S Pleasant St
Ashburnham MA
01430

Call Sign: N1YQH
Michael A Shear
39 School St
Ashburnham MA
01430

Call Sign: WA1NZH
Joseph J Frattallone
105 Sherbert Rd
Ashburnham MA
01430

Call Sign: WA1ACR
Dennis J Petalas
3 Valerie Cir
Ashburnham MA
01430

Call Sign: N1IUL
Rene H Roy Jr
8 Valerie Cir
Ashburnham MA
01430

Call Sign: WA1UNT
William J Nolan Jr
9 Valerie Cir
Ashburnham MA
01430

Call Sign: WB1FRW
Gary L Farhat
288 Winchendon Rd

Ashburnham MA
01430

Call Sign: KB1VUS
Olof Johnson
61 Young Rd
Ashburnham MA
01430

Call Sign: W1THV
Olof Johnson
61 Young Rd
Ashburnham MA
01430

FCC Amateur Radio Licenses in Ashby

Call Sign: N1CAX
John R Cauvel
414 Bennett Rd
Ashby MA 01431

Call Sign: KA1YUZ
Donna S Watson
Box 240a
Ashby MA 01431

Call Sign: KA1UIB
Norman B Pierce
Box 86
Ashby MA 01431

Call Sign: KA1WLB
Anthony M Gleason
496 County Rd
Ashby MA 01431

Call Sign: N1SHA
Theodore A Seppala
197 Crocker Rd
Ashby MA 01431

Call Sign: KB1VXH
George W Saari
1006 Foster Rd
Ashby MA 01431

Call Sign: N1HIG
David E Peterson
93 Hosmer Rd
Ashby MA 014312159

Call Sign: N1HXA

Michael I Traffie
421 Jones Hill Rd
Ashby MA 014311801

Call Sign: N1ZJX
Jonathan Traffie
421 Jones Hill Rd
Ashby MA 01431

Call Sign: KB1KAW
James M Traffie
421 Jones Hill Rd
Ashby MA 01431

Call Sign: KB1DPG
Andrew L Dik
421 Mayo Rd
Ashby MA 01431

Call Sign: W1NDP
Paul F Holmes Sr
569 New Ipswich Rd
Ashby MA 01431

Call Sign: KB1JKL
Philip C Hopkins
1166 New Ipswich Rd
Ashby MA 01431

Call Sign: K1ZOO
Matthew G Leonard
87 Piper Rd
Ashby MA 01431

Call Sign: W1ZOO
Gary E Leonard
87 Piper Rd
Ashby MA 01431

Call Sign: W2ZOO
Scholastic Arc
87 Piper Rd
Ashby MA 01431

Call Sign: KB1KEF
Nancy R Richards
1092 Richardson Rd
Ashby MA 014312183

Call Sign: KA1QYQ
Ernest F Lazette Jr
401 Simonds Rd
Ashby MA 014311821

Call Sign: K1KVJ
Richard M Tukianen
State Rd
Ashby MA 01431

Call Sign: KB1LOZ
Richard C Barbieri
2376 W State Rd
Ashby MA 01431

Call Sign: N1ZEY
Matthew F Johnson
603 Wheeler Rd
Ashby MA 01431

FCC Amateur Radio Licenses in Ashfield

Call Sign: N1ASC
Edward W Pepyne
134 Ashfield Mtn Rd
Ashfield MA 01330

Call Sign: N1UZI
Julius Kirn
502 Bug Hill Rd
Ashfield MA 01330

Call Sign: KB1NRQ
James S Ussailis
1797 Hawley Rd
Ashfield MA 01330

Call Sign: KA1WBO
James S Ussailis
1797 Hawley Rd
Ashfield MA 01330

Call Sign: WB1CXD
Andrea S Rizzo
2050 Hawley Rd
Ashfield MA 01330

Call Sign: WA1UOL
Ralph D Lovering Jr
501 Hill Rd
Ashfield MA 01330

Call Sign: KB1CMA
Isaac M Clark
16 S Cemetery Rd
Ashfield MA 01330

Call Sign: KA1STZ

Gerald W Lempicki
452 Williamsburg Rd
Ashfield MA 01330

Call Sign: KA1YJR
Robin L Lempicki
452 Williamsburg Rd
Ashfield MA 01330

Call Sign: KB1EZO
Susan B Urquhart
Ashfield MA
013300303

FCC Amateur Radio Licenses in Ashland

Call Sign: KB1JXE
Avner Kedmi
12 Ammetta Rd
Ashland MA 01721

Call Sign: K1OWF
Robert E Petherick
9 Bay Colony Dr
Ashland MA 01721

Call Sign: KB1CXH
Richard W Ohman
50 Bay Colony Dr
Ashland MA 01721

Call Sign: WB1DQB
Mary J Munroe
69 Captain Eames Cir
Ashland MA 01721

Call Sign: KB1NYH
Kevin C Smith
2 Carl Ghilani Cir
Ashland MA 01721

Call Sign: KB1NYI
Shaun T Smith
2 Carl Ghilani Cir
Ashland MA 01721

Call Sign: WA1DRT
Copeland W Hague
331 Cedar St
Ashland MA 01721

Call Sign: KA1SRY
David A Hansen Jr

337 Chestnut St
Ashland MA
017212239

Call Sign: KB1LOY
James T Cahill
2 Coburn Dr
Ashland MA 01721

Call Sign: K1RUW
Salvatore Greco
178 Cordaville Rd
Ashland MA 01721

Call Sign: KB1WMH
Scott D Wood
14 Crestwood Dr
Ashland MA 01721

Call Sign: K1UV
Charles R Green
66 Cross St
Ashland MA 01721

Call Sign: KB1BUC
Ashland High School
Radio Club
66 Cross St
Ashland MA 01721

Call Sign: N1PPU
Donald A Larick
145 Cross St
Ashland MA 01721

Call Sign: KA1HGL
Mary J Weiss
40 Cutler Dr
Ashland MA
017211201

Call Sign: W1NXC
Edmund A Weiss
40 Cutler Dr
Ashland MA
017211201

Call Sign: N1VYC
Kip Cooper
43 Cutler Dr
Ashland MA 01721

Call Sign: N1VYG

Alexander Y
Lubyansky
19 Dean Rd
Ashland MA 01721

Call Sign: KK1E
Stephen B Lewis
35 E Bluff Rd
Ashland MA
017212353

Call Sign: KA1UTI
Richard I Hoyte Jr
151 Eliot St
Ashland MA 01721

Call Sign: N1BPX
Chester B Marble
166 Fountain St
Ashland MA 01721

Call Sign: N1VYB
Michael A Catalano
361 Frankland Rd
Ashland MA 01721

Call Sign: KA1EPD
Rodney W Parker
17 Greenhalge Rd
Ashland MA 01721

Call Sign: N3HFK
Randolph A Krenz
7 Hayden Lane
Ashland MA 01721

Call Sign: KE1GE
Adam D Naiman
16 Indian Spring Rd
Ashland MA 01721

Call Sign: N1CSC
Thomas A Gray
6 Ivy Ln
Ashland MA 01721

Call Sign: KB5CBT
Blake C Westerman
8 Joanne Dr Apt 33
Ashland MA
017212284

Call Sign: WA1YJC
James R Wilner

33 Leland Farm Rd
Ashland MA 01721

Call Sign: W1SBF
Steven B Finks
35 Leland Farm Rd
Ashland MA 01721

Call Sign: KB1GSC
Terry C Shannon
135 Leland Farm Rd
Ashland MA 01721

Call Sign: W1YSA
Martin L Shapiro
659 Main St
Ashland MA 01721

Call Sign: KB1ISF
Mark S Walsh
2 Meadowbrook Ln
Ashland MA
017212209

Call Sign: WA1SHM
Mark S Walsh
2 Meadowbrook Ln
Ashland MA
017212209

Call Sign: N1QYL
Davide De Santis
49 Mountaingate Rd
Ashland MA 01721

Call Sign: N1EWG
Phyllis A Morse
16 Mt View Dr
Ashland MA 01721

Call Sign: NA1G
Peter Pollock
27 Nancy Dr
Ashland MA 01721

Call Sign: KB1SAS
Thomas V Seniuk
137 Oak St 13
Ashland MA 01721

Call Sign: KA1GXR
Thomas A D Orsay
24 Oakridge Ln
Ashland MA 01721

Call Sign: KB1VGX
Timothy A Emhoff
19 Pilgrim Rd
Ashland MA 01721

Call Sign: N1KFW
John M Elwell Jr
75 Pleasant St
Ashland MA 01721

Call Sign: N1PJJ
Paul B Cassidy
21 Raymond Marchetti
St
Ashland MA 01721

Call Sign: K1ACA
Frank L Ambrogio
10 Roberts Rd
Ashland MA 01721

Call Sign: KB1PEQ
Edwin J Robinson Jr
52 Roberts Rd
Ashland MA 01721

Call Sign: K1PAX
Edwin J Robinson Jr
52 Roberts Rd
Ashland MA 01721

Call Sign: WA1KYJ
Philip R Bosinoff
44 Roberts Rd
Ashland MA 01721

Call Sign: KA1PFC
Garry A Hennessy
7 Sherborne Cir
Ashland MA 01721

Call Sign: AJ1H
Fredric J Talmanson
38 Stagecoach Dr
Ashland MA 01721

Call Sign: KB1NRW
Igor Gueths
105 Sudbury Rd
Asland MA 01721

Call Sign: N5FHP
Daniel L Vanzo

243 Trailside Way
Ashland MA 01721

Call Sign: WA1BEZ
Lawrence H Hadley
228 Union St
Ashland MA 01721

Call Sign: KB1MCZ
Maxwell R David
306 Union St
Ashland MA 01721

Call Sign: W1KAN
Warren M Magee
186 West Union St
Ashland MA 01721

Call Sign: KB1RAQ
Callahan G Crehan
2 Woodland Rd
Ashland MA 01721

Call Sign: KB2OQN
Christopher E
Anderson
Ashland MA 01721

Call Sign: NT1L
Donald M Koch
Ashland MA
017210108

FCC Amateur Radio
Licenses in Ashley
Falls

Call Sign: KB1UIF
Andrew L Tedds
560 Clayton Rd
Ashley Falls MA
01222

Call Sign: KB1DNC
Edwin Barbiere Jr
150 E Main St
Ashley Falls MA
01222

Call Sign: KA1ODC
Michael D Agar
283 E Stahl Rd
Ashley Falls MA
01222

Call Sign: KB1BKA
Dale L Alden
Ashley Falls MA
01222

FCC Amateur Radio
Licenses in Assonet

Call Sign: KB1GJX
Brian M Pinault
20 Central Ave
Assonet MA
027021358

Call Sign: AA1Q
Gerald P Di Chiara
35 Central Ave
Assonet MA 02702

Call Sign: WT1U
Leslie E Eckhart
6 Chester Ave
Assonet MA 02702

Call Sign: N1IFY
Adolf W Arnold
34 Forge Rd
Assonet MA 02702

Call Sign: N1RGA
Debra J Souza
82 Forge Rd
Assonet MA 02702

Call Sign: WY1D
Daniel C Souza
82 Forge Rd
Assonet MA
027021128

Call Sign: AA1AN
John J Demetrius
15 Highland Ridge Rd
Assonet MA 02702

Call Sign: WG1U
Kenneth D Campbell
Jr
58 Howland Rd
Assonet MA 02702

Call Sign: KB1TRY
Quinn E Gagnon

95 Howland Rd
Assonet MA 02702

Call Sign: KA1WBJ
Richard D Meetis
8 Jeffrey Ln
Assonet MA 02702

Call Sign: N1SMO
David B Walker
32 Ledgeview Dr
Assonet MA 02702

Call Sign: KB1HRU
John T Rumbut
6 Matawa Dr
Assonet MA 02702

Call Sign: W1NET
John T Rumbut
6 Matawa Dr
Assonet MA 02702

Call Sign: KA1BNX
Lisa M Pereira
86 N Main St
Assonet MA
027021017

Call Sign: K1CBK
Christopher B Kendall
63 Narrows Rd
Assonet MA
027021637

Call Sign: KB1IWU
Carl D Cooperrider
6 Rocky Hill Rd
Assonet MA 02702

Call Sign: KA1CH
Calvin K Ellinwood
2 School St
Assonet MA 02702

Call Sign: WA1JDF
Harold W Hague
8 Simmons St
Assonet MA 02702

Call Sign: WA1JSZ
Margaret T Hague
8 Simmons St
Assonet MA 02702

Call Sign: KB1TRX
Luiz A Fernandes
221 Slab Bridge Rd
Assonet MA 02702

Call Sign: N1IFS
Kenneth D Campbell
III
Assonet MA 02702

Call Sign: KA1GG
Pilgrim Amateur
Wireless Assn
Assonet MA 02702

Call Sign: N1GWC
Cynthia Campbell
Assonet MA 02702

Call Sign: WB1DVG
John E Grandfield
Assonet MA 02702

Call Sign: KB1UHB
Pedro Aguiar
Assonet MA 02702

Call Sign: KB1WGX
Kimberly A Campbell
Assonet MA 02702

Call Sign: N1KIM
Kimberly A Campbell
Assonet MA 02702

FCC Amateur Radio
Licenses in Athol

Call Sign: KB1UHM
Kelvin D Bidwell
108 Briggs Rd
Athol MA 01331

Call Sign: N1AUU
Allen E Hastings
2894 Chestnut Hill
Athol MA 01331

Call Sign: KB1DPX
Calvin R Ballou
2086 Chestnut Hill
Ave
Athol MA 01331

Call Sign: N1KHW
Donald V Johnson
186 Crescent St
Athol MA 01331

Call Sign: N1LXP
Frederick A Richards
296 Crescent St
Athol MA 01331

Call Sign: K1FDR
Frederick A Richards
296 Crescent St
Athol MA 01331

Call Sign: KG4UQA
Robert J Coleman
739 Daniel Shays Hwy
C-30
Athol MA 01331

Call Sign: K1QED
Robert J Coleman
739 Daniel Shays Hwy
C-30
Athol MA 01331

Call Sign: KB1ONW
Timothy A Landry
742 Daniel Shays Hwy
Unit 4E
Athol MA 01331

Call Sign: KA1SIH
George E Goveia
38 Euclid St
Athol MA 013313604

Call Sign: N1HAK
Marshall C Tatro
165 Euclid St
Athol MA 01331

Call Sign: N1KKY
Thomas L Pratt
204 Freedom St
Athol MA 01331

Call Sign: KA1YTR
Matthew R Teto
67 Gage Rd
Athol MA 01331

Call Sign: KD1KI
Kent A Hager
51 Goddard St
Athol MA 01331

Call Sign: KK1H
Kent A Hager
51 Goddard St
Athol MA 01331

Call Sign: WA1FXY
Donald F Allen
66 Goddard St
Athol MA 01331

Call Sign: N1RSY
John F Rosati
122 Goddard St
Athol MA 013311934

Call Sign: N1HYI
Julie A Mc Guire
68 Hampstead Pl
Athol MA 01331

Call Sign: W1FZY
Paul D Pralinsky
259 High St
Athol MA 01331

Call Sign: N1WVG
Ann M Emery
120 Highland Ave
Athol MA 01331

Call Sign: N1WVH
Bruce A Emery
120 Highland Ave
Athol MA 01331

Call Sign: N1RJX
Paul Newcombe
76 Kelton St
Athol MA 01331

Call Sign: N1UIY
Roger J Allen
53 Lake Ellis Rd
Athol MA 013313520

Call Sign: KD1TK
Thomas F Hayden
141 Lake Ellis Rd
Athol MA 01331

Call Sign: N1LUO
William B Curtis Iii
301 Lake Ellis Rd
Athol MA 01331

Call Sign: WA1PFL
Leon W La Bombarde
86 Lakeview Ave
Athol MA 01331

Call Sign: WB1HHY
Gilbert S Brown
111 Lee St
Athol MA 01331

Call Sign: KC1OM
Roy M Lheureux
634 Lenox St
Athol MA 01331

Call Sign: N1KKX
Michael A Richards
1944 Main St
Athol MA 01331

Call Sign: KA1SN
David J Paradise
416 Main St Apt 411
Athol MA 01331

Call Sign: W1BJB
Bernard J Bevis
93 Marble St
Athol MA 01331

Call Sign: W1WGA
Esmonde J Bushey
95 Marshall
Athol MA 01331

Call Sign: KB1FCB
George W Bliss
23 Morton Meadows
Athol MA 013312123

Call Sign: N1FZV
Edward E Jennings
877 Old Keene Rd
Athol MA 01331

Call Sign: N1HYJ
Dennis P Richards Mr
22 Orange St

Athol MA 01331

Call Sign: KA1XR
Wesley F Laford
646 Pequoig Ave
Athol MA 01331

Call Sign: N1EWI
Bruce E Fessenden
362 Pleasant St
Athol MA 01331

Call Sign: W1MPY
Warner G Ellinwood
758 Pleasant St
Athol MA 01331

Call Sign: AA1WW
Jeffrey L Cooper
742 Pleasant St
Athol MA 01331

Call Sign: N1ZYG
Mark S Kimmel
347 Ridge Rd
Athol MA 01331

Call Sign: W1LMK
Lynda M Graves
Kimmel
347 Ridge Rd
Athol MA 01331

Call Sign: KA1ZFB
Phillip J Cote
85 Roosevelt Ave
Athol MA 01331

Call Sign: N1KWB
Paul A Batutis Jr
300 School St
Athol MA 01331

Call Sign: N1JAL
Robert C Defenderfer
Iv
503 School St
Athol MA 01331

Call Sign: W1FRH
Francis R Hughes
126 Silver Lake St
Athol MA 01331

Call Sign: KB1GKZ
Mohawk Contest Club
22 South Athol Rd
Athol MA 013312722

Call Sign: N1SVP
Brian V Paul
95 South St
Athol MA 01331

Call Sign: N1LBL
Wayne M Phillips
7 Tremont St
Athol MA 01331

Call Sign: AA1EY
Roland A Matthews Jr
338 Vine St
Athol MA 013313147

Call Sign: WT1S
Roland A Matthews Jr
338 Vine St
Athol MA 013313147

Call Sign: AA1FN
Ralph P Lapinskas
14 Wachusett Ave
Athol MA 01331

Call Sign: WB1HIN
Randal B King
59 Wallingford Ave
Athol MA 01331

Call Sign: WA2IFB
Ernest J Muglia
139 Western Ave
Athol MA 01331

Call Sign: K1JG
John A Gawronsky
72 Wilson Ave
Athol MA 01331

Call Sign: KA1RKK
Lorne K Johnstone
Athol MA 01331

Call Sign: N1JVQ
Vincent I Kulisanski
Athol MA 01331

Call Sign: N1QXW

Raymond J Ferrari
Athol MA 01331

Call Sign: KR1T
George F Fiske Jr
Athol MA 01331

Call Sign: N1LSR
Louis R Sulewski Iii
Athol MA 01331

Call Sign: WX1Y
David A Fisher
Athol MA 01331

**FCC Amateur Radio
Licenses in Attleboro**

Call Sign: K1JVA
Kenneth J Hathaway
19 3rd St
Attleboro MA 02703

Call Sign: N1SEC
Scott P Bumpus
16 Angell St Apt 3
Attleboro MA 02703

Call Sign: N1CMN
Robert A Rogers
137 Augsburg Dr
Attleboro MA 02703

Call Sign: KB1UMB
Richard C Morris
37 Bambury Lane
Attleboro MA 02703

Call Sign: K1EZM
Richard C Morris
37 Bambury Lane
Attleboro MA 02703

Call Sign: W1RMB
Robert M Braza
34 Beverly Circle
Attleboro MA 02703

Call Sign: KA1TR
Robert P Mc Auliffe
21 Burt St
Attleboro MA 02703

Call Sign: KD1QR

Michael J Audette
10 Carpenter St - 22
Attleboro MA 02703

Call Sign: KB1CTN
Edmund Burke
45 Central Av
Attleboro MA 02703

Call Sign: KB1EBY
Gregory L Morse
4 Chartley Brook Ln
Attleboro MA
027035304

Call Sign: K1LXJ
Ronald W Souza
121 Claire Dr
Attleboro MA
027031134

Call Sign: N9ZYF
Daniel C Guest
1 Cliff St Apt 1
Attleboro MA 02703

Call Sign: KB1JLL
Robert E Phillips
3 Commonwealth Ave
Apt B4
Attleboro MA 02703

Call Sign: K1CVB
Robert E Phillips
3 Commonwealth Ave
Apt B4
Attleboro MA 02703

Call Sign: N1TVZ
Steven J Lapierre
1421 County St
Attleboro MA 02703

Call Sign: N1LEO
Steven J Lapierre
1421 County St
Attleboro MA 02703

Call Sign: KB5TBB
Clayton L Coleman
12 Dale Ave
Attleboro MA 02703

Call Sign: KB1MMW

Attleboro Fm Repeater
Society
12 Dale Ave
Attleboro MA 02703

Call Sign: N1JZP
Timothy S Da Silva
17 Davis Ave
Attleboro MA 02703

Call Sign: KB1NBZ
Michael C Cohen
96 Dexter St
Attleboro MA 02703

Call Sign: W1MCC
Michael C Cohen
96 Dexter St
Attleboro MA 02703

Call Sign: KD1OQ
James B Dorrance
10 Doral Lane
Attleboro MA 02703

Call Sign: KA1EZH
Harold K Reynolds Iii
2 Douglas Ave
Attleboro MA 02703

Call Sign: N1MAF
Lisa M Doherty
8 Elizabeth St
Attleboro MA 02703

Call Sign: NX1X
William G Winnett
85 Evergreen Rd
Attleboro MA 02703

Call Sign: N1GJV
Richard Crowley
12 Forest St
Attleboro MA 02703

Call Sign: KB1JWJ
James M O Connor
10 Fuller Ave Unit 8
Attleboro MA 02703

Call Sign: N1OIO
James M O Connor
10 Fuller Ave Unit 8
Attleboro MA 02703

Call Sign: KB1SSM
Kenneth A Mclean
45 Hall Ave
Attleboro MA 02703

Call Sign: AB1LN
Kenneth A Mclean
45 Hall Ave
Attleboro MA 02703

Call Sign: AE1KM
Kenneth A Mclean
45 Hall Ave
Attleboro MA 02703

Call Sign: N1AT
Kenneth A Mclean
45 Hall Ave
Attleboro MA 02703

Call Sign: KB1VYH
Kathleen E Mclean
45 Hall Ave
Attleboro MA 02703

Call Sign: KC2MJI
Jonathan E Nitschke
17 Handy St
Attleboro MA 02703

Call Sign: WA1VEL
Paul F Moore Sr
25 Hanisch Rd
Attleboro MA 02703

Call Sign: KD5TVI
Jerry G Sweeton Jr
39 Harding Ave Unit 2
Attleboro MA 02703

Call Sign: AA1XH
Charles L Welsch
39 Hazelwood Ave
Attleboro MA 02703

Call Sign: W1CLW
Charles L Welsch
39 Hazelwood Ave
Attleboro MA 02703

Call Sign: AA1HP
Robert D Tella
12 Hickory Rd

Attleboro MA 02703

Call Sign: WA1PQQ
Eugene F Avallon
91 Hickory Rd
Attleboro MA 02703

Call Sign: KA1PQ
Robert L Johnson Jr
73 Holden St
Attleboro MA 02703

Call Sign: K1WHV
Henry C Martin
19 Hutchinson Rd
Attleboro MA 02703

Call Sign: KA1ZFN
Mohsen Khalifa
491 Locust St
Attleboro MA 02703

Call Sign: N1ZMV
Brian P Murphy
152 Maple St
Attleboro MA 02703

Call Sign: N1OIO
James M O Connor
109 Maple St Apt E6
Attleboro MA 02703

Call Sign: WA1WFH
Joseph P Agius
48 Marlise Dr
Attleboro MA 02703

Call Sign: AA1VB
Joseph P Agius
48 Marlise Dr
Attleboro MA 02703

Call Sign: W1TW
Joseph P Agius
48 Marlise Drive
Attleboro MA 02703

Call Sign: WZ1E
Michael J Hinckley
87 Middle St
Attleboro MA 02703

Call Sign: KA1YZY
David Teixeira

725 N Main St
Attleboro MA 02703

Call Sign: KB1RQU
Roy S Belcher
6 Nancy Ave
Attleboro MA 02703

Call Sign: KB1SAJ
William R Doyle
531 Newport Ave
Attleboro MA 02703

Call Sign: KF4UXP
Christine M Bonaguide
9 Nick Drive
Attleboro MA 02703

Call Sign: WA1VUG
Gregory M Bonaguide
9 Nick Drive
Attleboro MA 02703

Call Sign: KB1GVH
Geoffrey D Chase
48 Nick Rock Rd
Attleboro MA 02703

Call Sign: N1RYC
Stephen A Howe
North Ave
Attleboro MA
027031322

Call Sign: AA1LP
Rudolph W Pierce
51 Oak Ridge Ave
Attleboro MA 02703

Call Sign: K1BKS
Norman A Witherell
169 Patterson St
Attleboro MA 02703

Call Sign: N1DZY
Steven D Bassett
12 Paulette Ln
Attleboro MA 02703

Call Sign: K1CEY
Warren E Forbes
59 Payson St
Attleboro MA 02703

Call Sign: K1BOG
Blais M Klucznik
254 Phillips
Attleboro MA 02703

Call Sign: KA1TME
Domenic A Maio
135 Phillips St
Attleboro MA 02703

Call Sign: KA1GEK
Karen A Klucznik
254 Phillips St
Attleboro MA 02703

Call Sign: N1FSB
Marie R Klucznik
254 Phillips St
Attleboro MA 02703

Call Sign: AA1CQ
Richard G La Civita
506 Pike Ave
Attleboro MA 02703

Call Sign: KB1GJO
Edward C Peters Jr
28 Pine St Apt 2b
Attleboro MA 02703

Call Sign: N1YKJ
Ronald A Megna
174 Pleasant St
Attleboro MA 02703

Call Sign: KB1NCW
Gary R Piette
4 Presidential Blvd
Attleboro MA 02703

Call Sign: KA1VYD
Keith J Witherell
150 Read St
Attleboro MA 02703

Call Sign: N1OQM
Janine R Sprague
999 Read St Apt 304
Attleboro MA 02703

Call Sign: KA1YJY
James E Wiley Sr
999 Read St Apt 310
Attleboro MA 02703

Call Sign: K1JKB
James K Brown
21 Revere Terr
Attleboro MA
027031068

Call Sign: KC1UN
Kenneth A St Don
28 Richie Rd
Attleboro MA 02703

Call Sign: KA1SMX
Adolphe J Peter
63 Robinson Ave
Attleboro MA 02703

Call Sign: N1NA
Charles P Michaud
145 Robinson Ave
Attleboro MA 02703

Call Sign: KA1OLS
Milton L Knox Jr
9 Rocky Terrace
Attleboro MA
027034523

Call Sign: KA1YUF
Michael S Mac Kenzie
S Main St
Attleboro MA 02703

Call Sign: KA1ZHC
Robert D Santos
S Main St
Attleboro MA 02703

Call Sign: N1KNZ
Cindy A Santos
S Main St
Attleboro MA 02703

Call Sign: N1QWL
Samuel M Knight
51 Sargent Cir
Attleboro MA 02703

Call Sign: N1IIO
Helen O Hathaway
6 Short St
Attleboro MA 02703

Call Sign: WJ1K

Charles R Hathaway
6 Short St
Attleboro MA 02703

Call Sign: N2LMR
Adolfo E Sanchez
92 Slater St
Attleboro MA 02703

Call Sign: KC1JJ
John H Frost
313 Slater St
Attleboro MA 02703

Call Sign: N1MLL
Mark R April
327 Slater St
Attleboro MA 02703

Call Sign: K1WTP
Richard L Naslund
41 Solomon St
Attleboro MA 02703

Call Sign: N1VHL
Alain C Joly
24 South Ave
Attleboro MA 02703

Call Sign: KA1RXJ
Scott R Hathaway
307 South Main St
Attleboro MA 02703

Call Sign: K1URW
Leon N Robinson
8 Starkey Ave
Attleboro MA 02703

Call Sign: KA1ONA
William S Hazeldine
320 Steere St
Attleboro MA
027035318

Call Sign: WB1CCT
Robert J Brewer
572 Thacher St
Attleboro MA 02703

Call Sign: N1JMK
James M Kern
616 Thacher St
Attleboro MA 02703

Call Sign: KB1VKD
James M Kern
616 Thacher St
Attleboro MA 02703

Call Sign: KB1DRL
Martin L Pyne
704 Thacher St
Attleboro MA 02703

Call Sign: KA1RZX
John J Fontneau
743 Thacher St
Attleboro MA 02703

Call Sign: KA1SAM
Neil J Hathaway
19 Third St
Attleboro MA 02703

Call Sign: K1SKY
Michael P La Fratta
318 Tiffany St
Attleboro MA 02703

Call Sign: W1SN
Stephen D Nimiroski
356 Tiffany St
Attleboro MA 02703

Call Sign: KB1UZP
Nathan Stovall
73 Tondreau Ave
Attleboro MA 02703

Call Sign: WA3OFR
Mark A Koehnke
61 Turnstone Dr
Attleboro MA 02703

Call Sign: KB1JRS
Luke R Parker
24 Wamsutta Rd
Attleboro MA 02703

Call Sign: N1AZK
Stephen J Donovan
1526 West St
Attleboro MA
027034446

Call Sign: WB1EMT

Foxboro Company
Amat Rad Club
98 Wheaton Dr
Attleboro MA 02703

Call Sign: KB1TBK
Dale J Rheaume
25 Wood St
Attleboro MA 02703

Call Sign: KA1YDB
Donald F Dean
Attleboro MA 02703

Call Sign: WB1CQB
Betty R Gariepy
Attleboro MA
027630208

FCC Amateur Radio Licenses in Attleboro Falls

Call Sign: K1OZS
Mauran C Snow
273 Commonwealth
Ave
Attleboro Falls MA
02763

Call Sign: KB1VWK
Michael S Castiglioni
31 Freeman St
Attleboro Falls MA
02763

Call Sign: N1RJE
Richard A Gunther
999 Read St Apt # 310
Attleborough MA
02703

FCC Amateur Radio Licenses in Auburn

Call Sign: KB1LYH
Paul N Poirier
35 Appleton Rd
Auburn MA 01501

Call Sign: AB1ES
Paul N Poirier
35 Appleton Rd
Auburn MA 01501

Call Sign: KB1MVI
Lori J Hyde
24 Arlington St
Auburn MA 01501

Call Sign: K1LJH
Lori J Hyde
24 Arlington St
Auburn MA 01501

Call Sign: KB1QAQ
John J Donatelli Jr
61 Boyce St
Auburn MA 01501

Call Sign: W1JDJ
John J Donatelli Jr
61 Boyce St
Auburn MA 01501

Call Sign: N1IIU
Paul G Roy
12 Breezy Bend
Auburn MA 01501

Call Sign: KB1ILR
Richard O Gould
8 Brook Rd
Auburn MA 01501

Call Sign: KB1IOP
Juanita B Gould
8 Brook Rd
Auburn MA
015012000

Call Sign: KB1JBK
Brendan P O Dowd
80 Bryn Mawr Ave
Auburn MA 01501

Call Sign: K1WUK
Robert W Condon
4 Carriage Dr
Auburn MA 01501

Call Sign: N1YPT
Charles H Wilkicki Jr
19 Cedar St
Auburn MA 01501

Call Sign: KB1JFM
Edward R Olson

95 Central St
Auburn MA 01501

Call Sign: KB1MPC
Joseph M Jacques
187 Central St
Auburn MA 01501

Call Sign: WE1B
Joseph M Jacques
187 Central St
Auburn MA 01501

Call Sign: N1NYA
John J Mehrtens
12 Colonial Rd
Auburn MA 01501

Call Sign: N1JWL
Jonathan W Lacob
3 Crowl Hill Rd
Auburn MA 01501

Call Sign: K1QHD
Gary H Gustafson
28 Curtis St
Auburn MA 01501

Call Sign: WB1GSO
Gerald Finkle
3 Cutting Ave
Auburn MA 01501

Call Sign: K1QJM
Achille A Levesque
25 Davis Rd
Auburn MA
015013101

Call Sign: N1IQB
Wayne F Grabowski
15 Grandview St
Auburn MA 01501

Call Sign: N1LSK
Louis M Perron
Hampton St
Auburn MA 01501

Call Sign: KB1JBJ
Philip A Maio
5 Hanna Dr
Auburn MA 01501

Call Sign: WB1GIX
Charles B La Croix
1 Laurel St
Auburn MA
015011506

Call Sign: KA1QOK
Glen A Cleeton
13 Magna Vista Drive
Auburn MA
015011215

Call Sign: N1OGE
Bertha M Bonardi
18 Marilyn Dr
Auburn MA 01501

Call Sign: N1PAW
Joseph E Bonardi
18 Marilyn Dr
Auburn MA 01501

Call Sign: N1ZRF
Eric L Cove
24 Marilyn Dr
Auburn MA 01501

Call Sign: N1VKH
Matthew J Norgren
26 Marion Ave
Auburn MA 01501

Call Sign: N1XPA
John L Mousseau
4 Meadow St
Auburn MA 01501

Call Sign: KB1IUP
Jeno M Renner
2 Olde Colony Rd
Auburn MA 01501

Call Sign: KA1KWR
Francis J Roach
194 Oxford St
Auburn MA 01501

Call Sign: N1RNG
Michele M Adelinia
483 Oxford St N
Auburn MA 01501

Call Sign: KA1OXG
Glenn M Hanna

8 Packard Ave
Auburn MA 01501

Call Sign: W1VBF
Glenn M Hanna
8 Packard Ave
Auburn MA 01501

Call Sign: KB1APK
Cindy R Humphrey
2 Pakachoag St
Auburn MA 01501

Call Sign: N1IHS
John S Humphrey
2 Pakachoag St
Auburn MA 01501

Call Sign: KA1NLZ
Philip J Parker
384 Pakachoag St
Auburn MA 01501

Call Sign: KB1MPB
Paul H Ohman
5 Pakachoag Xing
Auburn MA 01501

Call Sign: WA1WOT
Russell A Johnson
1 Park St
Auburn MA 01501

Call Sign: KA1OGE
Joseph E Shenette Jr
4 Prospect Parkway
Auburn MA 01501

Call Sign: W1GGN
Stephen R Alpert
11 Ridgewood Dr
Auburn MA
015012316

Call Sign: KB1RVY
Michael E Fant
522 Rochdale St
Auburn MA 01501

Call Sign: KA1TZY
Bruce E Fant
522 Rochdale St
Auburn MA 01501

Call Sign: KB1UBQ
Randall L Davenport
41 Rockaway Rd
Auburn MA 01501

Call Sign: N1KVW
Elizabeth A Mahan
4 Rockland Rd
Auburn MA 01501

Call Sign: WG1K
Edmund F Dowd
81 Rockland Rd
Auburn MA 01501

Call Sign: N1MQF
Morris L Shelton
11 Shore Dr
Auburn MA 01501

Call Sign: K1WPO
Joseph E Shenette
129 South St
Auburn MA 01501

Call Sign: KA1OER
Portia J Shenette
129 South St
Auburn MA 01501

Call Sign: N1JET
Guy R Elliott Jr
3 Thayer Ave
Auburn MA 01501

Call Sign: N1GMI
Audwin J Benton
41125 Tuck Farm Rd
Auburn MA 01501

Call Sign: KB1HAX
Stanley J Slonski
Victoria Dr
Auburn MA 01501

Call Sign: K1UOT
Jerry H Laplante
1 Walsh Ave
Auburn MA
015012447

Call Sign: N1GMA
George M Jacobs
35 Walsh Ave

Auburn MA 01501

Call Sign: KB1QHO
Stephen Fant
40 Walsh Ave
Auburn MA 01501

FCC Amateur Radio Licenses in Auburndale

Call Sign: K1VKM
Charles Garabedian
95 Albert Rd
Auburndale MA 02166

Call Sign: WA1JSN
Richard L Freudberg
160 Aspen Ave
Auburndale MA
024663018

Call Sign: WA1IFF
Howard E Rummel Jr
11 Central Terrace
Auburndale MA 02166

Call Sign: NK1L
Frederick W Beihold
59 Charles St
Auburndale MA 02466

Call Sign: AA1FW
James W Peghiny
2202 Commonwealth
Ave
Auburndale MA 02166

Call Sign: KB1HBL
Jonathan M Soyt
2226 Commonwealth
Ave
Auburndale MA 02466

Call Sign: KA1BWN
Robert A Morris
40 Groveland St
Auburndale MA 02466

Call Sign: WA1LMJ
Mark E Becker
199 Lexington St
Auburndale MA
024661344

Call Sign: KB1SMJ
Matthew R Willis
155 Lexington St Apt
26
Auburndale MA 02466

Call Sign: WB9LNE
Kevin J Amundsen
18 Maple Ter
Auburndale MA 02166

Call Sign: W1LDY
Truman S Light
Seminary Ave Apt 239
Auburndale MA 02466

Call Sign: W1ERZ
Francis J Whalen Jr
17 Tudor Ter
Auburndale MA
021661509

Call Sign: KB1SXT
Sebastian J Courtney
68 West Pine St
Auburndale MA 02466

Call Sign: N1ERE
Joel L Lazewatsky
32 Woodland Rd
Auburndale MA 02466

Call Sign: KB1FPZ
Daniel A Lazewatsky
32 Woodland Rd
Auburndale MA 02466

Call Sign: KB1NXA
Daniel A Lazewatsky
32 Woodland Rd
Auburndale MA 02466

Call Sign: N1LAZ
Daniel A Lazewatsky
32 Woodland Rd
Auburndale MA 02466

Call Sign: N1AR
Andrea S Wasik
Auburndale MA 02466

FCC Amateur Radio Licenses in Avon

Call Sign: W1OQV
Fred W Wiley
14 Ballum Rd
Avon MA 02322

Call Sign: N1TWR
Robert S Hackett
300 Central St
Avon MA 02322

Call Sign: W1ZOC
Arthur C Toneatti Jr
252 East Spring St
Avon MA 02322

Call Sign: N1KHF
Robert H Mc Namara
35 Feeley St
Avon MA 02322

Call Sign: KA1ZEJ
Edward J Bevens
44 Malley Ave
Avon MA 02322

Call Sign: N1QHL
Frank L Tedesco Jr
15 Oliver St
Avon MA 02322

Call Sign: WA1JND
Ronald P Keswick Sr
504 South St
Avon MA 02322

Call Sign: N1LQK
David E Kaplan
Avon MA 023220674

FCC Amateur Radio Licenses in Ayer

Call Sign: K1FNA
Norman E Lariviere
10 Amandrey Way
Ayer MA 01432

Call Sign: KA1JIV
Denis R Parent
Antietam
Ayer MA 01433

Call Sign: N1JRI

John J Cadigan
203 Autumn Ridge Dr
Ayer MA 01432

Call Sign: KB1FTB
John J Medeiros
12 Brook St
Ayer MA 01432

Call Sign: KB1HDO
John A Griswold
34 Cambridge St
Ayer MA 01432

Call Sign: KK1X
John A Griswold
34 Cambridge St
Ayer MA 01432

Call Sign: WA2JTH
Philip A Zimmermann
36 Cambridge St
Ayer MA 01432

Call Sign: N1PZ
Philip A Zimmermann
36 Cambridge St
Ayer MA 01432

Call Sign: KA1RYE
Edward C Bergan
19 Douglas Dr
Ayer MA 014321002

Call Sign: KB1WI
Charles S Fisk
96 E Main St #6
Ayer MA 01432

Call Sign: KD1PI
James D Ford
26 Fletcher St
Ayer MA 01432

Call Sign: N1QOW
Mac Lean Woodbury
8 Forest St
Ayer MA 01432

Call Sign: W1DEA
Hector L Creamer Iii
18 Gardner Ln
Ayer MA 014321059

Call Sign: N1RPK
Jonathan Rose
31 Groton Harvard Rd
Ayer MA 01423

Call Sign: N1LBK
Norman R Cadorette
25 Groton School Rd 5
Ayer MA 01432

Call Sign: WA1WEB
Howard L Marshall
45 Groton School Rd
Rt 111
Ayer MA 01432

Call Sign: NR1G
Roland L Guilmet
10 High St Apt 1
Ayer MA 01432

Call Sign: KB1MTS
Michael J Loebl
55 Littleton Rd 19 B
Ayer MA 01432

Call Sign: KA1YBU
Dale Harmon
55 Littleton Rd Apt
21c
Ayer MA 01432

Call Sign: KB1OPT
Stephanie A Loebl
55 Littleton Rd Unit
19b
Ayer MA 01432

Call Sign: KB1SZE
Faisal J Mohammed
55 Littleton Rd Unit
19d
Ayer MA 01432

Call Sign: K1OGF
Erik J Thoresen
10 Mark St
Ayer MA 01432

Call Sign: N1OGS
Douglas P Ferguson
15 Mark St
Ayer MA 01432

Call Sign: KB1OGC
Luke A Perkins
7 Patricia Dr
Ayer MA 01432

Call Sign: WA1SMI
Robert S Isaacs
42 Pine Ridge Dr
Ayer MA 014321417

Call Sign: N1IXO
David M Podgorni
55 Pleasant St
Ayer MA 01432

Call Sign: N1FUI
Richard D Dusek
109 Pleasant St
Ayer MA 01432

Call Sign: WA1QZT
Jesse E Dow
18 Pond St
Ayer MA 01432

Call Sign: KO4YI
James G Watt
16 Pond St #2
Ayer MA 01432

Call Sign: KD4CHO
Carolyn Watt
16 Pond St #2
Ayer MA 01432

Call Sign: KB1GID
Ronald A Wood
49 Sandy Pond Rd
Ayer MA 014321420

Call Sign: N1OZN
Phillip W Shookman
8 Standish Ave
Ayer MA 01432

Call Sign: AJ6J
William L Principe Jr
Sunflower Ct
Ayer MA 014325503

Call Sign: K1NS
William L Principe Jr
Sunflower Ct
Ayer MA 014325503

Call Sign: N1DOK
Glenn C Glatfelter
3 Vernon St
Ayer MA 01432

Call Sign: KA1ZKV
Forrest J Macfarlane
41 W Main
Ayer MA 01433

Call Sign: N1MWF
Marvin L Tolf
6 Wachusett Ave East
Ayer MA 01432

Call Sign: KB1NNF
Andrew Paine
37 Washington St
Ayer MA 01432

Call Sign: KB1CZZ
Douglas A Winchester
97 Willard St
Ayer MA 01432

Call Sign: KB1FJZ
Johnpatrick K Marr
36 Wright Rd
Ayer MA 01432

Call Sign: KA1YID
Robert L Maxwell Jr
Ayer MA 01432

FCC Amateur Radio Licenses in Baldwinville

Call Sign: KB1FPK
Walter R Gallant Jr
Circle St
Baldwinville MA
01436

Call Sign: N1FDR
Thomas A Hurd
144 Main St
Baldwinville MA
01436

Call Sign: N1JIA
Kenneth D Baker
Main St

Baldwinville MA
014361107

Call Sign: KE6PRG
Susan F Frugoli
68 Norcross Hill
Baldwinville MA
01436

Call Sign: N1EWJ
Frank J Gorzkowicz Jr
53 Plesant St
Baldwinville MA
01436

Call Sign: N1KRX
Gregory W Abare
133 State Rd
Baldwinville MA
01436

Call Sign: W1KRX
Gregory W Abare
133 State Rd
Baldwinville MA
01436

Call Sign: N1JVR
Jayne S Thompson
30 Winchester St
Baldwinville MA
01436

Call Sign: KB1ETT
Joanne L Launier
78 Winchester St
Baldwinville MA
01436

Call Sign: KB1EZN
Wayne A Launier
78 Winchester St
Baldwinville MA
01436

Call Sign: N1LDP
Mary I Gorzkowicz
Baldwinville MA
01436

Call Sign: W1KMM
Kenneth C Mc Milleon
65 Forest St

Balldinville MA
021080143

FCC Amateur Radio Licenses in Barnstable

Call Sign: WA1JXS
William P Swift
46 Bow Ln
Barnstable MA 02630

Call Sign: N1MSV
Gareth P Crispell
225 Carriage Lane
Barnstable MA
026301506

Call Sign: WB1CMB
Edmund J Santos
11 George St
Barnstable MA 02630

Call Sign: KB1SOH
Ethan M Mcpherson
27 Jb Drive
Barnstable MA 02648

Call Sign: KB6QCV
Susan Angus
42 Locust Ln
Barnstable MA 02630

Call Sign: W1GM
Christopher H Moore
94 Marble Rd
Barnstable MA 02630

Call Sign: N1CDB
Bobbie Jo Cadman
477 Old Jail Ln
Barnstable MA 02630

Call Sign: WA1RC
David P Breski
120 Pine Lane
Barnstable MA 02630

Call Sign: W1GLE
Steven E Berglund
Barnstable MA 02630

Call Sign: KB1JUZ
Calvert F Eck

Barnstable MA 02630

FCC Amateur Radio Licenses in Barre

Call Sign: K1GDM
Christopher A Bjurling
120 Britton Rd
Barre MA 01005

Call Sign: K1PKA
Phyllis K Allen
115 Broad St
Barre MA 01005

Call Sign: K1YS
Robert M Doherty
74 Common St
Barre MA 01005

Call Sign: AB2CE
Lance B Smith
Dana Rd
Barre MA 01005

Call Sign: AA1FP
Gerald E Perry
35 Fellows Rd
Barre MA 01005

Call Sign: AE1B
John F Dould
41 Gauthier Rd
Barre MA 010059081

Call Sign: K1KMD
Kathleen M Dould
41 Gauthier Rd
Barre MA 010059081

Call Sign: N1WW
Mohawk Amateur
Radio Club Inc
41 Gauthier Rd
Barre MA 010059081

Call Sign: WW1DX
Mohawk Contest Club
41 Gauthier Rd
Barre MA 010059081

Call Sign: KB1RIG
Anthony P Curci
104 Glazier Rd

Barre MA 01005

Call Sign: KB1VGY
Michael P Laroche
65 High St N
Barre MA 01005

Call Sign: ND1W
Michael P Laroche
65 High St N
Barre MA 01005

Call Sign: N1XYW
Ward M Holloway Jr
57 Jackson Lane
Barre MA 01005

Call Sign: W1MWW
Paul L Bergquist
50 Lane Rd
Barre MA 01005

Call Sign: KB1KMN
John J Bielawski
115 Marsh Rd
Barre MA 01005

Call Sign: AB1EK
John J Bielawski
115 Marsh Rd
Barre MA 01005

Call Sign: KV1Z
John J Bielawski
115 Marsh Rd
Barre MA 01005

Call Sign: NI1T
Gary P Pearson
320 Oakham Rd
Barre MA 01005

Call Sign: KD4FOV
William W Rogers
559 Old Dana Rd
Barre MA 01005

Call Sign: KA1WKQ
Bryan C Bordeaux
Old Dana Rd
Barre MA 01005

Call Sign: K1NXM
Donald L Rich

33 Peach St
Barre MA 01005

Call Sign: K1YUK
David R Cutting
1090 Pleasant St
Barre MA 010059311

Call Sign: KB1RIF
Vernon A Chester Iii
18 School St No
Barre MA 01005

Call Sign: N1WVE
Charles E Hamilton Jr
93 South St
Barre MA 010050761

Call Sign: KB1TRM
James E Welsh V
451 Summer St
Barre MA 01005

Call Sign: K1DPB
Eugene C Brown Jr
899 West St
Barre MA 010050071

Call Sign: N1YWS
Brendan J Finn
511 Worcester Rd
Barre MA 01005

Call Sign: KB1QZC
Stanley E Andriski
669 Worcester Rd
Barre MA 01005

Call Sign: WA1YHW
Arthur R Brooks
973 Worcester Rd
Barre MA 01005

Call Sign: N1LQD
Arnold L Jackson
Barre MA 01005

Call Sign: W1QXE
Robert R Hunter Jr
Barre MA 01005

Call Sign: K1MGA
Mark G Allen
Barre MA 01005

FCC Amateur Radio Licenses in Barre Plains

Call Sign: K1DKX
Bernard Skrzypczak
20 Adams St
Barre Plains MA 01005

FCC Amateur Radio Licenses in Bass River

Call Sign: KB1GTG
Jorge J Colina
13 Mackenzie Rd
Bass River MA 02664

Call Sign: N1LVW
John A Hastings
31 Old Main St
Bass River MA 02664

FCC Amateur Radio Licenses in Becket Chester

Call Sign: KD1YJ
Ellen D Hoppe
61 Will Scarlet Drive
Becket Chester MA 01011

FCC Amateur Radio Licenses in Becket

Call Sign: KB1ADG
George A Crochiere
504 Brooker Hill Rd
Becket MA 01223

Call Sign: N1NKV
Morgan J Cohen
Camp Greylock
Becket MA 01223

Call Sign: KC5LPQ
Keith L Herzig
1134 Chester Rd
Becket MA 01223

Call Sign: KC1ZT
John E Thier
148 High St
Becket MA 01223

Call Sign: AA1IZ
Steven Rosenthal
84 Mystic Isle Way
Becket MA 01223

Call Sign: KB1TUC
Ruth Rosenthal
84 Mystic Isle Way
Becket MA 01223

Call Sign: K1DGA
Donald G Graves Sr
Pittsfield Rd
Becket MA 01223

Call Sign: KY1T
Michael S Lavery
331 Surriner Rd
Becket MA 01223

Call Sign: KB1NPB
David N Devane
313 Winter Dr
Becket MA 01223

Call Sign: KE2FE
Robert L Weinstein
Becket MA 01223

FCC Amateur Radio Licenses in Bedford

Call Sign: AA1UC
Byron T Burns
3 Alder Way
Bedford MA 01730

Call Sign: WA1PTZ
John Rheinstein
11 Andover Court
Bedford MA 01730

Call Sign: N1VXS
Howard D Cohen
5 Arbella Rd
Bedford MA 017301094

Call Sign: N1FPA

Phillip G Ahern
24 B Roberts Dr
Bedford MA 01730

Call Sign: KB1LSG
Kurt Rauschenbach
36 Battle Flag Rd
Bedford MA 01730

Call Sign: KB1ILF
Paul H P Christen
33 Battle Flagg Rd
Bedford MA 01730

Call Sign: W1CD
Robert E Browne
4 Birchwood Rd
Bedford MA 01730

Call Sign: KB1CKA
Alan L Cohn
17 Birchwood Rd
Bedford MA 01730

Call Sign: KB1WSP
Robert A Prescott Jr
1 Bridge St
Bedford MA 01730

Call Sign: KB1FXF
Katherine Durham
43 Brooksbie Rd
Bedford MA 01730

Call Sign: N1QVT
Richard A Cuti
28 Buehler Rd
Bedford MA 01730

Call Sign: KB1ITK
Katherine A Cuti
28 Buehler Rd
Bedford MA 01730

Call Sign: KB1ITL
Alexander R Cuti
28 Buehler Rd
Bedford MA 01730

Call Sign: N1HY
Richard A Cuti
28 Buehler Rd
Bedford MA 01730

Call Sign: W1ON
Mitre Corp - 202 Mitre
Bedford Amateur
Radio Club
Burlington Rd
Bedford MA 01730

Call Sign: KB1KXR
Eric M Renda Jr
202 Burlington Rd
E090
Bedford MA 01730

Call Sign: K1BAL
Cheryl A Balian
202 Burlington Rd S-
228
Bedford MA
017301420

Call Sign: KB1OCN
A Richard Leschack
8 Carlisle Rd
Bedford MA 01730

Call Sign: KB1OVI
Marta Portoles
201 Carlisle Rd
Bedford MA 01730

Call Sign: KB1OVP
Mark R Morwood
201 Carlisle Rd
Bedford MA 01730

Call Sign: W1LPG
Brendan J Welch
6 Cedar Ridge Ter
Bedford MA 01730

Call Sign: KB1ERJ
Vincent J Welch
6 Cedar Ridge Ter
Bedford MA 01730

Call Sign: KB1FCG
Francis Welch
6 Cedar Ridge Ter
Bedford MA 01730

Call Sign: KC0IIC
Christopher J Welch
6 Cedar Ridge Terrace
Bedford MA 01730

Call Sign: N1ILF
Robert D Logcher
12 Chestnut Ln
Bedford MA
017301052

Call Sign: KB1CPF
Colin Richardson
Concord Rd
Bed Ford MA 01730

Call Sign: KB1BDX
Christine M Campbell
267 Concord Rd
Bedford MA 01730

Call Sign: K1PJW
Ludger A Lucas
332 Concord Rd
Bedford MA 01730

Call Sign: N1CSL
Charles H Mazel
34 Dunelm Rd
Bedford MA 01730

Call Sign: AD1P
Daniel P Perez
11 Elmbrook Circle
Bedford MA
017301808

Call Sign: KB1FZ
Frank P Morrison
75 Essex Ct
Bedford MA 01730

Call Sign: KB1TEL
James H Cullen
5 Evans Ave
Bedford MA 01730

Call Sign: KB1JLE
James J Mosca
22 Evans Ave
Bedford MA 01730

Call Sign: KB1RG
Howard Sumner
7 Flintlock Dr
Bedford MA 01730

Call Sign: W1LZL

Anthony M Bille
6 Foster Rd
Bedford MA 01730

Call Sign: KB1KEO
Joseph A Holtgrefe
6 Foster Rd
Bedford MA 01730

Call Sign: W1LZL
Joseph A Holtgrefe
6 Foster Rd
Bedford MA 01730

Call Sign: K1SPE
Frederick W Klatt
30 Fox Run Rd
Bedford MA 01730

Call Sign: KA1PQN
Charles R Mahar Jr
1 Genetti Cir
Bedford MA 01730

Call Sign: W1SKT
Charles R Mahar Jr
1 Genetti Cir
Bedford MA 01730

Call Sign: WA1MQE
Thomas C Stockdale
5 Glenridge Dr
Bedford MA 01730

Call Sign: N1JWE
Beth E Bennett
42 Glenridge Dr
Bedford MA 01730

Call Sign: N1RTE
Megan O Bennett
42 Glenridge Dr
Bedford MA 01730

Call Sign: WN1K
Gang Zhang
25 Glenridge Drive
Bedford MA 01730

Call Sign: W1GBT
Robert R Pugh
7 Gould Rd
Bedford MA 01730

Call Sign: KC1OP
Stephen F Fusi
17 Gould Rd
Bedford MA
017301250

Call Sign: WA1MXO
James N O Boyle Jr
101 Great Rd #153
Bedford MA
017302715

Call Sign: N1WYN
Gregg Smith
18 Hemlock Lane
Bedford MA
017301327

Call Sign: K1TUB
Anthony L Baker
11 Hemlock Ln
Bedford MA 01730

Call Sign: W1GE
Harold R Ward
23 Hilltop Dr
Bedford MA 01730

Call Sign: KG1I
Gerald R Larocque
27 Hume Rd
Bedford MA 01730

Call Sign: N1XAM
Richard E Dolbec
5 Independence Rd
Bedford MA 01734

Call Sign: N1GJS
Stephen A Jamison
22 Independence Rd
Bedford MA 01730

Call Sign: KC1SJ
Stephen A Jamison
22 Independence Rd
Bedford MA 01730

Call Sign: KC1BG
Ronald M Cordes
3 Jeffrey Cir
Bedford MA 01730

Call Sign: K1CCL

Chester L Smith
2 Jonathan Lane
Bedford MA
017301848

Call Sign: N1PJD
Andrew J Brault
41 Liberty Ln
Bedford MA 01731

Call Sign: KB1WVQ
Gisela Kanne
Liberty Rd
Bedford MA 01730

Call Sign: N1BVN
Leo M Kenen
44 Loomis St
Bedford MA 01730

Call Sign: W1HEF
George F Dalrymple
3 Mae Rd
Bedford MA 01730

Call Sign: W1ULH
William E Gates
30 Marion Rd
Bedford MA 01730

Call Sign: W1QXX
John C Wilson Jr
28 Meadow Brook Rd
Bedford MA 01730

Call Sign: KA1JOE
Robert H Kress
8 Neillian St
Bedford MA 01730

Call Sign: WB2QJE
Douglas B Paul
6 Neillian Way
Bedford MA 01730

Call Sign: KD4AAN
Stephen P Brackett
56 Neillian Way
Bedford MA 01730

Call Sign: KD1GH
David W Dextradeur
63 Neillian Way
Bedford MA 01730

Call Sign: KB1YP
John A C Kleber Jr
110 North Rd
Bedford MA 01730

Call Sign: KD1DH
Allan Chertok
359 North Rd
Bedford MA
017301072

Call Sign: KA1RCV
John Paul Braud
463 North Rd
Bedford MA 01730

Call Sign: W1EMH
Thomas R Hirst
23 Notre Dame Rd
Bedford MA 01730

Call Sign: N1AYW
Richard A Gardner
49 Notre Dame Rd
Bedford MA 01730

Call Sign: N1ACA
Jose H Silva
50 Notre Dame Rd
Bedford MA
017302034

Call Sign: N1AQQ
Lucy W Silva
50 Notre Dame Rd
Bedford MA 01730

Call Sign: KD1TI
John W Gerdes
21 Page Rd
Bedford MA 01730

Call Sign: WA1FBP
Donald A Grassi
25 Page Rd
Bedford MA 01730

Call Sign: K1DZR
Joseph P Serra Jr
103 Page Rd
Bedford MA 01730

Call Sign: WB1HKU

Carroll R Bryan Iii
108 Page Rd
Bedford MA 01730

Call Sign: K1BK
Daniel L Smythe Jr
28 Pickman Dr
Bedford MA
017301005

Call Sign: W1JLR
Arthur W Barnes
13 Pine Hill Rd
Bedford MA 01730

Call Sign: N1HYE
Leon F Fairbanks
21 Putnam Rd
Bedford MA 01730

Call Sign: W1VAL
Colin M Valentine
26 Putnam Rd
Bedford MA 01730

Call Sign: KB1UKV
Albert R Vasso
12 Reed Ln
Bedford MA 01730

Call Sign: KB1UTP
Jay L Taft
10 Reeves Rd
Bedford MA 01730

Call Sign: N1GIM
Linden B Mercer
21 Roberts Dr
Bedford MA 01730

Call Sign: KA1VMQ
Russell D Hulbert
5 Robinson Dr
Bedford MA 01730

Call Sign: KB1GUE
Glenn E Graf
32 Selfridge Rd
Bedford MA 01730

Call Sign: W0UQ
Lee R Walus
37 Shawsheen Rd

Bedford MA
017301914

Call Sign: KB1HWS
Robert E Sulouff Jr
135 Shawsheen Rd
Bedford MA 01730

Call Sign: N1BHK
Daniel E Silverman
336 South Rd
Bedford MA 01730

Call Sign: KB1OVD
Robert L Batt
338 South Rd
Bedford MA 01730

Call Sign: KB1LOW
Steven J Morrow
548 Springs Rd
Bedford MA 01730

Call Sign: N1LOW
Steven J Morrow
548 Springs Rd
Bedford MA 01730

Call Sign: W1TRS
Allen D Ballentine
Springs Rd
Bedford MA 01730

Call Sign: KB1WIW
Charles J Reinhardt
35 Sunset Rd
Bedford MA 01730

Call Sign: N1JLD
Benjamin Bennett
10 Sweetwater Ave
Bedford MA 01730

Call Sign: KD1CO
John Bennett
10 Sweetwater Ave
Bedford MA 01730

Call Sign: K1VK
Paul W Pellegrini
22 Temple Terr
Bedford MA 01730

Call Sign: WS1H

Ronald N Morris
5301 Thompson Farm
Bedford MA 01730

Call Sign: WA1LBO
Robert L Collara
16 Walsh Rd
Bedford MA 01730

Call Sign: N3IRY
Roy M Kring
26 Washington St
Bedford MA
017302419

Call Sign: KD5QFP
Randy M Kring
26 Washington St
Bedford MA 01730

Call Sign: KD5QFQ
Ryan M Kring
26 Washington St
Bedford MA
017302419

Call Sign: K1TW
Thomas D Walsh
9 Wildwood Dr
Bedford MA 01730

Call Sign: W1GSG
William A Edwards
11 Wildwood Dr
Bedford MA 01730

Call Sign: N1NHE
Clarence Kenon
22 Wildwood Dr
Bedford MA 01730

Call Sign: W4BGV
Roger N Wallace
2 Willard Cir
Bedford MA 01730

Call Sign: KC1US
Bruce R Pigott
Bedford MA
017300004

Call Sign: N2OAU
Laurel D Riek
Bedford MA 01730

Call Sign: KB1KCG
Matthew W Bemis
Bedford MA
017300081

Call Sign: KB1MPZ
David H Comeau
Bedford MA 01730

FCC Amateur Radio Licenses in Belcherton

Call Sign: KB1NLM
Robert J Vanzandt Jr
148 S Washington St
Belcherton MA 01007

Call Sign: KB1AXW
Paul A Szczepanek
Belchertown MA
01007

Call Sign: KA3MGF
Eric W Bright
6a Westwood Drive
Belchertown MA
01007

Call Sign: NC1J
Philip M Langlois
45 Allen Rd
Belchertown MA
010079549

Call Sign: N1NMT
Anthony J Papirio Jr
211 Amherst Rd
Belchertown MA
01007

Call Sign: N1SIF
Francis F Leaf Iii
5 Azalea Way
Belchertown MA
01007

Call Sign: N1WGY
Diane L Leaf
5 Azalea Way
Belchertown MA
01007

Call Sign: N1HYD
Paul W Fenn
636 Bay Rd
Belchertown MA
01007

Call Sign: N1NGP
Laura Marks
646 Bay Rd
Belchertown MA
01007

Call Sign: KA1GVC
Eleanore E Gray
Box 924
Belchertown MA
01007

Call Sign: WA1DVU
Rodney W Gray
Box 924
Belchertown MA
01007

Call Sign: KA1TCZ
Robert L Mook Jr
52 Chadbourne St
Belchertown MA
01007

Call Sign: W1CSR
Alvah O Ericksberg
281 Chauncey Walker
St Lot 242
Belchertown MA
010079142

Call Sign: WB1DGP
James A Taylor
281 Chauncey Walker
St Lot5
Belchertown MA
010079250

Call Sign: KA1BCI
William E Ashby
281 Chauncy Walker
St Lot 535
Belchertown MA
01007

Call Sign: N1GUJ
Peter C Ferguson
19 Cheryl Circle

Belchertown MA
010079764

Call Sign: N1AAE
Alfred H Burns
13 Clear Brook Dr
Belchertown MA
01007

Call Sign: N1QCL
Ronald R Beaver
38 Cordner Rd
Belchertown MA
01007

Call Sign: KA1EBU
Gary F Vanasse
40 Daniel Shays
Highway
Belchertown MA
01007

Call Sign: KD1KW
John R Besse Jr
117 Daniel Shays Hwy
Belchertown MA
01007

Call Sign: N1NB
Louis P Zimmermann
490 Daniel Shays Hwy
Belchertown MA
01007

Call Sign: K1ORB
Florian B Czupkiewicz
59 Daniel Sq
Belchertown MA
01007

Call Sign: KB1LFF
Matthew D Allen
32 Depot St
Belchertown MA
010071251

Call Sign: N1UCV
Kenneth J Riley
41 Doe Hollow
Belchertown MA
010079469

Call Sign: KZ1U
John E Riley

41 Doe Hollow Rd
Belchertown MA
01007

Call Sign: KB1EFT
Tracey L Thompson
445 East St
Belchertown MA
01007

Call Sign: N1UZG
Charles E Bosworth Iii
28 Federal St
Belchertown MA
01007

Call Sign: WI1N
Charles F Tolpa
468 Federal St
Belchertown MA
01007

Call Sign: WB1FXI
George R Atkins
691 Federal St
Belchertown MA
01007

Call Sign: KB1MYA
John L St Onge
18 Greenwich Hill
Belchertown MA
010079366

Call Sign: WB1GLY
Frank J Walczak Jr
49 Hamilton St
Belchertown MA
01007

Call Sign: K8DJZ
Tilo R Schiffer
9 Heritage Dr
Belchertown MA
01007

Call Sign: N1RKY
Earl N Shepard
18 Ledgewood Dr
Belchertown MA
01007

Call Sign: N1DZH
David A Duquette

189 Michael Sears Rd
Belchertown MA
01007

Call Sign: N1YVH
James J Aliengena
451 Michael Sears Rd
Belchertown MA
01007

Call Sign: N1JFN
Denise M Cook
120 N Main St
Belchertown MA
01007

Call Sign: KB1JCI
Jeremy M Scott
121 N Main St Apt C2
Belchertown MA
01007

Call Sign: KA1CLZ
Debra J Smith
53 N Washington St
Belchertown MA
01007

Call Sign: N1AAX
Lawrence A Smith
53 N Washington St
Belchertown MA
01007

Call Sign: N1YRF
Matthew D Bein
257 N Washington St
Apt 5
Belchertown MA
01007

Call Sign: K1IQ
Paul J Lambert
73 Old Sawmill Rd
Belchertown MA
01007

Call Sign: N1VRK
Brian E Sklarski
418 Old Springfield Rd
Belchertown MA
01007

Call Sign: W1FAB

David E Cote
15 Pine St
Belchertown MA
01007

Call Sign: KB1CWT
David J Barnett Iii
34 Raymond Dr
Belchertown MA
01007

Call Sign: KA1ZW
V Kurian Thomas
83 Rockrimmon Rd
Belchertown MA
01007

Call Sign: N1HBZ
Benjamin F Perkins Iii
176 Rockrimmon St
Belchertown MA
01007

Call Sign: WA1JAE
John F Bachand Sr
296 S Liberty St
Belchertown MA
01007

Call Sign: KA1CDE
Patrick C Lees
151 Shea Ave
Belchertown MA
01007

Call Sign: KA1OWL
Christopher P Lees
151 Shea Ave
Belchertown MA
01007

Call Sign: N1YAZ
James W Sinclair
324 Springfield Rd
Belchertown MA
01007

Call Sign: KA1RJB
Edmond M Gingras
250 State St
Belchertown MA
01007

Call Sign: N1RWB

Richard A Plant
182 Warner Rd
Belchertown MA
01007

Call Sign: K1DFC
Philip J Carpenter
4 Westwood Dr
Belchertown MA
01007

Call Sign: W1EVJ
Schley A Warren Jr
Belchertown MA
01007

Call Sign: KB1UVG
Michele P Diamond
Belchertown MA
01007

Call Sign: W2BRY
Michele P Diamond
Belchertown MA
01007

Call Sign: KB1WXX
Alan K Perry Jr
Belchertown MA
01007

**FCC Amateur Radio
Licenses in
Bellingham**

Call Sign: KB1FIX
Roger E Dooley
17 Annmarie Dr
Bellingham MA 02019

Call Sign: N1TII
James P Dailey Jr
65 Blackstone St
Bellingham MA 02019

Call Sign: KB1EHW
Blackstone Valley Vhf
Society
72 Box Pond Dr
Bellingham MA 02019

Call Sign: N1RBY
Henry V Drummond
Iii

72 Box Pond Dr
Bellingham MA 02019

Call Sign: N1UYM
Christopher Walker
72 Box Pond Dr
Bellingham MA 02019

Call Sign: N1KML
Stephen M D Amelio
4 Brookside Rd
Bellingham MA 02019

Call Sign: KA1HEU
David M Fredericksen
17 Bucky Dr
Bellingham MA 02019

Call Sign: KB1HRJ
Dean P Dahlberg
47 Cedar Hill Rd
Bellingham MA 02019

Call Sign: W1AHO
Aulis W Aho
36 David Rd
Bellingham MA
020191610

Call Sign: K1UZQ
Walter D Vater
56 Depot St
Bellingham MA 02019

Call Sign: N1AJA
Thare E Gauthier
11 Easy St
Bellingham MA 02019

Call Sign: N1VYH
Matthew D Marino
90 Elbow St
Bellingham MA 02019

Call Sign: KA1ILA
Bert Guerin
39 Elvira St
Bellingham MA 02019

Call Sign: N1JIQ
Michael J Tarrasky
34 Farm St
Bellingham MA 02019

Call Sign: WA1SQC
Edmund F Walkowiak
9 Fifth Ave
Bellingham MA
020191409

Call Sign: N1DA
David J Allard
100 Florida Ave
Bellingham MA 02019

Call Sign: N1TEA
Jody M Allard
100 Florida Ave
Bellingham MA 02019

Call Sign: WB1EDE
Wagar Chin
8 Gaby Ln
Bellingham MA 02019

Call Sign: KF6WRZ
Brian D Clarke
24 Grove St
Bellingham MA
020191002

Call Sign: N1JMQ
Alvaro J Molina
379 Hartford Ave
Bellingham MA 02019

Call Sign: N1PYE
Richard A Lamphere
31 Irene Ct
Bellingham MA 02019

Call Sign: N1RDY
Susan J Abraham
31 Irene Ct
Bellingham MA 02019

Call Sign: KB1RYU
Paula M Desmarais
21 Irving St
Bellingham MA 02019

Call Sign: KB1JHR
Anthony J Durso
44 James St
Bellingham MA 02019

Call Sign: KB1MSO
Joseph G Fredette

26 Joyce Lane
Bellingham MA 02019

Call Sign: N1ZJH
Richard J Egan
53 Lakeshore Dr
Bellingham MA 02019

Call Sign: W1DUU
Russell G Nelson
71 N Main St
Bellingham MA 02019

Call Sign: KA1OMP
Michael B Sperry
147 North St
Bellingham MA 02019

Call Sign: N1IFG
David J Mancini
40 Oak St
Bellingham MA 02019

Call Sign: KA1RZQ
Albert E Honour Jr
117 Plymouth Rd
Bellingham MA 02019

Call Sign: WA1PJJ
Kevin J Keppler
19 Puddingstone Ln
Bellingham MA 02019

Call Sign: K1IRF
Raymond F
Archambault
541 Pulaski Blvd
Bellingham MA 02019

Call Sign: KA1OCJ
Steven R Carrier
1211 Pulaski Blvd
Bellingham MA 02019

Call Sign: N1MSK
Arthur C Motroni
51 Ray Ave
Bellingham MA 02019

Call Sign: N1NBA
Jacqueline V Casavant
161 S Main
Bellingham MA 02019

Call Sign: N1MSJ
Raymond J Casavant
161 S Main St
Bellingham MA 02019

Call Sign: KB1LXJ
Paul S Peluso
919 S Main St
Bellingham MA 02019

Call Sign: K1UZR
Earl J Vater
985 S Main St
Bellingham MA 02019

Call Sign: KA1HUY
William A Mac Leod
1068 S Main St
Bellingham MA 02019

Call Sign: W1XA
Frank S Jasinski
42 Saddleback Hill Rd
Bellingham MA 02019

Call Sign: WB1BZO
Jeffrey D Jasinski
42 Saddleback Hill Rd
Bellingham MA 02019

Call Sign: KB1HJY
Bernard R Cyr
10 Short St
Bellingham MA 02019

Call Sign: W1CYR
Bernard R Cyr
10 Short St
Bellingham MA 02019

Call Sign: KB1LUK
William E Bennett
59 Silver Ave
Bellingham MA 02019

Call Sign: KT1K
Robert F Drapeau
39 Steven Rd
Bellingham MA 02019

Call Sign: N1TEZ
Janet P Goodrich
18 Susan Ln
Bellingham MA 02019

Call Sign: WA1WIG
Gerald O Goodrich
18 Susan Ln
Bellingham MA 02019

Call Sign: K1RPI
Frances G Desillier
8 Taunton St
Bellingham MA 02019

Call Sign: N1BLC
Martin J Christie
75 Taunton St
Bellingham MA 02019

Call Sign: KB1KCK
Robert L Lussier
33 Trenton St
Bellingham MA 02019

Call Sign: WA1UMA
Thomas M Deffley
118 Twin Brook Lane
Bellingham MA 02019

Call Sign: W1YMW
Joseph Mason Jr
251 Wrentham Rd
Bellingham MA 02019

**FCC Amateur Radio
Licenses in Belmont**

Call Sign: KD1ZF
Brett A Mellor
18 Banks St
Belmont MA
024781214

Call Sign: WB1FGA
Edward Frazier
38 Barnard Rd
Belmont MA 02178

Call Sign: KB1QLT
Hiko M Yesiltepe
63 Bartlett Ave
Belmont MA 02478

Call Sign: KD1KY
Timothy J Shepard
122 Beech St
Belmont MA 02478

Call Sign: N1IZM
James B Murphy
181 Belmont St
Belmont MA 02178

Call Sign: W1AZH
William A Gianoukos
569 Belmont St
Belmont MA
024784420

Call Sign: K1OYD
David Coyle Sr
15 Bradford Rd
Belmont MA
024784249

Call Sign: KB1FRS
Robert Doebeli
9 Brentwood Rd
Belmont MA 02478

Call Sign: N1CVY
Kenneth A Stalberg
127 Brookside Ave
Belmont MA 02478

Call Sign: K1UIC
Harry Oteri
265 Channing Rd
Belmont MA
021783108

Call Sign: K1LUP
George W Doyle Jr
28 Chestnut St
Belmont MA 02178

Call Sign: WB1V
Edwin S Joiner
23 Chilton St
Belmont MA 02178

Call Sign: N1FWC
Cristofor M Cataudella
5 Claflin St
Belmont MA 02478

Call Sign: KB1SRY
Tieshun A Roquerre
89 Claflin St
Belmont MA 02478

Call Sign: KB1ETG
Arnold M Roquerre
89 Claflin St
Belmont MA 02478

Call Sign: KB1LKN
Kwan W Kim
11 Clarendon Rd
Belmont MA 02478

Call Sign: N1ZNS
Todd A Davis
386 Common St
Belmont MA 02178

Call Sign: KB1NCG
Marek J Kozubal
28 Crescent Rd
Belmont MA 02478

Call Sign: W1HIS
Charles C Counselman
Iii
42 Crestview Rd
Belmont MA
024782108

Call Sign: KC6EUY
Darren L Leigh
47 Cross St
Belmont MA 02478

Call Sign: N1ODR
Keith T Mc Lean
26 Cutter St
Belmont MA 02178

Call Sign: NM1X
Samuel L Norris
47 Davis Rd
Belmont MA
021781948

Call Sign: N1JKG
Thomas F Knight Jr
58 Douglas Rd
Belmont MA 02178

Call Sign: K1AQN
Francis J Kaszynski Jr
98 Douglas Rd
Belmont MA 02178

Call Sign: KB1OEY

Joseph H Allen
11 Drew Rd
Belmont MA 02478

Call Sign: AB1GO
Joseph H Allen
11 Drew Rd
Belmont MA 02478

Call Sign: K1SXS
Gordon B Greer
45 Fieldmont Rd
Belmont MA 02178

Call Sign: KA1GWK
Anne B Baddour
96 Fletcher Rd
Belmont MA 02178

Call Sign: N1WPZ
Luis C Gois
53 Foster Rd
Belmont MA 02478

Call Sign: KA8WFC
Christopher J Galbraith
39 Frederick St
Belmont MA 02478

Call Sign: N1RPA
Robert E Koch
47 Greensbrook Way
Belmont MA 02478

Call Sign: KA1RJM
Basil Kaloyanides
20 Grey Birch Park
Belmont MA 02178

Call Sign: W1MHL
Waltham Amateur
Radio Association Inc
24 Hamilton Rd
Belmont MA 02478

Call Sign: W1MJ
Eliot P Mayer
24 Hamilton Rd
Belmont MA
024784013

Call Sign: KB1KLA
Keith G Vetreno
63 Hamilton Rd

Belmont MA
024784038

Call Sign: W1CMC
Charles M Coldwell
46 Hammond Rd
Belmont MA
024782253

Call Sign: KB1GCZ
Thomas G Goodsell
3 Henry St
Belmont MA 02478

Call Sign: K1HBJ
Henry I Brugsch
30 Herman St
Belmont MA 02478

Call Sign: WB1ABD
Freda M Brugsch
30 Herman St
Belmont MA 02478

Call Sign: WA1RTT
Lawrence J Arone
30 Hermon St
Belmont MA
024782625

Call Sign: WA1RWN
John H Clements
30 Hermon St
Belmont MA 02478

Call Sign: KB1FIY
Phillip A Heller
22 Hill Rd
Belmont MA 02478

Call Sign: K1UCA
Raymond C Wanta
51 Hill Rd 509
Belmont MA 02478

Call Sign: N1PNM
Secondo Silvestri
88 Hillcrest Rd
Belmont MA 02478

Call Sign: N1VNR
Elpidio A Silvestri
88 Hillcrest Rd
Belmont MA 02178

Call Sign: W1HU
Harry D Gay
13 Horne Rd
Belmont MA 02178

Call Sign: N1GQE
Joseph Papandrea
9 Houghton Rd
Belmont MA
024784511

Call Sign: KB1NZC
Mario Pesce
5 Jeanette Ave
Belmont MA 02478

Call Sign: KB1EKZ
Justin M Seger
29 Jonathan St 2
Belmont MA 02478

Call Sign: N1DGK
Gerald C Garrity
23 Lamoine St
Belmont MA 02178

Call Sign: KB1QLP
Leo J Saidnawey
56 Lantern Rd
Belmont MA 02478

Call Sign: N1LJS
Leo J Saidnawey
56 Lantern Rd
Belmont MA 02478

Call Sign: KB1QLO
Nora A Ryan
53 Lawndale St
Belmont MA 02478

Call Sign: WX1GRL
Nora A Ryan
53 Lawndale St
Belmont MA 02478

Call Sign: KB1QLN
Maryann Nilsson
53 Lawndale St
Belmont MA 02478

Call Sign: KN1FTY
Maryann Nilsson

53 Lawndale St
Belmont MA 02478

Call Sign: WE1BBQ
Maryann Nilsson
53 Lawndale St
Belmont MA 02478

Call Sign: N1IR
Nathan L Cohen
2 Ledgewood Pl
Belmont MA 02478

Call Sign: W1YW
Nathan L Cohen
2 Ledgewood Pl
Belmont MA 02478

Call Sign: N1CVS
J Elliott Smith Jr
6 Leslie Rd
Belmont MA 02178

Call Sign: KD1BI
Walter L Littlewood Jr
212 Lexington St
Belmont MA 02179

Call Sign: KB1VCP
Leighton A Dolan
31 Lincoln St
Belmont MA 02478

Call Sign: KB1PFX
Leighton A Dolan
31 Lincoln St
Belmont MA 02478

Call Sign: K1QOO
Lesley Wilkins
74 Livermore Rd
Belmont MA 02178

Call Sign: WW1O
David D Smith
35 Loring St
Belmont MA 02478

Call Sign: KB1POT
Kirk D Kolenbrander
94 Louise Rd
Belmont MA 02478

Call Sign: KA1G

Kirk D Kolenbrander
94 Louise Rd
Belmont MA 02478

Call Sign: W1FA
Kirk D Kolenbrander
94 Louise Rd
Belmont MA 02478

Call Sign: N1DFK
Donald E Troxel
4 Madison St
Belmont MA 02178

Call Sign: N1SOA
Eileen M Troxel
4 Madison St
Belmont MA 02178

Call Sign: N1RYQ
Kathryn A Salter
1 Marion Rd Apt 1
Belmont MA 02478

Call Sign: W1ABR
Alfred B Roney
54 Marlboro St #2
Belmont MA 02478

Call Sign: AB1JK
Linn W Hobbs
12 Moore St
Belmont MA
024782502

Call Sign: W1LWH
Linn W Hobbs
12 Moore St
Belmont MA
024782502

Call Sign: W1MXI
Robert D Young
83 Oak Ave
Belmont MA
024782714

Call Sign: KB1QLQ
Brian S Saper
16 Old Middlesex Rd
Belmont MA 02478

Call Sign: KC1PZ
Thomas R Sciascia Dr

108 Oliver Rd
Belmont MA
024784633

Call Sign: N1FMJ
Katherine M Isaacs
140 Oliver Rd
Belmont MA 02478

Call Sign: K1BEX
Paul W Keating
285 Orchard St
Belmont MA 02478

Call Sign: KV1B
Robert V Pound
87 Pinehurst Rd
Belmont MA 02178

Call Sign: W1ZOI
Wilfred J Remillard
64 Pond St
Belmont MA 02178

Call Sign: KB1FDR
Richard Omohundro Jr
200 Prospect St
Belmont MA 02478

Call Sign: KA1KQG
Brooke Albert
38 Raleigh Rd
Belmont MA 02178

Call Sign: WA1UOU
James C Berets
44 Rayburn Rd
Belmont MA 02478

Call Sign: K8ZBE
Stephen D Umans
5 Regent Rd
Belmont MA 02178

Call Sign: KA1SVN
Denise S Umans
5 Regent Rd
Belmont MA 02178

Call Sign: KB1WLK
Nicholas C Veo
200 Rutledge Rd
Belmont MA 02478

Call Sign: KA1ZUG
Mary D Chamberlin
29 Selwyn Rd
Belmont MA 02178

Call Sign: W1PFX
Harold A Chamberlin
29 Selwyn Rd
Belmont MA 02178

Call Sign: W1PFX
Mary D Chamberlin
29 Selwyn Rd
Belmont MA 02178

Call Sign: KX1T
Ramon F Kolb
51 Simmons Ave
Belmont MA 02478

Call Sign: WB0PKX
Steven B Hargreaves
75 Slade St
Belmont MA 02178

Call Sign: N1GMO
Richard V Sailor
234 Slade St
Belmont MA 02478

Call Sign: KB1QZI
Jonathan Sailor
234 Slade St
Belmont MA 02478

Call Sign: W1DSZ
Morris H Rosenthal
56 Sycamore St
Belmont MA 02179

Call Sign: N1SZN
Yoshiyuki Takei
31 Tobey Rd
Belmont MA 02178

Call Sign: W1ESB
James H Nakashian
406 Trapelo Rd
Belmont MA
021781969

Call Sign: AB1MB
James A Krom
50 Trowbridge St

Belmont MA 02478

Call Sign: N1RTN
Erin B Seeling
55 Unity Ave
Belmont MA 02178

Call Sign: WK1O
Alexander Filippov
74 Vernon Rd
Belmont MA 02178

Call Sign: WB4SQV
Donald K Smith
10 Village Hill Rd
Belmont MA 02178

Call Sign: N1NUP
Herbert P Howe
37 Warwick Rd
Belmont MA 02178

Call Sign: N8BRF
Lubomyr Fedan
28 Watson Rd
Belmont MA 02178

Call Sign: N1WIM
Therese M Smith
55 Wellesley Rd
Belmont MA 02178

Call Sign: W1YBN
Lorenzo Falzarano
230 White St
Belmont MA 02178

Call Sign: WA0KAN
Barry Gaiman
53 Winslow Rd
Belmont MA 02478

Call Sign: KA1QNR
George E Battit
34 Woodbine Rd
Belmont MA 02178

Call Sign: KB1SPV
Ameya P Agaskar
52 Worcester St
Belmont MA 02478

FCC Amateur Radio Licenses in Berkley

Call Sign: WB1HLR
Abigail S Howes
105 Bayview Ave
Berkley MA 02779

Call Sign: KB1WXQ
Mark Whittaker
157 Bayview Ave
Berkley MA 02779

Call Sign: WA1DTN
Fred W Bopp
93 Bryant St
Berkley MA 02779

Call Sign: WA1WDP
Margaret M Bopp
93 Bryant St
Berkley MA 02779

Call Sign: W1RMN
Robert M Novack
43 Bryant St
Berkley MA 02779

Call Sign: N1IER
Kenneth E Stone
36 E Plain St
Berkley MA 02779

Call Sign: N1PRK
John B Wittey
55 E Plain St
Berkley MA 02779

Call Sign: N1ZZP
John M Logan
3 Elmwood Dr
Berkley MA 02779

Call Sign: N1JOX
Dennis P Maguire
20 Holloway St
Berkley MA 02779

Call Sign: N1OPN
Brian M Awalt
96 Myricks St
Berkley MA 02779

Call Sign: N1IYK
Tobe C Deutschmann
III

7 Parsons Walk
Berkley MA 02779

Call Sign: KB1UCN
Traci S Horton
710 Cheshire Rd
Berkshire MA 01224

Call Sign: KA1RSX
Richard V Carrow
Berkshire MA 01224

Call Sign: W1GCI
Arnold E Adelman
120 Ball Hill Rd
Berlin MA 01503

Call Sign: K1KH
Keith J Hanson
37 Brook Ln
Berlin MA 01503

Call Sign: N1IUP
Harold A Read Iii
32 Crosby Rd
Berlin MA 01503

Call Sign: AB1JP
Harold A Read Iii
32 Crosby Rd
Berlin MA 01503

Call Sign: K3FG
Harold A Read Iii
32 Crosby Rd
Berlin MA 01503

Call Sign: N1VPJ
Allan G Rodwell
227 Highland St
Berlin MA 01503

Call Sign: N1SFV
Robert F Mc Tague Jr
43 Lancaster Rd
Berlin MA 01503

Call Sign: W1ZMM

Richard B Sawyer
48 Linden St
Berlin MA 015030048

Call Sign: K1CZR
Leighton R Richardson
218 Linden St
Berlin MA 01503

Call Sign: KA1YFH
George A Pendergast
43 Peach Hill Rd
Berlin MA 01503

Call Sign: KB1FKQ
George A Pendergast
43 Peach Hill Rd
Berlin MA 01503

Call Sign: K1KV
William J Barry
121 Peach Hill Rd
Berlin MA 01503

Call Sign: WA1BMO
Lee R Mungeam
115 Pleasant
Berlin MA 01503

Call Sign: KB1TYF
David R De Mattia
Po Box 198
Berlin MA 01503

Call Sign: K1DVD
David R De Mattia
Po Box 198
Berlin MA 01503

Call Sign: WB2YTK
Douglas P Wiedeman
123 Randall Rd
Berlin MA 01503

Call Sign: N1QEV
Paul F Silvestri
283 Randall Rd
Berlin MA 01503

Call Sign: N1ZNQ
Karl K Karash
288 Randall Rd
Berlin MA 01503

Call Sign: KB1SMF
Andrew W Bezanson
171 River Rd West
Berlin MA 01503

Call Sign: W1ELU
Curtis P Hoffman
120 Sawyer Hill Rd
Berlin MA 01503

Call Sign: KB1FWR
David E Shevett
11 Village Lane
Berlin MA 01503

Call Sign: KA2CNN
Dwight A Ernest
20 Village Lane
Berlin MA 01503

Call Sign: KJ1H
Justin M Hughes
21 Village Lane
Berlin MA 01503

Call Sign: KB1WDE
Sawyer Hill Amateur
Radio Club
21 Village Lane
Berlin MA 01503

Call Sign: K1SCA
Heather F Cougar
30 Village Lane
Berlin MA 015031709

Call Sign: W1DRD
Harry E Miller Jr
16 West St
Berlin MA 015030062

Call Sign: KA1POP
Thomas O Thorburn
163 West St
Berlin MA 01503

Call Sign: KA1PPS
Carol A Thorburn
163 West St
Berlin MA 01503

Call Sign: N1SIP
William V Heyn
220 West St A

Berlin MA 01503

Call Sign: K1IW
Robert J De Mattia
Berlin MA 015030198

Call Sign: KB1BPY
Crocker Public Service
Group
Berlin MA 015030198

Call Sign: N1QPH
Joyce R De Mattia
Berlin MA 015030198

Call Sign: K1HHP
Crocker Public Service
Group
Berlin MA 015030198

Call Sign: KB1SXZ
Michael D Powell
Berlin MA 01503

Call Sign: W1KU
Michael D Powell
Berlin MA 01503

Call Sign: KB1VKE
Julia R Demattia
Berlin MA 01503

Call Sign: K1JLA
Julia R Demattia
Berlin MA 01503

Call Sign: N1YPS
Phillip R Grant
119 Hoeshop Rd
Bernardston MA
01337

Call Sign: KB1FNO
Brandon W Ovitt
199 Northfield Rd
Bernardston MA
01337

Call Sign: KB1FNP
Vickie L Ovitt

199 Northfield Rd
Bernardston MA
01337

Call Sign: KB1GNF
David F Powell
22 Purple Meadow Rd
Bernardston MA
01337

Call Sign: K1TYG
Marilyn M Pinson
111 South St
Bernardston MA
013379450

Call Sign: KB1FFS
William H Ovitt Jr
Bernardston MA
01337

Call Sign: K1WHO
William H Ovitt Jr
Bernardston MA
01337

**FCC Amateur Radio
Licenses in Beverly**

Call Sign: KB1QKR
Mass Task Force
Radio Club
43 Airport Rd
Beverly MA 01915

Call Sign: N1BYL
Arthur R Churchill Jr
47 Ashton St
Beverly MA 01915

Call Sign: KB1JFW
Donald E Cushing
101 Baker Ave
Beverly MA 01915

Call Sign: K1DEC
Donald E Cushing
101 Baker Ave
Beverly MA 01915

Call Sign: N1UTI
Ainsley D Randall
27 Baker Ave Apt 3r
Beverly MA 01915

Call Sign: N1CMQ
Shawn E Burke
Bancroft Ave
Beverly MA 01915

Call Sign: K1WXF
Norma L Knight
18 Bass River Rd
Beverly MA 01915

Call Sign: KB1IAN
John J Pottier
21 Bennett St Apt 1
Beverly MA 01915

Call Sign: KA1TMJ
Laura I Irwin
1 Beverly Commons
Dr Apt 37
Beverly MA 01915

Call Sign: N1URG
Richard B Taylor
24 Bisson St
Beverly MA
019154607

Call Sign: KB1RXY
Zachary D Spurr
26 Bisson St
Beverly MA 01915

Call Sign: WA1TKM
Bruce R Munson
31 Boyles St
Beverly MA 01915

Call Sign: K1EO
Whitney R Carter
57 Bridge St
Beverly MA
019152930

Call Sign: N4CZG
William M Rieker
14 Brimbal Hills Dr
Beverly MA 01915

Call Sign: AA1SI
Harry D Wilson
27 Broadway St #1
Beverly MA 01915

Call Sign: N3VII
Richard J Granger
505 Broughton Dr
Beverly MA 02925

Call Sign: KB1RXU
Matthew J Morris
2002 Broughton Dr
Beverly MA 01915

Call Sign: KB1OFG
Michael F Bookman
75 Cabot St
Beverly MA 01915

Call Sign: N1KYQ
Douglas A Wilson
726 Cabot St
Beverly MA 01915

Call Sign: KB1OFH
Paul M Couture
74 Chase St
Beverly MA 01915

Call Sign: KB1LKL
Gordon S Gravelese
9 Cobblers Ln
Beverly MA 01915

Call Sign: KB1LLZ
Alan J Gravelese
9 Cobblers Ln
Beverly MA
019151301

Call Sign: KX1KTY
Gordon S Gravelese
9 Cobblers Ln
Beverly MA 01915

Call Sign: W1OSU
Alan J Gravelese
9 Cobblers Ln
Beverly MA
019151301

Call Sign: KB1TQU
Andrew M Beaudry
18 Cole St
Beverly MA 01915

Call Sign: KB1WGB
Todd M Surette

1 Colgate Rd
Beverly MA 01915

Call Sign: KB1EGY
Bryan W Cunningham
112 Colon St
Beverly MA 01915

Call Sign: KA1GN
Arvid E Selin
17 Conant St Apt 38w
Beverly MA 01915

Call Sign: KZ1H
George Young
25 Cornell Rd
Beverly MA 01915

Call Sign: N1BLQ
Stephen E Woodbury
16 Corning St
Beverly MA 01915

Call Sign: W1DWY
Edwin F Dillaby
67 Corning St
Beverly MA 01915

Call Sign: N1NIG
John S Palaima
5 Cove Ave
Beverly MA
019154112

Call Sign: KB1GCJ
Michael C Jennings Jr
35 Crescent Ave
Beverly MA 01915

Call Sign: WB1HAS
Robert C Sant Fournier
5 Crescent Ct
Beverly MA 01915

Call Sign: W1EZZ
Malcolm E Barron
11 Dartmouth St
Beverly MA 01915

Call Sign: KB1LVC
Roger R Grey
5 Davis Rd
Beverly MA
019152307

Call Sign: W1RRG
Roger R Grey
5 Davis Rd
Beverly MA
019152307

Call Sign: KB1DSX
John A Nelson
10 Davis Rd
Beverly MA
019152308

Call Sign: N1KAH
Andrew J Terzakis
168 Dodge St
Beverly MA
019151215

Call Sign: W1PSG
John L Harrigan
13 Douglas Ave
Beverly MA 01915

Call Sign: KA1FKL
Michael J Mendalka
20 Dunham Rd
Beverly MA 01915

Call Sign: WB1FWE
Gordon J Essler
7 Eisenhower Ave
Beverly MA 01915

Call Sign: KB1BZQ
Plumfield School
Amateur Radio Club
449 Elliott St
Beverly MA 01915

Call Sign: N1XLQ
John F Koza
449 Elliott St
Beverly MA
019152330

Call Sign: N1ZOF
Stephen J Koza
449 Elliott St
Beverly MA 01915

Call Sign: KB1FIV
Anne E Koza
449 Elliott St

Beverly MA 01915

Call Sign: N1YMF
William J Mc
Donough
8 Elm Top Lane
Beverly MA 01915

Call Sign: N1GEK
Paul D Woodbury Jr
59 Essex St
Beverly MA 01915

Call Sign: WA1DTK
Edward P Pinanski
124 Essex St
Beverly MA
019153745

Call Sign: KB1OVR
Jacob D Pike
291 Essex St
Beverly MA 01915

Call Sign: W1JDP
Jacob D Pike
291 Essex St
Beverly MA 01915

Call Sign: N1ILP
Christopher J Jones
462 Essex St
Beverly MA 01915

Call Sign: WB1HEE
Philip R Cleversey
535 Essex St
Beverly MA
019151505

Call Sign: WA1NYP
John E Flynn
401 Essex St Apt 120
Beverly MA 01915

Call Sign: W1MHK
Arthur R Winter
401 Essex St Apt 312
Beverly MA 01915

Call Sign: KB1OFM
Daniel W Hering
460 Essex St Apt E
Beverly MA 01905

Call Sign: KA1FOD
Donald H Ames
7 Fayette St
Beverly MA 01915

Call Sign: KB1FHO
Robert A Clanton
22 Folger Ave
Beverly MA 01915

Call Sign: KB1OFK
Thomas W Brennan
1 Galloupe Ave
Beverly MA 01915

Call Sign: KB1OFL
Dennis A Amiro
34 Guild Rd
Beverly MA 01915

Call Sign: KB1AMY
Kiva Skolnick
202 Hale St
Beverly MA 01915

Call Sign: KB3FWZ
Alan B Strom
315 Hale St
Beverly MA 01915

Call Sign: N1DBO
Cecil C Blair
16 Harwood St
Beverly MA
019151414

Call Sign: K1GJE
Donald S Berman
66 Haskell St
Beverly MA 01915

Call Sign: K1DSB
Donald S Berman
66 Haskell St
Beverly MA 01915

Call Sign: KA1EUK
Robert L Haggstrom
12 High St
Beverly MA 01915

Call Sign: KA1NEC
Nancy E Haggstrom

12 High St
Beverly MA
019152104

Call Sign: KA1USI
David J Carnevale
25 Home St
Beverly MA 01915

Call Sign: KC2CQI
John J Puskarik
8 Lakeview Ave
Beverly MA 01915

Call Sign: N1GSP
Paul G Rudenberg
3 Lanthorn Ln
Beverly MA 01915

Call Sign: N1FMQ
Robert A Ward
6 Lanthorn Ln
Beverly MA 01915

Call Sign: KA1HQE
Allen G Torsey
14 Lincoln St
Beverly MA 01915

Call Sign: N1YAH
Michael D Salter
25 Linden Ave
Beverly MA
019154863

Call Sign: N1ZHJ
Kathleen E Salter
25 Linden Ave
Beverly MA
019154863

Call Sign: W1YZE
Richard P Lipman
136 Livingstone Ave
Beverly MA
019154045

Call Sign: WB1EFF
Harold E Proctor
3 Longfellow St
Beverly MA 01915

Call Sign: K1BDZ
Edward G Walsh

38 Lothrop St
Beverly MA 01915

Call Sign: N1IQN
Valerie L Passman
15 Lothrop St Apt 3
Beverly MA 01915

Call Sign: KB1PAW
Artur Orbinski
13 Lovett St
Beverly MA 01915

Call Sign: N1GSC
David G Earle
32 Mac Arthur Rd
Beverly MA 01915

Call Sign: W1GAX
Ernest F Tozier Jr
14 May St
Beverly MA 01915

Call Sign: W1BCN
Richard L Moroni
13 Memorial Drive
Beverly MA 01915

Call Sign: KB1NWL
Donald J Calnan
14 Micheal Rd
Beverly MA 01915

Call Sign: KB1HFI
Theodore R Mori
50 Middlebury Ln
Beverly MA 01915

Call Sign: WA1PNW
Mark C Foster
13 Morningside Dr
Beverly MA 01915

Call Sign: WC1ABV
Beverly Civil Defense
13 Morningside Dr
Beverly MA 01915

Call Sign: W1FXT
Ronald F Novello Sr
9 Museum Rd
Beverly MA 01915

Call Sign: KE6PO

Dan S Azlin
7 Myrtle St
Beverly MA
019153315

Call Sign: KA1GCQ
Howard M Rosenberg
6 Nelwood Terrace
Beverly MA 01915

Call Sign: KB1EWH
Kimberly S Rosenberg
6 Nelwood Terrace
Beverly MA 01915

Call Sign: W1DON
Donald J Czarnecki
37 Northern Ave
Beverly MA 01915

Call Sign: W1DG
Donald J Czarnecki
37 Northern Ave
Beverly MA 01915

Call Sign: WB1EPC
Mark F Rasmussen
16 Oakhurst Rd
Beverly MA 01915

Call Sign: KB1NGN
Mark A Watson
9 Ocean St
Beverly MA 01915

Call Sign: W1MAW
Mark A Watson
9 Ocean St
Beverly MA 01915

Call Sign: W1NDE
John F Burns Jr
38 Parramatta Rd
Beverly MA 07915

Call Sign: N1QCT
Alan D Kaplan
44 Pickman Rd
Beverly MA 01915

Call Sign: KA1SEZ
Mark H Round
4 Pierce Ave
Beverly MA 01915

Call Sign: KB1RXW
David R Perkins Jr
11 Pine Rd
Beverly MA 01915

Call Sign: KB1GCO
Curtis A Hall
2 Pinewood Ave
Beverly MA 01915

Call Sign: KB1JLI
Marc E Hall
27 Pleasant St
Beverly MA 01915

Call Sign: KA1OME
Albert F Moses
19 Pond St
Beverly MA 01915

Call Sign: KB1ILG
Michael S Boice
24 Pond St 2
Beverly MA 01915

Call Sign: WA1YFZ
Warren A Hartman Jr
1 Porter Ter
Beverly MA
019154021

Call Sign: W1LN
Warren A Hartman Jr
1 Porter Ter
Beverly MA
019154021

Call Sign: K1PTT
Peter K Fitzgibbons
18 Princeton Ave
Beverly MA
019155631

Call Sign: W1BVL
Richard S Briggs
9 Puritan Rd
Beverly MA 01915

Call Sign: N1OKX
Sylvia A Leftin
45 Railroad Ave
Beverly MA 01915

Call Sign: KB1GHQ
Lewis C Evans
12 Rantoul St
Beverly MA 01915

Call Sign: N1RSQ
Donald L Johnson
22 Roderick Ave
Beverly MA 01915

Call Sign: NN1A
Alfred W Cook
4 Ryan Pl
Beverly MA 01915

Call Sign: N1FMC
Kirk P Brown Sr
51 Sohier Rd
Beverly MA 01915

Call Sign: WA1HVX
John W Woodberry
4 Spring St
Beverly MA
019153628

Call Sign: KB1AMI
Pavel Jirka
35 Standley St
Beverly MA 01915

Call Sign: KB1ANP
Rachel E P Jirka
35 Standley St
Beverly MA 01915

Call Sign: KA1TTD
Andrew J Devitt
15 Sturtevant St
Beverly MA 01915

Call Sign: K1JE
Michael C Joens
4 Sunnycrest Ave
Beverly MA
019153932

Call Sign: KB1IQK
Anna L Joens
4 Sunnycrest Ave
Beverly MA
019153932

Call Sign: K1ALJ

Anna L Joens
4 Sunnycrest Ave
Beverly MA
019153932

Call Sign: KB1LAI
Norbert F Neidhardt
4 Sunnycrest Ave
Beverly MA 01915

Call Sign: ND2N
Norbert F Neidhardt
4 Sunnycrest Ave
Beverly MA 01915

Call Sign: N1EUO
Glenn P Scanlon
52 Sunset Dr
Beverly MA 01915

Call Sign: KB1WJB
Raymond R Page Jr
9 Swan St
Beverly MA 01915

Call Sign: KB1QKK
Scott E Butterfield
17 Swan St
Beverly MA 01915

Call Sign: KA1GQL
Keith E Weston
31 Taft Ave
Beverly MA 01915

Call Sign: KB1GCL
Jason E Comeau
15 Thompson Rd
Beverly MA 01915

Call Sign: KB1OFJ
Ryan J Comeau
15 Thompson Rd
Beverly MA 01905

Call Sign: KB1DDT
Robert W Renwick
5 Trask Ct Apt 32
Beverly MA
019155378

Call Sign: KB1TQW
Paulette K Brennan
8 Tyler Rd

Beverly MA 01915

Call Sign: KB1CIP
Thomas Grant
37 Walcott Rd
Beverly MA
019152344

Call Sign: W1ZT
George C Johnson
30 Washington St
Beverly MA 01915

Call Sign: KA1PPM
James A Hill
32 Whitney Ave
Beverly MA
019153476

Call Sign: KA1ACM
W Clark Goodchild Jr
1 Woodbury Dr
Beverly MA 01915

Call Sign: N1AIT
Thomas J Schalton
Beverly MA 01915

Call Sign: W1FCJ
Larry Van Walters
Beverly MA 01915

Call Sign: KB1JIM
Joseph E Tucker
Beverly MA 01915

**FCC Amateur Radio
Licenses in Beverly
Farms**

Call Sign: N1AXF
Charles B Kern
5 Beach
Beverly Farms MA
01915

Call Sign: KB1DRT
Adam B Seamans
840 Hale St
Beverly Farms MA
01915

**FCC Amateur Radio
Licenses in Billerica**

Call Sign: N1YEV
Russell M Callahan
50 Alexander Rd
Billerica MA 01821

Call Sign: KB1MVG
Kristan M Decesaro
72 Allen Rd
Billerica MA 01821

Call Sign: N1BRH
Robert R Leonard
230 Allen Rd
Billerica MA 01821

Call Sign: KB1HMT
Donald J Fitzreiter
7 Allen Rd Ext
Billerica MA 01821

Call Sign: KA1OOZ
Brian E Munier
32 Andover Rd
Billerica MA
018211916

Call Sign: K1NCN
Theodore N Colas
338 Andover Rd
Billerica MA 01821

Call Sign: KB1IWE
Paul M Juliano
15 Angela Ln
Billerica MA 01821

Call Sign: N1OZS
John W Landry Jr
1 Apollo Ave
Billerica MA 01821

Call Sign: N1SPB
Richard J Granfield
15 Applewood
Billerica MA 01821

Call Sign: KA1HYC
Arthur R Enos
17 Arakelian Dr
Billerica MA 01821

Call Sign: N1BCR
John J Granfield

2 Arborwood Rd
Billerica MA 01821

Call Sign: N1WSO
Brian D Zemba
6 Atherton Ave
Billerica MA 01821

Call Sign: KB1WIS
Christopher R Gray
83 Baldwin Rd
Billerica MA 01821

Call Sign: N1PJV
William Cordeiro Sr
8 Ben Pl
Billerica MA 01821

Call Sign: N1DEL
Maria E Atkinson
16 Biscayne Dr
Billerica MA 01821

Call Sign: K1SKK
John J Deeney
5 Blackhawk Rd
Billerica MA 01821

Call Sign: KB1MKZ
Billerica EMA
365 Boston Rd
Billerica MA 01821

Call Sign: KD1FZ
Frank E Sullivan
796 Boston Rd
Billerica MA 01821

Call Sign: N1DCM
Richard A Buxton
10 Boynton Ave
Billerica MA 01821

Call Sign: KF6TAZ
Eugene L Friedrich
37 Briarwood Ave
Billerica MA 01821

Call Sign: AA1DE
Harold J Sinclair Sr
23 Burlington Rd
Billerica MA 01866

Call Sign: KA1DO

Andrew J De Stefano
11 Cartwright Lane
Billerica MA 01821

Call Sign: N1YDI
Derrell Lipman
30 Champa Rd
Billerica MA 01821

Call Sign: KB1SEQ
James T Orsborn
43 Charme Rd
Billerica MA 01821

Call Sign: WA1VIA
Joseph L Medeiros Jr
50 Charme Rd
Billerica MA
018212126

Call Sign: K1FYJ
Anna D Di Lorenzo
54 Charme Rd
Billerica MA 01821

Call Sign: WA1FTA
James E Foye
54 Charme Rd
Billerica MA 01821

Call Sign: N1LHL
Scott R Dunham
63 Charme Rd
Billerica MA 01821

Call Sign: N2HWI
Edward E Erny
20 Charnstaffe Ln Apt
223
Billerica MA 01821

Call Sign: KB1MUV
Jay H Moore
40 Christina Ave
Billerica MA 01821

Call Sign: KA1WWK
Carlos R Morinico
6 Colby St
Billerica MA
018623214

Call Sign: N1PJY
Timothy E Johns

10 Comet Ln
Billerica MA 01862

Call Sign: N1QBW
Rita A Johns
10 Comet Ln
Billerica MA 01862

Call Sign: W1WQZ
Edgar O Parker Jr
46 Concord Rd
Billerica MA 01821

Call Sign: KG2MK
Joshua H Mayers
158 Concord Rd #M18
Billerica MA 01821

Call Sign: N1TYI
Rodney Ashworth
158 Concord Rd
Billirica MA 01821

Call Sign: KB1NEN
Joseph D Chapman
58 Concord Rd Apt
E24
Billerica MA 01821

Call Sign: KU1MAR
Ajit Kumar
Somasekharan Nair
158 Concord Rd Apt
H24
Billerica MA 01821

Call Sign: KB1IDZ
Charles E Ronayne
3 Connolly Rd
Billerica MA 01821

Call Sign: WI1O
Donald P Eriksen
27 Country Ln
Billerica MA 01821

Call Sign: N1VVP
Robert G Bland
3 Courtland Ln
Billerica MA 01821

Call Sign: N1TEV
Charles B Kitchin
26 Crystal St

Billerica MA 01821

Call Sign: WA1MEJ
William J Brosnahan
10 Cynthia Rd
Billerica MA 01866

Call Sign: WB1DTA
Kenneth P Gannon
4 Diane Dr
Billerica MA 01821

Call Sign: KB1GYN
William L Irvine
5 Dignon Rd
Billerica MA 01821

Call Sign: WA3AVU
Thomas R Posney
2 Doe Dr
Billerica MA 01821

Call Sign: W1RGX
Leonard D Hart
31 Dudley Rd
Billerica MA
018214106

Call Sign: KB1GP
Joseph P Bowker
54 Dyer St
Billerica MA
018623117

Call Sign: N1TML
Richard M Hajinlian
31 Fardon St
Billerica MA 01821

Call Sign: WA1GGU
Charles W Foye Jr
4 Fillmore Dr
Billerica MA 01821

Call Sign: KB1JKI
Eric R Johnson
11 Floyd St
Billerica MA 01821

Call Sign: WO1N
Kenneth J Caruso
20 Forest Park Ave
Billerica MA 01862

Call Sign: W1MJA
Donald E Pope
19 Forest St
Billerica MA
018215456

Call Sign: KB1OPP
Kenneth A Lambert
33 Fredrickson Rd
Billerica MA 01821

Call Sign: KB1NJS
Edmund P Howard Jr
33 George Brown St
Billerica MA 01821

Call Sign: WY2L
Kris A Francis
5 Glenwood Rd
Billerica MA 01821

Call Sign: N1GWT
David L Roy
10 Greenwood Rd
Billerica MA 01821

Call Sign: N1IWB
Helen F Roy
10 Greenwood Rd
Billerica MA 01821

Call Sign: WB1GCJ
John P Brady
22 Handel Rd
Billerica MA
018213719

Call Sign: KB1CVR
Cynthia A Fernandez
2 Harnden Rd
Billerica MA 01821

Call Sign: N1WKS
Charles E Folland Jr
108 High St
Billerica MA 01862

Call Sign: KD1TF
Gary S Wooster
14 Jef
Billerica MA 01821

Call Sign: N1DZM
Almon R Allard

3 Jeffrey Rd
Billerica MA 01821

Call Sign: KB1KEX
Sandra M Woodbury
3 Karen Circle #24
Billerica MA 01821

Call Sign: KD1BP
Mark L Perlmutter
8 Kirk Rd
Billerica MA 01821

Call Sign: K1MLP
Mark L Perlmutter
8 Kirk Rd
Billerica MA 01821

Call Sign: KA1WPC
Carol A Perlmutter
8 Kirk Rd
Billerica MA 01821

Call Sign: N1OSE
Karl C Cameron
9 Lakeside Rd
Billerica MA 01821

Call Sign: N1OAS
David J Lyons Jr
170 Leicester St
Billerica MA 01862

Call Sign: KB1LTT
Kristin L Wilson
41 Lexington Rd
Billerica MA 01821

Call Sign: W1BXI
Ralph W Burbank Jr
132 Lexington Rd
Billerica MA 01821

Call Sign: N1PJW
Richard Gemelli Sr
31 Lindsay Rd
Billerica MA 01821

Call Sign: KB1KQR
Robert M Orman
30 Little John Dr
Billerica MA 01821

Call Sign: N1IUY

Armand R Francoeur
44 Little John Dr
Billerica MA 01821

Call Sign: KA1HPP
Julia R Bosomworth
4 Maple Rd
Billerica MA 01821

Call Sign: KA1TNB
Leonard D Hodgkins Jr
75 Marshall St
Billerica MA 01821

Call Sign: KA1TNI
Leonard D Hodgkins
Sr
75 Marshall St
Billerica MA 01821

Call Sign: KA1TNJ
Matthew P Hodgkins
75 Marshall St
Billerica MA 01821

Call Sign: KA1MZH
Douglas H Goodwin
5 Melody Ln
Billerica MA 01821

Call Sign: KB1JKJ
James A Bradley
14 Meridien Way
Billerica MA 01821

Call Sign: KB1PMY
Claudia Beer
8 Michael Rd
Billerica MA 01862

Call Sign: KB1PMZ
Ralf Grzymalla
8 Michael Rd
Billerica MA 01862

Call Sign: N1HMR
Willard J Jasset Jr
413 Middlesex Tpke
Billerica MA 01821

Call Sign: KA1RKG
John J Hannafin
9 Montclair Cir
Billerica MA 01821

Call Sign: N1KFU
Martin J Bedard
6 Morningside Drive
Billerica MA 01821

Call Sign: KA1JDR
Wolfgang Stachuletz
1 Mt Vernon Ave
Billerica MA 01821

Call Sign: KS1T
Kenneth M Smalley
71 Nashua Rd
Billerica MA 01862

Call Sign: NT1S
William W Heiser
4 Ox Rd
Billerica MA 01821

Call Sign: WA1SXL
Edward W Mc Ginnis
19 Partridge Hill Rd
Billerica MA 01821

Call Sign: N1ZCA
Leigh J Gillespie
20 Pelham St
Billerica MA 01862

Call Sign: KA1TTG
Robert M Ankenbauer
Jr
15 Perreault Ave
Billerica MA 01821

Call Sign: KY1I
Robert P Hastings
2 Phillips Rd
Billerica MA
018211524

Call Sign: WA1ULH
Mary L Hastings
2 Phillips Rd
Billerica MA
018211524

Call Sign: WB1DPU
Norman A Poulin
13 Pichowicz Rd
Billerica MA 01821

Call Sign: K1TDS
Robert C Fuller
11 Pinehurst Ave
Billerica MA 01821

Call Sign: N1WAY
David J Mc Cleary Sr
22 Pinetree Rd
Billerica MA
018213446

Call Sign: KA1ZPH
James A Sullivan
9 Pinewood Ave
Billerica MA 01821

Call Sign: WA1CEY
Robert V Bedingfield
21 Poe Rd
Billerica MA 01821

Call Sign: N1SJE
Gary L Taylor
67 Pond St
Billerica MA 01821

Call Sign: KC0EBX
Andrew D Allan
23 Pondover Rd
Billerica MA
018211920

Call Sign: N1WRC
Gail M Musgrave
33 Pratt St
Billerica MA 01821

Call Sign: N1LMU
Allan F Galaid
64 Queensland Rd
Billerica MA 01862

Call Sign: W1AFG
Allan F Galaid
64 Queensland Rd
Billerica MA 01862

Call Sign: KB1KYS
Kimberley S Van
Auken
66 Rangeway Rd
Billerica MA 01862

Call Sign: W1LMV

Richard C Bejtlich
30 Ranlett Ln
Billerica MA 01821

Call Sign: KB1MJJ
Frank A Altobelli
31 Richardson St
Billerica MA 01821

Call Sign: W1VER
Frank A Altobelli Jr
31 Richardson St
Billerica MA 01821

Call Sign: KB1DFQ
John J Landy
39 Ridgeway Ave
Billerica MA 01821

Call Sign: N1MBP
John P Sullivan Sr
4 Ridgewood Rd
Billerica MA 01821

Call Sign: KA1IHP
Patricia A Wilcinski
188 River St
Billerica MA 01821

Call Sign: KB1QLA
James W Corell
181 River St Extension
Billerica MA 01821

Call Sign: AB1AF
Marc C Tinkler
50 Riverhurst Rd
Billerica MA 01821

Call Sign: K1UG
Marc Tinkler
50 Riverhurst Rd
Billerica MA 01821

Call Sign: N1QZX
Dan A Pascucci
21 Robinhood Ln
Billerica MA 01821

Call Sign: N1MOR
Philip D Gray
4 Robinwood Ave
Billerica MA 01821

Call Sign: KA1RHY
Richard H Young Ii
173 Salem Rd
Billerica MA 01821

Call Sign: WB1FZI
Alfred J Blouin
327 Salem Rd
Billerica MA 01821

Call Sign: KB1TSM
Allan M Ryan Jr
10 Shawnee Circle
Billerica MA 01821

Call Sign: N1WKR
Joel A Roush
5 Shawsheen Rd
Billerica MA 01821

Call Sign: KA1EAW
Robert J Perkins
35 Shawsheen Rd
Billerica MA 01821

Call Sign: AA1NA
Clement J Cote
8 Sheldon St
Billerica MA 01862

Call Sign: KA1NLI
Steven A Conatser
42 Sheridan St
Billerica MA
018215804

Call Sign: W1KHF
C Nelson Pike
37 Stag Dr
Billerica MA 01821

Call Sign: NA1R
Thomas H Windhorn
24 Sumac St
Billerica MA 01821

Call Sign: K1PAD
Richard P Beebe
6 Tracy Cir
Billerica MA 01821

Call Sign: N1UDZ
Daniel E Kane
406 Treble Cove Rd

Billerica MA 01862

Call Sign: N1DRZ
Joseph R Ruotolo
5 Vincent St
Billerica MA 01821

Call Sign: N1DSA
Sandra A Ruotolo
5 Vincent St
Billerica MA 01821

Call Sign: W7LSG
Kenneth M Olson Jr
22 Whipple Rd
Billerica MA 01821

Call Sign: W1WYU
Edward J Chanen
43 Whittier Rd
Billerica MA 01821

Call Sign: KD1HT
Arthur S Derfall
30 Wildcrest Ave
Billerica MA 01821

Call Sign: WA1ION
Mark V Connelly
30 William Rd
Billerica MA
018216079

Call Sign: N1RHZ
Kenneth R Sandler
2 Woodcrest Circle
Billerica MA 01821

Call Sign: W1HIY
Russell L Ashworth
41 Wyman Rd
Billerica MA 01821

Call Sign: K1KAZ
David L Babbidge
75 Wyman Rd
Billerica MA 01821

Call Sign: KA1NIT
Leo T Mc Cormack
90 Wyman Rd
Billerica MA 01821

Call Sign: KB1CKB

Fay S Hornstein
Billerica MA 01821

Call Sign: N1TMO
Kenneth C Barbush
Billerica MA 01821

Call Sign: NF1A
Arthur E Pizer
Billerica MA 01821

Call Sign: KB1HNA
Allan W Cortese
Billerica MA
018210437

Call Sign: KB1MVF
Michael D Melo
Billerica MA 01865

Call Sign: KB1PLD
Joseph F Regal
Billerica MA 01821

Call Sign: KB1VOQ
Tom Rezucha
Billerica MA 01821

FCC Amateur Radio Licenses in Blackstone

Call Sign: KC7IHG
George L Gallo
11 Bellingham Rd
Blackstone MA 01504

Call Sign: AB1EX
George L Gallo
11 Bellingham Rd
Blackstone MA 01504

Call Sign: K1ITS
Kurt W Train
324 Blackstone St
Blackstone MA 01504

Call Sign: W1JXI
John Seliga
15 Carrington St
Blackstone MA 01504

Call Sign: W1AUT
Normand R Thibault

15 Carter Ave
Blackstone MA 01504

Call Sign: KB1LTB
Daniel T Spulecki
5 Chestnut St
Blackstone MA 01504

Call Sign: K1DTS
Daniel T Spulecki
5 Chestnut St
Blackstone MA 01504

Call Sign: W1VAG
Edward V Fox
119 Elm St
Blackstone MA 01504

Call Sign: N1WLY
Peter L Jones
122 Elm St
Blackstone MA 01504

Call Sign: N1OQU
Brady Davison
129 Elm St
Blackstone MA 01504

Call Sign: WA1MJB
Michael J Buckley
227 Elm St
Blackstone MA 01504

Call Sign: KB1SXQ
Barbara A Connors
5 First Ave
Blackstone MA 01504

Call Sign: NP2FZ
Keithley R Sutton Jr
5 Hop Brook Ln
Blackstone MA 01504

Call Sign: N1YMC
Roberta R Solinko
10 Huntington Av
Blackstone MA
015042201

Call Sign: AI1Z
Donald R Savini
10 Huntington Ave
Blackstone MA 01504

Call Sign: KB1CMD
Joseph J Farrington
10 Huntington Ave
Blackstone MA 01504

Call Sign: KB1SNI
David J De Mello
10 Huntington Ave
Blackstone MA 01504

Call Sign: KA1QLO
SANDRA M
Farrington
10 Huntington Ave
2nd Fl
Blackstone MA 01504

Call Sign: KB1ITP
Teddy W Solinko
10 Huntington Ave
Black Stone MA
01504

Call Sign: N1YMC
Teddy W Solinko
10 Huntington Ave
Black Stone MA
01504

Call Sign: WB1GTI
Christopher J Ryan
21 Liberty Hill Dr
Blackstone MA 01504

Call Sign: N1KLF
Lawrence D Freitas
3 Mandy Drive
Blackstone MA 01504

Call Sign: KA1GXG
Ian M Newman
8 Mark Dr
Blackstone MA 01504

Call Sign: N1JNC
James J Coffey
22 May St
Blackstone MA 01504

Call Sign: N1UFV
Norman A Pennett
7 Milk St
Blackstone MA 01504

Call Sign: NA1Q
Matthew C Penttila
49 Miller St Apt 5
Blackstone MA
015042041

Call Sign: KB1PLN
Bryan A Marcotte
18 Milton St
Blackstone MA 01504

Call Sign: KF1D
Bryan A Marcotte
18 Milton St
Blackstone MA 01504

Call Sign: KB1LCH
Robert E Jean
19 Montcalm Ave
Blackstone MA 01504

Call Sign: KB1MTI
Dorothy A
Hetherington
Old Mendon St
Blackstone MA 01504

Call Sign: KB1SSL
John T Delaney
13 Orchard St
Blackstone MA 01504

Call Sign: KB1GUU
Arlene R Gagnon
57 Orchard St
Blackstone MA 01504

Call Sign: KB1QOT
Patricia L Vilnit
7 Park St
Blackstone MA 01504

Call Sign: W1AUT
Patricia L Vilnit
7 Park St
Blackstone MA 01504

Call Sign: N1VRM
James M Cunningham
1 Paul Drive
Blackstone MA 01504

Call Sign: NT4X
David R Wheatley

10 Rivers Edge Rd
Blackstone MA 01504

Call Sign: W2JIZ
Donald P Saladin
46 Rocco Dr
Blackstone MA 01504

Call Sign: WA1NY
Donald P Saladin
46 Rocco Dr
Blackstone MA 01504

Call Sign: KB1VGL
Bruce M Schaller
12 Saint Paul St Apt 3
Blackstone MA 01504

Call Sign: KB1RER
Robert W Caonette Jr
8 Saint Paul St Apt 5
Blackstone MA 01504

Call Sign: N1SMJ
Attila Marczin
7 St Germain Ave
Blackstone MA 01504

Call Sign: WA1URO
Peter A Christensen
112 Summer St
Blackstone MA
015041377

Call Sign: N1PSC
Lucille M Laliberte
133 Summer St
Blackstone MA
015040089

Call Sign: N1QJS
George W Millis
133 Summer St
Blackstone MA 01504

Call Sign: WA1CIG
Edward M Krajewski
5 William St
Blackstone MA 01504

Call Sign: KB1NJF
Christopher E Picanso
3 Windsong Dr
Blackstone MA 01504

Call Sign: KC2THF
Jennifer P Cormier
Blackstone MA 01504

FCC Amateur Radio Licenses in Blandford

Call Sign: WA1WZY
Craig M Stokowski
Blandford MA 01008

Call Sign: KB1DGW
Paul M Cotti
20 North St
Blandford MA 01008

Call Sign: WB1CPD
Gerald E Desroches
North St
Blandford MA 01008

Call Sign: N1TQS
Ronald J Cinq Mars
256 Otis Rd
Blandford MA 01008

Call Sign: KB1PHW
James A Wolfgang
166 Otis Stage Rd
Blandford MA 01008

Call Sign: N1TUZ
Dawn D Snow Cinq
Mars
256 Otis Rd
Blanford MA 01008

FCC Amateur Radio Licenses in Bolton

Call Sign: WB1FOB
David L Velardocchia
199 Annie Moore Rd
Bolton MA 01740

Call Sign: KB1WFC
Nicholas S Alberts
313 Berlin Rd
Bolton MA 01740

Call Sign: N1DHP
Richard M Klahne
339 Berlin Rd

Bolton MA 01740

Call Sign: WD8PTL
David J Sperry
141 Brown Rd
Bolton MA 01740

Call Sign: AA1S
William A Taylor
103 Burnham Rd
Bolton MA 01740

Call Sign: KB1JGT
Diane S Harris
44 Corn Rd
Bolton MA 01740

Call Sign: KB1JGW
Ethan F Harris
44 Corn Rd
Bolton MA 01740

Call Sign: W1GDW
Sallyann King
111 Coventry Wd Rd
Bolton MA 01740

Call Sign: W1CSM
Bruce A King
111 Coventry Wood
Rd
Bolton MA 01740

Call Sign: KB1RLO
William Dawson
34 Danforth Ln
Bolton MA 01740

Call Sign: WA1TMT
Richard J Corley
107 Fox Run Rd
Bolton MA 01740

Call Sign: N1BNJ
Kenneth E Egeland
153 Green Rd
Bolton MA 01740

Call Sign: N1XGH
Ralph D Barnie
13 Liberty Cir
Bolton MA 01740

Call Sign: WX8X

Marion W
Wannamaker
213 Long Hill Rd
Bolton MA 01740

Call Sign: KA1GFN
Kenneth A Horton
352 Longhill Rd
Bolton MA 01740

Call Sign: N1NVJ
Deborah D Horton
352 Longhill Rd
Bolton MA 01740

Call Sign: WA1HGA
Walter A Haslett Jr
198 Main St
Bolton MA 01740

Call Sign: K1JRA
Robert E Davis
1 Mc Nulty Rd
Bolton MA 01740

Call Sign: WA1RTI
Marie A Fusaro Davis
1 Mc Nulty Rd
Bolton MA 01740

Call Sign: N3JND
John R Mc Cullough
104 Nourse Rd
Bolton MA 01740

Call Sign: N1AOF
Richard A Bartlett
182 Nourse Rd
Bolton MA 01740

Call Sign: W1OJ
Dean R Perkins
Old Bay Rd
Bolton MA 01740

Call Sign: N1BCX
Michael M Hoeffler
43 Old Sugar Rd
Bolton MA 01740

Call Sign: WA1HMW
William W Cridland Sr
57 Pinewood Rd
Bolton MA 01740

Call Sign: N1TLD
David K Perry
Po Box 520
Bolton MA 01740

Call Sign: KB1VPW
Peter L Hoover
70 Quaker Ln
Bolton MA 01740

Call Sign: K1PLH
Peter L Hoover
70 Quaker Ln
Bolton MA 01740

Call Sign: N1ZNZ
Edward T Bissonnette
20 S Bolton Rd
Bolton MA 01740

Call Sign: N1LYD
Christopher J Siano
377 South Bolton Rd
Bolton MA 01740

Call Sign: K1AE
John D Allen
93 Spectacle Hill Rd
Bolton MA 01740

Call Sign: N1RWM
Linda A Allen
93 Spectacle Hill Rd
Bolton MA 01740

Call Sign: AA1EF
Richard F Du Fosse
11 Still River Rd
Bolton MA 01740

Call Sign: N1JEB
Daniel T Senie
324 Still River Rd
Bolton MA 01740

Call Sign: N1JIT
Faith M Senie
324 Still River Rd
Bolton MA 01740

Call Sign: KB1PCE
David J Perry
152 Sugar Rd

Bolton MA 01740

Call Sign: KB1RPY
Peter A Simmons
155 Sugar Rd
Bolton MA 01740

Call Sign: KB1FKP
Theodore O Grosch
242 Sugar Rd
Bolton MA 01740

Call Sign: KB1EMU
Robert R Blair
248 Sugar Rd
Bolton MA 01740

Call Sign: N4ADC
Gilbert A Burns
438 Sugar Rd
Bolton MA 01740

Call Sign: N1NQA
Walter A Mutti
12 Wattaquadock Hill
Rd
Bolton MA 01740

Call Sign: WB6VVA
Ernest W Swenson
299 Wattaquadock Hill
Rd
Bolton MA 01740

Call Sign: N1ONX
Alan D Parker
583 Wattaquadock Hill
Rd
Bolton MA 01740

Call Sign: N1QIM
Robert D Heinold
331 Wattaquadock Rd
Bolton MA 01740

Call Sign: K1KW
Charles D O Neal Iii
Bolton MA 01740

Call Sign: K1ANN
Mrithyunjaya K
Annapragada
Bolton MA 017400385

Call Sign: KB1OFY
Michael R
Courtemanche
3108 Main St
Bondsville MA 01009

Call Sign: KB1IEN
David L Smith
3012 Maple St
Bondsville MA 01009

Call Sign: KB1IAD
David L Smith Sr
Bondsville MA 01009

Call Sign: N1VBT
John P D Van
Schalkwyk
50 Melcher St
Bosotn MA 02210

Call Sign: AB1KG
Mitsugu Sato
-10484
Boston MA 02205

Call Sign: N3JX
Mitsugu Sato
-10484
Boston MA 022055071

Call Sign: WA1UAQ
John T Lu
13th Floor
Boston MA 02108

Call Sign: WB1GGF
Joseph P Wynne
15 Alcott St
Boston MA 02134

Call Sign: WA1QYQ
Franz E Keller
6 Alveston Terrace
Boston MA 02130

Call Sign: KB1NWW
Mathew R Ercoline

37 Anderson St 2
Boston MA 02114

Call Sign: N1SXQ
Jesse C Burstein
147 Appleton St #4
Boston MA 02116

Call Sign: WA1FYT
Edward P Anderson
3 Arborview Rd
Boston MA 02130

Call Sign: KB1MLB
Christopher C
Cummins
141 Arlington St Apt 5
Boston MA 02116

Call Sign: KA1GEB
Robert S White
Astor Station
Boston MA 021230441

Call Sign: W1TKS
Charles Hieken Esq
500 Atlantic Ave Unit
21a
Boston MA 022102257

Call Sign: KB1WFE
Massimo Forte
Ave De Lafayette
Boston MA 02111

Call Sign: KB1VZN
Guljed Birce
125 B St Unit 3c
Boston MA 02127

Call Sign: W1TUE
Nathaniel L Bell Sr
8 Bard Ave
Boston MA 02119

Call Sign: WB1AAU
Ford D Cavallari
50 Battery St 610
Boston MA 02109

Call Sign: KA1QZO
Matthew W Thompson
64 Bay State Rd
Boston MA 02215

Call Sign: KB1THG
Oliver K Yeh
97 Bay State Rd
Boston MA 02215

Call Sign: KB1GGA
David M Signoff
155 Bay State Rd
Boston MA 02215

Call Sign: KF4KJQ
Benjamin S Gelb
155 Bay State Rd
Boston MA 02215

Call Sign: KB1QWI
Daniel R Wieland
27 Bay State Rd Apt 2r
Boston MA 02215

Call Sign: KB1RBO
Erik S Beiser
86 Bayswater St
Boston MA 02128

Call Sign: KA1DEU
Gregory T Whitman
483 Beacan St 25
Boston MA 02115

Call Sign: KB1KFU
Isabel M Bernal
450 Beacon St
Boston MA 02115

Call Sign: KB1VDZ
Brian C Gardiner
526 Beacon St
Boston MA 02215

Call Sign: KB1GFR
Andrew G Greg
528 Beacon St
Boston MA 02215

Call Sign: KB1GFT
Mark B Harris
528 Beacon St
Boston MA 02215

Call Sign: KB1MLY
Adam R Vaccaro
528 Beacon St

Boston MA 02215

Call Sign: WB2CPU
Howard A Cahn
295 Beacon St 23
Boston MA 02116

Call Sign: W6CKB
Christophe C Assens
1600 Beacon St Appt
1110
Boston MA 02446

Call Sign: KB1GLF
William J Foley
147 Berkeley St
Boston MA 02116

Call Sign: KB1JMY
Salvation Army - 147
Masatern
Berkeley St
Boston MA 02116

Call Sign: W1MSA
Salvation Army - 147
Masatern
Berkeley St
Boston MA 02116

Call Sign: KB1HDK
David J Freedman
7 Bolton Pl
Boston MA 02129

Call Sign: KB1PJX
Taylor W Barton
43 Bowdoin St Apt 5f
Boston MA 02114

Call Sign: WN9T
G John Garrett
Box 35296
Boston MA 021350005

Call Sign: WA1NLG
Norman R Cantin
780 Boylston St
Boston MA 02199

Call Sign: W1UWB
Julian M Sobin
790 Boylston St
Boston MA 02199

Call Sign: KB8RLQ
Scott D Johnston
1395 Boylston St
Boston MA 02215

Call Sign: W1ALC
Andrew L Camarata
1330 Boylston St #404
Boston MA 02215

Call Sign: N1XZB
David P Goncalves
1197 Boylston St Apt
55
Boston MA 022153526

Call Sign: N1GDG
Joseph F Di Dio
158 Brandywyne Dr
Boston MA 02128

Call Sign: N1XBT
Stephen B Jeffries
12 Brimmer St
Boston MA 021081002

Call Sign: W1SBJ
Stephen B Jeffries
12 Brimmer St
Boston MA 021081002

Call Sign: KB1FPJ
Thaddeus J Stefanov
Wagner
170 Brookline Ave
Boston MA 02215

Call Sign: KB1HHX
David S Dodge
100 Calumet St
Boston MA 02120

Call Sign: KB1IXH
J Kent Post
Cambridge Center
Boston MA 02142

Call Sign: K1EDE
William H Spence
2426 Centre St W
Roxbury
Boston MA 02132

Call Sign: KC1SQ
Todd K Rodgers
25 Channel Center St
Boston MA 02210

Call Sign: KB1HDG
Neil A Hurst
25 Channel Center St
609
Boston MA 02210

Call Sign: WA1FNS
Ira G Deutsch
Charles St Sta
Boston MA 02114

Call Sign: K1TOC
Ira G Deutsch
Charles St Station
Boston MA 02114

Call Sign: K1YE
Ira G Deutsch
Charles St Station
Boston MA 02114

Call Sign: KB1VZJ
Joseph W Chapman
4 Charlesgate E Apt
608
Boston MA 02215

Call Sign: NV1W
Joseph W Chapman
4 Charlesgate E Apt
608
Boston MA 02215

Call Sign: W1JL
James R Lee
62 Chestnut St
Boston MA 02108

Call Sign: W1YAK
James R Lee
62 Chestnut St
Boston MA 02108

Call Sign: KB1VTT
James W Cook
70 Chestnut St
Boston MA 02108

Call Sign: W1BTC

James W Cook
70 Chestnut St
Boston MA 02108

Call Sign: KA1CPL
David B Arnold Jr
107 Chestnut St
Boston MA 02108

Call Sign: KC4NVS
Michael F Severini
62 Clarendon St Apt 8
Boston MA 02116

Call Sign: N1OOH
Michael R Lawrence
77 Cohasset St
Boston MA 02131

Call Sign: KB1FAT
Robert S Olszewski
300 Commercial St
#507
Boston MA 02109

Call Sign: KB1FAV
Robert S Olszewski
300 Commercial St
#507
Boston MA 02109

Call Sign: KB1MUU
Robert D Brown
357 Commercial St
Apt 819
Boston MA 02109

Call Sign: KB1NSP
David R Brown
253 Commonwealth
Av
Boston MA 02116

Call Sign: KB1WNM
Steven D Valdez
253 Commonwealth
Ave
Boston MA 02116

Call Sign: N3UCQ
John E Creighton
253 Commonwealth
Ave
Boston MA 02116

Call Sign: KB1CKG
Tibor Trunk
700 Commonwealth
Ave
Boston MA 02215

Call Sign: W1LGQ
Harold H Starr
1925 Commonwealth
Ave
Boston MA 02135

Call Sign: KB1SLM
Andrew B Ballantine
62 Commonwealth
Ave 5
Boston MA 02116

Call Sign: KB9LJQ
Michael R Sadowski
12 Commonwealth
Ave Apt 104
Boston MA 02116

Call Sign: N1SSO
Alan D Wilensky
1085 Commonwealth
Ave S 101
Boston MA 02215

Call Sign: N1KLN
Kenneth C Mc Milleon
30 Cornhill Ave Apt
802
Boston MA 02108

Call Sign: KB1WDZ
Richard M Orluk
163 Cottage St Apt 2f
Boston MA 02128

Call Sign: K1XRN
Richard M Orluk Rn
163 Cottage St Apt 2f
Boston MA 02128

Call Sign: WA1VMU
Boston University
Amat Rad Club
44 Cummington St
Boston Univ
Boston MA 02215

Call Sign: N1MIY
Ertha A Ikini
18 Dalrymple St
Boston MA 02130

Call Sign: KB1CXO
Leonard M Singer
271 Dartmouth St 6h
Boston MA 02116

Call Sign: W1CM
Charles V Madek
6 Dawes Ter
Boston MA 021251743

Call Sign: KB9IIA
Robbie I Furman
1 Devonshire Pl Apt
3509
Boston MA 02109

Call Sign: KB1EJK
Robbie I Furman
1 Devonshire Pl Apt
3509
Boston MA 021093513

Call Sign: KB1LWZ
John T Lu
90 Devonshire St -
16th Fl
Boston MA 02109

Call Sign: W1FYZ
Donald J Dalpe
2049 Dorchester Ave
Boston MA 02124

Call Sign: N1UTV
Daniel J Tocci
24 Dustin St
Boston MA 021352853

Call Sign: KB1OID
Peter E Satkus
58 Dwight St Apt 5
Boston MA 021183609

Call Sign: AB1NU
Peter E Satkus
58 Dwight St Apt 5
Boston MA 021183609

Call Sign: AB1OA

Peter E Satkus
58 Dwight St Apt 5
Boston MA 021183609

Call Sign: AB1PS
Peter E Satkus
58 Dwight St Apt 5
Boston MA 021183609

Call Sign: KB1BKZ
James P Mc Devitt
787 E Broadway
Boston MA 02127

Call Sign: KB1SVU
Benjamin B Zelno
65 E India Row Apt Ph
D
Boston MA 02110

Call Sign: KB1ENU
Chester Swanson Iii
33 Edgerly Rd Apt 13
Boston MA 021153029

Call Sign: N1VJQ
Carol M Novitsky
169 Endicott St 4
Boston MA 02113

Call Sign: KB0AQL
Janet G Staab
28 Exeter St Apt 303
Boston MA 02116

Call Sign: KC5NWL
Paul S Tocchio
30 Falcon St Apt 1
Boston MA 021281335

Call Sign: KB1SFV
Nicholas R Kathmann
35 Fay St Unit 214
Boston MA 02118

Call Sign: N4AKS
Giorgio Minguzzi
101 Federal St Ste
1900
Boston MA 02110

Call Sign: KD4QWC
Turkka O Makinen
Federal St Suite 302

Boston MA 02110

Call Sign: KB1VWF
Karl P Wiegand
7 Feneno Terrace Apt
2
Boston MA 02134

Call Sign: KB1RDJ
Theodore J Nemmers
Iii
162 Fisher Ave
Boston MA 02120

Call Sign: KB1UCD
Christian M Lanphere
99 Fulton St 5-2
Boston MA 02109

Call Sign: W1KDR
John J Homko
111 Gainsborough St -
Apt 403
Boston MA 02115

Call Sign: K1NIE
Almo P Bambini
120 Glenwood Ave
Hyde Park
Boston MA 02136

Call Sign: N1CQH
Darnley L Corbin Jr
Grove Hall Station
Boston MA 021210002

Call Sign: K1HB
Fred M De Bros
15 Hancock St
Boston MA 021144102

Call Sign: KB1ECS
Guy B Debros
15 Hancock St
Boston MA 021144102

Call Sign: KC0KIJ
Giampaolo Malin
5 Hanson St Apt 3
Boston MA 02118

Call Sign: WD1P
Jacques G Verly
16 Harcourt St Apt 8j

Boston MA 02116

Call Sign: KB1GLK
Edward E Stuart
860 Harrison Ave Apt
704
Boston MA 02118

Call Sign: KB1VOT
Jose G Venegas
2 Hawthorne Pl 15d
Boston MA 02114

Call Sign: KB1VOU
Magnolia M V
Venegas
2 Hawthorne Pl 15d
Boston MA 02114

Call Sign: KB9TRY
Joseph M Nehls
39 Haynes St 2
Boston MA 02128

Call Sign: K9VNR
Joseph M Nehls
39 Haynes St 2
Boston MA 02128

Call Sign: WA1ESZ
Joan M Morgan
25 Helena Rd
Boston MA 021221908

Call Sign: WA1GHL
William H Morgan
25 Helena Rd
Boston MA 02122

Call Sign: KB1WDV
Robert E Watson
108 Hemenway St Apt
B
Boston MA 02115

Call Sign: KB1NVJ
Michael L Benson
112 Hillside St -3
Boston MA 02120

Call Sign: N1LII
Fred E Hagan
21 Hopkins St
Boston MA 02124

Call Sign: W1PTC
Wentworth Institute Of
Tech Arc
550 Huntington Ave
Boston MA 02115

Call Sign: K9PKW
Karl P Wiegand
360 Huntington Ave
202
Boston MA 02115

Call Sign: KD4PNW
Nicholas S Mironov
331 Huntington Ave
Apt 51
Boston MA 02115

Call Sign: W1NAU
Timothy J Nau
550 Huntington Ave
Ms278
Boston MA 021155998

Call Sign: N1VJO
Wajana P Charlenkul
150 Huntington Ave
Nj8
Boston MA 02115

Call Sign: KA1BAN
Kendall W Guilford
John F Kennedy Sta
Boston MA 02114

Call Sign: KB7NHB
Kenyatta L Harris
62 Julian St Apt 3
Boston MA 02125

Call Sign: AB1CE
Ramon F Kolb
147 Kelton St 717
Boston MA 02134

Call Sign: AA1IU
Marco Fassiotto
Kenmore St
Boston MA 02215

Call Sign: KB1LZO
Paul J Kettle
14 Keswick St

Boston MA 02215

Call Sign: KB1LZP
Sonya Boggs
14 Keswick St 3
Boston MA 02215

Call Sign: AC5TB
Katsuhiko Morosawa
Kingston St (4f)
Boston MA 02111

Call Sign: KB1VWW
Ludwig H Castillo
34 Lagrange ST
Boston MA 02132

Call Sign: KI4NO
Leon Lane
1410 Lagrange St
Boston MA 02167

Call Sign: KA1WKN
Jia M Chen
92 Lawn St
Boston MA 02120

Call Sign: KB1VTW
Jay D Lowenstein
312 Lewis Wharf
Boston MA 02110

Call Sign: KZ3BMW
Jay D Lowenstein
312 Lewis Wharf
Boston MA 02110

Call Sign: W1VKE
Frank S Wozniak
9 Liberty Pl
Boston MA 02127

Call Sign: KA1HXV
Bernard F Start
4 Longfellow Pl 1805
Boston MA 02114

Call Sign: KB1SDT
Christiaan H Kelly
1 Longfellow Pl Apt
3224
Boston MA 02114

Call Sign: WH6APQ

Stephen L Macknik
Longwood Ave
Boston MA 02115

Call Sign: KB1NGJ
Volker H Kissling
Ludcke House Soldier
Field
Boston MA 02163

Call Sign: KI1SSI
Volker H Kissling
Ludcke House Soldier
Field
Boston MA 02163

Call Sign: KB1NAW
Matthew S Dunn
141 M St Apt 2
Boston MA 02127

Call Sign: KM1P
Joseph B Fitzgerald
170 Manthorne Rd
Boston MA 021321503

Call Sign: AD1I
Michael D Harnois
256 Marginal St
Boston MA 02128

Call Sign: KA7ZEE
Grenville P Byford
252 Marlborough St
Boston MA 02116

Call Sign: KB1HKA
Hector A Gonzalez
416 Marlborough St
209
Boston MA 02115

Call Sign: KE1CP
Michael L Glidewell
255 Mass Ave 318
Boston MA 02115

Call Sign: KB1EGW
David G Morris Jr
78 Mattapan St
Boston MA 02126

Call Sign: NB1X
Yachiyl Z Signorelli

92 Melville Ave
Boston MA 02124

Call Sign: KB1BRC
1053rd Judge
Advocate Generals
Dtchmnt Lso Rtu
85 Merrimac St
Boston MA 021142519

Call Sign: KB1QDS
Yachiyl Z Signorelli
92 Merville Ave
Boston MA 02124

Call Sign: AB1IS
Yachiyl Z Signorelli
92 Merville Ave
Boston MA 02124

Call Sign: N1SOT
James E Coyne
468 Metropolitan Ave
Boston MA 02136

Call Sign: W2KGA
Malvin C Teich
70 Montgomery St
Boston MA 02116

Call Sign: KI6FJS
Naushad Wahab
401 Mount Vernon St
Apt 918
Boston MA 02125

Call Sign: KB1KVQ
Gregory S Burd
83 Mount Vernon St
Unit 1
Boston MA 02108

Call Sign: N1PAZ
Timothy M Huntington
152 Mt Vernon St
Boston MA 02108

Call Sign: N1KUJ
Stephen H Dohrmann
35 Myrtle St Apt 9
Boston MA 02114

Call Sign: K1NDV
Lewis J Lipson

New Town Branch
Boston MA 02456

Call Sign: N1OAW
Evangelos
Athanasopoulos
304 Newbury St - Apt
388
Boston MA 02115

Call Sign: W1JXW
Borio J Magnani
184 Norfolk Ave
Boston MA 02119

Call Sign: WA1YAK
Paul A Mercauto Sr
11 North Sq
Boston MA 02113

Call Sign: KB1VOG
Mark J Gabrielson
350 North St Apt 601
Boston MA 02113

Call Sign: KB1BRL
Mark J Gabrielson
350 North St Apt 601
Boston MA 02113

Call Sign: N1YT
Brian H Guck
350 North St Apt 701
Boston MA 02113

Call Sign: KB1GFS
Brian H Guck
350 North St Apt 701
Boston MA 02113

Call Sign: KB1VZO
Marie M Tai
100 Norway St 12a
Boston MA 02115

Call Sign: W1TAI
Marie M Tai
100 Norway St 12a
Boston MA 02115

Call Sign: KC7GZB
Jan Marie Andersen
66 Nottinghill Rd #1
Boston MA 02135

Call Sign: KB1WNR
Stephen A Cass
13 Oakdale St Apt 3
Boston MA 02130

Call Sign: KB1LZG
Thomas A Poynter
2 Otis Place Apt 5
Boston MA 02108

Call Sign: KG4SDY
Nick Nathans
P O Box 52097
Boston MA 02205

Call Sign: KB1SPN
Angie M Covey
455 Park Dr 2
Boston MA 02215

Call Sign: KC1KK
Jack G Daubs
15 Park Dr Apt 10
Boston MA 02215

Call Sign: KB1QZJ
Peter A Berlin
131 Park Dr Apt 30
Boston MA 02215

Call Sign: WA1RFF
Jeffrey H Kline
51 Park Dr Apt 4
Boston MA 022155204

Call Sign: KB1CCJ
Austin E Wolfe
455 Park Dr Unit 2
Boston MA 02215

Call Sign: N1UVE
Noah I Hugenberger
3 Park St 7th Floor
Boston MA 02108

Call Sign: KC1MI
John F Rhilinger
37 Pearl St
Boston MA 021251815

Call Sign: KA1YSF
William H Vreeland
128 Pembroke St

Boston MA 02118

Call Sign: KB5RZR
Adam A Friedman
75 Peterborough St
#613
Boston MA 02215

Call Sign: K1ECD
Ernest A Cataldo
15 Phillips St
Boston MA 02114

Call Sign: KF1W
Mark J Greeley
15 Pinckney St Apt 2
Boston MA 02114

Call Sign: KA1HEK
Edwin L Prien Jr
145 Pinckney St Apt
306
Boston MA 02114

Call Sign: WO1S
Franklin H Stuart Ii
145 Pinckney St Apt
323
Boston MA 02114

Call Sign: KB1IYN
James J Kimbrough
400 Pond St
Boston MA 021303403

Call Sign: KA1FBM
Matthew M Cappello
Jr
144 Prince St
Boston MA 02113

Call Sign: KB1MQE
Michael H Coen
138 Prince St 9
Boston MA 02113

Call Sign: KA1NZQ
Nancy A Freed
1350 Prudential Tower
Boston MA 02199

Call Sign: W2IQD
Daniel L Fox
26 Rear Trenton St

Boston MA 02128

Call Sign: N1RSD
Richard J Curry
2 Redfield St
Boston MA 021223115

Call Sign: N1IJP
Jonathan R Metzger
80 Revere St 9
Boston MA 02114

Call Sign: W1PST
Justin L Wyner
20 Rowes Wharf Unit
507
Boston MA 02110

Call Sign: KB1VOP
Alejandro A Perez-
Hobrecker
24 Ruskin St
Boston MA 02132

Call Sign: KB1VOW
Armando Perez
24 Ruskin St
Boston MA 02132

Call Sign: KA1UEB
Benjamin P Grubin
39 Rutland St 1
Boston MA 02118

Call Sign: KB1WWJ
Siqing Li
75 Saint Alphonsus St
Apt 809
Boston MA 02120

Call Sign: N1AVF
William A Holbrook
9 Salman St
Boston MA 02132

Call Sign: N1QCW
David P Bard
21 Salutaton St
Boston MA 02109

Call Sign: KB1JZG
Stephan Harris
44 School St Pmb 186
Boston MA 02108

Call Sign: N1OQG
John E Lester
302 Shawmut Ave
Boston MA 02118

Call Sign: KB1UDM
Sachiko Fujiwara
448 Shawmut Ave
Boston MA 02118

Call Sign: AB1MJ
Toshiki Fujiwara
448 Shawmut Ave
Boston MA 02118

Call Sign: K1PP
Takashi Miyamoto
448 Shawmut Ave
Boston MA 02118

Call Sign: KB1UDL
Takashi Miyamoto
Shawmut Ave
Boston MA 02118

Call Sign: KB1U
Takashi Miyamoto
Shawmut Ave
Boston MA 02118

Call Sign: KB1VGV
Naomasa Nakamura
Shawmut Ave
Boston MA 02118

Call Sign: AB1MO
Katsuhiro Misumi
Shawmut Ave
Boston MA 02118

Call Sign: W1RAK
Katsuhiro Misumi
Shawmut Ave
Boston MA 02118

Call Sign: N1ZKR
Paul J Olivieri
39 Shepard St 3
Boston MA 02135

Call Sign: KB1GMO
Clifford B Brew-Smith
44 Sheridan St 3

Boston MA 02130

Call Sign: N1ATT
George S Brown
189 Sherrin St
Boston MA 021361851

Call Sign: N1TFW
William R Della Croce
Jr
33 Snow Hill St
Boston MA 02113

Call Sign: KJ6MWG
Edward B Guynn
2 Soldiers Field Park
Apt 618
Boston MA 02163

Call Sign: N1RTI
George N Riethof
36 Soley St
Boston MA 02129

Call Sign: N1XTX
Cheryl A Norsworthy
210 South St Unit 904
Boston MA 02111

Call Sign: WA1YGJ
Richard W Norsworthy
210 South St Unit 904
Boston MA 02111

Call Sign: KB1RFS
Boston University
Amateur Radio Club
8 St Mary S St Room
324c
Boston MA 02215

Call Sign: W1BUR
Boston University
Amateur Radio Club
8 St Marys St Room
324c
Boston MA 02215

Call Sign: N1AUW
Gerard Sarno
225 St Theresa Ave
Boston MA 02132

Call Sign: N1LYS

Stephen P Boudrot
150 Staniford St 626
Boston MA 021142525

Call Sign: KB1ULE
Peter N Allinson
4 Strong Pl
Boston MA 02114

Call Sign: N1VNU
Rodney L Singleton
17 Sunset St
Boston MA 02120

Call Sign: K1ASG
Peter F Crawford
36 Supple Rd
Boston MA 02121

Call Sign: AA1MA
Walter J Pienton
42 Sydney St
Boston MA 02125

Call Sign: N1NQK
James A Griffin Iii
77 Tampa St
Boston MA 02126

Call Sign: KB5SIY
Shaun P Duffy
28 The Fenway
Boston MA 02215

Call Sign: N1PSS
Joseph G Sullivan
9 Thurlow St
Boston MA 02132

Call Sign: KA1EXY
Joe I Ordia
690 Tremont St
Boston MA 02118

Call Sign: KB2VSV
Marc Pimentel
1575 Tremont St #510
Boston MA 02120

Call Sign: N1ZKT
Philip P Salkind
791 Tremont St W505
Boston MA 02118

Call Sign: N1RLZ
Allan G Sullivan
1036 Truman Hwy
Boston MA 021363319

Call Sign: WA5JTP
Alan W Pailet
Two Hawthorne Pl
Boston MA 02114

Call Sign: K1CHK
Byron A Aldridge
47 Tyndale St
Boston MA 02131

Call Sign: KB1KPK
Robert W Timmerman
Jr
25 Upton St
Boston MA 02118

Call Sign: W1TVW
George E Brady
5 Vincent Rd
Boston MA 02131

Call Sign: N1QPP
Selim S Vahas
80 W Cedar St Apt 2
Boston MA 02114

Call Sign: KB1TME
Daniel G Hechavarria
372 W Roxbury Pkwy
Boston MA 02132

Call Sign: KC0RPK
Kirk A Steele
46 Ward St Apt 3
Boston MA 02127

Call Sign: KA1HOO
Thomas M Chilton
155 Warren Ave
Boston MA 02116

Call Sign: N1IFM
JAMES C SWENSON
Mr
7 Warwick St
Boston MA 02120

Call Sign: K1CUF
Stanley W Floreskul

4360 Washington St
Boston MA 02131

Call Sign: W7IKO
Stephan Harris
276 Washington St
Pmb 186
Boston MA 02108

Call Sign: K1KIC
George T Bazinas
60 Wenham St
Boston MA 02130

Call Sign: KB1HGE
Erik J Pugh
320 West 3rd St Unit
206
Boston MA 02127

Call Sign: KB1VEX
Matthias W Andres
West 4th St 2
Boston MA 02127

Call Sign: AB1OO
Matthias W Andres
West 4th St 2
Boston MA 02127

Call Sign: AB1PV
Markus Weber
West 4th St 2
Boston MA 02127

Call Sign: KB1DWQ
Gordon Scott Shand
182 West Brookline St
Boston MA 02118

Call Sign: KA1RIS
Richard Y Yoon
46 Westland Ave 39
Boston MA 02115

Call Sign: KB1FQE
Pamela A Mallory-
Ricker
226 Westville St
Boston MA 02122

Call Sign: KB1KXU
Joseph A Walsh
40 Westwind Rd 305

Boston MA 02125

Call Sign: KG4NAG
Jacob D Baime
6 Whittier Pl Apt 10k
Boston MA 02114

Call Sign: N1LRT
Paul H Katz
8 Whittier Pl Apt 2f
Boston MA 02114

Call Sign: KB1WAG
Mark D Dymek
14 Willis St
Boston MA 021251946

Call Sign: N1SSP
Benjamin O Marte
35 Winchester St
Boston MA 02116

Call Sign: KG6HNY
Ash C Dyer
47 Winter St Fl 7
Boston MA 02108

Call Sign: W1FYE
Erik S T Scot
Winthrop
Boston MA 021520006

Call Sign: N1IJL
Edward A Lee
98 Winthrop St Apt #1
Boston MA 02119

Call Sign: W1FH
Charles Mellen
28 Woodley Ave
Boston MA 021324730

Call Sign: K1ZWQ
John T Yurewicz
16 Worthington St
Boston MA 02120

Call Sign: N1ANJ
Robert P Wotiz
34 Yarmouth St
Boston MA 02116

Call Sign: KA1ZQP
Deborah J Holt

Boston MA 02101

Call Sign: N1MXG
Vincent J Bono
Boston MA 02106

Call Sign: N1AFB
Shel H Peck
Boston MA 021990471

Call Sign: N1IRF
Stephen B Pankowicz
Boston MA 02196

Call Sign: N1SOC
William M Adams
Boston MA 02117

Call Sign: W1BOS
Boston Amateur Radio
Club
Boston MA 02215

Call Sign: KB1FED
Newton Amateur
Radio Club
Boston MA 02456

Call Sign: W1NDV
Newton Amateur
Radio Club
Boston MA 02456

Call Sign: KB1FQD
James Connors
Boston MA 02215

Call Sign: KB1GNN
K David Stahl
Boston MA 02127

Call Sign: NE1RI
James M Surprenant
Boston MA 02120

Call Sign: KB1NEA
Gregory P Dormitzer
Boston MA 021961989

Call Sign: KI4SIL
Nicholas D'apice
Boston MA 021350005

Call Sign: KB1QVZ

Christine M Spacone
Boston MA 02117

Call Sign: KB1RHK
Arcadio Delvalle
Boston MA 02123

Call Sign: K1SAW
James Connors
Boston MA 02215

Call Sign: N1AVI
Matthew H Trask
3 Canterbury Ln
Bourne MA
025324242

Call Sign: N1TB
Thomas E Burt
4 Daniel Webster Lane
Bourne MA 02532

Call Sign: KB1RGM
William J Corey Sr
57 Deseret Dr
Bourne MA 02532

Call Sign: KB1WKH
William J Corey Sr
57 Deseret Dr
Bourne MA 02532

Call Sign: N1BJC
William J Corey Sr
57 Deseret Dr
Bourne MA 02532

Call Sign: K1UUQ
Robert W Schertel
7 Dogwood Rd
Bourne MA 02532

Call Sign: KB1JKD
Daniel W Howard
40 Howard Ave
Bourne MA 02532

Call Sign: K1DYO
Daniel W Howard
40 Howard Ave
Bourne MA 02532

Call Sign: W1EEB
Earl E Emerick
62 Jefferson Rd
Bourne MA 02532

Call Sign: N1CHT
Harold J Ramsden Jr
201 Sandwich Rd
Bourne MA 02532

Call Sign: W1HTU
Harold J Ramsden Jr
201 Sandwich Rd
Bourne MA 02532

Call Sign: NI1Z
Stanley A Darmofalski
Jr
14 Sanford St
Bourne MA 02532

Call Sign: W1HCN
William G Morgan
51 Ships View Ter
Bourne MA 02532

Call Sign: N1UJV
Paul B Burt
46 Thom Ave
Bourne MA 02532

Call Sign: KA1AOM
Clark E Scammon
26 Waterhouse Rd
Bourne MA 02532

Call Sign: N1GJ
George B Jones
24 Weatherdeck Dr
Bourne MA 02532

Call Sign: KO1S
Donald F Landry
21 Weatherdeck Drive
Bourne MA 02532

Call Sign: N1LSC
Walter L Hoyt
130 Chester Rd
Boxboro MA 01719

Call Sign: KD6QEL
Peggy Barach
27 Fifers Lane
Boxboro MA 01719

Call Sign: WA2VAR
David R Barach
27 Fifers Ln
Boxboro MA 01719

Call Sign: W1HDX
John L Du Bois
873 Hill Rd
Boxboro MA 01719

Call Sign: N1PYF
Frank R Sibley
73 Liberty Square Rd
Apt 30a
Boxboro MA
017191609

Call Sign: WB7EEL
John F Woods
958 Massachusetts Ave
Boxboro MA 01719

Call Sign: W0JSB
Jason S Buchanan
301 Old Harvard Rd
Boxboro MA 01719

Call Sign: N1FQE
Joseph A Belliveau
188 Picnic St
Boxboro MA 01719

Call Sign: N1JKW
Michael A Marino Jr
69 Spencer Rd Apt J20
Boxboro MA 01719

Call Sign: N1TLC
Richard G Gullotti
58 Spencer Rd K12
Boxboro MA 01719

Call Sign: W1LUW

Harold C Jensen
119 Stow Rd
Boxboro MA
017191850

Call Sign: WB1GEY
Kenneth F Canfield Jr
628 Stow Rd
Boxboro MA 01719

Call Sign: KB1RPZ
Lamine Zeroual
300 Codman Hill Rd
Unit 5c
Boxborough MA
01719

Call Sign: KA1SZH
Benjamin S Scarlet
1001 Depot Rd
Boxborough MA
01719

Call Sign: KA1SZI
Richard I Scarlet
1001 Depot Rd
Boxborough MA
01719

Call Sign: N7NOD
Gregory W Sheets
121 Houghton Lane
Boxborough MA
01719

Call Sign: N1FRO
John F Borg
21 Joyce Lane
Boxborough MA
01719

Call Sign: N1OAB
J Daniel Geist
933 Liberty Square Rd
Boxborough MA
01719

Call Sign: AB1F
Richard C Winfrey
214 Littlefield Rd
Boxborough MA
01719

Call Sign: KB1FJQ
James R Mondor
240 Massachusetts Ave
Boxborough MA
01719

Call Sign: KB1PUC
Richard T Connolly
773 Massachusetts Ave
C10
Boxborough MA
01719

Call Sign: KB1RNK
John M Sorvari
275 Old Harvard Rd
Boxborough MA
01719

Call Sign: AB1KF
John M Sorvari
275 Old Harvard Rd
Boxborough MA
01719

Call Sign: K1ARG
John M Sorvari
275 Old Harvard Rd
Boxborough MA
01719

Call Sign: KB1SRW
Ann B Sorvari
275 Old Harvard Rd
Boxborough MA
01719

Call Sign: KA1PKB
Robert E Hatch
24 Prescott Rd
Boxborough MA
01719

Call Sign: AB1HW
Charles H Learoyd
128 Russet Lane

Boxborough MA
01719

Call Sign: K1PUB
Charles H Learoyd
128 Russet Lane
Boxborough MA
01719

Call Sign: N1OMU
Phillip C Smith
50 Spencer Rd L32
Boxborough MA
01719

Call Sign: W1MDD
Marvin D Drake
177 Summer Rd
Boxborough MA
017192000

Call Sign: KB1JQY
Richard A Green
59 Waite Rd
Boxborough MA
01719

Call Sign: W1RAG
Richard A Green
59 Waite Rd
Boxborough MA
01719

Call Sign: WB7EMD
Steven R Maislin
24 Whitney Lane
Boxborough MA
017191851

Call Sign: W0RES
Thomas E Myslinski
3 Andrews Farm Rd
Boxford MA 01921

Call Sign: N1FIO
Richard M Daniel Jr
128 Bare Hill Rd
Boxford MA 01921

Call Sign: W1MK
Robye L Lahlum

45 Brookview Rd
Boxford MA 01921

Call Sign: WV1Q
John West
17 Carleton Cir
Boxford MA 01921

Call Sign: KG4JSG
Grace A Rynk
18 Cedar St
Boxford MA 01921

Call Sign: KG4JSH
Barry R Rynk
18 Cedar St
Boxford MA 01921

Call Sign: K1FTE
Kenneth E Littlefield
Chandler Rd
Boxford MA 01921

Call Sign: W1BIT
Bruno Bitin
40 Chapman Rd
Boxford MA 01921

Call Sign: N1DGZ
Vernon H Young
65 Georgetown Rd
Boxford MA
019212109

Call Sign: N1FBM
Karsten Sorensen
88 Georgetown Rd
Boxford MA 01921

Call Sign: K1OID
Allan Titcomb
Georgetown Rd
Boxford MA 01921

Call Sign: KA1EFC
Ronald D Dole Sr
51 Highland Rd
Boxford MA 01921

Call Sign: KA1EFO
Ronald D Dole Jr
51 Highland Rd
Boxford MA 01921

Call Sign: NB1I
John E Levreault Jr
53 Highland Rd
Boxford MA 01921

Call Sign: KB1OCR
Joseph J Mcdonough
7 Hillside Rd
Boxford MA 01921

Call Sign: KB1DHB
Drew D Leavitt
15 Hunters Rd
Boxford MA 01921

Call Sign: N1DD
Gerald C Woodworth
Jr
132 Ipswich Rd
Boxford MA
019210193

Call Sign: W1USN
Michael P Rioux
132 Killam Hill Rd
Boxford MA 01921

Call Sign: KB1LOB
Scott S Rioux
132 Killam Hill Rd
Boxford MA 01921

Call Sign: W1SSR
Scott S Rioux
132 Killam Hill Rd
Boxford MA 01921

Call Sign: KB1UPQ
Nantuket Lightship
Amateur Radio Club
132 Killam Hill Rd
Boxford MA 01921

Call Sign: W1NLS
Nantucket Lightship
Amateur Radio Club
132 Killam Hill Rd
Boxford MA 01921

Call Sign: KB1UNG
Wayne A Mahon
53 King George Dr
Boxford MA 01921

Call Sign: N1EVW
Michael C Long
6 Lawrence Rd
Boxford MA 01921

Call Sign: W1KOX
Gordon A Russell
31 Main St
Boxford MA 01921

Call Sign: N1AZY
Priscilla E Harris
128 Main St
Boxford MA 01921

Call Sign: WA1KJZ
Kimball S Harris
128 Main St
Boxford MA 01921

Call Sign: N1NWC
Susan J Campbell
687 Main St
Boxford MA 01921

Call Sign: WA1HEX
Stephen J Campbell
687 Main St
Boxford MA 01921

Call Sign: W1OSG
John Hitchcock Jr
230 Middleton Rd
Boxford MA 01921

Call Sign: NG1W
George M Walk
20 Partridge Ln
Boxford MA 01921

Call Sign: KB1VKJ
Nicholas M
Mykulowycz
12 Porter Rd
Boxford MA 01921

Call Sign: N1CWN
Raymond G Moison
81 Porter Rd
Boxford MA 01921

Call Sign: KB1WDA
Gregory Sobczynski

15 Redington Ridge
Rd
Boxford MA 01921

Call Sign: WA1YLZ
Paul A Dube
8 Redwood Circle
Boxford MA 01921

Call Sign: N1RMW
Robert E Sloane
65 Spofford Rd
Boxford MA 01921

Call Sign: W1DYW
Gerald W Lawson
8 Sprucewood Cir
Boxford MA
019212096

Call Sign: N1HRJ
Sandra A Hamel
76 Surrey Lane
Boxford MA 01921

Call Sign: WA1UIW
Dana R Gould
8 Topsfield Rd
Boxford MA 01921

Call Sign: W1DPH
Douglas P Harvey
12 Towne Rd
Boxford MA 01921

Call Sign: K1MOK
James S Henrikson
105 Valley Rd
Boxford MA 01921

Call Sign: WA8NVD
David L Beauvais
54 Valley Rd
Boxford MA 01921

Call Sign: KA1SC
Kevin S O Hara
13 Wildmeadow Rd
Boxford MA
019212710

Call Sign: N1OQY
Joseph A Savasta Jr
72 Wildmeadow Rd

Boxford MA 01921

Call Sign: WA1IWQ
Joseph R Fallon
4 Wyndmere Dr
Boxford MA 01921

Call Sign: KB1PC
Philip S Rane
Boxford MA
019210325

Call Sign: KB1IAL
Paula J Hart
Boxford MA
019210182

Call Sign: W1VMH
Everett W Harrington
Box 603
Boylston MA 01505

Call Sign: KA1LXB
Peter R Woods
606 Edgebrook Dr
Boylston MA 01505

Call Sign: N1GMS
Steven P Grondin
608 Edgebrrok Dr
Boylston MA 01505

Call Sign: KB1MSJ
William J Collins
13 Flagg St
Boylston MA 01505

Call Sign: KA1LZS
John R Dennis
11 Fox Tail Way
Boylston MA 01505

Call Sign: WA1CJR
Clifford M Mac
Donald Sr
60 Linden St
Boylston MA 01505

Call Sign: N1IPH
Evelyn E Harrington
183 Main St

Boylston MA 01505

Call Sign: KA1REF
Richard D Buxton
115 Mill Rd
Boylston MA 01505

Call Sign: N1IXQ
John W Burkhardt
170 Mill Rd
Boylston MA 01505

Call Sign: KB1VUB
William R Belfield Sr
11 Oak Hill Ln
Boylston MA 01505

Call Sign: N1ADJ
James P Ancona
21 Scar Hill Rd
Boylston MA 01505

Call Sign: KB1JPP
Marie E Provenzano
394 School St
Boylston MA 01505

Call Sign: N1IJS
Nancy Ann M Filgate
149 Stiles Rd
Boylston MA 01505

Call Sign: WA1VPM
Bruce D Filgate
149 Stiles Rd
Boylston MA 01505

Call Sign: W1KH
Bruce D Filgate
149 Stiles Rd
Boylston MA 01505

Call Sign: KC1NM
William J Hakala
30 Stockton St
Boylston MA 01505

Call Sign: N0ADA
Kenneth A Hummel
128 Warren St
Boylston MA 01505

Call Sign: AG1G
Hans A Kvinlaug
441 Chadwick Rd
Bradford MA 01835

Call Sign: NC1H
Biagio A Di Pietro
86 Chadwick St
Bradford MA
018357372

Call Sign: N1VKY
Amanda J Belfiore
23 Curtis Ave
Bradford MA 01835

Call Sign: N1VKZ
Paul Belfiore
23 Curtis Ave
Bradford MA 01835

Call Sign: KA1DQZ
Arthur Olsen Jr
54 Farrwood Dr
Bradford MA 01835

Call Sign: W2IRW
Myles M Marcus
71 Farrwood Dr
Bradford MA 01835

Call Sign: KB1PPZ
Kenneth A Stein
3 Fernwood Ave
Bradford MA
018357705

Call Sign: KB1QLE
Eric A Stein
3 Fernwood Ave
Bradford MA 01835

Call Sign: KB1VFY
Darrell J Donati
16 Franzone Dr
Bradford MA 01835

Call Sign: N4DJD
Darrell J Donati
16 Franzone Dr
Bradford MA 01835

Call Sign: N1HIU

Bruce F Morse
360 Kingsbury Ave
Rfd 3
Bradford MA 01835

Call Sign: KB1OUO
Dennis W Gauvin
95 Leonard Ave
Bradford MA 01835

Call Sign: K1IKQ
William R Mitchell
32 Lexington Ave
Bradford MA 01835

Call Sign: KA1RDE
Lee M La Rivee
86 Lincolnshire Dr
Bradford MA 01830

Call Sign: KA1EEB
Andrew D Hay
14 S Kimball St
Bradford MA
018357418

Call Sign: N1ROP
Darlean R Augusta
61 S Kimball St
Bradford MA 01835

Call Sign: N1THS
Harold J Maupin
10 Shawmut Ave
Bradford MA
018357931

Call Sign: N1ZWK
Julia Christo
80 Sterling Ln
Bradford MA 01835

Call Sign: N1AMA
Gregory V Caliri
10 Tudor Ct
Bradford MA 01835

Call Sign: KB1UZU
Nicholas J Molloy
295 Willow Ave
Bradford MA 01835

Call Sign: KA1UCS
Dexter E Greer

298 Willow Ave
Bradford MA 01835

Call Sign: KB1LEG
Nicholas Finocchio
32 Addison St
Braintree MA 02184

Call Sign: WB1GON
Robert R Salvaggio
9 Alexander Rd
Braintree MA
021845020

Call Sign: W1DDO
Robert J Ruplenas
47 Andersen Rd
Braintree MA 02184

Call Sign: KB1MUA
Gilbert Yaker
138 Arnold St
Braintree MA 02184

Call Sign: N1TLJ
Kevin G Irving
169 Arnold St
Braintree MA 02184

Call Sign: KA1NVD
Jane K Elliott
101 Beech St
Braintree MA 02184

Call Sign: KB1AIZ
Paul L Anderson
133 Beechwood Rd
Braintree MA 02184

Call Sign: N1PAY
Robert F James
9 Beverly Ct
Braintree MA 02184

Call Sign: NK1Q
James F Cedrone
101 Blanchard Blvd
Braintree MA
021841502

Call Sign: KA1LAJ

Thomas J Spano
26 Bowditch St
Braintree MA 02184

Call Sign: KB1HSG
Susanne R Cantone
60 Bradley Rd Ext
Braintree MA 02184

Call Sign: KA1AZZ
Jeanette P Stahl
75 Brow Ave
Braintree MA
021846309

Call Sign: NJ5K
William D Krommes Jr
92 Cabot Ave
Braintree MA 02184

Call Sign: W1LZB
Wilmer D Lanoue
51 Cain Ave
Braintree MA 02184

Call Sign: N1IPS
Norman R Guivens
55 Calvin St
Braintree MA
021843813

Call Sign: N1SOU
Jon Soligan
95 Celia Rd
Braintree MA 02184

Call Sign: N1WEN
Matthew A Rapport
Mr
112 Celia Rd
Braintree MA 02184

Call Sign: W1FGD
Edward C Anders
129 Celia Rd
Braintree MA
021847738

Call Sign: K1DPE
Nicholas Mattia
232 Common St
Braintree MA 02184

Call Sign: KB1SMN

Glenn A Shiffer Jr
39 Connelly Cir
Braintree MA 02184

Call Sign: KB1UBW
Christine M Bowen
39 Connelly Circle
Braintree MA 02184

Call Sign: KA1HAI
Santo J Gozzo
45 Court Rd
Braintree MA 02184

Call Sign: W1SMT
Clifford I Spates
12 Crawford St
Braintree MA 02184

Call Sign: W1ACL
Gareth C E Linder
64 Davis Rd
Braintree MA 02184

Call Sign: N1KTU
Stephen T Wallace Jr
168 Edgehill Rd
Braintree MA 02184

Call Sign: AE1TH
Thomas J Holmes
157 Eleanor Drive
Braintree MA 02184

Call Sign: N1ADP
Arman J Del Pico
13 Fairview Ave
Braintree MA 02184

Call Sign: NB6H
Jonathan V Hays
288 Grove St #213
Braintree MA 02184

Call Sign: N1KSK
Paul Foley
128 Haucock St
Braintree MA 02184

Call Sign: N1BIY
James C Gill
39 Hawthorn Rd
Braintree MA
021841409

Call Sign: W1QVK
James C Gill
39 Hawthorn Rd
Braintree MA
021841409

Call Sign: W1ODL
Ralph L Thompson
9 Helen Rd
Braintree MA 02184

Call Sign: K1GUG
Richard W Jolls
10 Highland Ave East
Braintree MA 02184

Call Sign: W1ZST
Capeway Radio Club
Of Mass
10 Highland Ave East
Briantree MA 02184

Call Sign: W1YJG
Paul A Richmond Jr
35 Hillside Rd
Braintree MA 02184

Call Sign: K1OOI
James G Smith
100 Hillside Rd
Braintree MA 02184

Call Sign: WA1HSY
Robert C Bonang Jr
65 Howie Rd
Braintree MA 02184

Call Sign: KH2AB
John D Halter
41 Independence Ave
Apt 211
Braintree MA
021841735

Call Sign: K1FRF
Margaret H Weeks
28 Jersey Ave
Braintree MA 02184

Call Sign: KA1TOX
Thomas F Mc Gee
37 Kimball Rd

Braintree MA
021847513

Call Sign: N1QII
Jenny R Mc Gee
37 Kimball Rd
Braintree MA
021847513

Call Sign: N1DC
Richard C Pendleton
72 Lawnview Dr
Braintree MA 02184

Call Sign: N1XQY
Raymond E Folsom
97 Liberty St
Braintree MA 02184

Call Sign: N1OMX
Susan E Griffin
280 Liberty St
Braintree MA 02184

Call Sign: KB1RXS
Paul J Disher
6 Linda Rd
Braintree MA 02184

Call Sign: KA1GBL
Gerald L Pucillo
350 Lisle St
Braintree MA 02184

Call Sign: WD9CUU
Patrick J Clifford
401 Matthew Cir Apt
205
Braintree MA
021846663

Call Sign: W1KPX
Donald B Anderson
6 May Ave
Braintree MA
021844604

Call Sign: W1WNT
Evelyn J Anderson
6 May Ave
Braintree MA
021844604

Call Sign: KB1TXB

Robert D O'donnell Jr
51 Mccusker Drive #4
Braintree MA 02184

Call Sign: AG1S
Alexander M Golden
605 Middle St Apt 49
Braintree MA 02184

Call Sign: KF4CJR
Kathy E Golden
605 Middle St Apt 49
Braintree MA 02184

Call Sign: N1HFC
Thomas W Whalen
84 Oak St
Braintree MA 02184

Call Sign: KB1REB
Thomas Whalen
84 Oak St
Braintree MA 02184

Call Sign: N1HFC
Thomas Whalen
84 Oak St
Braintree MA 02184

Call Sign: K1DSW
John Milne Jr
67 Park Ave
Braintree MA
021847923

Call Sign: WA1AAO
Richard T Mezzetti
11 Parkside Ave
Braintree MA 02184

Call Sign: N1FHJ
David W Restrick
71 Partridge Hill Rd
Braintree MA
021843841

Call Sign: K1WN
William J Needham
62 Peach St
Braintree MA 02185

Call Sign: W1MFE
Paul B Sawyer
136 Pond St

Braintree MA 02184

Call Sign: KB1JZI
Stanley M Sigel
84 Poulos Rd
Braintree MA 02184

Call Sign: KA1LKB
Richard W Reuss
12 Primrose St
Braintree MA 02184

Call Sign: W1SM
Edward R Myrbeck
15 Primrose St
Braintree MA 02184

Call Sign: KA1VVB
Raymond D Stafford
71 Rome Dr
Braintree MA 02184

Call Sign: K1UDP
George O St Andre
120 School St
Braintree MA
021841843

Call Sign: N1ILS
Joseph F Brooks
83 Sheppard Ave
Braintree MA 02184

Call Sign: N1IWR
Sandra L Brooks
83 Sheppard Ave
Braintree MA 02184

Call Sign: KB1FNL
Boston Fire Radio
Group
83 Sheppard Ave
Braintree MA 02184

Call Sign: W1BFD
Boston Fire Radio
Group
83 Sheppard Ave
Braintree MA 02184

Call Sign: KB1HAF
William B Brown
50 Spring St

Braintree MA
021847212

Call Sign: KB1OSR
Richard A Wentzel
74 Spring St
Braintree MA 02184

Call Sign: N1LUD
John H Clark
19 Staten Rd
Braintree MA 02184

Call Sign: KB1KLP
Stephen E Lind
110 Sycamore Rd
Braintree MA 02184

Call Sign: KA1WKI
Shivaani A Selvaraj
23 Thetford Ave
Braintree MA 02184

Call Sign: KB1ICW
Ronald F O Loughlin
92 Town St
Braintree MA 02184

Call Sign: KA1WLX
Richard L De Paulo Jr
311 Union St
Braintree MA
021844928

Call Sign: K1DPH
Henry P Boivin
660 Union St 3d
Braintree MA 02184

Call Sign: W1BVV
Ralph F Simpson
130 Walnut St
Braintree MA 02184

Call Sign: KB1GLO
Chet A Michalak
601 Washington St
Braintree MA 02184

Call Sign: KA1FHP
Philip A Smith
1407 Washington St
Braintree MA 02184

Call Sign: N1GQI
Thomas A Sibbald
1996 Washington St
Braintree MA 02184

Call Sign: K1WQ
Kristen N Johnson
550 Washington St Apt
315
Braintree MA 02184

Call Sign: KA1BQ
Nicholas Finocchio
506 West St
Braintree MA 02184

Call Sign: KB1DZ
Rowland Young
37 Weston Ave
Braintree MA 02184

Call Sign: KA1DDS
Patricia A Rupprecht
24 Woodside Ave
Braintree MA 02184

Call Sign: W1DD
Robert A Rupprecht Jr
24 Woodside Ave
Braintree MA 02184

**FCC Amateur Radio
Licenses in Brant
Rock**

Call Sign: N1LMH
Daniel J Toomey
Brant Rock MA 02020

Call Sign: N1EWA
Dana B Blackman
Box 385
Brant Rock MA 02020

Call Sign: KB1FLZ
Jerry H Laplante
Brant Rock MA
020200156

**FCC Amateur Radio
Licenses in Brewster**

Call Sign: W1YQR
Peter D Wechter

36 A P Newcomb Rd
Brewster MA 02631

Call Sign: W2CKT
Raymond J Keogh
82 Ambergris Cir
Brewster MA
026311124

Call Sign: WA1TVH
Donald E Pelrine
119 Anawan Rd
Brewster MA 02631

Call Sign: WA1TVI
Ronald E Pelrine
119 Anawan Rd
Brewster MA 02631

Call Sign: KB1QOZ
Gregory J Scalise
23 Beachtree Drive
Brewster MA 02631

Call Sign: WA2SVY
Frank O Abbey
155 Bogpond Rd
Brewster MA 02631

Call Sign: KB1QDO
Michael A Steinmetz
51 Boulder Rd
Brewster MA 02631

Call Sign: K2JQC
John I Lough
114 Canoe Pond Dr
Brewster MA 02631

Call Sign: KB1RGO
Konrad L Schultz
13 Captain Fitts Rd
Brewster MA 02631

Call Sign: W1KON
Konrad L Schultz
13 Captain Fitts Rd
Brewster MA 02631

Call Sign: KA1VDS
Jason M Burke
13 Cedar Ln
Brewster MA 02631

Call Sign: N1PNO
Robert S Rea
10 Donahue Rd
Brewster MA 02631

Call Sign: KB1PCZ
Nicholas M Prisco
145 Eaton Ln
Brewster MA 02631

Call Sign: N1QJF
Clarence A Carlson
9 Fair Oak Dr
Brewster MA 02631

Call Sign: W1JTP
John T Pratt
Fletcher La
Brewster MA
026313032

Call Sign: WA1YVT
Douglas W Warner
Frederick Ct
Brewster MA 02631

Call Sign: W1MKW
Robert E J West
Frederick Ct
Brewster MA 02631

Call Sign: KB1QDI
Edward M Trainor
597 Great Fields Rd
Brewster MA 02631

Call Sign: N1YQE
Matthew C Wood
10 Great Oak Rd
Brewster MA 02631

Call Sign: N1MDA
Nelson F J Bramer
113 Greenland Pond
Rd
Brewster MA 02631

Call Sign: N1LZ
Nelson F J Bramer
113 Greenland Pond
Rd
Brewster MA 02631

Call Sign: W1HWO

Benjamin F Tillson Jr
186 Gulls Way
Brewster MA 02631

Call Sign: N1XIY
Abram L Fettig
418 Gulls Way
Brewster MA 02631

Call Sign: N1LVX
James R Mims
16 Hawser Ln
Brewster MA 02631

Call Sign: W2EBN
David E Bilton
411 Holly Ave Rr 2
Brewster MA 02631

Call Sign: N1CNC
Justin E Hill Jr
17 King Phillip Rd
Brewster MA 02631

Call Sign: N1FJD
Mark S Geisler
74 Locust Ln
Brewster MA 02631

Call Sign: N1AGT
Paul R Mangelinkx
766 Long Pond Rd
Brewster MA
026310390

Call Sign: KB1TLR
Barry D Hutchinson
1274 Long Pond Rd
Brewster MA 02631

Call Sign: KD1LK
James C Demetrion
25 Maclean Rd
Brewster MA 02631

Call Sign: KB1HEY
Pamela J Demetrion
25 Maclean Rd
Brewster MA 02631

Call Sign: K9PAM
Pamela J Demetrion
25 Maclean Rd
Brewster MA 02631

Call Sign: W1JCD
James C Demetrion
25 Maclean Rd
Brewster MA 02631

Call Sign: KD1LK
James C Demetrion
25 Maclean Rd
Brewster MA 02631

Call Sign: K1DCA
Donald C Arthur
1554 Main St
Brewster MA 02631

Call Sign: K1MWC
Mary W Chaffee
1554 Main St
Brewster MA 02631

Call Sign: KA2RHF
Barbara J Konecnik
69 Marlboro Rd
Brewster MA 02631

Call Sign: WB2PTP
Paul F Konecnik
69 Marlboro Rd
Brewster MA 02631

Call Sign: KB1TAN
Jeffrey V Eyestone
10 Mayflower Circle
Brewster MA 02631

Call Sign: KB1PXF
Tamson A Garran
314 Millstone Rd
Brewster MA
026312032

Call Sign: K1TAG
Tamson A Garran
314 Millstone Rd
Brewster MA
026312032

Call Sign: KA1KHP
Ruth E Redman
315 Millstone Rd
Brewster MA 02631

Call Sign: KA1KIC

Howard E Redman
315 Millstone Rd
Brewster MA
026312929

Call Sign: KB1BAM
Jamie J Pate
Millstone Rd
Brewster MA 02631

Call Sign: N1SGK
Stephanie L Erickson
32 Old Run Hill Rd
Brewster MA
026642332

Call Sign: KB1SOG
Jack B Perry
214 Oldlongpond Rd
Brewster MA 02631

Call Sign: N1AGC
Colleen M Maginniss
12 Oriole Cir
Brewster MA 02631

Call Sign: KB1PVV
Ronald E Reddick
120 Owl Pond Rd
Brewster MA 02631

Call Sign: KA1YUA
Frederick B Peach
39 Paddock Way
Brewster MA 02631

Call Sign: KB1ROB
Ralph P Marotti
61 Paddock Way
Brewster MA 02631

Call Sign: KT2I
John B Morris
101 Paddock Way
Brewster MA 02631

Call Sign: W2EUA
John B Morris
101 Paddock Way
Brewster MA 02631

Call Sign: KB1SJV
Felix G Banis Ii
21 Ranney Lane

Brewster MA 02631

Call Sign: N2EIE
Donald R Cooke
Route 6a Rd 1
Brewster MA 02631

Call Sign: KA1ZDW
A Murray Romme
31 Seamans Way
Brewster MA 02631

Call Sign: WA1DLU
Ira V Chapman
83 Sheep Pond Cir
Brewster MA 02631

Call Sign: W1VMG
John L Knight
99 Sheep Pond Dr
Brewster MA 02631

Call Sign: KA1SCA
Rachel E Johngren
98 Sheep Pond Drive
Brewster MA 02631

Call Sign: KB1CNM
Lloyd K Avery
83 Snow Rd
Brewster MA 02631

Call Sign: KB1MDV
Devin M Reynolds
141 Spring Lane
Brewster MA 02631

Call Sign: KB1FVM
Terry R Curran
26 State St
Brewster MA 02631

Call Sign: N1QBI
Donald V Bittenbender
210 State St
Brewster MA 02631

Call Sign: NF1W
Henry T Marcy
66 Stonybrook Rd
Brewster MA 02631

Call Sign: KA1HKB
Stefan Vogel

21 Susan Ln
Brewster MA 02631

Call Sign: W1NJV
Ernest J Chipman
92 Tower Hill Cir
Brewster MA 02631

Call Sign: W1IQX
George J Spada
93 Tower Hill Cir
Brewster MA 02631

Call Sign: N1BRX
Harold Stauffer
98 White Oak Trl
Brewster MA 02361

Call Sign: WB1AEO
Lois B Tillson
Brewster MA 02631

Call Sign: KA1RAP
Kimberly N
Mclaughlin
Brewster MA 02631

Call Sign: WA7QFS
Seymour B Hammond
Brewster MA 02631

Call Sign: WV1K
Matthew J Cassarino
Brewster MA
026317483

Call Sign: W1BCR
James R Hussey
Brewster MA 02631

**FCC Amateur Radio
Licenses in
Bridgewater**

Call Sign: K1AWP
Joseph T Amaral
30 Aldrich Rd
Bridgewater MA
02324

Call Sign: N1FEC
James E Blanchard
259 Aldrich St

Bridgewater MA
02324

Call Sign: KB1BTS
Priscilla A Imhoff
675 Auburn St
Bridgewater MA
02324

Call Sign: N1ZGS
Scott B Norris
160 Boxwood Ln
Bridgewater MA
02324

Call Sign: N1ZGT
Mark A Norris
160 Boxwood Ln
Bridgewater MA
02324

Call Sign: WB1FMA
Paul R Sellstone
12 Bridge St
Bridgewater MA
02324

Call Sign: KB1UFY
James S Allen
85 Brookside Dr
Bridgewater MA
02324

Call Sign: N1OOE
Joseph S Gomes
43 Clarence Ave
Bridgewater MA
02324

Call Sign: KB1CYV
Roy E Logan
51 Clover Dr
Bridgewater MA
02324

Call Sign: N1BRJ
Ronald J Sankunas
9 Crescent Dr
Bridgewater MA
02324

Call Sign: KB1GVD
Frank E Bibbins
159 Crescent St

Bridgewater MA
02324

Call Sign: WA1AKS
Robert C Mugherini
256 Cross St
Bridgewater MA
023242938

Call Sign: WB1DHT
Constance H Franciosi
675 Curve St
Bridgewater MA
02324

Call Sign: N1DIL
James F Ewas
237 East St
Bridgewater MA
02324

Call Sign: WA1JFB
Fred P Ewas
237 East St
Bridgewater MA
02324

Call Sign: KW1T
John T Kenney
105 Fox Hill Dr
Bridgewater MA
02324

Call Sign: KB1RXR
Gregory F Rodway
70 Grange Park
Bridgewater MA
02324

Call Sign: WB1CNX
Aldo R Tornari
56 Hammond St
Bridgewater MA
02324

Call Sign: KB1IUS
Dennis G Perry
294 Hemlock Dr
Bridgewater MA
02324

Call Sign: KD1HN
William W Wilder Sr

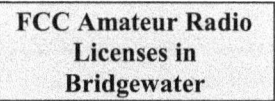

10 Heritage Circle -
101b
Bridgewater MA
023241545

Call Sign: KV1X
Bruce K Baresel
33 High Pond Drive
Bridgewater MA
02324

Call Sign: K1ZLI
Thomas E Gunnison Sr
454 High St
Bridgewater MA
02324

Call Sign: KC1ZW
Herbert J Lemon Jr
1004 High St
Bridgewater MA
02324

Call Sign: KB1EMT
Andrew Boisvert
1228 High St
Bridgewater MA
02324

Call Sign: N1NVL
Chris P Conti
31 High St Suite 1
Bridgewater MA
023241503

Call Sign: W1GRC
Gary R Cumiskey
15 Lakeview Lane
Bridgewater MA
02324

Call Sign: KB1RAA
Sharon L Cumiskey
15 Lakeview Park Ln
Bridgewater MA
02324

Call Sign: KA1FHL
Anthony C Cardello
60 Legge St
Bridgewater MA
02324

Call Sign: K1GJS

Gary R Cumiskey
180 Main St
Bridgewater MA
02324

Call Sign: N1OIQ
Ronald C Piche
38 Marianne Dr
Bridgewater MA
023242945

Call Sign: KA1ACL
Gerald E Maloney
31 Meadow Ln
Bridgewater MA
023241844

Call Sign: N1ZZR
Matthew R Connors
37 Miranda Way
Bridgewater MA
02324

Call Sign: KB1CKH
Ronald D Pagels
672 N St
Bridgewater MA
02324

Call Sign: K1JJJ
Alderico Fruzzetti Jr
1539 Old Pleasant St
Bridgewater MA
02324

Call Sign: KB1KSH
Carmelo Serrano Jr
54 Pleasant St
Bridgewater MA
02324

Call Sign: K1BAD
Carmelo Serrano Jr
54 Pleasant St
Bridgewater MA
02324

Call Sign: KA1KK
James G Butcher
796 Pleasant St
Bridgewater MA
02324

Call Sign: WA1OVG

Kevin A O Donnell
1101 Pleasant St
Bridgewater MA
02324

Call Sign: AA1TK
Leszek J Lechowicz
1755 Plymouth St
Bridgewater MA
02324

Call Sign: NI1L
Leszek J Lechowicz
1755 Plymouth St
Bridgewater MA
02324

Call Sign: KB1USG
Adam M Lechowicz
1755 Plymouth St
Bridgewater MA
02324

Call Sign: KB1UGJ
Viktoria Panagiotou
1755 Plymouth St
Bridgewater MA
02324

Call Sign: AB1MQ
Viktoria Panagiotou
1755 Plymouth St
Bridgewater MA
02324

Call Sign: K1YBS
Lawrence C Robbins
30 Prospect St
Bridgewater MA
02324

Call Sign: WB1AOZ
Nina D Robbins
30 Prospect St
Bridgewater MA
02324

Call Sign: KB1UVT
Joseph Tamarkin
12 Rainbow Cir
Bridgewater MA
02324

Call Sign: W1EID

Theodore R Haskell
14 Rodricks Terr
Bridgewater MA
023241646

Call Sign: KB1GOF
Martha E Haskell
14 Rodricks Terr
Bridgewater MA
02324

Call Sign: KA1PUX
Ronald R Leombruno
846 South St
Bridgewater MA
02324

Call Sign: KA1IKJ
Richard A Palleschi
58 Spring Hill Ave
Bridgewater MA
02324

Call Sign: N2LAF
Richard A Palleschi
58 Spring Hill Ave
Bridgewater MA
02324

Call Sign: N1FSA
Jean L Levasseur
473 Summer St
Bridgewater MA
02324

Call Sign: NV1H
Paul J Kruzona
571 Summer St
Bridgewater MA
02324

Call Sign: N1POO
Richmond P Carlson
1245 Summer St
Bridgewater MA
02324

Call Sign: KB1OAU
Alice L Carlson
1245 Summer St
Bridgewater MA
02324

Call Sign: K1MRH

Barbara A Rice
22 Tony Terrace
Bridgewater MA
02324

Call Sign: N1SGW
Maryanne C De Coster
74 Trailwood Dr
Bridgewater MA
02324

Call Sign: WA1CIM
Gary L De Coster
74 Trailwood Dr
Bridgewater MA
02324

Call Sign: KB1KVJ
Sandy-Joe Peluso
254 Vernon St
Bridgewater MA
02324

Call Sign: WA1IMS
Richard H Mc Ginn
945 Vernon St
Bridgewater MA
02324

Call Sign: WA1ZKK
Allen G Craddock
1200 Vernon St
Bridgewater MA
02324

Call Sign: K1SPP
Lee Garrison
245 Walnut St
Bridgewater MA
02324

Call Sign: KA1LGV
Herbert J Lemon Iii
Bridgewater MA
02374

Call Sign: N1ARL
James T Sanders
Bridgewater MA
023240474

**FCC Amateur Radio
Licenses in Brighton**

Call Sign: KC1FV
Richard A Parent
82 Academy Hill Rd
Brighton MA 02135

Call Sign: KB1WIR
Jeremiah F Ready
8 Atkins St
Brighton MA 02135

Call Sign: WA1ISK
Thomas M Costello
65 Beechcroft St
Brighton MA 02135

Call Sign: W1JJF
James J Flaherty
69 Bennett St
Brighton MA
021352601

Call Sign: KD5NFZ
Kyle L Vigil
84 Bennett St #2
Brighton MA 02135

Call Sign: KB1UDO
Jeffrey R Simpson
69 Breck Ave 2
Brighton MA 02135

Call Sign: KB1GYP
James J Flaherty
62 Brock St
Brighton MA
021352509

Call Sign: KB1UPF
Benjamin J Stubbs
6 Camelot Ct 5
Brighton MA 02135

Call Sign: N1NQC
Kevin L Norton
12 Carol Ave 5
Brighton MA 02135

Call Sign: N1NIA
Aram Falsafi
35 Chestnut Hill Ave
Apt 7
Brighton MA 02135

Call Sign: KA1BHZ

Wing S Choy
197 Chiswick Rd
Brighton MA 02135

Call Sign: KB1QVT
Donna M Suskawicz
1860 Commonwealth
Ave
Brighton MA 02135

Call Sign: KF6FKP
Dean E Samuels
2193 Commonwealth
Ave #333
Brighton MA 02135

Call Sign: KB1RHO
Anton Aboukhalil
1714 Commonwealth
Ave #4
Brighton MA 02135

Call Sign: KB1CZC
Stan W Bednarcyk
1626 Commonwealth
Ave Apt 23
Brighton MA 02135

Call Sign: N1SNZ
Robert L Morris
1848 Commonwealth
Ave Apt 47
Brighton MA 02135

Call Sign: N1ZRW
Thomas H Cumings
1662 Commonwealth
Ave Apt 62
Brighton MA 02135

Call Sign: KB1BFD
Ideale Salvucci
18 Cresthill Rd
Brighton MA
021351827

Call Sign: W1YZV
Charles A Forte
30 Donnybrook Rd
Brighton MA 02135

Call Sign: N1UZU
Louise Tocci
24 Dustin St

Brighton MA
021352853

Call Sign: KC8SXJ
Samuel M Jenkins
72 Englewood Ave
Apt 3
Brighton MA 02135

Call Sign: WA6YEP
Dennis J Geng
166 Foster St
Brighton MA
021353902

Call Sign: KB1CTK
Matthew F Ringel
80 Gardena St
Brighton MA 02135

Call Sign: KB1VXA
Nathan T Darling
76 Gordon St 11
Brighton MA 02135

Call Sign: KW1O
Perry C Donham
76 Gordon St Apt 14
Brighton MA 02135

Call Sign: KB1FEQ
Dawn N Skwersky
15 Henshaw St #2
Brighton MA 02135

Call Sign: WA1TBY
James W Hatherley
46 Hobson St
Brighton MA 02135

Call Sign: KK2R
Richard J Ayrovainen
77 Hobson St 1
Brighton MA 02135

Call Sign: N9XOG
Jay B Hancock
204 Lake Shore Rd 3
Brighton MA 02135

Call Sign: KB1NWQ
Benjamin A Lewis
26 Lake Shore Terrace
Brighton MA 02135

Call Sign: KA1MOM
Bill Mc Ininch Jr
26 Margo Rd
Brighton MA
021353025

Call Sign: KB1KBY
Melinda B Berkman
26 Margo Rd
Brighton MA 02135

Call Sign: KB2HEB
David P Biss
19 Oakland St
Brighton MA 02135

Call Sign: KB1KHG
Leo R Law
49 Parsons St
Brighton MA 02135

Call Sign: KA1ELR
Edwin G Warner
228 Parsons St
Brighton MA
021351867

Call Sign: N1JKD
Richard S Weld
79 R Union St
Brighton MA 02135

Call Sign: KA1WVF
George J Hamilton
91 Riverview Rd
Brighton MA 02135

Call Sign: KC0BZI
Paul A Bohn
39 Shepard St Apt 8
Brighton MA
021353327

Call Sign: KB1ULG
Theodore L Alevizos
70 South Hobart St
Brighton MA 02135

Call Sign: KF4SFT
Dieter Neu
8 South St 3
Brighton MA 02135

Call Sign: KF4SFS
Armin Reif
8 South St 3
Brighton MA 02135

Call Sign: KB1NUP
Mikhail V Golitsine
88 Strathmore Rd 3
Brighton MA 02135

Call Sign: KA1HLO
John T Casey
79 Surrey St
Brighton MA 02135

Call Sign: KB1RDZ
Aram W Babaian
89 Undine Rd
Brighton MA 02135

Call Sign: KA1ZLR
Michael G Marques
79 Union St
Brighton MA 02135

Call Sign: KB1VMZ
Sunil Dhungana
131 Washington St 45
Brighton MA 02135

Call Sign: KA1RBX
Rudolph L Bauer
88 Washington St Apt
23
Brighton MA 02135

Call Sign: KB1UPG
Dennis M Atwood Jr
589 Washington St Apt
3
Brighton MA 02135

Call Sign: AB1NX
Dennis M Atwood Jr
589 Washington St Apt
3
Brighton MA 02135

Call Sign: K4JOT
John J Ford Jr
91 Washington St Apt
4
Brighton MA
021354322

Call Sign: KE6UOH
Scott A Hirsch
15 Woodstock Ave
Brighton MA 02135

**FCC Amateur Radio
Licenses in Brimfield**

Call Sign: W1QVI
Thomas F Curry
5 Bridge Rd
Brimfield MA 01010

Call Sign: K1NBS
Granville F Lombard
15 Center St
Brimfield MA 01010

Call Sign: KA1GZA
Cheryl A Leary
31 Cubles Drive
Brimfield MA 01010

Call Sign: N1DYT
Christopher J Leary
31 Cubles Drive
Brimfield MA 01010

Call Sign: N1SSY
Mark Peters
12 Dix Hill Rd
Brimfield MA 01010

Call Sign: N1MHN
Shane C Thans
49 E Brimfield Rd
Brimfield MA 01010

Call Sign: WA1ZWE
Richard A Morris
36 E Hill Rd
Brimfield MA 01010

Call Sign: WB1ABE
Sandra P Morris
E Hill Rd
Brimfield MA 01010

Call Sign: KB1VXJ
Hans R Springer
50 Lyman Barnes Rd
Brimfield MA 01010

Call Sign: KB1CLX
David A Mc Intosh
96 Lyman Barnes Rd
Brimfield MA
010109621

Call Sign: KB1FBF
Ian A Mcintosh
96 Lyman Barnes Rd
Brimfield MA 01010

Call Sign: KB1HXS
John H Degnan
19 Paige Hill Rd
Brimfield MA
010109776

Call Sign: N2NWQ
Jeffrey D Luke
43 Tower Hill Rd
Brimfield MA 01010

Call Sign: N1RJJ
Ann M Mullen
144 Tower Hill Rd
Brimfield MA 01010

Call Sign: WA1ZUH
James A Mullen
144 Tower Hill Rd
Brimfield MA 01010

Call Sign: WB1HOF
Hampden County
Radio Association
144 Tower Hill Rd
Brimfield MA 01010

Call Sign: WB1Z
Hampden County
Radio Association
144 Tower Hill Rd
Brimfield MA 01010

Call Sign: KK1W
James A Mullen
144 Tower Hill Rd
Brimfield MA 01010

Call Sign: KA1MAJ
Jeffrey G Aptt
Brimfield MA 01010

Call Sign: N1NTD

TINA M Desrosiers
Brimfield MA 01010

Call Sign: KB1HXR
Karolyn K Koprowski
Brimfield MA
010100094

Call Sign: KB1WTT
TINA M Desrosiers
Brimfield MA 01010

FCC Amateur Radio Licenses in Brockton

Call Sign: WB1FNX
Philip S Cook
244 Ames St
Brockton MA 02302

Call Sign: W1LJL
Edward M Szachowicz
256 Ames St
Brockton MA 02402

Call Sign: K1ML
Michael L Landes
62 Anawan St
Brockton MA 02302

Call Sign: N1SZE
Richard A Schwartz
14 Annadea Rd
Brockton MA 02402

Call Sign: N1FRF
Kevin F Nolan Sr
94 Annella Rd
Brockton MA 02402

Call Sign: W1JOE
Joseph F Serrilla Iii
646 Ash St
Brockton MA
023015750

Call Sign: N1MAG
Wayne A Galvin
9 Auburn St
Brockton MA 02302

Call Sign: KA1UOJ
Frank J Erauth
11 Augustine St

Brockton MA 02401

Call Sign: KA1FYY
John O Nelson
50 Bailey Rd
Brockton MA 02402

Call Sign: WD1L
John O Nelson
50 Bailey Rd
Brockton MA
023024125

Call Sign: W1RXD
Robert N Dorrie
815 Belmont St
Brockton MA
024015664

Call Sign: W1LJT
George F Nowell
9 Blueberry Cir
Brockton MA 02402

Call Sign: K1JIY
Joel M Tenenbaum
20 Bourne St
Brockton MA 02402

Call Sign: N1JQJ
Salvatore A Saya
23 Bourne St
Brockton MA 02402

Call Sign: W1OEG
Robert E Selig
324 Boylston St
Brockton MA 02401

Call Sign: WB1DEJ
Keith G Anderson Sr
159 Braemoor Rd
Brockton MA 02401

Call Sign: KA1RSS
Warren R Nickerson
169 Braemoor Rd
Brockton MA 02401

Call Sign: K1UQH
Charles W English
17 Brookfield Dr
Brockton MA 02402

Call Sign: KB1CSB
Charles J Scrufutis
114 Cherry St - 2
Brockton MA 02301

Call Sign: W1TNK
Ronald Marshall
35 Christy Place
Brockton MA 02301

Call Sign: KA1YAY
Tina M Mahon
20 Clara Rd
Brockton MA 02402

Call Sign: N1PYN
John L Mahon
20 Clara Rd
Brockton MA 02402

Call Sign: WC1EOC
Brockton Emergency
Management Races
Club
20 Clara Rd
Brockton MA 02302

Call Sign: N1RYJ
Brian M Williams
6 Clarendon Ave
Brockton MA 02301

Call Sign: N1JOP
Robert A Clemens
Colonel Bell Dr
Brockton MA 02401

Call Sign: KB1EWC
Antonio Molina
80 Connell Ave
Brockton MA 02302

Call Sign: N1NTZ
Edward Meehan
19 Corcoran Rd
Brockton MA 02401

Call Sign: K1GSI
John F Pawlowski
1147 Court St
Brockton MA 02402

Call Sign: KA1LKK
Stephen P Calabro

246 Court St Apt H3
Brockton MA 02302

Call Sign: N1PI
Colonel C Blackwood
755 Crescent St 152a
Brockton MA 02402

Call Sign: K1EF
Evelyn L Foley
755 Crescent St 245a
Brockton MA
023023376

Call Sign: KB1NP
George F White
755 Crescent St 850a
Brockton MA 02042

Call Sign: K1HOL
Thomas L Barnard
20 Darby Rd
Brockton MA
023024402

Call Sign: N1SOK
Thomas H Smith
465 E Ashland St
Brockton MA 02402

Call Sign: K1BJG
Raymond L Moore
118 Edson St
Brockton MA 02402

Call Sign: WA1WED
Stephen Powers
41 Elsie Rd
Brockton MA
024021512

Call Sign: KA1DJA
Joseph J Gorgone
29 Emory St
Brockton MA 02401

Call Sign: N1AAU
Alfred L Handy
112 Emory St
Brockton MA 02301

Call Sign: KB1JWH
Jeffrey A Chabot
146 Errol Rd

Brockton MA 02302

Call Sign: KB1JWI
Debbie L Chabot
146 Errol Rd
Brockton MA 02302

Call Sign: N1JYL
Alfred U Bilunas
151 Field St
Brockton MA 02402

Call Sign: N1XFC
Kazimierz Szaflarski
44 First St
Brockton MA 02301

Call Sign: N1EDM
Robert E Mandeville
94 Florence St
Brockton MA 02301

Call Sign: N1SGT
Kathleen M
Mandeville
94 Florence St
Brockton MA 02401

Call Sign: W2SUB
Uss Submarine
Lionfish Radio Club
94 Florence St
Brockton MA 02401

Call Sign: N1TWN
Thomas J Crowe
49 Forest Rd
Brockton MA 02401

Call Sign: N1OIS
Victoria L Moore
94 Frankton Ave
Brockton MA 02401

Call Sign: KA1NCS
Edward R Anderson
31 Galen St
Brockton MA
024023337

Call Sign: KA1GBR
John J Yuskaitis
22 Glendale St
Brockton MA 02402

Call Sign: KB1VPU
Richard F Lindquist Jr
4 Hazel St
Brockton MA 02301

Call Sign: KA1TFC
Anthony L Manha
11 Henry St
Brockton MA
023023228

Call Sign: KA1HTC
John W Sliwa
176 Kathleen Rd
Brockton MA 02402

Call Sign: N1OQP
Michael Buiel
107 Leach Ave
Brockton MA 02401

Call Sign: KB1OMU
Juan R Mercado
12 Lenox St
Brockton MA 02301

Call Sign: W1GRN
Paul Sowsy
332 Linwood St
Brockton MA 02401

Call Sign: KA1IDK
Sharon B Gleason
369 Linwood St
Brockton MA 02301

Call Sign: KA1KY
Edward J Gleason
369 Linwood St
Brockton MA 02401

Call Sign: KA1WYX
Joseph E Faraca
78 Lynn Rd
Brockton MA 02402

Call Sign: KB1WWU
Olivia Davis
8 Madrid Square
Brockton MA 02301

Call Sign: KE4PIB
Henry C Gernhardt Iii

1315 Main St
Brockton MA 02301

Call Sign: N1FYZ
Carl A Aveni
89 Manners Ave
Brockton MA 02401

Call Sign: N1FY
Carl A Aveni
89 Manners Ave
Brockton MA 02401

Call Sign: N1LYP
Eric A Canha
95 Manners Ave
Brockton MA 02301

Call Sign: KA1BIN
Steven M Carlozzi
40 Market St
Brockton MA 02301

Call Sign: N1AMX
Anthony Carlozzi
48 Market St
Brockton MA 02401

Call Sign: KA1HTG
John C Adams Jr
197 Menlo St
Brockton MA 02401

Call Sign: WA3TMW
Ronald J Hallam Sr
15 Montello St Ext
Brockton MA 02401

Call Sign: KA1JDV
George E Mattson
361 Moraine
Brockton MA 02401

Call Sign: KB1EPJ
J Reuel Francis
97 North Leyden St
Brockton MA 02302

Call Sign: W1FAD
Gaston A Roy
28 Nye Ave
Brockton MA 02401

Call Sign: N1WEO

John W Gravlin
685 Oak St 21
Brockton MA 02401

Call Sign: KB1FVJ
Robert E Loring
221 Oak St Unit #195
Brockton MA
023011378

Call Sign: KA1BVY
Thomas J O Brien
28 Parker Ave
Brockton MA 02402

Call Sign: N1MHY
Ancee B Marchando
70 Parker St
Brockton MA 02402

Call Sign: KA1NTP
Thomas L Smith
218 Perkins Ave
Brockton MA 02402

Call Sign: W1KMS
Francis K Stevens Sr
68 Perkins St
Brockton MA 02402

Call Sign: KA1HTB
James F West Jr
22 Pineview Ter
Brockton MA 02401

Call Sign: N1OQW
Bernard A Snow
25 Porter St
Brockton MA 02301

Call Sign: K1MNO
Alton L Caldwell Jr
60 Reservoir St Apt
108
Brockton MA 02301

Call Sign: N1MPA
John J Rock Jr
60 Reservoir St Apt
303
Brockton MA
023011145

Call Sign: KA1HTF

Richard M Calnan
66 Richard St
Brockton MA 02401

Call Sign: WA1ZUG
Kenneth W Belcher Sr
42 Robert Rd
Brockton MA 02402

Call Sign: WB1DSL
John J Cassidy
84 Royal Rd
Brockton MA 02402

Call Sign: K1QJF
John J Lenkauskas
45 Ruth Rd
Brockton MA
024022511

Call Sign: WA1DDS
Joseph Gilback
227 Sawtell Ave
Brockton MA 02402

Call Sign: KC1PH
Joseph Stasaitis
136 Sawtelle Ave
Brockton MA 02402

Call Sign: KB1JCR
Brockton Races
45 School St
Brockton MA 02301

Call Sign: N1ZZQ
William C Gundel
71 South Leyden St
Brockton MA 02302

Call Sign: N1OED
Dwight F Kennedy
325 Southfield Dr
Brockton MA 02402

Call Sign: AB1C
Robert E Lee
136 Southworth St
Brockton MA
024017012

Call Sign: W1KGU
Sanford E Pope
294 Summer

Brockton MA 02402

Call Sign: KD7HVU
Thomas E Fuller
190 Summer St
Brockton MA
023023917

Call Sign: KD1NX
William A Foster
46 Sylvester St
Brockton MA 02402

Call Sign: WA1UMT
David N Darois
46 Temi Rd
Brockton MA 02402

Call Sign: WA1LXP
Frederick S Roog Jr
4 Thomas St
Brockton MA 02402

Call Sign: KB1NMG
Barbara A Anderson
48 Thompson Ave
Brockton MA 02301

Call Sign: KB1QKV
Michael R Anderson
48 Thompson Ave
Brockton MA 02301

Call Sign: KB1RXQ
Joseph S Casieri
4 Track St Apt 1n
Brockton MA 02301

Call Sign: KA1RQP
Edwin Ayala
6 Tufts Cir
Brockton MA 02402

Call Sign: KA1OHY
Robert J Plunkett
17 Vermont Ave
Brockton MA 02402

Call Sign: N1KQR
Paul B Foley
64 Walnut St
Brockton MA
023013441

Call Sign: N1KXD
Dennis K Foley
64 Walnut St
Brockton MA 02401

Call Sign: KB1VGF
Mark E Margolis
1087 Warren Ave
Brockton MA 02301

Call Sign: K1WQN
Heidi Balben
171 Wentworth Ave
Brockton MA 02301

Call Sign: KA1SXC
Albert L St George
7 Woodard Ave
Brockton MA 02401

Call Sign: N1MRG
David A Wilson
Brockton MA 02403

Call Sign: N1OAO
Joan M Wilson
Brockton MA 02405

Call Sign: K1RFB
Richard E Piantoni
Brockton MA 02303

Call Sign: KA1JUZ
Allan D Fillebrown
Brockton MA
023030767

Call Sign: N1OEH
Victor A Kairis
Brockton MA 02303

Call Sign: WA1MNQ
Michael R Valente Sr
Brockton MA
023052039

Call Sign: N1TWH
Michael P Dench
685 Oak St Bldg 4
Brocton MA 02401

FCC Amateur Radio
Licenses in
Brookfield

Call Sign: W1MQU
Walter F Burke
9 1st St Box N 10
Brookfield MA 01506

Call Sign: KA1CDJ
Sharon J Mach
Box 201
Brookfield MA 01506

Call Sign: N1DHR
Karen L Marini
4 Country Wood Circle
Brookfield MA 01506

Call Sign: KB1RIH
Albert J Difederico
5 Deer Run
Brookfield MA 01506

Call Sign: N1WLX
Marion E Burke
9 First St Box N 10
Brookfield MA 01506

Call Sign: KC0IYL
Paul N Lincoln
90 Long Hill Rd
Brookfield MA 01506

Call Sign: W1RVL
Boyd M Afton
37 Maple St
Brookfield MA 01506

Call Sign: N1SCG
Donald R Routhier Jr
65 Molasses Hill Rd
Brookfield MA 01506

Call Sign: N1UNN
Robert J Tibbetts
22 Pleasant St
Brookfield MA 01506

Call Sign: N1YUL
Ralph F Howe
54 Quaboag St
Brookfield MA 01506

Call Sign: N1XTM
Mitchell E Mateiko
Quaboag St

Brookfield MA 01506

Call Sign: K1RMS
James F Sniffen
28 Quaboag St 5
Brookfield MA 01506

Call Sign: KA1LNZ
Steven D Novak
71 Rice Corner Rd
Brookfield MA
015061804

Call Sign: WB1FCD
Michael J O Keefe
Brookfield MA 01506

Call Sign: NV1C
Michael J O Keefe
Brookfield MA 01506

Call Sign: KB1WYQ
Kevin J Guntor
Brookfield MA 01506

**FCC Amateur Radio
Licenses in Brookline**

Call Sign: KB1VEE
Scott Allen
239 A Walnut St
Brookline MA 02446

Call Sign: KA6WTZ
Cheryl J Mills
20 Abbottsford Rd
Brookline MA 02146

Call Sign: K1YL
Claire M Bardfield
16 Addington Rd
Brookline MA 02146

Call Sign: N1DDD
David A Bardfield
16 Addington Rd
Brookline MA 02445

Call Sign: N1LOU
Louis Y Bardfield
16 Addington Rd
Brookline MA 02445

Call Sign: W1FCC

Brookline Amateur
Radio Club
16 Addington Rd
Brookline MA 02146

Call Sign: W1RES
Edward I Bardfield
16 Addington Rd
Brookline MA 02445

Call Sign: W1UQ
Morton L Bardfield
16 Addington Rd
Brookline MA 02146

Call Sign: N1UQ
Edward I Bardfield
16 Addington Rd
Brookline MA 02445

Call Sign: KB1JFO
Melissa A Bardfield
16 Addington Rd
Brookline MA 02445

Call Sign: W1MEL
Melissa A Bardfield
16 Addington Rd
Brookline MA 02445

Call Sign: W1RES
Edward I Bardfield
16 Addington Rd
Brookline MA 02445

Call Sign: N1CYL
Cherienne D Bardfield
16 Addington Rd
Brookline MA 02445

Call Sign: N1SVW
Ian F Damm Luhr
71 Addington Rd
Brookline MA 02146

Call Sign: N1SVX
Toby F Damm Luhr
71 Addington Rd
Brookline MA 02146

Call Sign: KB2IPW
Jennifer L Patashnick
43 Addington Rd Apt 3
Brookline MA 02445

Call Sign: KB1RLJ
Farshid Varasteh
53 Alton Pl 6
Brookline MA 02446

Call Sign: KB4PRN
Jeremy M Isikoff
15 Alton Place 3
Brookline MA 02446

Call Sign: N1LRX
Martha Lonzana
260 Aspinwall Ave
Brookline MA 02146

Call Sign: WA1QVL
David C Jolly
15 Atherton Rd
Brookline MA 02146

Call Sign: KD1MU
Gregg A Lebovitz
57 Babcock St #3
Brookline MA 02446

Call Sign: KB1IMG
Adel Elazzouzi
34 Babcock St Apt 102
Brookline MA 02446

Call Sign: WA2VIU
Barry D Jacobson
134 Babcock St Apt 3
Brookline MA 02446

Call Sign: KB1VBS
Arthur E Plummer
60 Babcock St Apt 66
Brookline MA 02446

Call Sign: N9CXM
Carlton S Wood
1045 Beacon St
Brookline MA 02146

Call Sign: N1PHP
Harvey P Sattin
1871 Beacon St
Brookline MA 02445

Call Sign: N1PNN
Joshua A Sattin
1871 Beacon St

Brookline MA 02445

Call Sign: AB1GC
Koichi Nakase
1253 Beacon St / C-5
Brookline MA 02446

Call Sign: KI4ICY
Christopher T
Williams
1443 Beacon St 106
Brookline MA 02446

Call Sign: KB1WVY
Matthew A Berlow
1887 Beacon St 2
Brookline MA 02445

Call Sign: N1VIN
Henry J Hoffman Jr
1450 Beacon St 701
Brookline MA 02146

Call Sign: KB1FJY
Scott E Lanning
1215 Beacon St Apt #8
Brookline MA 02246

Call Sign: KB1BHN
Khem Wanglee
1735 Beacon St Apt
110
Brookline MA 02146

Call Sign: KB1REG
Sharman L Andersen
1731 Beacon St Apt
219
Brookline MA 02445

Call Sign: KA1JUT
Serge R J Fournier
1454 Beacon St Apt
343
Brookline MA 02146

Call Sign: KA1BJX
Gary D Perlman
1731 Beacon St Apt
907
Brookline MA 02445

Call Sign: N1IGT
Joseph R Siegel

1824 Beacon St Unit 4
Brookline MA 02445

Call Sign: KB1POM
Ronald Goodstein
29 Beresford Rd
Brookline MA
024672622

Call Sign: WA1QGC
David L Fox
Box 414
Brookline MA 02146

Call Sign: KB1HDM
Brian P Campbell
452 Boylston St
Brookline MA 02445

Call Sign: WK1C
Gregory P Guyton
19 Brook St
Brookline MA 02146

Call Sign: KB1FMO
Ruth Oconner
42 Browne St
Brookline MA 02446

Call Sign: N1KXS
David P Wong
Browne St
Brookline MA
024463408

Call Sign: N1UUD
William Osborn
115 Buckminster Rd
Brooklin MA 02146

Call Sign: W8PYN
Isadore Goodman
100 Center St Apt 422
Brookline MA 02446

Call Sign: KB1MJV
Kris J Lagadinos
62 Centre St
Brookline MA 02446

Call Sign: KB1CXJ
George R Bevis Jr
452 Chestnut Hill Ave
Brookline MA 02146

Call Sign: N1BCN
Frederick S Lebow
71 Colchester St
Brookline MA
024465439

Call Sign: KB1MDE
Robert J Dilibero
96 Craftsland Rd
Brookline MA 02467

Call Sign: K1UQM
Robert J Dilibero
96 Craftsland Rd
Brookline MA 02467

Call Sign: K1OP
Robert J Dilibero
96 Craftsland Rd
Brookline MA 02467

Call Sign: KB1WLJ
Douglas C Pearl
59 Crownshield Rd
Brookline MA 02446

Call Sign: N1FIC
Jozef Marsala
54 Cypress St
Brookline MA 02146

Call Sign: KB1LMH
Grenville P Byford
274 Dudley St
Brookline MA 02445

Call Sign: KA1SPZ
Cedric J Priebe Iii
44 Edgehill Rd
Brookline MA 02146

Call Sign: W1NL
Carl E Mascott
31 Englewood Ave
Brookline MA
024452022

Call Sign: KB1VEH
Jacqueline E Scott
27 Englewood Ave
Unit 3
Brookline MA 02445

Call Sign: NZ5H
Michael V Simonds
102 Franklin St Apt 2
Brookline MA 02445

Call Sign: N1UEO
Limor Fried
135 Fuller St
Brookline MA 02146

Call Sign: N1OES
Jascha A Franklin
Hodge
137 Gardner Rd
Brookline MA 02146

Call Sign: KA1SSL
Susan L Ivey
30 Gardner Rd 1g
Brookline MA 02146

Call Sign: N2SLK
Daniel J Debowy
60 Gardner Rd Apt 1
Brookline MA 02445

Call Sign: KB1REI
Gary A Toth
70 Gardner Rd Apt 1
Brookline MA 02445

Call Sign: N2CRT
Gary A Toth
70 Gardner Rd Apt 1
Brookline MA 02445

Call Sign: KB8UJW
Matthew R Lootens
50 Goddard Ave
Brookline MA 02445

Call Sign: K1GZZ
Ira E Leonard
50 Green St Apt 204
Brookline MA
024463316

Call Sign: N1OSA
William A White
64 Griggs Rd
Brookline MA 02146

Call Sign: KB1GIH
Mark C Mercer

19 Hamilton Rd Apt 2
Brookline MA
024465830

Call Sign: N2ESS
David L Leifer
32 Harrison St
Brookline MA 02446

Call Sign: WZ1C
David L Leifer
32 Harrison St
Brookline MA 02446

Call Sign: K1PEV
Michael B Silevitch
70 Harvard Ave
Brookline MA 02446

Call Sign: W1KBN
Northeastern
University Radio Club
70 Harvard Ave
Brookline MA 02446

Call Sign: WB1FVB
William J Letendre
258 Harvard St 117
Brookline MA 02146

Call Sign: KB1WWA
John H Kavanagh Jr
27 Heath St Unit 1
Brookline MA
024555909

Call Sign: N1EZP
Henry B Minsky
111 Ivy St
Brookline MA 02146

Call Sign: N1FQY
Milan Singh
111 Ivy St
Brookline MA 02146

Call Sign: N1YVW
Ronald R Hicks
240 Kent St
Brookline MA 02146

Call Sign: AF1D
Richard C Lanza
57 Kenwood St

Brookline MA 02446

Call Sign: KB1OBY
Martha Lonzana
151 Lancaster Terrace
Brookline MA 02446

Call Sign: KB1OBZ
Albert J Santoro
151 Lancaster Terrace
Brookline MA 02446

Call Sign: KA1UIW
Max V Rosenzweig
93 Lawton St
Brookline MA 02146

Call Sign: KB1JDP
Mark J Natale
41 Linden St
Brookline MA 02445

Call Sign: N1UTS
Henry W Winkleman
99 Marion St
Brookline MA 02446

Call Sign: KB1TNG
Terri N Gerber
90 Marion St Apt #4
Brookline MA 02446

Call Sign: N1UTR
Adam I Winkleman
99 Marion St #1
Brookline MA 02446

Call Sign: KB1VWG
Prakash Viswanathan
45 Marion St 32
Brookline MA 02446

Call Sign: AB1PN
Prakash Viswanathan
45 Marion St 32
Brookline MA 02446

Call Sign: KB1GMT
Terri N Gerber
90 Marion Stret 4
Brookline MA 02446

Call Sign: N1UVC
Brian C Matteson

12 Naples Rd
Brookline MA 02146

Call Sign: KB1LMO
Todd J Mondragon
12 Naples Rd
Brookline MA 02446

Call Sign: KV1M
Todd J Mondragon
12 Naples Rd
Brookline MA 02446

Call Sign: KA1ZAO
Philip C Mc Neill
16 Newell Rd
Brookline MA 02146

Call Sign: KB1LIL
Clay Center Amateur
Radio Club
20 Newton St
Brookline MA 02445

Call Sign: W1CLA
Clay Center Amateur
Radio Club
20 Newton St
Brookline MA 02445

Call Sign: KB1PFT
John W Briggs
20 Newton St
Brookline MA 02445

Call Sign: KB1SHH
Clay Center Amateur
Radio Club
20 Newton St
Brookline MA 02445

Call Sign: WX1CLA
Clay Center Amateur
Radio Club
20 Newton St
Brookline MA 02445

Call Sign: KB1EN
Gary M Arber
5 Park St
Brookline MA 02146

Call Sign: K2LAY
James M O Sullivan

55 Park St
Brookline MA 02446

Call Sign: KB1DXQ
Thomas W Martin Ii
162 Payson Rd
Brookline MA 02467

Call Sign: KB1KEP
Laura J Horstmann
40 Perry St Apt 3
Brookline MA 02445

Call Sign: N1GKW
Roger R Sullivan
58 Randolph Rd
Brookline MA
024672338

Call Sign: KB1QXW
Gil E Propp
77 Rawson Rd
Brookline MA 02445

Call Sign: KB1WVR
Joel S Shoner
16 Royal Rd
Brookline MA 02445

Call Sign: KA2NXF
Jason A Wirth
Russeel St
Brookline MA 08757

Call Sign: AA1CS
Richard A Siegel
201 Russett Rd
Brookline MA 02167

Call Sign: N1UUR
Matthew N Condell
259 Saint Paul St
Brookline MA 02146

Call Sign: N1UUS
Wandy Sae Tan
259 Saint Paul St
Brookline MA 02146

Call Sign: N1VAA
Masahiro Ishigami
259 Saint Paul St
Brookline MA 02146

Call Sign: KC7NBW
Kristoffer K Stokes
37 Saint Paul St #6
Brookline MA 02446

Call Sign: KB1SVP
Aaron Gettinger
80 Saint Paul St Apt1
Brookline MA 02446

Call Sign: WB1CXU
Milo W Grubb
160 Seaver St
Brookline MA 02146

Call Sign: KB1REH
Stephen J Walsh
15 Sherrin Rd
Brookline MA 02467

Call Sign: N1HDS
William D Hillis Ii
135 St Paul St
Brookline MA 02146

Call Sign: NU1N
Bryan P Bergeron
27 Stearns Rd #3
Brookline MA 02446

Call Sign: WA1KTY
Robert D Bello
30 Stearns Rd 104
Brookline MA 02146

Call Sign: WA1GR
Gary R Richard
111 Stedman St
Brookline MA 02446

Call Sign: KB1QHX
Nathaniel N Vishner
88 Tappan St
Brookline MA 02445

Call Sign: N1PPD
James K Hammerman
307 Tappan St #3
Brookline MA 02445

Call Sign: KB1EIP
Joseph Recht
15 Thatcher St 6
Brookline MA 02446

Call Sign: KB1FMT
Martha Recht
15 Thatcher St 6
Brookline MA 02446

Call Sign: KB1REN
Casey A Hatchett
84 Uiversity Rd
Brookline MA 02445

Call Sign: KB1SVB
Nicholas S Weber
30 Upland Rd
Brookline MA 02445

Call Sign: W3BER
Nicholas S Weber
30 Upland Rd
Brookline MA 02445

Call Sign: N2JFL
Alfred F Falk
3 Upland Rd 2
Brookline MA
024457733

Call Sign: KB1UKP
Daniel Epstein
779 Washington St
Brookline MA 02446

Call Sign: N1QEE
Kleanthes G Koniaris
797 Washington St
Brookline MA 02146

Call Sign: KB1VEF
Kingsley J Wong
803 Washington St 1
Brookline MA 02446

Call Sign: KB1REL
Colin R Mcardle
31 Weybridge Rd
Brookline MA 02445

Call Sign: KB1REM
Christine Mcardle
31 Weybridge Rd
Brookline MA 02445

Call Sign: N1OCI
Ryan W Mc Cue

35 White Pl 1
Brookline MA 02445

Call Sign: KB1VIX
Joshua A Einstein
189 Winchester St
Brookline MA 02446

Call Sign: N1GBS
Jesse D Roberts Jr
206 Winchester St
Brookline MA 02446

Call Sign: KS1W
Andre E Robatino
85 Winchester St Apt 1
Brookline MA
024462759

Call Sign: KB1WUV
David W Clark
78 Windsor Rd
Brookline MA 02445

Call Sign: WA1CHP
Michael J Hickey
44 Winslow Rd
Brookline MA 02146

Call Sign: WA1LXE
David L Fisher
127 Winthrop Rd
Brookline MA 02445

Call Sign: KB1VIW
Joshua S Koerpel
174 Winthrop Rd 1
Brookline MA 02445

Call Sign: WB2NDG
Gary L Elinoff
199 Winthrop Rd 32
Brookline MA 02146

Call Sign: N1LHR
Jacques J Lohr
Brookline MA 02146

Call Sign: KB1VEI
Desiree A Von Klis
Brookline MA 02446

Call Sign: KB1REO
Meei Li
Brookline Village MA
02447

Call Sign: KA1YDK
David P Lemanski
16 Jeanette Dr
Bryantville MA 02327

Call Sign: N1ILK
Mary D Lynch
130 Priscilla Dr
Bryantville MA 02327

Call Sign: N1HWX
Don E Michaud
Bryantville MA 02327

Call Sign: N1IIZ
John L Lynch
Bryantville MA 02327

Call Sign: N1PXX
Ronald R Smith
Bryantville MA 02327

Call Sign: KB1NAX
Joan Smith
Bryantville MA 02327

Call Sign: W1SDG
Stephen D Godfroy
154 Bray Rd
Buckland MA 01338

Call Sign: W1BPK
Charles W Manninen

17 Alma Rd
Burlington MA 01803

Call Sign: KB3DNG
Frank B De Fina
901 Arboretum Way
Burlington MA 01803

Call Sign: KB1WWN
Bruce R Jordan Jr
1333 Arboretum Way
Burlington MA 01803

Call Sign: N1NWS
Richard J Riendeau
1631 Arboretum Way
Burlington MA 01803

Call Sign: KA1ODK
Gerald W Baker
151 Bedford St
Burlington MA 01803

Call Sign: KB1DX
William L Le Comte
6 Boulder Dr
Burlington MA 01803

Call Sign: WB1GCK
Richard W Elliott
20 Boulder Dr
Burlington MA 01803

Call Sign: WO1O
Antonio Arini
124 Cambridge St
Burlington MA 01803

Call Sign: N1LAI
Charles A Reveal
2 Cathy Rd
Burlington MA 01803

Call Sign: W1KQZ
John T Murray
3 Cedarwood Ln
Burlington MA
018033706

Call Sign: W1UIO
George A Le Veille
59 Center St Unit 210
Burlington MA 01803

Call Sign: WA1EBH
Margaret H Narkewich
11 Central Ave
Burlington MA 01803

Call Sign: N1GYF
David L O Hearn
6 College Rd
Burlington MA 01803

Call Sign: KA1OVY
Diane M Rebello
Siguenza
9 Crawford Rd
Burlington MA 01803

Call Sign: N1CRI
Michael A Siguenza
9 Crawford Rd
Burlington MA 01803

Call Sign: W1MAS
Michael A Siguenza
9 Crawford Rd
Burlington MA 01803

Call Sign: W1QUX
Alfred L Stone
45 Cresthaven Dr
Burlington MA 01803

Call Sign: K1GXD
Walter E Bullock
11 Crowley Rd
Burlington MA
018036190

Call Sign: KB1UYP
Gregory S Danielius
32 Daniel Dr
Burlington MA 01803

Call Sign: W1ZHU
Joseph Baldrate
4 Dolores Dr
Burlington MA 01803

Call Sign: WA1IQT
Bernard W Heath Jr
43 Donald Rd
Burlington MA 01803

Call Sign: N1FEQ
Paul R Getchell

69 Donald Rd
Burlington MA 01803

Call Sign: KB1TKH
Bernard G Bowers
1 Donna Ln
Burlington MA 01803

Call Sign: KB1TNI
Bernard G Bowers
1 Donna Ln
Burlington MA 01803

Call Sign: KB1OSJ
Charles E Bobbish
82 Drake Rd
Burlington MA 01803

Call Sign: WA1ROG
Salvatore A Capotosto
12 Ellen Rd
Burlington MA 01803

Call Sign: KA1WWH
Richard E Mulcahy
7 Fairfax St
Burlington MA 01803

Call Sign: N1AQF
James T Sullivan
406 Farms Dr
Burlington MA 01803

Call Sign: KA1CJB
Kevin A Koffink
7 Foster Rd
Burlington MA 01803

Call Sign: N1QWJ
Janet S Finley
212 Fox Hill Rd
Burlington MA 01803

Call Sign: N8FZS
John F Porter
237 Fox Hill Rd
Burlington MA 01803

Call Sign: N1SOY
Michael A Proulx
76 Francis Wyman Rd
Burlington MA 01803

Call Sign: KB1OHD

Michael A Proulx
76 Francis Wyman Rd
Burlington MA 01803

Call Sign: KB1OKN
Ellen M Ferguson
76 Francis Wyman Rd
Burlington MA 01803

Call Sign: AB1HV
Michael A Proulx
76 Francis Wyman Rd
Burlington MA 01803

Call Sign: K1KIE
William J Flaherty
100 Francis Wyman
Rd
Burlington MA 01803

Call Sign: KA1TGN
Peter A Wyman
22 Gedick Rd
Burlington MA 01803

Call Sign: N1ZUO
Randall J Nowell
7 Greenwood Rd
Burlington MA
018032742

Call Sign: N1JZN
Kathy Lee
9 Hallmark Gardens 3
Burlington MA 01803

Call Sign: KB1APT
Douglas A Yates
18 Heritage Way
Burlington MA 01803

Call Sign: N1ERP
Charles E Foster
10 Kenmore Ave
Burlington MA 01803

Call Sign: KB1VSO
Victor M Modic
8 Kimball Ct 907
Burlington MA 01803

Call Sign: KG4IFG
Andrew J Modic
8 Kimball Ct Apt #907

Burlington MA 01803

Call Sign: KC2GH
Jacob Storfer
18 Knolwood Court
Burlington MA 01803

Call Sign: N6XKG
Mazal Storfer
18 Knolwood Court
Burlington MA 01803

Call Sign: WA3NFK
Arthur D Fisher
6 Lantern Lane
Burlington MA 01803

Call Sign: K1GPH
Erland R Babcock
38 Lantern Ln
Burlington MA 01803

Call Sign: KB1GHY
Stephen J
Consolmagno
24 Lexington St
Burlington MA 01803

Call Sign: K1SJC
Stephen J
Consolmagno
24 Lexington St
Burlington MA 01803

Call Sign: KB3ITI
Lindsay A Spriggs
6 Littles Brook Court
#131
Burlington MA 01803

Call Sign: W1WYC
Frederick N Garside
6 Manhattan Dr
Burlington MA 01803

Call Sign: N1IOI
Wayne P Mohler
16 Manhattan Dr
Burlington MA 01803

Call Sign: WA1MNJ
Michael S Viola
2 Mc Carthy Dr
Burlington MA 01803

Call Sign: KB1QWZ
John T Blathras
3 Mccafferty Way
Burlington MA 01803

Call Sign: K1ADW
Adam D Woodbury
10 Mildred Rd
Burlington MA 01803

Call Sign: KB1EGJ
George A Le Veille
10 Mountain Rd
Burlington MA 01803

Call Sign: KB1MQZ
Kelvin W Chan
11 Mowhawk Rd
Burlington MA 01803

Call Sign: W1SUN
Sun Microsystems
Laboratories
1 Network Drive -
Ubur-02
Burlington MA
018030902

Call Sign: WA1HZC
Norman A Martel
1 Old Colony Rd
Burlington MA 01803

Call Sign: N2MTD
Jason A Cline
80 Peach Orchard Rd
Burlington MA 01803

Call Sign: KA1FGY
Bruce R Frederick
14 Purity Springs Rd
Burlington MA 01803

Call Sign: N1RNW
Charles F Dubord Jr
1 Putnam Rd
Burlington MA 01803

Call Sign: N1SWJ
Lori A Du Bord
1 Putnam Rd
Burlington MA 01803

Call Sign: KB1NSK
Francis J Hart
2 Raymond Rd Ext
Burlington MA
018032828

Call Sign: K1FJH
Francis J Hart
2 Raymond Rd Ext
Burlington MA
018032828

Call Sign: W1TST
Charles B Correia
9 Richfield
Burlington MA 01803

Call Sign: K1WFZ
John E Tremblay
8 Ruthven Ave
Burlington MA 01803

Call Sign: W1RTT
Seward J Gray
34 Sandy Brook Rd
Burlington MA 01803

Call Sign: AA1M
Robert C Reiser
6 Savin St
Burlington MA
018032210

Call Sign: KB1UNA
Memorial Arc Uss
Essex Cv 9
6 Savin St
Burlington MA 01803

Call Sign: WW2CV
Memorial Arc Uss
Essex Cv 9
6 Savin St
Burlington MA 01803

Call Sign: N3YKR
Joshua I Kramer
Seven Springs Lane
Burlington MA 01803

Call Sign: KB1WIV
Michael L Judge Sr
6 Spring Valley Rd
Burlington MA 01803

Call Sign: W1LTC
Julio S Nobrega
5 Spruce Hill Rd
Burlington MA 01803

Call Sign: N1NCQ
Robert A De
Dominicis
8 Virginia Rd
Burlington MA 01803

Call Sign: N1BUB
Douglas R Purdy
3 Visco Rd
Burlington MA 01803

Call Sign: AA1GB
William C Rustenburg
12 Washington Ave
Burlington MA 01803

Call Sign: KA1MAP
Donald W Melanson
101 Wilmington Rd
Burlington MA
018032603

Call Sign: KA1CAB
Louis J Skarbek
153 Wilmington Rd
Burlington MA 01803

Call Sign: KA1ZVG
Edward W Howard
156 Wilmington Rd
Burlington MA 01803

Call Sign: K1UM
Thaddeus A Danley
Burlington MA 01803

**FCC Amateur Radio
Licenses in Buzzards
Bay**

Call Sign: KB1LQW
Mma Radio Club
101 Academy Dr - Box
669
Buzzards Bay MA
02532

Call Sign: KB1TRW

Kyle J St Onge
12 Cahoon Rd
Buzzards Bay MA
02532

Call Sign: W1DR
Radio Operators Assn
Of New Bedford
3 Clay Pond Rd
Buzzards Bay MA
02532

Call Sign: W1YN
Edward W Goodhue Jr
3 Clay Pond Rd
Buzzards Bay MA
02532

Call Sign: KA1TJT
Kathleen E Trant
12 Colonial Rd
Buzzards Bay MA
02532

Call Sign: K1SWT
Paul S Baillie
34 Howard Ave
Buzzards Bay MA
02532

Call Sign: KB1TZU
Max E Lantz Ii
5733 Johnson St
Buzzards Bay MA
02542

Call Sign: WA1KUL
Kenneth B Gordon
8 Little Bay Lane
Buzzards Bay MA
02532

Call Sign: WA1FQP
Joseph N Close
21 Little Bay Ln
Buzzards Bay MA
02532

Call Sign: WA1SCI
David L Sanford
228 Main St
Buzzards Bay MA
02532

Call Sign: W1OZ
David L Sanford
228 Main St
Buzzards Bay MA
02532

Call Sign: N1SGO
Anne J Murphy
25 Onset Ave
Buzzards Bay MA
02532

Call Sign: N1IPT
John H Ferguson
63 Pine Ridge Rd
Buzzards Bay MA
02532

Call Sign: N2FAC
Timothy M Johnson
11 Puritan Rd
Buzzards Bay MA
02532

Call Sign: K1RRF
Bruce A Selig
29 Puritan Rd
Buzzards Bay MA
02532

Call Sign: KB1FKW
Horst F Nitschke
115 Puritan Rd
Buzzards Bay MA
02532

Call Sign: AA1XG
Horst F Nitschke
115 Puritan Rd
Buzzards Bay MA
02532

Call Sign: KB1CZB
Richard M Menkello
152 Puritan Rd
Buzzards Bay MA
025325604

Call Sign: N1ZYS
Mark R Menkello
152 Puritan Rd
Buzzards Bay MA
02352

Call Sign: KB1TBA
David A Allen
16 Rip Van Winkle
Way
Buzzards Bay MA
02532

Call Sign: W1KIX
William J Staniewicz
Sr
1 Sandy Ln
Buzzards Bay MA
02532

Call Sign: K1VOY
John Andrade
1 Shamrock Ln
Buzzard Bay MA
02532

Call Sign: W1HYD
Kenneth E Nelson
4 Shanley Way
Buzzards Bay MA
02532

Call Sign: KA1GDQ
Joseph L Reynolds Iii
6 Sleepy Hollow Lane
Buzzards Bay MA
02532

Call Sign: WA1CQC
Michael F Brady
15 Sunset Ln
Buzzards Bay MA
025323451

Call Sign: KA1EAY
Annmarie O Brien
51 Tara Ter
Buzzards Bay MA
025323883

Call Sign: KA1EAZ
Robert C O Brien
51 Tara Ter
Buzzards Bay MA
025323883

Call Sign: KA1ZAI
Jonathan A Janulewicz
120 Valley Bars Rd N

Buzzards Bay MA
02532

Call Sign: N1KBV
William T Mc Inerney
20 Wallace Pt Rd
Buzzards Bay MA
02532

Call Sign: N1SGQ
William B Tyrie
38 Wenonah Rd
Buzzards Bay MA
02532

Call Sign: KA1HAH
Robert A Weller
12 Westerly Dr
Buzzards Bay MA
02532

Call Sign: N1EEN
Robert G Dietrich
18 Westerly Dr
Buzzards Bay MA
02532

Call Sign: KA1DHQ
Mark A Corio Sr
5 Whitecliff Rd
Buzzards Bay MA
02532

Call Sign: W1KHZ
Mark A Corio Sr
5 Whitecliff Rd
Buzzards Bay MA
02532

Call Sign: N1ZIZ
Genesis Amateur
Radio Society Inc
Buzzards Bay MA
02532

Call Sign: KB1EVY
John E Williams Ii
Buzzards Bay MA
02532

Call Sign: KB1LIP
Heavy Metal Radio
Group

Buzzards Bay MA
02532

Call Sign: W1HM
Heavy Metal Radio
Group
Buzzards Bay MA
02532

**FCC Amateur Radio
Licenses in Byfield**

Call Sign: KB1BDJ
David P Smart
1 Birch Ln
Byfield MA 01922

Call Sign: KB1TZG
Marco J Carnovale
12 Coleman Rd
Byfield MA 01922

Call Sign: KA1CPR
Wayne W Reetz
10 Courser Brook Dr
Byfield MA 01922

Call Sign: KA1RAT
Roger A Corbin
1 Elm St
Byfield MA 01922

Call Sign: KA1REC
David A Corbin
1 Elm St
Byfield MA 01932

Call Sign: K1BGK
Harold R Blackford
176 Elm St
Byfield MA 01922

Call Sign: K1WTF
Stanley Kaplan
28 Fatherland Dr
Byfield MA 01922

Call Sign: N1NEJ
Jarrod S Robertson
8 Larkin Rd
Byfield MA 01922

Call Sign: N1YQZ
Jonathan T Robertson

8 Larkin Rd
Byfield MA 01922

Call Sign: N1POI
Graeme S Godzyk
Byfield MA 01922

FCC Amateur Radio Licenses in Cambridge

Call Sign: N1XU
Ron M Hoffmann
20 Chestnut St Apt 305
Cambirdge MA
021394800

Call Sign: N1SUV
Theodore C Johnson
42 A Rindge Ave
Cambridge MA 02140

Call Sign: N1ZRN
Joseph T Foley
18 Acorn St
Cambridge MA 02139

Call Sign: KB1IRT
David D Diel
143 Albany St 412a
Cambridge MA 02139

Call Sign: KB1WNV
David A Wilson
235 Albany St Rm
3084c
Cambridge MA 02139

Call Sign: KB1WUA
Mary E Knapp
350 Allston St Apt 1
Cambridge MA 02139

Call Sign: KA1QZM
Louis J Toth
3 Ames St
Cambridge MA 02139

Call Sign: KB1ATB
Theresa V Iuzzolino
3 Ames St
Cambirdge MA 02139

Call Sign: KB1DDM

Joy J Nicholson
3 Ames St
Cambridge MA 02142

Call Sign: KB1DEL
Robert J Buckingham
3 Ames St
Cambridge MA 02139

Call Sign: KB1DJJ
Monica L Taylor
3 Ames St
Cambridge MA 02142

Call Sign: N1HFM
Carol K Chen
3 Ames St
Cambridge MA 02139

Call Sign: N1QIN
Ivano Gregoratto
3 Ames St
Cambridge MA 02139

Call Sign: N1QPY
Ian Seslick
3 Ames St
Cambridge MA 02142

Call Sign: N1ZXM
Andrew R Twyman
3 Ames St
Cambridge MA 02142

Call Sign: KB1GFX
James M Roewe
3 Ames St
Cambridge MA 02142

Call Sign: KB1HAJ
Hubert V Pham
3 Ames St
Cambridge MA 02142

Call Sign: KB1HTG
Lael U Odhner
3 Ames St
Cambridge MA 02141

Call Sign: KB1NCS
Matthew S Goldstein
3 Ames St
Cambridge MA 02142

Call Sign: KB1QED
Scott D Morrison
3 Ames St
Cambridge MA 02142

Call Sign: KB1SVR
Christopher P Merrill
3 Ames St
Cambridge MA 02142

Call Sign: N1UEK
Hong H Chen
4 Ames St
Cambridge MA 02139

Call Sign: N1NLF
Steve Mann
20 Ames St
Cambridge MA 02139

Call Sign: KB1EHH
Geoffrey L Goodell
3 Ames St #351
Cambridge MA
021421305

Call Sign: KB1VEA
Gustavo N Goretkin
3 Ames St 216
Cambridge MA 02142

Call Sign: KB1GFU
Leah E Hutchison
3 Ames St 253
Cambridge MA 02142

Call Sign: KB1WNN
Jessica M Parker
3 Ames St B309
Cambridge MA 02142

Call Sign: KB1WXI
Yuanyu Chen
3 Ames St B315
Cambridge MA 02142

Call Sign: KB1IAO
Jennifer M Selby
3 Ames St Box 199
Cambridge MA 02142

Call Sign: N1VAE
Diana C Buttz
3 Ames St Box 23

Cambridge MA 02142

Call Sign: N1UHU
Elaine C Yang
3 Ames St Box 308
Cambridge MA 02139

Call Sign: KB1DAF
Jose H Mercado Jr
3 Ames St Box 345
Cambridge MA 02142

Call Sign: KB1DCA
Timothy Y Dunn
3 Ames St Box 346
Cambridge MA
021421305

Call Sign: KC2IFL
Harold S Barnard
3 Ames St Box G
Cambridge MA 02142

Call Sign: KB1IYO
Mary M Lederer
70 Amherst St
Cambridge MA 02142

Call Sign: KB1DBZ
James L Waldrop Iii
70 Amherst St Rm 148
Cambridge MA 02142

Call Sign: KB1TZQ
Dmitry Turbiner
70 Amherst St Room
624
Cambridge MA 02142

Call Sign: KB1CTG
Albert C Lin
8 Amory St 1
Cambridge MA 02139

Call Sign: KB1KLX
Thomas D Sanfilippo
147 Amory St Apt 1
Cambridge MA 02139

Call Sign: W1ZH
Thomas D Sanfilippo
147 Amory St Apt 1
Cambridge MA 02139

Call Sign: KB1GJ
David R Karger
71 Antrim St
Cambridge MA
021391103

Call Sign: K3NA
Eric L Scace
89 Antrim St - Unit 2
Cambridge MA 02139

Call Sign: KB1TGJ
Fairhaven Operators
Club
89 Antrim St - Unit 2
Cambridge MA 02139

Call Sign: KM1W
Fairhaven Operators
Club
89 Antrim St - Unit 2
Cambridge MA 02139

Call Sign: KB1UFB
Radio Expeditions Inc
89 Antrim St Unit 2
Cambridge MA 02139

Call Sign: W1RXP
Radio Expeditions Inc
89 Antrim St Unit 2
Cambridge MA 02139

Call Sign: AJ1E
Charles R D Amico
185 Appleton St
Cambridge MA
021381330

Call Sign: AB1HL
Robert T Morris
28 Arlington St
Cambridge MA 02140

Call Sign: KA1RFE
Mary R Few
12 Arnold Cir
Cambridge MA 02139

Call Sign: N1TPR
Kyle A B Lapidus
25 Athens St 2
Cambridge MA 02138

Call Sign: KB1CTH
Matthew S De Bergalis
120 B Auburn St
Cambridge MA 02139

Call Sign: N3JUP
Jon M Steadman Jr
9 Banks St Apt 1
Cambridge MA 02138

Call Sign: N1HXL
David A Vallance
18 Bay St Apt 3
Cambridge MA 02139

Call Sign: K1BSO
David J Smith
4 Blanchard Rd
Cambridge MA 02138

Call Sign: KA1KDZ
James F Joyce Ii
80 Bolton St
Cambridge MA 02140

Call Sign: KA1HE
Lawrence J Kilgallen
Box 397081
Cambridge MA
021397081

Call Sign: KA1MQX
Nicholas Altenbernd
Box 425755
Cambridge MA 02142

Call Sign: W1IME
Frances R Cardullo
6 Brattle St
Cambridge MA 02138

Call Sign: KB1CIZ
Leah M Bateman
244 Brattle St 1
Cambridge MA 02138

Call Sign: WB1FFS
James H Flanders
35 Brewster St
Cambridge MA 02138

Call Sign: KB1IAA
Ellen Clegg
404 Broadway

Cambridge MA 02139

Call Sign: KA1REH
Edward J Burke Jr
16 Brookford St
Cambridge MA 02140

Call Sign: KC8AVS
Jessica A Durrum
186 Brookline St
Cambridge MA 02139

Call Sign: KB1VJC
Stefan A Devitt
256 Brookline St
Cambridge MA 02139

Call Sign: W8UPZ
Edward H Jacobsen
281 Brookline St
Cambridge MA 02139

Call Sign: KG6YOF
Jeffrey T Feldman
7 Brookline St Apt #3
Cambridge MA 02139

Call Sign: N1CGN
George W Waring Jr
7 Buckingham Pl
Cambridge MA 02138

Call Sign: N1XFZ
Gerald T Dang
160 Cabot Mail Center
Cambridge MA 02138

Call Sign: N1XGA
Thien T Huynh
188 Cabot Mail Center
Cambridge MA 02138

Call Sign: W6AXP
Rae F Stiening
75 Cambridge Parkway
E 903
Cambridge MA 02142

Call Sign: WB1BUZ
Joseph M Garfield
75 Cambridge Parkway
Unit E1103
Cambridge MA 02142

Call Sign: KA1GWS
Po Tsoi
471 Cambridge St
Cambridge MA 02141

Call Sign: AA9RB
Clayton M Nall
1737 Cambridge St
Cambridge MA 02138

Call Sign: KD4RBJ
Frank J Csar Iii
1699 Cambridge St
Apt 2
Cambridge MA 02138

Call Sign: KB1ROY
Brian J Julian
30 Cambridgepark Dr
Apt 4142
Cambridge MA 02140

Call Sign: KB1SSO
Alfred B Roney
10 Centre St Apt 3f
Cambridge MA 02139

Call Sign: KA1UD
Roger J Lightowler
4 Chauncy Ln
Cambridge MA
021382402

Call Sign: NI1H
Roger J Lightowler
4 Chauncy Ln
Cambridge MA
021382402

Call Sign: N1TPP
Sally M Pak
Chester St
Cambridge MA 02140

Call Sign: N1QL
Jeffrey S Willcox
69 Chestnut St
Cambridge MA 02139

Call Sign: KB1WXH
Rachel A Bowens-
Rubin
69 Chestnut St
Cambridge MA 02139

Call Sign: KB1RRC
Jeremy L Greene
130 Chestnut St
Cambridge MA 02139

Call Sign: KB1DEH
Jared P Hunter
180 Chestnut St
Cambridge MA 02139

Call Sign: N1UZY
Chieh S Lo
20 Chestnut St 402
Cambridge MA 02139

Call Sign: KB1TPA
Julien Godard
247 Chestnut St Apt 1
Cambridge MA 02139

Call Sign: N1QOD
John J Meehan Sr
60 Chilton St
Cambridge MA 02138

Call Sign: W1HFA
Paul Horowitz
111 Chilton St
Cambridge MA
021386844

Call Sign: N1PJX
Stephen J Beikman
118 Clay St Apt 3
Cambridge MA 02140

Call Sign: KB1OBB
Takeshi Nagatomi
4 Cogswell Ave -7
Cambridge MA 02140

Call Sign: W1SQI
Thomas A Synnott
3 Concord Ave
Cambridge MA
021383616

Call Sign: KB1HJU
Jeffrey A Liss
655 Concord Ave
Cambridge MA 02138

Call Sign: K1PS

Peter M Stonberg
346 Concord Ave #1
Cambridge MA 02138

Call Sign: KB1JPA
Dov Goldvasser
102 Coolidge Hill
Cambridge MA
021385522

Call Sign: K1RGM
Roger E Mascoll
25 Copley St
Cambridge MA 02138

Call Sign: N1ZRM
Elizabeth B Beeuwkes
48 Cottage St
Cambridge MA 02139

Call Sign: N1ZNN
Adam H Woodworth
Cottage St
Cambridge MA 02139

Call Sign: KA1VKO
Peter A Fried
1 Craigie St Apt 26
Cambridge MA 02138

Call Sign: AG4ZP
Ryan W Kingsbury
1 Crawford St Apt 11
Cambridge MA 02139

Call Sign: KE6REP
Jack E Dietz
17 Creighton St
Cambridge MA 02140

Call Sign: N1YJG
Daniel J B Clark
32 Crescent St
Cambridge MA
021381908

Call Sign: KB1CSC
Oliver R Oberdorf
30 Cushing St 1
Cambridge MA 02138

Call Sign: KB1MQH
Earl K Miller
45 D Museum St

Cambridge MA 02138

Call Sign: KB1EAD
Douglas D Plumer
27 Decatur St
Cambridge MA 02139

Call Sign: AC3T
Christian J Ternus
26 Ellery St
Cambridge MA 02138

Call Sign: KB1VGM
Ryan M Cooper
69 Elm St 2
Cambridge MA 02139

Call Sign: KB1RWA
Keith N Williams
98 Erie St Unit 12
Cambridge MA 02139

Call Sign: KA0QOM
David E Clark
14 Eustis St
Cambridge MA
021402204

Call Sign: AB1NC
David E Clark
14 Eustis St
Cambridge MA
021402204

Call Sign: KB1GML
Masashi Ijano
Fain Wood Cir 1
Cambridge MA 02139

Call Sign: KB1CHA
Jonathon B Weiss
26 Fairmont Ave
Cambridge MA 02139

Call Sign: KB1OEW
Kathryn A Hayes
26 Fairmont Ave
Cambridge MA 02139

Call Sign: KB1UPW
Marek K Kolodziej
20 Forest St Apt 1
Cambridge MA 02140

Call Sign: N1KOL
Marek K Kolodziej
20 Forest St Apt 1
Cambridge MA 02140

Call Sign: N1AMI
William H Bean
21 Foster St
Cambridge MA 02138

Call Sign: N1IPP
James D Koger
444 Franklin St
Cambridge MA 02139

Call Sign: N1PQF
Robert S Silvers
129 Franklin St 105
Cambridge MA 02139

Call Sign: KB1LQO
Richard M Ryde
411 Franklin St Apt
1005
Cambridge MA 02139

Call Sign: KE4NQN
Peter Z Bowen
129 Franklin St Apt
429
Cambridge MA 02139

Call Sign: N1WPF
Edward D Davis
411 Franklin St Apt
505
Cambridge MA 02139

Call Sign: N1AFH
Frank W Lo Gerfo
71 Fresh Pond Lane
Cambridge MA 02138

Call Sign: KB3EJD
Adam M Siegel
63 Fresh Pond
Parkway
Cambridge MA 02138

Call Sign: K2PNK
Arnold G Reinhold
14 Fresh Pond Pl
Cambridge MA 02138

Call Sign: N1RRX
David F Pincus
14 Fresh Pond Place
Cambridge MA 02138

Call Sign: N1VNT
Walter R Taylor
50 Frost St
Cambridge MA 02140

Call Sign: AB1BY
Riad S Wahby
7 Fulkerson St 3
Cambridge MA 02141

Call Sign: KA4IXB
Jonathan W Babb
130 Gore St 2
Cambridge MA 02141

Call Sign: N1IBU
Sedigheh Moosavihard
170 Gore St Apt 306
Cambridge MA 02141

Call Sign: AA1XB
Ali Talebinejad
170 Gore St Apt 306
Cambridge MA 02141

Call Sign: W5GSB
Gregory S Burd
5 Grant St 2
Cambridge MA 02138

Call Sign: KB1TZO
PAUL A Desimone
36 Gray St
Cambridge MA 02138

Call Sign: WB1ACH
PAUL A Desimone
36 Gray St
Cambridge MA 02138

Call Sign: KA1RBJ
Phillip T Ciaramitaro
29 Grozier Rd
Cambridge MA 02138

Call Sign: KB1IFT
Andrew M Heafitz
18 Hadley St
Cambridge MA 02140

Call Sign: N1NQO
Anthony W Gigante
80 Hampshire St
Cambridge MA 02139

Call Sign: N1XPD
Cyrus R Eyster
114 Hampshire St
Cambridge MA 02139

Call Sign: KB1MQF
Emil Sit
Hampshire St
Cambridge MA 02139

Call Sign: KB1CTI
Yonah Schmeidler
158 Hampshire St #1
Cambridge MA 02139

Call Sign: N1NDS
Benjamin P Avila
22 Hancock St
Cambridge MA 02139

Call Sign: KB1QVV
Jean L Tsutsumi
344 Harbard St Apt 9
Cambridge MA
021392002

Call Sign: AB1MK
Zachary J Weber
24 Harrison Ave
Cambridge MA 02140

Call Sign: N1HKR
James T Chao
17 Harvard College
Cambridge MA 02138

Call Sign: KA2QHM
Boris Dolgonos
Harvard College
Cambridge MA 02138

Call Sign: KB1NUU
Tomasz B
Mloduchowski
117 Harvard St
Cambridge MA 02139

Call Sign: N1NST

Stuart J Klein
378 Harvard St
Cambridge MA 02138

Call Sign: KG2IZ
Masahiko Ito
295 Harvard St #909
Cambridge MA 02139

Call Sign: N1CKL
Tetsuo Takigawa
Harvard St 12a
Cambridge MA 02139

Call Sign: KB1DMD
Matthew C Wakeman
287 Harvard St 25
Cambridge MA 02139

Call Sign: N1XPC
Paul H Janzen
351 Harvard St Apt 16
Cambridge MA 02138

Call Sign: KB1KGW
Michael C Axiak
351 Harvard St Apt 1a
Cambridge MA
021384220

Call Sign: WA2ICY
James F Butler
287 Harvard St Apt 53
Cambridge MA
021392368

Call Sign: KB1OXB
Iuliu Vasilescu
268 Harvard St Apt 6
Cambridge MA 02139

Call Sign: K1IV
Iuliu Vasilescu
268 Harvard St Apt 6
Cambridge MA 02139

Call Sign: WB9SWI
James F Babb
315 Harvard St Apt 6
Cambridge MA
021392015

Call Sign: N3NAF
Bradley E Cain

295 Harvard St Apt
611
Cambridge MA 02139

Call Sign: KB1MJN
Evan Sahlstrom
4 Hastings Sq
Cambridge MA 02139

Call Sign: K1HIE
Evan Sahlstrom
4 Hastings Sq
Cambridge MA 02139

Call Sign: N1KHJ
Stefan B Anninger
26 Healey St
Cambridge MA 02138

Call Sign: KA3ZOU
CYNTHIA Gilbert
29 Hews St
Cambridge MA 02139

Call Sign: K1KPS
Ernest H Taves
12 Hubbard Park Rd
Cambridge MA
021384731

Call Sign: KA1NIW
Shelby Pierce
231 Huron Ave
Cambridge MA
021381327

Call Sign: N1PPW
Tanya M Braginsky
700 Huron Ave 17f
Cambridge MA 02138

Call Sign: N1GIO
Vincent S Ng
91 Inman St
Cambridge MA 02139

Call Sign: KI1S
John G Rhoads
Inman St
Cambridge MA 02139

Call Sign: KB1RBT
Benjamin L Katz
36 Irving St 2

Cambridge MA 02138

Call Sign: N1EXQ
James D Allred
91 Jackson St
Cambridge MA 02140

Call Sign: N1VU
James D Allred
91 Jackson St
Cambridge MA 02140

Call Sign: WA1JPU
Thomas J Fitzgerald Jr
15 James Way
Cambridge MA 02141

Call Sign: KB3GAP
Jason B Alonso
Jay St Apt 2
Cambridge MA 02139

Call Sign: N1IZO
Stephen W Sauter
Kendall Sq
Cambridge MA 02142

Call Sign: N1ZQF
Thomas R
Fleischmann
1 Kendall Sq Bldg 600
Cambridge MA 02139

Call Sign: N1DHW
Francis X Murphy
84 Kinnaird St
Cambridge MA 02139

Call Sign: K1QWC
Stephen E Patten
87 Kinnaird St
Cambridge MA 02139

Call Sign: KC8UJJ
Joseph M Paxton
39 Kirkland St #1418
Cambridge MA 02138

Call Sign: N1HHN
Mark D Lindsay
41 Kirkland St 406b
Cambridge MA 02138

Call Sign: W1FS

Kris Markley
15 Lambert St Apt
1208
Cambridge MA 02141

Call Sign: W1LTL
George P Keich
15 Lambert St Apt
1708
Cambridge MA 02141

Call Sign: WA1ZSF
Gerald T Gannon
30 Langdon St
Cambridge MA 02138

Call Sign: W7HKW
William F Mann
105 Larch Rd
Cambridge MA 02138

Call Sign: N1OXI
Matthew J Gossett
61 Larchwood Dr
Cambridge MA 02138

Call Sign: AD5NV
Courtney E Waal
37 Lee St #1
Cambridge MA 02139

Call Sign: KB2HYC
Ernest R Post
37 Lee St Ste #1
Cambridge MA
021392217

Call Sign: N1XFY
Jimmy J Kang
401 Leverett Mail
Center
Cambridge MA 02138

Call Sign: KB1ODZ
Matthew R Tierney
450 Leverett Mail
Center
Cambridge MA 02138

Call Sign: KB1VPR
Nicholas A Hays
218 Lexington Ave
Cambridge MA 02138

Call Sign: KA1WPO
Dimitry Samarin
6 Linden St
Cambridge MA 02138

Call Sign: KA1WSS
Vladimir Alexandrov
6 Linden St
Cambridge MA 02138

Call Sign: W1AF
Harvard Wireless Club
6 Linden St
Cambridge MA 02138

Call Sign: N1IGF
Victor Stroganov
Linden St
Cambridge MA 02138

Call Sign: WB1EXO
Maurice J Martin
16 Locke St
Cambridge MA 02140

Call Sign: KB1ETU
David B O Connor
2 Longfellow Rd
Cambridge MA
021384736

Call Sign: KC1SW
Johnathan G Trumbull
Lowell B21
Cambridge MA 02138

Call Sign: KB1QKT
Diane L Christoforo
21 Madison Ave
Cambridge MA 02140

Call Sign: N1IDY
Sanjay Manandhar
24 Magazine 3
Cambridge MA 02139

Call Sign: K1GSN
Maxon J Buscher
47 Magazine St
Cambridge MA 02139

Call Sign: AA1WQ
William M Wells Iii
82 Magazine St

Cambridge MA 02139

Call Sign: NS1W
William M Wells Iii
82 Magazine St
Cambridge MA 02139

Call Sign: N1AOE
Maxon J Buscher
129 Magazine St
Cambridge MA 02139

Call Sign: KB1VIZ
Terrence Mckenna
180 Magazine St Apt 1
Cambridge MA 02139

Call Sign: KB1CJA
Marisa J Kirschbaum
790 Main St Apt 11
Cambridge MA 02139

Call Sign: KB1EDB
Joanne M Mikkelson
Market St
Cambridge MA
021391507

Call Sign: AF6EN
Vincent T Liao
56 Market St #2
Cambridge MA 02139

Call Sign: KB1NYR
Gregory A Marton
28 Marney St 3
Cambridge MA
021411654

Call Sign: N1RHP
Taylor M Smith
79 Martin St
Cambridge MA 02139

Call Sign: N1VAF
David K Critz
50 Mass Ave
Cambridge MA 02139

Call Sign: KB1GFY
Ziaieh C Sobhani
290 Mass Ave
Cambridge MA 02139

Call Sign: KB1HVZ
Katherine A Reid
290 Mass Ave
Cambridge MA 02139

Call Sign: KB1IAP
James K Whiting
290 Mass Ave
Cambridge MA 02139

Call Sign: N1JTO
George Hammel
848 Mass Ave
Cambridge MA 02139

Call Sign: AA1QG
Terje Arntzen
Mass Ave
Cambridge MA 02138

Call Sign: KB1EPK
Julio A Roque
2456 Mass Ave #105
Cambridge MA 02140

Call Sign: WB2PTZ
Ronald L Kalin
1600 Mass Ave 407
Cambridge MA 02138

Call Sign: KA5PJP
Seth D Berger
1105 Mass Ave Apt 8a
Cambridge MA 02138

Call Sign: KB1FAH
Bae Ian Wu
77 Mass Ave Rm 26
Cambridge MA 02139

Call Sign: W1MX
Mit Room 50 M I T
Radio Society
357 Massachusetts A
Cambridge MA 02139

Call Sign: N6WIT
Paul D Ashby
2130 Massachusetts
Apt 2c
Cambridge MA 02140

Call Sign: KB1MJO
You Zhou

290 Massachusetts Av
Cambridge MA
021394130

Call Sign: KB1QEE
Ekaterina S
Kuznetsova
290 Massachusetts Av
Cambridge MA 02139

Call Sign: KB1QEF
Kevin A Riggle
290 Massachusetts Av
Cambridge MA 02139

Call Sign: KB1QEH
Telmo L Correa Jr
290 Massachusetts Av
Cambridge MA 02139

Call Sign: KB1QEI
Joy C Perkinson
290 Massachusetts Av
Cambridge MA 02139

Call Sign: KB1QEK
Nickolas Koutsopoulos
290 Massachusetts Av
Cambridge MA 02139

Call Sign: KB1QMQ
Jasmine R Florentine
290 Massachusetts Av
Cambridge MA 02139

Call Sign: KB1QOE
Benjamin J Kaduk
84 Massachusetts Av
W20
Cambridge MA 02139

Call Sign: AB1EQ
Periclis Monioudis
77 Massachusetts Ave
Cambridge MA 02139

Call Sign: KI1E
Periclis Monioudis
77 Massachusetts Ave
Cambridge MA 02139

Call Sign: KA1QZL
Claudia U Ranniger
282 Massachusetts Ave

Cambridge MA 02139

Call Sign: KB1DEN
Liana F Lareau
290 Massachusetts Ave
Cambridge MA 02139

Call Sign: KB1DHK
Piotr F Mitras
290 Massachusetts Ave
Cambridge MA 02139

Call Sign: KB1GFO
Lanya M Dasilva
290 Massachusetts Ave
Cambridge MA 02139

Call Sign: KB1SVT
Jing Wang
290 Massachusetts Ave
Cambridge MA 02139

Call Sign: KC2MLF
Christian J Ternus
290 Massachusetts Ave
Cambridge MA 02139

Call Sign: AB1IU
Christian J Ternus
290 Massachusetts Ave
Cambridge MA 02139

Call Sign: KB2ERO
Susan L Loucks
897 Massachusetts Ave
Cambridge MA 02139

Call Sign: W4SCN
Thomas H Dupree
1100 Massachusetts
Ave
Cambridge MA 02138

Call Sign: KB1OEX
Luiz L Souza
2568 Massachusetts
Ave
Cambridge MA 02140

Call Sign: KB1KFL
Frank L Gerratana
632 Massachusetts Ave
#319
Cambridge MA 02139

Call Sign: WA1CXE
Frank L Gerratana
632 Massachusetts Ave
#319
Cambridge MA 02139

Call Sign: KB1FWS
Gerald S Ruderman
1008 Massachusetts
Ave #604
Cambridge MA
021385353

Call Sign: N1FQC
Michael J Maier
2130 Massachusetts
Ave 5d
Cambridge MA 02140

Call Sign: KA1SLM
Sachiko Yamaura
Massachusetts Ave 5d
Cambridge MA 02140

Call Sign: N1VNS
Scott J Limb
77 Massachusetts Ave
66
Cambridge MA 02139

Call Sign: N1NZV
Richard J Barbalace
84 Massachusetts Ave
W20-557
Cambridge MA 02139

Call Sign: N2WRW
Peter C Sample
1654 Massechusetts
Ave 46
Cambridge MA 02138

Call Sign: KB1MGQ
Michael A Hamburg
260 Mather House
Cambridge MA 02138

Call Sign: N2YYZ
Chris G Danis
10 Mcternan St #204
Cambridge MA 02139

Call Sign: KB1GFN

Jacinda L Clemenzi
410 Memoral Dr
Cambridge MA 02139

Call Sign: KB1EQB
Jacky Mallett
305 Memorial Dr
Cambridge MA 02139

Call Sign: KB1HFN
Christophe C Assens
305 Memorial Dr
Cambridge MA 02139

Call Sign: N1VAC
Nayana V Ghantiwala
320 Memorial Dr
Cambridge MA 02139

Call Sign: N1RRZ
Emily L Warlick
362 Memorial Dr
Cambridge MA 02139

Call Sign: N1UZZ
Nikhil Iyengar
362 Memorial Dr
Cambridge MA 02139

Call Sign: N1ZEO
Stanley R Hunter
362 Memorial Dr
Cambridge MA 02139

Call Sign: N1TCR
Seth E Webster
410 Memorial Dr
Cambridge MA 02139

Call Sign: N1UZX
David I Moreira
410 Memorial Dr
Cambridge MA 02139

Call Sign: KB1KFV
Craig D Morales
410 Memorial Dr
Cambridge MA 02139

Call Sign: KB1QMP
Evan M Broder
410 Memorial Dr
Cambridge MA 02139

Call Sign: N1UEF
Serkan Arslanalp
428 Memorial Dr
Cambridge MA 02139

Call Sign: N1VAB
Eric L Gravengaard
450 Memorial Dr
Cambridge MA 02139

Call Sign: N1VAD
George J
Delagrammatikas
450 Memorial Dr
Cambridge MA 02139

Call Sign: KB1FCL
Peter R Russo
450 Memorial Dr
Cambridge MA 02139

Call Sign: KB1GFZ
Michael D Seeman
450 Memorial Dr
Cambridge MA 02139

Call Sign: KB1MGP
Christopher R
Pentacoff
450 Memorial Dr
Cambridge MA 02139

Call Sign: KB1PBW
Emily R Pheiffer
450 Memorial Dr
Cambridge MA 02139

Call Sign: KB1MLX
Denny L Reyes
471 Memorial Dr
Cambridge MA 02139

Call Sign: N1QIL
Milton D Wong
473 Memorial Dr
Cambridge MA 02139

Call Sign: KA1VGC
Raphael H Ko
475 Memorial Dr
Cambridge MA 02139

Call Sign: KA1RBM
David B Wilson

500 Memorial Dr
Cambridge MA 02139

Call Sign: KB1GFL
Priya Agrawal
500 Memorial Dr
Cambridge MA 02139

Call Sign: KB1TZR
Zhen Li
550 Memorial Dr 11d3
Cambridge MA 02139

Call Sign: KB1NXX
Katonio A Butler
550 Memorial Dr -
22e4
Cambridge MA 02139

Call Sign: N1ZUV
Edwin R Karat
305 Memorial Dr 308c
Cambridge MA 02139

Call Sign: KB1DPL
Gisele M Proulx
320 Memorial Dr 317a
Cambridge MA 02139

Call Sign: KB1BMX
Steve S Lin
500 Memorial Dr 351
Cambridge MA 02139

Call Sign: N1KKG
Paul S Martin
305 Memorial Dr 417c
Cambridge MA 02139

Call Sign: N1HMB
David M Watt
305 Memorial Dr 604a
Cambridge MA 02139

Call Sign: KB1GFW
Sameera S Ponda
500 Memorial Dr 739
Cambridge MA 02139

Call Sign: N1UEI
Christine W Chan
450 Memorial Dr
A311
Cambridge MA 02139

Call Sign: KB1DMH
Bradford C Backus
305 Memorial Dr Apt
510b
Cambridge MA
021394303

Call Sign: KA1THV
Cyrus S Bamji
Memorial Dr Apt 516b
305
Cambridge MA 02139

Call Sign: WA1UVR
John J Morrison
100 Memorial Dr Apt
5-18a
Cambridge MA
021421328

Call Sign: N1TFY
Natalya Cohen
450 Memorial Dr
G423
Cambridge MA 02139

Call Sign: KA1VQL
Tanveer F Syeda
350 Memorial Dr Mit
Cambridge MA 02139

Call Sign: N1QIJ
Hao Chien
450 Memorial Dr Rm
G 325
Cambridge MA 02139

Call Sign: KB1HIK
Dava J Newman
362 Memorial Dr Ste
155
Cambridge MA 02139

Call Sign: KD1ODE
Jack W Holloway
305 Memorial Drive
Cambridge MA 02139

Call Sign: KB1WKE
Michael T Kelessoglou
410 Memorial Drive
Cambridge MA 02139

Call Sign: KB1WNU
Maxwell S Mann
471 Memorial Drive 5
Cambridge MA 02139

Call Sign: KB1IUL
Stephen J Hall
815 Memorial Drive
Apt 1705
Cambridge MA 02139

Call Sign: WU1V
Richard C St Clair
3 Michael Way
Cambridge MA 02141

Call Sign: KB1WXK
Danilo Roascio
194 Monsignor Obrien
Hwy
Cambridge MA 02141

Call Sign: KA1WL
Loredana Lignola
39 Montgomery St
Cambridge MA 02140

Call Sign: WO1G
Scott A Sminkey
22 Montgomery St Fl 1
Cambridge MA 02140

Call Sign: KG4JDC
Alan J Patterson Jr
191 Mount Auburn St
Cambridge MA 02138

Call Sign: KB1QAM
Barry J Briggs
169 Msgr Obrien Hwy
Apt 705
Cambridge MA 02141

Call Sign: K1BLB
Thomas A Poynter Dr
124 Mt Auburn St;
Suite 200
Cambridge MA
021385787

Call Sign: W1YTK
Paul K Simmons
50 Mt Pleasant St
Cambridge MA 02140

Call Sign: N1FMM
Richard Brezina
213 Munroe 3
Cambridge MA 02139

Call Sign: KF6SVX
Vincent C Auyeung
10 Museum Way #623
Cambridge MA 02141

Call Sign: WF1P
Charles M Foundyller
16 Myrtle Ave
Cambridge MA 02138

Call Sign: W1OMN
Robert E Mc Elroy
22 Norman St
Cambridge MA 02138

Call Sign: KB1QWH
Nicholas B Hambridge
62 Otis St Apt 3
Cambridge MA 02141

Call Sign: KB1WAE
Karl C Kulling
17 Otis St Unit 301
Cambridge MA 02141

Call Sign: KB1KNR
Leonard N Rodriguez
12 Oxford St Box 78
Cambridge MA 02138

Call Sign: AK0H
Riad S Wahby
70 Pacific St # 840b
Cambridge MA 02139

Call Sign: KC2CWI
Austin J Minnich
70 Pacific St Apt 216
Cambridge MA 02139

Call Sign: KE7SJE
Matthew E D Asaro
70 Pacific St Apt 363b
Cambridge MA 02139

Call Sign: AG4AI
Thomas B O Reilly
70 Pacific St Apt 904

Cambridge MA 02139

Call Sign: N1ROY
Dmitriy A
Rogozhnikov
70 Pacific St Apt 913
Cambridge MA 02139

Call Sign: KB1VED
Sung Wook Paek
70 Pacific St Rm 353a
Cambridge MA
021394204

Call Sign: KB1ALC
Glen F Spivak
2 Peabody Ter Unit
2004
Cambridge MA 02138

Call Sign: KB1OXN
Zachary B Sullivan
2 Peabody Tr Apt 503
Cambridge MA 02138

Call Sign: KB1QCU
Benjamin W Adams
42 Pearl St
Cambridge MA 02139

Call Sign: N1DRH
Belinda F Bacon
140 Pearl St
Cambridge MA
021394010

Call Sign: WB3LRY
Paul S Blum
162 Pearl St
Cambridge MA 02139

Call Sign: KR0TUS
Peter R Gamache
346 Pearl St Apt 1
Cambridge MA 02139

Call Sign: KB1PBX
David M Wentzlaff
279 Pearl St Apt 21
Cambridge MA 02139

Call Sign: N1NRU
Zagloul E Ayad
47 Pilgrim St #103

Cambridge MA 02139

Call Sign: N1RRY
Christopher A Kairis
24 Plymouth St
Cambridge MA 02141

Call Sign: AB1IZ
Quentin E Smith
86 Plymouth St #2
Cambridge MA 02141

Call Sign: KB1GGB
Michael J Walsh
89 Plymouth St 1
Cambridge MA 02141

Call Sign: KB1SDS
Jonathan L Morse
7 Portsmouth St
Cambridge MA 02141

Call Sign: KB1QYZ
Edward K Summers
24 Portsmouth St
Cambridge MA 02141

Call Sign: KB1SHV
Michael R Price
24 Portsmouth St
Cambridge MA
021411328

Call Sign: N1LYO
Julius Feinleib
12 Prentiss St
Cambridge MA 02140

Call Sign: KB1MVS
Victor Grau Serrat
15 Prentiss St
Cambridge MA 02140

Call Sign: KA1VGD
Maissam A Hazim
140 Prospect St
Cambridge MA 02139

Call Sign: N1HJT
Mohamad A Akra
140 Prospect St
Cambridge MA 02139

Call Sign: KB1HIQ

Terry G Lorber Ii
376 Prospect St 3
Cambridge MA 02139

Call Sign: KE1KA
Monty C Brandenberg
45 Putnam Ave
Cambridge MA 02139

Call Sign: KB1JPB
Jason W Pramas
32 Putnam Ave 3
Cambridge MA 02139

Call Sign: N1ZOT
Rafael H Schloming
102 R Inman St
Cambridge MA 02139

Call Sign: KG6EQE
Keith Manabe
Raymond
Cambridge MA 02140

Call Sign: KB1GMJ
Keith Manabe
Raymond
Cambridge MA 02140

Call Sign: AA1YX
Keith Manabe
Raymond
Cambridge MA 02140

Call Sign: KB1GMM
Makoto Kariyama
Raymond St
Cambridge MA 02140

Call Sign: W2KOY
Eugene P Simon
12 Remington St 206
Cambridge MA 02138

Call Sign: KB1VIU
Robert J Douglass
51 Reservoir St
Cambridge MA 02138

Call Sign: W1HGR
Richard J Levy
64 Richdale Ave
Cambridge MA
021402629

Call Sign: KB1RBV
Erik L Williams
320 Rindge Av 403
Cambridge MA 02140

Call Sign: K1ELW
Erik L Williams
320 Rindge Av 403
Cambridge MA 02140

Call Sign: W1CRU
Chastine B Carter
402 Rindge Ave 17a
Cambridge MA 02140

Call Sign: KA1RNM
Nathan R Lyczak
23 Rindgefield St
Cambridge MA 02140

Call Sign: K1DDL
Louis L Stoddard
183 River St
Cambridge MA 02139

Call Sign: KB1DDO
Gregory Cavanagh
168 River St Apt 2
Cambridge MA 02139

Call Sign: KD0AMG
Justin R Slepak
23 Rockingham St
Cambridge MA 02139

Call Sign: KB1TWG
Michael F Mccrory
10 Rockwell St
Cambridge MA 02139

Call Sign: KA8QDH
John R Barlow
2 Saint Paul St
Cambridge MA 02139

Call Sign: N1IHA
Nicholas A Maddix
14 Salem St 3
Cambridge MA 02139

Call Sign: KB3EFM
Eric M Hanson
20 Saville St

Cambridge MA 02138

Call Sign: W1HIT
Arthur A Davis
37 Saville St
Cambridge MA 02138

Call Sign: KB1WMK
Anna Fung
111 Sciarappa Str
Cambridge MA 02141

Call Sign: KB1EQA
Alejandro R Sedeno
18 Seven Pines Ave
Cambridge MA 02140

Call Sign: N1JZH
Noam I Weinstein
25 Sherman St
Cambridge MA 02138

Call Sign: W1PLJ
George W Jones
66 Sherman St Apt 328
Cambridge MA 02140

Call Sign: WA1ZEX
Joanne M Muolo
73 Sixth St
Cambridge MA 02141

Call Sign: KB1SVO
Robert J Freed
16 Soden St 3
Cambridge MA
021393154

Call Sign: W1RJF
Robert J Freed
16 Soden St 3
Cambridge MA
021393154

Call Sign: N1NHZ
Arthur N Ashley
10 Soden St Apt 42
Cambridge MA
021393130

Call Sign: KB1WXU
Kevin Gregory
58 Spring St
Cambridge MA 02141

Call Sign: KB1TZN
Luciano Boglione
127 Spring St
Cambridge MA 02141

Call Sign: WH6DSN
David L Cantrell Jr
32 Standish St #1
Cambridge MA 02138

Call Sign: KA1DPK
Kevin E Mascoll
10 Suffolk 6
Cambridge MA 02139

Call Sign: N1NLI
Andre M De Hon
545 Technology Sq
Cambridge MA 02139

Call Sign: N1TNO
Elmer S Hung
545 Technology Sq
Cambridge MA 02139

Call Sign: N1UEP
Gregory R Galperin
545 Technology Sq
Cambridge MA 02139

Call Sign: N1JEN
Michael Bolotski
703 Technology Sq
Cambridge MA 02139

Call Sign: N1DZE
Michael R Blair
545 Technology
Square Rm 788
Cambridge MA
021393594

Call Sign: KB1SHW
KATHLEEN D Mc
KENZIE
7 Temple St #420
Cambridge MA 02139

Call Sign: WB1FOE
Teri S Hanright
34 Tremont St
Cambridge MA 02139

Call Sign: KB1JSQ
Jennifer R Mills
44 Tremont St 2
Cambridge MA 02139

Call Sign: KB1WAH
Brandon W Hockle
84 Tremont St 2
Cambridge MA 02139

Call Sign: KB1IRF
Peter T Nigra
17 Upland Rd No 2
Cambridge MA 02140

Call Sign: N1NQJ
Barry R Jaspan
9 Valentine St
Cambridge MA 02139

Call Sign: N1NZU
Marc H Horowitz
9 Valentine St
Cambridge MA 02139

Call Sign: N1UPT
Jeremy H Brown
9 Valentine St
Cambridge MA 02139

Call Sign: W1CQB
Domenic T Ricci
14 Vandine St
Cambridge MA 02141

Call Sign: KC1VO
Joseph W Waddie
150 Vassal Ln
Cambridge MA 02138

Call Sign: N1UZV
Goro Tamai
60 Vassar 31
Cambridge MA 02139

Call Sign: KB1EMP
Shane A Dupree
20 Vineyard St
Cambridge MA 02138

Call Sign: KB1WNO
Eric B Munson
60 Wadsworth St Apt
24a

Cambridge MA 02142

Call Sign: K7ERS
Eric B Munson
60 Wadsworth St Apt
24a
Cambridge MA 02142

Call Sign: WA1RNO
Clyde E Layne
70 Walden St
Cambridge MA 02140

Call Sign: N1HDQ
Lewis W Tucker
109 Walden St
Cambridge MA 02140

Call Sign: KB1WNS
John C Keel
205 Walden St 4d
Cambridge MA 02140

Call Sign: KB1DAE
Calista E Tait
283 Washington St
Cambridge MA 02139

Call Sign: N1XPB
Karl C Ramm
283 Washington St
Cambridge MA
021393505

Call Sign: KB1EUQ
Sara C Pickett
283 Washington St
Cambridge MA 02139

Call Sign: KB0ZHZ
Adam J Serafin
361 Washington St
Cambridge MA 02139

Call Sign: N1JOL
Andrew W Howitt
409 Washington St
Cambridge MA 02139

Call Sign: KB1USD
Geoffrey S Wallick
45 Webster Ave
Cambridge MA 02141

Call Sign: WD0BIF
Donald F Raines
141 Western Ave 2
Cambridge MA 02139

Call Sign: N1NSP
Yan Ming Li
101 Western Ave Apt
74
Cambridge MA 02139

Call Sign: N1HPP
Mohammadali
Taalebinezhaad
1401 Westgate
Cambridge MA 02139

Call Sign: KB1NLO
Hideaki Nii
359 Windsor St 3
Cambridge MA 02141

Call Sign: W1WFK
John B Hopkins
30 Winslow St
Cambridge MA
021386735

Call Sign: KB3SMT
Sean R O'connor
85 Winter St Apt 2
Cambridge MA 02141

Call Sign: KB1UQY
Sean R O'connor
85 Winter St Apt 2
Cambridge MA 02141

Call Sign: W1SRO
Sean R O'connor
85 Winter St Apt 2
Cambridge MA 02141

Call Sign: N1XDB
Kanaka Pattabiraman
350 Winthrop Mail Ctr
Cambridge MA 02138

Call Sign: N1OSH
Eskinder Abebe
26 York St Apt 2
Cambridge MA 02141

Call Sign: K5MIT

Mark J Ralph
Cambridge MA
021397242

Call Sign: KA1UTE
Steven C Kirschner
Cambridge MA 02238

Call Sign: KA1WDQ
Catherine R Boyle
Cambridge MA 02238

Call Sign: KD1MC
Mark T Zimmerman
Cambridge MA 02139

Call Sign: N1HYW
Philip A Rizzo
Cambridge MA 02238

Call Sign: N1RQS
Thomas M Eche
Cambridge MA 02139

Call Sign: WA1VRB
Frank J Stefanov
Wagner
Cambridge MA
021410005

Call Sign: KA4FHJ
George E Clark
Cambridge MA
022381006

Call Sign: KB1CGZ
John A Hawkinson
Cambridge MA
021397103

Call Sign: KB1CJD
Brad Thompson
Cambridge MA 02139

Call Sign: KB1DBW
Lex Nemzer
Cambridge MA
021397274

Call Sign: KB1DQZ
Amy M Yu
Cambridge MA 02142

Call Sign: KC4YES

Terence S Sullivan
Cambridge MA 02142

Call Sign: N1GZN
James T Beaupre
Cambridge MA
022382101

Call Sign: N1PXP
Michael C Murphy
Cambridge MA
021420020

Call Sign: N1SCO
Franklin Jones
Cambridge MA
022381671

Call Sign: N1ZSV
Thomas L Yu
Cambridge MA 02142

Call Sign: W1GSL
Stephen L Finberg
Cambridge MA
021397082

Call Sign: W1XM
Mit Uhf Repeater Assn
Cambridge MA
021397082

Call Sign: KB1FBB
Martin D Connor
Cambridge MA 02139

Call Sign: KB1IZL
Brad Thompson
Cambridge MA 02139

Call Sign: KB1JLJ
Gregory D Watson
Cambridge MA 02238

Call Sign: KB1KFS
Susan E Born
Cambridge MA 02142

Call Sign: KB1KVP
Dean J Foulis
Cambridge MA 02238

Call Sign: KB1MMH
Dan Costa

Cambridge MA 02139

Call Sign: AA4AE
George E Clark
Cambridge MA
022381006

Call Sign: KB1MSD
Mark K Mondol
Cambridge MA 02142

Call Sign: AB1FK
David E Burmaster
Cambridge MA
022382069

Call Sign: W1XW
George E Clark
Cambridge MA
022381006

Call Sign: W2NRL
Michael Hirsch
Cambridge MA 02238

Call Sign: W1TM
David E Burmaster
Cambridge MA
022382069

Call Sign: W1DNA
Amy M Yu
Cambridge MA 02142

**FCC Amateur Radio
Licenses in Canton**

Call Sign: W1IBW
John G Milne
50 Autumn Cir
Canton MA 02021

Call Sign: AB1OK
James R Peverill
19 Autumn Circle
Canton MA 02021

Call Sign: K1BFD
Barry F Devine
17 Beatty St
Canton MA 02021

Call Sign: KB1JZJ
Janice M Devine

17 Beatty St
Canton MA 02021

Call Sign: KB1KIM
Canton Ema
Association
17 Beatty St
Canton MA 02021

Call Sign: KB1HKF
Charles J Hainley
7 Cedarcrest Rd
Canton MA
020211547

Call Sign: N1YLW
Robert Marquez
42 Church St
Canton MA 02021

Call Sign: W1REP
Robert L Gibbons
15 Everett St
Canton MA 02021

Call Sign: KB1KRP
James P Kondel
8 Fairview Rd
Canton MA 02021

Call Sign: KB1NHG
Vitaly I Pesikov
23 Fencourt Rd
Canton MA 02021

Call Sign: WA1CON
Henry F Robinson
352 G Neponset South
Canton MA 02021

Call Sign: N1TWI
John D Murphy Sr
1 Glendale Way
Canton MA 02021

Call Sign: N1NWZ
Charles S Crespi
51 Grand St
Canton MA 02021

Call Sign: WA1LEF
Stephen W Brigandi
1 Hillsview St
Canton MA 02021

Call Sign: KB1JJP
John R Chapin Iii
30 Kings Rd
Canton MA
020211706

Call Sign: WA1HFN
Joel M Peisach
1 Meadow Brook Way
Canton MA 02021

Call Sign: K1BRD
Ernest R Bryant
30 Mechanic St
Canton MA 02021

Call Sign: N1NRV
David Ruvich
31 Old Randolph St
Canton MA 02021

Call Sign: KA1LFP
Joseph J Elwood
27 Pleasant Cir
Canton MA 02021

Call Sign: N1XJF
Jerry Greenblatt
28 Pleasant Garden
Canton MA 02021

Call Sign: WA1IKI
William L Paull
1209 Pleasant St
Canton MA 02021

Call Sign: N1WGN
William D Kerr
1213 Pleasant St
Canton MA 02021

Call Sign: N1CBN
Todd C Weaver
18 Ponkapoag Way
Canton MA 02021

Call Sign: N1YSV
Eric J Melendez
3 Randolph St
Canton MA 02021

Call Sign: N1NJD
Edward J Buckley Sr

8 Randolph St
Canton MA 02021

Call Sign: N1OHL
Edward J Buckley Jr
8 Randolph St
Canton MA 02121

Call Sign: WB1GLC
Joseph A Anastasio
14 Randolph St
Canton MA 02021

Call Sign: N1BBC
John S Bassett
965 Randolph St
Canton MA 02021

Call Sign: W1YRV
Salvatore J Bertino
499 Sherman St
Canton MA 02021

Call Sign: W1RYE
William P Sullivan
30 Sumner St
Canton MA 02021

Call Sign: K1SRP
Donald J Bannister
16 Trudy Ter
Canton MA 02021

Call Sign: N1ZMC
Richard E Parker
34 Wardwell Rd
Canton MA 02021

Call Sign: N1SOW
Allan D Kallman
117 Washington St
Canton MA
020213805

Call Sign: KA1IPJ
George H Perkins
476 Washington St
Canton MA 02021

Call Sign: KA1SOR
Ronald M Hatch
29 Wentworth Rd
Canton MA 02021

Call Sign: N1SCZ
Russell A Mc Fatter
9 White Sisters Way
Canton MA
020212048

Call Sign: N1ZRY
Daniel Auger
1301 Windsor Woods
Lane
Canton MA 02021

Call Sign: K1DSS
Peter N Miller
45 York Brook Rd
Canton MA 02021

Call Sign: KB1DSS
Sara R Prenaveau
45 York Brook Rd
Canton MA 02021

Call Sign: KB1QVY
Howard M Faverman
Canton MA 02021

**FCC Amateur Radio
Licenses in Carlisle**

Call Sign: KA1YKJ
Kathryn A Lord
30 Baldwin Rd
Carlisle MA 01741

Call Sign: N1FGM
John H James
30 Baldwin Rd
Carlisle MA 01741

Call Sign: K1YM
John H James
30 Baldwin Rd
Carlisle MA 01741

Call Sign: K1DDD
Jonathon D Saphier
56 Bellows Hill Rd
Carlisle MA 01741

Call Sign: WA1DZL
Raymond A Modeen
48 Berry Cor Rd
Carlisle MA 01741

Call Sign: N1LGK
Ronald Kmiec
94 Bingham Rd
Carlisle MA 01741

Call Sign: N1ILZ
Jon W Mc Combie
296 Brook St
Carlisle MA 01741

Call Sign: KB1OKQ
Sharon D Ravan
511 Brook St
Carlisle MA 01741

Call Sign: KA1WCD
Sharon D Ravan
511 Brook St
Carlisle MA 01741

Call Sign: N1XYD
David C Shaver
123 Carlisle Pines Dr
Carlisle MA 01741

Call Sign: N1ICB
Robert J Spence Jr
145 Carlisle Pines Dr
Carlisle MA 01741

Call Sign: KB1JLA
Harold E Lane Jr
750 Concord St
Carlisle MA 01741

Call Sign: KB1JKZ
Adam W Macone
868 Concord St
Carlisle MA 01741

Call Sign: KB1JTW
Paul K Macone
868 Concord St
Carlisle MA 01741

Call Sign: W1CPD
Paul K Macone
868 Concord St
Carlisle MA 01741

Call Sign: KB1DML
Kenneth J Baker
48 Cottage St
Carlisle MA 02139

Call Sign: KB1UDQ
Kenneth J Cole
81 Craigre Circle
Carlisle MA 01741

Call Sign: W5DTQ
John V Terrey
498 Cross St
Carlisle MA 01741

Call Sign: N1CVB
Edward Lewis
864 Curve St
Carlisle MA
017411009

Call Sign: KB1MBX
Philip J Gladstone
1005 Curve St
Carlisle MA 01741

Call Sign: N1DQ
Philip J Gladstone
1005 Curve St
Carlisle MA 01741

Call Sign: NZ1O
Kunihiko Sano
1182 Curve St
Carlisle MA 01741

Call Sign: KB1NEZ
Alan L Lewis
282 E Riding Dr
Carlisle MA 01741

Call Sign: K1ALL
Alan L Lewis
282 E Riding Dr
Carlisle MA 01741

Call Sign: KD1GD
James H Elgin
331 E Riding Dr
Carlisle MA 01741

Call Sign: KB1WEG
Robert E Peary
32 East Riding Dr
Carlisle MA 01741

Call Sign: KB1MBT
Chris K Phillips

203 Fiske St
Carlisle MA
017411017

Call Sign: W3GLE
Edward J Sampson
315 Fiske St
Carlisle MA 01741

Call Sign: KB1OCK
Bruce D Metcalf
217 Heald Rd
Carlisle MA
017411440

Call Sign: KB1OYP
Tim Pierce
420 Heald Rd
Carlisle MA 01741

Call Sign: W1FMJ
John H Meyn
522 Heald Rd
Carlisle MA 01741

Call Sign: W1AON
David C Ives
555 Heald Rd
Carlisle MA 01741

Call Sign: KA1ETK
Lisa H Foote
61 Judy Farm Rd
Carlisle MA
017411491

Call Sign: N1AG
George B Foote Jr
61 Judy Farm Rd
Carlisle MA 01741

Call Sign: N1XGN
Tully B Foote
61 Judy Farm Rd
Carlisle MA 01741

Call Sign: KB1ITE
Tudor F Foote
61 Judy Farm Rd
Carlisle MA 01741

Call Sign: W1EO
David G Willard
39 Long Ridge Rd

Carlisle MA 01741

Call Sign: W1YCU
Judith G Willard
39 Long Ridge Rd
Carlisle MA 01741

Call Sign: WB1CQT
Arthur S Turner
175 Lowell St
Carlisle MA 01741

Call Sign: KB1JSM
Alexandra J Adrian
106 Maple St
Carlisle MA 01741

Call Sign: KB1JSN
Norman J Adrian
106 Maple St
Carlisle MA 01741

Call Sign: N1OXO
Norman J Adrian
106 Maple St
Carlisle MA 01741

Call Sign: N1AJA
Alexandra J Adrian
106 Maple St
Carlisle MA 01741

Call Sign: W1VIN
Calixte C Adrian
110 Maple St
Carlisle MA 01741

Call Sign: KB1VTN
William A Hamilton
491 Maple St
Carlisle MA 01741

Call Sign: W1IRH
Raymond P Pichulo
82 Mc Allister Dr
Carlisle MA
017411235

Call Sign: N1OKW
James F Davis
232 Munroe Hill Rd
Carlisle MA 01741

Call Sign: NZ1Q

Edward E Erny
923 North Rd
Carlisle MA 01741

Call Sign: KA1WRQ
David F Harris Jr
275 Nowell Farm Rd
Carlisle MA 01741

Call Sign: N1SEW
Eric N Balles
105 Nowell Farme
Carlisle MA 01741

Call Sign: W1FQ
Homer T Ash
163 Nowell Farme Rd
Carlisle MA 01741

Call Sign: W1PEB
Peter E Blankenship
233 Nowell Farme Rd
Carlisle MA 01741

Call Sign: WA1KTZ
Christopher M Leary
57 Pine Brook Rd
Carlisle MA 01741

Call Sign: KB3GFQ
John P Beckley
111 Pine Brook Rd
Carlisle MA 01741

Call Sign: K1PEK
Stephen F Davis
206 Prospect St
Carlisle MA 01741

Call Sign: N1JR
James S Robbins
156 River Rd
Carlisle MA 01741

Call Sign: KA1NWE
Jeffrey L Caruso
51 Robbins Dr
Carlisle MA 01741

Call Sign: K1CHI
Alan G Cameron
324 School St
Carlisle MA 01741

Call Sign: AA1O
William P Churchill Jr
333 School St
Carlisle MA
017410702

Call Sign: NA1Y
Robert R Herold
168 Stoney Gate
Carlisle MA 01741

Call Sign: AA1ZT
Jacques P Dumas
32 Suffolk Lane
Carlisle MA 01741

Call Sign: N1DBI
Kathleen J Wester
29 Suffolk Ln
Carlisle MA 01741

Call Sign: KA1WRJ
Paul R Courant
46 Virginia Farme Rd
Carlisle MA 01741

Call Sign: KA1RSJ
Robert C Pedersen
634 West St
Carlisle MA 01741

Call Sign: WA1EAZ
John M Stengrevics
1184 Westford Rd
Carlisle MA 01741

Call Sign: KB1JIW
Francis S Cassidy
252 Westford St
Carlisle MA 01741

Call Sign: WA1VBK
Elizabeth D Loutrel
105 Woodridge Rd
Carlisle MA 01741

Call Sign: WA1VBL
Stephen P Loutrel
105 Woodridge Rd
Carlisle MA
017411717

Call Sign: KB1HOM
Lionel A Williams

Carlisle MA 01741

Call Sign: KB1KDL
Chester A Osborne
Carlisle MA 01741

Call Sign: KB1OIT
William J Ho
Carlisle MA 01741

FCC Amateur Radio Licenses in Carver

Call Sign: KB1DAC
MICHELE L Goulet
7 Bouton St
Carver MA 02330

Call Sign: N1TIY
Peter A Brennan
1 Canterbury Path
Carver MA 02330

Call Sign: N1BJP
Andrew C Faire
78 Center St
Carver MA 02330

Call Sign: KA1TXM
Robert E Thibodeau Jr
23 Cranberry Cir
Carver MA 02330

Call Sign: K1EEL
Kristjan M Viise
84 Crescent St
Carver MA 02330

Call Sign: KB2AQH
David J Pollick
29 Cross St
Carver MA 02330

Call Sign: W1JOY
Robert E Joy
2 Daphne Way
Carver MA 023301556

Call Sign: KB1SBC
Derek F Olson
4 Dunham St
Carver MA 02330

Call Sign: K1IIL

Richard C La Cava
12 Edgewood Rd
Carver MA 02330

Call Sign: KA1UNU
Philip J Drosdik
15 Flax Pond Dr Box 415
Carver MA 02330

Call Sign: N1CIE
Benedict S Yuscavitch
26 Great Meadow Dr
Carver MA 02330

Call Sign: KA1UNP
Kevin M Sullivan
138 High St
Carver MA 02330

Call Sign: W1SM
Albert A Drollett Jr
19 Johns Pond Rd
Carver MA 02330

Call Sign: K1ZEH
Frank Beekes
47 Kennedy Dr
Carver MA 02330

Call Sign: K1EXM
William F Kingsbury Sr
9 Lincoln Cir
Carver MA 02330

Call Sign: N1TWK
Paul C Malley
133 Main St
Carver MA 02330

Call Sign: KA1TXS
Christopher B Clark
53 Meadow St
Carver MA 023301359

Call Sign: KB1TYH
William P Duggan
285 Meadow St
Carver MA 02330

Call Sign: WA1AZF
David L Centeio
301 Meadow St

Carver MA 02330

Call Sign: WA1ETQ
Alice R Centeio
301 Meadow St
Carver MA 02330

Call Sign: KA1IML
Edward J Keefe
7 Murdock St
Carver MA 02330

Call Sign: WA1GDB
Charles D Wilson
29 Pipers Way
Carver MA 02330

Call Sign: W1KXT
Walter S Schlieff
46 Pipers Way
Carver MA 02330

Call Sign: AA1MU
Christine A Coppellotti
25 Rickard St
Carver MA 023300451

Call Sign: N1BIO
Daniel F Hooley
57 Rickard St
Carver MA 02330

Call Sign: N1REV
Alden F Washburn
35 Roosevelt Ridge
Carver MA 02330

Call Sign: N1USE
David G Hoadley
4 S Meadow Village
Carver MA 02330

Call Sign: KA1HIS
Alfred L Snape Sr
41130 S Meadow Village
Carver MA 02330

Call Sign: N1IUN
Douglas A Caron
S Meadow Village
Carver MA 02330

Call Sign: W1IFX

William L Copeland Jr
3 S Meadow Vlg
Carver MA 02330

Call Sign: WA1JDE
Katherine H Thomas
So Meadow Village
Carver MA 02330

Call Sign: W1TL
Thomas D Larson
4 South Meadow Village
Carver MA 02330

Call Sign: K1REL
Robert E Loring
38 South Meadow Village
Carver MA 02330

Call Sign: KB1UML
Karen M Sharland
1 Swan Pond Lane
Carver MA 02330

Call Sign: WA1HIH
Everard N Dixon
26 Truman Court
Carver MA 02330

Call Sign: WA1POQ
Carol R Dixon
26 Truman Court
Carver MA 02330

Call Sign: N1CQO
Michael A Pinto
14 Woodlawn Dr
Carver MA 02330

Call Sign: KB1WWY
Richard A Hoadley
12 Woodlawn Drive
Carver MA 02330

Call Sign: N1PVP
Marino Coppellotti
Carver MA 023300451

Call Sign: KB1TDY
Jayson Tracy
Carver MA 02330

Call Sign: W1DJE
Robert A Mosher
64 Depot Rd
Cataumet MA 02534

Call Sign: KD1Y
Joseph Kiebala Jr
26 Pasture Rd Box 407
Cataumet MA 02534

Call Sign: KA1TX
Stephen P Liberatore
22 Whimbrel Drive
Cataum MA 02534

Call Sign: KB1LCZ
Eben M Olson
Cataumet MA
025340659

Call Sign: KB1VKO
Linda M Zuern
Cataumet MA 02534

**FCC Amateur Radio
Licenses in Center
Harbor**

Call Sign: K1EUF
Michael B Rukin
Center Harbor MA
032261156

**FCC Amateur Radio
Licenses in
Centerville**

Call Sign: KG4FRL
Wayne G Sellin
42 Ashley Drive
Centerville MA 02632

Call Sign: KB1IYS
Cynthia J Sellin
42 Ashley Drive
Centerville MA 02632

Call Sign: AB1LJ
Wayne G Sellin
42 Ashley Drive
Centerville MA 02632

Call Sign: N1HOQ
Shawn A Reed
65 Bridgets Path
Centerville MA 02632

Call Sign: K1FUR
June Carol Barr
201 Capt Crosby Rd
Centerville MA
026321605

Call Sign: K1ZFJ
Robert J Barr
201 Capt Crosby Rd
Centerville MA
026321605

Call Sign: K1SKN
Robert A Mckernan
48 Captain Lumbert
Lane
Centerville MA 02632

Call Sign: KA1UEG
John F Donovan
49 Captain Lumbert
Lane
Centerville MA 02632

Call Sign: KB1MDX
Jean-Philippe C
Beaudet
69 Clifton Lane
Centerville MA 02632

Call Sign: W1ZRP
Milton Roberts
86 Cottonwood Ln
Centerville MA 02632

Call Sign: K2OI
Lawrence E Rook
10 Fair Oaks Rd
Centerville MA 02632

Call Sign: KB1ZL
Joseph Kelley Jr
22 Goldenrod Ln
Centerville MA 02632

Call Sign: K1BIF
Robert D Thompson Sr
185 Great Marsh Rd

Centerville MA 02632

Call Sign: KB1VAA
William H Doherty
11 Helmsman Dr
Centerville MA 02632

Call Sign: NH0H
Timothy F Hayes
127 Highland Drive
Centerville MA 02632

Call Sign: W1OJY
Lester B Linsky
139 Holly Point Rd
Centerville MA 02632

Call Sign: WA1UWP
Douglas M Butler
191 James Otis Rd
Centerville MA 02632

Call Sign: KD5CLG
Richard K Mannal
99 Katherine Rd
Centerville MA 02632

Call Sign: KB1HEZ
John B Denahy Jr
22 Keefe Ct
Centerville MA 02632

Call Sign: W1ABS
John B Denahy Jr
22 Keefe Ct
Centerville MA 02632

Call Sign: KB1GSM
Leroy R Swayze
32 Lazarus Lovell Rd
Centerville MA 02632

Call Sign: KA1YRA
Michael J Fredericks
68 Longview Drive
Centerville MA 02632

Call Sign: K1DIZ
Kenneth W Howland
44 Nobadeer Rd
Centerville MA 02632

Call Sign: K1CB
Charles E Bresnahan

19 Nottingham Dr
Centerville MA 02632

Call Sign: N1HVB
Helen V Bresnahan
19 Nottingham Dr
Centerville MA 02632

Call Sign: KB1ORD
Timothy J Leonard
561 Old Stage Rd
Centerville MA 02632

Call Sign: KA1DFB
Philip E Larson
175 Pond View Dr
Centerville MA 02632

Call Sign: W1ORK
Austin R Banks
265 Prince Hinckley
Rd
Centerville MA 02632

Call Sign: N1PIC
Allan V Eisenhaur
9 Rachel Carson Ln
Centerville MA 02632

Call Sign: WA0FAM
John N Wilcox
67 Regatta Dr
Centerville MA 02632

Call Sign: KC6TDA
Fredrick L Bsharah
72 Scudder Bay Circle
Centerville MA 02632

Call Sign: KB1TAM
Donald J Donahue
640 Skunknet Rd
Centerville MA 02632

Call Sign: WA1KIJ
Allen R Nelson
104 Stoney Cliff Rd
Centerville MA 02632

Call Sign: K1VTW
Harold J Weber
411 Strawberry Hill Rd
Centerville MA
026320169

Call Sign: KC2GYP
Peter D Bregman
836 Strawberry Hill Rd
Centerville MA 02632

Call Sign: W3INE
Raymond E Shepherd
27 Victoria St
Centerville MA 02632

Call Sign: KB1USQ
Paul D Cooper
46 Wequaquet Lane
Centerville MA 02632

Call Sign: KC1VT
George Sinclair
68 Westminster Rd
Centerville MA 02632

Call Sign: WB4YHC
Phillip C Goelz
114 Wild Goose Way
Centerville MA 02632

Call Sign: KB1VMM
Lisa A Rimbach
Centerville MA 02632

**FCC Amateur Radio
Licenses in
Charlemont**

Call Sign: KB1GUI
May B Churchill
Jacksonville Stage Rd
Charlemont MA 01339

Call Sign: N1QXT
Christopher M Gilbert
Jacobs Rd
Charlemont MA 01339

Call Sign: W1LRX
Douglas K Webber
372 Maxwell Rd
Charlemont MA 01339

Call Sign: N1VVZ
Benjamin L Archambo
Mohawk Park
Charlemont MA 01339

Call Sign: KA1AEQ
Donna L Shepherd
Route 8a
Charlemont MA 01339

Call Sign: N1ALV
Lee F Shepherd
Route 8a
Charlemont MA 01339

Call Sign: N1SJV
David A Neumann
Charlemont MA
013390454

Call Sign: KB1KOO
Barbara Harris
Charlemont MA 01339

**FCC Amateur Radio
Licenses in
Charlestown**

Call Sign: WA1LOK
Joseph M Pollard Iii
128 Bunker Hill St 3
Charlestown MA
02129

Call Sign: KA1KN
Allan J Mac Donald
16 Chestnut St
Charlestown MA
02129

Call Sign: N1LWR
Robert W Mc Divitt
64 Constellation Wharf
Charlestown MA
02129

Call Sign: KA1RWU
Jack M Roberts
28 Constitution Rd
Charlestown MA
02129

Call Sign: N1HNI
David B Heeley
28 Constitution Rd
Charlestown MA
021290129

Call Sign: KG4LJJ

Andrew J Fowlie
28 Constitution Rd
Charlestown MA
02129

Call Sign: KA9SBN
Peter S Darby
255 Main St 2
Charlestown MA
021292923

Call Sign: KB1DKT
Patrick W Dever
6 Nearen Row
Charlestown MA
02129

Call Sign: N1FGO
James Whitlock
16 Parker St
Charlestown MA
02129

Call Sign: N1EVX
David M Hardy
16 Parker St
Charlestown MA
021291209

Call Sign: KC2PEI
Isaac Dekine
12 Pearl St Apt 4
Charlestown MA
02129

Call Sign: N1XSC
Chrystel L Claudio
46 Walker St
Charlestown MA
021292447

Call Sign: NK1G
Donald I Field
6 Wallace Ct
Charlestown MA
02129

Call Sign: N1PPE
David B Spaulding
28 Water St
Charlestown MA
02129

Call Sign: KF7QK

Peter C Schalock
14 Winthrop St #2
Charlestown MA
02129

Call Sign: WA1YHV
Kevin P Kelly
Charlestown MA
02129

**FCC Amateur Radio
Licenses in Charlton**

Call Sign: WB1HGL
James N Hague
67 Baypath Rd
Charlton MA
015070425

Call Sign: N1KRL
Joel D Desrochers
40 Berry Corner Rd
Charlton MA 01507

Call Sign: KB1KKT
Benjamin W Woodacre
55 Carroll Hill Rd
Charlton MA 01507

Call Sign: KB1JCF
Howard M Ranks Iii
10 Cranberry Shore Rd
Charlton MA 01507

Call Sign: WA1JCF
Donald A Loranger
12 Flint Rd
Charlton MA 01517

Call Sign: K1NDU
Donald R Engstrom
183 Gould Rd
Charlton MA 01507

Call Sign: KB0SEM
Michael S Sowter
8 Griffin Rd
Charlton MA 01507

Call Sign: KD6GPQ
John F Welch
60 H Putnam Rd
Charlton MA 01507

Call Sign: KB1LSN
William T Woodard
14 H Putnum Rd
Charlton MA 01507

Call Sign: WA1YSP
William T Woodard
14 H Putnum Rd
Charlton MA 01507

Call Sign: KB1KRR
Earl B Willey
62 Hanson Rd
Charlton MA 01507

Call Sign: KA1ZWS
Daniel E Cetin Sr
50 Harrington Rd
Charlton MA 01507

Call Sign: WA1OUZ
Casper W Hotaling
Masonic Home
Charlton MA 01507

Call Sign: KB1HF
Sophie G Quinlin
88 Masonic Home Rd
Charlton MA 01507

Call Sign: KB1CNT
Richard G Jensen
88 Masonic Home Rd
Apt H206
Charlton MA
015073312

Call Sign: W1QDR
Raymond B Barnes
88 Masonic Home Rd
Apt R214
Charlton MA 01507

Call Sign: KB1EGG
Roger R Dean
88 Masonic Home Rd
Box 1000
Charlton MA
045071000

Call Sign: K1LKW
Richard R Strack
88 Masonic Home Rd
T203

Charlton MA 01507

Call Sign: N1NVK
Clark R Conti
43 Morton Station Rd
Charlton MA 01507

Call Sign: N1VAN
Scott P Szretter
58 N Main St
Charlton MA 01507

Call Sign: KM1D
Raymond E Donadt
299 North Sturbridge
Rd
Charlton MA 01507

Call Sign: N1MHH
Ronald R Anderson
126 Nugget Dr
Charlton MA 01507

Call Sign: KB1BUK
Nynes
135 Old Worcester Rd
Charlton MA 01507

Call Sign: W1GH
William H Mc Guiness
66 Osgood Rd
Charlton MA 01507

Call Sign: KB1MTP
Kathy L Mcguiness
66 Osgood Rd
Charlton MA
015075341

Call Sign: KB1ILH
Jeffrey A Miller
148 Oxford Rd
Charlton MA 01507

Call Sign: KO1G
Jeffrey A Miller
148 Oxford Rd
Charlton MA 01507

Call Sign: KB1UUW
Joseph F Romagnano
166 Partridge Hill Rd
Charlton MA 01507

Call Sign: KA1RPY
Raymond J Higgins Sr
43 Prindle Hill Rd
Charlton MA 01507

Call Sign: K1QZ
Steven M Naticchioni
126 Ramshorn Rd
Charlton MA 01507

Call Sign: K1BVM
Raymond W Grenier
81 Sandersdale Rd
Charlton MA 01507

Call Sign: N1YUP
Peter J George
140 Saundersdale Rd
Charlton MA 01507

Call Sign: WB3DPZ
Kenneth F Krech
24 Stonybrook Rd
Charlton MA
015071809

Call Sign: W1QEA
John P Popiak
20 Willis Dr
Charlton MA
015076654

Call Sign: N1KNU
John P Popiak
24 Willis Dr
Charlton MA 01507

Call Sign: W0GMT
Glen C Birbeck
376 Worcester Rd Box
271
Charlton MA
015070271

Call Sign: KA1JRD
Lee R Amodeo
Charlton MA 01507

Call Sign: KB1EBA
Joseph E Holewa
Charlton MA
015070459

Call Sign: N1RWC

Matthew C Penttila
Charlton MA
015070038

Call Sign: N1VXR
Leland G Penttila
Charlton MA 01507

Call Sign: K1GTC
Leland G Penttila
Charlton MA 01507

FCC Amateur Radio Licenses in Charlton City

Call Sign: KD1PV
Ronald J Di Federico
Charlton City MA
01508

Call Sign: WA1ZRB
Dennis P Mach
Charlton City MA
01508

FCC Amateur Radio Licenses in Charlton Depot

Call Sign: N1FMZ
Allan F Taylor
Drawer F
Charlton Depot MA
01509

Call Sign: W1YPZ
Paul J Dobson
55 J Davis Rd
Charlton Depot MA
015090005

FCC Amateur Radio Licenses in Chartley

Call Sign: KB1OPR
Rickard J Sitte
Chartley MA 02712

FCC Amateur Radio Licenses in Chatham

Call Sign: KB1NGC

John O Fiebelkorn
46 Blueberry Lane
Chatham MA 02633

Call Sign: N1DFL
Patrick A Connolly Sr
303 Deer Meadow Ln
Chatham MA 02633

Call Sign: KB1JAL
Wcc Amateur Radio
Association
174 Eastward Rd
Chatham MA 02633

Call Sign: K1POP
Charles R Weidman
21 Eliphamets Ln
Chatham MA 02635

Call Sign: KD1EP
Frank C Schora
830 Fox Hill Rd
Chatham MA 02633

Call Sign: W1KL
William C Ryder
196 Joshua Jethro Rd
Chatham MA
026331219

Call Sign: N1MFW
Robert S Ryder
37 Monomoit Ln Box
315
Chatham MA 02633

Call Sign: N2KEQ
Edward F Quinn
91 Monomoyic Way
Chatham MA 02633

Call Sign: KB1QNC
Robert F Olson
54 Old Academy Rd
Chatham MA 02633

Call Sign: W1FZT
Francis C Doane
67 Old Academy Rd
Chatham MA 02633

Call Sign: N1MKB
Peter J Martin

51 Old Harbor Rd
Chatham MA 02633

Call Sign: K1EMO
John J Mc Carthy
679 Riverview Dr
Chatham MA 02633

Call Sign: N1BOQ
Barbara A Mc Carthy
679 Riverview Dr
Chatham MA 02633

Call Sign: KB1OMY
James O Mcpherson
157 Round Cove Rd
Chatham MA 02633

Call Sign: W1OE
James O Mcpherson
157 Round Cove Rd
Chatham MA 02633

Call Sign: N1VGP
Christopher J Kenely
27 Sachemas Way
Chatham MA 02633

Call Sign: KY1O
David D Bulkley
408 Stage Harbor Rd
Chatham MA 02633

Call Sign: KD5FGN
Caroline C Roberts
35 Stillwater Rd
Chatham MA 02633

Call Sign: W1RAM
Robert A Moss Jr
55 Trout Pond Lane
Chatham MA 02633

Call Sign: N1DZS
Douglas E Pierini
14 Woodpecker Valley
Rd
Chatham MA 02633

Call Sign: KA1WTV
Daniel W Lacroix
Chatham MA 02633

Call Sign: N1PUV

Douglas W Mac
Kenzie
Chatham MA 02633

Call Sign: N1EGN
Keith F Zibrat
Chatham MA 02633

FCC Amateur Radio
Licenses in
Chelmsford

Call Sign: KA1FAB
Lewis T Lloyd
19 Abbott Ln
Chelmsford MA 01824

Call Sign: KA1YVA
Ann E Wade
125 Acton Rd
Chelmsford MA 01824

Call Sign: KB1UTS
William C Wade
125 Acton Rd
Chelmsford MA 01824

Call Sign: AI1I
Aubrey Benstead
24 Amble Rd
Chelmsford MA 01824

Call Sign: KA1WUR
Richard G Berard
32 Ansie Rd
Chelmsford MA 01824

Call Sign: W1YFS
Richard G Berard
32 Ansie Rd
Chelmsford MA 01824

Call Sign: WA1IGA
Alexander W Gervais
5 Arbutus Ave
Chelmsford MA 01824

Call Sign: KB1ERL
Joshua R Christain
13 Arbutus Ave
Chelmsford MA 01824

Call Sign: WA1FWF
John M Rhude

15 Arbutus Ave
Chelmsford MA 01824

Call Sign: N1RTP
Donald J Desfosse
8 Autumn Ln
Chelmsford MA
018243362

Call Sign: KB1IYX
Gary B Mauser
3 Baldwin Rd
Chelmsford MA 01824

Call Sign: KA1EWK
John D Le Blanc Jr
9 Barry Dr
Chelmsford MA 01863

Call Sign: WB1HBE
John W Forrest Jr
37 Barton Hill Rd
Chelmsford MA 01824

Call Sign: KB1NOV
Daniel S Lindquist
6 Bentley Lane
Chelmsford MA 01824

Call Sign: KB1USE
Geoffrey O Stewart
27 Berkeley Dr
Chelmsford MA 01824

Call Sign: KB1PZG
Kimberly L Stewart
27 Berkeley Drive
Chelmsford MA 01824

Call Sign: N1XNW
ANITA P Bard
71 Billerica Rd
Chelmsford MA 01824

Call Sign: W1TGR
Stanley J Oczkowski
205 Billerica Rd
Chelmsford MA 01824

Call Sign: N1HXI
Richard H Edgar
7 Blaisdell Rd
Chelmsford MA 01824

Call Sign: KB1ILO
Richard H Edgar
7 Blaisdell Rd
Chelmsford MA 01824

Call Sign: KA1RHO
Keith H Erskine
160 Boston Rd
Chelmsford MA 01824

Call Sign: KB1PBD
May P Lam
70 Boston Rd Apt
F319
Chelmsford MA 01824

Call Sign: KB1NON
Courtney A Heffernan
11 Braeburn Rd
Chelmsford MA 01824

Call Sign: KB1LSC
Sharon K Buehrle
59 Brentwood Rd
Chelmsford MA 01824

Call Sign: KB1LSD
A Gregory Page
59 Brentwood Rd
Chelmsford MA 01824

Call Sign: KB1WAS
Jonathan Mackenzie
52 Brick Kiln Rd
Chelmsford MA 01824

Call Sign: K2LEB
Jonathan Mackenzie
52 Brick Kiln Rd
Chelmsford MA 01824

Call Sign: KB1TZK
Parthiv A Patel
57 Brick Kiln Rd
Chelmsford MA 01824

Call Sign: K1OTA
Kenneth E Cantrell
9 Brook St
Chelmsford MA 01824

Call Sign: W1OG
Gustave H N Fallgren
31 Byam Rd

Chelmsford MA 01824

Call Sign: KB1NBY
Rath N Chhun
14 Carlisle St
Chelmsford MA 01824

Call Sign: KB1PNT
Gary F Frascarelli
105 Carlisle St
Chelmsford MA 01824

Call Sign: W1GFF
Gary F Frascarelli
105 Carlisle St
Chelmsford MA 01824

Call Sign: KB1LQC
Bryce T Salmi
12 Carriage Dr
Chelmsford MA 01824

Call Sign: KB1LQD
Brenton J Salmi
12 Carriage Dr
Chelmsford MA 01824

Call Sign: KB1MGI
John E Salmi
12 Carriage Dr
Chelmsford MA 01824

Call Sign: N1RTQ
Samuel Black
16 Carriage Dr
Chelmsford MA 01824

Call Sign: KB1DES
Sean C Hennessey
14 Cathy Rd
Chelmsford MA 01824

Call Sign: KY1B
Joseph G O Neill
5 Central Square 10
Chelmsford MA 01824

Call Sign: N1MOX
David S Dodge
19 Chestnut Hill Rd
Chelmsford MA 01824

Call Sign: N1CHJ
Peter L Nelson

30 Chestnut Hill Rd
Chelmsford MA 01824

Call Sign: KB1AEQ
William B Burns
44 Chestnut Hill Rd
Chelmsford MA 01824

Call Sign: KA1YUV
Alan L Moyer
23 Clarissa Rd
Chelmsford MA 01824

Call Sign: N1LHQ
Pamela M Montella
Moyer
23 Clarissa Rd
Chelmsford MA 01824

Call Sign: KB1UKW
Samuel C Jones
29 Clover Hill Dr
Chelmsford MA 01824

Call Sign: W1XH
Albert H Bates
2 Coach Rd
Chelmsford MA 01824

Call Sign: WA2RIN
South Chelmsford Qrp
Club
2 Coach Rd
Chelmsford MA
018244208

Call Sign: K1SVC
Arthur J Smith Jr
211 Concord Rd
Chelmsford MA 01824

Call Sign: N1NGK
William W Plummer
7 Country Club Dr
Chelmsford MA 01824

Call Sign: N1OAR
Kevin D O Connell
4 Courtland Dr
Chelmsford MA 01824

Call Sign: W1YKH
Stephen A Slenker
10 Crabapple Ln

Chelmsford MA 01824

Call Sign: WA1CPG
Paul Higinbotham
9 Craig Rd
Chelmsford MA 01824

Call Sign: WA1FCD
Scott J Higinbotham
9 Craig Rd
Chelmsford MA
018244703

Call Sign: KB1NOU
Jessica A Tomas
6 Crescent Dr
Chelmsford MA 01824

Call Sign: KB1DAO
John N Rosenberger
8 Crockett Dr
Chelmsford MA 01824

Call Sign: KA1TAJ
Eric M Johnson
91 Crooked Spring Rd
Chelmsford MA 01863

Call Sign: KA1TDN
Dale M Johnson
91 Crooked Spring Rd
Chelmsford MA 01863

Call Sign: K1KOK
George R Flynn
160 Dalton Rd
Chelmsford MA 01824

Call Sign: WA1VNR
Francis J Tamilio Iii
9 Danforth Lane
Chelmsford MA 01824

Call Sign: KB1NSM
John P Rogers Jr
15 Davis Rd
Chelmsford MA 01824

Call Sign: WA1JKK
Walter J Ciesluk Jr
4 Draycoach Dr
Chelmsford MA 01824

Call Sign: W1AQE

Stephen H Morris
19 East Sheppard Ln
Chelmsford MA 01824

Call Sign: N1HWE
Henry H Zenzie
6 Eldorado Rd
Chelmsford MA 01824

Call Sign: WO1F
Ralph R Preston
1 Empire St
Chelmsford MA 01824

Call Sign: KB1AMS
Christopher J
Hannaford
4 Footpath Rd
Chelmsford MA 01824

Call Sign: KD1IV
Peter D Speen
7 Footpath Rd
Chelmsford MA 01824

Call Sign: K1SUB
Peter D Speen
7 Footpath Rd
Chelmsford MA 01824

Call Sign: KA1HER
Robert F Conway
22 Footpath Rd
Chelmsford MA 01824

Call Sign: KB1IOE
Steven J Miller
21 Gail St
Chelmsford MA 01824

Call Sign: N1FYF
Kenneth W Van
Tassell
5 Gallup Dr
Chelmsford MA 01824

Call Sign: KV1R
Kenneth W Van
Tassell
5 Gallup Dr
Chelmsford MA 01824

Call Sign: W1TVF
Stanley A Novak

3 Gary Rd
Chelmsford MA 01824

Call Sign: K1TGE
Edward S Carpenter
9 Gelding Rd
Chelmsford MA
018241917

Call Sign: N1GYG
Kenneth J Gudinas
10 George St
Chelmsford MA 01824

Call Sign: N1ISV
Judy A Gudinas
10 George St
Chelmsford MA 01824

Call Sign: KB1KYR
Kenneth D Elwell
142 Graniteville Rd
Chelmsford MA
018241122

Call Sign: WA8ZPF
John S Cole
154 Graniteville Rd
Chelmsford MA
018241122

Call Sign: WB3AHW
Vernon L Eshbaugh
216 Graniteville Rd
Chelmsford MA 01824

Call Sign: N1ISH
Alan D Mc Kersie
8 Gristone Rd
Chelmsford MA 01824

Call Sign: KA1KNR
Elizabeth Di Salvo
29 Grove St
Chelmsford MA
018243103

Call Sign: KA1WZ
Joseph Disalvo
29 Grove St
Chelmsford MA 01824

Call Sign: KB1JVV
Alex B Jordan

50 Hall Rd
Chelmsford MA 01824

Call Sign: WA2QET
James H Rutter Jr
6 Hart Rd
Chelmsford MA 01824

Call Sign: K1MGP
Frances S De Jager
4 Harvey Rd
Chelmsford MA
018244622

Call Sign: W1DBY
Melvin P De Jager
4 Harvey Rd
Chelmsford MA 01824

Call Sign: KB1NOL
Robert A Van Liew
6 Hemlock Dr
Chelmsford MA 01824

Call Sign: WB1AMY
Mark A Keller
6 Hidden Way
Chelmsford MA 01824

Call Sign: K1HDB
Donald B Hileman
22 Higate Rd
Chelmsford MA
018244440

Call Sign: K1VZK
William F Moloney Jr
29 High St
Chelmsford MA 01824

Call Sign: K1TWF
Michael N Raisbeck
85 High St
Chelmsford MA 01824

Call Sign: KB1DEF
Andrew G Raisbeck
85 High St
Chelmsford MA 01824

Call Sign: KB1DFJ
Daniel B Raisbeck
85 High St
Chelmsford MA 01824

Call Sign: N1QBV
Hilary E Hardy
85 High St
Chelmsford MA 01824

Call Sign: WT1E
Brian S Hardy
85 High St
Chelmsford MA 01824

Call Sign: WT1T
Scotch And Key
Society
85 High St
Chelmsford MA 01824

Call Sign: KB1KPB
Billerica Amateur
Radio Society
85 High St
Chelmsford MA 01824

Call Sign: N1ARM
George W Monsen
185 High St
Chelmsford MA 01824

Call Sign: K1TVV
Eric N Skoog
20 Hitchinpost Rd
Chelmsford MA 01824

Call Sign: KB1MKW
David M Steeves
66 Hunt Rd
Chelmsford MA 01824

Call Sign: KB1MPU
Alphonso J Firicano
66 Hunt Rd
Chelmsford MA
018243708

Call Sign: KB1HKX
Airvana Wireless
Association
25 Industrial Ave
Chelmsford MA 01886

Call Sign: KC1X
Kenneth L Weinbeck
20 Janet Rd
Chelmsford MA 01824

Call Sign: KB1NAO
Louis V De La Flor
34 Janet Rd
Chelmsford MA 01824

Call Sign: K1LVF
Louis V De La Flor
34 Janet Rd
Chelmsford MA 01824

Call Sign: WA1LSB
Elliott C Lea
14 Jonathan Ln
Chelmsford MA 01824

Call Sign: W1UGJ
James V Novak
13 Judith Rd
Chelmsford MA 01824

Call Sign: KB1OBF
Derek S White
9 Lafayette Terrace
Chelmsford MA 01824

Call Sign: K1SSN
Submarine Base
Amateur Radio Club
4 Lantern Lane
Chelmsford MA 01824

Call Sign: WA1VIE
Robert J Veth
4 Lantern Ln
Chelmsford MA 01824

Call Sign: K1RJV
Robert J Veth
4 Lantern Ln
Chelmsford MA 01824

Call Sign: K1TIH
James T Dossett
14 Lantern Ln
Chelmsford MA 01824

Call Sign: WA1URK
Alice L Dossett
14 Lantern Ln
Chelmsford MA 01824

Call Sign: N1CUH
Patrick J Calnan

16 Lantern Ln
Chelmsford MA 01824

Call Sign: W1DRS
Fortunato D Cavallari
18 Lantern Ln
Chelmsford MA 01824

Call Sign: WB1AAV
Elfrieda L Cavallari
18 Lantern Ln
Chelmsford MA 01824

Call Sign: N2TQV
Gilbert Burns
10 Lemay Way
Chelmsford MA 01863

Call Sign: KB1QBB
Nancy Araway
65 Littleton Rd
Chelmsford MA 01824

Call Sign: AB1IT
Nancy Araway
65 Littleton Rd
Chelmsford MA 01824

Call Sign: NK1A
Nancy Araway
65 Littleton Rd
Chelmsford MA 01824

Call Sign: W1ABR
Acton Boxborough
Amat Rad Club
181 Littleton Rd - Unit
433
Chelmsford MA 01824

Call Sign: KB1LSE
Gail R Held
175 Littleton Rd - Unit
B-6
Chelmsford MA 01824

Call Sign: K1LJN
Sheldon M Goldberg
270 Littleton Rd 148
Chelmsford MA
018243325

Call Sign: N1PUI
Gretchen B Goldberg

270 Littleton Rd 148
Chelmsford MA
018243325

Call Sign: W1CIW
Gretchen B Goldberg
270 Littleton Rd 148
Chelmsford MA
018243325

Call Sign: N1OHA
Virgil H Talbert
288 Littleton Rd 194
Chelmsford MA 01824

Call Sign: K1MFK
John P Verrill
288 Littleton Rd 241
Chelmsford MA 01824

Call Sign: N1OTO
Peter Iarossi
270 Littleton Rd 62
Chelmsford MA 01824

Call Sign: KB1EFO
Timothy M Patno
225 Littleton Rd Apt
30204
Chelmsford MA 01824

Call Sign: KA1PCE
Ralph J Bannister Sr
270 Littleton Rd Lot
53
Chelmsford MA 01824

Call Sign: WA8USB
Wesley T Dull
65 Locke Rd
Chelmsford MA 01824

Call Sign: WA1KYH
John D Chipman
6 Loiselle Ln
Chelmsford MA 01863

Call Sign: KB1SSA
Joseph G Mettee Jr
36 Long Meadow Rd
Chelmsford MA 01824

Call Sign: KB1NMT
Jacqueline A Mathews

12 Lovett Lane
Chelmsford MA 01863

Call Sign: N1FZM
Hugh L Southall
2 Luan Cir
Chelmsford MA 01824

Call Sign: KA1FAD
Lisa M Biro
162 Main St
Chelmsford MA 01863

Call Sign: KB8JDO
Andrew J Barber
21 Manning Rd
Chelmsford MA 01824

Call Sign: KA1TAI
Tom A Witt
8 Mansfield Dr
Chelmsford MA 01863

Call Sign: KD1AN
Harold A Witt
8 Mansfield Dr
Chelmsford MA 01824

Call Sign: N2NDE
Laura T Francis
13 Manwell Rd
Chelmsford MA 01824

Call Sign: KA1SBB
Daniel A Nakamoto
17 Marina Rd
Chelmsford MA 01824

Call Sign: KA1SWE
Karen A Nakamoto
17 Marina Rd
Chelmsford MA 01824

Call Sign: NH6IH
Shu Nakamoto
17 Marina Rd
Chelmsford MA 01824

Call Sign: KB1OHF
Bryan M Marcotte
8 Mcintosh Rd
Chelmsford MA 01824

Call Sign: N1DW

Donald F Wiggin
175 Mill Rd
Chelmsford MA
018244835

Call Sign: N1XBQ
Robert D Setterlund
187 Mill Rd
Chelmsford MA 01824

Call Sign: WF1F
Gregory M Mann
3 Moccasin Ln
Chelmsford MA 01824

Call Sign: KB1OIQ
Andrew M Stewart
25 Monument Hill Rd
Chelmsford MA 01824

Call Sign: KB1DAN
Moise Solomon
3 Mountain Laurel
Drive
Chelmsford MA 01824

Call Sign: W1SIE
Sing C Chin
22 Muriel
Chelmsford MA 01824

Call Sign: KB1NSV
Shashi S Parmar
2 Nashoba Dr
Chelmsford MA 01824

Call Sign: KB1NMX
Jennifer E Byrne
6 Natalie Rd
Chelmsford MA 01824

Call Sign: AB1W
Leonard R Flumerfelt
3 Nevada Dr
Chelmsford MA 01824

Call Sign: KB1LSF
John K Schindler
6 Nevada Dr
Chelmsford MA
018244514

Call Sign: KB1EKG
Garth G Brown Jr

170 North Rd
Chelmsford MA
018241668

Call Sign: KB1EKH
Scott G Brown
170 North Rd
Chelmsford MA 01824

Call Sign: KT1R
Lewis E Stafford
255 North Rd Unit 168
Chelmsford MA 01824

Call Sign: KB1JMS
Shirley Cool
4 Northview Ave
Chelmsford MA 01824

Call Sign: N1FIN
James Rose
89 Old Stage Rd
Chelmsford MA 01824

Call Sign: WB8CTF
Jerry R Van Wormer
146 Old Westford Rd
Chelmsford MA
018241252

Call Sign: WB1AAT
Michael W Ryan
301 Old Westford Rd
Chelmsford MA 01824

Call Sign: W1QVW
Charles F La Brecque
302 Old Westford Rd
Chelmsford MA 01824

Call Sign: KB1STQ
David E Couto
4 Overlook Dr
Chelmsford MA 01824

Call Sign: N5OA
Sons Of Sicily Contest
Club
5 Peachtree Lane
Chelmsford MA 01824

Call Sign: NJ1V
John Guida
5 Peachtree Lane

Chelmsford MA 01824

Call Sign: KB1HIU
Sons Of Sicily Contest
Club
5 Peachtree Ln
Chelmsford MA 01824

Call Sign: KB1OSC
Matthew D Medica
1 Peders Pl
Chelmsford MA 01824

Call Sign: KB1NOP
Tiffany Y Chao
1 Pendleton Rd
Chelmsford MA 01824

Call Sign: N1ISD
Edgar A Westbrook
6 Pennock Rd
Chelmsford MA 01824

Call Sign: KB1JHB
Charles L Weaver
5 Percheron Rd
Chelmsford MA 01824

Call Sign: N1RXR
Ivan La Garde
9 Pilgrim Rd
Chelmsford MA 01824

Call Sign: AA1BI
Raymond C Mc
Laughlin
40 Pine Hill Rd
Chelmsford MA
018242033

Call Sign: KE6BLJ
Timothy M Miller
11 Pleasant Ave
Chelmsford MA 01824

Call Sign: N1JUQ
Barbara J Ortler
4 Porter Rd
Chelmsford MA 01824

Call Sign: K1CL
Charles J Ludinsky
6 Prancing Rd
Chelmsford MA 01824

Call Sign: WQ1RP
New England Qrp
Club
6 Prancing Rd
Chelmsford MA 01824

Call Sign: N1TBR
Mark J Buliszak
92 Proctor Rd
Chelmsford MA
018244415

Call Sign: N1OS
Mark J Buliszak
92 Proctor Rd
Chelmsford MA
018244415

Call Sign: W1HET
Thomas W James
10 Purcell Dr
Chelmsford MA 01824

Call Sign: N1BC
Bruce W Carlile
24 Purcell Dr
Chelmsford MA 01824

Call Sign: N1TWY
Alan J Richer
12 Radcliff Rd
Chelmsford MA 01863

Call Sign: WA1YHY
Alan J Richer
12 Radcliff Rd
Chelmsford MA 01863

Call Sign: KB1NAY
Chelmsford High
School Amateur Radio
Club
200 Richardson Rd
Chelmsford MA 01863

Call Sign: N1CHS
Chelmsford High
School Amateur Radio
Club
200 Richardson Rd
Chelmsford MA 01863

Call Sign: KA1TUE

Edward Moor
24 Riverneck Rd
Chelmsford MA 01824

Call Sign: NC1C
David C Davies
35 Ruthellen Rd
Chelmsford MA 01824

Call Sign: KB1KGP
Gillian S Davies
35 Ruthellen Rd
Chelmsford MA 01824

Call Sign: N1OTR
Edwin Charnley
16 Samuel Rd
Chelmsford MA 01824

Call Sign: KV1F
Uve H W Lammers
5 San Mateo Dr
Chelmsford MA 01824

Call Sign: KB1NOM
Alayna I Tress
4 Santa Fe Rd
Chelmsford MA 01824

Call Sign: W4UIW
Howard A Baker
5 Santa Fe Rd
Chelmsford MA 01824

Call Sign: W1DU
James Buliszak
3 Sarah Ln
Chelmsford MA 01824

Call Sign: N1TWF
Michael G Salkins
116 School St
Chelmsford MA 01824

Call Sign: W1IWT
Burton E Salkins
116 School St
Chelmsford MA 01824

Call Sign: N1IAS
Marc C Bober
143 School St
Chelmsford MA 01824

Call Sign: W1SST
Zareh S Chutchian
4 Scott Dr
Chelmsford MA 01824

Call Sign: KA1NFA
Jeffory S Wright
37 Second St
Chelmsford MA
018620090

Call Sign: N1LRV
Stephen D Beyer
21 Sierra Dr
Chelmsford MA 01824

Call Sign: KB1DER
Theodore R Tang
42 Smith
Chelmsford MA 01834

Call Sign: KA1KEE
Diane Ng
19 Smith St
Chelmsford MA 01824

Call Sign: KE1KZ
Douglas D Tang
42 Smith St
Chelmsford MA 01824

Call Sign: KB1WEH
Dmytro Voloboy
16 Sprague Ave
Chelmsford MA 01824

Call Sign: W1UHJ
Richard L Taylor
6 Spruce St
Chelmsford MA 01824

Call Sign: WB2OSZ
John W Langner
115 Stedman St
Chelmsford MA
018241823

Call Sign: N1HPO
Peter N Baum
1 Steeple Dr
Chelmsford MA 01824

Call Sign: WB3DWA
George W Turner

3 Sunrise Ave
Chelmsford MA 01824

Call Sign: N1VKV
Brian A Walsh
6 Surrey Lane
Chelmsford MA 01824

Call Sign: WB1GBZ
Bruce C Pemberton
3 Thomas Dr
Chelmsford MA 01824

Call Sign: N1LMV
James R Metcalf
63 Thomas Dr
Chelmsford MA 01824

Call Sign: K1MHO
George E Michelsen
9 Topeka Rd
Chelmsford MA 01824

Call Sign: KB1NOO
Paulina N Tran
59 Turnpike Rd
Chelmsford MA 01824

Call Sign: WA1ZRY
Raymond H Gatti
175 Turnpike Rd
Chelmsford MA 01824

Call Sign: WA8TOP
David W Harmacek
116 Turnpike Rd 7
Chelmsford MA 01824

Call Sign: N1HKN
Charles E Ballantine
2 Village View Rd
Chelmsford MA 01824

Call Sign: KB1VIV
Nathan H Scollo
20 Wagontrail Rd
Chelmsford MA 01824

Call Sign: W1YM
Mason E Leggee
22 Walnut Rd
Chelmsford MA
018241143

Call Sign: N1KME
William J Warren
37 Walnut Rd
Chelmsford MA 01824

Call Sign: N1VUY
Nina C Warren
37 Walnut Rd
Chelmsford MA 01824

Call Sign: K1PGX
Paul F Sullivan
25 Warren Ave
Chelmsford MA 01824

Call Sign: KB1DEG
Hsiu Fan Wang
15 Warwick Dr
Chelmsford MA 01824

Call Sign: KC1KJ
Douglas S Rand
11 Waverly Ave
Chelmsford MA 01824

Call Sign: W2QZJ
Simon Rand
11 Waverly Ave
Chelmsford MA 01824

Call Sign: WA1HRT
Francis K Higson
9 Wedgewood Dr
Chelmsford MA 01824

Call Sign: WA1WDD
Eric A Rasmussen
142 Westford St
Chelmsford MA 01824

Call Sign: W1HH
Robert A Wallace
146 Westford St
Chelmsford MA
018242039

Call Sign: N1AAO
George F Flory
155 Westford St
Chelmsford MA 01824

Call Sign: WB1DFO
Albert E Smith
155 Westford St

Chelmsford MA 01824

Call Sign: N1HXJ
Eric D Ravenstein
9 Windsor St
Chelmsford MA 01824

Call Sign: W1FDR
Bob J Ravenstein
9 Windsor St
Chelmsford MA 01824

Call Sign: N1XNC
Raymond P Rosch
7 Winslow Rd
Chelmsford MA 01824

Call Sign: KB1NOQ
Thomas J Reale Iii
4 Woodlot Lane
Chelmsford MA 01824

Call Sign: WB1GSP
Thomas J Reale Jr
4 Woolot Ln
Chelmsford MA 01824

Call Sign: KA1HM
David W Roscoe
30 Worthen St Apt A9
Chelmsford MA 01824

Call Sign: KA1GTT
Andrew G Wallace
Chelmsford MA
018240395

Call Sign: N3AOA
David B Tweed
Chelmsford MA
018240442

Call Sign: KB1MCS
Richard Crisafulli
Chelmsford MA 01824

Call Sign: AB1HD
Richard Crisafulli
Chelmsford MA 01824

Call Sign: KA1JYA

Barbara A Bohn
51 Addison St
Chelsea MA 02150

Call Sign: N1NSA
Samuel Pagan Jr
78 Blossom St
Chelsea MA
021501932

Call Sign: KA1SVD
Mark T O Connor
421 Broadway
Chelsea MA 02150

Call Sign: WB1GBP
Joseph P Di Blasi
110 Central Ave
Chelsea MA 02150

Call Sign: K1ITH
Bronislaw P
Malachowski
55 Cherry St
Chelsea MA 02150

Call Sign: N1SOZ
David C Kezar
16 Columbus St
Chelsea MA 02150

Call Sign: KB1KUZ
Christopher J Kelley
160 Commamdants
Way 206
Chelsea MA
021504042

Call Sign: K1LVA
John E Fothergill
67 Cook Ave
Chelsea MA 02150

Call Sign: KB1LK
David Cleveland
397 Crescent Ave 2
Chelsea MA 02150

Call Sign: N1NDT
Richard J Nyhan
91 Crest Av
Chelsea MA 02150

Call Sign: KB1SDW

Michael J Carron
91 Crest Ave
Chelsea MA 02150

Call Sign: N3ZTS
Christopher M Miller
60 Dudley St Apt 327
Chelsea MA
021503035

Call Sign: N1CMM
Christopher M Miller
60 Dudley St Apt 327
Chelsea MA
021503035

Call Sign: WA1FJI
Luther A Studebaker
16 Fifth St 19
Chelsea MA 02150

Call Sign: N1LCQ
Mitchell Zybert
30 Gillooly Rd
Chelsea MA 02150

Call Sign: KA1YRQ
Robert P Botchie
129 Grove St
Chelsea MA 02150

Call Sign: K1BPN
Francis A Masucci
136 Grove St
Chelsea MA 02150

Call Sign: KA1SSI
Joseph A Vitale Iii
136 Grove St
Chelsea MA
021503317

Call Sign: KB1DJI
Strephon B Treadway
2 Laurel St
Chelsea MA 02150

Call Sign: KB1DGH
Robert E Griffin
48 Medford St
Chelsea MA
021502615

Call Sign: N1ESQ

Robert E Griffin
48 Medford St
Chelsea MA
021502615

Call Sign: K1DAA
Richard F Fleurant
64 Parker St
Chelsea MA 02150

Call Sign: N1QZY
Timothy A Mcbride
92 Sagamore Ave
Chelsea MA
021501305

Call Sign: N1GRA
Jose R Torres
48 Shawmut St
Chelsea MA 02150

Call Sign: KA1USM
Herbert M Siegel
302 Spruce St
Chelsea MA 02150

Call Sign: KA1OKL
Richard E Pilcher
61 Summit Ave
Chelsea MA 02150

Call Sign: N1SBO
Richard L Pilcher
61 Summit St
Chelsea MA 02150

Call Sign: WB1FQO
Carolyn Dailey
279 Wash Ave
Chelsea MA 02150

Call Sign: K1YYT
Gerard E Bachand
7 Atwood Ter
Cherry Valley MA
01611

Call Sign: N1WOG
Cheryl A Bachand
7 Atwood Terr

Cherry Valley MA
01611

Call Sign: N1AJC
Lorraine A Bachand
7 Atwood Terrace
Cherry Valley MA
01611

Call Sign: N1RGL
Jerald A Nichols Jr
118 Boyd St
Cherry Valley MA
01611

Call Sign: AB1LP
Jerald A Nichols Jr
118 Boyd St
Cherry Valley MA
01611

Call Sign: NG1I
Frank Mackenzie-
Lamb
21 Elmwood Ave
Cherry Valley MA
01611

Call Sign: KB1KEH
Michael S Wade
217 Main St
Cherry Valley MA
01611

Call Sign: KA1VEI
Richard E Jubinville
11 Michael Ave
Cherry Valley MA
01611

Call Sign: KA1PAE
Gerald Sherman
20 Monterey Dr
Cherry Valley MA
01611

Call Sign: N1EXS
Jonathan Sherman
20 Monterey Dr
Cherry Valley MA
01611

Call Sign: N1GDZ
Joseph Silipigni Ii

18 Tobin Rd
Cherry Valley MA
01611

FCC Amateur Radio
Licenses in Cheshire

Call Sign: KB1VNI
William E Rech
91 Briggs Dr
Cheshire MA 01225

Call Sign: K1LHI
Walter C Glass
20 Crest Rd
Cheshire MA 01225

Call Sign: N1LUY
Jeffery L Stutzman
74 Devonshire Dr
Cheshire MA 01225

Call Sign: KC2KTZ
William A Rech
35 Hampshire Dr
Cheshire MA 01225

Call Sign: N1AJI
Raymond P Fisher
68 Mallard Cove
Cheshire MA 01225

Call Sign: KA1IDC
Ronald F Mc Elroy
129 Outlook Ave
Cheshire MA 01225

Call Sign: KB1CJU
Gary B Trudeau
595 Outlook Ave
Cheshire MA 01225

Call Sign: N1GBT
Gary B Trudeau
595 Outlook Ave
Cheshire MA 01225

Call Sign: NS1M
Kenneth G Loynes Sr
1095 Outlook Ave
Cheshire MA 01225

Call Sign: WA1HTI
Joseph E Romano

320 Richmond Hill Rd
Cheshire MA 01225

Call Sign: W1HE
Thomas B Parkington
111 Richmond St
Cheshire MA
012250684

Call Sign: KD6PJA
Michael E Mc Cue
805 Savoy Rd
Cheshire MA 01225

Call Sign: N1NML
David A Nelson
81 South St
Cheshire MA 01225

Call Sign: KA1SLP
Emil R Schaffrick Jr
754 Stafford Hill
Cheshire MA 01225

Call Sign: WA1ZFR
Joseph E Sloane
69 Wells Rd
Cheshire MA
012250597

Call Sign: W1TO
William T Homewood
1610 Wells Rd
Cheshire MA
012259136

Call Sign: KB1AG
William R Vance
Cheshire MA 01225

Call Sign: KO1L
Catherine M Vance
Cheshire MA 01225

FCC Amateur Radio
Licenses in Chester

Call Sign: WA1ART
Arthur F Geary Jr
80 Route 20
Chester MA
010110308

Call Sign: KB1NKL

John W Noble
25 Taft Rd
Chester MA 01011

Call Sign: W1JWN
John W Noble Sr
25 Taft Rd
Chester MA 01011

Call Sign: KB1PLU
Rebecca T Noble
25 Taft Rd
Chester MA 01011

Call Sign: KB1DWM
Arthur F Geary
Chester MA
010110308

Call Sign: KB1NKE
Alex C Bricault
Chester MA 01011

FCC Amateur Radio
Licenses in
Chesterfield

Call Sign: KB2TUD
James F Saccento
206 Bryant St
Chesterfield MA
01012

Call Sign: N1TQR
Mathew R Jutras
67 Munson Rd
Chesterfield MA
01012

Call Sign: W1RSS
Randall S Smith
209 Old Chesterfield
Rd
Chesterfield MA
01012

Call Sign: KB1CWP
Kathleen E Brisbois
61 South St
Chesterfield MA
01012

Call Sign: KB1CWQ
James E Brisbois

Chesterfield MA
01012

Call Sign: KB1PLV
Jacob P Reed
Chesterfield MA
01012

FCC Amateur Radio Licenses in Chestnut Hill

Call Sign: WA1CYU
Joseph A Bergantino
16 Alberta Rd
Chestnut Hill MA
02467

Call Sign: KA1ZYN
John R Murnane
31 Algonquin Rd
Chestnut Hill MA
02167

Call Sign: KB1ADY
Schuyler M Costello
66 Algonquin Rd
Chestnut Hill MA
02167

Call Sign: N4ZZZ
George Schultz
206 Allandale Rd 1d
Chestnut Hill MA
02467

Call Sign: KD7CLB
Scott B Guthery
2400 Beacon Unit 208
Chestnut Hill MA
02467

Call Sign: KJ4JQV
Jacob R Chambers
757 Boylston St Apt# 1
Chestnut Hill MA
02467

Call Sign: KA1ZAC
Jason J Akbar
235 Commonwealth
Ave
Chestnut Hill MA
02167

Call Sign: KA1ZDG
Sheila S Akbar
235 Commonwealth
Ave
Chestnut Hill MA
02167

Call Sign: KA1ZZN
Andrew E Leibler
386 Commonwealth
Ave
Chestnut Hill MA
02167

Call Sign: WA1JKG
David N Robinson
77 Dale St
Chestnut Hill MA
02467

Call Sign: KB1WSY
Martin D Marris
59 Eliot Cres 1
Chestnut Hill MA
02467

Call Sign: W1UF
L Dennis Shapiro
24 Essex Rd
Chestnut Hill MA
02467

Call Sign: KA1WFR
Stanley E Weisman
77 Florence St 100n
Chestnut Hill MA
02467

Call Sign: KA1YYZ
Elliot L Servais
4 Garrison St
Chestnut Hill MA
02167

Call Sign: KA1ZXZ
Naomi R Nadelberg
11 Garrison St
Chestnut Hill MA
02167

Call Sign: KA1ZYA
Amanda R Nadelberg
11 Garrison St

Chestnut Hill MA
02167

Call Sign: N1YNN
Kaynam Hedayat
110 Hackensack Rd
Chestnut Hill MA
02167

Call Sign: W1ILP
Harvey Miller
250 Hammond Pond
Pkwy Apt 912N
Chestnut Hill MA
02167

Call Sign: KB1QVW
Jeffrey P Hutter
250 Hammond Pond
Pkwy Unit 111N
Chestnut Hill MA
02467

Call Sign: K1UN
Jordan L Ring
250 Hammond Pond
Pky Ph 170
Chestnut Hill MA
024671533

Call Sign: KB1WVU
Nora E Carr
935 Hammond St
Chestnut Hill MA
024672703

Call Sign: W1SGT
Robert M Whittemore
203 Heath St
Chestnut Hill MA
02167

Call Sign: KB1UHG
Kylie N Lucas
401 Heath St
Chestnut Hill MA
02467

Call Sign: K9DSD
David S Dill
308 Lagrange St
Chestnut Hill MA
02467

Call Sign: KA1ZYM
Joseph H Uchill
46 Malia Ter
Chestnut Hill MA
02167

Call Sign: N1EKR
Paul L Ross
24 Mayflower Rd
Chestnut Hill MA
02167

Call Sign: KA1YVQ
Gabriel S Eichler
93 Monadnock Rd
Chestnut Hill MA
02167

Call Sign: KA1YTA
Adam J Franklin
96 Monadnock Rd
Chestnut Hill MA
02167

Call Sign: KB1WWF
Robert M Rosengard
753 Newton St
Chestnut Hill MA
02467

Call Sign: NR1G
Bruno Bedetti
147 Payson Rd
Chestnut Hill MA
02167

Call Sign: WA1WZF
James R Fallon
128 Pond Brook Rd
Chestnut Hill MA
02467

Call Sign: KA1RQR
Claire E Ryan
234 Reservoir Rd
Chestnut Hill MA
02167

Call Sign: W1HLS
Lee L Selwyn
285 Reservoir Rd
Chestnut Hill MA
024671449

Call Sign: KB1WVZ
James H Philip
70 Shaw Rd
Chestnut Hill MA
024673122

Call Sign: KB1WVV
Beverly K Philip
70 Shaw Rd
Chestnut Hill MA
02467

Call Sign: WB1FGJ
Phillip Smith
55 Singletree Rd
Chestnut Hill MA
02167

Call Sign: WB1FGN
Karen F Smith
55 Singletree Rd
Chestnut Hill MA
02167

Call Sign: KA1ZAW
Rebecca K Schrage
11 Tudor Rd
Chestnut Hill MA
02167

Call Sign: KB1ADC
Kyra Z Norsigian
43 Waban Hill Rd N
Chestnut Hill MA
02167

Call Sign: KA1YVR
Seth W Herman
78 Waban Hill Rd N
Chestnut Hill MA
02167

Call Sign: KA1ZAA
Adam L Herman
78 Waban Hill Rd N
Chestnut Hill MA
02167

Call Sign: KB1ADX
Jacob I Broder Fingert
115 Waban Hill Rd N
Chestnut Hill MA
02167

Call Sign: WA1NNS
Thomas L Price
44 Westgate Rd 6
Chestnut Hill MA
02467

Call Sign: W1HYL
William H Schuette
34 Wolcott Rd Ext
Chestnut Hill MA
02167

Call Sign: KA1ZDB
Emily J Aronson
21 Woodchester Dr
Chestnut Hill MA
02167

Call Sign: K1YSO
James S Gessner
310 Woodland Rd
Chestnut Hill MA
02467

Call Sign: KA1YZZ
Jonathan I Nadel
25 Woodlawn Dr
Chestnut Hill MA
02167

Call Sign: KA1ZDP
Gabriel L Nadel
25 Woodlawn Dr
Chestnut Hill MA
02167

**FCC Amateur Radio
Licenses in Chicopee**

Call Sign: N1UCR
Thomas M Gill Iii
88 7th Ave
Chicopee MA
010202320

Call Sign: WB1FIP
Maurice L Beauchemin
56 Acrebrook Dr
Chicopee MA 01020

Call Sign: N1ZSF
Leo R Freeman
61 Abbey Memorial Dr
116

Chicopee MA 01020

Call Sign: KX1U
Paul C E Therrien
88 Acrebrook Dr
Chicopee MA 01020

Call Sign: N1OWH
Marc S Roberts
90 Ann St
Chicopee MA 01020

Call Sign: KB1OAP
Patrick H Goeckner
167 Applewood Dr
Chicopee MA 01022

Call Sign: KB1PQV
Joshua M Avery
17 Arimont St
Chicopee MA 01013

Call Sign: N7CVF
Jon A Avery
17 Arlmont
Chicopee MA
010133701

Call Sign: N1XOF
Ellen F Richard
22 Artisan St 12
Chicopee MA 01103

Call Sign: KB1QXK
Cynthia A Boutot
26 Artisan St 1st Floor
Chicopee MA 01013

Call Sign: KB1MXV
Paul M Heyl
38 Asselin St
Chicopee MA 01020

Call Sign: AA1LY
Roger Lapointe
24 Barby Ave
Chicopee MA 01020

Call Sign: KA0VCH
Stephen J Cook
35 Baril Ln
Chicopee MA 01013

Call Sign: N1KQG

Herb F Ewing
87 Beaudry Ave
Chicopee MA 01020

Call Sign: N1MHF
William N Stoner Jr
50 Bill St
Chicopee MA 01013

Call Sign: N1PLY
Cynthia A Stoner
50 Bill St
Chicopee MA 01013

Call Sign: W1QUS
Hugh E Cronin
49 Bonner St
Chicopee MA 01013

Call Sign: KB1TKT
Thomas K Walker
87 Boszwick Ln
Chicopee MA 01020

Call Sign: N1ISP
Thomas M Lazarz
180 Bridle Path Rd
Chicopee MA
010133826

Call Sign: KB1WCU
Michael R Smith
686 Britton St
Chicopee MA 01020

Call Sign: KB1MEB
Inc W1kk Wireless
Association
1 Broadcast Cir
Chicopee MA 01013

Call Sign: W1KK
Inc W1kk Wireless
Association
1 Broadcast Cir
Chicopee MA 01013

Call Sign: KB1QOQ
Inc W1kk Wireless
Association
1 Broadcast Ctr
Chicopee MA 01013

Call Sign: AA1KK

Inc W1kk Wireless
Association
1 Broadcast Ctr
Chicopee MA 01013

Call Sign: KA1ZIQ
Charlene G Murphy
621 Broadway
Chicopee MA 01020

Call Sign: N1SRI
Stephen J Miner Sr
283 Broadway St
Chicopee MA 01020

Call Sign: N1NJX
Christopher L Paton
566 Broadway St
Chicopee MA 01020

Call Sign: K1JIS
Ronald A La Rue
55 Bromont St
Chicopee MA 01020

Call Sign: W1QXV
Max H Voigt
1073 Burnett Rd
Chicopee MA
010204610

Call Sign: KB1AON
Louis Brodeur
1201 Burnette Rd
Chicopee MA 01020

Call Sign: KB1DYO
Robert B Cossaboom
11 Burton St
Chicopee MA 01013

Call Sign: W1AAW
Daniel M Bergeron
25 Calvin St
Chicopee MA 01013

Call Sign: W1DM
Catamount Amateur
Radio Club
25 Calvin St
Chicopee MA 01013

Call Sign: KB1LNS
David J Carabetta

31 Cardyn Terr
Chicopee MA 01020

Call Sign: KB1CQA
Charles P Caban
84 Champagne Ave
Chicopee MA 01013

Call Sign: WA1SCT
James E Burns
21 Chicomansett
Village
Chicopee MA 01013

Call Sign: KB1QHG
Daniel H Taney
362 Chicapee St
Chicapee MA 01013

Call Sign: N1CFU
Clifford A Madru
377 Chicopee St
Chicopee MA 01013

Call Sign: KB1QHI
Robert E Arnold
Chicopee St
Chicopee MA 01013

Call Sign: N1XXK
Paul M Platanitis Jr
573 Chicopee St 3r
Chicopee MA
010132161

Call Sign: KB1NFK
City Of Chicopee
Emergency
Management Races
Club
80 Church St
Chicopee MA 01020

Call Sign: N1MMS
James D Adam
89 Claire St
Chicopee MA 01020

Call Sign: W1FAB
Kenneth D Walker
99 Clarendon Ave
Chicopee MA 01013

Call Sign: N1QFN

Eugene F Landry Jr
118 Clark St
Chicopee MA 01013

Call Sign: KB1DVZ
Michael K Van Conant
229 College St
Chicopee MA 01020

Call Sign: W1BLL
Anthony J Lorraine
303 College St
Chicopee MA 01020

Call Sign: KA1QHG
Laurence E Wolanin
Colonial Circle
Chicopee MA 01020

Call Sign: AB1PC
John E Socha
40 Coolidge Rd
Chicopee MA 01013

Call Sign: N1BCH
Stephen J Buchanan
150 Cyran St
Chicopee MA
010202289

Call Sign: N1ABJ
Robert T Roy Sr
41 Dallaire Ave
Chicopee MA 01020

Call Sign: N1DOP
Marie A Roy
41 Dallaire Ave
Chicopee MA 01020

Call Sign: N1FDC
Phillip P Sowa
39 Deslauriers St
Chicopee MA
010202907

Call Sign: WB1FJK
Walter L Smith Jr
144 Deslauriers St
Chicopee MA
010202974

Call Sign: K1ZLB
Edward A Boisvert

93 Deslauries
Chicopee MA 01020

Call Sign: N1NYE
Emilio T Garcia
18 Douglas Cir
Chicopee MA 01013

Call Sign: WA1DZI
John C Gallagher
321 E Main St Apt 2
Chicopee MA
010203600

Call Sign: KE4TND
John C Gallagher
321 E Main St2
Chicopee MA 01020

Call Sign: KA1YAZ
Jose L Montanez
118 Elcon Dr
Chicopee MA 01013

Call Sign: N1LZF
Michael R Favreau
27 Emerald St 2nd
Floor
Chicopee MA 01013

Call Sign: KB1RNS
William P Cardinal
62 Fernwood St
Chicopee MA 01020

Call Sign: N1IFW
Mark S Formhals
14 Ferry St
Chicopee MA 01013

Call Sign: KA1CQK
Carl E Sittard
38 Fletcher Cir
Chicopee MA 01020

Call Sign: N1LYX
Ernest A Girard Jr
170 Fletcher Cir
Chicopee MA 01020

Call Sign: KA1ZMY
Guy F Delia
32 Fredette St
Chicopee MA 01022

Call Sign: KB1UYI
Richard G Thibault
84 Freedom St
Chicopee MA 01013

Call Sign: K1PKP
Michael W Griffin
93 Frink St
Chicopee MA 01020

Call Sign: KB1EIJ
Vincent M Lachendro
566 Front St
Chicopee MA 01013

Call Sign: K1YOU
Paul A Aubuchon
283 Fuller Rd Unit Z
Chicopee MA 01020

Call Sign: KB1HPG
David A Roy Sr
28 Gagne St
Chicopee MA 01013

Call Sign: KB1TBY
Colin J Lapierre
9 Gardner Rd
Chicopee MA 01013

Call Sign: KB1UYJ
Ann M Carroll
8 Gerard Ln
Chicopee MA 01020

Call Sign: W1QFS
John T Kopaczek
11 Glendale St
Chicopee MA
010203518

Call Sign: N1KQD
Frank T Knapp
20 Goodhue Ave
Chicopee MA 01020

Call Sign: N1TLK
Bradford G Alheim
749 Granby Rd
Chicopee MA
010201332

Call Sign: KB1OLT

Charles A Adams
1286 Granby Rd
Chicopee MA 01020

Call Sign: K1CAA
Charles A Adams
1286 Granby Rd
Chicopee MA 01020

Call Sign: W1LPC
George K Boutwell
37 Greenleaf St
Chicopee MA 01013

Call Sign: KB1MDR
Joseph E Conroy Iii
302 Grove St
Chicopee MA 01020

Call Sign: W1YMZ
George A Mattson
203 Hampden St
Chicopee MA 01013

Call Sign: KB1MZB
Joshua R Paul
239 Hampden St
Chicopee MA 01013

Call Sign: N1ZCK
Robert E Theroux
26 Holiday Cir
Chicopee MA 01020

Call Sign: N1TOS
Glen J Sharrow
86 Holiday Circle
Chicopee MA
010202896

Call Sign: KB1DEZ
Frank W Ilnicki
169 Irene St
Chicopee MA 01020

Call Sign: KB1JFT
Leonardo Samalot
424 Irene St
Chicopee MA 01020

Call Sign: KB1TCA
Jonathan M Rose
102 Jacob St
Chicopee MA 01020

Call Sign: AA1MM
David M Cayen
405 James St
Chicopee MA 01020

Call Sign: KB1GSD
Jill P Cayen
405 James St
Chicopee MA 01020

Call Sign: WN1E
David M Cayen
405 James St
Chicopee MA 01020

Call Sign: N1KRV
Richard Lacoste
1148 James St
Chicopee MA 01022

Call Sign: KB1WVB
Hampden Charter
School Of Science
Amateur Radio Club
20 Johnson Rd
Chicopee MA 01022

Call Sign: W1SCI
Hampden Charter
School Of Science
Amateur Radio Club
20 Johnson Rd
Chicopee MA 01022

Call Sign: W1CDZ
John L Dearness Mr
210 Johnson Rd Unit
#15
Chicopee MA 01022

Call Sign: N1JRS
George J Bergeron
20 Julia Ave
Chicopee MA 01020

Call Sign: N1JSK
Christine G Bergeron
20 Julia Ave
Chicopee MA 01020

Call Sign: KB1ODC
Joseph A Pelletier
12 Kane Dr

Chicopee MA 01013

Call Sign: KA1LMP
Allison P Bogia
45 Keddy Blvd
Chicopee MA 01020

Call Sign: KB1SHZ
Todd W Philbrick
58 Lafayette St
Chicopee MA 01020

Call Sign: KB1SIA
Zachary M Philbrick
58 Lafayette St
Chicopee MA 01020

Call Sign: N1BRS
Zachary M Philbrick
58 Lafayette St
Chicopee MA 01020

Call Sign: K1CFF
Todd W Philbrick
58 Lafayette St
Chicopee MA 01020

Call Sign: KB1MYC
Donald S Field
200 Lambert Terr Unit
20
Chicopee MA 01020

Call Sign: WB1Z
James R Allen Jr
56 Larchmont St
Chicopee MA
010133818

Call Sign: KB1PKI
Kenneth J Windyka
48 Lariviere Dr
Chicopee MA 01020

Call Sign: KA1ZLA
Todd J Richter
8 Lavallee Ave
Chicopee MA 01020

Call Sign: N1YIZ
Donald G Sansom
73 Lawrence Rd
Chicopee MA 01013

Call Sign: WA1DC
David E Cote
16 Liberty St
Chicopee MA 01013

Call Sign: K1RIB
Richard I Boyce Sr
32 Linden St
Chicopee MA
010202609

Call Sign: KA1QBI
Eugene L Corbeil
124 Mandalay Rd
Chicopee MA 01020

Call Sign: KB1OPU
Betsy A Jarmolowicz
38 Marble Ave
Chicopee MA 01013

Call Sign: KB1OPX
Betsy A Jarmolowicz
38 Marble Ave
Chicopee MA 01013

Call Sign: KB1LFB
Michael N Penna
15 Margaret St 2nd
Floor
Chicopee MA 01013

Call Sign: AA1OG
Ronald P Douillard
80 Maryland Ave
Chicopee MA 01020

Call Sign: N1OBG
Diane R Douillard
80 Maryland Ave
Chicopee MA 01020

Call Sign: N1FWR
Christopher J Barry
49 Massachusetts Ave
Chicopee MA 01013

Call Sign: WA1POB
David B Walker
518 Mc Kinstry Ave
Chicopee MA 01020

Call Sign: N1OBH
Norman Avondo Jr

817 Mc Kinstry Ave
Chicopee MA 01020

Call Sign: KB1JOQ
Stephen D Potvin
32 Mccarthy Ave
Chicopee MA 01020

Call Sign: KC8UXZ
Richard A Rinard
665 Mckinstry Ave
Chicopee MA 01020

Call Sign: KB1WKR
Ronald M Marchand
845 Mckinstry Ave
Chicopee MA 01020

Call Sign: N1YFQ
Arthur R Needham Ii
856 Mckinstry Ave
Chicopee MA 01020

Call Sign: KB1MTQ
John M Lapierre
213 Meadow Ct
Chicopee MA 01013

Call Sign: KA1FCU
Michael J Piecuch
4 Meetinghouse Rd
Chicopee MA 01013

Call Sign: KB1CWU
Gary A Tomestic
759 Mekinstry Ave
Chicopee MA 01020

Call Sign: KB1ANN
James Sheehan
67 Mellen St
Chicopee MA 01013

Call Sign: KB1SHC
Andrew K Peets
12 Mellenger Lane
Chicopee MA 01022

Call Sign: WA1VDE
Gerald E Overstreet
21 Mellinger Ln
Chicopee MA 01022

Call Sign: K1VEG

Albert F Le Tendre Sr
32 Mellinger Ln
Chicopee MA 01022

Call Sign: N1KQF
Scott C Hoiberg
41 Melvin St
Chicopee MA 01013

Call Sign: K1ETN
Austin A Lebert
53 Melvin St
Chicopee MA 01013

Call Sign: NE1Z
William J Didonna
735 Memorial Dr 58
Chicopee MA 01020

Call Sign: KD7LJB
James G Wheeler
1981 Memorial Drive
Chicopee MA 01020

Call Sign: KB1QYN
David E Neiford
203 Montcalm St
Chicopee MA 01020

Call Sign: KA1JDY
Robert R Archambault
33 Montclair St
Chicopee MA 01013

Call Sign: KB1VUT
Edward J Socha
77 Montgomery St
Chicopee MA 01020

Call Sign: W1MI
John B Sypek Jr
312 Montgomery St
Chicopee MA 01020

Call Sign: WA1ZRL
Shirley A Sypek
312 Montgomery St
Chicopee MA 01020

Call Sign: WA1CRV
Frank W Krol
963 Montgomery St
Chicopee MA 01013

Call Sign: KB1PRA
James D Machia Jr
145 Mt Vernon St
Chicopee MA 01013

Call Sign: KB1PRB
James D Machia
145 Mt Vernon St
Chicopee MA 01013

Call Sign: NN1Y
James D Machia
145 Mt Vernon St
Chicopee MA 01013

Call Sign: N1NPA
Walter A Bizon
92 Muzzy St
Chicopee MA 01020

Call Sign: N1ADL
Frank J Nally
11 Naomi St
Chicopee MA 01020

Call Sign: N1BAK
Max T Bobala Jr
11 Nelson St
Chicopee MA 01013

Call Sign: N1WGV
Charles W Doucette
152 Nelson St
Chicopee MA 01013

Call Sign: N1YWT
Laura M Doucette
152 Nelson St
Chicopee MA 01013

Call Sign: WA1MCK
Robert L Bray Jr
185 New Ludlow Rd
Apt 220
Chicopee MA 01020

Call Sign: N1LIQ
James M Sullivan
145 Newbury St
Chicopee MA 01013

Call Sign: N1VFK
Jerry L Pelkey
84 Nonotuck Ave

Chicpee MA 01013

Call Sign: N6MFG
John R Wilson
36 Northwood St
Chicopee MA 01013

Call Sign: N1HKJ
Howard B Plouf
150 Old Fuller Rd Ext
Chicopee MA 01020

Call Sign: WA1UIL
Frank S Furman
54 Parkwood Dr
Chicopee MA
010133538

Call Sign: NO1M
Kenneth E Doerpholz
Sr
686 Pendleton Ave
Chicopee MA
010202900

Call Sign: K1ZFD
Marcel R Lapierre
764 Pendleton Ave
Chicopee MA
010202950

Call Sign: AA1WH
Marcel R Lapierre
764 Pendleton Ave
Chicopee MA
010202950

Call Sign: N1ACS
Kathleen A Rodowicz
809 Pendleton Ave
Chicopee MA 01020

Call Sign: N1SR
Stefan J Rodowicz
809 Pendleton Ave
Chicopee MA 01020

Call Sign: KB1HVT
Region Iii Mema
Races Club
809 Pendleton Ave
Chicopee MA 01020

Call Sign: WC1MAC

Region Iii Mema
Races Club
809 Pendleton Ave
Chicopee MA 01020

Call Sign: KA1MBO
Marty Kandylakis
33 Penn Ave
Chicopee MA 01013

Call Sign: K1VXW
Thomas E Nallen
17 Peter St
Chicopee MA 01020

Call Sign: KB1RRP
Bradley M Scott
54 Pine St 2nd Floor
Chicopee MA 01020

Call Sign: N1VMF
Todd E Chartier
95 Quartus St
Chicopee MA
010134015

Call Sign: N1VMG
Aaron A Lolos
95 Quartus St
Chicopee MA 01013

Call Sign: N1VMI
Phillip A Dudas
95 Quartus St
Chicopee MA 01013

Call Sign: KA1CTU
Walter W
Waskelewicz
112 Quartus St
Chicopee MA 01013

Call Sign: WA1YFQ
Albert H Hodge
68 Rimmon Ave
Chicopee MA
010132826

Call Sign: KB1PQU
George C Fotopoulos
Iii
18 Rivest Court
Chicopee MA 01020

Call Sign: KB1FYU
Alex J Rock
64 Russell Terrace
Chicopee MA 01020

Call Sign: N1XPK
Michael J Leclair
24 Sandtrap Way
Chicopee MA 01020

Call Sign: KA1KEN
Edward A Fontaine
111 School House Rd
Chicopee MA 01020

Call Sign: WA1GXY
Philip W Gorman
36 Sesame Dr
Chicopee MA 01020

Call Sign: N1ONO
George A Garber Jr
118 Shepherd St
Chicopee MA 01013

Call Sign: KA1SFK
Duane A Renaldi
461 Sheridan St
Chicopee MA 01020

Call Sign: N1KXP
William C Theroux
500 Sheridan St
Chicopee MA 01020

Call Sign: N1KBX
Gary H Beaudry
85 Sherman Ave
Chicopee MA 01013

Call Sign: N1VWT
David A De Flumere
125 Silvin Rd
Chicopee MA 01013

Call Sign: KB1RNT
Matthew B Poe
117 Simonich Circle
Chicopee MA 01013

Call Sign: KB1RNR
Kyle E Mrozinski
138 Slate Rd
Chicopee MA 01020

Call Sign: W1MOK
Kyle E Mrozinski
138 Slate Rd
Chicopee MA 01020

Call Sign: KD1PU
Arthur A Breyare
31 Sophia St
Chicopee MA 01013

Call Sign: N1ZOL
Lisa M Hebert
421 Springfield St
Chicopee MA 01013

Call Sign: K1BW
Ronald J Grzelak
84 Stebbins St
Chicopee MA 01020

Call Sign: KC4KNG
David W Norman
84 Stephens St
Chicopee MA 01022

Call Sign: K1ZQB
John H Dumont
20 Surrey Ln
Chicopee MA 01013

Call Sign: WC1AAE
Chicopee Civil
Defense Agency
20 Surrey Ln
Chicopee MA 01020

Call Sign: N1UVS
Dennis A Cierpial
42 Swal St
Chicopee MA 01013

Call Sign: N1KJL
Donald J Cierpial
42 Swol St
Chicopee MA 01013

Call Sign: W1JEG
Henry R Glinka
125 Telegraph Ave
Chicopee MA 01020

Call Sign: N2HLA
Martin Oppenheimer

147 Theroux Dr
Chicopee MA 01020

Call Sign: W1GXS
Phillip F Brodacki
61 Van Horn St
Chicopee MA
010133420

Call Sign: K1AGL
Stanley I Partyka
141 Waite Ave
Chicopee MA 01020

Call Sign: KA1WGU
Gregg J Stefanik
79 Wanda St
Chicopee MA 01013

Call Sign: KB1JVM
Walter J Ziemba
105 Ward St
Chicopee MA
010210599

Call Sign: N1OWG
Mark A Robare
88 Wheatland Ave
Chicopee MA 01013

Call Sign: KD1UU
Earl F Chamberlin
173 Wildemere St
Chicopee MA 01020

Call Sign: KB1FXN
Jan J Lockhart
59 Wilmont St
Chicopee MA
010133851

Call Sign: KC1RY
Peter O Kandylakis
66 Wilmont St
Chicopee MA 01013

Call Sign: KB1MGR
Spencer J Lockhart
59 Wilmot St
Chicopee MA 01013

Call Sign: KB1CJW
Daniel F Tereso
122 Woodbridge Rd

Chicopee MA 01122

Call Sign: KB1KKW
James M Germana
145 Woodbridge Rd
Chicopee MA 01022

Call Sign: NX1M
Dennis C Syriac
21 Yorktown Ct
Chicopee MA 01020

Call Sign: KB1CIK
Gerald Gaouette
Chicopee MA 01013

Call Sign: KB1PSF
Philip Aelfwald
Chicopee MA 01021

Call Sign: W1ELF
Philip Aelfwald
Chicopee MA 01021

**FCC Amateur Radio
Licenses in Chicopee
Falls**

Call Sign: W1FXF
Albert J Gorzkowicz
41 Cortland St
Chicopee Falls MA
01020

Call Sign: KB1EPG
Robert J Hopkins
5 Garrity St
Chicopee Falls MA
01020

Call Sign: W1PHS
Robert J Hopkins
5 Garrity St
Chicopee Falls MA
01020

Call Sign: N1OZG
David L Wolanin
42 Sunnymeade Ave
Chicopee Falls MA
01020

Call Sign: KD1RV
Lawrence E Dziobek

77 Watson St
Chicopee Falls MA
01020

Call Sign: W1NPL
Edward J White
136 Woodlawn St
Chicopee Falls MA
01020

**FCC Amateur Radio
Licenses in Chilmark**

Call Sign: WA2KIV
Victor R Spelman
9 Beechtree Rd
Chilmark MA 02535

Call Sign: KA1WKY
Christian B Parker
Prospect Hill Box 477
Chilmark MA 02535

Call Sign: W1MIW
Donald G Beck
9 Shalers Way
Chilmark MA
025352851

Call Sign: N1QWY
Emma T Parker
Chilmark MA 02535

Call Sign: N1QWZ
J B R Parker
Chilmark MA 02535

Call Sign: KB1OCG
William H Smith
Chilmark MA 02535

**FCC Amateur Radio
Licenses in
Clarksburg**

Call Sign: WA1ZWX
James R Sweeney
120 Cross Rd
Clarksburg MA 01247

Call Sign: KB1EZB
George W Fischer
910 Daniels Rd
Clarksburg MA 01247

Call Sign: WB1CWX
Shirley M Collette
201 East Rd
Clarksburg MA 01247

Call Sign: KF4LHH
Marlene E Ansley
510 Walker St
Clarksburg MA
012472878

Call Sign: WB1CWW
William A Collette
Clarksburg MA 01247

**FCC Amateur Radio
Licenses in Clinton**

Call Sign: W1PFS
Paul F Silvestri
25 Arthur St
Clinton MA 01510

Call Sign: KB1FRZ
Mark S Ziko
213 Beacon St Unit 2
Clinton MA 01510

Call Sign: KB1NJR
Roger E Prather
290 Berlin St Apt 81
Clinton MA 01510

Call Sign: N1FBD
Charles J Audette
106 Cedar St
Clinton MA 01510

Call Sign: KB1FGA
Timothy L Noland
240 Chestnut St
Clinton MA 01510

Call Sign: KB1NEY
James H Evans
915 D Ridgefield
Circle
Clinton MA 01510

Call Sign: K1JAS
James H Evans
915 D Ridgefield
Circle

Clinton MA 01510

Call Sign: KB1PUF
Frank J Savell Sr
655 Devenwood Way
Clinton MA 01510

Call Sign: W1ULA
Frank J Savell Sr
655 Devenwood Way
Clinton MA 01510

Call Sign: KA1DFM
Michael J Kilcoyne
29 Dike Dr
Clinton MA 01510

Call Sign: W1LPF
Carroll M Collamore
1 Fairview St
Clinton MA 01510

Call Sign: N1AYK
Richard W Sowa
129 Flagg St
Clinton MA 01510

Call Sign: N1WOE
Robert J Kane
2 Goss St
Clinton MA 01510

Call Sign: KB1WPC
Theresa Kane
2 Goss St
Clinton MA 01510

Call Sign: N1RYI
Don A Black
2 Hamilton St
Clinton MA 01510

Call Sign: KA1YGO
Frank Dimase
437 High St
Clinton MA 01510

Call Sign: N1KXY
Jeffrey C Vaghini
74 Lancaster Rd
Clinton MA 01510

Call Sign: N1KJB
Constantino P Zapantis

37 Lane Ave
Clinton MA 01510

Call Sign: KB1GHH
Raymond J Nowak
43 Laurel St
Clinton MA 01510

Call Sign: WR1N
Raymond J Nowak
43 Laurel St
Clinton MA 01510

Call Sign: N1VFD
Joseph M Trautner
28 Lindberg St
Clinton MA 01510

Call Sign: N1PHE
Richard H Brown
664 Main St
Clinton MA 01510

Call Sign: N1GTA
Dennis M Williams
1028 Main St
Clinton MA 01510

Call Sign: KB1PZH
Albert P Modugno Jr
25 Nathan Drive
Clinton MA 01510

Call Sign: KB1JXD
Peter G Schaufus
35 Oak St
Clinton MA 01510

Call Sign: WA1CSP
Daniel F Paquette
208 Oak St
Clinton MA 01510

Call Sign: KB1DPE
George W Hamilton
218 Oak St
Clinton MA
015013713

Call Sign: KA1EEC
Eric S Johansson
147 Oak St Apt 2
Clinton MA 01510

Call Sign: WO1K
James P De Cesare
131 Park St
Clinton MA 01510

Call Sign: KB1EWP
Joseph A Puccia
20 Pond Ct
Clinton MA 01510

Call Sign: KA1KGN
Gaetano M Paganelli
19 Skyline Dr
Clinton MA 01510

Call Sign: KB1OSG
Gregory Coppenrath
27 Skyline Dr
Clinton MA 01510

Call Sign: KB1DWF
Rafael T Reyes
5 Spruce St
Clinton MA 07510

Call Sign: K1URP
Joseph A Pasquale
15 Thomas St
Clinton MA 01510

Call Sign: N1HMZ
Michael C Fontaine
27 Top
Clinton MA 01510

Call Sign: KB1UYY
Thomas R Kehn
138 Walnut St
Clinton MA 01510

Call Sign: N1NTB
Myron W Jokinen
24 Water St Apt 409
Clinton MA 01510

Call Sign: KB1MZH
Gerald W Rousseau
266 Wilson St
Clinton MA 01510

Call Sign: WJ1W
Steven R Duguay
236 Woodlawn St
Clinton MA 01510

Call Sign: W1YSB
Everett H Burgwinkle
Sr
71 Woodruff Rd
Clinton MA 01510

Call Sign: WC1ABR
Clinton Civil Defense
Dept
71 Woodruff Rd
Clinton MA 01510

Call Sign: N1VQJ
Karen S Mollica
Clinton MA 01510

FCC Amateur Radio Licenses in Cochituate

Call Sign: KA1DHV
Charles W Stevens
249 Main St
Cochituate MA 01778

FCC Amateur Radio Licenses in Cohasset

Call Sign: K1SSP
Andrew P Krueger
67 Aaron River Rd
Cohasset MA 02025

Call Sign: KB1IXI
Brian L James
19 Buttonwood Ln
Cohasset MA 02025

Call Sign: KB1JZH
Allen B Zenker
759 Cjc Highway #260
Cohasset MA 02025

Call Sign: KA1QYS
William P Fahy
203 Fair Oaks Ln
Cohasset MA 02025

Call Sign: KB1FDB
John K Bryant
251 Forest Ave
Cohasset MA 02025

Call Sign: WA1TJW
Ubaldo P Di Benedetto
32 Jerusalem Rd
Cohasset MA 02025

Call Sign: WA4QJN
John A Whealler Jr
619 Jerusalem Rd
Cohasset MA 02025

Call Sign: WA1PDY
George B Hovorka
38 Lantern Ln
Cohasset MA 02025

Call Sign: N3GGR
Thomas M Daley
11 Ledgewood Farm
Dr
Cohasset MA 02025

Call Sign: W1TMD
Thomas M Daley
11 Ledgewood Farm
Dr
Cohasset MA 02025

Call Sign: KA1MHK
Marjorie A Richards
N Main St
Cohasset MA 02025

Call Sign: KA1MKX
Deborah J Richards
N Main St
Cohasset MA 02025

Call Sign: KA1ZN
Fred W Quelle Jr
120 Nichols Rd
Cohasset MA
020251146

Call Sign: K1GLB
Nelson C Pratt Jr
246 North Main St
Cohasset MA 02025

Call Sign: N1AOR
Thomas N Dickson
111 Pond St
Cohasset MA 02025

Call Sign: W1TND

Thomas N Dickson
111 Pond St
Cohasset MA 02025

Call Sign: WA1J
Harold E Coughlin
25 Reservoir Rd
Cohasset MA 02025

Call Sign: N1FTO
Walter J Matherly Iii
30 Schofield Rd
Cohasset MA 02025

Call Sign: K1TK
David W Curry
24 Whitney Woods Ln
Cohasset MA
020251500

**FCC Amateur Radio
Licenses in Colrain**

Call Sign: N1NHA
Andrew S Gilbert
74 Adamsville Rd
Colrain MA 01340

Call Sign: N1QXU
Jeremy R Vight
22 Call Rd
Colrain MA 01340

Call Sign: KA1FVV
Lawrence M Dumas
142 Calvin Coombs Rd
Colrain MA 01340

Call Sign: WA1KJI
Theodore W Johnson
20 Coombs Hill Rd
Colrain MA 01340

Call Sign: KB1KFQ
Eva L Archambo
12 Dwight Cross Rd
Colrain MA 01340

Call Sign: KB1NOG
Harriet B Dyer
245 Ed Clark Rd
Colrain MA 01340

Call Sign: K1LVK

Robert M Shaw Sr
2 Griswoldville St
Colrain MA 01340

Call Sign: K1MQI
Norma J Shaw
2 Griswoldville St
Colrain MA 01340

Call Sign: W1ERK
Lloyd R Vight
24 Kings Bluff
Colrain MA 01340

Call Sign: KA1JRY
Elizabeth A Litskoski
10 Phillip Dr
Colrain MA 01340

Call Sign: WA1EDC
Richard A Litskoski
10 Phillip Dr
Colrain MA 01340

Call Sign: KB1WVA
Nina S Martin-
Anzuoni
17 Wilson Hill Rd
Colrain MA 01340

Call Sign: K1YCD
Walker T Miles
Colrain MA 01340

Call Sign: KB1FFT
Scott F Archambo
12 Dwight Cross Rd
Coltrain MA 01340

**FCC Amateur Radio
Licenses in Concord**

Call Sign: N1JLT
Robert G Bower
8 Anson Rd
Concord MA 01742

Call Sign: K1AKE
James M Moran Jr
93 Anson Rd
Concord MA 01742

Call Sign: WA1VOL
Lawrence L Parker

137 Arena Ter
Concord MA 01742

Call Sign: K1SAS
Lawrence L Parker
137 Arena Ter
Concord MA 01742

Call Sign: WB4RVA
Edward G Tiedemann
Jr
656 Barretts Mill Rd
Concord MA
017421524

Call Sign: N1ZYV
Sally A Gangloff
62 Bedford Ct
Concord MA 01742

Call Sign: KA1LQZ
Kathleen M Morris
423 Bedford St
Concord MA 01714

Call Sign: W1VXY
Fortunato N Rotondo
737 Bedford St
Concord MA 01742

Call Sign: W1FQG
Bernard R Olsen
42 Birch Dr
Concord MA 01742

Call Sign: W1PPK
William D K Burton
Box 621
Concord MA 01742

Call Sign: WB1AJL
Luke A Burnham
84 Bristers Hill Rd
Concord MA
017423502

Call Sign: KB1WHQ
Noah A Burnham
84 Bristers Hill Rd
Concord MA 01742

Call Sign: K1NAB
Noah A Burnham
84 Bristers Hill Rd

Concord MA 01742

Call Sign: N1AIR
John S Wurts
11 Cedar Way
Concord MA 01742

Call Sign: N1VYI
Christopher A Salerno
457 College Rd
Concord MA 01742

Call Sign: N1VYJ
Ricard G Salerno
457 College Rd
Concord MA 01742

Call Sign: KB1FGX
Jeremy A Salerno
457 College Rd
Concord MA 01742

Call Sign: KB1EMV
Fred W Harrington
28 Commerford Rd
Concord MA 01742

Call Sign: KB1JKU
Anita P Harrington
28 Commerford Rd
Concord MA 01742

Call Sign: KB1MBV
Heather A Harrington
28 Commerford Rd
Concord MA 01742

Call Sign: KB1JKV
Jimi Two Feathers
303 Commonwealth
Ave
Concord MA 01742

Call Sign: KB1JKW
Eugene A Hall
305 Commonwealth
Ave
Concord MA 01742

Call Sign: KB1JKX
Jesse Isaak-Ross
305 Commonwealth
Ave
Concord MA 01742

Call Sign: KB1JKY
Jeff Lowe
305 Commonwealth
Ave
Concord MA 01742

Call Sign: KB1JKR
Jocelyn A Hearnshaw
25 Concord Greene 7
Concord MA 01742

Call Sign: N1KYX
Colin G Trass
29 Concord Greene U4
Concord MA 01742

Call Sign: KB1HQB
Colin G Trass
29 Concord Greene U4
Concord MA 01742

Call Sign: KB1KAJ
Edward B Bokhour
67 Crest St
Concord MA 01742

Call Sign: KB1KUX
Frederic H Federlein
65 Deacon Haynes Rd
Concord MA 01742

Call Sign: N1FFF
Frederic H Federlein
65 Deacon Haynes Rd
Concord MA 01742

Call Sign: KG1F
Frederic H Federlein
65 Deacon Haynes Rd
Concord MA 01742

Call Sign: W1NCO
John E Sibel
80 Deaconess Rd
Concord MA
017424113

Call Sign: W1ZP
Donald Kaplan
80 Deaconess Rd Ne
Deaconess Rivercrest
Concord MA 01742

Call Sign: KE9AN
Patrick Dreher
66 Deer Grass Lane
Concord MA 01742

Call Sign: KB1UEZ
John P Gurski
15 Emerson Rd
Concord MA 01742

Call Sign: AB1MW
John P Gurski
15 Emerson Rd
Concord MA 01742

Call Sign: KB1WHO
Ashley J Briggs
33 Everett St
Concord MA 01742

Call Sign: KB1WHP
Jeffrey P Briggs
33 Everett St
Concord MA 01742

Call Sign: KB1OVE
Henry J Dane
58 Everett St
Concord MA 01742

Call Sign: KB1QAT
Gary W Schmitz
34 Everett St Apt 7a
Concord MA 01742

Call Sign: KB1MTF
Foster J Degiacomo
70 Farmers Cliff Rd
Concord MA 01742

Call Sign: WA3YKN
David J Braunegg
13 Garden Rd
Concord MA
017423409

Call Sign: W1OUN
Gordon H Pettengill
150 Garfield Rd
Concord MA 01742

Call Sign: N1DCA
R Hopkins Holmberg
385 Garfield Rd

Concord MA
017424906

Call Sign: N1HOP
Hopkins Holmberg
385 Garfield Rd
Concord MA
017424906

Call Sign: KB1OVG
Craig R Fontaine
62 Harrington Ave
Concord MA 01742

Call Sign: N1RTH
Leslie B Bates
519 Hayward Mill Rd
Concord MA 01742

Call Sign: WB1EYJ
Steven L Bates
519 Hayward Mill Rd
Concord MA 01742

Call Sign: K1SLB
Steven L Bates
519 Hayward Mill Rd
Concord MA 01742

Call Sign: KB1KAK
Jennifer E Bates
519 Hayward Mill Rd
Concord MA 01742

Call Sign: KB1LJM
Colonial Wireless
Association
519 Hayward Mill Rd
Concord MA 01742

Call Sign: N1CON
Colonial Wireless
Association
519 Hayward Mill Rd
Concord MA 01742

Call Sign: KA1SQQ
Carlton F Jablonski Sr
31 Highland St
Concord MA 01742

Call Sign: KB1MTG
Mark H Rubman
308 Holden Wood Rd

Concord MA 01742

Call Sign: KA1LOD
David G Zapol
182 Holdenwood Rd
Concord MA 01742

Call Sign: K1AZA
Francis B Magurn
204 Hubbard St
Concord MA
017423436

Call Sign: KB1VYQ
Ronald Jenssen
45 Hunters Ridge Rd
Concord MA 01742

Call Sign: WB4AMT
James K Hall Iii
26 Independence Rd
Concord MA 01742

Call Sign: W4BLX
James K Hall Iii
26 Independence Rd
Concord MA 01742

Call Sign: W1JUR
Morley J Lush
74 Independence Rd
Concord MA 01742

Call Sign: KF2FZ
Andrew P Valenti Jr
131 Indian Pipe Lane
Concord MA 01742

Call Sign: WA1VWE
Carl R Turnquist
106 Kenney Ln
Concord MA 01742

Call Sign: WB1ECO
Gerald F Sullivan
269 Laws Brook Rd
Concord MA 01742

Call Sign: WB1ECP
Francis J Sullivan
269 Laws Brook Rd
Concord MA 01742

Call Sign: K1AHY

Arlene C Gibson
477 Laws Brook Rd
Concord MA 01742

Call Sign: W1KPO
John W Teele
410 Lowell Rd
Concord MA 01742

Call Sign: N1MYK
Anne M Cayer
82 Macarthur Rd
Concord MA 01742

Call Sign: W1THQ
Richard I Gertz
1571 Main
Concord MA 01742

Call Sign: KC1IC
Harold F Soederberg
586 Main St
Concord MA 01742

Call Sign: KB1QAS
William B Whalen
1037 Main St
Concord MA 01742

Call Sign: KC9ADI
M Andrew Tucker
1995 Main St
Concord MA 01742

Call Sign: N3FVC
Gregory L Beyer Jr
2000 Main St
Concord MA 01742

Call Sign: KA1PMP
Elaine F Loomis
59 Marthas Point Rd
Concord MA 01742

Call Sign: WA1FOI
Vito J Augello
29 Meriam Rd
Concord MA 01742

Call Sign: K1UBB
Willis C Kellogg
104 Ministerial Dr
Concord MA
017424030

Call Sign: KB1MBO
Peter G Daigle
211 Monsen Rd
Concord MA 01742

Call Sign: N1EAS
Richard E Petersen
972 Monument St
Concord MA 01742

Call Sign: KB1STR
Drew D Peck
1200 Monument St
Concord MA 01742

Call Sign: K1DDP
Drew D Peck
1200 Monument St
Concord MA 01742

Call Sign: KB1KUY
Thomas C Ryde
1249 Monument St
Concord MA 01742

Call Sign: N1ZRK
Nancy J Beeuwkes
1360 Monument St
Concord MA 01742

Call Sign: W1BFM
Reinier Beeuwkes Iii
1360 Monument St
Concord MA 01742

Call Sign: KA1YKZ
Priscilla J Sneff
1732 Monument St
Concord MA 01742

Call Sign: KA1ES
Alva Morrison
229 Musketaquid Rd
Concord MA 01742

Call Sign: K1MZ
Michael J Zak
74 Musterfield Rd
Concord MA
017421613

Call Sign: W1MU
Michael J Zak

74 Musterfield Rd
Concord MA
017421613

Call Sign: W1OM
Kevin E Grant
134 Musterfield Rd
Concord MA 01742

Call Sign: KB1HKR
Lucien A Couvillon Jr
190 Nashawtuc Rd
Concord MA 01742

Call Sign: W1UM
Lucien A Couvillon Jr
190 Nashawtuc Rd
Concord MA 01742

Call Sign: KB1OVH
Dorothy Bernard
200 Nashoba Rd
Concord MA 01742

Call Sign: WB1HCD
Steven R Bussolari
129 Nimrod Dr
Concord MA 01742

Call Sign: KB1OCM
Thomas C Dawkins
21 Old Bridge Rd
Concord MA 01742

Call Sign: KA1ELJ
Michael A Hastie
82 Old Bridge Rd
Concord MA 01742

Call Sign: W1PJL
Alexander F Hastie
82 Old Bridge Rd
Concord MA
017423048

Call Sign: WA1NLL
George J Jakobsche
39 Old Farm Rd
Concord MA 01742

Call Sign: K1JS
John D Small
134 Old Marlboro Rd
Concord MA 01742

Call Sign: W1ELV
Walter B Hawes
192 Old Marlboro Rd
Concord MA 01742

Call Sign: KB1QAP
Dominic J Ingegneri
247 Old Marlboro Rd
Concord MA 01742

Call Sign: KB1QCT
Stephen J Ippolito
594 Old Marlboro Rd
Concord MA 01742

Call Sign: KB1NYF
Charles J Slagen
21 Old Mill Rd
Concord MA 01742

Call Sign: W1WJZ
James R Walker
847 Old Rd To 9
Concord MA 01742

Call Sign: WA1RPC
Roger J Walker
847 Ortnac
Concord MA
017424318

Call Sign: WA1UGW
James E Shepherd
210 Park Ln
Concord MA 01742

Call Sign: KC1ON
Alexander M Nicolson
226 Peter Spring Rd
Concord MA
017421945

Call Sign: K1YD
Alexander M Nicolson
226 Peter Spring Rd
Concord MA
017421945

Call Sign: N1SXZ
Robert P Harrison
51 Pilgrim Rd
Concord MA 01742

Call Sign: N1CRC
Richard E Mullen
83 Pilgrim Rd
Concord MA
017423410

Call Sign: N1DDW
Deborah J Mullen
83 Pilgrim Rd
Concord MA 01742

Call Sign: N1BDA
Steven W Telsey
40 Pine St
Concord MA 01742

Call Sign: N1PXA
Will J Bartlett
45 Pine St
Concord MA 01742

Call Sign: W1CB
Stephen A Smith
290 Powder Mill Rd
Concord MA
017424806

Call Sign: KB1JKS
Deborah E Bier
63 Prescott Rd
Concord MA 01742

Call Sign: WA1UDO
Paul S Nickelsberg
132 Prescott Rd
Concord MA 01742

Call Sign: KB1WHR
Roy A Westerberg
145 Range Rd
Concord MA 01742

Call Sign: KW1U
Marcia K Forde
44 Raymond Rd
Concord MA 01742

Call Sign: KB1AJ
Dale P Osborn Iii
44 Raymond Rd
Concord MA
017425733

Call Sign: N1PKT

Frank C Robey
144 Riverdale Rd
Concord MA 01742

Call Sign: N1AXX
James J Olsen
26 Robinwood Rd
Concord MA 01742

Call Sign: K7MRP
Richard A Flower
110 Rollingwood Lane
Concord MA 01742

Call Sign: KB1WTW
Sara Seager
28 Sevens St
Concord MA 01742

Call Sign: KB1NFB
Shen Y Shey
2 Shagbark Rd
Concord MA 01742

Call Sign: N1UUP
Samuel Wilensky
419 Silver Hill Rd
Concord MA 01742

Call Sign: N1JAJ
Charles A Ziering
263 Simon Willard Rd
Concord MA
017421625

Call Sign: N1JPR
Filippo C Cattaneo
52 Simon Willard Rd
Concord MA 01742

Call Sign: KB1VWD
Bettina M Warburg-
Johnson
4 South Meadow
Ridge
Concord MA 01742

Call Sign: N1NWD
William M Coan
39 Southfield Cir
Concord MA 01742

Call Sign: N1CQI
Robert J Magee

27 Southfield Rd
Concord MA 01742

Call Sign: K1QM
Joel H Malman
38 Staffordshire Ln
Concord MA 01742

Call Sign: KB1JKP
William C Sheehan
13 Stone Root Ln
Concord MA 01742

Call Sign: KB1JKQ
Donna B Salacuse
220 Stone Root Ln
Concord MA 01742

Call Sign: KB1VFH
Concord Rod And Gun
Club Arc
74 Strawberry Hill Rd
Concord MA 01742

Call Sign: WB1CRG
Concord Rod And Gun
Club Arc
74 Strawberry Hill Rd
Concord MA 01742

Call Sign: W1BW
Bruce J Walker
426 Strawberry Hill Rd
Concord MA 01742

Call Sign: KB1KMO
Frona B Vicksell
163 The Valley Rd
Concord MA 01742

Call Sign: WA1YRQ
Charles L Hanson Jr
245 The Valley Rd
Concord MA 01742

Call Sign: N1ONF
William J Duggan
115 Upland Rd
Concord MA 01742

Call Sign: K1EMT
George W Harvey
Walden Breezes
Concord MA 01742

Call Sign: KB1SBK
Timothy S Williams
572 Walden St
Concord MA 01742

Call Sign: KB1JKT
Robert M Foss
30 Walden Terrace
Concord MA
017423504

Call Sign: W1WME
Ralph D Stetson
450 Westford Rd
Concord MA 01742

Call Sign: N1DCV
John W Bottoms
26 Westvale Dr
Concord MA 01742

Call Sign: W1CUA
Robert Harper
Westvale Meadow
Concord MA 01742

Call Sign: KB1JHA
John W Wood Jr
132 Williams Rd
Concord MA 01742

Call Sign: AB1BZ
John W Wood Jr
132 Williams Rd
Concord MA 01742

Call Sign: K1ZY
John W Wood Jr
132 Williams Rd
Concord MA 01742

Call Sign: KB1SWZ
Robert Hayes
155 Williams Rd
Concord MA 01742

Call Sign: N1DPU
Mark W Eichin
76 Wood St
Concord MA 01742

Call Sign: KE4QYT
Robert L Hooper

16 Wright Farm Rd
Concord MA 01742

Call Sign: N1KVH
Chester C Larner Jr
Concord MA 01742

Call Sign: KB1KAL
Charles A Brown
Concord MA 01742

Call Sign: KB1NFA
James M Deas
Concord MA 01742

Call Sign: KB1TEM
Pamela Green
Concord MA 01742

Call Sign: KB1TEN
Arllen Acevedo
Concord MA 01742

Call Sign: KB1WHL
Claudio M Topolcic
Concord MA 01742

FCC Amateur Radio Licenses in Conway

Call Sign: W2GWI
Lloyd G Kent Jr
624 Bardwell Ferry Rd
Conway MA 01341

Call Sign: KB1NOB
Carl Meyer Ii
96 Hart Rd
Conway MA 01341

Call Sign: KB1NOE
Mary C Clayton-Jones
617 Hoosac Rd
Conway MA 01341

Call Sign: N1WNB
Winston S Burt
185 N Poland Rd
Conway MA 01341

Call Sign: KB1IPP
Nicholas Boisvert
949 Roaring Brook Rd
Conway MA 01341

FCC Amateur Radio Licenses in Cotuit

Call Sign: KB1TSE
Norman E Weill
35 Dewey Lane
Cotuit MA 02635

Call Sign: N1MKA
Hans W Sagemuehl
250 Eisenhower Dr
Cotuit MA 02635

Call Sign: N1ZWD
Richard Holmes
19 Forest Hills Rd
Cotuit MA 02635

Call Sign: N1IVS
James E Rockett
46 Forsyth Ct
Cotuit MA 02635

Call Sign: WM1L
Sean W Kelley
59 Grove St
Cotuit MA 02635

Call Sign: W1TNA
Sidney T Kimber
115 Grove St
Cotuit MA 02635

Call Sign: KB1QWP
Robert A Lancaster
21 Hannah Circle
Cotuit MA 02635

Call Sign: K1RAL
Robert A Lancaster
21 Hannah Circle
Cotuit MA 02635

Call Sign: N1LSQ
James K Mann
22 Narrows Way
Cotuit MA 02635

Call Sign: KB1FHH
Mary F Cicciu
87 Osprey Drive
Cotuit MA 02635

Call Sign: KB1FHI
John A Cicciu
87 Osprey Drive
Cotuit MA 02635

Call Sign: N1ZMY
William F Watt
29 Patience Ln
Cotuit MA 02635

Call Sign: W1GNV
John J Scanlon
9 Pineview Dr
Cotuit MA 02635

Call Sign: N1YFX
Matteo P Tromba
54 Roosevelt Rd
Cotuit MA 02635

Call Sign: KB1DGF
Jacob P Mastro
76 Trout Brook Rd
Cotuit MA 02635

Call Sign: K1FQY
Thomas O Hale
Cotuit MA 02635

Call Sign: KA1UZC
James N Le Clair
Cotuit MA 02635

Call Sign: KC1XE
Walter A Zilonis Jr
Cotuit MA 02635

Call Sign: KB1HJF
Paul Nevosh
Cotuit MA 02635

Call Sign: KB1UZY
Peter L Dudley
Cotuit MA 02635

FCC Amateur Radio Licenses in Cummaquid

Call Sign: K1QYV
Richard P Hooker
33 Midpine Rd
Cummaquid MA
02637

Call Sign: N1QWN
Kim M Bassett
Cummaquid MA
02637

Call Sign: WA1APR
Richard B Lewis
Cummaquid MA
02637

FCC Amateur Radio Licenses in Cummington

Call Sign: N1NMM
Gurdon E Arnold
Box 190
Cummington MA
01026

Call Sign: KA1WXM
David G Lynes
Box 95
Cummington MA
01026

Call Sign: KC4UMC
Diane R Bevan
83 Porter Hill Rd
Cummington MA
01026

Call Sign: WY1G
Mark G Bevan
83 Porter Hill Rd
Cummington MA
01026

Call Sign: KB1KKZ
Randall S Smith
10 Snow Rd
Cummington MA
01026

Call Sign: W2GPV
Frederick J Hunt
74 W Main St
Cummington MA
010269717

Call Sign: N1GYO
Harry J Fisher Jr
268 West St

Cummington MA
01026

Call Sign: KB1EHS
Linda L Merry
835 Windsor Bush Rd
Cummington MA
01026

FCC Amateur Radio Licenses in Dacut

Call Sign: N1UQI
Mark C Gooden
599 Arlington St
Dacut MA 01826

FCC Amateur Radio Licenses in Dalton

Call Sign: N1ESD
Leonard W Stroud
5 Bruce Dr
Dalton MA 01226

Call Sign: WB1AKW
Bruce L Johnston
95 Bruce Dr
Dalton MA 01226

Call Sign: KB1KQN
Raymond E Ferrin
59 Carson Ave
Dalton MA 01226

Call Sign: KB1AQI
James N Ward
6 Claremont Rd
Dalton MA 01226

Call Sign: W1WF
Willard Bridgham Sr
83 Curtis Ave
Dalton MA 01226

Call Sign: KB1EAA
David L Wendling
427 Dalton Division
Rd
Dalton MA 012262817

Call Sign: KB1EUH
Roann Wendling

427 Dalton Division
Rd
Dalton MA 01226

Call Sign: WA6CHT
Clifton P Bean
40 Daly Ave
Dalton MA 01226

Call Sign: KB1UVU
Ashley N Brewer
22 Deming St
Dalton MA 01226

Call Sign: K1DEJ
Joseph J Sakowski
40 Depot St
Dalton MA 01226

Call Sign: KB1AAD
Fred R Reinhold
80 Depot St
Dalton MA 01226

Call Sign: N1XRX
Robert R Merry
33 Ensign St
Dalton MA 01226

Call Sign: W1QCC
Russell W Merry
33 Ensign St
Dalton MA 012261016

Call Sign: KB1ARS
Robert J Kubli
53 Ensign St
Dalton MA 01226

Call Sign: KB1AAC
Glen R Reinhold
115 First St
Dalton MA 01226

Call Sign: KA1SON
Richard D Smith
60 Gertrude Rd
Dalton MA 01226

Call Sign: KB1JZC
Mary E Smith
60 Gertrude Rd
Dalton MA 01226

Call Sign: N1SYN
Richard D Smith
60 Gertrude Rd
Dalton MA 01226

Call Sign: KE3HT
Timothy P Ertl
128 Hale St Ext
Dalton MA 012261108

Call Sign: KB1UJQ
Martin V Myrick Sr
447 High St Apt 4c
Dalton MA 01226

Call Sign: KB1CXX
Paul R Silvernail
105 John St
Dalton MA 01226

Call Sign: KB1DDD
Allison M Silvernail
105 John St
Dalton MA 01226

Call Sign: N1SJR
Henry R Dondi
6 Judith Dr
Dalton MA 01226

Call Sign: W1NGE
Randel H Middlebrook
66 Judith Dr
Dalton MA 01226

Call Sign: KB1SVG
David P Mungo
66 Kimberly Dr
Dalton MA 01226

Call Sign: N1CZS
John J Weber Jr
839 Main St
Dalton MA 01226

Call Sign: W1WYS
Frederick C Lillpopp
956 Main St
Dalton MA 01226

Call Sign: W1VSR
R Chester Wisner
1014 Main St
Dalton MA 01226

Call Sign: KB1APX
Nancy E Clemo
373 North St
Dalton MA 012261219

Call Sign: N1MRS
John M Slade
91 Norwich Dr
Dalton MA 01226

Call Sign: N1MZU
Kimberly A Slade
91 Norwich Dr
Dalton MA 01226

Call Sign: WA1RZO
John M Slade
91 Norwich Dr
Dalton MA 01226

Call Sign: KA1OB
G Clinton Stowers
53 Oak St
Dalton MA 01226

Call Sign: KA1HFC
Donald E Harris Jr
274 Old Windsor Rd
Dalton MA 01226

Call Sign: KB2SCH
David M Thomas
500 Old Windsor Rd
Dalton MA 01226

Call Sign: KB1JDG
Dennis M Masengo
49 Orchard Rd
Dalton MA 01226

Call Sign: KB1VNG
Jacob J Pyra
226 Orchard Rd
Dalton MA 01226

Call Sign: KA1UH
Charles M Varney Jr
345 Orchard Rd
Dalton MA 01226

Call Sign: N1RMQ
Edward F Gero
53 Otis Ave

Dalton MA 01226

Call Sign: W1MEW
George Kardasen Jr
184 Park Ave
Dalton MA 012261425

Call Sign: N1LLR
George A Bishop Iv
90 Pine St
Dalton MA 01226

Call Sign: N1ISC
Michael P Cyr
297 Pleasant St
Dalton MA 01226

Call Sign: KA1VCR
Domenico Suppappola
120 Raymond Dr
Dalton MA 01226

Call Sign: KB1BIT
Darlene L T Chazey
1024 Rt 9
Dalton MA 012269601

Call Sign: N1RCK
William J Chazey Jr
1024 Rte 9
Dalton MA 01226

Call Sign: WA1DQK
Merle A Dodge
52 Tower Rd
Dalton MA 01226

Call Sign: W1HCF
Francis J Groleau
33 Woodside Ave
Dalton MA 01226

Call Sign: WA1ZBZ
Dennis T Croughwell
Dalton MA 01226

Call Sign: WB1ANU
Sharon D Croughwell
Dalton MA 01227

**FCC Amateur Radio
Licenses in Danvers**

Call Sign: W1LXF

Walter J Caron
6 Abington Rd
Danvers MA 01923

Call Sign: KB1BYI
James E Malionek
53 Adams St
Danvers MA 01923

Call Sign: WB2OVQ
Michael H Dawes
20 Alden St
Danvers MA 01923

Call Sign: KB1FPG
Michael H Dawes
20 Alden St
Danvers MA 01923

Call Sign: KB1GTI
Garry H Macdonald
3 Andover St
Danvers MA 01923

Call Sign: KA1EFM
James A Blanton
260 Andover St
Danvers MA
019231359

Call Sign: N1FLS
Alexander F Robb
267 Andover St
Danvers MA 01923

Call Sign: KB1KTJ
Colin A Campbell
353 Andover St
Danvers MA
019231346

Call Sign: W1CAC
Colin A Campbell
353 Andover St
Danvers MA
019231346

Call Sign: WA1AVC
Blake E Lloyd
111 Ash St
Danvers MA
019232727

Call Sign: KB1QKL

Heather E Tamilio
35 Bay View Terr 3
Danvers MA 01923

Call Sign: W1NKS
Heather E Tamilio
35 Bay View Terr 3
Danvers MA 01923

Call Sign: NE1X
Wlliam E Harding Sr
1 Belgian Rd
Danvers MA 01923

Call Sign: W1ZH
Richard L Gagnon Sr
12 Bradley Rd
Danvers MA
019233434

Call Sign: KB1JFV
John H Lang Jr
71 Bradstreet Ave
Danvers MA 01923

Call Sign: WB1FTK
Norman E Berry
15 Braman St
Danvers MA 01923

Call Sign: KA1RKW
Michael Rollnik
11 Bridge St Apt 2
Danvers MA 01923

Call Sign: KA1RKV
Holger Matzke
11 Bridge St Apt 3
Danvers MA 01923

Call Sign: AA1NN
Dana K Martin
98 Burley St
Danvers MA 01923

Call Sign: W1OPP
Charles H Dinsmore
14 Cabot Rd
Danvers MA 01923

Call Sign: KB1AZT
George M Putnam Jr
19 Cabot St
Danvers MA 01923

Call Sign: KX1N
Richard E Caldarone
21 Carolyn Dr
Danvers MA 01923

Call Sign: N1ACX
Raymond L Mac Neil
28 Central Ave
Danvers MA
019232908

Call Sign: KB1SCM
Jamie Stillings
7 Cherry St
Danvers MA 01923

Call Sign: W1YYJ
Horace A Snow
22 Cherry St
Danvers MA 01923

Call Sign: W1ZVU
Marian V Snow
22 Cherry St
Danvers MA 01923

Call Sign: KB1GCN
Lisa M Loreti
16 Choate Ave
Danvers MA 01923

Call Sign: KB1GGW
Alex E Howell
16 Choate Ave
Danvers MA 01923

Call Sign: WA1ZXB
Daniel I Rubin
18 Clark St
Danvers MA 01923

Call Sign: N1LWG
James J Crawford Iii
33 Clark St
Danver MA 01923

Call Sign: N1UZK
William K Hudson
44 Cohant St
Danvers MA 01923

Call Sign: N1DXK
Kenneth O Straney

118 Conant St
Danvers MA 01923

Call Sign: WZ1G
Joseph R Connolly
123 Conant St
Danvers MA 01923

Call Sign: N1HMT
Laurent J Bedard Jr
155 Conant St
Danvers MA 01923

Call Sign: K1WL
Warren P Lovell Jr
220 Conant St Apt 232
Danvers MA
019232588

Call Sign: KA1SXG
Gwen E Scottgale
47 Coolidge Rd
Danvers MA
019232360

Call Sign: N1VIY
Thomas N Scottgale
47 Coolidge Rd
Danvers MA
019232360

Call Sign: KA1OMF
Richard N Amnott
16 Cottage Ave
Danvers MA 01923

Call Sign: KB1FLC
Richard N Amnott
16 Cottage Ave
Danvers MA 01923

Call Sign: KB1UAD
Rose M Mahon
141 Dayton St
Danvers MA 01923

Call Sign: K1MXU
James A Steen
148 Dayton St
Danvers MA 01923

Call Sign: K1YXS
Beatrice C Carp
409 Ferncroft Tower

Danvers MA 01923

Call Sign: KT1V
J Stanley Carp
409 Ferncroft Tower
Danvers MA 01923

Call Sign: KB1MHA
Judith L Martel
13 Foster St
Danvers MA 01923

Call Sign: KB1MKJ
George W Martel
13 Foster St
Danvers MA 01923

Call Sign: N1AAZ
R Geoffrey Caldarone
18 Foxrun Rd
Danvers MA 01923

Call Sign: KB1SIF
James L Kingsley
17 Franklin St
Danvers MA 01923

Call Sign: W1CWU
James W Tumelty
2 Hickory Ln
Danvers MA 01923

Call Sign: KB1GCD
Mary K Baldini
70 High St
Danvers MA
019233147

Call Sign: N1WLK
Edwin J Wilkins
146 High St
Danvers MA 01923

Call Sign: KF6AIR
Kimberly A Mc
Murray Cathcart
21 Highland Meadows
Danvers MA 01923

Call Sign: N1USY
Carla M Van
Bennekom
35 Holton St
Danvers MA 01923

Call Sign: K1MOJ
Peter R Lovell
9 Innis Dr
Danvers MA
019231620

Call Sign: N1OQX
Andrew F Garrity Jr
4 Iroquois Rd
Danvers MA 01923

Call Sign: KA1RNQ
Eric J Rybicki
4 Kimball Ave
Danvers MA 01923

Call Sign: KB1UWM
Phyllis A Linane
2213 Kirkbride Dr 213
Danvers MA 01923

Call Sign: N1QGK
David R Gagnon
4 Lantern Lane
Danvers MA 01923

Call Sign: KA1DFO
Robert A Mc Leod
34 Ledgewood Dr
Danvers MA 01923

Call Sign: WA1RM
Robert A Mc Leod
34 Ledgewood Dr
Danvers MA 01923

Call Sign: KB1AZQ
Julie E Theiling
10 Lindall St
Danvers MA 01923

Call Sign: K1DFD
Gerald A Clark
64 Lindall St
Danvers MA 01923

Call Sign: N1QNJ
Beatrix M Clark
64 Lindall St
Danvers MA 01923

Call Sign: N1UGM
Mark A Caron

Linden Dr
Danvers MA 01923

Call Sign: KB1UWO
Gregg A Perry
87 Locust St
Danvers MA 01923

Call Sign: KB1RDU
David R Leblanc
92 Locust St
Danvers MA 01923

Call Sign: W1DLB
David R Leblanc
92 Locust St
Danvers MA 01923

Call Sign: N1EUC
Chester Macko
18 Loris Rd
Danvers MA
019231803

Call Sign: KB1FNI
Lawrence J Johnson
189 Maple St
Danvers MA
019232140

Call Sign: K2EBZ
Charles Wald
367 Maple St
Danvers MA 01923

Call Sign: KA1BNW
Daniel J Gingras
428 Maple St
Danvers MA 01923

Call Sign: N1DDP
Leonard T Lee
36 Mass Ave
Danvers MA 01923

Call Sign: KB1EAW
Matthew B Byrne
6 Mead St
Danvers MA
019232423

Call Sign: KA1PUC
Richard J Watson
21 Mello Pky

Danvers MA 01923

Call Sign: KB1PQC
David Juhola
10 Merrill St
Danvers MA 01923

Call Sign: W1JED
James H Power
15 Mildred Rd
Danvers MA 01923

Call Sign: NS1RA
Allan R Miller
15 Mohawk St
Danvers MA 01923

Call Sign: KB1ECP
Carl F Balsley Jr
6 Moulton Ter
Danvers MA 01923

Call Sign: NB1C
Carl F Balsley Jr
6 Moulton Ter
Danvers MA 01923

Call Sign: WA1ZOB
Angelo J Zakas
24 N Shetland Rd
Danvers MA 01923

Call Sign: W1MCC
William G Konos Sr
5 Neal Rd
Danvers MA
019231612

Call Sign: W1ZL
Nicholas G Konos
5 Neal Rd
Danvers MA 01923

Call Sign: K1GXG
Walter F Sorenson Sr
98 Newbury St 32a
Danvers MA 01923

Call Sign: AD5MW
Bernard G Lindsay
180 Newbury St Apt
2203
Danvers MA 01923

Call Sign: KH7MV
Donald R Speth
301 Newbury St
Danver MA 01923

Call Sign: WA1FPT
Lawrence G
Boudreault
119 North St
Danvers MA 01923

Call Sign: K1MXV
John F Zimmermann
3 Park St
Danvers MA 01923

Call Sign: WK1A
John B Lojko
13 Patricia Rd
Danvers MA 01923

Call Sign: W1HJ
Richard A Lutes Jr
9 Perry Dr
Danvers MA 01923

Call Sign: N1JFZ
Marlene R Connolly
18 Pickering St
Danvers MA 01923

Call Sign: WA1EAM
William G Drown
148 Pine St
Danvers MA 01923

Call Sign: KA1LQX
Mark C Hannon
6 Pond St
Danvers MA 01923

Call Sign: KB1UTQ
Henry R Dupuis Jr
10 Popes Ln
Danvers MA 01923

Call Sign: K1HRD
Henry R Dupuis Jr
10 Popes Ln
Danvers MA 01923

Call Sign: KB1GTJ
Timothy P Rider
7 Prince Place

Danvers MA 01923

Call Sign: WB1HAH
Burton Rubin
12 Princeton St
Danvers MA 01923

Call Sign: W1KPI
Richard L Moroni
5 R Bradstreet Ave
Danvers MA 01923

Call Sign: KB1CMH
Richard L Moroni
5 R Broadstreet Ave
Danvers MA 01923

Call Sign: N1GFX
Priscilla M Lindhout
3 Rainbow Terrace
Danvers MA 01923

Call Sign: N1GFY
Carol A Parsons
3 Rainbow Terrace
Danvers MA 01923

Call Sign: W1RLJ
Earle W Lymburner
4 Ralph Rd
Danvers MA 01923

Call Sign: N1HWA
Phillip E Knight
5 Ralph Rd
Danvers MA 01923

Call Sign: KB1EZM
Janna L Knight
5 Ralph Rd
Danvers MA 01923

Call Sign: WC1AAY
Danvers Mass Civil
Defense
4 Regent Dr
Danvers MA
019231617

Call Sign: W1UCF
Phillip J Campbell
12 Reservoir Dr
Danvers MA 01923

Call Sign: W1WFV
Neil F Dunn
5 Richards St
Danvers MA
019232104

Call Sign: N1IEQ
Tabitha L Carty
River Drive Apt 13b
Danvers MA 01923

Call Sign: KB1LNP
Daniel F Driscoll
9 Roman Ave
Danvers MA 01923

Call Sign: W1RAL
William J Sutherland
Jr
35 Roosevelt Ave
Danvers MA 01923

Call Sign: N1NGX
Earl W Almon
5 Shawmut Ave
Danvers MA 01923

Call Sign: W1EWA
Earl W Almon
5 Shawmut Ave
Danvers MA 01923

Call Sign: AA1OA
Neil E Henden
10 Shawmut Ave
Danvers MA 01923

Call Sign: N1ANV
Barbara A Skinner
7 Sheffield Rd
Danvers MA 01923

Call Sign: N1IQY
Daniel R Kelly
53 Sherwood
Danvers MA
019232322

Call Sign: W1HXO
Harvey L Chew
18 Shetland Rd
Danvers MA 01923

Call Sign: N1TBH

Robert P Dyserinck
50 Spring St
Danvers MA
019231545

Call Sign: W3GEE
George W Robinson
162 Summer St
Danvers MA 01923

Call Sign: N1RZR
Gregory S Woo
13 Sylvan St
Danvers MA
019232735

Call Sign: N1VTY
Brendan G Woo
13 Sylvan St
Danvers MA 01923

Call Sign: KB1FLH
Matthew Chaves
4 Tomahawk Lane
Danvers MA 01923

Call Sign: W1CKY
Matthew Chaves
4 Tomahawk Lane
Danvers MA 01923

Call Sign: WA1LIB
Edward Bornstein
19 Trask St
Danvers MA 01923

Call Sign: KB1LPX
Brian D Edmonds
6 Venice St Unit C6
Danvers MA 01923

Call Sign: K1LQN
Thomas E Persson
9 Wadsworth St
Danvers MA 01923

Call Sign: KA1SBR
Thomas C O Brien
15 Wellesley Rd
Danvers MA 01923

Call Sign: K1AFS
Thaddeus L Litchfield
9 Wellesly Rd

Danvers MA 01923

Call Sign: W1DX
Thaddeus L Litchfield
9 Wellesly Rd
Danvers MA 01923

Call Sign: W1VVY
Charles E Coffin
8 Whitfield Rd
Danvers MA 01923

Call Sign: K1LVV
Bruce A Birnie
15 Wildwood Rd
Danvers MA 01923

**FCC Amateur Radio
Licenses in
Dartmouth**

Call Sign: N1YCQ
Wheat K Kelley
14 Azalea Drive
Dartmouth MA
027475801

Call Sign: WB2ITX
Howard E Michel
45 Christine Dr
Dartmouth MA 02747

Call Sign: W1AEC
Southeastern Mass
Amat Rad Assn
54 Donald St
Dartmouth MA 02748

Call Sign: KB1ODF
Marcel L Dumont
17 Elizabeth Court
Dartmouth MA
027474046

Call Sign: W1MLD
Marcel L Dumont
17 Elizabeth Court
Dartmouth MA
027474046

Call Sign: KB1HFA
James M Aisenberg
424 Elm St
Dartmouth MA 02748

Call Sign: KB1JNI
Kathryn M Aisenberg
424 Elm St
Dartmouth MA 02748

Call Sign: KB1PTF
Raymond W Pease
465 Faunce Corner Rd
Dartmouth MA 02747

Call Sign: KA1WPH
Shawn S Goldstein
1116 Fisher Rd
Dartmouth MA 02747

Call Sign: W1VRP
Joseph P Frois
62 Huntington Ave
Dartmouth MA 02747

Call Sign: KB1FYS
Brian S Parent
1 Mary Crapo Way
Dartmouth MA 02748

Call Sign: KB1NZD
South Coastal Ma
Amateur Radio Group
24 Mishawum Dr
Dartmouth MA
027481213

Call Sign: W1RJC
Richard J Cabral
24 Mishawum Drive
Dartmouth MA
027481213

Call Sign: N1ETF
Stanley M Mickelson
17 Northfield Ln
Dartmouth MA 02747

Call Sign: KB1ODE
Marc M Dumont
16 Paul Rd
Dartmouth MA 02747

Call Sign: KB1VKU
Timothy J Klatt
53 Pinette St
Dartmouth MA 02747

Call Sign: N1YCR
David J Aguiar
178 Russells Mills Rd
Dartmouth MA 02748

Call Sign: KA1AW
Edward M Blouin
18 Seminole Rd
Dartmouth MA
027481259

Call Sign: W1EB
Edward M Blouin
18 Seminole Rd
Dartmouth MA
027481259

Call Sign: WB1ATO
John M Lima
46 Slades Corner Rd
Dartmouth MA 02714

Call Sign: KB1EBP
Christopher W White
64 Slocum Rd
Dartmouth MA 02747

Call Sign: WA1PLT
Donald A Mara
673 Tucker Rd
Dartmouth MA
027473576

Call Sign: KB1VKW
Michael L Dumont
288 W Mccabe St
Dartmouth MA 02747

Call Sign: N1XQL
Brian J Sladewski
8 Yankee Way
Dartmouth MA 02747

**FCC Amateur Radio
Licenses in Dedham**

Call Sign: KB1GNV
Carol A Campisano
93 Alden St
Dedham MA 02026

Call Sign: KB1URM
Joseph V Foppiano
30 Autumn Ln

Dedham MA 02026

Call Sign: KB1SAL
Roney Hawat
84 Booth Rd
Dedham MA 02026

Call Sign: W1LYL
Ralph L Berry
103 Brookdale Ave
Dedham MA 02026

Call Sign: WC1AAM
Dedham Civil
Preparedness Agency
103 Brookdale Ave
Dedham MA 02026

Call Sign: W1TLH
James M Tessitore
97 Bullard Rd
Dedham MA 01026

Call Sign: W1OEX
Ralph S Hawkins
10 Care Matrix Dr
Dedham MA 02126

Call Sign: N1DDU
James J Walsh
366 Cedar St
Dedham MA
020263743

Call Sign: WA1ETL
John P Mitchell
42 Churchill Pl
Dedham MA 02026

Call Sign: W1UOK
Samuel Rubin
73 Chute Rd
Dedham MA 02026

Call Sign: WD8OMY
Joel I Wolfe
35 Circuit Rd
Dedham MA 02026

Call Sign: WA1CKV
Jerome C Sumner
28 Colburn St
Dedham MA 02026

Call Sign: WA1SUS
Francis J Ryan
14 Crane St
Dedham MA 02026

Call Sign: KA1YFQ
Anita B Giunchetto
20 Durham Rd
Dedham MA 02026

Call Sign: K1UPY
Philip F Henneberry
28 Durham Rd
Dedham MA 02026

Call Sign: KA1WKJ
David J Finitsis
651 East St
Dedham MA 02026

Call Sign: W1WU
Alfred J Schwartz
710 East St
Dedham MA 02026

Call Sign: K1JUN
Jeffrey S Morris
762 East St
Dedham MA 02026

Call Sign: N1CCV
Harry D Woodlee
56 Fay Rd
Dedham MA 02026

Call Sign: W1KN
Tufts University
Amateur Radio Club
54 Hermaine Ave
Dedham MA 02026

Call Sign: KB1QNJ
Michael A Hart
54 Hermaine Ave
Dedham MA 02026

Call Sign: AD1B
Thomas M Hart
54 Hermaine Ave
Dedham MA 02026

Call Sign: WA1PXT
Donald A Freeland
10 Highland St

Dedham MA
020265802

Call Sign: AF1DF
Donald A Freeland
10 Highland St
Dedham MA
020265802

Call Sign: KB1MBG
Michael T Torchio
26 Hobart St
Dedham MA
020264921

Call Sign: N1SBZ
Eugene F Favret
53 Hooper Rd
Dedham MA 02026

Call Sign: K1KUZ
Herbert C Garber
65 Hooper Rd
Dedham MA 02026

Call Sign: WA1MIX
George R Hoell
116 Kimball Rd
Dedham MA 02026

Call Sign: K1TOX
Edward W Mc Hugh
63 Lancaster Rd
Dedham MA 02026

Call Sign: W1JAJ
Arthur J Nolan
188 Madison St
Dedham MA 02026

Call Sign: N1AJO
Thomas E Child
158 Monroe St
Dedham MA 02026

Call Sign: WB1CDR
Harry R Mahoney
39 Oak Tree Rd
Dedham MA
020267104

Call Sign: W1BWX
David A O Brien
11 Oakdale Ave

Dedham MA 02026

Call Sign: W1FLB
Marshall F F Knox Jr
21 O'neil Dr Apt 202
Dedham MA
020262065

Call Sign: AC1P
Donald E Ericsson
4 Parkway Court
Dedham MA 02026

Call Sign: K1RZN
Roger P Macie
29 Paul St
Dedham MA 02026

Call Sign: KB1IUK
David A O Brien
26 Reed St
Dedham MA 02026

Call Sign: N1SLN
John C Keane
74 Reed St
Dedham MA 02026

Call Sign: KB1NAA
Michael M Reich
7 S Stone Mill Dr 514
Dedham MA 02026

Call Sign: KW1B
John H Nichols Jr
225 Schoolmaster Ln
Dedham MA 02026

Call Sign: W1JLI
Louis H Schall
60 Shiretown Rd
Dedham MA 02026

Call Sign: N1IAV
Jeanie G Doran
49 Sprague St
Dedham MA 02026

Call Sign: W1JQC
Gary P Brefini
136 Stoney Lea Rd
Dedham MA 02026

Call Sign: W1RHN

Edward R Spadoni
91 Tower St
Dedham MA 02026

Call Sign: K1TGB
Ernest C Reid
46 Turner St
Dedham MA 02026

Call Sign: N1WCP
Martin J Schofield
79 Turner St
Dedham MA 02026

Call Sign: KB1VYS
Douglas M Brown
225 Walnut St
Dedham MA 02026

Call Sign: WA1HBK
Francis J Lynch
1003 Washington St
Dedham MA
020266713

Call Sign: WB1GAP
Patrick J Coughlin
9 Washington St 6
Dedham MA 02026

Call Sign: KB1MJ
Paul J Levesque
14 Wesley St
Dedham MA 02026

Call Sign: N1IWS
Edward E Watts Iii
311 West St
Dedham MA 02026

Call Sign: N1MNZ
Ross E Sherbrooke
414 Westfield St
Dedham MA 02026

Call Sign: WA1JDQ
George B Cudd Sr
479 Westfield St
Dedham MA
020265634

Call Sign: KA1NNX
Thomas J White Jr
23 Worthington St

Dedham MA 02026

Call Sign: KB1NSQ
Peter Gow
32 Worthington St
Dedham MA 02026

Call Sign: KA1QXJ
Martin J Geoghegan
Dedham MA 02026

FCC Amateur Radio Licenses in Deerfield

Call Sign: W1SRB
Robert B Solosko
22 Greenough
Crossing
Deerfield MA 01342

Call Sign: N1ZPZ
Wesley K Mason
297 Lower Rd
Deerfield MA 01342

Call Sign: WG1H
Albert F Mason Iii
297 Lower Rd
Deerfield MA 01342

Call Sign: KB1WTQ
Carolyn S Ness
10 Old Albany Rd
Deerfield MA 01342

Call Sign: N1JJB
Eugene R Klos
372 River Rd
Deerfield MA 01342

Call Sign: N1PAE
Paul F Dahowski
222 State Rd
Deerfield MA 01342

Call Sign: KA1SBN
John F Dubino
33 Upper Rd
Deerfield MA 01342

Call Sign: N1OMH
Edward V Hammond
Deerfield MA 01342

FCC Amateur Radio Licenses in Dennis

Call Sign: W1HHE
Wilson B Scofield
24 Bismark Way
Dennis MA 02638

Call Sign: WA1AOH
Robert L Motroni
66 Capt Prestons Rd
Dennis MA 02638

Call Sign: K1PQB
Robert F Quinlan
11 Erb Dr
Dennis MA 02638

Call Sign: W1CS
Spencer S Dodd Jr
50 Fieldstone Dr
Dennis MA 02638

Call Sign: WA1VWD
Robert F Foley
42 Grassy Pond Dr
Dennis MA 02638

Call Sign: KB1TLS
Sean M Mahoney
11 Independence Way
Dennis MA 02638

Call Sign: KB1TLT
Michael J Mahoney
11 Independence Way
Dennis MA 02638

Call Sign: N1JCI
Jean Braun
65 Long Hill Rd
Dennis MA 02638

Call Sign: W2RKB
Harry V N Braun
65 Long Hill Rd
Dennis MA 02638

Call Sign: KQ1K
Robert M Baker
469 Main St
Dennis MA 02638

Call Sign: KA1LQQ

Richard J Blaha
179 Nobscussett Rd
Dennis MA 02638

Call Sign: K2BAE
David A Dossin
62 Packet Dr
Dennis MA 02638

Call Sign: KB1THZ
David J Serloco
60 Pilgrim Rd
Dennis MA 02638

Call Sign: KB2YPM
Eric N Sheffer
71 Robbins Circle
Dennis MA 02638

Call Sign: N3JIR
Robert A Latimer
37 Run Pond Rd
Dennis MA 026382236

Call Sign: K1LKI
Robert S Bunar
22 Sassafras Rd
Dennis MA 02638

Call Sign: KB1UZW
Peter D Howes
58 Scarsdale Rd
Dennis MA 02638

Call Sign: W2YYS
Gregory J Mc Cauliff
44 Sou West Dr
Dennis MA 02638

FCC Amateur Radio Licenses in Dennisport

Call Sign: WB1ARO
Frank Lamparelli
31 Birch Hill Rd Box 1156
Dennis Port MA 02639

Call Sign: K1WT
Wallace C Turzyn
40 North St
Dennis Port MA 02639

Call Sign: WA1BEN
Alfred W Rebenklau
25 Upper County Rd
Dennis Port MA 02639

Call Sign: W1FYB
David W Swanson
101 Depot St
Dennisport MA 02639

Call Sign: KE6IDC
Nancy D Mather
33 Longell Rd
Dennisport MA 02639

Call Sign: AG0P
Theodore M Mather Jr
33 Longell Rd
Dennisport MA 02639

Call Sign: W1AQN
Jackson R Hibbert
24 South St
Dennisport MA 02639

Call Sign: WA1HWZ
Roger G Edwards
221 Upper County Rd
Dennisport MA 02639

Call Sign: N1JCR
William A Haskins
Dennisport MA 02639

FCC Amateur Radio Licenses in Dighton

Call Sign: KA1UHX
Manuel M Aguiar
1730 Cedar St
Dighton MA 02715

Call Sign: N1RHE
Nicholas J Biello
2113 County St Apt 1
Dighton MA 02715

Call Sign: N1DFD
Nicholas J Biello
2113 County St Apt 1
Dighton MA 02715

Call Sign: KA1RTN
Mark J Ready

1651 Elm St
Dighton MA 02715

Call Sign: N1ELF
James J Ready
1651 Elm St
Dighton MA 02715

Call Sign: KD1WT
Russell G James
1836 Elm St
Dighton MA 02715

Call Sign: WB1GYX
Nelson H Moore
221 Park Ave By63
Dighton MA 02715

Call Sign: KA1UDD
James R Varley
1247 Somerset Ave
Dighton MA 02715

Call Sign: KB5YND
David P Munding Jr
Dighton MA 02715

FCC Amateur Radio Licenses in Dorchester

Call Sign: N1XJC
David M Neely
2 A Pope's Hill St
Dorchester MA 02122

Call Sign: K1GQE
Patrick H Nugent
725 Adams
Dorchester MA 02122

Call Sign: KB1BEM
Isaac E Weekes
50 Alpha Rd
Dorchester MA 02124

Call Sign: N1QLS
Gregory C Richardson
496 Ashmont St
Dorchester MA 02122

Call Sign: N1VQY
Priscilla A Richardson
496 Ashmont St

Dorchester MA 02122

Call Sign: W1NF
Ralph E Benson
2 Barna Rd
Dorchester MA 02124

Call Sign: KB2MBD
Avrom W Smith
80 Beaumont St Apt 102
Dorchester MA 02124

Call Sign: KB1FXD
James F Sullivan
8 Brent St
Dorchester MA 02124

Call Sign: KA1TAN
Jeffrey J Klein
123 Cushing Ave
Dorchester MA 02125

Call Sign: N1KMK
Robert Clark
1392 Dorchester Ave
Dorchester MA 02122

Call Sign: K1PLX
Dennis E Mc Cormack
30 Dorset St
Dorchester MA 02125

Call Sign: N1MHD
John T Connolly
76 Downer Ave
Dorchester MA 02125

Call Sign: N3KRB
David M Dwiggins
65 Draper St #1
Dorchester MA 02122

Call Sign: W1KHP
Robert E Van Annan
337 Gallivan Blvd
Dorchester MA 02124

Call Sign: N1HKA
Call Sign: KB1OHQ
Jose Nova
165 Glenway St
Dorchester MA 02121

Call Sign: KA1KEP
James J Nicholson
23 Hamilton St
Dorchester MA 02125

Call Sign: N1WYP
Thomas L Peeples Sr
115 Harrishof St
Dorchester MA 02121

Call Sign: KB1WJN
Ahkym B Corbin
58 Holworthy St Apt 1
Dorchester MA 02121

Call Sign: KB1NXY
Lestroy A Brown
-5 Inwood St
Dorchester MA 02125

Call Sign: KB1RUQ
Jose A Velazquez
19 Irma St 3
Dorchester MA 02124

Call Sign: KE1L
Mark J Dulcey
24 Kenwood St
Dorchester MA
021242212

Call Sign: KB1LWR
Jose R Ulloa
23 Leroy St
Dorchester MA 02122

Call Sign: WC1Z
Robert J Williams Sr
31 Mayhew St
Dorchester MA 02125

Call Sign: WB3LEK
Mark Eisenberg
18 Melville Ave
Dorchester MA 02124

Call Sign: KB1HFK
Richard M Harris
40 Melville Ave
Dorchester MA 02124

Call Sign: KB1GQK
Joseph Juliano
6 Mill St Apt 2

Dorchester MA
021223517

Call Sign: N1HBX
Robert A Hayes
2 Moultrie St
Dorchester MA 02124

Call Sign: KA1LWF
Joseph E Giroux Jr
335 Norfolk Ave
Dorchester MA 02125

Call Sign: KB1HAD
Sarah Salter
19 Peverell St Apt 1
Dorchester MA
021252056

Call Sign: N1HTG
Mary F Murray
19 Regan Rd
Dorchester MA 02124

Call Sign: KB1IQE
Derek M Tobin
51 Sagamore St
Dorchester MA 02125

Call Sign: N1LRU
Norman W Green
11 Selden St
Dorchester MA 02124

Call Sign: K1TUR
Thomas M Corbett
2 Shenandoah St
Dorchester MA 02124

Call Sign: KB2NDQ
Scott M Queipo
37 South Munroe Ter
#3
Dorchester MA 02122

Call Sign: KA1JXM
Francis F Jandreau
18 South Munroe Terr
Dorchester MA 02122

Call Sign: N1ALF
Francis A Baker
176 Sydney St

Dorchester MA
021251257

Call Sign: N1JXY
Edward Doherty
10 Thelma Rd
Dorchester MA 02122

Call Sign: KC1ZI
James Worrell
25 Vaughan Ave
Dorchester MA 02121

Call Sign: KA1ZNL
Steven R Carlson
10 W Bellflower St
Dorchester MA 02125

Call Sign: WB1FRB
George Pinckney
495 Warren St
Dorchester MA 02121

Call Sign: KB1DZG
Nivaldo Stival
11 Wayne St
Dorchester MA 02121

Call Sign: W1SFV
Earl A Smith
7 Westglow St
Dorchester MA 02122

Call Sign: K1LCQ
Joseph F O Brien
31 Westglow St
Dorchester MA 02122

Call Sign: N1VUX
William D Ricker
226 Westville St
Dorchester MA 02122

Call Sign: KB1LNX
Louisa R Ricker
226 Westville St
Dorchester MA 02122

Call Sign: WR1S
William J Gallant
40 Westwind Rd Apt
604
Dorchester MA
021253510

Call Sign: N1GBF
Trevor V Comma
39 Wilcock St
Dorchester MA 02124

Call Sign: KB8YRC
Austin M Sutphin
145 Wrentham St
Dorchester MA 02124

Call Sign: KB1TTF
Richard E Williamson
Dorchester MA 02122

FCC Amateur Radio Licenses in Dorchester Center

Call Sign: W1LRY
James L Brown
2 Centervale Park
Dorchester Center MA
02124

FCC Amateur Radio Licenses in Douglas

Call Sign: N1SGD
David M Vergilis
15 Brookside Dr
Douglas MA 01516

Call Sign: KB1WPD
James K Fisher
11 Churchill Rd
Douglas MA 01516

Call Sign: KB1GIV
John C Snay
20 Cook St
Douglas MA 01516

Call Sign: KB1JHT
Robert K Mccann
1 Crescent Ln
Douglas MA 01516

Call Sign: KB1NMN
Matthew J Picanso
56 Davis St
Douglas MA 01516

Call Sign: KB1UDV

Andrew R Allard
9 Elm St
Douglas MA 01516

Call Sign: WA1NYV
William R Smith
56 Locust St
Douglas MA 01516

Call Sign: KB1EPB
Amanda M Smith
56 Locust St
Douglas MA
015162440

Call Sign: KB1EPC
Charles W Smith
56 Locust St
Douglas MA
015162440

Call Sign: W1OW
William R Smith
56 Locust St
Douglas MA 01516

Call Sign: W7AMS
Amanda M Smith
56 Locust St
Douglas MA
015162440

Call Sign: W7CWS
Charles W Smith
56 Locust St
Douglas MA
015162440

Call Sign: WB1FRP
John R Baca
45 Manchaug St
Douglas MA 01516

Call Sign: KB1KZR
Cynthia A Blondin
169 Martin Rd
Douglas MA 01516

Call Sign: N1CMH
Johannes A Bloemen
132 Nw Main St
Douglas MA
015162022

Call Sign: KA1SQA
Debra Mac Gregor
654 Nw Main St
Douglas MA 01516

Call Sign: KB1DXN
Amy C Nichols
101 Pine St
Douglas MA 01516

Call Sign: AA2S
William R Michalson
Po Box 673
Douglas MA 01516

Call Sign: N1TQ
Thomas L Qualtieri
4 Pond St
Douglas MA 01516

Call Sign: KB1JZK
Jeanne E Ridge
4 Pond St
Douglas MA 01516

Call Sign: N1JQ
Jeanne E Ridge
4 Pond St
Douglas MA 01516

Call Sign: N1QNO
Gerald G Bliss Jr
15 Riedell St
Douglas MA 01516

Call Sign: KB1WXE
Michael F O'brien
21 Royal Crest Drive
Douglas MA 01516

Call Sign: N1SMT
John P Moran
54 Se Main St
Douglas MA 01516

Call Sign: KB1DXO
Carl E Milton
350 Se Main St
Douglas MA 01516

Call Sign: W1QLF
Brandon N Auger
62 South St
Douglas MA 01516

Call Sign: N1VPI
Linda M Boothby
117 South St
Douglas MA 01516

Call Sign: KB1JFG
William Drew
311 South St
Douglas MA 01516

Call Sign: KB1NLI
Anthony J Valliere
24 Wallum Lake Rd
Douglas MA 01516

Call Sign: K1LDZ
Charles M Cheney
38 Wallum Lake Rd
Douglas MA 01516

Call Sign: W1WRS
Wayne R Shade
79 Webster Rd
Douglas MA 01516

Call Sign: N1NKT
Martha J Adams
50 Yew St
Douglas MA 01516

Call Sign: KE1IJ
Karen A Michalson
Douglas MA
015160673

Call Sign: KB1KZQ
John E Blondin
Douglas MA 01516

**FCC Amateur Radio
Licenses in Dover**

Call Sign: KB1KTK
Matthew E Mcneely Jr
29 Bretton Rd
Dover MA 02030

Call Sign: K1MCN
Matthew E Mcneely Jr
29 Bretton Rd
Dover MA 02030

Call Sign: WA1WER

John H Chapman
5 Brook Rd
Dover MA 02030

Call Sign: KB1HTV
Brenda Free
5 Centre St
Dover MA 02030

Call Sign: KB1NTJ
Theodore H Reimann
39 Draper Rd
Dover MA 02030

Call Sign: KB1PFS
Kurt H Reimann
39 Draper Rd
Dover MA 02030

Call Sign: AB1QG
William K Stewart
10 Glen St
Dover MA 02030

Call Sign: K5KEM
William K Stewart
10 Glen St
Dover MA 02030

Call Sign: KB1FHC
Douglas Garde
Hartford St
Dover MA 02030

Call Sign: KB1FHF
Ruth L Hill
Hartford St
Dover MA 02030

Call Sign: KB1WCF
John D French
8 Main St
Dover MA 02030

Call Sign: KB1KDJ
Walter E Clark
40 Main St
Dover MA 02030

Call Sign: W1WEC
Walter E Clark
40 Main St
Dover MA 02030

Call Sign: N1CHM
Thomas A Larson
85 Main St
Dover MA 02030

Call Sign: N1DAC
Sean A Wall
9 Old Meadow Rd
Dover MA 02030

Call Sign: KB1HTP
James R Repetti
14 Old Meadow Rd
Dover MA 02030

Call Sign: AB1AC
James R Repetti
14 Old Meadow Rd
Dover MA 02030

Call Sign: WJ1R
James R Repetti
14 Old Meadow Rd
Dover MA 02030

Call Sign: N1PYL
John F Sugden Jr
33 Pine St
Dover MA 02030

Call Sign: K2GP
Gordon H Piper
5 Pond St
Dover MA 02030

Call Sign: WB1EBS
Juris G Alksnitis
10 Rocky Brook Rd
Dover MA 02030

Call Sign: W1TIS
Bruce P Tis
20 Rocky Brook Rd
Dover MA 020302444

Call Sign: W1NWR
Kenneth T Lang
22 Rocky Brook Rd
Dover MA 02030

Call Sign: KA1VWF
Charles A Winans
15 Rolling Ln
Dover MA 02030

Call Sign: W1GAF
John H Sims
14 Tower Dr
Dover MA 02030

Call Sign: N1ENQ
Ruth J Connolly
20 Tubwreck Dr
Dover MA 02030

Call Sign: N1KJE
Donald D Hogg
12 Wakeland Rd
Dover MA 02030

Call Sign: W7CUT
Carleton G Lorig
65 Wilsondale St
Dover MA 02030

Call Sign: WA3RBN
Gary S Ambrosino
22 Yorkshire Rd
Dove MA 02030

Call Sign: W1EFV
Richard P Doyle
Dover MA 02030

Call Sign: K1PYI
Tobe C Deutschmann
Jr
Dover MA 02030

Call Sign: N1FR
Tobe C Deutschmann
Jr
Dover MA 02030

Call Sign: W1DG
Tobe C Deutschmann
Jr
Dover MA 02030

Call Sign: W1AT
Tobe C Deutschmann
Jr
Dover MA 02030

Call Sign: KB1GZH
Jon R Cave
Dover MA 02030

Call Sign: KB1JRV
Thomas J Repetti
Dover MA 02030

Call Sign: KB1JZV
Jack I London
Dover MA 020300265

Call Sign: W1JIL
Jack I London
Dover MA 020300265

Call Sign: KB1UHI
Brigitte A Berman
Dover MA 02030

Call Sign: KB1VYF
Alastair Bastian
Dover MA 02030

FCC Amateur Radio
Licenses in Dracut

Call Sign: KA1LKZ
Stephen J Kondziolka
8 A St
Dracut MA 01826

Call Sign: KB1DJC
Roberto S Machado
83 A St
Dracut MA 018265053

Call Sign: KA1GWV
Stephen M La Bella
21 Apple Blossom
Drive
Dracut MA 01826

Call Sign: KD1ZC
Marcel J Lamoureux
235 Arlington St
Dracut MA 01826

Call Sign: WB1DMN
Lucien J Asselin
17 B St
Dracut MA 01826

Call Sign: N1IGX
Mark H Litchfield
73 Bancroft St
Dracut MA 01826

Call Sign: N1INU
Robert Wroblewski
32 Barton Ave
Dracut MA 01826

Call Sign: W1PKC
Frank Blanchette
263 Bouchard Ave
Dracut MA 01826

Call Sign: WA1UER
Jean B Ippolito
1807 Bridge
Dracuf MA 01826

Call Sign: WB1BQC
Alan A Anganes
54 Camden St
Dracut MA 01826

Call Sign: WB1GEA
Susan J Anganes
54 Camden St
Dracut MA 018265718

Call Sign: KB1EIR
Andrew A Anganes
54 Camden St
Dracut MA 01826

Call Sign: KB1KNJ
Charles R Anganes
54 Camden St
Dracut MA 01826

Call Sign: KB1JUD
Bertus Weijers
78 Cottonwood Dr
Dracut MA 01826

Call Sign: K1OTH
Bertus Weijers
78 Cottonwood Dr
Dracut MA 01826

Call Sign: N1QN
Bertus Weijers
78 Cottonwood Dr
Dracut MA 01826

Call Sign: KB1MZZ
Brian P Daniels
61 Donohoe Rd
Dracut MA 01826

Call Sign: AB1MI
Brian P Daniels
61 Donohoe Rd
Dracut MA 01826

Call Sign: W1TFZ
Edward T Flynn
38 Emerson Ave
Dracut MA 01826

Call Sign: WB1GCD
David B Brown Sr
114 Fanning Ave
Dracut MA 01826

Call Sign: KB1HMS
Donna M Arcand
15 Fay Lane
Dracut MA 01826

Call Sign: W1WRA
William R Arcand
15 Fay Ln
Dracut MA 01826

Call Sign: KB1WWM
Thomas J Tremblay
60 Florry Drive Unit
20
Dracut MA 01826

Call Sign: KA1TTC
Laurie L Snyder
37 Fox Ave
Dracut MA 01826

Call Sign: KB1SYR
Brett N Rogers
56 Goodhue Ave
Dracut MA 01826

Call Sign: N1ALO
Peter L Norden
28 Greenridge Rd
Dracut MA 01826

Call Sign: KB1WIT
Corey A Hudson
136 Haverhill St
Dracut MA 01826

Call Sign: KB1PNU
Kendra R Jendro

24 Hillcrest Rd
Dracut MA 01826

Call Sign: KB1PNV
James N Jendro
24 Hillcrest Rd
Dracut MA 01826

Call Sign: KA1QCL
Jon A Marchand
28 Joseph Ave
Dracut MA 01826

Call Sign: K1CGJ
Jon A Marchand
28 Joseph Ave
Dracut MA 018265762

Call Sign: N1NHJ
Marcel J Jussaume
24 Keating Lane
Dracut MA 018261369

Call Sign: K8WVG
James L Jendro
135 Kenwood Rd
Dracut MA 01826

Call Sign: N1GUG
Kevin E Viera
50 Linden St
Dracut MA 01826

Call Sign: N1ZLB
Gary S Wooster Jr
89 Long Dr
Dracut MA 01826

Call Sign: KA1QBP
Vadim Schaldenko
15 Maria Ave
Dracut MA 01826

Call Sign: KA1QBQ
Diane F Schaldenko
15 Maria Ave
Dracut MA 01826

Call Sign: KN1T
Manfred A Matthews
35 Maria Ave
Dracut MA 01826

Call Sign: KB5AIS

Guy D Theodore Jr
100 Merrimack Ave
Unit 154
Dracut MA 01826

Call Sign: WA1LGY
Esther M Brown
59 Mill St 303
Dracut MA 018263248

Call Sign: W1YLO
Daniel A Bunce
146 Montaup Ave
Dracut MA 01826

Call Sign: KB1WOB
Daniel J Eno
73 Newbury St
Dracut MA 01826

Call Sign: KA1QYO
Francis E Bingham
15 O St
Dracut MA 01826

Call Sign: KA1HOY
David A Haggerty
49 Parker Ave Apt 13
Dracut MA 01826

Call Sign: WA1DTC
Germain L Bellemare
145 Passaconaway Dr
Dracut MA 01826

Call Sign: KA1AHT
Barbara A Flynn
204 Pleasant St #10-4
Dracut MA 01826

Call Sign: KB1CUL
Robert P Beatty
28 Poppy Ln
Dracut MA 01826

Call Sign: K1RC
John C Marchand
28 Prides Crossing Rd
Dracut MA 018262938

Call Sign: KB1GKF
Sean Saniuk
6 Rachel Rd
Dracut MA 01826

Call Sign: KA1LHA
Philip J Christian
8 Radcliff Rd
Dracut MA 01826

Call Sign: W1BJ
Paul F Mc Caffrey
13 Rebecca Ln
Dracut MA 018262590

Call Sign: N1YOQ
William R Granfield
93 Richardson Ave
Dracut MA 01826

Call Sign: KB1VUU
Robert K Wood
665 Robbins Ave Unit
3
Dracut MA 01826

Call Sign: KB1BKD
Charles P Alexander
189 Saw Mill Dr
Dracut MA 01826

Call Sign: KA1WSD
Paul W Rancourt
1030 Skyline Dr
Dracut MA 01826

Call Sign: N1CJE
Robert N Giffin
195 Sladen St
Dracut MA 01826

Call Sign: KB1HWU
Michael J Murphy
408 Sladen St
Dracut MA 01826

Call Sign: KB1SAI
William R Paquin
254 Sparks St
Dracut MA 01826

Call Sign: AA1RX
Lionel J Arsenault
27 Stonebridge Dr
Dracut MA 01826

Call Sign: N1MBV
Michelle M Martin

21 Superior Ave
Dracut MA 018263819

Call Sign: WK1V
James J Martin Jr
21 Superior Ave
Dracut MA 018263819

Call Sign: W6ZF
James J Martin Jr
21 Superior Ave
Dracut MA 018263819

Call Sign: WK1V
James J Martin Jr
21 Superior Ave
Dracut MA 018263819

Call Sign: W6ZF
James J Martin Jr
21 Superior Ave
Dracut MA 018263819

Call Sign: W1KQ
James J Martin Jr
21 Superior Ave
Dracut MA 018263819

Call Sign: N1QFB
Larry C Garneau Jr
94 Tennis Plaza Rd 31
Dracut MA 01826

Call Sign: KB1NYS
Andrew M Davenport
141 Thissell Av 11
Dracut MA 01826

Call Sign: KB1LJZ
James W Russell
114 Trout Brook Rd
Dracut MA 01826

Call Sign: WB1FRH
Robert E Corey
365 Tyngsboro Rd
Dracut MA 01826

Call Sign: KA1IKK
Stephen W York
330 Tyngsboro Rd
Dracut MA 01826

Call Sign: N1YJT

John D Messer
130 Varnum Rd
Dracut MA 018263030

Call Sign: KB1MDP
Kevin R Tucker
705 Wheeler Rd
Dracut MA 01826

Call Sign: KB1UKU
Russell Graves
Dracut MA 01826

FCC Amateur Radio Licenses in Drury

Call Sign: KB1UPN
Christopher R
Culpepper
56 South St
Drury MA 01343

Call Sign: N1EXF
Francis J Bergendahl
Drury MA 01343

FCC Amateur Radio Licenses in Dudley

Call Sign: K1ERB
Wayne T Kessler
1 Alton Dr
Dudley MA 01571

Call Sign: KB8VXF
Jerome M Skala
5 Ash Lane
Dudley MA 01571

Call Sign: N9XJY
Steven V Christensen
19 Ash Ln
Dudley MA
015713824

Call Sign: WA1VVS
Robert W
Ciabaszewski
148 Corbin Rd
Dudley MA
015716239

Call Sign: KA1KAC
William R Grovesteen

79 Cortis Rd
Dudley MA
015716811

Call Sign: K1GIS
Eugene C Jastrzebski
100 Dudley Oxford Rd
Dudley MA 01570

Call Sign: KA1SWI
Joseph B Mercier
10 Dudley Southbridge
Rd
Dudley MA
015716232

Call Sign: KB1MDG
Allen J Dumas
19 Fairview Ave
Dudley MA 01571

Call Sign: WA1ZXD
Ronald C Winslow
9 Hall Rd
Dudley MA 01571

Call Sign: W1PLH
Ronald C Winslow
9 Hall Rd
Dudley MA 01571

Call Sign: KB1MSP
Carl W Berger
34 Henry Marsh Rd
Dudley MA 01571

Call Sign: KB1CNV
Jeffrey A Miller
22 Jaybee Ave
Dudley MA 01571

Call Sign: KA1KVV
Lawrence K Doyle
39 June St
Dudley MA 01571

Call Sign: KB1FJR
Robert A Gallagher
7 Meadow Ln
Dudley MA
015713724

Call Sign: N1MQI
Thomas J Ladago

57 Mill Rd
Dudley MA 01571

Call Sign: KB1WTN
Donald C Wilson Jr
21 Mill St
Dudley MA 01571

Call Sign: N1FHA
Howard E Faneuf Jr
99 Ramshorn Rd
Dudley MA 01571

Call Sign: KE1JR
David R Stevens
158 Ramshorn Rd
Dudley MA 01571

Call Sign: N1OUT
Frank A Sampson
4 Saint Mary Ave
Dudley MA 01571

Call Sign: W1FAS
Frank A Sampson
4 Saint Mary Ave
Dudley MA 01571

Call Sign: KB1CLP
Kenneth R Kielinen
11 Sawmill Rd
Dudley MA 01571

Call Sign: K1ZBB
Ronald J Stachelek
5 School St
Dudley MA 01570

Call Sign: N1IJJ
Adam J Stachelek
5 School St
Dudley MA 01571

Call Sign: N1KYD
Amanda J Stachelek
5 School St
Dudley MA 01571

Call Sign: N1KYE
Juli Anne T Stachelek
5 School St
Dudley MA 01571

Call Sign: N1GPV

Michael M Barrette Sr
11 Sixth Ave
Dudley MA
015713458

Call Sign: N1TQM
Michael T Brodeur
7 Southbridge Rd
Dudley MA 01571

Call Sign: N1BEU
Donald A Baker Sr
146 W Main St
Dudley MA 01571

Call Sign: KB1TMS
Kevin Swanson
175 West Main St
Dudley MA 01571

Call Sign: N1IFC
Kenneth L Kendrick
Dudley MA
015711452

FCC Amateur Radio Licenses in Dunstable

Call Sign: KB1REJ
David F Spinosa
29 Century Way
Dunstable MA 01827

Call Sign: KB1CYT
Mark W Mc Donough
44 Century Way
Dunstable MA 01827

Call Sign: KB1OSH
Jeffrey Curtis
116 Century Way
Dunstable MA 01827

Call Sign: W1PAN
Carmen J Ferraro
641 Groton St
Dunstable MA 01827

Call Sign: AA1GZ
James P Kurdzo
166 Hall St
Dunstable MA
018272702

Call Sign: N1NKJ
Kathleen A Kurdzo
166 Hall St
Dunstable MA
018272702

Call Sign: KB1TSX
John W Cushion
141 Pond St
Dunstable MA 01827

Call Sign: WA1NWD
Cynthia B Sullivan
50 School St
Dunstable MA 01827

Call Sign: K1EFW
John L Heaton Iii
Westford St
Dunstable MA 01827

Call Sign: K1NLI
John F Elsbree Jr
Dunstable MA 01827

Call Sign: N1RKO
Mary Jane Sheldon
Dunstable MA 01827

Call Sign: NX1R
Thomas P Emery
Dunstable MA 01827

FCC Amateur Radio Licenses in Duxbury

Call Sign: W1RKS
Firmin J Bishop
32 Abrams Hill Rd
Duxbury MA 02332

Call Sign: KB1ILB
Donald G Gunster
190 Autumn
Duxbury MA 02332

Call Sign: N1ACN
Glenn A Brodie
331 Bay Rd
Duxbury MA 02331

Call Sign: K1TQ
H Walcott Brown Jr
511 Blackberry Path

Duxbury MA 02332

Call Sign: KA1RTB
Eric E Johnson
263 Bolas Rd
Duxbury MA 02332

Call Sign: K1JKA
George L Richards Ii
Box 1661
Duxbury MA 02332

Call Sign: N1GWA
Nina E Goodrich
66 Captains Hill Rd
Duxbury MA 02332

Call Sign: WT1Z
Carol D Neuger
286 Chandler St
Duxbury MA 02332

Call Sign: WU1B
Paul Neuger
286 Chandler St
Duxbury MA 02332

Call Sign: N1PN
Paul Neuger
286 Chandler St
Duxbury MA 02332

Call Sign: W1EQK
Arthur D Bradford
214 Chestnut
Duxbury MA 02332

Call Sign: WA1IAE
David A Bradford
214 Chestnut St
Duxbury MA 02332

Call Sign: K1HIR
Mary L Floyd
35 Cross St
Duxbury MA 02332

Call Sign: KB1NEU
David E Reed
97 Cross St
Duxbury MA 02332

Call Sign: KB1WEC
Peter J Capraro

62 Duxborough Trail
Duxbury MA 02332

Call Sign: N3QGF
Richard E Hanson
215 Elm St
Duxbury MA 02332

Call Sign: K1PJT
Stuart M Lee
421 Elm St
Duxbury MA 02332

Call Sign: N1XJN
Thomas J Sullivan
286 Enterprise St
Duxbury MA 02332

Call Sign: W1EEJ
Jerome P Janousek
531 Franklin St
Duxbury MA 02332

Call Sign: N1HHB
Bruce E Barrett
843 Franklin St
Duxbury MA 02332

Call Sign: K1HZL
Edmund P Frazar
98 Harrison St
Duxbury MA 02332

Call Sign: KA1RYS
Donald C Krafft
73 Heritage Ln
Duxbury MA 02331

Call Sign: KB1IKV
Linda M Phelan
140 Lake Shore Dr
Duxbury MA 02332

Call Sign: KB1IKW
Richard T Phelan
140 Lake Shore Dr
Duxbury MA 02332

Call Sign: W1MWQ
Ewald C Werner
2 Oceanwoods Dr
Duxbury MA 02332

Call Sign: WB8NEI

Robert M Jones
121 Park St Box M
Duxbury MA
023310614

Call Sign: W1BWP
Tingey H Sewall Mr
70 Parks St
Duxbury MA 02332

Call Sign: K9FLV
John J Bergin
121 Parks St
Duxbury MA 02331

Call Sign: N1RBV
Stephen T Delano
46 Pilgrim By Way
Duxbury MA 02332

Call Sign: W1CC
Thomas F Delano
46 Pilgrim By Way
Duxbury MA
023324437

Call Sign: N1DG
Donald R Greenbaum
27 Pill Hill Ln
Duxbury MA 02332

Call Sign: N1QMM
Micah B Greenbaum
27 Pill Hill Ln
Duxbury MA 02332

Call Sign: AB1GJ
Ken Tanuma
27 Pill Hill Ln
Duxbury MA 02332

Call Sign: KB1UFC
Yu Disong
27 Pill Hill Ln
Duxbury MA 02332

Call Sign: KB1JPG
Kevin W O Donnell
50 Roundtree Dr
Duxbury MA 02332

Call Sign: K1KOD
Kevin W O Donnell
50 Roundtree Dr

Duxbury MA 02332

Call Sign: N1NJE
Roger C Whipple
20 Sarahs Cir
Duxbury MA 02332

Call Sign: KJ1KJ
Kenneth A Johnston
63 St George St
Duxbury MA 02332

Call Sign: N1ILJ
Holcomb M Johnston
63 St George St
Duxbury MA 02332

Call Sign: KA1SND
Edward M Barrett
193 St George St
Duxbury MA 02332

Call Sign: NT1H
Edwin J Hacker Jr
1 Standish Rd
Duxbury MA 02332

Call Sign: KB1KSG
Angela M Scieszka
1 Summer St
Duxbury MA 02332

Call Sign: N1SDK
Stephen P Hearson
50 Summer St
Duxbury MA
023324748

Call Sign: WB1GEM
John P Hearson
50 Summer St
Duxbury MA 02332

Call Sign: KB1USN
James S Hartford
184 Surplus St
Duxbury MA 02332

Call Sign: WB1COI
William J Napier
67 Teakettle Ln
Duxbury MA 02332

Call Sign: WK1I

Daniel J Baer
76 Templewood Dr
Duxbury MA 02332

Call Sign: WA1CRT
Christopher E Coakley
33 Tinkertown Ln
Duxbury MA 02332

Call Sign: WA1YXM
Robert C Story
1345 Tremont St
Duxbury MA 02332

Call Sign: KB1PIX
Terrance C Reiber
1372 Tremont St
Duxbury MA 02332

Call Sign: W1DUX
Terrance C Reiber
1372 Tremont St
Duxbury MA 02332

Call Sign: N1IRT
Ashley N Vaughton
7 Winter St
Duxbury MA 02332

Call Sign: N1IRU
Jonathan P Mac
Callum
7 Winter St
Duxbury MA 02332

Call Sign: K1EHJ
Robert O Hutchinson
Duxbury MA
023310325

Call Sign: KH2Y
Toshikazu Kawanishi
Duxbury MA 02332

Call Sign: KH7Z
Dateline Dx
Association
Duxbury MA 02332

Call Sign: N1JBG
Douglas E Hart
Duxbury MA 02332

Call Sign: N1SUJ

Hilary G Stookey
Duxbury MA 02331

Call Sign: W1CXX
George E Kyller Jr
Duxbury MA 02331

Call Sign: W1EC
Robert B Enemark
Duxbury MA 02331

Call Sign: AD6VB
Neal J Dahlen
Duxbury MA 02331

Call Sign: KB1GRD
John M Dahlen
Duxbury MA 02331

**FCC Amateur Radio
Licenses in East
Boston**

Call Sign: KB1VIT
Edward Puglielli
1030 Bennington St
12a
East Boston MA 02128

Call Sign: N1KUK
Robert J Lotti
1193 Bennington St
Apt 1
East Boston MA
021281204

Call Sign: KA1SRP
David L Jeter Sr
326 Bremen St
East Boston MA 02128

Call Sign: KB1QGW
George R Strassburger
96 Byron St
East Boston MA 02128

Call Sign: WX1GRS
George R Strassburger
96 Byron St
East Boston MA 02128

Call Sign: KB9DWS
Michael D Bilica Ii
23 Chelsea St #2

East Boston MA
021281912

Call Sign: K1OFV
Robert E Hagemeister
177 Cowper St
East Boston MA 02128

Call Sign: KB1JUO
Mark C Vitale
90 Falcon St
East Boston MA 02128

Call Sign: KC1MH
Paul C Brooker
120 Gladstone St
East Boston MA 02128

Call Sign: KC1RZ
John Grana
196 Havre St
East Boston MA 02128

Call Sign: KA1LWV
Anthony L Pagliuca
37 Haynes St
East Boston MA 02128

Call Sign: KA1OET
Jerry Mazzarella
15 Horace St
East Boston MA 02128

Call Sign: K1JTF
Thomas A Guerra
12 Lamson Ct
East Boston MA 02128

Call Sign: N1YRJ
Edward J Gerwe
26 Lamson St
East Boston MA 02128

Call Sign: KB1LBG
Elizabeth F Gallagher
390 Meridian St 2
East Boston MA 02128

Call Sign: N1NMD
Kenneth J Fiandaca
86 St Andrew Rd
East Boston MA 02128

Call Sign: KB1DXS

Patricia A Berninger
25 Teragram St
East Boston MA 02128

Call Sign: WB1GUY
Michael E Maguire Sr
42 Webster St
East Boston MA 02128

FCC Amateur Radio Licenses in East Braintree

Call Sign: KB1AVX
Katherine J Murphy
134 Edgehill Rd
East Braintree MA
02184

Call Sign: W1GPL
Ralph B Toye
36 Hillside Rd
East Braintree MA
02184

Call Sign: KB1CL
Wilbur D Rhodes Jr
19 Hobart St
East Braintree MA
02184

FCC Amateur Radio Licenses in East Bridgewater

Call Sign: WB1COG
Paul E Rando
503 Bridge St
East Bridgewater MA
02333

Call Sign: W1VPM
Robert W Dennis Jr
530 Bridge St Box 534
East Bridgewater MA
02333

Call Sign: W1GQN
James W Havens
209 Broadmeadow Dr
East Bridgewater MA
02333

Call Sign: WA1MWF

Lawrence A Leblanc
210 Broadmeadow
Drive
East Bridgewater MA
023331568

Call Sign: KB1SJL
Frank Calogero Iii
667 Central St
East Bridgewater MA
02333

Call Sign: KB1KEN
Anthony J Rotondi Jr
50 Country Farm Rd
East Bridgewater MA
02333

Call Sign: WA1IRK
Bruce C Mc Kim
33 Crescent St
East Bridgewater MA
02333

Call Sign: W1IRK
Bruce C Mc Kim
33 Crescent St
East Bridgewater MA
02333

Call Sign: N1TWJ
Judith A Mc Colgan
292 Harvard St
East Bridgewater MA
02333

Call Sign: WA1POR
Carol A Whitaker
504 Harvard St
East Bridgewater MA
02333

Call Sign: KB1PVW
Brian L Kendrew
504 Harvard St
East Bridgewater MA
02333

Call Sign: WA1FVF
Cameron E Woodard
720 Harvard St
East Bridgewater MA
02333

Call Sign: KB1CWA
David P Hill
17 Meadowbrook Dr
East Bridgewater MA
02333

Call Sign: KA1DXE
Marguerite E Nelson
58 Metzler Rd
East Bridgewater MA
02333

Call Sign: KA1DXF
Arthur E Nelson
58 Metzler Rd
East Bridgewater MA
02333

Call Sign: N1LRC
Randy H Maille
856 N Bedford St
East Bridgewater MA
02333

Call Sign: KA1JBE
Joseph S Casieri
45 N Water St
East Bridgewater MA
02333

Call Sign: KB1HXB
Jutta Richter
45 N Water St
East Bridgewater MA
02333

Call Sign: N1XJD
Terrence J Smollett
2 Old Orchard Ln
East Bridgewater MA
02333

Call Sign: KA1HFB
James G Imlach
54 Park Ave
East Bridgewater MA
02333

Call Sign: N1EJP
Charles D Wilson Jr
102 Pleasant St
East Bridgewater MA
02333

Call Sign: KB1MOC
Kevin F Dykes
93 Plymouth St
East Bridgewater MA
02333

Call Sign: N1KXJ
Raymond E Wall Sr
37 Robins St
East Bridgewater MA
02333

Call Sign: N1VTI
Paul E Burbine
636 Summer St
East Bridgewater MA
02333

Call Sign: KB1SYU
Francis G Angelo
686 Summer St
East Bridgewater MA
02333

Call Sign: K1FGA
Francis G Angelo
686 Summer St
East Bridgewater MA
02333

Call Sign: KA1WJ
Frank P Flores Jr
13 Village Rd
East Bridgewater MA
02333

Call Sign: KB1DKO
David J Dick
1428 Washington St
East Bridgewater MA
023331673

Call Sign: WA1ZUF
Steven W Belcher
1825 Washington St
East Bridgewater MA
02333

Call Sign: W1TAV
Steven W Belcher
1825 Washington St
East Bridgewater MA
02333

Call Sign: KE1KR
George Pedro
62 Waterman St
East Bridgewater MA
02333

Call Sign: KA1JGL
Clayton R Hinds
404 West St
East Bridgewater MA
02333

Call Sign: WB1EYA
Scott A Henshaw
416 West St
East Bridgewater MA
02333

Call Sign: KB1OZN
Nancy Lauria
65 William Hersey
Lane
East Bridgewater MA
02333

Call Sign: KG4SEJ
Brian J Connors
East Bridgewater MA
02333

Call Sign: KB1LMP
Peter L Piana
East Bridgewater MA
02333

**FCC Amateur Radio
Licenses in East
Brookfield**

Call Sign: K1GI
John E Berthiaume
East Brookfield MA
01515

Call Sign: W1YQA
W Philip Woodard
East Brookfield MA
01515

Call Sign: W1CLO
Raymond D Hayden
Box 273
East Brookfield MA
01515

Call Sign: N1EOP
Michael J Shea
106 Court St
East Brookfield MA
01515

Call Sign: KA1RVN
Daniel P Millette
113 Cove St
East Brookfield MA
015150378

Call Sign: KB1CEC
Corey M Brodeur
209 E Main St
East Brookfield MA
01515

Call Sign: K1ZPQ
Lothrop Prouty
Harrington St
East Brookfield MA
01515

Call Sign: W1KWG
Arthur J Beauregard
Harrington St
East Brookfield MA
01515

Call Sign: N1ZKJ
Jason J Di Marzio
115 Oakwood Dr
East Brookfield MA
01515

Call Sign: N1ZKK
Nicholas J Treadwell
762 Podunk Rd
East Brookfield MA
01515

Call Sign: KB1VCD
James D Heller
190 West Sturbridge
Rd
East Brookfield MA
01515

**FCC Amateur Radio
Licenses in East
Dennis**

Call Sign: WA1PLV
Robert K Whitten
17 Boulder Dr
East Dennis MA 02641

Call Sign: N1NMB
Robert W Johnston
106 Greenland Cir
East Dennis MA 02641

Call Sign: KA1MR
Ronald R Marotta
4 Judy Dr
East Dennis MA 02641

Call Sign: WB1EAQ
Gilbert W Hardy
57 King James Dr
East Dennis MA 02641

Call Sign: W1AZF
Herman A Ausin
18 Marlboro Dr
East Dennis MA 02641

Call Sign: N1PIU
William Mc Elroy
87 Prince Way
East Dennis MA 02641

Call Sign: W1JCH
Norman E Carter
167 Sea St
East Dennis MA 02641

Call Sign: N1MJB
Norman W Badger
186 Sea St
East Dennis MA 02641

Call Sign: W1MPC
James J Donahue
435 Setucket Rd Box
507
East Dennis MA 02641

Call Sign: N1BXV
Earl B Haines
East Dennis MA 02641

**FCC Amateur Radio
Licenses in East
Douglas**

Call Sign: K1HIS
Paul W Peterson
30 Main St
East Douglas MA
01516

Call Sign: N1FUM
John A Muratore
55 Perry St
East Douglas MA
01516

FCC Amateur Radio Licenses in East Falmouth

Call Sign: W1CFI
Paul R Kranz
Airpark Dr
East Falmouth MA
02536

Call Sign: WB1DRS
Deborah A Valdes
63 Alderberry Ln
East Falmouth MA
02536

Call Sign: KB1CHP
Jamie Andrade
79 Altons Lane
East Falmouth MA
02536

Call Sign: K1RK
Falmouth Amateur
Radio Assn
91 Alton's Lane
East Falmouth MA
02536

Call Sign: WA1GPO
James R Valdes
91 Alton's Lane
East Falmouth MA
02536

Call Sign: KB1CER
Elizabeth A Dillon
18 Ashwood Ln
East Falmouth MA
02536

Call Sign: N1IVE

Hollis W Phinney
11 Bahia Ln
East Falmouth MA
02536

Call Sign: N1ZEN
Lee A Rand
5 Barque Dr
East Falmouth MA
02536

Call Sign: WA2BUX
Lawrence A Rachman
26 Ben Davis Lane
East Falmouth MA
02536

Call Sign: KB1IMN
Shaughnessy F Rogers
348 Blacksmith Shop
Rd
East Falmouth MA
02536

Call Sign: KB1JOT
Erin L Rogers
348 Blacksmith Shop
Rd
East Falmouth MA
02536

Call Sign: KB1HJJ
Robert J Lichtenstein
360 Boxberry Hill Rd
East Falmouth MA
02536

Call Sign: KB1QNE
Robin M Thompson
91 Brick Kiln Rd
East Falmouth MA
02536

Call Sign: KB1GHO
Gary V Vacon
40 Bridge St
East Falmouth MA
02536

Call Sign: K1MON
Gary V Vacon
40 Bridge St
East Falmouth MA
02536

Call Sign: KB1GSW
Janet L Vacon
40 Bridge St
East Falmouth MA
02536

Call Sign: W1KVX
Harold S Burns
19 Carl Landi Cir
East Falmouth MA
02536

Call Sign: KA1TUU
Anthony M Briana
10 Circle Rd
East Falmouth MA
02536

Call Sign: KA1UYH
Paula A Tavares
3 Clark St
East Falmouth MA
02536

Call Sign: N1JCQ
Robert D Tavares
3 Clark St
East Falmouth MA
02536

Call Sign: KA1YFO
Ethel B Levitz
10 Clearwater Dr
East Falmouth MA
02536

Call Sign: N1LNG
Meyer B Levitz
10 Clearwater Dr
East Falmouth MA
02536

Call Sign: K1ABW
Felice A Bonica
174 Coonamessett Cir
East Falmouth MA
02536

Call Sign: KB1JKE
Harry M Sloate
24 Deolinda Place
East Falmouth MA
02536

Call Sign: N1ZCF
Dwight D Meyer
121 East Falmouth
Highway Appt: 6f
East Falmouth MA
02536

Call Sign: KA1YIM
Eva D Nungesser
178 Edgewater Dr E
East Falmouth MA
02536

Call Sign: W1GKN
Rolla C Williamson Jr
79 Elizabeth Jean Dr
East Falmouth MA
02536

Call Sign: KB1CAF
Suzanne R O Leary
32 Fairfield Dr
East Falmouth MA
02536

Call Sign: KB1CAG
Susan M O Leary
32 Fairfield Dr
East Falmouth MA
02536

Call Sign: KB1FOH
Donna F Blanchette
87 Fordham Rd
East Falmouth MA
02536

Call Sign: N1YHS
Ralph K Swenson
99 Fox Run Ln
East Falmouth MA
02536

Call Sign: N1SAC
Culley J Parris
22 Gage Dr
East Falmouth MA
02536

Call Sign: N1YK
Peter S Grinnell Jr
90 Geggatt Rd

East Falmouth MA
02536

Call Sign: KC2EYI
Olga M M Mitchell
10 Glory Lane
East Falmouth MA
02536

Call Sign: KB1URJ
Timothy M Gray
18 Hampden Rd
East Falmouth MA
02536

Call Sign: W1TMG
Timothy M Gray
18 Hampden Rd
East Falmouth MA
02536

Call Sign: KB1VWC
Stephen M Harris
22 Hanson Circle
East Falmouth MA
02536

Call Sign: KB1HQQ
John G Fraser
442 Hayway Rd
East Falmouth MA
02536

Call Sign: W1IDE
John G Fraser
442 Hayway Rd
East Falmouth MA
02536

Call Sign: N1MZO
Paul D Godfrey Sr
132 Jamie Ln
East Falmouth MA
025365175

Call Sign: N1XOE
John P Gerbi
26 Jeffrey Ln
East Falmouth MA
02536

Call Sign: N1IVF
Brian J Guest Sr
61 John Parker Rd

East Falmouth MA
02536

Call Sign: N8UBD
Brent V Putnam
97 John Parker Rd
East Falmouth MA
02536

Call Sign: W1NCH
Brent V Putnam
97 John Parker Rd
East Falmouth MA
02536

Call Sign: KB1RAX
Dudley B Foster
19 Joshua Ln
East Falmouth MA
02536

Call Sign: N1CRN
John W Gillis
106 Lakeshore Dr
East Falmouth MA
02536

Call Sign: WB1DSG
Edward G Enos Jr
484 Locustfield Rd
East Falmouth MA
02536

Call Sign: KA1SGW
Craig A Flescher
621 Locustfield Rd
East Falmouth MA
02536

Call Sign: KA1SGY
Chris B Flescher
621 Locustfield Rd
East Falmouth MA
02536

Call Sign: N1IUE
William E Collins
18 Long Fellow Rd
East Falmouth MA
025367429

Call Sign: KC1IF
Norman L Darling
109 Madeline Rd

East Falmouth MA
025366235

Call Sign: N1SWX
Christopher Costa
465 Main St
East Falmouth MA
02536

Call Sign: KC0CVN
Kristopher B
Karnauskas
42 Meadow View
Drive
East Falmouth MA
02536

Call Sign: KA1SGX
Scott D Brown
110 N Bournes Pond
Rd
East Falmouth MA
02536

Call Sign: N1GMF
Charles F Day
126 Old Barnstable Rd
East Falmouth MA
02536

Call Sign: K1TV
Ralph G Siebert
158 Old Meeting
House Rd
East Falmouth MA
02536

Call Sign: W1BDS
Wilson E Burgess
24 Ormond Dr
East Falmouth MA
02536

Call Sign: N1VUW
Louis J Happas
20 Ovington Dr
East Falmouth MA
02536

Call Sign: KJ6ESZ
John A Smith
18 Owls Nest Rd
East Falmouth MA
02536

Call Sign: WA1WIS
Jay I W Moskow
32 Partridge Lane
East Falmouth MA
025366931

Call Sign: KB1NNH
Gerald D Campbell
43 Partridge Lane
East Falmouth MA
02536

Call Sign: N1HNF
George J Williams
23 Penny Royal Ln
East Falmouth MA
02536

Call Sign: NV1O
Linda A Blumer
23 Penny Royal Ln
East Falmouth MA
02536

Call Sign: KB1IHS
Frances R Harazi
153 Pinecrest Beach
Dr
East Falmouth MA
02536

Call Sign: K1BT
Thomas J Brion
210 Pinecrest Beach
Dr
East Falmouth MA
02536

Call Sign: KA1UYG
John L Bullister
18 Pondview Dr
East Falmouth MA
02536

Call Sign: N1GLC
Philip H Choate
46 Prince Henry Dr
East Falmouth MA
02536

Call Sign: WA1KPE
Lyman W Mix
36 Quashnet Way

East Falmouth MA
02536

Call Sign: K1PE
Lyman W Mix
36 Quashnet Way
East Falmouth MA
02536

Call Sign: N1JCT
Donald E Zaffini
33 Raffi Ave
East Falmouth MA
02536

Call Sign: K1PDH
Edgar A Schailler Jr
22 Reynolds St
East Falmouth MA
02536

Call Sign: KB1WSW
Robert E Conroy
113 Sam Turner Rd
East Falmouth MA
02536

Call Sign: W1HWU
Robert L Wagner
68 Sand Dollar Cir
East Falmouth MA
02536

Call Sign: N1TDM
Andrew J Mc Intosh
40 Sandpoint Shores
Dr
East Falmouth MA
02536

Call Sign: N1YRQ
Robert W Hendricks
11 Santa Maria Lane
East Falmouth MA
02536

Call Sign: K1WCC
Henry W Brown
19 Sao Paulo Dr
East Falmouth MA
02536

Call Sign: WW2MAN

Amateur Radio
Association Seehund
U-5075
19 Sao Paulo Dr
East Falmouth MA
02536

Call Sign: KA1TXW
Gregory E Dinsmore
279 Seacoast Blvd
East Falmouth MA
02536

Call Sign: KA1TXX
Matthew I Dinsmore
279 Seacoast Blvd
East Falmouth MA
02536

Call Sign: N1KKJ
Ernest J Marchisin
72 Seacoast Shores
East Falmouth MA
02536

Call Sign: KA1LII
Ernest I Kilkenny
55 Seatucket Rd
East Falmouth MA
02536

Call Sign: KE7QYD
Jesse B Bishop
17 Shorecrest Dr
East Falmouth MA
02536

Call Sign: K1QLG
Fred J Ravens Jr
17 Shoreview Ave
East Falmouth MA
02536

Call Sign: K1UFD
Kenneth G Goodman
141 Shorewood Dr
East Falmouth MA
02536

Call Sign: WA1WJY
Dorothy P Goodman
141 Shorewood Dr
East Falmouth MA
02536

Call Sign: W1TJW
Colin B Mac Dougall
35 Striper Ln
East Falmouth MA
02536

Call Sign: KB1CEQ
Ellysia H Amorim
150 Tanglewood Dr
East Falmouth MA
02536

Call Sign: N1TKZ
Alan T Gardner
65 Tasina Dr
East Falmouth MA
02632

Call Sign: KB1DOS
Philip Motta
875 Teaticket Hwy
East Falmouth MA
02536

Call Sign: K1TSL
Timothy S Little
18 Tiller Drive
East Falmouth MA
02536

Call Sign: KA1IOR
Geoffrey A Way
226 Trotting Park Rd
East Falmouth MA
025365647

Call Sign: W1REA
Leonard A Boutin
94 Turner Rd
East Falmouth MA
02536

Call Sign: KB1KFI
Clifford J Brennan
94 Turner Rd
East Falmouth MA
02536

Call Sign: K1KFI
Clifford J Brennan
94 Turner Rd
East Falmouth MA
02536

Call Sign: N1COW
Lawrence J Palmer
38 Twin Hill Rd
East Falmouth MA
02536

Call Sign: KA1KLH
William J Sellers
11 White Pine Ln
East Falmouth MA
02536

Call Sign: W1HCR
John F Barrows
East Falmouth MA
02536

Call Sign: WA1TEL
Adda S Barrows
East Falmouth MA
02536

Call Sign: N1UVW
Armen Garabedian
East Falmouth MA
02536

Call Sign: N1VDN
Sandra R Garabedian
East Falmouth MA
02536

Call Sign: KB1PTT
Armen Garabedian
East Falmouth MA
02536

**FCC Amateur Radio
Licenses in East
Freetown**

Call Sign: KB1IQR
Bradford E Paiva
71 Bullock Rd
East Freetown MA
027171017

Call Sign: W1BEP
Bradford E Paiva
71 Bullock Rd
East Freetown MA
027171017

Call Sign: WB1ERS
Adrien W Mercier Jr
113 Bullock Rd
East Freetown MA
02717

Call Sign: AA1AF
John B Cuzzone
258 Bullock Rd
East Freetown MA
02717

Call Sign: KB1WUW
71 Saf Amateur Radio
Club
Bullock Rd
East Freetown MA
02717

Call Sign: WA1IFN
Louis C Constantine
50 Chace Rd
East Freetown MA
02717

Call Sign: KB1MKQ
Montana Yergeau
50 Chace Rd
East Freetown MA
02717

Call Sign: KA1MEI
Robert S Spulock
14 Charbonneau Ave
East Freetown MA
02717

Call Sign: N1BZG
Frederick G Sterner
66 Chipaway Rd
East Freetown MA
02717

Call Sign: WB1FQP
Alan R Dulong
37 Chipway Rd
East Freetown MA
02717

Call Sign: KB1KZZ
Ernest E Breau Jr
126 Cty Rd
East Freetown MA
02717

Call Sign: KA1IB
Paul G Sadeck
90 Doctor Braley Rd
East Freetown MA
02717

Call Sign: K1PGS
Paul G Sadeck
90 Doctor Braley Rd
East Freetown MA
02717

Call Sign: KB1NMQ
Manuel Ferreira Iii
117 Dr Braley Rd
East Freetown MA
027171816

Call Sign: N1DNJ
Stephen R Mueller
34 Gurney Rd
East Freetown MA
02717

Call Sign: KA1NOH
Stanley M Boehler
5 Island Rd
East Freetown MA
02717

Call Sign: WB3IJO
Craig F Derewiany
4 Palmer Ct
East Freetown MA
02717

Call Sign: AB1FB
Craig F Derewiany
4 Palmer Ct
East Freetown MA
02717

Call Sign: N1ALN
Albert E Crook
20 Washburn Rd
East Freetown MA
02717

Call Sign: N1EHR
Betty L Crook
20 Washburn Rd
East Freetown MA
02717

Call Sign: N1LZY
Wayne A Braley
14 Winfield St
East Freetown MA
02717

Call Sign: K1NBA
Wayne A Braley
14 Winfield St
East Freetown MA
02717

Call Sign: N1OFW
Sherry L Morse
East Freetown MA
02717

Call Sign: KB1HPV
Hartland A Chadwick
East Freetown MA
02717

FCC Amateur Radio Licenses in East Hampton

Call Sign: W1HRV
Osborne R Mc
Keraghan
39 Ballard St
East Hampton MA
01027

Call Sign: N1WND
Alan J Gliniak
85 Briggs St
East Hampton MA
01027

Call Sign: KB1KKY
Mark R Bricault
34 Campbell Dr
East Hampton MA
01027

Call Sign: KB1NGI
Edward J Harnois Iii
65 Clark St
East Hampton MA
01027

Call Sign: KB1LWN
50 Northeast Vhf Club

Everett St
East Hampton MA
01027

Call Sign: KB1LYG
50 Northeast Vhf Club
Everett St
East Hampton MA
01027

Call Sign: N1WNE
Jonathan R Herbert
15 Hannum Brook Dr
East Hampton MA
01027

Call Sign: N1MHG
Timothy J Lukowski
Lincoln St
East Hampton MA
01027

Call Sign: N1YMJ
Peter A Di Rocco
5 Oak St
East Hampton MA
01027

Call Sign: N1WGW
Daniel R Cady
43 Ridgwood Terr
East Hampton MA
01027

FCC Amateur Radio Licenses in East Harwich

Call Sign: N1EJZ
Thomas A Currie Sr
153 Clearwater Dr
East Harwich MA
02645

Call Sign: W1BMW
Albert L Chesbro
1661 Orleans Rd
East Harwich MA
02645

Call Sign: W1VTX
Anthony Ross
1685 Orleans Rd

East Harwich MA
02645

Call Sign: W6DGD
John Wardell
303 Route 137
East Harwich MA
02645

Call Sign: W1JTL
Robert G Armstrong
26 Standish Woods Cir
East Harwich MA
02645

Call Sign: N1ECN
Arthur Heaton
1 Stevens Way
East Harwich MA
02645

Call Sign: KA1IR
John J Petersen
20 Sugar Hill Dr
East Harwich MA
02645

**FCC Amateur Radio
Licenses in East Long**

Call Sign: N1LZA
Steve N Rybacki
42 Hillside Dr
East Long MA 01028

**FCC Amateur Radio
Licenses in East
Longmeadow**

Call Sign: KA1GUC
Barbara B Panek
6 Alandale Dr
East Longmeadow MA
01028

Call Sign: WB1DLE
John F Panek
6 Alandale Dr
East Longmeadow MA
01028

Call Sign: KA1ZYE
Lesvia Basta
29 Amy Ln

East Longmeadow MA
01028

Call Sign: N1MOI
Frank M Doukellis
29 Amy Ln
East Longmeadow MA
01028

Call Sign: N1SBW
James F Da Silva
112 Braeburn Rd
East Longmeadow MA
01028

Call Sign: W1HGJ
Chester R Kruczek
29 Brookhaven Dr
East Longmeadow MA
01028

Call Sign: KA1CRG
Raymond A Morin
97 Brookhaven Dr
East Longmeadow MA
01028

Call Sign: KB1NNM
Christine P Sterritt
249 Canterbury Circle
East Longmeadow MA
01028

Call Sign: N1QKS
Alfred W Deyo Jr
403 Chestnut St
East Longmeadow MA
01028

Call Sign: KA1WER
Paul F Geng
25 Crescent Hill
East Longmeadow MA
01028

Call Sign: KB1CHE
Peter A Maserati
16 Day Ave
East Longmeadow MA
01028

Call Sign: KA1JWG
Gordon K Knight
42 Elm St

East Longmeadow MA
01028

Call Sign: KA1ONV
Janet O Knight
42 Elm St
East Longmeadow MA
01028

Call Sign: KB1HBO
Jason B Roath
43 Elm St
East Longmeadow MA
01028

Call Sign: KB1CSL
David E Pace
74 Elm St
East Longmeadow MA
01028

Call Sign: KA1EJS
Lura A Hawn
217 Elm St
East Longmeadow MA
01028

Call Sign: KA1EJT
Everett R Hawn
217 Elm St
East Longmeadow MA
01028

Call Sign: KA1ZKM
Harold L Bitzer
22 Elmcrest St
East Longmeadow MA
01028

Call Sign: KA1RFI
Theodor G Wallace
25 Fernwood Dr
East Longmeadow MA
01028

Call Sign: N1LZD
Louis A Calabrese Jr
16 Harris Dr
East Longmeadow MA
01028

Call Sign: N1LYZ
Preston R Wallace
330 Kibbe Rd

East Longmeadow MA
01028

Call Sign: AK1C
Olaf Passburg
37 Knollwood Dr
East Longmeadow MA
01028

Call Sign: K1LMY
Frank P Morrisino Jr
36 Lori Ln
East Longmeadow MA
01028

Call Sign: KB1JVB
David A Schunk
33 Lynwood Rd
East Longmeadow MA
010281258

Call Sign: W1WCV
Alan B Katze
231 Maple St
East Longmeadow MA
010282751

Call Sign: K1HBF
Frederick C Redin
185 Mapleshade Ave
East Longmeadow MA
010281226

Call Sign: K1JFB
Sylvia A Redin
185 Mapleshade Ave
East Longmeadow MA
010281226

Call Sign: KB1PAB
Elizabeth A Gorman
46 Melwood Ave
East Longmeadow MA
01028

Call Sign: N1NYC
Kevin J Gorman
46 Melwood Ave
East Long Meadow
MA 01028

Call Sign: KB1ANL
Paul E Paschetto
136 Melwood Ave

East Longmeadow MA
01028

East Longmeadow MA
01028

East Longmeadow MA
01028

East Longmeadow MA
010281652

Call Sign: KB1XG
Albert M Grimaldi
48 Millbrook Dr
East Longmeadow MA
01028

Call Sign: WA2PTR
Thomas J Franciosa
371 Pease Rd
East Longmeadow MA
01028

Call Sign: N1FEZ
Keith E Davis Sr
490 Somers Rd
East Longmeadow MA
010282906

Call Sign: N1EXG
Thomas J Sherry
11 Wedgewood Rd
East Longmeadow MA
01028

Call Sign: KB1TVO
Susan J Grimaldi
48 Millbrook Dr
East Longmeadow MA
010282650

Call Sign: KB1RGL
Christophe J Gerard
34 Pilgrim Rd
East Longmeadow MA
01028

Call Sign: KB1JVC
Martin J Bowen Jr
849 Somers Rd
East Longmeadow MA
01028

Call Sign: KB1IDH
Gary T Devine
11 William St
East Longmeadow MA
01028

Call Sign: WA1SJG
Susan J Grimaldi
48 Millbrook Dr
East Longmeadow MA
010282650

Call Sign: W1CLD
Charles L Dube
339 Porter Rd
East Longmeadow MA
01028

Call Sign: W1MJB
Martin J Bowen Jr
849 Somers Rd
East Longmeadow MA
01028

Call Sign: KB1KER
Nicholas J Devine
11 William St
East Longmeadow MA
01028

Call Sign: WW1A
Clyde A Llewellyn
88 Millbrook Dr
East Longmeadow MA
01028

Call Sign: W1AUF
William E Gourley
599 Prospect St
East Longmeadow MA
01028

Call Sign: KB2IVI
Melinda G Fant
9 Somerset St
East Longmeadow MA
01028

Call Sign: KB1HJS
Timothy M Rainey
87 Windham Dr
East Longmeadow MA
01028

Call Sign: K1LKT
James E Sullivan
154 Millbrook Dr
East Longmeadow MA
01028

Call Sign: KB1NPA
Richard W Forrest
642 Prospect St
East Longmeadow MA
01028

Call Sign: KB2KKE
Melanie G Maserati
9 Somerset St
East Longmeadow MA
01028

Call Sign: KB1WX
Ned S Schwartz
143 Windham Dr
East Longmeadow MA
010282671

Call Sign: WA1LRZ
Francis W King
156 Mountainview Rd
East Longmeadow MA
01028

Call Sign: KB1FHT
Richard J Brady
20 Pwder Hill Rd
East Longmeadow MA
01028

Call Sign: KE2SN
David L Fant
9 Somerset St
East Longmeadow MA
01028

Call Sign: KB1MIJ
Charles H Knorr
65 Worthy Ave
East Longmeadow MA
010282025

Call Sign: N1RJI
Martin A Kibbe
32 Oak Bluff Cir
East Longmeadow MA
01028

Call Sign: N1DXY
Ronald P Gaudreau
61 Quarry Hill
East Longmeadow MA
01028

Call Sign: KA1FDE
Cleborn L Woods
88 Thompkins Ave
East Longmeadow MA
01028

Call Sign: KP4BPR
Nelson R Figueroa
East Longmeadow MA
01028

Call Sign: KD1ZW
David W Baker
394 Parker St
East Longmeadow MA
01028

Call Sign: KB6MOM
Doris E Silloway
8 Savoy Ave
East Longmeadow MA
01028

Call Sign: KB1CSM
Norman B Ford Mr
3 Village Green
East Longmeadow MA
010281690

FCC Amateur Radio Licenses in East Lynn

Call Sign: WA1MKA
Robert P Nicholson
24 Lake Ave
East Lynn MA 01904

Call Sign: KA1IGC
Mark E Callahan
304 Pease Rd

Call Sign: N1LYY
Richard E Hawley
77 Somers Rd

Call Sign: N1UAO
Robert C Black
20 Vreeland Ave

FCC Amateur Radio Licenses in East Orleans

Call Sign: N1DIJ
Paul M Ware Jr
15 Barley Neck Rd
East Orleans MA
02643

Call Sign: KA1RAQ
Lester D Knisell Jr
Box 225
East Orleans MA
02643

Call Sign: W1NC
Jeffrey W Moore
29 Hayward Lane
East Orleans MA
02643

Call Sign: N1BMO
Harry S Earl
3 Mill Ln
East Orleans MA
02643

Call Sign: W1ZX
Robert A Hulick
8 Oak Lane
East Orleans MA
02643

Call Sign: K1MXF
Robert A Hulick
8 Oak Ln
East Orleans MA
02643

Call Sign: W1QP
Robert A Hulick
8 Oak Ln
East Orleans MA
02643

Call Sign: KB1KNQ
Mark E Duperron
East Orleans MA
02643

Call Sign: KK7ME
John E Nichols

East Orleans MA
02643

Call Sign: N1ZJZ
Edna M Smith
East Orleans MA
02643

Call Sign: W1DKI
Robert G Edwards
East Orleans MA
02643

Call Sign: W1KLV
Richard J O Hara
East Orleans MA
02643

Call Sign: K1IJV
D Jean Peacor
East Orleans MA
02643

Call Sign: AB1GQ
John E Nichols
East Orleans MA
02643

Call Sign: AB1IE
John E Nichols
East Orleans MA
02643

FCC Amateur Radio Licenses in East Otis

Call Sign: KB1HUY
Michael S Eades Sr
47 South Bay Rd
East Otis MA 01029

Call Sign: KB1HUZ
Suzanne R Eades
East Otis MA 01029

Call Sign: KB1UDA
Jeffrey C Davies
East Otis MA 01029

Call Sign: KB1WXW
Charles E Harner
East Otis MA 01029

FCC Amateur Radio Licenses in East Sandwich

Call Sign: KD1ZL
Vincent J Maio Jr
51 Beachway
East Sandwich MA
02537

Call Sign: WA1NHE
Vincent J Maio Jr
51 Beachway
East Sandwich MA
02537

Call Sign: KB1WVP
James D Redmond
3 Bluestone Terrace
East Sandwich MA
02537

Call Sign: KB1QDN
Anna T Burroughs-
Merrill
39 Boulder Brook Rd
East Sandwich MA
02537

Call Sign: WA1OPW
John J Brennan
5 Capt Towne Rd
East Sandwich MA
02537

Call Sign: K2TOM
Thomas Hartnett
17 Crestview Drive
East Sandwich MA
025371402

Call Sign: KB1TXI
Bart J Wesp
2 Easterly Dr
East Sandwich MA
02537

Call Sign: K1GRP
Edward J Cochran
7 Fox Hill Ln
East Sandwich MA
02537

Call Sign: K1ZJW

James F Robinson
14 Herring Run Rd
East Sandwich MA
025371713

Call Sign: WD8IWJ
Randolph A Lewis
35 Kiahs Way
East Sandwich MA
02537

Call Sign: WA1MWL
Stephen R Hall Jr
32 Kiahs Way Rd 2
East Sandwich MA
02537

Call Sign: KB1GSS
Robert A Dusseault
18 Longhill Dr
East Sandwich MA
02537

Call Sign: KB1GST
Barbara S Dusseault
18 Longhill Drive
East Sandwich MA
02537

Call Sign: KB1GSO
Barbara A Dougan
20 Madison Dr
East Sandwich MA
02537

Call Sign: N1NS
Barbara A Dougan
20 Madison Dr
East Sandwich MA
02537

Call Sign: K1XP
Cape Cod Vhf Society
21 Madison Dr
East Sandwich MA
02537

Call Sign: N1RCE
Carolyn M Walker
21 Madison Dr
East Sandwich MA
02537

Call Sign: W1LP

Clinton L Walker
21 Madison Dr
East Sandwich MA
02537

Call Sign: W1AA
Marconi Radio Club
2 Noel Henry Dr
East Sandwich MA
02537

Call Sign: K1VV
Robert J Doherty
2 Noel Henry Drive
East Sandwich MA
02537

Call Sign: KB1QDF
William A Lapine
126 North Shore Blvd
East Sandwich MA
02537

Call Sign: KB1NNO
Robert Marino
25 Oxford Rd
East Sandwich MA
02537

Call Sign: KA1OFP
John S Conroy
30 Oxford Rd
East Sandwich MA
025371341

Call Sign: KB1FL
John M Ranney
107 Quaker Meeting
House Rd
East Sandwich MA
02537

Call Sign: WA1MTI
Anthony La Scala
27 Quaker Village Ln
East Sandwich MA
025371347

Call Sign: W1VCW
David J W Parrott
374 Rt 6a
East Sandwich MA
02537

Call Sign: KB1UJL
Grayson B Mackenzie
119 Sevice Rd
East Sandwich MA
02537

Call Sign: N1VVC
Elwynn J Miller
13 Sheep Pasture Way
East Sandwich MA
02537

Call Sign: N1SAB
Maureen C Hall
27 Spectacle Rd
East Sandwich MA
02537

Call Sign: WB1CWI
Stephen A Hall
27 Spectacle Rd
East Sandwich MA
02537

Call Sign: W1ODO
Harry D Azadian
6 Stonefield Dr
East Sandwich MA
02537

Call Sign: W1TTY
Horace Schermerhorn
10 Village Dr
East Sandwich MA
025371418

Call Sign: W1UVN
Jocelyn M
Schermerhorn
10 Village Dr
East Sandwich MA
02537

Call Sign: W1TYZ
John N Cullity
East Sandwich MA
02537

Call Sign: N1AOS
John W Shay
East Sandwich MA
02537

Call Sign: KB1AKS
Mary E Mahoney
30 Bettsy Rd
East Taunton MA
02718

Call Sign: KB1KVM
James A Bardwell Jr
30 Birchwood Dr
East Taunton MA
02718

Call Sign: AA1JF
Keith J Leite
238 Bluejay Ln
East Taunton MA
02718

Call Sign: KA1YCV
James F Bowman Iii
8 Cotuit Rd
East Taunton MA
02718

Call Sign: W3ZYO
Robert M Bettinson
1797 County St
East Taunton MA
02718

Call Sign: KA1COL
Allen E Lipkind
15 King Fisher Way
East Taunton MA
02718

Call Sign: N1SXP
David N Costello
1620 Middleboro Ave
East Taunton MA
02718

Call Sign: KA1KMF
John H Rogers
275 Richmond St
East Taunton MA
02718

Call Sign: N1KSL
William D Ryder

49 Seaver St Box 508
East Taunton MA
02718

Call Sign: WA1GOV
Arthur J Arruda Jr
329 Seekell St
East Taunton MA
02718

Call Sign: KA1NFT
James D Frechette Jr
27 Staples St
East Taunton MA
02718

Call Sign: N1MPS
Westley C Estes
140 Strawberry Lane
East Taunton MA
02718

Call Sign: KB1FRQ
Amaro Cabral
365 Wren St
East Taunton MA
02718

Call Sign: K1UWJ
Thomas E Jeleniewski
357 S Main St
East Templeton MA
01468

Call Sign: N1FCB
Robert A Wilder
East Templeton MA
01438

Call Sign: N1KCU
Michael W Greene
East Templeton MA
01438

Call Sign: NY1L
David A Guy

10 Donnell Rd
East Walpole MA
02032

Call Sign: W1EJP
Edmund J Peshin
17 Donnell Rd
East Walpole MA
02032

Call Sign: AA1DU
Nita L Christopher
20 Gate Way
East Walpole MA
02032

Call Sign: WA1GCH
Allen L Bishop
Old Post Rd
East Walpole MA
02032

Call Sign: N1CAP
Daniel B Laferriere
1 Pall Mall
East Walpole MA
02032

Call Sign: AB1PH
W D Rolph Iii
8 Patty Ann Pl
East Walpole MA
020321346

Call Sign: WA1WDW
Robert J Roffinoli
21 Redwood Mews
East Walpole MA
02032

Call Sign: KB1MPA
Bryan G Buckley
48 Rustic Rd
East Walpole MA
02032

Call Sign: N1USD
Jeffrey M Padell
6 Sandra Rd
East Walpole MA
020321506

Call Sign: W1RI
Stanley F Crowhurst

9 Union St
East Walpole MA
02032

Call Sign: KB1UMD
Lawrence D Copeland
Ii
175 Union St
East Walpole MA
02032

Call Sign: KB1HNI
Marilyn L Connelly-
Lynn
17 Woodland Rd
East Walpole MA
02032

Call Sign: KB1HNJ
David E Lynn
17 Woodland Rd
East Walpole MA
02032

Call Sign: AA1ZL
David E Lynn
17 Woodland Rd
East Walpole MA
02032

Call Sign: AA1ZM
Marilyn L Connelly-
Lynn
17 Woodland Rd
East Walpole MA
02032

**FCC Amateur Radio
Licenses in East
Wareham**

Call Sign: N1ZYU
George F Spencer Jr
3036 Cranberry
Highway #16
East Wareham MA
02538

Call Sign: N1IDM
James T Regan
46 Sunset Blvd
East Wareham MA
02538

Call Sign: N1DGL
Robert C Da Silva
East Wareham MA
02538

Call Sign: N1TCW
Mary W Westgate
East Wareham MA
02538

Call Sign: W1IWK
Peter A Russett
East Wareham MA
025380875

Call Sign: WB1DNP
Ronald W Westgate
East Wareham MA
02538

**FCC Amateur Radio
Licenses in East
Weymouth**

Call Sign: N1BHH
Clyde D Ramsdell
691 Broad St
East Weymouth MA
02189

Call Sign: KB1TOJ
Douglas P Buchanan
50 Cedar St
East Weymouth MA
02189

Call Sign: W1DPB
Douglas P Buchanan
50 Cedar St
East Weymouth MA
02189

Call Sign: KA1YHY
Henry L O Brien
70 Cornish St
East Weymouth MA
02189

Call Sign: KA1WJQ
Phillip A Kawa
61 Curtis Cir
East Weymouth MA
02189

Call Sign: WA1VMX
Richard H Kream
53 Granite Post Ln
East Weymouth MA
02189

Call Sign: KB1TOI
Justin E Holstrom
39 Hawthorne St
East Weymouth MA
02189

Call Sign: W1BTC
Dora M La Gasse
53 Island View Rd
East Weymouth MA
02189

Call Sign: W1VOU
Hormidas A La Gasse
53 Island View Rd
East Weymouth MA
02189

Call Sign: K1YZQ
Francis J Barbuto Sr
60 Madison St
East Weymouth MA
021892202

Call Sign: WB1FRO
Warren H Minasian
70 Madison St
East Weymouth MA
02189

Call Sign: WC1ABD
Weymouth Civil
Defense
75 Middle St
East Weymouth MA
02189

Call Sign: N1ISS
Mark S Sullivan
54 Seaver Rd
East Weymouth MA
02189

Call Sign: N1JCA
Debra L Sullivan
54 Seaver Rd
East Weymouth MA
02189

Call Sign: N1PHH
William H James
27 Village Rd
East Weymouth MA
02189

Call Sign: W1WPG
Luther G Fulton
1 Wagon Rd
East Weymouth MA
021892712

Call Sign: K1HGT
Frank M Martin Jr
16 Woodbine Rd
East Weymouth MA
02189

**FCC Amateur Radio
Licenses in Eastham**

Call Sign: KA1SCN
Patricia M Hogg
Eastham MA 02642

Call Sign: KA1SCP
Joseph T Schiebel
Eastham MA 02642

Call Sign: KA1SCS
Jason R Nickerson
Eastham MA 02642

Call Sign: KA1SCT
Jeremy C Johnson
Eastham MA 02642

Call Sign: KA1SCW
Kristen E Ragusa
Eastham MA 02642

Call Sign: KA1SEN
Lindsay A Mc Dowell
Eastham MA 02642

Call Sign: KA1SEO
Jason T Hayes
Eastham MA 02642

Call Sign: KA1SGZ
Heidi A Eldredge
Eastham MA 02642

Call Sign: KA1SLO
Daniel M Kline
Eastham MA 02642

Call Sign: KA1TVI
Michelle N Fields
Eastham MA 02642

Call Sign: KA1VSH
Brian T Brady
Eastham MA 02642

Call Sign: KA1VTP
Jessica L Miller
Eastham MA 02642

Call Sign: KA1VXN
Daniel R Purtle
Eastham MA 02647

Call Sign: KA1WBV
Andrew E Young
Eastham MA 02642

Call Sign: KB1QDL
Larry R Jasper
10 Bens Way
Eastham MA 02642

Call Sign: K1LRJ
Larry R Jasper
10 Bens Way
Eastham MA 02642

Call Sign: KA1VSX
David J Sears
Box 104
Eastham MA 02642

Call Sign: KA1SDA
Emily B Wade
Box 1192
Eastham MA 02642

Call Sign: KA1SCO
Mozelle W Penney
Box 1297
Eastham MA 02642

Call Sign: KA1VSO
Jonathan F Farrell
Box 134
Eastham MA 02642

Call Sign: W1QQC
James A Harper
Box 150
Eastham MA 02642

Call Sign: KA1VTK
Jesse M Burt
Box 26a Lombard Ln
Eastham MA 02642

Call Sign: KA1SEB
David A
Meguerdichian
Box 271a
Eastham MA 02642

Call Sign: KA1TVU
Emily M Newton
Box 283
Eastham MA 02642

Call Sign: KA1SCL
Abby J Schoenberger
Box 32b Rr 1
Eastham MA 02642

Call Sign: KA1TVZ
Brian C Antel
Box 331
Eastham MA 02642

Call Sign: KA1SBY
Joseph J Gargolinski
Box 366
Eastham MA 02642

Call Sign: KA1SEQ
Daniel D Elliott
Box 41a Rr 1
Eastham MA 02642

Call Sign: KA1VSG
Andrew T Hoaglund
Box 437a
Eastham MA 02642

Call Sign: KA1VSW
Derek R Miller
Box 739
Eastham MA 02642

Call Sign: KA1TVT
Roya R Nassery
Box 80

Eastham MA 02642

Call Sign: KA1VSY
Najlla N Nassery
Box 80
Eastham MA 02642

Call Sign: KA1SEJ
Bobby J Derow Iv
Box 808
Eastham MA 02642

Call Sign: KA1YWH
Andrew B Wade
625 Bridge Rd
Eastham MA 02642

Call Sign: KB1AZW
Emily Ann Edwards
850 Bridge Rd
Eastham MA 02642

Call Sign: K2LP
Marvin D Hall Jr
70 Candlewood Dr
Eastham MA 02642

Call Sign: KB1BBE
Perry W Sparrow
190 Cross Cart Way
Eastham MA 02642

Call Sign: KB1PDA
Leanne Mclaughlin
15 Deepwood Rd
Eastham MA 02642

Call Sign: KA1VTI
Sarah D Elliott
100 Ellis Rd Rr 1
Eastham MA 02642

Call Sign: KA1VSN
Joshua P Murray
125 Foxwood Dr
Eastham MA 02542

Call Sign: KB1BAY
Kristin K O Hara
55 Garden Ln
Eastham MA 02642

Call Sign: KB1AEO
Marcy H Carlson

2 Geoffrey Rd
Eastham MA 02642

Call Sign: KA1SCE
Shannon O Neill
Gimlet Way
Eastham MA 02642

Call Sign: KB1BAD
Alexandria M Borrero
290 Goody Hallet Dr
Eastham MA 02642

Call Sign: KB1BHF
A W David La Vigne
30 Gov Brewster Rd
Eastham MA 02642

Call Sign: KA1TVW
Matthew S Sieger
60 Gov Prence Rd
Eastham MA 02642

Call Sign: KA1VTB
Hatfield Turner
385 Govener Prence
Rd
Eastham MA 02642

Call Sign: KA1YWQ
Jeffrey M Orcutt
88 Govornor Prence
Rd
Eastham MA 02642

Call Sign: KA1TVJ
James R Filliman
Grandfathers Way
Eastham MA 02642

Call Sign: KB1BAO
Blake E Petrick
580 Great Pond Rd
Eastham MA 02642

Call Sign: KA3RZZ
Anne F Marvin
845 Hay Rd
Eastham MA 02642

Call Sign: N1IJF
Donald G Coon
820 Herring Brook Rd
Eastham MA 02642

Call Sign: KA1VTH
Michael J
Meguerdichian
Indian Way Rr 1
Eastham MA 02642

Call Sign: KA1YWI
Charles H Wagner Iv
190 Ireland Way
Eastham MA 02642

Call Sign: KA1VST
Kathryn L Traut
280 Ireland Way
Eastham MA 02642

Call Sign: KA1YWM
Lucas C Strakele
Joshuas Way
Eastham MA 02642

Call Sign: KA1LLT
Henry P Burke
100 Kingsbury Beach
Rd
Eastham MA 02642

Call Sign: KB1AEN
Jenny F Handel
705 Kingsbury Beach
Rd
Eastham MA 02642

Call Sign: N1QJG
P Bishop Covell
185 Lawton Rd
Eastham MA 02642

Call Sign: KA1YVK
Erin E Covell
245 Lawton Rd
Eastham MA 02642

Call Sign: AE2D
Peter K Leather
130 Locust Rd
Eastham MA
026420645

Call Sign: KA1SCJ
Kimberly A Rogers
1120 Massasoit Rd
Eastham MA 02642

Call Sign: KA1SCZ
Earl J Weeks
Massasoit Rd Rr 2
Eastham MA 02642

Call Sign: KA1VTO
Sarah A Weeks
Massasoit Rd Rr 2
Eastham MA 02642

Call Sign: KB2SVJ
Joseph G Schneider
25 Mayflower Rd
Eastham MA 08012

Call Sign: KB1RPD
Nathan W Garran
180 Meadow Dr
Eastham MA
026426102

Call Sign: KB1LZV
Dryden E Clark
3 Nathaniel Swift Rd
Eastham MA 02642

Call Sign: KA1SDG
Meika Wahlstrom
Nauset Rd
Eastham MA 02642

Call Sign: KA1WDC
Karen Wahlstrom
Nauset Rd
Eastham MA 02642

Call Sign: KB1AEU
Carly D Richard
18 Nutmeg Ln
Eastham MA 02642

Call Sign: KA1VSL
Amber J Hall
Off Samoset Rd
Eastham MA 02642

Call Sign: KB1BAP
James T Rainey
2165 Old State High
Eastham MA 02642

Call Sign: KB1MDU
Paul M Niles

25 Pequod Lane
Eastham MA 02642

Call Sign: KA1VTJ
Jenna J Hollander
Essig
Pequod Ln Rd 1
Eastham MA 02642

Call Sign: N1NXV
Jack S Barritt
30 Perry Ln
Eastham MA 02642

Call Sign: N1LHF
David M Marr
13 Pilgrim Lane
Eastham MA 02642

Call Sign: NE8B
Morley A Marr
13 Pilgrim Ln
Eastham MA 02642

Call Sign: KA1SEI
Michael L Farrell
134 Pinewood Rd
Eastham MA 02642

Call Sign: N1BX
Peter Marrero
Po Box 534
Eastham MA 02642

Call Sign: KA1SEK
Ahnastasia S Jones
Route 6
Eastham MA 02642

Call Sign: KA1UAC
Allison M Welch
Rt 6 At Atlantic Oaks
Eastham MA 02642

Call Sign: KB1BAE
William H Allen Iv
95 S Eastham St
Eastham MA 02651

Call Sign: KA1ZEM
Mark R Vecchione
345 Schoolhouse Rd
Eastham MA 02642

Call Sign: KA1SED
Clay G Hachey
Sharon Cir
Eastham MA 02642

Call Sign: KB1BAK
Jennifer L Harris
4 Sibley Way
Eastham MA 02642

Call Sign: KA1YVJ
Kyle G Harris
4 Sibley Way Rr 1
Eastham MA 02642

Call Sign: KB1BBD
Erin L Fisk
10 Smith Ln Box 163
Eastham MA 02642

Call Sign: KA1YWX
Madeline L Baker
5 South East St
Eastham MA 02642

Call Sign: KB1BBA
Dana M Richardson
405 Squanto Rd 102
Eastham MA 02651

Call Sign: KA1WDA
Eben T Fogg
20 Starlight Ln
Eastham MA 02642

Call Sign: KA1VTN
Arien F Porter
3 Starlight Ln Rr 1
Eastham MA 02642

Call Sign: KB1AIU
Gerald A Harper Ii
595 State Hwy
Eastham MA 02646

Call Sign: KA1YVY
Edward R Chad
35 Surry Dr
Eastham MA 02642

Call Sign: KB1AZZ
John E Di Donato Iii
35 Swift Rd
Eastham MA 02651

Call Sign: N1JDG
Carl H Sylvester
80 Western Ave
Eastham MA 02642

Call Sign: K1RAL
John Spencer
190 Widgeon Dr
Eastham MA 02642

Call Sign: KA1SDW
Michelle L Monahan
10 Wilma Rd
Eastham MA 02642

Call Sign: KA1SDC
Joseph M Monahan
10 Wilma Rd Rr 2
Eastham MA 02642

Call Sign: KA1YWO
Kerrin A Ryan
275 Windjammer Ln
Rr 1
Eastham MA 02642

Call Sign: KA1SCD
Sean M Ambroult
Eastham MA 02642

Call Sign: KA1SCH
Regan M Cavaliere
Eastham MA 02642

Call Sign: KA1SCI
Michael C Miller
Eastham MA 02642

Call Sign: KA1SDD
Emily E Pechonis
Eastham MA 02642

Call Sign: KA1SDE
Jedediah D Carlson
Eastham MA 02642

Call Sign: KA1SDH
Andrew L Mc Mullen
Eastham MA 02642

Call Sign: KA1SDV
Joseph M Caivano
Eastham MA 02642

Call Sign: KA1TVL
Jonathan V Guardia
Eastham MA 02642

Call Sign: KA1TVO
Erica L Kimtis
Eastham MA 02642

Call Sign: KA1TVQ
Koert J Lyman
Eastham MA 02642

Call Sign: KA1TVY
Rosie M Albanese
Eastham MA 02642

Call Sign: KA1TWC
Scott E Brown
Eastham MA 02642

Call Sign: KA1TWF
William Buzzell
Eastham MA 02642

Call Sign: KA1TWY
Michael J Mc Donald
Eastham MA 02642

Call Sign: KA1VSP
Jennifer I Brown
Eastham MA 02642

Call Sign: KA1VTD
Cristina J Cepkauskas
Eastham MA 02642

Call Sign: KA1VTM
Brooke T Douglass
Eastham MA 02642

Call Sign: KA1WDB
James R Barnard
Eastham MA 02642

Call Sign: KA1YWK
Jeremy J Albanese
Eastham MA 02642

Call Sign: KA1YWR
Tara M Quinn
Eastham MA 02642

Call Sign: KA1YWV

Jonathan H Carlson
Eastham MA 02642

Call Sign: KA1ZEL
Joshua J Adams
Eastham MA 02642

Call Sign: KB1AEJ
Abigail L Deschamps
Eastham MA 02642

Call Sign: KB1BAB
Charles S Butler
Eastham MA 02542

Call Sign: KB1BAS
Erin M Brady
Eastham MA 02642

Call Sign: KB1BAW
Elizabeth C Lovelock
Eastham MA 02642

Call Sign: KB1BAX
Siobhan E O Brien
Eastham MA 02642

Call Sign: KA1CJY
Mark Coral
Eastham MA 02642

Call Sign: KA1YWC
Brendan C Adams
Eastham MA 02642

**FCC Amateur Radio
Licenses in
Easthampton**

Call Sign: N1BMA
Daniel J Ferreira Jr
4 Adams St
Easthampton MA
01027

Call Sign: KA1QGT
Ronald W Oatway
50 Adams St Apt A
Easthampton MA
01027

Call Sign: KB1MXW
Matt S Gangne
51 Ashley Circle

Easthampton MA
01027

Call Sign: KB1MXX
Laura M Gangne
51 Ashley Circle
Easthampton MA
01027

Call Sign: KB1PWQ
Juliusz Kirejczyk
18 Bayberry Dr
Easthampton MA
01027

Call Sign: W1WMA
Western Mass Amateur
Radio Group
34 Campbell Dr
Easthampton MA
01027

Call Sign: KB1QVQ
Emma M Bricault
34 Campbell Dr
Easthampton MA
01027

Call Sign: N1FSF
Harold J Woering
48 Campbell Dr
Easthampton MA
01027

Call Sign: N1FTP
Harold J Woering Sr
48 Campbell Dr
Easthampton MA
01027

Call Sign: N9ZHB
Joseph B Seitz
5 Chapman Ave 2
Easthampton MA
01027

Call Sign: KB1MXZ
Peter W Wintheiser
7 Chestnut St
Easthampton MA
01027

Call Sign: N1KIC
Gloria M Warnock

64253 Clapp St
Easthampton MA
01027

Call Sign: WA1KJD
Albert E Tilbe
14 Clark Ave
Easthampton MA
01027

Call Sign: KA1NDA
Daniel C Gallagher
101 Clark St
Easthampton MA
01027

Call Sign: N1XOH
Joseph Steele
11 Duda Dr
Easthampton MA
01027

Call Sign: KB1MMN
Mark T Sienkiewicz
51 East St
Easthampton MA
010271209

Call Sign: W1ZWZ
John W Ramsey Jr
111 East St
Easthampton MA
01027

Call Sign: N1RLX
Raymond E
Lendzioszek
46 Echo Ln
Easthampton MA
010272418

Call Sign: WB1CXC
Rudy J Zerdecki
3 Elliott St
Easthampton MA
01027

Call Sign: N1VAP
Stanley F Zygo Jr
50 Everett St
Easthampton MA
01027

Call Sign: N1WQX

Michelle L Zygo
50 Everett St
Easthampton MA
01027

Call Sign: KB1LJT
Nikoli A Zygo
50 Everett St
Easthampton MA
01027

Call Sign: KB1LNG
Demitria A Zygo
50 Everett St
Easthampton MA
01027

Call Sign: W1VAP
Nikoli A Zygo
50 Everett St
Easthampton MA
01027

Call Sign: W1MPG
Harvey J Vincent
55 Garfield Ave
Easthampton MA
01027

Call Sign: W1NDY
Lester J Vincent
55 Garfield Ave
Easthampton MA
01027

Call Sign: N1MUE
Bernt F Johansson
31 Glendale St
Easthampton MA
01027

Call Sign: KB1JOS
Robert A Donovan
13 Grant St
Easthampton MA
01027

Call Sign: K1BHA
Theodore F
Gratkowski
5 Gross Ln
Easthampton MA
01027

Call Sign: KB1MZJ
James E Torrey
15 Hampton Terrace
Easthampton MA
01027

Call Sign: AB1FC
Alexander J Rock
24 High St Apt 2r
Easthampton MA
01027

Call Sign: W1SEM
James D Allison
17 Holly Cir
Easthampton MA
010272705

Call Sign: KA1AMS
Joseph H Piorkowski
5 Kenneth Rd
Easthampton MA
01027

Call Sign: N1TPA
Lawrence J Boucher Jr
19 Lincoln St
Easthampton MA
01027

Call Sign: WA1LGU
Carol A Bernier Gawle
30 Line St
Easthampton MA
01027

Call Sign: W1LGU
Carol A Gawle
30 Line St
Easthampton MA
01027

Call Sign: KB1EXQ
Jeffrey D Ouellette
246 Londville Rd
Easthampton MA
01027

Call Sign: KB1HQO
Rebecca S Taft-
Childress
209 Loudville Rd
Easthampton MA
01027

Call Sign: N1AGV
Peter H Ouellette
246 Loudville Rd
Easthampton MA
01027

Call Sign: N1BIF
Elizabeth A Ouellette
246 Loudville Rd
Easthampton MA
01027

Call Sign: N1EOE
Stephen T Mc Grath
248 Loudville Rd
Easthampton MA
01027

Call Sign: N1PGV
Marilyn Mc Grath
248 Loudville Rd
Easthampton MA
01027

Call Sign: N1WCV
Dylan P Mawdsley
248 Loudville Rd
Easthampton MA
01027

Call Sign: AA1DX
Edward A Cadorette
9 Lownds Ave
Easthampton MA
01027

Call Sign: WA1CWI
Curtis R Cadorette
9 Lownds Ave
Easthampton MA
01027

Call Sign: AA1B
Robert L Barkowski
32 Lyman St
Easthampton MA
010271012

Call Sign: KF2JO
Richard B Wood
252 Main St
Easthampton MA
01027

Call Sign: KB1HV
Medora M Hunter
336 Main St
Easthampton MA
01027

Call Sign: KB1SHA
Edward H Hughes
8 Mckinley Ave
Easthampton MA
01027

Call Sign: KA1QYJ
Daniel L Constantine
17 Melinda Lane
Easthampton MA
01027

Call Sign: N1TTM
Leonard M Cocco
74 Oliver St
Easthampton MA
01027

Call Sign: KA1BG
Richard L La Barge
4 Pine Hill Rd
Easthampton MA
010279760

Call Sign: WB1HHA
Jack E Harris
21 Pine St
Easthampton MA
01027

Call Sign: KB1TAC
Jonathan D Frost
116 Pleasant St Suite
11
Easthampton MA
01027

Call Sign: KB1MMM
Bruce D Campbell
27 Pomeroy St
Easthampton MA
01027

Call Sign: KB1RRU
Joshua E Lafond
87 Pomeroy St

Easthampton MA
01027

Call Sign: KB1OIA
Maurice J Paul
Memorial Station
42 Ridgewood Terrace
Easthampton MA
01027

Call Sign: W1MGE
Maurice J Paul
Memorial Station
42 Ridgewood Terrace
Easthampton MA
01027

Call Sign: KB1WPG
David B Meunier
2 Summer St
Easthampton MA
01027

Call Sign: W1KYJ
Walter H Winsky
21 Summit Ave
Easthampton MA
01027

Call Sign: KA1AUI
Francis P Sturges
6 True Hart Dr
Easthampton MA
01027

Call Sign: WB1EHD
Dennis A Malone
29 Ward Ave Apt C
Easthampton MA
010272236

Call Sign: KB1PEE
Western Mass Amateur
Radio Group
29 Ward Ave Apt C
Easthampton MA
01027

Call Sign: WA1YZU
Frank W Furman Jr
45 West St
Easthampton MA
01027

Call Sign: N1LKU
Linda J Schmitter
20 Zabek Dr
Easthampton MA
01027

Call Sign: WX1Q
Brian W Baxa
Easthampton MA
010275474

FCC Amateur Radio Licenses in Easton

Call Sign: K1WMT
Robert F Mahoney
5 Chandler Way
Easton MA 02356

Call Sign: W1GFB
Edmund J Malley
87 Rockland St
Easton MA 02356

Call Sign: KC1XH
Francis S Mc Keen
6 Summer St
Easton MA 02356

FCC Amateur Radio Licenses in Edgartown

Call Sign: KB1LHR
35 Edgartown School
Amateur Radio Club
- Box 6
Edgartown MA 02539

Call Sign: K1MVY
35 Vineyard Amateur
Radio Assoc
- Box 6
Edgartown MA 02539

Call Sign: N1QDJ
Norman C Telles
Box 173a
Edgartown MA 02539

Call Sign: KB1IYT
Bill H Mackenty
Box 73z
Edgartown MA 02539

Call Sign: KA1SES
Nelson W Smith
29 Curtis Ln
Edgartown MA 02539

Call Sign: KB1IYU
Robert E Gilkes
77 Dodgers Hole Rd
Edgartown MA 02539

Call Sign: K1REG
Robert E Gilkes
77 Dodgers Hole Rd
Edgartown MA 02539

Call Sign: KB1QL
Bradford T Fligor
5 Marchants Path Box
2106
Edgartown MA 02539

Call Sign: N1MLO
Terence H Forde
50 North Neck Rd
Edgartown MA 02539

Call Sign: KB1OBJ
Jonathan K Dore
Rfd 203
Edgartown MA 02539

Call Sign: KB1BIN
Anna Elizabeth B
Villard Howe
Star Rt 81
Edgartown MA 02539

Call Sign: KA9UAX
Susan P Henley
1 Thames Court
Edgartown MA 02539

Call Sign: KB1IYR
Leslie J Freeman
5 Tower Ln
Edgartown MA 02539

Call Sign: K1IOC
William E Welch
7 Welch Way
Edgartown MA 02539

Call Sign: W1FC

Fred P Collins
42 Witchwood Lane
Edgartown MA 02539

Call Sign: WA1ZPA
Karen E Collins
42 Witchwood Lane
Edgartown MA 02539

Call Sign: KA1JII
Paul V Christian
Edgartown MA 02539

Call Sign: KA1JXL
Lorraine D Christian
Edgartown MA 02539

Call Sign: W1EOR
John L Henley
Edgartown MA 02539

Call Sign: KA1U
Stephen W Miller
Edgartown MA
025392335

Call Sign: KB1MJK
Hudson Lee
Edgartown MA 02539

Call Sign: KB1MKK
Conor J Smith
Edgartown MA 02539

Call Sign: KB1MKM
William T Fligor
Edgartown MA 02539

Call Sign: KB1OBI
William D Trapp
Edgartown MA
025391871

Call Sign: KB1OBK
Dylan M Rice
Edgartown MA 02539

Call Sign: KB1RFP
E Thor Farrish
Edgartown MA 02537

FCC Amateur Radio
Licenses in Erving

Call Sign: KB1PKK
Aaron D Budine
41 Forest St
Erving MA 01344

Call Sign: WB1HKN
Richard F Cunningham
46 High St
Erving MA 01344

Call Sign: KA1SIA
Donald R Calkins
12 North St
Erving MA 013449724

Call Sign: KB1FVW
Joseph A Bassett
5 Pleasant St
Erving MA 01344

Call Sign: N1JWW
Mark W Mc Cord
7 Wells St
Erving MA 01344

FCC Amateur Radio
Licenses in Essex

Call Sign: NK1K
Christopher H Taron
36 Belcher St
Essex MA 01929

Call Sign: K1VDE
Gilbert E Guerin
Box 4
Essex MA 01929

Call Sign: KB1RXV
Darrell R Perkins
35 Conomo Point Rd
Essex MA 01929

Call Sign: KB1KLY
Christopher A Jordan
143 Eastern Ave
Essex MA 01929

Call Sign: KA1VPF
Eric C Wilhelm
28 Western Ave
Essex MA 01929

Call Sign: N1CRX

Kurt A Wilhelm
28 Western Ave
Essex MA 01929

Call Sign: KA1ELN
Thomas E Skolfield
158 Western Ave
Essex MA 01929

Call Sign: N1VYQ
Mark A Jordan
164 Western Ave
Essex MA 01929

Call Sign: W1NIN
Ernest H Steadman
41 Wood Dr
Essex MA 01929

Call Sign: WB1GII
William C Steadman
41 Wood Dr
Essex MA 01929

Call Sign: WA1YRG
James N Lester
83 Wood Dr
Essex MA 01929

Call Sign: AA1XZ
James N Lester
83 Wood Dr
Essex MA 01929

Call Sign: KD1UX
Glenn R Pike
Essex MA 019290011

Call Sign: N1FMX
Barry B O'brien
Essex MA 01929

Call Sign: N1UIW
Deborah S Pike
Essex MA 019290011

Call Sign: WA1QWA
Barry V Hamilton
Essex MA 01929

Call Sign: KG1P
Glenn R Pike
Essex MA 019290011

Call Sign: N1YBF
Larry Meister
45 Adams Ave
Everett MA 02149

Call Sign: KA1GWU
John Philip Neal
27 Autumn St
Everett MA 02149

Call Sign: KB1JHZ
Frank V Permatteo
3 Baker Rd
Everett MA
021494913

Call Sign: WA1SVB
Frank V Permatteo
3 Baker Rd
Everett MA
021494913

Call Sign: KB1VKS
Joel H Chiet
18 Baker Rd
Everett MA 02149

Call Sign: W1JHC
Joel H Chiet
18 Baker Rd
Everett MA 02149

Call Sign: KB1JXH
Kashan Arshad
54 Baldwin Ave
Everett MA 02149

Call Sign: AA1XS
James F Sullivan
70 Baldwin Ave
Everett MA 02149

Call Sign: N1IWE
Richard J De Sisto
84 Baldwin Ave
Everett MA
021492133

Call Sign: KA1RDZ
Daniel J Malloy
Baldwin Ave

Everett MA
021492130

Call Sign: K1CKS
Hugo A N Semm
851 Broadway Apt 28
Everett MA 02149

Call Sign: N1UOZ
John J Moynihan
566 Broadway St
Everett MA 02146

Call Sign: N1RTD
Jeanne A Wilkens
25 Cabot St
Everett MA 02149

Call Sign: KB1WWC
Michael D Hussey
51 Central Ave
Everett MA 02149

Call Sign: KB1WWE
Mary Ellen C Hussey
51 Central Ave
Everett MA 02149

Call Sign: KB1CRY
Guy W Bzibziak
36 Church St
Everett MA 02149

Call Sign: N1ZFF
Hakim Madjid
36 Church St
Everett MA 02149

Call Sign: W1RYX
William W Beane
9 Courtland St
Everett MA 02149

Call Sign: KA1BMN
Paul M Hickey V
59 Dean St
Everett MA 02149

Call Sign: KI1Z
Mary A Walker
9 Dowse St
Everett MA 02149

Call Sign: KA1PHP

David E Moran
19 E Elm St
Everett MA 02149

Call Sign: KA1PHR
Mitzi Doherty
19 E Elm St
Everett MA 02149

Call Sign: KB1EEF
David A Goyette
34 Everett
Everett MA 02149

Call Sign: KB1KEK
Samuel Pagan Jr
442 Ferry St
Everett MA 02149

Call Sign: AA1TH
William M Knowles
15 Ferry St 7
Everett MA 02149

Call Sign: W1AFL
Charles F Pope
57 Forest Ave
Everett MA 02149

Call Sign: KA1NWD
Elizabeth M Arsenault
13 Gladstone St
Everett MA 02149

Call Sign: KB1QON
Gerald F Kelley
22 Hillside Ave
Everett MA 02149

Call Sign: KB1RFF
Gayle M Kelley
22 Hillside Ave
Everett MA 02149

Call Sign: N1BPB
Frank J De Caro
117 Irving St
Everett MA 02149

Call Sign: WA1FMW
Arthur A De Tore
51 Jackson Ave
Everett MA 02149

Call Sign: N1HFZ
Cheryl Cogliano
112 Linden St
Everett MA 02149

Call Sign: N1HGA
Robert W Cogliano
112 Linden St
Everett MA 02149

Call Sign: N1WWH
Neil N Stewart
12 Lynde St
Everett MA 02149

Call Sign: K1IIM
Donald B Demeritt
105 Lynn St
Everett MA 02149

Call Sign: N1GEN
Alexander K Galbraith
Jr
104 Main St
Everett MA 02149

Call Sign: KB1ICZ
Sean J Mangan
45 Malden St #3
Everett MA 02149

Call Sign: N1PQJ
Christian A Laquidara
6 Mead St
Everett MA 02149

Call Sign: KE1MB
Donald J Ball Iii
6 Mead St 2
Everett MA 02149

Call Sign: KB1WTM
Nicole N Edgecomb
6 Mead St 2
Everett MA 02149

Call Sign: N1HFY
Joseph J Nicotera
16 Parkview Rd
Everett MA 02149

Call Sign: N1PUJ
Stephen T Colameta
71 Pearl St

Everett MA 02149

Call Sign: N1PMF
Robert J Colameta Jr
73 Pearl St
Everett MA 02149

Call Sign: KB1KGC
Stephen J Muise
46 Peirce Ave Apt 1
Everett MA 02149

Call Sign: N1KCR
Lowell Wright
55 Preston St
Everett MA 02149

Call Sign: WA1WWI
Arthur R Fitzpatrick Jr
52 Reed Ave
Everett MA 02149

Call Sign: WA1YWZ
Arthur R Fitzpatrick Iii
52 Reed Ave
Everett MA 02149

Call Sign: KA1MON
Robert C Bishara
576 Second St
Everett MA 02149

Call Sign: N1GVY
Frank J Izzo
27 Spaulding St
Everett MA 02149

Call Sign: K1KQI
Barry L Allen
157 Springvale Ave
Everett MA 02149

Call Sign: N1PWZ
Michael J Moreschi
193 Springvale Ave
Everett MA 02149

Call Sign: W1KHA
Lawrence Parrish
18 Summer St
Everett MA 02149

Call Sign: KB1MWD
John G Young Jr

15 Summer St Apt 310
Everett MA 02149

Call Sign: WB3BBP
Jerry L Berrier
18 Trunfio Ln
Everett MA 02149

Call Sign: K1PDI
Charles A Di Sabatino
21 Tufts Ave
Everett MA
021492605

Call Sign: KC0MYM
Nathan T Glaser
37 Waters Ave Apt#2
Everett MA 02149

Call Sign: K0HOG
Timothy A Headle
32 Webster St
Everett MA 02149

Call Sign: K1NYQ
Raymond E Iapicca Sr
1 Winter St
Everett MA 02149

Call Sign: N1GRG
Calvin R Sprague Jr
Everett MA 02149

Call Sign: K1SQT
Joseph W Scully Jr
Everett MA 02149

Call Sign: N1CTN
William M Mullowney
Everett MA
021490403

**FCC Amateur Radio
Licenses in Fairhaven**

Call Sign: WA1AKR
Carl G Bissonnette
180 Adams Apt A26
Fairhaven MA 02719

Call Sign: N1VUG
Robert R Ambroult
257 Adams St
Fairhaven MA 02719

Call Sign: KA1YZM
John D Serpa
51 Akin
Fairhaven MA 02719

Call Sign: KB1SQG
Jeffrey G Kellogg
138 Alden Rd
Fairhaven MA 02719

Call Sign: K1JGK
Jeffrey G Kellogg
138 Alden Rd
Fairhaven MA 02719

Call Sign: K1JK
Jeffrey G Kellogg
138 Alden Rd
Fairhaven MA 02719

Call Sign: KB1VLH
Kevin W Gordon
400 Alden Rd
Fairhaven MA 02719

Call Sign: KB1KXX
Herbert Eddleston
26 Bay View Ave
Fairhaven MA
027191802

Call Sign: K1USW
Herbert Eddleston
26 Bay View Ave
Fairhaven MA
027191802

Call Sign: WA1NMD
Albert Sirois
6 Bernese
Fairhaven MA 02719

Call Sign: KB1SJY
David L Durfee Sr
11 Birchfield St
Fairhaven MA 02719

Call Sign: W1QKZ
David L Durfee Sr
11 Birchfield St
Fairhaven MA 02719

Call Sign: W1UCO

Ralph N Fuller
7 Blossom St
Fairhaven MA 02719

Call Sign: KA1WBH
Mark L Baron
36 Bluepoint Rd
Fairhaven MA 02719

Call Sign: KA1EYR
Charles Casmira
62 Boston Hill Rd
Fairhaven MA 02719

Call Sign: WB1FBP
Scott Jenney
43 Bridge St
Fairhaven MA 02719

Call Sign: K1AWX
Victor L Brunette
7 Brookview St
Fairhaven MA 02719

Call Sign: KB1TKU
Fairhaven Emergency
Management Agency
40 Center St
Fairhaven MA 02719

Call Sign: W1FEM
Fairhaven Emergency
Management Agency
40 Center St
Fairhaven MA 02719

Call Sign: K1NET
Stephen J Saunders
64 Cottage St
Fairhaven MA 02719

Call Sign: KB1CHR
Wayne C Edwards Sr
165 Ebony St
Fair Haven MA 02719

Call Sign: KA1ZEN
Ruben P Macedo
6 Elizabeth St
Fairhaven MA 02719

Call Sign: W1ZEI
Brownell Brightman
5 Elm Ave

Fairhaven MA 02719

Call Sign: W1HMS
James B Buckley
6 Fort St
Fairhaven MA 02719

Call Sign: KB1GZW
Robert M Gracia
20 Fort St
Fairhaven MA 02719

Call Sign: KB1KOP
Thomas R Dussault
21 Fort St
Fairhaven MA 02719

Call Sign: K1NEW
Thomas R Dussault
21 Fort St
Fairhaven MA 02719

Call Sign: KB1JUQ
Robert A Roderiques
Sr
31 Gellette Rd
Fairhaven MA 02719

Call Sign: KB1JUR
Robert A Roderiques
Jr
31 Gellette Rd
Fairhaven MA 02719

Call Sign: K1NSX
Kenneth Rapoza
19 Golf St
Fairhaven MA
027191720

Call Sign: WB3CEU
Grace M Nopper
Goulart Mem Dr
Fairhaven MA 02719

Call Sign: WB3CEV
Willis L Nopper
Goulart Mem Dr
Fairhaven MA 02719

Call Sign: KB1SJZ
Tammy Ann Moutinho
7 Grandview Ave
Fairhaven MA 02719

Call Sign: KB1EV
Emerson H Hiller
114 Green St
Fairhaven MA 02719

Call Sign: KB1MFE
Douglas E Johnson
39 Hathaway St
Fairhaven MA
027191744

Call Sign: W1RDJ
Douglas E Johnson
39 Hathaway St
Fairhaven MA
027191744

Call Sign: WA1WNO
Richard R Lauzon
22 Hill St
Fairhaven MA 02719

Call Sign: W1QJR
Kenneth F Gillum
15 Hiller Ave
Fairhaven MA 02719

Call Sign: N2HGU
Charles B Pear Iii
16 Hitch St
Fairhaven MA 02719

Call Sign: K1GMT
Charles B Pear Iii
16 Hitch St
Fairhaven MA 02719

Call Sign: WA1OMI
Michael Laronda
17 Hopkins St
Fairhaven MA 02719

Call Sign: WA1WPT
Joseph V Morgida
288 Huttleston Ave
Fairhaven MA
027195103

Call Sign: KB1RTJ
John Rogers
13 Jarvis Ave
Fairhaven MA 02719

Call Sign: N1NLV
Timothy P Duarte
8 Jenna Dr
Fairhaven MA
027195123

Call Sign: N1VDO
Ronald J Lessa
5 John St
Fairhaven MA 02719

Call Sign: W1RJL
Ronald J Lessa
5 John St
Fairhaven MA 02719

Call Sign: KA1KII
John L Chew
180 Main St
Fairhaven MA
027193259

Call Sign: KA1YZA
Thomas A Souza
327 Main St
Fairhaven MA 02719

Call Sign: KB1SKB
Nicholas L Gautreau
335 Main St
Fairhaven MA 02719

Call Sign: KB1AFR
John L Lienard
58 Main St Apt 1 E
Fairhaven MA 02719

Call Sign: WA1KDT
Norman L Benoit
275 Main St Apt 134
Fairhaven MA 02719

Call Sign: N1NDJ
Peter Szala
18 Mangham Way
Fairhaven MA 02719

Call Sign: KA1NMQ
Maurice Gagnon
10 Manuel St
Fairhaven MA 02719

Call Sign: KB1PNK
Bonnie J Brault

12 Maple Ave
Fairhaven MA 02719

Call Sign: KA1PCR
John L Tyson Jr
4 Marilaine Pl
Fairhaven MA 02719

Call Sign: KA1GXC
Michael W Correia
28 Mc Gann Terrace
Fairhaven MA 02719

Call Sign: WA1MQC
Alice M Bissonnette
100 Mcgann Terrace
Apt 218
Fairhaven MA 02719

Call Sign: N1ZGX
Stephen J Saunders
8 Middle St
Fairhaven MA 02719

Call Sign: W2RG
Richard A Griffiths
11 North St
Fairhaven MA 02719

Call Sign: N1VKB
Paul C Smith
69 North St
Fairhaven MA 02719

Call Sign: AA1GN
Bruce S Champoux
10 Oliver St
Fairhaven MA 02719

Call Sign: WB1DMQ
Raymond A Green
19 Paul St
Fairhaven MA 02719

Call Sign: KB1DOZ
Andrew T Perron
35 Phoenix St
Fairhaven MA 02719

Call Sign: WA1CQM
Paul J Lariviere
11 Pilgrim Ave
Fairhaven MA
027193373

Call Sign: KA1TK
Donald A Fowlie
119 Pleasant St
Fairhaven MA 02719

Call Sign: K1CDM
Alan J La Croix
11 Ridgecrest Ave
Fairhaven MA 02719

Call Sign: KA1JFI
Joseph Hampson Iii
375 Sconticut Neck Rd
Fairhaven MA
027191309

Call Sign: W1JFI
Joseph Hampson Iii
375 Sconticut Neck Rd
Fairhaven MA
027191309

Call Sign: KA1TP
John C Hadfield
16 Sconticut Neck Rd
288
Fairhaven MA 02719

Call Sign: N1NJI
John W O Brien Iii
16 Sconticut Neck Rd
323
Fairhaven MA 02719

Call Sign: N1IQU
John J Braz Jr
12 Sharon St
Fairhaven MA
027194402

Call Sign: N1VNC
Michael J Florio
4 Suzanne Way
Fairhaven MA 02719

Call Sign: WB1ATG
Dale G Kollars
89 Tootle Ln
Fairhaven MA
027195005

Call Sign: KB1KYM
William A Wood

33 Washburn Ave
Fair Haven MA 02719

Call Sign: KB1BEF
Frank A Cenerizio
47 Washburn Ave
Fairhaven MA 02719

Call Sign: K1DPI
Raymond Marshall
15 Weeden Pl
Fairhaven MA
027192514

Call Sign: KB1JUS
Bryan C Peirce
20 Welcome St
Fairhaven MA 02719

Call Sign: N1WKD
Alison L Savino
51 William St
Fairhaven MA 02719

Call Sign: N1WJI
Dennis G Bollea
57 Yale St
Fairhaven MA
027190450

Call Sign: KA1WBF
Marc N Jodoin
Fairhaven MA
027190423

Call Sign: KB1JUV
Liston G Kirkwood
Fairhaven MA 02719

Call Sign: KB1RTK
Martin B Higgins Iii
Fairhaven MA 02719

FCC Amateur Radio Licenses in Fairview

Call Sign: K1QVG
Norman R Derome
475 Montcalm St
Chicopee
Fairview MA 01020

FCC Amateur Radio Licenses in Fall River

Call Sign: WB1HGA
Ronald A Silvia
523 Aetna St
Fall River MA 02721

Call Sign: KB1ISK
Matthew Silvia
523 Aetna St
Fall River MA 02721

Call Sign: N1RHG
Lomer H Lapointe
40 Albion St
Fall River MA 02723

Call Sign: WA1LBK
Thomas J Lapointe
40 Albion St
Fall River MA 02723

Call Sign: KA1VXA
Paul Medeiros
367 America St
Fall River MA 02721

Call Sign: N1NOJ
Carol Medeiros
367 America St
Fall River MA 02721

Call Sign: K1VXA
Paul Medeiros
367 America St
Fall River MA 02721

Call Sign: KB1DYA
Michael T Silvia
199 Anthony St
Fall River MA
027213305

Call Sign: N1GXN
Donna Guindon
290 Anthony St
Fall River MA 02721

Call Sign: N1VDK
Brian Letendre
29 Ash St
Fall River MA 02724

Call Sign: N1WDJ
Eileen M Barillaro

8 B Rolling Green Dr
Fall River MA 02720

Call Sign: KB1LFK
Jason R Bertrand
186 Bark St
Fall River MA 02723

Call Sign: W1CGE
Marcel A Castonguay
125 Barlow St
Fall River MA 02723

Call Sign: N1JVI
George J Correia Jr
131 Barlow St
Fall River MA 02723

Call Sign: KB1TPG
John P Kusanagi-Cooney
12 Barrett St
Fall River MA 02724

Call Sign: KA1ZJU
Roberto M Couto
1915 Bay St
Fall River MA 02724

Call Sign: N1WFW
Frank Mello
143 Bayview St
Fall River MA 02724

Call Sign: W1FQU
Francis J Saunders Sr
55 Bigelow St
Fall River MA 02720

Call Sign: N1ZGV
John Zb Lozinski
651 Bowen St
Fall River MA 02724

Call Sign: WA1LET
Cyril Lievesley
142 Brightman St
Fall River MA 02720

Call Sign: WB1HFH
James Nascimento Jr
140 Broadway
Fall River MA 02721

Call Sign: W1FRY
Armand R Servant
793 Broadway
Fall River MA 02724

Call Sign: WA1PPQ
Theresa Servant
793 Broadway
Fall River MA 02724

Call Sign: N1ALW
James H Powell
199 Buffinton
Fall River MA 02721

Call Sign: K1EYG
Henry J Rodzen
287 Buffinton St
Fall River MA
027213939

Call Sign: KB1DID
Lydia L Heatherly
266 Buffinton St 2
Fall River MA
027213942

Call Sign: KB1UDH
Louis M Pacheco
82 Cedar St
Fall River MA 02720

Call Sign: N1XFT
Russell C Saucier
969 Charles St
Fall River MA 02724

Call Sign: K1IWE
Francis J Colaneri
986 Cherry Atreet
Fall River MA 02720

Call Sign: W1YHZ
Stanley W Tobol
86 Cherry St
Fall River MA 02720

Call Sign: KB1LKW
Shantae Martins
659 Cherry St
Fall River MA 02720

Call Sign: W1GTA
Larry L Beavers

297 Clarkson St
Fall River MA 02724

Call Sign: KB1PCF
Brittany Silvia
199 Columbia St
Fall River MA 02721

Call Sign: KB1NWX
Kevin E Franca
211 Columbia St
Fall River MA 02721

Call Sign: KB1OQC
Ceasar Braga Jr
173 Corbett St
Fall River MA 02720

Call Sign: AD1DX
Ceasar Braga Jr
173 Corbett St
Fall River MA 02720

Call Sign: KB1SES
Raymond J Levesque
Memorial Arc
173 Corbett St
Fall River MA 02720

Call Sign: K1ZZN
Raymond J Levesque
Memorial Arc
173 Corbett St
Fall River MA 02720

Call Sign: KB1FIR
Kris D Machado
76 Cottage St
Fall River MA 02721

Call Sign: N1RPX
John M Chaves
187 Cottage St
Fall River MA 02721

Call Sign: KB1WHJ
Kimberly A Rego
864 County St
Fall River MA 02723

Call Sign: KB1ALB
Antonio M Rebelo
424 Dale St
Fall River MA 02721

Call Sign: KB1MJE
James R Armstrong Jr
750 Davol St - Unit
819
Fall River MA 02720

Call Sign: NS5U
James W Benson
750 Davol St Apt 1122
Fall River MA
027201020

Call Sign: N1GFG
Omer D Harrison
667 Dickinson St
Fall River MA 02721

Call Sign: KA1JFK
Edward Martin
72 Dover St
Fall River MA 02721

Call Sign: KB1GJV
Chris A Gifford Jr
40 Duncan St
Fall River MA 02721

Call Sign: N1JQI
George W Kanuse
201 Durfee St
Fall River MA 02720

Call Sign: KB1NPM
Kaylee A Penland
557 Durfee St
Fall River MA 02720

Call Sign: KB1FIQ
Carlos Neves
424 Dwelly St
Fall River MA 02724

Call Sign: N1YCM
Edward A Dion
80 Earle St
Fall River MA
027233104

Call Sign: N1SMN
Donald J Perrault
112 Eastern Ave
Fall River MA 02723

Call Sign: KB1FIO
Michael R Pelletier
150 Eaton St
Fall River MA 02723

Call Sign: W1CMV
Joe E Velho
30 Edmond St
Fall River MA 02721

Call Sign: N1VHP
Manny Tavares
36 Edmund St
Fall River MA 02721

Call Sign: AA1QQ
Ellis W Deckey
140 Essex St 811
Fall River MA 02723

Call Sign: KB1LFX
Ronald W Barr
1 Ferry St
Fall River MA 02722

Call Sign: N1SMQ
James Voltas
405 Fifth St
Fall River MA 02721

Call Sign: N1TEN
Ann M Voltas
405 Fifth St
Fall River MA 02721

Call Sign: KB1LFL
Kyle D De Medeiros
81 Foster St
Fall River MA 02721

Call Sign: KB1LFP
Wei C Chen
153 Foster St
Fall River MA 02721

Call Sign: N1LSS
William J Mitz Jr
20 Freedom St
Fall River MA 02724

Call Sign: N1NJL
Kathleen M Correia
59 Freedom St
Fall River MA 02724

Call Sign: WA1FEQ
John C Ostapow
295 Frost St
Fall River MA 02721

Call Sign: N1SAO
Sherry A Martin
302 Frost St
Fall River MA 02721

Call Sign: WA1FER
Lawrence C Ostapow
375 Frost St
Fall River MA 02721

Call Sign: WB1EWZ
Everett R Costa
911 Globe St
Fall River MA 02724

Call Sign: KB1KVN
Alyssa M Manchester
1232 Globe St
Fall River MA 02721

Call Sign: KB1LFR
Justin D Xavier
298 Grinnell St
Fall River MA 02721

Call Sign: N1LMF
Glen A Pacheco
226 Haffard St
Fall River MA 02723

Call Sign: KB1AYQ
Lisa A Pacheco
226 Haffards St
Fall River MA 02723

Call Sign: N1WFX
John F Santos
54 Hanover St
Fall River MA
027205222

Call Sign: N1IOW
Antonio R Di
Benedetto
80 Hanover St
Fall River MA 02720

Call Sign: N1WGA

Joseph F Mc Grady
533 Hanover St
Fall River MA 02720

Call Sign: N1VBB
Jose H Carreiro
8 Harvard St
Fall River MA 02720

Call Sign: WA1AVS
Leonard M Lechan
349 Harvard St
Fall River MA 02720

Call Sign: KA1BTR
Stephen J Leite
190 Healy St
Fall River MA 02723

Call Sign: KB1HGM
Thomas J Eckersley
238 Henry St
Fall River MA 02721

Call Sign: N8LZD
Robert T Troutman Jr
1913 Highland Ave
Fall River MA 02720

Call Sign: N1ZCP
Alan G Bruce
2112 Highland Ave
Fall River MA
027204314

Call Sign: KB1MNK
JENNIFER De LEON
167 Hunter St 3rd
Floor
Fall River MA 02721

Call Sign: KB1FIN
Chris M Goncalo
521 Indiantown Rd
Fall River MA 02790

Call Sign: KB1NPJ
Markus Watson
232 John St
Fall River MA 02721

Call Sign: K1DLG
Arthur D Hubert
387 Johnson St

Fall River MA 02723

Call Sign: KB1GJZ
Ruben M Martinez
220 Johnson St Apt
29b
Fall River MA 02723

Call Sign: KC1HL
Edmond P Cote
179 Jones St
Fall River MA 02720

Call Sign: N1RQA
Mario J Paiva
549 Joseph Dr
Fall River MA 02720

Call Sign: WA1ZCB
Edmond F Duclos
4 Judge St
Fall River MA 02721

Call Sign: KB1JUY
Charles R Bardsley
529 June St
Fall River MA 02720

Call Sign: KA1UUF
Adoraldo P De
Almeida
747 June St
Fall River MA 02720

Call Sign: KB1GJW
Nicholas R Guerrier
55 Kellogg St
Fall River MA 02724

Call Sign: KB1LFM
Alan R Rogers
63 Kelly Dr
Fall River MA 02721

Call Sign: W1BOG
John H White
358 Kenyon St
Fall River MA 02720

Call Sign: KB1WHF
Karen L Masse
372 Lake Ave
Fall River MA 02721

Call Sign: KB1RDY
Joseph E Alston
227 Lawrence St
Fall River MA 02721

Call Sign: WA1DPB
Robert M Collins Sr
425 Linden St
Fall River MA 02720

Call Sign: N1SFG
Maurice A Pratt
489 Lindsey St
Fall River MA 02720

Call Sign: KB1LFN
Al-Amin Ahmed
130 Lowell St Apt 2wf
Fall River MA 02721

Call Sign: NJ1J
Arthur A Poulis
133 Madison St
Fall River MA 02720

Call Sign: N1KBJ
Steven Lawrence
689 Maple St
Fall River MA 02720

Call Sign: KB1AYS
Wayne Travis
709 Maple St
Fall River MA 02720

Call Sign: KB1FIK
David Carreiro Jr
19 Marble St
Fall River MA 02721

Call Sign: KB1AFF
Robert A D Arruda
185 Mason St
Fall River MA 02723

Call Sign: WB1CXA
George Botelho
154 Mc Gowan St
Fall River MA 02723

Call Sign: KB1NPK
Sarah Abren
52 Meadow St
Fall River MA 02720

Call Sign: N1BJY
Frederick Chew
158 Meridian St
Fall River MA 02720

Call Sign: KA1BJW
Eugene L Oliveira
1823 Meridian St
Fall River MA 02720

Call Sign: N1SAQ
Robert J Levesque
301 Milliken Blvd Apt
1701
Fall River MA 02721

Call Sign: K1NIO
Bruce A Mayall
124 Milton St
Fall River MA 02720

Call Sign: KB1LFQ
Brian Mota
157 Mt Hope Ave
Fall River MA 02724

Call Sign: KB1GKG
Kevin S Couto
438 Mt Hope Ave
Fall River MA 02724

Call Sign: N1WFV
Carl Mello
560 Mt Hope Ave
Fall River MA 02724

Call Sign: KA1KVG
Richard T Canole
145 Mt Pleasant St
Fall River MA 02720

Call Sign: WB1GYU
Michael J P Mc Grath
3853 N Main St
Fall River MA 02720

Call Sign: N1SMP
Peter A Belanger
4001 N Main St
Fall River MA 02720

Call Sign: KB1MJP
Thalita Xavier

68 N Main St - Apt 10
Fall River MA 02721

Call Sign: N1SAR
Matthew J Conlon
5500 N Main St #19-
211
Fall River MA 02720

Call Sign: KC0CLT
Christopher B Goff
5500 N Main St Apt
16-108
Fall River MA
027202092

Call Sign: W1JYR
Frank B Weaver
733 New Boston Rd
Fall River MA 02720

Call Sign: N1VFC
Arnold L Letendre
1355 Newhall St
Fall River MA 02724

Call Sign: N1NMY
Thomas C Medeiros Sr
514 Nichols St
Fall River MA 02720

Call Sign: K1GBA
Raymond H Martin
1241 North High
Fall River MA 02720

Call Sign: KB1GKE
Kyle D Levesque
1114 North Main St
Fall River MA 02720

Call Sign: WA1JTA
Daniel R Berger
22 Norwood St
Fall River MA 02723

Call Sign: N1NRW
James E Connors
57 O Grady St
Fall River MA 02720

Call Sign: N1HJY
James E Connors
57 O Grady St

Fall River MA 02720

Call Sign: KA1OEI
Alexander F Mc
Pherson
127 Oliver St Apt 3w
Fall River MA 02724

Call Sign: N1IXE
Richard A Ferreira
100 Palmer St
Fall River MA 02724

Call Sign: N1JZA
Debra L Ferreira
100 Palmer St
Fall River MA 02724

Call Sign: KB1LGZ
Lindsey A Ferreira
100 Palmer St
Fall River MA
027243236

Call Sign: KB1LNZ
Lindsey A Ferreira
100 Palmer St
Fall River MA
027243236

Call Sign: KB1HYT
John C Perry
503 Peckham St
Fall River MA 02721

Call Sign: N1RHS
Paul R Gosselin
370 Perry St
Fall River MA 02721

Call Sign: KB1FIM
Eric Bragan
724 Plymouth Ave
Fall River MA 02721

Call Sign: WO1L
David R Hague
10 Point West Dr
Fall River MA
027207911

Call Sign: KB1CNB
Arthur J Denault
443 President Ave

Fall River MA 02720

Call Sign: KB1IPJ
Robert J Souza
259 Prospect St
Fall River MA 02720

Call Sign: WB1CWY
Robert J Bedard
68 Prospect St Apt B
Fall River MA 02720

Call Sign: KB1APZ
Filomena M Vieira
133 Quarry St
Fall River MA 02723

Call Sign: KB1QIU
Joseph J Pietropaolo
151 Quequechan St
Fall River MA 02723

Call Sign: N1STF
Antonio Lazaro
75 Reney St
Fall River MA 02723

Call Sign: W1NKQ
James E Healey
225 Rich St
Fall River MA 02720

Call Sign: KB1OXK
Kenneth R Medeiros
133 Ridge
Fall River MA 02724

Call Sign: N1WVT
Jamie S Manuels
152 Riverview St
Fall River MA 02724

Call Sign: N1ODB
Donald L Desforges
1158 Robeson St
Fall River MA 02720

Call Sign: KB1NPL
Evan F Darmody
1769 Robeson St
Fall River MA 02720

Call Sign: KB1APY
Scott A Matton

743 Rodman St
Fall River MA 02721

Call Sign: KB1MJQ
Marissa G Matton
743 Rodman St
Fall River MA 02721

Call Sign: N1SRU
Harold R Solomon
791 Rodman St
Fall River MA 02721

Call Sign: N1WOM
John F Renn
929 Rodman St
Fall River MA
027213947

Call Sign: KB1NPO
Amanda L Tripp
462 S Beach St
Fall River MA 02724

Call Sign: KA1IVB
George Green Jr
341 S Beacon St
Fall River MA 02347

Call Sign: N1HSW
John Aguiar
2438 S Main St
Fall River MA 02724

Call Sign: WQ1S
Nan E Dolber
19 School Brook Rd
Fall River MA 02720

Call Sign: N1LSO
John R Andrade
26 School St
Fall River MA 02720

Call Sign: KA1ULR
Eduardo M Cabral
673 Second St
Fall River MA 02721

Call Sign: N1RWT
Louise A Chapdelaine
792 Second St
Fall River MA 02721

Call Sign: N1TVY
Alice M Des Jardins
792 Second St
Fall River MA 02721

Call Sign: KA1ZFV
Carol A Walsh
798 Second St
Fall River MA 02721

Call Sign: WV1L
Edward F Walsh
798 Second St
Fall River MA 02721

Call Sign: KB1WHK
Vanessa A Wicherski
66 Sevigny St
Fall River MA 02723

Call Sign: KB1FIJ
Kyle D Couture
15 Shannon St
Fall River MA 02721

Call Sign: K1ZAL
Albert Le Page Jr
700 Shore Dr Unit 912
Fall River MA 02721

Call Sign: N1RGB
Leo A Salva
377 Slade St
Fall River MA 02724

Call Sign: W1AUP
Louis T Krudys
1145 Slade St
Fall River MA 02724

Call Sign: KB1BVJ
Frederick C Walczyk
542 Smith St
Fall River MA 02721

Call Sign: WA1EST
Arthur Souza
255 So Beacon St
Fall River MA 02724

Call Sign: N1YNP
John Rocha Jr
94 Somerset St
Fall River MA 02721

Call Sign: KB1GKB
Jon E Robidoux
2213 South Main St
Fall River MA 02724

Call Sign: KB1BFV
Richard T Gallone
56 St Joseph St Apt
514
Fall River MA
027232022

Call Sign: KB1CNA
George M Lavoie
251 Stafford Rd
Fall River MA 02721

Call Sign: K1RFH
Stephen J Sorel
26 Stamford St
Fall River MA 02720

Call Sign: KB1GKD
Sarah A Reed
448 State Ave
Fall River MA 02724

Call Sign: KB1GJY
Jonathan J Albernaz
582 State Ave
Fall River MA 02724

Call Sign: NY1D
John S Ostapow
276 Stockton St
Fall River MA 02721

Call Sign: KB1LFJ
Richard R Bourheau Jr
278 Sunset Hill
Fall River MA 02724

Call Sign: KB1MGS
Victoria K Dombek
499 Tecumseh St
Fall River MA 02721

Call Sign: KB1GKA
Ian J Medeiros
283 Tower St
Fall River MA 02724

Call Sign: KA1YHK

David A Rosseter Jr
760 Valentine
Fall River MA 02720

Call Sign: KA1QXP
Faye Berube
70 Vestal St
Fall River MA 02720

Call Sign: N1EGJ
Edmond E Berube
70 Vestal St
Fall River MA 02720

Call Sign: KB1DKE
Joseph M Pires Jr
153 Walker St
Fall River MA 02723

Call Sign: W1CRN
Wendall B Sanford
560 Walnut St
Fall River MA 02720

Call Sign: KB1SDY
Jose Casimiro
797 Warren St
Fall River MA 02721

Call Sign: W1PFW
Arthur E Cate
16 Washngton Ct
Fall River MA
027205922

Call Sign: N1TZM
James R Cahill
2 Weaver St 519
Fall River MA 02720

Call Sign: N1MMW
Ronald G Breault
714 Weetamoe St
Fall River MA 02720

Call Sign: KB1LFO
John R Freitas
50 Weetamoe St Apt 2f
Fall River MA 02720

Call Sign: K1CJS
Chris J Smith
298 Whipple St

Fall River MA
027211728

Call Sign: KB1CDR
Matthew T St Amand
457 Whipple St
Fall River MA 02724

Call Sign: N1PRT
Leo A Dostou
457 Whipple St
Fall River MA 02724

Call Sign: N1TEB
Matthew L Dostou
457 Whipple St
Fall River MA 02724

Call Sign: KB1AHP
Alan A De Costa
357 Whipple St 1st
Floor
Fall River MA 02721

Call Sign: N1QOZ
Gilbert La Fleur Jr
20 Wiley St
Fall River MA 02720

Call Sign: N1IJT
Paul Lindo
229 Winter St
Fall River MA
027203317

Call Sign: KB1KLG
Tbc Amateur Radio
Association
Fall River MA 02722

Call Sign: KB1LBD
Uss Joseph P Kennedy
Jr Amateur Radio
Assoc
Fall River MA
027220111

Call Sign: NB1CR
Uss Joseph P Kennedy
Jr Amateur Radio
Assoc
Fall River MA
027220111

**FCC Amateur Radio
Licenses in Falmouth**

Call Sign: KC1RL
Richard M Gerace
12 Alma Rd
Falmouth MA 02541

Call Sign: KA1QNV
Timothy E Goslee
2 Arnold Gifford Rd
Falmouth MA 02540

Call Sign: N1CLC
David W Lovering
40 Barnabas Rd
Falmouth MA 02540

Call Sign: N1JCM
Mildred C Lovering
40 Barnabas Rd
Falmouth MA 02540

Call Sign: W1ULW
Nelson O Lindley
51 Barnabas Rd
Falmouth MA 02541

Call Sign: KA1UZI
Diana L Wald
23 Blair Ln
Falmouth MA 02540

Call Sign: N1HKS
David Wald
23 Blair Ln
Falmouth MA 02540

Call Sign: K1AK
Alexander T Johnston
Box 204
Falmouth MA 02541

Call Sign: W1HYN
Richard M Van Keuren
51 Carlson Ln D13
Falmouth MA 02540

Call Sign: WB1CQG
Robert E Conroy
15 Crofton Ln
Falmouth MA 02536

Call Sign: KA1YYL

David B Aronson
409 Currier Rd
Falmouth MA 02536

Call Sign: N1EZL
Thomas D Sweeny
50 Dove Cottage Rd
Falmouth MA 02540

Call Sign: KB1HJO
John H Gould
25 Garrison Rd
Falmouth MA
025403019

Call Sign: KB1ITW
Marilyn J Gould
25 Garrison Rd
Falmouth MA 02540

Call Sign: WX1K
John H Gould
25 Garrison Rd
Falmouth MA
025403019

Call Sign: N1LYN
Marilyn J Gould
25 Garrison Rd
Falmouth MA 02540

Call Sign: W1IAZ
Peter S Grinnell Jr
90 Geggatt Rd
Falmouth MA
025364004

Call Sign: W1GEW
Reed A Hamilton
94 Gifford St
Falmouth MA 02540

Call Sign: K1COG
John L Ham
176 Grand Ave
Falmouth MA 02540

Call Sign: KA1CYT
Nick P Fofonoff
6 Greengate Rd
Falmouth MA 02540

Call Sign: WA1JPF
Donald E Harris

3 Handy Ln
Falmouth MA
025403117

Call Sign: K1GM
George R Mc Farland
46 Harbor Ave
Falmouth MA 02540

Call Sign: KA1UZJ
Robert M Padden
5 Harvest Dr
Falmouth MA 02536

Call Sign: W1VAK
Edward A Denton
14 Holland Rd
Falmouth MA 02540

Call Sign: NN1Q
John R Mac Isaac
75 Lake Leaman Rd
Falmouth MA
025403633

Call Sign: WA1QLH
Marjorie M Bernklow
195 Lakeview Ave
Falmouth MA 02540

Call Sign: KB1FUR
Willaim J Dreyer
213 Lakeview Ave
Falmouth MA 02540

Call Sign: N1BLS
David I Bernklow Sr
195 Lakeview Ave
Falmouth MA 02540

Call Sign: W1GUR
Charles F Syverson
19 Loop Rd
Falmouth MA
025400810

Call Sign: N1WJJ
Richard L Boucher
7 Mbl St
Falmouth MA 02543

Call Sign: KA1FQX
John E Justason
29 Miami Ave

Falmouth MA 02540

Call Sign: W1HLL
Clayton W Collins Jr
126 Minot St
Falmouth MA 02540

Call Sign: N1JZE
Victor H Kester
297 Palmer Ave
Falmouth MA 02540

Call Sign: N1LTT
Clarence J Anderson
494 Palmer Ave
Falmouth MA 02540

Call Sign: KB1ELH
Robert B Jesus
5 Pennsylvania Court
Falmouth MA 02540

Call Sign: W1LKF
Lauren K Finn-Jesus
5 Pennsylvania Court
Falmouth MA 02540

Call Sign: KB1JOU
Matthew G Jull
18 Quissett Circle
Falmouth MA 02540

Call Sign: N1SAA
Pamela C Hart
53 Quonset Rd
Falmouth MA 02540

Call Sign: W1UU
Peter K Butler
5 Robinson Rd
Falmouth MA 02540

Call Sign: KB1FOG
Maureen Coughlin
58 Rosemorin Land
Apt 19
Falmouth MA 02540

Call Sign: W1BZA
James M Crossen
10 Salt Pond Rd
Falmouth MA 02540

Call Sign: KB1SSP

Christopher H Brown
19 Sao Paulo Dr
Falmouth MA 02540

Call Sign: KA1VQM
Ian P Mc Cullough
37 Saronesset Rd
Falmouth MA 02540

Call Sign: K2LYE
William B Fleck
36 Shore St
Falmouth MA 02540

Call Sign: NW1E
Elijah A White
170 Siders Pond Rd
Falmouth MA 02540

Call Sign: W1YCV
Marvin Tepper
17 Sippewissett Rd
Falmouth MA
025401870

Call Sign: W0RIO
Stuart R Wagner
120 Sippewissett Rd
Falmouth MA 02540

Call Sign: N1JCL
Michael Kramer
478 Sippewissett Rd
Falmouth MA 02540

Call Sign: KB1EPZ
Robert Bell
10 Spindrift Hill
Falmouth MA 02540

Call Sign: W1VZT
Peter B Carnevale
27 Teneycke Hill Rd
Falmouth MA
025563118

Call Sign: W1HZM
William H Horn
63 Two Ponds Rd
Falmouth MA 02540

Call Sign: W9MZD
Robert H Wilkie
3 Valley Rd

Falmouth MA 02540

Call Sign: KA1OKD
Lawrence F Palmer
12 Wachusett Ave
Falmouth MA 02540

Call Sign: K1OKD
Lawrence F Palmer
12 Wachusett Ave
Falmouth MA 02540

Call Sign: KB1PEB
James W Endress
210 Walker St
Falmouth MA 02540

Call Sign: W1GWN
Warren M Zapol
20 Whittemore Rd
Falmouth MA 02540

Call Sign: WA1YJV
Ernest H Mayberry
Falmouth MA 02541

Call Sign: KB1MLP
Matthew J Trott
Falmouth MA 02574

FCC Amateur Radio Licenses in Fayville

Call Sign: N1BGH
Isreal A Martin
15 Pleasant
Fayville MA 01745

Call Sign: NE1M
Roland C Suatengco
Fayville MA 01745

Call Sign: KB1RUM
Noel H Groves Jr
Fayville MA 01745

Call Sign: KB1DAD
Noel H Groves Jr
Fayville MA 01745

Call Sign: W1RSA
Noel H Groves Jr
Fayville MA 01745

FCC Amateur Radio Licenses in Feeding Hills

Call Sign: K1HFR
Jonathan D Kratovil
44 Annable St
Feeding Hills MA
010301802

Call Sign: WA1OTC
Charles A Camerlin
414 Barry St
Feeding Hills MA
01030

Call Sign: N1HIV
Robert D Mazeika
597 Barry St
Feeding Hills MA
01030

Call Sign: KA1GFX
Richard G Kana
727 Barry St
Feeding Hills MA
01030

Call Sign: K1PUP
Arthur E Von
Marschall
22 Briarcliff Drive
Feeding Hills MA
01030

Call Sign: KA2MCH
Lynne M Ledger
172 Cambridge St
Feeding Hills MA
01030

Call Sign: KA1RQL
Richard A Mazza
157 Clover Hill Dr
Feeding Hills MA
01030

Call Sign: KB1RBX
Kenneth A Labonte
244 Colemore St
Feeding Hills MA
01030

Call Sign: KA1EDE

Mark E Woods
69 Coronet Cir
Feeding Hills MA
01030

Call Sign: N1EUZ
David B Bertagnolli
16 Forest Hill Rd
Feeding Hills MA
01030

Call Sign: WA1BWF
Raymond N Rouillard
4 Granger Dr
Feeding Hills MA
01030

Call Sign: WA1OOF
Mary Ann Rouillard
4 Granger Dr
Feeding Hills MA
010301622

Call Sign: N1VGL
Adam B David
14 Granger Dr
Feeding Hills MA
01030

Call Sign: WA1NRI
David R Cote
66 Hayes Ave
Feeding Hills MA
01030

Call Sign: KB1FIT
James W Mccarthy
33 Henry St
Feeding Hills MA
01030

Call Sign: KA1VEH
Sarah E Platanitis
101 Highland St
Feeding Hills MA
01030

Call Sign: WC1L
James J Platanitis
101 Highland St
Feeding Hills MA
010302215

Call Sign: WC1O

Jeanette L Platanitis
101 Highland St
Feeding Hills MA
010302215

Call Sign: N1KNW
Mark A Weiner Sr
185 James St
Feeding Hills MA
01030

Call Sign: N1RL
Eric R Lindquist
32 Jessica Pl
Feeding Hills MA
01030

Call Sign: KB1JVD
Marian J Collier
32 Jessica Place
Feeding Hills MA
01030

Call Sign: N1QLM
John D Isham
14 Joanne Circle
Feeding Hills MA
01030

Call Sign: AA1I
John D Isham
14 Joanne Circle
Feeding Hills MA
01030

Call Sign: W1GVB
Gregory V Barber
31 Norman Terrace
Feeding Hills MA
01030

Call Sign: K1EPI
Florian R Di Roma
667 North St
Feeding Hills MA
01030

Call Sign: KB1QLC
Peter Lucia
480 North Westfield St
Feeding Hills MA
01030

Call Sign: N1INB

Stanley E Bates Sr
672 North Westfield St
Feeding Hills MA
01030

Call Sign: N1DUY
James R Sebolt
95 North Westfield St
Apt 39
Feeding Hills MA
010301665

Call Sign: WA1UDX
James R Sebolt
95 North Westfield St
Apt 39
Feeding Hills MA
010301665

Call Sign: ND1P
Kenneth R Grady Jr
274 Northwest St
Feeding Hills MA
01030

Call Sign: WA1URI
Gerald W Ledger
50 Partridge Ln
Feeding Hills MA
01030

Call Sign: KB1PQW
Jacob A Mccurdy
8 Paul Revere Dr
Feeding Hills MA
01030

Call Sign: N1CXT
Robert H Josephson
60 Pheasant Run Cir
Feeding Hills MA
01030

Call Sign: KB1FWN
Michael F
Dechristopher
73 Poplar Sr
Feeding Hills MA
01030

Call Sign: K1KAA
Michael F
Dechristopher
73 Poplar Sr

Feeding Hills MA
01030

Call Sign: KA1QJN
Dorothy M Johnson
63 Poplar St
Feeding Hills MA
01030

Call Sign: KA1VHA
Robert F Johnson Iii
63 Poplar St
Feeding Hills MA
01030

Call Sign: WB1HAB
Robert F Johnson
63 Poplar St
Feeding Hills MA
01030

Call Sign: KB1FWM
Thomas Dechristopher
73 Poplar St
Feeding Hills MA
01030

Call Sign: N0HI
Michael F
Dechristopher
73 Poplar St
Feeding Hills MA
01030

Call Sign: N1TA
Michael F
Dechristopher
73 Poplar St
Feeding Hills MA
01030

Call Sign: KB1WLV
The Gentlemans Radio
Society
73 Poplar St
Feeding Hills MA
01030

Call Sign: WA1J
The Gentlemans Radio
Society
73 Poplar St
Feeding Hills MA
01030

Call Sign: KA1HTJ
Antony F Albro
1059 Shoemaker Ln
Feeding Hills MA
01030

Call Sign: N1PLE
Kevin R Culverhouse
722 Southwest St
Feeding Hills MA
01030

Call Sign: KA1GPD
Patricia A Bouchard
650 Southwick St
Feeding Hills MA
01030

Call Sign: WA1VPT
Leonard A Gesualdo
619 Springfield St Apt
5
Feeding Hills MA
010302140

Call Sign: WB1BZW
Andre M Bouchard
93 Tobacco Farm Rd
Feeding Hills MA
01030

Call Sign: N1DPM
Fred M Stefanik
50 Witheridge St
Feeding Hills MA
01030

Call Sign: KA6MIG
Guerino A Mazza
100 Witheridge St
Feeding Hills MA
01030

Call Sign: KA1JUS
Joseph D Shaer
36 Woodcock Ct
Feeding Hills MA
01030

Call Sign: W1QA
Robert P Mccormick
Feeding Hills MA
010300017

Call Sign: KB1DVW
George P Nay
Feeding Hills MA
01030

Call Sign: KU1RT
Kurt J Dahdah
Feeding Hills MA
010300001

Call Sign: W1TTK
Lionel J Dupre Sr
10 Arnold Dr
Fiskdale MA 01518

Call Sign: N1PTF
Adrien T Dumont
30 Arnold Rd
Fiskdale MA 01518

Call Sign: KA1GEV
Stanley C Parzych
103 Brookfield Rd
Fiskdale MA 01518

Call Sign: KB1SIG
Edwin H Anderson Iii
125 Brookfield Rd
Fiskdale MA 01518

Call Sign: KB1OAO
Daniel L Desy
14 Camp Rd
Fiskdale MA 01518

Call Sign: KB1QGY
Peter Baldracchi
6 Cooper Rd
Fiskdale MA 01518

Call Sign: K3GM
Thomas J Hybiske
7 Cooper Rd
Fiskdale MA 01518

Call Sign: K1ICO
Philip W Paulhus
7 Crescent Way Unit
305
Fiskdale MA 01518

Call Sign: WA1HPN
Robert F La Barre Sr
100 Heritage Green Dr
Fiskdale MA 01518

Call Sign: N1LIS
Jonathan L Pevner
364 Leadmine Rd
Fiskdale MA 01518

Call Sign: KB1WLZ
Maxwell H Pevner
364 Leadmine Rd
Fiskdale MA 01518

Call Sign: W1WEL
Dennis J Kosakowski
Fiskdale MA 01518

Call Sign: KB1JCG
William S Stupski
Fiskdale MA 01518

Call Sign: N1ZMK
Everett H Fay
33 Adams St
Fitchburg MA 01420

Call Sign: N1RSR
Michael F Capone
321 Albee St
Fitchburg MA 01420

Call Sign: KA1SRD
Edward A Rauer
21 Allston Pl
Fitchburg MA 01420

Call Sign: N1WKM
Patrick W Faucher Jr
69 Almount Rd
Fitchburg MA 01420

Call Sign: N1NZZ
Ralph R Romano Iii
265 Arnhow Farm Rd
Fitchburg MA
014201374

Call Sign: W1OBU
Robert K Greenough
Ashburnham Hill Rd
Fitchburg MA 01420

Call Sign: KA1YOC
Karen Y Caponi
696 Ashburnham St
Fitchburg MA 01420

Call Sign: N1JUD
Arthur B Caponi
696 Ashburnham St
Fitchburg MA 01420

Call Sign: K1UTZ
Charles H Whitney
262 Ashby State Rd
Fitchburg MA 01420

Call Sign: WA2VXY
Michael J Moroney
483 Ashby State Rd
Fitchburg MA 01420

Call Sign: K1BBV
Gerard M Aubuchon
446 Beech St
Fitchburg MA 01420

Call Sign: KE4WUE
Jose M Melendez
32 Beekman St Apt 1
Fitchburg MA 01420

Call Sign: KB1IAM
Victor L Sanchez
42 Belmont St
Fitchburg MA 01420

Call Sign: KA1VTS
Catherine A Rochette
187 Bemis Rd Apt 8
Fitchburg MA 01420

Call Sign: KA1VTT
Robert J Rochette Jr
187 Bemis Rd Apt 8
Fitchburg MA 01420

Call Sign: KA1MQI
Denise M Barber
21 Bernap St
Fitchburg MA 01420

Call Sign: N1APY
Donald A P Le Court
4 Brigham St
Fitchburg MA 01420

Call Sign: KA1HXI
David A Barber
21 Burnap St
Fitchburg MA 01420

Call Sign: WA1ZBR
Edward L Stauff
26 Burnap St
Fitchburg MA 01420

Call Sign: KC1LU
James E Hebert
146 Buttrick Ave
Fitchburg MA 01420

Call Sign: KB1HBA
Aaron L Jones
8 Charleton St
Fitchburg MA 01420

Call Sign: K1QBA
Norman A Charette Sr
109 Charlton St
Fitchburg MA 01420

Call Sign: KB1LRL
Raymond P Lajoie
134 Clarendon St
Fitchburg MA 01420

Call Sign: KA1VOH
Jeffrey C Leger
399 Clarendon St
Fitchburg MA 01420

Call Sign: KA1VTV
Joseph R Caban
449 Clarendon St
Fitchburg MA 01420

Call Sign: KD1UZ
William D Leger
21 Clearview Ave
Fitchburg MA 01420

Call Sign: N1JKR
Cary P Harrison
77 Columbia Ave

Fitchburg MA
014207042

Call Sign: WA1AIC
Donald R Haaker
116 Culley St
Fitchburg MA 01420

Call Sign: W1CIA
Donald R Haaker
116 Culley St
Fitchburg MA 01420

Call Sign: K1GIG
Norman W Rice Sr
125 Day St
Fitchburg MA 01420

Call Sign: KB1FTN
Jeffrey R Newbro
67 Day St #4
Fitchburg MA 01420

Call Sign: WA1HVZ
Philip B Oliver
55 Electric Ave
Whalom Dist
Fitchburg MA 01420

Call Sign: W1MBL
William N Forman
270 Fisher Rd
Fitchburg MA 01420

Call Sign: W1LJZ
Marion F Mould
86 Fitch Hill Ave
Fitchburg MA 01420

Call Sign: KB1QAN
Anthony R Dipasquale
40 Forest Hill Ave
Fitchburg MA 01420

Call Sign: WN1E
Charles R Cayen
33 Forest St
Fitchburg MA 01420

Call Sign: K1MEB
Howard J Rivers
1029 Franklin Rd
Fitchburg MA 01420

Call Sign: KA1JL
Warren J Tuiskula
32 Gloria Ave
Fitchburg MA
014206128

Call Sign: N1JXA
Janet A Tuiskula
32 Gloria Ave
Fitchburg MA 01420

Call Sign: N1XYT
Benjamin W Tuiskula
32 Gloria Ave
Fitchburg MA 01420

Call Sign: N1ZML
Norman W Bowne Jr
34 Hannigan Ct
Fitchburg MA 01420

Call Sign: KD1ER
David A Andreucci
173 Heywood St
Fitchburg MA 01420

Call Sign: KE4IXV
Kurtis B Butterbaugh
64 Heywood St
Fitchburg MA 01420

Call Sign: N1KGZ
Sharon A Richard
810 High Rock Rd
Fitchburg MA 01420

Call Sign: N2CJT
James C Davis
935 John Fitch Hwy
Fitchburg MA 01420

Call Sign: W1LUG
Waldo H Nason
935 John Fitch Hwy
Fitchburg MA 01420

Call Sign: WA1NAQ
John N Fields
25 Lincoln St
Fitchburg MA 01420

Call Sign: KB1FXP
Raymond P Dean
401 Main St

Fitchburg MA 01420

Call Sign: N1GNJ
Louisa Medeiros
16 Maryland Ave
Fitchburg MA 01420

Call Sign: N1XWA
Thomas D Antil
182 Mechanic St
Fitchburg MA 01420

Call Sign: AB1GF
Thomas D Antil
182 Mechanic St
Fitchburg MA 01420

Call Sign: N1WRT
John J Aliskevicz
389 Mechanic St
Fitchburg MA 01420

Call Sign: N1RF
Malcolm D Coburn
29 Merriam Pkwy
Fitchburg MA 01420

Call Sign: WA1NDV
John J Mc Grath
29 Moran Hgts
Fitchburg MA 01420

Call Sign: AB1FT
Alan F Ingel
19 Mount Carmel Ave
Fitchburg MA 01420

Call Sign: KA1LFC
Jane S Beauregard
7 Mountain Ave
Fitchburg MA 01420

Call Sign: KB1AY
James E Beauregard
7 Mountain Ave
Fitchburg MA 01420

Call Sign: KB1GHI
Alan F Ingel
19 Mt Carmel Ave
Fitchburg MA 01420

Call Sign: AB1DE
Alan F Ingel

19 Mt Carmel Ave
Fitchburg MA 01420

Call Sign: KB1RPU
James P Cosgrove
141 Myrtle Ave
Fitchburg MA 01420

Call Sign: KB1LAR
Guy Edouard
63 Newton St
Fitchburg MA 01420

Call Sign: W1LXE
Norman B Lyons
9 Otis St
Fitchburg MA 01420

Call Sign: KB1OPS
David E Simonds
9 Park St
Fitchburg MA 01420

Call Sign: N1LNZ
Thomas H Nikitas
113 Pearl Hill Rd
Fitchburg MA 01420

Call Sign: KB1EYJ
Mary C Krueger
950 Pearl Hill Rd
Fitchburg MA 01420

Call Sign: KB1GKP
Kenneth M Andrews
1030 Pearl Hill Rd
Fitchburg MA
014201633

Call Sign: KB1MVY
Eric W Gustafson
64 Phillips Passway
Fitchburg MA 01420

Call Sign: KB1CLM
Rosemary Reynolds
112 Pleasant
Fitchburg MA 01420

Call Sign: W1MLF
Henry K Nacke
23 Prospect Ave
Fitchburg MA 01420

Call Sign: W1NQU
Arnold T Paulsen Jr
62 Richardson Dr
Fitchburg MA 01420

Call Sign: N1YWK
Joshua D Burchard
211 Richardson Rd
Fitchburg MA
014201303

Call Sign: N1NXO
Alan D Mazurka
393 Richardson Rd
Fitchburg MA 01420

Call Sign: WB1FJY
Harold F Desmond Jr
677 Rindge Rd
Fitchburg MA 01420

Call Sign: N1WHI
Jason S Nadeau
215 Rollstone Rd
Fitchburg MA 01420

Call Sign: KB1NXH
Nettie E Sears
28 Roosevelt St
Fitchburg MA 01420

Call Sign: KB1NTF
Randall L Peterman
126 Roosevelt St
Fitchburg MA 01420

Call Sign: N1YAK
Malcolm S Colgate
140 Saint Joseph Ave
Fitchburg MA 01420

Call Sign: KB1LGX
Lawrence K Murray
156 Sanborn St
Fitchburg MA 01420

Call Sign: KB1FOU
Wayne M Swanson
87 Scott Rd
Fitchburg MA 01420

Call Sign: N1CUW
Paula Cormier
366 South St

Fitchburg MA 01420

Call Sign: W1MDS
Alfred Schatz
89 Summer St
Fitchburg MA 01420

Call Sign: N1AGO
Helen G Savageau
395 Theresa St
Fitchburg MA 01420

Call Sign: N1AJQ
Robert A Savageau
395 Theresa St
Fitchburg MA 01420

Call Sign: K1YJT
William S Houghton
67 Valdalia Ave
Fitchburg MA 01420

Call Sign: N1IQO
David M Emery
24 Walnut St
Fitchburg MA 01420

Call Sign: N1STV
James M Kersch
203 Walton St
Fitchburg MA 01420

Call Sign: N1GNI
Kenneth E Bujold
1295 Water St
Fitchburg MA 01420

Call Sign: KA1FUV
Theresa A Turbide
350 Water St Apt 419
Fitchburg MA 01420

Call Sign: K1YEB
Raymond J Gagne
723 Westminster St
Fitchburg MA 01420

Call Sign: WB1HJA
Wilfred B Tessier
20 William St
Fitchburg MA 01420

Call Sign: K1SPX
Myron L Lavine

Fitchburg MA 01420

Call Sign: KA1VPK
R Cook
Fitchburg MA 01420

Call Sign: W1EAX
Roy E Miner
Fitchburg MA 01420

Call Sign: WB1EWS
Paul H Andrews
Fitchburg MA 01420

Call Sign: KB1FII
Bruce R Parsons
Fitchburg MA 01420

Call Sign: AB1GB
Francis Thompson
Fitchburg MA 01420

**FCC Amateur Radio
Licenses in Florence**

Call Sign: KA4NRF
Stephen J Tremblay
422 Acrebrook Dr
Florence MA 01062

Call Sign: N1HQM
Robert J Kolakoski
64 Austin Cir
Florence MA
010603506

Call Sign: KB1UNN
Maximilian J Krogius
42 Beacon St
Florence MA 01062

Call Sign: KB1LPN
Annunciation Amateur
Radio Club
87 Beacon St
Florence MA 01062

Call Sign: KA1LJO
James E Mc Nally
4 Cloverdale St
Florence MA 01060

Call Sign: KA1ZPG
Elsa C Vitols

216 Federal St
Florence MA 01060

Call Sign: N1HZV
Brett A Provost
280 Florence Rd
Florence MA 01062

Call Sign: KA1QFE
Robert J Gutowski
448 Florence Rd
Florence MA
010622624

Call Sign: KB1UAK
Peter E Olsen Iii
6 Gregory Ln
Florence MA 01062

Call Sign: KB1OIY
Robert J Bacon
20 Hawthorne Ter
Florence MA 01062

Call Sign: N1YQ
Robert J Bacon
20 Hawthorne Ter
Florence MA 01062

Call Sign: KB1RXD
Brian Johnson
9 Hickory Dr
Florence MA 01062

Call Sign: KB1SGZ
Joann L Berns
268 Locust St
Florence MA 01062

Call Sign: KB1SHB
Linda G Langlais
268 Locust St
Florence MA 01062

Call Sign: N1TOR
John R Koleszar
46 Middle St
Florence MA
010601920

Call Sign: N1IKD
Charles W De Rose
677 N Farms Rd
Florence MA 01062

Call Sign: KA1FKI
Robert R Luce
705 N Farms Rd
Florence MA 01060

Call Sign: N1AIY
Richard M Hirtle
108 North Main St
Florence MA
010621220

Call Sign: KA1WBO
Jim S Ussailis Jr
24 O Donnell Dr
Florence MA 01060

Call Sign: W1EQO
James S Ussailis
24 O Donnell Dr
Florence MA 01060

Call Sign: K1NWE
Robert C Young
23 Powell St
Florence MA 01060

Call Sign: K1UOR
Doris J Young
23 Powell St
Florence MA 01062

Call Sign: KB1TSD
Robin M Staples
36 Rick St
Florence MA 01062

Call Sign: N1LKA
Robert E De Carolis
648 Riverside Dr
Florence MA 01060

Call Sign: WB1EHE
Edward J Mc Carthy
94 Ryan Rd
Florence MA 01060

Call Sign: N1UOP
John J Glenowicz
405 Ryan Rd
Florence MA 01060

Call Sign: K1QQG
Ruth R Mc Conkey

418 Ryan Rd
Florence MA
010623435

Call Sign: KB1VXK
Stephen M Monska
817 Ryan Rd
Florence MA 01062

Call Sign: N1GGR
Stephen M Monska
817 Ryan Rd
Florence MA 01062

Call Sign: W1ODE
David Strachan
78 South Main St
Florence MA 01060

Call Sign: N2LRH
Geoffrey H Zukerman
5 Tiffany Ln
Florence MA 01062

Call Sign: N1FJ
Francis A Johnson
669 Westhampton Rd
Florence MA 01062

Call Sign: K1CBS
Robert D Doyle
1133 Westhampton Rd
Florence MA 01062

Call Sign: K1NQ
Robert D Doyle
1133 Westhampton Rd
Florence MA 01062

Call Sign: K1CBS
Robert D Doyle
1133 Westhampton Rd
Florence MA 01062

Call Sign: N1BPH
Ann U Carpenter
20 Winchester Ter
Florence MA 01062

Call Sign: KA1V
Ralph F Carpenter
20 Winchester Terr
Florence MA
010623542

Call Sign: KB1TLX
Bruce A Fuller
Florence MA
010620003

FCC Amateur Radio Licenses in Florida

Call Sign: KB1EQU
Craig A Gentes
47 Central Shaft Rd
Florida MA 01247

FCC Amateur Radio Licenses in Forestdale

Call Sign: N1BUZ
Joseph E Baggs Jr
11 Bramblebush Dr
Forestdale MA 02644

Call Sign: N1YHR
Richard C Waterfield
9 Craft Rd
Forestdale MA 02644

Call Sign: W1SGL
Cape Cod & Islands
Amat Rad Assn Inc
9 Craft Rd
Forestdale MA 02644

Call Sign: N1RCW
Richard C Waterfield
9 Craft Rd
Forestdale MA 02644

Call Sign: N1KSA
Gary A Gronlund
35 Deer Hollow Rd
Forestdale MA 02644

Call Sign: K4KTZ
Joseph A Fortin
22 Emerald Way
Forestdale MA 02644

Call Sign: N1RXZ
Gerald J Fortin
22 Emerald Way
Forestdale MA 02644

Call Sign: W2BQZ

Frederick Kirk
26 Emerald Way
Forestdale MA 02644

Call Sign: K1VGU
Philip B Midgley
16 Forest Rd
Forestdale MA 02644

Call Sign: N1YRT
Richard B Farrar
12 Friendly Rd
Forestdale MA 02644

Call Sign: W1RBF
Richard B Farrar
12 Friendly Rd
Forestdale MA 02644

Call Sign: N1KRT
Joseph J Pardo Jr
15 Joe Jay Ln
Forestdale MA 02644

Call Sign: KF4YEV
Michael T Martin
12 Ladyslipper Lane
Forestdale MA 02644

Call Sign: WA1MHG
John B Newton
19 Park Rd Box 34
Forestdale MA 02644

Call Sign: N1ODE
James F Gallagher
3 W Crossfield Rd
Forestdale MA 02644

Call Sign: N1HXY
Richard B Edson
3 West Rd
Forestdale MA
026441414

Call Sign: N1OQL
David M Smith
4 Woodvue Cir
Forestdale MA
026441012

Call Sign: KC1ZA
Richard A Servis Jr
Forestdale MA 02644

Call Sign: N1SYM
Andrew L Heckler
Forestdale MA
026440125

Call Sign: WA1ECF
James S Laine
Forestdale MA 02644

Call Sign: KB1GON
Michael R Servis
Forestdale MA 02644

Call Sign: W1LE
James S Laine
Forestdale MA 02644

FCC Amateur Radio Licenses in Fort Devens

Call Sign: KA1YBX
Mitchell J Dziduch
Adams Cir
Fort Devens MA
01433

Call Sign: AA1FT
Frankie Alvarez
Davao Cir
Fort Devens MA
01432

Call Sign: KA1ZMH
Michael E Newberg
Elliot Rd
Fort Devens MA
01433

Call Sign: KA1ZMI
Dina L Bonilla
I Co 112th Mi Bde
Box 1-1124
Fort Devens MA
01433

Call Sign: AA1BA
William B Colquhoun
Leyte Cir
Fort Devens MA
01433

Call Sign: KA1VVY

Ronald L Henry
Mid 10th Sfg A Bldg
P641
Fort Devens MA
01433

Call Sign: KA1ZZY
Todd M Harger
Mid 2nd Bn 10th Sfg
A
Fort Devens MA
01433

Call Sign: KA1ZNP
James D Murphy
Nttc Det Ft Devens
Fort Devens MA
01433

Call Sign: KA1ZMP
Forrest N Leamon
Nttcd Box 1769
Fort Devens MA
01433

Call Sign: KA1ZJG
Michelle L Bacon
Nttco Box 1881
Fort Devens MA
01433

Call Sign: N1IXX
Larry D Sweet
Perimeter Rd
Fort Devens MA
01433

Call Sign: KH6PE
John R Althouse
Salerno Cir
Fort Devens MA
01433

Call Sign: KA1SHT
Cathleen P Mulcair
Salerno Cir
Fort Devens MA
01433

Call Sign: N1HCR
Douglas S Boice Jr
Salerno Cir
Fort Devens MA
01433

Call Sign: KA1UKC
Pedro J Semidey
Salerno Cr
Fort Devens MA
01433

FCC Amateur Radio Licenses in Foxboro

See also FCC Amateur Radio Licenses in Foxborough

Call Sign: KC1PY
James A Shea Sr
15 Alexander Rd
Foxboro MA
020352209

Call Sign: KB1UOM
Timothy R Kennedy
6 Alger Rd
Foxboro MA 02035

Call Sign: WI1F
Timothy R Kennedy
6 Alger Rd
Foxboro MA 02035

Call Sign: W1MGL
Andrew R Leverone
54 B Main St
Foxboro MA 02035

Call Sign: KB1WAA
Edward J Reis
15 Boyden Dr
Foxboro MA 02035

Call Sign: AA1P
Richard G Brunner
10 Brookside Dr
Foxboro MA 02035

Call Sign: KA1JZM
Jud Graulich
2 Carter Rd
Foxboro MA 02035

Call Sign: W1MTI
Newell F Hicks
98 Central

Foxboro MA 02035

Call Sign: KB1GB
Roy N Carlson
7 Cheryl Dr
Foxboro MA
020351207

Call Sign: K1OVA
Roland J Blais
96 Chestnut
Foxboro MA 02035

Call Sign: W1BM
Robert G Miller
Chestnut Str Apt #5
Foxboro MA 02035

Call Sign: K1BMC
Brian M Clough
85 Cocasett St
Foxboro MA 02035

Call Sign: WA1CFQ
Glen A Hedderig
175 Cocasset St
Foxboro MA 02035

Call Sign: N1YKE
Cathy J Barnes
30 County St
Foxboro MA 02035

Call Sign: WA1WUE
Joyce E Cummings
2 Creighton Lane
Foxboro MA 02035

Call Sign: W1OX
Edward L Meade Jr
154 East St
Foxboro MA 02035

Call Sign: KB1FJN
Patrick P Mc Laughlin
18 Elm St
Foxboro MA 02035

Call Sign: N1AEU
Charles P Ouimet
9 Fairbanks Rd
Foxboro MA 02035

Call Sign: KD1LI

Neil B Sheer
2 Forest Rd
Foxboro MA 02035

Call Sign: KB1WTF
Nicholas K Duncan
100 Granite St
Foxboro MA 02035

Call Sign: K1RAA
Earl L Christie
3 Idlewild St
Foxboro MA 02035

Call Sign: KB1VAR
Kallol Dasgupta
14 Lyon Ln
Foxboro MA 02035

Call Sign: KB1UCG
Charles R Di Pompo
96 Main St D8
Foxboro MA 02035

Call Sign: N1MDX
Harris D Kagan
8 Maple Pl
Foxboro MA 02035

Call Sign: N1XBW
Gail H Kagan
8 Maple Pl
Foxboro MA 02035

Call Sign: K1YPZ
Raymond C Webb
131 Mechanic St
Foxboro MA 02035

Call Sign: W1RCW
Raymond C Webb
131 Mechanic St
Foxboro MA
020351539

Call Sign: KA1HPW
Scott F Molloy
24 Mechanic St Apt 3
Foxboro MA 02035

Call Sign: KJ4SWV
Richard L Mordaunt
29 Mirimichi Rd
Foxboro MA 02035

Call Sign: W1OJI
Maurice L Doiron
9 N High St
Foxboro MA 02035

Call Sign: N1HCS
James J Kershaw
176 North St
Foxboro MA 02035

Call Sign: KB1SGX
Andrew M Stone
11 Phyllis Rd
Foxboro MA 02035

Call Sign: KA1QVX
Jason J Lewicke
25 Prospect St
Foxboro MA 02035

Call Sign: W1HZS
Roger F Norian
37 Putnam Rd #6
Foxboro MA 02035

Call Sign: W1CZZ
Richard S Yahrmarkt
26 Putnam Rd Apt 8
Foxboro MA 02035

Call Sign: N1CYJ
Leonard Leonardi Jr
20 School St 7
Foxboro MA 02035

Call Sign: N1FQL
Thomas W Dineen
23 Shoreline Dr
Foxboro MA 02035

Call Sign: KA1OMZ
William J Everle
165 South St
Foxboro MA 02035

Call Sign: WO1Q
William C Euerle
165 South St
Foxboro MA 02035

Call Sign: WA1ZQT
John S Boynton
326 South St

Foxboro MA 02035

Call Sign: N2JMX
Andres T Navedo
Rivera
94 Spruce St
Foxboro MA 02035

Call Sign: N2JMY
Deborah D Navedo
94 Spruce St
Foxboro MA 02035

Call Sign: KB1GHX
Glenn A Field
7 Tiffney Rd
Foxboro MA 02035

Call Sign: W1QDX
Arthur D Porter
131 Washington St Lot
58
Foxboro MA 02035

Call Sign: KA1KM
George J Tardiff
131 Washington St
Rv2
Foxboro MA 02035

Call Sign: N1COU
Fred Foshey
72 West St
Foxboro MA 02035

Call Sign: KB1VXV
John H Ricker
Foxboro MA 02035

**FCC Amateur Radio
Licenses in
Foxborough**

**See also FCC
Amateur Radio
Licenses in Foxboro**

Call Sign: KA1HTO
Eric W Sorensen
53 Borrows Rd
Foxborough MA
02035

Call Sign: K3SVI

Ronald J Coyne
140 Cannon Forge
Drive
Foxborough MA
02035

Call Sign: KE1GU
Paul W Barnes
30 County St
Foxborough MA
02035

Call Sign: KB1CYO
Philip F Mclaughlin
18 Elm St
Foxborough MA
02035

Call Sign: KB1FVN
Joanne M Mclaughlin
18 Elm St
Foxborough MA
02035

Call Sign: N1MWA
Roger Nyren
3 Louise Dr
Foxborough MA
02035

Call Sign: N1VNH
Gerald L Kagan
8 Maple Pl
Foxborough MA
02035

Call Sign: KB1TXF
Philip C Moloney
14 Market St
Foxborough MA
02035

Call Sign: W1PCM
Philip C Moloney
14 Market St
Foxborough MA
02035

Call Sign: KA1KWG
Harold E Law
94 Mill St
Foxborough MA
02035

**FCC Amateur Radio
Licenses in
Framingham**

Call Sign: W1VIV
Sumner Weisman
43 Agnes Dr
Framingham MA
01701

Call Sign: N1HYM
Leo F Mc Auliffe Jr
8 Alan St
Framingham MA
01701

Call Sign: KA1WXY
Victor E Anderson
22 Anderson Rd
Framingham MA
01701

Call Sign: K1VEA
Victor E Anderson
22 Anderson Rd
Framingham MA
01701

Call Sign: KB1NIP
Ellen T Woodberry
22 Anderson Rd
Framingham MA
01701

Call Sign: N1ILY
Jeffrey F Perry
67 Angelica Dr
Framingham MA
01701

Call Sign: WA1LGO
Edward J Freeman
Arsenal Rd
Framingham MA
01701

Call Sign: N1JDV
Jeff C Good
10 Ashmont Dr
Framingham MA
01701

Call Sign: KB1TYG
Denise Corless

13 Ashmont Dr
Framingham MA
01701

Call Sign: N1IHB
Jenn Chorng Liou
63 Auburn St 9
Framingham MA
01701

Call Sign: N1MOZ
Stanley B Wernick
22 August Drive
Framingham MA
01701

Call Sign: KB1BXY
Freddy A Hernandez
31 B Interfaith Terr
Framingham MA
01701

Call Sign: N1GNY
Nancy Bowen
6 Bacon Rd
Framingham MA
01701

Call Sign: N1SKN
Carol J Tuthill
5 Bantry Rd
Framingham MA
01701

Call Sign: N1SKQ
Donald R Franklin
5 Bantry Rd
Framingham MA
01701

Call Sign: N1EXV
Neal H Shaffer
13 Barber Rd
Framingham MA
01702

Call Sign: N1ZAH
Nanci A Shaffer
13 Barber Rd
Framingham MA
01702

Call Sign: K1IKA
John F Kerns

90 Belknap Rd
Framingham MA
01701

Call Sign: KB1NIT
Jeffrey W T Buck
2 Belvidere Rd
Framingham MA
01702

Call Sign: KA1YBD
Dana E Clark
19 Berkeley Rd
Framingham MA
01701

Call Sign: KB1DHG
Brian J Gawronski
1 Birchmeadow Cir
Framingham MA
01701

Call Sign: KB1PVK
Christopher J Saia
94 Bishop Dr
Framingham MA
01702

Call Sign: KA1FOX
Christopher J Saia
94 Bishop Dr
Framingham MA
01702

Call Sign: N1VYF
Leo Laskin
12 Blackberry Ln
Framingham MA
01701

Call Sign: N1OMI
Edward J Barrett
37 Blackberry Ln
Framingham MA
01701

Call Sign: K3HI
Shawn R O Donnell
4 Blueberry Cir
Framingham MA
01701

Call Sign: KA1LJS
Beth A Markey

4 Blueberry Cir
Framingham MA
01701

Call Sign: N1EB
Ernest H Behrens Jr
3 Bosworth Rd
Framingham MA
017013703

Call Sign: N1JED
Paul V Mercurio
16 Brackett Rd
Framingham MA
01702

Call Sign: WA1IKA
Stanley L Markowitz
18 Bridle Path Cir
Framingham MA
01701

Call Sign: WA1LGP
Normand P Viens
156 Brook St
Framingham MA
01701

Call Sign: KB1MCY
Richard R Groleau
259 Brook St
Framingham MA
01701

Call Sign: W1GRO
Richard R Groleau
259 Brook St
Framingham MA
01701

Call Sign: WB1ECF
Joseph A Fitzpatrick
74 Brookfield Cir
Framingham MA
01701

Call Sign: N1XYB
John T Goodwin
25 Campello Rd
Framingham MA
01701

Call Sign: KB1TYL
Chris V Tarbassian

8 Capri Dr
Framingham MA
01701

Call Sign: KB1IRG
Stephen A Innis
9 Capri Dr
Framingham MA
01701

Call Sign: N1ZJO
Robin L Leone
19 Catherine Rd
Framingham MA
01701

Call Sign: WB1EUZ
David G Wilkie Sr
128 Cedar
Framingham MA
01701

Call Sign: K1KZE
Steven B Finks
14 Cedar St
Framingham MA
01701

Call Sign: N1TE
Robert E Richardson Jr
464 Central St
Framingham MA
01701

Call Sign: W1DL
Julius M Hoffer
24 Cherry Rd
Framingham MA
017017823

Call Sign: N1VYL
William J Smalley
132 Cherry St
Framingham MA
01701

Call Sign: N1YWN
Phyllis A Smalley
132 Cherry St
Framingham MA
017014401

Call Sign: N1XAR
Frederic F Schofield

23 Chubb Rd
Framingham MA
01701

Call Sign: KA1ZOS
Jean E Zack
34 Cider Mill Rd
Framingham MA
01701

Call Sign: N1IGG
Michael Zack
34 Cider Mill Rd
Framingham MA
01701

Call Sign: N1ZWF
Rene Souza
21 Clara Rd
Framingham MA
01701

Call Sign: KA1UUR
Albert L Mc Manus Jr
278 Concord St
Framingham MA
01701

Call Sign: KB1BKE
Steven F Harris
356 Concord St
Framingham MA
01701

Call Sign: W1CTO
Steven F Harris
356 Concord St
Framingham MA
01701

Call Sign: W1GAC
George Mouridian
1124 Concord St
Framingham MA
01701

Call Sign: N1KYC
Gary A Laundry
1359 Concord St
Framingham MA
01701

Call Sign: KA1SPX
Robert D Gross

4 Corregidor Rd
Framingham MA
01701

Call Sign: WA1GFY
Leonard J Hoffman
4 Corrine Dr
Framingham MA
017013210

Call Sign: AB1EH
Leonard J Hoffman
4 Corrine Dr
Framingham MA
017013210

Call Sign: WA1GFY
Leonard J Hoffman Ma
4 Corrine Drive
Framingham MA
017013210

Call Sign: KC1WD
Barry H Gold
11 Craig Rd
Framingham MA
01701

Call Sign: WA1VJG
Mal H Lemeshow
36 Crestwood Dr
Framingham MA
01701

Call Sign: KB1LWB
Randall S Cohen
Danforth St
Framingham MA
01701

Call Sign: W1CCE
Alan C Marshall
9 Daniels Rd
Framingham MA
017012703

Call Sign: K1GOQ
Harry C Andersen
27 Dartmouth Dr
Framingham MA
01701

Call Sign: KB1QDZ
Paul M Patriarca

10 Davidson Rd
Framingham MA
01701

Call Sign: K1PMP
Paul M Patriarca
10 Davidson Rd
Framingham MA
01701

Call Sign: N1LTM
William J Gardiner
9 Delmar Ave
Framingham MA
01701

Call Sign: W1JIT
William F Richardson
55 Dinsmore Ave Apt
305
Framingham MA
01702

Call Sign: KD5PEM
Nita K Madhav
50 Dinsmore Ave Apt
606
Framingham MA
01702

Call Sign: AD5EY
David J Holl Jr
50 Dinsmore Ave Apt
606
Framingham MA
01702

Call Sign: N1KQS
Steven M Goldberg
34 Donna Rd
Framingham MA
01701

Call Sign: KA1KNP
Stephen C Thierauf
17 Donovan Dr
Framingham MA
01701

Call Sign: N1IMX
Peter C Kliem
4 Doris Rd
Framingham MA
01701

Call Sign: N1HUN
Carlo P Belloli
41 Dow St
Framingham MA
01701

Call Sign: WB8MLD
Philip S Schwarz
14 Driscoll Dr
Framingham MA
01701

Call Sign: WA1TGK
Mary A Martel
12 Duffet Rd
Framingham MA
017017135

Call Sign: KB1GMP
Gregory S Berghorn
18 Duffett Rd
Framingham MA
01702

Call Sign: W1GSB
Gregory S Berghorn
18 Duffett Rd
Framingham MA
01702

Call Sign: KC1PI
Eric W Beasley
34 Eaton Rd
Framingham MA
01701

Call Sign: KB1KZO
George H Melton Jr
69 Eaton Rd
Framingham MA
01701

Call Sign: KA1RLR
Francis P Towne
51 Eaton Rd E
Framingham MA
01701

Call Sign: WB1CUK
Brian H Sherman
26 Edgell Drive
Framingham MA
01701

Call Sign: KA1ALT
John C Pacheco
66 Edgewater Dr
Framingham MA
01702

Call Sign: N1LAU
Robert P Stetson
159 Edgewater Dr
Framingham MA
01701

Call Sign: K1EII
Robert P Stetson
159 Edgewater Dr
Framingham MA
01702

Call Sign: KB1PNS
Jason A Kates
10 Edith Rd
Framingham MA
01701

Call Sign: K1JAK
Jason A Kates
10 Edith Rd
Framingham MA
01701

Call Sign: K1MEC
Michael E
Cunningham
28 Edith Rd
Framingham MA
01701

Call Sign: KB1ALK
Elliot S Korklan
580 Edmands Rd
Framingham MA
01701

Call Sign: K1UR
Nels J Anderson
585 Edmands Rd
Framingham MA
017013088

Call Sign: KB1TFR
Green Bean Mobile
Contest Club
585 Edmands Rd

Framingham MA
01701

Call Sign: NA1GB
Green Bean Mobile
Contest Club
585 Edmands Rd
Framingham MA
01701

Call Sign: K1ETY
Albert D Stadalski
11 Edmands Rd Apt 25
Framingham MA
017013076

Call Sign: WA1WXT
Ross A De Young
13 Eisenhower Rd
Framingham MA
01701

Call Sign: KB1GYL
Donald C Melanson
325 Elm St
Framingham MA
01701

Call Sign: N1MPI
Peter W Kung
10 Emily Rd
Framingham MA
01701

Call Sign: N1LYH
Stephen W Graveline
23 Fairbrook Rd
Framingham MA
01701

Call Sign: N1WWF
David E Grange
37 Fairbrook Rd
Framingham MA
01701

Call Sign: W1RYW
Arnold R Gilmore
43 Fenelon Rd
Framingham MA
01702

Call Sign: N1OMJ
Michael Giovannucci

17 Fenway Drive
Framingham MA
01701

Call Sign: KA1EKR
Michael E Demaree
26 Fenwood St
Framingham MA
01701

Call Sign: KB1CXF
Janice L Vaughn
56 Florissant Ave
Framingham MA
01701

Call Sign: N1BLZ
Mark D Vaughn
56 Florissant Ave
Framingham MA
01701

Call Sign: N1AIW
Robert S Thompson
89 Florissant Ave
Framingham MA
017014223

Call Sign: W1RST
Robert S Thompson
89 Florissant Ave
Framingham MA
017014223

Call Sign: N1IBT
William B Ware
12 Francine Rd
Framingham MA
01701

Call Sign: W1YVU
Maurice F Watson
342 Franklin St
Framingham MA
01701

Call Sign: KB1GMY
James S Redfield Iii
Franklin St
Framingham MA
01702

Call Sign: KB1GMZ
Kathy L Redfield

Franklin St
Framingham MA
01702

Call Sign: W1KAT
Kathy L Redfield
Franklin St
Framingham MA
01702

Call Sign: W1JSR
James S Redfield Iii
Franklin St
Framingham MA
01702

Call Sign: KB1JMP
Jonathan E Gaines
52 Frost St
Framingham MA
01701

Call Sign: KA1HL
Arnold M Fine
10 Gannon Ter
Framingham MA
01701

Call Sign: KB1CJI
Steven E Cohen
9 Garvey Rd
Framingham MA
01701

Call Sign: N1YKU
Jo Ann M Waithe
6 Greenview St Apt
117
Framingham MA
01701

Call Sign: W1BJS
Elmer M Goldman
52 Gregory Rd
Framingham MA
01701

Call Sign: KB1SCI
Johnathan C
Lamberson
61 Griffin Rd
Framingham MA
01701

Call Sign: K1ECK
Robert J Reed Sr
575 Grove St
Framingham MA
01701

Call Sign: W1IWA
George J Schneider
30 Hadley Rd
Framingham MA
01701

Call Sign: N1HYK
Armand J Larivee
9 Hallett Rd
Framingham MA
01701

Call Sign: KE1S
Gerard H Saunders
55 Harrington Rd
Framingham MA
01701

Call Sign: N1DHE
Sharon M Saunders
56 Harrington Rd
Framingham MA
01701

Call Sign: KB1QMH
Charles W Jensen
57 Harrison St
Framingham MA
01702

Call Sign: W1CWJ
Charles W Jensen
57 Harrison St
Framingham MA
01702

Call Sign: KD1BF
F Richard Cosma
95 Higgins Rd
Framingham MA
017014311

Call Sign: AA1VI
F Richard Cosma
95 Higgins Rd
Framingham MA
017014311

Call Sign: W1IOG
John J De Collibus Sr
23 Hodder Ln
Framingham MA
01701

Call Sign: KB1WAB
Hector L Vazquez
522 Hollis St
Framingham MA
01702

Call Sign: W1BAL
Thomas Bulbar
596 Hollis St
Framingham MA
01701

Call Sign: WA1LKF
Stephen A Moro
3 Huron Dr
Framingham MA
01701

Call Sign: K1BTF
Earle B Foote
13 Janebar Cir
Framingham MA
017013174

Call Sign: K1DGJ
Gerald J Dickie
47 Janebar Cir
Framingham MA
01701

Call Sign: K1HMM
Michael L Silk
6 Janice Cir
Framingham MA
01701

Call Sign: KA1ICV
Audrey M Ghidaleson
46 Jodie Rd
Framingham MA
01702

Call Sign: WA2KRS
Glenn D Ghidaleson
46 Jodie Rd
Framingham MA
01702

Call Sign: WA1MZC
Jeffrey C Slamin
John J Brady Dr
Framingham MA
01702

Call Sign: KA1USL
Lee J Gartenberg
31 Joseph Rd
Framingham MA
01701

Call Sign: KC1YR
Sharon M Gartenberg
31 Joseph Rd
Framingham MA
01701

Call Sign: K1GL
Lee J Gartenberg
31 Joseph Rd
Framingham MA
01701

Call Sign: WB1GCT
Donny Vecht
59 Joseph Rd
Framingham MA
017017638

Call Sign: KB1GMX
Allison J Parent
65 Joseph Rd
Framingham MA
01701

Call Sign: N1ZPE
Daniel Horvat
31 Joseph St
Framingham MA
01701

Call Sign: W1MEG
Gordon E Hopper
75 Kendall Ave
Framingham MA
01701

Call Sign: K1AIU
Gerald D Ceccarini
28 Kendall Ln
Framingham MA
01701

Call Sign: WA1TGJ
Regina B Ceccarini
28 Kendall Ln
Framingham MA
01701

Call Sign: K1IGD
Charles E Walbridge
6 Laclede Ave
Framingham MA
017014267

Call Sign: W1ZEN
Yankee Chapter
Quarter Century
Wireless Association
6 Laclede Ave
Framingham MA
01701

Call Sign: KB1LXN
Barry I Needalman
102 Lake Rd
Framingham MA
017014244

Call Sign: N1XAP
Jeffrey J Lance
1 Lakeside Dr
Framingham MA
017017201

Call Sign: KA1LFF
Eliott M Oven
83 Lanewood Ave
Framingham MA
017013664

Call Sign: KB1IUM
Michael Egan
159 Lincoln St 1st
Floor Rear
Framingham MA
01702

Call Sign: KB1WIQ
Michael Egan
159 Lincoln St 1st
Floor Rear
Framingham MA
01702

Call Sign: K1BTN
Lester T Dennis

56 Linda Ave
Framingham MA
01701

Call Sign: KA1RMD
Richard R Sliney
28 Livoli Rd
Framingham MA
017013852

Call Sign: K1RAW
Richard F Gregorio
178 Lockland Ave
Framingham MA
01701

Call Sign: W1RAW
Framingham High &
Low Club
178 Lockland Ave
Framingham MA
01701

Call Sign: N1CKB
Thomas Verra Jr
4 Lomas Cir
Framingham MA
01701

Call Sign: N1RUK
Christopher J
Lamberson
9 Lomas Drive
Framingham MA
01701

Call Sign: KA1LFV
Carolyn L Tompkins
29 Lyman Rd
Framingham MA
017013853

Call Sign: KC1JX
Martin H Green
35 Lyman Rd
Framingham MA
01701

Call Sign: WA1ZKZ
Risa S Green
35 Lyman Rd
Framingham MA
01701

Call Sign: KB1FHD
Joshua M Green
35 Lyman Rd
Framingham MA
01701

Call Sign: W1JMG
Joshua M Green
35 Lyman Rd
Framingham MA
01701

Call Sign: K1LV
Martin H Green
35 Lyman Rd
Framingham MA
01701

Call Sign: N1HT
Martin H Green
35 Lyman Rd
Framingham MA
01701

Call Sign: KB1UTK
Paul R O'neill
84 Mansfield St
Framingham MA
01702

Call Sign: WC1T
Hugh E Bowen
12 Maureen Rd
Framingham MA
01701

Call Sign: N1YXS
Paul C Hooper
9 Maymont Dr
Framingham MA
01701

Call Sign: AA1IA
Mark S Wilkins
9 Merlin St
Framingham MA
017014443

Call Sign: N1YWE
Brent H Otto
7 Merrill Dr
Framingham MA
01701

Call Sign: N1ZWE
Andrew H Otto
7 Merrill Dr
Framingham MA
01701

Call Sign: WA1QYW
Jeffrey C Otto
7 Merrill Dr
Framingham MA
01701

Call Sign: W1YTL
Charles W Hayden
5 Mohawk Dr
Framingham MA
01701

Call Sign: KA1TLA
Francis L Laviolette
400 Mt Wayte Ave
Framingham MA
01701

Call Sign: N1MPC
Dorothy A Buhrer
6 Murphy Cir
Framingham MA
01701

Call Sign: W1GNP
Carl F Buhrer
6 Murphy Cir
Framingham MA
01701

Call Sign: N1DFT
Howard A Gullbrand
5 Nadine Rd
Framingham MA
01701

Call Sign: N1TLB
Charles K Kaiden
15 Nadine Rd
Framingham MA
01701

Call Sign: N1QYV
V N Martin
20 Nadine Rd
Framingham MA
01701

Call Sign: KT4OK
Donald L Dygert
28 Oakcrest Dr
Framingham MA
017018904

Call Sign: KA1NSC
Sheldon P Golder
5 Oakwood Court
Framingham MA
01701

Call Sign: KB1HRF
Val Petrov
15 Oakwood Ct
Framingham MA
01701

Call Sign: WB1CVB
Stephen J Clements
14 Old Connecticut
Path
Framingham MA
017017802

Call Sign: KB1QDY
David J Longden Jr
1070 Old Connecticut
Path
Framingham MA
01701

Call Sign: W1BRA
Helzer P Paim
444 Old Connecticut
Path # 2
Framingham MA
01701

Call Sign: W6TCS
Frank H Timreck
Oran Rd
Framingham MA
01701

Call Sign: KB1OCI
Steven L Ostrovitz
19 Oroway St
Framingham MA
01702

Call Sign: N1SHJ
Alfred E Feuersanger
66 Overlook Dr

Framingham MA
01701

Call Sign: KB1WME
Benjamin E Greenwald
10 Pamela Rd
Framingham MA
01701

Call Sign: KB1DAK
Gerald H Naditch
16 Pamela Rd
Framingham MA
017013901

Call Sign: N1DOL
Mark J Shaffer
16 Perry H Henderson
Dr
Framingham MA
017014385

Call Sign: N4GJT
Herbert E Fickes
6 Picard Ter
Framingham MA
01701

Call Sign: AA1EL
Eric K Essigmann
4 Pincushion Rd
Framingham MA
01701

Call Sign: W1QX
Eric K Essigmann
4 Pincushion Rd
Framingham MA
01702

Call Sign: KB1GMU
Lawrence J Griffin
38 Pine Lane
Framingham MA
017013802

Call Sign: KA1NAK
Tony Suatengco
690 Pleasant St
Framingham MA
01701

Call Sign: KB1KPT
Tony Suatengco

690 Pleasant St
Framingham MA
01701

Call Sign: W1FOF
L Eloise Mc Lean
837 Pleasant St
Framingham MA
01701

Call Sign: WA1JNJ
Robert E Bosworth
837 Pleasant St
Framingham MA
01701

Call Sign: N2TNY
Clayton A Curry
168 Potter Rd
Framingham MA
01701

Call Sign: WA1HAM
Leo L Cantin
457 Potter Rd
Framingham MA
017013301

Call Sign: WA1NVC
Roger W Coulson
40 Prior Dr
Framingham MA
01701

Call Sign: KB1GMS
Bradley J Cauchon
118 Prospect St
Framingham MA
01701

Call Sign: WB1ATW
Edward F Kraft
10 Queens Way Apt 1
Framingham MA
017017729

Call Sign: N1UEZ
Angela R Tucker
19 Ridgefield Dr
Framingham MA
01701

Call Sign: N1JFO
Brian R Lees

31 Ridgefield Dr
Framingham MA
01701

Call Sign: N1JFP
Kristi E Lees
31 Ridgefield Dr
Framingham MA
01701

Call Sign: N1LOO
Beverly D Lees
31 Ridgefield Dr
Framingham MA
01701

Call Sign: N1SMS
Andrew C Lees
31 Ridgefield Dr
Framingham MA
01701

Call Sign: K1TY
David R Tucker
19 Ridgefield Dr
Framingham MA
01701

Call Sign: WB2KDX
Steven T Johnson
47 River St
Framingham MA
017025814

Call Sign: KB1OUU
Gary A Dubinsky
26 Riverview Rd
Framingham MA
01701

Call Sign: W1GAB
Thomas P Skinner
15 Rolling Dr
Framingham MA
01701

Call Sign: KA1FMF
Edward G Mc Faden
79 Roundtop Rd
Framingham MA
01701

Call Sign: WA1MPF
David B Hughes

4 Royal Meadow Lane
Framingham MA
01701

Call Sign: N1DDO
Burton Shaffer
73 Russell Rd
Framingham MA
01701

Call Sign: N1DDS
Toby L Shaffer
73 Russell Rd
Framingham MA
01701

Call Sign: KB1JCY
Douglas R Perry
9 Ruthellen Rd
Framingham MA
01701

Call Sign: WA1KRT
Alan R Kivnik
3 Sage Ln
Framingham MA
01701

Call Sign: WA1EAB
Lawrence S Hirsch
52 Salem End Ln
Framingham MA
01702

Call Sign: W1IAQ
Alfred S Mac Dermott
57 Salem End Ln
Framingham MA
01702

Call Sign: N1CXU
Anthony Carbone
567 Salem End Rd
Framingham MA
01701

Call Sign: KB1GLG
George F Coles Jr
37 Salem End Rd Apt
17
Framingham MA
01702

Call Sign: KA1WZS

Richard A Jewell Ii
28 Simpson Dr
Framingham MA
01701

Call Sign: KA1SYL
Cheryl A Bird
41 Simpson Dr
Framingham MA
01701

Call Sign: W1GEU
Gary C Hicks Sr
26 Spring Lane
Framingham MA
01701

Call Sign: W1DNE
Gerald B Carvin
19 Spring Ln
Framingham MA
01701

Call Sign: KB1KKG
Gregory J Andrews
32 Springhill Rd
Framingham MA
01701

Call Sign: KB1KKH
Hilary A Sullivan
Andrews
32 Springhill Rd
Framingham MA
01701

Call Sign: N1TDF
Hilary A Sullivan
Andrews
32 Springhill Rd
Framingham MA
01701

Call Sign: W1TDF
Gregory J Andrews
32 Springhill Rd
Framingham MA
01701

Call Sign: N1YNT
Eric J Tarini
20 Spruce St
Framingham MA
01701

Call Sign: N1FXE
Mark A Weingart
70 Spruce St
Framingham MA
01701

Call Sign: K1TJZ
June L Ungvary
236 Summer
Framingham MA
01701

Call Sign: KB1LCK
Helzer P Paim
169 Summer St
Framingham MA
01701

Call Sign: AB1GE
Helzer P Paim
169 Summer St
Framingham MA
01701

Call Sign: KM1L
Helzer P Paim
169 Summer St
Framingham MA
01701

Call Sign: W1KSK
Robert L Ungvary
236 Summer St
Framingham MA
017017903

Call Sign: KA1UST
Cheryl A Deckert
11 Swanson Rd
Framingham MA
01701

Call Sign: N1PTT
Robert Green
7 Sylvester Dr
Framingham MA
01701

Call Sign: N1MPH
Ralph C Moore Jr
10 Sylvester Dr
Framingham MA
01701

Call Sign: K1NDF
Neal Lipson
10 Tartufi Circle
Framingham MA
01701

Call Sign: N1SVY
Charles E Latham
Brown
40 Temple St
Framingham MA
017018815

Call Sign: WN1O
George E James
14 Temple St Apt 3-B
Framingham MA
01702

Call Sign: KI4HVJ
Judith E Plummer
14 Temple St Apt 3d
Framingham MA
01702

Call Sign: WA2AQI
Glenn S Small
14 Temple St Apt 7g
Framingham MA
01702

Call Sign: KA1ZXX
J John Moreira
13 Thomas Dr
Framingham MA
01701

Call Sign: KB1AVY
Joao C Cabral
13 Thomas Drive
Framingham MA
01701

Call Sign: N1KRH
Jeffrey A Morrissey
7 Tomkins Lane
Framingham MA
01702

Call Sign: WB1AVY
William Zimmer
30 Travis Dr

Framingham MA
01701

Call Sign: K1KMN
Frederick V Dixon
23 Turner Rd
Framingham MA
01701

Call Sign: N1XXZ
Lorraine A Laforce
23 Turner Rd
Framingham MA
01701

Call Sign: KB1JSY
Rogerio Sa
258 Union Ave
Framingham MA
01701

Call Sign: AA8QU
Motoyuki Seta
2 Victory St
Framingham MA
01702

Call Sign: N1CYS
John Pezzlo
5 Walkers Way
Framingham MA
01701

Call Sign: W1ZOP
Charles F Rousseau
552 Water St
Framingham MA
01701

Call Sign: KA1GEN
Fred Rosebury
747 Water St 248
Framingham MA
017013222

Call Sign: N1RTS
Sheldon W Rothstein
5 Waveney Rd
Framingham MA
01701

Call Sign: N1EHN
Michael D Shaffer
13 Waveney Rd

Framingham MA
01701

Call Sign: N2AWG
David L Kent
43 Wayside Inn Rd
Framingham MA
01701

Call Sign: KC1DS
Malcolm H Chellquist
90 Wayside Inn Rd
Framingham MA
01701

Call Sign: KB1LTM
Robert V Deleon
4 Wellington Ave
Framingham MA
01702

Call Sign: WA1ZRH
David B Kirschen
8 Westview Rd
Framingham MA
01701

Call Sign: K1RP
Robert B Platt
43 Whittemore Rd
Framingham MA
01701

Call Sign: W1KPZ
William H Mc Sheehy
501 Windsor Dr
Framingham MA
01701

Call Sign: KB1HIL
William H Mc Sheehy
501 Windsor Dr
Framingham MA
01701

Call Sign: W1KPZ
William H Mc Sheehy
501 Windsor Dr
Framingham MA
01701

Call Sign: KB1NIV
Stephen C Hewlett
44 Winter Park Rd

Framingham MA
017026208

Call Sign: N4GNV
Gregg Askin
110 Winter St
Framingham MA
017022432

Call Sign: WA1PYF
Enzo F Rotatori
550 Winter St
Framingham MA
01701

Call Sign: N1JTN
William C Stamm Jr
607 Winter St
Framingham MA
01701

Call Sign: KF4EYL
Clayton L Juckett
121 Winter St Apt #4
Framingham MA
017022433

Call Sign: KA1EPR
Leonard J Salafia
31 Woodmere Rd
Framingham MA
01701

Call Sign: N1OJX
George R Barnes
38 Woodmere Rd
Framingham MA
017012880

Call Sign: WC1AAR
Massachusetts Emerg
Mngmnt Agency
400 Worcester Rd
Framingham MA
01701

Call Sign: WC1ABL
Massachusetts
Emergency
Management Agency
400 Worcester Rd
Framingham MA
01701

Call Sign: WC1CAA
Massachusetts Emerg
Mngmnt Agency
400 Worcester Rd
Framingham MA
01701

Call Sign: KB1HUL
Mema Hq Races Club
400 Worcester Rd
Framingham MA
017025399

Call Sign: WC1MA
Mema Hq Races Club
400 Worcester Rd
Framingham MA
017025399

Call Sign: KA1RQK
Sidney Geller
1450 Worcester Rd
Framingham MA
01701

Call Sign: KO1N
Irving Geller
1450 Worcester Rd
Framingham MA
01701

Call Sign: KD1FX
Yutaka Umebayashi
1500 Worcester Rd
Framingham MA
01701

Call Sign: W8JCD
Jack C Dietz
555 Worcester Rd #25
Framingham MA
01701

Call Sign: KD8CNP
Bayhas M Kana
1612 Worcester Rd
#622A
Framingham MA
01702

Call Sign: KB1FEU
Mark F TRUE
1450 Worcester Rd
122b

Framingham MA
01702

Call Sign: KA1WIW
Christina H Sefranek
1186 Worcester Rd
631
Framingham MA
01702

Call Sign: KA1HIA
Marjorie J Stern
1400 Worcester Rd
7616
Framingham MA
017028936

Call Sign: KA1VZV
Robert E Crisler
1640 Worcester Rd
Apt 231
Framingham MA
01701

Call Sign: N1FIS
Aniruddha Mukherjee
1630 Worcester Rd
Apt 406
Framingham MA
01701

Call Sign: KB1KLL
Sushmita Sengupta
1622 Worcester Rd
Apt 424b
Framingham MA
01702

Call Sign: KF4DRA
Jeremy R Phillips
1400 Worcester Rd
Apt 7318
Framingham MA
01702

Call Sign: WA1R
Marc J Stern
1400 Worcester Rd
Apt 7616
Framingham MA
017028936

Call Sign: N1YER
Michael R Kass

1325 Worcester Rd D6
Framingham MA
01701

Call Sign: AA1GQ
Mark A Chase
Framingham MA
01701

Call Sign: KA1WSM
Howard M Thompson
Framingham MA
01701

Call Sign: KC5AWV
Mary J Craver
Framingham MA
017053103

Call Sign: N1SFX
Duane M Tesorero
Framingham MA
01701

Call Sign: W1FY
Framingham Amateur
Radio Association
Framingham MA
01705

Call Sign: W2MM
Quarter Century
Wireless Assn Inc
Framingham MA
01705

Call Sign: KB1LRA
Quarter Century
Wireless Association
Inc
Framingham MA
017053247

Call Sign: KB1QEA
Doe West
Framingham MA
01701

Call Sign: W1DOE
Doe West
Framingham MA
01701

Call Sign: W2CVF

Quarter Century
Wireless Association
Inc
Framingham MA
017053247

Call Sign: KB1VLS
David Levenson
Framingham MA
01701

FCC Amateur Radio Licenses in Franklin

Call Sign: WB1BZP
Steven J Jasinski
24 A Elm St
Franklin MA 02038

Call Sign: N1VKR
Derek Clougherty
247 A Pond St
Franklin MA 02038

Call Sign: KB1VUC
Bruce E Erickson
1 Acorn Pl
Franklin MA 02038

Call Sign: N1TQC
William J Gilbert
20 Beaver St
Franklin MA 02038

Call Sign: K1COQ
Roy G Cornelius Jr
25 Bridle Path
Franklin MA 02038

Call Sign: WA1PWS
Stephen J Reynolds
30 Brook St
Franklin MA 02038

Call Sign: AB1HJ
John K Samolyk
60 Charles River Dr
Franklin MA 02038

Call Sign: W1JKS
John K Samolyk
60 Charles River Dr
Franklin MA 02038

Call Sign: KA1ZDY
Carie E Robinson
230 Chestnut St
Franklin MA 02038

Call Sign: KB1HLR
Michael D Dubois
41 Crescent St
Franklin MA 02038

Call Sign: W1EGV
James K Hosford Sr
54 Crocker Ave
Franklin MA 02038

Call Sign: WD4LXO
Melanie R Payne
22 Cypress Lane
Franklin MA 02038

Call Sign: N1UWF
Jay R Volner
49 Dean Ave E
Franklin MA 02038

Call Sign: KD1FG
Thomas Pilis
9 Donato Dr
Franklin MA 02038

Call Sign: WA3NQW
John W Lemansky
10 Donato Dr
Franklin MA 02038

Call Sign: N1YXP
Thomas R Di Francia
655 E Central St
Franklin MA 02038

Call Sign: WA1OLV
Richard M Vito
522 Eagles Nest Way
Franklin MA 02038

Call Sign: KC1R
Richard E Ferland
496 East Central St
Franklin MA 02038

Call Sign: N1LRZ
Brian J D Amelio
36 Everett St
Franklin MA 02038

Call Sign: K1MVO
John Tamasco
4 Forge Hill Rd
Franklin MA 02038

Call Sign: WN1C
Ann M Bellinger
430 Franklin Village
Dr 178
Franklin MA 02038

Call Sign: N1LSA
John F Manning
9 Glen Dr
Franklin MA 02038

Call Sign: KA1GGG
Arthur T Donahue
14 Greensfield Rd
Franklin MA 02038

Call Sign: KA1KRF
Mary V Donahue
14 Greensfield Rd
Franklin MA 02038

Call Sign: K1UKM
Irving C Davis
79 Grove St
Franklin MA 02038

Call Sign: WN1N
Barry M Kasindorf
1 Heights Rd
Franklin MA 02038

Call Sign: KB1GVG
Jon M Chalk
28 High St
Franklin MA 02038

Call Sign: W1FFD
Jon M Chalk
28 High St
Franklin MA 02038

Call Sign: WA1HII
Bradford N Dixon
130 Highwood Drive
Franklin MA 02038

Call Sign: WA1QMY
Kenneth G Wood

200 Irondequoit Rd
Franklin MA 02038

Call Sign: WB1ADB
Douglas A Robar
230 Irondequoit Rd
Franklin MA
020382908

Call Sign: KA1NGP
Jeffrey L Greer
22 Jackson Cir
Franklin MA 02038

Call Sign: N1OUX
Richard A Gavel
7 Joval Ct
Franklin MA 02038

Call Sign: KA3BOB
Robert J Shaw Mr
27 Lenox Dr
Franklin MA 02038

Call Sign: K1JEN
Americo D Santoro
64 Lewis St
Franklin MA 02038

Call Sign: K1RGZ
Thomas C Rocheleau
477 Lincoln St
Franklin MA 02038

Call Sign: KB1SGI
Vincent J Barba
31 Lockewood Dr
Franklin MA 02038

Call Sign: AD1AD
Chiyoon C An
32 Lorraine Metcalf
Rd
Franklin MA 02038

Call Sign: WB8TSL
Paul R Swedberg
10 Lucius St
Franklin MA 02038

Call Sign: KB1KQH
Lauren A Henchy
5 Lydia Lane
Franklin MA 02038

Call Sign: W1LAH
Lauren A Henchy
5 Lydia Lane
Franklin MA 02038

Call Sign: KB1EFS
Steven J Henchy
5 Lydia Ln
Franklin MA 02038

Call Sign: KA1BOS
Gary R Stucchi
65 Maple St
Franklin MA 02038

Call Sign: N1DVE
Jaclyn K Swenson
485 Maple St
Franklin MA 02038

Call Sign: K1JKS
Jaclyn K Swenson
485 Maple St
Franklin MA 02038

Call Sign: W1IDF
Charles H Dancy
440 Martello Rd
Franklin MA 02038

Call Sign: KC1JB
Peter N Spotts
9 Martha S Way
Franklin MA 02038

Call Sign: W1PNS
Peter N Spotts
9 Martha S Way
Franklin MA 02038

Call Sign: N2EZF
Matthew A Roth
48 Newell Drive
Franklin MA 02038

Call Sign: KB1OBE
John R Amell Jr
31 Oak St
Franklin MA 02038

Call Sign: KA1UIG
Matthew E Allard
225 Oak St

Franklin MA 02038

Call Sign: KA1VVT
Robert J Shaw
392 Old Farm Rd
Franklin MA 02038

Call Sign: K4YX
Pamela R Rathmell
11 Pear Tree Lane
Franklin MA
020383936

Call Sign: W2AXL
Jack E Rathmell
11 Pear Tree Lane
Franklin MA 02038

Call Sign: WB1CTO
Richard J Whitten
97 Pine Ridge Dr
Franklin MA 02038

Call Sign: K1AAP
James E Morris
136 Pleasant St
Franklin MA 02038

Call Sign: KB1RLS
Alan R Earls
222 Pond St
Franklin MA 02038

Call Sign: N1YWD
Glenna H Richards
372 Pond St
Franklin MA 02038

Call Sign: N1FUP
Elizabeth A Valero
1082 Pond St
Franklin MA
020382635

Call Sign: ND1Z
Vernon C Valero
1082 Pond St
Franklin MA 02038

Call Sign: KB1BHW
Amanda M Lacouture
103 Populatic
Franklin MA 02038

Call Sign: WV1T
Thomas A Lacouture
103 Populatic St
Franklin MA 02038

Call Sign: K1KQC
John H Potter
47 Quince Landing
Franklin MA
020382581

Call Sign: AA1UZ
Drew D Leavitt
46 Silver Fox Rd
Franklin MA 02038

Call Sign: N1FYQ
Gerald L Price
7 Stanwood Drive
Franklin MA 02038

Call Sign: N1OAT
John S Kenney
143 Stone Ridge Rd
Franklin MA 02038

Call Sign: KA1YQC
Mark P Hofstra
212 Summer St
Franklin MA 02038

Call Sign: AB1OY
Chiyoon C An
15 Summer St 104
Franklin MA 02038

Call Sign: KA1UIF
Frank E Suchanek
349 Union St
Franklin MA 02038

Call Sign: N1YUR
David J Sciolto
711 Washington St
Franklin MA 02038

Call Sign: KB1BLW
Jeffrey G Cody
64 West St
Franklin MA 02038

Call Sign: W1ZLQ
George E Crawford Jr
Franklin MA 02038

Call Sign: KB1ULZ
Erinn M Knowles
Franklin MA 02038

Call Sign: N1ZQZ
Vincent T Doliveira
44 Huron Ave
Freetown MA 02717

Call Sign: K1APL
Thomas G Reese
10 Bancroft St
Gardner MA 01440

Call Sign: K1KDW
G Luther Cheney
40 Banner Rd
Gardner MA 01440

Call Sign: NM1C
Matthew F Tatro
3 Beech St Apt 2
Gardner MA 01440

Call Sign: K4IWN
David H Arens
62 Bickford Hill Rd
Gardner MA 01440

Call Sign: KB1DPD
Robert A Bradshaw Iii
151 Blanchard St Suite
B
Gardner MA
014402073

Call Sign: KD1LH
Bruce R Gibbs
84 Century Way
Gardner MA
014404308

Call Sign: WJ1I
Bruce R Gibbs
84 Century Way
Gardner MA
014401233

Call Sign: KD1LH
Bruce R Gibbs
84 Century Way
Gardner MA
014401233

Call Sign: K1RPZ
Jean E Dube
17 Chapel St
Gardner MA 01440

Call Sign: KA1GMA
Barbara A Dube
17 Chapel St
Gardner MA 01440

Call Sign: N1LQI
Michael L Kudravetz
90 Cherry St
Gardner MA
014402361

Call Sign: KB1KVT
Gardner Civil Defense
Radio Club
31 City Hall Ave
Gardner MA 01440

Call Sign: W1GCD
Gardner Civil Defense
Radio Club
31 City Hall Ave
Gardner MA 01440

Call Sign: KB1BQD
Sheldon R Perry
1 Clairmont St
Gardner MA 01440

Call Sign: KB1BYX
Felix Izquierdo
300 Clark St
Gardner MA 01440

Call Sign: N1ERS
Kevin T Erickson
194 Conant St
Gardner MA
014403158

Call Sign: KB1QCG
Walter C Penzinski
189 Connors St

Gardner MA 01440

Call Sign: KB1EOV
Gary F Conboy
40 Crawford St
Gardner MA 01440

Call Sign: KB1GJD
Elizabeth L Johnson
35 Dyer St
Gardner MA 01440

Call Sign: KB1GJE
D Alan Johnson
35 Dyer St
Gardner MA 01440

Call Sign: K1LBJ
Kingsley D Locke
197 Elm St
Gardner MA 01440

Call Sign: KA1IMO
Nils D Anderson
346 Elm St
Gardner MA
014403916

Call Sign: K1FLW
Raymond Faucher
156 Green
Gardner MA 01440

Call Sign: KB1TGN
Erich J Kaiser
118 Greenwood St
Gardner MA 01440

Call Sign: KB1DPI
Joshua J May
349 High St
Gardner MA 01440

Call Sign: KA1QGB
Donald L Landry Jr
339 High St
Gardner MA 01440

Call Sign: KD2GT
Jeffrey L Cooper
28 Jonathan St
Gardner MA 01440

Call Sign: K1JMD

James M Daly
888 Kelton St
Gardner MA
014401152

Call Sign: AD1L
James M Daly
888 Kelton St
Gardner MA
014401152

Call Sign: N1STT
Richard J Tatro
47 Lake St Apt A302
Gardner MA 01440

Call Sign: W1SEX
Paul A Topolski
153 Logan St
Gardner MA 01440

Call Sign: KA1MWP
Charles W Partain
403 Lovewell St
Gardner MA 01440

Call Sign: KB1TPN
Keegan N Mehrtens
89 Maple St
Gardner MA 01440

Call Sign: N1LEF
William E Wilson Iii
3 Maple St Apt 2r
Gardner MA 01440

Call Sign: W1CJI
Eino I Taavitsainen
376 Mathews St
Gardner MA 01440

Call Sign: N1MXV
David E Jenkins
52 Norman St
Gardner MA
014401916

Call Sign: K1UJG
Robert C Stroscio
51 Old Colonial Dr
Gardner MA 01440

Call Sign: K1EZP
Harry O Miller

216 Park St
Gardner MA 01440

Call Sign: KB1QCB
Marlene A Erickson
176 Pleasant St 3
Gardner MA 01440

Call Sign: KA1GCN
Frederick J Erickson Jr
176 Pleasant St Apt #3
Gardner MA 01440

Call Sign: KB1SVW
Matthew S Cohen
73 Prospect St
Gardner MA 01440

Call Sign: WI1Q
Daniel W Gaumond
17 Red Fox Crossing
Gardner MA 01440

Call Sign: N1NUW
George F Bucenko
17 Regan St
Gardner MA 01440

Call Sign: KB1QCC
Debbie A Bilodeau
27 Ridgewood Ln Unit
24
Gardner MA 01440

Call Sign: KB1IYW
Charles S Thompson
173 Sand St
Gardner MA 01440

Call Sign: N6BRP
James D Bargnesi
12 Stephanie Dr
Gardner MA 01440

Call Sign: N1BRP
James D Bargnesi
12 Stephanie Dr
Gardner MA 01440

Call Sign: KB1ISJ
Ian A Kinloch
318 Union St
Gardner MA 01440

Call Sign: N1JYW
Norman A Bourgeois
99 Washington St
Gardner MA 01440

Call Sign: N1SOR
Robert W Clark
33 Wateford St
Gardner MA 01440

Call Sign: N1IPZ
Donald L Landry Sr
46 Water St
Gardner MA 01440

Call Sign: KA1WHX
Dennis E Cormier
46 Waterford St
Gardner MA 01440

Call Sign: N1FCA
Hector A Poirier
209 Waterford St
Gardner MA 01440

Call Sign: KB1GIX
Walter E Lacey
12 West End Ave
Gardner MA 01440

Call Sign: N1GKU
Heidi G Heck
93 West End Ave
Gardner MA 01440

Call Sign: N1IXN
David W Walters
137 West St
Gardner MA 01440

Call Sign: WA1QZV
Steven M Naticchioni
961 West St
Gardner MA
014401521

Call Sign: KD4YSU
Susan E Rayles
163 Whitney St
Gardner MA 01440

Call Sign: KE4BKD
Ron Rayles
163 Whitney St

Gardner MA 01440

Call Sign: N1RSX
Adam P Brodeur
182 Willis Rd
Gardner MA 01440

Call Sign: KA1QGE
Edmund H Damon
196 Woodland Ave
Gardner MA 01440

Call Sign: N1KQC
Milton H Taylor
Gardner MA 01440

Call Sign: KB1SNG
Nicholas T Lapointe
Gardner MA 01440

FCC Amateur Radio Licenses in Georgetown

Call Sign: KA1ZNN
Max A Shapiro
90 Baldpate Rd
Georgetown MA
01833

Call Sign: KA1JMX
Gerald E Finnigan
2 Boardman St
Georgetown MA
01834

Call Sign: N1CNE
Robert P Rudolph
39 Brook St
Georgetown MA
01833

Call Sign: KB1GPS
Matthew L Brodie
7 Brownfield Ln
Georgetown MA
01833

Call Sign: KA1ACN
Colin L Wheeler
9 Canterbury Dr
Georgetown MA
01833

Call Sign: W1AFJ
Everett A Spaulding
90 East Main St
Georgetown MA
01833

Call Sign: KB1GNM
Robert G Wilson
140 Elm St
Georgetown MA
018332517

Call Sign: KB1LOC
Alfred A Nicotra
5 Hawk Way
Georgetown MA
01833

Call Sign: KB1EDJ
Aubrey R Bishop Jr
15 Horsemint Cir
Georgetown MA
018331111

Call Sign: KB1LSW
Helen L Lee
1 Jewett St
Georgetown MA
01833

Call Sign: KB1LSX
Daniel F Lee
1 Jewett St
Georgetown MA
01833

Call Sign: W1DFL
Daniel F Lee
1 Jewett St
Georgetown MA
01833

Call Sign: N1BYJ
Robert J Crawford
56 Jewett St
Georgetown MA
01833

Call Sign: N1KYM
Christian Y Roop
58 Jewett St
Georgetown MA
018331210

Call Sign: KA1FET
Robert W Sprague
1 Juniper Ln
Georgetown MA
018331614

Call Sign: NG1L
Richard J De Sisto
2 Marlboro Rd
Georgetown MA
018331701

Call Sign: KA1UQ
William A Lawless Jr
18 Marlboro Rd
Georgetown MA
01833

Call Sign: K1UQ
William A Lawless Jr
18 Marlboro Rd
Georgetown MA
018331703

Call Sign: KB1MIZ
Charles R Cunningham
23 Marlboro Rd
Georgetown MA
01833

Call Sign: KB1QJV
Cory D Cunningham
23 Marlboro Rd
Georgetown MA
01833

Call Sign: WB1GZK
Charles A Davis
30 Marlboro Rd
Georgetown MA
018332203

Call Sign: K1CAD
Charles A Davis
30 Marlboro Rd
Georgetown MA
018332203

Call Sign: KB1MIA
Laurent R Palardy
59 North St
Georgetown MA
01833

Call Sign: KD1EI
David P Meader
68 North St
Georgetown MA
01833

Call Sign: N1JUO
Richard A Lutes Jr
553 North St
Georgetown MA
01833

Call Sign: K1GBX
Arthur S Greenberg
123 Pond St
Georgetown MA
01833

Call Sign: KB1NEQ
Michael S Lee
7 Silvermine Ln
Georgetown MA
01833

Call Sign: W1MSL
Michael S Lee
7 Silvermine Ln
Georgetown MA
01833

Call Sign: N1YRV
Rebecca A Murphy
104 Thurlow St
Georgetown MA
01833

Call Sign: W1UXX
Bruce W Miller
142 Thurlow St
Georgetown MA
01833

Call Sign: N1FBA
James C Mood
27 Warren St
Georgetown MA
01833

Call Sign: N1FOQ
Peter R Kelly
90 West Main St
Georgetown MA
01833

Call Sign: N1LPB
Lewis D Grasso
8 West St
Georgetown MA
01833

Call Sign: N1LCI
John D Starr
22 West St
Georgetown MA
01833

Call Sign: N1WLE
James J Shalkoski Jr
1 Whiffletree Ln
Georgetown MA
01833

Call Sign: N1PZL
Peter M Langevin
Georgetown MA
01833

FCC Amateur Radio Licenses in Gilbertville

Call Sign: WB9LAA
Tamar R Berthiaume
15 Dow Rd
Gilbertville MA 01031

Call Sign: N1XOO
James J Gadbois Sr
511 Main St
Gilbertville MA 01031

FCC Amateur Radio Licenses in Gill

Call Sign: N1VOZ
Earl F Tetreault
151 Aa Barney Hale
Rd
Gill MA 01376

Call Sign: N1OOU
Wayne F Tetreault
Barney Hale Rd
Gill MA 01376

Call Sign: N1LJZ
Darryl A Wesso
Box 177

Gill MA 01376

Call Sign: KB1QAD
Steven P Connell
102 Center Rd
Gill MA 01354

Call Sign: KB1MFM
Stuart F Elliott
27 Franklin Rd
Gill MA 01354

Call Sign: KB1PCH
Frank J Clark
44 French King Hwy
Gill MA 01354

Call Sign: N1KRR
Robert J Koolkin
6 Mountain Rd
Gill MA 01376

Call Sign: KB1HAV
David A Balise
4 S Cross Rd
Gill MA 013549719

FCC Amateur Radio Licenses in Gloucester

Call Sign: KB1WFZ
Doris F Cole
24 Acacia St
Gloucester MA 01930

Call Sign: W1LF
Robert G Crockett
25 Adams Hill Rd
Gloucester MA 01930

Call Sign: AB1JL
Stanley W Stone
20 Andrews St
Gloucester MA 01930

Call Sign: W4HIX
Stanley W Stone
20 Andrews St
Gloucester MA 01930

Call Sign: KA1ZMM
Mario M Marnoto
Arthur St Unit 1

Gloucester MA 01930

Call Sign: KB1GRO
Daniel D Lanciani
185 Atlantic Rd
Gloucester MA 01930

Call Sign: W1NBA
Daniel D Lanciani
185 Atlantic Rd
Gloucester MA 01930

Call Sign: N1RTK
Douglas B Kenny
73 Atlantic St
Gloucester MA 01930

Call Sign: KB1PGH
Dean J Burgess
21 Bass Ave
Gloucester MA 01930

Call Sign: WA1BWR
Wilfred L Burke
34 Bass Ave
Gloucester MA
019303118

Call Sign: KA1OH
Kenneth D Ekstrom
1 Bickford Way
Gloucester MA 01930

Call Sign: N1URH
Muriel J Burke
Box 1553
Gloucester MA
019311553

Call Sign: KB1RUI
Judith A Knickle
48 Bray St
Gloucester MA 01930

Call Sign: KB1LKK
Ronald J Beckley
60 Causeway St
Gloucester MA 01930

Call Sign: N1RJB
Ronald J Beckley
60 Causeway St
Gloucester MA 01930

Call Sign: WA9TEP
Michael D Ronan
18 Centennial Ave
Gloucester MA 01930

Call Sign: KA1ZLG
Bayard J Pless
35 Chapel St
Gloucester MA 01930

Call Sign: KB1VSU
Jacqueline M Hardy
29 Cherry St
Gloucester MA 01930

Call Sign: WV1A
Robert P Quinn
150 Cherry St
Gloucester MA 01930

Call Sign: KB1BTY
Matthew C Howden
152 Cherry St
Gloucester MA 01930

Call Sign: N1WVI
Philip A Howden
152 Cherry St
Gloucester MA 01930

Call Sign: WZ1B
Richard C Maybury
152 Cherry St
Gloucester MA 01930

Call Sign: KB1TOL
Erin C Maybury
152 Cherry St
Gloucester MA 01930

Call Sign: W1ERN
Erin C Maybury
152 Cherry St
Gloucester MA 01930

Call Sign: KA1YSD
Earl L Montgomery Jr
11 Cleveland Pl
Gloucester MA 01930

Call Sign: KB1VSS
Robert B Cavender Sr
Colburn St
Gloucester MA 01930

Call Sign: KB1TRF
Christine M Maney
3 Compass Way
Gloucester MA 01930

Call Sign: KB1TRG
John P Maney
3 Compass Way
Gloucester MA 01930

Call Sign: N1CF
William F Collins Iii
364 Concord St
Gloucester MA 01930

Call Sign: W1RSW
Herbert C Batten
13 Corliss Ave
Gloucester MA 01930

Call Sign: WB1FVK
Bruce R Parsons
5 Crafts Rd
Gloucester MA 01930

Call Sign: KA1LRR
Bradley R Parsons
5 Crafts Rd
Gloucester MA 01930

Call Sign: KA1UCC
Elaine A Bleau
Richards
9 Crowell Ave
Gloucester MA 01930

Call Sign: WB1EAZ
Ronald B Richards
9 Crowell Ave
Gloucester MA 01930

Call Sign: KB1WGA
Brian A Cutler
89 Dennison St
Gloucester MA 01930

Call Sign: KB1VSZ
Michael E Mcmahon
9 Digby Ln
Gloucester MA 01930

Call Sign: KB1VSY
Carol A Mcmahon

9 Digley Ln
Gloucester MA 01930

Call Sign: KE1IR
Pierre E Besson
35 Dory Rd
Gloucester MA 01930

Call Sign: KA1IRE
Loren E White
121 E Main St
Gloucester MA 01930

Call Sign: K1UZX
Thomas H Simmonds
Jr
263 E Main St
Gloucester MA
019304141

Call Sign: KB1GLB
Andrew Campbell
243 East Main St
Gloucester MA 01930

Call Sign: N1XRU
Jamin S Edwards
114 Eastern Ave
Gloucester MA 01930

Call Sign: N1FMS
John A Davis Jr
Edgemoor Rd
Gloucester MA 01930

Call Sign: KA1LKY
Nicholas P Guarrasi
14 Ellery St
Gloucester MA
019302208

Call Sign: N1UIU
Bruce E Tarr
80 Essex Ave
Glouster MA 01930

Call Sign: WA1LXV
George D Hurd
567 Essex Ave
Gloucester MA 01930

Call Sign: AB1OJ
James D Hurd
581 Essex Ave

Gloucester MA 01930

Call Sign: K1LDL
James D Hurd
581 Essex Ave
Gloucester MA 01930

Call Sign: KA1GTA
Thomas S Andrew
5 Ferry St N
Gloucester MA 01930

Call Sign: KA1SFD
Nancy M Andrew
5 Ferry St N
Gloucester MA 01930

Call Sign: WW1N
Ruth E Hodsdon
67 Friend St Unit 7
Gloucester MA 01930

Call Sign: KA1LKX
David Linsky
34 Gee Ave
Gloucester MA 01930

Call Sign: K0TB
Thomas S Bernie Iii
4 Gerring Rd
Gloucester MA 01930

Call Sign: WU1S
Francis A Vidal
9 Harborview Court
Gloucester MA 01930

Call Sign: N1KYP
Joan Vidal
26 Harrison Ave
Gloucester MA 01930

Call Sign: KB1UWI
Michael M Faivre
1120 Heights At Cape
Ann
Gloucester MA 01930

Call Sign: W1RK
Ralph E Karcher Jr
157 Hesperus Ln
Gloucester MA 01930

Call Sign: WB1CHJ

Joseph A Pallazola
3 Highland Ct
Gloucester MA 01930

Call Sign: K1UPK
Robert P Koller
10 Horton St
Gloucester MA 01930

Call Sign: KB1IGN
Richard F Ray
33 King Philip Rd
Gloucester MA 01930

Call Sign: KB1IGO
Judith M Ray
33 King Philip Rd
Gloucester MA 01930

Call Sign: KB1SFR
Charles G Symonds
9 Langsford St
Gloucester MA 01930

Call Sign: W1HRA
Charles G Symonds
9 Langsford St
Gloucester MA 01930

Call Sign: KB1VSV
David F Hayes
28 Langsford St
Gloucester MA 01930

Call Sign: KB1VSW
Joan R Hayes
28 Langsford St
Gloucester MA 01930

Call Sign: KB1SLR
Edward V Tarsook
15 Larose Ave
Gloucester MA 01930

Call Sign: KA1RBR
Emery D Dukette
33 Laurel St
Gloucester MA 01930

Call Sign: KB1WGM
James W O Hara Jr
55 Lexington Ave
Gloucester MA 01930

Call Sign: W1GDT
Frederick J Sallah
18 Liberty
Gloucester MA 01930

Call Sign: KA1CHZ
Albert G Joseph
127 Magnolia Ave
Gloucester MA 01930

Call Sign: N1YDC
Jamin M Jones
39 Mansfield St
Gloucester MA 01930

Call Sign: K1MB
Michael C Burke Sr
152 Maplewood Ave
Gloucester MA 01930

Call Sign: N1KTG
Jeanne F Burke
152 Maplewood Ave
Gloucester MA 01930

Call Sign: N1CJO
Joseph A Enos Jr
33 Maplewood Ave
Unit 214
Gloucester MA 01930

Call Sign: KB1NLA
John H Mceachern
16 Mceachern Place
Gloucester MA 01930

Call Sign: W1JHM
John H Mceachern
16 Mceachern Place
Gloucester MA 01930

Call Sign: KB1PTK
Edwin R Waldsmith Jr
43 Middle St
Gloucester MA 01930

Call Sign: KA1VPH
David C Ham
2 Middle St 3rd Floor
Gloucester MA 01930

Call Sign: N1YGI
Jon W Dahlmer
34 Millett St

Gloucester MA 01930

Call Sign: KB1HVS
Edward P Keyes
15 Mondello Sq
Gloucester MA 01930

Call Sign: N1CPC
Genevieve G Dionne
18 Mondello Square
Unit #1
Gloucester MA 01930

Call Sign: KB1OMI
Peter S Tibbetts
22 Morgan Ave
Gloucester MA 01930

Call Sign: K1WZE
Peter S Tibbetts
22 Morgan Ave
Gloucester MA 01930

Call Sign: KB1DBD
Patrick J Mclaughlin
34 Mount Vernon St
Gloucester MA
019302967

Call Sign: AB1HQ
Patrick J Mclaughlin
34 Mount Vernon St
Gloucester MA
019302967

Call Sign: N1UVF
Albert Haselgard
12 N Kilby St
Gloucester MA 01930

Call Sign: N1OPG
Jean B O Gorman
16 N Kilby St
Gloucester MA 01930

Call Sign: KD1MS
Kenneth R Pearson
34 Norman Ave
Gloucester MA 01930

Call Sign: WD9GHN
Robert C Jagel
9 Old Nugent Farm
Gloucester MA 01930

Call Sign: W4RIG
Henry N Mc Carl
28 Old Nugent Farm
Rd
Gloucester MA
019303167

Call Sign: KB1WGG
Mary Mccarl
28 Old Nugent Farm
Rd
Gloucester MA 01930

Call Sign: KB1WGH
Troy R Petrillo
73 Perkins St
Gloucester MA 01930

Call Sign: KB1WGI
Ronald E Beck
2 Pierce Ave
Gloucester MA 01930

Call Sign: KB1UFZ
Robert A Chadbourne
4 Pierce Ave
Gloucester MA 01930

Call Sign: K1LJO
Robert A Chadbourne
4 Pierce Ave
Gloucester MA 01930

Call Sign: N1MAU
Greville Balzarini
6 Pigeon Ln
Gloucester MA
019301279

Call Sign: N1VNX
Sara C Balzarini
6 Pigeon Ln
Gloucester MA 01930

Call Sign: W1IO
Pendleton Radio Assn
Of The North Shore
6 Pigeon Ln
Gloucester MA
019301279

Call Sign: AK1U
Edward G Araujo

43 Pleasant St
Gloucester MA 01930

Call Sign: N1VUU
Ann Margaret Ferrante
11 Proctor St
Gloucester MA 01930

Call Sign: WA1HRJ
David E Murphy
172 R Atlantic St
Gloucester MA 01930

Call Sign: KB1RYB
Pamela Burton
1193 R Washington St
Gloucester MA 01930

Call Sign: KB1HYP
Paul F Frontiero Jr
32 Riverview Dr
Gloucester MA 01930

Call Sign: K1MDJ
Lester F Olson Sr
7 Rockmoor Terrace
Gloucester MA 01930

Call Sign: KB1RYE
Leslie W Milne
50 Rowley Shore
Gloucester MA 01930

Call Sign: KB1WGJ
James R Capillo
5 Sayward St
Gloucester MA 01930

Call Sign: W1VCA
James R Capillo
5 Sayward St
Gloucester MA 01930

Call Sign: N3DUO
Steven J Raher
8 Stage Font Acres
Gloucester MA 01930

Call Sign: W1GLO
Cape Ann Amateur
Radio Assn
6 Stanwood St
Gloucester MA 01930

Call Sign: N1TKH
David E Mitchell
3 Stone Ct
Gloucester MA 01930

Call Sign: KB1HTT
Barbara W Black
6 Sumac Lane
Gloucester MA 01930

Call Sign: KB1HTZ
John D O'connell
6 Sumac Lane
Gloucester MA 01930

Call Sign: KB1TRD
Beverly R Johnson
50 Summer St 3
Gloucester MA 01930

Call Sign: W1ZBE
Lawrence E Sargent
Thatcher Rd
Gloucester MA 01930

Call Sign: WA1BEV
James R Cooney
51 Thurston Pt Rd
Gloucester MA 01930

Call Sign: KB1PQQ
Paul E Lawson Jr
34 Warner St Apt 1
Gloucester MA 01930

Call Sign: KB1PVN
Sandra E Downey
34 Warner St Apt 1
Gloucester MA 01930

Call Sign: KB1VST
Nathaniel H Dewolfe
289 Washington St
Gloucester MA 01930

Call Sign: N1RC
Robert M Clarke
301 Washington St
Gloucester MA 01930

Call Sign: N1JEI
Anthony A Marks
350 Washington St
Gloucester MA 01930

Call Sign: KB1SLS
Peter V Cherry
497 Washington St
Gloucester MA 01930

Call Sign: KA1TTR
Ronald T Theriault
519 Washington St
Gloucester MA 01930

Call Sign: WA1GCO
Ralph H Knight
542 Washington St
Gloucester MA 01930

Call Sign: KA1SFF
Chandler D Pearce
722 Washington St
Gloucester MA 01930

Call Sign: WB1DGM
Ross A Burton
Washington St
Gloucester MA 01930

Call Sign: KB1WBR
Anthony T Ciulla
109 Washington St Fl
2
Gloucester MA 01930

Call Sign: AB2NJ
Briggs Longbothum
1 Wesley St
Gloucester MA 01930

Call Sign: N1RYP
David J Colarusso
39 Western Ave
Gloucester MA 01930

Call Sign: N1ZSZ
Joshua P Noseworry
53 Wheeler St
Gloucester MA 01930

Call Sign: KG4TLB
Carol A Martini
Wingaersheek Rd
Gloucester MA 01930

Call Sign: KC1GE
John M Clayton

47 Winthrop Ave
Gloucester MA 01930

Call Sign: N1CBL
Christopher M Cook
20 Witham St
Gloucester MA 01930

Call Sign: W1MVM
Robert E Mc Kechnie
10 Wolf Hill Rd
Gloucester MA 01930

Call Sign: KB1FRO
Dakota B Hamill
11 Woodward Ave
Gloucester MA 01930

Call Sign: WB1GYM
Kenneth M Burdsall
46 Woodward Ave
Gloucester MA 01930

Call Sign: KA1MXK
Jayne M Wilson
12 Youngs Rd
Gloucester MA 01930

Call Sign: KF6QZQ
Daniel E Salo
18 Youngs Rd
Gloucester MA 01930

Call Sign: KA1UCE
Clarence W Wood
Gloucester MA 01930

Call Sign: KA1YMV
Ann W Banks
Gloucester MA 01930

Call Sign: N1JFW
Harry Lenchitz
Gloucester MA 01930

Call Sign: N1GPX
Terrill J Malvesti
Gloucester MA 01931

Call Sign: N1HWY
Deaken K Banks
Gloucester MA 01931

Call Sign: N1HWZ

Catherine M Banks
Gloucester MA 01931

Call Sign: N1RSP
George R Burke Jr
Gloucester MA
019311553

Call Sign: KB1NEH
James P Mondello
Gloucester MA 01930

Call Sign: W1DDX
James P Mondello
Gloucester MA 01930

Call Sign: KB1SXO
Ruth E Hodsdon
Gloucester MA
019313231

Call Sign: N1ZYH
Trevor J Bates
612 Essex Ave #10
Gloucester MA MA
019302039

Call Sign: KB1HOA
Thomas W Watson
16 Hope Dr
Gorham MA 04038

Call Sign: KB1FWL
David Lutz
Goshen MA 01032

Call Sign: N1PGA
John E Vogel
39 Barbara Jean St
Grafton MA 01519

Call Sign: KA1OCL
John S Wilson Iii
66 Brigham Hill Rd
Grafton MA 01519

Call Sign: K1OYJ
Robert M Misterka

11 Cheryl Dr
Grafton MA 01519

Call Sign: KB1LIX
Russell E Beebe
1 Coventry Rd
Grafton MA 01519

Call Sign: KB2CRY
Joseph B Maselli
16 Danielle Dr
Grafton MA 01519

Call Sign: K1URA
Robert W Froment
56 Follette St
Grafton MA 01536

Call Sign: KB1HEQ
William P Hassinger
48 George Hill Rd
Grafton MA 01519

Call Sign: KB1JSL
Michael G Perry
1 Greta Ln
Grafton MA
015191554

Call Sign: W1HNG
Roger M Corey
34 Keith Hill Rd
Grafton MA 01519

Call Sign: KB1ESX
David S Walsh
111 Keith Hill Rd
Grafton MA 01519

Call Sign: KA1FBE
Richard A Jasmin
71 Londonderry Rd
Grafton MA 01519

Call Sign: K1KAL
Jeremy F Swett
17 Meadowbrook Rd
Grafton MA 01519

Call Sign: WA1ZRC
Peter F Pombo
20 Pigeon Hill Dr
Grafton MA 01519

Call Sign: WB1DOA
Edward J Collins
25 Pleasant St
Grafton MA 01519

Call Sign: N1IFA
Stephen P Poirier
45 Potter Hill Rd
Grafton MA 01519

Call Sign: N1JXD
Diane R Poirier
45 Potter Hill Rd
Grafton MA 01519

Call Sign: N1HBW
Gary L Smith
168 Upton Rd
Grafton MA 01519

FCC Amateur Radio Licenses in Granby

Call Sign: NZ1N
Kazuo Yana
153 Amherst St
Granby MA 01033

Call Sign: KA1BS
Roy L Dupuis Jr
20 Barton St
Granby MA 01033

Call Sign: KB1GHC
Stephen M Zemanek
247 Batchelor St
Granby MA 01033

Call Sign: WA1HSK
Richard K Sturtevant
18 Cedar Drive
Granby MA 01033

Call Sign: WA2IOS
Mark D Paquette
24 Cedar Drive
Granby MA 01033

Call Sign: N1LIP
Susan E Cronin
52 Center St
Granby MA 01033

Call Sign: N1DAR

David A Johnson
52 Cold Hill
Granby MA 01033

Call Sign: N1GUI
Charles Ferguson
59 Cold Hill
Granby MA 01033

Call Sign: KB1TH
Michael S Ribeiro
25 Green Meadow Ln
Granby MA 01033

Call Sign: KB1FBG
Larry I Dansky
39 Harris St
Granby MA 01033

Call Sign: KA1BEZ
Roelof Moes
21 High St
Granby MA 01033

Call Sign: KB1WPI
James P O'connell
8 Ken Lane
Granby MA 01033

Call Sign: N1MOL
Anthony V Cerini
7 Lyman St
Granby MA 01033

Call Sign: KB1ATV
Stewart A Warren
20 Lyn Dr
Granby MA 01033

Call Sign: KA1GIP
Russell E La Morder
33 New Ludlow Rd
Granby MA 01033

Call Sign: N1CQ
William A Shaheen
49 South St
Granby MA 01033

Call Sign: N1TQT
Dwight D Witter
93 South St
Granby MA 01033

Call Sign: N1ZNT
Ann M Royal
102 South St
Granby MA
010330187

Call Sign: N1TTN
Douglas V Mac Brien
24 Truby St
Granby MA
010339539

Call Sign: KB1GJR
Jeffrey R Coopee
6 Virginia Dr
Granby MA 01033

Call Sign: NX1X
Jeffrey R Coopee
6 Virginia Dr
Granby MA
010339434

Call Sign: N1PMC
Eric J Gagne
111 West St
Granby MA 01033

Call Sign: N1MON
John W Carroll Sr
Granby MA 01033

FCC Amateur Radio Licenses in Granville

Call Sign: KB1LFA
Rushton J Brown
87 Barnard Rd
Granville MA
010349314

Call Sign: N1QOR
Jeanette F Brown
192 Barnard Rd
Granville MA 01034

Call Sign: WM1N
Robert G Brown
192 Barnard Rd
Granville MA 01034

Call Sign: KC1TP
James H Duval Sr
18 Julia La

Granville MA
010349717

Call Sign: N1PAH
Clarke C Boynton
15 Old Westfield Rd
Granville MA 01034

Call Sign: KA1WMK
Marilyn Z Tkaczuk
186 South Ln
Granville MA
010340341

Call Sign: KA1WML
Stanley J Tkaczuk
186 South Ln
Granville MA
010340341

Call Sign: KA1WMM
Adam S Tkaczuk
186 South Ln
Granville MA
010340341

Call Sign: WA1JUJ
Kevin C Stromgren
529 South Ln
Granville MA 01034

FCC Amateur Radio Licenses in Great Barrington

Call Sign: KB1VNK
Keon E Diggs
84 Alford Rd
Great Barrington MA
01230

Call Sign: N1OK
John R Brownell
11 Benton Ave
Great Barrington MA
01230

Call Sign: KB1SQF
William M Brinker
37 Blue Hill Rd
Great Barrington MA
01230

Call Sign: K1WMB

William M Brinker
37 Blue Hill Rd
Great Barrington MA
01230

Call Sign: KD2DW
Elliot B Lowell
Box 50
Great Barrington MA
01230

Call Sign: KB1VNF
Paul A Kakley
71 Castle St
Great Barrington MA
01230

Call Sign: W1TM
William T Lowe
14 Commonwealth
Ave
Great Barrington MA
01230

Call Sign: KB1INV
Jacob R Stone
1 Copper Beech Lane
Great Barrington MA
01230

Call Sign: WA1MJE
Thomas P Jaworski
101 Cottage St
Great Barrington MA
01230

Call Sign: K2BUS
Arthur H Seidman
1624 County Rd
Great Barrington MA
01230

Call Sign: KA1SKT
Janos J Keseru Jr
210 Division St
Great Barrington MA
01230

Call Sign: KB1VNE
Gary N Harrington
27 Egremont Plain Rd
Great Barrington MA
01230

Call Sign: WB1CSI
John F Whalen Jr
Egremont Rd
Great Barrington MA
01230

Call Sign: W1WQ
Robert R Parrish
Green River Hill Rd3
Great Barrington MA
01230

Call Sign: KB1GFJ
Brian S Rice
62 Grove St
Great Barrington MA
01230

Call Sign: KA1SKW
Brian E Trombley
66 Grove St
Great Barrington MA
01230

Call Sign: KB1THE
Edward G Mccormick
10 Haley Rd
Great Barrington MA
01230

Call Sign: W1EGM
Edward G Mccormick
10 Haley Rd
Great Barrington MA
01230

Call Sign: W1BJJ
Ernest Gannett
9 Laurel St
Great Barrington MA
01230

Call Sign: N1USA
Edward T Courtney
180 Main Rd
Great Barrington MA
01230

Call Sign: KB1TOB
Walter F Atwood Iii
370 Maple Ave
Great Barrington MA
01230

Call Sign: WA1II
Walter F Atwood Iii
370 Maple Ave
Great Barrington MA
01230

Call Sign: KB1FXV
Hunter J Mccormick
403 Monterey Rd
Great Barrington MA
01230

Call Sign: W6ZNL
Orville H Thornall
27 Peter Menaker Rd
Great Barrington MA
012303001

Call Sign: KA1ARU
James N Parrish
Rd 3
Great Barrington MA
01230

Call Sign: KA1QWZ
Allen E Hale
610 S Egremont Rd
Great Barrington MA
01230

Call Sign: WA1HFB
Harold C Shaw
5 Seekonk Rd
Great Barrington MA
012301562

Call Sign: KA1OA
Robert E Drennan
10 South St
Great Barrington MA
01230

Call Sign: N1FNG
Rose L Tannenbaum
10 South St
Great Barrington MA
01230

Call Sign: W1VC
Rolfe S Tessem
Great Barrington MA
01230

Call Sign: KB0RQN
Cheryl W Ring
P O Box 9
Green Harbor MA
020410009

Call Sign: N1EA
David J Ring Jr
19 Pearl St
Green Harbor MA
02041

Call Sign: WA1DRR
David J Ring
19 Pearl St
Green Harbor MA
020410199

Call Sign: WA1ZLQ
Richard E Paret Jr
79 Pownal St
Green Harbor MA
02041

Call Sign: W1NXF
Robert G Spinney
Green Harbor MA
020410277

Call Sign: WA1JID
Michael S Doolittle
Green Harbor MA
02041

Call Sign: KB1GXW
Ethan Maass
Green Harbor MA
02041

FCC Amateur Radio Licenses in Greenbush

Call Sign: K1QAV
Henry F Rogers
9 Jenkins Pl
Greenbush MA 02040

Call Sign: K1PA
Paul D Le Blanc

Greenbush MA 02040

Call Sign: WG1E
John W Wilson Sr
Greenbush MA
020400316

FCC Amateur Radio Licenses in Greenfield

Call Sign: KB1NQJ
Amber Ortiz
136 -3b Main St
Greenfield MA 01301

Call Sign: WA1TLM
Michael D Leonard
389 Adams Rd
Greenfield MA
013011361

Call Sign: W1UXI
Curtis H Dean
42 Adams Rd #58
Greenfield MA 01301

Call Sign: KB1FVV
Peter R Letson
29 Allen St
Greenfield MA
013012336

Call Sign: K1LHS
James B Waterman
602 Bernardston Rd
Greenfield MA 01302

Call Sign: W1WDU
George H Mayberry
26 Brookside Ave
Greenfield MA 01301

Call Sign: N1WQY
David B Roy
41 Burnham Rd
Greenfield MA 01301

Call Sign: KB1MBL
John M Michelson
13 Cedar St
Greenfield MA 01301

Call Sign: N1EWL

Perry E Cole Sr
170 Chapman St
Greenfield MA 01301

Call Sign: N1NGZ
Kenneth W Vight
52 Chapman St Apt
302
Greenfield MA 01301

Call Sign: N1KHK
Warren J Gould
10 Congress St Apt
303
Greenfield MA 01301

Call Sign: KB1KFR
Michael D Seredejko
569 Country Club Rd
Greenfield MA 01301

Call Sign: KB1VPN
Jacob D Emond
772 Country Club Rd
Greenfield MA 01301

Call Sign: N1IUM
Bertram M Phillips
14 Cypress St
Greenfield MA 01301

Call Sign: K8HSF
Ronald D Niswander
6 Emily Lane
Greenfield MA 01301

Call Sign: K1RWC
Richard W Briggs
390 Federal St
Greenfield MA 01301

Call Sign: KB1ARI
Jorge C Leon
46 Forest Ave
Greenfield MA 01301

Call Sign: KB1TWA
Michael J King
12 Fort Square East
Greenfield MA 01301

Call Sign: KB1BSS
Franklin County
Amateur Radio Club

18 Freeman Dr
Greenfield MA 01301

Call Sign: KB1DCG
Betty M Boutwell
18 Freeman Dr
Greenfield MA 01301

Call Sign: N1EWK
Willard R Boutwell
18 Freeman Dr
Greenfield MA 01301

Call Sign: KC4WMU
Theodore T Poppke
15 George St
Greenfield MA
013013010

Call Sign: KB1NOH
John F Berrigan
77 Hastings St
Greenfield MA 01301

Call Sign: KB1NOI
Barbara C Berrigan
77 Hastings St
Greenfield MA 01301

Call Sign: N1FOM
George D Hague
25 Haywood St
Greenfield MA 01301

Call Sign: KA1TA
Edward H Hug
80 High St
Greenfield MA 01301

Call Sign: WA2IFI
Christopher I Connolly
25 High St Apt 1
Greenfield MA 01301

Call Sign: KB1TCJ
Wendy S C Marsden
8 Highland Ave
Greenfield MA 01301

Call Sign: KA1EMR
Frank F Benedetti
28 Kenwood St
Greenfield MA 01301

Call Sign: WB1EDA
Daniel T De
Lesdernier
725 Lampblack Rd
Greenfield MA 01301

Call Sign: KA1GVO
Michael J Bassett
71 Laurel St
Greenfield MA 01301

Call Sign: KC5KKS
Kevin R Tracy
146 Laurel St
Greenfield MA 01301

Call Sign: KB1MSU
Greenfield High
School 1 Greenfield
High School Amateur
Radio Club
Lenox Ave
Greenfield MA 01301

Call Sign: KB1NQK
Milo M Thompson Jr
366 Leyden Rd
Greenfield MA 01301

Call Sign: K1PCW
Ely W Wyman
316 Log Plain Rd
Greenfield MA 01301

Call Sign: KB1SHY
Hal G Dwyer
344 Log Plain Rd
Greenfield MA 01301

Call Sign: N1VFN
Daniel P Field
252 Log Plain Rd E
Greenfield MA 01301

Call Sign: N1LYW
Scott F Conti
88 Lovers Ln
Greenfield MA 01301

Call Sign: KB1HBS
Jason M Boduch
3 Maple St
Greenfield MA 01301

Call Sign: N1NUF
Viorel Bobe
22 Maple St
Greenfield MA 01301

Call Sign: KA1AIJ
Joanne T Teague
53 Maple St
Greenfield MA 01301

Call Sign: KB1ENT
Stanley J Ambo
126 Maple St
Greenfield MA 01301

Call Sign: KB1AKU
Gary A Roy
112 Meadow Ln
Greenfield MA 01301

Call Sign: AC1L
Richard C Burnham
15 Meridian St
Greenfield MA 01301

Call Sign: N1JJJ
Brian E Tower
140 Meridian St
Greenfield MA 01301

Call Sign: KB1WTP
Julie A Page
9 Miner St
Greenfield MA 01301

Call Sign: N1MXT
Jeffrey S Norwood
124 Munson St
Greenfield MA 01301

Call Sign: AA1YY
Peter A Barnes
10 Myrtle St
Greenfield MA 01301

Call Sign: N1EKF
George Nardacci
12 North St
Greenfield MA 01301

Call Sign: KA1VLP
Thomas J Chevalier
35 Oak Hill Acres
Greenfield MA 01301

Call Sign: N1KVZ
Kathryn M Chevalier
35 Oak Hill Acres
Greenfield MA 01301

Call Sign: KB1MFL
Ben R Damery
28 Old Albany Rd
Greenfield MA 01301

Call Sign: W1CBN
Robert H Kugell
75 Overland Rd
Greenfield MA
013011139

Call Sign: KB1MFK
Kane W Kurtyka
305 Plain Rd
Greenfield MA 01301

Call Sign: N1LYV
Kenneth S Ketchum
387 Plain Rd
Greenfield MA 01301

Call Sign: KB1MFI
Luke H Ketchum
387 Plain Rd
Greenfield MA 01301

Call Sign: KB1MFJ
Eli R Ketchum
387 Plain Rd
Greenfield MA 01301

Call Sign: N1YMI
Michael A Field
58 Plantation Circle
Greenfield MA
013019736

Call Sign: KA1PPR
Jean E Corso
34 Plum Tree Ln
Greenfield MA 01301

Call Sign: KB1UQZ
Cassie L Hatch
39 Prospect St
Greenfield MA 01301

Call Sign: KB1UWA

Douglas S Downham Ii
98 Shelburne Rd
Greenfield MA 01301

Call Sign: NK1H
Ronald S Szulborski
192 Silver St
Greenfield MA 01301

Call Sign: WA1FBI
Douglas R Bassett
40 Summer St
Greenfield MA 01301

Call Sign: KB1JWZ
William H Pease Jr
5 Sunrise Ave
Greenfield MA 01301

Call Sign: KB1DCC
Janice M Peeters
5 Temple Ave
Greenfield MA 01301

Call Sign: KE1IM
Richard G Peeters
5 Temple Ave
Greenfield MA 01306

Call Sign: AA1XU
Richard G Peeters
5 Temple Ave
Greenfield MA 01301

Call Sign: AB1JY
Janice M Peeters
5 Temple Ave
Greenfield MA 01301

Call Sign: KB1NOF
David J James
96 Thayer Rd
Greenfield MA 01301

Call Sign: KB1NEJ
Andre I Melcuk
102 Thayer Rd
Greenfield MA 01301

Call Sign: N3BFV
Constantine N Aloupis
50 Union St
Greenfield MA 01301

Call Sign: N1IMU
Christopher C Slack
15 Valley View Dr
Greenfield MA 01301

Call Sign: KB1DCH
Mildred T Burnham
24 Washburn Ave
Greenfield MA
013011826

Call Sign: KB1SNA
Cathleen M Mitchell
358 Wells St
Greenfield MA 01301

Call Sign: KF4DRE
Daniel S Root
40 White Birch Ave
Greenfield MA
013019606

Call Sign: N1XZ
Thomas W Root
40 White Birch Ave
Greenfield MA 01301

Call Sign: K1QKY
Daniel S Root
40 White Birch Ave
Greenfield MA
013019606

Call Sign: N1OTS
Thomas J Foxwell
191 Wisdom Way
Greenfield MA 01301

Call Sign: KB1FBC
Ellen A Foxwell
191 Wisdom Way
Greenfield MA 01301

Call Sign: KU1N
Keith T Rowley
Greenfield MA
013021216

Call Sign: KB1JXV
David J Walker
Greenfield MA 01302

Call Sign: KB1RCG
Mark L Holland

Greenfield MA 01301

FCC Amateur Radio Licenses in Greenwood

Call Sign: W1EKT
Quannapowitt Radio
Assoc Inc
18 Crosby Rd
Greenwood MA 01880

FCC Amateur Radio Licenses in Groton

Call Sign: NO1A
Frank L Less
75 Ames Rd
Groton MA 014501963

Call Sign: KE1EC
Herman D Raymond
19 Balsam Walk
Groton MA 01450

Call Sign: WW1HR
Herman D Raymond
19 Balsam Walk
Groton MA 01450

Call Sign: N1LLG
Daniel J Daigneault
112 Birchwood Ave
Groton MA 01450

Call Sign: N1NXQ
Rayna L Daigneault
112 Birchwood Ave
Groton MA 01450

Call Sign: KB1ELE
Lee T Davy
290 Boston Rd
Groton MA 01450

Call Sign: W1MOH
Edwin A Fisher
429 Boston Rd
Groton MA 01450

Call Sign: KB1VHV
Morgan T Mcclure
446 Boston Rd
Groton MA 01450

Call Sign: KB1PZK
Steven J Roux
451 Boston Rd
Groton MA 01450

Call Sign: WA1CW
Steven J Roux
451 Boston Rd
Groton MA 01450

Call Sign: W1JZD
Charles E Ruckstuhl
496 Boston Rd
Groton MA 01450

Call Sign: KB1BVZ
Ingrid E Hersh
8 Bridge St
Groton MA 01450

Call Sign: WA1TAC
Rodney R Hersh
8 Bridge St
Groton MA 01450

Call Sign: KB1LUA
Rudolf T Hersh
8 Bridge St
Groton MA 01450

Call Sign: KB1KWP
Steven D Morlock
136 Broadmeadow Rd
Groton MA 01450

Call Sign: N1FOO
Steven D Morlock
136 Broadmeadow Rd
Groton MA 01450

Call Sign: W1ZZ
Edward H Stratton
93 Castle Dr
Groton MA 01450

Call Sign: KB1BGI
Dan R Schulman
39 Chicopee Row
Groton MA 01450

Call Sign: K1KZU
Clifford L Maxwell
439 Chicopee Row

Groton MA 014501461

Call Sign: KB1KAZ
Robert C Johnson
43 Common St
Groton MA 014501330

Call Sign: AB1CV
Robert C Johnson
43 Common St
Groton MA 014501330

Call Sign: WA1QHQ
Mark W Donaldson
20 Cypress Rd
Groton MA 01450

Call Sign: WU1F
Joel M Magid
47 Drumlin Hill Rd
Groton MA 01450

Call Sign: W1JMM
Joel M Magid
47 Drumlin Hill Rd
Groton MA 01450

Call Sign: N1JAN
Lester L Burdick Jr
518 Farmers Row
Groton MA 01450

Call Sign: KA1JVU
Karen D Reif
20 Flavell Rd
Groton MA 01450

Call Sign: N1LHE
Paul C Nuccio
82 Flavell Rd
Groton MA 014501537

Call Sign: WB1GCE
Arthur B Beal
75 Floyd Rd
Groton MA 01450

Call Sign: KA1TTZ
George M Gogas Iii
130 Gratuity Rd
Groton MA 01450

Call Sign: KA1TUA
George M Gogas Jr

130 Gratuity Rd
Groton MA 01450

Call Sign: N3UTM
Sam Mohan
151 Gratuity Rd
Groton MA 01450

Call Sign: KB1BGL
Peter A Gogas
130 Gratvity Rd
Groton MA 01450

Call Sign: KB1ESR
Lawrence W Swezey
Sr
39 Indian Hill Rd
Groton MA 01450

Call Sign: W2YLV
David K Snodgrass
414 Longley Rd
Groton MA 01450

Call Sign: N1OJP
Verell D Boaen
523 Longley Rd
Groton MA 01450

Call Sign: N1JDE
Mark T Hollinger
365 Lost Lake Dr
Groton MA 014502120

Call Sign: KB1ILQ
Michael J Heinser
924 Lowell Rd
Groton MA 01450

Call Sign: KB1AST
Bronwen M Wallens
952 Lowell Rd
Groton MA 01450

Call Sign: KB1ATG
Jeffrey A Wallens
952 Lowell Rd
Groton MA 01450

Call Sign: KB1ATH
Benjamin J H Wallens
952 Lowell Rd
Groton MA 01450

Call Sign: N1QOB
Gwenneth H Wallens
952 Lowell Rd
Groton MA 01450

Call Sign: KC2AOQ
Anne E Bohan
711 Martins Pond Dr
Groton MA 01450

Call Sign: KF2GH
James W Luening Jr
711 Martins Pond Dr
Groton MA 01450

Call Sign: N1IGN
Barry D Weeks
65 Martins Pond Rd
Groton MA 01450

Call Sign: KB1WAQ
Gregory S Cote
21 Nashua Rd
Groton MA 01450

Call Sign: N1VGQ
James P Judge
Off Prescott St
Groton MA 01450

Call Sign: WB1HMA
Mauro A Accomazzo
499 Old Dunstable Rd
Groton MA 01450

Call Sign: KA1TOR
Michele H Browne
28 Pacer Way
Groton MA 01450

Call Sign: KA1TOS
Douglas J Browne
28 Pacer Way
Groton MA 01450

Call Sign: N1FXD
Hans C Henning
68 Pleasant St
Groton MA 01450

Call Sign: N1JRJ
Clifford A Drubin
76 Pleasant St
Groton MA 01450

Call Sign: KB1BGK
Scott J Sivak
85 Raddin Rd
Groton MA 01450

Call Sign: N1SEV
Carla Langdon Sivak
85 Raddin Rd
Groton MA 01450

Call Sign: N1SEY
James M Sivak
85 Raddin Rd
Groton MA 01450

Call Sign: N1BSQ
Thomas P Baillio
147 Reedy Meadow
Rd
Groton MA 01450

Call Sign: W1PKX
Thomas P Baillio
147 Reedy Meadow
Rd
Groton MA 01450

Call Sign: N1RLM
Glen R Horton Sr
178 Reedy Meadow
Rd
Groton MA 01450

Call Sign: N1SVH
Glen R Horton Jr
178 Reedy Meadow
Rd
Groton MA 01450

Call Sign: N1TTD
Andrew J Horton
178 Reedy Meadow
Rd
Groton MA 01450

Call Sign: N1TZY
Susan I Horton
178 Reedy Meadow
Rd
Groton MA 01450

Call Sign: N1DVC
Robert J Mignard

15 Rhodenda Rd
Groton MA 01450

Call Sign: N1MNC
Robert E Mc Cauley
2 Rooks Run
Groton MA 01450

Call Sign: KB1BNW
Sarah J Moskow
Rustic Trl
Groton MA 01450

Call Sign: KG6UH
Louis N Anciaux
203 Sand Hill Rd
Groton MA 01450

Call Sign: N1QPC
David W Dearborn
172 Shelters Rd
Groton MA 01450

Call Sign: KB1BGN
David A French
13 Skyfield Dr
Groton MA 01450

Call Sign: N1UMN
Phyllis V Polhemus
36 Skyfields Dr
Groton MA 01450

Call Sign: N1UMP
Richard E Polhemus Sr
36 Skyfields Dr
Groton MA 01450

Call Sign: WR1Y
Earl D Russell Mr
98 Skyfields Dr
Groton MA 01450

Call Sign: KB1NJW
Daniel Rasmussen
21 Spaulding Ln
Groton MA 01450

Call Sign: N1KMR
Jason A Back
769 Townsend Rd
Groton MA 01450

Call Sign: KB1IDA

Steven N Bastarache
38 Valliria Dr
Groton MA 01450

Call Sign: KB1OPO
Daniel T Sullivan
167 Wharton Row
Groton MA 01450

Call Sign: KB1OJI
Stephen Faust
164 Whiley Rd
Groton MA 01450

Call Sign: KB1EKV
James V Picone
176 Whitman Rd
Groton MA 01450

Call Sign: AA1PO
James R Western
Groton MA 01450

Call Sign: KB1BGC
Philip B Pallian
Groton MA 01450

Call Sign: N1RZW
Kerry A Mc Connell
Groton MA 01450

Call Sign: W1XP
Robert H Reif
Groton MA 01450

Call Sign: KB1KEG
William J Grennell
Groton MA 01450

FCC Amateur Radio Licenses in Groveland

Call Sign: KB1OSQ
Richard N York
7 Abbott Circle
Groveland MA 01834

Call Sign: N1EMG
Richard N York
7 Abbott Circle
Groveland MA 01834

Call Sign: KB1HAZ

Michael D Dwyer
6 Alpha Rd
Groveland MA 01834

Call Sign: KB1EVA
Michael G Mcdermott
Mr
24 Balch Ave
Groveland MA 01834

Call Sign: KD1NA
David A Robertson
8 Blueberry Hill
Groveland MA 01834

Call Sign: KB1HHA
Frank E Majewski Jr
8 Cannon Hill Ext
Groveland MA 01834

Call Sign: KB1UUJ
William K Lorenz
21 Carlida Rd
Groveland MA 01834

Call Sign: K1BIQ
John D Wormald
38 Center St
Groveland MA
018341001

Call Sign: KB1PQB
Jason J Sample
40 Center St
Groveland MA 01834

Call Sign: KB1QXC
Stephen R Sample
40 Center St
Groveland MA 01834

Call Sign: KB1QKI
Christopher M Sample
40 Center St
Groveland MA 01834

Call Sign: WA1WYE
William F Kaczor
228 Center St
Groveland MA 01834

Call Sign: W1WLW
Calvin M Watson Jr
243 Center St

Groveland MA
018341712

Call Sign: NZ1S
Robert H Colburn
320 Center St
Groveland MA 01834

Call Sign: WA1HRO
Robert M Cattan
66 Centre St
Groveland MA 01834

Call Sign: K1KKM
Pentucket Radio Assc
25 Elm Park
Groveland MA 01834

Call Sign: KB1NQD
Ryan P Maloney
38 Elm Park
Groveland MA 01834

Call Sign: KC8CUK
Michael A Balistreri
7 Evergreen Lane
Groveland MA 01834

Call Sign: W1MAB
Michael A Balistreri
7 Evergreen Lane
Groveland MA 01834

Call Sign: N1AQH
Robert E Clisbee
1 Garrison St
Groveland MA 01834

Call Sign: W1TFM
Thomas F Marsters Jr
12 Groveland
Commons Way
Groveland MA 01834

Call Sign: KB1EUR
Donald R Broderick
155 King St
Groveland MA 01834

Call Sign: N1BTG
Brian C Smith
85 Main St
Groveland MA 01834

Call Sign: KB1PBK
Steven A Spaulding
257 Main St
Groveland MA 01834

Call Sign: KA1CRA
Audrey J Lawrence
383 Main St
Groveland MA 01834

Call Sign: N1YZB
Ronald A Reade
398 Main St
Groveland MA
018341112

Call Sign: KB1QBV
Stephen M Sargent
3 Marjorie St
Groveland MA 01834

Call Sign: W1EMG
Stephen M Sargent
3 Marjorie St
Groveland MA 01834

Call Sign: W1MNG
Henry H Balboni
2 Mill St Ext
Groveland MA 01834

Call Sign: KB1SRQ
Michael B Mcclelland
48 R Center
Groveland MA 01834

Call Sign: KB1SRR
Christopher M
Mcclelland
48 R Center St
Groveland MA 01834

Call Sign: N1ZQQ
James Cicatello
26 Rollins St
Groveland MA 01834

Call Sign: KB1BGW
Ernest A Gilford
22 Union St
Groveland MA 01834

Call Sign: KA2JGB
Donald J Boye Jr

21 Uptack Rd
Groveland MA 01834

Call Sign: KB1IY
Norman H Baker
163 Washington St
Groveland MA 01834

Call Sign: W1ZYX
William E Slusher
180 Washington St
Groveland MA 01834

Call Sign: N1RIQ
Henry H Balboni
12 Yale St
Groveland MA 01834

Call Sign: K9MUT
Douglas D Laustsen
Groveland MA 01834

Call Sign: W1RFW
Philip J Lawrence
Groveland MA
018340234

**FCC Amateur Radio
Licenses in Hadley**

Call Sign: KA1QDO
Paul A Corbeil
63 Aqua Vitae Rd
Hadley MA 01035

Call Sign: WB1EHS
Barbara A Murnane
54 Bay Rd
Hadley MA
010359427

Call Sign: N1RPF
Siddhartha Arora
114 Bay Rd
Hadley MA 01035

Call Sign: KA1MCW
John H Heins
26 Breckenridge Rd
Hadley MA 01035

Call Sign: W1ZI
John L Ragle
12 Cold Spring Ln

Hadley MA 01035

Call Sign: KA1SWV
Tony S Kulas
64 East St
Hadley MA 01035

Call Sign: WB3CDL
Wayne H Comstock
30 Greenleaves Rd
Hadley MA 01035

Call Sign: NR1X
Frank A Chapman
14 Highland Cir
Hadley MA
010350730

Call Sign: N1PNP
David J Michalak
93 Huntington Rd
Hadley MA 01035

Call Sign: KB1CLW
Aaron A Lastowski
41 Mountain Rd
Hadley MA 01035

Call Sign: N1GNS
Kenneth R Walsh Jr
26 N Maple St
Hadley MA 01035

Call Sign: N1GGM
Joseph T Koski
7 Roosevelt St
Hadley MA 01035

Call Sign: W1YI
Alfred T Purseglove
241 Russell St
Hadley MA
010350558

Call Sign: AI4FC
David L Whitney
167 S Maple St
Hadley MA 01035

Call Sign: KB1MYB
Philip F Cooper
47 Spruce Hill Rd
Hadley MA 01035

Call Sign: AI4XP
Christopher C Slack
8 Wampanoag Dr
Hadley MA 01035

Call Sign: N1IMU
Christopher C Slack
8 Wampanoag Drive
Hadley MA 01035

Call Sign: N1KKO
Frederick P Kucharski
Hadley MA 01035

Call Sign: W1BCQ
Frederick P Kucharski
Hadley MA
010350462

**FCC Amateur Radio
Licenses in Halifax**

Call Sign: K1HJQ
Andrew M Forsyth
129 Beechwood Rd
Halifax MA 02338

Call Sign: KB1TEG
Jeffrey A Boltz
177 Cranberry Dr
Halifax MA 02338

Call Sign: AD1R
David L Whitney
38 East St
Halifax MA 02338

Call Sign: KB1SJR
Mark V Campbell
65 Highland Circle
Halifax MA 02338

Call Sign: N1AWQ
Richard F Cubi
261 Holmes St
Halifax MA 02338

Call Sign: WB2SIQ
Gene B Lunderman
129 Hudson St
Halifax MA 02338

Call Sign: N1COP
Robert F Woodbury Jr

65 Lingan St
Halifax MA 02338

Call Sign: WA1GAN
David R Pierce
Lydon Ln
Halifax MA 02338

Call Sign: KB1NCY
Paul M Bauer
26 Marilyn Way
Halifax MA 02338

Call Sign: KB1WFN
Michael K Rogers
25 Ninth Ave
Halifax MA 02338

Call Sign: K1JRH
William F Doherty
189 Oak St
Halifax MA 02338

Call Sign: KA1RTD
Paul T Clougherty
90 Redwood Drive
Halifax MA 02338

Call Sign: N1BVV
Keith W Mc Elman
52 Ridge Rd
Halifax MA 02338

Call Sign: KB1ODL
Glyn O Staples
366 River St
Halifax MA 02338

Call Sign: KB1WFP
Derek M Bennett
66 South St
Halifax MA 02338

Call Sign: KB1WFS
Michael D Bennett
66 South St
Halifax MA 02338

Call Sign: W1GPX
William D Perkins
80 South St
Halifax MA
023380133

Call Sign: W1IBA
Ruth V Perkins
80 South St
Halifax MA
023380133

Call Sign: K1MLS
Charles N Bauer
36 Sycamore Dr
Halifax MA 02338

Call Sign: W1DWD
William J Key
58 Sycamore Dr
Halifax MA 02338

Call Sign: W1ULJ
William H Ward
63 Sycamore Dr
Halifax MA 02338

Call Sign: W1FGI
Franklin H Page
68 Sycamore Drive
Halifax MA 02338

Call Sign: N1IXW
Jean A Dickinson
373 Thompson St
Halifax MA 02338

Call Sign: WB1FMN
Donna M Nordgren
23 White Island Rd
Halifax MA 02338

Call Sign: AE1P
Robert W Govoni
Halifax MA 02338

Call Sign: KA1WHQ
Robert W Johnson
Halifax MA 02338

Call Sign: KB1VIY
Louis L Stone
Halifax MA 02338

FCC Amateur Radio
Licenses in Hamilton

Call Sign: N1YUD
Harry W Carlson
139 Asbury St

Hamilton MA
019821859

Call Sign: KA1VPD
John H Parslow
20 Baker Ave
Hamilton MA 01982

Call Sign: KA1VPE
David L Parslow
20 Baker Ave
Hamilton MA 01982

Call Sign: KA1VPG
Allen P Parslow
20 Baker Ave
Hamilton MA 01982

Call Sign: N1VTX
Nancy M Strunk
489 Bridge St
Hamilton MA 01982

Call Sign: KB1HTS
David T Marsh
5 Crescent Rd
Hamilton MA 01982

Call Sign: N1KKK
David T Marsh
5 Crescent Rd
Hamilton MA 01982

Call Sign: W7WPD
David T Marsh
5 Crescent Rd
Hamilton MA 01982

Call Sign: N1IFV
Ellen M Ames
250 Cutler Rd Box 430
Hamilton MA 01936

Call Sign: AA1GS
Jonathan R Senning
353 Essex St
Hamilton MA 01982

Call Sign: N1PGU
Karen K Senning
353 Essex St
Hamilton MA 01982

Call Sign: N1KKS

Karen K Senning
353 Essex St
Hamilton MA 01982

Call Sign: N1KYF
David T Marsh
324 Highland St
Hamilton MA 01982

Call Sign: N1GW
Richard J Conrad
52 Meyer Rd
Hamilton MA 01936

Call Sign: KD1HFD
Daniel E Parsons
22 Norman Rd
Hamilton MA 01982

Call Sign: KD1JQ
Ernst F Scherer
6 Old Cart Rd
Hamilton MA 01982

Call Sign: N1RZI
Dana M Scherer
6 Old Cart Rd
Hamilton MA 01982

Call Sign: KB1BVG
Angus D Mc Intyre
3 Patton Dr
Hamilton MA 01982

Call Sign: KB1ITC
Daniel E Parsons
Hamilton MA 01982

FCC Amateur Radio
Licenses in Hampden

Call Sign: W1GLM
Melha Radio Club
24 Allen Ct
Hampden MA
010369790

Call Sign: W1UPH
Donald S Johnson
24 Allen Ct
Hampden MA 01036

Call Sign: N1TUX
Edward W Brittain Jr

11 Allen Pl
Hampden MA 01036

Call Sign: N1LZK
Paul A Liapis
252 Allen St
Hampden MA 01036

Call Sign: N1ZLU
Timothy A Clark
398 Allen St
Hampden MA 01036

Call Sign: KB1DVX
Joseph T Mascaro
245 Bennett Rd
Hampden MA 01036

Call Sign: N1LJY
Donald R Talbot
39 Carmody Rd
Hampden MA 01036

Call Sign: W1DRT
Donald R Talbot
39 Carmody Rd
Hampden MA
010369609

Call Sign: K1RBS
George W Walsh
199 Chapin Rd
Hampden MA 01036

Call Sign: KB6FPB
Nancy J Hickman
30 Crestwood Ln
Hampden MA 01036

Call Sign: N1XOL
Kerri E De Nucci
5 Erica Cir
Hampden MA 01036

Call Sign: N1ZLT
Jeffrey M Zamorski
29 Fernwood Dr
Hampden MA 01036

Call Sign: K1YXX
Philip W Gorman Jr
14 Forest Hills Rd
Hampden MA 01036

Call Sign: KA1NTK
Michael J Cooney
231 Glendale Rd
Hampden MA 01036

Call Sign: AA1BH
Susan C Donoghue
542 Glendale Rd
Hampden MA 01036

Call Sign: W2EPE
Stan D Degen
Hampden Station
Hampden MA 01036

Call Sign: N1AZW
Le Mont E Evans
3 Hickory Ln
Hampden MA 01036

Call Sign: KB1WHB
Bruce R Foss
47 Kelly Ln
Hampden MA 01036

Call Sign: K1MAP
Mark Casey
303 Main St
Hampden MA 01036

Call Sign: W1LZA
Ellsworth M Frey
203 N Monson Rd
Hampden MA 01036

Call Sign: W1VKY
Willard J Flynn
59 North Rd
Hampden MA 01036

Call Sign: KA1UFL
Seth R Hedlund
43 Rock A Dundee Rd
Hampden MA 01036

Call Sign: K1ILZ
Lawrence F Smith
130 Scantic Rd
Hampden MA 01036

Call Sign: N1CET
Patricia G Smith
130 Scantic Rd
Hampden MA 01036

Call Sign: KA1OPN
Robert O Bluteau
33 Sessions Dr
Hampden MA 01036

Call Sign: KA1QDE
Sally J Bluteau
33 Sessions Dr
Hampden MA 01036

Call Sign: N1VMS
Erik J A Pori
132 Sessions Dr
Hampden MA 01036

Call Sign: KB1GPF
John W Plaster
181 South Monson Rd
Hampden MA 01036

Call Sign: K1VOI
John W Plaster
181 South Monson Rd
Hampden MA 01036

Call Sign: K1CPS
Christine P Sterritt
181 South Monson Rd
Hampden MA 01036

Call Sign: K1BXE
Yorke P Phillips
15 Southwood Circle
Hampden MA 01036

Call Sign: WB1FIQ
Elizabeth A Phillips
15 Southwood Circle
Hampden MA 01036

Call Sign: KA1GWQ
Richard S Nichols
7 Wilbraham Rd
Hampden MA 01036

Call Sign: KB1FLJ
Marc P Maserati
367 Wilbraham Rd
Hampden MA 01036

Call Sign: KB1PMC
Matthew T Brewer
388 Wilbraham Rd

Hampden MA 01036

Call Sign: KB1FHU
Ellsworth M Frey
Hampden MA 01036

FCC Amateur Radio
Licenses in Hancock

Call Sign: N1CD
Carlene M Drake
11 Main St
Hancock MA 01237

Call Sign: WA1RKS
Ellis C Foley Jr
11 Main St
Hancock MA 01237

Call Sign: KC2HNE
Linda C Burdick
Hancock MA 01237

Call Sign: K1LMB
Marc F Burdick
Hancock MA 01237

FCC Amateur Radio
Licenses in Hanover

Call Sign: KB1CKJ
Arnold J Stenborg
37 Broad Oak Way
Hanover MA 02339

Call Sign: W1JXZ
Arnold J Stenborg
37 Broad Oak Way
Hanover MA 02339

Call Sign: AC1N
Francis J Di Sabatino
742 Broadway
Hanover MA 02339

Call Sign: WC1ACF
Hanover Emergency
Management Agency
742 Broadway
Hanover MA 02339

Call Sign: KB1GVB
William L Morse Ii
1505 Broadway

Hanover MA 02339

Call Sign: KB1SVX
Stephen M Girardi
94 Brook Bend Rd
Hanover MA 02339

Call Sign: N1TLI
Amy A Fulton
204 Brook Cir
Hanover MA 02339

Call Sign: N1OYL
Timothy E Fulton
204 Brook Circle
Hanover MA 02339

Call Sign: K1AWB
Steven C Laroe
362 Center St
Hanover MA
023392614

Call Sign: KB1QKW
Christopher S Laroe
362 Center St
Hanover MA 02339

Call Sign: N1QPT
Raymond F Fennessey
426 Center St
Hanover MA 02339

Call Sign: K1WNJ
Sherman K Paige
846 Circuit St
Hanover MA 02339

Call Sign: N1JQR
Elwood B Turner
866 Circuit St
Hanover MA 02339

Call Sign: KB1BCL
Charles L Whelan
118 Cross St
Hanover MA 02339

Call Sign: KB1FON
Chris W Laidler
168 Dillingham Way
Hanover MA 02339

Call Sign: KB1SZY

Andrew E Nixon
41 Evergreen Lane
Hanover MA 02339

Call Sign: K1AEN
Andrew E Nixon
41 Evergreen Lane
Hanover MA 02339

Call Sign: W1GXV
Garth R Nelson
30 Fieldstone Ln
Hanover MA 02339

Call Sign: K1GRN
Garth R Nelson
30 Fieldstone Ln
Hanover MA 02339

Call Sign: N1OHM
James F Conway
65 Franks Ln Apt 407
Hanover MA 02339

Call Sign: KB1CQK
David A Jones
68 Gail Rd
Hanover MA
023392519

Call Sign: KB1EGU
James A Jones
68 Gail Rd
Hanover MA
023392519

Call Sign: N1YRN
Raymond W Limbert
103 Grove St
Hanover MA
023392126

Call Sign: N1QXY
SHERYL A Foster
129 Grove St
Hanover MA 02339

Call Sign: KA1HWB
Mildred A Fraser
107 Hacketts Pond Dr
Hanover MA 02339

Call Sign: KB1FKX
Susan O Remick

515 Hanover St
Hanover MA 02339

Call Sign: KB1FKY
Jason D Remick
515 Hanover St
Hanover MA 02339

Call Sign: KB1FKZ
Donald H Remick
515 Hanover St
Hanover MA 02339

Call Sign: W1EQU
Arthur W Murray
99 Heritage Way
Hanover MA 02339

Call Sign: N1IAQ
John N Fogg Jr
269 King St
Hanover MA 02339

Call Sign: KF1M
Dennis M Sproul
1136 Main St
Hanover MA 02339

Call Sign: KB1GEY
Bonnie L Dehner
170 Maplewood Drive
Hanover MA 02339

Call Sign: W1KXY
David M Walsh
116 Meadowbrook Rd
Hanover MA 02339

Call Sign: KA1FL
John F Keane
361 Myrtle St
Hanover MA 02339

Call Sign: NU1V
Eric E Hahn
515 Old Town Way
Hanover MA 02339

Call Sign: WA1YDG
Leroy M Bertolo
119 Plain St
Hanover MA
023392169

Call Sign: N1QML
Matthew A Eppich
290 Plain St
Hanover MA 02339

Call Sign: KC1II
Donald Cirasuolo
115 Richard Dr
Hanover MA 02339

Call Sign: KA1GTS
Stephen F O Brien
33 Roberts Rd
Hanover MA
023391124

Call Sign: KB1SGF
Jonathan S Demeo
60 Rosaria Ln
Hanover MA 02339

Call Sign: KB1KVH
Edward G Salvas
18 Rose Hill Rd
Hanover MA 02339

Call Sign: W1RRR
Charles F Dare Sr
24 Shingle Mill Ln
Hanover MA 02339

Call Sign: K6RAL
Thomas S Burr
157 Spring Meadow
Lane
Hanover MA 02339

Call Sign: KB1SGE
Matthew B Dunn
96 Wahington St
Hanover MA 02339

Call Sign: KA2SCA
Koney W Carlsen
142 Walnut St
Hanover MA 02339

Call Sign: KB1GYF
Phillip A Doucette
263 Webster St
Hanover MA 02339

Call Sign: WA1ENO
Anthony G Manna

614 Webster St
Hanover MA 02339

Call Sign: WB1ARU
Anne E Manna
614 Webster St
Hanover MA
023391180

Call Sign: W1HRL
Russell H Vargus
875 Webster St
Hanover MA 02339

Call Sign: N1ZMD
Leonard L Trainer Jr
203 Woodland Dr
Hanover MA 02339

FCC Amateur Radio Licenses in Hanscom AFB

Call Sign: N1XAQ
Larry L Alexander
75 Grenier St 348
Hanscom Afb MA
01731

Call Sign: NL7OT
Jackson R Dobbins
122 Offutt Rd
Hanscom Afb MA
01731

FCC Amateur Radio Licenses in Hanson

Call Sign: KA1RJX
Francis J Crowley
261 Adams Cir
Hanson MA 02341

Call Sign: N1PZA
Ralph J Collins
2 Baker Sr
Hanson MA 02341

Call Sign: N1WAI
Edwin H Mc Caw
267 Brook St
Hanson MA 02341

Call Sign: KB1QPR

Kenneth E Duty
257 County Rd
Hanson MA 02341

Call Sign: N1UJP
Donald E Cahill
381 County Rd
Hanson MA 02341

Call Sign: N2DEC
Donald E Cahill
381 County Rd
Hanson MA 02341

Call Sign: K1ZKX
Kenneth P Wassmouth
123 Crescent Pl
Hanson MA 02341

Call Sign: N1CWW
Madeleine I Russell
32 Donna Drive
Hanson MA 02341

Call Sign: WB1CNM
James A Russell
32 Donna Drive
Hanson MA 02341

Call Sign: KB1GHA
Gilbert W Grabowski
248 E Washington St
Hanson MA 02341

Call Sign: N1ZZN
Jeffrey J Lehmann
52 Forest Trail
Hanson MA 02341

Call Sign: N1ZZM
Thomas J Lehmann
52 Forest Trl
Hanson MA 02341

Call Sign: KB1PHN
John J Murphy Jr
363 Gorwin Dr
Hanson MA 02341

Call Sign: K1GVM
Glenn D Howard
314 High St
Hanson MA 02341

Call Sign: KB1QMX
David C Beauvais Sr
149 Holmes St
Hanson MA 02341

Call Sign: KB1OEM
Brian Mc Keen
104 Independence Ave
Hanson MA 02341

Call Sign: KB1OEN
Deborah Frye Mckeen
104 Independence Ave
Hanson MA 02341

Call Sign: KB1SGB
Joshua T Stenstrom
761 Main St
Hanson MA 02341

Call Sign: KB1OOG
Mark W Bemis
335 Maquan St
Hanson MA 02341

Call Sign: KB1SGH
Michael S Arlin
443 Maquan St
Hanson MA 02341

Call Sign: N1OIU
James C Wolf
113 Pleasant St
Hanson MA 02341

Call Sign: N1JCW
James C Wolf
113 Pleasant St
Hanson MA 02341

Call Sign: KB1JOR
Michael J Wolf
294 Pleasant St
Hanson MA 02341

Call Sign: KB1WFQ
Michelle M Derochers
385 Pleasant St
Hanson MA 02341

Call Sign: W1XD
Louis G Marcarelli
31 Stonebridge Drive
Hanson MA 02341

Call Sign: WA1DUZ
Kenneth E Garren Jr
182 W Washington St
Hanson MA 02341

Call Sign: KB1CVN
John G Seamans
41 Winter Terr
Hanson MA
023411222

Call Sign: N1MJI
Michael L Gilligan
Hanson MA 02341

Call Sign: N1LKE
Mark C
Wojciechowski
Hanson MA 02341

Call Sign: W1ZHX
Richard J Smith
Hanson MA 02341

Call Sign: NN1MF
Marshfield Fair Radio
Club
Hanson MA 02341

**FCC Amateur Radio
Licenses in Hardwick**

Call Sign: KA1QDR
George A Anderson Iii
Hardwick MA 01037

Call Sign: N1IIW
Robert M Wood
Hardwick MA 01037

Call Sign: KA1PYD
Julia Mankowsky
Barre Rd Box 222
Hardwick MA 01037

Call Sign: N1NRX
Zachary L Brown
Charity Hill Rd
Hardwick MA 01037

Call Sign: N1NRY
Newell Pledger Shinn
Fleming Rd

Hardwick MA 01037

Call Sign: KA1QDQ
Gail Anderson
Hardwick MA 01037

Call Sign: NC1Z
George A Anderson Jr
Hardwick MA 01037

**FCC Amateur Radio
Licenses in Harvard**

Call Sign: N1NOV
Melinda A Kuong
10 Abbot Lane
Harvard MA 01451

Call Sign: WA1SCS
Allan P Kuong
10 Abbot Lane
Harvard MA 01451

Call Sign: WB1EEB
Earl E Emerick
88 Ann Lee Rd
Harvard MA 01451

Call Sign: AB1FI
Earl E Emerick
88 Ann Lee Rd
Harvard MA 01451

Call Sign: N1FXK
Warren R Keene
132 Ayer Rd
Harvard MA
014510373

Call Sign: N1XGM
Robert E Daniels
133 Ayer Rd
Harvard MA 01451

Call Sign: N1GNB
Richard B Watson Jr
310 Ayer Rd
Harvard MA 01451

Call Sign: WA1SLX
Stephen R Klein
17 Blanchard Rd
Harvard MA 01451

Call Sign: K1BG
Bruce D Blain
40 Blanchard Rd
Harvard MA 01451

Call Sign: WA2TBA
Gary J Helmstetter
48 Blanchard Rd
Harvard MA 01451

Call Sign: WA1ZJG
Robert M Barrett
146 Bolton Rd
Harvard MA 01451

Call Sign: W1JHR
George H Vaccaro
68 Brown Rd
Harvard MA 01451

Call Sign: KA1UEA
Malcolm M Allison
24 Deerfoot Trail
Harvard MA 01451

Call Sign: KA1UEN
Thomas W Cotton
186 E Bare Hill Rd
Harvard MA 01451

Call Sign: KB1BDO
Michael E Judy
194 E Bare Hill Rd
Harvard MA 01451

Call Sign: KB1SCE
Christopher Dahlstrom
113 East Bare Hill Rd
Harvard MA 01451

Call Sign: AA1SD
John M Dumser Jr
19 Eldridge Rd
Harvard MA
014510375

Call Sign: KB1NNW
John B Ayer
8 Finn Rd
Harvard MA 01451

Call Sign: KB1CAY
Stephen J Keville
38 Finn Rd

Harvard MA 01451

Call Sign: N1BRC
Paul M Kuell
40 Finn Rd
Harvard MA 01451

Call Sign: N1UPZ
Alfred R Towle
225 Littleton County
Rd
Harvard MA 01451

Call Sign: N1PVR
Theodore J Stefanik
283 Littleton County
Rd
Harvard MA 01451

Call Sign: KA1CCC
Dorothy L Herbert
295 Littleton Rd
Harvard MA 01451

Call Sign: WA1IDT
David E Herbert
295 Littleton Rd
Harvard MA 01451

Call Sign: KB3GXY
Susan Morris
14 Lovers Lane
Harvard MA 01451

Call Sign: AA3SD
Paul J Morris
14 Lover's Lane
Harvard MA 01451

Call Sign: N1LBO
John W Truett
31 Lovers Ln
Harvard MA 01451

Call Sign: W9RUW
Karl R Kreeb
72 Massachusetts Ave
Harvard MA 01451

Call Sign: N9RE
John H Oglesby
91 Old Littleton Rd
Harvard MA
014511420

Call Sign: K1EA
Kenneth T Wolff
221 Old Littleton Rd
Harvard MA 01451

Call Sign: W1AKD
John M Johnson
38 Peninsula Rd Box
484
Harvard MA 01451

Call Sign: N1PQ
Peter C Quinn Jr
16 Poor Farm Rd
Harvard MA
014511450

Call Sign: KA1FXM
Mark H Etzel
9 Quarry Ln
Harvard MA
014511210

Call Sign: W1HVV
James R Hannigan
Shaker Glen Farm
Ayer Rd
Harvard MA 01451

Call Sign: KB1HFO
Andrew T Hebb
17 Sherry Rd
Harvard MA 01451

Call Sign: K1DKR
Martin W Schramm Jr
45 Sherry Rd
Harvard MA
014510353

Call Sign: KE1CQ
John R Roe
29 Simon Atherton
Harvard MA 01451

Call Sign: K1JIX
Janet M Zimmer
57 Slough Rd
Harvard MA 01451

Call Sign: W2BVU
John T Zimmer
57 Slough Rd

Harvard MA 01451

Call Sign: K1OLM
Joyce I Garrick
73 Slough Rd
Harvard MA 01451

Call Sign: K1OLN
Wilmer S Garrick
73 Slough Rd
Harvard MA 01451

Call Sign: KA1VGO
Mark S Dewandel
3 Stonecutters Path
Harvard MA 01451

Call Sign: WB9JBM
Gerald R Benitz
314 Stow Rd
Harvard MA 01451

Call Sign: W1NQ
Gerald R Benitz
314 Stow Rd
Harvard MA 01451

Call Sign: K4LSX
John E Owings
82 Tahanto Trl
Harvard MA 01451

Call Sign: KA1KIY
Gail S Owings
82 Tahanto Trl
Harvard MA 01451

Call Sign: WB2RCN
Michael E Lipman
129 W Bare Hill Rd
Harvard MA
014511626

Call Sign: N1PPS
Donald B Strang
25 Warren Ave
Harvard MA 01451

Call Sign: N1OMR
J Brinton Ferguson
11 Willow Rd
Harvard MA 01451

Call Sign: W1DVC

Harvard Repeater Club
16 Withington Lane
Harvard MA 01451

Call Sign: N1TMD
Susan A Tokay
16 Withington Ln
Harvard MA 01451

Call Sign: WA9WTK
Gordon J Weast
16 Withington Ln
Harvard MA 01451

Call Sign: K1YOW
Joseph A Dzekevich Jr
17 Withington Ln
Harvard MA
014511921

Call Sign: AJ1S
Milo P Hnilicka
Harvard MA 01451

Call Sign: K1VF
Vincent Fedele
Harvard MA
014510061

Call Sign: KA1CDP
Lili P Hnilicka
Harvard MA 01451

Call Sign: N1GNW
Lawrence E
Christensen
Harvard MA 01451

Call Sign: W4LVG
John C Clemmer
Harvard MA 01451

Call Sign: K1HMN
Robert R Mc Nerney
Sr
Harvard MA 01451

Call Sign: N1PIF
Joan A Watson
Harvard MA 01451

Call Sign: NO1D
Douglas H Theriault
Harvard MA 01451

Call Sign: W1RPM
Edward F Dillard
Harvard MA
014510112

Call Sign: KB1OZX
James B Riley
Harvard MA 01451

**FCC Amateur Radio
Licenses in Harwich**

Call Sign: WA1GZK
Robert J Dowling
15 Alder Ln
Harwich MA 02645

Call Sign: W1DGB
Leon H Baumlin
129 Azalea Dr
Harwich MA 02645

Call Sign: K4WDH
Warren D Hayes Jr
14 Cannon Hill Drive
Harwich MA 02645

Call Sign: N2KNL
William A Kretschmer
6 Captains Lane
Harwich MA 02645

Call Sign: KB1VAJ
Elaine Mason
6 Captains Ln
Harwich MA 02645

Call Sign: KC1OQ
Francis J Bigda
16 Courtney Rd
Harwich MA
026451835

Call Sign: KB1ROF
Peter L Benson
35 Derby Lane
Harwich MA 02645

Call Sign: N1KJD
Christopher R Pistel
43 Driftwood Ln
Harwich MA 02645

Call Sign: W1HVM
Russell I Carter
28 Fairways Drive
Harwich MA 02645

Call Sign: N1OON
Paul F Kelly
20 Fern Wood Cir
Harwich MA
026456644

Call Sign: W1VPB
A Charles Puzo
18 Forsythia Dr
Harwich MA 02645

Call Sign: KA1TPG
David R Fee
56 Glenwood Dr
Harwich MA 02645

Call Sign: KB1UZX
Donald J Gutt
19 Hillcrest Dr
Harwich MA 02645

Call Sign: KA1RWW
Andrew J Usowski
25 Indigo Ln
Harwich MA 02645

Call Sign: KA1UHF
George E Mannix
26 John Joseph Rd
Harwich MA 02645

Call Sign: W1NP
Paul M Laconto
7 Katies Pond Lane
Harwich MA 02645

Call Sign: WA1AC
Alan M Curran
9 Lakeview Dr
Harwich MA 02645

Call Sign: W1IKU
William H Fishback
6 Locust Grove Rd Rfd
1
Harwich MA 02645

Call Sign: N1ENR
Dudley F Blanchard

228 Long Pond Dr
Harwich MA 02645

Call Sign: WB4FVK
Julius F Nugent Iii
34 Lynch Lane
Harwich MA 02645

Call Sign: KI4WLB
Paul M Kozar
12 Maple Lane
Harwich MA 02645

Call Sign: W1RD
William A Martin
13 Mary Willet Ct
Harwich MA 02645

Call Sign: K1YZY
Richard C Johnson
1073 Oak St
Harwich MA 02645

Call Sign: N1CVR
Joseph Ross
1685 Orleans Rd
Harwich MA 02645

Call Sign: WB2SOU
Richard A Flink
3 Oyster Pond Rd
Harwich MA 02645

Call Sign: KB1VAC
Thomas E Leach
224 Pleasant Bay Rd
Harwich MA 02645

Call Sign: KB1UME
Sarah H Byron
457 Pleasant Lake Ave
Harwich MA 02645

Call Sign: KB1RQT
Patrick Donnelly
22 Randolph Lane
Harwich MA 02645

Call Sign: WA1ITY
Robert S Ford Sr
17 Robert Rd
Harwich MA 02645

Call Sign: W1HXI

Harold A Kotzum
15 Samoset Rd
Harwich MA 02645

Call Sign: K1GGI
Edwin C Moxon
67 Seymour Rd
Harwich MA 02645

Call Sign: WA1WCC
Wcc Amateur Radio
Association
67 Seymour Rd
Harwich MA 02645

Call Sign: KB1TPU
Wcc Amateur Radio
Association
67 Seymour Rd
Harwich MA 02645

Call Sign: W1WIM
Wcc Amateur Radio
Association
67 Seymour Rd
Harwich MA 02645

Call Sign: KB1QOF
Brian Z Zayatz
53 Sherwood Rd
Harwich MA 02645

Call Sign: KB1UJM
John J Zayatz
53 Sherwood Rd
Harwich MA 02645

Call Sign: N1JUJ
Wicke Walsh
Sidney Rd
Harwich MA 02645

Call Sign: WC1AAZ
183 Harwich
Emergency Radio Club
Sisson Rd
Harwich MA 02645

Call Sign: N1KEL
Frank O Nicolay
6 Tonis Way
Harwich MA 02645

Call Sign: K1BGY

Gordon D Benoit
Harwich MA 02645

Call Sign: KA1SCF
Joan G Hensler
Harwich MA 02645

Call Sign: WW1RF
Richard A Formato
Harwich MA 02645

Call Sign: KA1ZNJ
H Christian Witte Iv
Harwich MA 02645

Call Sign: KK1Q
Phillip E Davison
Harwich MA 02645

Call Sign: W1HZV
Eugene E Hawkins
Harwich MA 02645

Call Sign: KB1SFE
Melissa A Clayton
Harwich MA 02645

FCC Amateur Radio Licenses in Harwich Port

Call Sign: W2JJM
James Q Montress
6 Doane Way
Harwich Port MA
026461611

Call Sign: KA1IKX
Lester F Childs Iii
23 Hoyt Rd
Harwich Port MA
02646

Call Sign: KB1JYC
Pieter A Stienstra
371 Rt 28 Apt 10
Harwich Port MA
02646

Call Sign: KA1UHD
Arthur P Doane Jr
Harwich Port MA
026460423

Call Sign: N1JFE
Gregor M Weremey
13 Kildee Rd
Harwichport MA
026461612

Call Sign: KC1KM
James A Leavitt
19 Meadowbrook Ln
Harwichport MA
02646

Call Sign: KA1NSV
Richard L Eressy
124 Miles St
Harwichport MA
02646

FCC Amateur Radio Licenses in Hatchville

Call Sign: N1JCU
Robert L Elder
34 Deep Pond Dr
Hatchville MA 02536

FCC Amateur Radio Licenses in Hatfield

Call Sign: N1ROV
Charles W Lundberg
Abbott Pleasant Dr
Hatfield MA 01038

Call Sign: N1TDX
David W Biddle
96 Bridge St
Hatfield MA 01038

Call Sign: N1HVN
Francis J Purcell
76 Bridge St Box 145
Hatfield MA 01038

Call Sign: N1YVS
Donald L Brooks
11 Circle Dr
Hatfield MA 01038

Call Sign: KD1LN
Jason P O Brien
151 West St Apt F
Hatfield MA 01088

FCC Amateur Radio Licenses in Hathorn

Call Sign: K1KIN
Alfred V Carbone
Hathorn MA 01937

FCC Amateur Radio Licenses in Harverhill

Call Sign: KB1VZC
John A D'aoust
57 16th Ave
Haverhill MA 01830

Call Sign: W1JAD
John A D'aoust
57 16th Ave
Haverhill MA 01830

Call Sign: KA1CRT
Gerald F Ritchie
94 8th Ave
Haverhill MA 01830

Call Sign: W1VI
Michael J Wheeler
29 Alice St
Haverhill MA 01830

Call Sign: KE4PGY
Ria F Van Der Auwera
29 Alice St
Haverhill MA 01830

Call Sign: KE4QNA
Carl S De Ryck
29 Alice St
Haverhill MA 01830

Call Sign: KA1TDJ
Christopher R Marston
2 Alpine Dr
Haverhill MA 01830

Call Sign: N1OUH
Joseph J Bagshaw Jr
189 Amesbury Rd
Haverhill MA 01830

Call Sign: KA1CHL
George A Patnaude
818 Amesbury Rd
Haverhill MA 01830

Call Sign: WA2YHR
Allan M Wilson
865 Amesbury Rd
Haverhill MA 01830

Call Sign: N1MYY
Andrew J Denoncour
989 Amesbury Rd
Haverhill MA 01830

Call Sign: N1GXA
Wayne R Lescarbeau
69 Ashworth Ter
Haverhill MA 01832

Call Sign: KA1RCB
Wayne D Rodger
15 Auburn St
Haverhill MA 01830

Call Sign: KB1FWD
John S Cardran
75 Bateman St
Haverhill MA
018322551

Call Sign: KA1RKY
Linda A Pride
86 Bateman St
Haverhill MA 01830

Call Sign: KB1ATW
Jesus Nieves
51 Bellevue Ave
Haverhill MA 01830

Call Sign: KA1VIZ
Michael W Malvers
14 Bennington St
Haverhill MA 01830

Call Sign: WA1JF
Joseph E Ferrero
40 Brandon Rd
Haverhill MA
018323000

Call Sign: KB1BCE
Garry C Psaros
180 Brickett Hill
Haverhill MA 01830

Call Sign: N1CFR

Charles E Eastman
1393 Broadway
Haverhill MA
018321051

Call Sign: N1NLO
James A Slauter
1448 Broadway
Haverhill MA 01832

Call Sign: KB1IAH
Mark A Burgess
75 Brockton Ave
Haverhill MA 01830

Call Sign: KO1U
Mark A Burgess
75 Brockton Ave
Haverhill MA 01830

Call Sign: WA1SLC
Clifton W Houston
40 Buttonwoods Ave
Apt 215
Haverhill MA 01830

Call Sign: N1TYL
Bryon S Uloth
43 Cedar St
Haverhill MA 01831

Call Sign: K1KGW
Donald E Boucher
212 Cedar St
Haverhill MA 01830

Call Sign: KB1CYQ
Lawrence A Dysart Iii
5 Cornell Rd
Haverhill MA
018323762

Call Sign: K1DNY
John J Walsh
6 Cottage St
Haverhill MA 01830

Call Sign: KB1FNH
Glenn P Keenan
19 Country Hill Lane
Haverhill MA 01832

Call Sign: W1GPK
Glenn P Keenan

19 Country Hill Lane
Haverhill MA 01832

Call Sign: N1CXS
Steven M Lambrou
127 Crosby St Ext
Haverhill MA 01830

Call Sign: WA1UTP
Jean J Comeau
Crystal Lake Rd
Haverhill MA 01832

Call Sign: W1IQI
George E Adams
21 Crystal St
Haverhill MA 01832

Call Sign: N1WPN
Wayne P Nakata
5 Dawn Cir
Haverhill MA 01832

Call Sign: KB1PTY
Thomas J Hashem
13 Dawn Circle
Haverhill MA 01832

Call Sign: KB1PTZ
James D Hashem
13 Dawn Circle
Haverhill MA 01832

Call Sign: K1PFS
Raymond D Smith
5 Dustin St
Haverhill MA 01830

Call Sign: KB1RIQ
BRIAN P Mccabe
46 Dwight St
Haverhill MA 01830

Call Sign: W1BMC
BRIAN P Mccabe
46 Dwight St
Haverhill MA 01830

Call Sign: KB1QZ
Brian R Wells
721 E Braodway
Haverhill MA
018301811

Call Sign: N1SJM
Richard R Plourde
38 E Broadway
Haverhill MA
018306508

Call Sign: KA1YTU
Paul E Boucher
62 E Broadway
Haverhill MA 01830

Call Sign: N1GEI
Lori J Bisenti
172 E Broadway
Haverhill MA 01830

Call Sign: N1HSX
Lynn A Vaine
170 East Broadway
Haverhill MA 01830

Call Sign: N1GEJ
Arthur C Bisenti Jr
172 East Broadway
Haverhill MA 01830

Call Sign: N1DTN
David P Naylor Sr
11 Edgewood Ave
Haverhill MA 01832

Call Sign: KB1KHV
Daniel W O Brien
69 Edgewood Ave
Haverhill MA 01832

Call Sign: W1MAR
Mark A Roope
15 Fox Run Dr
Haverhill MA
018321054

Call Sign: N1HDG
Anthony J Zukas
33 Garrison Ave
Haverhill MA 01830

Call Sign: W1STA
Gordon B Moran
25 Germain Ave
Haverhill MA
018357123

Call Sign: KB1NSE

Sharon A Stevens
15 Greenhill Farm Rd
Haverhill MA 01832

Call Sign: K1MVJ
Raymond L Marino
212 Groveland St
Haverhill MA 01830

Call Sign: N1UZQ
Paul A Marino
212 Groveland St
Haverhill MA 01830

Call Sign: W1HAV
Raymond L Marino
212 Groveland St
Haverhill MA 01830

Call Sign: K1HAV
Paul A Marino
212 Groveland St
Haverhill MA 01830

Call Sign: KB1PVJ
Douglas P White
72 Hamilton Ave
Haverhill MA 01830

Call Sign: AB1IQ
Douglas P White
72 Hamilton Ave
Haverhill MA 01830

Call Sign: AB1MF
Douglas P White
72 Hamilton Ave
Haverhill MA 01830

Call Sign: AB1MG
Douglas P White
72 Hamilton Ave
Haverhill MA 01830

Call Sign: KB1PNX
Lee A Morgan
12 Hancock St
Haverhill MA 01832

Call Sign: KC2BPA
Robert T Klenk
44 Hanscom Ave
Haverhill MA 01839

Call Sign: N1QWB
Thomas F Marinis Jr
45 Hermon Ave
Haverhill MA 01832

Call Sign: N1SNJ
Christopher T Marinis
45 Hermon Ave
Haverhill MA 01832

Call Sign: KA1WJY
George H Kutromanos
106 High St
Haverhill MA 01830

Call Sign: KB1BKV
Luis Cerezo
83 High St Apt 3
Haverhill MA 01831

Call Sign: WA1MKK
Paul D Comeau
207 Hilldale Ave
Haverhill MA 01830

Call Sign: KB9VDF
Todd A Mccoy
398 Hilldale Ave
Haverhill MA 01832

Call Sign: N1KMC
Emil G K Geithner
68 I St
Haverhill MA 01835

Call Sign: WA1GEI
Malcolm G Johnston
16 Iris Way
Haverhill MA
018308700

Call Sign: N1FKE
James F Dupre
33 Isabel St
Haverhill MA 01830

Call Sign: AA1NO
Charles M Magras
19 Janet Rd
Haverhill MA 01832

Call Sign: KC1QA
Frank Arcidiacono
20 Janet Rd

Haverhill MA 01832

Call Sign: KB1WEY
William D Brennan
37 Jordan St
Haverhill MA 01830

Call Sign: KA1QKW
Jeanne M Lundell
266 Lake St
Haverhill MA 01830

Call Sign: KB1MKB
Paul C Macmullin
53 Lakeview Ave
Haverhill MA 01830

Call Sign: KA1RCT
William F Mooney
23 Lamoille Ave
Haverhill MA 01835

Call Sign: K1WIP
Frank W Marshall
45 Lansing Ave
Haverhill MA
018323721

Call Sign: KB1MVD
John L Schulman
33 Leroy Ave
Haverhill MA 01835

Call Sign: KA1VYY
William A Gould
22 Littlefield Ct
Haverhill MA 01832

Call Sign: WA1NTH
Robert T David
730 Main St
Haverhill MA 01830

Call Sign: KA1QFX
Stevan A Shapiro
16 Margerie St
Haverhill MA
018301626

Call Sign: KA1UAB
William A Vlahos
58 Marshland St
Haverhill MA 01830

Call Sign: KA1AUN
Diane Y Forte
3 Mary St
Haverhill MA 01830

Call Sign: KI1K
John J Forte
3 Mary St
Haverhill MA 01830

Call Sign: KA1YFT
James Antonopoulos
24 Mt Dustin Ave
Haverhill MA 01832

Call Sign: KA1EZ
Walter W Wilson Jr
103 Murie Ter
Haverhill MA 01835

Call Sign: KE2MQ
Henry J Muller
31 N Broadway
Haverhill MA 01832

Call Sign: WA1EBJ
Richard L Davis
40 N Broadway
Haverhill MA
018322956

Call Sign: N1YLJ
Emanuel Tickelis
314 North Ave
Haverhill MA 01830

Call Sign: KA1WP
Richard T Dunn
440 North Ave 34
Haverhill MA 01830

Call Sign: KA1WRN
Jeannette B Frechette
11 North St
Haverhill MA 01830

Call Sign: KA1WRO
Roland E Frechette
11 North St
Haverhill MA 01830

Call Sign: KB1WAZ
Michael J Zylinski
5 Oak Hill Rd

Haverhill MA 01830

Call Sign: AB1PX
John L Jorgensen
81 Old Ferry Rd
Haverhill MA 01830

Call Sign: KA1YGE
Michael S Kostojohn
50 Park St
Haverhill MA 01830

Call Sign: KD1XY
Daniel J Morelle
21 Parsonage Hill Rd
Haverhill MA 01832

Call Sign: KA1NOC
Charles Patras
34 Parsonage Hill Rd
Haverhill MA
018321237

Call Sign: KC4AWP
Danny L Becker
10 Pear Tree Rd
Haverhill MA 01830

Call Sign: KT1S
Michael S Lambrou
6 Philip St
Haverhill MA 01830

Call Sign: N1CXQ
Cathy Lambrou
6 Philip St
Haverhill MA 01830

Call Sign: W1JSP
James S Plummer
20 Pleasant View Ave
Haverhill MA 01832

Call Sign: W1GSP
Gabriella Plummer
20 Pleasant View Ave
Haverhill MA 01832

Call Sign: KA1CQY
Patricia J Dewhirst
73 Powderhouse Ave
Haverhill MA 01830

Call Sign: WP3NN

Malquiel Linares-Soto
649 Primrose St
Haverhill MA 01830

Call Sign: KB1IRY
Sylvia D Leonard
10 Primrose Way
#8303
Haverhill MA 01830

Call Sign: N1RTB
Albert E Fischer
10 Primrose Way Apt
6102
Haverhill MA 01830

Call Sign: KB1DZZ
David A Crockford
52 Rockland St
Haverhill MA 01832

Call Sign: W1OLN
Henry P Weber
36 S Central St
Bradford
Haverhill MA
018357548

Call Sign: KT1B
James S Currier
77 S Riverview St
Haverhill MA 01835

Call Sign: N1SNB
Jeff B Demers
187 Salem St
Haverhill MA 01835

Call Sign: N1REQ
Thomas E Tracy
7 Shapleigh Ave
Haverhill MA 01830

Call Sign: N1LTZ
Robert F Piepiora Ii
65 Shattuck St
Haverhill MA 01830

Call Sign: KA1RSW
Marcelle Greenbaum
5 Sheridan St
Haverhill MA
018303318

Call Sign: W1RQ
Bradley M Roope
11 Singingwood Dr
Haverhill MA 01830

Call Sign: KB1AJO
John Kakavitsas
32 Standish Rd
Haverhill MA 01832

Call Sign: N1GQW
Carol T Paraskos
30 Sterling Ln
Haverhill MA
018358403

Call Sign: KA1BSH
James W Thomson
75 Talmouth Ave
Haverhill MA 01830

Call Sign: KV1H
Charles T Sapienza
76 Talmuth Ave
Haverhill MA 01830

Call Sign: N1VDX
Steven H Woodward
32 Taylor St
Haverhill MA
018322531

Call Sign: K1OSG
Donald A Sicard
6 Tyler Pk
Haverhill MA 01830

Call Sign: K1QMW
Martin I Kriegsman
25 Victory Ave
Haverhill MA
018302836

Call Sign: KA1CNU
Ernest W Arnold Jr
6 Village Ln
Haverhill MA 01832

Call Sign: KB1SFG
Aldrin J Dinero
30 W Parish Ct 31-D
Haverhill MA 01832

Call Sign: W1SIX

Ernest R Senter Jr
Ward Hill
Haverhill MA 01835

Call Sign: KD1DN
Joseph L Melanson
721 Washington St
Haverhill MA 01832

Call Sign: N1NUL
Allen R Norris
100 Water St
Haverhill MA 01830

Call Sign: N8SBU
James M Daly
645 West Lowell Ave
#1
Haverhill MA 01832

Call Sign: WB1CLP
Jonathan C Goldfield
2 West Meadow Rd
Haverhill MA
018321180

Call Sign: N1TKO
Gerald D Colton
120 West Rochambault
St
Haverhill MA 01832

Call Sign: KB1PWY
Matthew L Daniels
21 Westford St
Haverhill MA 01832

Call Sign: K1MDF
Matthew L Daniels
21 Westford St
Haverhill MA 01832

Call Sign: KB1JPD
Lawrence G Caruso
77 Whittier Rd
Haverhill MA 01830

Call Sign: K1LGC
Lawrence G Caruso
77 Whittier Rd
Haverhill MA 01830

Call Sign: KB1MKA
Drew P Caruso

77 Whittier Rd
Haverhill MA 01830

Call Sign: KA1VFO
Ioannis E Souliotis
35 Willie St
Haverhill MA 01830

Call Sign: WB2DSH
Brian C Longwell
45 Wingate St
Haverhill MA 01832

Call Sign: KB1HFS
Charles P Donovan
21 Wingate St Unit
705
Haverhill MA 01832

Call Sign: WB1EAF
Charles P Demeris
111 Winona Ave
Haverhill MA
018302156

Call Sign: KA1VF
Robert H Smith
128 Winona Ave
Haverhill MA
018302139

Call Sign: KB1QMN
Anthony L Dicicco
25 Winston Circle
Haverhill MA 01830

Call Sign: KA1MUV
Andy A Boyd
107 Winter St
Haverhill MA 01830

Call Sign: N0YGQ
Jonathan S Harada
35 Woodcock Ave Apt
20
Haverhill MA 01832

Call Sign: K1FPV
William R Bibeau
15 Woodman Ave
Haverhill MA
018301422

Call Sign: KB1CSH

Serafim Makris
Haverhill MA
018311339

Call Sign: KB1DOP
Harry V Ellis
Haverhill MA 01830

Call Sign: KB1MMO
James A Dawkins
Haverhill MA 01830

Call Sign: N1IDI
Bruce P Hansen
1100 N Broad
Haverill MA 01832

FCC Amateur Radio Licenses in Hawley

Call Sign: WB1DVK
Charles H Riggott
12 Ashfield Rd
Hawley MA 01339

Call Sign: N2YMR
Michael King
62 Labelle Rd
Hawley MA 01339

Call Sign: N1SWY
George M Turner
118 Leon Ct
Hawson MA 02341

FCC Amateur Radio Licenses in Haydenville

Call Sign: KB1MXY
Matthew P Thibodeau
18 Hatfield St
Haydenville MA
01039

Call Sign: N1OUC
Matthew P Thibodeau
18 Hatfield St
Haydenville MA
01039

Call Sign: WA1WDT
Robert E Pomeroy
33 High St

Haydenville MA
01039

Call Sign: KC1NW
Steven E Weinstein
3 Westbrook Rd
Haydenville MA
01039

FCC Amateur Radio Licenses in Heath

Call Sign: KB1RCF
Ellen L Jenkins
51 Bray Rd
Heath MA 01346

Call Sign: N1AMW
Robert T Markert
Hosmer Rd
Heath MA 01346

Call Sign: AB1JX
Alan R Corey
12 Schoolhouse Rd
Heath MA 01346

Call Sign: W1HPQ
Russell E Johnson
South Rd
Heath MA 01346

FCC Amateur Radio Licenses in Hingham

Call Sign: N1FMY
Frederick J Herzig
21 Andrews Isle
Hingham MA 02043

Call Sign: KB2WY
Marc E Snyder
23 Backriver Rd
Hingham MA 02043

Call Sign: AB1KT
David M Tenenbaum
9 Beach Rd
Hingham MA 02043

Call Sign: KB1PUN
Richard J Hart
29 Beach Rd
Hingham MA 02043

Call Sign: KB1VTU
Luke C Goodman
53 Beal St
Hingham MA 02043

Call Sign: K1IPB
William F Downey
1 Bradley Park Dr
Hingham MA 02043

Call Sign: WA1KSF
Brian P Downey
1 Bradley Park Dr
Hingham MA
020432101

Call Sign: KB1EKN
Mark J Duff
37 Bradley Park Dr
Hingham MA 02043

Call Sign: KB1ISG
Geraldine Duff
37 Bradley Park Dr
Hingham MA 02043

Call Sign: N1LJU
John D Barrett
42 Bradley Park Dr
Hingham MA 02043

Call Sign: W1VPR
Hingham Amateur
Radio Club
37 Bradley Park Drive
Hingham MA 02043

Call Sign: N9DKC
Dwight Crowther
12 Bradley Woods Dr
Hingham MA 02043

Call Sign: WA1AUR
Richard L Nicholson
31 Brewster Rd
Hingham MA 02043

Call Sign: KB1PVC
Michael J Dowd
63 Canterbury St
Hingham MA 02043

Call Sign: N1GMX

Robert G Karlis
160 Central St
Hingham MA 02043

Call Sign: KF2HO
Simon J Collinge
93 Chief Justice
Cushing Hwy
Hingham MA 02043

Call Sign: KG2CO
Julie P Collinge
93 Chief Justice
Cushing Hwy
Hingham MA 02043

Call Sign: N1GBZ
Kevin G Ricketts
16 Clifford Ct
Hingham MA 02043

Call Sign: K1SQL
Frank P Bellofatto
412 Cushing St
Hingham MA 02043

Call Sign: K1WYF
C Ronald Johnson
43 Fearing Rd
Hingham MA
020431836

Call Sign: KB1RUS
John M Kasznica
10 Flintlock Circle
Hingham MA 02043

Call Sign: KB1FHS
Eric D Dresser
24 French St
Hingham MA 02043

Call Sign: WA1AMP
Edward R Moore
37 Gilford Rd
Hingham MA 02043

Call Sign: WA1IAH
Robert P Smith
17 Golf View Dr
Hingham MA 02043

Call Sign: W1DDH
Dudley W Burke

54 Governor Long Rd
Hingham MA 02043

Call Sign: WA1YZJ
Thomas C Jantzen
23 Hancock Rd
Hingham MA 02043

Call Sign: W1SXN
Richard A Nese
52 Hersey St
Hingham MA 02043

Call Sign: KB1NMJ
Steven J Hawker
182 Hersey St
Hingham MA 02043

Call Sign: N1IXR
John J Barbuto
145 High St
Hingham MA 02043

Call Sign: K1BBM
John J Barbuto
145 High St
Hingham MA 02043

Call Sign: WY1S
John F Mc Kendry
207 High St
Hingham MA 02043

Call Sign: KB1UTB
Newton D Swain
2506 Hockley Dr
Hingham MA 02043

Call Sign: N3NBP
Eric B Sansone
35 Howland Lane
Hingham MA
020433349

Call Sign: WB1AIR
Gerald T Leibenguth
16 Hull St
Hingham MA 02043

Call Sign: KA1SVH
Dieter Wittkowski
9 Huntley Rd
Hingham MA 02043

Call Sign: KA1AT
Richard A Butterworth
14 Kents Ln
Hingham MA 02043

Call Sign: N1HMF
Eric F Weld
47 Kimball Beach Rd
Hingham MA 02043

Call Sign: WA1NXY
Allan E Pratt
138 Leavitt St
Hingham MA 02043

Call Sign: KB1IOT
Michael A Ide
207 Leavitt St
Hingham MA 02043

Call Sign: N1GBY
Glenn A Shaw
250 Leavitt St
Hingham MA 02043

Call Sign: W1GAS
Glenn A Shaw
250 Leavitt St
Hingham MA 02043

Call Sign: K1GAS
Glenn A Shaw
250 Leavitt St
Hingham MA 02043

Call Sign: N1ECQ
Norman J Wilbur
134 Lincoln St
Hingham MA 02043

Call Sign: KB1SXX
Linden Ponds Amateur
Radio Club
301 Linden Ponds Way
- Bc-411
Hingham MA 02043

Call Sign: W1LPH
Linden Ponds Amateur
Radio Club
301 Linden Ponds Way
- Bc-411
Hingham MA 02043

Call Sign: K1JV
Joseph I Volpe Jr
301 Linden Ponds Way
Apt 411
Hingham MA 02043

Call Sign: W1LOU
Raleigh J Martin
303 Linden Ponds Way
Et319
Hingham MA 02043

Call Sign: W1NWI
William H Hurd Sr
302 Linden Ponds Way
Unit 301
Hingham MA 02043

Call Sign: KA1TBQ
William B Kirby
302 Linden Ponds Way
Wc-102
Hingham MA 02043

Call Sign: KB1KDH
David M Berkin
452 Main St
Hingham MA 02043

Call Sign: K0OSZ
Ivan D Frantz Iii
971 Main St
Hingham MA 02043

Call Sign: KB1PVA
Timothy P Thomas
319 North St
Hingham MA 02043

Call Sign: WA1OOM
William F Becker
7 Palmers Ln
Hingham MA 02043

Call Sign: KB1VGN
Harold S Rydell
7 Patriots Way
Hingham MA 02043

Call Sign: K1LC
Lindsley D Colclough
11 Patriots Way
Hingham MA 02043

Call Sign: K1HDH
James S Rice
9 Presidents Rd
Hingham MA 02043

Call Sign: WB1FIR
Daniel D Sheehan
5 Rosewood Lane
Hingham MA 02043

Call Sign: KA1MIJ
Harold S Goldstein
12 S Pleasant St
Hingham MA 02043

Call Sign: KC1FZ
George I Davis
10 Sanborn Rd
Hingham MA 02043

Call Sign: K1BA
Allan L Bacon
73 School St
Hingham MA
020432915

Call Sign: N1KXH
Craig J Trudell
14 Spring St
Hingham MA 02043

Call Sign: W1AUZ
Richard E Trudell
14 Spring St
Hingham MA 02043

Call Sign: N1SEP
Michael P Lynch
11 Studley Rd
Hingham MA 02043

Call Sign: KB1URG
Timothy M Dawson-
Townsend
68 Thaxter St
Hingham MA 02043

Call Sign: N1VDZ
Ronald D Middendorf
30 Thaxter St 71
Hingham MA 02043

Call Sign: W1BIY
Laurence B Stein Jr

86 Turkey Hill Ln
Hingham MA 02043

Call Sign: WB1APA
Lester D Meserve
Turkey Hill Ln
Hingham MA 02043

Call Sign: K1VDQ
H James Gorman Jr
4 Upland Dr
Hingham MA 02043

Call Sign: AB1MN
Robert W Kembel
12 Water St
Hingham MA 02043

Call Sign: KB1HFJ
Charles R Creighton Jr
9 Whitcomb Ln
Hingham MA 02043

Call Sign: KB1UBX
Karen L Trask
311 Whiting St
Hingham MA 02043

Call Sign: KB1IPV
Lisa A Ragone
1 Winona Way
Hingham MA
020431137

Call Sign: KB1IPW
Andrew E Clark
1 Winona Way
Hingham MA
020431137

Call Sign: N1KTD
Michael S Antoine
132 Wompatuck Rd
Hingham MA 02043

Call Sign: W1HFG
John L Procter
7 Woodbine Lane
Hingham MA 02043

FCC Amateur Radio
Licenses in Hinsdale

Call Sign: N1EMT

Michael J Majchrowski
256 Bilodeau Brook
Rd
Hinsdale MA 01235

Call Sign: KB1PDS
Raymond R Bolduc
520 Creamery Rd
Hinsdale MA 01235

Call Sign: W1TTT
David A Foley
77 Curtis St
Hinsdale MA 01235

Call Sign: W1OAZ
Donald L Coleman Jr
21 Lakeview Rd
Hinsdale MA 01235

Call Sign: W1FVT
Ralph T Simmons
Hinsdale MA 01235

Call Sign: KB1VGB
Keith F Beebe
Hinsdale MA 01235

FCC Amateur Radio
Licenses in Holbrook

Call Sign: K1UCY
Allan G Dunn
68 Abington Ave
Holbrook MA
023431522

Call Sign: N1VPU
John H Dunn
68 Abington Ave
Holbrook MA 02343

Call Sign: KB1IKH
Elayne G Tovet
115 Abington Ave
Holbrook MA 02343

Call Sign: KA1EUI
James D Tovet
115 Abington Ave
Holbrook MA 02343

Call Sign: W1JT
James D Tovet

115 Abington Ave
Holbrook MA 02343

Call Sign: KB1GUZ
Jeannemarie Bacon
6 Arch Rd
Holbrook MA 02343

Call Sign: KB1KVI
Joseph P Renna
135 Belcher St
Holbrook MA 02343

Call Sign: KB1GN
Michael J Sheehan
66 E Shore Rd
Holbrook MA 02343

Call Sign: N1MYF
Irene M Visocchi
9 Ell Rd
Holbrook MA 02343

Call Sign: KE1KY
James J Curran Jr
19 Fargo Rd
Holbrook MA
023431249

Call Sign: N1XNV
Phu V Truong
4 George Rd
Holbrook MA 02343

Call Sign: WA1GUN
Ernest H Davy
17 Hillsdale Rd
Holbrook MA 02343

Call Sign: K1RAK
Louis E Savoie
29 Hillsdale Rd
Holbrook MA 02343

Call Sign: WA1BJM
Howard G Mayers
30 Johns Ave
Holbrook MA 02343

Call Sign: W1MGB
Howard G Mayers
30 Johns Ave
Holbrook MA 02343

Call Sign: KB1OCB
Belonny Michel
28 Linfield St
Holbrook MA 02343

Call Sign: KB1NAV
Laurence J Stewart
156 Longmeadow Dr -
203
Holbrook MA 02343

Call Sign: N1NRN
Myron F Holbrook
156 Longmeadow Dr
Apt 101
Holbrook MA 02343

Call Sign: K1LEO
Leo V Mc Gonagle Jr
144 Longmeadow
Drive
Holbrook MA 02343

Call Sign: N1TRY
Joseph B Marsala
32 Morgan Rd
Holbrook MA 02343

Call Sign: WA1YKF
Warren J Dickie
270 N Franklin St
Holbrook MA 02343

Call Sign: KA1OGU
Robert J Larkin Jr
19 Orchard St
Holbrook MA 02343

Call Sign: KB1FRR
James Burrell
41 Pleasant St
Holbrook MA 02343

Call Sign: KA1BBU
Robert J Egles
546 Plymouth St
Holbrook MA 02343

Call Sign: N1QEU
William A Cantin
735 Plymouth St
Holbrook MA 02343

Call Sign: KA1OGV

John A Murrin Jr
186 Pond St
Holbrook MA 02343

Call Sign: N1WIH
John R Greene
52 Rose Way
Holbrook MA 02343

Call Sign: KA1HPG
Gary E Montgomery
53 S Shore Rd
Holbrook MA 02343

Call Sign: KB1EKR
Saraswathi Kakileti
16 Scott St
Holbrook MA 02343

Call Sign: KB1EKS
Kishore Kumar
Kakileti
16 Scott St
Holbrook MA 02343

Call Sign: KA1CD
Philip E Molloy
34 Sherrick Ave
Holbrook MA 02343

Call Sign: W1RWI
Wesley L Fowler
330 South St
Holbrook MA 02343

Call Sign: N1PTK
Richard Borowicz
499 South St
Holbrook MA 02343

Call Sign: KB1UCE
Peter D Blaher Jr
31 Spring St
Holbrook MA 02343

Call Sign: N1VUQ
Keith L Kennedy
48 Summit Rd
Holbrook MA 02343

Call Sign: N1KLK
Keith L Kennedy
48 Summit Rd
Holbrook MA 02343

Call Sign: N1TQK

Call Sign: KA1KIJ
Robert S Azanow
35 William Rd
Holbrook MA 02343

Call Sign: W1OHB
John H Mackinaw
25 Woodlawn Ave
Holbrook MA 02343

Call Sign: N1DZD
William G Ryan
Holbrook MA
023430163

Call Sign: KB1GRY
Keith F Lazaron Ii
Holbrook MA 02343

Call Sign: KB1IKX
Victoria J Ryan
Holbrook MA
023430163

Call Sign: KB1SMW
James W Doyle
Holbrook MA 02343

Call Sign: AB1OZ
James W Doyle
Holbrook MA 02343

**FCC Amateur Radio
Licenses in Holden**

Call Sign: KA1UTT
Liliane M J A
Lindberg
55 A Sawyer Ln
Holden MA 01520

Call Sign: WE1C
John J Henrion Iii
195 Bailey Rd
Holden MA 01520

Call Sign: N1AUP
Christopher A Shustak
Box 585
Holden MA
015200585

William R Moran
49 Brattle St
Holden MA 01520

Call Sign: N1HCG
Alan E Siddons
6 Brewer Way
Holden MA 01520

Call Sign: KA1PYE
Janetta Petkus
Brewer Way
Holden MA 01520

Call Sign: K1YZE
William F White
9 Briarcliff Ln
Holden MA 01520

Call Sign: KB1EZF
Scott W Olsen
101 Bullard St
Holden MA 01520

Call Sign: KA1SZZ
Edward H Hudson Jr
366 Bullard St
Holden MA 01520

Call Sign: KB1MSI
Andrew J Demarco
455 Bullard St
Holden MA 01520

Call Sign: KB1GX
Rufus M Franklin
54 Centerwood Dr
Holden MA 01520

Call Sign: W1RV
Richard P Vitello
7 Clark St
Holden MA 01520

Call Sign: KJ6NSB
Steven R Parr
9 Country Hill Rd
Holden MA 01522

Call Sign: KB1UBL
THOMAS Macdonald
66 Cranbrook Dr
Holden MA 01520

Call Sign: KA1VKK
Robert F Tonning Jr
64 Crestview Dr
Holden MA 01520

Call Sign: N1NZY
Allen W Smith
88 Doyle Rd
Holden MA 01520

Call Sign: WA1SCG
John F Meyers
150 Doyle Rd
Holden MA 01520

Call Sign: N1MQJ
George E Burgwinkle
32 Edgewood Dr
Holden MA 01520

Call Sign: N1QYG
George P Guertin Jr
10 Flager Dr
Holden MA 01520

Call Sign: K1ULW
Alden H Wood
41 Glenwood St
Holden MA
015202033

Call Sign: N1GR
Gary A Rodgers
14 Greenbriar Ln
Holden MA 01520

Call Sign: K1HVJ
Edmund H Clouatre
365 Highland St
Holden MA 01520

Call Sign: K1IC
Edward H Leonard
184 Holden St
Holden MA 01520

Call Sign: WA1KLN
Kevin R Sullivan
28 Homestead Rd
Holden MA 01520

Call Sign: K1DVL
Edsel E Ross
87 Homestead Rd

Holden MA 01520

Call Sign: KA1NED
William T Dolan
56 John Alden Rd
Holden MA 01520

Call Sign: K1RWZ
Peter L Ettenberg
15 Kris Alan Drive
Holden MA 01520

Call Sign: WA1NQF
William B Deedy Jr
6 Lexington Circle
Holden MA 01520

Call Sign: KD4DYV
Jason B Feifer
1306 Main St
Holden MA 01520

Call Sign: WA1IXX
Robert D Price
11 Malden St
Holden MA 01520

Call Sign: KD4LXN
Joseph S Gulachenski
18 Meadow Wood Dr
Holden MA 01520

Call Sign: W1RL
Walter R Szarek
80 Mixter Rd
Holden MA 01520

Call Sign: WA1CDY
Theodore Le Blanc
94 Mt View Dr
Holden MA 01520

Call Sign: WA1IMI
David Cyganski
94 Newell Rd
Holden MA 01520

Call Sign: N1TID
Christopher A Peskin
106 Newell Rd
Holden MA 01520

Call Sign: N1FJP
Paul M Piscitelli

187 Newell Rd
Holden MA 01520

Call Sign: K1RZQ
Frederick W Paul
124 Nola Dr
Holden MA 01520

Call Sign: W1CVO
John H Nieman
172 Nola Drive
Holden MA 01520

Call Sign: WB1ANA
Thomas K Kerxhalli
9 Oakwood St
Holden MA 01520

Call Sign: WA1IOD
John A Nilson
9 Osgood Ave
Holden MA 01520

Call Sign: N1TNV
Timothy K Samara
114 Parker Ave
Holden MA 01520

Call Sign: WA1ZUC
Stephen A Breed
150 Parker Ave
Holden MA 01520

Call Sign: WA6ILT
David S Reinhart
82 Parker Ave
Holden MA 01520

Call Sign: W1PDW
Robert G Ferguson
90 Phillips Rd
Holden MA 01520

Call Sign: WJ1S
Henry H Enman Jr
36 Pinecroft Ave
Holden MA 01520

Call Sign: KB1LMW
James A Young
156 Putnam Rd
Holden MA 01520

Call Sign: W1WER

James A Young
156 Putnam Rd
Holden MA 01520

Call Sign: N1ENX
Norman T Hanney Jr
84 Raymond St
Holden MA 01520

Call Sign: K1VLZ
Walter D Solodyna
218 Reservoir St Unit
331
Holden MA 01520

Call Sign: KA1QHR
Otto R Lies
564 Salisbury St
Holden MA 01520

Call Sign: W1TAG
John K Andrews
48 Sandy Glen Dr
Holden MA 01520

Call Sign: N1FIU
Paul W Sundquist
456 Shrewsbury St
Holden MA 01520

Call Sign: N1MPY
Wayne M Mc Mahon
605 Shrewsbury St
Holden MA 01520

Call Sign: W1ANE
Wayne M Mc Mahon
605 Shrewsbury St
Holden MA 01520

Call Sign: K1CTU
Gordon B Dodge
16 Somerset Ln
Holden MA 01520

Call Sign: KB1MHI
Ryan D Peterson
37 Steppingstone Dr
Holden MA 01520

Call Sign: N1LSH
Brent N Hiller
141 Wachusett St
Holden MA 01520

Call Sign: KB1GNB
Thomas C Mina
30 Woodland Rd
Holden MA 01520

Call Sign: AA1AA
John L Giasi
50 Woodland Rd
Holden MA 01520

Call Sign: KB1BPW
Vastese American
Radio Club
50 Woodland Rd
Holden MA 01522569

Call Sign: KB1BSD
Casertano American
Radio Assn
50 Woodland Rd
Holden MA
015202569

Call Sign: WA4DDH
William C Latimer
Holden MA 01520

Call Sign: KI6AKA
Massachusetts State
Guard Radio Club
Holden MA 01520

Call Sign: KA1ZUE
Alan R Twichell
22 Woodland Rd
Holdon MA 01520

Call Sign: WA1LFR
Joseph M Kosinski
Box 1323
Holland MA 01521

Call Sign: N1SIH
Melvin P Langley
Box 85
Holland MA 01521

Call Sign: KB1MNN
Kyle J Ebersold
33 Brimfield Rd

Holland MA
015213011

Call Sign: KB1UPX
John R Ebersold
33 Brimfield Rd
Holland MA 01521

Call Sign: WA1JGN
George J Hemingway
34 Forest Dr
Holland MA
015212448

Call Sign: N1KYW
Michael J Wrona
129 Sturbridge Rd
Holland MA 01521

Call Sign: N1NTE
Robert R Bellville
Holland MA
015210104

Call Sign: W1SC
Stephen D Coleman
261 Adams St
Holliston MA 01746

Call Sign: KB1MKC
Thomas K Killoren
449 Adams St
Holliston MA 01746

Call Sign: KB1PZN
Thomas K Killoren
449 Adams St
Holliston MA 01746

Call Sign: N1EMU
Kenneth T Mac Keil
80 Baker St
Holliston MA 01746

Call Sign: N1CGO
Ray E Givens
5 Birchwood Rd
Holliston MA 01746

Call Sign: KB5GC
Charles E Wyatt Jr

53 Birchwood Rd
Holliston MA 01746

Call Sign: W1CEW
Charles E Wyatt Jr
53 Birchwood Rd
Holliston MA 01746

Call Sign: KB1UCF
Jeffery A Pinterparson
45 Briarcliff Ln
Holliston MA 01746

Call Sign: KA1AL
Alan E Kunian
47 Carl Rd
Holliston MA 01746

Call Sign: N3LBW
Martin W Flohr
114 Central St
Holliston MA 01746

Call Sign: KB6WDL
Elissa R Sanford
196 Central St
Holliston MA 01746

Call Sign: KB1MLT
Henry W Piel
523 Central St
Holliston MA 01746

Call Sign: KA1IYV
Joseph A Cibotti
44 Christopher Rd
Holliston MA 01746

Call Sign: K1HK
Harold S Kost
30 Concord St
Holliston MA 01746

Call Sign: N1HVI
Paul L Guyon
233 Concord St
Holliston MA 01746

Call Sign: KB1VLR
Paul F Kaufman
616 Concord St
Holliston MA 01746

Call Sign: AA1BU

Joseph A Gagliardi Jr
20 Country Rd
Holliston MA 01746

Call Sign: N1YFR
Susan B Gagliardi
20 Country Rd
Holliston MA 01746

Call Sign: KB1RLT
Paul D Kaitz
6 Day Rd
Holliston MA 01746

Call Sign: K1PDK
Paul D Kaitz
6 Day Rd
Holliston MA 01746

Call Sign: KB1IBI
Charles A Camiel
73 Dodd Dr
Holliston MA 01746

Call Sign: K1MT
David J Talmanson
81 Dodd Dr
Holliston MA 01746

Call Sign: N1QY
Ronald C Evett
18 Elm St
Holliston MA
017462123

Call Sign: N1EVZ
Jay E Green
71 Goulding St
Holliston MA 01746

Call Sign: KB1JTY
Thomas R Amlicke Jr
61 Gregory Rd
Holliston MA 01746

Call Sign: N1FUT
Wayne E Field
134 High St
Holliston MA 01746

Call Sign: N1FUU
Marianne F Field
134 High St
Holliston MA 01746

Call Sign: KB1PQA
Andrew J Brockert
184 High St
Holliston MA 01746

Call Sign: WA1JIR
Joseph M Mc Grath
648 Highland St
Holliston MA 01746

Call Sign: N1UGL
Matthew D Brennan
133 Holly Lane
Holliston MA 01746

Call Sign: KA1FVG
Richard S Packer
109 Jerrold St
Holliston MA 01746

Call Sign: N1LE
Lewis H Elias
10 Johnson Dr
Holliston MA 01746

Call Sign: KB1RDK
Michael J Craren
107 Juniper Rd
Holliston MA 01746

Call Sign: WI1M
Michael J Craren
107 Juniper Rd
Holliston MA 01746

Call Sign: KB1LCP
Richard I Kilpatrick
162 Karen Cir
Holliston MA 01746

Call Sign: N1SNL
Gerald M Bergeron
181 Locust St
Holliston MA 01746

Call Sign: N1XCK
Stephen D Haynes Jr
91 Maple St
Holliston MA 01746

Call Sign: KB1IBH
Michael C Haynes
91 Maple St

Holliston MA 01746

Call Sign: WB1DQD
Philip I Thombs
137 Maple St
Holliston MA 01746

Call Sign: W1DQD
Philip I Thombs
137 Maple St
Holliston MA 01746

Call Sign: W1HAZ
Donald L Underwood
125 Marilyn St
Holliston MA 01746

Call Sign: KA1UJW
Juana E Brewster
124 Marked Tree Rd
Holliston MA 01746

Call Sign: KA1KHS
Warren B Brewster
124 Marked Tree Rd
Holliston MA 01746

Call Sign: W1YHY
Lance O Hobson
136 Marked Tree Rd
Holliston MA 01746

Call Sign: N1TQA
Peter W Vernon
26 Mechanic St
Holliston MA 01746

Call Sign: K1ESW
Eugenia S Ware
230 Mellen St
Holliston MA 01746

Call Sign: K1JCB
John C Barstow
230 Mellen St
Holliston MA
017461139

Call Sign: KB1ETA
Siobhan A Sheehy
79 Morton St
Holliston MA 01746

Call Sign: N1UDS

Jeffrey R Gregor
194 N Mill St
Holliston MA
017461043

Call Sign: N1UTN
Elizabeth A Bourque
Theiler
17 Norland St
Holliston MA 01746

Call Sign: N1UTO
Willie J Theiler
17 Norland St
Holliston MA 01746

Call Sign: KB1MCW
James L Mcgrath
49 Northway St
Holliston MA 01746

Call Sign: KB1NJZ
James J Cavan
68 Northway St
Holliston MA 01746

Call Sign: W1OJN
Bedros Kamitian
93 Orchard Ln
Holliston MA
017461112

Call Sign: N1RDX
Quentin J Greeley
81 Pilgrim Rd
Holliston MA 01746

Call Sign: WD8DAE
David L Keating
56 Pinecrest Rd
Holliston MA 01746

Call Sign: KA1RVM
William H Hawley
368 Prentice St
Holliston MA 01746

Call Sign: N1XPO
Benjamin S Tartakoff
118 Prospect St
Holliston MA 01746

Call Sign: W1BIP
Earl W Herzog

31 Robert Rd
Holliston MA 01746

Call Sign: W1HSS
Robert I Rudko
4 Short Rd
Holliston MA 01746

Call Sign: WB1FIY
Leo A Parker Jr
22 Skyview Ter
Holliston MA 01746

Call Sign: KB1NUQ
Alexander Smirnov
111 South St
Holliston MA 01746

Call Sign: W1STI
N Bradford Carey Jr
196 South St
Holliston MA 01746

Call Sign: W1VLK
George E Stronach
60 Stony Brook Dr
Holliston MA 01746

Call Sign: N1YWG
Brian A Maeder
78 Stony Brook Dr
Holliston MA 01746

Call Sign: W4LKR
George E Stronach
60 Stony Brook Drive
Holliston MA 01746

Call Sign: KB1ECU
Harold E Baldwin
100 Summer St Apt
217
Holliston MA
017462263

Call Sign: K1VHD
Chester J Tillson
25 Travis Rd
Holliston MA 01746

Call Sign: K1ZUA
Ruth E Tillson
25 Travis Rd

Holliston MA
017461244

Call Sign: KA1WIB
Joan F Legee
43 Travis Rd
Holliston MA 01746

Call Sign: KD1BC
Warren L Legee Jr
43 Travis Rd
Holliston MA 01746

Call Sign: KA1SF
Clement T Lambert
379 Underwood St
Holliston MA 01746

Call Sign: KT2E
Jay S Falk
465 Underwood St
Holliston MA
017461510

Call Sign: N1HXE
Wendy M Gruber
465 Underwood St
Holliston MA 01746

Call Sign: KB1FXG
Richard L Brumber
16 Union St
Holliston MA 01746

Call Sign: K1AXK
Robert H Mann
110 Union St
Holliston MA 01746

Call Sign: KB1JLQ
Richard W Williams
1874 Washington St
Holliston MA 01746

Call Sign: WA1PNZ
Louis R Raneri
492 Washington St Apt
66
Holliston MA
017461920

Call Sign: N1KQT
Francis G Kelley Jr
31 Wedgewood Dr

Holliston MA 01746

Call Sign: WA2DLT
Howard K Hager
425 Winter St
Holliston MA 01746

Call Sign: WA1NPN
John L Pratt
715 Winter St
Holliston MA
017461129

Call Sign: WA1TCX
Cynthia A Pratt
715 Winter St
Holliston MA 01746

Call Sign: N1UTQ
Edward P Foss Jr
41 Winthrop St
Holliston MA 01746

Call Sign: KA1AXY
Peter Z Simpson
Holliston MA 01746

Call Sign: N1FOF
Catherine M Simpson
Holliston MA 01746

Call Sign: KA1CTL
John H Kosian
Holliston MA
017466198

Call Sign: N1NVU
Anita Mc Fadden
Holliston MA
017466198

Call Sign: N1VZW
Michael W Simpson
Holliston MA
017466634

Call Sign: N1XAG
Elizabeth A Simpson
Holliston MA
017466634

Call Sign: N1ZFG
John M Nelson

Holliston MA
017466531

FCC Amateur Radio Licenses in Holyoke

Call Sign: KB1BBW
Carolyn L Overlock
8 Alderman St
Holyoke MA 01040

Call Sign: KB1WQ
William A Johnston
391 Apremont Hwy
Holyoke MA 01040

Call Sign: KB1NOX
Richard R Stewart Jr
3 Beacon Ave
Holyoke MA 01040

Call Sign: N1XSA
Andrew C Bail
62 Beacon Ave
Holyoke MA 01040

Call Sign: KB1GJQ
Jeffrey E Bail
62 Beacon Ave
Holyoke MA 01040

Call Sign: KB1HPF
Derick A Demers
485 Beech St
Holyoke MA 01040

Call Sign: K1VDJ
Michael Gemelli
75 Belvidere Ave
Holyoke MA 01040

Call Sign: KC1TV
John J Le Moine
66 Berkshire St
Holyoke MA 01040

Call Sign: KA1VWW
Ronald A Fournier
21 Bowers St Apt 705
Holyoke MA 01040

Call Sign: KB1RXO
Karl A Krassler
165 Brown Ave

Holyoke MA
010403618

Call Sign: KB1LNU
Edward C Mandigo Jr
101 Cabot St 603
Holyoke MA 01040

Call Sign: N1TOT
Brian A Balise
49 Chapin St
Holyoke MA 01040

Call Sign: N1NYB
Ron J Stebbins
19 Cherry St
Holyoke MA 01040

Call Sign: KB1DEU
Damian L Nowak
19 Clark St
Holyoke MA
010402903

Call Sign: KE1DF
Tristam I Greaney
11 Columbus Ave
Holyoke MA 01040

Call Sign: N1GYN
Norman R Jacques
25 Columbus Ave
Holyoke MA 01040

Call Sign: KA1HCF
Gilberto Sotolongo
15 Dale St
Holyoke MA 01040

Call Sign: N1AFY
Norman A Cournoyer
77 Dupuis Rd
Holyoke MA 01040

Call Sign: KB1JGD
Holyoke Emergency
Management Races
Club
536 Dwight St
Holyoke MA 01040

Call Sign: KB1EVB
Jennifer L Wilkerson

20 Easthampton Rd
Apt C-5
Holyoke MA 01040

Call Sign: KB1GEH
Shaun J Murphy
20 Easthampton Rd
Apt M9
Holyoke MA 01040

Call Sign: N1MHL
Manuel Padilla
62 Ely St
Holyoke MA 01040

Call Sign: KB1RIE
Elijah B Harris
67 Francis Ave
Holyoke MA 01040

Call Sign: N1ELI
Elijah B Harris
67 Francis Ave
Holyoke MA 01040

Call Sign: KA1TPL
Donald T Proulx
26 George St
Holyoke MA 01040

Call Sign: KA1PAJ
George L Bach
5 Glen St
Holyoke MA 01040

Call Sign: KA1TVA
Melvin Gonzalez
955 Hampden St Apt
3a
Holyoke MA 01040

Call Sign: KB1PVF
Fredrick P Grundman
128 High St
Holyoke MA 01040

Call Sign: KC8WRR
Thomas G Ferguson
48 Holy Family Rd
Apt 103
Holyoke MA 01040

Call Sign: W1TGF
Thomas G Ferguson

48 Holy Family Rd
Apt 103
Holyoke MA 01040

Call Sign: W1RDC
Walter R Walczak
917 Homestead Ave
Holyoke MA 01040

Call Sign: KM5MG
Ralph D Higginbotham
155 Huron Ave
Holyoke MA 01040

Call Sign: N1KFG
Ian R Mc Leish
415 Ingleside St
Holyoke MA 01040

Call Sign: KA1ZYK
Miguel A Medina
30 James St
Holyoke MA 01040

Call Sign: N1JOI
Donald J Mish
125 Jarvis Ave
Holyoke MA 01040

Call Sign: N1JOJ
Elizabeth A Mish
125 Jarvis Ave
Holyoke MA 01040

Call Sign: WA2OQF
Glenn Koger
298 Jarvis Ave Apt A8
Holyoke MA 01040

Call Sign: KB1QHJ
LAWRENCE E Jodoin
39 King St
Holyoke MA 01040

Call Sign: W1LEJ
LAWRENCE E Jodoin
39 King St
Holyoke MA 01040

Call Sign: AA1NE
David A Wilbur
22 Lexington Ave
Holyoke MA 01040

Call Sign: W1NYP
Robert G Gadbois
297 Linden St
Holyoke MA 01040

Call Sign: KB1RID
Christopher R Hodges
77 Lynch Dr
Holyoke MA 01040

Call Sign: KB1BBV
Angel R Pabon
348 Maple St
Holyoke MA 01040

Call Sign: KB1BCG
Jason N Bermudez
462 Maple St
Holyoke MA 01040

Call Sign: W1CJK
William F Werenski
35 Mayer Dr
Holyoke MA
010401434

Call Sign: KA1MDP
Charles B Crean
19 Mc Grady St
Holyoke MA 01040

Call Sign: AA1CR
Owen F Kelly Jr
22 Mclellan Dr
Holyoke MA 01040

Call Sign: KB1BEJ
Donna M O Brien
16 Meggison Ln
Holyoke MA 01040

Call Sign: N1IVT
Daniel J O Brien
16 Meggison Ln
Holyoke MA 01040

Call Sign: KA1IOS
Theodore R Kuc Sr
36 Merrick Ave
Holyoke MA 01040

Call Sign: W1TDO
Alfred I Haberman
129 Morgan St

Holyoke MA 01040

Call Sign: W1EYC
Richard H Loescher
71 Mountain Rd
Holyoke MA 01040

Call Sign: WB1EQS
Robert K Berger
225 Mountain View Dr
Holyoke MA 01040

Call Sign: KB1QHH
Robert F Zajac
39 Mt Tom Ave
Holyoke MA 01040

Call Sign: KB1ARJ
Agustin P Rodriguez
63 Newton St
Holyoke MA 01040

Call Sign: KV1C
Leo F Tourigny
11 Park View Ter
Holyoke MA 01040

Call Sign: N1QCK
Matthew T Washburne
95 Pearl St
Holyoke MA 01040

Call Sign: N1VRJ
Gary S Gaulin
7 Philip Dr
Holyoke MA 01040

Call Sign: KA1MDO
Gary A Bennett
91 Pleasant St
Holyoke MA 01040

Call Sign: K1WJZ
Walter J Ziemba
297 Pleasant St
Holyoke MA 01040

Call Sign: NB1Q
Edward Mc Hugh
71 Reservation Rd
Holyoke MA 01040

Call Sign: N1OVY
James D Schell

8 Richard Eger Drive
Holyoke MA 01040

Call Sign: K1IYT
Ernest D Sias
95 Ridgewood Ave
Holyoke MA 01040

Call Sign: WA1GVV
Vincent R Falardeau
39 Roland St
Holyoke MA 01040

Call Sign: WA1OCL
Northampton High
School Amateur Radio
Clb
39 Roland St
Holyoke MA 01040

Call Sign: WP4EKB
Natividad Pagan
526 South St
Holyoke MA 01040

Call Sign: W1UWX
Clifford E Junkins Jr
485 South St Apt 321
Holyoke MA 01040

Call Sign: KB1GFB
James M Kane
206 Southampton Rd
Holyoke MA 01040

Call Sign: KB1JFP
Kristen L Golonka
129 St Jerome Ave
Holyoke MA
010402220

Call Sign: KB1JFQ
Charles R Carriere
129 St Jerome Ave
Holyoke MA
010402220

Call Sign: KB1BBX
Jesse J Torres
210 Suffolk St
Holyoke MA 01040

Call Sign: KB1ERR

Iso Ne Amateur Radio
Club
1 Sullivan Rd
Holyoke MA
010402841

Call Sign: N1WYC
Philip H Scott
71 Sun Valley Rd
Holyoke MA 01040

Call Sign: KB1CIS
Christine A Balise
11 Temple St
Holyoke MA 01040

Call Sign: KA1AZO
Richard C Rondeau
398 Tokeneke Rd
Holyoke MA 01040

Call Sign: W1JK
Jordan Koltz
121 W Meadowview
Rd
Holyoke MA 01040

Call Sign: WB1ETT
Robert E Shattuck
238 Walnut St
Holyoke MA 01040

Call Sign: W1AKB
Clifford Bennett
94 Westfield Rd
Holyoke MA 01040

Call Sign: KA1ZEI
Andrew F Metroske
25 Woodland St
Holyoke MA 01040

FCC Amateur Radio Licenses in Hopedale

Call Sign: N1CAV
Roger V Calarese
80 Adin St
Hopedale MA 01747

Call Sign: K1RWS
Richard T Mac Donald
20 Ballou Rd
Hopedale MA 01747

Call Sign: KA1SNA
Jay B Appell
125 Dutcher St
Hopedale MA 01747

Call Sign: K1CCS
Ian D Mac Donald Jr
170 Dutcher St
Hopedale MA 01747

Call Sign: NE1P
Michael J Hill
208 Freedom St
Hopedale MA 01747

Call Sign: W1YUW
William F Kimball
114 Hartford Ave
Hopedale MA 01747

Call Sign: WA1UEH
Cecil J Boates
31 Hill St
Hopedale MA 01747

Call Sign: K1GRA
Bernard A Rogers
32 Inman
Hopedale MA 01747

Call Sign: WB1EPG
Michael B Rowe
21 Laurelwood Dr
Hopedale MA 01747

Call Sign: KA1DXV
Carl W Olson
52 Laurelwood Dr
Hopedale MA 01747

Call Sign: N1PQK
Maru R Robinson
150 Mendon St
Hopedale MA 01747

Call Sign: WA1MSW
Reno J Cervassi
6 Oakwood Ave
Hopedale MA
017471807

Call Sign: W1YDU
Charles H Nixon

8 Warfield St
Hopedale MA 01747

FCC Amateur Radio Licenses in Hopkinton

Call Sign: N1EZV
Kenneth D Dietz
44 Alexander Rd
Hopkinton MA
017482400

Call Sign: K1SAD
Donald E Bresse
47 Ash
Hopkinton MA 01748

Call Sign: WJ1D
Howard A Lawrence
127 Ash St
Hopkinton MA 01748

Call Sign: KA1FRV
Dorothy E Wood
Box 72
Hopkinton MA 01748

Call Sign: WA2YYF
John P Sullivan Jr
21 Briarcliff Dr
Hopkinton MA 01748

Call Sign: KB1DDU
Patience M Umina
24 Chestnut St
Hopkinton MA 01748

Call Sign: N1ZNX
Michael P Umina Sr
24 Chestnut St
Hopkinton MA
017482520

Call Sign: KB1HBJ
Jon H Umina
24 Chestnut St
Hopkinton MA 01748

Call Sign: WA2PNQ
Kevin J Norby
1 Cubs Path
Hopkinton MA 01748

Call Sign: KB1KAM
Ryan K Norby
1 Cubs Path
Hopkinton MA 01748

Call Sign: K1FE
Robert E Pierce
1 D J Murphy Ln
Hopkinton MA 01748

Call Sign: K1DAD
Royce N Sawyer
14 Downey St
Hopkinton MA 01748

Call Sign: WA1PQY
William E Downing
8 Doyle Ln
Hopkinton MA 01748

Call Sign: W1LHF
Martin F J Duffy
4 Duffield Rd
Hopkinton MA 01748

Call Sign: KA1KTE
Leonard A Coffey
157 E Main St
Hopkinton MA 01748

Call Sign: K5LVE
John A Daniel
89 Front St
Hopkinton MA 01748

Call Sign: K2YOW
David S Goldman
20 Fruit St
Hopkinton MA 01748

Call Sign: AA1ON
Martin W Bayes
106 Hayden Rowe St
Hopkinton MA 01748

Call Sign: KB1BIJ
Kathyrn G Le Pelley
294 Hayden Rowe St
Hopkinton MA
017482806

Call Sign: KB1QOU
David B Bartolini Jr
11 Huckleberry Rd

Hopkinton MA 01748

Call Sign: N1VWM
John P Ryan Jr
5 Joseph Rd
Hopkinton MA 01748

Call Sign: WB1DXR
Brian W Branscomb
8 Kerry Ln
Hopkinton MA 01748

Call Sign: KA5GGV
Lynda G Sims
6 Leonard St
Hopkinton MA 01748

Call Sign: KB5CBS
William C Conway
7 Linden St
Hopkinton MA
017481921

Call Sign: N1DKC
Gerald E Tammi
1 Maria Ln
Hopkinton MA 01748

Call Sign: KB1WJR
Frank Iuso
5 Morse Ln
Hopkinton MA 01748

Call Sign: N1AHA
Edward J Rooney
8 Park St
Hopkinton MA 01748

Call Sign: W1HYA
John J Loncar
60 Pleasant St
Hopkinton MA 01748

Call Sign: WA1JKI
Stephen J Webber
34 Priscilla Rd
Hopkinton MA 01748

Call Sign: K1ST
Steven K Tolf
3 Ridge Rd
Hopkinton MA 01748

Call Sign: WA1RCA

Linda M Tolf
3 Ridge Rd
Hopkinton MA 01748

Call Sign: KE1GF
William P Smith
2 Robbern Rd
Hopkinton MA 01748

Call Sign: N1XAS
James J Smith
2 Robbern Rd
Hopkinton MA 01748

Call Sign: N1NUR
Stephen G Meier
40 S Mill St
Hopkinton MA 01748

Call Sign: KB1VXY
John J Iwuc
6 South Barn Rd
Hopkinton MA 01748

Call Sign: W1OLD
Anthony P Umina
64 South Mill St
Hopkinton MA 01748

Call Sign: W1EMC
Emc Amateur Radio
Club
176 South St
Hopkinton MA 01748

Call Sign: KA1TW
Trevor L Barron
8 Stewart St
Hopkinton MA 01748

Call Sign: KB1BEQ
Jeannine A Smith
2 Stonegate Rd
Hopkinton MA 01748

Call Sign: KD1T
Rudolph M Stucchi
2 Stonegate Rd
Hopkinton MA 01748

Call Sign: KB1CQI
Edward D Collins
1 Valentine Cir

Hopkinton MA
017482688

Call Sign: N1CTK
Paul A St Jean
27 Valleywood Rd
Hopkinton MA
017481634

Call Sign: K1SG
Stephen M Gilbert
75 W Elm St
Hopkinton MA
017482126

Call Sign: AB1LB
Mike Chirkov
75 W Elm St
Hopkinton MA 01748

Call Sign: KZ1R
Mike Chirkov
75 W Elm St
Hopkinton MA 01748

Call Sign: K1ODW
Robert W Smith
271 W Main St
Hopkinton MA
017482110

Call Sign: K1IOQ
Baldassare S Brunetta
27 Walcott St
Hopkinton MA 01748

Call Sign: N1XAN
George B Foster
29 Walcott Valley Dr
Hopkinton MA 01748

Call Sign: N1QWP
Cuong P Le
5 Westcott Dr
Hopkinton MA 01748

Call Sign: N1MYP
Michael D De Sousa
339 Wood St
Hopkinton MA 01748

Call Sign: KA1MOZ
Thomas C Keefe Jr
Hopkinton MA 01748

Call Sign: N1WLN
Jay M Broderick
Hopkinton MA 01748

Call Sign: KB1QEB
Zhuo Yang
Hopkinton MA 01748

Call Sign: KB1QGR
Digital ARC
Hopkinton MA 01748

Call Sign: W1DSR
Digital ARC
Hopkinton MA 01748

FCC Amateur Radio Licenses in Housatonic

Call Sign: KB1HSA
Alan J Soto
4 Linda Ln
Housatonic MA 01236

Call Sign: KB1GZR
Maggie Fuller
32 Pixley Hill Rd
Housatonic MA 01236

Call Sign: KB1BXG
Dennis C Johnson
Housatonic MA 01236

Call Sign: KB1MWN
Charles A Burger
Housatonic MA 01236

FCC Amateur Radio Licenses in Hubbardson

Call Sign: KA1PNP
Matthew D Aubuchon
101 Williamsville Rd
Hubbardson MA
01440

Call Sign: KB1PZI
Peter H Laitinen
63 Gardner Rd
Hubbardston MA
01452

Call Sign: W1EYB
John D Cortelli
27 Grimes Rd
Hubbardston MA
01452

Call Sign: K1COW
David W Penttila
105 Hale Rd
Hubbardston MA
01452

Call Sign: KA1SLS
Joshua A Beauvais
20 Kruse Rd
Hubbardston MA
01452

Call Sign: N1VYK
Carl J Silkey
41 Kruse Rd
Hubbardston MA
01452

Call Sign: KB1FGU
Brendan J Silkey
41 Kruse Rd
Hubbardston MA
01452

Call Sign: N1TSL
Robert A Duris
36 Lombard Rd
Hubbardston MA
01452

Call Sign: N1AMM
Rudolf C Helenius
37 Madison Way
Hubbardston MA
014521610

Call Sign: KC1PJ
Dan J Jones
Mayo Rd
Hubbardston MA
01452

Call Sign: KA1MSY
Randy J Mizereck
102 New Templeton
Rd

Hubbardston MA
01452

Call Sign: KB1GQD
Andrew P Stachura
147 New Westminster
Rd
Hubbardston MA
01452

Call Sign: N1UZ
William D Leger
131 Old Westminster
Rd
Hubbardston MA
01452

Call Sign: KA1OOU
Martha B Holgerson
12 Ragged Hill Rd
Hubbardston MA
01452

Call Sign: N1RRU
John E Gardner
101 Ragged Hill Rd
Hubbardston MA
01452

Call Sign: KB1MAA
Norman A Hebert
149 Ragged Hill Rd
Hubbardston MA
01452

Call Sign: WX1W
Phillip D Buso
43 Williamsville Rd
Hubbardston MA
01452

Call Sign: NA1Q
Robert M Taylor
70 Williamsville Rd
Hubbardston MA
01452

Call Sign: W1CE
Robert M Taylor
70 Williamsville Rd
Hubbardston MA
01452

Call Sign: KB1HYC

Michael R Savasta
87 Williamsville Rd
Hubbardston MA
01452

Call Sign: KB1CFH
43 Hubbardston
Firefighters Radio
Club
Williamsville Rd
Hubbardston MA
01452

Call Sign: KA1LPZ
Colleen M Higgins
Hubbardston MA
01452

Call Sign: N1VXI
Dan R Slocum
Hubbardston MA
01452

FCC Amateur Radio Licenses in Hudson

Call Sign: K1DZS
Bruce J Davidson
13 Avon Dr
Hudson MA
017491124

Call Sign: N1WCD
Stephen B Hoffman
4 B Autumn Drive
Hudson MA 01749

Call Sign: KB1PZL
Andrea E Shauger
7 Birchwood Rd
Hudson MA 01749

Call Sign: KO1RGI
Andrea E Shauger
7 Birchwood Rd
Hudson MA 01749

Call Sign: KE6GLW
Timothy P Ikeda
7 Birchwood Rd
Hudson MA 01749

Call Sign: KA1OS
Timothy P Ikeda

7 Birchwood Rd
Hudson MA 01749

Call Sign: N1KBC
Cynthia C Gregoire
23 Blueberry Ln
Hudson MA 01749

Call Sign: KB1VCM
Margaret S Cahoon
7 Brigham Circle 10
Hudson MA 01749

Call Sign: W1MW
Lawrence E Ober
Brigham St
Hudson MA 01749

Call Sign: N1ZOX
David F Greenwood
34 Broad St
Hudson MA 01749

Call Sign: KA1QH
Michael J Hermann
30 Carlton St
Hudson MA 01749

Call Sign: AD1X
Anthony D J Rock
4 Causeway St
Hudson MA 01749

Call Sign: N1DKJ
Geoffrey R Mowry
25 Causeway St
Hudson MA 01749

Call Sign: KD3FM
Carole A Hetzler
30 Causeway St
Hudson MA 01749

Call Sign: N1QOK
Gary P Vaillette
7 Champlain Dr
Hudson MA 01749

Call Sign: N1GYP
Gino L Tebaldi
19 Champlain Dr
Hudson MA 01740

Call Sign: AA1BE

Elizabeth A Lord
125 Chapin Rd Apt 3c
Hudson MA 01749

Call Sign: WB1S
David H Edwards Jr
290 Chestnut St
Hudson MA
017493235

Call Sign: N1HBR
Walter S Ching
296 Chestnut St
Hudson MA
017493235

Call Sign: N1HQB
Drew B Harvey
47 Church St
Hudson MA 01749

Call Sign: N1NOM
Horace E Mulhern Jr
50 Church St
Hudson MA 01749

Call Sign: WA1SWK
Peter A Draymore
5 Claire Circle
Hudson MA
017491857

Call Sign: AB1AW
Michael J Polia
23 Cortland Dr
Hudson MA 01749

Call Sign: WB4WXT
Melissa Rathmell
47 Deer Path
Hudson MA 01749

Call Sign: KA1NDH
John L Corcoran
3 Drew Cir
Hudson MA 01749

Call Sign: WA1UDH
Stephen E Press
49 Eaton Dr
Hudson MA 01749

Call Sign: K1XG
Stephen E Press

49 Eaton Drive
Hudson MA 01749

Call Sign: KN6OT
William M Johnson
1 Elm St
Hudson MA 01749

Call Sign: N1MGJ
Gayle A Francis
10 Erie Dr
Hudson MA 01749

Call Sign: K1TXH
Elizabeth A Mc Carthy
128 Forest Ave
Hudson MA 01749

Call Sign: W1BK
Charles D Mc Carthy
128 Forest Ave
Hudson MA 01749

Call Sign: N1SPA
DERYL H Clune
140 Forest Ave
Hudson MA 01749

Call Sign: KA1MZN
James R Blais
57 Fort Meadow Dr
Hudson MA 01749

Call Sign: N1KTW
Joan E Fortmiller
72 Fort Meadow Dr
Hudson MA 01749

Call Sign: N1KTZ
Edward G Fortmiller Jr
72 Fort Meadow Dr
Hudson MA 01749

Call Sign: N1JTM
Edwin E Hastings
93 Fort Meadow Dr
Hudson MA 01749

Call Sign: W1EOW
Richard E Morin
121 Fort Meadow Dr
Hudson MA 01749

Call Sign: W1BIZ

George D Melideo
7 Four Bridges Rd
Hudson MA 01749

Call Sign: N1EWB
Edwin J Kroeker
4 Hickory Ln
Hudson MA
017492723

Call Sign: KA1CCB
Gary R Fredrickson
101 Hosmer St
Hudson MA 01749

Call Sign: KA1CLX
Scott R Bullock
8 Howard Rd
Hudson MA
017491004

Call Sign: N1RBS
Patrick J O Kane
53 Hunter Ave
Hudson MA 01749

Call Sign: WA1SON
Oscar J Bedigian Jr
40 Laurel Dr
Hudson MA 01749

Call Sign: N1RIM
Deborah A Jansky
6 Lincoln St
Hudson MA 01749

Call Sign: N1XDQ
Robert C Haynes
11 Lincoln St
Hudson MA 01749

Call Sign: KB1UGQ
Randall P Mason
425 Main St
Hudson MA 01749

Call Sign: WA1FXD
Paul R Olin
605 Main St
Hudson MA
017493036

Call Sign: N1HKY
Robert M Langdon Jr

425 Main St Unit 17b
Hudson MA 01749

Call Sign: W1GFN
Robert M Langdon Jr
425 Main St Unit 17b
Hudson MA 01749

Call Sign: KB1QYH
Jason R Henning
278 Manning St Unit
103
Hudson MA 01749

Call Sign: KB1GNA
Neil R Salamack
36 Marlboro St
Hudson MA 01749

Call Sign: AJ1I
Yankee Clipper
Contest Club
11 Michigan Dr
Hudson MA 01749

Call Sign: K1XM
Paul J Young
11 Michigan Dr
Hudson MA 01749

Call Sign: KQ1F
Charlotte L Richardson
11 Michigan Dr
Hudson MA 01749

Call Sign: NY1K
Rolf Rasp
11 Michigan Dr
Hudson MA 01749

Call Sign: W2PV
Yankee Clipper
Contest Club
11 Michigan Dr
Hudson MA 01749

Call Sign: N1GPW
William A Siler
35 Murphy Rd
Hudson MA 01749

Call Sign: WA1MFR
Robert P Allison
72 Old Bolton Rd

Hudson MA 01749

Call Sign: KB1IJO
Carl J Patterson
7 Oneida Pl
Hudson MA 01749

Call Sign: KB1MJG
Patrick J Kelley
66 Ontario Dr
Hudson MA 01749

Call Sign: KB1FNN
Michael P Neilsen
5 Otsego Dr
Hudson MA
017493127

Call Sign: W1MPN
Michael P Neilsen
5 Otsego Dr
Hudson MA
017493127

Call Sign: KB1NVK
Laura Nelson
5 Otsego Dr
Hudson MA 01749

Call Sign: WA2YTO
Lawrence L Gutter
12 Otsego Dr
Hudson MA 01749

Call Sign: KB1BMT
Casmer C Ziemlak Jr
14 Packard St
Hudson MA 01749

Call Sign: KA2VDT
Donald J Volk
40 Park St
Hudson MA 01749

Call Sign: KA2VDU
Lucia E Miller
40 Park St
Hudson MA 01749

Call Sign: N1FSS
Joseph W Provost
7 Parmenter Rd
Hudson MA 01749

Call Sign: N1GRC
Douglas M Spiller
9 Parmenter Rd
Hudson MA 01749

Call Sign: N1SUP
Yong Hee Spiller
9 Parmenter Rd
Hudson MA 01749

Call Sign: N1FTD
Roland A Belanger
51 Pine St
Hudson MA 01749

Call Sign: WA1YHE
Billy R Cronos
19 Richard Rd
Hudson MA 01749

Call Sign: N1RBN
Timothy F Mc Coy
25 Richardson Rd
Hudson MA 01749

Call Sign: N1NIE
Seumas Soltysik
59 River St
Hudson MA 01749

Call Sign: K1NOQ
Robert E Donaldson
76 River St
Hudson MA 01749

Call Sign: W1HIG
Colleen M Higgins
135 River St
Hudson MA 01749

Call Sign: WB1ABK
William F Kellicker
278 River St
Hudson MA 01749

Call Sign: N1QQP
Robert H Freedman
Rotherham Way
Hudson MA
017492869

Call Sign: N1ICS
Stephen R Moore
21 Seneca Dr

Hudson MA 01749

Call Sign: WA1RKO
Russell L Moore
21 Seneca Dr
Hudson MA 01749

Call Sign: KB1NYO
Emily Shriver
24 Seneca Drive
Hudson MA 01749

Call Sign: N1PIO
James P Saenz
8 Shawmut Ave
Hudson MA
017491410

Call Sign: KA1ZTU
John W Nugent Jr
13 Still Dr
Hudson MA 01749

Call Sign: W1JAI
John W Nugent Sr
13 Still Dr
Hudson MA 01749

Call Sign: W1CRZ
William P Sullivan
22 Still Dr
Hudson MA 01749

Call Sign: KB1TTE
Sandor Toth
104 Tower St
Hudson MA 01749

Call Sign: NB1N
Sandor Toth
104 Tower St
Hudson MA 01749

Call Sign: KB1AVE
Jose Carneiro
144 Washington St
Hudson MA 01749

Call Sign: WD8BKZ
Mark C Helton
48 Washington St 18
Hudson MA 01749

Call Sign: N1LSI

John C Cabral Jr
28 Water St
Hudson MA 01799

Call Sign: N1CYL
Richard A Sonsini
223 White Pond Rd
Hudson MA 01749

Call Sign: KB1ENQ
Russell E Roberto
107 White Pond Rd
Hudson MA 01749

Call Sign: N1ZCB
Paul A Cabral
10 Wilson St
Hudson MA
017491512

Call Sign: N1OFP
William A Murtoff
9 Worcester Rd
Hudson MA 01749

Call Sign: N1LSG
Brian E Simaneao
Hudson MA 01749

Call Sign: KB1MOU
Stephen Isacoff
Hudson MA
017490465

FCC Amateur Radio Licenses in Huggardston

Call Sign: N1XXC
Matthew J Boutin
66 Grimes Rd
Huggardston MA
01452

FCC Amateur Radio Licenses in Hull

Call Sign: KB1VBG
James P Seal
23 A St
Hull MA 02045

Call Sign: W1OLE
John F Martini

81 Atlantic Ave
Hull MA 02045

Call Sign: N1MYE
Brian J Kelly
233 Atlantic Ave
Hull MA 02045

Call Sign: K1LWI
F Wendell Boyden Jr
1 Atlantic House Ct
Apt 3
Hull MA 02045

Call Sign: K1DKP
Ruth E Campbell
19 Bay Ave E
Hull MA 02045

Call Sign: N1AVN
Robert F Hegner
109 Bay St
Hull MA 02045

Call Sign: KB1RSF
Michael Holodinski
87 Beach Ave
Hull MA 02045

Call Sign: N1CUV
Barry Hass
145 Beach Ave
Hull MA 02045

Call Sign: N1GMW
Allen Bernstein
223 Beach Ave
Hull MA 02045

Call Sign: K1HLP
Marc Cadoff
22 C St
Hull MA 020451939

Call Sign: N1FTM
Everett W Lutzy
16 Clifton Ave
Hull MA 02045

Call Sign: KB1DNV
Frank Terrazzano
78 Clifton Ave
Hull MA 02045

Call Sign: W1SAI
Morris Allen
31 E St
Hull MA 02045

Call Sign: KB1HIM
Katie Condo
19 Fair St
Hull MA 02045

Call Sign: N1STW
Norman A Britting
7 Gallops Hill Rd
Hull MA 02045

Call Sign: KA1FJN
Peter K Eldredge
155 George
Washington Blvd 314
Hull MA 02045

Call Sign: KB1WVN
Stephen J Somario
32 Guild St
Hull MA 02045

Call Sign: K1BTH
Blake T Haskell
13 Halvorsen Ave
Hull MA 020452008

Call Sign: KB1QFI
Eric G Burns
15 Halvorsen Ave
Hull MA 02045

Call Sign: K1ZNY
Thomas J Homer Sr
32 Harbor View Rd
Hull MA 02045

Call Sign: KC8PIN
John K Giffin
102 Highland Ave
Hull MA 02045

Call Sign: KB1HGF
Catherine Condo
83 Main St
Hull MA 02045

Call Sign: N1FVI
Michael J Gallagher
156 Manomet Ave

Hull MA 02045

Call Sign: KC1AZ
David J Hammond
12 Maple Lane
Hull MA 02045

Call Sign: N1JOS
Cheryl M Yasi
196 Nantasket Rd
Hull MA 02045

Call Sign: NS1C
Kenneth F Yasi
196 Nantasket Rd
Hull MA 02045

Call Sign: K1ABT
George H Fox
9 Park Ave Apt 202
Hull MA 02045

Call Sign: N1PDG
Adam W Iversen
45 Point Allerton Ave
Hull MA 02045

Call Sign: N1DKH
Kenneth G Tong
13 Q St
Hull MA 02045

Call Sign: KG4RNR
David M Johnson
12 Rivers Edge Rd
Hull MA 020453410

Call Sign: N1HWH
Justin P Mc Carthy
34 Rockland House Rd
Hull MA 02045

Call Sign: K1FWC
Martin W Liben
51 Samoset Ave
Hull MA 02045

Call Sign: N1GQN
Francisco Gonzalez
63 Samoset Ave
Hull MA 02045

Call Sign: N1PTS
Susan P Gonzalez

63 Samoset Ave
Hull MA 02045

Call Sign: AE1EA
Francisco Gonzalez
63 Samoset Ave
Hull MA 02045

Call Sign: NT1M
Arthur W Anderson
21 Spring Valley Rd
Hull MA 020453227

Call Sign: W6JMB
Jack M Baringer
5 State Park Rd #1
Hull MA 02045

Call Sign: W1DFW
Donald C Russell
46 Sunset Ave
Hull MA 02045

Call Sign: KB1KFG
John A Baksys
16 V St
Hull MA 02045

Call Sign: W1ABN
John A Baksys
16 V St
Hull MA 02045

Call Sign: NT1G
Laurits S Flem
Hull MA 020450815

Call Sign: N1WNT
Louis C Vanderstreet
22 R Newport St
Humarock MA
020470257

Call Sign: N2NDY
Dale M Minnis
Humarock MA 02047

Call Sign: KB1RLN
Brandon R Stiles
151 Bromley Rd
Huntington MA 01050

Call Sign: KG4UOF
James F Jones
Cresent St
Huntington MA 01050

Call Sign: KA1MZP
David S Norton
11 E Main St
Huntington MA
010500373

Call Sign: KB1NIF
Barbara Luchini
219 Goss Hill Rd
Huntington MA 01050

Call Sign: KB1NEI
Stephen G Luchini Ii
219 Gosshill Rd
Huntington MA 01250

Call Sign: KA1GPH
Laurie A Slowick
11 Harlo Clark Rd
Huntington MA 01050

Call Sign: K1TVX
Daniel C Damkauskas
Huntington MA 01050

Call Sign: N1KXL
W Paul Hoppe
Huntington MA 01050

Call Sign: N1NFL
Stephen G Luchini
Huntington MA 01050

Call Sign: W1MRB
Mark R Bricault
Huntington MA 01050

Call Sign: WA2EXQ
Lloyd S Montcalm
93 Arbor Way

Hyannis MA 02601

Call Sign: N1ZKQ
John N Daby
191 Bishops Ter
Hyannis MA 02601

Call Sign: KA1UZB
Charles A Harkins
20 Bodfish Pl
Hyannis MA 02601

Call Sign: N1JOA
Donald P Snyder
49 Breakwater Sh Dr
Hyannis MA 02601

Call Sign: W1SPQ
Edward H Bill Jr
219 Castlewood Cir
Hyannis MA 02601

Call Sign: WA1KCC
Kenneth J Bradbury Jr
56 Cook Cir
Hyannis MA
026014619

Call Sign: KB1ECL
Robert P G Daniels
16 George St
Hyannis MA
026011274

Call Sign: KB1ROG
Doris M Menard
69 Goat Field Lane
Hyannis MA 02601

Call Sign: W1ODM
Joseph F Pepi
27 Grove St
Hyannis MA 02601

Call Sign: KB1VAH
Gerald J Somers
55 Hampshire Ave
Hyannis MA 02601

Call Sign: WA1MJO
John Neves
149 Hinckley Rd
Hyannis MA 02601

Call Sign: KB1PCI
Benjamin J Runnels
29 Lafrance Ave
Hyannis MA 02601

Call Sign: KA1MVD
Bruce A Carver
420 Main St
Hyannis MA 02601

Call Sign: N1XXA
Thomas C Smith
70 Main St #13
Hyannis MA 02601

Call Sign: KB1ORF
Robert A Johnson Ii
597 Main St 1st Floor
Hyannis MA 02601

Call Sign: KA1MNR
Robert A Johnson Ii
597 Main St 1st Floor
Hyannis MA 02601

Call Sign: KB1TKL
Faith A Wood
500 Old Colony Rd -
317
Hyannis MA 02601

Call Sign: KA1HUO
Mark W Small
117 Old Town Rd
Hyannis MA 02601

Call Sign: KB1HAM
Karl R Hemr
19 Owen St
Hyannis MA 02601

Call Sign: KB1PXB
Cape Cod Hospital
27 Park St
Hyannis MA 02601

Call Sign: W1CCH
Cape Cod Hospital
27 Park St
Hyannis MA 02601

Call Sign: KB1TAW
Jonathan K O'neil
127 Pine Ave

Hyannis MA 02601

Call Sign: KB1SFF
Taylor C White
98 Pine St
Hyannis MA 02601

Call Sign: WA1CVO
Frederic A White
98 Pine St
Hyannis MA 02601

Call Sign: KA1FAQ
Kevin J A Perry
721 Pitchers Way
Hyannis MA
026012578

Call Sign: N1XTO
Skip Egan
12 Priscilla Way
Hyannis MA 02601

Call Sign: W1YAN
Sally A Norris
57 Snows Creek Dr
Hyannis MA 02601

Call Sign: N1GIK
Geraldine H Trudeau
160 Spring St
Hyannis MA 02601

Call Sign: NU1X
George H Trudeau
160 Spring St
Hyannis MA 02601

Call Sign: KB1TJT
Ralph W Hansen
157 Straightway
Hyannis MA 02601

Call Sign: N1FJO
Larry L Mc Atee
189 Sudbury Ln
Hyannis MA 02601

Call Sign: KD1SI
George Laurinaitis
253 Sudbury Ln
Hyannis MA 02601

Call Sign: KB1EXZ

Darryl W Breffe
6 Sunny Knoll Dr
Hyannis MA 02601

Call Sign: KB1QQS
Vicki Breffe
6 Sunny Knoll Drive
Hyannis MA 02601

Call Sign: N1SYE
Jeffrey L Pimentat
93 Uncle Willies Way
Hyannis MA 02601

Call Sign: K1ZSR
Rose I Capelle
148 West Main St Apt
D 206
Hyannis MA
026485814

Call Sign: KC1AP
Charles E Goode
Hyannis MA
026010685

Call Sign: W1KBV
Earle R Drake
Hyannis MA 02601

FCC Amateur Radio Licenses in Hyannis Port

Call Sign: KB1TAL
Linda L Doll
Hyannis Port MA
02647

Call Sign: KB1TAY
Neil S Tanger
Hyannis Port MA
02647

FCC Amateur Radio Licenses in Hyde Park

Call Sign: N1EHU
Bobbie Raines
74 Blake St
Hyde Park MA 02136

Call Sign: KB1BCH

Zenen Ramos Jr
47 Charles St
Hyde Park MA 02136

Call Sign: N1BWM
Joseph T Rogers
141 Child St
Hyde Park MA 02136

Call Sign: N1OBI
Catherine A Keller
109 Clare Ave
Hyde Park MA 02136

Call Sign: WB9MUP
Kevin W Keller
109 Clare Ave
Hyde Park MA 02136

Call Sign: N1XNE
Ricot Cadet
132 Crownpoint Dr
Hyde Park MA 02136

Call Sign: W1DAV
David M Mcclelland
180 Dana Ave
Hyde Park MA 02136

Call Sign: W1MRM
David Bloom
21 Dodge Rd
Hyde Park MA 02136

Call Sign: KB1WBL
Bronislav Batkilin
172 Fairmount Ave
Hyde Park MA 02136

Call Sign: N1UQF
Carleton W Jones
225 Fairmount Ave
Hyde Park MA
021363507

Call Sign: W1ASI
Joseph A Mullen
84 Farrar Ave
Hyde Park MA 02136

Call Sign: WB1FIV
Thomas J Mc Bride
10 Forestvale Rd
Hyde Park MA 02136

Call Sign: KB1DBX
Charles E Suprin
19 Maida Terr
Hyde Park MA
021363723

Call Sign: KA1UNI
Paul D Amara
29 New Bedford St
Hyde Park MA 02136

Call Sign: KA1ZOV
Ralph N Dean
25 Norway Pk
Hyde Park MA 02136

Call Sign: KA1DHN
Stephen M Collier
7 Pond St Apt 1
Hyde Park MA 02136

Call Sign: N1NSQ
James M Joseph
11 Readville St
Hyde Park MA 02136

Call Sign: KA1SGU
Steven E Hillson
21 Riley Rd Apt 5
Hyde Park MA
021362444

Call Sign: KB1GLI
Richard N Gunn
1016 River St
Hyde Park MA 02136

Call Sign: K1OCN
Nello A Bambini
38 Tyler St
Hyde Park MA 02136

Call Sign: W1DWF
Joseph A Mulligan Sr
124 Warren Ave
Hyde Park MA 02136

FCC Amateur Radio Licenses in Indian Orchard

Call Sign: KB1NTQ
Warren W Hudson

1050 Berkshire Ave
Indian Orchard MA
01151

Call Sign: W1KPQ
Irving L Mallett
68 Brittany Rd
Indian Orchard MA
01151

Call Sign: KB1UPZ
Robert W Cowdrey
29 Daniel St
Indian Orchard MA
01151

Call Sign: WA1OIR
William M Hampton Jr
93 Grochmal Ave Lot
95
Indian Orchard MA
01151

Call Sign: N1XDS
Lilianne Narreau
3 Hampden St 3
Indian Orchard MA
01151

Call Sign: W1TTL
Edward H Foster
156 Hampshire St
Indian Orchard MA
011511506

Call Sign: N1PAV
Jayson P Nunes
86 Holly St
Indian Orchard MA
01151

Call Sign: N1TER
Ken P Nunes
86 Holly St
Indian Orchard MA
01151

Call Sign: W1MGY
Inc Titanic Historical
Society
208 Main St
Indian Orchard MA
011510053

Call Sign: N1XOG
Cassandra D Manley
241 Main St
Indian Orchard MA
01151

Call Sign: KA1BQU
Barbara L Ladue
56 Midway St
Indian Orchard MA
011511325

Call Sign: WA1VCQ
William G Boilard
495 Oak St
Indian Orchard MA
01151

Call Sign: KB1DFL
Stephen A Chmura
264 Parker St
Indian Orchard MA
01151

Call Sign: KB1LTC
John J Lenville Jr
98 Pinevale St
Indian Orchard MA
011511500

Call Sign: KI1A
John J Lenville Jr
98 Pinevale St
Indian Orchard MA
011511500

Call Sign: N1SFF
Gregory J Fontaine
37 Steuben St
Indian Orchard MA
01151

Call Sign: KB1TRQ
Jeffrey R Rostron
45 Wing St
Indian Orchard MA
01151

Call Sign: W1JRR
Jeffrey R Rostron
45 Wing St
Indian Orchard MA
01151

Call Sign: KB1VTB
Daniel C Morris
16 Appleton Pk Unit
C2
Ipswich MA 01938

Call Sign: K1DCM
Daniel C Morris
16 Appleton Pk Unit
C2
Ipswich MA 01938

Call Sign: K1GCV
Andrew D Clapp
161 Argilla Rd
Ipswich MA 01938

Call Sign: N3WIG
Mike Brophey
28 Birch Lane
Ipswich MA 01938

Call Sign: KB1KHP
Mike Brophey
28 Birch Lane
Ipswich MA 01938

Call Sign: WA1DRY
Charles H Wilson
17 Birch Ln
Ipswich MA 01938

Call Sign: N1RQE
Pierre J Doucet
22 Brownville Ave
Ipswich MA 01938

Call Sign: KA1RKC
Walter J Petrowicz
44 Brownville Ave
Ipswich MA 01938

Call Sign: N1EDI
J Royce Brown
55 Clark Rd
Ipswich MA 01938

Call Sign: KB1OSP
Robert W Mulloy
400 Colonial Dr 36
Ipswich MA 01938

Call Sign: KB1CMP
Ralph E Milroy
27 Edge St
Ipswich MA 01938

Call Sign: KB1KHO
Town Of Ipswich
Public Safety
Emergency
Management
15 Elm St
Ipswich MA 01938

Call Sign: KB1KIC
Town Of Ipswich
Public Safety
Emergency
Management
15 Elm St
Ipswich MA 01938

Call Sign: W1IEM
Town Of Ipswich
Public Safety
Emergency
Management
15 Elm St
Ipswich MA 01938

Call Sign: KB1DB
Jeffrey D Ingalls
25 Heard Dr
Ipswich MA 01938

Call Sign: W1PMG
Peter Fowler
2 Herring Way
Ipswich MA 01938

Call Sign: KB1MUY
Steven R Hatch
23 High St
Ipswich MA 01938

Call Sign: KE1II
Andrew Eppler
28 Hodgkins Dr
Ipswich MA
019381631

Call Sign: K1TWK
Kenneth W Nokes
10 Island Park Rd

Ipswich MA 01938

Call Sign: N1DFH
Juanita M Simons
101 Jeffrey Neck Rd
Ipswich MA
019381413

Call Sign: KB1DAH
Geoffrey L Whalen
65 Jeffreys Neck Rd
Ipswich MA 01939

Call Sign: K1VTH
Peter R Hull
22 Kings Way
Ipswich MA 01938

Call Sign: KB1JWO
Richard E Slavin
82 Linebrook Rd
Ipswich MA 01938

Call Sign: K1OWM
James Mc Cormack
155 Linebrook Rd
Ipswich MA
019382914

Call Sign: KB1WGC
Matthew D Allred
200 Linebrook Rd
Ipswich MA 01938

Call Sign: W1WNK
David W Savage
291 Linebrook Rd
Ipswich MA 01938

Call Sign: W1OCY
Everett E Chapman
352 Linebrook Rd
Ipswich MA
019381056

Call Sign: KA1ICC
Thomas J Blakely
Linebrook Rd
Ipswich MA 01938

Call Sign: N1KYG
John T Glencross Sr
98 Little Neck Rd
Ipswich MA 01938

Call Sign: N1LUA
Ena A Griswold-
Glencross
98 Little Neck Rd
Ipswich MA 01938

Call Sign: N1LUA
John T Glencross Sr
98 Little Neck Rd
Ipswich MA 01938

Call Sign: N1ITX
John R Beirne
108 Little Neck Rd
Ipswich MA 01938

Call Sign: KA1YMM
Joseph M Pecoraro
5 Mulholland Dr
Ipswich MA 01938

Call Sign: KN1B
John R Fleming Jr
23 Mulholland Dr
Ipswich MA 01938

Call Sign: N1PSF
Dirk Van Ligtenberg
55 N Ridge Rd
Ipswich MA 01938

Call Sign: W1DVL
Dirk Van Ligtenberg
55 N Ridge Rd
Ipswich MA 01938

Call Sign: K1NLQ
Angelo M Johnson
81 N Ridge Rd
Ipswich MA
019381456

Call Sign: KA1OTB
Mildred E Johnson
81 N Ridge Rd
Ipswich MA 01938

Call Sign: W1PYT
Leon S Dorr
36 New March
Ipswich MA 01938

Call Sign: W7DRB

James A Strunk
10 New Mill Pl
Ipswich MA 01938

Call Sign: N1BYK
Walter E Koster
53 Newmarch St
Ipswich MA 01938

Call Sign: WB1EOP
Edward C Jones
31 Northgate Rd
Ipswich MA 01938

Call Sign: N1CDC
Edward P Murphy Sr
4 Paradise Rd
Ipswich MA 01938

Call Sign: W1EPM
Edward P Murphy Sr
4 Paradise Rd
Ipswich MA 01938

Call Sign: W1YLW
William G Mavroides
9 Poplar
Ipswich MA 01938

Call Sign: KA1GKY
Charles H Cooper
4 Poplar St
Ipswich MA 01938

Call Sign: K1YZW
Walter Schreuer
4 Riverbank Ln
Ipswich MA 01938

Call Sign: NX1J
Kirk B Jackman
3 Riverside Dr
Ipswich MA 01938

Call Sign: W1SFK
Richard G Edmonds
7 Sunset Dr
Ipswich MA 01938

Call Sign: KB1MVM
Jonathan M Hubbard
99 Topsfield Rd
Ipswich MA 01938

Call Sign: W1HUB
Jonathan M Hubbard
99 Topsfield Rd
Ipswich MA 01938

Call Sign: KA1OTC
Virginia M Lyman
55 Turkeyshore Rd
Ipswich MA 01938

Call Sign: WA1WMS
Willis G Lyman Jr
55 Turkeyshore Rd
Ipswich MA
019382333

FCC Amateur Radio Licenses in Islington

Call Sign: NF0AZ
Joseph V Foppiano
484 Canton St
Islington MA 02090

FCC Amateur Radio Licenses in Jamaica Plain

Call Sign: W0JF
Yardley Beers
44 Allandale St 139
Jamaica Plain MA
02130

Call Sign: KB1WTY
Vadim Pokotilov
231 Amory St
Jamaica Plain MA
02130

Call Sign: KA1EXR
Walter K Eastman
19 Bournedale Rd
Jamaica Plain MA
02130

Call Sign: N1LBW
Joseph F Wright
21 Boynton St
Jamaica Plain MA
02130

Call Sign: KB1RBP
Linda M Blair

545 Center St 316
Jamaica Plain MA
02130

Call Sign: NA1I
Linda M Blair
545 Centre St 316
Jamaica Plain MA
02130

Call Sign: KD5ESS
Joshua K Bratton
122 Day St
Jamaica Plain MA
02130

Call Sign: AB1KM
Hugh L Medal
86 Forest Hill St Apt 1
Jamaica Plain MA
02130

Call Sign: N1QPX
Nikolai Krusenstiern
40 Halifax 2
Jamaica Plain MA
02130

Call Sign: N1EPX
Byron Sharbetian Jr
14 Hampstead Rd
Jamaica Plain MA
02130

Call Sign: N1IDL
Shirley A Sharbetian
14 Hampstead Rd
Jamaica Plain MA
02130

Call Sign: KB1IZK
David A Jones
25 Hillcroft Rd
Jamaica Plain MA
02130

Call Sign: KB1WWB
Mondakini B Walsh
31 Hopkins Rd
Jamaica Plain MA
02130

Call Sign: K6AUS
Scott A Robson

21 John A Andrew St
#1
Jamaica Plain MA
02130

Call Sign: KB1WEW
Ryan J Conway
14 Lakeville Rd 12a
Jamaica Plain MA
02130

Call Sign: N1CJH
James Ryan
264 Lamartine St
Jamaica Plain MA
021302214

Call Sign: N1NIF
Tamas Szabo
51 Parkton Rd
Jamaica Plain MA
02130

Call Sign: KA1AO
John G Spritzler
35 Parley Ave
Jamaica Plain MA
02130

Call Sign: KE0MY
Richard E Brown
95 Paul Gore St
Jamaica Plain MA
02130

Call Sign: WA3TTI
Craig A James
42 Paul Gore St
Jamaica Plain MA
02130

Call Sign: N1ZFY
Christine E Barnhart
15 Paul Gore St #1
Jamaica Plain MA
02130

Call Sign: KB1WLL
Ronald F Dantowitz
464 Pond St
Jamamica Plain MA
02130

Call Sign: N1YAI

Michael W Abruzzese
284 Pond St
Jamaica Plain MA
021302443

Call Sign: N1FRH
Nahum W Morse
150 S Huntington Ave
Jamaica Plain MA
02130

Call Sign: N1VCH
Jessie Zoldak
36 S St
Jamaica Plain MA
02130

Call Sign: KB8IIR
Katie A Kowall
69 Sedgwick St 3
Jamaica Plain MA
02134

Call Sign: K1PAV
Elliot M Belin
11 Segel St
Jamaica Plain MA
021304419

Call Sign: N1RFA
James E Jones Jr
293 Wachusett St
Jamaica Plain MA
021304276

Call Sign: KB1WAJ
Sally J Gorrill
1 Warren Square
Jamaica Plain MA
02130

Call Sign: KA1WJZ
Gregory S Rakauskas
97 Williams St 2
Jamaica Plain MA
02130

Call Sign: KE7EHE
Richard G Salvin
11 Wyman St 3b
Jamaica Plain MA
02130

Call Sign: KA4IFL

Jorge G Arroyo Jr
8 Zamora St
Jamaica Plain MA
02130

FCC Amateur Radio Licenses in Jefferson

Call Sign: KC8WMX
Norbert T Maly
31 Diamond Hill Rd
Jefferson MA 01522

Call Sign: ND1D
Doug Maly
31 Diamond Hill Rd
Jefferson MA 01522

Call Sign: KE1GY
Lee A Horton
72 Heather Cir
Jefferson MA 01522

Call Sign: N1GOC
Marjorie A Sullivan
79 Heather Cir
Jefferson MA 01522

Call Sign: KB1ETI
Kevin P Taylor
83 Heather Cir
Jefferson MA 01552

Call Sign: N1KXZ
Michael R Freeman
201 High St
Jefferson MA 01522

Call Sign: WE1L
Erick Andrews
189 Jackson St
Jefferson MA 01522

Call Sign: KB1JMB
Carl H Raatikainen
1775 Main St
Jefferson MA 01522

Call Sign: KA1GWL
Stephen J Bigelow
Manning St
Jefferson MA 01522

Call Sign: KB1PSA

Paul J Trimby
60 North St
Jefferson MA 01522

Call Sign: KB1PZX
Jeffrey L Summit
8 Quaker Rd
Jefferson MA 01522

Call Sign: K1WNQ
Joseph R Welsh Jr
1268 Wachusett St
Jefferson MA 01522

Call Sign: N1XYZ
Gwen E Ackley
1410 Wachusett St
Jefferson MA 01522

Call Sign: KB1PSD
Christopher B Lyons
8 Windsor Court
Jefferson MA 01522

Call Sign: KB1IYY
Wayne F Rocheleau
20 Wood St
Jefferson MA 01522

Call Sign: KA1WNX
Daniel Lorusso
Jefferson MA 01522

Call Sign: N1WXC
Dianne D Carpenter
Jefferson MA 01522

**FCC Amateur Radio
Licenses in Kingston**

Call Sign: KD1PS
Ralph A Sodersjerna
36 Bay Hill Rd
Kingston MA
023643036

Call Sign: KB1UKR
Scott J Nevins
16 Bayview Ave
Kingston MA 02364

Call Sign: WA1RZT
Francesca O Regan Sr
363 Bishops Hwy

Kingston MA
023642035

Call Sign: KW1H
Peter J Giberti
6 Blue Jay Way
Kingston MA 02364

Call Sign: WB1EVP
David L Newman
7 Chestnut St
Kingston MA 02364

Call Sign: KB1JSD
Eric J Haas
10 Clifton Drive
Kingston MA 02364

Call Sign: KA1YRB
Barbara C Odell
11 Foster Ln
Kingston MA 02364

Call Sign: N1SJA
David E Clinton
13 Foxtail Dr
Kingston MA
023641807

Call Sign: N1DAZ
Robert J Gomersall
129 Grove St
Kingston MA 02364

Call Sign: WA1DIB
Linda D Gomersall
129 Grove St
Kingston MA 02364

Call Sign: AA1DC
Sergio M Camargo
8 Grove St Extension
Kingston MA 02364

Call Sign: KB1JSE
Donald R Howard
14 High Pines Dr
Kingston MA 02364

Call Sign: WA1PJI
Charles A Sanborn
55 Lake St
Kingston MA 02364

Call Sign: K1WPC
James J Farrell Sr
101 Lake St
Kingston MA 02364

Call Sign: N1EKT
James J Farrell Jr
101 Lake St P O Box 2
Kingston MA 02364

Call Sign: N1NXA
Mando A Aldrovandi
11 Loring Ave
Kingston MA 02364

Call Sign: N1OEC
Sheri R Caron
12 Main St
Kingston MA 02364

Call Sign: WW1US
Guy H Chandler
26 Main St #9
Kingston MA 02364

Call Sign: KB1MP
Guy H Chandler
26 Main St 9
Kingston MA 02364

Call Sign: KA1YQZ
Alton Borghesani
39 Mayflower St
Kingston MA 02364

Call Sign: N1SUY
George N Johnston
4 Milliken Dr
Kingston MA 02364

Call Sign: KA1RTF
David L Abbruzzese
10 Paradise Ln
Kingston MA 02364

Call Sign: KA1RYR
Andrea M Abbruzzese
10 Paradise Ln
Kingston MA 02364

Call Sign: KA1SDJ
Robert A Mulliken
31 River St
Kingston MA 02364

Call Sign: W1HTX
Manas Manasian
19 Rosewood Dr
Kingston MA
023642152

Call Sign: WA1RWK
Sr Ida Mary Lutz
Route 80
Kingston MA 02364

Call Sign: W1LJH
Stanley E Rogers
16 Second Brook St
Kingston MA
023642118

Call Sign: N1DTX
Ralph L O Leary
4 Sherwood Ln Apt
417
Kingston MA 02364

Call Sign: N1DXI
Peter P Krzyzewski
43 Smith Ln
Kingston MA
023642225

Call Sign: N1KXA
Roy D Frazee
15 Spruce St
Kingston MA 02364

Call Sign: KD1UN
Roger C Mitchell
4 St Francis Ave
Kingston MA 02364

Call Sign: N1DCP
Ruth V Mitchell
4 St Francis Ave
Kingston MA 02364

Call Sign: N9HUU
Julia Y Mitchell
4 St Francis Ave
Kingston MA 02364

Call Sign: N1MOY
Robert V Tohosky
6 Stonewall Ter

Kingston MA
023641045

Call Sign: KA1YRC
Roger J La Greca
150 Summer St
Kingston MA 02364

Call Sign: KA1QXN
George S Buhl Jr
5 Sunset Rd
Kingston MA 02364

Call Sign: KB1WNY
Victor J Silenzi Jr
7 Sycamore Dr
Kingston MA 02364

Call Sign: KE1KQ
Lester E Swanson
10 Torrey Ln
Kingston MA 02364

Call Sign: WB1FLA
Thomas E Bolus
33 West St
Kingston MA 02364

Call Sign: KB1HKD
Janis L Bolus
33 West St
Kingston MA 02364

Call Sign: KB1IKG
Richard C Seibert
101 Wolf Pond Rd
Kingston MA
023642144

Call Sign: KN1IRP
David R Buhl
Kingston MA 02364

Call Sign: N3YIP
Deborah A Smith
Kingston MA 02364

**FCC Amateur Radio
Licenses in Lakeville**

Call Sign: KB1TDU
Martin A Turco
14 Bedford St
Lakeville MA 02347

Call Sign: KB1TDW
Jennifer M Burke
14 Bedford St
Lakeville MA 02347

Call Sign: W1SXU
Harry A Pierce Sr
139 Bedford St
Lakeville MA
023471353

Call Sign: AF1H
Joseph P Bessette
430 Bedford St
Lakeville MA 02347

Call Sign: WA1BGQ
Evelyn T Mc Manus
687 Beechwood Ave
Lakeville MA 02347

Call Sign: K1MCY
George H Sutcliffe
4 Blueberry Dr Apt 5
Lakeville MA 02347

Call Sign: KB1OET
John M Bell
1 Central Ave
Lakeville MA 02347

Call Sign: KB1WXA
Gerald A Sferruzza Jr
9 Cherry St
Lakeville MA 02347

Call Sign: NN1D
Donald V Tanguay
8 Cicero Dr Apt 2
Lakeville MA 02347

Call Sign: KB1IDJ
Ara Uss Joseph P
Kennedy Jr Dd-850
8 Cicero Dr Apt 2
Lakeville MA 02347

Call Sign: KB1HUK
Amateur Radio
Association Seehund
U-5075
153 County St - 1193
Lakeville MA 02347

Call Sign: WA1YPT
Joanne E Mullen
21 Forest Park Dr
Lakeville MA 02347

Call Sign: W1DW
John L Mullen
21 Forest Pk Dr
Lakeville MA 02347

Call Sign: K1SKQ
Francis W Mc Dermott
Huckleberry Shores
Lakeville MA 02346

Call Sign: KB1EAH
Paul J Tanguay
18 Keith Ave
Lakeville MA 02347

Call Sign: N1ZHZ
William W Hunt
6 King Philip Rd
Lakeville MA 02347

Call Sign: KB1WCK
Joseph A Messaline Jr
21 Lakeside Ave
Lakeville MA 02347

Call Sign: KA1ZGR
Myer S Bornstein
5 Lang St
Lakeville MA 02347

Call Sign: KB1WIX
David M Singer
57 Long Point Rd
Lakeville MA 02347

Call Sign: N1PPY
David M Singer
57 Long Point Rd
Lakeville MA 02347

Call Sign: KA1ALO
Edward L Higginson
179 Main St
Lakeville MA 02346

Call Sign: KA1WVJ
Steven Souza Jr
44 Malbone St

Lakeville MA 02347

Call Sign: KA1WVK
Thelma R Souza
44 Malbone St
Lakeville MA 02347

Call Sign: WZ1U
Steven Souza
44 Malbone St
Lakeville MA 02347

Call Sign: KB1GKH
Glen Bredberg
12 Margeaux Dr
Lakeville MA 02347

Call Sign: N1NVO
Nelson E Woodward
1 Merigold Ln
Lakeville MA
023472312

Call Sign: KB1SRZ
Alex Luch
8 Old Stonewall Rd
Lakeville MA 02347

Call Sign: K1FSK
Charles J Hainley
5 Paddock Hill Dr
Lakeville MA
023471233

Call Sign: N1FLT
Christopher Harrison
1 Pierce Ave
Lakeville MA 02347

Call Sign: WA1BNF
Phillips C Baird
11 Southworth St
Lakeville MA 02347

Call Sign: WA1PFC
John A Bosse
73 Taunton St
Lakeville MA
023471209

Call Sign: N1GYA
Harold Wood Jr
4 Tinkham Lane

Lakeville MA
023472216

Call Sign: WB1ANX
Paul Laliberte
3 Tinkham Ln
Lakeville MA 02347

Call Sign: K1DUT
Ray O Delano Jr
1 Vaughn St
Lakeville MA 02347

Call Sign: W1DL
Peter Secakusuma
9 Wagon Trail
Lakeville MA 02347

Call Sign: KB1WHG
Peter M Maguire
2 Woodview Dr
Lakeville MA 02347

Call Sign: KB1GMA
Uss Submarine
Lionfish Radio Club
Lakeville MA 02347

Call Sign: KB1GQI
Marconi Cape Cod
Memorial Radio Club
Lakeville MA 02347

Call Sign: KB1WKQ
Timothy D Fletcher
Lakeville MA 02347

**FCC Amateur Radio
Licenses in Lancaster**

Call Sign: N1PST
David L Harvie
74 Brockelman Rd
Lancaster MA 01523

Call Sign: N1PHD
Mark T Harvie
114 Brockelman Rd
Lancaster MA 01523

Call Sign: KA1SOL
Albert D Carnali
210 Bull Hill Rd
Lancaster MA 01523

Call Sign: K1KNH
James G Richards
9 Burbank Ln
Lancaster MA 01523

Call Sign: KB1REX
Pierre E Omeler
172 Center Bridge Rd
Lancaster MA 01523

Call Sign: N1NKL
David B Shumway
431 Centerbridge Rd
Lancaster MA 01523

Call Sign: N1ZUZ
Efrain Gonzalez
37 Chace Hill Rd
Lancaster MA 01523

Call Sign: KB1GYM
Ana E Gonzalez
37 Chace Hill Rd
Lancaster MA
015231862

Call Sign: WA1JXR
Louis G Algieri
22 Chacehill Rd
Lancaster MA 01523

Call Sign: KB1KKS
Michael P Algieri
22 Chase Hill Rd
Lancaster MA 01523

Call Sign: KN1F
Robyn L Prentiss
140 Deershorn Rd
Lancaster MA 01523

Call Sign: N1OLZ
Thomas P Markham Jr
34 Donelle Way
Lancaster MA 01523

Call Sign: KB1RUX
John M Lewis
19 Evelyn Pl
Lancaster MA 01523

Call Sign: KA1JLR
Philip J Eugene

565 Langen Rd
Lancaster MA 01523

Call Sign: KB1IVY
Neal J Marigliano
15 Lawson Ave
Lancaster MA 01523

Call Sign: N1VFV
Karen A Cardamone
8 Magnolia Ave
Lancaster MA 01523

Call Sign: WA1MDD
John W Spencer
674 Main St
Lancaster MA
015230184

Call Sign: KA1QWF
Masanao Shinmura
922 Main St
Lancaster MA 01523

Call Sign: KA1QWG
Maki Shinmura
922 Main St
Lancaster MA 01523

Call Sign: KA1OJT
Jonathan Goulding
780 Main St #2
Lancaster MA 01523

Call Sign: KD4ZQD
Allan C Broskowitz
780 Main St Apt 2
Lancaster MA 01523

Call Sign: W1ERJ
Jerome L Hartke
240 Mary Catherine Dr
Lancaster MA 01523

Call Sign: W9MO
Robert J Hamel
136 Mill St
Lancaster MA 01523

Call Sign: KB5MHK
Michael J Schexnaydre
437 Mill St Ext
Lancaster MA 01523

Call Sign: N1LSB
Roy D Fulton
2201 N Main St
Lancaster MA 01523

Call Sign: W1GUI
Ellis G Holden
2500 N Main St
Lancaster MA 01523

Call Sign: K1EEO
Richard A Guenther
24 Neck Rd
Lancaster MA 01523

Call Sign: KB1ID
Evan H Suits
469 Neck Rd
Lancaster MA
015232275

Call Sign: KB1OKF
David M Anderson
387 Nicholas Dr
Lancaster MA 01523

Call Sign: KB1GHG
Gary H Evans
223 Old Common Rd
Lancaster MA 01523

Call Sign: KB1MSG
Susan E Smiley
183 Packard St
Lancaster MA 01523

Call Sign: KB1GUY
Roger A Fleming
181 Parker Rd
Lancaster MA
015231912

Call Sign: KB1JHS
Edward B Rixford
171 Shirley Rd
Lancaster MA 01523

Call Sign: K1PTF
James T Francis
121 Sterling Rd
Lancaster MA 01523

Call Sign: KB1GBB
Lester H Mclean

47 Sterling St
Lancaster MA 01523

Call Sign: N1NUU
Timothy A Minko
Lancaster MA 01523

| FCC Amateur Radio
Licenses in
Lanesboro |

Call Sign: KB1VUD
Matthew R Montini
40 Baker St
Lanesboro MA 01237

Call Sign: WA1RZO
Robert E Flood
347 Baker St
Lanesboro MA 01237

Call Sign: N1JJK
Edward C Piacenti
8 Irwin St
Lanesboro MA 01237

Call Sign: N1VPD
Michael J Weber
6 Monica Dr
Lanesboro MA 01237

Call Sign: WA1SFU
Jerry W Christopher
57 Old State Rd
Lanesboro MA 01237

Call Sign: W1JWC
Jerry W Christopher
57 Old State Rd
Lanesboro MA 01237

Call Sign: NI1K
Harry D Evans Iii
93 Prospect St
Lanesboro MA 01237

Call Sign: WA1KVL
Chester J Laston
514 S Main St
Lanesboro MA 01237

Call Sign: AA1ZW
Luciano G Guadagno
514 South Main St D2

Lanesboro MA 01237

Call Sign: K1UTV
Cornelius R Wells
14 Victoria Ln
Lanesboro MA
012379606

Call Sign: KB1AHG
Gavin J Chapman
47 Victoria Ln
Lanesboro MA 01237

Call Sign: W1GG
Gareth B Gaudette
21 Westview Rd
Lanesborough MA
01237

Call Sign: KA1MUK
Harry D Evans Iv
Lanesboro MA 01237

Call Sign: KB1FPV
Christina A Cruz
Lanesboro MA 01237

| FCC Amateur Radio
Licenses in Lawrence |

Call Sign: K1DI
Ernest A Robillon
97 Ames St
Lawrence MA 01841

Call Sign: N1GIZ
Louis H Mc Aloon
535 Andover St
Lawrence MA 01843

Call Sign: WA1YAU
George P Young
10 Andover Ter
Lawrence MA 01843

Call Sign: N1KDX
Jeffrey S Patterson
161 Arlington St
Lawrence MA 01841

Call Sign: KA1TEM
Esteban Bruno
4 Basswood St
Lawrence MA 01841

Call Sign: KA1HDM
William A Marciello
137 Beacon St
Lawrence MA 01843

Call Sign: KB1KMG
Juan M Gonzalez
5 Bennington St
Lawrence MA 01841

Call Sign: NO1X
Alfred G Rouff
9 Carleton St
Lawrence MA 01843

Call Sign: N1CXP
Mary B Smeesters
64 Columbus Ave
Lawrence MA 01841

Call Sign: KB1WDB
Richard L Russell
34 Cross St
Lawrence MA 01841

Call Sign: N1RLR
Richard L Russell
34 Cross St
Lawrence MA 01841

Call Sign: WA1WLV
Joseph P Demers
61 Eaton St 2nd Flr
Lawrence MA 01843

Call Sign: N1KMD
Ralph A Lebron
8 Forest St
Lawrence MA 01841

Call Sign: KB1BLZ
Julio C Rodriguez
107 Greenwood St
Lawrence MA 01841

Call Sign: K1ICE
James F Gentile
4 Hale St
Lawrence MA 01842

Call Sign: KB1KMH
Danilo A Gonzalez
87 Haverhill St

Lawrence MA 01841

Call Sign: KA1WXQ
Luis A Nieves
436 Haverhill St
Lawrence MA 01841

Call Sign: KA1CQI
Ernest C Maroun
189 High St
Lawrence MA 01841

Call Sign: WA1WJW
Paul W Kiesling Iii
7 Hillside Ave
Lawrence MA 01841

Call Sign: W1ILD
Manuel A Vargas
4 Katherine St
Lawrence MA 01841

Call Sign: KB1BCS
Shirley H Vargas
4 Kathrine St
Lawrence MA 01841

Call Sign: N1KJN
Daniel R Rajczyk
20 Knox St Apt 14
Lawrence MA 01841

Call Sign: KB1KMK
Jhohanne A Cabrera
16 Linden St
Lawrence MA 01841

Call Sign: N1ORC
Arthur Z Rowe
30 Linden St
Lawrence MA
018414545

Call Sign: W1SSZ
John L Gilbo
193 Maple St Apt 5f
Lawrence MA
018413711

Call Sign: KB1MVH
John S Miller
4 Marc Lane
Lawrence MA 01843

Call Sign: WB1CHU
Vernon T Mitchell Jr
40 Market St
Lawrence MA 01843

Call Sign: KB1KML
Oscar Del Toro
41 Mechanic St
Lawrence MA 01841

Call Sign: KB1WKD
Alfredo Rolon
36 Milton St 3
Lawrence MA 01841

Call Sign: KA1ZYS
Angel Colon
24 Montgomery St 3rd
Lawrence MA 01841

Call Sign: W1GOW
John A Peterson
133 Mt Vernon St
Lawrence MA 01843

Call Sign: KB1UWN
Jean J Najm
72 Nesmith St
Lawrence MA 01841

Call Sign: KB1PID
Christopher A
Donovan
180 Olive Ave
Lawrence MA
018414420

Call Sign: N1HPT
Rafael J Fuchu
6 Osgood St
Lawrence MA 01843

Call Sign: KB1SFH
Delfin Alicea
147 Oxford St
Lawrence MA 01840

Call Sign: WP4IZU
Aurelio Burgos
152 Oxford St
Lawrence MA 01841

Call Sign: KB1KDS
Antonio A Ramos

18 Park St
Lawrence MA 01841

Call Sign: KB1EVI
James P Dudley
172 Parker St Fl-3
Lawrence MA
018431525

Call Sign: KB1ALS
Manuel L Troncoso
17 Platt St 2nd Floor
Lawrence MA 01841

Call Sign: K1ZVM
James A La Torre Jr
29 Ridge Rd
Lawrence MA 01841

Call Sign: KA1VNI
James M Conlon
9 Roberta Ln
Lawrence MA 01843

Call Sign: KB1JMA
Joseph A Peralta
32 Rollins St
Lawrence MA 01841

Call Sign: KA1MGN
George Conrad
151 Salem St
Lawrence MA
018431517

Call Sign: N1UDF
Lawrence R Lambert
398 Salem St
Lawrence MA 01843

Call Sign: KB1BRY
Daisy Troncoso
14 Sargent St
Lawrence MA 01841

Call Sign: W1BEY
Kermit H Spitz
41 Sargent St
Lawrence MA 01841

Call Sign: W1IFB
Irwin W Spitz
41 Sargent St
Lawrence MA 01841

Call Sign: W1KNU
Walter A Wilkie
23 Saunder
Lawrence MA 01841

Call Sign: N1TKW
Doris M Mitchell
38 Shattuck St
Lawrence MA 01843

Call Sign: AB1KS
William P Ouelette
47 South Bowdoin St
Lawrence MA 01843

Call Sign: KB1KDP
Jose Martinez
65 Union St Apt 407
Lawrence MA 01840

Call Sign: K7UIK
Peter W Cole
6 Wachusett Ave
Lawrence MA 01841

Call Sign: N1RUL
William L Olivieri
223 Water St
Lawrence MA 01841

Call Sign: N1RCB
Gordon S Collupy Jr
31 Winthrop Ave
Lawrence MA 01843

Call Sign: N1UZN
Lillian E Jackson
31 Winthrop Ave
Lawrence MA 01843

Call Sign: N1KDY
Beth Ann Patterson
Siviter
26 Wyman St
Lawrence MA 01841

Call Sign: ND1F
Robert J De Felice
Lawrence MA 01842

Call Sign: N1SWD
Angel V Mencia
Lawrence MA 01841

Call Sign: KB1KDO
Jose Rosario
Lawrence MA 01842

Call Sign: KB1NNE
Daniel G Davison
Lawrence MA 01842

FCC Amateur Radio Licenses in Lee

Call Sign: N1JZB
Mark G Plaquet
21 Center St
Lee MA 01238

Call Sign: K1URJ
Henry B Farina
70 Columbia St
Lee MA 01238

Call Sign: KB1URT
Richard B Brittain
15 Davis St
Lee MA 01238

Call Sign: K1RBB
Richard B Brittain
15 Davis St
Lee MA 01238

Call Sign: KB1EAB
Linda L Taylor
405 Devon Rd
Lee MA 01238

Call Sign: N1PTZ
Timothy O Taylor
405 Devon Rd
Lee MA 01238

Call Sign: WA1ZLE
William F Roche
840 Fairview St
Lee MA 01238

Call Sign: WA9NOZ
Philip J Arndt
365 Greylock St
Lee MA 01238

Call Sign: K1SXA
Gary R Kleinerman

195 Mandalay Rd
Lee MA 01238

Call Sign: N1DCX
Alan B Corcoran
19 Olive St
Lee MA 01238

Call Sign: KR1R
Willard B Lunt
14 Park Place
Lee MA 01238

Call Sign: WA1IUX
John W Herbert
300 Theresa Ter
Lee MA 01238

Call Sign: K1AWT
Walter J Terlik
41 Theresa Terrace
Lee MA 01238

Call Sign: KB1JTP
Peter J Markavage
Tyringham Rd
Lee MA 01238

Call Sign: WB2VVQ
Timothy A Martin
171 W Park St
Lee MA 01238

Call Sign: KB2DXE
Sara A Hopp
120 Wood Duck Rd
Lee MA 012380002

Call Sign: WA2HVZ
Richard L Hopp
120 Wood Duck Rd
Lee MA 012380002

Call Sign: N3OEW
Christopher T Ertl
Lee MA 01238

FCC Amateur Radio Licenses in Leeds

Call Sign: NF1G
Paul G Kelliher
520 Audubon Rd
Leeds MA 01053

Call Sign: N1GMJ
Robert L Ansaldo
521 Audubon Rd
Leeds MA 01053

Call Sign: N1ZHV
Randy L Lahr
48 Evergreen Rd 113
Leeds MA 01053

Call Sign: KB1DCE
Celeste R Jeffway
37 Front St
Leeds MA 01053

Call Sign: WA1OJN
Robert W Jeffway Jr
37 Front St
Leeds MA 01053

Call Sign: KB1ERQ
Bear Hill Arc
421 N Main St
Leeds MA 010539714

Call Sign: KB1IVF
James M Bethke
421 N Main St 26
Leeds MA 01053

Call Sign: N1HNA
Harold S Bauver
Leeds MA 01053

Call Sign: KA1MDA
Thomas S Rowinski
Leeds MA 01053

FCC Amateur Radio Licenses in Leicester

Call Sign: W8ZW
Fred J Looft Iii
12 Baldwin St
Leicester MA 01524

Call Sign: KA1UKN
Keith A Desautels
16 Brookside Dr
Leicester MA 01524

Call Sign: N1KWL
Robert E Cutting

5 Crestwood Rd
Leicester MA 01524

Call Sign: N1IQL
Richard W Duquette
27 Deer Pond Dr
Leicester MA 01524

Call Sign: K1AGR
Francis C Margadonna
51 Grove St
Leicester MA 01524

Call Sign: KA1NHZ
Philip J Metcalf Jr
7 Hyland Ave
Leicester MA 01524

Call Sign: WB1GSB
Donald T Brown
23 King Ct
Leicester MA 01524

Call Sign: AB1LE
Charles H Jordan Iv
62 King St
Leicester MA 01524

Call Sign: WG1S
Lawrence R Day Jr
9 King St Extension
Leicester MA 01524

Call Sign: NH6XW
Wayne E Anderson
1074 Main St
Leicester MA 01524

Call Sign: KC5SPF
William J Duntzee Iii
1274 Main St
Leicester MA 01524

Call Sign: K1KDZ
George J Emmett
1075 Main St Apt 102
Leicester MA 01524

Call Sign: W1GMS
David S Tibbetts
120 Manville St
Leicester MA 01524

Call Sign: W1OVT

George Jerome
18 Massasoit Dr
Leicester MA 01524

Call Sign: N1KWX
Eugene U Bouchard
23 Mayflower Cir
Leicester MA 01524

Call Sign: KB1JQO
Ian A Underwood
30 Mayflower Rd
Leicester MA 01524

Call Sign: N1MQH
Rene A Duval
9 Park Ln
Leicester MA 01524

Call Sign: N1RBT
Robert H Dupuis
200 Pine St
Leicester MA 01524

Call Sign: W1LZK
Sigmund J Caika
228 Pine St
Leicester MA 01524

Call Sign: W1BWL
Benn P Malesky
289 Pine St
Leicester MA 01524

Call Sign: K1ESX
Randall L Rogers
2 Tanglewood Rd
Leicester MA
015241618

Call Sign: N1NTC
Levon N Kachadoorian
1894 W Main St
Leicester MA 01524

Call Sign: KD0FEK
Michael R Murzycki
67 Waite St
Leicester MA 01524

Call Sign: KC2YQK
Michael R Murzycki
67 Waite St
Leicester MA 01524

Call Sign: N1FIY
Brian G Arsenault
900 Whittemore St
Leicester MA 01524

Call Sign: N1ITZ
Tracy A Arsenault
900 Whittemore St
Leicester MA 01524

Call Sign: N1RPE
Frank R Reale
14 Winslow Ave
Leicester MA 01524

Call Sign: N1WNZ
Ronald W Laconto Sr
Leicester MA 01524

**FCC Amateur Radio
Licenses in Lenox**

Call Sign: KA1ATO
Richard A Levasseur
21 Bracelan Ct
Lenox MA 01240

Call Sign: KA1BND
Doris M Jones
26 Brunell Ave
Lenox MA 01240

Call Sign: KA1ARO
Robert L Jones
38 Brunell Ave
Lenox MA 012402025

Call Sign: N1LAL
Keith W Cahalan
44 Brunell Ave
Lenox MA 01240

Call Sign: N1DAY
Norman Steven
Hubbard
103 Cliffwood St
Lenox MA 01240

Call Sign: W1RBP
Ross B Perreault
176 East St
Lenox MA 01240

Call Sign: N1MDE
Peter K Kurdzionak
582 East St
Lenox MA 012402238

Call Sign: KA1ARN
John F Roosa
169 Housatonic St
Lenox MA 012402549

Call Sign: WB1AUV
Thomas P Sullivan
380 Housatonic St
Lenox MA 01240

Call Sign: W1AUV
Thomas P Sullivan
380 Housatonic St
Lenox MA 01240

Call Sign: W1EOT
Harold F Allan
14 Hutchinson Ln
Lenox MA 012402217

Call Sign: N1VGM
John Church
4 Lee Dr
Lenox MA 01240

Call Sign: W1ARX
Percival L Williams Jr
27 Martha Ln
Lenox MA 01240

Call Sign: N1QOU
John V Lason
260 Pittsfield Rd 10c
Lenox MA 01240

Call Sign: K1RYO
Ralph Hansen
3 Sullivan Ln
Lenox MA 01240

Call Sign: KB2WOW
Robert L Delaney
17 Tucker St
Lenox MA 01240

Call Sign: K1ZHJ
Francis J Vahle
91 W Mtn Rd
Lenox MA 01240

Call Sign: KA1RIR
Linda J Caldwell
85 Walker St
Lenox MA 01240

Call Sign: K1AU
Grier B Miller
96 West St
Lenox MA 01240

**FCC Amateur Radio
Licenses in Lenoxdale**

Call Sign: KB1FEZ
Benjamin E Losaw
12 Lawton St
Lenoxdale MA 01242

Call Sign: N1PUA
Paul E Losaw
Lenox Dale MA
012420119

Call Sign: KA1YMS
William F Sheehan
Lenoxdale MA 01242

Call Sign: KA1PIJ
Stephen J Jezak
Lenoxdale MA 01242

**FCC Amateur Radio
Licenses in
Leominster**

Call Sign: KB1MCK
Douglas B Lepisto
68 4th St # 1
Leominster MA 01453

Call Sign: KB1AXK
David P Mc Neill Ii
30 Abbey Rd Apt 201
Leominster MA 01453

Call Sign: KC1L
Wesley A Johnson
28 Aloe Dr
Leominster MA 01453

Call Sign: N1APX
Alberta C Johnson
28 Aloe Dr

Leominster MA 01453

Call Sign: WB1FXJ
Kenneth J Turchin
43 Arlington St
Leominster MA 01453

Call Sign: W1QUO
James M Moran
53 Austin St
Leominster MA 01453

Call Sign: AA2T
Jerry J Rogich
69 Beth Ave
Leominster MA 01453

Call Sign: KB1EIL
Jerome J Rogich
69 Beth Ave
Leominster MA 01453

Call Sign: K1SON
Jerome J Rogich
69 Beth Ave
Leominster MA 01453

Call Sign: WB1HIB
Gerard L Breault
14 Birchcroft Rd
Leominster MA 01453

Call Sign: W3DEC
Donald E Carlton Jr
141 Birchcroft Rd
Leominster MA 01453

Call Sign: N1CUJ
Sharon A Kubik
160 Birchcroft Rd
Leominster MA 01453

Call Sign: N1DOM
Christopher S Kronick
160 Birchcroft Rd
Leominster MA 01453

Call Sign: W1BYH
Norman L Rivers
112 Bonnydale Rd
Leominster MA 01453

Call Sign: KB1RWD
Cris Tibbert

89 Boutelle St
Leominster MA 01453

Call Sign: KB1UYB
Timothy A Wortley
68 Brown Ave
Leominster MA 01453

Call Sign: KQ1Y
Timothy A Wortley
68 Brown Ave
Leominster MA 01453

Call Sign: KB1DPW
Greg Hanlon
97 Buttermilk Rd
Leominster MA 01453

Call Sign: K1OYE
Joseph P Coyle
18 Campbell Ave
Leominster MA 01453

Call Sign: W1QPM
Richard L Miller Sr
39 Carolyn St
Leominster MA
014534641

Call Sign: N1DVF
Oliver E Parker
556 Central St 116
Leominster MA 01453

Call Sign: KA1MQH
Carl G Rosen
556 Central St Lot 155
Leominster MA 01453

Call Sign: KB1NID
Victor R Torres
740 Central St T-1
Leominster MA 01453

Call Sign: KB1VGW
John J Caron
175 Chapman Pl
Leominster MA 01453

Call Sign: K1JJC
John J Caron
175 Chapman Pl
Leominster MA 01453

Call Sign: WB1FBS
Anthony J Jordan
145 Chapman Place
Leominster MA 01453

Call Sign: K1JHC
Thomas B Duffy
14 Cherry St
Leominster MA 01453

Call Sign: W1MM
Qcwa Pioneer Chapter
183
14 Cherry St
Leominster MA 01453

Call Sign: N1VQI
Arnold A Kelly
12 Cloverleaf Rd
Leominster MA 01453

Call Sign: KB1SXK
Larry Dufresne
25 Coolidge Place
Leominster MA 01453

Call Sign: K1LOL
Larry Dufresne
25 Coolidge Place
Leominster MA 01453

Call Sign: N1EGM
Michael D Kelly
85 Cortland Cir
Leominster MA 01453

Call Sign: KB1AKR
Simon M Braune
21 Crescent Rd
Leominster MA 01453

Call Sign: W1IBJ
Donald E Montrym
40 Dennis Drive
Leominster MA
014537014

Call Sign: KB1HRC
John R Fors
65 Dewey Ave
Leominster MA 01453

Call Sign: N1YLD
Jeffrey D Cavaioli

35 Ebury Court
Leominster MA 01453

Call Sign: WB1AVC
James I Watts
1199 Elm St
Leominster MA 01453

Call Sign: K1NX
Mark J Darrigo
1354 Elm St
Leominster MA 01453

Call Sign: N1OBP
Melinda L M C
Darrigo
1354 Elm St
Leominster MA 01453

Call Sign: KB1FOV
David L Holbrook
18 Evans Ct
Leominster MA 01453

Call Sign: AA1LC
Jonathan J Taku
65 Fairview St
Leominster MA 01453

Call Sign: N1SOP
Fumio Taku
65 Fairview St
Leominster MA 01453

Call Sign: KB1TDN
Jeffrey M Peters
4 Farm Hill Rd
Leominster MA 01453

Call Sign: KA1ZGW
Carlos M Schawillie
22 Fifth Ave
Leominster MA 01453

Call Sign: N1GNH
Richard A Roberge
223 Fifth St
Leominster MA 01453

Call Sign: KA1ACH
Dennis C Farnsworth
19 Foster Ct
Leominster MA
014533105

Call Sign: N1UDY
Lee J Merrill
60 Fourth St
Leominster MA 01453

Call Sign: N2EON
Brian Kennedy
60 Fox Meadow Rd
Unit H
Leominster MA 01453

Call Sign: N1QU
Brian Kennedy
60 Fox Meadow Rd
Unit H
Leominster MA
014531955

Call Sign: N1KCW
Richard G Di Mascio
Foxmeadow Rd
Leominster MA 01453

Call Sign: W1PQW
Dieter H Keller
36 George Ter
Leominster MA 01453

Call Sign: N1WGC
Robert D Ethier
67 George Terr
Leominster MA 01453

Call Sign: N1ACV
Paul A Melanson
100 Gordon St
Leominster MA 01453

Call Sign: N1QEW
Bradford J Snow
164 Grafton St
Leominster MA 01453

Call Sign: N1KWR
James Foshin
111 Granite St
Leominster MA 01453

Call Sign: N1COF
Edmund F Murphy
2 Haskell Ave
Leominster MA 01453

Call Sign: WB1AER
Judith A Hebert
119 Helena St
Leominster MA 01453

Call Sign: N1XYH
Barry P Machado
33 Highland Ave
Leominster MA 01453

Call Sign: W1YCT
Barry P Machado
33 Highland Ave
Leominster MA 01453

Call Sign: KB1FCA
Megan B Gentry
22 Hill Top Drive
Leominster MA 01453

Call Sign: N1RET
Walter A Deery
11 J State St
Leominster MA 01453

Call Sign: KB1HMQ
John C Barnwell Iii
140 Jamestown Rd
Leominster MA 01453

Call Sign: N1MQ
John C Barnwell Iii
140 Jamestown Rd
Leominster MA 01453

Call Sign: KB1HNB
Richard A Leclair
217 Johnny Appleseed
Ln
Leominster MA 01453

Call Sign: KB1IVC
Richard F Loiselle
8 Judy Dr
Leominster MA
014531732

Call Sign: KB1DGA
Lema
145 Lancaster St
Leominster MA
014534376

Call Sign: WC1LEO

Lema
145 Lancaster St
Leominster MA
014534376

Call Sign: KF0VH
Ted J Dunker
49 Larson Ave
Leominster MA 01453

Call Sign: KB1NTG
Cassie Jeon
103 Laurel St
Leominster MA 01453

Call Sign: KD1PL
Gregory T Wasik
202 Lincoln St
Leominster MA 01453

Call Sign: W1DRF
Roy D Smith
113 Lindell Ave
Leominster MA 01453

Call Sign: KA1VTU
Anthony J Lemmo
10 Longwood Ave
Leominster MA 01453

Call Sign: N1FJT
John J Murphy
41 Lorchris St
Leominster MA 01453

Call Sign: WU1X
Robert M Young
8 Lynnhaven Rd
Leominster MA 01453

Call Sign: W1UD
William C Voedisch Jr
240 Main St
Leominster MA 01453

Call Sign: K1IKD
Thomas Thomasian
732 Main St
Leominster MA 01453

Call Sign: W1TQB
Howard R Keeney Jr
100 Main St Apt 212
Leominster MA 01453

Call Sign: K1AGK
William T Gavin
86 Maple Ave
Leominster MA 01453

Call Sign: KB1VVF
Peter Chromiak
136 Maple Ave
Leominster MA 01453

Call Sign: N1ONE
William H Hahn Iii
35 Mc Kinley St
Leominster MA 01453

Call Sign: KA1AKD
Albert G Faul Jr
449 Mechanic St
Leominster MA 01453

Call Sign: KB1TNN
Albert G Faul Jr
449 Mechanic St
Leominster MA 01453

Call Sign: KA1TWQ
Roy J Bilodeau
478 Mechanic St
Leominster MA 01453

Call Sign: KA1VWY
Melissa M Bilodeau
478 Mechanic St
Leominster MA 01453

Call Sign: N1JKP
Chrystal J Brosseau
478 Mechanic St
Leominster MA 01453

Call Sign: W1WTZ
James W Sullivan
431 Merriam Ave
Leominster MA 01453

Call Sign: N1MXK
Vincent J Spingola Jr
534 Merriam Ave
Leominster MA 01453

Call Sign: KA1OYL
Ramon Sierra
789 Merriam Ave

Leominster MA 01453

Call Sign: KA1EUX
John P Allen
67 Mooreland Ave
Leominster MA 01453

Call Sign: KA1VOU
Wolfgang H Seidlich
93 Mooreland Ave Apt
7
Leominster MA 01453

Call Sign: WA1ONI
Emerson W Grant Ii
45 Morningside St
Leominster MA
014536808

Call Sign: KB1JAZ
Duane P Mohney
115 Morningside St
Leominster MA 01453

Call Sign: KB1HNC
Rick D Leclair
12 Mount Pleasant Ave
Leominster MA 01453

Call Sign: AB1PM
Rick D Leclair
12 Mount Pleasant Ave
Leominster MA 01453

Call Sign: KB1EZG
Rudolph Johnson
46 Musket Dr B5
Leominster MA 01453

Call Sign: K1KAY
Thomas R Moore
602 N Main St Lot 18
Leominster MA 01453

Call Sign: WA1DWS
Philip N Oliver
109 Nelson St
Leominster MA
014532161

Call Sign: N1NWA
James A Biker
18 Norman Rd
Leominster MA 01453

Call Sign: KA1MQG
Roger E Hill
193 North St
Leominster MA 01453

Call Sign: WI1W
Mark D Schneider
39 Norwood Ave
Leominster MA 01453

Call Sign: WB1HJS
Mark D Schneider
39 Norwood Ave
Leominster MA 01453

Call Sign: KB1NTI
Anastasia Alexander
85 Old Farm Rd
Leominster MA 01453

Call Sign: WA1ANA
Barry S Tuttle
50 Old Willard Rd
Leominster MA
014535212

Call Sign: KA1BVM
Mario V Medeiros
64 Olde Tavern Rd
Leominster MA
014532067

Call Sign: WA1JCK
Ronald D Robichaud
255 Pierce St
Leominster MA 01453

Call Sign: W1UDK
James E Basque
262 Pierce St
Leominster MA 01453

Call Sign: KC5RUP
Kenneth P Daby
264 Pleasant St
Leominster MA
014536228

Call Sign: N1KFT
Kenneth P Daby
264 Pleasant St
Leominster MA
014536228

Call Sign: WB1HIP
Eugene J Shepard
372 Pleasant St
Leominster MA 01453

Call Sign: N1FHB
Gerry A Marini
152 Pleasant Ter
Leominster MA 01453

Call Sign: N2DV
Robert H Woodside
9 Powder House Ln
Leominster MA 01453

Call Sign: KB1JKG
David E Bauer
115 Princeton St
Leominster MA 01453

Call Sign: WB1GAB
Sandra A Helenius
139 Princeton St
Leominster MA 01453

Call Sign: N1TIZ
Samuel J Giadone
11 Prospect Ave
Leominster MA 01453

Call Sign: WB1COR
William A Malenfant
167 Prospect St
Leominster MA 01453

Call Sign: W1IJI
Daniel E Paquette
12 Regina Dr
Leominster MA 01453

Call Sign: KB1PZM
Robert E Caponi
30 Revolution Drive
Leominster MA
014532508

Call Sign: KA1BUL
George H Beaulieu
121 Ridgewood Dr
Leominster MA 01453

Call Sign: K1JGZ
Wilfred R Houle

238 Ridgewood Dr
Leominster MA 01453

Call Sign: KC0CE
Charles A Milhans Jr
54 Rose Ave
Leominster MA 01453

Call Sign: KB1MMJ
Kim E Brown
4 Saint Jean Ave
Leominster MA 01453

Call Sign: KA1UFP
Lena Petitto
16 Salisbury St
Leominster MA 01453

Call Sign: NX1U
Rocco C Petitto Jr
16 Salisbury St
Leominster MA 01453

Call Sign: WA1GCY
John R Cromwell
45 Scenic Dr
Leominster MA 01453

Call Sign: W1PQO
Wilfred A Lemoine
11 Sixth St
Leominster MA 01453

Call Sign: N1GNK
Joseph J D Le Blanc
182 Spruce St
Leominster MA 01453

Call Sign: K1VQR
George J Ciriello
62 Stetson St
Leominster MA
014531740

Call Sign: KB1QQV
Christopher J Petrie
8 Steuben Circle
Leominster MA 01453

Call Sign: KB1SQW
Stephen W O'malley
112 Sycamore Dr
Leominster MA 01453

Call Sign: KB1QWR
Mark S Turmaine
44 Sylvan Ave
Leominster MA 01453

Call Sign: WB2SZC
Gary S Casaburri
5 Tanagers Landing
Leominster MA 01453

Call Sign: WR1T
David C Besnia
38 Third St
Leominster MA 01453

Call Sign: N1YWH
Daniel M Kronick
90 Union St
Leominster MA 01453

Call Sign: KD1KT
Keith O Brown
227 Union St
Leominster MA 01453

Call Sign: KD1BA
Thomas J Tefft Jr
671 Union St
Leominster MA 01453

Call Sign: WA1FIA
Chatmon Houston Jr
42 Valleyview Rd
Leominster MA
014536634

Call Sign: N1AP
Raymond W St Jean
8 Veronica St
Leominster MA 01453

Call Sign: W1GMC
Ian M Mac Donald
38 Veronica St
Leominster MA 01453

Call Sign: KB1TKD
Giulio G Greco
175 Washington St
Leominster MA 01453

Call Sign: K1DOP
Theodore J Symonds
360 West

Leominster MA 01453

Call Sign: N1ABF
Robert M Elder
381 West St
Leominster MA 01453

Call Sign: N1RDC
David J Sheridan
13 Wheeler St
Leominster MA 01453

Call Sign: N1MGO
Gordon A La Point
144 Wilder Rd
Leominster MA 01453

Call Sign: KB1JXJ
Pauline R Carulli
144 Wilder Rd
Leominster MA 01453

Call Sign: KA1MWQ
Paul P Piermarini Jr
450 Willard St
Leominster MA 01453

Call Sign: WA1HLX
Robert H Lizotte
626 Willard St
Leominster MA
014535930

Call Sign: KB1DBP
Anthony C Demmons
175 Willard St Apt 304
Leominster MA 01453

Call Sign: KB1WUG
Paul L Woodcome Jr
166 Willow St
Leominster MA 01453

Call Sign: KA1UGZ
Stephen A Spinak
Leominster MA 01453

Call Sign: N2OGM
Christopher J
Campbell
Leominster MA
014531028

Call Sign: W2SX

Christopher J
Campbell
Leominster MA
014531028

FCC Amateur Radio Licenses in Leverett

Call Sign: N1NVI
Bernard P Morin Jr
27 6th Rd
Leverett MA 01054

Call Sign: N1RES
Mary M Morin
27 6th Rd
Leverett MA 01055

Call Sign: N1TGX
Stephanie A Blombach
27 6th Rd
Leverett MA 01055

Call Sign: N1RUS
Scott W Allen
133 Depot Rd
Leverett MA 01054

Call Sign: KB1MJX
Stephen S Ball
62 N Leverett Rd
Leverett MA 01054

Call Sign: N1FSP
Mary A Smith
226 N Leverett Rd
Leverett MA 01054

Call Sign: K1RIF
Christopher B Emery
71 Teawaddle Hill Rd
Leverett MA 01054

Call Sign: KA1CMA
Carol A Emery
71 Teawaddle Hill Rd
Leverett MA 01054

FCC Amateur Radio Licenses in Lexington

Call Sign: N1MKF
Robert T Sanford
9 Alcott Rd

Lexington MA
024201901

Call Sign: N1MKE
George J Primes
3 Appletree Ln
Lexington MA 02420

Call Sign: NB1R
James M Surprenant
15 April Lane
Lexington MA 02421

Call Sign: N1MKI
M Colin Godfrey
2 Balfour St
Lexington MA 02173

Call Sign: KJ1L
Herbert G Weiss
28 Barberry Rd
Lexington MA 02173

Call Sign: N1BQV
Ruth S Weiss
28 Barberry Rd
Lexington MA 02173

Call Sign: N1YWL
Teddy I Ben Harav
36 Bartlett Ave
Lexington MA 02173

Call Sign: N1YXN
Ronn Ben Harav
36 Bartlett Ave
Lexington MA 02173

Call Sign: KA1HF
Christopher B Walker
22 Baskin Rd
Lexington MA 02173

Call Sign: W2QC
Charles W Lamb
55 Baskin Rd
Lexington MA
024216928

Call Sign: KB1KDK
Christopher M
Morrison
13 Bedford St
Lexington MA 02420

Call Sign: K1BXX
William F Mc Bride
121 Bedford St
Lexington MA
021734403

Call Sign: N1JKY
Thomas J Murphy
149 Bedford St
Lexington MA 02420

Call Sign: KB1REK
Michael R Sowle
338 Bedford St
Lexington MA 02420

Call Sign: N1YFV
Harry B Scott Jr
440 Bedford St
Lexington MA 02420

Call Sign: NK1B
Adam G Pennington
72 Bertwell Rd
Lexington MA 02420

Call Sign: N1FVW
Robert H Gould
30 Blake Rd
Lexington MA 02173

Call Sign: N1LBN
Paul Nesbeda
10 Blodgett Rd
Lexington MA 02173

Call Sign: W1EQG
Thomas Maier
29 Bloomfield St
Lexington MA
021735607

Call Sign: WA1EVH
Frank J Rosato
12 Blueberry Ln
Lexington MA 02173

Call Sign: KB1WPN
William A Wright
15 Blueberry Ln
Lexington MA 02420

Call Sign: WW1P

William A Wright
15 Blueberry Ln
Lexington MA 02420

Call Sign: W1CNS
Emanuel E Landsman
3 Brookwood Rd
Lexington MA 02173

Call Sign: W1AIH
Alan R Adolph
7 Buckman Drive
Lexington MA
024215915

Call Sign: KA1NIA
Frank J Belinowiz
167 Burlington St
Lexington MA 02420

Call Sign: KB1WAK
Christopher J Wysopal
17 Carol Ln
Lexington MA 02420

Call Sign: N1OBJ
Christopher J Wysopal
17 Carol Ln
Lexington MA 02420

Call Sign: WA2YZK
Stephen A Youngwirth
24 Carriage Dr
Lexington MA 02420

Call Sign: N1AXG
Earl F Sunderland Jr
55 Cary Ave
Lexington MA 02421

Call Sign: KJ1P
William Bertozzi
8 Castle Rd
Lexington MA
024203527

Call Sign: KA9REY
Bradford L Terrell
148 Cedar St
Lexington MA 02421

Call Sign: N6GJL
Toshihiko Okubo
24 Circle Rd

Lexington MA 02420

Call Sign: AA1SJ
Sheldon S Sandler
34 Colony Rd
Lexington MA 02173

Call Sign: WB1FQW
Jose Varon
546 Concord Ave
Lexington MA 02421

Call Sign: W1DUW
Alfred R Prudhomme
Jr
12 Coolidge Ave
Lexington MA 02420

Call Sign: K1SHY
Howard E Dow
50 Coolidge Ave
Lexington MA 02420

Call Sign: N1MLN
Michael C Coln
33 Dawesroad
Lexington MA 02421

Call Sign: N1SFY
Richard T Rigby
23 Deering Ave
Lexington MA 02173

Call Sign: KA1MOH
George W Wong
5 Demar Rd
Lexington MA 02173

Call Sign: N1FVT
John M Frankovich
19 Dewey Rd
Lexington MA 02173

Call Sign: KB1DJH
Peter S Litwack
15 Dexter Rd
Lexington MA 02173

Call Sign: N6KCJ
Suzanne M Grant
Lewis
18 Dexter Rd
Lexington MA 02173

Call Sign: NZ6B
Paul Lewis
18 Dexter Rd
Lexington MA 02173

Call Sign: WA1DBM
Fred L Niemann
11 Diamond Rd
Lexington MA 02173

Call Sign: N9FJO
James B Tinkler
22 Donald St
Lexington MA
024201411

Call Sign: N9JBT
James B Tinkler
22 Donald St
Lexington MA
024201411

Call Sign: KB1EIG
Lee R Minardi
37 Downing Rd
Lexington MA
024216918

Call Sign: KB1FMJ
James B Osborn
50 Downing Rd
Lexington MA 02421

Call Sign: N1VKU
Cynthia C Baird
19 Drummer Boy Way
Lexington MA 02173

Call Sign: KE1FW
Joseph A Knight Jr
172 East St
Lexington MA 02173

Call Sign: N1UEL
Philip C Davis
191 East St
Lexington MA 02173

Call Sign: W1GFH
Joseph M Tyburczy
172 East St
Lexington MA 02420

Call Sign: N1MKG

Martin J Grossman
5 Elena Rd
Lexington MA 02173

Call Sign: N1YWM
Charles S Howe
22 Eliot Rd
Lexington MA 02173

Call Sign: K1MC
Malcolm F Crawford
19 Ellison Rd
Lexington MA
024217407

Call Sign: W1QGL
William R Weiss Jr
16 Estabrook Rd
Lexington MA
021737539

Call Sign: WA1FGO
Janet D Melcher
29 Fairlawn Ln
Lexington MA 02173

Call Sign: K1CLO
Anthony Fantasia
34 Fairlawn Ln
Lexington MA 02173

Call Sign: AE1F
Brian G Connelly Mr
18 Farmcrest Ave
Lexington MA 02421

Call Sign: N1JAR
David G Kanter
48 Fifer Ln
Lexington MA
024201224

Call Sign: KB1QEL
David K Lewis
31 Fletcher Av Unit 10
Lexington MA 02420

Call Sign: W1ZEK
Robert C Dalrymple
20 Fletcher Ave
Lexington MA 02173

Call Sign: WA1LAI
Edward A Ganshirt

48 Fletcher Ave
Lexington MA 02173

Call Sign: N1AKH
Donald G Bell
15 Flintlock Rd
Lexington MA 02173

Call Sign: KA1RHP
John M Fletcher
22 Flintlock Rd
Lexington MA 02173

Call Sign: N3JBC
Joseph P Campbell Jr
49 Follen Rd
Lexington MA
024215921

Call Sign: N1XJZ
Alexandra L Treadway
205 Follen Rd
Lexington MA 02173

Call Sign: N1TFV
Randall G Seed
16 Fox Run Lane
Lexington MA 02420

Call Sign: KB1OVC
Karl R Mckinney
31 Garfield St
Lexington MA 02421

Call Sign: N1YOX
Paul C Davidson
31 Gleason Rd
Lexington MA
021733354

Call Sign: KA1RKF
Coelynn E Mc Ininch
102 Gleason Rd
Lexington MA 02173

Call Sign: N1GIX
Robert F Prongay
37 Grant St
Lexington MA 02173

Call Sign: K1BC
Robert C Clements
100 Grant St
Lexington MA 02420

Call Sign: W1GYY
Norman B Stetson
194 Grant St
Lexington MA
024202127

Call Sign: N1RYB
Glenn E Comeau
11 Grape Vine Ave
Lexington MA 02173

Call Sign: N1SBT
Deborah J Comeau
11 Grapevine Ave
Lexington MA 02173

Call Sign: WM1K
Michael P Perry
24 Grassland St
Lexington MA 02421

Call Sign: KB1GRQ
Henry L Buccigross
146 Grove St
Lexington MA 02420

Call Sign: K1QK
Henry L Buccigross
146 Grove St
Lexington MA 02420

Call Sign: N1INT
William P Kenealy
7 Hancock Ave
Lexington MA 02173

Call Sign: KB1QVR
Ian F Page
43 Hancock St
Lexington MA 02420

Call Sign: KD1IK
Anthony Michel
52 Hancock St
Lexington MA 02173

Call Sign: WH2B
John A Taylor
21 Harbell St
Lexington MA 02421

Call Sign: N1DIF
Russell W Corkum Sr

22 Hathaway Rd
Lexington MA
024201806

Call Sign: WA1TTV
Russell W Corkum Jr
22 Hathaway Rd
Lexington MA 02173

Call Sign: W1OLK
Ralph R Richardi
11 Hibbert St
Lexington MA 02421

Call Sign: WA1IPQ
Theresa M Richardi
11 Hibbert St
Lexington MA 02173

Call Sign: N1TWG
Ansel Singer Barnum
17 Highland
Lexington MA 02173

Call Sign: N1CWY
Bruce R Ellis
3 Hill St
Lexington MA 02173

Call Sign: W1KDG
Arthur W Collins
79 Hill St
Lexington MA 02421

Call Sign: K1PZK
Robert C Di Pietro
94 Hill St
Lexington MA 02421

Call Sign: W1UDU
John F Frazer
50 Hillcrest Ave
Lexington MA 02173

Call Sign: WA1VBV
Kenneth R Lewis
9 Holmes Rd
Lexington MA 02420

Call Sign: N1DVK
Matthew Proujansky
7 James St
Lexington MA 02173

Call Sign: N1QLO
Jonah Proujansky Bell
7 James St
Lexington MA 02173

Call Sign: KB1WSO
Chirag Y Bhatt
201 Katahdin Dr
Lexington MA 02421

Call Sign: N1FKD
Daniel P Perez
307 Katahdin Dr
Lexington MA 02173

Call Sign: W1LEY
Paul H P Christen
210 Katahdin Drive
Lexington MA 02421

Call Sign: KC0GQK
Christopher W
Reichert
218 Katahdin Drive
Lexington MA 02421

Call Sign: K1FSH
Daniel P Perez
307 Katahdin Drive
Lexington MA 02421

Call Sign: KB1MBS
Robert L Sheridan
34 Lawrence Ln
Lexington MA 02421

Call Sign: N1WJG
Erik E Wang
10 Lexington Ave
Lexington MA 02421

Call Sign: KA2GOL
Daniel M Sheff
17 Lexington Ave
Lexington MA 02421

Call Sign: WB9RDM
Craig W Davidson
53 Liberty Ave
Lexington MA 02420

Call Sign: KT1D
Timothy Y Dunn
32 Liberty Ave

Lexington MA 02420

Call Sign: KB1ETJ
Dawn Perlner
32 Liberty Ave
Lexington MA 02420

Call Sign: W1AJ
John B Porter
19 Lillian Rd
Lexington MA 02173

Call Sign: KB1VHZ
Joseph R Mostika
127 Lincoln St
Lexington MA 02421

Call Sign: W1LSI
Frederick D Tighe
243 Lincoln St
Lexington MA 02173

Call Sign: N1KTT
Robert C Boucher
252 Lincoln St
Lexington MA 02173

Call Sign: WA1GQX
George R Mooza
32 Locust Ave
Lexington MA 02421

Call Sign: W1EUJ
David P Goncalves
111 Lowell St
Lexington MA
024202819

Call Sign: N1MKK
Kathleen F Bell
264 Lowell St
Lexington MA 02173

Call Sign: KD6IZG
Jason R Bosinoff
663 Lowell St Unit 34
Lexington MA 02420

Call Sign: W1BSX
Albert M Wentworth
280 Marrett Rd
Lexington MA 02173

Call Sign: N1FXT

Adam M Alevy
290 Marrett Rd
Lexington MA
024217009

Call Sign: KA1BTJ
Gary Brookner
9 Marshall Rd
Lexington MA
024202303

Call Sign: KB1MVL
James L Frankel
29 Mason St
Lexington MA
024216327

Call Sign: W1JLF
James L Frankel
29 Mason St
Lexington MA
024216327

Call Sign: WB1CNW
Arthur W Stead
250 Massachusetts Ave
Lexington MA 02133

Call Sign: N1PFX
Barbara J Rutledge
284 Massachusetts Ave
Lexington MA 02173

Call Sign: KB1QMG
Nick B Parker
859 Massachusetts Ave
Lexington MA 02420

Call Sign: N1WPC
Anton V Denissov
1024 Massachusetts
Ave
Lexington MA 02173

Call Sign: N2CYN
Jonathan L Burstein
64 Middle St
Lexington MA 02421

Call Sign: W1SZH
John P Mullen
11 Muster Ct
Lexington MA 02173

Call Sign: W1CVT
Walter A Kmiec
27 N Hancock St
Lexington MA 02173

Call Sign: WA1NKW
Lawrence C Madoff
27 Normandy Rd
Lexington MA 02173

Call Sign: W1ENO
William E Bicknell
50 Oak St
Lexington MA 02421

Call Sign: N1PNG
Paul O Perry
38 Parker St
Lexington MA 02421

Call Sign: WA1MOP
Perry Pollins
14 Peachtree Rd
Lexington MA 02173

Call Sign: KA1RHM
Daniel P Goodwin
9 Pearl St
Lexington MA 02173

Call Sign: KB1IIN
Patrick M Toscano
14 Phinney Rd
Lexington MA
024217717

Call Sign: N1SOH
Ethan Handwerker
17 Pine Knoll Rd
Lexington MA
024201206

Call Sign: N1UEQ
Jason Handwerker
17 Pine Knoll Rd
Lexington MA 02173

Call Sign: W1FM
Jacob Handwerker
17 Pine Knoll Rd
Lexington MA
024201206

Call Sign: K1XW

Wayne D Warren
64 Pleasant St
Lexington MA
024216115

Call Sign: W1CZF
J Harper Blaisdell Jr
12 Plymouth Rd
Lexington MA 02173

Call Sign: KB7UAA
Mauro Mandara
17 Potter Pond
Lexington MA 02421

Call Sign: KB1RUN
Jason R Cerundolo
6 Powers Court
Lexington MA 02421

Call Sign: KB1CPC
Cori R Benson
64 Prospect Hill Rd
Lexington MA 02173

Call Sign: N1MKJ
Lawrence S Aulenback
28 Ricard Rd
Lexington MA 02173

Call Sign: W1MR
Jason H Woodward
11 Robbins Rd
Lexington MA 02173

Call Sign: K1JTP
Robert F Mason
33 Robinson Rd
Lexington MA 02173

Call Sign: N1TMQ
Steven M Isenberg
9 Ross Rd
Lexington MA 02421

Call Sign: N1EKV
Byron E Blanchard
16 Round Hill Rd
Lexington MA 02420

Call Sign: KA1BTX
Leslie H Rudnick
39 Sanderson Rd
Lexington MA 02420

Call Sign: KA1FEH
Karen B Rudnick
39 Sandeson Rd
Lexington MA 02173

Call Sign: K2RWE
Russell W Elliot
22 Skyview Rd
Lexington MA 02420

Call Sign: AB1BP
Scott D Hankin
27 Skyview Rd
Lexington MA
024201123

Call Sign: N6MR
Robert S Schneider
12 Stevens Rd
Lexington MA
024214127

Call Sign: N1IPE
John P Keyes
14 Thoreau Rd
Lexington MA
024201942

Call Sign: N1RSA
Nicholas A Lauriat
2 Tricorne Rd
Lexington MA 02421

Call Sign: KB1BWU
Jeremy I Silber
8 Tricorne Rd
Lexington MA 02173

Call Sign: N1HLZ
Dan C Hazen
15 Trotting Horse Dr
Lexington MA 02173

Call Sign: KB1EEV
Pavlik Mintz
23 Turning Mill Rd
Lexington MA
024201317

Call Sign: KB1ORA
Carol R Siegel
30 Turning Mill Rd
Lexington MA 02420

Call Sign: KO1O
William T Vetterling
35 Turning Mill Rd
Lexington MA 02173

Call Sign: N1TDI
Mary Anne L
Vetterling
35 Turning Mill Rd
Lexington MA 02173

Call Sign: WA1HQC
Nathan O Sokal
4 Tyler Rd
Lexington MA 02420

Call Sign: W1UG
John G Jelatis
27 Tyler Rd
Lexington MA 02173

Call Sign: W1DRH
Arthur J Pennell
6 Upland Rd
Lexington MA
021733610

Call Sign: N1SHG
Richard M Corazzini
19 Utica St
Lexington MA 02173

Call Sign: K1PHT
Harold F Hemond
104 Vine St
Lexington MA 02173

Call Sign: KA1SRA
Michael S Hemond
104 Vine St
Lexington MA
024202217

Call Sign: N1MKH
Brian D Hemond
104 Vine St
Lexington MA 02420

Call Sign: KB1OEZ
Christopher C Hemond
104 Vine St
Lexington MA 02420

Call Sign: KB1BVY
Kathryn R Vogel
11 Volunteer Way
Lexington MA 02173

Call Sign: N1XNB
Jennifer N Laukien
19 Volunteer Way
Lexington MA 02173

Call Sign: KB1RCR
Susan C Gillmor
4 Wachusett Circle
Lexington MA 02421

Call Sign: KA1RHL
Richard H Leon
Wachusett Dr
Lexington MA 02173

Call Sign: W2FLO
Melvin A Snyder
342 Waltham St
Lexington MA 02421

Call Sign: KB1IDL
John G Bell
405 Waltham St #164
Lexington MA 02421

Call Sign: KB1IDM
Jil A Westcott
405 Waltham St #164
Lexington MA 02421

Call Sign: KB1IDN
Lauren J Bell
405 Waltham St #164
Lexington MA 02421

Call Sign: N1VBW
Frank R Parsons
12 Warren St
Lexington MA
021735625

Call Sign: KA1WNH
Daniel B Wells
9 Washington St
Lexington MA 02173

Call Sign: NX1Y
Robert A Charlantini
10 Watertown St

Lexington MA
024216320

Call Sign: K1IMP
Herbert D Kline
25 Webster Rd
Lexington MA 02173

Call Sign: WA1MHF
Irving Bosinoff
11 Welch Rd
Lexington MA 02173

Call Sign: KA1PGL
Charles C Perez
3 Westwood Rd
Lexington MA 02173

Call Sign: AB1N
Kenneth E Palm
12 Westwood Rd
Lexington MA
021731834

Call Sign: KE1AR
Mark D Manuelian
1 Whipple Rd
Lexington MA 02173

Call Sign: W1OHJ
Fred G Benkley Jr
35 Whipple Rd
Lexington MA 02173

Call Sign: K1SOP
Nathaniel H Swartz
44 Williams Rd
Lexington MA
024203232

Call Sign: AB1NL
Marja Riitta Koivunen
68 Winter St
Lexington MA 02420

Call Sign: AB1NO
Mauri A Niininen
68 Winter St
Lexington MA 02920

Call Sign: AG1LE
Mauri A Niininen
68 Winter St
Lexington MA 02420

Call Sign: KB1NCR
Kendrick A Goss
75 Winter St
Lexington MA 02420

Call Sign: KA1IIR
James A Scott
85 Woburn St
Lexington MA 02420

Call Sign: W1QBA
Salvatore J Abbadessa
131 Woburn St
Lexington MA 02173

Call Sign: K1UKT
Albert G Hale
41 Woodcliffe Rd
Lexington MA 02173

Call Sign: K3AHM
Arthur L Fox
30 Woodland Rd
Lexington MA
024202016

Call Sign: KI4MRU
Adam N Jenkins
Worthen Rd Apt 1
Lexington MA
024214819

Call Sign: AB1N
Adam N Jenkins
Worthen Rd Apt 1
Lexington MA
024214819

Call Sign: KB1OJZ
Elliot R Ranger
7 Young St
Lexington MA 02420

Call Sign: K1JZZ
Nicholas Hay
Lexington MA
024200003

Call Sign: WA1YVK
Richard D Close
Lexington MA 02420

Call Sign: KB1VYL

Ellen Jervis
Lexington MA 02420

**FCC Amateur Radio
Licenses in Leyden**

Call Sign: N1AW
Albert S Woodhull
199 Eden Trail Rd
Leyden MA 01337

Call Sign: N1WYU
Dennis C Rolstad
202 W Leyden Rd
Leyden MA 01337

**FCC Amateur Radio
Licenses in Lincoln**

Call Sign: K1MCH
Glenn O Gustavson
Lincoln MA
017736176

Call Sign: N1RYD
Adam V Donovan
76 Bedford Rd
Lincoln MA 01773

Call Sign: WA1GEP
Andrew E Donovan
76 Bedford Rd
Lincoln MA 01773

Call Sign: N1RTC
Walter M Hollister
139 Bedford Rd
Lincoln MA 01773

Call Sign: AB1FP
John G Zornig
6 Brooks Rd
Lincoln MA 01773

Call Sign: N1ZJ
John G Zornig
6 Brooks Rd
Lincoln MA 01773

Call Sign: AA1TR
Petr Doudera
27 Conant Rd
Lincoln MA 01773

Call Sign: W1TEC
John A Klobuchar
27 Conant Rd
Lincoln MA 01773

Call Sign: N1SEU
Joseph A Wheelock Iii
7 Deer Run Rd
Lincoln MA 01773

Call Sign: KB1KVA
Joseph A Wheelock Iii
7 Deer Run Rd
Lincoln MA 01773

Call Sign: N1UUQ
John P Solman
16 Deerhaven Rd
Lincoln MA 01773

Call Sign: N1PBB
Chauncey C Chu Sr
43 Deerhaven Rd
Lincoln MA 01773

Call Sign: N1DEA
James R Henderson
6 Giles Rd
Lincoln MA 01773

Call Sign: KB1TEQ
Nancy S Henderson
6 Giles Rd
Lincoln MA 01773

Call Sign: W1MUA
J Frank Lane
6 Goose Pond Rd
Lincoln MA 01773

Call Sign: N1SNM
Jesse V Gray
9 Goose Pond Rd
Lincoln MA 01773

Call Sign: KC2FZH
Moshe N Kushnir
44 Greenridge Lane
Lincoln MA 01773

Call Sign: N1MQZ
John R Almeida
362 Hemlock Circle
Lincoln MA 01773

Call Sign: N1HWF
David G Hunter
Indian Camp Ln
Lincoln MA 01773

Call Sign: KB1UED
Morgan
Santhamoorthy
138 Lexington Rd
Lincoln MA 01773

Call Sign: K1AHN
James Olivieri
152 Lexington Rd
Lincoln MA 01773

Call Sign: KB1UUE
Christopher S Zurenko
168 Lincoln Rd
Lincoln MA 01773

Call Sign: KA2CDO
Steven D Lipsey
195 Lincoln Rd
Lincoln MA 01773

Call Sign: K1BRG
Anthony J Cotoia
Lincoln Rd
Lincoln MA 01773

Call Sign: KA1DWR
Donald H Wilson
11 Linway Rd
Lincoln MA 01773

Call Sign: KB1LY
Joseph R Smulowicz
7 Moccasin Hill
Lincoln MA 01773

Call Sign: KA1PLY
Curtis A Risley Jr
21 Old Concord Rd
Lincoln MA 01773

Call Sign: WA2GFZ
Curtis A Risley
21 Old Concord Rd
Lincoln MA 01773

Call Sign: WC1AAL

Lincoln Civil Defense
Agency
21 Old Concord Rd
Lincoln MA 01773

Call Sign: KB1VYJ
Austin R Brown
79 Old Sudbury Rd
Lincoln MA 01773

Call Sign: KB1USK
Ellen S Withrow
14 Page Farm Rd
Lincoln MA 01773

Call Sign: WA3FCZ
Robert L Steinbrook
8 Peirce Hill Rd
Lincoln MA
017733202

Call Sign: W1FSB
Michael T O Brien
163 S Great Rd
Lincoln MA
017734120

Call Sign: KB1UYN
Nicholas D Andre
286 S Great Rd
Lincoln MA 01773

Call Sign: KA1VRR
Peter A Barnes
5 Sandy Pond Rd
Lincoln MA 01773

Call Sign: KB1GTY
Peter A Barnes
5 Sandy Pond Rd
Lincoln MA 01773

Call Sign: AB1NP
Stephen A Fairfax
148 South Great Rd
Lincoln MA 01773

Call Sign: N1WVV
Matthew L Revis
5 Stonehedge Rd
Lincoln MA 01773

Call Sign: WA1GRJ
Edmund W Lang

5 Tabor Hill Rd
Lincoln MA 01773

Call Sign: N8KEI
Andrew C Payne
83 Tower Rd
Lincoln MA 01773

Call Sign: K1NJ
Edward A Johnson
127 Tower Rd
Lincoln MA
017734402

Call Sign: KB1FQJ
Eric C Klem
168 Trapelo Rd
Lincoln MA 01773

Call Sign: KB1DXH
Frederick S Kimberk
137 Weston Rd
Lincoln MA 01773

Call Sign: K1VR
Fred Hopengarten
6 Willarch Rd
Lincoln MA
017735105

Call Sign: KB1TKJ
Radivoje Lazarevic
6 Willarch Rd
Lincoln MA 01773

Call Sign: KB1UDN
Connor M Mccann
7 Winchelsea Lane
Lincoln MA 01773

Call Sign: W1GUQ
John S Hammond Iii
46 Winter St
Lincoln MA 01773

Call Sign: K9YB
Fred J Solman Iii
Lincoln MA 01773

Call Sign: K1WES
Thomas J Aprille Jr
Lincoln MA
017730701

Call Sign: KA1PLW
Claire F Solman
Lincoln MA 01773

Call Sign: W1MMT
William F Ryan
Lincoln MA 01773

Call Sign: KB1GPJ
William L Papp
Lincoln MA 01773

Call Sign: KB1HRD
Matthew D Von Hone
Lincoln MA
017730044

Call Sign: KB1MTT
Eric M Gustavson
Lincoln MA 01773

FCC Amateur Radio
Licenses in Lincoln
Center

Call Sign: K1PBL
Robert M Fraser
Lincoln Center MA
01773

Call Sign: N1FVU
Patricia A Morten
Lincoln Center MA
01773

FCC Amateur Radio
Licenses in Littleton

Call Sign: KA1LDW
Carole L Hansen
8 Abenaki Trail
Littleton MA 01460

Call Sign: K1JKR
Kenneth E Atkins
19 Adams St
Littleton MA 01460

Call Sign: KB1JTX
Richard E Landers
27 Andrea St
Littleton MA 01460

Call Sign: WA1OJS

William J Cronin Jr
9 Apple Ridge Lane
Littleton MA 01460

Call Sign: WA1DKH
John A Dundas
239 Ayer Rd 30
Littleton MA 01640

Call Sign: KB1IKE
John P Carlson
239 Ayer Rd 35
Littleton MA 01460

Call Sign: W1JPC
John P Carlson
239 Ayer Rd 35
Littleton MA 01460

Call Sign: KB1WSQ
John R Sousa
239 Ayer Rd Lot 78
Littleton MA 01460

Call Sign: K1TPM
Guy P Bonfiglio Sr
239 Ayer Rd Lot 95
Littleton MA
014601015

Call Sign: W1CAN
John W Hathaway
28 Baldwin Hill Rd
Littleton MA 01460

Call Sign: N1MPJ
Kurt J Kraemer
32 Baldwin Hill Rd
Littleton MA 01460

Call Sign: N1FII
Barry L Sullivan
2 Beaver Brook Rd
Littleton MA 01460

Call Sign: KB1GOH
Amy M Lanning
66 Bruce St
Littleton MA
014601013

Call Sign: N1XUY
Thomas R Lanning
66 Bruce St

Littleton MA
014601013

Call Sign: N1AMY
Amy M Lanning
66 Bruce St
Littleton MA
014601013

Call Sign: N1KTX
Mark S Hickox
11 Colburn Ln
Littleton MA
014601288

Call Sign: W1PEI
Mark S Hickox
11 Colburn Ln
Littleton MA
014601288

Call Sign: KB1EKE
Marc J Tessler
94 Cricket Ln
Littleton MA 01460

Call Sign: N1VKW
Joseph E Rock
4 David Way
Littleton MA
014606205

Call Sign: N1GGI
Mitchel I Friedman
7 Dog Wood Rd
Littleton MA 01460

Call Sign: N1LDL
Thomas C Searle Jr
7 Dogwood Rd
Littleton MA 01460

Call Sign: KA4DGF
John E Bielefeld
19 Ernie Dr
Littleton MA 01460

Call Sign: AA1UW
John E Bielefeld
19 Ernie Dr
Littleton MA 01460

Call Sign: K1JEB
John E Bielefeld

19 Ernie Dr
Littleton MA 01460

Call Sign: KA1DR
James L Carozza
116 Foster St
Littleton MA 01460

Call Sign: W1GHC
Perry L Schwartz
171 Foster St
Littleton MA 01460

Call Sign: N1OGX
Kenneth J Lind Jr
41 Goldsmith St
Littleton MA 01460

Call Sign: KB1LZH
Peter F Barbella
62 Goldsmith St
Littleton MA 01460

Call Sign: W1WX
Patrick Taber
291 Goldsmith St
Littleton MA
014601948

Call Sign: KB1MBR
Richard F Lyons
12 Hartwell Ave
Littleton MA
014601206

Call Sign: W1LTN
Richard F Lyons
12 Hartwell Ave
Littleton MA
014601206

Call Sign: KB1PRE
David H Green Jr
45 Hartwell Ave
Littleton MA 01460

Call Sign: WA1WYX
John P Sullivan Jr
218 Hartwell Ave
Littleton MA 01460

Call Sign: K1MGY
Mark R Richards
29 Juniper Rd

Littleton MA 01460

Call Sign: KB1PSC
Keilin Bickar
147 King St
Littleton MA 01460

Call Sign: NM5A
Patrick Taber
147 King St #312
Littleton MA 01460

Call Sign: N1VSJ
Edward J Burg
20 Mannion Pl
Littleton MA 01460

Call Sign: WA1VAB
Henry G Christle Sr
18 Mill Ln
Littleton MA 01460

Call Sign: K1UHX
Philip A Swenson
181 Mill Rd
Littleton MA 01460

Call Sign: WB1ACU
Cyril A Carhoun
50 Mill Rd Apt 205
Littleton MA 01460

Call Sign: K1SRG
Scott R Glorioso
87 Nashoba Rd
Littleton MA 01460

Call Sign: KB1FSV
Lesley T Glorioso
87 Nashoba Rd
Littleton MA 01460

Call Sign: K1LTG
Lesley T Glorioso
87 Nashoba Rd
Littleton MA 01460

Call Sign: KB1FNA
Scott R Glorioso
87 Nashobu Rd
Littleton MA 01460

Call Sign: KB1NEV
Grant C Mills

604 Newtown Rd
Littleton MA
014602117

Call Sign: WA1LDJ
William C Brown Jr
7 Old Orchard Ln
Littleton MA 01460

Call Sign: KA1LAQ
Wendy A Mc Dougall
47 Orchid Dr
Littleton MA 01460

Call Sign: KD1MI
Michael T Burke
8 Porter Rd
Littleton MA 01460

Call Sign: KB1LJL
Daniel P Noe
18 Porter Rd
Littleton MA 01460

Call Sign: KB1KAI
Karen A Rosado
15 Roxbury Dr
Littleton MA 01460

Call Sign: W1ARR
Robert J Hill
28 Roxbury Dr
Littleton MA
014601641

Call Sign: W1EHP
Allen L Grant
19 Shattuck St Apt 28
Littleton MA 01460

Call Sign: KA1UYQ
Brad W Johnson
40 Snow Dr
Littleton MA 01460

Call Sign: KD1QM
Wayne M Johnson
40 Snow Dr
Littleton MA 01460

Call Sign: KB7YAM
Curtis N Bingham
35 Snow Drive
Littleton MA 01460

Call Sign: KB7YPB
Becky W Bingham
35 Snow Drive
Littleton MA 01460

Call Sign: WA1PWT
Peter W Tierney
153 Tahattawan Rd
Littleton MA
014601656

Call Sign: KB1RNW
Kim P Van Der Riet
174 Tahattawan Rd
Littleton MA 01460

Call Sign: K1ZA
Kim P Van Der Riet
174 Tahattawan Rd
Littleton MA 01460

Call Sign: KB1FTQ
Peter W Tierney
153 Tuhattawun Rd
Littleton MA 01460

Call Sign: N1JKL
Ronald D Thornton
10 Uplands Rd
Littleton MA
014601117

Call Sign: N1LDM
Carol V Conroy
10 Uplands Rd
Littleton MA 01460

Call Sign: K1MS
Ivan G Pagacik
123 Whitcomb Ave
Littleton MA 01460

Call Sign: KC1JY
Roger H Hauck
147 Whitcomb Ave
Littleton MA
014601429

Call Sign: KB1NT
Paul H Budlong
19 Woodridge Rd
Littleton MA 01460

Call Sign: N1HVA
Donald P Gallant
89 Wychwood Height
Littleton MA 01460

Call Sign: N1OQH
Rachel R Gallant
89 Wychwood Height
Littleton MA 01460

Call Sign: KA1GIF
Richard M Sawdo
Littleton MA 01460

Call Sign: KA1RCC
William R Colbert
Littleton MA
014603296

Call Sign: KA1YUW
John W Hathaway Ii
Littleton MA 01460

Call Sign: K1ZCY
John W Hathaway Ii
Littleton MA 01460

**FCC Amateur Radio
Licenses in
Longmeadow**

Call Sign: KB1LFG
Timothy D Peet
123 Albemarle Rd
Longmeadow MA
01106

Call Sign: WB1GLZ
Alfred A Tedeschi
132 Albemarle Rd
Longmeadow MA
01106

Call Sign: KB1WXY
David J Krahm
76 Barrington Rd
Longmeadow MA
01106

Call Sign: WB1DEA
Samuel Horowitz
52 Bel Air Dr
Longmeadow MA
01106

Call Sign: WA1HFF
Steven M Berg
174 Bel Air Dr
Longmeadow MA
01106

Call Sign: KB1CPZ
Elizabeth C Gregoire
510 Bliss Rd
Longmeadow MA
01106

Call Sign: W1BMK
Normand R Gregoire
510 Bliss Rd
Longmeadow MA
01106

Call Sign: KB1AAB
Irving I Ser
11 Blueberry Hill Rd
Longmeadow MA
011061625

Call Sign: KB1HWG
Jeffrey W Hulbert
236 Burbank Rd
Longmeadow MA
01106

Call Sign: K1AJH
Jeffrey W Hulbert
236 Burbank Rd
Longmeadow MA
01106

Call Sign: KB1WCT
Warren Myers
91 Chiswick St
Longmeadow MA
01106

Call Sign: KB1VKY
Jeffrey A Myers
136 Colton Pl
Longmeadow MA
01106

Call Sign: N1TOW
Joshua C Randall
38 Crescent Rd
Longmeadow MA
01106

Call Sign: WA3SLJ
Albert B Pleet
276 Deepwoods Dr
Longmeadow MA
01106

Call Sign: WB3EAU
Rochelle E Pleet
276 Deepwoods Dr
Longmeadow MA
01106

Call Sign: N3IMU
Alan W Dove
248 Deepwoods Dr
Longmeadow MA
011062137

Call Sign: WA1FJV
Rodney M Riker Jr
17 Drury Ln
Longmeadow MA
01106

Call Sign: KA1WSC
Niel J Prankus
37 Elmwood Ave
Longmeadow MA
01106

Call Sign: K1JDL
Richard P Diefenderfer
779 Frank Smith Rd
Longmeadow MA
01106

Call Sign: N1MSY
Douglas W Barron
43 Franklin Ter
Longmeadow MA
01106

Call Sign: KB1AYC
Jason D Shapiro
264 Green Hill Rd
Longmeadow MA
01106

Call Sign: KB1KEU
David M Koffman
264 Green Hill Rd
Longmeadow MA
01106

Call Sign: K1DRD
David M Koffman
264 Green Hill Rd
Longmeadow MA
01106

Call Sign: NJ1E
William C Sample
43 Hillside Ter
Longmeadow MA
01106

Call Sign: KB1FTU
Christopher M
Mirabello
108 Homestead Blvd
Longmeadow MA
01106

Call Sign: KB1KQM
David B Slitzky
441 Inverness Ln
Longmeadow MA
01106

Call Sign: WB1DBY
Larry Krainson
100 Kenmore Dr
Longmeadow MA
011062759

Call Sign: KB1NSN
Jacob E Krainson
100 Kenmore Dr
Longmeadow MA
01106

Call Sign: KA1AGQ
Steven E Horowitz
242 Kenmore Dr
Longmeadow MA
01106

Call Sign: KB1JXP
James M Whitehouse
99 Knollwood Dr
Longmeadow MA
011062713

Call Sign: WA1LUV
James A Whitehouse
99 Knollwood Drive

Longmeadow MA
011062713

Call Sign: K1JAW
James A Whitehouse
99 Knollwood Drive
Longmeadow MA
011062713

Call Sign: KA1PEQ
Frank T Chidsey
172 Longview Dr
Longmeadow MA
01106

Call Sign: KA1HTI
David M D Antonio
81 Madow Rd
Longmeadow MA
01106

Call Sign: KA1BSG
Robert L Beaudoin
728 Maple Rd
Long Meadow MA
01006

Call Sign: W1WBH
Roland M Douillard
133 Massachusetts Ave
Longmeadow MA
01106

Call Sign: KB1WCS
Christopher M Grello
110 Meadow Rd
Longmeadow MA
01106

Call Sign: WB1BZG
Donald C Shukan
358 Merriweather Dr
Longmeadow MA
01106

Call Sign: KB1UYH
Samuel M Epstein
80 Mill Rd
Longmeadow MA
01106

Call Sign: KB1HAA
Eric Rubenstein
32 Morningside Dr

Longmeadow MA
01106

Call Sign: KB1KNK
John E Taylor
27 Norway St
Longmeadow MA
01106

Call Sign: KB1ANM
Stanley Glasser
320 Pine Wood Dr
Longmeadow MA
01106

Call Sign: N1CAS
William T Mc Gurk
70 Riverview Ave
Longmeadow MA
01106

Call Sign: N1JJI
John D Colton
15 Roseland Ter
Longmeadow MA
01106

Call Sign: N1LJX
Jeff A Setterstrom
75 Roseland Terrace
Longmeadow MA
01106

Call Sign: KB1VIC
Caerwyn B Jones
33 Rosemore St
Longmeadow MA
01106

Call Sign: N1OBD
Mohan R Kottamasu
112 Twin Hills Dr
Longmeadow MA
01106

Call Sign: WB1HKE
Mark E Lantzakis
45 Whitmun Rd
Longmeadow MA
01106

Call Sign: KA1YHT
Robert J Bye
109 Wild Grove Ln

Longmeadow MA
01106

Call Sign: KB1MTR
Michael N Taniwha
48 Willett Dr
Longmeadow MA
01106

Call Sign: NZ1MT
Michael N Taniwha
48 Willett Dr
Longmeadow MA
01106

Call Sign: N1KFD
John I Shyloski
16 Williams Ct
Longmeadow MA
01106

Call Sign: NU1O
Christopher J Scibelli
226 Wimbleton Dr
Longmeadow MA
01106

Call Sign: W6IS
Irving Slitzky
119 Yarmouth St
Longmeadow MA
011063226

Call Sign: KB1PBI
James R Cook
Longmeadow MA
01116

**FCC Amateur Radio
Licenses in Lowell**

Call Sign: N1PRV
Jason E Bunker Sr
49 2nd St Apt 1
Lowell MA 01852

Call Sign: N1DBJ
Robert R Di Padua
58 3rd St
Lowell MA 01850

Call Sign: N1SWB
Cary L Renault
35 7th St

Lowell MA 018502153

Call Sign: KA1RMA
Henry L Pare
107 Alcott St
Lowell MA 01852

Call Sign: N1GRD
Michael R Hereth
305 Andover St
Lowell MA 01852

Call Sign: N1MYZ
Jeanne M Hereth
305 Andover St
Lowell MA 01852

Call Sign: KA1OPJ
George C Rapp
30 Angle St Unit 49
Lowell MA 01851

Call Sign: KB1MUW
Albert R Perkinson
153 Appleton St
Lowell MA 01852

Call Sign: KB1PNW
Christine M Green
86 Arbor Rd
Lowell MA 01852

Call Sign: N1DYQ
David P Naylor Jr
52 Arlington St
Lowell MA 01854

Call Sign: N1VZK
Carlos J Gonzalez
49 Arnold Ave
Lowell MA 01852

Call Sign: KB1AIT
Bernard P Rayball
148 B St
Lowell MA 01851

Call Sign: N1HAN
David R Leclair
70 Barbara St
Lowell MA 01854

Call Sign: W1MKX
Francis M Mc Grath

21 Belmont St
Lowell MA 01851

Call Sign: KB1TKC
Christian St Cyr
35 Bernier St Apt 10
Lowell MA 01852

Call Sign: N1KTS
Lenny A Ricupero
140 Bowden St Apt#
204
Lowell MA 01852

Call Sign: KB1OHM
Samuel Sanabria
51 Bownton St
Lowell MA 01850

Call Sign: NZ1R
Robert D Berube
849 Bridge St
Lowell MA 01850

Call Sign: WB1AKN
Louis B Nelson
735 Broadway St Apt
308
Lowell MA 01854

Call Sign: KB1MVE
Clayton L Leblanc
7 Butman Rd
Lowell MA 01852

Call Sign: WA1VNA
Rita L Hogan
120 Campbell Dr
Lowell MA 018513926

Call Sign: WB1BRW
Francis W Hogan
120 Campbell Dr
Lowell MA 018513926

Call Sign: KA1JMT
Carmen I Rinne
152 Carlisle St
Lowell MA 01852

Call Sign: N1EGG
Francis M Hojlo
26 Charant Rd
Lowell MA 018541045

Call Sign: KA1OJW
Sydney G Jump
610 Chelmsford St
Lowell MA 01851

Call Sign: N1YOP
Mark E Holmes
260 Christian St
Lowell MA 01850

Call Sign: N1VRU
Kim N Delinsky
107 Clarendon St
Lowell MA 01851

Call Sign: N1VRY
Jason S Delinsky
107 Clarendon St
Lowell MA 01851

Call Sign: KB1JXM
Marco S Sandoval
118 Corinthian Dr
Lowell MA 01854

Call Sign: K1MPS
Marco S Sandoval
118 Corinthian Dr
Lowell MA 01854

Call Sign: N1NNC
Brian R O Keefe
26 Crawford St
Lowell MA 01854

Call Sign: N1UFT
Cherylle J Hird
244 Cumberland Rd
Lowell MA 01850

Call Sign: KB1ORH
Walter H Hird
244 Cumberland Rd
Lowell MA 01850

Call Sign: N1ZVA
Angel J Reyes
139 Cumberland Rd
Apt 1
Lowell MA 01850

Call Sign: N1QVU
Arnaldo Mejias

68 Dalton St
Lowell MA 01850

Call Sign: KB1RHH
Michael S Colon
10 Dane St
Lowell MA 01854

Call Sign: KB1RHI
Cathy L Colon
10 Dane St
Lowell MA 01854

Call Sign: AB1EE
James Cadorette
26 Doane St Apt G
Lowell MA 01851

Call Sign: AB1FH
James Cadorette
26 Doane St Apt G
Lowell MA 01851

Call Sign: KB1RLW
Jason W Sweeney
30 Dracut St 2nd Fl
Lowell MA 01854

Call Sign: N1PZN
Steve T Tingas
18 E Meadow Ln 120
Lowell MA 01854

Call Sign: KA1VDZ
Carlos L Johnson
694 E Merrimack St
Lowell MA 01852

Call Sign: N1JGE
George A De Amicis
80 Ellis Ave
Lowell MA 01854

Call Sign: KB1SNB
Richard A Lavigne
170 Ennell St
Lowell MA 01850

Call Sign: N1ZRX
Stanley Sawlan
Farmland Rd
Lowell MA 01850

Call Sign: AI1E

Elmer W Carlson
37 Featherstom Ave
Lowell MA 01852

Call Sign: KA1WUA
Christopher T Ryder
98 Florence St
Lowell MA 01852

Call Sign: WP4AKE
Fernando Suarez
21 Floyd St
Lowell MA 01852

Call Sign: KA1VCL
Richard C Snyder
53 Fowler Rd
Lowell MA 01854

Call Sign: WB9IIS
Marc W Ditz
40 Garden Rd
Lowell MA 01852

Call Sign: AA1RB
James Cadorette
3 Gates St
Lowell MA 01851

Call Sign: KB1KRG
Ronald P Quattrochi
68 Geana Ln
Lowell MA 018521427

Call Sign: WQ1Z
Ronald P Quattrochi
68 Geana Ln
Lowell MA 018521427

Call Sign: WB1CAX
Gerald D Colton
218 Gibson St
Lowell MA 01851

Call Sign: KA1WZI
Robin E Chestna
25 Glenellyn Rd W
Lowell MA 01852

Call Sign: AB1G
Bernard C Perron
151 Glenwood St
Lowell MA 01852

Call Sign: KB2KWB
Juan A Santiago
400 Gorham St Apt A2
Lowell MA 01852

Call Sign: KB2PUU
Julia M Rivera
400 Gorham St Apt A2
Lowell MA 01852

Call Sign: KB1SMH
Erinn C Makary
230 Gorham St Unit 14
Lowell MA 01852

Call Sign: WA7YVA
Lewis S Keele
1506 Gorham St Unit
308
Lowell MA 01852

Call Sign: KA1WTZ
Eric M Ryder
30 Haines Ave
Lowell MA 01852

Call Sign: K1PRQ
Joseph A Landry
27 Hampshire St
Lowell MA 01850

Call Sign: N1AUQ
James W Clark
12 Hampton Ave
Lowell MA 018543106

Call Sign: N1JEE
Richard E De Paulis
36 Harris Ave
Lowell MA 01851

Call Sign: AA1HO
Arthur L Walsh Jr
73 Hawthorn St
Lowell MA 01851

Call Sign: N1PZK
Conrad P Dion Sr
117 High St
Lowell MA 01852

Call Sign: KB1NYG
Marcos Dias
428 High St

Lowell MA 01852

Call Sign: KA1OLA
David F Hadley
34 Hildreth St
Lowell MA 01850

Call Sign: N1MRJ
George Matusiak
91 Hildreth St
Lowell MA 01850

Call Sign: KB1MUX
Andrew J Bullock
271 Humphrey St - 18
Lowell MA 01850

Call Sign: KA1RDR
Norman E Morin
15 Johnson St
Lowell MA 01854

Call Sign: WA1IPA
Norman R Gauthier
5 Joiners Ct
Lowell MA 01852

Call Sign: KB1IOH
Keri A Demers
22 Lisa Ln
Lowell MA 018541218

Call Sign: KB1GYJ
Candace M Levesque
9 Ludlam St
Lowell MA 01850

Call Sign: KB1GYK
Steven J Levesque
9 Ludlam St
Lowell MA 01850

Call Sign: K1ZKA
James J Lee
390 Mammoth Rd
Lowell MA 01854

Call Sign: KB1LTS
Sarah J Clark
256 Mansur St
Lowell MA 01852

Call Sign: KB1HMB
Carl G Greenbaum

200 Market St Unit
311
Lowell MA 01852

Call Sign: WM3E
Carl G Greenbaum
200 Market St Unit
311
Lowell MA 01852

Call Sign: N1PMQ
Charles P Boudreau
37 Marlboro St Apt 2
Lowell MA 01851

Call Sign: N1LUC
Evelyn M Hojlo
30 Marlborough St
Lowell MA 01851

Call Sign: N1DGP
Ronald E Matthews
118 Marshall Rd
Lowell MA 01852

Call Sign: KB1HLX
Edward J Dicroce
200 Massmills Dr Apt
402
Lowell MA 01852

Call Sign: AA1VS
Charles E Suprin
75 Merrill Ave
Lowell MA 01850

Call Sign: N1SIY
Conrad R Monty
657 Merrimack St Apt
207
Lowell MA 01854

Call Sign: KB1NFX
Richard A Harvey
657 Merrimack St Apt
728
Lowell MA 01854

Call Sign: WT1Q
Michael J Munro
23 Methuen St
Lowell MA 01850

Call Sign: KA1UKW

Leonard J Sicard
84 Methuen St
Lowell MA 01850

Call Sign: KB1RBA
Mark J Micire
172 Middle St Apt 206
Lowell MA 01852

Call Sign: WA2YUI
Stephen Moses
Middlesex St
Lowell MA 01851

Call Sign: KC1QM
Don W O Brien
159 Moore St
Lowell MA 01852

Call Sign: KB1WSS
Andrew J Garabedian
51 Morningside Dr
Lowell MA 01852

Call Sign: K1ROL
George D Gatzimos
17 Mt Vernon St
Lowell MA 018543325

Call Sign: N1ARO
Earl A Le Bourdais
149 Orleans St
Lowell MA 01850

Call Sign: N1KGC
William J Wyatt
341 Pawtucket Blvd 13
Lowell MA 01854

Call Sign: N1KOW
Diogenes J Guimaraes
611 Pawtucket Blvd 9
Lowell MA 01854

Call Sign: KA1RIG
Leo Perlmutter
1461 Pawtucket Blvd
E6
Lowell MA 01854

Call Sign: KB1FY
Dexter C Atkinson
24 Perron Way
Lowell MA 01854

Call Sign: N1TT
Stanley A White
26 Phoebe Ave
Lowell MA 01854

Call Sign: KB1GZN
Nicholas J Papadonis
31 Photine Dr
Lowell MA 018541247

Call Sign: N1MNG
Bernard Shapiro
451 Pine St
Lowell MA 01851

Call Sign: N1UWS
Diana M Shapiro
451 Pine St
Lowell MA 01851

Call Sign: KA1WPB
Ernest J Demopolos
145 Po Square Apt
A809
Lowell MA 01852

Call Sign: WU1C
Kenneth J Stranc
58 Prescott St Unit #6
Lowell MA 018521936

Call Sign: WB1GGE
Glenn L Wallace
27 Princeton Blvd
Lowell MA 01851

Call Sign: N1TRE
Kenneth A Zeller
182 Princeton Blvd
Lowell MA 01851

Call Sign: N1LYN
Edward L Salsgiver Jr
725 Princeton Blvd 13
Lowell MA 01851

Call Sign: N2PSC
Michael L Franzino
620 Princeton Blvd
Unit 17
Lowell MA 01851

Call Sign: KC7MOE

Edward R Kopacz Sr
4 Puffer Ave
Lowell MA 08185

Call Sign: KA1MNF
Edward R Kopacz Sr
4 Puffer Ave
Lowell MA 01850

Call Sign: N1IJG
Brian C Ryder
11 Roberta Ln
Lowell MA 01852

Call Sign: NE1X
Andrew J Brockert
85 Royal St
Lowell MA 01851

Call Sign: N1GYB
Timothy J Sherman
170 S Good St Apt 2
Lowell MA 01851

Call Sign: WB8WGY
Steven M Schultz
145 Sanders Ave
Lowell MA 018513416

Call Sign: W1LOW
David W Mc Laughlin
61 Saratoga St
Lowell MA 01852

Call Sign: KE1JI
Hipolito Masa
231 School St
Lowell MA 01854

Call Sign: N1MEQ
Charles E Lowder
88 Sixth Ave
Lowell MA 01854

Call Sign: KA1HIU
Henry N Dozois
24 Smith St
Lowell MA 01851

Call Sign: KA5DSX
Robert P Fisk
63 Stanley St
Lowell MA 01852

Call Sign: N1LNM
Harold F Larock
38 Starbird St
Lowell MA 01854

Call Sign: KB1FFI
Frank E Harrington
38 Staveley St
Lowell MA 01852

Call Sign: N1VWF
Edwin Encarnacion
293 Stevens St
Lowell MA 01851

Call Sign: K1YZB
Daniel J Toohey
355 Stevens St
Lowell MA 01851

Call Sign: KA1JNT
Rodney R Minklein
272 Trotting Park Rd
Lowell MA 01854

Call Sign: KB1CAJ
U Mass Lowell
Amateur Radio Club
1 University Ave E E
Dept
Lowell MA 01854

Call Sign: KB1NEW
James T Silva
1142 Varnum Ave
Lowell MA 01854

Call Sign: N1UGN
John F Dennis Iii
15 Veterans Way
Crescent Bldg 204
Lowell MA 01852

Call Sign: KA1RZN
Kathleen S Fox
Williams
99 Walker St
Lowell MA 01854

Call Sign: N1FVC
Richard J Williams
99 Walker St 2nd Flr
Rear
Lowell MA 01854

Call Sign: KB1RHJ
Hector Gonzalez
27 Ware St
Lowell MA 01851

Call Sign: KB1VSB
Amy M Haskins
40 Warnock St
Lowell MA 01852

Call Sign: K1VKT
Francis Mc Namara
51 Wedge St
Lowell MA 01851

Call Sign: KB1OKR
Gary R Chandonnet
22 Weed St
Lowell MA 01852

Call Sign: KB1MGG
Stephen C Farley
25 Weed St
Lowell MA 01852

Call Sign: KB1OPM
Mark L Farley
25 Weed St
Lowell MA 01852

Call Sign: KA1WNJ
Richard C Duhamel
509 Wentworth Ave
Lowell MA 01852

Call Sign: N1XJI
Christopher C Damren
1001 Westford At Apt
2
Lowell MA 01851

Call Sign: N1NSA
Sharon M Jacobus
562 Westford St
Lowell MA 01851

Call Sign: N1HGY
David M Stevens
606 Westford St
Lowell MA 01851

Call Sign: N1UVU
Robert A Landoni Jr

1003 Westford St Apt
5
Lowell MA 01851

Call Sign: WA1BNA
Leon R Morency
159 White St
Lowell MA 01854

Call Sign: WB1DKE
Shadow M Clark
18 Whitehead Ave
Lowell MA 01852

Call Sign: N1OSU
John J Mullen
85 Wightman St
Lowell MA 01851

Call Sign: KA1VKP
Constantina A
Panagakos
340 Wilder St
Lowell MA 01851

Call Sign: KB1NXL
Richard J Tedesco
20 Woodland Dr 346
Lowell MA 01852

Call Sign: N1CVO
Shawn K Dodds
20 Woodland Drive
Unit 328
Lowell MA 01852

**FCC Amateur Radio
Licenses in Ludlow**

Call Sign: WB1AIK
Michael J Rybak Jr
116 Americo St
Ludlow MA 01056

Call Sign: AA1AW
Joseph J Martin
22 Berkshire St
Ludlow MA
010563557

Call Sign: N1PVW
Diane M Hall
81 Bondsville Rd
Ludlow MA 01056

Call Sign: KA1ZHF
Robert A Hall
81 Bondsville Rd
Ludlow MA 01056

Call Sign: KB1BIC
Richard A Langlais
37 Brookhaven Dr
Ludlow MA 01056

Call Sign: K1QMV
William Jaciow
783 Center St
Ludlow MA 01056

Call Sign: N1XLF
Robert F Edelmann
848 Center St
Ludlow MA 01056

Call Sign: KA1LXT
Allan R Leto
530 Chapin St
Ludlow MA 01056

Call Sign: N1GJU
Richard I Boyce
144 Coolidge Ave
Ludlow MA 01056

Call Sign: N1UCY
Paul S Lizak
21 Davis St
Ludlow MA 01056

Call Sign: K1IQA
William B Leonard
17 Deponte Drive
Ludlow MA 01056

Call Sign: WA1WTK
Louis J Regnier
136 East Akard St
Ludlow MA 01056

Call Sign: N1RFQ
Joseph R Gazialle
138 East St
Ludlow MA
010563409

Call Sign: W1VNE
Leo H J Brodeur

1032 East St
Ludlow MA 01056

Call Sign: KB1GPI
Terrance E
Chandonnet
1064 East St
Ludlow MA 01056

Call Sign: KB1IQQ
Evan J Chandonnet
1064 East St
Ludlow MA 01056

Call Sign: W1TER
Terrance E
Chandonnet
1064 East St
Ludlow MA 01056

Call Sign: W1EVN
Evan J Chandonnet
1064 East St
Ludlow MA 01056

Call Sign: K1EAX
J Bernard Syriac
41 Eden St
Ludlow MA 01056

Call Sign: KA1WAH
Michael A Doda
39 Electric Ave
Ludlow MA 01056

Call Sign: WQ1X
Ronald L Chartier
68 Fairview St
Ludlow MA 01056

Call Sign: N1VRG
Brian L Bedard
14 Fairway Dr
Ludlow MA 01056

Call Sign: K1GXU
Laurence J Langevin
22 Fern St
Ludlow MA 01056

Call Sign: WA1WKE
Linda F Langevin
22 Fern St
Ludlow MA 01056

Call Sign: KB1PQY
Robert Larkin
668 Fuller
Ludlow MA 01056

Call Sign: KB1UYK
Kyle T Grondalski
132 Fuller St
Ludlow MA 01056

Call Sign: KB1UYL
Thomas J Grondalski
132 Fuller St
Ludlow MA 01056

Call Sign: KB2DWB
Lisa J Doiron
84 Fuller St 9
Ludlow MA 01056

Call Sign: WB1HFZ
Paul V Roberts
372 Holyoke St
Ludlow MA 01056

Call Sign: N1LLJ
Robert E Goddeau
143 Kendall St
Ludlow MA 01056

Call Sign: N1IVM
Bert D Ramage
101 Lavoie Ave
Ludlow MA 01056

Call Sign: W1MLJ
Bert D Ramage
101 Lavoie Ave
Ludlow MA 01056

Call Sign: KB1MIE
Lucy A Rae
122 Lyon St
Ludlow MA 01056

Call Sign: KB1MIF
James C Rae
122 Lyon St
Ludlow MA 01056

Call Sign: K0RAE
James C Rae
122 Lyon St

Ludlow MA 01056

Call Sign: K9LAR
Lucy A Rae
122 Lyon St
Ludlow MA 01056

Call Sign: KD1HB
Brian T Fillion
48 Lyons St
Ludlow MA 01056

Call Sign: KB1DCF
Eric W King
31 Maple St
Ludlow MA 01056

Call Sign: KB1JVA
Charles H Zelck
223 Marion Circle
Ludlow MA 01516

Call Sign: KA1ECJ
Murel A Gover
6 May Rd
Ludlow MA 01056

Call Sign: WB1EOR
Orlando D Batista
503 Meadowe Crest
Ludlow MA 01056

Call Sign: KB1FFK
Ernest J Bramucci
506 Meadowe Crest
Drive
Ludlow MA 01056

Call Sign: K1EJB
Ernest J Bramucci
506 Meadowe Crest
Drive
Ludlow MA 01056

Call Sign: WB1GIZ
William H Martin
82 Michael St
Ludlow MA 01056

Call Sign: W1CIP
Anastasios D Kinanis
159 Michael St
Ludlow MA 01056

Call Sign: KD1IR
Thomas B Fillion
360 Munsing St
Ludlow MA 01056

Call Sign: N1KNY
Thomas N Gibeau
984 Poole St
Ludlow MA 01056

Call Sign: W1DGJ
Michael W Ludkiewicz
143 Richmond Rd
Ludlow MA 01056

Call Sign: K1XZ
Paul R Duquette
66 Rood St
Ludlow MA 01056

Call Sign: KB1RXC
Antonio S Martins
29 Roy St
Ludlow MA 01056

Call Sign: N1MAR
Antonio S Martins
29 Roy St
Ludlow MA 01056

Call Sign: W3SYB
Harold D Fonner
83 Stivens Terr
Ludlow MA 01056

Call Sign: KB1WGY
James R Shatzer
104 Warwick Dr
Ludlow MA 01056

Call Sign: N1HZZ
Everett E Kerr
350 West St
Ludlow MA 01056

Call Sign: KB1GDI
John L Minerich
522 West St
Ludlow MA 01056

Call Sign: N1OWK
Christopher R Vyce
350 West St Lot 36
Ludlow MA 01056

Call Sign: W1KOA
Henry J Cristina
279 Winsor St
Ludlow MA
010563533

Call Sign: KB1MIL
Robert S Marek
Ludlow MA 01056

FCC Amateur Radio Licenses in Lumenburg

Call Sign: N1GKX
Stephen A Ruggles
48 Cliffview Ter
Lunenburg MA 01462

Call Sign: N1UDQ
David J Boisvert
22 Cove Rd
Lunenburg MA 01462

Call Sign: KB1DYS
Kevin J Fish
70 Eastern Ave
Lunenburg MA 01462

Call Sign: KB1TUV
David J Smith Jr
183 Elmwood Rd
Lunenburg MA 01462

Call Sign: KB1OZM
Justin A Brzozoski
21 Francis Ave
Lunenburg MA
014622023

Call Sign: KB1LJJ
Edward J Hendershaw
90 Gilchrest St
Lunenburg MA 01462

Call Sign: N1EJH
Edward J Hendershaw
90 Gilchrest St
Lunenburg MA 01462

Call Sign: KD1EF
William G Brown Jr
2 Goodrich St

Lunenburg MA 01462

Call Sign: N1FYW
Kenneth J Chenis
230 Holman St
Lunenburg MA 01462

Call Sign: N1DJB
James H Donalds
492 Holman St
Lunenburg MA 01462

Call Sign: K1SNX
Mark H Feinberg
130 Houghtons Mill
Rd
Lunenburg MA 01462

Call Sign: KB1RUU
Devin J Carroll
803 Leominster Rd
Lunenburg MA 01462

Call Sign: KA1LOA
James M Novak
43 Longwood Drive
Lunenburg MA
014622161

Call Sign: N1RDD
Christopher M Gibson
438 Mass Ave
Lunenburg MA 01462

Call Sign: N1IRC
Robert L Groves
572 Mass Ave
Lunenburg MA 01462

Call Sign: N1THX
John D Hallisey
739 New W Townsend
Rd
Lunenburg MA 01462

Call Sign: N1THY
Diane S Bouvier
739 New W Townsend
Rd
Lunenburg MA 01462

Call Sign: N1QKK
Thongchai Hongsmatip
80 Northfield Rd

Lunenburg MA 01462

Call Sign: KC2KDT
Michael J Meier
216 Northfield Rd
Lunenburg MA 01462

Call Sign: KB1MOE
Paul J Charpentier
6 Peninsula Dr
Lunenburg MA 01462

Call Sign: N1PFZ
Edward P Dextraze
25 Rangeley Rd
Lunenburg MA 01462

Call Sign: W1QXG
Henry G Root
180 Rolling Acres
Lunenburg MA 01462

Call Sign: KB1WKI
Christopher
Handwerker
161 Rolling Acres Rd
Lunenburg MA 01462

Call Sign: KB1HIB
Paul R Marichal
108 Royal Fern Dr
Lunenburg MA 01462

Call Sign: AA1BF
Leonard D Marsolais
44 Sunny Hill Rd
Lunenburg MA 01462

Call Sign: KB1GHZ
Eric J Koslowski
271 Sunset Lane
Lunenburg MA 01462

Call Sign: KD1SM
Ralph R Swick
113 Townsend Harbor
Rd
Lunenburg MA 01462

Call Sign: N1QIT
Jeanine E Swick
113 Townsend Harbor
Rd
Lunenburg MA 01462

Call Sign: KB1UVP
Kenneth K Bailey Jr
157 Townsend Harbor
Rd
Lunenburg MA 01462

Call Sign: N1QDX
Paul J Doherty
214 Townsend Harbor
Rd
Lunenburg MA 01462

Call Sign: KB1JZU
Robert E Montemerlo
362 Townsend Harbor
Rd
Lunenburg MA 01462

Call Sign: N1HFW
Barbara L Vienneau
570 Townsend Harbor
Rd
Lunenburg MA 01462

Call Sign: WB1B
James C Vienneau
570 Townsend Harbor
Rd
Lunenburg MA 01462

Call Sign: WB1CLI
James W Prescott
78 Turkeyhill Rd
Lunenburg MA 01462

Call Sign: KA1DTF
Kenneth A Reed
77 Upland Ave
Lunenburg MA 01462

Call Sign: KB1JCE
George H Oliver
33 Wallis Park
Lunenburg MA 01462

Call Sign: N1UDR
Ian G Martin
427 Whalom Rd
Lunenburg MA
014622240

Call Sign: WT1A
Dana B Fraser

131 White St
Lunenburg MA 01462

Call Sign: KB1HNK
Ronald E Kiuru
192 White St
Lunenburg MA 01462

Call Sign: KB1OOI
Ronald E Kiuru
192 White St
Lunenburg MA 01462

Call Sign: WT1Y
Ronald E Kiuru
192 White St
Lunenburg MA 01462

Call Sign: N1KRQ
Edward A Markham
Lunenburg MA 01462

Call Sign: KB1HWT
Kevin Mcdonald
Lunenburg MA 01462

Call Sign: N1EJJ
Jean Joseph Cote
371 Northfield Rd
Lunengurg MA 01462

**FCC Amateur Radio
Licenses in Lynn**

Call Sign: KB1ICX
Richard F Courtney
6 Adams St
Lynn MA 01902

Call Sign: N1RYT
William J Bridgham
197 Allen Ave
Lynn MA 01902

Call Sign: KB1GMQ
Debra A Bridgham
197 Allen Ave
Lynn MA 01902

Call Sign: KB1GMR
Daniel T Bridgham
197 Allen Ave
Lynn MA 01902

Call Sign: WC1H
Michael J Barry
26 Apple St
Lynn MA 019022710

Call Sign: KB1FLD
Robert W Haddow Sr
16 Archer St
Lynn MA 01902

Call Sign: N1XBA
Dana F Cyr
26 Archer St
Lynn MA 01902

Call Sign: N1XBS
Michael S Karpinski
27 Ashland St
Lynn MA 019052023

Call Sign: N1KYI
Vincent L Fure
65 Ashland St
Lynn MA 01905

Call Sign: KB1HQI
Paul L Mcdonough
67 Ashland St
Lynn MA 01905

Call Sign: W1PLM
Paul L Mcdonough
67 Ashland St
Lynn MA 01905

Call Sign: W1TVG
Frank J Eckert
25 Atlantic Terr
Lynn MA 01902

Call Sign: KB1UEA
Zackary B Mackay
9 Audubon Park
Lynn MA 01902

Call Sign: KA1NCE
Lawrence W Bishop
55 B St
Lynn MA 01905

Call Sign: KA1AMO
Christopher J Carroll
66 Belleaire Ave
Lynn MA 01904

Call Sign: KA1AYF
Elisabeth A Carroll
66 Belleaire Ave
Lynn MA 01904

Call Sign: W1UYL
James M Carroll
66 Belleaire Ave
Lynn MA 01904

Call Sign: WA1PGG
Kathleen S Kraemer
66 Belleaire Ave
Lynn MA 01904

Call Sign: WB1GYE
Joanna M Carroll
66 Belleaire Ave
Lynn MA 01904

Call Sign: N1FQV
Peter J Di Forte
30 Bonavesta St
Lynn MA 01905

Call Sign: N1OHW
Thomas F Marsters Jr
796 Boston St
Lynn MA 01905

Call Sign: K1LTP
Charles Kokinos
63 Briar Hill Dr
Lynn MA 01902

Call Sign: N1CKH
Eileen J Kokinos
63 Briar Hill Dr
Lynn MA 01902

Call Sign: KB1VWU
Pantelis C Thomadis
28 Brookvale St
Lynn MA 01905

Call Sign: N1DXA
Bruce J Forrest
24 Bruce Place
Lynn MA 01902

Call Sign: N1PIW
George P Doonan Sr
15 Buchanan Cir

Lynn MA 01902

Call Sign: KB1PZY
Scott H Addison
84 Burrill Ave
Lynn MA 01902

Call Sign: KB1ODG
James G Barrett
55 Burrill Ave #2
Lynn MA 01902

Call Sign: W1OPI
Guy R Gianino
60 Casco Rd
Lynn MA 01904

Call Sign: WB1HBU
Eric A Cottrell
37 Centre St
Lynn MA 019052248

Call Sign: N1EVH
Michael A Naselroad
73 Centre St
Lynn MA 019052246

Call Sign: KB1LLY
Samuel D White Iii
112 Chatham St
Lynn MA 01902

Call Sign: N1GEM
Stephen C Calder
319 Chatham St
Lynn MA 01902

Call Sign: N1TVW
Vasilios Migos
18 Cherry St
Lynn MA 01902

Call Sign: K1UIW
John J Cull
12 Cherry Tree Lane
Lynn MA 01904

Call Sign: WA1TFJ
Eli C Hancock
14 Chestnut Ave
Lynn MA 01905

Call Sign: N1UGT
Daniel E Quinn

34 Clifton Ave
Lynn MA 01902

Call Sign: N1XWU
Frank Nelson
55 Collins St
Lynn MA 01902

Call Sign: W1DFO
Herbert R Ricker
50 Colonial Ave
Lynn MA 01904

Call Sign: KB1MBC
Joseph C Canizaro
52 Conomo Ave
Lynn MA 01904

Call Sign: N1KYR
Eric R Burns
11 Coolidge Rd
Lynn MA 01902

Call Sign: W1DVG
George E Webber Iii
72 Cottage St
Lynn MA 01905

Call Sign: WA1WGY
George E Webber Iv
72 Cottage St
Lynn MA 01905

Call Sign: WA1WKY
Denise L Webber
72 Cottage St
Lynn MA 01905

Call Sign: N1RMF
Mark S Theriault
44 Cowdrey Ave
Lynn MA 01904

Call Sign: KA1DIN
Earl G Bacon
42 Dearborn Ave
Lynn MA 01905

Call Sign: KA1FLD
Linda C Bacon
42 Dearborn Ave
Lynn MA 01905

Call Sign: KA1FLE

Pauline E Bacon
42 Dearborn Ave
Lynn MA 01905

Call Sign: KA1AHD
John C Lennerton
17 Dona Rd
Lynn MA 01904

Call Sign: W1JCL
John C Lennerton
17 Dona Rd
Lynn MA 01904

Call Sign: N1THV
Stephen J Evans
11 Duke St
Lynn MA 01902

Call Sign: K9PUG
Stephen J Evans
11 Duke St
Lynn MA 01902

Call Sign: KB1STZ
Christopher A Wright
373 Eastern Ave
Lynn MA 01902

Call Sign: KB1FRP
Kenneth A Stover
130 Eastern Ave Apt
727
Lynn MA 01902

Call Sign: WC1K
Philip D Theriault
102 Emerald Dr
Lynn MA 01904

Call Sign: N1YPO
Kimne Ngem
201 Essex Apt 310
Lynn MA 01402

Call Sign: WA1PVK
William F Voigt
57 Estes
Lynn MA 01920

Call Sign: N1VGJ
Arcadio Guzman
157 Euclid Ave
Lynn MA 01902

Call Sign: KB1TEJ
Toni A Sloan
305 Euclid Ave
Lynn MA 01904

Call Sign: K1DJL
Augustus M Bowzer
158 Eutaw Ave
Lynn MA 019022121

Call Sign: N1UVD
Herbert A Doumanian
65 Eutaw Ave Apt #3
Lynn MA 01902

Call Sign: N4ACZ
James E Mcleod
65 Eutaw Ave Apt 3
Lynn MA 019022136

Call Sign: KB1FCK
Amy M Doumanian
65 Eutaw Ave Apt 3
Lynn MA 01902

Call Sign: KB1WDC
Steven Connolly
20 Fearless Ave
Lynn MA 01902

Call Sign: KA1ZLD
Julie E Rice
57 Fiske Ave
Lynn MA 01902

Call Sign: W1ADD
Ellsworth H Gibson
9 Goodridge St
Lynn MA 01902

Call Sign: W1LMJ
Adolphe J Boudreau
17 Hancock St
Lynn MA 01904

Call Sign: N1EYW
Edward F Gillon
44 Harmon St
Lynn MA 01905

Call Sign: N1VFR
William J Mullarkey
48 Hawthorne St

Lynn MA 01902

Call Sign: N1VFS
Barbara L Mullarkey
48 Hawthorne St
Lynn MA 019023506

Call Sign: KA1RKH
Robert H Foster
134 Holyoke St
Lynn MA 01905

Call Sign: KA1AAI
Wayne M Redmond
45 Hood St
Lynn MA 01905

Call Sign: K1VJY
James A Reed
18 Hudson St
Lynn MA 01904

Call Sign: KA1JSV
Robinson B Nunez
9 Jackson St
Lynn MA 01902

Call Sign: W1SWR
Steven W Ryback
111 Jenness St
Lynn MA 01904

Call Sign: N1WNJ
Thomas A Martinez
56 Johnson St 8
Lynn MA 01902

Call Sign: KA1VAD
Arthur J Hynes
105 Kernwood Dr
Lynn MA 01904

Call Sign: N1JKJ
Jeffrey M Kemp
41 Kings Hill Dr
Lynn MA 01905

Call Sign: KB1TKE
Irving F Brown
26 Lafayette Park - 1
Lynn MA 01902

Call Sign: KB1BFI
I F Brown

26 Lafayette Park 1
Lynn MA 01902

Call Sign: KD1ZR
Ronald W Prendergast
Jr
78 Laurel St
Lynn MA 01905

Call Sign: KA1LAW
Edgar S Doliber Jr
35 Lawrence Rd
Lynn MA 01904

Call Sign: KB1FCJ
Christine E Scanlon
81 Lexington St
Lynn MA 01902

Call Sign: N1YNL
Ramon D J Duran
148 Liberty St 205
Lynn MA 01902

Call Sign: N1KWQ
Darryl W Flint
14 Like View Ave Apt
A6
Lynn MA 01904

Call Sign: KB1FCW
Robert G Wilson
198 Locust St 403
Lynn MA 019042940

Call Sign: K1GDE
Stephen R Gorski
40 Lowell St
Lynn MA 01905

Call Sign: KA1HKY
Christine P Smith
271 Lynn Shore Dr
Lynn MA 01902

Call Sign: KA1TLW
James J Donohue
Mall St Apt 8
Lynn MA 01905

Call Sign: WB1ERC
Oscar Robinson
55 Merrill Ave
Lynn MA 01902

Call Sign: KA1SUY
Richard E Lemme
45 Moffett Rd
Lynn MA 01905

Call Sign: KB1QKH
Matthew J Adolph
48 Mt Pleasant St
Lynn MA 01902

Call Sign: N1ASW
George W Poole Jr
77 Myrtle St
Lynn MA 01905

Call Sign: N1FRD
James G Leavey
30 Nicholson St
Lynn MA 01905

Call Sign: N1TMN
Charles W Noble
17 Oakville St
Lynn MA 01905

Call Sign: N1KFJ
Angelo G Self
25 Oneida St
Lynn MA 01902

Call Sign: KB1FSM
Ronald F Healey
71 Pacific St
Lynn MA 01902

Call Sign: KB1KGE
Colin A Mccannon
45 Park Rd
Lynn MA 01904

Call Sign: KB1PZW
Mike W Ledoux
6 Parrott St
Lynn MA 01902

Call Sign: W1GIZ
Arthur H Graham
12 Pattys Way
Lynn MA 019022435

Call Sign: KB1IVU
Paul J Houlihan
10 Pickering Terrace

Lynn MA 01904

Call Sign: W1DUD
Paul J Houlihan
10 Pickering Terrace
Lynn MA 01904

Call Sign: KA1EFP
Kenneth V Nagy
29 Piedmont St
Lynn MA 01904

Call Sign: KB1PUO
Kenneth V Nagy
29 Piedmont St
Lynn MA 01904

Call Sign: KA1EFP
Kenneth V Nagy
29 Piedmont St
Lynn MA 01904

Call Sign: KB1QBW
Geoffrey D Allen
86 President St
Lynn MA 01902

Call Sign: N1GDA
Geoffrey D Allen
86 President St
Lynn MA 01902

Call Sign: N1YME
Victor R Scalona
114 President St
Lynn MA 01902

Call Sign: KB1SCK
James R Lucier
20 Quinn Rd
Lynn MA 01904

Call Sign: KB1CHQ
Michael A Reale
45 Reservoir Rd
Lynn MA 01905

Call Sign: W1QQL
William C Woods
43 Richardson Rd
Lynn MA 01904

Call Sign: KA1RSD
Brian C Burns

61 Robinson St
Lynn MA 01905

Call Sign: KB1KOG
Michael W Doane
69 Robinson St
Lynn MA 01905

Call Sign: KB1NZA
Richard J Grindrod
31 Saratoga St
Lynn MA 01902

Call Sign: WR1CK
Richard J Grindrod
31 Saratoga St
Lynn MA 01902

Call Sign: KG1U
Benjamin D Roiter
5 Seaside Ter
Lynn MA 01902

Call Sign: WA1PMI
Marion W Rousseau
67 Silsbee St Apt 514
Lynn MA 01901

Call Sign: KB1EHJ
Robert B Sewell
39 South St
Lynn MA 01905

Call Sign: KE1V
Donald F Mac
Comisky
10 Springview Dr
Lynn MA 01904

Call Sign: KA1DGH
Patricia A Testa
32 Sutcliffe Rd
Lynn MA 01904

Call Sign: KA1DLC
Charles J Testa
32 Sutcliffe Rd
Lynn MA 01904

Call Sign: W1EYP
Paul C Demergy
50 The Lynnway Apt
325
Lynn MA 01902

Call Sign: KB1LGW
Robert J Bermani
8 Trevett Ave
Lynn MA 01904

Call Sign: N1IWH
Peter F Margeson
67 Tudor St 10
Lynn MA 01902

Call Sign: KA1FTA
John J Calnan
32 Virginia Ter
Lynn MA 01904

Call Sign: KA1LWW
Lawrence A Cyr
202 Walnut St
Lynn MA 01905

Call Sign: W1WUE
Victor C Wishneusky
634 Walnut St
Lynn MA 019051038

Call Sign: N1LMY
Harvey B Wiggin
86 Washington St
Lynn MA 01902

Call Sign: KA1SSB
David J Morin
80 Webster St
Lynn MA 01902

Call Sign: WA1ZWD
Jean M Rawding
12 Wellington St
Lynn MA 01902

Call Sign: W1WOZ
Herbert A Dukett
12 Wells Pl
Lynn MA 01902

Call Sign: KB1HGI
John J Fleury
127 Western Ave
Lynn MA 01904

Call Sign: N1WCZ
John F Russell
14 William St

Lynn MA 01904

Call Sign: KB1KZL
Kevin Spearman
155 Williams Ave
Lynn MA 01902

Call Sign: WB1DLT
Douglas C Hunter
5 Williams Pl
Lynn MA 01902

Call Sign: KB1TRJ
John W Russell
14 Williams St
Lynn MA 01904

Call Sign: K1TNS
Robert J Albanese
10 Woodlawn St
Lynn MA 01904

Call Sign: K1VOQ
Robert M Shyavitz
Lynn MA 019030654

Call Sign: KB1DJ
Alan D Kline
Lynn MA 01904

Call Sign: N1KBD
Joseph P Harden
Lynn MA 01903

Call Sign: WA1UGA
Paul J Mahoney Jr
Lynn MA 019031067

Call Sign: KB1PKB
James M Dicrescenzo
Lynn MA 01903

Call Sign: KB1PKD
Amanda B
Dicrescenzo
Lynn MA 01903

Call Sign: KQ1D
Alan D Kline
Lynn MA 01904

Call Sign: KA1DVQ
Marc S De Rosa
9 Atherton Cir
Lynnfield MA 01940

Call Sign: KA1BBL
Henry G Jacobsen
65 Carter Rd
Lynnfield MA 01940

Call Sign: W1KNS
William A Yahn
2 Doncaster Rd
Lynnfield MA 01940

Call Sign: KC1YN
Woodrow S Jackson Jr
22 Edward Ave
Lynnfield MA 01940

Call Sign: KB1KNN
Steven E Presser
49 Edward Ave
Lynnfield MA 01940

Call Sign: W1KEK
Richard W Doremus
177 Essex
Lynnfield MA 01940

Call Sign: WA1MYJ
Clifton E Rawcliffe
14 Gerry Rd
Lynnfield MA 01940

Call Sign: K1VIO
Ralph J Caruso
2 Goldenrod Ln
Lynnfield MA
019401620

Call Sign: KA1RLZ
Arthur V Sarazini
6 Heath Cir
Lynnfield MA 01940

Call Sign: KB1DIZ
Daniel C Mc Lemore
12 Hunting Ln
Lynnfield MA 01940

Call Sign: W1WXJ
Daniel C Mc Lemore
12 Hunting Ln

Lynnfield MA 01940

Call Sign: KE1FN
Paul M Keefe
12 Ivanhoe Dr
Lynnfield MA 01940

Call Sign: N1WMB
Richard J Keefe
12 Ivanhoe Dr
Lynnfield MA
019401739

Call Sign: KB1HMW
Vipul J Shah
10 Kimberly Terr
Lynnfield MA 01940

Call Sign: W1KC
Charles R Kaliris
3 Knoll Rd
Lynnfield MA
019402025

Call Sign: N1KXV
Charles P Pike
69 Locksley Rd
Lynnfield MA 01940

Call Sign: AA1HL
Richard E Jones
93 Locksley Rd
Lynnfield MA 01940

Call Sign: KA1VMC
Christopher A Talbot
179 Locksley Rd
Lynnfield MA 01940

Call Sign: WA1EGL
Geoffrey A Talbot
179 Locksley Rd
Lynnfield MA 01940

Call Sign: W1KXQ
Victor G Jarvis
505 Lowell St
Lynnfield MA
019401647

Call Sign: W1EHQ
Terence T Ringer
3 Maiden Ln
Lynnfield MA 01940

Call Sign: W1BJM
John P Cushman Jr
27 Melch Rd
Lynnfield MA 01940

Call Sign: WA1BGI
John Lecouras
34 Munroe St
Lynnfield MA 01940

Call Sign: K1HZP
Richard J Shafner
67 Pillings Pond Rd
Lynnfield MA 01940

Call Sign: N1UPX
Miriam A Shafner
67 Pillings Pond Rd
Lynnfield MA
019401317

Call Sign: W1MTP
John D De Luca
4 Pine St
Lynnfield MA 01940

Call Sign: W1PLA
Ira J Dilts Jr
6 Richards Rd
Lynnfield MA 01940

Call Sign: W1PZC
Henry J Zimmermann
14 Russet Ln
Lynnfield MA 01940

Call Sign: W1LEV
John A Rose
6 Saunders Rd
Lynnfield MA 01940

Call Sign: N1HOG
Robert E Langan
3 Squire Ln
Lynnfield MA 01940

Call Sign: N1FXM
Angelo De Giovanni
333 Summer St
Lynnfield MA 01940

Call Sign: N1YBE
Paul J Orlowski

849 Summer St
Lynnfield MA 01940

Call Sign: AA1KI
Donald R Hyer
41 Vokes Ter
Lynnfield MA 01940

Call Sign: N1GFN
William L Moreton
21 Walnut St
Lynnfield MA 01940

Call Sign: K1LJT
Theodore E Ginsberg
174 Walnut St
Lynnfield MA
019402106

Call Sign: KB1MKI
Michael C Walsh
Lynnfield MA 01940

FCC Amateur Radio Licenses in Lynnfield Center

Call Sign: W1PDH
Eugene M Gutowski
355 Main
Lynnfield Center MA
01940

FCC Amateur Radio Licenses in Magnolia

Call Sign: KA1SFB
Howard Moulton Sr
10 Field Rd
Magnolia MA 01930

Call Sign: WA1EVO
Aubrey L Ruggles
165 Hesperus Ave
Magnolia MA 01930

Call Sign: W1LTS
Loring A Cook Jr
16 Lake Rd
Magnolia MA
019305235

Call Sign: N1NGY
Roberta L Colameta

58 Lexington Ave
Magnolia MA 01930

Call Sign: W1DCB
Joshua Horwitz
85 Lexington Ave
Magnolia MA 01930

Call Sign: N1HRT
John J Ronan
5 Magnolia Ave
Magnolia MA 01930

Call Sign: WA1UCG
Robert W Spanks Jr
4 St Peters Ln
Magnolia MA 01930

Call Sign: K1DBX
Maxwell G Jacobs
765 Western Ave
Magnolia MA 01930

Call Sign: KA1NDB
Kurt A Gustafson
Magnolia MA 01930

FCC Amateur Radio Licenses in Mahapoisett

Call Sign: KB1NBW
Robert F Spink
32 Driscoll Lane
Mahapoisett MA
02739

FCC Amateur Radio Licenses in Malden

Call Sign: WB1AKZ
Eugene T Leary
116 Adams St
Malden MA 02148

Call Sign: N1DEY
William H
Commerford
171 Adams St
Malden MA
021486306

Call Sign: KB1JXG
Gerald Gillis

97 Alden St
Malden MA 02148

Call Sign: KA1YRR
Thomas E Barnacle
21 Andrew St
Malden MA 02148

Call Sign: N1YVP
Christopher J Holley
20 Arlington St
Malden MA 02148

Call Sign: N1JDU
Richard G Amirault
44 Bainbridge St
Malden MA 02148

Call Sign: W1LNM
Sidney F Shernan
339 Bainbridge St
Malden MA 02148

Call Sign: K1ONE
Norman D Lang
82 Beltran St
Malden MA 02148

Call Sign: N1HQL
Thomas C Murphy
55 Blomerth St
Malden MA 02148

Call Sign: N2QEK
Daniel W Zeman
61 Boylston St
Malden MA 02148

Call Sign: W1QJF
Benjamin H Littlefield
Jr
685 Broadway Lot 58
Malden MA 02148

Call Sign: KB1GDP
Jeffrey A Berg
181 Clifton St
Malden MA
021482452

Call Sign: K0RIG
Jeffrey A Berg
181 Clifton St

Malden MA
021482452

Call Sign: KB1URL
Brandon Cunningham
307 Clifton St
Malden MA 02148

Call Sign: KC1HX
Philip J Feeley
99 Crystal St
Malden MA 02148

Call Sign: KB1RRV
Daniel J O'connell
21 Desmond Rd Apt 1
Malden MA 02148

Call Sign: N1GWW
Harry C Liskowsky
66 Devir St Apt 311
Malden MA 02148

Call Sign: N1TBL
Montgomery P Mc
Guire
26 Dexter St
Malden MA 02148

Call Sign: W1LQX
Angelo J Moro Sr
48 Emerald St
Malden MA 02148

Call Sign: N1QLT
Ernst Jean
46 Everett St
Malden MA 02148

Call Sign: W1VCF
Jacob Abelow
99 Florence St 222
Malden MA
021483954

Call Sign: K1LVA
Jarrod A Fothergill
30 Franklin Court
Malden MA 02148

Call Sign: W1SAC
Anthony Tortorella
33 Garland Ave
Malden MA 02148

Call Sign: KB1AXU
Derek S Scuteri
83 Glenrock Ave
Malden MA 02148

Call Sign: N1JGV
Charles Tumasz
136 Hadley St
Malden MA
021488005

Call Sign: KA1KJM
John D De Luca Jr
15 Hanover St
Malden MA 02148

Call Sign: KB1FER
Joseph F Fitzgerald
21 Harnden Rd
Malden MA 02148

Call Sign: KB1JMO
Raymond M Frangiosa
12 Havelock St
Malden MA 02148

Call Sign: KB1QME
John F Forestier
61 Havelock St
Malden MA 02148

Call Sign: N1YRK
Robert W Keyes
112 Highland Ave 2nd
Floor
Malden MA 02148

Call Sign: KA1FDJ
Anthony Micalizzi
79 Home St
Malden MA 02148

Call Sign: KB1GZO
David A Cuscuna
55 Hunting St
Malden MA 02148

Call Sign: K1DAC
David A Cuscuna
55 Hunting St
Malden MA 02148

Call Sign: N1PHM

Donald J Mirley
84 Jacob St
Malden MA 02148

Call Sign: K1GJF
Ernest B Andrade
89 Lawrence St
Malden MA 02148

Call Sign: KA1TSJ
Francesco P D Amato
392 Lebanon St
Malden MA 02148

Call Sign: WC1A
Jonathan A Cohen
75 Linden Ave #2
Malden MA
021488208

Call Sign: KA1KVQ
James E Mulvey
36 Lyle Ter
Malden MA 02148

Call Sign: KB1FMP
Ben M Artin
38 Lyme St Apt 302
Malden MA 02148

Call Sign: KA1PWQ
Carl F Stead
28 Mc Comack St
Malden MA 02148

Call Sign: KB1OFD
John J Dion
117 Mount Vernon St
Malden MA 02148

Call Sign: NM1J
John J Dion
117 Mount Vernon St
Malden MA 02148

Call Sign: K1RAN
Frederick L Curtis
120 Mountain Ave Apt
B14
Malden MA 02148

Call Sign: KB1SDR
James L Hall
5 Nanpashemer Ave

Malden MA 02148

Call Sign: N1FAS
Arthur B Kingsley
69 Nichols Rd
Malden MA 02148

Call Sign: WB1GDV
Paul V Colella
138 Oakland St
Malden MA 02148

Call Sign: N1KNE
James M Govoni
85 Oliver St
Malden MA 02148

Call Sign: N1WLH
Dennis J La Frenier
438 Pleasant St
Malden MA
021488103

Call Sign: N1GBC
John A Sica
557 Pleasant St Apt
214
Malden MA 02148

Call Sign: KA1KNB
John H Mc Gurk
117 Porter St
Malden MA 02148

Call Sign: KB1OCH
Mark E Bolls
61 Rockland Ave
Malden MA 02148

Call Sign: K1KGG
Mark E Bolls
61 Rockland Ave
Malden MA 02148

Call Sign: AA1RR
Paul F Kuhn
1156 Salem St
Malden MA 02148

Call Sign: K1RHH
Thomas L Reid Jr
280 Salem St Apt 809
Malden MA
021484262

Call Sign: N1GDL
Richard E Teague
284 Summer St
Malden MA 02148

Call Sign: KB1PHO
Richard E Teague
284 Summer St
Malden MA 02148

Call Sign: KB1IUQ
Shigeru Ueda
82 Summer St 302
Malden MA 02148

Call Sign: W1LD
Orin D Hood Sr
31 Tuft St
Malden MA 02148

Call Sign: N1OOM
David R Cluff
87 Upham St
Malden MA 02148

Call Sign: KB1KAP
Jarrod A Fothergill
47 Vernon St
Malden MA 02148

Call Sign: KA1OFZ
Kenneth G Lake Jr
115 Washington St
Malden MA
021483718

Call Sign: N1KGL
Kenneth G Lake Jr
115 Washington St
Malden MA
021483718

Call Sign: WC1I
Salvatore J Lo Piccolo
176 Washington St
Malden MA 02148

Call Sign: WB1FOL
Richard J Rock
77 Wentworth St
Malden MA 02148

Call Sign: N1IST

Michael L Ardai
41 Williams St
Malden MA 02148

Call Sign: N1GJE
Joseph A Bellitti Jr
36 Wolcott St
Malden MA 02148

Call Sign: KB1WES
Richard E Vinciguerra
Malden MA 02148

FCC Amateur Radio Licenses in Manchaug

Call Sign: KZ1M
James P Dalterio
18 Mumford Rd
Manchaug MA 01526

Call Sign: N1XXH
David V De Costa Jr
Manchaug MA
015260415

Call Sign: W1YCW
Donald A King
Manchaug MA 01526

FCC Amateur Radio Licenses in Manchester

Call Sign: N1PBK
Sage H Cole
Manchester MA 01944

Call Sign: N1OCT
Charles E Downey
23 A Desmond Ave
Manchester MA 01944

Call Sign: WB1FJD
Thomas M Beaton
2 Birch Ln
Manchester MA 01944

Call Sign: KA1MHP
Augustine P O Keeffe
14 Boardman Ave
Manchester MA 01944

Call Sign: N1PKB
Nicky Hardenbergh
Box 1514
Manchester MA 01944

Call Sign: N1AAM
Richard J Kerry
29 Central St
Manchester MA 01944

Call Sign: N1XQW
Susan J Downey
Desmond Ave
Manchester MA 01944

Call Sign: W1OKD
William J Canty
22 Hickory Hill Rd
Manchester MA
019441576

Call Sign: KB1GCF
Alan Reed
5 Highwood Rd
Manchester MA 01994

Call Sign: WA1JG
John H Graves Ii
4 Kings Way
Manchester MA 01944

Call Sign: W1DFG
James B Carroll
18 Loading Place Rd
Manchester MA
019441276

Call Sign: N1FXA
Paul D Shuwall
2 Masconomo St
Manchester MA 01944

Call Sign: AB1QF
Kurt A Melden
42 Masconomo St
Manchester MA 01944

Call Sign: K1SEA
Kurt A Melden
42 Masconomo St
Manchester MA 01944

Call Sign: N1IDD
James Z Wielgorecki

23 Norwood Ave
Manchester MA 01944

Call Sign: KD1IW
Garrick F Cole
Off Crooked Ln
Manchester MA
019440860

Call Sign: KB1SJW
Thomas P Eddy
15 Old Neck Rd
Manchester MA 01944

Call Sign: N1HAA
Richard L Wilhelm
129 Pine St
Manchester MA 01944

Call Sign: WB1EHL
John H Graves Ii
498 R Summer St
Manchester MA 01944

Call Sign: KB1NRK
Kathy Bacsik
21 Union St
Manchester MA 01944

Call Sign: KA1CHY
Daniel J Ferreira
30 Vine St
Manchester MA 01944

Call Sign: K1BUF
Dorothy H Jodice
15 Woodcrest Rd
Manchester MA 01944

Call Sign: KD1JH
Forrester H Cole
Manchester MA
019440860

Call Sign: W1ZQM
James A Jodice
Manchester MA
019440616

FCC Amateur Radio Licenses in Manomet

Call Sign: W1WMZ
Joseph F Poplosky

31 Arnold Ave
Manomet MA 02345

Call Sign: K1IDU
Sidney F Pell
Box 601
Manomet MA 02345

Call Sign: N1PCD
George S Mariner
26 Earl Rd
Manomet MA 02345

Call Sign: N1TSD
Leo P Ariagno
17 Manomet Point Rd
Manomet MA 02345

Call Sign: KA1CGQ
Claire J Graham
164 Old Field Rd
Manomet MA 02345

Call Sign: WA1YTL
John B Graham Jr
164 Old Field Rd
Manomet MA 02345

Call Sign: KA1VBM
William P O Day
Woodland Ave
Manomet MA 02345

Call Sign: KA1YDR
Paul W Ginnett
Manomet MA 02345

Call Sign: N1RAQ
Fred Taylor Jr
Manomet MA 02345

Call Sign: K1VTE
Anthony Tamosaitis
Manomet MA
023452349

FCC Amateur Radio Licenses in Mansfield

Call Sign: WA1JBJ
Alfred J Kuplast Jr
10 Atwood St
Mansfield MA 02048

Call Sign: N1JQN
Walter A White
12 Avon St
Mansfield MA 02048

Call Sign: N1KJZ
Helena G White
12 Avon St
Mansfield MA 02048

Call Sign: KB1HRB
Frank J Svoboda
14 Beech St
Mansfield MA 02048

Call Sign: WA1KCI
Charles A Norton
27 Bellview Dr
Mansfield MA 02048

Call Sign: KB1UGE
Robert R Allen
16 Birch Bark Lane
Mansfield MA 02048

Call Sign: KB1UGG
Valeria M Allen
16 Birch Bark Lane
Mansfield MA 02048

Call Sign: KB1UGH
Michael D Allen
16 Birch Bark Lane
Mansfield MA 02048

Call Sign: WB1GON
Robert R Allen
16 Birch Bark Lane
Mansfield MA 02048

Call Sign: KB1UGF
Alissa M Allen
16 Birch Bark Ln
Mansfield MA 02048

Call Sign: KB1MWL
Brian S St Aubin
69 Branch St
Mansfield MA 02048

Call Sign: KB1WNP
John J Kane Jr
23 Bungay Rd
Mansfield MA 02048

Call Sign: KB1RS
Richard C Leavitt
48 Carpenter Ave
Mansfield MA 02048

Call Sign: KB1REQ
Jeremy E Breef-Pilz
154 Church St
Mansfield MA 02048

Call Sign: KA1MIZ
John M Paine
72 Court St
Mansfield MA 02048

Call Sign: KA1YSZ
Victor F Romanul
15 Curtin St
Mansfield MA 02048

Call Sign: KA1FUJ
David H Longendorfer
10 Danielle Ln
Mansfield MA
020482846

Call Sign: KB1LPA
Guy C Resh
6 Deer Path Circle
Mansfield MA 02048

Call Sign: N1TVS
Robert B Button
63 East St
Mansfield MA 02048

Call Sign: KA1TDX
Arthur R Birman
1327 East St
Mansfield MA 02048

Call Sign: K1TKI
Albert O Keyworth
328 Elm St
Mansfield MA 02048

Call Sign: AA1TI
Richard J Cantin
525 Elm St
Mansfield MA 02048

Call Sign: N1XPQ
Cynthia J Cantin

525 Elm St
Mansfield MA 02048

Call Sign: N1OLE
Edward F Fitzgerald
181 Essex St
Mansfield MA 02048

Call Sign: N1PFP
Joan M Fitzgerald
181 Essex St
Mansfield MA 02048

Call Sign: KB1BDU
Siobhan Shea
197 Essex St
Mansfield MA 02048

Call Sign: WB1COT
Mark W Shachat
374 Essex St
Mansfield MA 02048

Call Sign: KB1VJA
Maxim Chtangeev
23 Fisher Ln
Mansfield MA 02048

Call Sign: W1HHX
William F Kaphaem Jr
288 Gilbert St
Mansfield MA 02048

Call Sign: KB1NDA
Kenneth A Thompson
Sr
21 Henry St
Mansfield MA 02048

Call Sign: K1YAW
Konrad C Brown
158 High St
Mansfield MA 02048

Call Sign: WA1HVS
Donald F Chesley
240 Hope St
Mansfield MA 02048

Call Sign: W1YIA
Raymond F Bedard
4 John St
Mansfield MA 02048

Call Sign: KB1NES
Richard M Kelly
23 Kerry Dr
Mansfield MA 02048

Call Sign: KB1NHF
Michael R Kelly
23 Kerry Dr
Mansfield MA 02048

Call Sign: KB1GSK
Lazar K Lazarov Iii
54 King St
Mansfield MA
020481418

Call Sign: KB1HIY
Elaine M Sciog
Lazarov
54 King St
Mansfield MA
020481418

Call Sign: KB1GUV
Allan M Cox Jr
150 Lawndale Rd
Mansfield MA
020481622

Call Sign: K2VQH
Allan M Cox Jr
150 Lawndale Rd
Mansfield MA
020481622

Call Sign: K1VQ
Allan M Cox Jr
150 Lawndale Rd
Mansfield MA
020481622

Call Sign: WA1KYK
Richard J Gleason
14 Lewis Rd
Mansfield MA 02048

Call Sign: KB1MDI
Victor F Romanul
807 Maple St
Mansfield MA 02048

Call Sign: WB1GOL
Rene R Chevalier
150 Mill St

Mansfield MA 02048

Call Sign: KA1JSR
Frank R Guardabascio
220 Mill St
Mansfield MA 02048

Call Sign: KB1HMR
Carol M Richie
296 N Main
Mansfield MA 02048

Call Sign: KB2WIL
Daniel Austin
Horowitz
539 N Main St
Mansfield MA 02048

Call Sign: N1GCE
Gerald R Mailly Jr
11 Newell Ln
Mansfield MA 02048

Call Sign: KB1SQV
Richard A Strano
59 North St
Mansfield MA 02048

Call Sign: KB1OSV
Matthew A Paine
149 Oakland St Apt
130 Bled D3
Mansfield MA 02048

Call Sign: W1AXB
Matthew A Paine
149 Oakland St Apt
130 Bled D3
Mansfield MA 02048

Call Sign: KA1JGQ
Warren G Shadrick
1 Old Colony Way
Apti1
Mansfield MA 02048

Call Sign: K1PZB
Alice S Pillsbury
55 Old Elm St
Mansfield MA 02048

Call Sign: WA1AZA
Walter R Chace
109 Otis St

Mansfield MA 02048

Call Sign: N1HDA
Geraldine A Cabral
101 Park St
Mansfield MA 02048

Call Sign: KB1UPP
Wpi Radio Club
60 Park St 2
Mansfield MA 02048

Call Sign: W1LNL
WPI Lnl Radio Club
60 Park St 2
Mansfield MA 02048

Call Sign: KB1CGY
Benjamin E Feller
59 Pilgrim Rd
Mansfield MA 02048

Call Sign: KT1H
Benjamin E Feller
59 Pilgrim Rd
Mansfield MA 02048

Call Sign: KB1WNX
Steven A Lyons
22 Pleasant St
Mansfield MA 02048

Call Sign: KB1FGY
Anthony J Pasquino
129 Rumford Ave
Mansfield MA 02048

Call Sign: WB2BUP
Howard P Rosenof
150 Rumford Ave
Mansfield MA 02048

Call Sign: KE3UE
Vincent J Bonsaint
150 Rumford Ave -
Apt 222
Mansfield MA 02048

Call Sign: KE1MN
Vincent J Bonsaint
150 Rumford Ave -
Apt 222
Mansfield MA 02048

Call Sign: N1IPQ
William H Howell
150 Rumford Ave Apt
124
Mansfield MA 02048

Call Sign: KB1NER
Ken E Cramer
55 Stearns Ave
Mansfield MA 02048

Call Sign: KB1NHH
Harvey D Cramer
55 Stearns Ave
Mansfield MA 02048

Call Sign: KC1XP
John P Rooney
18 Thomas St
Mansfield MA 02048

Call Sign: KA1PYT
Thomas M Martone
5 Trowbridge Ln
Mansfield MA 02048

Call Sign: KA2PFY
Terry J Yoder
8 Twin Oaks Village
Mansfield MA 02048

Call Sign: KB1FYC
Terry J Yoder
8 Twin Oaks Village
Mansfield MA 02048

Call Sign: KB1HYY
William J Morocco
14 Van Gemert Dr
Mansfield MA 02048

Call Sign: N1LRH
Michael F Ahern Jr
41 Walnut St
Mansfield MA 02048

Call Sign: KB1DPA
Philip N Stocking
105 Ware St
Mansfield MA 02048

Call Sign: K1NTR
Alan M Foskett
287 Ware St

Mansfield MA 02048

Call Sign: KB1LRJ
Gregory E Raynard
171 Ware St - Apt 3
Mansfield MA 02048

Call Sign: KA1MNP
James M Rakiey
765 Warl St
Mansfield MA 02048

Call Sign: KB1JJE
Mansfield Ema
Communications
50 West St
Mansfield MA 02048

Call Sign: KB1UGX
Robert S Bokleman
861 West St
Mansfield MA 02048

Call Sign: KB1UMC
Ronald J Bokleman
861 West St
Mansfield MA 02048

Call Sign: WB1FCV
David W Farrington
211 Willow St
Mansfield MA 02048

Call Sign: W1DWF
David W Farrington
211 Willow St
Mansfield MA
020482717

Call Sign: WA1LOL
Steven A Sousa
26 Windchime Dr
Mansfield MA 02048

Call Sign: KA1ULZ
Miguel A Gabutti
Mansfield MA 02048

Call Sign: KA1MY
William Beardsworth
Jr
Mansfield MA 02048

Call Sign: WB1FJQ

James T Doty
Mansfield MA 02048

Call Sign: WB1GIW
Gary P Nelson
Mansfield MA 02048

**FCC Amateur Radio
Licenses in
Marblehead**

Call Sign: KA1OUG
Michael H Bomacorso
Jr
12 Amgemica Ter
Marblehead MA 01945

Call Sign: KB1QEU
David M Walker
114 Atlantic Ave
Marblehead MA 01945

Call Sign: W1BVV
David M Walker
114 Atlantic Ave
Marblehead MA 01945

Call Sign: KB1CNY
Ronald W Tracy
190 Atlantic Ave
Marblehead MA
019452912

Call Sign: K1XML
Alexander Falk
452 Atlantic Ave
Marblehead MA
019452759

Call Sign: N1TAV
David W Graham
7 Batchelder Rd
Marblehead MA 01945

Call Sign: W1DWG
David W Graham
7 Batchelder Rd
Marblehead MA 01945

Call Sign: N1XJG
Lawrence H Lessard
45 Bayview Rd
Marblehead MA 01945

Call Sign: W1GKX
Michael L Ferber
64 Bayview Rd
Marblehead MA 01945

Call Sign: W1FIN
Robert W Bradley
44 Beach St
Marblehead MA 01945

Call Sign: KA1RNS
Henry E Cooper Iii
103 Beacon St
Marblehead MA 01945

Call Sign: KB1ENV
John P Campbell
19 Beverly Ave
Marblehead MA 01945

Call Sign: W1IXO
Samuel W Thomas
12 Birch St
Marblehead MA 01945

Call Sign: KB1MWF
David A Shaw
16 Birch St
Marblehead MA 01945

Call Sign: W1CKP
David A Shaw
16 Birch St
Marblehead MA 01945

Call Sign: N1PQG
Michael M Mentuck
13 Blueberry Rd
Marblehead MA 01945

Call Sign: KE1AO
John B Sledge Iii
31 Cedar St
Marblehead MA 01945

Call Sign: KD1KH
Margaret A Jameson
33 Central St
Marblehead MA 01945

Call Sign: N1JCC
Dana H Mc Carriston
2 Charlette Rd
Marblehead MA 01945

Call Sign: N1TDE
Paul H Shiner
34 Chestnut St
Marblehead MA 01945

Call Sign: W1VRK
Eugene H Hastings
18 Churchill Rd
Marblehead MA 01945

Call Sign: W1EQE
Donald S Yeaple
11 Circle St
Marblehead MA 01945

Call Sign: N1SGX
Matthew L Plauche
2 Clark Lane
Marblehead MA 01945

Call Sign: N1ZET
Daniel L Sullivan
22 Cliff St
Marblehead MA 01945

Call Sign: KB1LOS
Richard A Benua
7 Dennett Rd
Marblehead MA 01945

Call Sign: WB2OSY
Susan E Benua
7 Dennett Rd
Marblehead MA
019453712

Call Sign: WB2PJU
David Benua
7 Dennett Rd
Marblehead MA
019453712

Call Sign: KA1EGA
Edward J Robinson
114 Elm St
Marblehead MA 01945

Call Sign: N1HOM
Wendy C Ciarletta
141 Elm St #2
Marblehead MA 01945

Call Sign: W1ELB

Daniel A Packard
107 Farrell Ct
Marblehead MA 01945

Call Sign: N1GYR
Joseph C Roper Jr
9 Faye Cir
Marblehead MA 01945

Call Sign: WA1SSI
Frederic M Bauer
6 Fountain Inn Ln
Marblehead MA 01945

Call Sign: KB1VBT
Alexander Falk
9 Fox Run Ln
Marblehead MA 01945

Call Sign: KD6TQY
Philip G Blaisdell
72 Front St
Marblehead MA 01945

Call Sign: KA1PHS
David M Reid
112 Front St
Marblehead MA 01945

Call Sign: W1RNO
Alfred H Feffer
1 Frost Ln
Marblehead MA 01945

Call Sign: W1PPZ
Harvey H Chamberlain
6 Ft Beach Way
Marblehead MA 01945

Call Sign: KA1LQW
Russell Goldsmith
38 Gallison Ave
Marblehead MA 01945

Call Sign: KA1DHC
Richard C Mc Cluskey
10 Garfield St
Marblehead MA 01945

Call Sign: N1OWW
Helen J Mc Cluskey
10 Garfield St
Marblehead MA 01945

Call Sign: KB1RFH
Lanning L Levine
30 Gerald Rd
Marblehead MA 01945

Call Sign: WA1LNY
Lanning L Levine
30 Gerald Rd
Marblehead MA 01945

Call Sign: KB1VN
Peter D Aery
25 Green St Ct
Marblehead MA 01945

Call Sign: AI1S
Peter D Aery
25 Green St Ct
Marblehead MA 01945

Call Sign: KI1P
Peter D Aery
25 Green St Ct
Marblehead MA 01945

Call Sign: N1BER
Margareta A Bartlett
4 Haley Rd
Marblehead MA 01945

Call Sign: N1BES
Sumner B Bartlett
4 Haley Rd
Marblehead MA 01945

Call Sign: KA1ECD
Mark S Sedgwick
6 Highland Terr 1
Marblehead MA 01945

Call Sign: N1RSC
William R Main Jr
22 Hillside Ave
Marblehead MA 01945

Call Sign: K1BJZ
Carolyn G Thompson
Hillside Ave
Marblehead MA 01945

Call Sign: KB1GFA
Keith D Jones
149 Humphrey St
Marblehead MA 01945

Call Sign: WA1ZDW
Todd J Barbera
74 Jersey St
Marblehead MA 01945

Call Sign: KB1VTS
Stephen D Coleman
129 Jersey St
Marblehead MA 01945

Call Sign: KB1HXL
Duane Marshall
2 Kimball St
Marblehead MA 01945

Call Sign: AB1BJ
Duane Marshall
2 Kimball St
Marblehead MA 01945

Call Sign: W1EQP
Ralph W Anthony
31 Lafayette St
Marblehead MA 01945

Call Sign: N1BTY
Elwin D Mills
52 Lafayette St
Marblehead MA 01945

Call Sign: KB1EJR
Christopher H Teague
13 Lattimer St
Marblehead MA 01945

Call Sign: KB1HMU
Jonathan P Teague
13 Lattimer St
Marblehead MA 01945

Call Sign: K2FCC
Jonathan P Teague
13 Lattimer St
Marblehead MA 01945

Call Sign: K1GFK
John J Vytal
8 Lee St
Marblehead MA 01945

Call Sign: N1WOC
Christopher T Hartley
14 Leggs Hill Rd

Marblehead MA 01945

Call Sign: N1YDZ
Judy J Miller
62 Leicester Rd
Marblehead MA 01945

Call Sign: KA1JLG
Richard M Seibel
53 Londonderry Rd
Marblehead MA 01945

Call Sign: K1RNO
Goodwin G Mills
71 Maverick St
Marblehead MA 01945

Call Sign: KB1TON
Joseph M Naroski
4 Meadow Lane
Marblehead MA 01945

Call Sign: KB1SVV
Corey S Tapper
8 Miles Standish Rd
Marblehead MA 01945

Call Sign: K1CST
Corey Tapper
8 Miles Standish Rd
Marblehead MA 01945

Call Sign: W1PXK
Joseph M Paresky
10 Monroe Rd
Marblehead MA 01945

Call Sign: WB1CIJ
Standley H Goodwin
33 Norman St
Marblehead MA 01945

Call Sign: N1UOY
Clement B Sledge
279 Ocean Ave
Marblehead MA 01945

Call Sign: N1BRR
Wilbur T Moulton
10 Orchard St
Marblehead MA 01945

Call Sign: W1FMS
William F Genett

75 Overlook Rd
Marblehead MA 01945

Call Sign: KB1HUE
Frederick R Williams
80 Overlook Rd
Marblehead MA 01945

Call Sign: W1BNH
Laurence T Hogan
8 Peach Highlands
Marblehead MA 01945

Call Sign: WA1TZE
Edward Kabadian Jr
59 Peach Highlands
Marblehead MA 01945

Call Sign: W1BRJ
Stanley A Fierston
7 Pickwick Rd
Marblehead MA 01945

Call Sign: N1DAE
Theodore T Fligor
15 Pickwick Rd
Marblehead MA 01945

Call Sign: KB1KKR
Michael D Osattin
44 Pinecliff Dr
Marblehead MA 01945

Call Sign: W1AAZ
Edward A Pacyna Jr
72 Pitman Rd
Marblehead MA 01945

Call Sign: W1JJ
Russell E Small
224 Pleasant St
Marblehead MA 01945

Call Sign: KB1OCS
Nathaniel A
Henricksen
266 Pleasant St
Marblehead MA 01945

Call Sign: KC2REP
Peter T Catalfamo
48 Pleasant St Apt 4
Marblehead MA 01945

Call Sign: KA1LEL
Robert S Goldman
15 Preston Beach Rd
Marblehead MA 01945

Call Sign: KA1RWB
Richard L Ashley Jr
19 Preston Beach Rd
Marblehead MA 01945

Call Sign: KC1TA
Richard E Thornton
46 Prospect St Unit 1
Marblehead MA 01945

Call Sign: K1DTG
Ruth M Keyes
25 Rainbow Rd
Marblehead MA 01945

Call Sign: W1SKQ
Arthur Zolot
82 Rockaway Ave
Marblehead MA 01945

Call Sign: N1ENT
Douglas F Hulsman
8 Roosevelt Ave
Marblehead MA 01945

Call Sign: W1RNM
S Lyle Hall
25 Rose Ave
Marblehead MA 01945

Call Sign: W1UNA
Thomas J Eichelberger
26 Seaview Ave
Marblehead MA 01945

Call Sign: W1AGE
Paul H Silbert
44 Seaview Ave
Marblehead MA 01945

Call Sign: N1LJS
David Koh
14 Shuman Rd
Marblehead MA 01945

Call Sign: KE1LY
David Koh
14 Shuman Rd
Marblehead MA 01945

Call Sign: WA1BZE
Richard B Wilson
25 Skinners Path
Marblehead MA 01945

Call Sign: KB1BEG
Benjamin W Loveland
15 Sparhawk Ter
Marblehead MA 01945

Call Sign: N1ULH
Peter B Loveland
15 Sparhawk Ter
Marblehead MA
019451522

Call Sign: KB1GRP
William R Walsh-
Rogalski
5 Spray Ave
Marblehead MA 01945

Call Sign: KB1WTV
Raymond W Waitekus
6 Stoney Brook Rd
Marblehead MA 01945

Call Sign: K1RWW
Raymond W Waitekus
6 Stoney Brook Rd
Marblehead MA 01945

Call Sign: KA1YRG
Joseph L Brophy
9 Taft St
Marblehead MA 01945

Call Sign: N1WBN
Elizabeth B Morris
6 Union St
Marblehead MA 01945

Call Sign: KA1TUG
Paul C Marshall
54 Village St
Marblehead MA 01945

Call Sign: K9POB
Kenneth J Bures
16 Washington Sq
Marblehead MA 01945

Call Sign: N1CGD

Paul L Lausier
147 Washington St
Marblehead MA 01945

Call Sign: N1XLO
Paul M Milone
4 Winslow Sq Lane
Marblehead MA 01945

Call Sign: N1ICF
Brent A Arnold
Marblehead MA
019450289

Call Sign: KB1GCG
Karen L Whalen
Marblehead MA 01945

Call Sign: NG1Z
Nathaniel A
Henricksen
Marblehead MA 01945

**FCC Amateur Radio
Licenses in Marion**

Call Sign: KC1MS
John A Arcuri
4 Autumn Lane
Marion MA 02738

Call Sign: N1DFS
Diana G Tottenham
10 Bay Rd
Marion MA 02738

Call Sign: W1LND
Gordon C Avery Sr
49 County Rd
Marion MA 02738

Call Sign: WA1ITP
Thomas C Ireland
77 County Rd
Marion MA 02738

Call Sign: K1OQM
James C Archer Sr
151 County Rd
Marion MA 02738

Call Sign: KB1IYQ
Matthew E Farrell
97 County Rd 02738

Marion MA 02738

Call Sign: KC2GDY
Peter T Francis
107 Cove Circle
Marion MA 02738

Call Sign: K1LAD
Richard T Giberti
30 Cranberry Way
Marion MA 02738

Call Sign: KA1YZT
Michael G Thompson
601 Deland Rd
Marion MA 02738

Call Sign: KJ4NLK
Randy L Parker
552 Front St
Marion MA 02738

Call Sign: AD1M
Roy H Rehbein
602 Front St
Marion MA
027381438

Call Sign: WB1GZE
Scott D Rehbein
602 Front St
Marion MA 02738

Call Sign: N1ULA
Mary H Pierce
606 Front St
Marion MA 02738

Call Sign: KA1MTU
Margaret C Hiller
680 Front St
Marion MA 02738

Call Sign: KC1UY
Eldredge M Hiller
680 Front St
Marion MA 02738

Call Sign: N1ULB
Eric V Pierce
77 Holmes St
Marion MA 02738

Call Sign: WB1DUT

Roger E Ouellette
16 Inland Rd
Marion MA 02738

Call Sign: N1ZKU
John F Molander
4 Jenna Dr
Marion MA 02738

Call Sign: WA1GMD
Fredric C Danhauser
40 Lewis
Marion MA 02738

Call Sign: K1FSU
Frederic S Bacon Jr
100 Main St
Marion MA
027380287

Call Sign: WA1MRH
Frederic S Bacon Iii
100 Main St
Marion MA 02738

Call Sign: N1TF
Frederic S Bacon Iii
100 Main St
Marion MA 02738

Call Sign: KB1OIB
Robert M Stanton
21 Oak Ave
Marion MA 02738

Call Sign: W1UJ
Joseph T Carson
10 Oakdale Ave
Marion MA 02738

Call Sign: KB1OPY
Leslie M Dole
5 Olde Sheepfield Rd
Marion MA 02738

Call Sign: N1ZOD
Megan M Tarini
38 Parkway Ln
Marion MA 02738

Call Sign: W3AAF
Aurelio E Vivino
34 Register Rd
Marion MA 02738

Call Sign: KB1JYE
Christopher W
Washburn
45 Rocky Knook Ln
Marion MA 02738

Call Sign: N1DAL
Edward C Brainard Ii
23 Roger's Dr
Marion MA 02738

Call Sign: W1PKE
Ralph G Washburn
325 Wareham
Marion MA 02738

Call Sign: KB1JUP
Marinus Vander Pol Iii
Marion MA 02738

Call Sign: W1EAV
Christopher W
Washburn
Marion MA 02738

**FCC Amateur Radio
Licenses in Marlboro**

**See also FCC
Amateur Radio
Licenses in
Marlborough**

Call Sign: K1TCV
Roger N Tessier
716 Berlin Rd
Marlboro MA 01752

Call Sign: WD6ATD
Edward A Cotterell Jr
596 Boston Post Rd
Marlboro MA 01752

Call Sign: N2BLS
William Y Chan
Boston Post Rd
Marlboro MA 01752

Call Sign: KA1IMW
Jeffrey S Pearlstein
460 Boston Post Rd
Apt B402
Marlboro MA 01752

Call Sign: KD1QS
John P Simoneau Iii
107 Broad St Apt D
Marlboro MA 01752

Call Sign: WA1MTN
Herbert C Edmunds
270 Broadmeadow Rd
Marlboro MA 01752

Call Sign: WB1EKX
Bruno B S Resteghini
1 Chandler St
Marlboro MA 01752

Call Sign: N1XYC
Thomas D Dossa
45 Collins Dr
Marlboro MA 01752

Call Sign: N1YWJ
Carol M Dossa
45 Collins Dr
Marlboro MA 01752

Call Sign: WQ1C
Paul W Gallier
988 Concord Rd
Marlboro MA 01752

Call Sign: KB1HRE
William T Mcmanus
Cook Ln
Marlboro MA 01752

Call Sign: N1OUU
Brian S Corfield
39 Cortland St
Marlboro MA 01752

Call Sign: N1RBM
David E Kirkpatrick
19 Crescent St
Marlboro MA 01752

Call Sign: WA3UKI
Zvili Berman
Curtis Ave
Marlboro MA 01752

Call Sign: KB1AMW
David S Cassidy Sr
68 E Lincoln St

Marlboro MA 01752

Call Sign: KB1AOM
Lillian M Cassidy
68 E Lincoln St
Marlboro MA 01752

Call Sign: W1SLH
Carl S Field
23 Eager Ct
Marlboro MA 01752

Call Sign: KA1GOA
Albert L Senecal Sr
139 Edinboro St
Marlboro MA 01752

Call Sign: KB1DWE
William G Carlson
217 Elm St
Marlboro MA 01752

Call Sign: KD1OA
Michael J Ryan
12 Ewald Ave
Marlboro MA 01752

Call Sign: W1YGS
Edgar G Evers
21 Fay Ct
Marlboro MA 01752

Call Sign: N1HBQ
Jeffrey A Fasulo
24 Foley Rd
Marlboro MA 01752

Call Sign: K1GIR
James F Hopkins
151 Framingham Rd
Marlboro MA 01752

Call Sign: N1LLI
James C Palmer
29 Front St
Marlboro MA 01752

Call Sign: N1HZN
George R Kossuth
36 Girard St
Marlboro MA 01752

Call Sign: N1NVY
Rene A Rusche

212 Glenstreet
Marlboro MA 01752

Call Sign: W1SEF
Albert R Skrzypczak
54 Goodale St
Marlboro MA 01752

Call Sign: WA1GBN
Donald R Taranto
126 Helen Dr
Marlboro MA 01752

Call Sign: WB1HMB
Electro-Optics Center
Ham Radio Club
126 Helen Dr
Marlboro MA 01752

Call Sign: N1JAG
Thomas G Vallas
11 High St
Marlboro MA 01752

Call Sign: N1RER
Michael G Zichella
79 Highland St
Marlboro MA 01752

Call Sign: N1ONW
Charles C Lai
355 Hosmer St
Marlboro MA 01752

Call Sign: K1ZFH
Quincy A Spear
519 Hosmer St
Marlboro MA 01752

Call Sign: KA1VZZ
Christopher A Spear
519 Hosmer St
Marlboro MA 01752

Call Sign: KB1EPN
Anthony J Roberto
629 Hosmer St
Marlboro MA 01752

Call Sign: WB1FLT
Ronald J Achin
23 Houde St
Marlboro MA 01752

Call Sign: WB1FOG
Earlon A Kenney
12 Hurley Cir
Marlboro MA 01752

Call Sign: AA1WX
Thomas J Gluszczak
83 Jacobs Rd
Marlboro MA 01752

Call Sign: N1MGG
Sheila F Sussman
70 Kosmas St
Marlboro MA 01752

Call Sign: WA1VCP
Daniel W Cahill Jr
157 Lakeshore Dr
Marlboro MA 01752

Call Sign: WA1IKM
Richard H
Archambeault
7 Lincoln St
Marlboro MA 01752

Call Sign: N1LMI
Dennis J Maroney Sr
91 Lincoln St
Marlboro MA
017522370

Call Sign: KB1HHK
Gregory P Militello
80 Lodi Rd
Marlboro MA 01752

Call Sign: N1MEY
Keith C Boudreau
280 Main St
Marlboro MA 01752

Call Sign: KA1VLO
Jack J Forman
26 Maurice Dr
Marlboro MA 01752

Call Sign: N1KLU
Charles L Larsen
49 Meadowbrook Rd
Marlboro MA 01752

Call Sign: KA1YJQ
James H Dowd

21 Melody Ln
Marlboro MA 01752

Call Sign: WA1ZBP
Camille Mowry
16 Minehan Ln
Marlboro MA 01752

Call Sign: KB1DEK
Chris J Di Rado
126 Mt Pleasant St
Marlboro MA 01752

Call Sign: KA1FSQ
William S Cameron
14 Mt Pleasant St Apt
4
Marlboro MA 01752

Call Sign: K1KCG
David V Marino
11 Orchard St
Marlboro MA 01752

Call Sign: WA1KGA
Hq Co A 726th Maint
Bn Maarng
26 Pembroke St
Marlboro MA 01752

Call Sign: N1OBZ
Bryan D Newman
55 Phelps St
Marlboro MA 01752

Call Sign: AA1WK
Bryan D Newman
55 Phelps St
Marlboro MA 01752

Call Sign: KV1J
Eric A Williams
763 Pleasant St
Marlboro MA 01752

Call Sign: AE1M
Robert A Levine
32 Queens View Rd
Marlboro MA 01752

Call Sign: KA1WRW
Carol V Levine
32 Queens View Rd
Marlboro MA 01752

Call Sign: W1YDK
Joseph J Hughes Sr
110 Ridge Rd
Marlboro MA 01752

Call Sign: WB1AST
Richard P Smith
48 Russell St
Marlboro MA 01752

Call Sign: WA1CMH
Murad Mooradian
394 Stow Rd
Marlboro MA 01752

Call Sign: WA1AGQ
Emile L Dumais
46 Tavitian Blvd
Marlboro MA
017523438

Call Sign: WA1GEG
Eleanor L Dumais
46 Tavitian Blvd
Marlboro MA
017523438

Call Sign: KB1JXC
Douglas D Sylvester
111 Wagonhill Rd
Marlboro MA
017524913

Call Sign: K1IX
Frank E Mcinnis
162 Woodland Dr
Marlboro MA 01752

Call Sign: WD4BWB
Beverly Ann Seidler
Marlboro MA 01752

**FCC Amateur Radio
Licenses in
Marlborough**

**See also FCC
Amateur Radio
Licenses in Marlboro**

Call Sign: KA1NOI
William A Ledder
9 Wellington St

Marlborogh MA 01752

Call Sign: KA1PON
Ann L Weldon
14 A Emmett St
Marlborough MA
017524325

Call Sign: KA1RZS
Won H Bae
105 Anderson Rd
Marlborough MA
01752

Call Sign: KA1DBA
Carl L Crockford
144 Anderson Rd
Marlborough MA
01752

Call Sign: KB1LUJ
Christopher L David
1409 Applebriar Lane
Marlborough MA
01752

Call Sign: K1AGE
David K Wolfe
12 Avalon Dr Apt 10
Marlborough MA
017523573

Call Sign: KG1H
David K Wolfe
12 Avalon Dr Apt 10
Marlborough MA
017523573

Call Sign: W1NR
Michael A Mc Carthy
4 Barnes Cir
Marlborough MA
01752

Call Sign: KB1LIV
Ray E Speitel
29 Belmore Pl
Marlborough MA
01752

Call Sign: KA1GCB
James M Niro
85 Berlin Rd

Marlborough MA
01752

Call Sign: N1CW
Raymond A Shoop Iii
98 Bigelow St
Marlborough MA
01752

Call Sign: KB1OEI
Keith E Wheeler
191 Bolton St
Marlborough MA
01752

Call Sign: N1DKI
Wayne M Duval
397 Bolton St Apt E7
Marlborough MA
01752

Call Sign: KB1PAO
Raytheon Company -
1001 Raytheon-
Marlborough Amateur
Radio Club
Boston Post Rd
Marlborough MA
01752

Call Sign: N1WCT
Paul F Hurley
45 Boston Post Rd 4
Marlborough MA
017523505

Call Sign: KB1WTL
Richard C Metro
Boston Post Rd Apt
W103
Marlborough MA
01752

Call Sign: KB1JFJ
Tomer T Jackman
849 Boston Post Rd E
9a
Marlborough MA
01752

Call Sign: KB1NQE
Kevin M Colomey
547 Boston Post Rd
Lot 23

Marlborough MA
01752

Call Sign: KB1KIK
Chris J L Moore
849 Boston Post Rd
Unit 6g
Marlborough MA
01752

Call Sign: N1HYL
Ernest R Borden Jr
270 Broad Meadow Rd
Lot 254
Marlborough MA
01752

Call Sign: N1ZCD
Richard G Mahoney
22 Broad St - 108
Marlborough MA
01752

Call Sign: W1OJF
John E Wood
Broadmeadow Rd
Marlborough MA
01752

Call Sign: KB1EIK
Mani Sundaram
Broadmeadow St #4
Marlborough MA
01752

Call Sign: KB1PBE
Peter E Skrzypczak
172 C Cook Lane
Marlborough MA
017522765

Call Sign: W1SEF
Peter E Skrzypczak
172 C Cook Lane
Marlborough MA
017522765

Call Sign: N1LTO
John S Ebb
11 Carver Hill Rd
Marlborough MA
01752

Call Sign: KB1IYK

John N Houghton
44 Concord Rd
Marlborough MA
01752

Call Sign: KA2CKC
Norman R Wicklman
959 Concord Rd
Marlborough MA
01752

Call Sign: KB1JYD
Alexander J Sayegh
Crystal Brook Way
Marlborough MA
01752

Call Sign: N1NVS
Lauryn A Chabot
49 E Curtis Ave
Marlborough MA
017522641

Call Sign: N1MYT
John R Duncan
332 E Main St
Marlborough MA
017525400

Call Sign: K1DIN
Edmund P L Fitzgerald
95 East Dudley St
Marlborough MA
01752

Call Sign: N1FIP
Daniel L Bloch
909 Elm St
Marlborough MA
01752

Call Sign: W1RCJ
Walter S Woodward
14 Emmett
Marlborough MA
01752

Call Sign: KA1NOJ
Dianne M Cook
Emmett St
Marlborough MA
01752

Call Sign: N1DFQ

James D Weldon
Emmett St
Marlborough MA
01752

Call Sign: N1FJQ
David B Weldon
Emmett St
Marlborough MA
01752

Call Sign: K1PWE
Katherine E Nunes
685 Farm Rd
Marlborough MA
01752

Call Sign: KB1WBT
David J Blanchard
Farm Rd
Marlborough MA
01752

Call Sign: N1BHI
Andrew L Morrison
740 Farm Rd 24
Marlborough MA
01752

Call Sign: K1NR
Eugene W Balinski
51 Farrington Lane
Marlborough MA
01752

Call Sign: N1KCQ
James M Gosse
36 Fontaine St
Marlborough MA
01752

Call Sign: N1PHG
Thomas J Gosse
36 Fontaine St
Marlborough MA
01752

Call Sign: WX1YZ
Thomas J Gosse
36 Fontaine St
Marlborough MA
01752

Call Sign: KA1RVP

Jay S Field
26 Franklin St
Marlborough MA
01752

Call Sign: N1DNX
John L Snyder
137 Frye St
Marlborough MA
01752

Call Sign: KA1NQN
Parker C Allinson
72 Glen St
Marlborough MA
01752

Call Sign: WB2HRB
Christopher F De
Angelis
57 Goodale St
Marlborough MA
01752

Call Sign: K1CRT
Christopher F De
Angelis
57 Goodale St
Marlborough MA
01752

Call Sign: KA1BK
Michael A Tyo
108 Goodale St
Marlborough MA
01752

Call Sign: KA1FJB
Manuel B Garcia
43 Greenwood St
Marlborough MA
01752

Call Sign: W1HGU
Ned L Fenstermacher
35 Hayden St
Marlborough MA
01752

Call Sign: KC7MIF
Joel B Rosenzweig
16 Heath St
Marlborough MA
01752

Call Sign: K2HA
Charles R Cross
400 Hemenway St Apt
134
Marlborough MA
017526773

Call Sign: W1EU
J Francis Bartlett
400 Hemenway St Ste
241
Marlborough MA
01752

Call Sign: KB1CQF
Margaret D Sahagian
146 Hildreth St
Marlborough MA
01752

Call Sign: W1CDA
William T Muise Jr
230 Hildreth St
Marlborough MA
01752

Call Sign: KA1YLW
Kimberly C Moore
84 Howland St
Marlborough MA
01752

Call Sign: KB1IGQ
Gregory J O Brien
50 Hunter Ave
Marlborough MA
017521162

Call Sign: NE1OB
Gregory J O Brien
50 Hunter Ave
Marlborough MA
017521162

Call Sign: WB1FJS
Steven W Symes
27 Kelber Dr
Marlborough MA
01752

Call Sign: KB1UQK
Steven W Symes
27 Kelber Drive

Marlborough MA
01752

Call Sign: KB1PKA
Kenneth A Backman
32 Kevork Ave
Marlborough MA
01752

Call Sign: W1KAB
Kenneth A Backman
32 Kevork Ave
Marlborough MA
01752

Call Sign: N1ETO
Clarence Baker
190 Kings Grant Rd
Marlborough MA
01752

Call Sign: KA1EWM
John P Sullivan
231 Kings Grant Rd
Marlborough MA
01752

Call Sign: KB1SAT
Stephen P Mccall
14 Kirby St
Marlborough MA
01752

Call Sign: N1MGH
Rhonda S Sussman
70 Kosmas St
Marlborough MA
01752

Call Sign: W1QFD
Anthony J Yuoska
105 Lincoln St
Marlborough MA
01752

Call Sign: N1JNT
Byron H Kiser Jr
4 Lodi Rd
Marlborough MA
01152

Call Sign: KB1HXI
Richard L Landau
276 Main St Apt 1

Marlborough MA
01752

Call Sign: KS1N
Eric J St Cyr
185 Main St Apt 7
Marlborough MA
01752

Call Sign: KA1HIH
Louis R Tramontozzi
2 Masciarelli Drive
Marlborough MA
01752

Call Sign: WA1EJY
James J Lynch
205 Miles Standish Dr
Marlborough MA
01752

Call Sign: W1NNX
Donald A Boyle
163 Millham St
Marlborough MA
01752

Call Sign: KA1ZKB
Suzanne L De Millar
250 Millham St
Marlborough MA
01752

Call Sign: KZ1D
Dennis J Brevik
250 Millham St
Marlborough MA
017521025

Call Sign: KA1YQJ
Elizabeth R Mowry
16 Minehan Ln
Marlborough MA
01752

Call Sign: KB1RO
Ronald C Mowry
16 Minehan Ln
Marlborough MA
01752

Call Sign: WA1WXN
Michael J Sowa
61 Morrissey Rd

Marlborough MA
01752

Call Sign: N8XEQ
Victor D Grund
34 Muir Way
Marlborough MA
01752

Call Sign: KB1IGR
Mark I Niedzielski
41 Obrien Rd
Marlborough MA
01752

Call Sign: N4CMX
Renee S Norton
55 O'malley Rd
Marlborough MA
01752

Call Sign: N1LCX
James E Chaffee
11 Orchard St
Marlborough MA
017524311

Call Sign: K1KTW
Woodrow A Wilson
36 Patricia Rd
Marlborough MA
017521554

Call Sign: N1FOR
Ann L Williams
763 Pleasant St
Marlborough MA
01752

Call Sign: KB1JFI
Matthew D Williams
763 Pleasant St
Marlborough MA
01752

Call Sign: W1MAT
Matthew D Williams
763 Pleasant St
Marlborough MA
01752

Call Sign: KB1JLP
Jennie Williams
763 Pleasant St

Marlborough MA
01752

Call Sign: W1JNE
Jennie Williams
763 Pleasant St
Marlborough MA
01752

Call Sign: KB1OFN
Hewlett Packard New
England Radio Club
763 Pleasant St
Marlborough MA
01752

Call Sign: NE1HP
Hewlett Packard New
England Radio Club
763 Pleasant St
Marlborough MA
01752

Call Sign: KB1CHK
Peter A Lothian
155 Pleasant St 14b
Marlborough MA
01752

Call Sign: KB1VWL
Douglas J Steinfeld
72 Prendiville Way
Marlborough MA
01752

Call Sign: WB1ATX
Anti Algonquin Radio
League
32 Queensview Rd
Marlborough MA
017521501

Call Sign: N2IOF
Charles C Read Iv
14 Ridge Rd
Marlborough MA
01752

Call Sign: KB1GBZ
Emilie R Read
14 Ridge Rd
Marlborough MA
01752

Call Sign: KB1TYN
James C Read
14 Ridge Rd
Marlborough MA
01752

Call Sign: N1AGW
Paul A Sittard
255 Robert Rd
Marlborough MA
017526532

Call Sign: KA1PIQ
Neal S Pressman
175 Roundtop Rd
Marlborough MA
01752

Call Sign: KA1NLX
Dennis J Sulewski
2 Royal Crest Dr 3
Marlborough MA
01752

Call Sign: WB8RUN
Klaes W Daley
27 Royal Crest Dr Apt
10
Marlborough MA
01752

Call Sign: KB1HFM
Richard R Wolf
14 Shawmut Ave
Marlborough MA
01752

Call Sign: N1OW
Richard R Wolf
14 Shawmut Ave
Marlborough MA
01752

Call Sign: W1OLF
Richard R Wolf
14 Shawmut Ave
Marlborough MA
01752

Call Sign: W1JDD
Joshua D Dick
159 Silver Leaf Way
Apt 34

Marlborough MA
01752

Call Sign: KA1OUI
Gerald J Mc Garry
371 Simpson Rd
Marlborough MA
01752

Call Sign: KB1SFZ
Erick Andrews
19 South St
Marlborough MA
01752

Call Sign: KB1SMI
Erick Andrews
19 South St
Marlborough MA
01752

Call Sign: KB1TSY
Katherine Karwoski
338 Stearns Rd
Marlborough MA
01752

Call Sign: KB1ISN
Jennifer L O Rourke
427 Stearns Rd
Marlborough MA
01752

Call Sign: W1LZY
Jennifer L O Rourke
427 Stearns Rd
Marlborough MA
01752

Call Sign: KB1RGX
David L Haralambou
427 Stearns Rd
Marlborough MA
01752

Call Sign: W1SHK
David L Haralambou
427 Stearns Rd
Marlborough MA
01752

Call Sign: N1IZ
Paul H Hansen
54 Stow Rd

Marlborough MA
01752

Call Sign: N1CEW
Augustus E Pierce
80 Tremont
Marlborough MA
01752

Call Sign: N1TIP
Edward M Rogers
77 Tremont St
Marlborough MA
01752

Call Sign: WB1EGE
Kenneth J Sloan
38 Victoria Ln B2
Marlborough MA
01752

Call Sign: N1KQV
Lee S Snow
102 Warren Ave #5
Marlborough MA
017520004

Call Sign: N1ZOW
Laurence N Ladd
22 Whispering Brook
Rd
Marlborough MA
01752

Call Sign: KB1UFR
Dean Zach
20 Wilkens Way
Marlborough MA
01752

Call Sign: W1UE
Dennis G Egan
166 Wilson St
Marlborough MA
01752

Call Sign: WA0LOZ
Michael W Shields
47 Woodridge Rd
Marlborough MA
01752

Call Sign: WQ1D
Jeffrey S Cohen

22 Wright Drive
Marlborough MA
01752

Call Sign: N1EM
Algonquin Amateur
Radio Club
Marlborough MA
017520258

Call Sign: N1UWL
Nora A Semmel
Marlborough MA
01752

Call Sign: W1GBE
Raytheon Company
M/S1-2-1934
Raytheon-Marlborough
Amateur Radio Club
Marlborough MA
01752

**FCC Amateur Radio
Licenses in
Marshfield**

Call Sign: K1EGR
Archibald M Mack
152 Acorn Box 23
Marshfield MA 02050

Call Sign: KA1FAN
Helen L Demers
Box 207
Marshfield MA 02050

Call Sign: K1VS
Norby Comeau
142 Careswell St
Marshfield MA
020504166

Call Sign: N1VFA
Gerard O Crawley
44 Carolina Tr
Marshfield MA 02050

Call Sign: W1PXC
Vaino A Kestila
44 Carolyn Cir
Marshfield MA 02050

Call Sign: KB1DDP

Ronald D Montgomery
122 Croos St Box 860
Marshfield MA 02050

Call Sign: KA1AQ
James H Rafuse Jr
145 Damons Point Rd
Marshfield MA 02050

Call Sign: WB1BQN
Constantine
Courtoglous
Deer Hill Ln
Marshfield MA 02050

Call Sign: KB1UCC
Dianne J Stark
104 Donald Rd
Marshfield MA 02050

Call Sign: N1IZK
Norby Comeau
7 Fletcher Dr
Marshfield MA 02050

Call Sign: WA1NZA
Philip A Reeves
Flower Hill Ln
Marshfield MA 02050

Call Sign: KB1QEM
John R O Neill
20 Fox Run Unit 10
Marshfield MA 02050

Call Sign: KB1HDJ
Robert C Flynn
21 Hatch St
Marshfield MA
020502449

Call Sign: W1NMF
Robert C Flynn
21 Hatch St
Marshfield MA
020502449

Call Sign: N1LDJ
Mark W Tomkins
77 Holly Dr
Marshfield MA 02050

Call Sign: KB1TUB
Linda M Evans

108 Holyoke Ave
Marshfield MA 02050

Call Sign: WB1FTL
Bernard F Pesce Ii
56 Ireland Rd
Marshfield MA 02050

Call Sign: WA1QCZ
Paul F Melia
4 Lady Slipper Ln
Marshfield MA 02050

Call Sign: KD1IQ
Robert E Dyer
Ma 02050
Marshfield MA 02050

Call Sign: KB1WWG
James R Ellsworth
76 Magoun Path
Marshfield MA 02050

Call Sign: KB1WSX
Daniel I Brannum
205 Main St
Marshfield MA 02050

Call Sign: KA1DH
Robert A Demers
571 Main St
Marshfield MA 02050

Call Sign: WQ1L
John R Coombs
633 Main St
Marshfield MA 02050

Call Sign: KB1LZM
John E Plunkett Jr
600 Moraine St
Marshfield MA 02050

Call Sign: K1JEP
John E Plunkett Jr
600 Moraine St
Marshfield MA 02050

Call Sign: W1DCF
Gustavus C Lane
1681 Ocean St Box
184
Marshfield MA 02050

Call Sign: KB1CHW
John R Coombs Jr
1801 Ocean St S-31
Marshfield MA 02050

Call Sign: KA1WKL
Melissa A Tedone
20 Old Barn Path
Marshfield MA 02050

Call Sign: N1KGG
James A Logue
134 Old Colony Ln
Marshfield MA 02050

Call Sign: KB1CHU
Stephen H Black
99 Orchard Rd
Marshfield MA 02050

Call Sign: KA1AQU
Carolyn S Richards
300 Parsonage St
Marshfield MA
020501139

Call Sign: WA1OEX
Barry M Richards
300 Parsonage St
Marshfield MA
020501139

Call Sign: K1TJS
Thomas J Sullivan
401 Parsonage St
Marshfield MA 02050

Call Sign: N1BSO
John P Laiosa
301 Pine St
Marshfield MA 02050

Call Sign: KB1AKZ
Patrick J Smith
66 Pioneer Trl
Marshfield MA 02050

Call Sign: KA1PS
George L Mc Carron
3 Rayfield Rd
Marshfield MA 02050

Call Sign: WA4PSC
Martha W Watjen

30 Settlers Pathe
Marshfield MA 02050

Call Sign: KB1OJC
Jonathan H Walzer
864 South River St
Marshfield MA
020502550

Call Sign: KB1DNA
Richard L Seeg
46 Stagecoach Dr
Marshfield MA
020504141

Call Sign: AE1L
Paul T Fata Sr
165 Stagecoach Drive
Marshfield MA
020504161

Call Sign: KB1NA
Dennis A Watts
201 Stonybrook Rd
Marshfield MA 02050

Call Sign: W1DT
Neal J Dahlen
93 Summer St
Marshfield MA 02050

Call Sign: KE1HN
Joe Beals Iv
979 Summer St
Marshfield MA 02050

Call Sign: KB1MRI
David A Copeland
25 Tea Rock Gardens
Marshfield MA 02050

Call Sign: AA1A
David F Riley
11 Walnut St
Marshfield MA 02050

Call Sign: W1AAI
Judith L Riley
11 Walnut St
Marshfield MA 02050

Call Sign: KB1HER
Uscg Radsta Nmf
11 Walnut St

Marshfield MA 02050

Call Sign: K1NMF
Uscg Radsta Nmf
11 Walnut St
Marshfield MA 02050

Call Sign: KB1ILV
Reginald A Fessenden
Ars
11 Walnut St
Marshfield MA 02050

Call Sign: W1FRV
Reginald A Fessenden
Ars
11 Walnut St
Marshfield MA 02050

Call Sign: WA1LJH
Alan L Robbins
356 Webster St
Marshfield MA 02050

Call Sign: K1CLA
Paul V Malley
466 Webster St
Marshfield MA 02050

Call Sign: KB1WVL
Thomas A Scott
23 Woodbine Rd
Marshfield MA 02050

Call Sign: N1QGI
Michael R Johnson
Marshfield MA 02050

Call Sign: K1FW
Frederick A Wasti
Marshfield MA 02050

Call Sign: W1EDP
David J Shain
Marshfield MA 02050

Call Sign: N1NO
David J Hammond
Marshfield MA
020501042

**FCC Amateur Radio
Licenses in
Marshfield Hills**

Call Sign: AA1FD
Peter P Roper
34 Deerhill Ln
Marshfield Hills MA
02051

Call Sign: N1KBQ
Mark E Roper
34 Deerhill Ln
Marshfield Hills MA
02051

Call Sign: WA1TBA
Peter O Swanson
23 Pinehurst Rd
Marshfield Hills MA
020510237

Call Sign: KA1BCV
Marilee A Cantelmo
35 Robert Ave
Marshfield Hills MA
02051

Call Sign: WB1FWS
N Frank Cantelmo Jr
35 Robert Ave
Marshfield Hills MA
02051

Call Sign: N1LXQ
Christerpher Perry
846 Summer St
Marshfield Hills MA
02051

Call Sign: N1SEO
Bradford C Swanson
Marshfield Hills MA
02051

Call Sign: KB1PBU
Joel P Clark
Marshfield Hills MA
02051

Call Sign: KB1QCH
Daniel K Ryan
Marshfield Hills MA
02051

Call Sign: KA1VUS
Debra E Lincoln
170 Asa Meigs
Marstons Mills MA
02648

Call Sign: N1RTJ
Jane K Frost
253 Asa Meigs Rd
Marstons Mills MA
02648

Call Sign: KA1VUU
John E Lincoln Sr
170 Asameigs Rd
Marstons Mills MA
02648

Call Sign: KB1TAI
Stephen S Alongi
10 Aster Lane
Marstons Mills MA
02648

Call Sign: KB1VAL
John W Kourafas
160 Audreys Ln
Marstons Mills MA
02648

Call Sign: N1HNZ
Albert A Amerigian
61 Barnicle Dr
Marstons Mills MA
02648

Call Sign: W1RF
Michael N Coulter
84 Baxter Neck Rd
Marstons Mills MA
02648

Call Sign: KB1VHT
Warren J Volk
93 Blueberry Ln
Marstons Mills MA
02648

Call Sign: W1PSS
Donald F Varnum Sr

28 Calvin Hamblin Rd
Marstons Mills MA
02648

Call Sign: KB1BFB
Sophie G Chestnut
110 Camelback Rd
Marstons Mills MA
02648

Call Sign: N1JNF
Roy H Thomas
115 Camelback Rd
Marstons Mills MA
02648

Call Sign: N1XYY
Mark S Conway
17 Cranberry Ridge Rd
Marstons Mills MA
02648

Call Sign: KB1VAE
Gordon T Woods
60 Deer Hollow Rd
Marstons Mills MA
02648

Call Sign: KB1VAF
Daria Lewis
60 Deer Hollow Rd
Marstons Mills MA
02648

Call Sign: KA1GDZ
Andrew F Picariello
103 Dory Cir
Marstons Mills MA
02648

Call Sign: WA1WSP
Frederick H Prip
115 Evergreen Dr
Marstons Mills MA
026481289

Call Sign: W1OLP
George A Wilson Jr
82 Frazier Way
Marstons Mills MA
02648

Call Sign: W1QON
Eleanor L Wilson

82 Frazier Way
Marstons Mills MA
02648

Call Sign: KC1UA
Scott A Halligan
15 Gooseberry Ln
Marstons Mills MA
02648

Call Sign: KA1TJU
Kimberley A Phu
20 Gristmill Path
Marston's Mills MA
02648

Call Sign: KB1TNR
Aaron M Tokarz
49 High Point Rd
Marstons Mills MA
02648

Call Sign: KB1UKO
Cory M Mac Donald
78 Huckleberry Ln
Marstons Mills MA
02648

Call Sign: W1CMM
Cory M Mac Donald
78 Huckleberry Ln
Marstons Mills MA
02648

Call Sign: KC1TI
James D Mitchell
900 Lumbert Mill Rd
Box 135
Marstons Mills MA
026480135

Call Sign: KB1KMB
Jennifer L D Elia
193 Mockingbird Ln
Marstons Mills MA
02648

Call Sign: W1CRK
Calvert F Eck
1351 Old Post Rd
Marstons Mills MA
026480036

Call Sign: N1BAD

Kenneth J Soares Sr
P O Box 1065
Marstons Mills MA
02648

Call Sign: N1IUI
Stephen J Finocchi
37 Pebble Path
Marstons Mills MA
02648

Call Sign: KA1UQF
Robert D Heller
59 Pebble Path
Marstons Mills MA
02648

Call Sign: K1FFR
Robert D Burd
24 Prince Ave
Marston Mills MA
02648

Call Sign: KB1LFW
Joseph Chretien
1605 Race Ln
Marstons Mills MA
02648

Call Sign: W1JJC
Joseph Chretien
1605 Race Ln
Marstons Mills MA
02648

Call Sign: NX1V
Edward G Schwarm
251 Regency Dr
Marstons Mills MA
02648

Call Sign: KB1HQP
Thomas E Collis
408 Regency Dr
Marstons Mills MA
02648

Call Sign: KB1HVO
Thomas E Collis
408 Regency Dr
Marstons Mills MA
02648

Call Sign: AB1AX

Thomas E Collis
408 Regency Dr
Marstons Mills MA
02648

Call Sign: KB1LNY
Matthew R Muller
495 River Rd
Marstons Mills MA
02648

Call Sign: W1KJD
Russell R Lanoue
149 School St
Marstons Mills MA
02648

Call Sign: W1MXB
Harvey F Sinnett
193 School St
Marstons Mills MA
02648

Call Sign: W1BBK
Anthony P Capelle
566 Wakeby Rd
Marstons Mills MA
02648

Call Sign: N2JWW
Michael J Wilbur
603 Wakeby Rd
Marstons Mills MA
02648

Call Sign: W1KM
Gregory M Cronin
484 Whistleberry Dr
Marstons Mills MA
02648

Call Sign: W4LME
John J Regan
380 Whistleberry
Drive
Marstons Mills MA
02648

Call Sign: WQ1O
Francis M O Laughlin
Marstons Mills MA
02648

Call Sign: K1UA

Jay K Chesler
Marstons Mills MA
02648

Call Sign: KB1NNN
Andrew D Newton
Marstons Mills MA
02648

**FCC Amateur Radio
Licenses in Mashpee**

Call Sign: N1GMK
Geraldine K Maikath
63 Algonquin Ave
Mashpee MA 02649

Call Sign: KA1THC
Kyle K Maikath
230 Algonquin Ave
Mashpee MA 02649

Call Sign: W1IQW
Theodore A Bergstrom
50 Bayshore Drive
Mashpee MA 02649

Call Sign: KB1PGX
Michael S Spivack
73 Blue Spruce Way
Mashpee MA 02649

Call Sign: K1VTR
Michael S Spivack
73 Blue Spruce Way
Mashpee MA 02649

Call Sign: W1ABV
Floyd Campbell
85 Blue Spruce Way
Mashpee MA 02649

Call Sign: N1GML
Paul F Trask
52 Brewster Rd
Mashpee MA 02649

Call Sign: KB1KMP
Richard S Heinrich
7 Butler Lane
Mashpee MA
026496210

Call Sign: KB1BSR

Matt R Taylor
43 Cambridge Dr
Mashpee MA 02649

Call Sign: N1RAP
Peter R Taylor
43 Cambridge Dr
Mashpee MA 02649

Call Sign: KD1SD
Allan Mac Donald Jr
1 Carleton Drive Apt
211
Mashpee MA 02649

Call Sign: KB1NNP
Arthur J Raymond
20 Coombs Ln
Mashpee MA 02649

Call Sign: N1HEW
Ziv Sirkes
Deer Crossing C21
Mashpee MA 02649

Call Sign: N1LEG
David R Allan
11 Deer Ridge Rd
Mashpee MA 02360

Call Sign: N1XWR
Timothy S Little
74 Degrass Rd
Mashpee MA 02649

Call Sign: KA1QMA
Alan Costa
2 Essex Rd
Mashpee MA 02649

Call Sign: KC6LFP
A J Pulley
195 Falmouth Rd #8e
Mashpee MA 02649

Call Sign: KA1SV
Daniel P Schaaf Sr
65 Forest Dr
Mashpee MA 02649

Call Sign: W1PPY
Christopher J Lynch
2 Forest Rd

Mashpee MA
026494709

Call Sign: KB1HCS
Mark R Walden
46 Gia Ln
Mashpee MA 02649

Call Sign: N1HQZ
Scott A Fronius
1178 Great Hay Rd
Mashpee MA 02649

Call Sign: KB1SFS
Jeremy M Thomas
32 Gunters Lane
Mashpee MA 02649

Call Sign: N1OEI
Douglas E Thomas
32 Gunters Ln
Mashpee MA 02649

Call Sign: KB1TAJ
Ray E Bowman
38 Hilltop Rd
Mashpee MA 02649

Call Sign: KB1QIT
Edwin Theis
223 Hooppole Rd
Mashree MA 02649

Call Sign: N1PPV
Jan L Borden
26 Kells Pond Cir
Mashpee MA 02649

Call Sign: KD1SK
Harold J Almeida
9 Lakeview Dr
Mashpee MA 02649

Call Sign: W1NA
Pier L Iovino
302 Main St
Mashpee MA 02649

Call Sign: KB1NNQ
Alessandro D'onofrio
302 Main St
Mashpee MA 02649

Call Sign: N3AN

Alessandro D'onofrio
302 Main St
Mashpee MA 02649

Call Sign: KF1P
Luigi Attaianese
304 Main St
Mashpee MA 02649

Call Sign: N2UR
Luigi Attaianese
304 Main St
Mashpee MA 02649

Call Sign: N1WAT
Robert J Courtemanche
386 Mashpee Neck Rd
Mashpee MA 02649

Call Sign: W1XR
James T Welch
29 Meadow Haven Dr
Mashpee MA 02649

Call Sign: N1LNI
Robert L Thomas
222 Meetinghouse Rd
Mashpee MA 02649

Call Sign: NQ1L
Robert L Thomas
222 Meetinghouse Rd
Mashpee MA
026492615

Call Sign: N1JCO
Barbara C Priestly
73 Neshobe Rd
Mashpee MA 02649

Call Sign: KB1QDM
Richard J Riley
51 Park Place Way
Mashpee MA 02649

Call Sign: N1RMH
Mathieu M Landry
44 Pequot Rd
Mashpee MA 02649

Call Sign: KA1YHL
David C Whiting
62 Polaris Dr
Mashpee MA 02649

Call Sign: KB1COX
Stephen J Greelish
130 Pond Cir
Mashpee MA 02649

Call Sign: KB2CQM
William J Henry
15 Rachelle Ct
Mashpee MA 02649

Call Sign: KB1BRR
William R Sabatini
29 Ships Anchor Dr
Mashpee MA 02049

Call Sign: KB1CAB
Derek C Sabatini
29 Ships Anchor Dr
Mashpee MA 02649

Call Sign: N2KTC
Robert B Adams Jr
277 South Sandwich
Rd
Mashpee MA 02649

Call Sign: N1AM
John T Flynn
24 Starboard Dr
Mashpee MA 02649

Call Sign: WB2LWY
Walter F Phillips
32 Sunset Circle
Mashpee MA
026494999

Call Sign: KB1TAS
Judith M Matson
121 Sunset Strip
Mashpee MA 02649

Call Sign: KB1TAT
Stephen D Matson
121 Sunset Strip
Mashpee MA 02649

Call Sign: N1TCV
Daniel P Martin
4 Tradewind Dr
Mashpee MA 02649

Call Sign: KB1HMM

Susan Mazzucchi
24 Tradewind Dr
Mashpee MA 02649

Call Sign: KA1BXB
Donald J Mazzucchi
24 Tradewind Drive
Mashpee MA 02649

Call Sign: N1UGD
Chad M Nichols
9 Tricia Ln
Mashpee MA 02649

Call Sign: KC2AFH
Paul D Mascott
11 Webquish Ln
Mashpee MA 02649

Call Sign: KA1MDQ
Paul D Mascott
11 Webquish Ln
Mashpee MA 02649

Call Sign: WG3U
John L Griener
252 Wheeleer Rd
Mashpee MA
026494316

Call Sign: KB1EYQ
Lincoln D Kraeuter
92 Whippoorwill
Circle
Mashpee MA 02649

Call Sign: KB1LIO
Arthur A Jacobson
50 Wilann Drive
Mashpee MA 02632

Call Sign: K1BPM
Arnold Zunick
20 Yardarm Dr
Mashpee MA 02649

Call Sign: KA1DUF
Susan F Zunick
20 Yardarm Dr
Mashpee MA 02649

Call Sign: KB1QDH
Marleen C Burton
6 Yellow Perch Circle

Mashpee MA 02649

Call Sign: K2CHM
Michael S Gutman
Mashpee MA
026491108

Call Sign: N1ZOQ
Julia M Umina
Mashpee MA 02649

Call Sign: WB1DSF
James V Oliveto Jr
Mashpee MA 02649

Call Sign: KB1FVS
Christopher J Lynch
Mashpee MA
026441994

Call Sign: KB1GEJ
Paul E Mills
Mashpee MA 02649

Call Sign: W1CWO
James V Oliveto Jr
Mashpee MA 02649

Call Sign: N1ALD
Paul E Mills
Mashpee MA 02649

FCC Amateur Radio Licenses in Mattapan

Call Sign: KA1YTG
Edward V Lanczi
58 Cedar St
Mattapan MA 02126

Call Sign: KB1VKI
Robert Perello
92 Hazelton St
Mattapan MA 02126

Call Sign: N1QED
Eustace F Benjamin
1094 Morton St
Mattapan MA 02126

Call Sign: KA1HTL
Canute Byfield Sr
34 Ormond St
Mattapan MA 02126

Call Sign: K1YNL
Louis W Thompson
705 River St Apt 106
Mattapan MA 02026

FCC Amateur Radio Licenses in Mattapoisett

Call Sign: WB2MKA
Timothy J Brown
9 Abby Ln
Mattapoisett MA
02739

Call Sign: W1MKA
Timothy J Brown
9 Abby Ln
Mattapoisett MA
02739

Call Sign: K1KVV
Robert B Kelley
51 Angelica Ave
Mattapoisett MA
02739

Call Sign: K1ZFX
John T Mc Manus
60 Fairhaven Rd Apt
2w
Mattapoisett MA
02739

Call Sign: KA1SQD
Howard C Chadwick
Iii
12 Grand Ave
Mattapoisett MA
02739

Call Sign: KB1IYM
Morgan C Hiller
8 Harbor Rd
Mattapoisett MA
02739

Call Sign: N1GFS
Ronald M Ellis Jr
1 Highland View Ave
Mattapoisett MA
02739

Call Sign: K1RON
Ronald M Ellis Jr
1 Highland View Ave
Mattapoisett MA
02739

Call Sign: KB1LMQ
Matthew D Grossi
13 Hitching Post Rd
Mattapoisett MA
02739

Call Sign: N1COD
John W Folino Jr
2 Holmes St
Mattapoisett MA
02739

Call Sign: KB1LFY
Weston V Cantor
29 Main St
Mattapoisett MA
02739

Call Sign: KB8MNS
James B Hein
7 Marion 1
Mattapoisett MA
02739

Call Sign: W1BLR
Old Rochester
Regional Jr High
School Radio Clb
133 Marion Rd
Mattapoisett MA
02739

Call Sign: N1NVT
Raymond Rose
11 Meadowbrook Ln
Mattapoisett MA
02739

Call Sign: KB1SKA
David A Ellis
30 Park St
Mattapoisett MA
02739

Call Sign: K1AI
Clifford J Snell Jr
5 Reservation Rd

Mattapoisett MA
02739

Call Sign: N1BTQ
Timothy R Smith
3 Riverside Drive
Mattapoisett MA
02739

Call Sign: N1TI
Timothy R Smith
3 Riverside Drive
Mattapoisett MA
02739

Call Sign: KB1IZI
Richard K Hiller
Mattapoisett MA
02739

FCC Amateur Radio Licenses in Maynard

Call Sign: N4JKT
David C Watkins
95 Acton St
Maynard MA
017541257

Call Sign: KC1BC
Ellis J Clark
8 Allan Dr
Maynard MA 01754

Call Sign: N1UGU
Barbara A Schlichter
Apple Rdg
Maynard MA 01754

Call Sign: WA1CFG
Timothy C Shea
Apple Ridge Rd
Maynard MA 01754

Call Sign: KA2ARK
John K Iler
Appleridge Rd
Maynard MA 01754

Call Sign: KC2OZT
John R Edson
2 Brian Way
Maynard MA 01754

Call Sign: WA1NAR
Jeffrey D Loeb
35 Brooks St
Maynard MA 01754

Call Sign: KB1UUG
Douglas T Lally
46 Brooks St
Maynard MA 01754

Call Sign: N0DUG
Douglas T Lally
46 Brooks St
Maynard MA 01754

Call Sign: W1NVL
Donald J Moreau
62 Butler Ave
Maynard MA 01754

Call Sign: K1TOW
John B Zancewicz
7 Cindy Ln
Maynard MA 01754

Call Sign: N1LYM
Michael B Chapman
35 Crane Ave
Maynard MA 01754

Call Sign: KA1LJV
Margaret L Gallagher
226 Dawn Rd
Maynard MA 01754

Call Sign: KB1FHP
William T Muise Jr
312 Dawn Rd
Maynard MA
017543407

Call Sign: KB1DNU
Donald F Bistany
22 Dix Rd
Maynard MA 01754

Call Sign: KB1DAA
Jon H Holtham
39 Durant Ave
Maynard MA 01754

Call Sign: W1FV
John E Kaufmann
47 Durant Ave

Maynard MA 01754

Call Sign: KB1AIH
Benjamin E Thorburn
8 Elaine Ave
Maynard MA 01754

Call Sign: KD1TE
Gary W Thorburn
8 Elaine Ave
Maynard MA 01754

Call Sign: WA1FHO
Paul A Newsham
6 Ethelyn Cir
Maynard MA 01754

Call Sign: W1TRC
James T Hanson
8 Ethelyn Cir
Maynard MA 01754

Call Sign: KB1SCG
Claudia R Stewart
3 Garfield St
Maynard MA 01754

Call Sign: N1VHX
John H Van
Kuilenburg
39 Great Rd
Maynard MA 01754

Call Sign: KA1CBX
John D Kelly
252 Great Rd
Maynard MA 01754

Call Sign: KB1ACY
Douglas J Meyer
32 Howard Rd
Maynard MA 01754

Call Sign: WZ0C
Michael T Ford
32 Lincoln St
Maynard MA 01754

Call Sign: KC1WA
John F Boothroyd
3 Loring Ave
Maynard MA
017541127

Call Sign: N1KMJ
Kevin P Hall
Main St Ste 317
Maynard MA 01754

Call Sign: KB1GUF
Michael J Polia
1 Marlboro St
Maynard MA 01754

Call Sign: WA1SLQ
John E Magoon
29 Mc Kinley St
Maynard MA 01754

Call Sign: KP4M
John M Comella
2 Mockingbird Ln
Maynard MA 01754

Call Sign: WA1OSJ
Edward B Hanfling
26 Mockingbird Ln
Maynard MA 01754

Call Sign: WB1AQA
Robert I Macomber
16 North St
Maynard MA 01754

Call Sign: KD1PD
Paul D Guthrie
Oak Ridge Dr
Maynard MA 01754

Call Sign: KA1WZM
Judith A Johnson
4 Oak St
Maynard MA 01754

Call Sign: W1UJQ
Harry F Chapell
41 Old Marlboro Rd
Maynard MA
017542145

Call Sign: KA1PGJ
William C Wade
61 Old Marlboro Rd
Maynard MA 01754

Call Sign: W1EPH
Martin R O Connell
7 Old Mill Rd

Maynard MA 01754

Call Sign: KB1PZJ
Thomas G Boerman
12 Oscar Way
Maynard MA 01754

Call Sign: KB1WKJ
Matthew D Truch
189 Parker St
Maynard MA 01754

Call Sign: K1MDT
Matthew D Truch
189 Parker St
Maynard MA 01754

Call Sign: N1ZNP
Mary A Dewar
24 Railroad St
Maynard MA
017541512

Call Sign: K1MWK
John D Barbagallo
18 Reo Rd
Maynard MA 01754

Call Sign: WA1ACA
Janice H Barbagallo
18 Reo Rd
Maynard MA 01754

Call Sign: KA1AZH
Herbert R Drury Jr
5 Shore Ave
Maynard MA 01754

Call Sign: N1PBM
Thomas L Rizzo
1 Sudbury St
Maynard MA 01754

Call Sign: W1VCX
Edward J Brennan
100 Summer
Maynard MA 01754

Call Sign: N1GWY
William T Drago Jr
57 Summer Hill Glen
Maynard MA 01754

Call Sign: KA1QDZ

Kevin J Stockwood
10 Summer Hill Rd
Maynard MA
017541547

Call Sign: N1IPL
Francesca C Pitt
146 Summer St
Maynard MA 01754

Call Sign: WD8LOC
Stuart H Pitt
146 Summer St
Maynard MA 01754

Call Sign: KA1SKV
Judith A Duehring
24 Walnut St
Maynard MA 01754

Call Sign: KB1FQG
John A Flood
79 Waltham St
Maynard MA 01754

Call Sign: N1JHW
Joakim Karlsson
11 Wood Ln Apt 1
Maynard MA 01754

Call Sign: N1KFX
Julie A Schoenfeld
9 Woodridge Rd
Maynard MA 01754

Call Sign: N1KFZ
John C Schoenfeld
9 Woodridge Rd
Maynard MA 01754

Call Sign: WA1SEN
Richard R Hurd
Maynard MA 01754

FCC Amateur Radio Licenses in Medfield

Call Sign: W1DKN
Richard H Bates
40 Adams St
Medfield MA 02052

Call Sign: KA1PPG
Neil I Grossman

17 Brastow Dr
Medfield MA 02052

Call Sign: N1MLP
Diane B Grossman
17 Brastow Dr
Medfield MA 02052

Call Sign: KB1VGZ
Nathan D Grossman
17 Brastow Dr
Medfield MA 02052

Call Sign: KB1JSW
Richard S Mckinney
40 Bridge St
Medfield MA 02052

Call Sign: N1OVZ
Blair R March
74 Bridge St
Medfield MA 02052

Call Sign: KE6BID
David C Steele
19 Bridlefield Lane
Medfield MA 02052

Call Sign: W1LIO
Arline F Berry
6 Causeway Ln
Medfield MA 02052

Call Sign: N1BID
Robert H Gibbs
7 Causeway St
Medfield MA 02052

Call Sign: W1HIV
Patrick S Harris
198 Causeway St
Medfield MA 02052

Call Sign: K1KG
Warner G Harrison
234 Causeway St
Medfield MA 02052

Call Sign: KB1KFK
Ryan J Orvedahl
13 Cross St
Medfield MA 02052

Call Sign: K1RJO

Ryan J Orvedahl
13 Cross St
Medfield MA 02052

Call Sign: N1LIH
Jeffrey A Orvedahl
13 Cross St
Medfield MA
020522722

Call Sign: WB1C
Charles R Mapps
22 Elm St
Medfield MA 02052

Call Sign: KB1RYN
Alexander I Mykyta
2 Forest St
Medfield MA 02052

Call Sign: KB1QDX
Domenic A Dicicco
51 Frairy St
Medfield MA 02052

Call Sign: N1KBU
Vincent M Cellucci
1 Granite St
Medfield MA 02052

Call Sign: N1SSN
Christopher J Fusco
10 Green St 12a
Medfield MA 02052

Call Sign: N1XAH
Neal R Olsen
74 Harding St
Medfield MA 02052

Call Sign: KB1HWZ
Robert A
Frankenthaler
22 Hawthorne Dr
Medfield MA 02446

Call Sign: N8DDI
David L Darmofal
58 High St
Medfield MA
020523110

Call Sign: K1YAE
Carl W Heine

21 Hillcrest Rd
Medfield MA 02052

Call Sign: WA1LJF
Alan R Beckwith
4 Larkspur Lane
Medfield MA 02052

Call Sign: W1JF
Alan R Beckwith
4 Larkspur Lane
Medfield MA 02052

Call Sign: KB1PWU
Brendan T Mcloughlin
7 Mahave Rd
Medfield MA 02052

Call Sign: N1QZV
John B Kinsellagh
3 Marsh Drive
Medfield MA 02052

Call Sign: W1SR
George R Wood
8 Nauset St
Medfield MA
020523021

Call Sign: WA1ZAZ
George G Wood
8 Nauset St
Medfield MA 02052

Call Sign: W1DE
Edward J Drozdick
30 Nebo St
Medfield MA 02052

Call Sign: KB1LBS
David M Wang
339 North St
Medfield MA 02052

Call Sign: W1ANG
David M Wang
339 North St
Medfield MA 02052

Call Sign: AL7GD
Harold R Economos
121 North St Apt 12
Medfield MA
020521650

Call Sign: N1COY
Robert R Downer
99 Philip St
Medfield MA 02052

Call Sign: K1GMF
Gayle F Manning
4 Pilgrim Lane
Medfield MA 02052

Call Sign: KA1CNP
Richard H Ryder
9 Pilgrim Lane
Medfield MA 02052

Call Sign: KB1NZT
David M Cronin
5 Rocky Lane
Medfield MA 02052

Call Sign: NE1A
David M Cronin
22 School St
Medfield MA 02052

Call Sign: WD8MFG
Darin S Oliver
229 South St
Medfield MA 02052

Call Sign: KB1PRI
Darin S Oliver
229 South St
Medfield MA 02052

Call Sign: W1YOU
Darin S Oliver
229 South St
Medfield MA 02052

Call Sign: KA1WWB
Frederick L Schultz
81 Spring St
Medfield MA 02052

Call Sign: W1ETB
Grant G Paul Jr
7 Tubwreck Dr
Medfield MA 02052

Call Sign: WF1V
Richard E Kumpf
12 Whichita Rd

Medfield MA 02052

Call Sign: K1JHU
Michael J Cronin
19 Wight St
Medfield MA 02052

Call Sign: KB1GLP
Joshua J Burton
1003 Wilkins Glen Rd
Medfield MA 02052

Call Sign: WB1GWG
Eric M Aker
5 Willow Circle
Medfield MA 02052

Call Sign: N1KUE
Ray M Burton Jr
Medfield MA 02052

Call Sign: N1BLR
Judith C Harris
Medfield MA 02052

FCC Amateur Radio Licenses in Medford

Call Sign: KD6EOK
Megan E Mower
84 1st St 2nd Floor
Medford MA 02155

Call Sign: KB1WVW
Rachel E Brown
15 A Tucker St
Medford MA 02155

Call Sign: KB1NLE
Steven W Winkler Jr
25 Alexander Ave
Medford MA 02155

Call Sign: KA1WGQ
Michael J Barry Ii
20 Allen Court
Medford MA 02155

Call Sign: N1IJZ
Donald R Haley
60 Almont St
Medford MA 02155

Call Sign: N1PNC

Mary G Haley
60 Almont St
Medford MA 02155

Call Sign: K1AKA
Rose C Hoebeke
106 Andrews St
Medford MA 02155

Call Sign: KA1EDX
David J Hegarty
41 Aquavia Rd
Medford MA 02155

Call Sign: N1HDR
Anthony S Knight
98 Arlington St
Medford MA 02155

Call Sign: KB1IQW
Ray L Thompson
68 Ashland St
Medford MA 02155

Call Sign: KB1NQT
John E Davis
14 Auburn St
Medford MA 02155

Call Sign: KA1NNY
Ralph L West
43 Belle Ave
Medford MA 02155

Call Sign: WA1ZRQ
Joseph A Pinto
25 Billing Ave
Medford MA 02155

Call Sign: KB1WXS
Harusuke Yoneyama
389 Boston Ave
Medford MA 02155

Call Sign: KE6MVF
Michael J Augusteijn
620 Boston Ave #5e
Medford MA 02155

Call Sign: KD4SFS
Michael Egan
30 Bower St
Medford MA 02156

Call Sign: AB1GN
Luiz L Souza
71 Bower St
Medford MA 02155

Call Sign: KB1TMM
Terri L Spencer
21 Bradlee Rd - 22
Medford MA 02155

Call Sign: W2GY
Christina M Rea
32 Brainard St
Medford MA 02155

Call Sign: WA1DXI
Paul J Planchet
16 Burget Ave
Medford MA 02155

Call Sign: N1CKN
Paula J Couture
50 Canal St
Medford MA 02155

Call Sign: WA1RTR
Robert P Newell
88 Central Ave
Medford MA 02155

Call Sign: N1EMZ
Stephen A Cabral
21 Chandler Rd
Medford MA 02155

Call Sign: N1RNC
James A Carbone
118 Circuit Rd
Medford MA 02155

Call Sign: K1GVJ
Alfonso J Falco Sr
49 Cobb St
Medford MA 02155

Call Sign: W1JPT
Isadore Werlin
39 Coolidge Rd
Medford MA 02155

Call Sign: WA1JRK
Paul L Cabral
16 Corinne Rd
Medford MA 02155

Call Sign: KB1WMD
Abby Bailey
49 Dearborn St
Medford MA 02155

Call Sign: N1HDU
Edward F Keeley
37 Dexter St
Medford MA 02155

Call Sign: K1UXB
Nicholas E Adiletto Jr
63 Doonan St
Medford MA 02155

Call Sign: N1OSB
Ishantha J Lokuge
60 Dwyer Cir
Medford MA 02155

Call Sign: N1JAO
Robert M Marotta
22 Early Ave
Medford MA 02155

Call Sign: W1NVX
Everett A Cook
56 Elm
Medford MA 02155

Call Sign: N1RND
David S Carbone
15 Everlyn Ave
Medford MA 02155

Call Sign: N1MJV
Gaetano La Terza
100 Fells Ave
Medford MA 02155

Call Sign: N1MJW
Guy M La Terza
100 Fells Ave
Medford MA 02155

Call Sign: KC1ZP
Peter Anda
41 Franklin St
Medford MA 02155

Call Sign: KA1FII
George C Finnegan
66 Frederick Ave

Medford MA 02155

Call Sign: KB1VQE
Arthur A Mancusi
207 Fulton St
Medford MA 02155

Call Sign: WA1EPK
Dwight E Perkins
559 Fulton St
Medford MA
021551230

Call Sign: N1FEV
Salvatore J Arria
8 G Walkling Ct
Medford MA 02155

Call Sign: W1HRW
Vincent Messina
99 Grant Ave
Medford MA 02155

Call Sign: N1JOM
Leigh Ann Polverelli
20 Greenhalge St
Medford MA 02155

Call Sign: KB1THF
Judd L Shapiro
22 Greenleaf Ave
Medford MA 02155

Call Sign: K1SQK
Judd L Shapiro
22 Greenleaf Ave
Medford MA 02155

Call Sign: KB1UQR
Ebc Radio Club
22 Greenleaf Ave
Medford MA 02155

Call Sign: K1EBC
Ebc Radio Club
22 Greenleaf Ave
Medford MA 02155

Call Sign: N1ADF
Arnold R Mac Collum
336 Grove St
Medford MA 02155

Call Sign: N1RXL

Bruno G Caruso
50 Hicks Ave #4
Medford MA 02155

Call Sign: N1GIB
Carole T Roberts
348 High St
Medford MA 02155

Call Sign: W1NOG
Patrick E De Salvatore
190 High St Apt 301
Medford MA 02155

Call Sign: WB1APS
Kenneth G Taylor
81 Hillsdale Rd
Medford MA 02155

Call Sign: KC1MA
Nicholas J Magliano
12 Kilsyth Rd
Medford MA 02155

Call Sign: KB1BDN
Adam S Harold
3 Laird Rd
Medford MA 02155

Call Sign: WA1EWL
Richard S Harold
3 Laird Rd
Medford MA 02155

Call Sign: N1PXB
Rodrigo C Santos
20 Lawler Rd
Medford MA 02155

Call Sign: KA1EEU
Rena M Wallace
363 Lawrence Rd
Medford MA 02155

Call Sign: KC1LT
David S Mcqueen
67 Lincoln Rd
Medford MA 02155

Call Sign: K1CHT
Chester Swanson Iii
27 Locust St Apt 8
Medford MA 02155

Call Sign: W1AAV
Peter A Pietropaolo
544 Main St
Medford MA 02155

Call Sign: KA1VQH
Tena C Lee
27 Manning St
Medford MA 02155

Call Sign: K1VUZ
Charles D Ranieri
49 Marion St
Medford MA 02155

Call Sign: N1TMK
Thomas A Amoroso
70 Marion St
Medford MA 02155

Call Sign: W1HHL
Edward S Scovel
15 Marston St
Medford MA 02155

Call Sign: K1BJ
Peter E Powers
48 Mc Cormack Ave
Medford MA 02155

Call Sign: W1YNF
Clifford E Dunbrack
163 Middlesex Ave
Medford MA 02155

Call Sign: N1KWP
Ralph Di Fonzo Ii
164 Middlesex Ave
Medford MA 02155

Call Sign: KA1VBO
Donna M Cooney
40 Morrison St
Medford MA 02155

Call Sign: KB1AMQ
Heather M Cooney
40 Morrison St
Medford MA 02155

Call Sign: K1ZOE
Andrew J Costa
2500 Mystic Valley
Parkway #701

Medford MA 02155

Call Sign: K1NGQ
Theodore L Filteau
2500 Mystic Valley
Pkwy 903
Medford MA 02155

Call Sign: N2YIC
Mitchell E Berger
Newbern Ave
Medford MA 02155

Call Sign: N1RMT
Frank K Berthold
86 Orchard St #3
Medford MA 02155

Call Sign: KA1SSC
Martin Cohen
6 Osborne Rd
Medford MA
021551515

Call Sign: KA1FZQ
Lawrence S Bacow
161 Packard Ave
Medford MA 02155

Call Sign: N1FDS
Joseph A Bellitti Sr
60 Palmer St
Medford MA 02155

Call Sign: K1WYJ
Leonard D Hanley
102 Park St
Medford MA
021553901

Call Sign: N1EYQ
David J Di Russo
52 Piggott Rd
Medford MA 02155

Call Sign: KB1LLO
Fred R Ziegler
16 Pineridge Rd
Medford MA 02155

Call Sign: KB1WUK
Lewis H Warren
31 Pleasant St
Medford MA 02155

Call Sign: W1EAU
Lewis H Warren
31 Pleasant St
Medford MA 02155

Call Sign: N1ZSU
Theodore Y Tso
43 Pleasant St
Medford MA 02155

Call Sign: KB1POS
Devasenapathi P
Seetharamakrishnan
19 Quincy St
Medford MA 02155

Call Sign: W1SHX
Thurston F Ackerman
62 Quincy St
Medford MA 02155

Call Sign: KB1TOY
David G Brozzell Jr
20 Renfrew St
Medford MA 01255

Call Sign: N1XTL
Lisa M Rigazio
13 Revere Pl
Medford MA 02155

Call Sign: W1NBV
Maynard E Wentzel
24 Robinson Rd
Medford MA 02155

Call Sign: KB9ZBY
Joshua L Wardell
183 Salem St
Medford MA 02155

Call Sign: KB1MSE
Karen E Robinson
85 Sharon St
Medford MA 02155

Call Sign: KB1WTB
James R Doyle
125 Sheridan Ave 1
Medford MA 02155

Call Sign: KB1NMY
Robert A Tarani

61 Sherwood Rd
Medford MA 02155

Call Sign: KB1NBG
Ricky A Chiampi
65 Sherwood Rd
Medford MA 02155

Call Sign: N1AJT
Ricky A Chiampi
65 Sherwood Rd
Medford MA 02155

Call Sign: K1MRI
Michael R Iacono
168 Spring St
Medford MA
021554068

Call Sign: N1QHC
Daniel P Joy
15 Stearns Ave
Medford MA 02155

Call Sign: KB1MKD
Roger M Borlase
43 Summer St
Medford MA 02155

Call Sign: N1PBA
Edward R Hennessy
11 Trainer Ave
Medford MA
021551716

Call Sign: N1ACE
Michael J Cronin
59 Victor St
Medford MA 02155

Call Sign: KB1NUS
William J Adams Jr
22 Waddell St
Medford MA 02155

Call Sign: KB1QMM
Christopher J Adams
22 Waddell St
Medford MA 02155

Call Sign: KO1M
Frank Comfort
14 Walsh St
Medford MA 02155

Call Sign: W1GF
Frederick W Brown Sr
157 Walsh St
Medford MA 02155

Call Sign: N1DDG
Joseph F Crowley
3 Washington St
Medford MA 02155

Call Sign: KB1OKP
Thomas S Bertolino
21 Water St
Medford MA 02155

Call Sign: KA1BKO
Carl E Waltman
203 Willis Ave
Medford MA 02155

Call Sign: W1YVT
Robert M Rizza
48 Winchester St
Medford MA 02155

Call Sign: KB1SVS
David S Phillips
186 Woburn St
Medford MA 02155

Call Sign: KB1UMH
Ronald S Senykoff Jr
99 Woods Rd
Medford MA 02155

Call Sign: N1TDL
Oanh J Dang
542 Wren Hall Tufts
Univ
Medford MA 02155

Call Sign: KB1EUP
Geoffrey C Bartlett
Medford MA 02153

**FCC Amateur Radio
Licenses in Medway**

Call Sign: K1EI
Joseph K Mulcahey
15 Alder St
Medway MA
020532268

Call Sign: NC1N
Charles H Ross Jr
5 Blueberry Hill Rd
Medway MA
020532168

Call Sign: W1URV
Robert P Bernard
5 Coffee St
Medway MA 02053

Call Sign: WA1ULY
Valerie L Bernard
5 Coffee St
Medway MA 02053

Call Sign: WA1ZIC
Frederick L Covell
4 Deerfield Rd
Medway MA 02053

Call Sign: W1ZZA
Terrence P Mc
Gillicuddy Rev
40 Dogwood Lane
Medway MA 02053

Call Sign: WB1BVK
Edythe R Hallinan
Elm St
Medway MA 02053

Call Sign: W1EGE
Richard V Robertson
42 Fisher St
Medway MA 02053

Call Sign: KB1OJK
Donald G Bergmann
53 Fisher St
Medway MA 02053

Call Sign: WA2TXQ
Donald G Bergmann
53 Fisher St
Medway MA 02053

Call Sign: KB1ITG
Keith R Wolfe
13 Florence Circle
Medway MA 02053

Call Sign: KW0LFE

Keith R Wolfe
13 Florence Circle
Medway MA 02053

Call Sign: KC1GB
Jeffrey M Hodge
4 Fuller Brook Ln
Medway MA
020531410

Call Sign: K1GBD
William T Harty
12 Highland St
Medway MA 02053

Call Sign: K1FV
Sheila M Hassan
50 Highland St
Medway MA 02053

Call Sign: W1KG
Richard J Hughes
3 Hillview Terrace
Medway MA 02053

Call Sign: WA1SBL
Herbert Rivkin
135 Holliston St
Medway MA 02053

Call Sign: KB1KZN
Robert F Phinney
24 Howe St
Medway MA 02053

Call Sign: K5TEC
Robert F Phinney
24 Howe St
Medway MA 02053

Call Sign: KE1HV
Richard A Fisher
4 Iroquois St
Medway MA 02053

Call Sign: N1XCP
Marie T Fisher
4 Iroquois St
Medway MA 02053

Call Sign: W1AWP
Peter E Parchesky
14 Karen Ave
Medway MA 02053

Call Sign: KD1IY
Dennis J Birch
2 Kings Ln
Medway MA 02053

Call Sign: KA1NU
Daniel E Yasi
3 Ledgewood Rd
Medway MA 02053

Call Sign: N1LKQ
Todd M Gallagher
15 Lincoln St
Medway MA 02053

Call Sign: KB1ONY
Domenic M Padula Iii
8 Longmeadow Ln
Medway MA 02053

Call Sign: K1DMP
Domenic M Padula Iii
8 Longmeadow Ln
Medway MA 02053

Call Sign: K1DP
Domenic M Padula Iii
8 Longmeadow Ln
Medway MA 02053

Call Sign: N2HSG
James E Phillips
6 Lost Hill Dr
Medway MA 02053

Call Sign: N1RDN
Dennis G Driscoll
16 Lovering St
Medway MA 02053

Call Sign: N1TBS
Paul B Driscoll
16 Lovering St
Medway MA 02053

Call Sign: KB1ACU
Danelle K Haynes
170 Main St
Medway MA 02053

Call Sign: KB1CUJ
Norman A Schneider
187 Main St

Medway MA 02053

Call Sign: KB1CUK
Barbara A Schneider
187 Main St
Medway MA 02053

Call Sign: W1RRP
Richard B Brown Iii
9 Massasoit St
Medway MA
020531214

Call Sign: N1RZM
Theodore L Davis
21 Meryl St
Medway MA 02053

Call Sign: N1KTC
Mark E Robinson
26 Milford St
Medway MA 02053

Call Sign: W1IJJ
Andrew J Cofelice Jr
122 Milford St
Medway MA 02053

Call Sign: KB1QDV
Roland A Burke
8 Oakland St
Medway MA 02053

Call Sign: WA1RGY
John C Simcox
11 Ohlson Cir
Medway MA 02033

Call Sign: KA1RLT
Scott H Ledder
8 Overlook Dr
Medway MA 02053

Call Sign: N1NRM
John J Ritter
8 Pheasant Run Rd
Medway MA
020536105

Call Sign: KB1MZK
Richard K Wasnewski
22 Populatic St
Medway MA 02053

Call Sign: WA1TBD
David A Newton
5 Rob Way
Medway MA 02053

Call Sign: WD4JQQ
Pace G Willisson
4 Spruce Rd
Medway MA 02053

Call Sign: W1CMR
Robert W Wilmarth
27 Summer Hill Rd
Medway MA 02053

Call Sign: WB1EWD
Lester J Seal
4 Temple St
Medway MA 02053

Call Sign: KA1UIH
Craig P Allen
8 Temple St
Medway MA 02053

Call Sign: KA1EW
William A
Christopherson
21 Vernon Rd
Medway MA 02053

Call Sign: KA1ZLV
Peter E Parchesky
86 Village St
Medway MA 02053

Call Sign: N1JUI
Robert W Mac Swain
284 Village St
Medway MA 02053

Call Sign: KA1ZTW
John C Codman
405 Village St
Medway MA 02053

Call Sign: KB1UIB
Brian M Clough
146 Village St Unit 1
Medway MA 02053

Call Sign: W1KXR
Harold W Jack
111 Winthrop St

Medway MA 02053

Call Sign: N1WER
Thomas S Hamano
138 Winthrop St
Medway MA 02053

Call Sign: K1SM
William A Hassan
Medway MA 02053

Call Sign: N1DLN
William S Mc Donald
Medway MA 02053

FCC Amateur Radio Licenses in Mellbury

Call Sign: N1QZE
Ann M Beausoleil
Mellbury MA 01527

FCC Amateur Radio Licenses in Melrose

Call Sign: KA1RPG
Roberta J Bailey
28 Albion St
Melrose MA 02176

Call Sign: N1YEX
Michael R Harris
19 Bartlett St
Melrose MA 02176

Call Sign: W1OUL
Leonard M Newberry
43 Baxter St
Melrose MA 02176

Call Sign: K1ZAJ
Bruno V Segalini
35 Bay State Rd
Melrose MA 02176

Call Sign: N1GEL
Edward A Sherman Jr
121 Beech Ave
Melrose MA 02176

Call Sign: KA1DNO
Richard B Bell
20 Belmont Place
Melrose MA 02176

Call Sign: W1QXS
Stuart J Tuma
17 Briggs St
Melrose MA 02176

Call Sign: WA1NWC
Stuart J Tuma
17 Briggs St
Melrose MA 02176

Call Sign: WB1DVI
Louise G Tuma
17 Briggs St
Melrose MA 02176

Call Sign: KB1BVR
Randy L Wohlen
17 Burnett St
Melrose MA 02176

Call Sign: W1FJL
Carl H Gylfphe Jr
2 Clarendon St
Melrose MA 02176

Call Sign: K2IRO
James H Singleton
77 Cochrane St
Melrose MA 02176

Call Sign: N1VGN
Ransom T Rowe
100 Cottage St
Melrose MA 02176

Call Sign: KA1PZQ
Edith A Trainor
159 Florence St
Melrose MA 02176

Call Sign: KA1PZR
Charles Trainor
159 Florence St
Melrose MA 02176

Call Sign: W1UZK
James H Chetwynd
124 Forest St
Melrose MA 02176

Call Sign: N1ICA
Daniel L Franklin
20 Garfield Rd

Melrose MA 02176

Call Sign: N1WBG
Dennis N Crouse
12 Gould St
Melrose MA 02176

Call Sign: W1WUL
Charles N Evans
24 Groveland Rd
Melrose MA 02176

Call Sign: KB1FXX
Kevin K Foss
17 Hancock St
Melrose MA 02176

Call Sign: KB1HEL
Kevin K Foss
17 Hancock St
Melrose MA 02176

Call Sign: AC1F
Norman H Blaney
106 Highview Ave
Melrose MA 02176

Call Sign: KA1ULO
Steven Giangregorio
49 Howard St
Melrose MA 02176

Call Sign: WB1DVH
Elmer N Wolf
158 Howard St
Melrose MA
021762008

Call Sign: W1CIW
Russell A Berg
192 Howard St
Melrose MA
021762022

Call Sign: WB4ELX
James E Mulvey
9 Howie St
Melrose MA 02176

Call Sign: N1FMK
Daniel L Cerys
22 Ledgewood Ave
Melrose MA
021765203

Call Sign: W1FRX
Richard Hardwick
186 Lincoln St
Melrose MA 02176

Call Sign: K1BCO
Elizabeth L Mullett
29 Lynde Ave
Melrose MA 02176

Call Sign: KB1KG
William S Mack
744 Lynn Fells Pky
Melrose MA 02176

Call Sign: N1TRC
Michael J Mc Cormack
990 Main St 4
Melrose MA 02176

Call Sign: W1LML
Leo A Green
471 Main St Apt 1
Melrose MA
021763837

Call Sign: KB1MWE
Christopher Thullen
585 Main St Apt 301
Melrose MA
021763146

Call Sign: KB1QKF
Maxwell J Titelbaum
49 Maple St
Melrose MA 02176

Call Sign: N1ULF
Stanford R Fredericks
22 Martin St
Melrose MA 02176

Call Sign: W1RMQ
John C Doherty
109 Marvin Rd
Melrose MA 02176

Call Sign: W1UNT
Philip A Russo
85 Meridian St
Melrose MA
021764830

Call Sign: N1LQZ
Jerzy W Krol
51 Oakland St
Melrose MA 02176

Call Sign: KB1WYC
Robert B Wall
131 Orris St
Melrose MA 02176

Call Sign: W1WJH
John R Sundquist
86 Otis St
Melrose MA 02176

Call Sign: WB1DMP
Stephen J Fitzpatrick
46 Pearl St
Melrose MA 02176

Call Sign: K1ILR
Francis M Walsh
96 Pleasant St
Melrose MA 02176

Call Sign: KB1PRT
Fairlie A Dalton
96 Pleasant St
Melrose MA 02176

Call Sign: K1DLC
Daniel L Cerys
14 Richardson Rd
Melrose MA
021761221

Call Sign: KE1GX
Charles Makredes
59 Richardson Rd
Melrose MA 02176

Call Sign: KE1X
Charles Makredes
59 Richardson Rd
Melrose MA 02176

Call Sign: W1FYV
Antenori H Tassinari
18 Sharon Rd
Melrose MA 02176

Call Sign: WB1DWS
Albert T Payson Jr
9 Sheffield Rd

Melrose MA 02176

Call Sign: N1USS
Ronald G Perry
34 Summer St
Melrose MA 02176

Call Sign: W1LOR
Francis T Wittmann
62 Summer St
Melrose MA 02176

Call Sign: KB1IPF
Jason M Marshall
196 Sylvan St #3
Melrose MA 02176

Call Sign: W1NOL
Vito J Di Benedetto
68 Upham St
Melrose MA 02176

Call Sign: K4IWX
Peter I Navarra
39 Vine St #3
Melrose MA 02176

Call Sign: KB1RWJ
Roderick E
Mangalonso
86 Vinton St
Melrose MA 02176

Call Sign: AB1KO
Roderick E
Mangalonso
86 Vinton St
Melrose MA 02176

Call Sign: KA1EHI
Kenneth D Mac
Donald
330 W Emerson St
Melrose MA 02176

Call Sign: KA1CKV
John F Short Jr
109 W Highland Ave
Melrose MA 02176

Call Sign: WF1T
Nathanael Y Waller
158 W Wyoming Av

Melrose MA
021763743

Call Sign: NC1V
Richard T Meuse
189 W Wyoming Ave
Melrose MA 02176

Call Sign: N1QMD
Thomas M
Thorndycraft
147 W Wyoming Ave
Apt 3
Melrose MA 02176

Call Sign: KA1FMV
Janet L Adamec
15 Warren St
Melrose MA
021761641

Call Sign: N1PFO
Thomas D Adamec
15 Warren St
Melrose MA 02176

Call Sign: KB1FEC
Thomas D Adamec
15 Warren St
Melrose MA 02176

Call Sign: W1PL
Leslie S Radnay
66 Wheeler Ave
Melrose MA
021765026

Call Sign: KB1VBF
Brian W Denley
75 Whitman Ave
Melrose MA 02176

Call Sign: W1KLG
George D Jones
25 Willard St
Melrose MA 02176

Call Sign: KD1VT
Wolfgang Lindner
150 Youle St
Melrose MA 02176

Call Sign: AB1DW
Wolfgang Lindner

150 Youle St
Melrose MA 02176

Call Sign: KG2DG
Norbert E Kremer
Melrose MA 02176

Call Sign: WB1F
Scott A Kingsley
Melrose MA 02176

Call Sign: KB1MOX
John A Mahon
Melrose MA 02716

Call Sign: KB1RCS
Pamela J Montanya
3 A Spring Brook Ct
Mendon MA 01756

Call Sign: K6NDV
Pamela J Angenent
3 A Spring Brook Ct
Mendon MA 01756

Call Sign: KN6DV
High Desert 160m Salt
Rats
3 A Springbrook Ct
Mendon MA 01756

Call Sign: K6ND
Willem A Angenent
3 A Springbrook Ct
Mendon MA 01756

Call Sign: NU5Y
Mladen Bogdanov
3 A Springbrook Ct
Mendon MA 01756

Call Sign: AE2W
Mladen Bogdanov
3 A Springbrook Ct
Mendon MA 01756

Call Sign: KB1WKF
Iliya S Getsov
3 A Springbrook Ct
Mendon MA 01756

Call Sign: KD1UY
Carolyn D Peterson
13 Ashkins Dr
Mendon MA 01756

Call Sign: KD1OK
Michael D Peterson
13 Ashkins Drive
Mendon MA 01756

Call Sign: W1MDP
Puddingstone Amateur
Radio Club
13 Ashkins Drive
Mendon MA 01756

Call Sign: W1LSH
Clinton York
5 Bates St
Mendon MA 01756

Call Sign: N1DXF
Richard L Earle
16 Bates St
Mendon MA 01756

Call Sign: N1GFB
Ralph F Archambault
41 Bellingham St
Mendon MA 01756

Call Sign: K1MDV
Ralph F Archambault
41 Bellingham St
Mendon MA 01756

Call Sign: N1NUE
Susan V Aurelio
7 Bicknell Dr
Mendon MA
017561184

Call Sign: N1SEB
Joseph V Aurelio
7 Bicknell Dr
Mendon MA
017561184

Call Sign: W1GDI
Vincent A Langelo
112 Blackstone St
Mendon MA 01756

Call Sign: N1HCX

Nancy Ann Jenkins
9 Blackstone St Apt C-1
Mendon MA 01756

Call Sign: KA1BYH
Lewis T Cronis
24 Colonial Drive
Mendon MA 01756

Call Sign: AE1C
James R Podsiadlo
8 Forest Park Drive
Mendon MA 01756

Call Sign: KT1U
Vivian M Podsiadlo
8 Forest Park Drive
Mendon MA 01756

Call Sign: N1UTW
Jean M Vendetti
16 George St
Mendon MA 01756

Call Sign: N1EIE
Richard A Skinner
143 Hartford Ave E
Mendon MA 01756

Call Sign: K1KAR
Herbert W Smith Jr
15 Hartford Ave West
Mendon MA 01756

Call Sign: KB9MH
Howard H Tarnoff
16 Lovell St
Mendon MA 01756

Call Sign: KA2UUP
Alberto L Rodriguez
6 Massasoit Way
Mendon MA
017560057

Call Sign: W1NGS
Dominic Grillo
28 Millville St
Mendon MA 01756

Call Sign: W1RZF
Arthur W Holmes Jr
48 N Av

Mendon MA 01756

Call Sign: KA1NFR
MARGUERITE L
Girard
116 North Ave
Mendon MA
017560220

Call Sign: KB1LNI
Sean M Luck
6 Talbott Farm Dr
Mendon MA 01756

Call Sign: W1SML
Sean M Luck
6 Talbott Farm Dr
Mendon MA 01756

Call Sign: K1CSU
J E Marcone
39 Washington St
Mendon MA 01756

Call Sign: KE1AP
William J Cote
74 Washington St
Mendon MA 01756

Call Sign: KA1LXK
Cheryl F Kearsley
Mendon MA 01756

Call Sign: KA1VN
George R Kearsley
Mendon MA 01756

Call Sign: K1JQF
John E Starbird
11 Bear Hill Rd
Merrimac MA 01860

Call Sign: N1AHM
Lawrence W Hardy
1 Broad St
Merrimac MA 01860

Call Sign: N1IVU
John C West
6 Carriage Court
Merrimac MA 01860

Call Sign: KA1VAA
Lorin M Maloney
15 Church St
Merrimac MA 01860

Call Sign: W1SRH
Melvin R Randall
27 High
Merrimac MA 01860

Call Sign: N1LOF
Robert K Heusser
82 Highland Rd
Merrimac MA 01860

Call Sign: N1GOZ
Ronald E Wilson
10 Oak Cir
Merrimac MA
018601625

Call Sign: K2CSX
Dana M Scott
17 Red Oak Acres
Merrimac MA 01860

Call Sign: KB1QYY
Daniel R O'sullivan
6 Shore Rd
Merrimac MA 01860

Call Sign: N1ERV
Daniel R O'sullivan
6 Shore Rd
Merrimac MA 01860

Call Sign: KB1TUK
James E Smith
8 Sunset Ter
Merrimac MA 01860

Call Sign: WA1NOS
John S Mason
Merrimac MA 01860

FCC Amateur Radio Licenses in Metheun

Call Sign: KB1PBF
Louis A Gemellaro
34 Sugar Hill Circle
Metheun MA 01844

Call Sign: KA1KDK
Henry P Ouellette
91 Adams Ave
Methuen MA 01844

Call Sign: K1NHQ
Robert E Evans
5 Albion St
Methuen MA 01844

Call Sign: N1KWC
Mark A Long
21 Almont St
Methuen MA 01844

Call Sign: KB1KDQ
Victor M Torres
45 Arnold St
Methuen MA 01844

Call Sign: N1IUQ
Michael D Gearan
34 Arrowood St
Methuen MA 01844

Call Sign: N1JES
David A Mauceri
39 Arrowwood St
Methuen MA 01844

Call Sign: KA1MBG
C Robert Doucot
47 Baremeadow St
Methuen MA 01844

Call Sign: WA1REI
Daniel J Dodson
10 Belmont St
Methuen MA
018442916

Call Sign: K1MMI
Edmund J Hajjar
8 Blackberry Ln
Methuen MA 01844

Call Sign: N1OZP
Gerald L Coller
6 Brandywine Lane
Methuen MA 01844

Call Sign: N1LMW
David M Piscopo
35 Bridgham St

Methuen MA 01844

Call Sign: N1LMX
Priscilla D Piscopo
35 Bridgham St
Methuen MA 01844

Call Sign: KA2WME
Ruben D Puello
175 Broadway Apt 10
Methuen MA 01844

Call Sign: KA1IXH
Victor Cirella
40 Brook St
Methuen MA 01844

Call Sign: W1BDY
Donald M Gagnon
51 Butternut Ln
Methuen MA 01844

Call Sign: N1QMN
Pauline G Bergeron
91 Butternut Ln
Methuen MA 01844

Call Sign: KB1SCJ
William J Schadlick
81 Clayton Ave
Methuen MA 01844

Call Sign: AB1KU
William J Schadlick
81 Clayton Ave
Methuen MA 01844

Call Sign: KA1JEH
Emmanuel J
Spampinato
19 Clinton St
Methuen MA 01844

Call Sign: N1TZQ
Mildred J Greenler
67 Cochrane Cir
Methuen MA 01844

Call Sign: WA1CBH
Michael L Greenler
67 Cochrane Cir
Methuen MA 01844

Call Sign: KB1WSN

Mark R Peglow
83 Comet Rd
Methuen MA 01844

Call Sign: W1UDR
William R Irving Jr
36 Coolidge St
Methuen MA 01844

Call Sign: NG1N
William P Toomey
73 Cross St
Methuen MA
018441612

Call Sign: KB1QOM
Christopher J Rock
96 Cross St
Methuen MA 01844

Call Sign: N1CYV
William F Mc
Donough Jr
3 Dow St
Methuen MA 01844

Call Sign: KD6PNZ
Jonathan M Ziel
171 E St 373f
Methuen MA 01844

Call Sign: N1FTY
Ross S Frey
30 East St
Methuen MA 01844

Call Sign: KB1AXM
Emil J Theriault
5 Echo Ln
Methuen MA 01844

Call Sign: N1NRT
Thomas J Oliveri
11 Emsley Ter
Methuen MA 01844

Call Sign: KB1KRF
William Fallon
22 Falcon St
Methuen MA
018442750

Call Sign: N1ZV
William Fallon

22 Falcon St
Methuen MA
018442750

Call Sign: N1CXR
Dora M Janos
524 Forest St
Methuen MA
018441940

Call Sign: W1JDU
Russell G Gagne Sr
20 Glen Ave
Methuen MA 01844

Call Sign: WA1BFN
Ronald Clamp
8 Glenwood Ave
Methuen MA 01844

Call Sign: N1BTO
Henry G Dupuis Jr
347 Hampshire Rd
Methuen MA 01844

Call Sign: KB1PIA
Roger F Perreault
21 Hampshire Rd Unit
316
Methuen MA 01844

Call Sign: KB1MSH
Peter J Perreault
21 Hampshire Rd Unit
316
Methuen MA 01844

Call Sign: KB1DJW
Steven H Douglass
83 Hampstead St
Methuen MA
018441206

Call Sign: AA1OD
Robert J Lacey Jr
201 Hampstead St
Methuen MA
018441234

Call Sign: N1VQL
Laura M Lacey
201 Hampstead St
Methuen MA
018441234

Call Sign: N1ZBU
Humberto I Zelic
20 Hancock Cir
Methuen MA 01844

Call Sign: W1IVW
Robert T Tataronis
Hawthorne Ave
Methuen MA 01844

Call Sign: K1BVX
Richard A De Feo
4 Hazel St
Methuen MA 01844

Call Sign: AA1JJ
Bruce A Cormier
22 High St
Methuen MA 01844

Call Sign: N1JLU
Michael J Spitalere
18 Hobart Rd
Methuen MA 01844

Call Sign: WJ1O
Victor J R Duphily Jr
32 Howe St
Methuen MA 01844

Call Sign: N1MXF
Donald Albanese
332 Howe St
Methuen MA 01844

Call Sign: N1BBB
James F Landers Sr
6 Hudson St
Methuen MA 01844

Call Sign: KB1IXD
Paul R Messineo
19 Huntress Ave
Methuen MA 01844

Call Sign: N1WAV
David M Collupy
18 Jasper St
Methuen MA 01844

Call Sign: WA1QEK
Dale R Dallon
11 Kimball Cir

Methuen MA 01844

Call Sign: WA1RNE
Christopher P Harris
4 Lady Slipper Lane
Methuen MA 01844

Call Sign: N1RZN
Valerie H Lowe
40 Landing Dr
Methuen MA 01844

Call Sign: W1DJS
Daniel J Shine
28 Landing Drive
Methuen MA
018445824

Call Sign: K1ALA
Adam J Buika
7 Longwood Dr
Methuen MA 01844

Call Sign: KB8DPV
James F Kennedy
40 Lowell St
Methuen MA 01844

Call Sign: W1PZR
Alfred J Walker
381 Lowell St
Methuen MA 01844

Call Sign: KB1RQP
Richard D Lafferty
708 Lowell St
Methuen MA 01844

Call Sign: N1JDJ
Armando Valadao
33 Marshall St
Methuen MA 01844

Call Sign: N1GAV
Harry A Paraskos
1 Melrose St
Methuen MA
018446517

Call Sign: KB1HMN
Emil P Pacula
40 Memorial Dr
Methuen MA 01844

Call Sign: KA1WKZ
Gerald J Leone
375 Merrimack St
Methuen MA 01844

Call Sign: WB1CXB
Robert H Feather
89 Milk St
Methuen MA 01844

Call Sign: N1AFQ
Paul A Miller
47 Milk St
Methuen MA
018445181

Call Sign: KA1WXS
Ramon G Matias
71 Mystic St Apt 5
Methuen MA 01844

Call Sign: N1IYE
Armand J De Roche
146 North St
Methuen MA 01844

Call Sign: W1OHZ
Emile J Desrosiers
10 Noyes St
Methuen MA 01844

Call Sign: KB1TJY
Lyman G Deliguori Sr
1 Oak Knoll Rd
Methuen MA 01844

Call Sign: N1CPH
Ronald R Messina
107 Oakland Ae
Methuen MA
018443649

Call Sign: KA1PXE
Clifford J Duhamel
133 Oakland Ave
Methuen MA 01844

Call Sign: NP4AZ
Ruben Gines Nieves
90 Oakland Ave 2nd Fl
Methuen MA 01844

Call Sign: KA1FS
James P Murphy

27 Overlook Dr
Methuen MA
018442372

Call Sign: KA1BDK
Daniel P Barrows
30 Overlook Dr
Methuen MA 01844

Call Sign: KB1CIO
Alexander F Vannett
314 Pelham St
Methuen MA 01844

Call Sign: KB1EFZ
William R Arcand
119 Pleasant Valley St
Methuen MA 01844

Call Sign: WD4FZJ
Albert E Grant Jr
4 Quebec St
Methuen MA 01844

Call Sign: K1UJA
Albert E Grant Jr
4 Quebec St
Methuen MA 01844

Call Sign: KB1RHG
Sixto Bobadilla
30 Riverdale St
Methuen MA 01844

Call Sign: N1AJJ
William M Kaupinis
95 Riverdale St
Methuen MA 01844

Call Sign: KB1TSO
John J Murphy
19 Riverview Ave
Methuen MA 01844

Call Sign: K1NZQ
Allan R Muise
22 Riverview Ave
Methuen MA
018441910

Call Sign: KB1USP
David Boucher
6 Russel Farm Dr
Methuen MA 01844

Call Sign: N1UIV
Sam F Di Noto
3 Savin Ave
Methuen MA 01844

Call Sign: W1HFF
Joseph F Ferullo
9 Sharon St
Methuen MA 01844

Call Sign: KB1RSS
John A Sullivan
113 Temple Dr
Methuen MA 01844

Call Sign: K1TTC
Ronald A Zelle
120 Tyler St
Methuen MA 01844

Call Sign: KB1FSR
Edward J Rhodes
7 Tyler St
Methuen MA 01844

Call Sign: WB1FOK
Gary Keltz
70 Union St
Methuen MA 01844

Call Sign: WA1TFG
Nunzio M Cavallaro
45 Washington St 38
Methuen MA 01844

Call Sign: N1ICT
John M Quinn
26 West St
Methuen MA
018441318

Call Sign: N1JDN
William L Lugli Jr
132 West St
Methuen MA 01844

Call Sign: N1YLX
Richard P Bradley
56 Weybossett St
Methuen MA 01844

Call Sign: KX1D
John Mc Andrew

19 Winthrop Ave
Methuen MA 01844

Call Sign: W1SUU
Ralph R Spidale Sr
76 Woburn St
Methuen MA 01844

Call Sign: W1TJC
Sam S Spidale
76 Woburn St
Methuen MA 01844

Call Sign: K1TNQ
Joseph A Salvo
107 Woodburn Dr
Methuen MA 01844

Call Sign: N1EXC
Juan M Jerez
Methuen MA 01844

Call Sign: KB1OHN
Juan B Malena
Methuen MA 01844

Call Sign: N1OZQ
Gilbert S Edwards
65 North St
Methuer MA 01844

Call Sign: K1PCN
Joseph A Milone
35 Canobieola Rd
Metuen MA 01844

FCC Amateur Radio Licenses in Middleboro

See also FCC Amateur Radio Licenses in Middleborough

Call Sign: KB1TED
Bart J Devine
1 Benton St
Middleboro MA 02346

Call Sign: KB1WFO
Earl R Casey
3 Benton St
Middleboro MA 02346

Call Sign: WS1LWS
Earl R Casey
3 Benton St
Middleboro MA 02346

Call Sign: N1VEG
Arthur Fontes Jr
12 Benton St
Middleboro MA 02346

Call Sign: WA1YKE
Forney R Johnson
806 Crystal Way
Middleboro MA 02346

Call Sign: N1IPO
Christopher J Lannan
23 Deebee Circle
Middleboro MA 02346

Call Sign: W1DLS
David L Sanford
41 E Main St
Middleboro MA 02346

Call Sign: WA1SCI
David L Sanford
41 E Main St
Middleboro MA 02346

Call Sign: W1AP
David L Sanford
41 E Main St
Middleboro MA 02346

Call Sign: KB1TEA
Patrick M Franey
54 Fernway
Middleboro MA 02346

Call Sign: KB1CJO
Daniel B Farquharson
57 Fieldstone Cir
Middleboro MA 02346

Call Sign: AA1VZ
Daniel B Farquharson
57 Fieldstone Cir
Middleboro MA 02346

Call Sign: KB1SEZ
John T Buckley
52 Forest St

Middleboro MA 02346

Call Sign: W1AKN
John T Buckley
52 Forest St
Middleboro MA 02346

Call Sign: KB1JUU
David T Masten
90 Highland St
Middleboro MA 02346

Call Sign: KB1TEI
Jeanne C Spalding
168 Highland St
Middleboro MA 02346

Call Sign: N1SKR
John A Hardy
5 Metacomet Rd
Middleboro MA 02346

Call Sign: KA1WBD
Frederick F Martins
335 Miller St
Middleboro MA 02346

Call Sign: KB1JMI
Linda A O Brien
608 Oak Point Dr
Middleboro MA 02346

Call Sign: KB1JMJ
Robert E O Brien
608 Oak Point Dr
Middleboro MA 02346

Call Sign: N1ECR
Stephen R Gross
81 Oak St
Middleboro MA 02346

Call Sign: KB1SFT
Christopher W Gross
81 Oak St
Middleboro MA 02346

Call Sign: KB1TDZ
Donna C Bernabeo
165 Old Miller St
Middleboro MA 02346

Call Sign: KB1TDV

Bejamin J Mackiewicz Jr
3 Park St
Middleboro MA 02346

Call Sign: KB1RTI
Roger E Desmarais Mr
Peirce St
Middleboro MA 02346

Call Sign: W1QPS
Kenneth F Blandin Jr
63 Pleasant St
Middleboro MA
023461009

Call Sign: N1REO
John J Hamm Ii
153 Plymouth St
Middleboro MA 02346

Call Sign: KA1UAE
Stuart A White
256 Plymouth St
Middleboro MA 02346

Call Sign: KA1OZ
Richard A Roth
319 Plymouth St
Middleboro MA 02346

Call Sign: KB1DKP
Peter W Murdy
4 Plympton St
Middleboro MA 02346

Call Sign: KB1TDX
Peter J Sgro Jr
15 Rainbow Circle
Middleboro MA 02346

Call Sign: N1FDX
James Zappulla
120 Rivers Edge Dr
Middleboro MA 02346

Call Sign: N1YAM
Michael J Day
86 Rocky Meadow St
Middleboro MA 02346

Call Sign: WA1DDN
Edward J Clark Jr
102 Rocky Meadow St

Middleboro MA 02346

Call Sign: K1VUT
David A Clemons
148 Rocky Meadow St
Middleboro MA 02346

Call Sign: K1RBD
Thomas A Perry
208 Rocky Meadow St
Middleboro MA 02346

Call Sign: KA1MAE
Michael W Duggan
7 Star Ave
Middleboro MA 02346

Call Sign: KA1AVA
William W Dresner Jr
3 Starrett Ave
Middleboro MA 02346

Call Sign: N1BCA
Walter A Zeronsky
26 Summit
Middleboro MA
023462523

Call Sign: WA1UEC
Norman L Diegoli
5 Sunset Ave
Middleboro MA 02346

Call Sign: KB1OZO
Richard A May
231 Thomas St
Middleboro MA 02346

Call Sign: K1KJL
Richard S Maguire
21 Towerview Dr
Middleboro MA 02346

Call Sign: KA1TXK
William R Burke
61 Walnut St
Middleboro MA 02346

Call Sign: KB1TEE
Richard J Emord
135 Wareham St
Middleboro MA 02346

Call Sign: N1YOY

Ralph V Hunt
581 Wareham St
Middleboro MA 02346

Call Sign: KD1DG
John L Lemmo
34 Woodlawn St
Middleboro MA 02346

Call Sign: W1MV
Massasoit Amateur
Radio Assn
Middleboro MA 02346

Call Sign: WA1SCI
David L Sanford
Middleboro MA 02346

FCC Amateur Radio
Licenses in
Middleborough

See also FCC
Amateur Radio
Licenses in
Middleboro

Call Sign: N1GJO
Thomas F Mc
Laughlin
107 Beach St
Middleborough MA
02346

Call Sign: KB1KYW
James D Strader
74 Miller St
Middleborough MA
02346

Call Sign: KB1KNI
Joseph E Walsh Sr
4101 Pheasant Lane
Middleborough MA
02346

Call Sign: W1SF
Stuart A Forman
5707 Pheasant Lane
Middleborough MA
02346

Call Sign: N1FKQ
Russell J Gershman

93 Plymouth St
Middleborough MA
02346

Call Sign: N1TWM
William D Arneson
46 Summer St
Middleborough MA
02346

Call Sign: N1WVQ
Jay N Rogers
288 Wareham St
Middle Borough MA
023462906

Call Sign: N1XTB
Philip G Mcnamara
Middleborough MA
023460687

FCC Amateur Radio Licenses in Middlefield

Call Sign: K1DCS
Howard L
Knickerbocker Jr
Middlefield MA 01243

FCC Amateur Radio Licenses in Middleton

Call Sign: WA1QZK
Ronald J Draper
6 Acorn St
Middleton MA 01949

Call Sign: KB1HSE
Jay H Ballard
39 Boston St
Middleton MA 01949

Call Sign: W1JHB
Jay H Ballard
39 Boston St
Middleton MA 01949

Call Sign: WA1KOP
David L Smith
7 Deacon Dr
Middleton MA
019492257

Call Sign: KB1WVJ
Michael P Nigrelli
34 Donovans Way
Middleton MA 01949

Call Sign: KB1ITD
James M Armitage
62 East St
Middleton MA 01949

Call Sign: KB1NMB
Ariel Perez Sanchez
4 Hills Rd
Middleton MA 01948

Call Sign: N1VWP
Diana L Ballard
155 Lake St
Middleton MA 01949

Call Sign: N1LQ
David H Hammond
140 Liberty St
Middleton MA 01949

Call Sign: KA1CXW
Thomas W Powers
69 Maple St
Middleton MA 01949

Call Sign: K8MF
Marc S Fuller
8 Maytum Way
Middleton MA 01949

Call Sign: N1CXW
Richard L Mc Grane
15 Mills Point
Middleton MA 01949

Call Sign: WB1CVA
Daniel G Condon
55 N Liberty St
Middleton MA 01949

Call Sign: W1AGX
William E Morrison
61 N Main St Apt 4f
Middleton MA 01949

Call Sign: KB1NXI
Sean J Langford
33 North Liberty St
Middleton MA 01949

Call Sign: KA1AWH
Ernest J Sandoe
14 Northwoods Rd
Middleton MA 01949

Call Sign: KD1JY
Duane C Long
17 Oak Rd
Middleton MA
019492226

Call Sign: NF1T
Bernard G Och
25 Peabody St
Middleton MA 01949

Call Sign: KM6OP
Jon L Coad
17 Perkins Rd
Middleton MA 01949

Call Sign: KB1AMO
Doris A Mitchell
127 River St
Middleton MA 01949

Call Sign: N1OUF
Rodney G Mitchell
127 River St
Middleton MA 01949

Call Sign: K1MTS
James F Shanley
150 River St
Middleton MA 01949

Call Sign: N1TDJ
William R Mugford
151 S Main St
Middleton MA 01949

Call Sign: KA1JPE
Joseph W Pesce
Middleton MA 01949

Call Sign: KA1PVJ
Lawrence A Parker
Middleton MA 01949

Call Sign: KB1HEF
Theodore H Butler
48 School St

Middletown MA
01949

FCC Amateur Radio Licenses in Milford

Call Sign: K4BRA
Marcio R Moura
2 Shadowbrook Ln Apt 28
Milford MA 01757

Call Sign: KA1UMD
John J Bonnell
29 Alfred Rd
Milford MA 01757

Call Sign: KB1SXY
Edward W Hunter
2 Alfred Rd Apt M
Milford MA 01757

Call Sign: N1MPE
Anthony A Iacovelli
8 Beach St
Milford MA 01757

Call Sign: KB1PQE
Donald E Eastlake Iv
155 Beaver St
Milford MA 01757

Call Sign: K1NFA
Donald E Eastlake Iv
155 Beaver St
Milford MA 01757

Call Sign: WA1WOS
Thaddeus F Cichanowicz
22 Blanchard Rd
Milford MA 01757

Call Sign: KB1IMK
Richard G Jonasch
68 Bowdoin Dr
Milford MA
017571246

Call Sign: KA1PHE
Carol A Cleveland
8 Bruno Dr
Milford MA 01757

Call Sign: N1EYY
Dave M Cleveland
8 Bruno Dr
Milford MA 01757

Call Sign: WA1QGU
George S Cleveland
8 Bruno Dr
Milford MA 01757

Call Sign: N1TBP
Lori A Belliveau
5 Capitol Rd #5
Milford MA 01757

Call Sign: N1KRB
Klaus J Schneller
3 Clarridge Cir
Milford MA 01757

Call Sign: K1HMC
John J Moore
25 Claudette Dr
Milford MA 01757

Call Sign: N1AIC
Svein H Jakobsen
Country Club Lane
Bue
Milford MA 01757

Call Sign: W1BRI
Bryan H Cerqua
Country Club Ln
Milford MA 01757

Call Sign: KB1IBD
Jon T Ruscitti
31 Courtland St
Milford MA 01757

Call Sign: KA1UAR
Joseph D Hysong
117 E Main St
Milford MA 01757

Call Sign: N1MMY
Dana K Heath
134 E Main St
Milford MA 01757

Call Sign: N1IQQ
Albert L Brackett
195 E Main St Ste 284

Milford MA 01757

Call Sign: N1OAQ
Henry G Semmel
50 East Main St
Milford MA 01757

Call Sign: KA4FRH
Francis L Belliveau
20 Elizabeth Rd
Milford MA 01757

Call Sign: N1TBO
Adam A Belliveau
20 Elizabeth Rd
Milford MA 01757

Call Sign: WB1EOJ
Bruce A Beauchemin
11 Esther Dr
Milford MA 01757

Call Sign: N1SZH
Brian L Semmel
21 Fairfield Court
Milford MA 01757

Call Sign: W1BLS
Brian L Semmel
21 Fairfield Court
Milford MA 01757

Call Sign: W7HV
Louis Hlousek
21 Field Pond Rd
Milford MA 01757

Call Sign: W1WH
William J Hanrahan
57 Forest St
Milford MA 01757

Call Sign: KA1YAO
Jane T Hanrahan
57 Forest St
Milford MA 01757

Call Sign: N1UFM
Robert J Anderson Sr
36 Franklin St
Milford MA 01757

Call Sign: N9ZWS
Theodore R Grevers Jr

4 Geneseo Circle
Milford MA 01757

Call Sign: KB1LTN
Scott D Carter
19 Geneseo Circle
Milford MA 01757

Call Sign: N1JDS
Joseph W Morgado Jr
53 Grove St
Milford MA 01757

Call Sign: KB1KGF
Timothy J Nau
30 Hancock St
Milford MA 01757

Call Sign: KA1SHX
Joseph E Monty Jr
7 Harding St
Milford MA 01757

Call Sign: N1CPE
Thomas M Kinahan Jr
58 Harding St
Milford MA 01757

Call Sign: W1ZIY
Ronald W Kimball
8 Hawthorne Path
Milford MA 01757

Call Sign: K1AWH
Dominic E Creasia
92 High St
Milford MA 01757

Call Sign: KB3PFW
Richard A Hooker
196 Highland St
Milford MA 01757

Call Sign: N1FOE
David P Recchia
37 Iadarola Ave
Milford MA 01757

Call Sign: KB1IBC
Wayne R Tessicini
3 Ivy Ln
Milford MA 01757

Call Sign: N1GDF

Barbara E Corley
3 Janock Rd
Milford MA 01757

Call Sign: N1FQN
Donald V Gallahue
16 Janock Rd
Milford MA 01757

Call Sign: K1ETP
Richard A Leverone
9 Jencks Rd
Milford MA 01757

Call Sign: WA1DSZ
James B Harden
39 Jillson Cir
Milford MA 01757

Call Sign: AB1LF
Brent G Dewitt
6 Julie Circle
Milford MA 01757

Call Sign: KA1RTO
Henry I Hatch
2 Kennedy Ln
Milford MA 01757

Call Sign: N1EYV
Lynda L Slocomb
2 Kennedy Ln Apt 43
Milford MA 01757

Call Sign: N1AYC
Robert E Fitzgerald
30 Leonard St
Milford MA 01757

Call Sign: N1VTH
Thomas F Bonina
9 Manguso Ave
Milford MA 01757

Call Sign: KA1JYW
David M Tangredi
3 Manoogian Cir
Milford MA 01757

Call Sign: KB1IIF
Mass Nat'l Guard
Amateur Radio Club
50 Maple St
Milford MA 01757

Call Sign: WA1AWR
John J Paganelli
55 Mt Pleasant St
Milford MA 01757

Call Sign: KA1NKW
Jeffrey P Manosh
15 Packard Rd
Milford MA 01757

Call Sign: KB1VKG
Shawn E Volpicelli
34 Parkhurst St
Milford MA 01757

Call Sign: KF6JFD
AMI C Bellefeuille
36 Pearl St
Milford MA 01757

Call Sign: W1MNP
Charles A Gray
6 Penny Ln
Milford MA 01757

Call Sign: KC1KD
William R Greene
11 Penny Ln
Milford MA 01757

Call Sign: N2KNJ
Robert K Bridges
85 Purchase St
Milford MA 01757

Call Sign: KB1NKW
David A Cocuzzi
21 Ramble Rd
Milford MA 01757

Call Sign: N1PRH
Andrew R Leverone
5 Redwood Dr
Milford MA 01757

Call Sign: KB1JRT
Peter Secakusuma
45 S Central St
Milford MA
017573673

Call Sign: N1KIL
Martin S Pachomski

27 Shadowbrook Ln
Apt 24
Milford MA 01757

Call Sign: KB1ECQ
Michael J Cameron
24 Sherwood Dr
Milford MA 01757

Call Sign: N1OWA
John H Cameron
24 Sherwood Dr
Milford MA 01757

Call Sign: KB1JWK
Peter Secakusuma
45 South Central St
Milford MA
017573673

Call Sign: AB1CS
Peter Secakusuma
45 South Central St
Milford MA
017573673

Call Sign: K1QF
Peter Secakusuma
45 South Central St
Milford MA
017573673

Call Sign: KB1OLH
Katherine M High
29 South Main St
Milford MA 01757

Call Sign: KB1TYK
Kenneth L Poole
2 Temple St
Milford MA 01757

Call Sign: N1CTY
Robert H Flumere
47 Village Circle
Milford MA 01757

Call Sign: KA1FXK
Harry M Platcow
158 W Spruce St
Milford MA 01757

Call Sign: KA1OPI
George C Gagnon

45 Water St
Milford MA 01757

Call Sign: NE1R
Thomas C Carrigan
161 West St (Rte 140)
Milford MA 01757

Call Sign: KB1OYY
Brennan J Murray
38 Whitewood Rd
Milford MA 01757

Call Sign: N1HHD
Quyen G Dam
5 Woodhill Rd
Milford MA 01757

Call Sign: KB1RDS
Steven J Terrill
46 Woodridge Rd
Milford MA 01757

Call Sign: WA1JWE
Harry Miller
31 Yale Dr
Milford MA 01757

Call Sign: KA1PU
David M Ruscitti
Milford MA 01757

FCC Amateur Radio
Licenses in Mill River

Call Sign: KA1WHV
Michael J Britton
78 Mill River Great
Barrington Rd
Mill River MA 01244

Call Sign: KB1UCI
Lucy Ann J Britton
Mill River MA 01244

FCC Amateur Radio
Licenses in Millbury

Call Sign: K1VNP
Roger A Lavallee
14 Auburn Rd
Millbury MA 01527

Call Sign: WB1FXF

Eugene D Lavallee
23 Braney Rd
Millbury MA
015273944

Call Sign: KB1VTZ
Geoff C Gerhardt
8 Brian Circle
Millbury MA 01527

Call Sign: KB1TQD
Stephen M Choiniere
8 Broadmeadow Ave
Millbury MA 01527

Call Sign: N1SMC
Stephen M Choiniere
8 Broadmeadow Ave
Millbury MA 01527

Call Sign: KB1IHA
Ray P Ford
65 Canal St Apt 222
Millbury MA 01527

Call Sign: W1GLD
Alderic J Melanson
6 Colonial Dr
Millbury MA 01527

Call Sign: KC1YS
Steven E Ballard
11 Curve St
Millbury MA 01527

Call Sign: N1OJT
Melissa A Adams
6 Cyndy Lane
Millbury MA 01527

Call Sign: KB1FDS
Steven W Tatro
351 Greenwood St
Millbury MA
015271527

Call Sign: W1EDL
Eugene D Lavallee
54 Horne Way
Millbury MA 01527

Call Sign: N1TCZ
Richard L Morgan O
Connor

1 Lindy St
Millbury MA 01527

Call Sign: N1ZCU
Martyn E Wright
120 Mac Arthur
Millbury MA
015273536

Call Sign: W1COU
Martyn E Wright
120 Macarthur Dr
Millbury MA
015273536

Call Sign: NB1H
Benjamin T Holmes
Main St
Millbury MA 01527

Call Sign: KB1AFI
Cara M Rucci
19 Maple Lane
Millbury MA 01527

Call Sign: N1CNT
Stephen J Howard
42 Maple St
Millbury MA 01527

Call Sign: KB1RTB
David R Charette
34 Middleton St
Millbury MA 01527

Call Sign: W1RBC
David R Charette
34 Middleton St
Millbury MA 01527

Call Sign: K1VML
Paul A Sweet Sr
80 Millbury Ave
Millbury MA 01527

Call Sign: N1YUQ
Raymond S Allen
92 N Main St
Millbury MA 01527

Call Sign: N1IEX
Ronald E Richard
23 Prospect St
Millbury MA 01527

Call Sign: WA1DNZ
Wesley R Army
15 Rhodes St
Millbury MA 01527

Call Sign: N1EKO
James A Singer
16 Rindge St
Millbury MA 01527

Call Sign: KB1OKL
Robert Young Jr
33 S Main 2b
Millbury MA 01527

Call Sign: N1XYU
Gary F Carey
67 S Main St
Millbury MA
015273148

Call Sign: KB1IBJ
Mark J Belliveau
75 S Oxford Rd
Millbury MA 01527

Call Sign: W1KXD
Joseph J Krula Sr
59 South Main St
Millbury MA 01527

Call Sign: KB1MRX
Richard J Harris
123 Wheelock Ave
Millbury MA 01527

Call Sign: AA1RH
Richard J Harris
123 Wheelock Ave
Millbury MA 01527

Call Sign: N1KNQ
Mark L Dyberg
2 Wingfoot Lane
Millbury MA 01527

Call Sign: KA1PML
Charles C Divris
34 Woodland St
Millbury MA 01527

Call Sign: KA1OTQ
Robert A Beausoleil

Millbury MA 01527

FCC Amateur Radio Licenses in Millers Falls

Call Sign: KB1BYY
Gerald A Bergeron
6 Gunn St
Millers Falls MA
01349

Call Sign: N1LXR
Frederick J Erickson Sr
13 Pleasant St
Millers Falls MA
01349

Call Sign: KA1ZEH
Charles A Waseleski
47 Poplar Mtn Rd Box
14
Millers Falls MA
01349

FCC Amateur Radio Licenses in Millis

Call Sign: KA1UCR
Jeffrey A Neal
6 Bogastow Cir
Millis MA 02054

Call Sign: NU6Q
Henry P Ames
28 Brookview Rd
Millis MA 020541000

Call Sign: N1FUG
David A Carlson
4 Concord Cir
Millis MA 02054

Call Sign: WA1HNW
John T Kosinski
4 Crestview Dr
Millis MA 02054

Call Sign: KA1WNY
John J Olstead
244 Exchange St
Millis MA 02054

Call Sign: K3JO

Velimir Deric
Exchange St
Millis MA 02054

Call Sign: N8BO
Markovic Milovan
Exchange St
Millis MA 02054

Call Sign: W1SFJ
Frederick G May
156 Farm St
Millis MA 02054

Call Sign: N1DGT
Paul W Bacchiocchi
12 Hemlock Circle
Millis MA 02054

Call Sign: KB1SAO
Anne M Bacchiocchi
12 Hemlock Circle
Millis MA 02054

Call Sign: KB1GGD
Raymond M Saulnier
58 Heritage Path
Millis MA 02054

Call Sign: K1GTD
Walter E Brasier Jr
4 Hilltop Dr
Millis MA 02054

Call Sign: WA1QLJ
Lynn E Feuling
14 Independence Ln
Millis MA 02054

Call Sign: N1MPD
Jeffry J Steele
4 Ironwood Ln
Millis MA 02054

Call Sign: KB1QNG
Valeri E Neytchev
448 Main St
Millis MA 02054

Call Sign: KB1QNH
Vessela Neytcheva
448 Main St
Millis MA 02054

Call Sign: KB1QNZ
Elitza Neytcheva
448 Main St
Millis MA 02054

Call Sign: K1VAL
Valeri E Neytchev
448 Main St
Millis MA 02054

Call Sign: K1ELZ
Elitza Neytcheva
448 Main St
Millis MA 02054

Call Sign: K1VES
Vessela Neytcheva
448 Main St
Millis MA 02054

Call Sign: W1SXL
James H Hurley
612 Main St
Millis MA 02054

Call Sign: W1FNM
Herman F Downing
45 Mc Gabe Ave
Millis MA 02054

Call Sign: KB1QYA
Richard J Becherer
7 Meadow Brook Rd
Millis MA 02054

Call Sign: N1RBX
Richard J Becherer
7 Meadow Brook Rd
Millis MA 02054

Call Sign: K1QMX
Lawrence P Gentili
83 Middlesex St
Millis MA 020541015

Call Sign: K1DAT
Kenneth J Jones
84 Middlesex St
Millis MA 02054

Call Sign: KE1GK
Vincent H Gannon
121 Plain St
Millis MA 020541519

Call Sign: N1LED
Francis X Spinoza
351 Plain St
Millis MA 02054

Call Sign: KB1GMV
Joseph D Hersey
354 Plain St
Millis MA 02054

Call Sign: W1LEX
Joseph D Hersey
354 Plain St
Millis MA 02054

Call Sign: WA1UPP
Harold R Howe
202 Pleasant
Millis MA 02054

Call Sign: WB8ZJZ
Richard C Sack
34 Pleasant St
Millis MA 02054

Call Sign: KB1TBJ
Kevin R Knehr
176 Pleasant St
Millis MA 02054

Call Sign: W1KRK
Kevin R Knehr
176 Pleasant St
Millis MA 02054

Call Sign: N1JKF
Richard J Donovan
224 Pleasant St
Millis MA 02054

Call Sign: AB1GH
Paul Hilton
225 Pleasant St
Millis MA 02054

Call Sign: KA1IYX
Charles H Grant
47 Railroad Ave
Millis MA 02054

Call Sign: KA1KMQ
Paul N Robinson Sr
91 Ridge St

Millis MA 02054

Call Sign: WB1GQX
Robert E Eaton
94 Ridge St
Millis MA 02054

Call Sign: KB1EGV
Eugene D Smith
53 Spencer St
Millis MA 02054

Call Sign: KB1OJD
Michael D Damiano
82 Spring St
Millis MA 02054

Call Sign: N1ECI
Anne M Bacchiocchi
39 Stoney Brook Dr 10
Millis MA 02054

Call Sign: KB1FZB
Joel R Lempicki
54 Stoneybrook Drive
Apt 6
Millis MA 02054

Call Sign: KB1SAK
Christopher D Howie
42 Union St
Millis MA 02054

Call Sign: N1AKM
Kenneth R Drew
233 Village St
Millis MA 02054

Call Sign: AJ1W
Julius J Rosen
333 Village St
Millis MA 02054

Call Sign: KA1IYY
Mary Jane H Simpson
6 Wainwright Cir
Millis MA 02054

Call Sign: N1FPW
Wayne A Simpson
6 Wainwright Cir
Millis MA 02054

Call Sign: WB6YDS

Gregg M Kamilar
14 Walnut St
Millis MA 020541032

FCC Amateur Radio Licenses in Millville

Call Sign: N1WOI
Keith A Mercure
14 Bow St
Millville MA 01529

Call Sign: N1VWN
Timothy P Ryan
163 Chestnut Hill Rd
Millville MA 01529

Call Sign: KC1LM
Timothy J Mcnamara
201 Chestnut Hill Rd
Millville MA 01529

Call Sign: N1WBY
Jamie R Martin
378 Chestnut Hill Rd
Millville MA 01529

Call Sign: KD1YM
Russell R Desjourdy
83 Fisher St
Millville MA 01529

Call Sign: W1RUS
Russell R Desjourdy
83 Fisher St
Millville MA 01529

Call Sign: N1LLH
Michael J Buckley
17 Forest View Dr
Millville MA 01529

Call Sign: N1IMS
David J Golden
7 Joe's Way
Millville MA 01529

Call Sign: KB1JDA
Joel T Plasse
8 Old Coach Rd
Millville MA 01529

Call Sign: N1REL
Mark M Renaud

Millville MA 01529

Call Sign: W2RWF
Dean L Graves Sr
173 Adams St
Milton MA 02187

Call Sign: NG1A
Frederick J Butts
90 Antwerp St
Milton MA 02186

Call Sign: W1CDA
Edward H Corning
133 Blue Hills Pkwy
Milton MA 02186

Call Sign: KE3IG
Mike K Blackwell
357 Blue Hills Pky
Milton MA 021862700

Call Sign: KA1YHJ
James E Stallions
379 Central Ave
Milton MA 02186

Call Sign: KC1SZ
George A Geary
59 Centre Ln
Milton MA 02186

Call Sign: N1NLS
Vincent K Butler
36 Cheever St
Milton MA 021861127

Call Sign: N1MV
Mystic Valley Amateur
Radio Group
95 Clapp St
Milton MA 02186

Call Sign: N1ZMB
Walter L Mc Dermott
Jr
95 Clapp St
Milton MA 021863245

Call Sign: WG1W
Georges L Desroches

144 Craig St
Milton MA 02186

Call Sign: W1JUP
Eliot Young
66 Cypress Rd
Milton MA 02186

Call Sign: WA1BPL
Paul J Mc Grath
82 Dyer Ave
Milton MA 02186

Call Sign: KB1NTR
Alexander K Richman
305 Eliot St
Milton MA 02186

Call Sign: KB1SPW
Benjamin S Richman
305 Eliot St
Milton MA 02186

Call Sign: KB1TXA
Wade L Morse
63 Grafton Ave
Milton MA 02186

Call Sign: N1WNK
Daniel Cuevas
58 Grove St
Milton MA 02186

Call Sign: KB1JPH
Thomas H Wilson
59 Gulliver St
Milton MA 02186

Call Sign: AA1NG
John W Mc Cue
67 Harborview Rd
Milton MA 02186

Call Sign: KB1JJR
David P Brady
142 Hinckley Rd
Milton MA 02186

Call Sign: W1OUT
Stanley R Perry Jr
21 Houston Ave
Milton MA 02186

Call Sign: K1KHE

David A Johnson Sr
5 Howard St
Milton MA 02186

Call Sign: W1DAJ
David A Johnson Sr
6 Howard St
Milton MA 02186

Call Sign: K1KHE
David A Johnson Jr
6 Howard St
Milton MA 02186

Call Sign: KB1BPL
Joseph F Thomas
4 Lafayette St
Milton MA 02186

Call Sign: WB1EMS
Joseph F Thomas
4 Lafayette St
Milton MA 02186

Call Sign: KA1YIE
Alan L Pullman
28 Lincoln St
Milton MA 02186

Call Sign: WA1DDD
Kenneth C Whitney
15 Maple St
Milton MA 02186

Call Sign: WB1DRH
Harriet Goldman
7 Marshall Rd
Milton MA 02186

Call Sign: N1OIL
Paul J Hopkins
87 Meagher Ave
Milton MA 02186

Call Sign: N1SET
Joel P Moerschel
10 Pope Hill Rd
Milton MA 02186

Call Sign: N1KQX
Jack S Treger
21 Pope Hill Rd
Milton MA 02186

Call Sign: W1KMW
William E Pike
7 Sheridan Dr
Milton MA 02186

Call Sign: N1KUL
Michael P Kenney
54 Thistle Ave
Milton MA 02186

Call Sign: K1EQC
V Charles Primpas
348 Truman Pkwy
Milton MA 02186

Call Sign: N1HBJ
Jean Raynal Fougy
40 Victoria St
Milton MA 02186

Call Sign: K1LPJ
William E Haynes
102 Whitelawn Ave
Milton MA 02187

Call Sign: KB1TZL
John J Hackett Jr
109 Wood St
Milton MA 02186

Call Sign: K1CEM
John J Hackett Jr
109 Wood St
Milton MA 02186

Call Sign: W1OSJ
Sydney G Millen
Milton MA 02187

Call Sign: N1CGB
John A Hill Iii
156 Hinckley Rd
Milton Village MA
02187

Call Sign: KB1SRN

Brian M Bruzzese
75 Milford St
Monponsett MA 02350

Call Sign: KB1UQQ
Tyler C Kindy
Monponsett MA 02350

Call Sign: KB1WMO
Power Radio Club
Monponsett MA 02350

Call Sign: K1BU
Power Radio Club
Monponsett MA 02350

FCC Amateur Radio Licenses in Monson

Call Sign: N1MHM
Todd R Panico
31 Ayers Rd
Monson MA 01057

Call Sign: KA1SWK
Russell E Partlow
187 Beebe Rd
Monson MA 01057

Call Sign: W1OLS
Robert E Pease
106 Brimfield Rd
Monson MA 01057

Call Sign: N1KSU
Ralph S Rinaldi
26 Butler Rd
Monson MA 01057

Call Sign: K1IQI
Chester Zalewski
369 C Cedar Swamp
Rd
Monson MA 01057

Call Sign: N1MMT
Gregory Dill
16 Cote Rd
Monson MA 01057

Call Sign: N1SZB
Dennis G Parent
109 Cote Rd

Monson MA
010579211

Call Sign: WB1BPN
Wilfred E Marion
119 Cote Rd
Monson MA 01057

Call Sign: W1CEU
Frederick L Sherman
47 Country Clb Dr
Monson MA 01057

Call Sign: KA1OUX
William F Donovan
28 Country Club Dr
Monson MA 01057

Call Sign: KB1TF
Richard A Behrens
39 E Hill Rd
Monson MA 01057

Call Sign: N1TQP
David J Pelletier
31 East Hill Rd
Monson MA 01057

Call Sign: NM1I
Howard L Bacon Iii
20 Elm St
Monson MA 01057

Call Sign: KA1RPH
Lawrence P Meacham
21 Ely Rd
Monson MA 01057

Call Sign: N1NPC
Stephen Dill
Green St
Monson MA 01057

Call Sign: KB1KSY
Monson Emergency
Management
110 Main St
Monson MA
010571343

Call Sign: N1BNV
Stephen Kozloski Jr
110 Main St
Monson MA 01057

Call Sign: NL7BV
Charles E Brightman
173 Main St
Monson MA 01057

Call Sign: N1OLK
Charles S Brightman
175 Main St
Monson MA 01057

Call Sign: KB1RND
Michael A Allen Sr
86 Margaret St
Monson MA 01057

Call Sign: KB1RNE
Mellisa A Allen
86 Margaret St
Monson MA 01057

Call Sign: KB1GPH
Neil C Hansen Sr
88 Maxwell Rd
Monson MA
010579428

Call Sign: KA1HSP
Joseph C Plante
47 Moulton Hill Rd
Monson MA 01057

Call Sign: K3FGO
Gary Wolf
205 Moulton Hill Rd
Monson MA 01057

Call Sign: KB1LLX
David M Wulfing
30 Old Wales Rd
Monson MA 01057

Call Sign: KB1UPY
David G Tait Iv
232 Palmer Rd
Monson MA 01057

Call Sign: KB1WPK
Raymond J Grassetti
57 Paradise Lake Rd
Monson MA 01057

Call Sign: KB1EJW
Jeremy T Bedson

7 Silva St
Monson MA 01057

Call Sign: N1RJM
William B Wood
35 Stafford Hollow Rd
Monson MA 01057

Call Sign: K1TRP
Todd R Panico
126 Stafford Hollow
Rd
Monson MA 01057

Call Sign: KC1P
John M B Wilson
139 Stafford Rd
Monson MA
010579315

Call Sign: KB1SIB
Douglas E Fox Sr
31 State St
Monson MA 01057

Call Sign: N1AND
Douglas E Fox Sr
31 State St
Monson MA 01057

Call Sign: NW1R
Carlo A Grassetti
77 Thayer Rd
Monson MA
010579445

Call Sign: WC1G
Tom M Grassetti
81 Thayer Rd
Monson MA 01057

Call Sign: KC1BO
Ira A Bonett Jr
91 Town Farm Rd
Monson MA 01057

Call Sign: K1VKD
James R Caldwell Jr
193 Wales Rd
Monson MA 01057

Call Sign: WB1ESW
Ralph W Wood Sr
19 Wilbraham Rd

Monson MA 01057

Call Sign: KB1JVE
Marilyn G Gorman
Monson MA 01057

FCC Amateur Radio Licenses in Montague

Call Sign: K1PBW
James C Hemingway
Box 316
Montague MA 01351

Call Sign: N1KKP
Jonathan C Burgess
9 Central St
Montague MA 01351

Call Sign: W1TZZ
Carle Ellis
36 Central St
Motague MA 01351

Call Sign: N1ATD
Robert W Walker
102 Chestnut Hill
Loop
Montague MA 01351

Call Sign: N1SXG
Aaron M Crowell
6 Grout Circle
Montague MA
013491355

Call Sign: KD1OE
John W Gilman
39 Hillside Rd
Montague MA
013519617

Call Sign: KB1BEZ
Jesse A Kroin
26 J St
Montague MA 01376

Call Sign: WA1YDB
Mark C Beaubien
15 N Taylor Hill Rd
Montague MA 01351

Call Sign: W1TTC
Mark C Beaubien

15 N Taylor Hill Rd
Montague MA 01351

Call Sign: N1HKG
Daniel J Chevalier
58 Randall Wood
Drive
Montague MA 01351

Call Sign: KD1XE
Alan E Kurkulonis
38 Taylor Hill Rd
Montague MA 01351

Call Sign: KB1GGC
Thomas C Kurtyka
426 Turner Falls Rd
Montague MA 01351

Call Sign: KB2BG
William C Conner Jr
Montague MA 01351

FCC Amateur Radio Licenses in Monterey

Call Sign: N1HS
Ian O Mcalister
72 Chestnut Hill Rd
Monterey MA 01245

Call Sign: KB1AAA
Kathleen Purcell
Monterey MA 01245

Call Sign: KD4UBU
Mark W Bennett
Monterey MA 01245

Call Sign: KE4AWA
Rita A Bennett
Monterey MA 01245

Call Sign: KF2SX
William Purcell
Monterey MA
012450044

FCC Amateur Radio Licenses in Montgomery

Call Sign: N1SZC
Teresa E Mc Clellan

196 Pitcher St
Montgomery MA
01085

Call Sign: N1SRF
David F Mc Clellan Sr
196 Pitcher St
Montgomery MA
01085

Call Sign: N1EFQ
John E Grabowski
1631 Russell Rd
Montgomery MA
01085

Call Sign: KB1JVF
James L Harrington Jr
80 Upper Pomeroy Rd
Montgomery MA
01085

FCC Amateur Radio Licenses in Monument Beach

Call Sign: KB1ORG
Bruce P Ambuter
43 Beach St
Monument Beach MA
02553

Call Sign: KA1KMD
Theodore P Lindberg
Jr
Box 362
Monument Beach MA
02553

Call Sign: WA1ZKB
Ronald K Roth
33 Cliff Rd
Monument Beach MA
02553

Call Sign: KA1HEZ
David B Major
316 Shore Rd
Monument Beach MA
02553

Call Sign: KA1HFA
George R Major
316 Shore Rd

Monument Beach MA
02553

Call Sign: KA1WBX
Ogden H Hammond Jr
395 Shore Rd
Monument Beach MA
02553

Call Sign: N1LNC
Mark C Tutuny
Monument Beach MA
02553

Call Sign: KB1RLF
Steven J Chapman
Monument Beach MA
02553

FCC Amateur Radio Licenses in Morwood

Call Sign: KB1QWD
Nick C Lento
410 Prospect St
Morwood MA 02062

FCC Amateur Radio Licenses in Mount Washington

Call Sign: KB1IKT
Stephen H Kimpel
38 East St
Mount Washington
MA 01258

FCC Amateur Radio Licenses in Nagog Woods

Call Sign: WA2GJH
Daniel S Klein
537 Old Stone Brook
Nagog Woods MA
017181008

FCC Amateur Radio Licenses in Nahant

Call Sign: KB1TUM
John W Standish Jr
19 Baker Rd

Nahant MA 01908

Call Sign: K1EFU
Paul Lospennato
34 Bass Point Rd
Nahant MA 01908

Call Sign: N1FZO
Joseph V Benson
5 Cottage St
Nahant MA 01908

Call Sign: KB1PCA
Daniel P O'brian
4 Fenno Way
Nahant MA 01908

Call Sign: W1HNW
Francis J Murphy
17 Greystone Rd
Nahant MA 01908

Call Sign: KF4NSC
Neal F Sullivan
86 Lennox Rd
Nahant MA 01908

Call Sign: KA1BYG
Charles Cronis
5 Linda Ln
Nahant MA 01908

Call Sign: N1VFQ
Nancy L B Gilman
8 Little Nahant Rd
Nahant MA
019081120

Call Sign: N1VSK
Jeffrey C G Bigler
8 Little Nahant Rd
Nahant MA
019081120

Call Sign: KB1QES
Charles H Briggs
32 Little Nahant Rd
Nahant MA 01908

Call Sign: N1DMJ
Lawrence J Scaglione
Jr
71 Maolis Rd
Nahant MA 01908

Call Sign: KA1QDU
Robert D D Amico
39 Maple Ave
Nahant MA 01908

Call Sign: K1VTB
Howland S Warren
409 Nahant Rd
Nahant MA 01908

Call Sign: KB1WMI
Paul A Wilson
50 Ocean St
Nahant MA 01908

Call Sign: K1ZJG
Frederick J Hyde
11 Pond St Ct
Nahant MA 01908

Call Sign: KA1WMV
Brian P O Neill
21 Range Rd 3
Nahant MA 01908

Call Sign: N1GDO
Frank W Pitzi
Sea Breeze Lane
Nahant MA 01908

Call Sign: N1LOD
Robert F Myers Sr
80 Willow Rd
Nahant MA 01908

Call Sign: KA1EF
William Caldwell Jr
96 Willow Rd
Nahant MA 01908

Call Sign: W1RUD
Robert P Rafuse
167 Willow Rd
Nahant MA
019081435

Call Sign: WA1MBT
David L Mac Duff
125 Wilson Rd
Nahant MA
019081040

Call Sign: N1NBR
Glenn A Mc Garvey
82 A Old South Rd
Nantucket MA 02554

Call Sign: N1JYV
Edward E Benham
55 A Polpis Rd
Nantucket MA 02554

Call Sign: W1QDZ
Antone F Sylvia
Cato Ln Bx 1214
Nantucket MA 02554

Call Sign: KB1WOT
David O Small
23 Daffodil Ln
Nantucket MA 02554

Call Sign: WA1RWB
Albert W Jenkins
5 Daley Ct
Nantucket MA 02554

Call Sign: KB1ECD
Jedediyah F Williams
13 Dennis Dr
Nantucket MA 02554

Call Sign: W1QLL
Harry W Rex Jr
13 Derrymore Rd
Nantucket MA 02554

Call Sign: N1YFW
Andrew B Butler
16 Federal St
Nantucket MA 02554

Call Sign: N1YFF
David C Gray Sr
11 Friendship Ln
Nantucket MA 02554

Call Sign: W1ACK
David C Gray Sr
11 Friendship Ln
Nantucket MA 02554

Call Sign: KB1MCF

Joseph M Swain Jr
19 Friendship Ln
Nantucket MA 02554

Call Sign: N1YFE
Robert J Thompson
3 Golf View Dr
Nantucket MA
025542767

Call Sign: KB1QIS
Bradford C Ames
10 Green Meadows Ln
Nantucket MA 02554

Call Sign: K1NGJ
Eldridge B Norton
39 Hooper Farm Rd
Nantucket MA 02554

Call Sign: K1JKV
Francis W Pease
166 Hummock Pond
Rd
Nantucket MA 02554

Call Sign: KB1IHE
Linda R Natsis
Hummock Pond Rd
Nantucket MA 02554

Call Sign: KB1KYO
Robert B Lang
10 Hussey Farm Rd
Nantucket MA 02554

Call Sign: K1RBL
Robert B Lang
10 Hussey Farm Rd
Nantucket MA 02554

Call Sign: W2BTA
Robert B Lang
10 Hussey Farm Rd
Nantucket MA 02554

Call Sign: W1UYU
Richard S Szymczak
7 Joy St
Nantucket MA 02554

Call Sign: KA1YMJ
James A Ozias
22 Lovers Ln

Nantucket MA 02554

Call Sign: N1OYC
Louise L Ozias
22 Lovers Ln
Nantucket MA 02554

Call Sign: KA1WFX
Lore M Richard
12 Madaket Rd
Nantucket MA 02554

Call Sign: KB1NG
David J Leggett
262 Madaket Rd
Nantucket MA 02554

Call Sign: K1CKR
Josiah S Barrett
3 Martins Ln
Nantucket MA 02554

Call Sign: W2BTA
Harold M Lang
11 Monomoy Rd
Nantucket MA 02554

Call Sign: W1WJP
William J Pittman
P O Box 3629
Nantucket MA
025843629

Call Sign: KC1OI
Chris T Wilson
76 Pleasant St
Nantucket MA 02554

Call Sign: K1ACK
Chris T Wilson
76 Pleasant St
Nantucket MA 02554

Call Sign: K2LEK
Michael Wodynski
Po Box 854
Nantucket MA 02554

Call Sign: N1KDG
Robert R Hall
65 Polpis Rd
Nantucket MA 02554

Call Sign: WA1DQJ

Valerie A Hall
65 Polpis Rd
Nantucket MA 02554

Call Sign: W1RRH
Robert R Hall
65 Polpis Rd
Nantucket MA 02554

Call Sign: W1NQT
Kenneth T Blackshaw
4 Sandwich Rd
Nantucket MA 02554

Call Sign: W1PJR
Phillip J Raneri
1 Sheep Commons
Lane
Nantucket MA 02554

Call Sign: WA2LKB
Phillip J Raneri
1 Sheep Commons Ln
Nantucket MA 02554

Call Sign: KB1VMC
Maryanne R Worth
14 Somerset Ln
Nantucket MA 02584

Call Sign: K1NON
Robert L Burnham
Surfide Rd
Nantucket MA 02584

Call Sign: KB1POC
Daniel Rezendes
30 Tashma Ln
Nantucket MA 02554

Call Sign: WE1I
Terrence H Laundry
3 Thurstons Ct
Nantucket MA 02554

Call Sign: N1JEA
Bernard L Walsh Jr
5 Trotters Ln
Nantucket MA 02554

Call Sign: W1TJM
Terrill J Malvesti
20 Vesper Ln Unit A1
Nantucket MA 02554

Call Sign: KB1IHF
Ronald E Russell
4 Washaman Ave
Nantucket MA 02554

Call Sign: N1NBP
Frank P Brooks
18 Washington Ave
Nantucket MA 02554

Call Sign: KB1OWM
William J Pittman
38 West Chester St
Nantucket MA 02554

Call Sign: N1NBQ
George F Allen
Nantucket MA
025540727

Call Sign: KB1EPW
Paul Connelly
Nantucket MA
025843344

Call Sign: KB1ILC
Jonathan Thayer
Nantucket MA 02584

Call Sign: KB1KYN
Andrew H Bennett
Nantucket MA 02554

Call Sign: KB1OWL
Charles B Gibson
Nantucket MA 02584

Call Sign: KB1QNF
Max S Perkins
Nantucket MA 02584

Call Sign: KB1VBD
Burton J Balkind
Nantucket MA 02584

Call Sign: KB1VBE
Barry G Rector
Nantucket MA 02584

Call Sign: KB1VMB
Linda M Barrett
Nantucket MA 02584

Call Sign: KB1WOU
Sarah B Sylvia
Nantucket MA 02554

Call Sign: K1NBG
Sarah B Sylvia
Nantucket MA 02554

FCC Amateur Radio Licenses in Nashua

Call Sign: K1IHM
Oliver B Mc Mahon
106 Ash St
Nashua MA 03060

FCC Amateur Radio Licenses in Natick

Call Sign: KB1QDW
Anthony M Caruso
22 A Walnut St
Natick MA 01760

Call Sign: W1KIN
Gregory J Kinchla
14 Appleton Rd
Natick MA 01760

Call Sign: WA1ZLN
Richard A Ruggiero
11 Avon St
Natick MA 01760

Call Sign: N1XAT
Michael K Rosebury
133 Bacon St
Natick MA 01760

Call Sign: K1LIX
Robert D Garvey
19 Barnesdale Rd
Natick MA 01760

Call Sign: WA1VIL
Gregory J Magarie
33 Barnesdale Rd
Natick MA 01760

Call Sign: KB1EC
Walter E Nold
24 Birch Rd
Natick MA 01760

Call Sign: KA1VRP
Clifford S Firth
2 Border Rd
Natick MA 01760

Call Sign: KB1ALT
Jerry R Wilder
13 Bunker Lane
Natick MA 017604203

Call Sign: N1IHC
Robert H Hedges
3 Cabot St
Natick MA 01760

Call Sign: KB2KOZ
Robert J Migliore
15 Church St Apt 5
Natick MA 01760

Call Sign: KB1GMW
Henry L Mittelman
1 Clearview Drive
Natick MA 01760

Call Sign: N1YWC
Russell J Sandow
61 Cottage Rd
Natick MA 01760

Call Sign: KB1LPD
Joseph D Dick
32 Cottage St
Natick MA 017605840

Call Sign: KA1NHF
Sean T Goguen
1 Countryside Rd
Natick MA 01760

Call Sign: KA1UFW
Donna M Elliot
3 Curtis Rd
Natick MA 01760

Call Sign: KB1KKM
Nicholas P Rosato
16 Eastleigh Ln
Natick MA 01760

Call Sign: K0PIJ
Stephen L Watson
102 Eliot St
Natick MA 01760

Call Sign: KB1NH
Yo Y Cho
52 Elliot Hill Rd
Natick MA 01760

Call Sign: K1NIX
Raymond L Gereau
4 Euclid Ave
Natick MA 01760

Call Sign: N1JEC
Albert A Miller
64 Fairway Cir
Natick MA 01760

Call Sign: NQ1F
Steven J Ciavarini
56 Fairway Circle
Natick MA 01760

Call Sign: W1DAN
Daniel D Brown
34 Felch Rd
Natick MA 017601202

Call Sign: NM1C
Leonard W Geier
51 Felch Rd
Natick MA 01760

Call Sign: KA1RLQ
Elaine I Getter
58 Felch Rd
Natick MA 01760

Call Sign: W1MIJ
Carl M Getter
58 Felch Rd
Natick MA 01760

Call Sign: W1VSS
Antipode Radio
Research Society
16 Fieldstone Lane
Natick MA 01760

Call Sign: W5IQJ
William G Sievers
16 Fieldstone Lane
Natick MA 01760

Call Sign: KB1DMG
Mark F Poyant

11 Fiske Ln
Natick MA 017604234

Call Sign: KP2AS
Geoffrey D Edmands
38 Glen St
Natick MA 01760

Call Sign: N1FWO
Anthony B Payne
53 Grove Rd
Natick MA 01760

Call Sign: W1PLW
Ronald A Wood
4 Harrison St
Natick MA 01760

Call Sign: N1MGI
Jacob E Richardson
20 Harrison St
Natick MA 01760

Call Sign: KA1LQP
Dwight A Blaha
2 Harwood Cir
Natick MA 01760

Call Sign: KB1FWQ
Randy Blue
13 Harwood Rd
Natick MA 01760

Call Sign: N1FU
Randy Blue
13 Harwood Rd
Natick MA 01760

Call Sign: KB1JQZ
David L Bursch
34 Hemlock Dr
Natick MA 01760

Call Sign: KB1FHJ
Lowell M Bursch
34 Hemlock Drive
Natick MA 01760

Call Sign: W9CKB
Charles K Brown
10 High St Apt 1
Natick MA 01760

Call Sign: K1CQV

Donald J Curns
2 Hopewell Farm Rd
Natick MA 01760

Call Sign: KB1EW
Robert N Press
25 Indian Ridge Rd
Natick MA 01760

Call Sign: KA1TUB
John F Forsyth
24 Irving Rd
Natick MA 01760

Call Sign: KA1TUF
Marilyn M Forsyth
24 Irving Rd
Natick MA 01760

Call Sign: KA1WWG
Michelle G Mac
Kenzie
13 Jackson Ct
Natick MA 01760

Call Sign: WB1DNZ
Stephen G Mac Kenzie
13 Jackson Ct
Natick MA 01760

Call Sign: KB1KAX
David Schafer
87 Kendall Ln
Natick MA 01760

Call Sign: KA1AXX
Dennis L Reagan Sr
8 Lakeshore Rd
Natick MA 01760

Call Sign: KB1FHE
David A Harrow Jr
55 Lakeview Ave
Natick MA 01760

Call Sign: KB1LCN
Thomas G Woods
3 Lakeview Gardens
403
Natick MA 01760

Call Sign: KB1SPX
Vishwanath Iyer
4 Larkspur Way 10

Natick MA 01760

Call Sign: KA1HDJ
Martha B Gawthrop
12 Larkspur Way Apt
3
Natick MA 01760

Call Sign: KB1YR
Roy V Crossman
9 Leighton St
Natick MA 01760

Call Sign: WB4EJR
James H Irby
6 Liberty St
Natick MA 017601218

Call Sign: WR1P
Nathan S Keedy
4 Mac Arthur Rd
Natick MA 01760

Call Sign: K1NCJ
Joseph F Sweeney
67 Mac Arthur Rd
Natick MA 01760

Call Sign: N1QYW
Stephen D Gartrell
19 Morningside Ave
Natick MA 017605407

Call Sign: N1YXR
James R Gartrell
19 Morningside Ave
Natick MA 017605407

Call Sign: KA1OMS
Christopher D Clark
1 Murdoch Rd
Natick MA 01760

Call Sign: KA1SAS
Edward F Newdorf
5 Naples Rd
Natick MA 01760

Call Sign: KB1LWY
Donna A La Roche
19 New Hampshire
Ave
Natick MA 01760

Call Sign: K1LZ
Krassimir D Petkov
118 North Ave
Natick MA 01760

Call Sign: N1GTB
Elaine R Chase
40 Oak Knoll Rd
Natick MA 01760

Call Sign: KA1SYQ
Stella M Ash
223 Oak St
Natick MA 01760

Call Sign: N1DGC
Gerald E Ash
223 Oak St
Natick MA 01760

Call Sign: KB1JSX
Raymond L Patriacca
Jr
7 Pleasantview Rd
Natick MA 01760

Call Sign: N1RLP
Raymond L Patriacca
Jr
7 Pleasantview Rd
Natick MA 01760

Call Sign: W1JDM
James J Mello
49 Pond St
Natick MA 01760

Call Sign: W1EWN
James M Crump Iii
54 Pond St
Natick MA 01760

Call Sign: W1HAI
Joseph W Weisse
75 Pond St
Natick MA 01760

Call Sign: N1YWF
Marilyn Mc Cormick
110 Pond St
Natick MA 01760

Call Sign: WA1WDE
John A Mc Reynolds

3 Prescott Ave
Natick MA 01760

Call Sign: KA1RLY
Richard P Winchester
29 Ranger Rd
Natick MA 01760

Call Sign: KA1RNC
Robert J Winchester
29 Ranger Rd
Natick MA 01760

Call Sign: N1ZWI
James Billings
55 Rathbun Rd
Natick MA 01760

Call Sign: KA1QAS
Scott A Cohen
26 Reynolds Ave
Natick MA 01760

Call Sign: KA1MHR
Patricia E Smith
31 Ridge Ave
Natick MA 01760

Call Sign: W1VAB
Peter J Burrel
105 Rockland St
Natick MA 01760

Call Sign: N1XPP
Mark D Longworth
65 School St Ext
Natick MA 01760

Call Sign: K1PR
Mark R London Mr
11 Sherman St Apt 1
Natick MA 01760

Call Sign: W1GUF
John B Hawkes
2 Sherwood Rd
Natick MA 01760

Call Sign: W1RQP
Maurice A Meyer
19 Sherwood Rd
Natick MA 01760

Call Sign: WA1QWF

Stephen M Diamond
42 Silver Hill Ln
Natick MA 01760

Call Sign: KB1DFN
Natick Emergency
Radio Group
168 Speen St
Natick MA 01760

Call Sign: N1DM
Domenic M Mallozzi
168 Speen St
Natick MA 01760

Call Sign: KI5CZ
Terence J Bordelon
5 Stonebridge Circle
Natick MA 01760

Call Sign: KA1SKE
Leo J Poisson
22 Stratford Rd
Natick MA 01760

Call Sign: KG6CHX
VIJAY S Reddy
9 Strathmore Rd
Natick MA 01760

Call Sign: K1VTX
Loretta H Szretter
Federico
41 Sylvester Rd
Natick MA 01760

Call Sign: KB1TZM
Douglas C Cooney
52 Travis Rd
Natick MA 01760

Call Sign: KB1FGZ
Tobias G Leiner
9 Union St
Natick MA 01760

Call Sign: WB1CCA
Margaret M Staines
19 Union St Apt 2
Natick MA 01760

Call Sign: N1VYD
Mark C Dixon
17 Village Hill Ln 3

Natick MA 01760

Call Sign: N1FJZ
William J Carrigan Jr
17 Village Way 2
Natick MA 01760

Call Sign: N1MDJ
Gregory J Dinning
251 W Central St Ste
146
Natick MA 01760

Call Sign: KB1UTW
Claudius W Li
36 Washington Ave 1
Natick MA 01760

Call Sign: N1GNR
Martin D Stevens
31 Water St
Natick MA 01760

Call Sign: KB1KZM
David A Resmini
23 Wellesley Ave
Natick MA 01760

Call Sign: AJ2X
Mark R Nelson
17 Wentworth Rd
Natick MA 01760

Call Sign: KB1PJN
Eric Taylor Jr
220 West Central St
Natick MA 01760

Call Sign: NK1T
James M Welch
40 West Central St # 6
Natick MA 017604516

Call Sign: K1NHS
Natick High School
Amateur Radio Club
15 West St
Natick MA 01760

Call Sign: N1YRM
James J Mello
15 Western Ave
Natick MA 01760

Call Sign: N1KRF
Robert N Sciretta
29 Windsor Ave
Natick MA 01760

Call Sign: N1FTB
Thomas J Malloy Jr
28 Winnemay St
Natick MA 017602845

Call Sign: N1SHF
Kenneth J Fitzgerald Jr
10 Woodbine Rd 3
Natick MA 01760

Call Sign: K1RG
Robert E Greim
59 Woodland St
Natick MA 01760

Call Sign: KB1TYJ
Mark R Lenci
18 Woronoco Dr
Natick MA 01760

Call Sign: KA1HBC
Judy A Anderson
Natick MA 01760

Call Sign: KA1HBD
Robert T Anderson
Natick MA 01760

Call Sign: N1FOD
Andrew W Luke
Natick MA 01760

Call Sign: N1FOG
Patricia D Luke
Natick MA 01760

Call Sign: N1MQG
Phillip A Leavitt
Natick MA 01760

Call Sign: WA1IDA
S Robert Salow
Natick MA 01760

Call Sign: KA1YSA
Robert D Bastien
Natick MA 01760

Call Sign: N1NUS

Roger R Prive
Natick MA 01760

Call Sign: N1VOJ
Julie A Love
Natick MA 01760

FCC Amateur Radio
Licenses in Needham

Call Sign: N1RDU
James F Malzone
16 Aletha Rd
Needham MA 02192

Call Sign: WB1CAL
Jay R Englander
104 Aletha Rd
Needham MA 02492

Call Sign: KB1LFS
Gretchen Vernon
7 Avalon Rd
Needham MA 02492

Call Sign: KG1C
Sergio Marino
20 Avalon Rd
Needham MA 02192

Call Sign: N1HII
Rosella Marino
20 Avalon Rd
Needham MA 02192

Call Sign: NV1N
Edgardo Petronzio
20 Avalon Rd
Needham MA 02192

Call Sign: WB1FCZ
Edward F Gallagher
87 Beaufort Ave
Needham MA 02192

Call Sign: N1KBL
Theo V S Van Dinter
44 Birch St
Needham MA
024941216

Call Sign: KA1LQO
Georges A Vedie
85 Blake St

Needham MA 02192

Call Sign: KB1RVW
Anthony J Silveri
22 Bonwood Rd
Needham MA 02492

Call Sign: KA1SBM
James C Benoit
73 Bradford St
Needham MA 02192

Call Sign: KB1PWD
Edward B Walk
98 Bridle Trail Rd
Needham MA 02492

Call Sign: K0XOX
Edward B Walk
98 Bridle Trail Rd
Needham MA 02492

Call Sign: N1RDM
David W Boston
334 Brookline St
Needham MA 02192

Call Sign: KU4XC
Henry A Pasternack
34 Brookline St
Needham MA 02492

Call Sign: N1BCP
Vincent C Dwyer
865 Central Ave A506
Needham MA 02192

Call Sign: KA5QQW
Everett F Warner Sr
865 Central Ave I 108
Needham MA 02192

Call Sign: N2BAF
Frank H Waldecker
Chambers St
Needham MA 02192

Call Sign: N4KIV
Peter L Godino
30 Chambers St Apt-A
Needham MA 02492

Call Sign: K2BAC
Walter C Cummings

207 Charles Ct East
Needham MA 02192

Call Sign: W1NZV
Bernard J Welsch
93 Clarke Cir
Needham MA 02192

Call Sign: KD1VA
Timothy G Huemiller
104 Clarke Cir
Needham MA 02192

Call Sign: KB1QMA
Karl D Huemiller
104 Clarke Circle
Needham MA 02492

Call Sign: KB1QIE
Jason H Hurvitz
30 Concord St
Needham MA 02494

Call Sign: KB1DQR
Michael P Anzalone
33 Coulton Pk
Needham MA
024923301

Call Sign: KC6MJV
Andrea B Hawkins
35 Dale St
Needham MA 02494

Call Sign: WA1ACD
Alan L Kosow
28 David Rd
Needham MA 02494

Call Sign: KD1FP
Joseph J Miceli Sr
81 Dedham Ave
Needham MA 02192

Call Sign: N1OOO
Donna L Hawkes
409 Dedham Ave
Needham MA 02192

Call Sign: N1OPE
George Hawkes
409 Dedham Ave
Needham MA 02192

Call Sign: KA1GIL
Peter J Hussey
33 Dunster Rd
Needham MA
024941926

Call Sign: KD1ZB
Carl H Gundel
59 Ellicott St
Needham MA 02492

Call Sign: N1WEQ
Arthur E Spiller
165 Fair Oaks Prk
Needham MA 02192

Call Sign: KA1RDQ
Debra M Bergin
108 Fairfield St
Needham MA 02192

Call Sign: KB1BVE
Peter P Forge
37 Gay St
Needham MA 02192

Call Sign: KB1OTR
Wolfgang K Floitgraf
80 Grant St
Needham MA 02492

Call Sign: N1SYJ
Norma E Mc Evoy
114 Grant St
Needham MA 02192

Call Sign: K1ZAF
Richard E Smith
264 Greendale Ave
Needham MA
021942028

Call Sign: KA1UII
Francis D Garrity
1180 Greendale Ave
Needham MA 02192

Call Sign: WA1ONB
James A Pasco-Anderson
389 Grove St
Needham MA 02492

Call Sign: WA2SXI

Neil M Spooner
31 Hamlin Ln Apt A24
Needham MA 02192

Call Sign: N1CKQ
Eugene R Molter
10 Hawthorne Ave
Needham MA 02192

Call Sign: W1TUG
Walter B Mills Sr
15 Hawthorne Ave
Needham MA 02192

Call Sign: WA1FRK
Lawrence C Wetmore
398 High Rock St
Needham MA 02492

Call Sign: KA1VE
Donald C Lockhart
506 High Rock St
Needham MA 02192

Call Sign: WB2AVC
Robert O Landry
9 High St
Needham MA 02194

Call Sign: KB1PMH
Joey Mansour
875 Highland Ave
Needham MA 02494

Call Sign: KB1CJ
Joseph C Hutcheson Ii
384 Hillcrest Rd
Needham MA 02492

Call Sign: KA1ZPP
Jean Salamone
210 Hillside Ave
Needham MA 02194

Call Sign: N1FWS
Ronald R Guerriero
14 Holland St
Needham MA 02192

Call Sign: KB1MR
Thomas L Hawkridge
68 Hoover Rd
Needham MA 02194

Call Sign: WB2PID
James N Kile
342 Hunnewell St
Needham MA 02494

Call Sign: KA1WYA
Richard C Stoddart
41 Jarvis Cir
Needham MA 02192

Call Sign: KA1CHW
Robert O Bylaska
12 Laurel Dr
Needham MA 02192

Call Sign: N1BPV
John J Carr
27 Locust Ln
Needham MA 02192

Call Sign: WA1ISQ
John J Carr
27 Locust Ln
Needham MA 02192

Call Sign: KA1HDF
David P Wilsey
28 Maple St
Needham MA 02192

Call Sign: K3ZKK
J Thomas Gehman
141 Marked Tree Rd
Needham MA 02192

Call Sign: KA1QIY
Joel M Sturman
262 Marked Tree Rd
Needham MA 02492

Call Sign: N1RDL
John C Balconi
26 Mason Rd
Needham MA 02192

Call Sign: KB1SVQ
Benjamin C Kroop
Mb 553
Needham MA 02492

Call Sign: KB1MAE
Joshua H Rothenberg
15 Meadow Ln
Needham MA 02492

Call Sign: N1QIQ
Charles J Treciokas Jr
146 Meetinghouse Cir
Needham MA 02192

Call Sign: KB1KDU
Thomas C Ajamian
47 Meetinghouse
Circle
Needham MA 02492

Call Sign: K1ZQW
David L Tannozzini
57 Melrose Ave
Needham MA 02192

Call Sign: KA1YAU
Matthew M Hughes
6 Morningside Rd
Needham MA 02192

Call Sign: N1OAV
Steven J Goldman
82 Morton St
Needham MA 02194

Call Sign: WA1ZOD
Gerald K Goodwin
60 Nehoiden St
Needham MA 02192

Call Sign: W1IBV
Allan B Macquarrie
93 Newell Ave
Needham MA 02192

Call Sign: N1UPV
William M Leblanc
15 Norfolk St
Needham MA 02192

Call Sign: W1JOT
Theodore Simmington
Jr
88 Old Farm Rd
Needham MA
021924117

Call Sign: W1LDG
William T Burke
14 Otis St
Needham MA 02192

Call Sign: WB3AHS
Matthew B Kirk
65 Otis St
Needham MA 02492

Call Sign: KA1AUP
Michele K Wolfman
31 Paine Rd
Needham MA 02492

Call Sign: N1ZCE
Gary D Schwartz
14 Parish Rd
Needham MA
024941022

Call Sign: KB7FXT
Charles D Butler
170 Parish Rd
Needham MA 02192

Call Sign: N1CZT
Americo Procopio
17 Peacedale Cir
Needham MA 02192

Call Sign: N1CRK
Maurice B Polayes
82 Pine Grove St
Needham MA 02194

Call Sign: W1JIM
James Blumenfeld
19 Pine St
Needham MA 02492

Call Sign: N1KCX
Robert A Jeffery
18 Prince St
Needham MA
024923719

Call Sign: W1MIC
James M O Connor
84 Prince St
Needham MA
021923719

Call Sign: WA1BGP
John K Ross
51 Redington Rd
Needham MA 02192

Call Sign: KB1OEB

Michael L Cooper
103 Richdale Rd
Needham MA 02494

Call Sign: K1LLQ
Robert K Novak
11 River Park St
Needham MA 02494

Call Sign: N1UFF
Gregory J Kinchla
10 Riverside St
Needham MA 02494

Call Sign: N1HSK
Hans P Batra
53 Robinwood Ave
Needham MA 02492

Call Sign: AA1ZV
Laurence M Coyle
100 Rolling Ln
Needham MA
024921323

Call Sign: N1JKZ
Robert F Giovannucci
Jr
29 Rosalie Rd
Needham MA 02494

Call Sign: KB1FLP
Robert E Roman
298 Rosemary St
Needham MA 02494

Call Sign: K1IIR
Gloria J Sessler
22 Seabeds Way Apt 9
Needham MA 02194

Call Sign: N3EAN
Dhananjay G Wadekar
381 South St
Needham MA 02192

Call Sign: KB1OYO
Sean A Wall
1095 South St
Needham MA 02492

Call Sign: W1QZG
Louis C Remond
74 Stewart Rd

Needham MA 02192

Call Sign: KB6YRZ
Thomas E Morf
120 Stratford Rd
Needham MA
021921432

Call Sign: WB7CUT
Carleton G Lorig
10 Sunset Rd
Needham MA 02494

Call Sign: KA1MKB
William J Gaudaitis
67 Taylor St
Needham MA
024941815

Call Sign: KC1ZS
David A Hill Jr
83 Thornton Rd
Needham MA 02492

Call Sign: KA1ANT
James L Bond
95 Thornton Rd
Needham MA 02192

Call Sign: N1OCF
Lee Ann Mazzaferro
7 Trout Pond Ln
Needham MA 02192

Call Sign: N1OCG
Ted W Hasenfus
7 Trout Pond Ln
Needham MA 02192

Call Sign: K1GNY
Leigh B Macquarrie
15 Tudor Rd
Needham MA 02192

Call Sign: W1IBV
Leigh B Macquarrie
15 Tudor Rd
Needham MA 02192

Call Sign: WA1PBU
Kim O Peck
29 Wachusett Rd
Needham MA 02192

Call Sign: N1TPU
John J Logan Jr
277 Warren St
Needham MA 02192

Call Sign: KA1SBJ
Mark T Devlin Jr
45 Washington Ave
Needham MA 02192

Call Sign: N1FVY
Joseph T De
Bettencourt
137 Washington Ave
Needham MA 02192

Call Sign: NV1T
Gerard A Driscoll
101 Whiting Way
Needham MA
024921123

Call Sign: KB1TKS
William C Wall
20 Wilshire Park
Needham MA 02492

Call Sign: N1EZB
Leon F Kaufman
27 Winfield St
Needham MA 02492

Call Sign: K1RGX
Patricia A Paulson
Needham MA 02492

Call Sign: W1UOP
Roger C Paulson
Needham MA 02492

Call Sign: KB1RRW
Mark Silveri
Needham MA 02492

Call Sign: KJ1H
Jack Levy
286 Greendale Ave
Needham Heights MA
02194

Call Sign: W1EYA
Carmen C Mastropieri
1081 Highland Ave
Needham Heights MA
02494

Call Sign: KB1IBF
Elaine C Kile
342 Hunnewell St
Needham Heights MA
024941330

Call Sign: N1BD
Bruce A Dean
366 Hunnewell St
Needham Heights MA
02494

Call Sign: WA1JGU
Lawrence Milesky
250 Hunting Rd
Needham Heights MA
02194

Call Sign: AF1R
Leandra S Mac Lennan
4 Pershing Rd
Needham Heights MA
02494

Call Sign: KB1TYM
Stanley T Yamane
119 Webster St
Needham Heights MA
02494

Call Sign: K1SIF
Edward J Le Febvre
110 Beach Hill Rd
New Ashford MA
01237

Call Sign: N1FGY
Edmond B Grosso
70 Route 7
New Ashford MA
01237

Call Sign: W1WGN
George D Rogers Jr
14 Abalone St
New Bedford MA
027441302

Call Sign: N1ZDP
Manuel P Medeiros
14 Abbott St
New Bedford MA
02744

Call Sign: WP4KZZ
Hilario Gonzalez Soto
57 Acorn St
New Bedford MA
027404623

Call Sign: N1XTT
Edward F Gadue
24 Acushnet Ave
New Bedford MA
02744

Call Sign: N1YCD
Gayle A Gadue
24 Acushnet Ave
New Bedford MA
02744

Call Sign: K1MTK
Kenneth S Pickering
3506 Acushnet Ave
New Bedford MA
02745

Call Sign: KB1WHI
Wayne Ignacio
3526 Acushnet Ave
New Bedford MA
02745

Call Sign: WA1OAJ
Glenn M Silverberg Sr
3628 Acushnet Ave
New Bedford MA
027454010

Call Sign: N1XKL
Michael R Burke

4038 Acushnet Ave
New Bedford MA
02746

Call Sign: WA1IUA
Arthur Motta
4045 Acushnet Ave
New Bedford MA
02745

Call Sign: AC7RB
Mark A Pereira
4633 Acushnet Ave
New Bedford MA
027454728

Call Sign: WA1CXC
Stanley J Skozolek
29 Agnes St
New Bedford MA
027451703

Call Sign: N1BLE
John F Santos
378 Allen St
New Bedford MA
02740

Call Sign: N1TEH
Richard Cunha
432 Allen St
New Bedford MA
02740

Call Sign: W1GYL
Henry R Blanchett Jr
115 Alva St
New Bedford MA
02740

Call Sign: K1JNM
Mary L Whelan
79 Appleton St
New Bedford MA
027452748

Call Sign: K1BKR
Edward Baker
213 Aquidneck St 1st
New Bedford MA
02744

Call Sign: N1AS
Lawrence E Purcell

146 Armour St
New Bedford MA
02740

Call Sign: N1IPF
Eccleston A Franklin
16 Atlantic St
New Bedford MA
02740

Call Sign: KA1QV
Emile E Martel Jr
330 Austin St
New Bedford MA
02740

Call Sign: N1GLU
Kenneth D Cameron
76 Babbitt St
New Bedford MA
02740

Call Sign: KA1BHH
Danielle Lygren
153 Bates St
New Bedford MA
02745

Call Sign: KB1FRL
Charles W
Moszczenski
1055 Becket St
New Bedford MA
02745

Call Sign: W1ATI
Norman F Riley
527 Bedford St
New Bedford MA
02740

Call Sign: WB1EEM
Richard F Torrey Jr
180 Belleville Rd
New Bedford MA
027455221

Call Sign: AI1Q
Richard F Torrey
180 Belleville Rd
New Bedford MA
027455221

Call Sign: K1OO

John P Aguiar Jr
54 Bellevue St
New Bedford MA
027441902

Call Sign: N1BGX
Carl Thornhill
174 Bellevue St
New Bedford MA
02744

Call Sign: N1USF
Ronald R Cabral
67 Blaze Rd
New Bedford MA
02745

Call Sign: K1RRC
Ronald R Cabral
67 Blaze Rd
New Bedford MA
02745

Call Sign: N1VKT
Janice M Jaworski
75 Blueberry Ter
New Bedford MA
02745

Call Sign: KB1ASD
Fernando A Teixeira
233 Bolton St
New Bedford MA
02740

Call Sign: N1VUE
Jay J Lewis
23 Bourne St
New Bedford MA
02740

Call Sign: W1EVW
Richard B Nopper
980 Brantwood St
New Bedford MA
02745

Call Sign: WA1KKI
Georgette J Nopper
980 Brantwood St
New Bedford MA
02745

Call Sign: K1WIU

Raymond J Loiselle
366 Bream St
New Bedford MA
027441312

Call Sign: N1MXY
Glenn J Martin
65 Brock Ave
New Bedford MA
027441314

Call Sign: KE1FL
Lucilio J Caneira
14 Brownell St
New Bedford MA
02740

Call Sign: KE1AN
Richard A Netinho
10 Canterberry St
New Bedford MA
02746

Call Sign: KA1VSA
Frank M Macedo
96 Capitol St
New Bedford MA
02744

Call Sign: N1QWW
Mark J Bento
33 Carlisle St
New Bedford MA
02745

Call Sign: N1TEJ
Joanne M Bento
33 Carlisle St
New Bedford MA
02745

Call Sign: KA1OOG
John Agrelo
343 Cedar St
New Bedford MA
02740

Call Sign: WA1GDE
Louis S Whitlow Jr
373 Cedar St
New Bedford MA
027404534

Call Sign: WA1GDD

Kathleen G Whitlow
373 Cedar St Apt 2
New Bedford MA
027404534

Call Sign: AA1QH
Manuel S Bernardo
132 Central Ave
New Bedford MA
02745

Call Sign: KA1SBF
Maurice D Scheinman
13 Chancery St
New Bedford MA
02740

Call Sign: KB1DLR
Gabriel S Da Silva
250 Chancery St
New Bedford MA
02740

Call Sign: KB1EAK
Antonio S Barreiros
250 Chancery St
New Bedford MA
02740

Call Sign: KA1IQG
Amilcar Raposo
126 Chestnut St
New Bedford MA
02740

Call Sign: W1KBK
Eugene H Sasseville
240 Chestnut St
New Bedford MA
02740

Call Sign: N1SSB
Robert J Majka
41 Chime St
New Bedford MA
02746

Call Sign: KB0WNA
Jacob N Freeman
1098 Church St
New Bedford MA
02745

Call Sign: KB1ODA

Jacob N Freeman
1098 Church St
New Bedford MA
02745

Call Sign: N1LIW
Charles K Gaspar
24 Circuit St
New Bedford MA
02740

Call Sign: KB1OQB
Stanley J Chmielewski
68 Clifford St
New Bedford MA
02745

Call Sign: KB1JVU
Robert T Branco
359 Coggeshall St
New Bedford MA
02746

Call Sign: N1SZI
Ruth M Babigian
520 Coggeshall St
New Bedford MA
02746

Call Sign: KB1JCQ
Arthur P Motta Jr
642 Coggeshall St
New Bedford MA
027461335

Call Sign: W1APM
Arthur P Motta Jr
642 Coggeshall St
New Bedford MA
027461335

Call Sign: KA1WOJ
Peter J Carreiro
710 Coggeshall St
New Bedford MA
02746

Call Sign: KA1YUH
Patricia Carreiro
710 Coggeshall St
New Bedford MA
02746

Call Sign: KB1WHE

Robert J Bardsley
16 Columbia St
New Bedford MA
02740

Call Sign: N1XXQ
Theodore K
Przymierski
606 Cottage St 2
New Bedford MA
027405542

Call Sign: N1LTV
Henry B Riley
408 County St
New Bedford MA
02740

Call Sign: W1AQS
Harold F Riley
408 County St
New Bedford MA
02740

Call Sign: WA1FYF
William Field
774 County St
New Bedford MA
02740

Call Sign: WA1ZXG
Robert C Petitpas
806 County St
New Bedford MA
02740

Call Sign: KB5IJE
David P Leaver
717 County St Apt 4
New Bedford MA
02740

Call Sign: N1EXA
Peter W Kodis Iii
735 County Steet
New Bedford MA
02740

Call Sign: N1MWD
Raul A Arede
88 Covell St
New Bedford MA
02745

Call Sign: N1XPF
Antonio F Debrito
88 Covell St
New Bedford MA
02745

Call Sign: KE1GC
Fernando C Branco
49 Dartmouth St
New Bedford MA
02740

Call Sign: N1MUK
Matthew D White
103 Davis St 2
New Bedford MA
02746

Call Sign: N1ZE
Walter T Schneider
208 Dawson St
New Bedford MA
02745

Call Sign: WA1CRA
Richard F Simpkin
69 Dewolf St
New Bedford MA
02740

Call Sign: KA1KRI
Vandal A Johnson
16 Dudley St
New Bedford MA
027441503

Call Sign: KA1WHZ
Cheryl J Johnson
16 Dudley St
New Bedford MA
02744

Call Sign: KA1ZDT
Frank S Gadomski
62 Durfee St
New Bedford MA
02740

Call Sign: N1XZJ
Robert W Metivier
169 E Clinton St
New Bedford MA
02740

Call Sign: N1YJO
Susan C Metivier
169 E Clinton St
New Bedford MA
02740

Call Sign: N1ZGR
Scott E Liberty
70 Earle St
New Bedford MA
02746

Call Sign: KA1EYS
Roger A Rioux
188 Earle St
New Bedford MA
02746

Call Sign: N1TLF
Norman J Jacques
349 Earle St
New Bedford MA
02746

Call Sign: N1YRS
Antonio F De Almeida
14 Eastland Ter
New Bedford MA
02740

Call Sign: KB1AFQ
Fernando B De
Oliveira
38 Easton St
New Bedford MA
02746

Call Sign: N1WXV
Manuel A Deoliveira
38 Easton St
New Bedford MA
027461138

Call Sign: N1MAO
Manuel A Deoliveira
38 Easton St
New Bedford MA
027461138

Call Sign: K1KKC
Roland L Jodoin
31 Edna St
New Bedford MA
027455640

Call Sign: N1ZAY
Antonio V Mendes
27 Elaine Ave
New Bedford MA
02745

Call Sign: N1ZMW
Mark P Raposo
47 Elaine Ave
New Bedford MA
02745

Call Sign: KB1IQC
Delilah Maldonado
First St Apt 2
New Bedford MA
02740

Call Sign: N1BGR
Joseph A Nunes Sr
132 Frank St
New Bedford MA
02740

Call Sign: WB1GJU
Lawrence Teixeira
176 Frank St
New Bedford MA
02740

Call Sign: N1WXX
Francisco M Araujo
31 Frederick St
New Bedford MA
02744

Call Sign: N1DGS
Francisco M Araujo
31 Frederick St
New Bedford MA
02744

Call Sign: WA1NBL
John B Bento
136 Garfield
New Bedford MA
02746

Call Sign: KD1YZ
David A De Costa
28 Grant St
New Bedford MA
02740

Call Sign: KA1WNR
Evelyn F Robitaille
148 Greenbrier Dr
New Bedford MA
02745

Call Sign: N1PQX
David V Velazquez
12 Harmony St
New Bedford MA
02746

Call Sign: KA1RSY
Edward A Caron
119 Hatch St
New Bedford MA
027456026

Call Sign: N1MWI
Arthur Calheta
166 Hathaway St
New Bedford MA
02746

Call Sign: KA1WMH
Rita R Gadomski
459 Hawes St
New Bedford MA
02745

Call Sign: WA1CNO
Leonard F Gadomski
459 Hawes St
New Bedford MA
02745

Call Sign: N1MSL
Zelia M Correia
259 Hawthorn St
New Bedford MA
02740

Call Sign: KA1HXT
Richard Cabral
178 Hemlock
New Bedford MA
02740

Call Sign: N1TEI
Cheryl H Holmes
55 Heritage Ct
New Bedford MA
027452125

Call Sign: N1VUF
Brad F Anselmo
424 Hersom St
New Bedford MA
02745

Call Sign: KB1MKP
Dennis M Morris
108 Highland St Apt 2
N
New Bedford MA
02740

Call Sign: N1WNM
Joao L Camara
941 Hillcrest Rd
New Bedford MA
02745

Call Sign: KK1JC
Joao L Camara
941 Hillcrest Rd
New Bedford MA
02745

Call Sign: N1ZAZ
Steven A Almeida
136 Holly St
New Bedford MA
02746

Call Sign: KA1WIM
Sharon M Goldstein
32 Hollyhock St
New Bedford MA
02740

Call Sign: WB1GJO
Morris R Fogaren
159 Holyoke St
New Bedford MA
02745

Call Sign: KA1SME
Elizabeth A Dias
22 Homer St
New Bedford MA
02740

Call Sign: KA1WIY
Kathleen A Coulombe
56 Hudson St

New Bedford MA
02744

Call Sign: KA1YVI
Richard Houghton
174 Hudson St
New Bedford MA
02744

Call Sign: WA1CXG
Richard D Houghton
174 Hudson St
New Bedford MA
02744

Call Sign: N1WXW
Carlos J Barbeiro
228 Hudson St
New Bedford MA
02744

Call Sign: KA2CIK
Jose Demedeiros
44 Hussey St
New Bedford MA
02740

Call Sign: KA1ARL
David F Constantine
50 Illinois St
New Bedford MA
02745

Call Sign: KK1I
Carlos M Santos
17 Irene St
New Bedford MA
02745

Call Sign: KA1YZR
Philip H Viall
20 Irvington St
New Bedford MA
02745

Call Sign: KA1YZS
Claudette A Roy Viall
20 Irvington St
New Bedford MA
02745

Call Sign: WA1VAN
Waldo W Peckham
206 James St

New Bedford MA
02740

Call Sign: WA1CQJ
Henry W Deslaurier
22 Jarry St
New Bedford MA
02745

Call Sign: N1SVR
Robert Gomes
63 Jonathan St
New Bedford MA
02740

Call Sign: KA1OSN
David J Almeida
78 Jonathan St
New Bedford MA
02740

Call Sign: WA1WMH
Paul Gaudreau
27 Leland St
New Bedford MA
02745

Call Sign: N1BOA
Clifford J Snell Sr
36 Lemos St
New Bedford MA
02740

Call Sign: N1LIF
Jeffrey S Peckham
35 Liberia Lane
New Bedford MA
02746

Call Sign: N1QLA
Martin J Butler
60 Liberty St
New Bedford MA
02740

Call Sign: KA1PUY
David C Beauregard
47 Locust St
New Bedford MA
02740

Call Sign: N1XLB
Julio O Pinto
327 Loftus St

New Bedford MA
027461347

Call Sign: N1OMB
Robert A Lincoln
965 Ludlow St
New Bedford MA
02745

Call Sign: N1XFV
Christopher Buchanan
987 Ludlow St
New Bedford MA
02745

Call Sign: KB1BTF
Taunton Skywarn
Amateur Radio Club
50 Mandell St
New Bedford MA
02740

Call Sign: WX1BOX
Taunton Skywarn
Amateur Radio Club
50 Mandell St
New Bedford MA
02740

Call Sign: KD1CY
Robert D Macedo
50 Mandell St
New Bedford MA
02740

Call Sign: N1MWG
Gil F Martin
1 Margin St
New Bedford MA
02744

Call Sign: KB1JGB
Hugh J Murray
195 Maryland St
New Bedford MA
027452555

Call Sign: K1HJM
Hugh J Murray
195 Maryland St
New Bedford MA
027452555

Call Sign: W1ZPE

Paul A Bernard
255 Maryland St
New Bedford MA
027452565

Call Sign: KA1YLP
Alfredo Penalvert
Santiago
493 Maxfield St
New Bedford MA
02740

Call Sign: N1BZZ
Joseph Rodriques
624 Maxfield St
New Bedford MA
02740

Call Sign: N1KXC
Michael G Driscoll
146 Maywood St
New Bedford MA
02745

Call Sign: N1JXZ
Anthony A Gomes
439 Mill St
New Bedford MA
02740

Call Sign: N1ZSD
Rui Batista
69 Mosher St
New Bedford MA
02744

Call Sign: N1PMB
Donald T Manley
24 Myrtle St   Apt 1
New Bedford MA
027407024

Call Sign: WA1DDU
Muriel H Purcell
39 N 6th St Apt 1h
New Bedford MA
02740

Call Sign: N1ZNR
Jose L Silva
65 Nash Rd
New Bedford MA
02746

Call Sign: KA1YZO
Paul M Boucher
346 Natick St
New Bedford MA
02745

Call Sign: KB1UAM
Anthony J Lessa Jr
7 Nelson St
New Bedford MA
02744

Call Sign: WC1MAB
Area Ii Mema Races
Club
64 Nestles Ln
New Bedford MA
02745

Call Sign: N1ZYT
Gerald R Lemos
80 Oesting St
New Bedford MA
02740

Call Sign: KD1QQ
Richard P Loiselle
466 Oliver St
Newbedford MA
02745

Call Sign: KB1VLJ
Ian J Rymszewicz
250 Oregon St Apt 2
New Bedford MA
02745

Call Sign: KB1UDU
Melissa C Wesember
263 Palmer
New Bedford MA
02740

Call Sign: KB1UJN
Tomas M Tavares
263 Palmer St
New Bedford MA
02740

Call Sign: WA1ETG
Irving R Snyder
38 Park St
New Bedford MA
02740

Call Sign: KA1WRG
John D Barlow
68 Park St
New Bedford MA
02740

Call Sign: KB1ADL
Joseph G Ribeiro
1399 Phillips Rd 103
New Bedford MA
02745

Call Sign: N1WBV
Benjamin B Jackson
1940 Phillips Rd Unit -
17
New Bedford MA
02745

Call Sign: W1FXH
Ernest W Lavalette
50 Pierce St
New Bedford MA
02740

Call Sign: N1IEP
Mark M Mahoney
261 Pine Grove St
New Bedford MA
02745

Call Sign: N1YAL
Joseph P Frois
775 Pine Hill Dr
New Bedford MA
02745

Call Sign: W1JPF
Joseph P Frois
775 Pine Hill Dr
New Bedford MA
027451934

Call Sign: AB1CP
Joseph P Frois
775 Pine Hill Dr
New Bedford MA
027451934

Call Sign: N1PGN
Samuel S Wagstaff
942 Pine Hill Dr

New Bedford MA
02745

Call Sign: KA1AP
Herve J Bertrand
850 Pleasant St Apt
707
New Bedford MA
02740

Call Sign: W1VF
Edmund A Harrington
Jr
800 Pleasant St Apt
803
New Bedford MA
02740

Call Sign: KA1WIK
Arthur De Mello Jr
800 Pleasant St
Regency 16th Floor
New Bedford MA
02740

Call Sign: W1UH
Arthur De Mello Jr
800 Pleasant St
Regency 16th Floor
New Bedford MA
02740

Call Sign: WB1ASD
Francis O Fonseca Sr
800 Pleasent St Apt
1408
New Bedford MA
02740

Call Sign: N1WXU
Leonel V Pereira
176 Portland St
New Bedford MA
02744

Call Sign: W1PWL
Antone L Oliveira
94 Potomska St
New Bedford MA
027405722

Call Sign: KA1FAT
Roger M Quintin
107 Princeton St

New Bedford MA
02745

Call Sign: KB1RBU
Danilo B Pao
208 Princeton St
New Bedford MA
02745

Call Sign: N1VDM
Robert H Marchant
20 Princeton St Apt 3w
New Bedford MA
02745

Call Sign: W1AQX
James Lopes
1959 Purchase St Apt
S305
New Bedford MA
02740

Call Sign: WB1BUG
Armand F Augustine
37 Query St
New Bedford MA
02745

Call Sign: W1BUG
Armand F Augustine
37 Query St
New Bedford MA
02745

Call Sign: KB1SJK
April D Oliveira
238 Reed St
New Bedford MA
02740

Call Sign: K1EEQ
Arthur Fortin
232 Richmond
New Bedford MA
02740

Call Sign: KB1RLX
Samuel J Simoes
515 Rivets St
New Bedford MA
02740

Call Sign: W1AIQ
Deo Z Brunette

137 Rochambeau St
New Bedford MA
02745

Call Sign: N1EBW
Raymond A Guillotte
1107 Rockdale Ave
New Bedford MA
02740

Call Sign: KB1PQF
Andrew J Guillotte
1107 Rockdale Ave
New Bedford MA
02740

Call Sign: KD1DA
Charles W Pelletier Jr
23 Rogers St
New Bedford MA
02740

Call Sign: KB1TBC
John J Murphy Iii
93 Rotch St
New Bedford MA
02740

Call Sign: KH6HZ
Michael P Deignan
706 S Rodney French
Blvd
New Bedford MA
02744

Call Sign: KA1YDF
Anthony Arruda Jr
1446 Sassaquin Ave
New Bedford MA
02745

Call Sign: KA1LV
George S Pereira
139 Seabury St
New Bedford MA
027455149

Call Sign: W1CGR
George S Pereira
139 Seabury St
New Bedford MA
027455149

Call Sign: KA1KX

George S Pereira
139 Seabury St
New Bedford MA
027455149

Call Sign: KB1RTH
Roger A Gautreau
181 Shawmut Ave
New Bedford MA
02740

Call Sign: KA1CCQ
Andre G Poirier
760 Shawmut Ave
New Bedford MA
027461109

Call Sign: K1RFP
Alexander J Duff
829 Shawmut Ave
New Bedford MA
02746

Call Sign: W1QUE
Ralph C Morris
1077 Shelburne St
New Bedford MA
027452632

Call Sign: N1DT
Donald V Tanguay
1077 Shelburne St
New Bedford MA
02745

Call Sign: WA1GCN
Lawrence J Drayton
203 Smith St
New Bedford MA
02740

Call Sign: N1KKL
Russell R Bonneau
158 Somerset St
New Bedford MA
02745

Call Sign: N1ITQ
Michael R Miller
347 South 2nd St
New Bedford MA
02740

Call Sign: WA1ZHV

Daniel Ferreira
407 Summer St
New Bedford MA
02740

Call Sign: AA1FS
Lawrence R Houbre Jr
63 Sycamore St
New Bedford MA
02740

Call Sign: N1QEG
Lisa P Houbre
63 Sycamore St
New Bedford MA
02740

Call Sign: KB1MFF
Lawrence R Houbre Iii
63 Sycamore St
New Bedford MA
02740

Call Sign: KB1AKT
Doreen A Cloutier
54 Tallman St
New Bedford MA
02746

Call Sign: KA1NYU
Edward Longworth Jr
472 Tarkiln Hill Rd
New Bedford MA
02745

Call Sign: KA1ZYT
Manuel R Jorge
69 Tremont St
New Bedford MA
02740

Call Sign: KB1WGR
Marcilio V Raposo
246 Tremont St Apt 2
New Bedford MA
02740

Call Sign: K1EJX
William N Whelan
39 Turner St
New Bedford MA
02740

Call Sign: KD1H

Barry L Miller
3 Vernon St
New Bedford MA
02745

Call Sign: KB1BUN
Luis Rodriguez
7 Walker St
New Bedford MA
02746

Call Sign: N1HGX
Wallace R Houtman
46 Walker St
New Bedford MA
02746

Call Sign: N1XTP
Peter R Feldmar
242 Walnut St
New Bedford MA
02740

Call Sign: K5MLK
Matthew L Kuhl
75 Wamsutta St S117
New Bedford MA
02740

Call Sign: N1ZCS
Bernard P Desrosiers
1137 Westgate St
New Bedford MA
02745

Call Sign: N1VZN
Daniel A Alves
140 Willow St
New Bedford MA
02740

Call Sign: N1HCV
Daniel A Souza
278 Wilson St
New Bedford MA
02746

Call Sign: N1VDP
James A Souza
278 Wilson St
New Bedford MA
02746

Call Sign: N1OHI

James M Stewart
284 Wilson St
New Bedford MA
02746

Call Sign: KA1ESG
Manuel C Mello Jr
240 Wood St
New Bedford MA
02745

Call Sign: W1ESG
Manuel C Mello Jr
240 Wood St
New Bedford MA
02745

Call Sign: KB1NAR
Steve F Silvestre
42 Worcester St
New Bedford MA
02745

Call Sign: K1XTB
Steve F Silvestre
42 Worcester St
New Bedford MA
02745

Call Sign: KA1WDG
Jose X Magalhaes
6 Wordinton St
New Bedford MA
02745

Call Sign: KB1BWN
Luso American
Amateur Radio
Association
6 Wordinton St
New Bedford MA
02745

Call Sign: K1JXM
Jose X Magalhaes
6 Wordinton St
New Bedford MA
02745

Call Sign: NB1MA
Luso American
Amateur Radio
Association
6 Worthington St

New Bedford MA
027451013

Call Sign: KB1HKJ
Juan M Ramirez
51 Yale St
New Bedford MA
02746

Call Sign: K1EZ
Joseph A Barros
New Bedford MA
02745

Call Sign: KA1BJF
Victor R Hebert
New Bedford MA
02742

Call Sign: WB1DBX
Lawrence Lygren
New Bedford MA
02745

Call Sign: WB1AQX
James Lopes
New Bedford MA
02741

FCC Amateur Radio Licenses in New Braintree

Call Sign: KB1NDP
Wesley Anderson
452 Wine Rd
New Braintree MA
01531

Call Sign: W1AWA
Wesley Anderson
452 Wine Rd
New Braintree MA
01531

Call Sign: KB1PUU
Jakob Anderson
452 Wine Rd
New Braintree MA
01531

Call Sign: W1JFA
Jakob Anderson
452 Wine Rd

New Braintree MA
01531

FCC Amateur Radio Licenses in New Marlboro

Call Sign: KB1FBD
Robert F Vaughan
98 Harbville New
Marlboro Rd
New Marlboro MA
01230

Call Sign: KB1JOD
Russell H Silver
78 Knight Rd
New Marlborough MA
01230

Call Sign: WB1CGG
David F Brigham
784 Rhodes & Bailey
Rd
New Marlborough MA
01244

FCC Amateur Radio Licenses in New Salem

Call Sign: N1LAY
Roderick A Raubeson
16 Cooleyville Rd
New Salem MA 01355

Call Sign: WB1FBV
Dale R Monette
111 Wendell Rd
New Salem MA 01355

FCC Amateur Radio Licenses in New Seabury

Call Sign: KA1LIK
James J Priestly
73 Neshobe Rd
New Seabury MA
02649

FCC Amateur Radio Licenses in Newbury

Call Sign: KA2FUF
Charles R Mead
8 Hanover St
Newbury MA 01951

Call Sign: KB1AIB
Zacky Youcef Toumi
13 Hay St
Newbury MA 01951

Call Sign: N1RMV
Robert W Scanlon
22 Hay St
Newbury MA 01951

Call Sign: K1VVE
Barry L Johnson
43 Hay St
Newbury MA 01951

Call Sign: WB2GDC
Michael Fried
178 Hay St
Newbury MA 01951

Call Sign: N1AQZ
Arthur R Evans
150 High Rd
Newbury MA 01951

Call Sign: KC9JKB
Kenneth P Ayotte
209 High Rd
Newbury MA 01951

Call Sign: KB1JKO
John M Bogert
6 Independence Way
Newbury MA 01951

Call Sign: N1LOY
Daniel V La Rue
94 Northern Blvd
Newbury MA 01951

Call Sign: KB1VIO
Roger A Daniel
56 Old Point Rd
Newbury MA 01951

Call Sign: N1VWQ
Frederick S Hurlburt
48 Old Rowley Rd

Newbury MA 01951

Call Sign: KA1RNO
Robert A Gouldthorpe
Sr
7 Plum Island Blvd
Newbury MA 01950

Call Sign: KB1EFP
James S Velonis Jr
101 Scotland Rd
Newbury MA 01951

Call Sign: KL7LK
Luke H Smith
49 Southern Blvd
Newbury MA 01951

FCC Amateur Radio Licenses in Newburyport

Call Sign: N1RBO
Arthur W Woods
10 78th St Plum Island
Newburyport MA
01950

Call Sign: KB1UAF
Harold E Babcock
28 B Merrill St
Newburyport MA
01950

Call Sign: KB1UWH
Donald P Degloria Jr
2 Bourbeau Terrace
Newburyport MA
01950

Call Sign: KR1H
Thomas A Norman
Box 376
Newburyport MA
01950

Call Sign: N1XRM
Joseph C Dondero
5 Briggs Ave
Newburyport MA
01950

Call Sign: KB1KR
David E Suuronen

6 Brooks Ct
Newburyport MA
01950

Call Sign: KI4AM
Robert C Shook
6 Brooks Ct
Newburyport MA
01950

Call Sign: N1JAZ
Lynne E Suuronen
6 Brooks Ct
Newburyport MA
01950

Call Sign: KC1GQ
Richard L Hopkinson
9 Buck St
Newburyport MA
01950

Call Sign: WB1DFP
Hartwell Flemming Jr
14 Carter St
Newburyport MA
01950

Call Sign: N1YQX
Mark T Brophy
4 Cherry St
Newburyport MA
01950

Call Sign: N1JMR
Adolf Benca
25 Cherry St
Newburyport MA
01950

Call Sign: W1PGN
Harry L Thornton Jr
95 Clipper Way
Newburyport MA
01950

Call Sign: W1LLU
James E Mc Cobb Jr
65 Coffin St
Newburyport MA
019851209

Call Sign: KF1V
Mark W Olsen

141 Crow Ln
Newburyport MA
01950

Call Sign: KB1UWJ
Allan B Gates
25 Dove St
Newburyport MA
01950

Call Sign: WA1BET
John H Morrill Sr
73 Federal St
Newburyport MA
019502814

Call Sign: KA1TKI
Richard J Cataldo
5 Fenders Ave
Newburyport MA
01950

Call Sign: K1CEQ
Alfred E Price
30 Ferry Rd
Newburyport MA
01950

Call Sign: WB1EMV
Harry L Moore
32 Ferry Rd
Newburyport MA
01950

Call Sign: KA1UI
James T Connolly
49 Green St
Newburyport MA
01950

Call Sign: KB1JGV
John M Douglass
11 Greenleaf St
Newbury Port MA
01950

Call Sign: KB1VIN
Robert J Mckeown
3 Hallisey Dr
Newburyport MA
01950

Call Sign: KB1DZF
Philip J Kubat Jr

78 High St
Newburyport MA
01950

Call Sign: NI1P
Frank E Miller Jr
202 High St
Newburyport MA
01950

Call Sign: K2RYW
Philip A Hurzeler
252 High St
Newburyport MA
019503827

Call Sign: N1AHB
Raymond B Richard Jr
9 Hunter Dr
Newburyport MA
01950

Call Sign: N1UQX
Clifford P Martellini
33 Inn St
Newburyport MA
01950

Call Sign: W1GXZ
Edward L Ramsdell
32 Kent St
Newburyport MA
019502305

Call Sign: KA1TGR
Robert M Hutton
23 Lafayette St
Newburyport MA
01950

Call Sign: KB1AMR
James S Arnette
Liberty St
Newburyport MA
01950

Call Sign: N1XQV
William L Kelleher
111 Low St
Newburyport MA
01950

Call Sign: N1YDB
Margaret M Kelleher

111 Low St
Newburyport MA
01950

Call Sign: KB1TOU
Jacob P Descheneaux
155 Low St
Newburyport MA
01950

Call Sign: KB1SWS
Daniel E Bennett
500 Merrimac St
Newburyport MA
01950

Call Sign: KB1TDA
Philisity K Kitson
500 Merrimac St
Newburyport MA
01950

Call Sign: N1ZAG
Ralph K York
518 Merrimac St
Newburyport MA
01950

Call Sign: KB1DFO
Ricahrd V Grillo
126 Merrimac St 55
Newburyport MA
01950

Call Sign: K1BRQ
Richard H Daly
126 Merrimac St Unit
51
Newburyport MA
01950

Call Sign: KA1USE
Christopher G
Raymond
402 Merrimack St
Newburyport MA
01950

Call Sign: KB1FRI
Bruce F Offhaus
22 Milk St
Newburyport MA
01950

Call Sign: KB1DYH
Steven J Lewis
78 Moseley Ave
Newburyport MA
01951

Call Sign: KB1JBA
James C Janson
6 Moulton St
Newburyport MA
01950

Call Sign: W1JCJ
James C Janson
6 Moulton St
Newburyport MA
01950

Call Sign: KB1VEK
Beth Van Belle
45 Moulton St
Newburyport MA
01950

Call Sign: N7LXR
David A Strohschein
Noble St
Newburyport MA
019501824

Call Sign: KA1KIZ
Bruce A Seiger
4 Peters Rd
Newburyport MA
01950

Call Sign: WA1ESU
Joseph F Beaulieu
49 Plummer Ave
Newburyport MA
01950

Call Sign: N1CQM
William Angelos
13 Prospect St
Newburyport MA
01950

Call Sign: K1AN
John P O Connell
43 Prospect St
Newburyport MA
01950

Call Sign: W2EEK
Harold D Mack Jr
357 R High St
Newburyport MA
01950

Call Sign: KA1HHG
Creighton L Conner
1 Rawson Hill Rd
Newburyport MA
01950

Call Sign: KB1VSX
Nadine E Lavender
10 Rawson Hill Rd
Newburyport MA
01950

Call Sign: W1AGF
William H Bryant
4 Reilly Ave
Newburyport MA
01950

Call Sign: WA4ORG
James M Mc Carthy
17 Russia St
Newburyport MA
01950

Call Sign: AA1XJ
Pierre E Besson
4 Stanley Tucker Dr
Newburyport MA
01950

Call Sign: W1JCA
James F Ronan
25 Summit Place
Newbury Port MA
01950

Call Sign: N1KNA
Paul J Gerry
81 Turkey Hill Rd
Newburyport MA
01950

Call Sign: KB1LST
Donna George
18 Walnut St
Newburyport MA
01950

Call Sign: W1EOC
Claude A Woodward
13 Windward Dr
Newburyport MA
01950

Call Sign: KB1UWL
Daniel J Kmiec
12 Zabriskie Dr Apt B
Newburyport MA
01950

Call Sign: K1DJK
Daniel J Kmiec
12 Zabriskie Dr Apt B
Newburyport MA
01950

Call Sign: KB1BPO
Michael J Comparone
Jr
Newburyport MA
019506136

Call Sign: N1UXH
Anita Rossi
Newburyport MA
01950

Call Sign: N1WBM
Ray Pike
Newburyport MA
01959

Call Sign: KB1OUC
Glenn Obey
Newburyport MA
01950

Call Sign: KB1TJS
Thomas P Savastano
Newburyport MA
01950

FCC Amateur Radio Licenses in Newton

Call Sign: KA1WKK
Thanh C Tran
308 Adams St
Newton MA 02158

Call Sign: N1LIK
Daniel A Bianchi

322 Adams St
Newton MA 02158

Call Sign: WA3RPG
Neil J Halin
138 Albemarle Rd
Newton MA
024601135

Call Sign: WA1URF
Harold R Fisher
62 Alexander
Newton MA 02161

Call Sign: N1RZL
William Z Zisi
60 Allerton Rd
Newton MA 02159

Call Sign: KB1VWZ
Noah M Goldstein
97 Annawan Rd
Newton MA 02468

Call Sign: N1CBO
Leslie H Spaulding
60 Anthony Cir
Newton MA 02130

Call Sign: KA1EIZ
Stacy W Nichols
427 Auburn St
Newton MA 02166

Call Sign: N1LKO
Edward R Horowitz
64 Baldpate Hill Rd
Newton MA 02459

Call Sign: WA1NDE
Peter L Hansen
Baldwin St
Newton MA 02158

Call Sign: KB1QMB
Bill Yee
671 Beacon St
Newton MA 02459

Call Sign: W1YEE
Bill Yee
671 Beacon St
Newton MA 02459

Call Sign: N2DJC
A Richard Rosenberg
831 Beacon St
Newton MA 02459

Call Sign: KB1KRU
Martin Himmelfarb
108 Beaumont Ave
Newton MA 02460

Call Sign: W1RFD
Robert F Dugas
15 Beech St
Newton MA
024581040

Call Sign: KB1HTN
Boris Dynkin
7 Beecher Ter
Newton MA 02459

Call Sign: WB2DDC
Andrew M Higgins
45 Bellevue St
Newton MA 02158

Call Sign: KA1WFS
Benjamin G Ledsham
40 Bemis St
Newton MA 02160

Call Sign: WB2RIG
William H Ledsham
40 Bemis St
Newton MA 02160

Call Sign: AB1QR
John Koczera
57 Bennington St
Newton MA 02458

Call Sign: KB1HAE
David A Carlen
135 Berkley St
Newton MA 02465

Call Sign: W1EUY
David A Belsley
33 Bolton Rd
Newton MA
024602130

Call Sign: N1IXY
Harold A Bailey Jr

957 Boylston St
Newton MA 02161

Call Sign: KA1ZAX
Andrew S Dignan
46 Brackett Rd
Newton MA 02158

Call Sign: N1MYH
Walter A Brown
29 Brewster Rd
Newton MA 02161

Call Sign: N1OLL
Kenneth W Halpern
325 Brookline St
Newton MA 02159

Call Sign: K1ECC
Richard Boltrus
61 Brush Hill Rd
Newton MA 02161

Call Sign: KA1ZCI
Matthew A Caplan
8 Burrage Rd
Newton MA 02159

Call Sign: K1SYG
Charles R Murray
102 Cabot St
Newton MA 02158

Call Sign: KC0MGI
Michael N Mang
184 Cabot St #1
Newton MA 02458

Call Sign: KC0MGJ
Andrew G Mang
184 Cabot St #1
Newton MA 02458

Call Sign: N1ZGZ
Peter F Judge
1112 Centre St
Newton MA 02459

Call Sign: N1ZXN
Kris D Van Alstine
505 Centre St 11
Newton MA
024582062

Call Sign: WB4OGB
Andrew B Littman
15 Channing Rd
Newton MA 02159

Call Sign: K8HGZ
Yehuda M Cern
79 Chapel St
Newton MA 02458

Call Sign: KB1OWZ
Kenneth J Groves
229 Chapel St Apt -1
Newton MA 02458

Call Sign: AA1IM
Ara N Knaian
90 Cherry St
Newton MA 02465

Call Sign: KA1HDR
Gary L Irving
48 Chesley Rd
Newton MA 02459

Call Sign: KB1QYJ
John F Sterk
16 Chesterfield Rd
Newton MA 02465

Call Sign: KE1IQ
Alan Schneiderman
192 Christina St
Newton MA 02461

Call Sign: KA1IZP
Louis Copman
16 Cibel Path
Newton MA 02159

Call Sign: N1EQN
Joel F Nevin
55 Circuit Ave
Newton MA 02461

Call Sign: WA1SZY
Robert L Devine Iii
90 Circuit Ave
Newton MA
024611603

Call Sign: KA1NJP
George E Macnair Jr
151 Clark St

Newton MA 02159

Call Sign: KB1STO
David W Yellen
47 Clements Rd
Newton MA 02458

Call Sign: KA1ZDF
Adam M Taub
55 Clements Rd
Newton MA 02158

Call Sign: W4RD
Willie J Goldwasser
70 Clements Rd
Newton MA 02458

Call Sign: K8EP
Edward D Sawyer
92 Clinton Pl
Newton MA 02459

Call Sign: KB1NZY
John O Mullaney
4 Clinton St
Newton MA 02458

Call Sign: K1BOS
John O Mullaney
4 Clinton St
Newton MA 02458

Call Sign: WO1Y
Michael P Walker
47 Clinton St
Newton MA 02458

Call Sign: N1SOF
Joseph Blanchard
48 Clinton St
Newton MA 02158

Call Sign: KB1MSK
Henry B Minsky
67 Clyde St
Newton MA 02460

Call Sign: AE1G
Steven J Henry
1337 Commonwealth
Ave
Newton MA
024652912

Call Sign: N1WYO
Shih Chao Lin
2171 Commonwealth
Ave
Newton MA 02166

Call Sign: K1IO
Fred R Goldstein
69 Commonwealth Pk
W
Newton MA 02459

Call Sign: KA1YVS
Timothy M Rooney
15 Cotton St
Newton MA 02158

Call Sign: KA1ZCL
Stacey P Faneuil
56 Cotton St
Newton MA 02158

Call Sign: KA1ZXB
Seth L Rosenbloom
142 Cotton St
Newton MA 02158

Call Sign: KB1RLI
Vadim A Afonkin
53 Countryside Rd
Newton MA 02459

Call Sign: WA2DHN
Jenifer Nesin
101 Crafts St
Newton MA 02160

Call Sign: AB1JF
Arthur Tong
85 Dartmouth St
Newton MA 02465

Call Sign: AK1FT
Arthur Tong
85 Dartmouth St
Newton MA 02465

Call Sign: W1VAN
Earl M Burtman
Dedham St
Newton MA 02159

Call Sign: K1KOO
Charles A Valentine

34 Eliot Memorial Rd
Newton MA 02158

Call Sign: KB1VWE
Edward T Gardner
216 Elliot St
Newton MA 02464

Call Sign: KB1UPH
Nathaniel F Gilbert
55 Ellis Rd
Newton MA 02465

Call Sign: WM1V
Henry L Dorkin Md
75 Evergreen Ave
Newton MA
024661702

Call Sign: K1ZDB
Harold G De Wolfe
29 Faxon St
Newton MA 02158

Call Sign: KB1LNA
Charles A Geis
41 Fellsmere Rd
Newton MA 02459

Call Sign: N1QEB
Robert H Brown
41 Fenno Rd
Newton MA 02159

Call Sign: WB1GFQ
Eleanor G Palais
58 Ferncroft Rd
Newton MA 02168

Call Sign: W1BFO
Giovanni G Fazio
244 Franklin St
Newton MA 02458

Call Sign: KB1JMK
Gayle V Salemme
93 Freeman St
Newton MA 02466

Call Sign: KB1JML
John A Salemme
93 Freeman St
Newton MA 02466

Call Sign: KA1ZCJ
Alexandra K Smith
140 Grant Ave
Newton MA 02159

Call Sign: WA2GUY
Robert P Schreiber
28 Grayson Ln
Newton MA 02162

Call Sign: KB1BOJ
Jared D Friedman
29 Greenwood St
Newton MA 02159

Call Sign: KA1ZWI
Lorna W Rawlings
581 Grove St
Newton MA 02162

Call Sign: KA1ZWJ
Nancy W Rawlings
581 Grove St
Newton MA 02162

Call Sign: N1FCY
Michael E Weissel
99 Hagen Rd
Newton MA 02459

Call Sign: KA1TUD
Martin J Rossman
239 Harvard Cir
Newton MA
024602216

Call Sign: K1FFX
Bruce L Rosen
23 Hazelhurst Ave
Newton MA
024651342

Call Sign: W1UVE
A Stewart Johnson
11 Hemlock Rd
Newton MA
021641206

Call Sign: KA1ZY
Gary B Ruvkun
120 Herrick Rd
Newton MA 02459

Call Sign: KB2VGF

Michael E Mesolella
21 Herrick Rd Apt 6
Newton MA 02459

Call Sign: KA1ENP
Arthur T Thompson
91 High St Apt Rear
Newton MA
024641239

Call Sign: KA1ZCM
Miriam S Udler
41 Hobart Rd
Newton MA 02159

Call Sign: W1APB
Warren F Davis
43 Holden Rd
Newton MA
024651909

Call Sign: N1IBB
Matthew Chao
48 Hollis St 2
Newton MA 02458

Call Sign: KB1PHC
Pamela M Westrom
9 Howard St
Newton MA 02458

Call Sign: KB1RYQ
Pamela M Westrom
9 Howard St
Newton MA 02458

Call Sign: WA1KDS
Michael J Sherman
85 Huntington Rd
Newton MA 02158

Call Sign: N1CJK
Allan H Ropper
6 Ivanhoe St
Newton MA 02158

Call Sign: WA1DX
Allan H Ropper
6 Ivanhoe St
Newton MA 02458

Call Sign: KA1ZXC
Aaron T Kriss
36 Ivanhoe St

Newton MA 02158

Call Sign: W1EKK
Joseph D Di Loffi
181 Jackson Rd
Newton MA 02158

Call Sign: KA1NML
Jason E Kimenker
35 Juniper Ln
Newton MA 02459

Call Sign: K3KLQ
Stuart J Lipoff
192 Kirkstall Rd
Newton MA 02160

Call Sign: N1QGF
Samuel H Lipoff
192 Kirkstall Rd
Newton MA
021602441

Call Sign: N1NIB
Vladimir Khaynovsky
24 Knowles St
Newton MA 02159

Call Sign: KA1SA
Richard S Lindzen
301 Lake Ave
Newton MA 02161

Call Sign: WO1I
Richard S Lindzen
301 Lake Ave
Newton MA 02461

Call Sign: KA1ZZM
Emily A Apsell
11 Lancaster Rd
Newton MA 02158

Call Sign: KB1WAC
Paul N Dahlstrand
287 Langley Rd 28
Newton MA 02459

Call Sign: KB1LZN
Robert K Tendler
19 Lawrence Ave
Newton MA 02467

Call Sign: W1RKT

Robert K Tendler
19 Lawrence Ave
Newton MA 02467

Call Sign: KB1ADZ
William A Fossey
37 Lewis St
Newton MA 02158

Call Sign: N1CEO
Peter L Dabos
181 Lexington St Apt
29
Newton MA 02166

Call Sign: WA1UIY
Robert N Drukman
23 Locksley Rd
Newton MA 02159

Call Sign: N1BFA
Milton L Weiss
500 Lowell Ave
Newton MA 02160

Call Sign: KA1ZCH
Andrew B Pascal
56 Mandalay Rd
Newton MA 02159

Call Sign: KB1FQL
Andrew L Yeats
36 Maple Ave
Newton MA 02158

Call Sign: KB1HEK
Andrew L Yeats
36 Maple Ave
Newton MA
024581904

Call Sign: AB1CX
Andrew L Yeats
36 Maple Ave
Newton MA
024581904

Call Sign: KA1PSG
John W Tuckerman
91 Moulton St
Newton MA
021621407

Call Sign: KE6YVI

Asher Hsu
89 Needham St Apt
2160
Newton MA 02461

Call Sign: KB1AZP
David R Wood
51 Newtonville Ave
Newton MA 02158

Call Sign: KB1TZ
Michael T Rosenbaum
33 Nonantum St
Newton MA 02158

Call Sign: AA1FL
Burton J Stein
128 Old Farm Rd
Newton MA 02459

Call Sign: KB1HRT
Peter A Rothberg
226 Park St
Newton MA 02458

Call Sign: KB1BIF
Todd L Friedman
26 Philmore Rd
Newton MA 02158

Call Sign: W1AT
William B Dean
55 Playstead Rd
Newton MA 02158

Call Sign: KA1UTR
Martin S Osman
212 Plymouth Rd
Newton MA 02161

Call Sign: N1GKT
Stephen F Bart
26 Rochester Rd
Newton MA
024582517

Call Sign: KB1HDL
Philip J Knodle
74 Rockland Pl
Newton MA 02464

Call Sign: N1LZJ
Daniel A Quintiliani
10 Rockland St

Newton MA 02458

Call Sign: KJ4DWT
Matthew J Vildzius
29 Royce Rd
Newton MA 02459

Call Sign: N1ETL
Steven I Garson
54 Saint Marys St
Newton MA
024621019

Call Sign: KB1ETK
Andrew T Mcafee
42 Selwyn Rd
Newton MA 02461

Call Sign: KB1FFW
Andrew T Mcafee
42 Selwyn Rd
Newton MA 02461

Call Sign: KA1PYJ
Richard E Barnett
42 Sevland Rd
Newton MA 02159

Call Sign: KB1MZE
James M Bloom
56 Sherrin Rd
Newton MA
024621124

Call Sign: W1RPI
Francisco Da Costa
265 Spiers Rd
Newton MA 02159

Call Sign: K1JTO
John C Hepburn
132 Stanley Rd
Newton MA 02168

Call Sign: W1ZHH
David G Hawkins
151 Stanton Ave
Newton MA 02166

Call Sign: KA1UHN
Sharon M Mc Kenna
14 Sylvan Ave
Newton MA 02165

Call Sign: KB1BIE
Benjamin E Green
41 Travis Dr
Newton MA 02167

Call Sign: N1EDT
Wellington B
Fairweather Jr
24 Vernon St
Newton MA 02158

Call Sign: KB1BIV
Sarah A Feldberg
85 Waban Hill Rd N
Newton MA 02167

Call Sign: W1HYQ
Ross S Feldberg
85 Waban Hill Rd N
Newton MA 02167

Call Sign: KA1ZCK
Sarabeth Broder
Fingert
115 Waban Hill Rd N
Newton MA 02467

Call Sign: WA1GIO
Mark N Horenstein
49 Wade St
Newton MA 02161

Call Sign: K1DXJ
Joseph M Sanroma
1000 Walnut St
Newton MA 02461

Call Sign: KB1QVX
Robert Staulo
1155 Walnut St
Newton MA 02461

Call Sign: WA3BBF
Israel B Zibman
423 Ward St
Newton MA 02459

Call Sign: WA2LXL
Daniel N Ozick
131 Warren St
Newton MA 02159

Call Sign: N1KUM

Leslie A Morris-
Cassidy
Washington St
Newton MA
024621427

Call Sign: KA1MVL
Lynn W Chernoff
3 Wauwinet Rd
Newton MA 02165

Call Sign: K4BSX
Arthur L Wardwell
3 Wauwinet Rd
Newton MA 02465

Call Sign: KA1THR
Alexander J Wei
420 Waverley Ave
Newton MA 02158

Call Sign: KA1SJL
Mark W Eagle
69 Wayne Rd
Newton MA 02159

Call Sign: N1KWY
Robert L Barnett
34 Westminster Rd
Newton MA 02159

Call Sign: N1QDM
John P Gately
4 Wilson Cir
Newton MA 02161

Call Sign: WB1GBG
Jeffrey A Ashur
24 Wiswall St
Newton MA 02465

Call Sign: KA1ACZ
John L Vaccaro
291 Woodland Rd
Newton MA 02166

Call Sign: KB1CJB
Daniel R Keylor
289 Woodward St
Newton MA 02468

Call Sign: KB1CLT
Sonesta Radio Club

Newton MA
021680001

Call Sign: KB1FXI
Larry A Nathanson
Newton MA
024610164

Call Sign: KB1LTO
Harold I Binder
Newton MA 02466

Call Sign: KB1NIU
Robert D Solomon
Newton MA 02459

Call Sign: KB1QHP
Nathan Colena
Newton MA 02461

Call Sign: N1IFU
Nathan Colena
Newton MA 02461

**FCC Amateur Radio
Licenses in Newton
Center**

Call Sign: KB1NJI
Larry Speiser
27 Hamlin Rd
Newton Center MA
024591001

Call Sign: KB1SSQ
Eli Cohn
132 Homer St
Newton Center MA
02459

Call Sign: KB1VEG
David Wihl
155 Homer St
Newton Center MA
02459

Call Sign: W1HEB
Middlesex Amateur
Radio Club
23 Locksley Rd
Newton Center MA
02459

Call Sign: KB1UON

Middlesex Amateur
Radio Club
23 Locksley Rd
Newton Center MA
02459

Call Sign: W1LJO
Middlesex Amateur
Radio Club
23 Locksley Rd
Newton Center MA
02459

Call Sign: KA1ZCN
Yonathan A Nuta
27 Lorna Rd
Newton Center MA
02159

Call Sign: KA1TUZ
Richard C Doherty
46 Moreland Ave
Newton Center MA
02159

Call Sign: KA1ZDD
Adam P Caplan
8 Burrage Rd
Newton Centre MA
02159

Call Sign: KA1ZDE
Saskia E Ziolkowski
930 Centre St
Newton Centre MA
02159

Call Sign: KA1ZYL
Ada M Ziolkowski
930 Centre St
Newton Centre MA
02159

Call Sign: KC1RQ
Bradford K Hammer
439 Commonwealth
Ave
Newton Centre MA
02459

Call Sign: N1GCY
Harry Baum
79 Drumlin Rd

Newton Centre MA
02459

Call Sign: KA1ZDC
Nicholas C Wexler
22 Exmoor Rd
Newton Centre MA
02159

Call Sign: W1DIX
Gilbert Davidson
23 Exmoor Rd
Newton Centre MA
02159

Call Sign: KA1SAX
Edward W Friedman
29 Greenwood St
Newton Centre MA
02459

Call Sign: W1NYI
Lawrence Mc
Donough
23 Keller Path
Newton Centre MA
02159

Call Sign: WB2EBA
Michael N Weinstein
71 Morton St
Newton Centre MA
02459

Call Sign: KA1MXS
R Scott Perry
178 Morton St
Newton Centre MA
02159

Call Sign: N1AGK
Michael A Taricano
21 Nathan Rd
Newton Centre MA
02159

Call Sign: WA1VAV
William E Marchant Jr
34 North St
Newton Centre MA
02159

Call Sign: KA1ZAB
Sean J Bradley

3 Nottingham St
Newton Centre MA
02159

Call Sign: W1LJO
Paul E Dumais
36 Parker St
Newton Centre MA
02459

Call Sign: KA1ZYO
Rachel F Stein
41 Stuart Rd
Newton Centre MA
02159

Call Sign: W1DDN
Southard Lippincott
74 Tyler Terr
Newton Centre MA
021591814

Call Sign: WC1ABI
City Of Newton Dept
Of Cd
47 Wayne Rd
Newton Centre MA
02159

Call Sign: KA1RHQ
Mark J Walters
36 Willow St
Newton Centre MA
02159

Call Sign: WD0BDI
John K Waterman
274 Tremont St
Newton Corner MA
02158

Call Sign: N1RHO
Robert E Tracy Jr
166 Waverley Ave
Newton Corner MA
02158

Call Sign: AB1IA
Howard L Bleich
152 Hagen Rd
Newton Ctr MA
024592755

Call Sign: W3CW

Howard L Bleich
152 Hagen Rd
Newton Center MA
024592755

Call Sign: W1MLG
Laurence R Berk
19 Andrew St
Newton Highlands MA
02461

Call Sign: N1KCS
Marshall C Schneider
1042 Boylston St
Newton Highlands MA
02161

Call Sign: N1OBE
John S Davis
18 Chester St
Newton Highlands MA
02161

Call Sign: AB1KY
Bruce R Adams
52 Puritan Rd
Newton Highlands MA
02461

Call Sign: KA1SDL
Stephen R Buckman
21 Standish St
Newton Highlands MA
02461

Call Sign: KA1HSQ
Harry W Klebanow
1242 Walnut St
Newton Highlands MA
02161

Call Sign: KA1KMX
Martha H Johnson
1377 Walnut St
Newton Highlands MA
02161

Call Sign: KA1KMY
Winston R Johnson
1377 Walnut St

Newton Highlands MA
02161

Call Sign: WB2ZXD
Roger S Putnam
Walnut St
Newton Highlands MA
02161

Call Sign: K2TZD
John G Kassakian
31 Berkshire Rd
Newtonville MA
02160

Call Sign: KA1RFV
Louis Di Dino
50 Broadway St
Newtonville MA
02160

Call Sign: WA1QPT
Laurence F Cleveland
24 Fairfield St
Newtonville MA
02160

Call Sign: KE1KK
Stephen P Vaglica
79 Madison Ave
Newtonville MA
02460

Call Sign: WA1PPM
Donato A Delicata
352 Nevada St
Newtonville MA
02160

Call Sign: W1ENS
Donald A Foster
390 Newtonville Ave
Newtonville MA
024601941

Call Sign: KA1UGD
Hillel R Alpert
18 Vineyard Rd
Newtonville MA
02160

Call Sign: KA1UET
Paul B Campanis
37 Walnut Pl
Newtonville MA
02160

Call Sign: KB1PIE
Michael S Jasper
203 Walnut St
Newtonville MA
02460

Call Sign: KB1GBU
Jacqueline Sonnabend
321 Walnut St 411
Newtonville MA
024601927

Call Sign: N1VJP
Paul W Musow
221 Walnut St Apt 2
Newtonville MA
02460

Call Sign: KA1AXW
Charles R Reynolds Jr
33 Washington Park
Newtonville MA
02160

Call Sign: KA1ZLW
Norman J Darish
843 Watertown St
Newtonville MA
02465

Call Sign: KA2TMT
Richard D Goldstein
Newtonville MA
02160

Call Sign: WA1FEF
John F Olivieri Jr
4 Barrell Pl
Norfolk MA 02056

Call Sign: WB1FLI
David H Lawry
20 Boardman St
Norfolk MA 02056

Call Sign: W1NJI
John Olivieri
99 Boardman St
Norfolk MA 02056

Call Sign: W1LOS
George C Wright
113 Boardman St
Norfolk MA 02056

Call Sign: W1MPD
Richard M Wright
113 Boardman St
Norfolk MA
020561058

Call Sign: WA1JRR
Scott A Bushway
14 Brookside Ln
Norfolk MA 02056

Call Sign: KB1MHX
Michael C Lazdowsky
11 Cleveland St
Norfolk MA 02056

Call Sign: WA2EDY
Gregory D Jay
3 Crossbow Rd
Norfolk MA 02056

Call Sign: KB1QFN
Christopher D
Bergerson
2 Fox Hill Ln
Norfolk MA 02056

Call Sign: KB1EHA
Morgan Bent
14 Holbrook St
Norfolk MA 02056

Call Sign: KA1WOQ
Richard F Conlin
1 Hunter Ave
Norfolk MA 02056

Call Sign: KB1RCC
Jeffrey T Eszlari
77 King St
Norfolk MA 02056

Call Sign: N1CMK

Edward H Eszlari
77 King St
Norfolk MA 02056

Call Sign: KB1NO
John Nuhibian
3 Knoll Dr
Norfolk MA 02056

Call Sign: N1OMC
David A Nuhibian
3 Knoll Dr
Norfolk MA 02056

Call Sign: K1WOW
Richard P Peters
27 Lafayette Ln
Norfolk MA 02056

Call Sign: KB1WXJ
Benjamin Gallup
22 Lake St
Norfolk MA 02056

Call Sign: N1HPR
Richard B Stillman
33 Lake St
Norfolk MA 02056

Call Sign: N1KVD
Diane O Stillman
33 Lake St
Norfolk MA 02056

Call Sign: K1DOB
Diane O Stillman
33 Lake St
Norfolk MA 02056

Call Sign: K1VFY
Howard J Brown Jr
19 Lois Lane
Norfolk MA
020561823

Call Sign: N1SHI
Gary G Ravinski
230 Main St
Norfolk MA 02056

Call Sign: KA1LZB
Bernard A Brule
12 Malcolm
Norfolk MA 02056

Call Sign: WA1LRK
Paul J Hurd
2 Maple St
Norfolk MA 02056

Call Sign: KA1YBE
Elizabeth S Oxley
10 Marshall St
Norfolk MA 02056

Call Sign: KB1ENE
Robert W Delano
5 Meadowbrook Way
Norfolk MA 02056

Call Sign: N1KZA
David E Robsham
69 Medway St
Norfolk MA 02056

Call Sign: KI1O
Robert T Burke
82 Myrtle St
Norfolk MA 02056

Call Sign: KB1PEP
Gary E Power
98 North St
Norfolk MA 02056

Call Sign: WB1GZP
Dennis A Lynch
46 Pine St
Norfolk MA 02056

Call Sign: KB1RRO
Jonathan W Smith
26 Robin Rd
Norfolk MA 02056

Call Sign: NY2H
Warren H Ziegler Jr
55 Rockwood Rd
Norfolk MA 02056

Call Sign: N1HOE
Jenifer L Coburn
76 Rockwood Rd
Norfolk MA 02056

Call Sign: W1IW
Charles F Pyne
187 Seekonk St

Norfolk MA 02056

Call Sign: W1OW
Albert A Leverone
4 Spring St
Norfolk MA 02056

Call Sign: KB1HMO
Steven R Foster
12 Stacey Rd
Norfolk MA 02056

Call Sign: AB1ID
Alexander T Farkas
20 Tucker Rd
Norfolk MA 02056

Call Sign: W1IMM
Robert P Levreault
Norfolk MA 02056

Call Sign: W1EIK
Andrew Phillips
85 Pattison St
North Abington MA
02351

Call Sign: KA1ILR
Richard H Burnham
122 Wales St
North Abington MA
023511825

Call Sign: N1KXI
Karl W Kemp
North Abington MA
02351

Call Sign: N1MJL
Jeanne E Kemp
North Abington MA
02351

Call Sign: N1UZJ
Michael A Reopell
53 Autumn Dr

North Adams MA
01247

Call Sign: N1TQW
William E Roberts
37 Beacon St
North Adams MA
01247

Call Sign: N1PYQ
Paul A Lepel
144 Bradley St
North Adams MA
01247

Call Sign: KB1CJT
Toby M Alves
120 Brooklyn St
North Adams MA
01247

Call Sign: WA1KMW
Paul H Howcroft Sr
148 Brooklyn St
North Adams MA
01247

Call Sign: KB1LAL
Renee L Wlodyka
11 Burnhams St
North Adams MA
01247

Call Sign: N1XBL
Linda C Wlodyka
86 Cady St
North Adams MA
01247

Call Sign: WA1VHC
William W Chandler
119 Chantilly Ave
North Adams MA
01247

Call Sign: KB3DKS
William N Courtright
3 Chase Hill
North Adams MA
01247

Call Sign: N1FBP
Harold Taskin
101 Chen Aille Ter

North Adams MA
01247

Call Sign: KA1CN
John H Choquette
68 Cherry St
North Adams MA
01247

Call Sign: KA1QAZ
Martha C Choquette
68 Cherry St
North Adams MA
01247

Call Sign: KB1TWU
Michael L Follett
192 Church St
North Adams MA
01247

Call Sign: W1WLS
Walter L Smith Jr
410 Church St Apt 3
North Adams MA
01247

Call Sign: WA1ZFM
Richard J La Vigne
344 E Main St
North Adams MA
01247

Call Sign: WA1WMN
Stephen W Konopka
676 E Main St
North Adams MA
01247

Call Sign: WA1ZNM
Anita M Konopka
676 E Main St
North Adams MA
01247

Call Sign: N1RMP
Milton J Overlock
205 E Main St Apt 1b
North Adams MA
01247

Call Sign: N5PNM
Cecil E Oxford Jr
164 E Quincy

North Adams MA
01247

Call Sign: WA1UQK
Isabelle G King
85 Eagle St Apt 310
North Adams MA
01247

Call Sign: WB1EPR
Robert E Brownsword
62 East Ave
North Adams MA
01247

Call Sign: W1VMK
Felix A Puccio
138 East Ave
North Adams MA
01247

Call Sign: WA1OOI
Sonia A Puccio
138 East Ave
North Adams MA
01247

Call Sign: WA1PNH
Michael G Downey
350 Franklin
North Adams MA
01247

Call Sign: KA1AY
Anthony J Saltamartini
83 Furnace St
North Adams MA
01247

Call Sign: KA1QAY
Marilyn A Saltamartini
83 Furnace St
North Adams MA
01247

Call Sign: W1GKK
George L De Grenier
109 Gallup St
North Adams MA
01247

Call Sign: KE1KM
Nicholas J Mantello
86 Hathaway St

North Adams MA
01247

Call Sign: N1AZJ
Thomas Beall
36 Highland Ave
North Adams MA
01247

Call Sign: WA1VRX
JOHN R DE MARCO
Mr
164 Houghton St
North Adams MA
01247

Call Sign: NI1V
Jeffrey J Kemp
295 Houghton St
North Adams MA
012472435

Call Sign: KB1VNN
Matthew D Parker
365 Houghton St
North Adams MA
01247

Call Sign: N1MDB
Albert W St Cyr
20 Hudson St
North Adams MA
01247

Call Sign: KA1KTT
David A Brown
14 Iroquois Drive
North Adams MA
01247

Call Sign: KG4ZBH
Gordon R Long
1080 Massachusetts
Ave
North Adams MA
01247

Call Sign: N1NMO
Peter A Dickinson
1527 Massachusetts
Ave
North Adams MA
012472240

Call Sign: KB1UCJ
David S O'neil
132 Meadow St
North Adams MA
01247

Call Sign: WA1DSY
Kenneth P Boillat
56 Mohawk Trl
North Adams MA
01247

Call Sign: N1SJS
Joseph R Overlock
28 Navajo Dr
North Adams MA
01247

Call Sign: KB1HZM
Frank M Davignon Jr
147 North St
North Adams MA
01247

Call Sign: KB1NFL
Ann M Davignon
147 North St
North Adams MA
01247

Call Sign: N1YFG
David L Belanger
3 Palmer Ave
North Adams MA
01247

Call Sign: N1YCW
Bruce E Pierce
183 Prospect St
North Adams MA
01247

Call Sign: KB1HZL
Francis J Morandi Sr
126 Protection Ave
North Adams MA
01247

Call Sign: KA1ELK
Joseph R Bolus
140 Protection Ave
North Adams MA
01247

Call Sign: W1EBK
A Paul Willey
372 Reservoir Rd
North Adams MA
01247

Call Sign: N1MGA
Michael F Gagne
79 Richview Ave
North Adams MA
01247

Call Sign: WA1NQI
Harold S Briggs
21 Rickard St
North Adams MA
01247

Call Sign: WA1SPY
George L De Rosier
6 Seminole Drive
North Adams MA
012470122

Call Sign: WA1YQG
Herbert E Blake
13 Seminole Drive
North Adams MA
01247

Call Sign: KB1VNM
Robert H Allard
320 State Rd
North Adams MA
012473012

Call Sign: KB1ABB
Enid V Shields
31 Veazie St Apt 203
North Adams MA
01247

Call Sign: N1HGE
Vernon E Shields Jr
91 W Main St
North Adams MA
01247

Call Sign: WA1ABL
David G Thompson
121 W Shaft Rd
North Adams MA
01247

Call Sign: WA1VYO
Louise F Thompson
121 W Shaft Rd
North Adams MA
01247

Call Sign: K1ABL
David G Thompson
121 W Shaft Rd
North Adams MA
01247

Call Sign: K1WEZ
Louise F Thompson
121 W Shaft Rd
North Adams MA
01247

Call Sign: N1LLP
Ralph C Montgomery
Jr
444 W Shaft Rd
North Adams MA
01247

Call Sign: N1CKT
Arthur F Barry Jr
102 Walker St
North Adams MA
01247

Call Sign: KB1RAO
Michael A Mariani
363 Walker St
North Adams MA
01247

Call Sign: KO1L
Michael A Mariani
363 Walker St
North Adams MA
01247

Call Sign: WA1EKR
Frederick E Crosier
89 Wells Ave
North Adams MA
01247

Call Sign: WA1YQF
Barbara A Blake
North Adams MA
01247

Call Sign: N1UZF
John B Oxford
North Adams MA
01247

Call Sign: KA1IUQ
Norman A Kessler
North Amherst MA
010599480

Call Sign: KB1WAM
Michael F Kotarba
North Amherst MA
01059

Call Sign: N1WBE
Peter V Gatto
417 Abbott
North Andover MA
01845

Call Sign: K1IUG
Thomas D Ippolito
338 Abbott St
North Andover MA
01845

Call Sign: N1WBH
Vinny J Gatto
417 Abbott St
North Andover MA
01845

Call Sign: KE6ZQR
Pramode C Kandpal
95 Amberville Rd
North Andover MA
01845

Call Sign: N1UIN
John S Mitchell Jr
32 Andrew Cir
North Andover MA
01845

Call Sign: KC4CIE

Linda Gundal
22 Annis St
North Andover MA
01845

Call Sign: KB1PPS
David J Mitton
370 Appleton St
North Andover MA
018453118

Call Sign: W1MMX
David J Mitton
370 Appleton St
North Andover MA
018453118

Call Sign: W1DI
Bradford A Smith
419 Bear Hill Rd
North Andover MA
01845

Call Sign: N1IXS
William M Hastings
19 Beaver Brook Rd
North Andover MA
01845

Call Sign: KA1XC
John F Kay
208 Boston St
North Andover MA
01845

Call Sign: K1HKQ
Richard P Slade
21 Bradford St
North Andover MA
018451103

Call Sign: W1AGA
Albert J Le Bel
97 Bradford St
North Andover MA
01845

Call Sign: KB1UTO
Joseph A Mangano
340 Bradford St
North Andover MA
01845

Call Sign: KB1RDN

Robert G Cerchione
173 Bridges Lane
North Andover MA
01845

Call Sign: N1AFE
Steven E Tessler
308 Campbell Rd
North Andover MA
018455715

Call Sign: AC1AA
Steven E Tessler
308 Campbell Rd
North Andover MA
018455715

Call Sign: WA1JAM
Samuel F Gagliano
43 Candlestick Rd
North Andover MA
01845

Call Sign: AA2TX
Anthony J Monteiro
25 Carriage Chase
North Andover MA
01845

Call Sign: N1HND
Raymond J Hamel Jr
25 Castlemere Place
North Andover MA
01845

Call Sign: KB1IFE
Brian M Lambert
91 Chadwick St
North Andover MA
01845

Call Sign: AB1CA
Brian M Lambert
91 Chadwick St
North Andover MA
01845

Call Sign: KA1WB
Anthony J Carbone
145 Chadwick St
North Andover MA
01845

Call Sign: KC6SEW

Jeanne M Rudy
252 Chestnut St
North Andover MA
01845

Call Sign: KB1KMM
Rigoberto B Nina
23 Concord St
North Andover MA
01845

Call Sign: KA1SYR
Hilton P Cormey
171 Cotuit St
North Andover MA
01845

Call Sign: KJ4FBE
John P Harrod Iv
7 Court St
North Andover MA
01845

Call Sign: N6BD
Chris M Rines
90 Crossbow
North Andover MA
01845

Call Sign: AC6UT
Stephen B Davis
21 Delucia Way
North Andover MA
01845

Call Sign: K1IOS
Robert E Anderson
163 Farnum St
North Andover MA
01845

Call Sign: W1UW
Sidney B Coleman
247 Farnum St
North Andover MA
01845

Call Sign: K1BZT
David A Higginbottom
250 Farnum St
North Andover MA
01845

Call Sign: W8SPI

John W Livermore
103 Farrwood Ave Apt
3
North Andover MA
01845

Call Sign: KB1MUZ
Frank P Monastiero
3 Fernview Ave
North Andover MA
01845

Call Sign: KA1JXY
Joseph A Palladino Jr
667 Forest St
North Andover MA
01845

Call Sign: KA1ZNC
Carol Ann G Dulong
701 Forest St
North Andover MA
01845

Call Sign: KB1PUA
John Z Chmielecki
242 Foster St
North Andover MA
01845

Call Sign: K1ETT
Joseph F Marcin
475 Foster St
North Andover MA
01845

Call Sign: N1MVE
Elizabeth M Kramer
19 Francis St
North Andover MA
01845

Call Sign: N1GQX
Jane F Cuozzo
190 Granville Ln
North Andover MA
01845

Call Sign: N9TFP
Simon G Spanier
1160 Great Pond Rd
North Andover MA
01845

Call Sign: KA1TQS
Claire J Donnelly
83 Hewitt Ave
North Andover MA
01845

Call Sign: KB1GFV
Timothy W D
Macdonald
180 Hickory Hill Rd
North Andover MA
01845

Call Sign: W1WCI
Timothy W D
Macdonald
180 Hickory Hill Rd
North Andover MA
01845

Call Sign: N1UIT
Haris
Karamehmedovic
1 High St
North Andover MA
01845

Call Sign: KB1IRH
Warren A Zimmer
113 High St
North Andover MA
01845

Call Sign: K1GGZ
Edmond R Becotte
136 Hillside Rd
North Andover MA
01845

Call Sign: N1OTP
David R Delaney
9 Ingalls St
North Andover MA
01845

Call Sign: N1FDI
Wendy L Gale
30 Jay Rd
North Andover MA
01845

Call Sign: N1UUZ
David H De Witt
34 Johnson St

North Andover MA
01845

Call Sign: KA1FYN
Robert E Maurer
88 Johnson St
North Andover MA
01845

Call Sign: KA1IPL
Marion E Maurer
88 Johnson St
North Andover MA
01845

Call Sign: W1DJB
John J Coco
695 Johnson St
North Andover MA
01845

Call Sign: KB1UEC
Shawn E Stevens
9 Kingston St
North Andover MA
01845

Call Sign: KA1VFU
Tracy W Tarin
Kingston St
North Andover MA
01845

Call Sign: W1RAP
Gerard J Rowen
23 Lyman Rd
North Andover MA
01845

Call Sign: WA1OEC
William F Sherlock
60 Lyman Rd
North Andover MA
01845

Call Sign: KA1PNY
Eugene R Ducheneau
36 Main St
North Andover MA
01845

Call Sign: KB1JMR
Donald R Elliott
266 Main St

North Andover MA
01845

Call Sign: N1FDZ
Thomas D Ippolito Jr
514 Mass Ave
North Andover MA
01845

Call Sign: W1LVA
Leonard Somers
401 Massachusetts Ave
North Andover MA
01845

Call Sign: KB1UHK
Thomas D Ippolito
514 Massachusetts Ave
North Andover MA
01845

Call Sign: N1WIW
William T Godden
25 Morningside Ln
North Andover MA
01845

Call Sign: W1ZZO
William T Godden
25 Morningside Ln
North Andover MA
01845

Call Sign: N2UA
Thomas Varga
208 Old Cart Way
North Andover MA
01845

Call Sign: KB1SCL
Federico Padovan
120 Old Farm Rd
North Andover MA
01845

Call Sign: KB1PY
Paul D Weinstein
52 Olympic Ln
North Andover MA
01845

Call Sign: N1IJA
Cameron T Holland
7 Parker St

North Andover MA
01845

North Andover MA
018451325

North Andover MA
01845

North Andover MA
01845

Call Sign: N1IJB
Nicole Y Holland
7 Parker St
North Andover MA
01845

Call Sign: WB0YXC
Jeffrey M Cornblatt
1070 Salem St
North Andover MA
01845

Call Sign: KB1HLW
Peter G Bolis
26 Tolland Rd
North Andover MA
01845

Call Sign: KD1PG
Ruth A Seltzer
129 Weyland Cir
North Andover MA
018454935

Call Sign: N1SIW
Christopher H Neff
24 Patton Ln
North Andover MA
01845

Call Sign: N1LKR
Duane W Hurlburt
1187 Salem St
North Andover MA
01845

Call Sign: K1YB
Peter G Bolis
26 Tolland Rd
North Andover MA
01845

Call Sign: KI8II
Dennis A Atkins
77 Weyland Circle
North Andover MA
01845

Call Sign: WB7WOG
Neal H Neff
24 Patton Ln
North Andover MA
01845

Call Sign: KB1QYF
David A Dolben
114 Spring Hill Rd
North Andover MA
01845

Call Sign: KB1OKU
Gabriel Ricker
733 Turnpike St
North Andover MA
01845

Call Sign: N1UV
Maurice Martini
91 Weyland Circle
North Andover MA
01845

Call Sign: N1PRX
Paul R Teplitz
92 Quail Run
North Andover MA
01845

Call Sign: N1LRB
Stephen J Jaskela
37 Sullivan St
North Andover MA
01845

Call Sign: KA1SWT
Benjamin S Farnum
1370 Turnpike St
North Andover MA
01845

Call Sign: N1SUU
Alden K Coolidge Jr
11 Woodlea Rd
North Andover MA
01845

Call Sign: KA1OIL
Arthur L Schmitt Jr
416 Raleigh Tavern Ln
North Andover MA
01845

Call Sign: KB1WCZ
Paul Spencer
272 Summer St
North Andover MA
01845

Call Sign: KB1OUZ
Richard N Lee
42 Vest Way
North Andover MA
01845

Call Sign: KA1YKY
Celeste J Kneeland
North Andover MA
01845

Call Sign: N2AEO
Ron Zeheb
134 Rosemont Drive
North Andover MA
01845

Call Sign: AE1PS
Paul Spencer
272 Summer St
North Andover MA
01845

Call Sign: KB1EHI
Charles M Woods
5 Walker Rd Apt 2
North Andover MA
018453830

**FCC Amateur Radio
Licenses in North
Attleboro**

Call Sign: KN1N
Bradford S Gaudreau
336 Allen Ave
North Attleboro MA
02760

Call Sign: KB1HVM
Laurier A St Onge
43 Royal Crest Dr 12
North Andover MA
01845

Call Sign: KB1HAN
Bartley C Johnson
399 Summer St
North Andover MA
01845

Call Sign: N1PSA
Philip Westerhuijs
148 Waverly Rd
North Andover MA
01245

Call Sign: KA1WES
Carl G Quilitzsch Iii
227 Arnold Rd
North Attleboro MA
02760

Call Sign: W1QIH
Mark F TRUE
1 Royal Crest Dr Apt 7
North Andover MA
01845

Call Sign: KA1RIE
William P Krueger
204 Sutton Hill Rd
North Andover MA
01845

Call Sign: KB1IKD
John W Shea
158 Waverly Rd
North Andover MA
01845

Call Sign: W1WZ
Michael A Arminio
12 Brick Kiln Rd
North Attleboro MA
02760

Call Sign: W1JT
Emil J Tanana
10 Russett Ln

Call Sign: KB1UMU
Benson T Caswell
30 Tanglewood Lane

Call Sign: AB1BH
Maurice Martini
91 Weyland Cir

Call Sign: N1WIL
John A Rogers
115 Broad St
North Attleboro MA
02760

Call Sign: KB1NHP
Katherine Mae J
Rogers
115 Broad St
North Attleboro MA
02760

Call Sign: K1WIZ
John A Rogers
115 Broad St
North Attleboro MA
02760

Call Sign: KA1SAN
Steven T Hathaway
85 Broad St Apt 2
North Attleboro MA
02760

Call Sign: N1JCD
William C Farrell
360 Broadway
North Attleboro MA
02760

Call Sign: N1MPT
Glen S Downing
80 Broadway Unit 6
North Attleboro MA
02760

Call Sign: N1PRU
Patricia A Downing
80 Broadway Unit 6
North Attleboro MA
02760

Call Sign: KB1TQE
Shawn M Fontneau
15 Cedar Rd
North Attleboro MA
02760

Call Sign: KA1IG
Bruce B Alexander
39 Church St Apt 3
North Attleboro MA
02760

Call Sign: N1ATE
Walter T Karaniuk
287 Cumberland Ave
North Attleboro MA
02760

Call Sign: K1XE
Richard B Wall Jr
447 Cushman Rd
North Attleboro MA
02760

Call Sign: K1MUC
Wayne A Perzan
232 Draper Ave
North Attleboro MA
02760

Call Sign: N1KLE
Andrew P Young
317 E Washington St
C6
North Attleboro MA
02760

Call Sign: KB1JIX
James S Boyd
130 E Washington St
Unit 93
North Attleboro MA
02760

Call Sign: K1CIE
James S Boyd
130 E Washington St
Unit 93
North Attleboro MA
02760

Call Sign: N1IPR
Lawrence W Haines Iii
136 East St
North Attleboro MA
02760

Call Sign: N1LH
Lawrence W Haines Iii
136 East St
North Attleboro MA
02760

Call Sign: K1DSY
David J Bitar

633 East Washington
St
North Attleboro MA
027602494

Call Sign: N1DPG
Dana P Gaboury
64 Eddy St Apt 2
North Attleboro MA
02760

Call Sign: KB1QKX
Walter Cekala
105 Fales Rd
North Attleboro MA
02760

Call Sign: KB1WMU
Richard A Heaton
158 Fisher St Apt 1
North Attleboro MA
02760

Call Sign: N2SDF
GEORGE A RAGON
Jr
7 Franklin Ave
North Attleboro MA
02760

Call Sign: KB1TMK
Christopher C Mantia
27 George St
North Attleboro MA
027604159

Call Sign: W1CFR
Christopher C Mantia
27 George St
North Attleboro MA
027604159

Call Sign: KA1POJ
Diane L Fontaine
47 Glenfield Rd
North Attleboro MA
02760

Call Sign: N1LRJ
Thomas J Wainwright
70 Grove St
North Attleboro MA
02760

Call Sign: N1ZPJ
Glenn W Laflamme
92 Grove St
North Attleboro MA
02760

Call Sign: AA1ZX
Edward G Corbett
47 Haduk
North Attleboro MA
02760

Call Sign: N1SYP
Tim E Hutchins
317 High St
North Attleboro MA
02760

Call Sign: KA1EWN
John V Bellissimo
376 High St
North Attleboro MA
02760

Call Sign: W1SMH
Sturdy Memorial
Hospital Arc
376 High St
North Attleboro MA
02760

Call Sign: WB1DJM
William F Tomlinson
586 High St
North Attleboro MA
02760

Call Sign: KB1BA
Michael L
Worthington
704 Holmes Rd
North Attleboro MA
02760

Call Sign: N1ROO
William A Anderson
131 Horace Darling
Drive
North Attleboro MA
02760

Call Sign: KA1LKG
Gloria M Jordan
32 Johnson St

North Attleboro MA
02760

Call Sign: KB1DQU
David M Markt
50 Juniper Rd C3
North Attleboro MA
02760

Call Sign: K1DMM
David M Markt
50 Juniper Rd C3
North Attleboro MA
02760

Call Sign: K1SMT
Dana G Seaman
492 Kelley Blvd
North Attleboro MA
02760

Call Sign: KB1RWT
Toyoji Hirai
12 Kingsley Rd
North Attleboro MA
02760

Call Sign: N1CWS
David L O Brien
17 Lakeshore Dr Apt
A12
North Attleboro MA
02760

Call Sign: KB1WML
Ranjith Unnikrishnan
42 Landry Ave
North Attleboro MA
02760

Call Sign: W1YOW
Thomas J Klimiata Jr
975 Longview Dr
North Attleboro MA
02760

Call Sign: KB1LWH
Donald N Dupuis
984 Longview Dr
North Attleboro MA
02760

Call Sign: KB1MOY
Benjamin W Hodgkins

327 Mansfield Rd
North Attleborough
MA 02760

Call Sign: WA1QFV
Theodore S Oven
380 Mansfield Rd
North Attleboro MA
02760

Call Sign: KD1WW
Stuart A Daniels
30 Mc Keon Dr
North Attleboro MA
02760

Call Sign: WA1WNQ
Donald R Cleveland
195 Mc Keon Dr
North Attleboro MA
02760

Call Sign: W1CSG
Howard Gomes
259 Mendon Rd
North Attleboro MA
02760

Call Sign: N1NVE
Peter J Lamb
19 Metcalf Circle
North Attleboro MA
02760

Call Sign: KA1UE
Jeffrey P Davis
40 Monticello Dr
North Attleboro MA
02760

Call Sign: KA1FSV
Robert A Seguin
258 Mount Hope St
North Attleboro MA
027603939

Call Sign: WB1FEA
Fern E Lake
621 Mount Hope St
North Attleboro MA
02760

Call Sign: KD1TC
Daniel M Lampron

83 Mt Hope St
North Attleboro MA
02760

Call Sign: K1PKI
James M La Fratta
198 Mt Hope St
North Attleboro MA
02760

Call Sign: KB1NCX
James M Moriarty
595 Mt Hope St
North Attleboro MA
02760

Call Sign: KA1OZJ
Ronald J Desrosier
971 Mt Hope St
North Attleboro MA
02760

Call Sign: K1RII
Ronald J Desrosier
971 Mt Hope St
North Attleboro MA
02760

Call Sign: N1EZT
Pierre J Guimond
195 Mt Hope St
North Attleboro MA
02760

Call Sign: KB1MHY
Stephen C Vermette
68 N Washington St -
Unit 514
North Attleboro MA
02760

Call Sign: W1PAC
Stephen C Vermette
68 N Washington St -
Unit 514
North Attleboro MA
02760

Call Sign: KB1X
Robert A Benoit
785 Old Post Rd
North Attleboro MA
02760

Call Sign: N1BUV
Raymond A Howell
35 Old Wood Rd
North Attleboro MA
02760

Call Sign: K1KEJ
Frederick G Oakley
3 Orchard Dr
North Attleboro MA
02760

Call Sign: N1CNX
Arthur H Murphy
531 Paine Rd
North Attleborough
MA 02760

Call Sign: N1VKS
Kenneth A Oufour
47 Pleasant
North Attleboro MA
02760

Call Sign: N1FFE
David T Sturtevant
13 Prospect St
North Attleboro MA
02760

Call Sign: K1JMG
Charles W Doran
52 Rocky Knoll Dr
North Attleboro MA
02760

Call Sign: W1XS
Thomas A Bell
64 Scout Ln
North Attleboro MA
027604714

Call Sign: KB1WWV
Robert J Smith
389 Smith
North Attleboro MA
02760

Call Sign: KB1JLU
Alexander S Rullo
81 Spruce St
North Attleboro MA
02760

Call Sign: N1IKY
Kathleen Viveiros
21 Spruce St Apt 4
North Attleboro MA
02760

Call Sign: N1IKZ
James C Viveiros
21 Spruce St Apt 4
North Attleboro MA
02760

Call Sign: KB1HEP
Bradley E Read
35 Taylor St
North Attleboro MA
02760

Call Sign: WF1H
Bruce B Callahan
71 Towne St
North Attleboro MA
02760

Call Sign: KA1QID
Jonathan D Maslen
Towne St
North Attleborough
MA 02760

Call Sign: KA1FTW
Kevin M Rose
9 Tracy Beth Dr
North Attleboro MA
02760

Call Sign: WB1DJR
Ora C Belcher
130 W Washington St
Lot 33
North Attleboro MA
027602340

Call Sign: N1SSG
John L Parsons
177 West St
North Attleboro MA
02760

Call Sign: KA1PES
Arthur J Higginbotham
Jr
142 Westside Ave

North Attleboro MA
027601438

Call Sign: WC1AAW
Attleboro Emergency
Management
142 Westside Ave
North Attleboro MA
02760

Call Sign: N1ODA
Steven M Jankowski
33 William Tanner
Ave
North Attleboro MA
02760

Call Sign: KB1KLJ
North Attleboro High
School Amateur Radio
Club
1 Wilson W Whitty
Way
North Attleboro MA
02760

Call Sign: NA1HS
North Attleboro High
School Amateur Radio
Club
1 Wilson W Whitty
Way
North Attleboro MA
02760

Call Sign: K1FWA
Robert L Martell
1 Woodchip Square
North Attleboro MA
02760

**FCC Amateur Radio
Licenses in North
Billerica**

Call Sign: KB1CIC
Bruce G Mc Ardle
39 Mason Ave
North Billercia MA
018621143

Call Sign: KA1BGI
Richard G Beatty
Amherst St

North Billerica MA
01862

Call Sign: KB1WWK
Steve J Gauger
60 Brandon St
North Billerica MA
01862

Call Sign: N1MZN
Christopher R Eastman
45 Chelmsford Rd
North Billerica MA
01862

Call Sign: N1PRZ
George A Johns
10 Comet Ln
North Billerica MA
01862

Call Sign: KA1LEP
Thomas P Costas
29 Donna Rd
North Billerica MA
01862

Call Sign: WA1NYR
Alan D Tasker
64 Dyer St
North Billerica MA
018623118

Call Sign: WB1FUH
Edward S Jablonski
1 Green Meadow Dr
North Billerica MA
01862

Call Sign: WA1DCL
Bruce C Stacey
203 High St
North Billerica MA
01862

Call Sign: N1JZK
Michael J Paradie
12 Holt St
North Billerica MA
01862

Call Sign: N1IGZ
Murry G Marcano
16 Horman Rd

North Billerica MA
01862

Call Sign: N1VXH
Branden C Loizides
6 Ipswich St
North Billerica MA
01862

Call Sign: KA4PKU
Paul A La Fave Jr
7 Ipswich St
North Billerica MA
01862

Call Sign: N1HEZ
Fred B Kenyon
39 Letchworth Ave
North Billerica MA
01862

Call Sign: AC6YM
Gerd R Sapper
37 Liberty Dr
North Billerica MA
018623219

Call Sign: KB1DMO
Laura I Mellen
39 Mason Ave
North Billerica MA
018621143

Call Sign: KB1GNP
Jennifer Russo
43 Oak St
North Billerica MA
01862

Call Sign: KB1GRZ
Tara M Kirby
67 Old Elm St
North Billerica MA
01862

Call Sign: KB1FTL
Scot J Weisman
67 Old Elm St
North Billerica MA
018621439

Call Sign: N2VRS
Matthew M Lug
142 Parlmont Park

North Billerica MA
01862

Call Sign: N1ISG
Paul M Ware Iii
Parlmont Pk Apt 34
North Billerica MA
01862

Call Sign: KB1KTR
Kevin G Fallon
66 Rangeway Rd
North Billerica MA
01862

Call Sign: W6TOH
Russell Noftsker
288 Rangeway Rd
North Billerica MA
018622015

Call Sign: K1DOY
James H Peers
30 Rexhame St
North Billerica MA
01862

Call Sign: KB1FQK
Daniel D Hunt
6 Salem Rd
North Billerica MA
01862

Call Sign: K1XLO
Daniel D Hunt
6 Salem Rd
North Billerica MA
01862

Call Sign: WB1GHC
Stephen G Hunt
6 Salem Rd
North Billerica MA
01862

Call Sign: K1YA
Stephen G Hunt
6 Salem Rd
North Billerica MA
01862

Call Sign: WB1GAQ
George F Adam Iii
5 Stage Rd

North Billerica MA
018620211

Call Sign: KC1HC
William T Smith
North Billerica MA
01862

Call Sign: N1DRY
Gregory R Wright
North Billerica MA
018620090

Call Sign: KA1LFD
Paul H Whitman Iii
80 Rio Vista St
North Bllarica MA
01862

**FCC Amateur Radio
Licenses in North
Brookfield**

Call Sign: KA1RJY
Ronald L Karbowski
15 Birch Hill Rd
North Brookfield MA
01535

Call Sign: KB1GII
Jason A Thomas
39 Brookfield Rd
North Brookfield MA
01535

Call Sign: W1BUP
Walter W Nelson Jr
3 Central St
North Brookfield MA
01535

Call Sign: KB1HRL
Thomas J Ahearn
100 Downey Rd
North Brookfield MA
01535

Call Sign: N1ZSJ
James J Murphy
7 Forest St
North Brookfield MA
015350081

Call Sign: N1FRY

James A Flamand
23 Fullam Hill Rd
North Brookfield MA
01535

Call Sign: N1FSH
Lawrence H Soucie
73 Gilbert St
North Brookfield MA
01535

Call Sign: K1KCN
Arthur L Lindsey Jr
22 Main St
North Brookfield MA
01535

Call Sign: KB1KFN
Kevin S Parker
33 Mt Pleasant St
North Brookfield MA
01535

Call Sign: K1KCO
Elizabeth A Lindsey
22 S Main St
North Brookfield MA
015351435

Call Sign: KA1ONE
George J Sullivan
60 Shore Rd
North Brookfield MA
01535

**FCC Amateur Radio
Licenses in North
Cambridge**

Call Sign: KA1PTX
Paul R Viera
121 Clay St
North Cambridge MA
02140

**FCC Amateur Radio
Licenses in North
Chatham**

Call Sign: K1LJS
Lewis H Masson
33 Cove Hill Rd
North Chatham MA
02650

Call Sign: N1BTR
Douglas L Brunell
374 Orleans Rd
North Chatham MA
02650

Call Sign: W1VB
Vern J Brownell
661 Orleans Rd
North Chatham MA
02650

Call Sign: KB1VLI
Carol S Fano
44 Woodland Way
North Chatham MA
02650

Call Sign: K1CSF
Carol S Fano
44 Woodland Way
North Chatham MA
02650

Call Sign: N2HGP
Edward W Edwards Jr
111 Woodland Way
North Chatham MA
02650

Call Sign: W1SCD
William E Pyne
North Chatham MA
02650

**FCC Amateur Radio
Licenses in North
Chelmsford**

Call Sign: KB1OIR
Michael A Clancy
22 Arbor Rd
North Chelmsford MA
01863

Call Sign: WB1FHT
Robert W Chin
11 Augusta Way
North Chelmsford MA
018632050

Call Sign: K1KSY
John R Biro

18 Augusta Way
North Chelmsford MA
018632000

Call Sign: N1ATQ
Douglas N Chandler
47 Augusta Way
North Chelmsford MA
01863

Call Sign: K1AAJ
Darrel D Mallory
10 Berkshire Rd
North Chelmsford MA
018632113

Call Sign: K1EJ
Darrel D Mallory
10 Berkshire Rd
North Chelmsford MA
018632113

Call Sign: N1YDJ
Darrel D Mallory
10 Berkshire Rd
North Chelmsford MA
018632113

Call Sign: KB1NOR
Dro J Gregorian
3 Blueberry Lane
North Chelmsford MA
01863

Call Sign: KB1WIU
Alan L Teubner
90 Crooked Spring Rd
North Chelmsford MA
01863

Call Sign: KB1WNF
Patrick W Landrigan
7 Doral Dr
North Chelmsford MA
01863

Call Sign: KB1WNG
Robert W Landrigan
7 Doral Dr
North Chelmsford MA
01863

Call Sign: WA1GSF
David A Wallace

154 Dunstable Rd
North Chelmsford MA
018631202

Call Sign: N1RBE
Maureen D Polson
23 Edgelawn Ave
North Chelmsford MA
01863

Call Sign: N1RBP
Paul C Polson
23 Edgelawn Ave
North Chelmsford MA
01863

Call Sign: N1TPY
Emerson C Reed Jr
25 Edgelawn Ave
North Chelmsford MA
01863

Call Sign: N1VI
Emerson C Reed Jr
25 Edgelawn Ave
North Chelmsford MA
01863

Call Sign: W1AYC
Maurice T Martineau
37 Highland Ave
North Chelmsford MA
01863

Call Sign: KB1NOT
Laura M Desrochers
11 Kelshill Rd
North Chelmsford MA
01863

Call Sign: KB1NOS
Sara T Dion
6 Lamplighter Lane
North Chelmsford MA
01863

Call Sign: KB1HFT
George Kavanagh
1 Mansur St
North Chelmsford MA
018631710

Call Sign: N1TIN
Gerald A Bass

8 Penni Lane
North Chelmsford MA
018632330

Call Sign: N1DQE
Larry S Vidoli
55 Prescott Dr
North Chelmsford MA
01803

Call Sign: W1LSV
Larry S Vidoli
55 Prescott Dr
North Chelmsford MA
01863

Call Sign: KB0ZRU
Jonathan W Dixon
Scotty Hollow Dr
North Chelmsford MA
01863

Call Sign: AA1VO
Jonathan W Dixon
Scotty Hollow Dr
North Chelmsford MA
01863

Call Sign: AB1LA
Andrew J Anderson
1 Shore Dr
North Chelmsford MA
01863

Call Sign: W1VKZ
Andrew J Anderson
1 Shore Dr
North Chelmsford MA
01863

Call Sign: KB1WUI
Joao C Almeida
1 Technology Dr Apt
2121
North Chelmsford MA
01863

Call Sign: WN1V
Susan L Raisbeck
1 Technology Dr Apt
4125
North Chelmsford MA
01863

Call Sign: N1CLN
Paul A Simpson
24 Tobin Ave
North Chelmsford MA
01863

Call Sign: KA1TTT
Joy H Welsh
235 Wellman Ave
North Chelmsford MA
01863

Call Sign: N1JIR
Robert D Lansing
251 Wellman Ave
North Chelmsford MA
01863

Call Sign: N1CHZ
Timothy S Tait
817 Wellman Ave
North Chelmsford MA
01863

Call Sign: KB1OBL
Chad R Elliott
820 Wellman Ave
North Chelmsford MA
01863

Call Sign: WA1MGQ
Neil A Harmon
234 Wellman Ave
North Chelmsford MA
018631362

Call Sign: N1KMN
Anthony J Penta
903 Wellman Ave
North Chelmsford MA
01863

Call Sign: N1FFI
Richard D Coffman
North Chelmsford MA
01863

FCC Amateur Radio Licenses in North Dartmouth

Call Sign: KB1WGU
Madelyn C Gregory
87 Alpha St

North Dartmouth MA
02747

North Dartmouth MA
02747

North Dartmouth MA
027471151

North Dartmouth MA
02747

Call Sign: WA1VQA
Robert L Whitlow
4 Bartlett St
North Dartmouth MA
02747

Call Sign: W1ZYV
John G Carreiro
15 Crescent Dr
North Dartmouth MA
027473507

Call Sign: WB1ATN
Michel Chiron
603 Hixville Rd
North Dartmouth MA
027471562

Call Sign: WA1FAR
Robert W Bairos
868 Old Fall River Rd
North Dartmouth MA
027471204

Call Sign: KA1SPP
Matthew J Rovas
29 Bellevue St
North Dartmouth MA
02747

Call Sign: N1LMG
Dimas Amaral
280 Duane Ave
North Dartmouth MA
02747

Call Sign: W1MLN
Joseph Rogers
33 Holly Dr
North Dartmouth MA
02747

Call Sign: KB1AFS
Antero M Paiva
1212 Old Fall River Rd
North Darmouth MA
02747

Call Sign: WA1VXY
Edmund J Rovas
29 Bellevue St
North Dartmouth MA
027471981

Call Sign: K1JGV
David G Dean
21 Elizabeth St
North Dartmouth MA
02747

Call Sign: N1BLF
Robert R Zeida
37 Juliette St
North Dartmouth MA
02747

Call Sign: K1IBR
William M Miller Jr
49 Old Westport Rd
North Dartmouth MA
02747

Call Sign: KC1OG
David J Goldstein
45 Birchwood Terrace
North Dartmouth MA
02747

Call Sign: KB1VAN
Alexander L Davis
461 Faunce Corner Rd
North Dartmouth MA
02747

Call Sign: W1YEG
Henry C Zeitler
83 Longview Dr
North Dartmouth MA
02747

Call Sign: KA1BZE
Margaret M Gaffney
1 Orchard St
North Dartmouth MA
02747

Call Sign: W1DJG
David J Goldstein
45 Birchwood Terrace
North Dartmouth MA
02747

Call Sign: N1ZCQ
Michael R Martin
26 Goldfinch Dr
North Dartmouth MA
02747

Call Sign: WB1GJR
Susan E Ponte
357 Lucy Little Rd
North Dartmouth MA
02747

Call Sign: N1OHV
Theodore T Wright
1 Orchard St
North Dartmouth MA
02747

Call Sign: KA1UNN
David R Dirk
5 Brownell Ave
North Dartmouth MA
02747

Call Sign: KA1YDH
Kenneth J Lent
171 Hathaway Rd
North Dartmouth MA
02747

Call Sign: K1DIY
Matthew C Howland
51 Massachusetts Ave
North Dartmouth MA
027471622

Call Sign: KA1YDG
Robert J Peckham
112 Pine Island Rd
North Dartmouth MA
02747

Call Sign: N1NJF
Dorothy A Szala
111 Chase Rd
North Dartmouth MA
02747

Call Sign: KB1EBQ
Alan R Carrier
162 High Hill Rd
North Dartmouth MA
02747

Call Sign: K1BOC
Milton V Francis
37 Mc Cormick St
North Dartmouth MA
027472615

Call Sign: N1LIE
Karen L Peckham
112 Pine Island Rd
North Dartmouth MA
02747

Call Sign: W1EV
Scott E Szala
111 Chase Rd
North Dartmouth MA
02747

Call Sign: W1UID
Arthur J Valois
716 High Hill Rd
North Dartmouth MA
02747

Call Sign: K1VJZ
Octave S Pimentel
66 Morton Ave
North Dartmouth MA
02747

Call Sign: K1SLI
John C Rogers Sr
22 Pinehurst
North Dartmouth MA
02747

Call Sign: N1IXC
Joseph E Krisnosky Jr
76 Colonial Way

Call Sign: KB1NB
Michael J Mc Donald
113 Highland Ave

Call Sign: N1KXG
Charles F Crooks
538 Old Fall River Rd

Call Sign: KB1WGS
Rakesh Kannan
2 Pinehurst St

North Dartmouth MA
02747

Call Sign: KB1WGT
Margaret J Kannan
2 Pinehurst St
North Dartmouth MA
02747

Call Sign: W1GJD
David G Black
535 Reed Rd
North Dartmouth MA
02747

Call Sign: WA1CXH
Frank A Queripal
818 Reed Rd
North Dartmouth MA
02747

Call Sign: KE1EZ
Manuel L Leite
1233 Reed Rd
North Dartmouth MA
02747

Call Sign: N1XPG
Manuel N Alcobia
466 Reed Rd
North Dartmouth MA
027471819

Call Sign: N1NRH
Michael D Patnode
14 Richard Alan Rd
North Dartmouth MA
02747

Call Sign: W1BMQ
Edward R Lopes
9 Robert St
North Dartmouth MA
02747

Call Sign: WA1HJD
Edward J Magiera
5 Sable Ave
North Dartmouth MA
02747

Call Sign: N1ADW
Richard P D Auteuil
179 Slocum Rd

North Dartmouth MA
02747

Call Sign: KB1JTR
Joseph J Luiz
5 Strawberry Ln
North Dartmouth MA
02747

Call Sign: KA1THM
Mathew Vangel
15 Sundance Rd
North Dartmouth MA
02747

Call Sign: W1JPN
Jean Pierre Nuss
63 Tucker Lane
North Dartmouth MA
02747

Call Sign: KB1JHV
Jean-Pierre Nuss
63 Tucker Ln
North Dartmouth MA
02747

Call Sign: K1AHA
Richard J Halliwell
934 Tucker Rd
North Dartmouth MA
02747

Call Sign: N1DEW
Bertha B Rogers
1057 Tucker Rd
North Dartmouth MA
027473119

Call Sign: W1EB
Earle K Rogers
1057 Tucker Rd
North Dartmouth MA
02747

Call Sign: N1MVY
Joseph E Demers Jr
91 Wilbur Ave
North Dartmouth MA
02747

Call Sign: N1OTH
David J Banville

26 William Bradford
Rd
North Dartmouth MA
02747

FCC Amateur Radio Licenses in North Dighton

Call Sign: KA1KTM
William R Pruitt
228 Chase St
North Dighton MA
02764

Call Sign: WA1OHA
Alan M Huntress
2321 Fieldstone Dr
North Dighton MA
02764

Call Sign: KB1CYP
John S Windle
244 Forest St
North Dighton MA
02764

Call Sign: WA1GUS
John T Daley Jr
300 Lincoln Ave E40
North Dighton MA
02764

Call Sign: K1SX
David A Eckerson
751 Oak St
North Dighton MA
02764

Call Sign: KA1YLL
Alfred Pacheco Jr
925 Oak St
North Dighton MA
02764

Call Sign: KA1KDH
Christopher W Ready
484 Old Somerset Ave
North Dighton MA
027641815

Call Sign: N1KQZ
Douglas C Cugini
Po Box 245

North Dighton MA
02764

Call Sign: WA1LNV
John S Kimpton
454 Spring St
North Dighton MA
02764

Call Sign: AE1R
John S Kimpton
454 Spring St
North Dighton MA
02764

Call Sign: KB1LVZ
Michael J Harwood
1317 Susan Rd
North Dighton MA
02764

Call Sign: WA1VED
Theodore M Small
974 Windfield Ln
North Dighton MA
02764

Call Sign: WA1GLK
Russell E Rothwell
North Dighton MA
02764

Call Sign: KB1KDI
Nancy D Cugini
North Dighton MA
02764

FCC Amateur Radio Licenses in North Eastham

Call Sign: KA1SBX
Elizabeth A Sheptyck
North Eastham MA
02651

Call Sign: KA1SCB
Wesley G Rogers
North Eastham MA
02651

Call Sign: KA1SCC
Benjamin T Andrulot

North Eastham MA
02651

Call Sign: KA1SCK
Mary Kate Sandblom
North Eastham MA
02651

Call Sign: KA1SCM
Ryan T Kennedy
North Eastham MA
02651

Call Sign: KA1SCQ
Randy B Garry Jr
North Eastham MA
02651

Call Sign: KA1SCU
Mark W Shakliks
North Eastham MA
02651

Call Sign: KA1SCV
Rachael T Sapp
North Eastham MA
02651

Call Sign: KA1SCX
Raegan M Frazier
North Eastham MA
02651

Call Sign: KA1SCY
Philip C Burt
North Eastham MA
02651

Call Sign: KA1SDF
Michael P Riordan Jr
North Eastham MA
02651

Call Sign: KA1SDX
Timothy W Lloyd
North Eastham MA
02651

Call Sign: KA1SDZ
Sarah M Delaney
North Eastham MA
02651

Call Sign: KA1SEC

Marco G Cestaro
North Eastham MA
02651

Call Sign: KA1SEH
John T Hilferty Jr
North Eastham MA
02651

Call Sign: KA1SEP
James C Mc Makin Jr
North Eastham MA
02651

Call Sign: KA1SFM
Adam E Bohannon
North Eastham MA
02651

Call Sign: KA1SII
Michael D Carlsen
North Eastham MA
02651

Call Sign: KA1TVD
Tessa J Szedlak
North Eastham MA
02651

Call Sign: KA1TVE
Jeremy A Turner
North Eastham MA
02651

Call Sign: KA1TVF
Kristi K Turowski
North Eastham MA
02651

Call Sign: KA1TVG
Hollie A Zimmer
North Eastham MA
02651

Call Sign: KA1TVH
Elizabeth R Dumas
North Eastham MA
02651

Call Sign: KA1TVP
Kimberly E Levasseur
North Eastham MA
02651

Call Sign: KA1TVR
Shannon L Mac
Donald
North Eastham MA
02651

Call Sign: KA1TVV
Kelley A Sexton
North Eastham MA
02651

Call Sign: KA1TWA
Gregory A Bartz
North Eastham MA
02651

Call Sign: KA1TWB
Matthew T Bartz
North Eastham MA
02651

Call Sign: KA1TWE
Abby M Burt
North Eastham MA
02651

Call Sign: KA1TWG
Aaron G Cestaro
North Eastham MA
02651

Call Sign: KA1VSI
Kathrine M Sheptyck
North Eastham MA
02651

Call Sign: KA1VSJ
Justin C Bohannon
North Eastham MA
02651

Call Sign: KA1VSK
Brian C Reeves
North Eastham MA
02651

Call Sign: KA1VSR
Patrick W Varley
North Eastham MA
02651

Call Sign: KA1VSS
Brian E Rossi

North Eastham MA
02651

Call Sign: KA1VSU
Fawn A Wright
North Eastham MA
02651

Call Sign: KA1VTA
Daniel C Mokrycki
North Eastham MA
02651

Call Sign: KA1VTF
Matthew J Riordan
North Eastham MA
02651

Call Sign: KA1VTL
Rory P Kennedy
North Eastham MA
02651

Call Sign: KA1YWA
Heather S Pearston
North Eastham MA
02651

Call Sign: KA1YWD
Bryan D Berg
North Eastham MA
02651

Call Sign: KB1BAN
Elizabeth M Pecce
North Eastham MA
02651

Call Sign: KB1BAR
Kristen E Badera
North Eastham MA
02651

Call Sign: KA1WCY
William W Barnes
5350 State Hwy
North Eastham MA
02642

Call Sign: KB1BAU
Christopher R Burt
185 Alston Ave
North Eastham MA
02651

Call Sign: KB1BBB
Amy C Watson
130 Anne Rd
North Eastham MA
02651

Call Sign: KA1VWZ
Larasa E Mc Makin
Barrow House Rd
North Eastham MA
02651

Call Sign: KA1WDD
Kristina M M Lee
1266 Bayside Dr
North Eastham MA
02051

Call Sign: KA1VTC
Patricia A Anderson
Box 1377
North Eastham MA
02651

Call Sign: KA1SEG
Teresa M Roza
Box 287
North Eastham MA
02651

Call Sign: KA1VSZ
Ian D Hatch
Box 381
North Eastham MA
02651

Call Sign: KA1VTG
Kate E Douglas
Box 398
North Eastham MA
02651

Call Sign: WA1WLS
Glenn A Boyd
Box 681
North Eastham MA
02651

Call Sign: KA1SEF
James C Barnes
Box Ah
North Eastham MA
02651

Call Sign: KA1TWD
Damon J Brunelle
Brackett Rd
North Eastham MA
02642

Call Sign: KB1BAJ
Jason D Gritzbach
125 Circle Dr
North Eastham MA
02651

Call Sign: KA1TWH
Matthew H Cole
Drawer D
North Eastham MA
02651

Call Sign: KB1BAT
Shannon M Burke
16 Gile Rd
North Eastham MA
02651

Call Sign: KA1VSQ
Timothy P O Neill
Gimlet Way
North Eastham MA
02651

Call Sign: W1BEE
Gary Derman
55 Harding Rd
North Eastham MA
026511792

Call Sign: KB1AZX
Todd N Bohannon
170 Higgin Rd
North Eastham MA
02651

Call Sign: KB1BAL
David G Hill
20 Hill Rd
North Eastham MA
02651

Call Sign: KB1BAV
Brian A Jalbert
480 Massasoit Rd
North Eastham MA
02651

Call Sign: KA1YWE
Patrick B Savin
1850 Massasoit Rd
North Eastham MA
02651

Call Sign: KA1FZA
Angelo F Addona
2455 Nauset Rd
North Eastham MA
02651

Call Sign: KB1BAA
Kim M Coakley
2660 Nauset Rd
North Eastham MA
02651

Call Sign: KA1VSM
Tabitha L Kreber
Ne Q651
North Eastham MA
02651

Call Sign: KA1SDY
Philip G Becotte
Pine Needle Way
North Eastham MA
02651

Call Sign: KB1BAC
Rachael E Burns
20 Roscoe Ave
North Eastham MA
02651

Call Sign: W1FHS
Frank Schumann
Seaward Way
North Eastham MA
02651

Call Sign: KA1WEU
Erin E Oberist
Snow Rd
North Eastham MA
02651

Call Sign: KB1BAI
Tiffany L Gremila
80 Toland Dr
North Eastham MA
02651

Call Sign: KB1BAQ
Andrew J Varley
Welpley Rd
North Eastham MA
02651

Call Sign: KB1AEL
Christian A Reichers
155 Whelpley Rd Rr 2
North Eastham MA
02642

Call Sign: KA1VTE
Justin A Reichers
155 Whepley Rd Rr 2
North Eastham MA
02651

Call Sign: KA1WCZ
Carrie E Led Duke
North Eastham MA
02691

Call Sign: KA1YWF
James N Goodrich
North Eastham MA
02651

Call Sign: KA1YWG
Katherine Duff
North Eastham MA
02651

Call Sign: KA1YWJ
Alexander J Cestaro
North Eastham MA
02651

Call Sign: KA1YWN
Sarah B Radke
North Eastham MA
02651

Call Sign: KA1YWP
Nicole M Ness
North Eastham MA
02651

Call Sign: KA1YWS
Teresa A Lind
North Eastham MA
02651

Call Sign: KA1YWT
Erin L Haggerty
North Eastham MA
02651

Call Sign: KA1YWU
Kevin M Goodrich
North Eastham MA
02651

Call Sign: KA1YWW
Ricky L Carlsen
North Eastham MA
02651

Call Sign: KA1YWY
Ian B Mack
North Eastham MA
02651

Call Sign: KA1ZGB
Jared L Souther
North Eastham MA
02651

Call Sign: KB1AEI
Nicholas H Canu
North Eastham MA
02651

Call Sign: KB1AEK
Matt O Johnston
North Eastham MA
02651

Call Sign: KB1AEM
Phillip J Wetmore
North Eastham MA
02651

Call Sign: KB1AZY
Emily K Dumas
North Eastham MA
02651

Call Sign: KB1BAF
David C Adams
North Eastham MA
02651

Call Sign: KB1BAZ
Carol A Pearston
North Eastham MA
02651

Call Sign: N1QWO
Kevin J Varley
North Eastham MA
02651

Call Sign: KB1BBC
Michael J Plakas
North Eastham MA
02651

FCC Amateur Radio Licenses in North Easton

Call Sign: KA1WYV
David A Gibbs
224 Bay Rd
North Easton MA
02356

Call Sign: KB1LMZ
Jason D Goveia
20 Canton St
North Easton MA
023561345

Call Sign: N1RYN
Robert J Amoroso
126 Chestnut St
North Easton MA
02356

Call Sign: K1AD
The Brown Radio Club
9 Day St
North Easton MA
02356

Call Sign: NN1P
Gregory J Galer
9 Day St
North Easton MA
02356

Call Sign: KA1OGK
Donald J Dion
430 Foundry St
North Easton MA
02356

Call Sign: N1CTO
David Finstein
15 Harlow St

North Easton MA
02356

Call Sign: N1DH
J Daniel Heather
27 Heritage Dr
North Easton MA
02356

Call Sign: KB1TMB
Stephen M Daigle
8 Hillington Ave
North Easton MA
02356

Call Sign: K1ESQ
Colin W Gillis
8 Hillington Drive
North Easton MA
02356

Call Sign: KA1VNL
Thomas M Dupont
88 Lincoln St
North Easton MA
02356

Call Sign: W1KEE
George E Dupont
88 Lincoln St
North Easton MA
023561712

Call Sign: W1LQB
Joseph F Goveia
192 Lincoln St
North Easton MA
02356

Call Sign: KB1FBM
Robert A Klane
270 Lincoln St
North Easton MA
02356

Call Sign: N1CPR
Kenneth M Klane
270 Lincoln St
North Easton MA
02356

Call Sign: N1YSQ
Henri C Acacia
302 Lincoln St

North Easton MA
02356

Call Sign: N1XE
Richard P Freeman
10 Littlefield Lane
North Easton MA
023563634

Call Sign: KB1KZG
Jon S Gilmore
12 Main St
North Easton MA
023561430

Call Sign: KB1KZJ
Jon S Gilmore
12 Main St
North Easton MA
023561430

Call Sign: W1JSG
Jon S Gilmore
12 Main St
North Easton MA
023561430

Call Sign: WA1BHF
John J Marshall
7 Marshall Rd
North Easton MA
023561006

Call Sign: W1DCY
Merrill E Spiller Jr
3 Oak Ridge Dr
North Easton MA
02356

Call Sign: N1MSM
Carl Peters
2 Olde Stable Ln
North Easton MA
02356

Call Sign: K1NFO
Edward M Eidelman
81 Poquanticut Ave
North Easton MA
02356

Call Sign: K1AL
Alan W Pond
6 Robin Lane

North Easton MA
02356

Call Sign: KA1BUZ
John J St Onge
11 Scott Dr
North Easton MA
02356

Call Sign: W1EYY
Robert O De Witt
54 Sheridan St
North Easton MA
02356

Call Sign: WB1GVB
Michael J Freeman
194 Sheridan St
North Easton MA
02356

Call Sign: KB1SAM
Michael J Freeman
194 Sheridan St
North Easton MA
02356

Call Sign: NS1R
Steven E Hershman
10 Truman Dr
North Easton MA
02356

Call Sign: N1XJJ
Erkki E Haikola
35 Western Ave
North Easton MA
02356

Call Sign: K1BHR
William J Walsh
42 Western Ave
North Easton MA
02356

Call Sign: N1LVY
David P Odabashian
59 Williams St
North Easton MA
02356

**FCC Amateur Radio
Licenses in North
Egremont**

Call Sign: N7DIS
Diane L Fratalone
24 Boice Rd
North Egremont MA
012520046

Call Sign: N1ZNV
Alan F Carter
42 Millard Rd
North Egremont MA
01252

Call Sign: KB1GDS
Peter D Campbell
North Egremont MA
01252

Call Sign: KB1PDC
Peter D Campbell
North Egremont MA
01252

**FCC Amateur Radio
Licenses in North
Falmouth**

Call Sign: N1DGO
Bernard J Nolan
24 Althea Rd
North Falmouth MA
02556

Call Sign: KB1HJM
Paul V Kenneally
40 Althea Rd
North Falmouth MA
02556

Call Sign: AA6PN
Richard E Currier
119 Althea Rd
North Falmouth MA
025563121

Call Sign: W6ZEN
Richard E Currier
119 Althea Rd
North Falmouth MA
025563121

Call Sign: AA1FB
Richard E Currier
119 Althea Rd

North Falmouth MA
025563121

Call Sign: W1DO
W Ernest Bosselman
19 Arthur Hennessey
Rd
North Falmouth MA
025560035

Call Sign: K1MGH
Richard A Wiklund
Md
79 Bay Rd
North Falmouth MA
02556

Call Sign: W1YRS
George H Holmes
39 Bay Rd 598
North Falmouth MA
02556

Call Sign: N1JNY
Earl R Ottey Jr
Box 537
North Falmouth MA
02556

Call Sign: N1MRM
Alan T Fowler
Box 850
North Falmouth MA
02556

Call Sign: KA1TNK
Alfred S Kuntz
416 Boxberry Hill Rd
North Falmouth MA
02556

Call Sign: W1LJD
Herbert R Davenport
30 Cameron Rd
North Falmouth MA
02556

Call Sign: N1DOX
Robert E Liddell
33 Cameron Rd
North Falmouth MA
02556

Call Sign: KA1QPB

David A Rugg
25 Crowell Pond Ln
North Falmouth MA
025562833

Call Sign: N1PIB
Elizabeth H Renaghan
44 Deer Run Ln
North Falmouth MA
02556

Call Sign: N1PIT
Peter W Renaghan
44 Deer Run Ln
North Falmouth MA
02556

Call Sign: N1DAX
Willis M Partridge Jr
4 Eldredge Dr
North Falmouth MA
02556

Call Sign: N1LNJ
Ralph N Lorson Jr
40 Fernwood Rd
North Falmouth MA
02556

Call Sign: N1JCJ
John C Hotchkiss Jr
104 Heather Ln
North Falmouth MA
02556

Call Sign: N1JUZ
Walter L Bzibziak
23 Old Forge Rd
North Falmouth MA
02556

Call Sign: N1ILO
John D Todd
30 Old Forge Rd
North Falmouth MA
02556

Call Sign: KA1FLP
Albert M Bradley
160 Old Main Rd
North Falmouth MA
02556

Call Sign: KA1UJU

Deborah T Bradley
160 Old Main Rd
North Falmouth MA
02556

Call Sign: N1GJJ
Ronan F Chartois
160 Old Main Rd
North Falmouth MA
02556

Call Sign: KC2F
Don J Dudley
52 Pebble Ln
North Falmouth MA
02556

Call Sign: KB1UDW
Benjamin J Polloni
48 Wild Harbor Rd
North Falmouth MA
02556

Call Sign: WA1TGL
James J Tomlin
North Falmouth MA
02556

Call Sign: N1LNK
Janice M Lorson
North Falmouth MA
02556

Call Sign: KB1JXF
Richard A Wiklund
North Falmouth MA
02556

Call Sign: AA1EN
Sallye A Davis
North Falmouth MA
025561467

Call Sign: N1KNS
L Barry Evans
North Falmouth MA
02556

Call Sign: N1LND
Frederick L Pratt
North Falmouth MA
02556

Call Sign: N1RZY

Eugene R Coe
North Falmouth MA
02556

Call Sign: KB1GSN
Terrence K Hinds
North Falmouth MA
02556

Call Sign: KB1HJK
Leslie R Lichtenstein
North Falmouth MA
02556

FCC Amateur Radio Licenses in North Grafton

Call Sign: KA1CTH
Wayne B Warwick
40 Airport Rd
North Grafton MA
01536

Call Sign: W1VMS
Henry R Bernier
18 Bedford Dr
North Grafton MA
01536

Call Sign: N1TQL
Charles T Glodas
34 Bernard Rd
North Grafton MA
01536

Call Sign: K1GLR
Louis E Kuchinsky
211 Brigham Hill Rd
North Grafton MA
01536

Call Sign: N1FRU
Michael J Paradise Sr
215 Brigham Hill Rd
North Grafton MA
01536

Call Sign: KB1BUF
Grafton Middle School
Amateur Radio Club
215 Brigham Hill Rd
North Grafton MA
01536

Call Sign: W1JI
Roger D Demers
215 Brigham Hill Rd
North Grafton MA
01536

Call Sign: KA1WON
Christopher J Mead
217 Brigham Hill Rd
North Grafton MA
01536

Call Sign: KB1NBF
Clare J Garabedian
2 Christmas Tree Lane
North Grafton MA
01536

Call Sign: WA1KRJ
Charles A Butkus
60 Countryside Rd
North Grafton MA
01536

Call Sign: KB1VIM
John P Inman
10 Creeper Hill Rd
North Grafton MA
01536

Call Sign: KA1IXQ
Peter L Ballantyne
68 East St
North Grafton MA
01536

Call Sign: KB1VCN
Michelle L Fournier
8 Elm St Apt 3
North Grafton MA
01536

Call Sign: WA1HFJ
Charlotte L Pinfield
Forest Ln
North Grafton MA
01536

Call Sign: KB1LYL
Robert E Havasy
6 Glen St
North Grafton MA
01536

Call Sign: W1REH
Robert E Havasy
6 Glen St
North Grafton MA
01536

Call Sign: WA1OPN
Gayle A Sabonaitis
17 Hawthorne St
North Grafton MA
01536

Call Sign: W1ONA
Anthony P Kuklierus
6 Hingham Rd
North Grafton MA
01536

Call Sign: KC6NWH
Richard M Green
5 Hitchings Rd
North Grafton MA
01536

Call Sign: K1KQS
John G Chenis
8 Kay St
North Grafton MA
01536

Call Sign: N1UWH
David S Walsh
9 Lordvale Blvd
North Grafton MA
01536

Call Sign: N1GAH
Jonathan W Lacob
7 Martin Dr
North Grafton MA
015361236

Call Sign: KB1PPW
Matt P Batchelder
134 Old Westboro Rd
North Grafton MA
01536

Call Sign: WA1OII
Peter D Morico
154 Old Westborough
Rd

North Grafton MA
01536

Call Sign: WB1FEM
Edward H Thorne Iv
2 Paxton Court
North Grafton MA
01536

Call Sign: KA1PVK
Timothy E Roberts
24 Samuel Dr
North Grafton MA
01536

Call Sign: KB1LYQ
Roger Will
8 Whitney St
North Grafton MA
01536

Call Sign: W1LLR
Roger Will
8 Whitney St
North Grafton MA
01536

FCC Amateur Radio Licenses in North Hampton

Call Sign: KB1GCU
David L Kinner
37 Prospect Ave
North Hampton MA
01060

FCC Amateur Radio Licenses in North Harwich

Call Sign: KA1KYC
Robert C Goodrich
19 Herring Run Rd
North Harwich MA
02645

FCC Amateur Radio Licenses in North Hatfield

Call Sign: N1GJX
Paul J Lapinski
169 Pantry Rd

North Hatfield MA
010660115

Call Sign: WA1UWX
James M O Brien
337 West St
North Hatfield MA
01066

Call Sign: KB1IAC
Justin F Herzig
North Hatfield MA
010660214

FCC Amateur Radio Licenses in North Oxford

Call Sign: KB1LXM
Daniel J Butler
36 Comins Rd
North Oxford MA
01537

Call Sign: N1BEA
Carl O Olson
89 Leicester St
North Oxford MA
01537

Call Sign: W1MED
Craig R Gagner
152 Southbridge Rd
North Oxford MA
01537

Call Sign: W1MMG
Maria M Gagner
152 Southbridge Rd
North Oxford MA
01537

Call Sign: W1MSG
Craig R Gagner
152 Southbridge Rd
North Oxford MA
01537

Call Sign: N1INW
William N Halcrow
North Oxford MA
01537

Call Sign: KB1TJK

Kapriel Arakelian
North Oxford MA
01537

Call Sign: K1KAP
Kapriel Arakelian
North Oxford MA
01537

FCC Amateur Radio Licenses in North Pembroke

Call Sign: W1AZ
George B Gardner
North Pembroke MA
02358

FCC Amateur Radio Licenses in North Quincy

Call Sign: KC1XI
George A Clisham
126 Billings St
North Quincy MA
02171

Call Sign: W1YR
George A Clisham
126 Billings St
North Quincy MA
02171

Call Sign: KA1UFT
Lawrence A Otis
35 Birch St
North Quincy MA
02171

Call Sign: KB1SGO
BRIAN F Mc NAMEE
133 Commander Shea
Blvd 304
North Quincy MA
02171

Call Sign: KB1BLK
Kamalakar Gulukota
30 French St 412
North Quincy MA
02171

Call Sign: KB1NZZ

John W Chetwynd Sr
36 Glover Ave
North Quincy MA
02171

Call Sign: N1NQN
Timothy E Lynch Jr
93 Glover Ave
North Quincy MA
02171

Call Sign: K1TOZ
Lawrence Sava
17 Holyoke St
North Quincy MA
02171

Call Sign: K1ZOK
W Edwin Lambert Jr
234 Newbury Ave
North Quincy MA
02171

Call Sign: N1XNY
Hsi Hsun Wu
115 W Squantum St
1012
North Quincy MA
02171

Call Sign: WA1IZW
Mihailo Repovich
55 Walnut St
North Quincy MA
02171

FCC Amateur Radio Licenses in North Reading

Call Sign: N1YDF
Jonathan F Belinowiz
3 Adrian Drive
North Reading MA
018641553

Call Sign: W1CWZ
Philip W Sewall
33 Bow St
North Reading MA
01864

Call Sign: KB1MWC
William J Piper

6 Burditt Rd	141 Elm St	1 James Millen Rd	258 Main St Apt 12
North Reading MA	North Reading MA	North Reading MA	North Reading MA
018642115	01864	01864	01864

Call Sign: W1BRX
William J Piper
6 Burditt Rd
North Reading MA
018642115

Call Sign: W1HFX
Frank M Mason
225 Elm St
North Reading MA
01864

Call Sign: KB1WAY
Richard D Ward
1 James Millen Rd
North Reading MA
01864

Call Sign: KA1QJJ
William C Connors Jr
279 Main St Apt 16
North Reading MA
018641351

Call Sign: WA1SIV
John W Gleason
6 Burditt St
North Reading MA
01864

Call Sign: N1DCW
Frank M Mason
225 Elm St
North Reading MA
01864

Call Sign: W1HYG
Philip K Hathaway
1 Larchmont Rd
North Reading MA
01864

Call Sign: W1ZGI
Russell E Morris
103 Marblehead St
North Reading MA
01864

Call Sign: N1YQW
Alexander D Mc Leod
56 Burroughs Rd
North Reading MA
018641103

Call Sign: WB1FAB
Etta F Mason
225 Elm St
North Reading MA
01864

Call Sign: N1FOS
William R Matyuf
12 Leclair Rd
North Reading MA
01864

Call Sign: N1OHT
Scott E Harrison
3 Mentus Farm Lane
North Reading MA
01864

Call Sign: N1UIO
Robert K Pierce
4 Caroline Rd
North Reading MA
01864

Call Sign: N1QEC
Alan Walker
11 Flash Rd
North Reading MA
01864

Call Sign: KA1HDT
Penny J Richards
15 Leland Rd
North Reading MA
01864

Call Sign: KD1Q
Scott E Harrison
3 Mentus Farm Lane
North Reading MA
01864

Call Sign: KB1WNB
Scott R Pepi
63 Central St Unit 205
North Reading MA
01864

Call Sign: KB1NNA
Jacqulyn L Jones
9 Flint St
North Reading MA
018642805

Call Sign: WB1FYH
David M Richards
15 Leland Rd
North Reading MA
01864

Call Sign: WD1G
John Nicosia
85 North St
North Reading MA
01864

Call Sign: N1CHF
Steven L Boomhower
9 Chester St
North Reading MA
01864

Call Sign: N1SWE
Alfred L Lisby
25 Gordon Rd
North Reading MA
01864

Call Sign: N1STE
Robert J Van Laethem
37 Lindor Rd
North Reading MA
01864

Call Sign: N1DBE
William D Mc Donnell
158 North St
North Reading MA
01864

Call Sign: N1GET
Marcial Bones Jr
20 Country Club Rd
North Reading MA
01864

Call Sign: WA1HTP
Philip P Maguire Jr
1 Greenbriar Dr 107
North Reading MA
018643124

Call Sign: KB1TKK
Michael P Callahan Sr
10 Macarthur Rd
North Reading MA
01864

Call Sign: WM1X
William D Mc Donnell
158 North St
North Reading MA
01864

Call Sign: N1CQU
Susan M Gillespie
141 Elm St
North Reading MA
01864

Call Sign: AB1HF
Bruce D Wedlock
25 Hickory Lane
North Reading MA
01864

Call Sign: K1MPC
Michael P Callahan Sr
10 Macarthur Rd
North Reading MA
01864

Call Sign: WA1ZFG
Charles M Imbracsio
62 Northridge Drive
North Reading MA
018643162

Call Sign: N1CSO
Edward J Gillespie

Call Sign: KB1WAX
John P Ward

Call Sign: N1PJR
Christopher J Woods

Call Sign: KB1TQV
Karl E Berg

241 Park St
North Reading MA
01864

Call Sign: WA1DDZ
William C Blatchley
23 Pine Ridge Rd
North Reading MA
01864

Call Sign: KA1BKS
Donald F Gonzalo
7 Sachem St
North Reading MA
01864

Call Sign: N1YPJ
Donald L Holden
9 Southwick Rd
North Reading MA
01864

Call Sign: N1MGV
Steven L Green
53 Southwick Rd
North Reading MA
018642113

Call Sign: K1EP
Edward C Parish
9 Spoon Way
North Reading MA
01864

Call Sign: W1KNI
Kenneth W Robbins Sr
18 Sunset Ave
North Reading MA
018641427

Call Sign: KA1BKR
John E Joyce Iii
9 Sylvia Rd
North Reading MA
01864

Call Sign: N1ESG
Warren R Pearce
5 Tower Hill Rd
North Reading MA
01864

Call Sign: N1IUS
Kimberly F Smith

North Reading MA
01864

Call Sign: N1JBJ
William P N Smith
North Reading MA
01864

**FCC Amateur Radio
Licenses in North
Scituate**

Call Sign: K1AAO
Edward C Kimpton
15 Mordecal Lincoln
Rd
North Scituate MA
02066

**FCC Amateur Radio
Licenses in North
Truro**

Call Sign: K1SNV
Ronald F Friese
North Truro MA
02652

Call Sign: KB1BOE
Luther A Bumps
10 Bay View Dr
North Truro MA
026520277

Call Sign: K1BMU
F Wesley Garran
Box 2
North Truro MA
02652

Call Sign: KB1HVX
Mark B Adams
Route 6
North Truro MA
02652

Call Sign: N1XIX
William J Painter
North Truro MA
026520031

Call Sign: KB1OYX
Thomas Pires

North Truro MA
02652

**FCC Amateur Radio
Licenses in North
Uxbridge**

Call Sign: KB1VU
John V Picchioni Sr
114 E Hartford Ave
North Uxbridge MA
015380425

Call Sign: NE1CU
John V Picchioni Sr
114 E Hartford Ave
North Uxbridge MA
015380425

Call Sign: KB1VU
John V Picchioni Sr
114 E Hartford Ave
North Uxbridge MA
015380425

Call Sign: KE1MJ
John V Picchioni Sr
114 E Hartford Ave
North Uxbridge MA
015380425

Call Sign: KB1VU
John V Picchioni Sr
114 E Hartford Ave
North Uxbridge MA
015380425

Call Sign: N1DBA
Lewis L Stead
Elm St
North Uxbridge MA
01538

Call Sign: KB1TBH
Uxbridge Cert Team
North Uxbridge MA
01538

Call Sign: W1UXB
Uxbridge Cert Team
North Uxbridge MA
01538

**FCC Amateur Radio
Licenses in North
Weymouth**

Call Sign: K1RN
Raymond E Neiland
11 Athens St
North Weymouth MA
02191

Call Sign: N1CWE
Patricia A Connelly
44 Bartlett St
North Weymouth MA
02191

Call Sign: NA1XX
Michael J Connelly
44 Bartlett St
North Weymouth MA
02191

Call Sign: W1OKE
John L Josephs
103 Birchbrow Ave
North Weymouth MA
02190

Call Sign: KB1TXD
Matthew J Walsh
51 Broad Reach T84a
North Weymouth MA
02191

Call Sign: WA1OWQ
Raymond N Witt
62 Caldwell St
North Weymouth MA
02191

Call Sign: N1MJU
Damaso E Gomez
26 Doris Dr
North Weymouth MA
02191

Call Sign: W1IKI
John E O Neill
33 Great Hill Dr
North Weymouth MA
02191

Call Sign: KA1YSB
William N Johnson

36 Great Hill Dr
North Weymouth MA
02191

Call Sign: WA1MHH
John F Nelson Jr
70 Great Hill Dr
North Weymouth MA
02191

Call Sign: KB1UCA
Robert L Keaney
395 Green St
North Weymouth MA
02191

Call Sign: WB1GFB
Mitchell J Fijol
94 Moreland Rd
North Weymouth MA
021911728

Call Sign: WN1NZB
Jane M Forrester
160 Neck St
North Weymouth MA
02191

Call Sign: KB1ETW
James M Halpin
135 River St
North Weymouth MA
02191

Call Sign: WA1YII
Joyce E Schneiderhan
32 Sea St
North Weymouth MA
02191

Call Sign: WB1CKC
Richard L
Schneiderhan
32 Sea St
North Weymouth MA
02101

Call Sign: W1KQJ
William F West
28 Sherwood Rd
North Weymouth MA
02191

Call Sign: WG1L

James P O Rourke
64 Weybosset St
North Weymouth MA
02191

Call Sign: KC6EXM
Carette Y Mc Farlane
North Weymouth MA
02191

Call Sign: KB1SET
Thomas J Laliberte
North Weymouth MA
02191

Call Sign: N1AVY
Thomas J Laliberte
North Weymouth MA
02191

FCC Amateur Radio Licenses in Northampton

Call Sign: KB1CLZ
Tristan M Chambers
73 Barrett St 3113
Northampton MA
010601417

Call Sign: KB1ISP
Luke R Dyson
73 Barrett St 5174
Northampton MA
01060

Call Sign: KB1PHI
Karl A Hathaway
73 Barrett St Apt 1023
Northampton MA
01060

Call Sign: KB1TCL
Matthew S Wilhelm
64 Belmont Ave
Northampton MA
01060

Call Sign: KB1URX
Sota Jerks
64 Belmont Ave
Northampton MA
01060

Call Sign: K2YMR
Dederick L Snyder
101 Bridge Rd
Northampton MA
01060

Call Sign: KA3UCG
Allison S Crawford
13 Carpenter Ave
Northampton MA
01060

Call Sign: W1YD
Neal H Mc Coy
25 Coles Meadow Rd
Northampton MA
01060

Call Sign: N1WIP
Robert W Jeffway
225 Elm St
Northampton MA
01060

Call Sign: WA1NTI
John D Spencer
149 Elm St Apt 7
Northampton MA
01060

Call Sign: KA1ZPF
Edward F O Connor
6 Garfield Ave
Northampton MA
01060

Call Sign: WA1PCJ
Charles H Hemminger
20 Harrison Ave
Northampton MA
01060

Call Sign: N1NJW
Gregory R Skibiski
50 Hastings Hgts
Northampton MA
01060

Call Sign: N1CBF
Colleen B Finnegan
14 Jewett St
Northampton MA
010602808

Call Sign: KB1EZP
S L Johnston
14 Jewett St
Northampton MA
01060

Call Sign: W1SLJ
S Lacey Johnston
14 Jewett St
Northampton MA
01060

Call Sign: WB1ACQ
Donna M Shotwell
39 Kingsley Ave
Northampton MA
01060

Call Sign: N1COH
Michael R Fuller Esq
7 Longfellow Dr
Northampton MA
01062

Call Sign: WA1VEI
Paul M Koplow
Lyman Rd
Northampton MA
010604247

Call Sign: NM1DR
Daniel Ruddy
26 Maynard Rd
Northampton MA
01060

Call Sign: KA1IJV
Paul H Langheld Sr
50 North St
Northampton MA
01060

Call Sign: N1QBS
Jeffrey W Naus
107 North St
Northampton MA
01060

Call Sign: KC1JW
Sanford P Scharmer
154 North St
Northampton MA
01060

Call Sign: W1UPR
Michael A Woolf
39 Olander Dr
Northampton MA
010603631

Call Sign: KB1TCK
Christopher T Flynn
24 Phillips Pl
Northampton MA
01060

Call Sign: N1QOO
Michael J Haggert
351 Pleasant St Ste 210
Northampton MA
01060

Call Sign: KB1CIR
Brett A Treganowan
129 Prospect St
Northampton MA
01060

Call Sign: WA1WRM
Joseph J Deyette
159 Riverside Dr
Northampton MA
01060

Call Sign: AB1QO
Peter M St Marie
163 Roundhill Rd
Northampton MA
01060

Call Sign: K1MAL
Marvin E Mc Conkey
418 Ryan Rd
Northampton MA
010623435

Call Sign: K1JUO
Kenneth T Mc Kown
278 South St
Northampton MA
01060

Call Sign: N1NOY
Sharon L Rowinski
292 South St
Northampton MA
01060

Call Sign: KA2QIB
Cindy E Hill
243 South St Apt 1
Northampton MA
01060

Call Sign: N1TLP
Walter L Colby
61 South St Apt 8
Northampton MA
01060

Call Sign: KB1MIM
Kevin C Collins
29 Stoddard St - 1st Fl
Northampton MA
01060

Call Sign: KA1SUA
Edward J Manwell
20 Ward Ave
Northampton MA
01060

Call Sign: KB1WVO
Joseph P Henefield
14 Wilson Ave
Northampton MA
01060

Call Sign: KG6GZN
Claire E Cantwell
26 Wright
Northampton MA
01060

Call Sign: WA1OZQ
Edward S Cimek
9 Wright Ave
Northampton MA
01060

Call Sign: N1KXR
Richard H Wheeler
Northampton MA
010610482

Call Sign: N1VOY
Gerald F O Donnell
Northampton MA
010610223

Call Sign: N1VRF
Chris W Biddle

Northampton MA
01061

Call Sign: KB1REF
Cathleen M Wheeler
Northampton MA
01061

FCC Amateur Radio Licenses in Northboro

See also FCC Amateur Radio Licenses in Northborough

Call Sign: KB1PLP
John E Shaffer
18 Assabet Hill Circle
Northboro MA 01532

Call Sign: K1ONN
Harvey A Thomasian
369 Brigham St
Northboro MA 01532

Call Sign: KA1RUN
Michael C Bongarzone
55 Chesterfield Rd
Northboro MA 01532

Call Sign: K1LNY
Ralph W Snell
9 Chestnut Hill Rd
Northboro MA 01532

Call Sign: KB1RHZ
Kenneth J Maclean
92 Coolidge Circle
Northboro MA 01532

Call Sign: K1WVU
Robert L Shafner
258 Crawford St
Northboro MA 01532

Call Sign: W1LNG
Louis W Rydant
53 Crestwood Dr
Northboro MA 01532

Call Sign: AA1WA

Prabhasadanam G
Sadhujan
83 Davis St
Northoboro MA 01532

Call Sign: K1VVN
Joseph A Mc Caffrey
1 Hamilton Rd
Northboro MA 01532

Call Sign: WA1RQF
William R Armstrong
386 Howard
Northboro MA 01532

Call Sign: KA1VRD
Henry L Mossman
363 Hudson St
Northboro MA 01532

Call Sign: N6RFM
Robert J Mattaliano
15 Increase Ward Dr
Northboro MA 01532

Call Sign: KA4ZMM
Esther A Zocco
149 Indian Meadow Dr
Northboro MA 01532

Call Sign: W1RLV
Ronald L Vanosdol
1 Kent Dr
Northboro MA 01532

Call Sign: N1HLR
Charles F Cassidy
21 Lexington Rd
Northboro MA 01532

Call Sign: WA1HCX
Thomas P Ferris
44 Lincoln St
Northboro MA 01532

Call Sign: K1EYN
Sean D Mcenroe
59 Newton St
Northboro MA 01532

Call Sign: KD1HL
Maurice A Richesson
57 Oak Ave
Northboro MA 01532

Call Sign: N1JAI
Raymond F Kirally
64 Ridge Rd
Northboro MA 01532

Call Sign: WA1GNE
Joseph P Lonergan
90 Ridge Rd Box 381
Northboro MA 01532

Call Sign: KA1OJ
Mark B Foster
3 Ruth Rd
Northboro MA 01532

Call Sign: W1PJQ
Mesack H Sagerian
22 Washington Rd
Northboro MA 01532

Call Sign: KA1GVN
Edward G Prentice
25 Wiles Farm Rd
Northboro MA 01532

**FCC Amateur Radio
Licenses in
Northborough**

**See also FCC
Amateur Radio
Licenses in
Northboro**

Call Sign: N1BFF
Edward C Soomre
1 Alcott Dr
Northborough MA
015322703

Call Sign: W1ECS
Edward C Soomre
1 Alcott Dr
Northborough MA
015322703

Call Sign: KB1PIB
Gerald Isaacson
14224 Avalon Drive
Northborough MA
01532

Call Sign: N1AVY

Barbara A Ercolani
112 Bartlett St
Northborough MA
01532

Call Sign: KE3KK
Ronald M Rothman
9 Blueberry Lane
Northborough MA
01532

Call Sign: K1OJH
Richard W Eastman
55 Brigham St
Northborough MA
01532

Call Sign: KX1M
James J Whelan
80 Brigham St
Northborough MA
01532

Call Sign: N1ZQY
Greta C Whelan
80 Brigham St
Northborough MA
01532

Call Sign: N1QAN
Brian S Dextradeur
14 Catharine Dr
Northborough MA
02052

Call Sign: WA1NVS
Thomas C Carrigan
5 Catherine Drive
Northborough MA
01532

Call Sign: KB1DSN
Leon J Cormier
43 Cedar Hill Rd
Northborough MA
01532

Call Sign: N1SE
Roland L Erikson
62 Chesterfield Rd
Northborough MA
01532

Call Sign: KB1OTV

Daniel A Rowe
66 Chesterfield Rd
Northborough MA
01532

Call Sign: KB1JPU
Benjamin A Tober
27 Corey Way
Northborough MA
01532

Call Sign: W1WRV
Edward W White
224 Crawford St
Northborough MA
01532

Call Sign: W1JNS
Emil N Du Pont
297 Crawford St
Northborough MA
01532

Call Sign: KB1VXZ
Sidharth Sadhujan
83 Davis St
Northborough MA
01532

Call Sign: KA1SAW
Neal H Swenor
23 Deacon St
Northborough MA
015321677

Call Sign: N1HXP
Carole A David
25 Deacon St
Northborough MA
01532

Call Sign: KC6NHK
Laura L Green
28 E Main 2
Northborough MA
01532

Call Sign: N1VNG
Andrew R Lee
1 Edmunds Way
Northborough MA
01532

Call Sign: KA1SRS

Jeffrey L Woodard
2 Eliot Rd
Northborough MA
01532

Call Sign: KB1GBY
Roger W Pageau
5 Garrison Circle
Northborough MA
015322710

Call Sign: W1NMM
Roger W Pageau
5 Garrison Circle
Northborough MA
015322710

Call Sign: N1SOI
Peter M Mc Bride
16 Greenwood Rd
Northborough MA
015322702

Call Sign: N1MZM
William D Cobb
17 Greenwood Rd
Northborough MA
01532

Call Sign: N1RYK
Robert Y Dien
77 Howard St
Northborough MA
01532

Call Sign: KB1WTO
Bruce E Rickard
218 Howard St
Northborough MA
01532

Call Sign: K1ZG
David E Mc Curdy
491 Howard St
Northborough MA
01532

Call Sign: KA1PCA
Kurt G Schneider
200 Hudson St 22
Northborough MA
015321666

Call Sign: N1SXF

George M Conrad
113 Indian Meadow Dr
Northborough MA
01532

Call Sign: N1DDK
James M Lee
49 Lincoln St
Northborough MA
01532

Call Sign: KA1ZWF
Adrian M Burk
81 Lincoln St
Northborough MA
01532

Call Sign: K1LCT
Donald R Brennan
91 Maple St
Northborough MA
01532

Call Sign: KB1TTD
John D Mauro Jr
3 Memorial Dr
Northborough MA
01532

Call Sign: W1PMA
John D Mauro Jr
3 Memorial Dr
Northborough MA
01532

Call Sign: N0LF
Mark E Sheffield
8 Newton St
Northborough MA
01532

Call Sign: KB1FGV
John E Wilson
8 Northgate Rd
Northborough MA
015232233

Call Sign: KB1PWN
Seth E Mendelson
48 Pinehaven Dr
Northborough MA
01532

Call Sign: W1DXH

Steven L Jobes
90 Ridge Rd
Northborough MA
01532

Call Sign: KB1EHL
University Of Maine
Alumni Radio Club
3 Ruth Rd
Northborough MA
01532

Call Sign: W1XAH
University Of Maine
Alumni Radio Club
3 Ruth Rd
Northborough MA
01532

Call Sign: W1VKA
Richard I Bemis
16 School St
Northborough MA
015322618

Call Sign: KB1CS
William J Spurlin
9 Spruce Hill Drive
Northborough MA
01532

Call Sign: WA1QON
William Myerson
22 Thoreau Rd
Northborough MA
01532

Call Sign: KJ1Y
Robert S Finley
25 Tomahawk Dr
Northborough MA
01532

Call Sign: KA1PZ
William K Gross
35 Treetop Cir
Northborough MA
01532

Call Sign: KB1VKF
David E Jusseaume
7 Warren Dr
Northborough MA
01532

Call Sign: KR1COL
Dr David E Jusseaume
7 Warren Dr
Northborough MA
01532

Call Sign: KM2P
Alan Gonsenhauser
254 West St
Northborough MA
01532

Call Sign: N8VUO
Jonathan D Krause
16 Woodlawn St
Northborough MA
01532

Call Sign: KB1IJN
Jonathan D Krause
16 Woodlawn St
Northborough MA
01532

FCC Amateur Radio Licenses in Northbridge

Call Sign: NR1E
Steven R Horsefield
187 Brookway Dr
Northbridge MA
01534

Call Sign: AB2NE
Robert Evans
243 Brookway Drive
Northbridge MA
01534

Call Sign: KB1PPU
Robert V Dumont
234 Church Ave
Northbridge MA
01534

Call Sign: KB1LPT
James M Babineau
453 Cooper Rd
Northbridge MA
01534

Call Sign: N1VZH

Colleen M Hicks
55 Mc Quades Ln
Northbridge MA
01534

Call Sign: K2KRI
Leonard H Duey
102 Mendon Rd
Northbridge MA
01534

Call Sign: WB8JES
Carl J Ostoin
491 Moon Hill Rd
Northbridge MA
01534

Call Sign: K1JWB
John W Bacon
14 Pine St
Northbridge MA
01588

Call Sign: KB1AZJ
Catherine M Hewett
53 School St
Northbridge MA
01534

Call Sign: KB1GTW
Thomas M Brown
67 South Main St
Northbridge MA
01534

Call Sign: N1TUE
Kevin W Stolte
544 Sutton St
Northbridge MA
01534

Call Sign: WA1NJQ
Joseph H Boisvert
649 Sutton St
Northbridge MA
01534

Call Sign: KB1VPA
Richard A Arsenault
793 Sutton St
Northbridge MA
01534

Call Sign: KB1UJF

Michael R Murzycki
Northbridge MA
01534

FCC Amateur Radio Licenses in Northfield

Call Sign: WA1QKT
Robert L Dickerman
32 Alexander Hill Rd
Northfield MA 01360

Call Sign: KB1IAE
Cynthia A Dickerman
32 Alexander Hill Rd
Northfield MA 01360

Call Sign: KB1SMY
Christopher R
Dickerman
32 Alexander Hill Rd
Northfield MA 01360

Call Sign: KB1SMZ
Jenna A Dickerman
32 Alexander Hill Rd
Northfield MA 01360

Call Sign: K1SMY
Christopher R
Dickerman
32 Alexander Hill Rd
Northfield MA 01360

Call Sign: W1CAD
Cynthia A Dickerman
32 Alexander Hill Rd
Northfield MA 01360

Call Sign: K1UUE
Estelle J Smith
Box 69
Northfield MA 01360

Call Sign: AB1PA
Jens C Beesen
177 Capt Beers Plain
Rd
Northfield MA 01360

Call Sign: KB1LUP
Warren D Ondras
364 Four Mile Brook
Rd

Northfield MA 01360

Call Sign: KB1LUQ
Lisa A Mcloughlin
364 Four Mile Brook
Rd
Northfield MA 01360

Call Sign: KH2WK
David C Rhenow
14 Glenwood Ave
Northfield MA 01360

Call Sign: WB1HJG
Bruce C Magliola
129 Gulf Rd
Northfield MA 01360

Call Sign: KB1NNZ
William W Schweikert
39 Highland Ave Apt 3
Northfield MA 01360

Call Sign: W1MHS
Lewis H Wood
154 Main St
Northfield MA 01360

Call Sign: KB1SHU
Benjamin D Johnson
167 Main St
Northfield MA 01360

Call Sign: WA1WHE
G Louis Johnson
88 Main St 14
Northfield MA 01360

Call Sign: KB1TKB
Andrew K Rogers
471 Millers Falls Rd
Northfield MA 01360

Call Sign: WA1RHE
Kenneth H Short
46 Old Bernardston Rd
Northfield MA
013609502

Call Sign: KB1CIQ
Dennis H Williams
50 Parker Ave
Northfield MA
013601004

Call Sign: K1LRB
Russell F Newton
363 S Mountain Rd
Northfield MA 01360

Call Sign: N1TEU
Russell C Fisher Jr
457 S Mtn Rd
Northfield MA 01360

Call Sign: KB1IPU
Norma I Fisher
457 S Mtn Rd
Northfield MA 01360

Call Sign: KB1FXO
David F Nadeau
8 South Mountain Rd
Northfield MA 01360

Call Sign: W1IPN
Northfield Mount
Hermon School
Amateur Rad Cl
16 Warwick Rd
Northfield MA 01360

Call Sign: W1ZPB
Walton G Congdon
16 Warwick Rd
Northfield MA 01360

FCC Amateur Radio Licenses in Norton

Call Sign: N1PTM
Jeffrey S Robertson
14 Arrow Rd
Norton MA 02766

Call Sign: KB1OPL
Joel R Sitte
14 Barrows Ct
Norton MA 02766

Call Sign: K1WTU
Elias J Demas
3 Beach St
Norton MA 02766

Call Sign: WA1SLD
Gerard A Plasse
3 Berkshire Ave

Norton MA 02766

Call Sign: WA1JOS
Sumner J Eagerman
14 Boutas Dr
Norton MA 02766

Call Sign: KA1BMA
Carol S Spaziano
45 Cross St
Norton MA 02766

Call Sign: WA1KWZ
Arthur R Spaziano
45 Cross St
Norton MA 02766

Call Sign: KA1ZRL
Robert J Bellitti
12 E Hodges St
Norton MA 02766

Call Sign: W1RJB
Robert J Bellitti
12 E Hodges St
Norton MA 02766

Call Sign: KK1M
Kenneth P Kibilda
69 E Main St
Norton MA 02766

Call Sign: KB1POE
Brandon D Deal
37 Essex St
Norton MA 02766

Call Sign: KB1HTO
Charles S Lippmeier
57 Evergreen Rd
Norton MA 02766

Call Sign: KB1QMS
Betsey P Lippmeier
57 Evergreen Rd
Norton MA 02766

Call Sign: W1BPL
Betsey P Lippmeier
57 Evergreen Rd
Norton MA 02766

Call Sign: KA1TNQ
Herbert L Chisholm

9 Freeman St
Norton MA 02766

Call Sign: WA1RIW
Richard W Carnes
121 Godfrey Drive
Norton MA 02766

Call Sign: KB1ASR
Lauren M Buckman
7 Goodwin Dr
Norton MA 02766

Call Sign: KD1HF
Michael K Galloway
Sr
7 Goodwin Dr
Norton MA 02766

Call Sign: N1MWT
Diana R Galloway
7 Goodwin Dr
Norton MA 02766

Call Sign: KB1EZK
Michael K Galloway Jr
7 Goodwin Dr
Norton MA 02766

Call Sign: KB1PAP
Marissa J Galloway
7 Goodwin Dr
Norton MA 02766

Call Sign: K1MJG
Marissa J Galloway
7 Goodwin Dr
Norton MA 02766

Call Sign: KB1GRC
Kristopher M
Buckman
7 Goodwin Dr
Norton MA 02766

Call Sign: KB1POF
Anthony J Mazzaferro
11 Hadley Rd
Norton MA 02766

Call Sign: N1TD
Thomas M De Luca
5 John F Kennedy Dr
Norton MA 02766

Call Sign: N1MDY
Charles W Mc Donald
11 John F Kennedy Dr
Norton MA 02766

Call Sign: N1MGM
Charles J Mc Donald
11 John F Kennedy Dr
Norton MA 02766

Call Sign: K1JWP
John W Pompei
19 Kingsley Rd
Norton MA 02766

Call Sign: K1TGM
Edrick A Smith
250 Mansfield Ave
Norton MA 02766

Call Sign: N1TWL
Wilford G Miller
250 Mansfield Ave
#35
Norton MA 02766

Call Sign: N1HNX
Lawrence H Lahey
250 Mansfield Ave
150c
Norton MA 02766

Call Sign: W1WIZ
Lawrence H Lahey
250 Mansfield Ave
150c
Norton MA 02766

Call Sign: W1HYR
Harold A Brabbin
250 Mansfield Ave
Unit 50
Norton MA 02766

Call Sign: KB1PFM
Robert J Mcdowell
30 Maple St
Norton MA 02766

Call Sign: N1SRM
Steven R Mcdowell
30 Maple St
Norton MA 02766

Call Sign: K1MLZ
Louis Coburn Jr
166 N Worcester St
Norton MA 027662031

Call Sign: N1NWG
Robert W Garber
102 Newcomb St
Norton MA 02766

Call Sign: WA1WJZ
Horace E Osborne
55 Newland St
Norton MA 02766

Call Sign: N1SLL
Jeffrey R Lori
18 Norton Glen 98
Norton MA 02766

Call Sign: KB1SRM
Stuart W Studley
11 Noyes St
Norton MA 02766

Call Sign: W1BON
Stuart W Studley
11 Noyes St
Norton MA 02766

Call Sign: KB2SRV
Jerry L Brooks
98 Oak St
Norton MA 02766

Call Sign: KA1EWZ
Michael Halko
4 Olympia St
Norton MA 02766

Call Sign: WB0OCV
Kenneth J Sejkora
136 Pine St
Norton MA 02766

Call Sign: WB1FAW
Larry Cherner
95 Plain St
Norton MA 02766

Call Sign: W1JVW
Howard B Baker
258 Plain St Rr 5

Norton MA 02766

Call Sign: KB1NPQ
Jonathan M Bevis
10 Renwick Dr
Norton MA 02766

Call Sign: N1LTP
Edward J Capone
16 Renwick Dr
Norton MA 02766

Call Sign: N1YHE
Eugene P Shade
301 Reservoir St
Norton MA 02766

Call Sign: N1YHF
Leona A Shade
301 Reservoir St
Norton MA 02766

Call Sign: KG1G
William D Daunt
261 Resevoir St
Norton MA 02766

Call Sign: KA1SAL
Kurt J Hathaway
14 Richardson Ave
Norton MA 02766

Call Sign: KA1UNG
Kathleen E Hathaway
14 Richardson Ave
Norton MA 02766

Call Sign: NZ1L
Donald F Hathaway
14 Richardson Ave
Norton MA 02766

Call Sign: KD0IHJ
Don M Veale
4 Robin Circle
Norton MA 02766

Call Sign: K1HF
Henry R Fortin
274 S Worcester St
Norton MA 02766

Call Sign: K1KKG
Ann L Fortin

274 S Worcester St
Norton MA 02766

Call Sign: K2TGX
Raymond B Cord Jr
316 S Worcester St
Norton MA 02766

Call Sign: KB1IQM
Norton Emcom Team
316 S Worcester St
Norton MA 02766

Call Sign: WC1NOR
Norton Emcom Team
316 S Worcester St
Norton MA 02766

Call Sign: N1ZMF
Erik A Nolette
244 S Worcester St 1
Norton MA 02766

Call Sign: K1SMH
Attleboro Fm Repeater
Society
316 So Worcester St
Norton MA 02766

Call Sign: KB1TWJ
Rebecca L Howarth
249 South Worcester
St Apt 3
Norton MA 02766

Call Sign: KB1KZV
George L Pereira
13 Stanley Rd
Norton MA 02766

Call Sign: WA1DAH
Philip R Wilson
Norton MA 02766

Call Sign: WA1RGA
Christopher K Wiles
Norton MA 027660703

Call Sign: WA1ZJE
Robert S Feltmate
Norton MA 02766

Call Sign: KB1IDR
Edward M Elliott

Norton MA 027660624

Call Sign: KB1KLE
New Testament
Knights A R C
Norton MA 02766

Call Sign: NT1CS
New Testament
Knights A R C
Norton MA 02766

Call Sign: KB1PFG
Carl E Duchaine
Norton MA 02766

Call Sign: KB1WOZ
Alexander D Henning
29 Birchwood Ln
Norwell MA 02061

Call Sign: KA1OKT
John C Slupski Jr
225 Brigantine Cir
Norwell MA 02061

Call Sign: KB1PSB
Colin W Mccarthy
212 Brigantine Circle
Norwell MA 02061

Call Sign: KB1FZJ
Robert C Thompson
219 Brigantine Circle
Norwell MA 02061

Call Sign: KB1WTA
Christopher Scheer
10 Douglas Ave
Norwell MA 02061

Call Sign: K1YAI
David E Stevens
115 Forest St
Norwell MA 02061

Call Sign: K1BU
James E Power Sr
145 Grove St
Norwell MA 02061

Call Sign: KA1R
Matthew H Power
145 Grove St
Norwell MA 02061

Call Sign: WU1ITU
Valley Swamp
Amateur Radio Club
145 Grove St
Norwell MA 02061

Call Sign: KB1JFN
Alexandra S Barlow
439 Grove St
Norwell MA 02061

Call Sign: K1TBP
Joseph T Lo Sciuto
510 Grove St
Norwell MA
020611102

Call Sign: W1ARO
Dennis A Hart
194 High St
Norwell MA 02061

Call Sign: KD1JA
Donald E Reed
1093 Main St
Norwell MA 02061

Call Sign: W1SON
William J Monahan
1098 Main St
Norwell MA
020611443

Call Sign: N1ZGU
Richard A Caldwell
1150 Main St
Norwell MA
010611458

Call Sign: KB1QLR
Clarence W Scott
36 Samuel Woodworth
Rd
Norwell MA 02061

Call Sign: K1JZX
Clarence W Scott
36 Samuel Woodworth
Rd

Norwell MA 02061

Call Sign: N1TFX
Thomas J Mc Alear
44 Simon Hill Rd
Norwell MA 02061

Call Sign: N1XUK
Thomas J Mc Alear
44 Simon Hill Rd
Norwell MA 02061

Call Sign: W1UOE
John J Neary
9 Stanley Rd
Norwell MA 02061

Call Sign: W1AY
Bradford M Wilson
22 Tiffany Rd
Norwell MA 02061

Call Sign: KA1KIK
Tileston C Power
15 Trout Brook Ln
Norwell MA 02061

Call Sign: AB1BK
John P Cunningham
335 Washington St
Norwell MA
020611900

Call Sign: W1YOR
Richard P Johnson
399 Washington St
Unit 4
Norwell MA 02061

Call Sign: KB1JGR
Robert J Manning Jr
Norwell MA 02061

Call Sign: K1QAR
Theodore N Robinson
189 Access Rd
Norwood MA 02062

Call Sign: AA1MM
Theodore N Robinson
Access Rd

Norwood MA 02062

Call Sign: N1JFK
Jerry D Spingarn
168 Albemarle Rd
Norwood MA 02062

Call Sign: WC1Y
Carl R Carter
Bahama Dr Apt 405c
Norwood MA 02062

Call Sign: KA1VRB
Andrew C Nicholas
77 Bond St
Norwood MA 02062

Call Sign: N1UZC
Daniel A Fields
Box 769
Norwood MA 02062

Call Sign: N1RYZ
James E Conton
41 Brookview Circle
Bldg 4 Apt 50
Norwood MA
020622653

Call Sign: N1HUF
Barry M Glassman
46 Bruce Rd
Norwood MA 02062

Call Sign: N1BAW
Mark S Damish
20 Burnley Rd
Norwood MA 02062

Call Sign: KA1LFR
Roy E Hill
51 Codman Rd
Norwood MA 02062

Call Sign: WE1N
Francis W Kaseta
45 Concord Ave
Norwood MA 02062

Call Sign: KB1VWR
Anthony R Lasalvia
21 Cross St
Norwood MA 02062

Call Sign: N1QFR
Peter J Hand
61 Cypress St
Norwood MA 02062

Call Sign: KB1NGX
Jeffrey O Lind
55 David Terrace Apt
18
Norwood MA 02062

Call Sign: N1CWA
Robert F Wyman
75 Dean St
Norwood MA 02062

Call Sign: N1IFF
Andrew P Thompson
170 Dean St
Norwood MA 02062

Call Sign: N1PUF
Christopher L
Bingham
22 Dorset St
Norwood MA 02062

Call Sign: KB1DJQ
Emergency Radio
Group
25 E Hoyle St 216
Norwood MA 02062

Call Sign: KB1JPN
Suzanne M Lowe
69 Elliott St
Norwood MA 02062

Call Sign: W1UXL
Robert A Arnold
40 Endicott St
Norwood MA
020623007

Call Sign: N1OEF
John F O Keeffe
31 Fairview Rd
Norwood MA 02062

Call Sign: KB1JRA
Norwood Ema Radio
Association
31 Fairview Rd
Norwood MA 02062

Call Sign: WC1NWD
Norwood Ema Radio
Association
31 Fairview Rd
Norwood MA 02062

Call Sign: WA1PIK
Edward R Spadoni Jr
43 Fieldbrook Dr
Norwood MA 02062

Call Sign: W1JPL
Edmund F Kinsman
47 Florence Ave
Norwood MA 02062

Call Sign: N1LRE
David R Packard
15 Franklin St
Norwood MA 02062

Call Sign: AK1R
Dorothy M Kempainen
7 Grant Ave
Norwood MA 02062

Call Sign: KB1EDE
David B Marshall
53 Hampden Dr
Norwood MA 02062

Call Sign: KB1WKK
Andre V Heil
19 Harrow Rd
Norwood MA 02062

Call Sign: K1JMR
Norwood Amateur
Radio Club
20 Hemlock St
Norwood MA 02062

Call Sign: W1MA
Edward V Lajoie
20 Hemlock St
Norwood MA 02062

Call Sign: KB1ENA
Thomas W Lawler
22 Highland St
Norwood MA 02062

Call Sign: WA1MZJ

Richard L Sawyer
19 Hill St Apt 5-3
Norwood MA 02062

Call Sign: W1LA
Stanley B Pierce
4 Inverness Rd
Norwood MA 02062

Call Sign: N1UWG
John R Jones
600 Lansdowne Way
Apt 204
Norwood MA 02062

Call Sign: W1WHM
Vincent J Kasauskas
294 Lenox St
Norwood MA
020623434

Call Sign: K1HAB
George W Abely
25 Margaret
Norwood MA 02062

Call Sign: KB1DMK
Thomas M Nee
63 Marlboro St
Norwood MA 02062

Call Sign: K1SEC
Paul E Petherick
12 Maxwell Ave
Norwood MA 02062

Call Sign: KA1GKW
Maurice C Weiner
8 Mayfair Cir
Norwood MA
020621223

Call Sign: KA1GKX
Alan S Weiner
8 Mayfair Cir
Norwood MA 02062

Call Sign: N1DKE
John F Cusick Jr
50 Monroe St
Norwood MA 02062

Call Sign: KB1IBQ
Rickey Davis

68 Nahatan St
Norwood MA 02062

Call Sign: AB1DN
Rickey Davis
68 Nahatan St
Norwood MA 02062

Call Sign: KB1CEM
Joseph P O Riordan
265 Nahatan St
Norwood MA 02062

Call Sign: KB1TTL
Matthew B Murphy
267 Nahatan St
Norwood MA 02062

Call Sign: W1LIS
John T Soderlund Sr
290 Nahatan St
Norwood MA 02062

Call Sign: KA1PGI
Brian P Woolley
220 Nahatan St Suite H
Norwood MA 02062

Call Sign: N1ELI
David P Provencher
89 Neponset St
Norwood MA 02062

Call Sign: KM1G
Richard A Booth
133 Neponset St
Norwood MA 02062

Call Sign: N1BTC
Gail E Scott
74 Nichols St
Norwood MA
020622133

Call Sign: N1XNG
Geoffrey C K Sluicer
398 Normandy Dr
Norwood MA 02062

Call Sign: AA1DN
Gary P Singer
4 Norwich Rd
Norwood MA 02062

Call Sign: KB1KRM
Alexander L Chalmers
51 Oak Rd
Norwood MA 02062

Call Sign: KA1FNM
Norma C Herig
95 Pellana Rd
Norwood MA 02062

Call Sign: W1GOF
Paul H Zenis
535 Pleasant St
Norwood MA 02062

Call Sign: WA1WGX
Charlotte E Alman
82 Plymouth Dr Apt 1c
Norwood MA
020625473

Call Sign: WN1TKD
Harold Alman
82 Plymouth Dr Apt 1c
Norwood MA
020625473

Call Sign: N1SGV
Terrence P Mc
Gillicuddy Dr
74 Plymouth Dr Apt C
Norwood MA 02062

Call Sign: WB1CAM
Joel M Gould
24 Prescott Rd
Norwood MA 02062

Call Sign: KV1Y
David M Goonan
323 Prospect St
Norwood MA 02062

Call Sign: W1EDI
Edward L Collins
230 Richland Rd
Norwood MA
020625528

Call Sign: KA1CNR
Claude E Lockwood
227 Ridgewood Dr
Norwood MA 02062

Call Sign: K1MSA
Francis B Kiley
268 Ridgewood Dr
Norwood MA 02062

Call Sign: W1TBX
Thomas P Burns
132 Roosevelt Ave
Norwood MA 02062

Call Sign: KA1TMK
Matthew N Roy
30 Rosemary St
Norwood MA 02062

Call Sign: KB1KRN
John J Haggerty
31 Roxana St
Norwood MA 02062

Call Sign: KB1PI
Bronius M Davis
26 Saint Joseph Ave
Norwood MA
020624311

Call Sign: N1UYO
Suzanne E Bartlett
136 Saunders Rd
Norwood MA 02062

Call Sign: KB1BTN
John B Stadalnick
40 Savin Ave
Norwood MA 02062

Call Sign: KA1ISY
George E Thompson
25 Shaw St
Norwood MA 02062

Call Sign: KA1FTV
Joseph A Catalano Jr
17 Stratford Rd
Norwood MA 02062

Call Sign: KB1IBP
Antonio Pinheiro
111 Sumner St
Norwood MA 02062

Call Sign: KB1NYX
Matthew J Mccarthy
65 Sycamore St

Norwood MA 02062

Call Sign: KA1VGE
Brian A Swanson
160 Vernon St
Norwood MA 02062

Call Sign: KA1HMW
John S Manteiga
11 Victoria Cir
Norwood MA 02062

Call Sign: KB1EPX
Lauren K Jesus
196 Walpole St
Norwood MA 02062

Call Sign: W1CAW
Henry W Diggs
439 Washington
Norwood MA 02062

Call Sign: N1TQE
Stephen J Libbey
31 West St
Norwood MA 02062

Call Sign: KI1J
Irving Sall
47 Westover Pkwy
Norwood MA 02062

Call Sign: KB1JLS
Richard J Weiner
102 Westover Pkwy
Norwood MA 02062

Call Sign: N2BWM
Brian W Morrison
16 Williams St
Norwood MA 02062

Call Sign: KA1WFM
Richard R Farnsworth
Jr
35 Winfield St
Norwood MA 02062

Call Sign: W1LK
Guy S Costa
20 Worcester Dr
Norwood MA 02062

Call Sign: KB1CWB

Sonia B Skricki
32 Yarmouth Rd
Norwood MA 02062

Call Sign: KB1CWC
John W Skricki
32 Yarmouth Rd
Norwood MA
020621040

Call Sign: AK1S
Eric A Kempainen
Norwood MA 02062

Call Sign: N1OP
Norwood Amateur
Radio Club
Norwood MA 02062

Call Sign: WB1ALT
Brian T Caramanica
Norwood MA 02062

Call Sign: KB1FGT
Joseph A Vinci
Norwood MA
020620278

Call Sign: KB1GNW
Edward J Campisano
Norwood MA 02062

Call Sign: KB1NHL
Norwood Amateur
Radio Club Repeaters
Norwood MA 02063

Call Sign: KB1NIW
Norwood Amateur
Radio Club Repeaters
Norwood MA 02063

Call Sign: KB1ESU
Charles F Sharkey
Nutting Lake MA
01865

Call Sign: KB1NNB
Heather I Trauthwein

Nutting Lake MA
01865

Call Sign: W1HH
Billerica Amateur
Radio Society
Nutting Lake MA
01865

Call Sign: KB1EBR
John L Stenroth
180 Barnes Rd
Oak Bluffs MA 02557

Call Sign: K1ADX
John L Stenroth
180 Barnes Rd
Oak Bluffs MA 02557

Call Sign: N1RFB
Mark W Crossland
2310 County Rd
Oak Bluffs MA 02557

Call Sign: W1VJ
Mark W Crossland
2310 County Rd
Oak Bluffs MA 02557

Call Sign: W1VWZ
Robert E Scott
1 Forest Hill & First
Aves Box 1507
Oak Bluffs MA 02557

Call Sign: AD1U
Lawrence A Gelzer
New York Ave
Oak Bluffs MA 02557

Call Sign: K0RMH
Lloyd A Henke
Wing Rd
Oak Bluffs MA 02557

Call Sign: N1KVF
Alan J Muckerheide
Oak Bluffs MA 02557

Call Sign: KA1RPZ

John F Zietlow Jr
Oak Bluffs MA 02557

Call Sign: KA1SJT
James C Walton
Oak Bluffs MA 02557

Call Sign: N1SGU
Joseph A Deree
Oak Bluffs MA 02557

Call Sign: KB1NPS
Joseph M Osterhoudt
Jr
Oak Bluffs MA 02557

Call Sign: KB1RLE
Richard A Washington
Oak Bluff MA 02552

Call Sign: KA1OJI
Phillip B Warbasse
485 East Hill Rd
Oakham MA 01068

Call Sign: K1OJI
Phillip B Warbasse
485 East Hill Rd
Oakham MA 01068

Call Sign: KA1YDO
George S Smichinski
28 East Hill Rd E
Oakham MA 01068

Call Sign: KB1MPQ
Michelle M Boudreau
275 Edson Rd
Oakham MA 01068

Call Sign: N1KMF
Adam M Perrott
172 Hunt Rd
Oakham MA 01068

Call Sign: KA1WOK
David J Richard
98 N Brookfield Rd
Oakham MA 01068

Call Sign: KD6AJO

Gregg A Josephson
1366 Old Turnpike Rd
Oakham MA 01068

Call Sign: K1KBU
Robert W Mann
711 Spencer Rd
Oakham MA 01068

Call Sign: WA1WTQ
John F Kennedy
758 Spencer Rd
Oakham MA 01068

Call Sign: W1YR
John A Pagliarini Jr
Box 2458
Ocean Bluff MA
02065

Call Sign: KA1ALE
Ann M Martin
432 Ocean St
Ocean Bluff MA
02065

Call Sign: KA1AKZ
Kathleen D Ramsey
661 Ocean St
Ocean Bluff MA
02065

Call Sign: W1IWP
Benedict J Parisi
12 7th
Onset MA 02558

Call Sign: N1GXU
John C Rogers Jr
42 Amos Way
Onset MA 02558

Call Sign: KA1YZQ
Jason J Andrade
Box 1092
Onset MA 02558

Call Sign: N1SYD
Robert A Tibbetts
22 Highland Ave
Onset MA 025580646

Call Sign: N1VOA
Nancy R Smith
60 Longwood Ave
Onset MA 025580373

Call Sign: KB1HJQ
Elizabeth A Gerald
14 Pleasant Ave
Onset MA 02558

Call Sign: KA1SOQ
Ronald G Mc Coy
2 Tradewinds Dr
Onset MA 02558

Call Sign: KE1CN
Scott R Smith
Onset MA 02558

Call Sign: KB1JGM
William C Hobbs
Onset MA 02558

Call Sign: KB1LJN
Barry Sumner
Onset MA 02558

Call Sign: KB1NWO
Mikal Entzminger
Onset MA 025580686

Call Sign: KB1VOR
Anita C Rigassio
Smith
Onset MA 02558

Call Sign: KB1VOS
R Todd Smith
Onset MA 02558

**FCC Amateur Radio
Licenses in Orange**

Call Sign: W1JGV
John G Vanbobo
73 B Pleasant St
Orange MA
013641621

Call Sign: KB1OUE
Evan E Songer
1 Cove Rd
Orange MA 03164

Call Sign: N1OFU
Sharon A Batutis
519 E River Lot 67
Orange MA 01364

Call Sign: K1TOM
Thomas R Mc Dowell
Sr
383 E River St
Orange MA 01364

Call Sign: N1JSS
Patricia J Mc Dowell
383 E River St
Orange MA 01364

Call Sign: N1QXX
D Robert De Pratti Sr
625 E River St
Orange MA 01364

Call Sign: N1KLI
Ira E Baker
383 E River St Apt 105
Orange MA 01364

Call Sign: AA1AX
Paul A Batutis
519 E River St Lot 67
Orange MA
013642107

Call Sign: AA1CP
Douglas K Clark
519 East River St Lot
107
Orange MA 01364

Call Sign: KB1PKM
Diane M Field
519 East River St -124
Orange MA 01364

Call Sign: N1YPU
Tina M Streeter
519 East River St Lot
123
Orange MA 01364

Call Sign: N1RMZ
John E Field
519 East River St Tlr
#124
Orange MA 01364

Call Sign: W1WWX
John E Field
519 East River St Tlr
124
Orange MA 01364

Call Sign: N1NET
Arthur D Hicks
519 East River Stree
Lot 122
Orange MA 01364

Call Sign: W1URM
Dominic J Bruno
40 Lake Ave
Orange MA 01364

Call Sign: WB1CPY
Barry R Cormier
21 Logan Ave
Orange MA 01364

Call Sign: K1SQF
Robert H Cormier Sr
140 Mechanic St
Orange MA 01364

Call Sign: N1ZXI
Ida Gwendolyn Peavy
115 Memory Lane
Orange MA 01364

Call Sign: N1ZXH
Barbara J Sawyer
115 Memory Ln
Orange MA 01364

Call Sign: N1WLB
Dennis C Tucci
87 New Athol Rd
Orange MA 01364

Call Sign: N1VRC
John G Vanbobo
39 Pleasant St
Orange MA
013641621

Call Sign: N1XYV
Monica J Williams
73 Pleasant St (Apt B)
Orange MA
013641623

Call Sign: N1YJB
Ronnie P Cherichetti
68 Pleasant St 2
Orange MA 01364

Call Sign: N1IAM
John B Johnson Iii
745 S Main St
Orange MA 01364

Call Sign: N1LDN
Darlene A Maroni
745 S Main St
Orange MA 01364

Call Sign: NA1P
Louis Maroni Jr
745 S Main St
Orange MA 01364

Call Sign: KA1YSN
Thomas M Deam
83 Sandrah Dr
Orange MA 01364

Call Sign: N1MPX
Charlene J Deam
83 Sandrah Drive
Orange MA 01364

Call Sign: N1KLG
Michael D Phillips
80 Tully Rd
Orange MA 01364

Call Sign: N1RMY
Keith F Bergeron
90 W River St Apt 1
Orange MA 01364

Call Sign: N1LDO
Thomas R Mc Dowell
Jr
90 W River St Apt 4
Orange MA 01364

Call Sign: KB1TTX
John M Bergquist

190 Walnut Hill Rd
Orange MA 01364

Call Sign: W1TTX
John M Bergquist
190 Walnut Hill Rd
Orange MA 01364

Call Sign: KB1WMP
Lorne Johnstone
54 Ward Rd
Orange MA 01364

Call Sign: KA1QEW
Ernest T Moriarty
Warwick Rd
Orange MA 01364

Call Sign: AA1BY
Marian L Batchelor
35 Wheeler Ave
Orange MA 01364

Call Sign: WE1B
Richard D Batchelor
35 Wheeler Ave
Orange MA 01364

Call Sign: KB1SKU
Darlene A Maroni
Orange MA 01364

Call Sign: N1DMJ
Darlene A Maroni
Orange MA 01364

**FCC Amateur Radio
Licenses in Orleans**

Call Sign: N1MJQ
David A Riccio
Box 1094
Orleans MA 02653

Call Sign: KA1TVX
Elise M Costa
Box 263
Orleans MA 02653

Call Sign: K1YTY
Walter E Lenk
205 Brick Hill Rd
Orleans MA 02653

Call Sign: KW4W
James H Feick
79 Capt Linnell Rd
Orleans MA 02653

Call Sign: K1KED
Martin W Essigmann
25 Childs Homestead
Rd
Orleans MA 02653

Call Sign: WB1API
Rita L Essigmann
25 Childs Homestead
Rd
Orleans MA 02653

Call Sign: W1CJR
Donald W Howe Jr
29 Clayton Cir
Orleans MA 02653

Call Sign: KB1WDD
Michael N Elliott
25 Ellis Rd
Orleans MA 02653

Call Sign: N1BIQ
A Rives Mc Ginley
27 Heritage Dr
Orleans MA
026534601

Call Sign: WB2YSJ
Bernard Spieker
24 Hidden Valley Rd
Orleans MA 02653

Call Sign: KB1PCY
Logan A Wells
9 Kescayogansett Rd
Orleans MA 02653

Call Sign: KB1AAM
William F Mac Donald
62 Locust Rd
Orleans MA 02653

Call Sign: KB1MKN
David F Mccarthy
170 Main St
Orleans MA 02653

Call Sign: KN1P

Frank E White
175 Main St
Orleans MA 02653

Call Sign: W1YHQ
Robert E Collins
9 Main St Apt 5n
Orleans MA 02653

Call Sign: K1UWV
S Edwin Bevans
77 Nickerson Rd Box
1085
Orleans MA 02653

Call Sign: KA1VLX
David N Marshall Iii
115 Old Chatham
Orleans MA 02653

Call Sign: KB3KSO
Fred C Novello Jr
35 Pond Rd
Orleans MA 02653

Call Sign: KB1OJF
Fred C Novello Jr
35 Pond Rd
Orleans MA 02653

Call Sign: K1CJ
Robert J Edmonson
55 Rock Harbor Rd
Orleans MA 02653

Call Sign: KA1DXC
Douglas S Velie
105 Rock Harbor Rd
Orleans MA 02653

Call Sign: KD1PC
Edward A Finlay
Rock Harbor Rd
Orleans MA 02653

Call Sign: WA1SIY
Timothy P Call
190 Rt 6a 9d
Orleans MA 02653

Call Sign: W2AUG
Meredith W Elliott
19 Safe Harbor Ln
Orleans MA 02653

Call Sign: W1HZQ
Coleman W Thacher
20 Snow Way
Orleans MA 02653

Call Sign: KA1NMM
Eleanor S Blake
22 Twiss Rd
Orleans MA 02653

Call Sign: KZ1V
Henry H Fales Jr
Twiss Rd
Orleans MA
025633713

Call Sign: KA1DLR
Stephen B Elmer
3 Uncle Bens Way
Orleans MA 02653

Call Sign: N6POH
Felix A Conte
18 West Rd Unit 101
Orleans MA 02653

Call Sign: KA1SBZ
Michele C Ferreira
Orleans MA 02653

Call Sign: KA1SCR
Lucas J Potts
Orleans MA 02653

Call Sign: KA1SDB
Billiejo Ferreira
Orleans MA 02653

Call Sign: KA1SEM
Derek C Mickle
Orleans MA 02653

Call Sign: KA1TVK
Ian W Grant
Orleans MA 02653

Call Sign: KA1TVM
Dale N Hunter
Orleans MA 02653

Call Sign: KA1TVN
Andrew E Heard
Orleans MA 02653

Call Sign: KA1TVS
Faith A Mahoney
Orleans MA 02653

Call Sign: N1FXR
George W Fowler
Orleans MA 02653

Call Sign: N1OWD
Sr Mary Mag
Buddington
Orleans MA 02653

Call Sign: N1RIV
Kevin R Cronin
Orleans MA 02653

Call Sign: KB1MDY
Jack F Bicker
33 Barley Neck Rd
Orleans MA 02653

Call Sign: W1RCA
Roger C Albiston
49 Barley Neck Rd
Orleans MA 02653

Call Sign: KA1SEA
Allison L Hunter
Orleans MA 02653

Call Sign: KA1VSV
Nathan Doyen Charon
Orleans MA 02653

Call Sign: KA1YVZ
Jacquelyn A Heard
Orleans MA 08653

Call Sign: KA1YWB
Nicholas S Giordano
Orleans MA 02653

Call Sign: KB1BAH
Kathryn R Heard
Orleans MA 02653

Call Sign: K1CKK
Carl A Johngren
Orleans MA
026530931

Call Sign: K1LYQ

Ralph D Sawyer
Orleans MA 02653

Call Sign: KA1SEL
William A Sullivan
Orleans MA
026531118

Call Sign: KA1WSW
Richard W Davis
Orleans MA 02653

Call Sign: N1YRU
James R Hussey
Orleans MA 02653

Call Sign: W1JQL
Raymond E Simonds
Orleans MA 02653

Call Sign: WB1EBK
Robert A Marsella
Orleans MA 02653

**FCC Amateur Radio
Licenses in Osterville**

Call Sign: KB1CYC
Cape Cod Packet
Group Inc
176 Bumps River Rd
Osterville MA 02655

Call Sign: WA1YKN
Frank M Hill
176 Bumps River Rd
Osterville MA 02655

Call Sign: K1FH
Frank M Hill
176 Bumps River Rd
Osterville MA 02655

Call Sign: K1LEG
Cape Cod Packet
Group Inc
176 Bumps River Rd
Osterville MA 02655

Call Sign: KB1IHT
David E Bowman
523 Bumps River Rd
Osterville MA
026551301

Call Sign: W1OII
John A Anderson Jr
26 Chine Way
Osterville MA 02655

Call Sign: N1VBV
Townsend Hornor
239 Eel River Rd
Osterville MA 02655

Call Sign: K1JWF
Arthur J Balian
91 Falling Leaf La
Osterville MA 02655

Call Sign: WA1CML
Carl L Wolsieffer Jr
60 Fire Station Rd
Osterville MA 02655

Call Sign: W1CPJ
Ralph F Atwood
130 Hickory Hill Cir
Osterville MA 02655

Call Sign: N1MRF
Maurice R Pinard
26 Hidden Lane
Osterville MA 02655

Call Sign: K1PBO
Barnstable Amateur
Radio Club
44 Jasons Lane
Osterville MA 02655

Call Sign: KB1TFY
Barnstable Amateur
Radio Club
44 Jasons Lane
Osterville MA 02655

Call Sign: W1EXP
Barnstable Amateur
Radio Club
44 Jasons Lane
Osterville MA 02655

Call Sign: WA1JSE
Paul J Finnegan
44 Jasons Ln
Osterville MA 02655

Call Sign: N1VBU
Theodore A Swanson
17 Jonathans Way
Osterville MA 02655

Call Sign: NI1G
Alexander W Bishop
109 Marquand Dr
Osterville MA
026551803

Call Sign: NW1D
Stephen C Rich
131 Marquand Drive
Osterville MA 02655

Call Sign: WB1FUF
Odber R Mc Lean Jr
69 Meadowlark Ln
Osterville MA
026552020

Call Sign: KC1AB
Henry S France
51 Old Mill Rd
Osterville MA 02566

Call Sign: K1CLN
Laurel Welch
49 Parker Rd
Osterville MA
026550425

Call Sign: W1DPN
Charles E Kitson
22 Poplar Dr
Osterville MA 02655

Call Sign: W1ESM
Philip L Warren
46 Tanglewood Dr
Osterville MA 02655

Call Sign: KB1EPY
Michael J Kowalski
46 Third Ave
Osterville MA 02655

Call Sign: KA1RMK
Cyril F Wells
141 Tower Hill Rd
Osterville MA 02655

Call Sign: W1DJK

Lawrence E Keander
194 Tower Hill Rd
Osterville MA
026551623

Call Sign: KB1KFJ
Lori A Feenstra
194 Tower Hill Rd
Osterville MA 02655

Call Sign: W1FGG
Damon L Getman
327 Tower Hill Rd
Osterville MA 02655

Call Sign: KB1ORC
Paul R Wills
9 West Wind Circle
Osterville MA 02655

Call Sign: K1CN
William R Welch
Osterville MA
026550425

Call Sign: KN1EPL
Uss Massachusetts
Amateur Radio Assn
Osterville MA 02655

Call Sign: N1UXJ
Christopher J Nardi
Osterville MA 02655

Call Sign: N1EPL
Uss Massachusetts
Amateur Radio Assn
Osterville MA 02655

FCC Amateur Radio Licenses in Otis

Call Sign: W1WYN
Peter J Caden
Otis MA 01253

Call Sign: KB1NIE
Norman J Gelinas
Otis MA 01253

FCC Amateur Radio Licenses in Otis AFB

Call Sign: KD1MK

Bradly J Lockhart
Ogle Cir
Otis Afb MA 02542

Call Sign: N1FRK
Michael J Abad
Carpenter Ave
Otis A N G B MA
02542

Call Sign: KA1SHC
Herbert E Anderson
Prince Cir
Otis Angb MA 02542

FCC Amateur Radio Licenses in Otter River

Call Sign: N1OAA
Randy L Brown
116 Main St
Otter River MA 01436

Call Sign: KA1SZX
Amy R Duplessis
214 State Rd
Otter River MA 01436

Call Sign: N1RO
Lawrence G Fleming
349 State Rd
Otter River MA
014361124

FCC Amateur Radio Licenses in Oxford

Call Sign: KG4PZW
Mark C Harrison
32 Bailey Rd
Oxford MA 01540

Call Sign: KD1BX
James H Haskell Sr
16 Bartlett St
Oxford MA 01540

Call Sign: KA1SRZ
Ronald L Fisher Sr
3 Bird Ct
Oxford MA 01540

Call Sign: W1COU

Martyn E Meservey
1 Bounty Rd
Oxford MA
015402426

Call Sign: K1AOI
Richard C Olney
Box 191
Oxford MA 01540

Call Sign: WB3CUU
Leon J Cahill
16 Charlton St
Oxford MA 01540

Call Sign: KB1SBH
Phil J Sointu
162 Charlton St
Oxford MA 01540

Call Sign: K1LOW
Phil J Sointu
162 Charlton St
Oxford MA 01540

Call Sign: KA3EHP
Donald H Burd
14 Conlin Rd
Oxford MA
015401401

Call Sign: KB1RUT
Joseph C Perry Sr
27 Conlin Rd
Oxford MA 01540

Call Sign: KB1IEO
Anne-Marie Donohue
92 Dana Rd
Oxford MA 01540

Call Sign: N1MQD
Karen L Mc Intire
44 Depot Rd
Oxford MA 01540

Call Sign: KB1PPV
Ralph J Standring Jr
9 Dudley Rd
Oxford MA
015402233

Call Sign: W1LGD
Ralph J Standring Jr

9 Dudley Rd
Oxford MA
015402233

Call Sign: N1KNV
Darrell A Orcutt
59 Forest St
Oxford MA 01540

Call Sign: N1LLM
Kimberly A Orcutt
59 Forest St
Oxford MA 01540

Call Sign: K1OTW
Howard R
Worthington
17 Fremont St
Oxford MA 01540

Call Sign: KB1KSU
Charles A Garabedian
105 Huguenot Rd
Oxford MA 01540

Call Sign: KA1LVE
Paul H Murphy
18 June St
Oxford MA 01540

Call Sign: K1JWL
Philip K Spinney
20 June St
Oxford MA 01540

Call Sign: KB1ILD
Peter J Kosel
8 Larned Rd
Oxford MA 01540

Call Sign: W1PJK
Peter J Kosel
8 Larned Rd
Oxford MA 01540

Call Sign: AB1PK
Peter J Kosel
8 Larned Rd
Oxford MA 01540

Call Sign: N1QX
Peter J Kosel
8 Larned Rd
Oxford MA 01540

Call Sign: K1LCO
Claire A Plasse
53 Main St
Oxford MA
015402837

Call Sign: KA1CHA
Bruce P Plasse
53 Main St
Oxford MA 01540

Call Sign: W1HJC
Gerard C Plasse
53 Main St
Oxford MA
015402837

Call Sign: N1ZNW
Christine D Munger
464 Main St
Oxford MA 01540

Call Sign: N1XGY
Carol S Colena
1 Matthew Circle
Oxford MA 01540

Call Sign: KB1JUH
Deborah D Steele
6 Mayfair Cir
Oxford MA 01540

Call Sign: WK1H
Gilbert W Hayes
61 Old Worcester Rd
Oxford MA
015401249

Call Sign: KB1VBJ
Zachary T Robinson
8 Pine St
Oxford MA 01540

Call Sign: KB1VBL
Jason T Robinson
8 Pine St
Oxford MA 01540

Call Sign: KB1VCO
Amy L Robinson
8 Pine St
Oxford MA 01540

Call Sign: W1BHF
Patrick J Hester Jr
12 Quobaug Ave
Oxford MA 01540

Call Sign: KB1NBB
Jeremy T Whorton
17 Russell Lane
Oxford MA 01540

Call Sign: W1NOX
Jeremy T Whorton
17 Russell Lane
Oxford MA 01540

Call Sign: K1ICU
Richard P Casagranda
26 Walcott St
Oxford MA 01540

Call Sign: WA1WPX
Phyllis A Naramore
7 Walcott St
Oxford MA 01540

Call Sign: N1GNQ
Craig N Rollins
68 Walnut St
Oxford MA 01540

Call Sign: N1KKR
Robert M Smith
Oxford MA 01540

Call Sign: N1MQK
Anna H Shea
Oxford MA 01540

Call Sign: W1USA
Gregory R Bares
Oxford MA
015400014

Call Sign: WA1WJJ
Daniel F Shea
Oxford MA 01540

Call Sign: KB1GCC
Ismael Rosado
Oxford MA 01540

Call Sign: W0IRR
Ismael Rosado
Oxford MA 01540

FCC Amateur Radio Licenses in Palmer

Call Sign: KB1JVI
Eric G Richardson
215 Breckenridge St
Palmer MA 01069

Call Sign: N1NBT
Clayton L Thomas
Dingley Dell Rfd 1
Palmer MA 01069

Call Sign: KH6RF
Reese L Jones
37 E Palmer Pk Dr
Palmer MA 010691939

Call Sign: WH6OZ
Diane E Jones
37 East Palmer Park
Drive
Palmer MA 01069

Call Sign: KA1UMF
Bruce J Coburn
115 Flynt St
Palmer MA 01069

Call Sign: N1MFL
David V Scarpa
285 Gates St
Palmer MA 01069

Call Sign: N1RLW
Christopher P Adeletti
16 King St
Palmer MA 01069

Call Sign: KB1DVU
Gary M Larzazs
17 Lathrop St
Palmer MA 010691009

Call Sign: KB1DWL
Debra A Larzazs
17 Lathrop St
Palmer MA 010691009

Call Sign: KB1QCK
Michael R Larzazs
17 Lathrop St
Palmer MA 01069

Call Sign: KA1NYA
Michael L Deyorio
116 Mason St
Palmer MA 01069

Call Sign: KD1P
Dennis G Parent
146 Mason St
Palmer MA 010699211

Call Sign: KA1DQI
Helen C Sutty
Meadowbrook Acres
20
Palmer MA 01069

Call Sign: KA1DNZ
William C Stoddard
26 Meadowbrook Ln
Palmer MA 01069

Call Sign: N1KHV
Russel A Brown
53 Mt Dumplin Rd
Palmer MA 01069

Call Sign: KA1WVM
John D Lane
1644 North Main St
Palmer MA 01069

Call Sign: N1QOP
Christopher S Tracy
3 Old Farm Rd
Palmer MA 01069

Call Sign: KA1TFU
Edward W Midura
528 Old Warren Rd
Palmer MA 01069

Call Sign: WA1VHU
William R Riley
55 Park St Box 330
Palmer MA 01069

Call Sign: N1WCW
Dennis J Mallette
69 Quaboag Valley
Park
Palmer MA 01069

Call Sign: N1QOQ

Paul W Shepardson Sr
20 Shaw
Palmer MA 01069

Call Sign: KB1RBZ
Rory L Bacon
80 Squier St
Palmer MA 01069

Call Sign: N1RNR
Rory L Bacon
80 Squier St
Palmer MA 01069

Call Sign: WC1Y
Rory L Bacon
80 Squier St
Palmer MA 01069

Call Sign: WB1FKT
Douglas A Auvine
35 St John St
Palmer MA 01069

Call Sign: WT1W
Edward R Libera Jr
1586 Ware Rd
Palmer MA 01069

Call Sign: KD1OR
Paul R Bukowski
185 Ware St
Palmer MA 01069

Call Sign: N1WHB
Matthew J Lovell
Palmer MA 010690245

**FCC Amateur Radio
Licenses in Paxton**

Call Sign: W1OBQ
Kurt R Jackson
82 Asnebumskit Rd
Paxton MA 01612

Call Sign: W1XOJ
Yankee Network /
Nynes
82 Asnebumskit Rd
Paxton MA 016121349

Call Sign: KB1BB
Daniel F Kelleher

10 Brooks Rd
Paxton MA 01612

Call Sign: W1FIX
Richard G Bedard
10 Burtenmar Cir
Paxton MA 01612

Call Sign: WA1RMP
Daniel J Lucey
17 Burtenmar Cir
Paxton MA 01612

Call Sign: K1UOB
Samuel T Sespaniak
35 Crowningshield Dr
Paxton MA 016121253

Call Sign: KB1HYA
Lawrence H Pray
17 Cutler Rd
Paxton MA 016121423

Call Sign: W1RIL
Kenneth Schofield
21 Forestdale Rd
Paxton MA 01612

Call Sign: WA1ZOE
Lorraine D Sullivan
277 Grove St
Paxton MA 01612

Call Sign: W2DYQ
Charles J Glassbrenner
380 Grove St
Paxton MA 016121143

Call Sign: K1WGN
Steven W Siter
488 Marshall St
Paxton MA 01612

Call Sign: WA1HDY
Harry Kiremitjian
3 Monticello Dr
Paxton MA 01612

Call Sign: K1AUB
William M Foley
346 Pleasant St
Paxton MA 01612

Call Sign: N1KOO

Michael J Foley
346 Pleasant St
Paxton MA 01612

Call Sign: WA1RMU
J Arden Woodall
580 Pleasant St
Paxton MA 016121365

Call Sign: WB1CLD
Glenn E Miller
1110 Pleasant St
Paxton MA 01612

Call Sign: AB2IX
Adrian M Zeffert
6 Pond St
Paxton MA 016121127

Call Sign: KB1WMR
Ethan E Foley
2 Ridgewood Rd
Paxton MA 01612

Call Sign: KB1WMS
Michael J Foley
2 Ridgewood Rd
Paxton MA 01612

Call Sign: WA1NDT
Ralph V Hovanesian
12 Streeter Rd
Paxton MA 01612

Call Sign: WB1GBK
John T Le Fave
84 Suomi St
Paxton MA 016121212

Call Sign: KA1JKY
Katherine M Stannard
3 Whitney Dr
Paxton MA 016121101

Call Sign: KE1D
George E Stannard
3 Whitney Dr
Paxton MA 01612

**FCC Amateur Radio
Licenses in Peabody**

Call Sign: KA1ZMN
Orlando J Belo

49 Aborn St
Peabody MA 01960

Call Sign: KB1KEL
Theodore L Kowalski
76 Andover St
Peabody MA 01960

Call Sign: K1LOX
Frederick F Mc Elroy
Jr
199 Andover St
Peabody MA 01960

Call Sign: AA1DR
Kenneth M Smith
300 Andover St #116
Peabody MA 01960

Call Sign: N1RQH
Michael W Daniels
20 Anthony Rd
Peabody MA 01960

Call Sign: WA1BAJ
Gilbert R Odom
3111 Avalon Drive
Peabody MA 01960

Call Sign: KD1RA
Frank Toste
17 Ayer St
Peabody MA 01960

Call Sign: N1SYI
Maria C Toste
17 Ayer St
Peabody MA 01960

Call Sign: KB1GBQ
Peter O Laubner
2 Azalea Lane
Peabody MA 01960

Call Sign: KA1SBK
Milton L Cottrell
1 Azalea Ln
Peabody MA 01960

Call Sign: KB1LSZ
Robert P Manning
18 Beacon Blvd
Peabody MA 01960

Call Sign: KB1RPM
Robert P Manning
18 Beacon Blvd
Peabody MA 01960

Call Sign: WA1ROU
John E Agurkis Sr
16 Belfast Rd
Peabody MA
019603625

Call Sign: KA1SUZ
Robert D Sullivan
8 Birchwood Ave
Peabody MA 01960

Call Sign: W1BOU
William J Tremblay
43 Blaney Ave
Peabody MA 01960

Call Sign: W3BVC
Alexander J Bogash Jr
47 Blaney Ave
Peabody MA 01960

Call Sign: KD1SF
Anthony W Hoffmann
26 Boulderbrook Drive
Peabody MA
019604936

Call Sign: KA1NCF
Eric N Horwitz
12 Bourbon St Unit 16
Peabody MA
019607403

Call Sign: N1NFY
Mark A Gallant
12 Bourbon St Unit 16
Peabody MA 01960

Call Sign: W1UKC
Edward C Papski
201 Brooksby Vil Dr
514
Peabody MA 01960

Call Sign: KB1QET
Thomas O Moore
201 Brooksby Village
Dr
Peabody MA 01916

Call Sign: K1NNA
Thomas O Moore
201 Brooksby Village
Dr
Peabody MA 01916

Call Sign: K1MSS
Milton V Ratynski
301 Brooksby Village
Dr 216
Peabody MA 01960

Call Sign: N1AU
William F Santelmann
Jr
304 Brooksby Village
Dr Apt 415
Peabody MA 01960

Call Sign: KB1SDU
Brooksby Radio
Amateur Radio Group
304 Brooksby Village
Dr Apt 415
Peabody MA 01960

Call Sign: W1BBV
Brooksby Radio
Amateur Group
304 Brooksby Village
Dr Apt 415
Peabody MA 01960

Call Sign: W2HDN
William L Folkerts
103 Brooksby Village
Dr Apt 523
Peabody MA 01960

Call Sign: W1VYI
Robert A Wood
304 Brooksby Village
Dr Apt 602
Peabody MA
019608588

Call Sign: W1CNR
George O Lewis
302 Brooksby Village
Dr Unit 220
Peabody MA 01960

Call Sign: W1QEC

William G Hooper Jr
303 Brooksby Village
Dr Unit 316
Peabody MA
019608574

Call Sign: W1YBT
Warner L Smith
202 Brooksby Village
Dr Unit 420
Peabody MA
019608503

Call Sign: WA2IOR
Dorothy Halpern
101 Brooksby Village
Dr Unit 507
Peabody MA
019601454

Call Sign: KB1RFE
Dorathy F Stewart
103 Brooksby Village
Dr Unit 608
Peabody MA 01960

Call Sign: W1VYH
Elizabeth Wood
304 Brooksby Village
Drive 602
Peabody MA 01960

Call Sign: KA2HSU
Rogers B Finch
202 Brooksby Village
Drive Apt 304
Peabody MA 01960

Call Sign: N1DYO
William L Kierstead
302 Brooksby Village
Drive Unit 121
Peabody MA 01960

Call Sign: W2GDS
Arnold L Halpern
101 Brooksby Village
Drive Unit 507
Peabody MA 01960

Call Sign: N1MIZ
Charles H Johnson
202 Brooksby Village
Unit 213

Peabody MA 01960

Call Sign: KB1TOV
Lois S Robblee
101 Brooksby Vlg Dr
Apt Tg408
Peabody MA 01960

Call Sign: KB1TKI
Joshua M Monaco
12 Burke St
Peabody MA 01960

Call Sign: N1QYX
Manuel F Gomes
15 Calumet
Peabody MA 01960

Call Sign: N1JNU
Jonathan J Duprez
5 Castle Cir
Peabody MA 01960

Call Sign: KB1KYL
Michael T Higgins
7 Catherine Dr
Peabody MA 01960

Call Sign: K1RHB
Lawrence M Ball
15 Charles St
Peabody MA 01960

Call Sign: KB1CFN
Grufo Radio Luis
Camoes Grlc
10 Collins St
Peabody MA 01960

Call Sign: N1SLU
Samuel S Kenner
4 Country Club Rd
Peabody MA
019602715

Call Sign: KB1HKP
Ira W Wyman
14 Crane Ave
Peabody MA 01960

Call Sign: N1ONP
Alec Dluznieski
12 Crowninshield Apt
704

Peabody MA 01960

Call Sign: KA1MID
Thomas J Mc Nulty Iii
24 Dale St
Peabody MA 01960

Call Sign: KB1FLB
Thomas J Mc Nulty Iii
24 Dale St
Peabody MA 01960

Call Sign: K1TIM
Thomas J Mc Nulty Iii
24 Dale St
Peabody MA 01960

Call Sign: N1WOD
Glenn S Watkins
6 Dalton Ct
Peabody MA 01960

Call Sign: KB1VAP
Timothy E Steffens
7 Dartmouth St
Peabody MA 01960

Call Sign: K1FEV
Daniel E Bowman
28 Downing Rd
Peabody MA 01960

Call Sign: N1TAU
Linda M Smith
48 Downing Rd
Peabody MA 01960

Call Sign: N1HCN
Leslie E Awrach
20 Dublin Rd
Peabody MA 01960

Call Sign: KA1SSN
Leslie E Awrach
20 Dublin Rd
Peabody MA 01960

Call Sign: KB1ITF
James F Cooper
27 Dublin Rd
Peabody MA 01960

Call Sign: KA1WZH
Frank E Downey

6 Elm Place #2
Peabody MA 01960

Call Sign: N1IIM
Bonnie S Decosta -
Downey
6 Elm Place 2nd Floor
Peabody MA 01960

Call Sign: KB1OUN
Patricia E Rotondo
6 Elm Place 2nd Floor
Peabody MA 01960

Call Sign: K1ATO
Patricia E Rotondo
6 Elm Place 2nd Floor
Peabody MA 01960

Call Sign: N1ATI
Roger W Smith
28 Elmwood Cir
Peabody MA 01960

Call Sign: KB1UQO
Matthew J Harrington
19 Emily Ln
Peabody MA 01960

Call Sign: N1CAY
Lawrence P Mc Cauley
6 Endicott St
Peabody MA 01960

Call Sign: N1AE
Alfred E Smith
23 Felton St
Peabody MA 01960

Call Sign: W1HOO
Charles King
96 Forest St
Peabody MA 01960

Call Sign: N1GTP
Edwin R Hutson
22 Franklin St
Peabody MA 01960

Call Sign: KB1JPR
John V Winbun
22 Franklin St
Peabody MA 01960

Call Sign: KB1OKT
Herbert P Morrison
86 Franklin St
Peabody MA 01960

Call Sign: KB1JPL
Joseph E Conlon
16 Gemma Drive
Peabody MA 01960

Call Sign: KB1NND
Thomas J Lyons
35 Glen Dr
Peabody MA 01960

Call Sign: WA1LYK
Melvin G Morris
34 Glendale Ave
Peabody MA 01960

Call Sign: KB1EEC
Stephen M Fleet
95 Goodale St
Peabody MA 01960

Call Sign: WA1RIY
Frank J Carp
108 Goodale St
Peabody MA
019601257

Call Sign: N1YJC
Howard D Burnett Jr
29 Griffin Rd
Peabody MA 01960

Call Sign: W1FBI
Edward P Gustat
21 Hamilton Rd
Peabody MA
019602129

Call Sign: K1RSO
Robert S Olszewski
Harris St
Peabody MA 01960

Call Sign: W1OK
Dennis C Walach
40 Highland Park
Peabody MA
019603203

Call Sign: KB1KQW

James R Palmer
24 Highland St
Peabody MA 01960

Call Sign: KB1PAL
Ycc-Bsa Venture Crew
47
24 Highland St
Peabody MA 01960

Call Sign: KA1JBP
Thomas L Coletti
1 Hopi Cir
Peabody MA 01960

Call Sign: NX1Z
John J O'brien
19 Johnson Ave
Peabody MA 01960

Call Sign: N1IQW
Edward R Skelley
1 Joyce Rd
Peabody MA 01960

Call Sign: KB1NEE
Ray E Fraley
16 Keyes Drive -11
Peabody MA 01960

Call Sign: KB1JIL
Jonathan R Austin
34 Keys Dr Apt 9
Peabody MA 01960

Call Sign: KA1E
Ralph J Gandolfo
5 Lake St
Peabody MA 01960

Call Sign: KA1OL
Ann F Gandolfo
5 Lake St
Peabody MA 01960

Call Sign: KA1PLN
Lawrence L Jacobson
15 Larrabee Terrace
Peabody MA 01960

Call Sign: W1ADF
Robert L Gove
1 Ledgewood Way Apt
14

Peabody MA 01960

Call Sign: KB1AMZ
Benjamin Sousa
23 Lenox Rd
Peabody MA 01960

Call Sign: WA1ITR
Byron T Nichols
162 Lowell
Peabody MA 01960

Call Sign: KA1ZQL
Frederick L Mercer
193 Lowell St
Peabody MA 01960

Call Sign: KB1CQJ
Jeffrey W Mercer
193 Lowell St
Peabody MA
019604258

Call Sign: N1DKO
Robert C Mahoney
657 Lowell St
Peabody MA 01960

Call Sign: N1XWT
Christopher R
Odonnell
735 Lowell St
Peabody MA 01960

Call Sign: N1ZAF
Christopher J Jasper
737 Lowell St
Peabody MA 01960

Call Sign: KB1MSR
David I Titelbaum
Lowell St - 2
Peabody MA
019604288

Call Sign: WN1X
William J Jones
127 Lynn St
Peabody MA 01960

Call Sign: KB1OUM
Christopher D Boles
188 Lynn St
Peabody MA 01960

Call Sign: W1ZLX
Christopher D Boles
188 Lynn St
Peabody MA 01960

Call Sign: N1PQH
Jeffrey D Boles
188 Lynn St
Peabody MA 01960

Call Sign: KB1GCH
Arthur W Athas
26 Lynnfield St
Peabody MA 01960

Call Sign: KA1EDT
Arthur W Cole
369 Lynnfield St
Peabody MA 01960

Call Sign: KB1DT
Irving M Taub
240 Lynnfield St Apt
443
Peabody MA 01960

Call Sign: KA1CXF
Linda L Hebert
28 Martinack Ave
Peabody MA 01960

Call Sign: N1EQT
John F Bowman Jr
10 Maryvale Ln
Peabody MA 01960

Call Sign: W1WLD
John F Bowman Jr
10 Maryvale Ln
Peabody MA 01960

Call Sign: KQ1C
Wade L Wilson
86 N Central St
Peabody MA 01960

Call Sign: KA1PGD
Robert B Kohn
4 Nathans Way
Peabody MA 01960

Call Sign: N1PXY
James F Marrs

6 Nelson Rd
Peabody MA 01960

Call Sign: KB1DWB
William A Caperci
266 Newbury St Apt
17
Peabody MA
019601318

Call Sign: KA1GCD
James M Sheffield
278 Newbury St Lot 12
Peabody MA
019601319

Call Sign: KD1FW
James H Cavanaugh
286 Newbury St Lot
131
Peabody MA 01960

Call Sign: KB1OFI
Stuart W Whenal
261 Newbury St Lot
49b
Peabody MA 01960

Call Sign: N1CIC
Danny R Parris
286 Newbury St Lot 84
Peabody MA 01960

Call Sign: KA1NKL
Tara L Wright
266 Newbury St Park
42
Peabody MA 01960

Call Sign: AA1TG
Donald R Boland
154 Newbury St Trlr
23
Peabody MA 01960

Call Sign: KB1HVQ
William J Hyslip
161 Newbury St Trlr
25
Peabody MA
019603842

Call Sign: N2WEX
Nancy D Mangraviti

8 Normandy Drive
Peabody MA 01960

Call Sign: KE1AG
Victor M Silva
40 Paleologos St
Peabody MA 01960

Call Sign: WA1ZQE
James M Kelly
17 Paul Ave
Peabody MA 01960

Call Sign: N1YKQ
Adalberto M Santos
23 Perkins St
Peabody MA 01960

Call Sign: KB1RXZ
Leigh A Mansberger
2002 Pheasant Creek
Lane
Peabody MA
019604748

Call Sign: W1FLD
Kenneth A Schaffer
4 Philip Ave
Peabody MA
019602629

Call Sign: N1JWN
Ronald A Michalak
41 Pine St 43
Peabody MA 01960

Call Sign: K1LRX
Leo Morgan
1 Pond St
Peabody MA 01960

Call Sign: K1AZQ
Spiro Zakas
6 Putnam St
Peabody MA 01960

Call Sign: K1IUH
Carol A Zakas
6 Putnam St
Peabody MA 01960

Call Sign: KA1UUU
Charleen A Libby
6 Putnam St

Peabody MA 01960

Call Sign: WA1RQG
Jon S Zakas
6 Putnam St
Peabody MA
019606113

Call Sign: KB1QKG
Douglas Z Blanchette
Quail Rd
Peabody MA 01960

Call Sign: W1NCM
Arnold M Werlin
16 Raymond Cir
Peabody MA 01960

Call Sign: WA1DTI
Eleanore M Hynes
4 Reo Rd
Peabody MA 01960

Call Sign: WA1UIB
Robert A Ditty Sr
6 Rose Circle
Peabody MA
019605254

Call Sign: N1KTH
Joel P Heusser
15 Russell St
Peabody MA 01960

Call Sign: N1FBG
Stuart H Silverman
155 Russell St
Peabody MA 01960

Call Sign: KA1TOM
Leonard C Levesque
Sr
12 Sabino Farm Rd
Peabody MA 01960

Call Sign: AA1RV
Paulo J Giraldes
5 Shamrock
Peabody MA 01960

Call Sign: KB1LPY
John M Mendonca Jr
6 Shamrock St
Peabody MA 01960

Call Sign: N1NXP
Leonard P Robichau
7 Shaws Ln
Peabody MA 01960

Call Sign: KB1BCW
Cathy A Russell
13 Shillaber St
Peabody MA 01960

Call Sign: KQ1V
George D Johnston
Shore Dr
Peabody MA 01960

Call Sign: K1JZS
Wilfred Collier Jr
14 Southwick Ave
Peabody MA 01960

Call Sign: KB1DWC
Elmer L Andrew
26 Squanto Rd
Peabody MA 01960

Call Sign: W1UQP
Edward F Caramanica
24 Surrey Ln
Peabody MA 01960

Call Sign: KB1DHU
John M Partaledis
9 Swampscott Ave 4
Peabody MA 01960

Call Sign: KB1BGB
Anthony R Gravallese
3 Symphony Rd
Peabody MA 01960

Call Sign: N1ECX
Steven N Kemp
2 Tammie Ln
Peabody MA 01960

Call Sign: N1AZI
Gerald M Pressman
8 Tara Rd
Peabody MA
019606262

Call Sign: KB1UQN
Jeremy A Jacobson

5 Taylor St
Peabody MA 01960

Call Sign: N1DHZ
Wayne D Prost
3 Theresa Rd
Peabody MA 01960

Call Sign: KA1OEU
Howard P Freedman
3 Travis Terrace
Peabody MA 01960

Call Sign: KB1QKN
Roger J Schmidt
15 Truman Rd
Peabody MA 01960

Call Sign: N1FWV
Jeffrey Arnold
13 Tumelty Rd
Peabody MA
019602509

Call Sign: K1EMS
Jeffrey Arnold
13 Tumelty Rd
Peabody MA
019602509

Call Sign: KB1OHR
Peabody Weather
Amateur Radio Club
13 Tumelty Rd
Peabody MA 01960

Call Sign: WX1PBD
Peabody Weather
Amateur Radio Club
13 Tumelty Rd
Peabody MA 01960

Call Sign: KB1RRA
Dan S Foss
75 Walnut St Unit 316
Peabody MA 01960

Call Sign: KB1SZZ
Brian F Shea
8 Walsh Ave
Peabody MA 01960

Call Sign: N1QEH
Allison T Williams

147 Washington Apt 2
Peabody MA 01960

Call Sign: W1VOE
Elwyn E Ayers
11 Water St
Peabody MA 01960

Call Sign: KB1NTD
Jody N Barden
2 Wayne Rd
Peabody MA 01960

Call Sign: KB1NEG
Andrew J Barden
2 Wayne Rd
Peabody MA 01960

Call Sign: W1EGJ
Lawrence H Wright
7 Wheatland St
Peabody MA 01960

Call Sign: N1VSI
David A Pais
14 Winthrop St
Peabody MA 01960

Call Sign: N1BNX
Chester M Nibby Jr
Peabody MA
019613602

Call Sign: WA1RRK
Donna M Stella
Peabody MA 01960

Call Sign: WA1RRN
John C Stella
Peabody MA 01960

Call Sign: N2MV
Matthew W Vania
Peabody MA
019613908

Call Sign: KB1OHO
Jose Morales Arroyo
Peabody MA 01960

**FCC Amateur Radio
Licenses in Pelham**

Call Sign: KA1GLR

Lindsay E Stromgren
106 Amherst Rd
Pelham MA
010029706

Call Sign: KB1UPB
Douglas L Anderton
10 Boyden Rd
Pelham MA 01002

Call Sign: W1DLA
Douglas L Anderton
10 Boyden Rd
Pelham MA 01002

Call Sign: N1XSY
Seth Seeger
44 Boyden Rd
Pelham MA 01002

Call Sign: KB1EWQ
Katharine E Jensen
9 Harkness Rd
Pelham MA
010029704

Call Sign: KZ1T
Keith R Carver
49 S Valley Rd
Pelham MA 01002

FCC Amateur Radio Licenses in Pembroke

Call Sign: N1ISR
William J Carter
25 Adams Ave
Pembroke MA 02359

Call Sign: N1NLW
David P Smith
35 Alvern Rd
Pembroke MA 02359

Call Sign: N1OYH
Carleton W Davis
262 Center St
Pembroke MA 02359

Call Sign: KB1OVF
Michael P Skillings
349 Center St
Pembroke MA 02359

Call Sign: KB1KRO
Anthony P Oteri
694 Center St
Pembroke MA 02359

Call Sign: KB1PFL
James R Madden
10 Dunn Lane
Pembroke MA 02359

Call Sign: KA1BGK
Cynthia L Proctor
25 Edgewater Dr
Pembroke MA 02359

Call Sign: N1JBZ
James P Shea Iii
195 Elm St
Pembroke MA 02359

Call Sign: N1IQI
Loren S Pimentel
5 Evan Rd
Pembroke MA 02359

Call Sign: N1TXJ
Gail E Manning
16 Forest St
Pembroke MA
023591506

Call Sign: KB1KSE
David G Crooker
268 Forest St
Pembroke MA 02359

Call Sign: KB1ODS
John A Chase
76 Harvard St
Pembroke MA 02359

Call Sign: KB1PFU
Daniel L Chase
76 Harvard St
Pembroke MA 02359

Call Sign: KB1SPB
Daniel L Chase
76 Harvard St
Pembroke MA 02359

Call Sign: KA1TPC
Frederick J Spargo
78 High St

Pembroke MA 02359

Call Sign: W1KOI
Frank P Rivelli
12 Holly Hill Ln
Pembroke MA 02359

Call Sign: KB1AFG
Kevin W Cook
38 Indian Trail
Pembroke MA 02359

Call Sign: N1ZZL
William A Litchfield
22 Johnson St
Pembroke MA 02359

Call Sign: N1JOR
Gordon E Hayward Jr
55 Lake St
Pembroke MA 02359

Call Sign: K1MRG
Michael P Canney Jr
31 Macdonald Way -
Bldg D
Pembroke MA
023591838

Call Sign: N1OYG
Kevin P Fairclough Sr
19 Malinda Ln
Pembroke MA 02359

Call Sign: WA1KPF
Kevin P Fairclough Sr
19 Malinda Ln
Pembroke MA 02359

Call Sign: KB1SRL
Arthur L Phillips
45 Mayflower Rd
Pembroke MA 02359

Call Sign: KA1PUT
Arthur L Phillips
45 Mayflower Rd
Pembroke MA 02359

Call Sign: N1MJJ
Todd M Proctor
187 Monroe St
Pembroke MA 02359

Call Sign: N1MJK
John R Proctor
187 Monroe St
Pembroke MA 02359

Call Sign: KA1ILQ
Paul R Burke
141 Old Pelham St
Pembroke MA 02359

Call Sign: KB1VXL
William H Wormald
65 Old Washington
Pembroke MA 02359

Call Sign: K1CG
George A Manning
128 Old Washington St
Pembroke MA 02359

Call Sign: K8BIT
Michael S Day
27 Parker Rd
Pembroke MA 02359

Call Sign: KA1WPF
Beverly A Clements
171 Priscilia Dr
Pembroke MA 02359

Call Sign: KA1ZHL
Ronnie A Michaud
57 Priscilla Dr
Pembroke MA 02359

Call Sign: KA1ZHM
Valerie A Michaud
57 Priscilla Dr
Pembroke MA 02359

Call Sign: KA1WPG
Robert E Smith
171 Priscilla Dr
Pembroke MA 02359

Call Sign: N1IIY
Bartholomew F
Clements
171 Priscilla Dr
Pembroke MA 02359

Call Sign: N1IHN
Margaret Michaud
136 Priscilla Drive

Pembroke MA 02359

Call Sign: N1RQR
Declan K Kelly
35 S Boundary Rd
Pembroke MA 02359

Call Sign: K1VHE
Rudolph W Kalns
19 Spring St
Pembroke MA 02359

Call Sign: WA2RWZ
Jane M Hodge
140 Spring St
Pembroke MA
023592001

Call Sign: N1MJT
Richard A Hall Jr
48 Standford Hill Rd
Pembroke MA 02359

Call Sign: WB1EJF
Frederick W O Brien
68 Sudmi Rd
Pembroke MA 02359

Call Sign: KA1MUW
Clement G Burt
163 Taylor St
Pembroke MA 02359

Call Sign: KB1UIA
David S Elswer
24 Victoria Ln
Pembroke MA 02359

Call Sign: AB1NA
David S Elsner
24 Victoria Ln
Pembroke MA 02359

Call Sign: N1GXV
David F Hill Sr
166 W Elm St
Pembroke MA 02359

Call Sign: N1JBY
Robert P Carter
Wampatuck St
Pembroke MA 02359

Call Sign: N1IDE

John R De Freitas
161 Water St
Pembroke MA 02359

Call Sign: KB1OWN
Elaine H Thompson
166 West Elm St
Pembroke MA 02359

Call Sign: W1EHT
Elaine H Thompson
166 West Elm St
Pembroke MA 02359

Call Sign: W1JGR
John G Rupple Iii
56 Yale Rd
Pembroke MA 02359

Call Sign: KA1RSZ
David S Elsner
Pembroke MA 02359

Call Sign: N1LUM
David N Spalding
Pembroke MA
023590296

Call Sign: KB1OTS
Daniel S Hatton
Pembroke MA 02359

Call Sign: KB1PMN
John G Rupple Iii
Pembroke MA 02359

Call Sign: KB1UYV
William J Malinowski
Pembroke MA 02359

Call Sign: W1MAL
William J Malinowski
Pembroke MA 02359

FCC Amateur Radio Licenses in Pepperell

Call Sign: KN6LX
Robert B Keeter
34 Bayberry St
Pepperell MA
014631014

Call Sign: WA1ZYD

Ernest M Preisig
1 Beaver Creek Circle
Pepperell MA 01463

Call Sign: W1HFD
David M Taylor
6 Blood St
Pepperell MA 01463

Call Sign: AA1VX
Dave Glow
24 Brookline St
Pepperell MA 01463

Call Sign: KC1AW
Mark D Holbrook
33 Brookline St
Pepperell MA 01463

Call Sign: WA1TNY
Frederick J
Courtemarche Jr
136 Brookline St
Pepperell MA
014631141

Call Sign: KB1IFF
Brian L Bagby
Brookline St
Pepperell MA 01463

Call Sign: N1VAW
Patricia S Rice
11 Celestial Way
Pepperell MA 01463

Call Sign: N1SUE
David L Banks
5 Countryside Rd
Pepperell MA 01463

Call Sign: N1XOT
David L Banks
5 Countryside Rd
Pepperell MA 01463

Call Sign: N1JGA
Jonathan P Kinney
28 Cranberry St
Pepperell MA 01463

Call Sign: KB1SLB
Roland L Guilmet
9 Elm St

Pepperell MA 01463

Call Sign: W1RLG
Roland L Guilmet
9 Elm St
Pepperell MA 01463

Call Sign: KB1IIW
Robert A Sweeney
27 Elm St
Pepperell MA 01463

Call Sign: N1DDE
Stephen C Bourgeois
91 Elm St
Pepperell MA 01463

Call Sign: K1KKS
Harvey B Serreze
93 Elm St
Pepperell MA 01463

Call Sign: W1OCL
Herbert D Cooper
3 First Ave
Pepperell MA 01463

Call Sign: N1NIX
Peter A Quintin
14 Groton St
Pepperell MA 01463

Call Sign: WA1KVJ
Daniel R Piantaggini Jr
32 Groton St
Pepperell MA 01463

Call Sign: KB1AWE
Jeremy T Bisbo
122 Groton St
Pepperell MA 01463

Call Sign: N1OJW
Roger W Bisbo
122 Groton St
Pepperell MA 01463

Call Sign: N1UPR
Linda E Bisbo
122 Groton St
Pepperell MA 01463

Call Sign: WC1D
Richard A Lewis

101 Harbor St
Pepperell MA 01463

Call Sign: WA1KVK
Donald L Piantaggini
34 Haskell Rd
Pepperell MA 01463

Call Sign: WA1ULK
Leo J Hunter
52 Heald St
Pepperell MA 01463

Call Sign: K1LK
Leo J Hunter
52 Heald St
Pepperell MA 01463

Call Sign: N1ZRG
Peter N Nordberg Sr
61 Heald St
Pepperell MA
014631254

Call Sign: WA1VVH
Harold F Chase
166 Heald St
Pepperell MA 01463

Call Sign: WA2AOI
Richard L Rosenbaum
170 Heald St
Pepperell MA 01463

Call Sign: NM1Z
Christopher R Ogren
5 Hog Hill Rd
Pepperell MA 01463

Call Sign: AB1GA
Dale R Sinclair
30 Hog Hill Rd
Pepperell MA 01463

Call Sign: N1LBA
Jan A Malouin
140 Hollis St
Pepperell MA
014631434

Call Sign: N1THO
Virginia I Malouin
140 Hollis St

Pepperell MA
014631434

Call Sign: KB1EOW
Donald E Crim
Hollis St
Pepperell MA 01463

Call Sign: N1NWE
Donald I Campbell
17 Hyacinth Dr
Pepperell MA 01463

Call Sign: W1LLB
Peter I Morley
101 Jewett St
Pepperell MA 01463

Call Sign: KZ1L
Andrew S Morrison
2 Joan St
Pepperell MA
014631322

Call Sign: N1UGG
Virginia E Wellwood
2 Joan St
Pepperell MA
014631322

Call Sign: KB1UYX
Jackson P Rea
1 Kayla Lane
Pepperell MA 01463

Call Sign: KA1VQW
Beverley M Poulin
92 Lawrence St
Pepperell MA 01463

Call Sign: N1TIB
Russell A Leclerc
24 Lowell St
Pepperell MA 01463

Call Sign: W1VBO
Roger R Lorrey
28 Lowell St
Pepperell MA
014631257

Call Sign: W1EII
Timothy F Casey
28 Main St

Pepperell MA 01463

Call Sign: KA1AVH
Joseph Mills Jr
159 Main St
Pepperell MA 01463

Call Sign: K1FLU
Eugene P Tracey
6 Mason St
Pepperell MA 01463

Call Sign: W1NOS
Elwood E Gaskill Jr
6 Mason St Lot 48
Pepperell MA 01463

Call Sign: W1ZBT
Erik A Stromsted
36 Mt Lebanon St
Pepperell MA 01463

Call Sign: N8VIM
James F Hein
80 Nashua Rd
Pepperell MA
014631404

Call Sign: WA1FOQ
David K Bell
119 Nashua Rd
Pepperell MA 01463

Call Sign: KD2S
Dennis T Connors
Nashua Rd
Pepperell MA
014631404

Call Sign: N1MYI
Martin A Gill
22 Nissitissit Ln
Pepperell MA 01463

Call Sign: KD1TX
Kent H Springer
43 Oak Hill Rd
Pepperell MA 01463

Call Sign: KA1ZCV
Amy F Grondin
18 Park St
Pepperell MA 01463

Call Sign: N1VAV
Gregory J Rice
49 Parkwood Dr
Pepperell MA 01463

Call Sign: N1YEZ
Lenny Story
Po Box 734
Pepperell MA 01463

Call Sign: WA2CUN
Gary D Myers
23 River Rd
Pepperell MA 01463

Call Sign: W1GXC
William C Wilder
79 River Rd
Pepperell MA 01463

Call Sign: K1ERQ
Alfred Nickerson
18 River Rd Apt 13
Pepperell MA 01463

Call Sign: WA1CPC
Roger W Nichols
38 River Rd Lot 4
Pepperell MA
014631623

Call Sign: KA1WCL
Adam G Merrifield
Sartelle St
Pepperell MA 01463

Call Sign: KA1WEW
William M Driscoll
57 Shattuck St
Pepperell MA 01463

Call Sign: N1PQV
Charles E Hayden
18 Shawnee Rd
Pepperell MA 01463

Call Sign: KB1LVU
Charly Smith
107 South Rd
Pepperell MA 01463

Call Sign: WA1VMG
Joseph W Bonfiglio
122 South Rd

Pepperell MA 01463

Call Sign: N1ZHC
John J Surprenant
31 Tarbell St
Pepperell MA 01463

Call Sign: KX1G
Anthony P Di Cenzo
19 Village Rd
Pepperell MA 01463

Call Sign: N1UMK
Anthony M Sampas
51 W St
Pepperell MA 01463

Call Sign: KA1PRR
William S Mc Donald
105 West St
Pepperell MA
014631273

Call Sign: KA1ISB
Harold J Durocher
West St
Pepperell MA 01463

Call Sign: KB1IH
Mark L Stevens
90 Wheeler Rd
Pepperell MA 01463

Call Sign: AB1X
Mark L Hald Jr
60 Wheeler Rd
Pepperell MA 01463

Call Sign: WA1MFY
Mark J Giubardo
9 Wheeler St
Pepperell MA 01463

Call Sign: W1MJG
Mark J Giubardo
9 Wheeler St
Pepperell MA 01463

Call Sign: KB1JSG
Thomas J Olsen
76 Wheeler St
Pepperell MA 01463

Call Sign: KA1TGO

David B Meade
Pepperell MA 01463

Call Sign: KD1LE
Stanley W Pozerski Jr
Pepperell MA 01463

Call Sign: N1OMM
Scott M Pozerski
Pepperell MA 01463

Call Sign: N1PBL
Lynda J Pozerski
Pepperell MA 01463

Call Sign: KB1WT
Richard L Hodge
Pepperell MA 01463

Call Sign: N1MNX
David K Peabody
Pepperell MA 01463

Call Sign: N1NC
Nashoba Valley
Amateur Radio Club
Pepperell MA 01463

Call Sign: KB1JXT
Frank W Barnaby
Pepperell MA 01463

Call Sign: KB1KFZ
Kenneth E Young
Pepperell MA 01463

Call Sign: KB1NTH
Matthew Dion
Pepperell MA 01463

**FCC Amateur Radio
Licenses in Peru**

Call Sign: K1TTT
David R Robbins
15 Baumann Rd
Peru MA 01235

Call Sign: N1SDM
Earle L Locke
95 E Main Rd
Peru MA 01235

Call Sign: N1ESX

Rudolph D Kaatz
48 E Windsor Rd
Peru MA 01235

Call Sign: K1UNF
John J Mc Hugh
7 Pierce Rd
Peru MA 01235

**FCC Amateur Radio
Licenses in
Petersham**

Call Sign: KA1DWM
Robert F Laford
276 West Rd
Petersham MA 01366

Call Sign: KB1ESS
Mark H Hager
Petersham MA 01366

Call Sign: N1WLM
John M Ritchie
20 Shattuck St
Petterell MA 01463

**FCC Amateur Radio
Licenses in
Phillipston**

Call Sign: KB1TPB
Susan Malouin
30 Petersham Rd
Phillipston MA 01331

Call Sign: KF4GAF
David P Bramhall
55 Williamsville RD
Phillipston MA
013319414

**FCC Amateur Radio
Licenses in Pittsfield**

Call Sign: W1DWA
Donald N Davis
27 Adam St
Pittsfield MA 01201

Call Sign: K1MRP
Charles E Caldwell
32 Alba Ave
Pittsfield MA 01201

Call Sign: W1BEG
John A Laurent
84 Alfred Dr
Pittsfield MA 01201

Call Sign: KB1FN
Richard D Le Blanc
252 Allengate Ave
Pittsfield MA 01201

Call Sign: KB1FLL
Wayne J Giroux
219 Appleton Ave
Pittsfield MA 01201

Call Sign: K2XV
Ronald D Gagnon
104 Appleton Ave Apt
E
Pittsfield MA 01201

Call Sign: KA1TKC
Robert M Czerwinski
142 April Ln
Pittsfield MA 01201

Call Sign: N1QDC
Gregg G Quadrozzi
15 Arch St
Pittsfield MA 02101

Call Sign: W1UFR
Joseph A Condi Sr
40 Backman Ave
Pittsfield MA 01201

Call Sign: KB1CYA
William E Morrison
23 Balance Rock Rd
Pittsfield MA 01201

Call Sign: N1MBU
Susan B Wilansky
71 Balance Rock Rd
Pittsfield MA 01201

Call Sign: NU1P
Stewart M Wilansky
71 Balance Rock Rd
Pittsfield MA 01201

Call Sign: N1QIW
H Lee Stern

120 Bartlett Ave
Pittsfield MA 01201

Call Sign: KA1SKR
Stephen F T Miller
16 Bay State Rd
Pittsfield MA 01201

Call Sign: KB1QWG
Joann S Wagner
19 Bay State Rd
Pittsfield MA 01201

Call Sign: AB1KD
Joann S Wagner
19 Bay State Rd
Pittsfield MA 01201

Call Sign: WB1HIZ
Robert G Herd
34 Bellmore Dr
Pittsfield MA 01201

Call Sign: KB1WNE
Robert E Flood
15 Belvidere Ave
Pittsfield MA 01201

Call Sign: W1RZO
Robert E Flood
15 Belvidere Ave
Pittsfield MA 01201

Call Sign: KA1WRK
Linda D Dutcher
321 Benedict Rd
Pittsfield MA 01201

Call Sign: KA1WRL
James A Dutcher
321 Benedict Rd
Pittsfield MA 01201

Call Sign: N1PTY
William C Plumb
385 Benedict Rd
Pittsfield MA 01201

Call Sign: N1LLQ
Daniel J Bromback
7 Bentley Ter
Pittsfield MA 01201

Call Sign: KD1GX

John A Kazura
55 Bishop Pky
Pittsfield MA 01201

Call Sign: KB1BHG
Richard J Ranti
Box 1504
Pittsfield MA 01202

Call Sign: N1MDF
Kurt A Gabel Sr
100 Boylston St
Pittsfield MA 01201

Call Sign: KB1EHR
Kim T Rivers
35 Boylston St 2nd Flr
Pittsfield MA 01201

Call Sign: KB1PWG
Edward R Vidal Jr
45 Branch St
Pittsfield MA 01201

Call Sign: N1TGY
Richard E Knower
35 Brenton Ter
Pittsfield MA 01201

Call Sign: W1FLX
Joseph F Koziol
20 Britton St
Pittsfield MA 01201

Call Sign: KA1ZVO
Mary F Mazzeo
121 Broadview Ter
Pittsfield MA 01201

Call Sign: KE1P
Ronald R Mazzeo Sr
121 Broadview Ter
Pittsfield MA 01201

Call Sign: K1ZOY
Ernest F Charbonneau
14 Brooks Ave
Pittsfield MA 01201

Call Sign: N1VES
Richard A Jacob
33 Brown St
Pittsfield MA 01201

Call Sign: K1MQX
William F Bancroft
98 Bryan St
Pittsfield MA 01201

Call Sign: KB1CXY
Derek A Wood
174 Bryant St
Pittsfield MA 01201

Call Sign: KB1UDT
William J Slater Iii
52 Burke Ave
Pittsfield MA 01201

Call Sign: N1LZH
Patricia C Pietrowsky
117 Bushey Rd
Pittsfield MA 01201

Call Sign: W1BS
Joseph F Pietrowsky
117 Bushey Rd
Pittsfield MA 01201

Call Sign: AA1AR
Michael J Pietrowsky
117 Bushey Rd
Pittsfield MA
012014432

Call Sign: AA1ZA
Douglas R Crittendon
41 Cecelia Terr
Pittsfield MA 01201

Call Sign: KB1AAE
Donna M Crittendon
41 Cecelia Terrace
Pittsfield MA 01201

Call Sign: NJ1T
Douglas R Crittendon
41 Cecelia Terrace
Pittsfield MA 01201

Call Sign: KA1YDY
David L Wick
60 Cherry St
Pittsfield MA 01201

Call Sign: KB1JGE
Karen M Lemieux
221 Cheshire Rd

Pittsfield MA 01201

Call Sign: N1VJT
Gregory J Tatro
68 Chickering St
Pittsfield MA 01201

Call Sign: WA1QGW
Thomas C Nolan
20 Clarendon St
Pittsfield MA 01201

Call Sign: WA1KFN
Henry W Bak
31 Clarendon St
Pittsfield MA 01201

Call Sign: WA1MVP
Rita A Bak
31 Clarendon St
Pittsfield MA 01201

Call Sign: KA1TYD
Peter D Muir
61 Clarendon St
Pittsfield MA 01201

Call Sign: N1BT
David A Leone
106 Clarendon St
Pittsfield MA 01201

Call Sign: WA1LUX
Thomas C Nolan
120 Clarendon St
Pittsfield MA 01201

Call Sign: KB1ATP
Terry C Lampiasi
35 Clark Rd
Pittsfield MA 01201

Call Sign: KA1SDT
Joseph E Giard Bell
9 Cliff Ave
Pittsfield MA 01201

Call Sign: WA1ZYK
Leo A Lazits
174 Cole Ave
Pittsfield MA 01201

Call Sign: K1OEM

City Of Pittsfield
Emergency
Management
74 Columbus Ave
Pittsfield MA 01201

Call Sign: N1EIP
A Richard Chretien
176 Columbus Ave
Apt 215a
Pittsfield MA 01201

Call Sign: W1PHZ
Joseph F Crippa
176 Columbus Ave
Apt 215a
Pittsfield MA
012015065

Call Sign: KB1BLH
Bruce M Powell
59 Concord Pkwy
Pittsfield MA 01201

Call Sign: KD1FC
Richard L Hamel
713 Crane Av
Pittsfield MA 01201

Call Sign: KA1ATM
Lorenzo M Briggs
56 Crystal St
Pittsfield MA 01201

Call Sign: KB1AQV
Carol R Tetlow
38 Dalton Ave
Pittsfield MA 01201

Call Sign: W1IDJ
Richard J Conklin
408 Dalton Ave
Pittsfield MA 01201

Call Sign: WA1ZHM
John F Lindley
881 Dalton Ave
Pittsfield MA 01201

Call Sign: KB1DMR
Pierre E Gaviorno
25 Danforth Ave
Pittsfield MA
012020737

Call Sign: KB1IN
Benjamin V Catinella
82 Danforth Ave
Pittsfield MA 01201

Call Sign: N1TQX
Stanley B Clark
114 Danforth Ave
Pittsfield MA 01201

Call Sign: N1QOV
Jan C O Bryan
26 Davis St
Pittsfield MA 01201

Call Sign: KA1UKK
Stephen I Siff
257 Dawes Ave
Pittsfield MA 01201

Call Sign: KB1IST
Steven F Smith
30 Day St
Pittsfield MA 01201

Call Sign: KB1DGZ
John F Laplante
12 Delaware Ave
Pittsfield MA
012013616

Call Sign: N1MBS
Richard F Harwood
175 E Housatonic St
Pittsfield MA 01201

Call Sign: KB1HUF
Richard F Harwood
175 E Housatonic St
Pittsfield MA 01201

Call Sign: KB1PDT
Richard F Harwood
175 E Housatonic St
Pittsfield MA 01201

Call Sign: KB1CTA
Clifford F Carmel
49 Eleanoa Rd
Pittsfield MA
012015801

Call Sign: K1NM

Brian E Mc Cue
43 Eleanor Rd
Pittsfield MA 01201

Call Sign: W1CCC
Clifford F Carmel
49 Eleanor Rd
Pittsfield MA
012015801

Call Sign: K1SGK
Roy E Himes
247 Eleanor Rd
Pittsfield MA 01201

Call Sign: KE1HT
William R Mac
Farlane Ii
31 Elmview Terr
Pittsfield MA 01201

Call Sign: KA1ZVM
Ronald R Mazzeo Jr
36 Essex St
Pittsfield MA 01201

Call Sign: KA1ZVN
John J Mazzeo
36 Essex St
Pittsfield MA 01201

Call Sign: KB1IQP
John H Bartini Jr
36 Euclid Ave
Pittsfield MA 01201

Call Sign: WA1VCM
Robert R Secord
155 First St
Pittsfield MA 01201

Call Sign: WB2KEW
Ferdinand T Wiehl
51 Flintstone Dr
Pittsfield MA 01201

Call Sign: NJ1T
Douglas R Crittendon
105 Francis Ave
Pittsfield MA 01201

Call Sign: KB1CXZ
David L Benoit
26 Garden St

Pittsfield MA 01201

Call Sign: WA1RZQ
Joseph J Ferraro
75 Greylock Ter
Pittsfield MA 01201

Call Sign: WA1WDL
John F Sheerin Jr
89 Greylock Terrace
Pittsfield MA 01201

Call Sign: WA1ZNE
Hildegarde E Sheerin
89 Greylock Terrace
Pittsfield MA 01201

Call Sign: KA1LLW
Richard E Flood
21 Grove St
Pittsfield MA 01201

Call Sign: N1PBU
Gary J Rossin
62 Grove St
Pittsfield MA 01201

Call Sign: WA1WMG
James V Pivero
37 Hawthorne Ave
Pittsfield MA
012016009

Call Sign: N1GHC
Steven D Hickson
40 Hawthorne Ave
Pittsfield MA
012016010

Call Sign: WB1DSP
Chandler T Pilsbury
35 Hazelwood Ter
Pittsfield MA 01201

Call Sign: K1NWO
Henry G Bertini
31 Henry Ave
Pittsfield MA 01201

Call Sign: KA1PNW
Jeffrey L Mizell
2 Herie Ave
Pittsfield MA 01201

Call Sign: WA1DHI
Herbert F Plouffe
69 High St
Pittsfield MA 01201

Call Sign: KB1KZE
Ronald M Adriance
14 Hollister St
Pittsfield MA 01201

Call Sign: WA1WSB
Arthur Stein
497 Holmes Rd
Pittsfield MA 01201

Call Sign: KA1SKS
Daniel M Niedzwiecki
576 Holmes Rd
Pittsfield MA 01201

Call Sign: KD1SE
Jeffrey L Reopell
32 Hopewell Dr
Pittsfield MA 01201

Call Sign: N1MBT
Laura A Reopell
32 Hopewell Dr
Pittsfield MA 01201

Call Sign: N1CCF
Christopher C Foley
59 Howard St
Pittsfield MA 01201

Call Sign: NK1E
Kenneth M Kellogg
101 Joseph Drive
Pittsfield MA 01201

Call Sign: KB1GLA
Luciano G Guadagno
15 Lake St
Pittsfield MA 01201

Call Sign: KA1CFE
Donald J Coudert Jr
68 Lakeview St
Pittsfield MA 01201

Call Sign: N1MDC
Margaret I Szobesky
580 Lakeway Drive
Pittsfield MA 01201

Call Sign: N1VJS
Carl A Jerome
29 Lakewood Dr
Pittsfield MA 01201

Call Sign: KB1PAX
Nancy A Schaffer
16 Lathers Ave
Pittsfield MA 01201

Call Sign: KB1UCK
Katherine M Farias
48 Lebanon Ave
Pittsfield MA 01201

Call Sign: KB1BNZ
Ellen E Rud
400 Lebanon Ave
Pittsfield MA 01201

Call Sign: N1ZKM
Bridget A
Romanowicz
73 Lenox Ave
Pittsfield MA 01201

Call Sign: N1SAV
Jeffrey W Carmel Sr
119 Lenox Ave
Pittsfield MA 01201

Call Sign: N1LLO
Michael A Desrosiers
12 Leslie Dr
Pittsfield MA 01201

Call Sign: N1EQC
Ken P Masoero
6 Lillybrook Rd
Pittsfield MA 01201

Call Sign: KA1RRF
Roland R Hand
27 Lucia Dr
Pittsfield MA 01201

Call Sign: KB1EVC
Shane N Gerwaski
58 Madison Ave
Pittsfield MA 01201

Call Sign: N1BOR
Thomas J Leslie

40 Maple Grove Dr
Pittsfield MA 01201

Call Sign: KB1HZO
Gary J Costigan
67 Maplewood Ave
Pittsfield MA 01201

Call Sign: KA1SIW
Gary J Costigan
67 Maplewood Ave
Pittsfield MA 01201

Call Sign: W1ERF
Anthony E Simeone
9 Maryland Ave
Pittsfield MA 01201

Call Sign: N1NMN
Wilbur W Burchard
87 Maryland Ave
Pittsfield MA 01201

Call Sign: W1NWO
Wilbur W Burchard
87 Maryland Ave
Pittsfield MA 01201

Call Sign: AB1Y
Wilbur W Burchard
87 Maryland Ave
Pittsfield MA 01201

Call Sign: KB1CWR
Timothy A Burnell
51 Mc Kinley Terrace
Pittsfield MA 01201

Call Sign: N1VSM
James A Currie
31 Meadow Ridge Dr
Pittsfield MA 01201

Call Sign: WA1HSO
Leo O Robillard
148 Meadow View Dr
Pittsfield MA 01201

Call Sign: WA1PGP
Maria S C Robillard
148 Meadow View Dr
Pittsfield MA 01201

Call Sign: KA1AXQ

James O Kenney
135 Meadowview Dr
Pittsfield MA
012011923

Call Sign: K2MQ
Pierre P Turillon
140 Melbourne Rd
Pittsfield MA
012018544

Call Sign: N1WCF
Joel W Miller
164 Melbourne Rd
Pittsfield MA 01201

Call Sign: AB1MH
Joel W Miller
164 Melbourne Rd
Pittsfield MA 01201

Call Sign: K2HFM
James W Kerr
118 Morningview Dr
Pittsfield MA 01201

Call Sign: W1HEM
John W Valiasek
90 Mountain Dr
Pittsfield MA 01201

Call Sign: N1LTN
Randall A Mais
37 Newell St
Pittsfield MA 01201

Call Sign: KB1JNZ
Brian S Schultz
85 Oak Rd RR3
Pittsfield MA 01201

Call Sign: N1DQU
Walter L Smith Jr
194 Onota St
Pittsfield MA 01201

Call Sign: W1OIV
Erwin P Currier
306 Onota St
Pittsfield MA
012013150

Call Sign: KA1DYX
William R Pellows

127 Ontario
Pittsfield MA 01201

Call Sign: KB1AQL
Francis A Tremblay
19 Orchard Ave
Pittsfield MA 01201

Call Sign: NZ1Z
Charles W Lowery Jr
83 Osceola St
Pittsfield MA 01201

Call Sign: N1YCY
Mark W Johnson
114 Parker St
Pittsfield MA 01201

Call Sign: KA1GRJ
Mark W Johnson
114 Parker St
Pittsfield MA 01201

Call Sign: W1CVI
George N Becker
120 Parker St
Pittsfield MA 01201

Call Sign: KB1HFG
Kerry L Couchman
189 Partridge Rd
Pittsfield MA
012011720

Call Sign: N1NGA
William R Theroux
20 Patricia Ave
Pittsfield MA 01201

Call Sign: N1ONT
John J Kowach
10 Paula Ave
Pittsfield MA 01201

Call Sign: KA1ZMD
David J Andrews
261 Pecks Rd
Pittsfield MA 01201

Call Sign: N1SAW
Sean M Clark
363 Pecks Rd
Pittsfield MA 01201

Call Sign: WS1T
Ralph W Lake
753 Pecks Rd
Pittsfield MA 01201

Call Sign: N1BKA
John M Ellery
82 Pinegrove Dr
Pittsfield MA 01201

Call Sign: KB1HZN
Arthur F Fitzpatrick
24 Plastics Ave
Pittsfield MA 01201

Call Sign: N2EPV
Dave L Goodfellow
43 Plinn St
Pittsfield MA 01201

Call Sign: W1HER
Daniel P Lorusso
Po Box 3918
Pittsfield MA
012023918

Call Sign: KB1UCM
Timothy E Kelly
96 Pollock Ave
Pittsfield MA 01201

Call Sign: KA1SAY
Donald M Hayford
215 Pomeroy Ave
Pittsfield MA 01201

Call Sign: KA1LKQ
John J Kirby
Pondview Drive
Pittsfield MA 01201

Call Sign: KA1ZUU
Francis J Baumgartner
48 Preston Ave
Pittsfield MA 01201

Call Sign: KB1JZD
Jeremy D Farmer
11 Rhode Island Ave
Pittsfield MA 01201

Call Sign: KB2VLC
Diane L Bourassa
21 Richmond Ave

Pittsfield MA 01201

Call Sign: N1XHR
Todd A Shoff
37 Richmond Ave
Pittsfield MA 01201

Call Sign: W1BKG
Milton A George
35 Ridgeway Ave
Pittsfield MA
012012843

Call Sign: WB1DBN
Edward M Prezenik
41 Ridgeway Ave
Pittsfield MA 01201

Call Sign: KA1OKP
Adrian H Bissaillon
106 Robbins Ave
Pittsfield MA 01201

Call Sign: K3SQQ
George G Bodnar
24 Roberta Rd
Pittsfield MA 01201

Call Sign: KB1LTK
Mark G Bodnar
24 Roberta Rd
Pittsfield MA 01201

Call Sign: K1SQQ
Mark G Bodnar
24 Roberta Rd
Pittsfield MA 01201

Call Sign: KA1ZUP
Helen E Kimpel
62 Rockland Dr
Pittsfield MA 01201

Call Sign: KJ1K
Sigurd E Kimpel
62 Rockland Dr
Pittsfield MA 01201

Call Sign: N1MDD
Edward L Kinsella
273 Second St
Pittsfield MA 01201

Call Sign: KA1KUV

Tracy E Woodstock
42 Spring St
Pittsfield MA 01201

Call Sign: K1DWU
Frank E Woodstock
42 Spring St
Pittsfield MA 01201

Call Sign: N1FZH
Stephen E Flood
31 Summit Ave
Pittsfield MA 01201

Call Sign: KB1URU
Benjamin J Lapine
49 Taconic St Apt 2
Pittsfield MA 01201

Call Sign: KA1ZXK
George W Castell Jr
18 Taubert Ave
Pittsfield MA 01201

Call Sign: KB1WCX
Alex J Bassett
20 Taylor St
Pittsfield MA 01201

Call Sign: N1UJM
Alexander F Koldys
11 Taylor St
Pittsfield MA 01201

Call Sign: N1UVR
Raymond J Koldys
11 Taylor St
Pittsfield MA 01201

Call Sign: KB1NBA
Gerard M Krupka
83 Thomas Island Rd
Pittsfield MA 01201

Call Sign: KB1DJP
City Of Pittsfield
Emergency
Management
235 Tyler St
Pittsfield MA 01201

Call Sign: KB1PDR
Roberta E Newberry
68 Union St

Pittsfield MA 01201

Call Sign: KB1NWR
Christopher J Read
68 Union St Apt 2
Pittsfield MA 01201

Call Sign: KA1OKH
Larry P Kratka
55 Velma Ave
Pittsfield MA 01201

Call Sign: N1UZH
Michael E Williams
716 W Housatonic St
Pittsfield MA 01201

Call Sign: KI4BFL
Duane A Broga
335 Wahconah St
Pittsfield MA 01201

Call Sign: N1IN
William C Sexton
7 Walden Ln
Pittsfield MA 01201

Call Sign: WA1ZYJ
John L Bak
26 Walnut St
Pittsfield MA 01201

Call Sign: KA1PWB
Stuart H Coolbroth
22 Wealthy Ave
Pittsfield MA 01201

Call Sign: N1SRW
Nancy D Morin
37 Wealthy Ave
Pittsfield MA 01201

Call Sign: N1XSL
Joseph E Bourquard
61 Wealthy Ave
Pittsfield MA 01201

Call Sign: N1FJI
Joseph C Lysonski Jr
15 Weller Ave
Pittsfield MA 01201

Call Sign: KB1W
Leonard D Bean

62 Wellington Ave
Pittsfield MA 01201

Call Sign: WA1UBZ
John W Fitzpatrick
65 Wellington Ave
Pittsfield MA 01201

Call Sign: KB1JCJ
Michael J Dottavio
828 West Housatonic
St
Pittsfield MA 01201

Call Sign: KB1OJT
Roger A Armstrong
1089 West St
Pittsfield MA 01201

Call Sign: K1RAA
Roger A Armstrong
1089 West St
Pittsfield MA 01201

Call Sign: W1WCC
Henry N Decelles
90 West Union St Apt
2
Pittsfield MA 01201

Call Sign: W1DDW
Thomas D Legault
61 Whittier Ave
Pittsfield MA 01201

Call Sign: W1TAD
Alan H Cooper
77 Whittier Ave
Pittsfield MA 01201

Call Sign: N1ELM
Perry F Pavolko
45 Willard Pl
Pittsfield MA 01201

Call Sign: KA1KRY
Lawrence H Kirchner
739 Williams St
Pittsfield MA
012017401

Call Sign: KB1EXR
Thomas G Grizey
1 Willow Rd Rr3

Pittsfield MA 01201

Call Sign: N1UZE
Colleen P Mayo
67 Wilson St
Pittsfield MA 01201

Call Sign: W1UUJ
Llewellyn P Hannigan
53 Winship Ave
Pittsfield MA 01201

Call Sign: KA1LZC
David A Foley
Pittsfield MA 01202

Call Sign: K1FFK
Northern Berkshire
Ama Rad Club
Pittsfield MA
012022097

Call Sign: K1WEJ
Carroll B French
Pittsfield MA
012022673

Call Sign: N1NSJ
Gary C Engwer
Pittsfield MA 01202

Call Sign: N1TQV
Richard W Farmer
Pittsfield MA 01202

Call Sign: N1WM
Northern Berkshire
Amateur Radio Club
Pittsfield MA
012022097

Call Sign: W1FGV
William E Scully Sr
Pittsfield MA 01201

Call Sign: KB1PDQ
Charles G Griffin
Pittsfield MA 01201

Call Sign: KB1SNN
Northern Berkshire
Amateur Radio Club
Pittsfield MA 01202

Call Sign: KA1OA
Northern Berkshire
Amateur Radio Club
Pittsfield MA 01202

FCC Amateur Radio
Licenses in Plainfield

Call Sign: KB1FAQ
Leonard A Benoit
43 Campbell Rd
Plainfield MA 01070

Call Sign: W1NSD
John O Copley
149 Pleasant St
Plainfield MA 01070

Call Sign: KB1ELM
Michael A Woolf
8 Warner Hill Rd
Plainfield MA 01070

FCC Amateur Radio
Licenses in Plainville

Call Sign: N1PZG
Brian P Gaucher
11 Azalea Dr
Plainville MA 02762

Call Sign: N1LJR
Bruce E Altfeter
45 Berry St
Plainville MA 02762

Call Sign: W1KSS
Bruce E Altfeter
45 Berry St
Plainville MA 02762

Call Sign: N1BUW
John P Toresco
49 Cowell St
Plainville MA 02762

Call Sign: W1III
John P Toresco
49 Cowell St
Plainville MA 02762

Call Sign: KA1MYE
Eric C Paul
138 E Bacon St

Plainville MA 02762

Call Sign: KB1VYR
Timothy C Brooks
18 Evergreen Rd
Plainville MA 02762

Call Sign: KA1YUG
Ruthann Le Blanc
13 Fremont St
Plainville MA 02762

Call Sign: WA1EUU
Richard J Yuryan
95 Grove St
Plainville MA 02762

Call Sign: N1SHE
John C Strang
11 Hancock St
Plainville MA 02762

Call Sign: N1UTX
Gordon W Spencer
41 High St
Plainville MA 02762

Call Sign: KB1FLR
Richard K Myers
4 Highland Ave
Plainville MA 02762

Call Sign: WB1FIG
Edmund P Chin
8 Highland Ave
Plainville MA 02762

Call Sign: N1ACT
Peter J B Teague
6 Hillcrest Drive
Plainville MA 02762

Call Sign: N1OFC
Bruce R Bumpus
2 June St
Plainville MA 02762

Call Sign: N1DPV
William J Dorothy
8 Mathurin Rd
Plainville MA 02762

Call Sign: WB1DJP
Edward P Brown

82 Messenger St
Plainville MA 02762

Call Sign: KB1CUR
Lewis J Martin
71 Messenger St Box 1005
Plainville MA 02762

Call Sign: N1WSQ
David S Bernazzani
10 Morningside Rd
Plainville MA 027625029

Call Sign: KB1ECT
Jennifer A Bernazzani
10 Morningside Rd
Plainville MA 02762

Call Sign: KB1HCL
Donald A Claiborne
4 Oakridge Dr
Plainville MA 02762

Call Sign: KA1EIV
James W Duarte
93 Pleasant St
Plainville MA 027621900

Call Sign: N1IV
James W Duarte
93 Pleasant St
Plainville MA 02762

Call Sign: KB1ILW
Plainville EMA
93 Pleasant St
Plainville MA 02762

Call Sign: WC1PLV
Plainville EMA
93 Pleasant St
Plainville MA 02762

Call Sign: N1NKS
Patrick A Truitt
26 Redcoat Ln
Plainville MA 02762

Call Sign: AA1X
Joseph A Arruda
8 Shady Ln

Plainville MA 02762

Call Sign: KB1WFR
Kevin D Laliberte
24 Sharlene Ln
Plainville MA 02762

Call Sign: W1FRM
Guy E Devine
18 Taunton St Lot 40
Plainville MA 02762

Call Sign: WB1ETW
Raymond W Merigold Jr
18 Taunton St Unit 43
Plainville MA 02762

Call Sign: N1TQB
Richard W Payne
120 W Bacon St
Plainville MA 02762

Call Sign: K1ICJ
Paul E Ares
45 Washington St
Plainville MA 027622698

Call Sign: KA1ZUI
Emil C Wilbur Sr
45 Washington St Box 112
Plainville MA 02762

Call Sign: N8SF
Steven J Faulkingham
160 Washington St Unit 19
Plainville MA 027621316

Call Sign: KA1RNE
Meredith R Detwiler
10 Wisteria Dr
Plainville MA 02762

Call Sign: N1KND
Roland P Lizotte Jr
13 Fremont St
Planville MA 02762

FCC Amateur Radio Licenses in Plymouth

Call Sign: KD1CG
Joseph O Donnell
105 1620 Dr
Plymouth MA 02360

Call Sign: KB1JGA
Gerald R Flaherty
63 Agawam Rd
Plymouth MA 02360

Call Sign: N1KXF
Arthur W Policelli
6 Albert Rd
Plymouth MA 02360

Call Sign: W1HHZ
Michael R Rocchi
77 Alden St
Plymouth MA 02360

Call Sign: K1NXH
Gerald A Ouellette
87 Andrews Way
Plymouth MA 023601641

Call Sign: KB1HJG
Edward M Mello
56 B Wallwind Dr
Plymouth MA 02360

Call Sign: W1HNO
Peter B Koch
53 Bay Shore Dr
Plymouth MA 02360

Call Sign: KB1TXG
Marshall M Kennard
17 Bayberry Rd
Plymouth MA 02360

Call Sign: KB1TXH
Donna M Donovan
17 Bayberry Rd
Plymouth MA 02360

Call Sign: N1FWX
Lauren E Foster
134 Beaver Dam Rd
Plymouth MA 02360

Call Sign: N1YCE
Robert J Burns

136 Beaver Dam Rd
Plymouth MA 02360

Call Sign: N1BLK
Edmund T Lavin Sr
184 Beaver Dam Rd
Plymouth MA 02360

Call Sign: KA1RNL
Sarah W Flood
183 Bettencourt Rd
Plymouth MA 02360

Call Sign: KB1KBN
Richard G West
158 Billington St
Plymouth MA
023603580

Call Sign: KB1KVF
Richard G West
158 Billington St
Plymouth MA
023603580

Call Sign: KA1YGQ
Robert J Meharg Iii
Boot Pond Rd
Plymouth MA 02360

Call Sign: KB1ACH
Sean F Mc Neill
177 Bourne Rd
Plymouth MA 02360

Call Sign: W1SUR
John L Koukol
16 Boutemain Ave
Plymouth MA 02360

Call Sign: N1OYJ
John J Waitner
121 Brentwood Cir
Plymouth MA 02360

Call Sign: N1AOR
Thomas N Dickson
25 Bridge Gate
Plymouth MA 02360

Call Sign: WA1WQC
David L Whelan
11 Bruce Rd
Plymouth MA 02360

Call Sign: KA1ZZ
Paul F Gavoni
72 Carver Rd
Plymouth MA 02360

Call Sign: KB1ERW
Sylvan Pierre
205 Carver Rd
Plymouth MA 02360

Call Sign: KB9ACL
Sarah E De Lair
Carver Rd
Plymouth MA 02360

Call Sign: KB1KMA
David P Gilbert
10 Chapel Hill Dr Unit
10
Plymouth MA 02360

Call Sign: N1JAM
Steven F Leone
5 Chapel Hill Dr Unit
8
Plymouth MA 02360

Call Sign: K1YAN
Gary T Meyn
8 Charlotte Dr
Plymouth MA 02360

Call Sign: KB1CYW
Sean B Montgomery
18 Charlotte Drive
Plymouth MA 02360

Call Sign: KA1WCE
Marie L Wood
21 Cherry St
Plymouth MA 02360

Call Sign: KE1ER
Lebon A Pinto
76 Cherry St
Plymouth MA 02360

Call Sign: WA1GDN
David N Swinney
8 Chestnut St
Plymouth MA 02360

Call Sign: KA1OYZ

Stephen J Keris Jr
20 Columbia Cir
Plymouth MA 02360

Call Sign: KB1WSV
Mark R Shean
76 Columbia Circle
Plymouth MA 02360

Call Sign: N1ORA
Ronald F Gear Jr
1 Cordage St
Plymouth MA 02360

Call Sign: KA1RTA
Richard A Wood
22 Cordage Ter
Plymouth MA 02360

Call Sign: K1BFJ
John M Kenealy
128 Court St - Apt C-
37
Plymouth MA 02360

Call Sign: KB1GDQ
Wesley B Holmes Jr
39 Crabtree Rd
Plymouth MA 02360

Call Sign: N1WH
Wesley B Holmes Jr
39 Crabtree Rd
Plymouth MA 02360

Call Sign: N1BLI
Robert Girvan
8 Dartmouth Rd
Plymouth MA 02360

Call Sign: KB1HKH
Eric P Sears
30 Davis St
Plymouth MA 02360

Call Sign: WA1FRL
Lawrence A Laspesa
9 Downey St
Plymouth MA 02360

Call Sign: KB1ERV
Edward B Maccaferri
Jr
25 E Russell Mills Rd

Plymouth MA 02360

Call Sign: KA1QOD
John F Maguire Jr
8 Eel River Cir
Plymouth MA 02360

Call Sign: KA1YIH
Jeremy M Davis
27 Eel River Cir
Plymouth MA 02360

Call Sign: WA1VIM
Arthur J Rossi
20 Ellisville Green
Plymouth MA 02360

Call Sign: KC1HO
K Stephen Johnson Jr
103 Esta Rd
Plymouth MA
023604911

Call Sign: KB1RGN
William T Tilden
38 Fairway Dr
Plymouth MA 02360

Call Sign: KB1QDT
William F Seale Iii
10 Fathom Rd
Plymouth MA 02360

Call Sign: W1ZZR
William F Seale Iii
10 Fathom Rd
Plymouth MA 02360

Call Sign: KB1QVA
Richard G Tavas
21 Federal Furnace Rd
Plymouth MA 02360

Call Sign: KB1WWZ
Calvin L Wilson
18 Flying Jib Lane
Plymouth MA 02360

Call Sign: N1SZU
Clayson L Nicholson
23 Garrett Place
Plymouth MA 02360

Call Sign: W1LM

Mayflower Amateur
Radio Club
6 Gate Rd
Plymouth MA 02360

Call Sign: WS1K
Jonathan H Jesse
6 Gate Rd
Plymouth MA 02360

Call Sign: W1JHJ
Jonathan H Jesse
6 Gate Rd
Plymouth MA 02360

Call Sign: WS1K
Jonathan H Jesse
6 Gate Rd
Plymouth MA 02360

Call Sign: WX1DOG
Robert J Simcik
18 Great Wind Dr
Plymouth MA 02360

Call Sign: N1LRD
Alan P Wolcott
30 Halyard Rd
Plymouth MA
023602754

Call Sign: KB1UAZ
Matthew R Trimberger
49 Harborlight Dr
Plymouth MA 02360

Call Sign: KB1PND
Jennifer A Sullivan
10 Harvard Dr
Plymouth MA 02360

Call Sign: KV1T
Robert A Hickey
33 Headlands Dr
Plymouth MA 02360

Call Sign: N1XJK
Myron E Winders Jr
233 Hedges Pond Rd
Plymouth MA
023602215

Call Sign: N1XQD
James W Dimodica

14 Hillside Drive
Plymouth MA 02360

Call Sign: KB1UUS
Robert J Power
31 Home Depot Dr
Suite #244
Plymouth MA 02360

Call Sign: NS1X
Jeffrey J Alves
4 Hood Dr
Plymouth MA 02360

Call Sign: WB1DQS
Paul C Stasinos
32 Howard Dr
Plymouth MA 02360

Call Sign: KB1EAG
Alan M Costello
41 Huntington Rd
Plymouth MA 02360

Call Sign: KC1BY
Henry F Washington
Iii
18 Independence St
Plymouth MA 02360

Call Sign: KB1DE
Robert M Mattson
2 Indian Tr Plym Mob
Est
Plymouth MA 02360

Call Sign: KB1ACJ
Janine M Haley
20 James Cir
Plymouth MA 02360

Call Sign: KB1UYW
William S Wennerberg
Jr
23 Jan Marie Dr
Plymouth MA 02360

Call Sign: W1HTY
Leslie A Harlow
35 Jane Bar Cir
Plymouth MA 02360

Call Sign: W1FSZ
William R Bradford

19 Janebar Cir
Plymouth MA 02360

Call Sign: N1SZF
Christopher E Johnson
19 Janet St
Plymouth MA 02360

Call Sign: N1IR
Christopher E Johnson
19 Janet St
Plymouth MA 02360

Call Sign: KB1HJI
Stephen J Main
26 Janet St
Plymouth MA 02360

Call Sign: KA1WGV
Peter A Shakalis
9 John Alden Rd
Plymouth MA 02360

Call Sign: KD1BJ
Edward G Shakalis
10 John Alden Rd
Plymouth MA 02360

Call Sign: KB1BDQ
Stephen R Pennington
49 Justine Rd
Plymouth MA 02360

Call Sign: KB1ACE
Erin M Doherty
50 Justine Rd
Plymouth MA 02360

Call Sign: KB1ACF
Chrissy R Doherty
50 Justine Rd
Plymouth MA 02360

Call Sign: N1GRX
Dennis A Silva
69 Kenwood Dr
Plymouth MA 02360

Call Sign: K1OTM
Donald H Erickson
147 Lake Dr
Plymouth MA 02360

Call Sign: KB1SVA

Douglas A Loud
52 Liberty St Apt K3
Plymouth MA 02360

Call Sign: KB1MHW
Wesley B Holmes
222 Long Pond Rd
Plymouth MA 02360

Call Sign: W1WQ
Robert P G Daniels
871 Long Pond Rd
Plymouth MA
023621371

Call Sign: KB1ACI
Michael A Savino
1120 Long Pond Rd
Plymouth MA 02360

Call Sign: N1KXB
John B Flattery
1167 Long Pond Rd
Plymouth MA 02360

Call Sign: N1VIW
Mary Lou Flattery
1167 Long Pond Rd
Plymouth MA 02360

Call Sign: N1XXM
Carlos T B Fragata
27 Lucys Path
Plymouth MA 02360

Call Sign: W1COD
Bernard E Mc Peck
396 Lunns Way
Plymouth MA 02360

Call Sign: KB1NGB
Mark W Tomkins
459 Lunns Way
Plymouth MA 02360

Call Sign: K1MWT
Mark W Tomkins
459 Lunns Way
Plymouth MA 02360

Call Sign: WA1CHH
John W Prescott
22 Lydia Dr
Plymouth MA 02360

Call Sign: N1VIP
Paulo C Silva
53 Main St
Plymouth MA 02360

Call Sign: N1MJM
Jonathan M Le Bretton
9 Marscot Way
Plymouth MA 02360

Call Sign: W1CUY
Robert L Parker
81 May Hill Rd
Plymouth MA 02360

Call Sign: WA2MHY
Russel L Appleyard
31 Megansett Drive
Plymouth MA 02360

Call Sign: WB1AAJ
Charles H Mc Leavy
62 Melix Ave
Plymouth MA 02360

Call Sign: N1TBI
Paul F Moriarty
54 Micajah Ave
Plymouth MA 02360

Call Sign: KA1WRF
William F Adamski
107 Micajah Pond Rd
Plymouth MA 02360

Call Sign: KA2SJF
Claude P Boudwin
3 Mimosa Circle
Plymouth MA 02360

Call Sign: KA1NMA
Robert A Johnson
7 Morton Park Rd
Plymouth MA
023621418

Call Sign: N1JKO
Christopher P Querze
9 Muster Field Rd
Plymouth MA 02360

Call Sign: KB1VKC
Christopher P Querze

9 Muster Field Rd
Plymouth MA 02360

Call Sign: K1TH
Thomas W Hurley
109 N Triangle Dr
Plymouth MA 02360

Call Sign: N1YWW
William T Hurley
109 N Triangle Dr
Plymouth MA 02360

Call Sign: WB2BYO
Linda J Hurley
109 N Triangle Dr
Plymouth MA 02360

Call Sign: W1BIH
John H Thompson
19 Newfield St C5
Plymouth MA 02360

Call Sign: KB1GLC
Arthur J Dupuis Jr
27 Nicks Rock Rd
Plymouth MA
023604170

Call Sign: N1IOU
Darren D Clark
28 Oar And Line Rd
Plymouth MA 02360

Call Sign: KB1RAV
Plymouth EOC
44 Obery St
Plymouth MA 02760

Call Sign: KB1RVV
Kevin R Johnson
26 Palmer Rd
Plymouth MA 02360

Call Sign: KB1ACD
Jessica A Slowey
64 Pawtuxet Rd
Plymouth MA 02360

Call Sign: WS1M
Leopold Bric
134 Pine Mountain Dr
Plymouth MA 02360

Call Sign: N1KCN
George D Le Brun
63 Pinehurst Dr
Plymouth MA 02360

Call Sign: NC1K
Mervyn J Mc Kee
15 Plantation Rd
Plymouth MA 02360

Call Sign: N1NDO
John E White
27 Plantation Rd
Plymouth MA 02360

Call Sign: KA1VAX
Mary E Sproles
17 Pleasant St
Plymouth MA 02360

Call Sign: N1HMH
William R Sproles
17 Pleasant St
Plymouth MA 02360

Call Sign: AH6NN
Kenneth W Cannon
4 Pokanoket Rd
Plymouth MA 02360

Call Sign: N1WNR
Richard H Cicchetti Sr
144 Raymond Rd
Plymouth MA 02360

Call Sign: N1WNS
Phyllis E Cicchetti
144 Raymond Rd
Plymouth MA 02360

Call Sign: N5OAI
Donald M Moore Jr
65 River St
Plymouth MA 02360

Call Sign: N1WJH
Richard B Condron
173 Rocky Hill Rd
Plymouth MA 02360

Call Sign: N1WPA
Cathryn J Condron
173 Rocky Hill Rd
Plymouth MA 02360

Call Sign: KA1UJP
Courtney A Ford
194 Rocky Hill Rd
Plymouth MA 02360

Call Sign: NM1F
James E Ford
194 Rocky Hill Rd
Plymouth MA 02360

Call Sign: KB1LOO
Christopher F Babbitt
711 Rocky Hill Rd
Plymouth MA 02360

Call Sign: WA1CGO
Henry A Coveney
Rocky Hill Rd
Plymouth MA 02360

Call Sign: W1SCA
John H Steele
181 Roxy Cahoon Rd
Plymouth MA 02360

Call Sign: W1VVW
Doris I Steele
181 Roxy Cahoon Rd
Plymouth MA 02360

Call Sign: N1MJO
Robynn L Sampson
2 S Cherry St
Plymouth MA 02360

Call Sign: N1ZIZ
Raymond V Govoni
151 S Meadow
Plymouth MA 02360

Call Sign: N1RGM
William A Mc Donald
64 S Meadow Rd
Plymouth MA 02360

Call Sign: W1QKR
Francis A Pineau
85 S Meadow Rd
Plymouth MA
023604750

Call Sign: N1MJS
John C Chandler

6 S Spooner St
Plymouth MA 02360

Call Sign: N1OEE
Roberta E Chandler
6 S Spooner St
Plymouth MA 02360

Call Sign: WB1GZB
Colin C Moran
37 Sachem Rd
Plymouth MA 02360

Call Sign: N1NZD
Scott A Carroll
58 Sanderson Dr
Plymouth MA 02360

Call Sign: WA1KFQ
Steven P Gallagher
221 Sandwich St
Plymouth MA 02360

Call Sign: KD6EYE
Steve Delaney
232 Sandwich St
Plymouth MA 02360

Call Sign: KA1RTE
Douglas H Armstrong
274 Sandwich St
Plymouth MA
023602131

Call Sign: KB1CGP
Owen V Malaguti
293 Sandwich St
Plymouth MA 02360

Call Sign: KA1RTG
Carl F Mattson
345 Sandwich St
Plymouth MA 02360

Call Sign: KB1WGW
Robert Mcganty
38 Sandy Beach Rd
Plymouth MA 02360

Call Sign: KD1BZ
Thomas F Williams
11 Savin Rd
Plymouth MA 02360

Call Sign: K1THS
Rodney C Schonland
9 Sever St
Plymouth MA 02360

Call Sign: K1QKE
Francis L Pizzano Sr
209 Ship Pond Rd
Plymouth MA 02360

Call Sign: KB1SEV
Dominic T Lentini
81 South Meadow Rd
Plymouth MA 02360

Call Sign: N1DTL
Dominic T Lentini
81 South Meadow Rd
Plymouth MA 02360

Call Sign: AA1DD
Jure J Skvarc
1985 Sr
Plymouth MA 02360

Call Sign: WB1GUS
Dale M Webber
20 Stafford St
Plymouth MA 02360

Call Sign: W1III
David F Crowley Jr
68 State Rd
Plymouth MA 02360

Call Sign: KB1JGN
Scott A Berna
802 State Rd
Plymouth MA 02360

Call Sign: KC1ML
Mark E Loring
1028 State Rd
Plymouth MA 02360

Call Sign: N1UHS
Robert T Samuelson
1555 State Rd
Plymouth MA 02360

Call Sign: WA1DEE
James M Moores Jr
1632 State Rd

Plymouth MA
023605192

Call Sign: N1AMP
Paul F Willard
1661 State Rd
Plymouth MA 02360

Call Sign: N1YCP
John R Turner Jr
4 Stephens Ln Unit B
Plymouth MA
023603368

Call Sign: KD4OFZ
Ricardo Diaz
5 Stephens St
Plymouth MA 02360

Call Sign: N1SYC
Robert E Holland Jr
58 Stockade Path
Plymouth MA 02360

Call Sign: N1JKI
Richard L Hatch Sr
4 Tadpole
Plymouth MA 02360

Call Sign: KA1VBN
Herman J Hunt Jr
205 Taylor Ave
Plymouth MA
023606326

Call Sign: KB1PVD
David K Hood
70 Thoreau Rd
Plymouth MA 02360

Call Sign: W1KB
David K Hood
70 Thoreau Rd
Plymouth MA 02360

Call Sign: KA2EPV
Andrew M Simon
15 Valley Front
Plymouth MA 02360

Call Sign: N1NVV
Peter J Curley
10 Vernon St
Plymouth MA 02360

Call Sign: KA1KYT
Diane M Baldwin
49 W Long Pond Rd
Plymouth MA 02360

Call Sign: N1HMJ
Paul J Mello
56 Wall Wind Dr
Plymouth MA 02360

Call Sign: N1SYB
Edward M Mello
56 Wall Wind Dr
Plymouth MA 02360

Call Sign: W1PJM
Paul J Mello
56 Wall Wind Dr
Plymouth MA 02360

Call Sign: N1OEA
Robert B Mc Kenna
12 Wamsutta Ave
Plymouth MA 02360

Call Sign: W1EIF
Charles E Winkley Jr
81 Warren Ave
Plymouth MA 02360

Call Sign: N1MJN
Roger A Perry
10 Washington St
Plymouth MA 02362

Call Sign: W1AG
Bernard T Lee
6 Wellingsley Ave
Plymouth MA
023602933

Call Sign: W1CFH
Ralph F Goldman
7 West Trevor Hill
Plymouth MA 02360

Call Sign: N1DFJ
Brian P Mitchell
9 White St
Plymouth MA 02360

Call Sign: W1OFK
Joseph J De Sousa Jr

29 Whiting St
Plymouth MA 02360

Call Sign: N1MSG
David K Kapell
15 Winding Ln
Plymouth MA 02360

Call Sign: N1JTY
Peter M Flynn
2 Winding Way
Plymouth MA 02360

Call Sign: N1KF
Peter M Flynn
2 Winding Way
Plymouth MA 02360

Call Sign: WW1U
Roger V Burns Jr
91 Winding Way
Plymouth MA
023602028

Call Sign: N1EH
Eugene M Harriman Ii
Plymouth MA
023620903

Call Sign: N1LRF
Timothy J Donovan
Plymouth MA
023621166

Call Sign: N1MJP
Samantha J Harriman
Plymouth MA
023620903

Call Sign: N1SLM
Warren E Hart
Plymouth MA 02362

Call Sign: KB1SRO
Judith A Attaya-Harris
Plymouth MA 02360

Call Sign: KB1UHV
Anthony M Attaya-
Harris
Plymouth MA 02360

Call Sign: KB1VDE
Robert M Lloyd

Plymouth MA 02362

Call Sign: KB1AKL
Christopher W Hunt
24 Center St
Plympton MA 02367

Call Sign: WA5GZI
Carl T Brummett
164 County Rd
Plympton MA 02367

Call Sign: N1OXJ
John Kennedy
5 Lake St
Plympton MA 02367

Call Sign: KB1KPQ
Stephen J Mattern
10 Lemuel Cobb Rd
Plympton MA 02367

Call Sign: K1MVT
James H Chisholm
149 Main St
Plympton MA 02367

Call Sign: KB1KVO
Jacob H Matern
113 Maple St
Plympton MA 02367

Call Sign: W1XRA
Robert R Smith
6 Trout Farm Ln
Plympton MA 02367

Call Sign: KK3P
Robert R Smith
6 Trout Farm Ln
Plympton MA 02367

Call Sign: KB1TEB
Elizabeth M Krance
103 Upland Rd
Plympton MA 02367

Call Sign: KB1TEF
Deborah Anderson
Plympton MA 02367

Call Sign: W1BTL
Joseph P Galvani
121 Bellavista Dr
Pocasset MA 02559

Call Sign: N1PDJ
Anthony A Gargano
149 Bellavista Drive
Pocasset MA
025592017

Call Sign: KB1GFH
George W Weinert
20 Cedar Point Dr
Pocasset MA 02559

Call Sign: KB1GFI
Jo Ann Weinert
20 Cedar Point Dr
Pocasset MA 02559

Call Sign: W1JSS
Joseph F Dineen
260 Circuit Ave
Pocasset MA 02559

Call Sign: WJ1A
Joseph B Thornton
81 Clubhouse Dr
Pocasset MA 02559

Call Sign: N1HXM
Anthony G Vallance
119 Elgin Rd
Pocasset MA 02559

Call Sign: N1GEU
David G Curran
3 Mame Cir
Pocasset MA
025590328

Call Sign: W1MHG
Donald N Crowell
20 Observatory Ln
Box 456
Pocasset MA 02559

Call Sign: W1UAN
Robert S Sabin
49 Old North Rd

Pocasset MA
025593075

Call Sign: N1SIC
Donald A Deluca
41 Portside Drive
Pocasset MA
025591929

Call Sign: KA1THA
Richard L Penney
13 Second Ave
Pocasset MA
025590606

Call Sign: N1UGE
Charles E Bresnahan
110 Tahanto Rd
Pocasset MA
025593502

Call Sign: WA1RSP
Donald F Bolles
183 Tahanto Rd
Pocasset MA 02559

Call Sign: KA1ZAJ
Christopher J O
Donnell Jr
20 Vesper Dr
Pocasset MA 02559

Call Sign: N1ILH
Jeffrey P Moon
25 Vesper Dr Rd 1
Pocasset MA 02559

Call Sign: K1ZLF
Robert J Kilduff
8 Wenaumet Bluff Dr
Pocasset MA 02559

Call Sign: W1JSS
Thomas N Dineen
25 Wing Rd
Pocasset MA 02559

Call Sign: KB1JAF
William P Fahy
260 Wings Neck Rd
Pocasset MA
025591768

Call Sign: KB1WPF

William P Fahy
260 Wings Neck Rd
Pocasset MA
025591768

Call Sign: KA1YDZ
Neil M Mc Phee
Pocasset MA 02559

Call Sign: N1JTS
William R Goranson
Pocasset MA 02559

Call Sign: N1MMG
Carol E Goranson
Pocasset MA 02559

Call Sign: N1QAH
Maureen R Goode
Pocasset MA 02559

Call Sign: KA1NBN
George H Tupper
Pocasset MA 02559

Call Sign: N1CFV
Ernest A Larsen
Pocasset MA
025590422

Call Sign: KB1KMC
Helen V Bresnahan
Pocasset MA
025593502

FCC Amateur Radio Licenses in Polton

Call Sign: KA1QDS
Eric A R Gallini
308 Perlin Rd
Polton MA 01740

FCC Amateur Radio Licenses in Prides Crossing

Call Sign: N1TCU
Charles S Dunne
16 Greenwood Ave
Prides Crossing MA
01965

Call Sign: KA1KFN

Richard Olney Iii
425 Hale St
Prides Crossing MA
01965

Call Sign: N1UAY
Pierce Nichols
Prides Crossing MA
01965

FCC Amateur Radio Licenses in Princeton

Call Sign: W1BR
Roger H Prince
18 Bigelow Rd
Princeton MA
015411916

Call Sign: KA1PZJ
Timothy M Boilard
36 Bigelow Rd
Princeton MA 01541

Call Sign: KA1RPP
Judith H Boilard
36 Bigelow Rd
Princeton MA 01541

Call Sign: NQ1N
Roger B Boilard
36 Bigelow Rd
Princeton MA 01541

Call Sign: N2TEO
Dale A Faraday
113 Calamint Hill Rd
North
Princeton MA
015410224

Call Sign: WB1AEL
Shawn C Kelley
50 Coal Kiln Rd
Princeton MA 01541

Call Sign: N1RDV
Brian T Long
7 Goodnow Rd
Princeton MA
015411602

Call Sign: WA1YVL
Douglas E August

122 Hobbs Rd
Princeton MA 01541

Call Sign: AB1GG
Douglas E August
122 Hobbs Rd
Princeton MA 01541

Call Sign: N1TNP
Michael R Lafountain
131 Houghton Rd
Princeton MA 01541

Call Sign: W1JPA
John P Allen
173 Mountain Rd
Princeton MA 01541

Call Sign: KB1WCQ
Kohji Shino
227 Mountain Rd
Princeton MA 01541

Call Sign: K1YI
Francis J Furmanick
Princeton MA 01541

Call Sign: KA1ISH
Norma J Furmanick
Princeton MA 01541

FCC Amateur Radio Licenses in Provincetown

Call Sign: N1RIW
Timothy W Caldwell
58 Bradford St
Provincetown MA
02657

Call Sign: KB1ADA
Daniel J Notaro
512 Commercial St
Provincetown MA
02657

Call Sign: W1JBW
Powell Murchison
2 Commercial St Box
543
Provincetown MA
02657

Call Sign: K1CUD
Anthony S Roda
Conwell St
Provincetown MA
02657

Call Sign: KA2RGL
Susan M Leven
Franklin St
Provincetown MA
02657

Call Sign: KD1DQ
Frank E Thompson
9 Johnson St
Provincetown MA
02657

Call Sign: K1TCO
Walter R Harding
6 Pleasant St
Provincetown MA
02657

Call Sign: W1PY
Carl B Black
6 Priscilla Alden Rd
Provincetown MA
02657

Call Sign: NW1F
Chester A Jones
56 W Vine St
Provincetown MA
02657

Call Sign: WA1KZT
Earle H Chaddock
Provincetown MA
02657

Call Sign: WZ1O
William A Von Der
Heydt
Provincetown MA
02657

FCC Amateur Radio Licenses in Qunicy

Call Sign: N1EIA
Jerrol E Quillin Jr
1 Adams St Unit 207

Quincy MA
021692005

Call Sign: WA2IWC
Donald J Breda
1 Adams St Unit 404
Quincy MA
021692005

Call Sign: N1PIG
Fu S Tham
217 Arlington St
Quincy MA
021701705

Call Sign: N1DAN
James B Walker
24 Bell St
Quincy MA 02169

Call Sign: WA1CBI
Warren E Houghton
26 Bellevue Rd
Quincy MA 02171

Call Sign: N1MYQ
John P Foley
350 Belmont St
Quincy MA 02170

Call Sign: KD1HR
Stephen M Carousso
19 Branch St
Quincy MA 02169

Call Sign: N1VIO
Kwok Lung W Lee
73 Bromfield St
Quincy MA 02170

Call Sign: N1VSL
Jackson Lee
73 Bromfield St
Quincy MA 02170

Call Sign: KB1LWL
Amy P Keung
70 Buckingham Rd
Quincy MA 02170

Call Sign: KB1QPO
Joseph Duffy
12 Bunker Hill Lane
Quincy MA 02169

Call Sign: KB1IXK
Joseph A Harris
113 Burgin Pkwy 3rd
Floor
Quincy MA 02169

Call Sign: WA1GTB
Frank J Carroll
26 Calumet St
Quincy MA
021702107

Call Sign: KB1SWD
Jason M Courtemanche
2 City View Ln Apt
303
Quincy MA 02169

Call Sign: KB1SWC
Edward T
Courtemanche
2 Cityview Ln Apt 303
Quincy MA 02169

Call Sign: K1EEK
John B Gilmore
37 Colonial Drive
Quincy MA 02169

Call Sign: KB1KZI
Jimmy Devarie
95 Columbia St
Quincy MA 02169

Call Sign: WA1JIM
Jimmy Devarie
95 Columbia St
Quincy MA 02169

Call Sign: KA1FTY
Joseph F Fernandez
205 Copeland St
Quincy MA 02169

Call Sign: KA1FWB
Mary A Fernandez
205 Copeland St
Quincy MA 02169

Call Sign: KB1NWZ
Tenley T Mckee
195 Copeland St Unit J
Quincy MA 02169

Call Sign: N1WPT
Hugh C Kelley
119 Cranch St
Quincy MA 02169

Call Sign: KB1OJB
Kristjan M Viise
84 Crescent St
Quincy MA 02169

Call Sign: WA1NIX
Louis S Venturelli
64 Cross St
Quincy MA 02169

Call Sign: KE1GD
Patricia E Allen
43 Cummings Ave
Quincy MA 02170

Call Sign: KA1FXX
John S Lyons
5 Curtis Ave
Quincy MA 02169

Call Sign: KB1IUR
Tzu-Fang Lee
35 Des Moines Rd 403
Quincy MA 02169

Call Sign: N5NBA
Alfred J Bird Phd
138 E Elm Ave
Quincy MA
021702422

Call Sign: KB2NXU
Alexander J Skrabut
86 E Howard St Unit
107
Quincy MA 02169

Call Sign: KB1TXC
Craig J Ingram
50 E Squantum St Apt
#13a
Quincy MA 02171

Call Sign: KA1TRD
George F Doherty Jr
85 Edison Pk
Quincy MA 02169

Call Sign: N1KQY
Frank J Colantonio Jr
26 Edison St
Quincy MA 02169

Call Sign: KA1QDX
Edward C Budreau
41 Ellington Rd
Quincy MA
021701905

Call Sign: N1SOX
William C Moynihan
Jr
17 Elm St 8
Quincy MA
021695405

Call Sign: N1KUF
Brian P Mahoney Jr
31 Elmwood Ave
Quincy MA 02170

Call Sign: KB1PMI
David P Mcnally
92 Elmwood Ave
Quincy MA
021701503

Call Sign: N1HRR
Daniel M Smith
34 Emerald
Quincy MA 02169

Call Sign: N1OCN
Carole A Smith
34 Emerald St
Quincy MA 02169

Call Sign: KB1WEE
Brian A Labrecque
35 Estabrook Rd
Quincy MA 02170

Call Sign: K1UEK
Francis R Stec
14 Euclid Ave
Quincy MA 02169

Call Sign: K1PRO
Patrick O'malley
71 Fenno St Apt 9
Quincy MA 02170

Call Sign: KC1KV
John C Crowley Sr
34 Field St Apt F
Quincy MA 02169

Call Sign: W1DXQ
John E Schmock
40 Franklin St
Quincy MA 02169

Call Sign: W1LZW
William H Pitts
175 Gardiner Rd
Quincy MA 02169

Call Sign: KA1HCJ
Hollis G Watlington
57 Gay St
Quincy MA 02169

Call Sign: KB1MEH
Steve T Kondo
74 Glendale Rd Apt 2
Quincy MA 02169

Call Sign: KA2POE
Charles A Antonelli
25 Gothland St Unit G
Quincy MA
021691841

Call Sign: N1WIK
Joseph M Zero
15 Grace Rd
Quincy MA 02169

Call Sign: K1FZC
Ralph W Kief
125 Granite St
Quincy MA 02169

Call Sign: WB0ADV
Terry T Steeden
2 Hancock St Apt 401
Quincy MA
021711767

Call Sign: WB0WGV
Marylou L Steeden
2 Hancock St Apt 401
Quincy MA
021711767

Call Sign: KB1VSR

Marylou L Steeden
2 Hancock St Apt 401
Quincy MA
021711767

Call Sign: N1TTS
Terry T Steeden
2 Hancock St Apt 401
Quincy MA
021711767

Call Sign: AA1CC
Alan J Atkinson
32 Hilda St
Quincy MA 02169

Call Sign: KE4PGE
Lucille W Jansen Mrs
36 Hilda St
Quincy MA 02169

Call Sign: KE4PGJ
Peter Z Jansen
36 Hilda St
Quincy MA 02169

Call Sign: W1KRN
Henry V Maher Jr
71 Hobart St
Quincy MA
021701631

Call Sign: W1ACB
Charles F Anderson
106 Hobart St
Quincy MA 02170

Call Sign: K1YWI
Paul V Doherty
14 Homestead Ave
Quincy MA 02169

Call Sign: KA1DPN
Theresa M Mc Niel
28 Hudson St
Quincy MA 02169

Call Sign: KB1DDJ
Thomas H Allen
1 Hughes St
Quincy MA
021698901

Call Sign: AA1JZ

William J Hennessy
56 Hughes St
Quincy MA 02169

Call Sign: KB1GRX
Patrick T Odonnell
72 Hughes St
Quincy MA
021698932

Call Sign: KB1CHV
Richard F Giguere
225 Independence Ave
#33
Quincy MA 02169

Call Sign: N1TWO
Bernard L Warshauer
20 James St
Quincy MA
021696914

Call Sign: W1PKQ
Ernest A Smith
17 Lebanon St
Quincy MA 02169

Call Sign: N1INY
Herbert R Driscoll
53 Liberty St
Quincy MA 02169

Call Sign: KB1TWZ
Donna M Lymneos
216 Liberty St
Quincy MA 02169

Call Sign: N1IVQ
Andrew D Merliss
2001 Marina Dr 411w
Quincy MA 02171

Call Sign: W1SOJ
Leo F Burke
1 Marlboro St
Quincy MA 02170

Call Sign: N1QIK
William J Corbett
20 Mascoma St
Quincy MA 02170

Call Sign: KB1EKK
Krikor Kolandjian

80 Mc Grath Hwy
Quincy MA 02169

Call Sign: KB1THI
Fred E Reynolds
8 Mechanic St
Quincy MA 02169

Call Sign: W1BZE
Fred E Reynolds
8 Mechanic St
Quincy MA 02169

Call Sign: N1AWX
John J O Brien
65 Merry Mount Rd
Quincy MA 02169

Call Sign: N1KUG
William E Dunn Jr
178 Milton St
Quincy MA 02170

Call Sign: KB1JFU
Metro Boston Disaster
Medical Assistance
Team
178 Milton St
Quincy MA 02170

Call Sign: ND1MA
Metro Boston Disaster
Medical Assistance
Team Ma-1
178 Milton St
Quincy MA
021702504

Call Sign: N1VCZ
Paul V Minezzi
50 Monmouth St
Quincy MA 02171

Call Sign: N1YIA
David R Polk
31 Mt Ararat Rd
Quincy MA 02169

Call Sign: KB1WVM
Daniel J Kane
63 Norton Rd
Quincy MA 02169

Call Sign: KA1NGT

Ervin L Crandell
75 Palmer St
Quincy MA 02169

Call Sign: KC1GI
David M Tenenbaum
75 Palmer St
Quincy MA 02169

Call Sign: WA2HNI
David J Reich
26 Phillips St
Quincy MA 02170

Call Sign: KB1MJM
Francis G Fell
93 Piermont St
Quincy MA 02170

Call Sign: N1FGF
Francis G Fell
93 Piermont St
Quincy MA 02170

Call Sign: KB1NWV
Donald J Timmins
221 Pine St
Quincy MA 02170

Call Sign: N1YZU
Richard E Eames Jr
168 Plymouth Ave
Quincy MA 02169

Call Sign: K1VKV
Fausto G De Santis
22 Presidential Dr
Quincy MA 02169

Call Sign: N1QIF
William A Puzo
Presidential Dr
Quincy MA 02169

Call Sign: N1ALR
Henry Niklas
145 Presidents Ln
Quincy MA 02169

Call Sign: N1QKI
Mongkol Horburapa
162 Presidents Ln
Quincy MA 02169

Call Sign: N1CVI
Ronald L Mc Kim
243 Presidents Ln
Quincy MA 02169

Call Sign: N1LG
Ronald L Mc Kim
243 Presidents Ln
Quincy MA 02169

Call Sign: AB1II
Jay M Tarantino
87 Princess Eve Drive
Quincy MA 02170

Call Sign: KB1KNM
Walter H Macneil
270 Quarry St Apt 30
Quincy MA 02169

Call Sign: W1WMN
Walter H Macneil
270 Quarry St Apt 30
Quincy MA 02169

Call Sign: KB1QMO
Kevin E Macleod
57 Quincy St
Quincy MA 02169

Call Sign: K1LTD
Kevin E Macleod
57 Quincy St
Quincy MA 02169

Call Sign: KA1EQS
Stephen F Mc
Donough
36 Ratchford St
Quincy MA 02169

Call Sign: K1LOE
Walter D Sellers
70 Raycroft
Quincy MA 02169

Call Sign: KB1TOM
Thomas H Wilson
175 Rhoda St
Quincy MA 02169

Call Sign: W1ICU
Thomas H Wilson
175 Rhoda St

Quincy MA 02169

Call Sign: KB1UOE
Michael T Wilson
175 Rhoda St
Quincy MA 02169

Call Sign: KB1NAN
Steven M Papile
23 Ridgeway Dr
Quincy MA 02169

Call Sign: WA1EAT
Joseph F Daley
39 Riverbank Rd
Quincy MA 02169

Call Sign: KB1VJT
Chester R Freeman
42 Samuset Ave
Quincy MA 02169

Call Sign: N1ZGW
James J Quinn
45 Shed St
Quincy MA 02169

Call Sign: KB1WEM
Thomas J Whalen
128 Shore Ave
Quincy MA 02169

Call Sign: KB1TRE
George R Johnson
11 Shoreham St
Quincy MA 02171

Call Sign: KF6NWP
Robert P Bell
69 Sims Rd
Quincy MA 02170

Call Sign: K1PFT
Howard Reid Ward
1000 Southern Artery
730
Quincy MA 02169

Call Sign: N0GVI
Gary J Ludlam
1055 Southern Artery
Apt 305
Quincy MA 02169

Call Sign: N1BNW
Paul T Devine
999 Southern Artery
Apt 309
Quincy MA
021698405

Call Sign: KB1OVS
David M Mcclelland
29 Sunrise Rd
Quincy MA 02171

Call Sign: N1WSP
Erik W Johnson
19 Warwick St
Quincy MA 02170

Call Sign: KC4FRC
CARLY L Bridden
211 West St Unit 4b
Quincy MA 02169

Call Sign: W2HUG
Philip J Reich
10 Weston Ave Apt
423
Quincy MA 02170

Call Sign: KA1ONC
Jack Wolper
43 Whitney Rd
Quincy MA 02169

Call Sign: N1WIN
Ronald R Di Bella
55 Whiton Ave
Quincy MA 02169

Call Sign: N1ZEV
Mark N Mossbacker
64 Willard St 410
Quincy MA 02169

Call Sign: WA1TSL
Ralph V Lanzetta Jr
230 Willard St Unit
710
Quincy MA 02169

Call Sign: KB1GLJ
James W Robbins
46 Winter St 20
Quincy MA 02169

Call Sign: N1CMC
John D Smith
22 Winthrop Ave
Quincy MA
021703310

Call Sign: AA1FX
Barry J Bueler
18 Woodcliff Rd
Quincy MA
021697446

Call Sign: NB1B
Barry J Bueler
18 Woodcliff Rd
Quincy MA
021697446

Call Sign: N1LMD
Ronald S Walker
Quincy MA 02169

Call Sign: KD4VIL
Francklin Blaise
Quincy MA 02171

FCC Amateur Radio Licenses in Quincy Point

Call Sign: KB1RPR
William L Mills
73 Arnold St
Quincy Point MA
02169

FCC Amateur Radio Licenses in Randolph

Call Sign: N1LCY
Robert E Keene Jr
56 Adelaide St
Randolph MA 02368

Call Sign: N1ALP
Melvin Miller
15 Barbara Rd
Randolph MA 02368

Call Sign: KA1WIZ
Bruce W Kneller
29 Birch Dr
Randolph MA 02368

Call Sign: N1HLF
David M Kneller
29 Birch Dr
Randolph MA 02368

Call Sign: K1ATY
Joel L Richmond
30 Birch Drive
Randolph MA 02368

Call Sign: KB1DNL
Michele A Freedman
1 Boothby Cir
Randolph MA 02368

Call Sign: KB1ELG
Arthur M Mann
12 Boylston St
Randolph MA 02368

Call Sign: K1YM
Arthur M Mann
12 Boylston St
Randolph MA 02368

Call Sign: KB1PFN
Ben Kuipers
230 Centre St
Randolph MA 02368

Call Sign: K1KRD
Ben Kuipers
230 Centre St
Randolph MA 02368

Call Sign: KY2A
Ben Kuipers
230 Centre St
Randolph MA 02368

Call Sign: W1RQW
Irving Spector Mr
1 Charlotte Ln
Randolph MA 02368

Call Sign: N1NLL
Daniel R Mc Eleney
514 Decelle Drive
Randolph MA 02368

Call Sign: WA1ZID
Thomas J Holmes
19 Devine Rd
Randolph MA 02368

Call Sign: KB1DVA
Emily A Younie
93 Emily Jeffers Rd
Randolf MA 02368

Call Sign: N3UAN
Patrick J Younie
93 Emily Jeffers Rd
Randolf MA 02368

Call Sign: N1IJN
George A Joseph
15 Fencourt Ave
Randolph MA 02368

Call Sign: KA1KTN
Mark S Ross
6 Frederickson Dr
Randolph MA 02368

Call Sign: KB1JAJ
Stuart A Forman
43 Frederickson Dr
Randolph MA 02368

Call Sign: KB1JUL
Seth R Forman
43 Frederickson Dr
Randolph MA 02368

Call Sign: WA1SAF
Stuart A Forman
43 Frederickson Drive
Randolph MA 02368

Call Sign: W1SAF
Stuart A Forman
43 Frederickson Drive
Randolph MA 02368

Call Sign: W1PVJ
Abraham Bahm
21 Glen Ln
Randolph MA 02368

Call Sign: N1TDF
William G Sullivan
29 Grove Square
Randolph MA
023684027

Call Sign: N1NQR
Stephen C Cohn

10 Hemlock Ter
Randolph MA 02368

Call Sign: KA1YTY
Eric S Goldman
63 Highland Ave
Randolph MA 02368

Call Sign: KA1TTS
Emily J Avillan
14 Hildegarde St
Randolph MA
023682023

Call Sign: KA1EDO
John A Kespert
17 Hildegarde St
Randolph MA 02368

Call Sign: KD5LLS
Mohamed F Noamany
25 Jacobs Rd
Randolph MA 02368

Call Sign: KB1UBZ
Joan Cooper Zack
30 Knights Crescent
Randolph MA 02368

Call Sign: N1EVT
Carl R Rey
34 Lantern Ln
Randolph MA 02368

Call Sign: KA1USN
Gregorio Batista
42 Lantern Ln
Randolph MA 02368

Call Sign: W1IZH
Joseph A Schindler
1 Lisa Rd
Randolph MA
023683511

Call Sign: N1BKP
David H Ellis
5 Lisa Rd
Randolph MA 02368

Call Sign: KB1MVN
David S Odess
5 Macauley Way
Randolph MA 02368

Call Sign: W1ETF
Bruno D Puglia
27 Maitland Ave
Randolph MA 02368

Call Sign: W1UTG
Louis W Rovner
34 Maitland Ave
Randolph MA 02368

Call Sign: N1PNQ
Donald J Mahoney
24 Martin Ter
Randolph MA 02368

Call Sign: K1DWA
Ralph R Richardi
27 Morse St
Randolph MA 02368

Call Sign: W1IC
George H Foley
1241 No Main St
Randolph MA 02368

Call Sign: K1NKQ
Domenic A Conca
5 Norfolk Rd
Randolph MA 02368

Call Sign: KB1MQW
Zu Yen Lieng
41 Norfolk Rd
Randolph MA 02368

Call Sign: KA1NAH
Howard L Mariotti
368 North St
Randolph MA 02368

Call Sign: W1SCB
Carleton M Lang
480 North St
Randolph MA 02368

Call Sign: K1KZY
Charles L Mugherini
8 Plain St
Randolph MA 02368

Call Sign: KG4BVJ
O Neal Isom Jr
8 Powdrell Ave

Randolph MA 02368

Call Sign: KB1KKA
Gary A Reich
11 Randolph Rd
Randolph MA 02368

Call Sign: N1LWK
Kenneth J Desruisseau
34 Reed St
Randolph MA 02368

Call Sign: WY1B
Leonard H Lit
13 Reservoir Dr
Randolph MA 02368

Call Sign: W1IHS
Samuel Smith
19 Reservoir Dr
Randolph MA 02368

Call Sign: WA1WDQ
Donald F Mofford
39 Reynolds Ave
Randolph MA
023683739

Call Sign: N1RSO
Michael P Mc Eleney
10 Roy Croft Dr
Randolph MA 02368

Call Sign: N1HKW
Anthony M Lesniak
1 Royal Crest Dr
Randolph MA 02368

Call Sign: N1VEQ
James B Brennan Jr
2 Smith Rd
Randolph MA 02368

Call Sign: W1TPB
Theodore N Smith
81 Stearns Dr
Randolph MA
023683138

Call Sign: N2HQC
Jack E Mooney
49 Thomas Patten Dr
218
Randolph MA 02368

Call Sign: WB1EEA
Howard L Cohen
50 Union Square
Randolph MA 02368

Call Sign: KB1VBM
Michael P Mclaughlin
11 Velma Rd
Randolph MA 02368

Call Sign: KB1SQP
Bonnie L Marshall
41 Vesey Rd
Randolph MA 02368

Call Sign: K1WGU
Robert A Bass
7 Virginia Cir
Randolph MA 02368

Call Sign: KB1WED
Bryan C Michalski
46 Waldo St
Randolph MA 02368

Call Sign: WB1EZC
Leo St John Alves
7 Walsh St
Randolph MA 02368

Call Sign: NR1T
Robert R Cross Jr
4 Washington Dr
Randolph MA 02368

Call Sign: WA1YDP
James J Albertsen
94 Wilmarth Rd
Randolph MA 02368

Call Sign: N1NLC
Arnold J Galina
Randolph MA 02368

Call Sign: WB1O
Donald J Naphen
Randolph MA
023681250

FCC Amateur Radio Licenses in Raynham

Call Sign: KA1RTL

Warren D Pillsbury
500 Britton St
Raynham MA 02767

Call Sign: KA1RJH
Ronald E Vieira
373 Broadway
Raynham MA 02767

Call Sign: N1LHD
Walter C Fitzgerald
99 Center St
Raynham MA
027671741

Call Sign: W1WCF
Walter C Fitzgerald
99 Center St
Raynham MA
027671741

Call Sign: KA1RFJ
Alfred Machado Jr
481 Center St
Raynham MA 02767

Call Sign: W1EP
Edgar H Adler
Center St
Raynham MA 02767

Call Sign: N1PWJ
Ricardo L Gonzalves
101 Diniz Drive
Raynham MA 02767

Call Sign: WA1AZR
Frederick S Celli
160 Easy St
Raynham MA 02767

Call Sign: KA1CGK
George Phillips
38 Elm St East
Raynham MA 02767

Call Sign: K1BL
Wayne F Martyniak
398 Elm St East
Raynham MA 02767

Call Sign: N1IFH
Grant R Waterman
109 Everett Dr

Raynham MA 02767

Call Sign: KA1ZNT
Holly Hobart
36 Forge River Pky
Raynham MA 02767

Call Sign: KA1GSH
John Welch
43 Gilmore St
Raynham MA 02767

Call Sign: KA1BLP
George D Bradford Jr
383 Hall
Raynham MA 02767

Call Sign: N1LGL
Jeffery H T Clay
408 Hall St
Raynham MA 02767

Call Sign: N1IAL
James D Brackett
26 Hidden Valley Dr
Raynham MA 02767

Call Sign: KB1FGJ
George M
Dechambeau
595 Hill St
Raynham MA 02760

Call Sign: W1DMD
John D Alley
48 Judson St
Raynham MA 02767

Call Sign: N1LEH
Brian J Parry
784 King St
Raynham MA 02767

Call Sign: WA1HOS
Henry P Crombie
918 King St
Raynham MA 02767

Call Sign: N1WSS
David W Thomas
239 Locust St
Raynham MA
027671115

Call Sign: KB1RSR
Andrew V Niles Sr
606 Locust St
Raynham MA 02767

Call Sign: KB1SRP
Andrew V Niles Jr
606 Locust St
Raynham MA 02767

Call Sign: N1OPM
William G Bastiansen
646 Locust St
Raynham MA 02767

Call Sign: KC1S
David Rubin
933 Locust St
Raynham MA 02767

Call Sign: NI1X
Bruce D Hayden
1000 Locust St
Raynham MA 02767

Call Sign: WA1NPO
Whitman Amateur
Radio Club Inc
1000 Locust St
Raynham MA
027671130

Call Sign: N1NPB
James A Tilbe
18 N Main St
Raynham MA 02767

Call Sign: W1TI
Robert J Mc Guire Jr
613 N Main St
Raynham MA 02767

Call Sign: KB1VWT
Anthony J Vandermeel
847 N Main St
Raynham MA 02767

Call Sign: N1MII
Leonard J Amabile
100 New State Hwy
245
Raynham MA 02767

Call Sign: WA1IOZ

Anthony L Neves
663 Orchard St
Raynham MA 02767

Call Sign: KB2UIJ
Jared A Hollenbeck
202 Park Place
Raynham MA 02767

Call Sign: W1SJM
Henry S Kaminski
111 Paul St
Raynham MA 02767

Call Sign: N1HLD
Euclides L Bala
103 Peter St
Raynham MA 02767

Call Sign: N1LKJ
James T Ward
27 Phyllis Rd
Raynham MA
027671907

Call Sign: KB1BZF
David J O Malley
140 Pine St
Raynham MA 02767

Call Sign: WA1RII
Edward M Flanagan
365 Ramblewood Dr
Raynham MA 02767

Call Sign: ND1N
James H S Melville Ii
60 River St
Raynham MA 02767

Call Sign: KA1RJI
Aubrey L Redford
265 S Main St
Raynham MA 02767

Call Sign: KA1DFG
Norman C Poirier
198 Stonybrook Rd
Raynham MA 02767

Call Sign: KB1NVX
Brent T Dukes
218 Titicut Rd
Raynham MA 02767

Call Sign: KA1FAO
Edward O Hall
67 Tucker Terrace
Raynham MA 02767

Call Sign: W1CBK
Michael S Cucinotta
302 W Elm St
Raynham MA 02767

Call Sign: KB1SKF
Brian J Estano
176 Wilbur St
Raynham MA 02767

**FCC Amateur Radio
Licenses in Raynham
Center**

Call Sign: KA1ZVR
Alan W Kenney
Raynham Center MA
02768

Call Sign: N1OIP
Robert A Pribusauskas
Raynham Center MA
02768

**FCC Amateur Radio
Licenses in Reading**

Call Sign: AA1MN
Charles O Parshley
7 Alden Cir
Reading MA 01867

Call Sign: N0XZ
Matthew A Morton
4 Archstone Cir Unit
305
Reading MA 01867

Call Sign: N1YPH
Chester F Tyminski
17 Balsam Rd
Reading MA 01867

Call Sign: KB1QQF
Bernard R Horn Jr
99 Beaver Rd
Reading MA 01867

Call Sign: W1CKH
Jeffrey S Hollis
46 Bond St
Reading MA
018672432

Call Sign: KB1IQJ
Robert L Galante
95 Border Rd
Reading MA 01867

Call Sign: WA1PWZ
Robert L Galante
95 Border Rd
Reading MA 01867

Call Sign: KB1EQS
Anthony Dougas
1 Brentwood Dr
Reading MA 01867

Call Sign: N1AKG
James T Chamberlain
5 California Rd
Reading MA 01867

Call Sign: W1YCN
Russell B S Greene
31 Cape Cod Ave
Reading MA 01867

Call Sign: KA1AS
Albert S Bolduc
37 Catherine Ave
Reading MA 01867

Call Sign: KB1KMI
Jose Candelario
15 Center
Reading MA 01867

Call Sign: KB1KMJ
Edwin Vega
15 Center Ave
Reading MA 01867

Call Sign: N1XCI
Matthew C Mc
Laughlin
62 Charles St
Reading MA 01867

Call Sign: WA1NUY

Thomas H Grosvenor
Iii
1 Charles St Unit Y
Reading MA 01867

Call Sign: W1DKM
Harvey P Poore
6 Chestnut Rd
Reading MA 01867

Call Sign: N1SRE
Erwin K Leder
10 Colburn Rd
Reading MA 01867

Call Sign: KA1UJA
Christopher M Ahearn
84 Dana Rd
Reading MA 01867

Call Sign: KA1WIH
Brian P Moynihan
93 Dana Rd
Reading MA 01867

Call Sign: WA1SNM
Simon J Hubbard
3 Elderberry Ln 208
Reading MA
018671004

Call Sign: KB1MVK
Richard J Moore
5 Elm St
Reading MA 01867

Call Sign: N1KUH
Robert B Mark
14 Fairview Ave
Reading MA
018673417

Call Sign: W1KAE
Roy L Parsons Jr
13 Forest St
Reading MA 01867

Call Sign: W1ILS
Leslie M Vant
51 Forest St
Reading MA 01867

Call Sign: N1YPI
Stephen R Smith

163 Forest St
Reading MA
018671634

Call Sign: W2GGG
Robert B Solosko
224 Forest St
Reading MA
018671413

Call Sign: KA1EWJ
Philip F Logsdon
15 Francis Dr
Reading MA 01867

Call Sign: KB1JFL
Robert J Walcott
25 Francis Dr
Reading MA 01867

Call Sign: K1QON
Robert H Conner
124 Franklin St
Reading MA 01867

Call Sign: KB1CCI
Chester P Gunn
237 Franklin St
Reading MA
018671030

Call Sign: N1AKI
Chester P Gunn
237 Franklin St
Reading MA
018671030

Call Sign: NR1R
Reynolds A Sylvester
Jr
20 Gardner Rd
Reading MA 01867

Call Sign: KB1BPM
Ronald W Baker
62 Glenmere Cir
Reading MA 01867

Call Sign: WA1RTB
Stephen A Dresser
167 Green St
Reading MA 01867

Call Sign: KA1TII

John J Mc Crae
272 Haven St
Reading MA 01867

Call Sign: W1DEU
Henry D Minich
127 Haverhill St
Reading MA 01867

Call Sign: WB1FAJ
Margaret E Middleton
711 Haverhill St
Reading MA 01867

Call Sign: N1KFI
Kevin S Larimore
25 Hemlock Rd
Reading MA 01867

Call Sign: W1HFR
Michael J Riordan
38 Highland St
Reading MA 01867

Call Sign: KB1HCT
Joseph M Nicosia
68 Hopkins St
Reading MA 01867

Call Sign: KA1ZOC
Wilfrid J Dufresne
33 Howard St
Reading MA 01867

Call Sign: KA1NKG
Leonard P Callahan
7 Indiana Ave
Reading MA 01867

Call Sign: KB1CQT
Mark R Harrison
25 Indiana Ave
Reading MA 01867

Call Sign: KB1CPG
Patricia A Sheets
12 Jere Rd
Reading MA
018673346

Call Sign: W1SYA
Redmond G Sheets
12 Jere Rd
Reading MA 01867

Call Sign: K1ZWB
Carol A Glowacki
Wasilewski
36 Johanna Dr
Reading MA 01867

Call Sign: AB1FA
Patrick S Sudbay
107 John Carver Rd
Reading MA
018671601

Call Sign: AA1AT
Patrick S Sudbay
107 John Carver Rd
Reading MA
018671601

Call Sign: WU1H
Lawrence L De Renne
17 John St Ct
Reading MA 01867

Call Sign: WB1FST
Philip G Dole Sr
25 Kingston St
Reading MA 01867

Call Sign: KB1CCG
William J Mc Laughlin
37 Knollwood Rd
Reading MA 01867

Call Sign: NZ1X
Thomas F
Charbonneau
22 Latham Ln
Reading MA 01867

Call Sign: WA1ZWC
Carol A Charbonneau
22 Latham Ln
Reading MA 01867

Call Sign: KB1MID
George A Vetter
26 Lee St
Reading MA
018672439

Call Sign: W1VAE
George A Vetter
26 Lee St

Reading MA
018672439

Call Sign: WA1RHN
John L Pineau
6 Libby Ave
Reading MA 01867

Call Sign: KB1GHW
Scott N Fillmore
25 Linden St
Reading MA 01867

Call Sign: KB1MIC
Erik J Kramer
22 Lindsay Ln
Reading MA 01867

Call Sign: KE1V
Erik J Kramer
22 Lindsay Ln
Reading MA 01867

Call Sign: N1PSB
David Kieran
87 Lowell St
Reading MA 01867

Call Sign: KB1JXL
Stephen F Napolitano
98 Lowell St
Reading MA 01867

Call Sign: N1AAN
Stephen F Napolitano
98 Lowell St
Reading MA 01867

Call Sign: K1FKL
Raymond P Jackson
316 Lowell St
Reading MA 01867

Call Sign: KC1PR
David I Bush
354 Lowell St
Reading MA 01867

Call Sign: KB1NFW
Adrian L Pyke
34 Lynn Village Way
Reading MA 01867

Call Sign: KB1VKR

Benjamin D Pyke
34 Lynn Village Way
Reading MA 01867

Call Sign: KA1DKB
Albert F Shumilla
1490 Main St
Reading MA 01867

Call Sign: KB1FAU
Scott E Campbell
5 Margaret Rd
Reading MA 01867

Call Sign: N1HIC
Steven P Surette
21 Middlesex Ave
Reading MA 01867

Call Sign: KA1RAL
Maureen M Stafford
26 Middlesex Ave
Reading MA 01867

Call Sign: N1XVN
Brian C Wedell
73 Mount Vernon St
Reading MA 01867

Call Sign: W1DXD
Otis E Simms
14 Nichols Rd
Reading MA 01867

Call Sign: KB1KGB
Matthew C Applin
3 Norman Rd
Reading MA 01867

Call Sign: KA1GIJ
Paul Anderson
753 Pearl St
Reading MA 01867

Call Sign: N1SUR
James A Wilcox
127 Pine Ridge Rd
Reading MA 01867

Call Sign: AE1E
Joseph A Maggiore
14 Pitman Dr
Reading MA
018671958

Call Sign: KB1LKR
Stephen L Crook
137 Pleasant St
Reading MA
018673020

Call Sign: WB1CUB
David A Rawding
11 Prospect St
Reading MA 01867

Call Sign: KB1PUP
Michael J Rawding
11 Prospect St
Reading MA 01867

Call Sign: KB1JPI
Stephen A Whittaker
6 Puritan Rd
Reading MA 01867

Call Sign: N1SJB
David B Libby
7 Rachel Rd
Reading MA 01867

Call Sign: KB1VMR
Laurier A Beaulieu Jr
62 Red Gate Ln
Reading MA 01867

Call Sign: AB1PO
Laurier A Beaulieu Jr
62 Red Gate Ln
Reading MA 01867

Call Sign: AJ1Z
Laurier A Beaulieu Jr
62 Red Gate Ln
Reading MA 01867

Call Sign: WA1WEC
Francis R De Angelis
121 Rustic Ln
Reading MA
018671152

Call Sign: N1FYS
Michael T Higgins
32 Shackford Rd
Reading MA 01867

Call Sign: W1UKS

Stanley M Karandanis
197 South St
Reading MA 01867

Call Sign: KB1WMC
Ethan M Schwartz
282 South St
Reading MA 01867

Call Sign: W1ZMJ
Raymond H Swain
428 South St
Reading MA
018674004

Call Sign: KB1LVB
Andrew L Camarata
126 Summer Ave
Reading MA 01867

Call Sign: KB1JYG
Karen-Ann Daly
503 Summer Ave
Reading MA 01867

Call Sign: WD1B
John D Kierstead
2 Summit Dr Apt 55
Reading MA
018674045

Call Sign: KA3VUK
Jason A Small
62 Sunnyside Ave
Reading MA 01867

Call Sign: N3DSX
George A Small Jr
62 Sunnyside Ave
Reading MA 01867

Call Sign: KB1BKO
Linda M H Bolle
66 Temple St
Reading MA 01867

Call Sign: N1IRS
Edward N Bolle
66 Temple St
Reading MA 01867

Call Sign: N1PHF
Richard A Federico
20 Victoria Ave

Reading MA
018673452

Call Sign: KE1HL
Anthony J Garratt
Reed
64 Wakefield St
Reading MA
018671851

Call Sign: KC1AH
Raymond B Higgins
175 Walnut St
Reading MA 01867

Call Sign: W1BMR
Raymond B Higgins
175 Walnut St
Reading MA 01867

Call Sign: W1JUS
Raymond B Higgins
175 Walnut St
Reading MA 01867

Call Sign: KC1MR
Raymond B Higgins
175 Walnut St
Reading MA 01867

Call Sign: WB2HTO
David S Kruh
3 Wescroft Rd
Reading MA 01867

Call Sign: KB1TSU
Jennifer S Kruh
3 Wescroft Rd
Reading MA 01867

Call Sign: N1LOG
Frederick R Felone
495 West St
Reading MA 01867

Call Sign: KB1VZI
Timothy J Marquardt
61 Whitehall Ln
Reading MA 01867

Call Sign: N1XAL
Michael A Brothers
38 Willow St

Reading MA
018671548

Call Sign: K1MAB
Michael A Brothers
38 Willow St
Reading MA
018671548

Call Sign: KA1KDD
Daniel G Carusi
118 Willow St
Reading MA 01867

Call Sign: KB1CRK
Wallace H Langell Jr
Reading MA 01867

Call Sign: W1JDR
Wallace H Langell Jr
Reading MA 01867

FCC Amateur Radio Licenses in Readville

Call Sign: WA1TNF
Anthony F Zollo Jr
48 Como Rd
Readville MA 02136

Call Sign: N1TYK
Richard S Spada
131 Neponset Valley
Pky
Readville MA 02136

Call Sign: K1MZP
Paul M Regan
97 W Milton St
Readville MA 02136

FCC Amateur Radio Licenses in Rehoboth

Call Sign: N1EEQ
Carl F Chace Sr
133 Anawan St
Rehoboth MA 02769

Call Sign: KB1NCB
William H Balme
24 Ashlynn Way
Rehoboth MA 02769

Call Sign: KB1NCC
Laurie Balme
24 Ashlynn Way
Rehoboth MA 02769

Call Sign: KB1LAA
Matthew M Bomes
31 Bay State Rd
Rehoboth MA 02769

Call Sign: W1LUN
Theodore C Hamlin
35 Bay State Rd
Rehoboth MA
027692317

Call Sign: KB1KZT
Vincent A Vinniti Jr
184 Bay State Rd
Rehoboth MA 02769

Call Sign: WA1VEC
Edmond R Couture
140 Brook St
Rehoboth MA 02769

Call Sign: KA1NJ
Peter F Cardosi
247 Brook St
Rehoboth MA 02769

Call Sign: N1STX
Edward P Jastram Iii
80 Carpenter St
Rehoboth MA 02769

Call Sign: N1XGF
Teresa M Jastram
80 Carpenter St
Rehoboth MA 02769

Call Sign: W7OT
Michael R Zeug
120 Danforth St
Rehoboth MA 02769

Call Sign: K7UQT
Lisa M Zeug
120 Danforth St
Rehoboth MA 02769

Call Sign: K1UQT
Lisa M Zeug
120 Danforth St

Rehoboth MA 02769

Call Sign: W1YM
Michael R Zeug
120 Danforth St
Rehoboth MA 02769

Call Sign: N1CEI
John King Jr
122 Davis St
Rehoboth MA
027691604

Call Sign: KA1UAJ
Charles A Greaves
20 Dewey Ave
Rehoboth MA 02769

Call Sign: KB1MNL
Michelle Laxer
37 Elm St
Rehoboth MA 02769

Call Sign: W1VQ
John Record
76 Fairview Ave
Rehoboth MA 02769

Call Sign: WC1ACR
Rehoboth Civil
Defense
76 Fairview Ave
Rehoboth MA 02769

Call Sign: KA1UYM
Bernadette I Maynard
418 Fairview Ave
Rehoboth MA 02769

Call Sign: KA1UYN
Timothee J Maynard
418 Fairview Ave
Rehoboth MA 02769

Call Sign: KB1NPN
Mark R Thomsen
9 Greenwood Dr
Rehoboth MA 02769

Call Sign: WA1BZJ
Michael Ponte
10 Greenwood Drive
Rehoboth MA 02769

Call Sign: W1BZJ
Michael Ponte
10 Greenwood Drive
Rehoboth MA 02769

Call Sign: KB1KYY
Gary A Kloss Sr
45 Lake St
Rehoboth MA 02769

Call Sign: WA1QBR
Bradley A Backman
92 Martin St
Rehoboth MA 02769

Call Sign: KA1HTU
Jeffrey S Greenberg
135 New St
Rehoboth MA 02769

Call Sign: KB1DC
Jon C Klinkhamer
10 Nichols St
Rehoboth MA 02769

Call Sign: KB1HXJ
Erik J Klinkhamer
10 Nichols St
Rehoboth MA 02769

Call Sign: KB1WBB
Emma J Klinkhamer
10 Nichols St
Rehoboth MA 02769

Call Sign: W1NOR
Carroll A Philbrook
139 Pine St
Rehoboth MA 02769

Call Sign: KB1LXL
Neal V Harrington Sr
24 Plain St
Rehoboth MA
027692516

Call Sign: KB1TCO
Scott A Laverdiere
250 Plain St
Rehoboth MA 02769

Call Sign: K1KUG
Frank P Cardoza
88 Pleasant St

Rehoboth MA 02769

Call Sign: N1SGE
Thomas P Greaves
39 Pond St
Rehoboth MA 02769

Call Sign: KB1HYU
Steven V Cabral
46 Pond St
Rehoboth MA 02769

Call Sign: KB1WSB
Ernest C Boren
28 Providence St
Rehoboth MA 02769

Call Sign: KB1KZA
Roland Aubin
222 Providence St
Rehoboth MA
027691023

Call Sign: KB1LAC
Alan P Larson
88 Rocky Hill Rd
Rehoboth MA 02769

Call Sign: KB1LAD
Carl A Larson
88 Rocky Hill Rd
Rehoboth MA 02769

Call Sign: KB1LAE
Scott N Larson
88 Rocky Hill Rd
Rehoboth MA 02769

Call Sign: WA1UFH
Donald F Heitzmann
150 Rocky Hill Rd
Rehoboth MA 02769

Call Sign: KC8MDW
Nicole M Belk
196 Rocky Hill Rd
Rehoboth MA 02769

Call Sign: KC8MDX
Matthew H Belk
196 Rocky Hill Rd
Rehoboth MA
027691426

Call Sign: N1IIA
Steven C Robinson
Rocky Hill Rd
Rehoboth MA 02769

Call Sign: KA1RES
Gerard C Leger
294 Summer St
Rehoboth MA 02769

Call Sign: W1UPS
Gabriel G Melo
312 Summer St
Rehoboth MA 02769

Call Sign: KB1SMV
Glenn L Doucette
356 Tremont St
Rehoboth MA 02769

Call Sign: KB1KYZ
David A Drowne
45 Williams St
Rehoboth MA 02769

Call Sign: KB1LAG
Thomas F Rose
Rehoboth MA
027690305

Call Sign: KB1QIO
James E Tynan
Rehoboth MA 02769

Call Sign: KC1JET
James E Tynan
Rehoboth MA 02769

Call Sign: KB1UNU
Alexander P Kozatek
Rehoboth MA 02769

Call Sign: W1KOZ
Alexander P Kozatek
Rehoboth MA 02769

**FCC Amateur Radio
Licenses in Revere**

Call Sign: KA1LBD
Stanley A Andrews
58 Bateman Ave
Revere MA 02151

Call Sign: N1GKB
Jonathan P Bazemore
675 Beach St
Revere MA 02151

Call Sign: KB1QVS
Samuel P Ranger
45 Belle Isle Ave 34
Revere MA 02151

Call Sign: N1KYH
Ronald Bardaro
51 Bennington St
Revere MA 02151

Call Sign: N1MHK
Yusuf A Hassan
77 Bennington St 305
Revere MA 02151

Call Sign: KB1SYL
John H Driscoll
56 Bosson St
Revere MA 02151

Call Sign: KB1GPY
Elvis Mendez
150 Campbell Ave
Revere MA 02151

Call Sign: KA1YPM
Martin P Knab
Campbell Ave Apt 1
Revere MA 02151

Call Sign: WA1UZU
Sarah Yanow
44 Chamberlain Ave
Revere MA 02151

Call Sign: N1PUG
Pamela I Mitchell
115 Cooledge St
Revere MA 02151

Call Sign: KB1FOT
Adrianus M Van Der
Weiden
212 Crescent Ave
Revere MA 02151

Call Sign: KB1DBT
Terran K Melconian
216 Crest Ave

Revere MA 02151

Call Sign: KB1LPW
Kathleen G Savage
10 Dale St
Revere MA 02151

Call Sign: W1QD
Edward J Michalski
120 Derby Rd
Revere MA 02151

Call Sign: WA1RVJ
Stella M Michalski
120 Derby Rd
Revere MA 02151

Call Sign: N1GNX
Edward I Baker Jr
60 Fernwood Ave
Revere MA 02151

Call Sign: N1FOH
Thomas C Tonelli
26 Folsom St
Revere MA 02151

Call Sign: KA1KMQ
Thomas C Tonelli
26 Folsom St
Revere MA 02151

Call Sign: AB1FO
Thomas C Tonelli
26 Folsom St
Revere MA 02151

Call Sign: KC1Q
Thomas C Tonelli
26 Folsom St
Revere MA 02151

Call Sign: N1EOB
Americo H Arpino
94 Gage Ave
Revere MA 02151

Call Sign: KB1QEG
Richard Montanino
4 Green St
Revere MA 02151

Call Sign: KD8BKE
Richard J Finn

14 Griffin St
Revere MA 02151

Call Sign: KB1FTE
Brian Piccolo
290 Grover St
Revere MA 02151

Call Sign: N1CLK
Henry C Chorlian
55 High St
Revere MA 02151

Call Sign: N1INQ
Erwin A Rosen
39 Highland St
Revere MA 02151

Call Sign: N1GRB
Francis D Leonard
74 Hillside Ave
Revere MA 02151

Call Sign: N1ZKS
Ifeanyi O Nwobodu
259 Lantern Rd 21
Revere MA 02151

Call Sign: KB1TUJ
Vito Sabella
72 Lincoln St
Revere MA 02151

Call Sign: KB1LYJ
Richard Savage
16 Madison St
Revere MA 021515801

Call Sign: WA1DFL
Steven J Rich
35 Mc Clure St
Revere MA 02151

Call Sign: N1ZXB
Patrick J Mcbrien Jr
Mermaid Ave
Revere MA 02151

Call Sign: KB1LHX
Michelle A Gabutti
361 Mountain Ave
Revere MA 02151

Call Sign: N1GQH

Antonio P Maglione Jr
366 Mountain Ave
Revere MA 02151

Call Sign: KB1LJE
Michelle A Gabutti
398 Mountain Ave
Revere MA 02151

Call Sign: KA1OFQ
Alexander R Glimcher
211 N Shore Rd
Revere MA 02151

Call Sign: KA1SBS
Gerard A Martinez
1022 N Shore Rd
Revere MA 02151

Call Sign: KB1KLK
Charles E Fadely Iv
364 Ocean Ave #1201
Revere MA 02151

Call Sign: KB1VDU
Adam R Davis
364 Ocean Ave Apt
1201
Revere MA 02151

Call Sign: W1THT
Arthur S Tomkinson
9 Oliver Ter
Revere MA 021512718

Call Sign: W1KUC
Roger N Fielding
5 Oliver Terrace
Revere MA 02151

Call Sign: N1ZFU
Theresha M Brinig
46 Page
Revere MA 021510002

Call Sign: N1ZFT
Raymond F Brinig
46 Page St
Revere MA 02151

Call Sign: KA1SGM
Sherman E Foster
287 Park Ave
Revere MA 02151

Call Sign: W1XMJ
Joseph J Mcdonough
126 Pemberton St
Revere MA 02151

Call Sign: KA1OFV
Bebe K Wunderlich
35 Pines Rd
Revere MA 02151

Call Sign: N1YAN
Donald Carasso
41 Proctor Ave
Revere MA 02151

Call Sign: K1CRY
Victor A Lospennato Jr
95 Proctor Ave
Revere MA 021512912

Call Sign: W1NZJ
Frederick V Leyden
454 Proctor Ave
Revere MA 02151

Call Sign: KB1EJM
Michael P Dakin
74 Prospect Ave
Revere MA 021513815

Call Sign: K1VLK
Frank P Di Pesa
265 Revere
Revere MA 02151

Call Sign: W1HKU
John D Ahern
350 Revere Bch Blvd
Revere MA 02151

Call Sign: KB1RXT
Marlene L Piazza
662 Revere Beach
Blvd
Revere MA 02151

Call Sign: WA1OBD
William J Martin
418 Revere Beach
Pkwy
Revere MA 021514089

Call Sign: WA1MTS

Raymond P Lambert
250 Revere St
Revere MA 02151

Call Sign: KA1MHS
Alexandria L Di Pesa
265 Revere St
Revere MA 02151

Call Sign: WB1GHO
Amateur Radio Assn
19-79
265 Revere St
Revere MA 02151

Call Sign: KB1RPS
Girard J Simon
321 Revere St
Revere MA 02151

Call Sign: K1RAP
John F Kelleher Jr
138 Ridge Rd
Revere MA 02151

Call Sign: N1SYH
John J Guarino
Ridge Rd
Revere MA 02151

Call Sign: K1SKV
Edward D Terrell
70 Sewall St
Revere MA 02151

Call Sign: K1KXW
Ralph F Hooper
34 Shawmut St
Revere MA 02151

Call Sign: KA1LWN
Herbert Cummings
46 Temple St
Revere MA 02151

Call Sign: KA1LXA
Shirley E Guillette
46 Temple St
Revere MA 02151

Call Sign: KD1QY
Denise R Finley
8 Warren St
Revere MA 02151

Call Sign: N1JTP
Richard F Orluk
575 Washington Ave
Revere MA 02151

Call Sign: KB1JJO
Michael J Wilton
679 Washington Ave
Revere MA 02151

Call Sign: KA1LWY
Robert La Porta
926 Winthrop Ave
Revere MA 02151

Call Sign: N1DHG
Annette A La Porta
926 Winthrop Ave
Revere MA 02151

Call Sign: N1ROX
Vallilius Vutsadakis
10 Yeamans 24
Revere MA 02151

Call Sign: N1NUI
Gary S Cohen
Revere MA 02151

Call Sign: W1GSC
Gary S Cohen
Revere MA 02151

FCC Amateur Radio Licenses in Richmond

Call Sign: KB1UCL
Patrick J Seckler
151 Canaan Rd Route
295
Richmond MA 01254

Call Sign: KE1LD
Donald M Clemett
68 Chesnut Rd
Richmond MA 01254

Call Sign: KA1JVO
Eric C Weber
Notch Rd
Richmond MA 01254

Call Sign: KB1BSO

James M Weber
248 Osceola Notch
Richmond MA 01254

Call Sign: KB1DDA
Allison E Edwards
932 State Rd
Richmond MA
012549434

Call Sign: KB1DDB
William F Edwards
932 State Rd
Richmond MA
012549434

Call Sign: KB1AQX
Sam C Morse
2040 State Rd
Richmond MA 01254

Call Sign: N1ZNU
Harry Hartford
3050 State Rd
Richmond MA 01254

Call Sign: AF1S
William M Malumphy
Richmond MA 01254

Call Sign: KB1AQP
Gloria D Morse
Richmond MA 01254

FCC Amateur Radio Licenses in Rochdale

Call Sign: KB1CK
Philip J Wiley
45 Carleton Rd
Rochdale MA 01542

Call Sign: KB1GSJ
Harold G Carlson Jr
20 Clark St
Rochdale MA 01542

Call Sign: N1ZC
Harold G Carlson Jr
20 Clark St
Rochdale MA 01542

Call Sign: N1VXJ
Robert L Wirtanen Jr

847 Stafford St
Rochdale MA 01542

Call Sign: KB1LGF
Craig A Swindel
Rochdale MA 01542

Call Sign: KB1LGG
N L Sheilds
Rochdale MA 01542

**FCC Amateur Radio
Licenses in Rochester**

Call Sign: W1AST
Harold A Dorschug
61 Cross Rd
Rochester MA 02770

Call Sign: KA1FAW
Geraldine R Correia
25 Cushman Rd
Rochester MA 02770

Call Sign: KA1WBG
James M Correia
25 Cushman Rd
Rochester MA 02770

Call Sign: KB1FRK
John A Stroscio
11 Forster Rd
Rochester MA 02770

Call Sign: N1ZTV
Harold W Crapo
11 Hathaway Pond
Circle
Rochester MA
027704135

Call Sign: KA1GAG
Hodges S Martin
77 Marion Rd Route
105
Rochester MA 02770

Call Sign: KB1MIT
Leonard S Silverberg
547 Marys Pond Rd
Rochester MA 02770

Call Sign: WA1WXI
Alvey R Smith Jr

593 Mary's Pond Rd
Rochester MA 02770

Call Sign: KC0JUT
Thomas A Blais
21 Neck Rd
Rochester MA 02770

Call Sign: KQ1G
Thomas A Blais
21 Neck Rd
Rochester MA 02770

Call Sign: K1VFB
Paul R Dion
63 New Bedford Rd
Rochester MA 02770

Call Sign: KA1WME
Steven R Coulombe
472 New Bedford Rd
Rochester MA 02770

Call Sign: N1WEP
Donald H Loader
34 North Ave
Rochester MA 02770

Call Sign: KC6PYS
Dennis C Maxey
544 North Ave
Rochester MA 02770

Call Sign: KB1TEH
Richard J Metcalf
14 Randall Rd
Rochester MA 02770

Call Sign: KA1MYZ
Conrad O Bernier
84 Robinson Rd
Rochester MA 02770

Call Sign: KA1MCQ
Sherman W Fearing
299 Rounseville Rd
Rochester MA 02770

Call Sign: N1SGP
Nicholas M Bolintiam
11 Snipatuit Rd
Rochester MA 02770

Call Sign: WA1GXV

Lawrence J Ferreira
370 Snipatuit Rd
Rochester MA 02770

Call Sign: WA1ZDQ
Paul Ciaburri
265 Walnut Plain Rd
Rochester MA 02770

Call Sign: KA1FEE
Henry M Chapman
Rochester MA 02770

Call Sign: KA1KLA
Richard L Coulombe
Rochester MA 02770

Call Sign: WA1DSR
Arthur L Doyle
Rochester MA 02770

Call Sign: K1KLA
Richard L Coulombe
Rochester MA 02770

**FCC Amateur Radio
Licenses in Rockland**

Call Sign: KB1WSZ
Charles J Amico Jr
704 Brookline Way
Rockland MA 02370

Call Sign: W1KP
Brian M Stephens
319 Centre Ave 166
Rockland MA 02370

Call Sign: WF1Y
Douglas E Schofield
44 Everett St
Rockland MA 02370

Call Sign: KB1IGY
Michael D Schofield
44 Everett St
Rockland MA 02370

Call Sign: KB1KFF
James S Kenworthy
39 Exchange St
Rockland MA 02370

Call Sign: KB1VOX

Stephen M Powers
146 French Rd
Rockland MA 02370

Call Sign: N1DKN
Walter P Hayward
7 Grasswood Cir
Rockland MA 02370

Call Sign: K1DKT
Beverly A Keefe
20 Grasswood Ln
Rockland MA 02370

Call Sign: W1NRW
John R Keefe
20 Grasswood Ln
Rockland MA 02370

Call Sign: WA1AXJ
Fred Naples
103 Grove St Apt 341
Rockland MA 02370

Call Sign: KB1SEW
Steven P Buckley
50 Harlow Rd
Rockland MA 02370

Call Sign: W1BTS
Steven P Buckley
50 Harlow Rd
Rockland MA 02370

Call Sign: KB1UQM
Michael C Collins
27 Highland St
Rockland MA 02370

Call Sign: K1KWA
Richard H Johnson
68 Liberty Square
Rockland MA 02370

Call Sign: KB1GVC
Stephen T Bradford
513 Liberty St
Rockland MA 02370

Call Sign: KB1KVK
William W Patterson
270 Market St
Rockland MA
023701933

Call Sign: KA1FSN
Robert A Fisher Sr
680 Market St
Rockland MA 02370

Call Sign: N1PXW
John A Korejwa
174 North Ave
Rockland MA 02370

Call Sign: KB1EPO
Francis A Sheputa
122 Pacific St
Rockland MA
023702233

Call Sign: KB1SGG
Shawn M Benduzek
303 Pond St
Rockland MA 02370

Call Sign: K1WHR
Clarence A Moore
520 Salem St
Rockland MA 02370

Call Sign: KD4ZIO
Ted L Geiger
323 Spring St
Rockland MA 02370

Call Sign: N1PDO
Terri L Geiger
323 Spring St
Rockland MA 02370

Call Sign: WB1EEN
Patricia A Torrey
542 Summer St
Rockland MA 02370

Call Sign: W1LJM
Frank A Sheputa
567 Summer St
Rockland MA
023707219

Call Sign: KC1ZX
Richard C Turner
14 Townsend St
Rockland MA 02370

Call Sign: KB1PBT

Daniel G Chiasson Jr
21 Warren Ave
Rockland MA
023701115

Call Sign: KB1UWF
Evan R Davis-Drennan
10 White Rd
Rockland MA 02370

Call Sign: WF3RRY
Evan R Davis-Drennan
10 White Rd
Rockland MA 02370

Call Sign: KB1NPH
William J Anstead
Rock Land MA 02370

Call Sign: N1PGC
Norman J Cedarstrom
Rockland MA 02370

Call Sign: KB1FRT
Eric J Larsen
Rockland MA 02370

Call Sign: KB1FUI
Linda M Ellis
Rockland MA 02370

**FCC Amateur Radio
Licenses in Rockport**

Call Sign: KB1NJY
James J Cavan Jr
13 Broadway Ave Apt
1
Rockport MA 01966

Call Sign: KB1TRL
Joan E Thompson
9 Broadway Ave Unit
B
Rockport MA 01966

Call Sign: N1AJB
Arthur E Curry
3 Cathedral Ave
Rockport MA 01966

Call Sign: AA1ZG
Arthur E Curry
3 Cathedral Ave

Rockport MA 01966

Call Sign: WB1CHF
Joseph E Perry
Country Club Rd
Rockport MA 01966

Call Sign: KB1WJC
Robert D Claypool
25 Curtis St
Rockport MA 01966

Call Sign: N1YGJ
Nels M Story
31 Curtis St
Rockport MA
019661232

Call Sign: WI1U
Charles E Anderson
Drumlin Rd
Rockport MA 01966

Call Sign: W1AAU
Raymond A Brown Jr
11 Granite St
Rockport MA 01966

Call Sign: K1UFY
Ronald M Straka
40 Granite St
Rockport MA 01966

Call Sign: W1VEC
Edgar F Whittaker Jr
90 Granite St
Rockport MA 01966

Call Sign: WA1SQR
Julian Soshnick
111 Granite St
Rockport MA 01966

Call Sign: N1DWA
Clifford J Wheeler
215 Granite St
Rockport MA 01966

Call Sign: KA1SFA
Timothy A Robinson
230 Granite St
Rockport MA 01966

Call Sign: KA1SFC

Stephen J Robinson
230 Granite St
Rockport MA 01966

Call Sign: N1OPH
Richard D Stoloff
227 Granite St 1a
Rockport MA 01966

Call Sign: KB1RYC
John F Kasten
31 High St
Rockport MA 01966

Call Sign: KB1RYD
Sayles D Kasten
31 High St
Rockport MA 01966

Call Sign: KA1SFE
Arthur P Alves Jr
64 High St
Rockport MA 01966

Call Sign: K1TP
Jon P Cunningham
41 Jerdens Lane
Rockport MA 01966

Call Sign: KB1IDU
Allen S Stanish
17 King St
Rockport MA 01966

Call Sign: K1GCZ
Guy J Micalizzi
32 King St
Rockport MA
019661460

Call Sign: KB1GHP
Giacomo A Terzo
175 Main St
Rockport MA 01966

Call Sign: KA1QAO
Vernon E Nulk
Main St
Rockport MA 01966

Call Sign: KA1HV
Robert M C Smith
88 Marmion Way
Rockport MA 01966

Call Sign: KA1NET
Sally L Costello
6 Mill Ln
Rockport MA 01966

Call Sign: N1RBG
John A Malcolmson Jr
Norwood Ave
Rockport MA 01966

Call Sign: KB1UWP
Mark W Schmink
6 Ocean Ave
Rockport MA 01966

Call Sign: AI2X
Bruce P Bogert
16 Penryn Way
Rockport MA
019662319

Call Sign: KB9YOZ
David M Delakas
70 Pigeon Hill St
Rockport MA 01966

Call Sign: KB1GBP
Scott W Story
1 Rail Rd Ave
Rockport MA 01966

Call Sign: AA3JE
Curtis Wright Iv
14 Ruthern Way
Rockport MA 01966

Call Sign: KB1MWG
Linda J Wright
14 Ruthern Way
Rockport MA 01966

Call Sign: KA1MBJ
Leonidas Aggelakis
511 Sandy Bay Estate
Rockport MA 01966

Call Sign: KD1QB
Paul G Lucas
8 Shetland Rd
Rockport MA 01966

Call Sign: KB1JGY
Ernest E Allen

181 South St
Rockport MA 01966

Call Sign: KA1BTM
Sylvia C Bernard
12 South St Ct
Rockport MA 01966

Call Sign: K1VRA
Richard H Ober
7 Spring Lane
Rockport MA
019662169

Call Sign: KB1HNL
Derek Morrison
22 Squam Rd
Rockport MA
019661467

Call Sign: KB1SIK
Jonathan G Estabrook
22 Stockholm Ave
Rockport MA 01966

Call Sign: KC1PT
Ronald C Petoff
Rockport MA 01966

FCC Amateur Radio Licenses in Rocks Village

Call Sign: KB1NYP
David A Marchand
29 East Main St
Rocks Village MA
01830

FCC Amateur Radio Licenses in Rookland

Call Sign: N1WCS
Henry E Dion
32 Crestview St
Rookland MA 02470

FCC Amateur Radio Licenses in Roslindale

Call Sign: KB1OYI
Paul M Lydon
5 Aldrich St - Apt 2r
Roslindale MA 02131

Call Sign: N1QZP
Vergel M Blake
865 American Legion
Hwy 4c
Roslindale MA 02131

Call Sign: N1QFM
Daniel E O Connell
39 Arborough Rd
Roslindale MA 02130

Call Sign: N1YZK
John Baez
40 Augustus Ave
Roslindale MA 02131

Call Sign: KB1BNC
Ryan P Fasanello
19 Basto Ter
Roslindale MA 02131

Call Sign: N1TBK
John T Fasanello
19 Basto Ter
Roslindale MA 02131

Call Sign: KB1LNB
Joyce A Fasanello
19 Basto Terr
Roslindale MA 02131

Call Sign: N1WPS
Daniel F Long
33 Bateman St
Roslindale MA 02131

Call Sign: KB1OEJ
Sam Vernon Iii
461 Beech St 3
Roslindale MA 02131

Call Sign: WB1AJA
Bruno F Vasil
58 Bradeen St
Roslindale MA 02131

Call Sign: W1QY
Arthur J Raymond
88 Colberg Ave
Roslindale MA 02131

Call Sign: K1AJA
Donna J Marshall

52 Cornell St
Roslindale MA 02131

Call Sign: KB1ANT
David T Marshall
52 Cornell St
Roslindale MA 02131

Call Sign: W1JTX
Joseph M Welby
42 Florence St
Roslindale MA 02131

Call Sign: KA1TPZ
Kenneth L Matthews Jr
61 Hawthorne St
Roslindale MA 02131

Call Sign: KB1NIY
Michael Glaum
27 Hillock St
Roslindale MA 02131

Call Sign: N1ZDQ
Jovanny G Pimentel
50 Jewett St Apt 2
Roslindale MA 02131

Call Sign: KC1GM
Paul A Ward
Kittredge St
Roslindale MA 02131

Call Sign: N1OZL
Ronald C J Ward Sr
Kittredge St
Roslindale MA 02131

Call Sign: KC4IWO
Donald J Ball Iii
86 Knoll St
Roslindale MA 02131

Call Sign: KA1JNY
Valmore A Girardi
13 Montvale St
Roslindale MA 02131

Call Sign: K1PLU
Robert W Callahan
65 Penfield St
Roslindale MA 02131

Call Sign: KA1SFP

Rafael James
22 Pleasantview St
Roslindale MA 02137

Call Sign: KB1VTK
Matthew R Anderson
79 Poplar St 14
Roslindale MA 02131

Call Sign: KB1POU
Kathryn M Gallagher
68 Seymour St
Roslindale MA 02131

Call Sign: KB1DPK
Jacob A Strauss
1055 South St
Roslindale MA 02131

Call Sign: N1TEW
Nancy L Walsh
968 South St 2
Roslindale MA 02131

Call Sign: KQ1S
Grant R Mc Keehan
843 South St Apt 2
Roslindale MA 02131

Call Sign: KB2DYL
David C Bozzo
128 Sycamore St 1
Roslindale MA 02131

Call Sign: WA1GSB
Charles T Marshall
758 W Roxbury Pkwy
Roslindale MA 02131

Call Sign: N1GZT
Fadi H Daou
4050 Washington St
Roslindale MA 02131

Call Sign: KA1QYA
Kevin J Hallinan
4324 Washington St
Roslindale MA 02131

Call Sign: N1RZO
Qui V Lai
87 Wellsmere Rd
Roslindale MA 02131

Call Sign: KD1JL
Alice C Fontaine
Roslindale MA
021310001

Call Sign: N1DUW
Robert G Parna
Roslindale MA 02131

FCC Amateur Radio Licenses in Rowe

Call Sign: N1TEP
Gary D Clark
159 Number 9 Rd
Rowe MA 01367

Call Sign: KB1WEK
Daniel J Miller
Rowe MA 01367

FCC Amateur Radio Licenses in Rowley

Call Sign: KA1ZBA
Johanna C Blasi
Rowley MA 01969

Call Sign: KB1VQF
Joseph J Perry
7 Bennett Hill Rd
Rowley MA 01969

Call Sign: N1NXR
Gary R Pond
10 Boxford Rd 3
Rowley MA 01969

Call Sign: KA1YKF
Nerissa R Pacenka
Central Ter
Rowley MA 01969

Call Sign: KA1WLM
William C Nakis
9 Central Way
Rowley MA 01969

Call Sign: KB1GIY
Shawn M Pothier
9 Cooper Pond Rd
Rowley MA 01969

Call Sign: W1NRY

Thomas J Potts Jr
27 Fenno Dr
Rowley MA
019691009

Call Sign: KA1NWS
Betty J Cooke
Glen Mills
Rowley MA 01969

Call Sign: WA1SNH
Peter T Baldwin
185 Haverhill St
Rowley MA 01969

Call Sign: KB1KTM
Scott A Marquis
509 Haverhill St
Rowley MA 01969

Call Sign: N1ZTZ
Christopher W Pringle
865 Haverhill St
Rowley MA 01969

Call Sign: KB1AID
Jennifer M L
Harrington
970 Haverhill St
Rowley MA 01969

Call Sign: NE9X
Timothy H Dick
870 Haverhill St Apt D
Rowley MA 01969

Call Sign: KB1CYU
Michael G Bussone
60 Hillside St
Rowley MA 01969

Call Sign: N1YQY
Adam J Donofrio
6 Isabelle Cir
Rowley MA 01969

Call Sign: KA1EEG
William A Faughnan Jr
17 Jellison Rd
Rowley MA 01969

Call Sign: KB1QQY
Thomas J Howell
28 Kathleen Cir

Rowley MA 01969

Call Sign: K1NKA
Thomas J Howell
28 Kathleen Cir
Rowley MA 01969

Call Sign: KB1RBR
Jake N Howell
28 Kathleen Cir
Rowley MA 01969

Call Sign: KB1RBS
Thomas J Howell Jr
28 Kathleen Cir
Rowley MA 01969

Call Sign: KB1CAW
Jeffrey A Petrowicz
36 Kittery Ave
Rowley MA 01969

Call Sign: KB1NU
John P Petrowicz
36 Kittery Ave
Rowley MA 01969

Call Sign: N1DIN
Kathleen M Petrowicz
36 Kittery Ave
Rowley MA 01969

Call Sign: KB1GVE
Michael D Petrowicz
36 Kittery Ave
Rowley MA 01969

Call Sign: KB1JSC
Michael B Welenc
11 Leslie Rd
Rowley MA 01969

Call Sign: N1KUT
Glen W Robertson
Long Hill Rd
Rowley MA 01969

Call Sign: N1NTR
Michael C Ciman
118 Newbury Rd
Rowley MA 01969

Call Sign: WT1H
Charles L Ciman

118 Newbury Rd
Rowley MA 01969

Call Sign: WB1FVY
James L Di Marino
160 Newbury Rd
Rowley MA 01969

Call Sign: KB1LWM
James L Dimarino
164 Newbury Rd
Rowley MA 01969

Call Sign: WB1FVY
James L Dimarino
164 Newbury Rd
Rowley MA 01969

Call Sign: W1LN
James W Farmer
165 Newbury Rd
Rowley MA 01969

Call Sign: KA2GXJ
Charles J Pencinger
23 Saunders Lane
Rowley MA 01969

Call Sign: KB1JOY
John E Pinette
15 Schoolhouse Ln
Rowley MA 01969

Call Sign: N1YLE
Richard P Shanahan
16 Wethersfield St
Rowley MA 01969

Call Sign: N1GSE
Anne B Kelliher
81 Wethersfield St
Rowley MA 01969

Call Sign: ND1S
James L Kelliher
81 Wethersfield St
Rowley MA 01969

Call Sign: WX1R
Warren A Grimes
176 Wethersfield St
Rowley MA 01969

Call Sign: N1TXQ

Ben T Draper
243 Wethersfield St
Rowley MA 01969

Call Sign: KD7ZG
Britton E Cooke
50 Wethersfield St
Rowley MA 01969

FCC Amateur Radio Licenses in Roxbury

Call Sign: KA1UGE
Harold J Sealls
32 Thornton St
Roxbury MA 02119

FCC Amateur Radio Licenses in Roxbury Crossing

Call Sign: N1KOI
Ralph W Walton
10 Alleghany St
Roxbury Crossing MA
021203408

Call Sign: KB1SPU
Mark Williams
31 Hayden St
Roxbury Crossing MA
02120

Call Sign: N2PZB
Grant K Chang
108 Hillside St Apt 2
Roxbury Crossing MA
02120

FCC Amateur Radio Licenses in Royalston

Call Sign: KK1DX
Michael H Lajoie
101 Athol Rd
Royalston MA
013688933

Call Sign: KA1ITL
Russell L Martin
Athol Rd
Royalston MA 01368

Call Sign: AB1PY

Joseph M Steim
159 Athol Richmond
Rd
Royalston MA 01368

Call Sign: KB1TGO
Linelle K Vaughn
187 Bliss Hill Rd
Royalston MA 01368

Call Sign: K1VVI
Linelle K Vaughn
187 Bliss Hill Rd
Royalston MA 01368

Call Sign: KE1ID
Herve J Bosse
43 Laurel Lake Rd
Royalston MA 01368

Call Sign: KB1QCF
Jon H Hardie
119 N Fitzwilliam Rd
Royalston MA 01368

Call Sign: WR1X
Paul C Bolduc
26 Stewart Rd
Royalston MA 01368

Call Sign: KB1QCA
Mary C Barclay
The Anchorage
Royalston MA 01368

Call Sign: W1KKM
Mary C Barclay
The Anchorage
Royalston MA 01368

Call Sign: KA1TLT
Goyola O Shackelford
The Common
Royalston MA 01368

Call Sign: KA1TLU
Lynn A Shackelford
The Common
Royalston MA 01368

Call Sign: KB1FCC
Harley L Smith Sr
Royalston MA 01368

Call Sign: KB1FPW
Janice Bosse
Royalston MA 01368

Call Sign: AB1IM
James M Barclay
Royalston MA 01368

Call Sign: NS1J
James M Barclay
Royalston MA 01368

Call Sign: KB1QHZ
Royalston Emergency
Operations
Royalston MA 01368

FCC Amateur Radio Licenses in Russell

Call Sign: KA1GPU
Maureen A Baillargeon
17 Hillcrest Ln
Russell MA 01071

Call Sign: N1TOV
Steve E Rettie
184 Main St
Russell MA 01071

Call Sign: N1UOU
Lori J Ordog
Main St
Russell MA 01071

FCC Amateur Radio Licenses in Rutland

Call Sign: N1YQL
Edward G Kofton
1 Anthony Dr
Rutland MA 01543

Call Sign: N1NCD
Robert W Piltzecker Jr
344 E County Rd
Rutland MA 01543

Call Sign: N1ZTD
John D Richard
25 Edson Ave
Rutland MA 01543

Call Sign: N1JDR

John D Richard
25 Edson Ave
Rutland MA 01543

Call Sign: W1JKQ
Tauno Ketonen
Glenwood Rd
Rutland MA 01543

Call Sign: KB1HMV
Roxy L Wallace
5 Hope Way
Rutland MA 01543

Call Sign: K1GCM
Gerald C Mcdonald Jr
17 Jackson Ave
Rutland MA 01543

Call Sign: KB1KCC
Melissa A Mcdonald
17 Jackson Ave
Rutland MA 01543

Call Sign: N1IPY
William P Orrico
1 Joanna Drive
Rutland MA
015430676

Call Sign: K1SOG
George L Gershman
10 Johnson Way
Rutland MA 01543

Call Sign: KB1LMV
Ted J Carlson
3 Jonathan Circle
Rutland MA 01543

Call Sign: K1KMA
Edward G Kofton
5 Olivia Lane
Rutland MA 01543

Call Sign: W1JLC
Francisco A Herrera
318 Pommagussett Rd
Rutland MA
015431403

Call Sign: KB1FEV
Douglas L Farber
249 Pommogussett Rd

Rutland MA 01543

Call Sign: KB1DFI
David M Plante
351 Pommogussett Rd
Rutland MA 01543

Call Sign: K1VNT
John C Smith
Rutland MA 01543

**FCC Amateur Radio
Licenses in Sagamore**

Call Sign: KA1KLD
Peter Connor
65 Pleasant St
Sagamore MA 02561

Call Sign: KB1ACG
Adrienne L Boffetti
16 Westdale Pk
Sagamore MA 02561

Call Sign: WA1BJV
Benjamin B Coleman
Jr
29 Williston Rd
Sagamore MA 02532

Call Sign: KB1EAJ
Ritchey L Guild
Sagamore MA
025610535

Call Sign: KB1JZE
Stanley W Lukas
Sagamore MA
025610095

**FCC Amateur Radio
Licenses in Sagamore
Beach**

Call Sign: WB2ORC
James J Fitzpatrick
6 Homestead Rd Ext
Sagamore Beach MA
025622437

Call Sign: KB1OXM
Timothy L Blegen
26 Norris Rd

Sagamore Beach MA
02562

Call Sign: WB1EOK
Kevin F Lacina
93 Norris Rd
Sagamore Beach MA
025620044

Call Sign: NW1X
Lawrence E Palmer
33 Sachem Drive
Sagamore Beach MA
02562

Call Sign: KB1RPB
Andrew J Fair
42 Savery Ave
Sagamore Beach MA
02562

Call Sign: KB1VKQ
Paul J Sullivan
48 Siasconset Dr
Sagamore Beach MA
02562

Call Sign: N1MJR
Robert H Mainey
73 Squanto Rd
Sagamore Beach MA
02562

Call Sign: N1RZZ
Thomas A Mc Michen
100 Standish Rd
Sagamore Beach MA
02562

Call Sign: KA1KVY
Lester E Geary
Sagamore Beach MA
02562

Call Sign: AA1DG
Roger A Blaisdell
Sagamore Beach MA
02562

Call Sign: KB1NPR
Stephen Angelique
Sagamore Beach MA
02562

**FCC Amateur Radio
Licenses in Salem**

Call Sign: N1KNG
Florence L Carty
10 Arthur St
Salem MA 01970

Call Sign: N1GFW
Wilfred N Julien
1 Barnes Ave
Salem MA 019701705

Call Sign: KA1KFJ
Edward M Piecewicz
8 Barnes Ave
Salem MA 01970

Call Sign: KA1KFP
Edward P Piecewicz
8 Barnes Ave
Salem MA 019701706

Call Sign: KA1EPP
Edward P Piecewicz
8 Barnes Ave
Salem MA 019701706

Call Sign: KA1EXZ
Joseph E Carty
6 Barton Square Apt
301
Salem MA 01970

Call Sign: KA1ROB
David J Featherstone
88 Bay View Ave
Salem MA 01971

Call Sign: KA1RPF
Julita R Compton
88 Bayview Ave
Salem MA 01971

Call Sign: N1NHW
Richard K Stauffer
28 Beckford St
Salem MA 019703239

Call Sign: N1HVK
Daniel P Smith
21 Belleview Ave
Salem MA 01970

Call Sign: N1FOU
Glenn E Schroeder
Belleview Ave
Salem MA 019701143

Call Sign: KA1VUX
Lisa D Anthony
21 Bellwview Dr
Salem MA 01970

Call Sign: N1IIJ
Michael P La Bonte
78 Bridge St
Salem MA 01970

Call Sign: WA4S
Andrew Nucci
190 Bridge St 1401
Salem MA 01970

Call Sign: NN1NN
Clifford O Thomson
29 Brittania Cir
Salem MA 01970

Call Sign: KB1NIR
Benjamin K Delong
25 Broad St
Salem MA 019703140

Call Sign: K3GRN
Benjamin K Delong
25 Broad St
Salem MA 019703140

Call Sign: KB1OUL
James G Brown
Buffum St Extension
Salem MA 01970

Call Sign: N1JLC
Richard J Calvani
45 Calumet St
Salem MA 019701142

Call Sign: WA1OSZ
Stephen R Nickerson
5 Cedarcrest Ave
Salem MA 01970

Call Sign: WU1T
Damon Z Cassell
35 Cedarcrest Ave
Salem MA 01970

Call Sign: KB1VZH
Jason C Kentros
20 Central St Apt 215
Salem MA 01970

Call Sign: KA1LCU
Otis F Putnam Jr
27 Charter St A1007
Salem MA 01970

Call Sign: W1UBB
Edward A Millen
103 Columbus Ave
Salem MA 019705771

Call Sign: KB1CWW
Gary E Richards
73 Congress St
Salem MA 01970

Call Sign: K1KAS
Robert H Johnson
23 Cross St
Salem MA 01970

Call Sign: KA1FOR
June C Clark
21 Crowdis St
Salem MA 01970

Call Sign: W1OAY
Frank N Clark
21 Crowdis St
Salem MA 01970

Call Sign: KA1ZIT
Elaine M Verrette
28 Crowdis St
Salem MA 01970

Call Sign: KB1WYB
Allen M Lighthiser
102 Derby St Apt 1
Salem MA 01970

Call Sign: N1ZOS
Richard G Carlton
7 Devereaux St
Salem MA 01970

Call Sign: KB1JMQ
Robert R Dehate
3 Essex St

Salem MA 01970

Call Sign: N1ZSX
Warren D Sauders
416 Essex St
Salem MA 01470

Call Sign: KB1HHL
Donald J Warnock Jr
15 First St
Salem MA 01970

Call Sign: K1JVQ
Donald J Warnock Jr
15 First St
Salem MA 01970

Call Sign: KB1KNG
Allison H Feldhusen
2 Flying Cloud Lane
Salem MA 01970

Call Sign: K1YNW
Marie A Erps
8 Forest Ave
Salem MA 01970

Call Sign: W1RJS
Mac E Erps
8 Forest Ave
Salem MA 01970

Call Sign: KB1EF
Otto F Persson Jr
151 Fort Ave
Salem MA 01970

Call Sign: W1TTQ
John J Moore
8 Fowler St
Salem MA 019703214

Call Sign: W1AYD
Fernand E Rioux Sr
8 Gardner St
Salem MA 01970

Call Sign: W1EKL
Joseph F Kerwin
21 Glendale St
Salem MA 01970

Call Sign: N1HDO
Richard D Hatfield Jr

38 Greenway Rd
Salem MA 01970

Call Sign: N1HIY
Thomas H Pszenny
8 Harmony St
Salem MA 019702314

Call Sign: KA1SWU
Eric V Schroeder
15 Harrison Ave
Salem MA 01970

Call Sign: KA1ANC
Edward L Smith
Hart Way
Salem MA 01970

Call Sign: NJ1L
Carmine F
Mastrogiovanni
6 Hartford St
Salem MA 01970

Call Sign: W1BOA
Edward S Mansfield
14 Hemenway Rd
Salem MA 01970

Call Sign: KB2SSA
Michael C Sensabaugh
10 Heritage Dr #33
Salem MA 01970

Call Sign: KB1IRI
Mohamed K Rahman
5 Heritage Dr Apt 22
Salem MA 01970

Call Sign: AB1BN
Mohamed K Rahman
5 Heritage Dr Apt 22
Salem MA 01970

Call Sign: KB1GCM
Matthew A Vita
2 Heritage Drive Apt
25
Salem MA 01970

Call Sign: N1KYK
Michael R Chandler
8 Hersey St
Salem MA 01970

Call Sign: N3PDE
Christian A Murphy
19 High St
Salem MA 01970

Call Sign: KB1EKT
John J Stavros
79 Highland Ave
Salem MA 01970

Call Sign: KA1EFZ
Richard J Cox
Highland Ave
Salem MA 01970

Call Sign: KB1PCN
Dennis J Eberl
Highland Ave Apt 104
Salem MA 01970

Call Sign: K2YTJ
Dennis J Eberl
Highland Ave Apt 104
Salem MA 01970

Call Sign: N1KGA
Thomas A Gilligan
7 Hillside Ave
Salem MA 01970

Call Sign: WA1YGC
George L Bouchard
28 Lafayette Pl
Salem MA 01970

Call Sign: W1DNZ
Fred J Harney
474 Lafayette St
Salem MA 01970

Call Sign: N1YVO
Jason N Chalifour
245 Lafayette St Apt
3e
Salem MA 01970

Call Sign: KA1GXE
Gerald F Gilrain
77 Leach St
Salem MA 01970

Call Sign: KA1SLX
Elizabeth E Lessard

3 Lightning Ln
Salem MA 01970

Call Sign: KA1LJ
George C Brackett
16 Lincoln Rd
Salem MA 019704456

Call Sign: KB1OHZ
Michael J Griffin
39 Linden St
Salem MA 01970

Call Sign: N1SNI
William B Bushong
79 Linden St
Salem MA 01970

Call Sign: W1QLB
Roger E Chagnon
492 Loring Ave
Salem MA 019704218

Call Sign: W1EHX
Stuart W Martin
1 Lowell St
Salem MA 01970

Call Sign: KA1YPP
Donald R Masella Jr
40 Marlborough Rd
Salem MA 01970

Call Sign: AA1BR
Paul E Morin
44 Memorial Dr
Salem MA 01970

Call Sign: N1OPF
Ronald L Sirois
2 Messervy St
Salem MA 01970

Call Sign: KB1ORT
John L Tachuk
1 Moffatt Rd
Salem MA 01970

Call Sign: KD1YP
Mark Sullivan
1 Moffatt Rd
Salem MA 01970

Call Sign: WG9W

Mark Sullivan
1 Moffatt Rd
Salem MA 01970

Call Sign: KB1FYV
James V Dunning
80 Moffatt Rd
Salem MA 01970

Call Sign: K1KLI
James V Dunning
80 Moffatt Rd
Salem MA 01970

Call Sign: KB1GCE
Neil M Moynihan
14 Naples Rd
Salem MA 01970

Call Sign: N1LIM
Leeanne B Swift
10 Norman St Unit 101
Salem MA 01970

Call Sign: W1VUO
Arthur L Russell Jr
206 North St
Salem MA 01970

Call Sign: N1URI
Jorge O Goulart
7 Oakland St
Salem MA 01970

Call Sign: KB1TPR
Michael Bencal
26 Oakland St
Salem MA 01970

Call Sign: KA1KFQ
Charles F Bergman
139 Ocean Ave
Salem MA 01970

Call Sign: KB1MLR
Frederick P Christian
5 Olde Village Drive
Salem MA 01970

Call Sign: KB1TJR
Tyler L Semmel
5 Paul Ave
Salem MA 01970

Call Sign: KB1TJU
Nora A Mcneil
5 Paul Ave
Salem MA 01970

Call Sign: KB1OHY
Richard F Ringer
91 Proctor St
Salem MA 01970

Call Sign: KA1ZKQ
Cheryl A La Pointe
34 Raymond Ave
Salem MA 01970

Call Sign: WD1Q
Andrew J La Pointe
34 Raymond Ave
Salem MA 01970

Call Sign: KB1TRK
Frederick J Stone Iii
6 Red Jacket Ln
Salem MA 01970

Call Sign: KB1HRN
Richard P Clement
5 Salem St
Salem MA 01970

Call Sign: KB1QKM
Ralph W Sherrick
45 School St
Salem MA 01970

Call Sign: K1QAX
Ralph W Sherrick
45 School St
Salem MA 01970

Call Sign: KA1ZJB
Norman P La Pointe
5 St Paul St
Salem MA 01970

Call Sign: N1KGH
David C Moisan
45 St Peter St 311
Salem MA 01970

Call Sign: K1VZX
Nelson L Dionne Sr
12 Sumner Rd
Salem MA 019704467

Call Sign: KC1TB
William A Claffey
40 Walter St
Salem MA 01970

Call Sign: KB1RYA
Nancy Tenbroeck
74 Washington Sq East
Salem MA 01970

Call Sign: KB1HKQ
Joseph I Wyman
257 Washington St Apt 9
Salem MA 01970

Call Sign: ND1G
William E Skeffington Jr
17 Woodside St
Salem MA 01970

Call Sign: AA1MO
Nelson L Dionne Jr
Salem MA 01920

Call Sign: N1UGA
Jane A Dionne
Salem MA 01970

FCC Amateur Radio Licenses in Salisbury

Call Sign: KA1LLN
Ralph J Sweeney
25 Beach Rd
Salisbury MA 01952

Call Sign: KB1VOZ
Dana Freeman
170 Beach Rd Unit 49
Salisbury MA 01952

Call Sign: KB1OGM
Reginald B Santos
8 Brooks Rd
Salisbury MA 01952

Call Sign: K1GFP
Matthew Chimioga
87 Cable Ave
Salisbury MA 01952

Call Sign: KB1FLA
John S Clarke
130 Cable Ave
Salisbury MA 01952

Call Sign: KA1ZBD
Kevin S Thomas
91 Dock Ln
Salisbury MA 01952

Call Sign: K1WOC
William R Dickie
377 Elm St
Salisbury MA 01950

Call Sign: KA1YKE
Gabrielle A Dillon
36 Ferry Rd
Salisbury MA 01952

Call Sign: KB1JAD
Todd D Williams
65 Ferry Rd
Salisbury MA 01952

Call Sign: KB1JGO
Todd D Williams
65 Ferry Rd
Salisbury MA 01952

Call Sign: KB1TCS
Todd D Williams
65 Ferry Rd
Salisbury MA 01952

Call Sign: KB1TQZ
Robert E Cook Sr
78 Ferry Rd
Salisbury MA 01952

Call Sign: N1WFE
Matthew Knowlton
165 Ferry Rd
Salisbury MA 01952

Call Sign: KB1MGC
Randy M Hitchcock
12 First St
Salisbury MA 01952

Call Sign: N1IPM
Shawn W Perkins
18 First St
Salisbury MA 01952

Call Sign: W1TLX
Clayton E Perkins
18 First St Rings Island
Salisbury MA 01950

Call Sign: N1ZNM
Evelyn I Barrett
1 Forest Rd
Salisbury MA 01952

Call Sign: KA1NRJ
Anthony E Girardi
10 Fowler St
Salisbury MA 01950

Call Sign: KA1ZJI
Akio Takahashi
3 Gerrish Rd
Salisbury MA 01952

Call Sign: N1VEH
Don C Coleman
1 High St
Salisbury MA 01952

Call Sign: KB1JAC
Terrence A Marengi Sr
85 Lafayette Rd
Salisbury MA 01952

Call Sign: AB1BS
Terrence A Marengi Sr
85 Lafayette Rd
Salisbury MA 01952

Call Sign: W1TCS
Terrence A Marengi Sr
85 Lafayette Rd
Salisbury MA 01952

Call Sign: KA1WKP
Shawn E Stevens
264 Lafayette Rd
Salisbury MA 01952

Call Sign: KB1FDE
Gordon F Blaney
37 Main St
Salisbury MA 01952

Call Sign: KB1CVQ
Mark J Gaudette
1 Meaders Ln

Salisbury MA 01952

Call Sign: N1PZS
Frederick J Gaudette
1 Meaders Ln
Salisbury MA 01952

Call Sign: KB1QOV
Igor Kosvin
3 Michelle Drive
Salisbury MA 01952

Call Sign: N1YX
Igor Kosvin
3 Michelle Drive
Salisbury MA 01952

Call Sign: W1GOE
Robert L Bowlen
13 Mudnock Rd
Salisbury MA 01952

Call Sign: W1YAS
Jesse W Shaw
80 Mudnock Rd
Salisbury MA 01952

Call Sign: KB1SAD
George M Mckenna III
2 Niko Way
Salisbury MA 01952

Call Sign: KB1AYD
Joseph R Perusse
12 Odin St
Salisbury MA 01952

FCC Amateur Radio Licenses in Sandisfield

Call Sign: N1MVN
Frank W Dwyer
Box 49
Sandisfield MA 01255

Call Sign: N2KJN
Peter B Levine
97 N Main St
Sandisfield MA 01255

Call Sign: KJ1N
Peter B Levine
97 N Main St

Sandisfield MA 01255

Call Sign: KC2ZBW
James T Dollard
7 Sandisfield Rd
Sandisfield MA 01255

Call Sign: KB1TWH
Andre P D Andrea
12 Silverbrook Rd
Sandisfield MA 01255

Call Sign: KB1UGI
Constance E D'andrea
12 Silverbrook Rd
Sandisfield MA 01255

FCC Amateur Radio Licenses in Sandwich

Call Sign: WT1O
Robert G Melvin Ii
4 Arbutus Ln
Sandwich MA 02563

Call Sign: N1RIX
Warren S Harriman
8 Bowmans Way
Sandwich MA 02563

Call Sign: KB1VL
Stephen Q Day
2 Buckingham Dr
Sandwich MA
025632483

Call Sign: N1YHT
Norman R Hollis
7 Chadwell Ave
Sandwich MA 02563

Call Sign: W1NYR
John F Collins
48 Chipman Rd
Sandwich MA 02563

Call Sign: KA1VBQ
Samantha A Fisher
163 Cotuit Rd
Sandwich MA 02563

Call Sign: K1OIK
Burton E Fisher
163 Cotuit Rd

Sandwich MA 02563

Call Sign: WA2HIF
Barbara J Hichar
219 Cotuit Rd
Sandwich MA 02563

Call Sign: N1BWK
John A Howard
8 Coventry Place
Sandwich MA 02563

Call Sign: KA1SGK
Ira B Carmel
Dewey Ave Rfd 1
Sandwich MA 02563

Call Sign: N1WRK
Marc A Muir
9 Dukes Dr
Sandwich MA
025632420

Call Sign: KB1HJC
Alton E Robbins
5 Evergreen Dr
Sandwich MA 02563

Call Sign: KB1ECM
Paul F Howard
201 Farmersville Rd
Sandwich MA 02563

Call Sign: W2LDM
Robert L Gunshor
10 Grove St
Sandwich MA 02563

Call Sign: W9OPF
Wayne E Hoover
1 Haystack Ln
Sandwich MA 02563

Call Sign: KB1VPJ
Sean P Grady
17 Highfield Drive
Sandwich MA 02563

Call Sign: W1EZV
James H Nye
38 Highview Dr
Sandwich MA
026352312

Call Sign: KB1PEA
Rory C Gibbons
4 Holder Ln
Sandwich MA 02563

Call Sign: K1RCG
Rory C Gibbons
4 Holder Ln
Sandwich MA 02563

Call Sign: KB1PRH
Matthew R Powderly
9 Holder Ln
Sandwich MA 02563

Call Sign: N0NXJ
Matthew R Powderly
9 Holder Ln
Sandwich MA 02563

Call Sign: N1LIT
Matthew R Powderly
9 Holder Ln
Sandwich MA 02563

Call Sign: N1AJR
Carl E Swanson
21 Holly Ridge Dr
Sandwich MA 02563

Call Sign: WD6BMB
William D Durgan
8 Ink Berry Cir
Sandwich MA 02563

Call Sign: N1YHZ
Jeffrey A Kettell
3 Katies Way
Sandwich MA 02563

Call Sign: N1ACQ
Jeffrey R Cohen
25 Kensington Dr
Sandwich MA 02563

Call Sign: WA1DRQ
Robert J Zylinski
4 Kings Row
Sandwich MA 02563

Call Sign: KB1UGK
Ellen M Zylinski
4 Kings Row
Sandwich MA 02563

Call Sign: K1JL
Gerald L Selby
7 Lands End Lane
Sandwich MA 02563

Call Sign: W8FLJ
Robert H Dillon
108 Lyndsey Way
Sandwich MA 02563

Call Sign: KA1BPH
Richard A Carey
Merchants Way
Sandwich MA 02563

Call Sign: W1LNO
Harold C Wolfe Jr
66 Old Fields Rd Rfd 2
Sandwich MA 02563

Call Sign: KB1VBR
James A Della Morte
221 Old Main St
Sandwich MA 02563

Call Sign: WA1ZAU
John O Della Morte Jr
221 Old Main St
Sandwich MA 02563

Call Sign: WA1EKQ
Elmer F Carlson
163 Route 6a
Sandwich MA
025632052

Call Sign: KB1MJZ
Jesse B Marrs
94 Rt 130
Sandwich MA 02644

Call Sign: KB1QDJ
Barbara Shaner
91 Rt 6a
Sandwich MA 02563

Call Sign: KB1SLI
Michael A Mcginty
13 Sedgewick Ln
Sandwich MA 02563

Call Sign: W2FBI
Michael A Mcginty

13 Sedgewick Ln
Sandwich MA 02563

Call Sign: KB1QDK
Donald J Donahue III
12 Sherwood Lane
Sandwich MA 02563

Call Sign: K1YZO
James I Sammons
8 Summer St
Sandwich MA 02563

Call Sign: W9PQS
Anthony J Tamulis
2 Surrey Lane
Sandwich MA 02563

Call Sign: N1CKR
Jonas R Bielkevicius
2 Swann Hill Ln
Sandwich MA 02563

Call Sign: KB1WGQ
Andrew W Brown
26 Triangle Circle
Sandwich MA 02563

Call Sign: KB1MJY
Patrick M Fandel
22 Tyler Dr
Sandwich MA 02563

Call Sign: KB1TAQ
Garvin F Kelley
3 Viking Ln
Sandwich MA 02563

Call Sign: KC4NAO
Roberts G Hannegan
Iii
8 Woodspring Farm
Lane
Sandwich MA
025632789

Call Sign: W1KNW
Elbert F Powell
Sandwich MA 02563

Call Sign: KB1VWS
Heather L Gallant
Sandwich MA 02563

Call Sign: KB1VYT
Brian J Gallant
Sandwich MA 02563

Call Sign: K1BOH
Heather L Gallant
Sandwich MA 02563

Call Sign: KB1WBF
Sandwich Emergency
Management Club
Sandwich MA 02563

Call Sign: N5EMD
Brian J Gallant
Sandwich MA 02563

Call Sign: W1SEM
Sandwich Emergency
Management Club
Sandwich MA 02563

**FCC Amateur Radio
Licenses in Saugus**

Call Sign: K1KDF
James V Howard Jr
145 Adams Ave
Saugus MA 01906

Call Sign: K1JML
Ronald F Meuse
6 Alvah St
Saugus MA 01906

Call Sign: WA1WYA
Frank D Thomas
58 Auburn St
Saugus MA 01906

Call Sign: KA1PWY
Robin A Pisano
Austin Ct
Saugus MA 01906

Call Sign: W1JZU
W Phillip Heath
10 Birch
Saugus MA 01906

Call Sign: N1SBS
John R Surette Iii
20 Biscayne Ave
Saugus MA 01906

Call Sign: KB1TDO
Nicholas W
Melanchook
44 Boulder Rd
Saugus MA 01906

Call Sign: KB1TKG
Elizabeth A
Melanchook
44 Boulder Rd
Saugus MA 01906

Call Sign: KB1SZW
Nicholas V
Melanchook
44 Boulder Rd
Saugus MA 01906

Call Sign: K1INE
Chester L Bejtlich
19 Bow St
Saugus MA 01906

Call Sign: KF6DGP
William F Ingersoll
47 Bow St
Saugus MA 01906

Call Sign: KB1EZL
Michael A Coffey
1753 Broadway
Saugus MA 01906

Call Sign: K1OZR
Joseph Taddonio Jr
9 Broadway 211
Saugus MA
019061035

Call Sign: K1COS
Lloyd W Locke
104 Broadway L13
Saugus MA 01906

Call Sign: N1ZQB
John P Burkhardt
20 C Austin Ct
Saugus MA
019063565

Call Sign: KB1UAB
Wayne K Mcclintock
Jr

462 Central St
Saugus MA 01906

Call Sign: WA1NTA
George E Falardeau Jr
8 Cherry St
Saugus MA
019063402

Call Sign: W1JCJ
Kenneth S Campbell
9 Cherry St
Saugus MA 01906

Call Sign: N1FXL
James J Murphy Jr
18 Clifton Ave
Saugus MA 01906

Call Sign: W1TTS
Walter S Pisiak
87 Clifton Ave
Saugus MA 01906

Call Sign: WA1AAA
Harry A Woodland Sr
9 Cottage St
Saugus MA 01906

Call Sign: N1XLN
Paul C Agersea
42 Denver St
Saugus MA 01906

Call Sign: N1SOE
Robert J Loder
28 Endicott
Saugus MA 01906

Call Sign: KB1ANA
Karen L Sullivan
141 Essex St
Saugus MA 01906

Call Sign: WA1JKP
Ernest W Chadwick
210 Essex St
Saugus MA 01906

Call Sign: KB1ITY
John R Sullivan
217 Essex St
Saugus MA 01906

Call Sign: K1NSI
Donald R Ballard
16 Fairchild Ave
Saugus MA 01906

Call Sign: KA1SMB
Dean E Cook Jr
20 Fairchild Ave
Saugus MA 01906

Call Sign: WW1E
Thomas J Thibault
12 Fairmount Ave
Saugus MA 01906

Call Sign: KA1WLF
Domenic A Correggio
Iii
20 Ferncliff Ave
Saugus MA 01906

Call Sign: WA1AYY
Domenic A Correggio
Jr
20 Ferncliff Ave
Saugus MA 01906

Call Sign: KG1E
Alex M Jozsa
31 Glendale Ave
Saugus MA 01906

Call Sign: KA1DUI
Louise M Rees
15 Grandview Av
Saugus MA 01906

Call Sign: WA1LEZ
Charles A Rees
15 Grandview Ave
Saugus MA
019062748

Call Sign: N1INX
Edward A Whelan
22 Granite Rd
Saugus MA 01906

Call Sign: KA1GXW
Paul H Arsenault
91 Great Woods Rd
Saugus MA 01906

Call Sign: KA1AYL

Carolyn F Hashem
100 Hamilton St
Saugus MA 01906

Call Sign: KA1F
Thomas C Hashem
100 Hamilton St
Saugus MA 01906

Call Sign: K1SVP
Francis A Cascio
240 Hamilton St
Saugus MA 01906

Call Sign: W1NO
Nite Owl Radio Club
240 Hamilton St
Saugus MA 01906

Call Sign: W1TYM
Malden Amateur Radio
Assn Inc
240 Hamilton St
Saugus MA 01906

Call Sign: W1VGE
Harold A Strick
30 Harrison Ave
Saugus MA 01906

Call Sign: K1QQA
William R Fairfield
56 Harrison Ave
Saugus MA 01906

Call Sign: WA1CBN
John W Coffey Sr
10 Hemingway Ter
Saugus MA 01906

Call Sign: W1WUD
George J Wishneusky
32 Herbert Ave
Saugus MA 01906

Call Sign: W1VGZ
Thomas Di Milla Jr
8 High St
Saugus MA
019063618

Call Sign: K1FXZ
Ralph J Knowlton
7 Horton St

Saugus MA 01906

Call Sign: K1YWW
Sidney Shanbar
35 Howard St
Saugus MA 01906

Call Sign: WA1YXD
Victor J Cann
9 Jackson St
Saugus MA
019063707

Call Sign: KB1JPS
Thomas W Linehan Jr
8 Lake Dam Rd
Saugus MA 01906

Call Sign: N1HOL
Paul C Ciarletta
17 Ledgewood Rd
Saugus MA 01906

Call Sign: KB1MLS
Harlan D Tapley Jr
307 Main St
Saugus MA 01906

Call Sign: N1ZHI
Ronald A Cook
7 Montgomery St
Saugus MA
019062632

Call Sign: W1OGK
Andrew J Donovan
16 Montgomery St
Saugus MA 01906

Call Sign: KB1TUI
Kevin P Merlina
31 Morton Ave
Saugus MA 01906

Call Sign: AB1QM
Kevin P Merlina
31 Morton Ave
Saugus MA 01906

Call Sign: W1KPM
Kevin P Merlina
31 Morton Ave
Saugus MA 01906

Call Sign: W1SCH
John J Di Troia Sr
5 Mt Pleasant St
Saugus MA 01906

Call Sign: KB1DKU
Allen E Humphries
19 Myrtle St
Saugus MA
019064325

Call Sign: N1GQY
Waldemar Chomicki
33 Newcomb Ave
Saugus MA 01906

Call Sign: N1XEV
Walter J Koschen Iii
77 Newhall Ave 107
Saugus MA 01906

Call Sign: KD1KA
Raymond A Sprague
31 Oaklandvale Ave
Saugus MA 01906

Call Sign: KB1QMC
Paul O Penachio
17 Palmer Ave
Saugus MA 01906

Call Sign: N1JEJ
Frederick Mc Garry
42 Palmetto St
Saugus MA 01906

Call Sign: KB1PCV
Kevin C Meagher
2 Pearl Rd
Saugus MA 01906

Call Sign: KM1BFM
Kevin C Meagher
2 Pearl Rd
Saugus MA 01906

Call Sign: KA1YGI
Stephen J Twohig
26 Pearson St
Saugus MA 01906

Call Sign: N1GWG
Joseph W Kushlan
2 Pranker Rd

Saugus MA 01906

Call Sign: N1ZEB
Ralph C Pugh
17 Prospect St
Saugus MA
019062154

Call Sign: N1ZDZ
David M Di Gennaro
23 Prospect St
Saugus MA
019062154

Call Sign: KB1IAG
Cindy L Pearson
8 Saugus Ave
Saugus MA 01906

Call Sign: KB1GCI
Donald R Dipietro
113 Saville St
Saugus MA 01906

Call Sign: WA1DFL
Donald R Di Pietro
113 Saville St
Saugus MA 01906

Call Sign: W1JKF
Richard B Kendall
10 Stocker St
Saugus MA
019061638

Call Sign: KB1RQL
Alan E Drozdowicz
35 Summer St
Saugus MA 01906

Call Sign: K1BIG
Alan E Drozdowicz
35 Summer St
Saugus MA 01906

Call Sign: KA1ENK
William H Cox Jr
23 Susan Dr
Saugus MA
019061262

Call Sign: KE4BQJ
Jean Y King
19 Talbot St #615

Saugus MA
019063468

Call Sign: N1IXT
Martin A Zardeskas
75 Vine St
Saugus MA 01906

Call Sign: K1RPM
Virgil A Savary Sr
51 Waban St
Saugus MA 01906

Call Sign: KB1RHX
Michael S Cammarata
29 Westford St
Saugus MA 01906

Call Sign: N1CBR
Charles P Rocheleau
12 Woodland Ave
Saugus MA
019061244

Call Sign: W1CPR
Charles P Rocheleau
12 Woodland Ave
Saugus MA
019061244

FCC Amateur Radio Licenses in Savoy

Call Sign: KB1EXN
David N Maisonneuve
100 Hawley
Savoy MA 01256

Call Sign: WA1WHA
Robert L Ryan
Haskins Rd
Savoy MA 01256

Call Sign: WA1TFV
David R Armstrong
67 Jackson Rd
Savoy MA 01256

Call Sign: KA1SUN
Eric J Mazur
763 Main Rd
Savoy MA 012569202

Call Sign: N1MBR

John J Bromback
1107 Main Rd
Savoy MA 01256

Call Sign: KA1ZXR
Lauralee J
Cunningham
1204 Main Rd
Savoy MA 01256

Call Sign: W1SJV
Clifford G Ey
1204 Main Rd
Savoy MA 01256

Call Sign: W1TGE
William A Sakowski
125 Old Main Rd
Savoy MA 01256

Call Sign: AA1TZ
Kimberly A Yarter
10 Windsor Rd
Savoy MA 01256

FCC Amateur Radio Licenses in Saxonville

Call Sign: KA1UTO
Joseph F Lynch
14 Eaton Rd
Saxonville MA 01705

Call Sign: K1MTD
Stanley J Szretter
Saxonville MA 01701

Call Sign: AA1EA
Lawrence R Brandt
Saxonville MA 01701

FCC Amateur Radio Licenses in Scituate

Call Sign: N1KZB
Michael J Monaco
53 Acorn St
Scituate MA 02066

Call Sign: W1QWT
Robert E Callahan
56 Acorn St
Scituate MA 02066

Call Sign: KS1C
Charles J Mac Pherson
36 Briarwood Ln
Scituate MA 02066

Call Sign: N1SOJ
Donald S Cook
29 Bridge Ave
Scituate MA 02066

Call Sign: KA1AMR
James F Dillon
66 Brook St
Scituate MA 02066

Call Sign: N1VCE
Sean P Fay
236 Cairo Cir
Scituate MA 02066

Call Sign: W1AAX
Harry D Wilson
88 Captain Pierce Rd
Scituate MA 02066

Call Sign: KB1JJQ
George H Cavanagh Iii
82 Clapp Rd
Scituate MA 02066

Call Sign: W1DKD
Robert W Jennings
15 Cliff Ave
Scituate MA 02066

Call Sign: WA1HEJ
Stephen A Jennings
15 Cliff Ave
Scituate MA 02066

Call Sign: K1NOK
Robert J Marchese
63 Cobb Ln
Scituate MA 02066

Call Sign: KA1RDT
Adam S Marchese
63 Cobb Ln
Scituate MA 02066

Call Sign: KB1REP
Michael L Fitzmaurice
102 Country Way
Scituate MA 02066

Call Sign: KA1KUM
Arthur E Nichols
153 Country Way
Scituate MA
020663714

Call Sign: W1RQS
William F Krusell
275 Country Way
Scituate MA 02066

Call Sign: W1UKZ
David P Allen
19 Damon Rd
Sandhills
Scituate MA 02066

Call Sign: KA1IBM
Richard K Walbridge
Sr
15 Edgewood Rd
Scituate MA 02066

Call Sign: K1RMO
Terence J Gorman
12 Edith Holmes Dr
Scituate MA
020662664

Call Sign: N1XJE
Thomas M Reilly
1 Ermine Rd
Scituate MA 02066

Call Sign: WB1ANL
Anthony D Fusco
20 Fay Rd
Scituate MA 02066

Call Sign: K1DJ
Richard L Hoffman
15 Fifth Ave
Scituate MA 02066

Call Sign: N1GNE
Kai M Hoffman
15 Fifth Ave
Scituate MA 02066

Call Sign: KB1KPR
Albert J Monaco
293 First Parish Rd
Scituate MA 02066

Call Sign: KB1FBA
Robert J Mahoney
5 Foam Rd
Scituate MA 02066

Call Sign: N1QVN
William E Verge
19 Garden Rd
Scituate MA 02066

Call Sign: WA1YKT
Robert P Loyot
26 Gilson Rd
Scituate MA 02066

Call Sign: KB1QPP
Melissa Y Sieminski
11 Jay Rd
Scituate MA 02066

Call Sign: N1OOF
Jason W Rhodes
17 Jay Rd
Scituate MA 02066

Call Sign: W1FBT
Kenneth J Walsh
12 Laurel Dr
Scituate MA 02066

Call Sign: N1ZZO
George L Kelly
108 Lawson Rd
Scituate MA 02066

Call Sign: KE1U
Brian J Poole
80 Lighthouse Rd
Scituate MA 02066

Call Sign: KA1RTC
Ralph H Brown
92 Lighthouse Rd
Scituate MA
020663538

Call Sign: WA1JAD
Mark J Radding
45 Marys Ln
Scituate MA 02066

Call Sign: W1HIL
Richard H Eckhouse

12 Meeting House Ln
103
Scituate MA
020664206

Call Sign: KB1MYP
Brian G Draves
272 Old Oaken Bucket
Rd
Scituate MA 02066

Call Sign: KB1JUK
George F Grimes
114 Pratt Rd
Scituate MA
020662035

Call Sign: NS1N
Karl S Johnson Sr
39 Richfield Rd
Scituate MA 02066

Call Sign: W1NEL
Robert M Sylvester
7 Stenbeck Pl
Scituate MA 02066

Call Sign: K1CWS
Bruce E Billings
10 Stockbridge Rd
Scituate MA 02066

Call Sign: AA1V
Donald F Mikes
32 Summer St
Scituate MA 02066

Call Sign: W1TMC
James K Howard
11 Three Ring Rd
Scituate MA 02066

Call Sign: NJ1P
Joseph W Parskey
4 Winslow Ave
Scituate MA 02066

Call Sign: N1QZR
Paul A Deibel
21 Woodbine Way
Scituate MA
020660871

Call Sign: N1ZWQ

Ralph E Butler Jr
Scituate MA
020660238

Call Sign: W1BT
Ralph E Butler Jr
Scituate MA
020660238

**FCC Amateur Radio
Licenses in Seekonk**

Call Sign: WZ1K
Mario J Veiga
490 Arcade Ave
Seekonk MA 02771

Call Sign: WA1JYF
Anthony Sears Jr
74 Back St
Seekonk MA 02771

Call Sign: N1SYO
Barry Figara
Bittersweet Dr
Seekonk MA 02771

Call Sign: KB1UNK
Matthew M Owens
140 Bloomfield St
Seekonk MA 02771

Call Sign: AA1RO
Myron T Dourado
45 Border Ave
Seekonk MA 02771

Call Sign: KB1OHU
Wayne T Stone
87 Brook Hill Dr
Seakonk MA 02721

Call Sign: W1WTS
Wayne T Stone
87 Brook Hill Dr
Seekonk MA 02771

Call Sign: KB1RMM
Thomas J Hannigan
75 Brookside Ct
Seekonk MA 02771

Call Sign: NG1U
Stephen C Healy

214 Central Ave
Seekonk MA 02771

Call Sign: N1SAS
William E Stone
360 Central Ave
Seekonk MA 02771

Call Sign: WB1FAI
Charles L Harris
24 Chantilly Ct
Seekonk MA 02771

Call Sign: W1CLH
Charles L Harris
24 Chantilly Ct
Seekonk MA 02771

Call Sign: N1ZZK
Christopher N Abell
97 Elm St
Seekonk MA 02771

Call Sign: WA1IZM
Lester E Potter
559 Fall River Ave
Seekonk MA
027715418

Call Sign: KA1ZXO
John A Buono
61 Forest Ave
Seekonk MA 02771

Call Sign: K1CZB
Tanis J Tavernier Sr
28 French Dr
Seekonk MA 02771

Call Sign: KA1WNB
David M Melo
7 Garden St
Seekonk MA 02771

Call Sign: WA1JHW
Gregory M La Rocque
10 Gardner St
Seekonk MA 02771

Call Sign: KB1DFD
David J Welch
2 Greenhalgh Dr
Seekonk MA
027713806

Call Sign: KA1PBF
Omer R Goulet
6 Gregory Dr
Seekonk MA 02771

Call Sign: W1JES
Joseph E Sirois
5 Ivy Ln
Seekonk MA 02771

Call Sign: KB1EWD
Nathaniel E Sirois
5 Ivy Ln
Seekonk MA 02771

Call Sign: N1OCD
Renee K Eghian
115 Lake St
Seekonk MA 02771

Call Sign: N1BKV
John F Lovett
80 Leonard St
Seekonk MA 02771

Call Sign: W1PM
Anthony J Medeiros Jr
462 Lincoln St
Seekonk MA 02771

Call Sign: K1CH
Curtis H Heuberger
51 Maynard Ave
Seekonk MA 02771

Call Sign: KE1FT
Philip J Terrien
2 Milton St
Seekonk MA 02771

Call Sign: N1YDS
Priscilla A Terrien
2 Milton St
Seekonk MA 02771

Call Sign: KB1EGF
James R Salvatore
148 Monarch Dr
Seekonk MA 02771

Call Sign: N1OQT
Ralph Pallotta Jr
365 N Wheaton Ave

Seekonk MA 02771

Call Sign: N1RR
Charles Morrison
1287 Newman Ave
Seekonk MA 02771

Call Sign: WZ1R
Seekonk Contest Club
1287 Newman Ave
Seekonk MA 02771

Call Sign: W1KUQ
Egidio J Policastri
25 Noble
Seekonk MA 02771

Call Sign: KB1QCN
Peter D Kirchmann
59 Oakhill Ave
Seekonk MA 02771

Call Sign: N1ICX
Gary K Mc Nally
46 Oakland Ave
Seekonk MA 02771

Call Sign: W1DBC
Dan Costa
46 Oakland Ave
Seekonk MA 02771

Call Sign: WA2KFE
Martin D Chapman
41 Pheasant Ridge Rd
Seekonk MA 02771

Call Sign: K1JI
John W Isidoro
46 Pheasant Ridge Rd
Seekonk MA 02771

Call Sign: KA1QIE
John R Isidoro
46 Pheasant Ridge Rd
Seekonk MA 02771

Call Sign: WA1LAD
William E Frankland
49 Pimental Dr
Seekonk MA 02771

Call Sign: N1WSG
Glenn H Britland

665 Pine St
Seekonk MA 02771

Call Sign: KA1ZEA
David C Cooney
993 Pine St
Seekonk MA 02771

Call Sign: KB1JQE
Dennis W Welch
10 Prospect St
Seekonk MA 02771

Call Sign: K1FD
David J Welch
41 Read St
Seekonk MA 02771

Call Sign: N1PR
Michael P Rego
30 Sunset Dr
Seekonk MA 02771

Call Sign: K1UGE
Timac Amateur Radio
Club
204 Taunton Ave
Seekonk MA 02771

Call Sign: WA1TCR
Robert E Tella Jr
12 Tee Jay Dr
Seekonk MA 02771

Call Sign: KB1VYI
Tyler M Turcotte
17 Tullson Ave
Seekonk MA 02771

Call Sign: WB1DGB
Robert L Allen
38 Tullson Ave
Seekonk MA 02771

Call Sign: KM1X
Robert L Allen Jr
38 Tullson Ave
Seekonk MA 02771

Call Sign: W1AQ
Associated Rad Amts
Of S New England Inc
38 Tullson Ave
Seekonk MA 02771

Call Sign: KB1JEC
Douglas M Harrington
13 Wagonwheel Rd
Seekonk MA 02771

Call Sign: N1MSS
Richard F Savignano
43 Walker St
Seekonk MA 02771

Call Sign: KA1TOB
Raymond E O Neill
37 Washington St
Seekonk MA 02771

Call Sign: N1HLT
Raymond G O Neill
37 Washington St
Seekonk MA 02771

Call Sign: W1FNH
Paul E Dunn
11 Wesley St
Seekonk MA 02771

**FCC Amateur Radio
Licenses in Sharon**

Call Sign: KA1MIT
Mitchell J Bogart
3 Abbott Ave
Sharon MA 02067

Call Sign: WA1LAW
James L Gleason
5 Abbott Ave
Sharon MA 02067

Call Sign: WA1OCI
Gerald H Gleason
5 Abbott Ave
Sharon MA 020672310

Call Sign: WA1OCJ
Madeleine M Gleason
5 Abbott Ave
Sharon MA 02067

Call Sign: WA1SNR
Jeffrey H Shapiro
18 Azalea Rd
Sharon MA 02067

Call Sign: KA1HNR
Stanley Jacobs
2 Barefoot Hill Rd
Sharon MA 02067

Call Sign: N1FRP
Charles F Williams
1425 Bay Rd
Sharon MA 02067

Call Sign: WB1ELU
Jeffrey C Lane
53 Beach St
Sharon MA 02067

Call Sign: KA1LHN
Jacqueline Chados
Kramer
77 Beach St
Sharon MA 02067

Call Sign: N1AJ
Richard I Kramer
77 Beach St
Sharon MA 02067

Call Sign: KB1SRE
Stephen G Rabinovitz
93 Billings St
Sharon MA 02067

Call Sign: K1BFO
Stephen G Rabinovitz
93 Billings St
Sharon MA 02067

Call Sign: W1COO
Robert F London
30 Bishop Rd
Sharon MA 02067

Call Sign: N1RCF
William F Sanford
18 Borderland Rd
Sharon MA 02067

Call Sign: W9NRS
Stephen Machinton
8 Burnt Bridge Rd
Sharon MA 02067

Call Sign: WA1ZFD
Edward A Levine
6 Carlton Rd

Sharon MA 02067

Call Sign: WB9FKD
Steve A Bogen
35 Cheryl Dr
Sharon MA 020671118

Call Sign: W1RTS
Robert T Snyder
28 Colburn Dr
Sharon MA 02067

Call Sign: W1AC
Ernest W Horne
43 Deerfield Rd
Sharon MA 020672301

Call Sign: N1HME
R Michel Zilberstein
58 Deerfield Rd
Sharon MA 02067

Call Sign: KQ1W
Kenneth P Dono
6 Dogwood Rd
Sharon MA 02067

Call Sign: WB8JMV
Mark A Tinianow
25 Dunbar St
Sharon MA 02067

Call Sign: N1OII
Frank W Bagley Sr
444 E Foxboro St
Sharon MA 02067

Call Sign: KB1HQH
Sean E Cloherty
9 Eagle Dr
Sharon MA 02067

Call Sign: KA1KMK
Francis M Magro
34 East St
Sharon MA 02067

Call Sign: KA1LHP
Richard W Reuss
6 Elliot St
Sharon MA 02067

Call Sign: KB1LNC
David W Wetherell

20 Elliot St
Sharon MA 020671711

Call Sign: K1DWW
David W Wetherell
20 Elliot St
Sharon MA 020671711

Call Sign: KA1JLM
Harry L Bakerman
40 Essex Rd
Sharon MA 02067

Call Sign: KD1GY
Art R Jonkers
21 Everett St
Sharon MA 02067

Call Sign: K1HLZ
Alan H Carp
6 Fales Rd
Sharon MA 020671086

Call Sign: KA1CAZ
Linda F Carp
6 Fales Rd
Sharon MA 020671086

Call Sign: N1COX
Norman B Bernstein
24 Foxfire Dr
Sharon MA 02067

Call Sign: K1YZ
Steven T Meserve
71 Gavins Pond Rd
Sharon MA 02067

Call Sign: KD1EL
Tzvi Rubinstein
214 Hampton Rd
Sharon MA 02067

Call Sign: AK2N
Michael J Delman
44 Harold St
Sharon MA 02067

Call Sign: WA1WDI
Michael S Corman
43 High St
Sharon MA 02067

Call Sign: N1PWL

Beverly L Newman
High St
Sharon MA 02067

Call Sign: WM1G
Mark A Stone
29 Juniper Rd
Sharon MA 02067

Call Sign: W1MCF
Marilyn C Francer
9 Lyndon Rd
Sharon MA 02067

Call Sign: N1FGL
Peter D Rhodes
33 Lyndon Rd
Sharon MA 02067

Call Sign: KB1NRM
Kenneth M Zoller
3 Manning Way
Sharon MA 02067

Call Sign: K1KMZ
Kenneth M Zoller
3 Manning Way
Sharon MA 02067

Call Sign: KA1ANW
Sydney M Baron
6 Marcus Rd
Sharon MA 02067

Call Sign: K1CNX
Bernard M Rosenberg
72 Massapoag Ave
Sharon MA 02067

Call Sign: WB1FEK
Barry R Zlotin
130 Massapoag Ave
Sharon MA 02067

Call Sign: N1WSR
Ken D Olum
156 Massapoag Ave
Sharon MA 02067

Call Sign: KA1DPW
J David Goldblatt
13 Middlesex Rd
Sharon MA 02067

Call Sign: WB1EYE
Carl Gelormini
427 N Main St
Sharon MA 02067

Call Sign: KB1TMN
Sheila J Halper
178 North Main St
Sharon MA 02067

Call Sign: KA1HPD
Dominic J Butanowicz
105 Oakhill Dr
Sharon MA 02067

Call Sign: WA2ACU
William L Schweber
58 Pleasant St
Sharon MA 02067

Call Sign: KB1UOL
Victor L Dowdell
23 Pole Plain Rd
Sharon MA 02067

Call Sign: AB1NQ
Victor L Dowdell
23 Pole Plain Rd
Sharon MA 02067

Call Sign: KC1FH
Gary Buchwald
59 Pond St
Sharon MA 02067

Call Sign: WA1YAT
Alan R Shapiro
149 Pond St
Sharon MA 02067

Call Sign: K1FNX
Michael I Polimer
20 Roberta Rd
Sharon MA 02067

Call Sign: KD1UD
Hyman I Stramer
5 Robin Rd
Sharon MA 02067

Call Sign: KC4IRV
Ashley M Marx
143 S Main St
Sharon MA 02067

Call Sign: KB1HQV
Eli A Geller
143 S Main St
Sharon MA 02067

Call Sign: K1CNX
Norfolk County
Repeater Association
217 S Main St
Sharon MA 01067

Call Sign: KB1EDV
Sharon Civil Defense -
217 Norfolk County
Repeater Association
S Main St
Sharon MA 01067

Call Sign: WB3LCN
Andrew Beckerman
Rodau
17 School St
Sharon MA 02067

Call Sign: WC1C
Wayne M Bethoney
5 Sherwood Cir
Sharon MA 020672205

Call Sign: WN2GTF
Henry Gitter
10 Sherwood Circle
Sharon MA 02067

Call Sign: WA1RBQ
Richard J Van Hooft
17 Webb Rd
Sharon MA 02067

Call Sign: K1AMU
Victor Ellins
14 West St
Sharon MA 02067

Call Sign: W1IAE
Merrill Callum
Sharon MA 02067

Call Sign: KB1NNC
Christos Zabounidis
Sharon MA 02067

Call Sign: N1ZYE
David B Rogers
875 Barnum St
Sheffield MA 01257

Call Sign: KA2OZM
Wesley G Mc Cain
400 Boardman St
Sheffield MA 01257

Call Sign: K2KR
Merle W Wynn
839 Bow Wow Rd
Sheffield MA 01257

Call Sign: W1DDZ
Merle A Wynn Sr
839 Bow Wow Rd
Sheffield MA 01257

Call Sign: W1XB
Noel C Anderson
23 Cobble Lane East
Sheffield MA
012570242

Call Sign: KB1PLF
John M Schmearer
128 Glen Ana Way
Sheffield MA 01257

Call Sign: AA1OK
Stephen M Greenspan
353 Miller Ave
Sheffield MA
012579776

Call Sign: KA1DYE
Thomas E Carey
North Main St
Sheffield MA 01257

Call Sign: N1XHQ
Michael J Romanowicz
132 Oak St
Sheffield MA 01257

Call Sign: N1UES
Stephen R Hyer
25 Shunpike Rd
Sheffield MA 01257

Call Sign: KA1ARR
Robert S Schoenfeld
24 Spring Hollow Ln
Sheffield MA 01257

Call Sign: KB1AHD
Douglas C Mac
Donald
Sheffield MA 01257

Call Sign: KA1PLT
Mary S Woods
Sheffield MA 01257

Call Sign: KB1MZM
Berkshire School Rd -
Attn Paul O Brien Mt
Everett Amateur Radio
Club
Sheffield MA 01257

Call Sign: W1XTV
Berkshire School Rd -
Attn Paul O Brien Mt
Everett Amateur Radio
Club
Sheffield MA 01257

FCC Amateur Radio Licenses in Shelburne

Call Sign: KA1SZD
Robert L Nichols
Bardwells Ferry Rd
Shelburne MA 01370

FCC Amateur Radio Licenses in Shelburne Falls

Call Sign: KB1QYO
Eric A Parham
34 Ashfield St
Shelburne Falls MA
01370

Call Sign: AB1JW
Eric A Parham
34 Ashfield St
Shelburne Falls MA
01370

Call Sign: W1BAN

Eric Parham
34 Ashfield St
Shelburne Falls MA
01370

Call Sign: KB1CBC
Justin C Schuman
Box 532
Shelburne Falls MA
01370

Call Sign: K1HNJ
Edwin B Moseley
99 Colrain Shelburne
Rd
Shelburne Falls MA
013709808

Call Sign: W1HND
Howard S Fish
10 Dungarvin Dr
Shelburne Falls MA
01370

Call Sign: N1UOQ
Robert D Howson
75 Elm St
Shelburne Falls MA
013701520

Call Sign: N2DMV
Theodore B Merrill Jr
30 High St
Shelburne Falls MA
01370

Call Sign: N1LUP
Howard A Field
7 Laurel St
Shelburne Falls MA
01370

Call Sign: KA3QCS
Julie R Goldman
202 Lower St
Shelburne Falls MA
01370

Call Sign: W1DKY
Robert F Bessette
34 Main St
Shelburne Falls MA
01370

Call Sign: N1SCC
William J Campbell
35 Main St
Shelburne Falls MA
013701122

Call Sign: W2HMD
Harry M Dunning Sr
44 Main St
Shelburne Falls MA
013701112

Call Sign: WA1UST
Jonathan F George Sr
89 Main St
Shelburne Falls MA
01370

Call Sign: KB1NEK
Christopher A Myers
52 Maple St
Shelburne Falls MA
01370

Call Sign: KA1QBH
Joseph A Corbeil
40 Mechanic St
Shelburne Falls MA
01370

Call Sign: N1QOT
Richard M Caiander
Shelburne Falls MA
01370

FCC Amateur Radio Licenses in Sheldonville

Call Sign: K3KDP
Richard L P Custer
1420 West St
Sheldonville MA
02070

Call Sign: KA1LHQ
Pamela A Powell
Sheldonville MA
02070

Call Sign: N1DPW
Paul G Freeman
Sheldonville MA
02070

Call Sign: W1KRS
Francis D Doucette
Sheldonville MA
02070

Call Sign: KB1MQA
Dean C Hodgkins
Sheldonville MA
02070

FCC Amateur Radio Licenses in Sherborn

Call Sign: K1LRK
John W Lovell
1 Bridle Path
Sherborn MA 01770

Call Sign: K1ODB
Spiros G Pantazi
14 Coolidge St
Sherborn MA 01770

Call Sign: NF1Z
Gerald W Weare
26 Dopping Brook Rd
Sherborn MA 01770

Call Sign: WB1BVA
Frances B Garfield
27 Dopping Brook Rd
Sherborn MA 01770

Call Sign: N1PGR
Thomas N Dineen
91 Eliot St
Sherborn MA 01770

Call Sign: N1ZBG
Meghan A Dineen
91 Eliot St
Sherborn MA 01770

Call Sign: N1CTW
Charlotte E Ludington
8 Everett St
Sherborn MA
017701526

Call Sign: KA1MUS
George J Kerins Jr
47 Everett St
Sherborn MA 01770

Call Sign: KA1MYO
Elaine G Teran
68 Farm Rd
Sherborn MA 01770

Call Sign: KA1GWY
Barbara M Wood
137 Forest Ln
Sherborn MA 01770

Call Sign: KB1DXR
Thomas W Martin
37 Great Rock Rd
Sherborn MA
017701609

Call Sign: N1KZE
William A Hall
42 Great Rock Rd
Sherborn MA 01770

Call Sign: KB1LOL
Benjamin R Urmston
79 Hollis St
Sherborn MA
017701253

Call Sign: KB1LVL
Thomas H Urmston
79 Hollis St
Sherborn MA 01770

Call Sign: KB1VYA
Michael C Williamson
27 Parks Dr
Sherborn MA 01770

Call Sign: K1BAF
Aaron J Fishman
32 Parks Dr
Sherborn MA 01770

Call Sign: N1UWI
Gabriel A Matlin
137 S Main St
Sherborn MA 01770

Call Sign: KB1QLB
Brendan R Waldron
8 Surrey Lane
Sherborn MA 01770

Call Sign: KA1AYJ

Patricia A Narowski
10 Towne Lyne Rd
Sherborn MA 01770

Call Sign: K4DAD
E Douglas Jensen
Sherborn MA 01770

Call Sign: KA1RUO
Eric D Martin
Sherborn MA 01770

Call Sign: W1YJI
Lloyd J Teran
Sherborn MA 01770

Call Sign: W1NGS
Thomas C Keefe Jr
Sherborn MA 01770

Call Sign: W1NGY
Zhuo Yang
Sherborn MA 01770

**FCC Amateur Radio
Licenses in Shirley**

Call Sign: KB1RYO
Kenneth M Lee
8 Ayer Rd
Shirley MA 01464

Call Sign: N1NKU
Elizabeth A Beecher
Ayer Rd
Shirley MA 01464

Call Sign: N1IXP
Steven D Jackson
53 B Chapel St
Shirley MA 01464

Call Sign: WB1GFZ
Milton E Westover
8 Benjamin Rd
Shirley MA
014642600

Call Sign: WW1MW
Milton E Westover
8 Benjamin Rd
Shirley MA
014642600

Call Sign: WI1Y
Milton E Westover
8 Benjamin Rd
Shirley MA
014642600

Call Sign: N1WOF
Shawn M Denoncour
58 Brook Trail
Shirley MA 01464

Call Sign: W1FKB
William G Burnley
2 Brown Rd
Shirley MA 01464

Call Sign: N1UYJ
Charles F Yanconish
8 Brown Rd
Shirley MA 01464

Call Sign: KB1CII
Matthew C Mc Neal
10 Caleb Rd
Shirley MA 01464

Call Sign: K1BEZ
James E Keefe
11 Carriage Lane
Shirley MA 01464

Call Sign: N1JWR
Norman R Kashdan
109 Center Rd
Shirley MA 01464

Call Sign: N1SAI
Elizabeth A Wade
161 Center Rd
Shirley MA 01464

Call Sign: N1MRI
Joseph J Paul
28 Clark Rd
Shirley MA 01464

Call Sign: KD1NU
Douglas A Johnson
59 Front St
Shirley MA
014640563

Call Sign: AB1EI
Douglas A Johnson

59 Front St
Shirley MA
014640563

Call Sign: N1ZRE
Verna M Sefranek
112 Great Rd
Shirley MA 01464

Call Sign: WA1RHP
Thomas C Sefranek
112 Great Rd
Shirley MA 01464

Call Sign: KB1RCW
Christina Sefranek
112 Great Rd
Shirley MA 01464

Call Sign: KA1WIW
Christina Sefranek
112 Great Rd
Shirley MA 01464

Call Sign: N1MZH
Antonio F Rondeau
117 Great Rd
Shirley MA 01464

Call Sign: KB1OKM
Thomas A Farnsworth
130 Great Rd
Shirley MA 01464

Call Sign: K1NNJ
Thomas A Farnsworth
130 Great Rd
Shirley MA 01464

Call Sign: N2MRX
Mary L Bolton
102 Groton Rd
Shirley MA 01464

Call Sign: KB3SHA
Cathy I Pedtke
102 Groton Rd
Shirley MA 01464

Call Sign: KW2T
Daniel F Pedtke
102 Groton Rd
Shirley MA 01464

Call Sign: KB3RWM
Benjamin D Pedtke
102 Groton Rd
Shirley MA 01464

Call Sign: KB1OZQ
Suzanne Williams
Harvard Rd
Shirley MA 01464

Call Sign: N1XRQ
Cynthia J Sefranek
9 Hill Lane
Shirley MA 01464

Call Sign: W1IPZ
Gerald L Jubb Sr
21 Holden Rd
Shirley MA 01464

Call Sign: KE6UQO
John E Keesee
44 Holden Rd
Shirley MA
014642113

Call Sign: N1STD
Eric C Capucci
73 Holden Rd
Shirley MA 01464

Call Sign: N1BWX
Jerry K Bean
80 Holden Rd
Shirley MA 01464

Call Sign: N1ZRO
Lorraine M Toth
Schwartz
31 Horse Pond Rd
Shirley MA
014642713

Call Sign: W1CYC
Cyclotron Radio
Isodopes
31 Horse Pond Rd
Shirley MA
014642713

Call Sign: W1TE
Charles R Schwartz
31 Horse Pond Rd

Shirley MA
014642713

Call Sign: KB1GHT
Central Ma Wpx
Group
31 Horse Pond Rd
Shirley MA
014642713

Call Sign: WR1TE
Central Ma Wpx
Group
31 Horse Pond Rd
Shirley MA
014642713

Call Sign: WA1VUI
Alfred P Armstrong
2 Hunter Ln
Shirley MA
014642329

Call Sign: KB1FJ
Bennie D Akins
15 Kittredge Rd
Shirley MA
014642801

Call Sign: KA1ZTS
Steven R Woods
96 Leominster Rd
Shirley MA 01464

Call Sign: WA1INU
Frederick H Hyde
4 Maple St
Shirley MA 01464

Call Sign: K9MR
Paul A Davis
13 Pumpkin Brook Rd
Shirley MA 01464

Call Sign: KB1IRX
Tamara L Davis
13 Pumpkin Brook Rd
Shirley MA 01464

Call Sign: K9JRT
Tamara L Davis
13 Pumpkin Brook Rd
Shirley MA 01464

Call Sign: WA1RCH
Charles M Oliveira
72 Squannacook Rd
Shirley MA 01464

Call Sign: KB1CKE
Greg L Andrews
83 Squannacook Rd
Shirley MA 01464

Call Sign: N1FVB
Donald L Andrews
83 Squannacook Rd
Shirley MA 01464

Call Sign: KA1GNU
Philip A Mc Gibney
17 Tolman Ave
Shirley MA 01464

Call Sign: KA1TOY
Charles F Madden Jr
Shirley MA 01464

Call Sign: KA1VTY
Marianne E Boss
Shirley MA 01464

Call Sign: WB5VPY
Mary A Carlson
Shirley MA 01464

Call Sign: KA1ZSO
Shaundra I Woods
Shirley MA 01464

Call Sign: WB1FWW
William A Henry Jr
Shirley MA 01464

Call Sign: KB1UNH
Rick J Luddy Jr
Shirley MA 01464

Call Sign: KA1RED
Rick J Luddy Jr
Shirley MA 01464

Call Sign: KB1WYG
Douglas Y Armstrong
Shirley MA 01464

**FCC Amateur Radio
Licenses in
Shrewsbury**

Call Sign: K1ZT
Sakaaki Ashikawa
4224 Avalon Way
Shrewsbury MA 01545

Call Sign: N1IPV
Gary D Hebblethwaite
28 Bellridge Dr
Shrewsbury MA 01545

Call Sign: N1GEX
Raymond Pavlak Jr
60 Beverly Hill Dr
Shrewsbury MA 01545

Call Sign: W1BGL
Nicholas E Gatzios
8 Birch Ln
Shrewsbury MA 01545

Call Sign: N1NVX
Eric J Fitch
11 Bittersweet Cir
Shrewsbury MA 01545

Call Sign: N1VX
Eric J Fitch
11 Bittersweet Cir
Shrewsbury MA 01545

Call Sign: KA1VWX
Alexander T Syriac
465 Boston Tpk Apt
H-2
Shrewsbury MA 01545

Call Sign: KB1IZC
Adam D Woodbury
465 Boston Tpke M6
Shrewsbury MA 01545

Call Sign: N1EOB
Sandra M Woodbury
465 Boston Tpke M-6
Shrewsbury MA 01545

Call Sign: W1JWM
Howard J Fuller
99 Boylston Cir

Shrewsbury MA
015451812

Call Sign: KB1FIU
Paul M Bardash
10 Brightside Ave
Shrewsbury MA 01545

Call Sign: KA1OVM
Paul M Drapeau
21 Brookdale Circle
Shrewsbury MA 01545

Call Sign: N1CPV
Allen A Cramer
29 Brookway Dr
Shrewsbury MA 01545

Call Sign: K1DNU
William A Carruth
6 Broushane Cir
Shrewsbury MA 01545

Call Sign: KB1PHY
Matthew Rublesky
36 C Shrewsbury
Green Dr
Shrewsbury MA 01545

Call Sign: K1WEO
Mabel M Lambert
21 Canna Dr
Shrewsbury MA 01545

Call Sign: KB1TDQ
Stephen Kunkel
111 Clinton St
Shrewsbury MA 01545

Call Sign: KB1QWK
Daniel L Satrom
20 Coachman Ridge
Rd
Shrewsbury MA 01545

Call Sign: KB1PEM
Bharath S Pingali
35 Commons Dr Apt
29
Shrewsbury MA 01545

Call Sign: KA1PMR
Joseph E Prochilo
55 Commons Dr Apt 7

Shrewsbury MA 01545

Call Sign: KV1GS
Glenn S Small
65 Commons Dr Unit
509
Shrewsbury MA 01545

Call Sign: KB1UTV
Arthur A Minklein
39 Cortland Grove Dr
Shrewsbury MA 01545

Call Sign: N2GBZ
Neil S Heim
5 Crane Cir
Shrewsbury MA 01545

Call Sign: WA1WSL
Kurt A Melden
29 Cross St
Shrewsbury MA 01545

Call Sign: KA1TAX
Weston Clarke
42 E Brandywine Dr
Shrewsbury MA 01545

Call Sign: N1IPX
Pearl M Heck
69 Edgemere Blvd
Shrewsbury MA 01545

Call Sign: N1PBI
Prashanth Ram
10 Everett Ave
Shrewsbury MA 01545

Call Sign: WA2HLK
Jerome B Favata
14 Farmington Dr E
Shrewsbury MA 01545

Call Sign: W7HGP
Thomas R Gurski
25 Fifth Ave R D W
Shrewsbury MA 01545

Call Sign: WA1OAU
John S Kay
43 Gage Ln
Shrewsbury MA 01545

Call Sign: KA1ZIY

Edward W Anderson
89 Grace Ave
Shrewsbury MA 01545

Call Sign: N1KVU
Timothy J Keenan
60 Hapgood Way
Shrewsbury MA 01545

Call Sign: K1DX
George R L Woods
3 Harriet Ln
Shrewsbury MA
015452707

Call Sign: KA1MBI
Sidney Liberfarb
54 Harrington Farms
Shrewsbury MA 01545

Call Sign: KB1LGH
Robert A Babin
15 Harvard Ave
Shrewsbury MA 01545

Call Sign: WX1L
James C Colonies
40 Harvard Ave
Shrewsbury MA 01545

Call Sign: KB1TPQ
Daniel T Jones
28 Hillando Dr
Shrewsbury MA 01545

Call Sign: KB7WZE
Bruce R Beckmann
4 Hobblebush Rd
Shrewsbury MA 01545

Call Sign: KB1KGZ
Bruce R Beckmann
4 Hobblebush Rd
Shrewsbury MA 01545

Call Sign: KB1OJL
Brandon M Morreale
49 Holden St
Shrewsbury MA 01545

Call Sign: KB1ILT
Robert C Labonte
28 Hunter Circle
Shrewsbury MA 01545

Call Sign: W1HLC
Robert C Labonte
28 Hunter Circle
Shrewsbury MA 01545

Call Sign: N1PCH
James M Carelli
2 Ireta Rd
Shrewsbury MA 01545

Call Sign: KB1MJU
Michael C Follo
66 Janet Circle
Shrewsbury MA 01545

Call Sign: KA1HAL
Stina B Long
30 Julio Dr
Shrewsbury MA 01545

Call Sign: N2CTJ
Mark Addison
30 Julio Dr Apt 514
Shrewsbury MA 01545

Call Sign: W1RUH
Bradford Marple
30 Julio Dr Apt 620
Shrewsbury MA 01545

Call Sign: N1AYZ
Donald G Mac Millan
30 Julio Drive Apt 472
Shrewsbury MA 01545

Call Sign: N1CDQ
Mark W Fisher
12 Kemble Drive
Shrewsbury MA 01545

Call Sign: W1AQM
Clarence C Margerum
15 Knowlton Ave
Shrewsbury MA 01545

Call Sign: KB1UBM
Andrew I Nehring
2 Lahinch Lane
Shrewsbury MA 01545

Call Sign: KB1OBG
Kevin J Lisciotti
7 Laurel Ridge Lane

Shrewsbury MA 01545

Call Sign: N1GCP
Ronald J Korzon
49 Liberty Dr
Shrewsbury MA
015453333

Call Sign: KB1FPY
Rita G Korzon
49 Liberty Dr
Shrewsbury MA 01545

Call Sign: N1OZC
Edward C Orrizzi
195 Main St
Shrewsbury MA 01545

Call Sign: KB1IYJ
Lynne M Perreault
633 Main St
Shrewsbury MA 01545

Call Sign: KB1KFM
David L Merchant
3 Mangs Dr
Shrewsbury MA 01545

Call Sign: KB1JPJ
Shrewsbury
Emergency
Management Races
Club
100 Maple Ave
Shrewsbury MA 01545

Call Sign: W1SHR
Shrewsbury
Emergency
Management Races
Club
100 Maple Ave
Shrewsbury MA 01545

Call Sign: K1TE
Bradshaw B Lupton Jr
227 Maple Ave
Shrewsbury MA 01545

Call Sign: N1EOG
Paula S Lupton
227 Maple Ave
Shrewsbury MA
015452731

Call Sign: WA1DRE
Arthur E Berg Jr
11 Meadowbrook Cir
Shrewsbury MA
015455035

Call Sign: NT1U
David B Siegrist
34 Millwood Dr
Shrewsbury MA 01545

Call Sign: WB1FOW
Lee A Collier
17 Minuteman Way
Shrewsbury MA 01545

Call Sign: KB1UBK
Elizabeth V Alexander
35 Old Laxfield Rd
Shrewsburg MA 01545

Call Sign: K1WZC
Hubert W Davis Jr
30 Olde Colony Drive
Shrewsbury MA 01545

Call Sign: KA1UFJ
Matthew C Leonard
43 Olympia Ave
Shrewsbury MA 01545

Call Sign: KB1EFU
Jacob J Rosen
225 Prospect St
Shrewsbury MA 01545

Call Sign: KA1ZEU
Samantha L Davis
34 Rawson Hill Dr
Shrewsbury MA 01545

Call Sign: N1OGZ
David Farber
39 Rawson Hill Drive
Shrewsbury MA 01545

Call Sign: W1LMP
Lynne M Perreault
21 Raymond Ave
Shrewsbury MA
015455624

Call Sign: KB1LOU

Ronald W Diprofio
32 Redland St
Shrewsbury MA 01545

Call Sign: N1TYH
Steven A Olivieri
24 Richard Ave
Shrewsbury MA
015455326

Call Sign: N1KRD
Michael V Pasquale
9 Roman Dr
Shrewsbury MA 01545

Call Sign: W1MVP
Michael V Pasquale
9 Roman Dr
Shrewsbury MA 01545

Call Sign: KB1SRI
Carol Szabo
26 Roman Dr
Shrewsbury MA 01545

Call Sign: K1KWP
Kevin W Paetzold
30 Roman Dr
Shrewsbury MA 01545

Call Sign: W6QHY
Carl H Hafstrom
23 Saturn Dr
Shrewsbury MA 01545

Call Sign: K1ANA
William H Gagen
46 Saybrook Rd
Shrewsbury MA 01545

Call Sign: N1OHB
Robert P Leo
26 Sewall Drive
Shrewsbury MA 01545

Call Sign: KB1JQV
Gerald C Mcdonald Jr
5 Shirley Rd
Shrewsbury MA 01545

Call Sign: KB9UJM
Rangarajan Sudharsan
40 Shrewsbury Green
Dr Apt H

Shrewsbury MA 01545

Call Sign: KA1SPO
John M Kapinos
86 South
Quinsigamond Ave
Shrewsbury MA
015454254

Call Sign: WF1E
Patrick J Foley
15 South St
Shrewsbury MA 01545

Call Sign: KB1RCM
Stephen C Daukas
2 Spring Meadow Dr
Shrewsbury MA 01545

Call Sign: KB1SCD
Stephen C Daukas
2 Spring Meadow Dr
Shrewsbury MA 01545

Call Sign: N1HCL
Jeff H St Pierre
12 Spruce St
Shrewsbury MA 01545

Call Sign: KB1VAQ
Ernest Peter
24 Stoney Hill Rd
Shrewsbury MA 01545

Call Sign: AB1QH
Ernest Peter
24 Stoney Hill Rd
Shrewsbury MA 01545

Call Sign: KB1HKL
Patricia A Aschoff
7 Sycamore Rd
Shrewsbury MA 01545

Call Sign: KB1SGA
Subbiah
Muthukalayappan
7 Toblin Hill Dr
Shrewsbury MA 01545

Call Sign: N1KYA
David W Easterbrook
1 Trowbridge Ln
Shrewsbury MA 01545

Call Sign: WA1PIQ
Paul L Reddy Sr
Turnpike Station
Shrewsbury MA 01545

Call Sign: KB1GPK
Christopher J
Arsenault
12 Turtle Creek Circle
Shrewsbury MA 01545

Call Sign: W1PGB
Michael J Sacco
9 View
Shrewsbury MA 01545

Call Sign: N1CUF
Walter J Condon
509 W Main St
Shrewsbury MA 01545

Call Sign: KA2OGE
Eugene J Brady
44 Wachusett Ave
Shrewsbury MA 01545

Call Sign: N1LPL
Ronald R Duff Jr
9 Weagle Farm Rd
Shrewsbury MA 01545

Call Sign: KA1HNL
Patricia M Jones
30 Wesleyan Terrace
Shrewsbury MA 01545

Call Sign: K1QZE
Edward P Roman
19 Westport Dr
Shrewsbury MA 01545

Call Sign: KA1YCN
Marc E Roman
19 Westport Dr
Shrewsbury MA 01545

Call Sign: NV1E
Christopher W Kirk
40 Westwood Rd
Shrewsbury MA 01545

Call Sign: N3EVL
Peter J Thompson

12 Whitehall Cir
Shrewsbury MA 01545

Call Sign: N1WK
Matthew F Tatro
26 Yorkshire Terrace
#9
Shrewsbury MA 01545

Call Sign: W1ZTK
Bernard J Seastrom
Shrewsbury MA
015450335

FCC Amateur Radio Licenses in Shutesbury

Call Sign: KC4ABE
Homer J Susmuth
9 Haskins Way
Shutesbury MA
010729730

Call Sign: N1LYU
Steven C Svoboda
30 Lake Dr
Shutesbury MA 01072

Call Sign: N1XLE
Richard J Strangman Jr
87 Leverett Rd
Shutesbury MA 01072

Call Sign: WB1GWA
Theodore P De
Lesdernier
Leverett Rd
Shutesbury MA 01072

Call Sign: K1JRW
Richard S Robinson
Pelham Hill Rd
Shutesbury MA 01072

Call Sign: K1VCK
F Ellen Mc Kay
314 W Pelham Rd
Shutesbury MA
010720001

Call Sign: KB1FSE
Kevin J Sousa
168 Wendell Rd

Shutesbury MA 01072

Call Sign: N1NBD
Ruth Ann Hatt
Shutesbury MA 01072

Call Sign: WA1MBA
Thomas D Williams
Shutesbury MA 01072

Call Sign: AA1EC
Richard E Hatt
Shutesbury MA 01072

Call Sign: WB1FSV
Louis F De Lesdernier
Shutesbury MA
010720281

FCC Amateur Radio Licenses in Siasconset

Call Sign: WA1IOW
Joseph B Horodyski
Siasconset MA
025640115

Call Sign: W1AWB
Andrew W Bullington
Siasconset MA 02564

Call Sign: W1JBH
Joseph B Horodyski
Siasconset MA
025640115

Call Sign: KB1IHG
Andrew W Bullington
Siascouset MA 02564

FCC Amateur Radio Licenses in Somerset

Call Sign: KA1VNT
Russell L Estrella
96 Beach Ave
Somerset MA 02726

Call Sign: KA1VQS
Manuel S Estrela
96 Beach Ave
Somerset MA 02726

Call Sign: N1NN

Roger A Hentershee
82 Berube Ave
Somerset MA 02726

Call Sign: KA1SFJ
David D Chapman
61 Beverly St
Somerset MA
027263503

Call Sign: KB1JNJ
Alan J Costa
26 Buffington St
Somerset MA 02726

Call Sign: N1QLC
Carl A Merrill
22 Buxton Ave 2
Somerset MA 02726

Call Sign: WA1JXM
Raymond A Mc
Connell
31 Cardinal Rd
Somerset MA 02726

Call Sign: KB1DAI
Cornelis Y Blom
55 Carey St
Somerset MA 02725

Call Sign: KB1IQS
Lorens N Kulla
211 Compos St
Somerset MA 02726

Call Sign: W1DZQ
Gennaro R Lopriore
90 Connecticut Ave
Somerset MA 02726

Call Sign: N1ZMH
William J Robinson
1628 County St
Somerset MA 02726

Call Sign: WB3GNI
Darryl Umland
2244 County St
Somerset MA 02726

Call Sign: WA1ZCA
William H Crabtree
122 Dwelly Rd

Somerset MA 02726

Call Sign: WA1KFB
Charles F Rowe Jr
239 Eastview Ave
Somerset MA
027263907

Call Sign: WA1LLN
Emanuela A Rowe
239 Eastview Ave
Somerset MA 02726

Call Sign: WA1MIC
Nancy J Rowe Dowd
239 Eastview Ave
Somerset MA 02726

Call Sign: N1TVT
Joseph V Mulready
140 Evans St
Somerset MA 02726

Call Sign: KB1FGI
Byron J Piette
36 Florida Ave
Somerset MA 02726

Call Sign: K1YCQ
Byron J Piette
36 Florida Ave
Somerset MA 02726

Call Sign: N1LVV
Jay J Alexander
240 Folsom Ave
Somerset MA 02726

Call Sign: KB1SDZ
Richard Couto
24 Grove Ave
Somerset MA 02726

Call Sign: KB1USF
Richard Couto
24 Grove Ave
Somerset MA 02726

Call Sign: KB1FBH
William H Langfield Jr
67 Harrington Ln
Somerset MA 02726

Call Sign: AA1XR

William H Langfield Jr
67 Harrington Ln
Somerset MA 02726

Call Sign: KA1NSU
John E Leary
30 Holly Ln
Somerset MA 02726

Call Sign: KA1OST
Edward R Cote
81 Jackson Ave
Somerset MA 02725

Call Sign: WB1GYT
Marcel J Dionne
380 Kaufman Rd
Somerset MA 02726

Call Sign: KA1QEC
Michael K Modlowski
106 Leahy Ave
Somerset MA 02726

Call Sign: W1GDJ
Arnold J Molloy
167 Massachusetts Ave
Somerset MA 02726

Call Sign: KB1WHH
Richard L Branco
134 Millers Ln
Somerset MA 02726

Call Sign: KB1KKN
Chris A Rowland
723 Mohawk Rd
Somerset MA 02726

Call Sign: K1EPP
Alfred Silvia Jr
164 Mt Hope Rd
Somerset MA 02726

Call Sign: N1OFV
Michael D Muldoon
394 Mt Hope Rd
Somerset MA 02726

Call Sign: WA1MZL
Steven E Lempke
102 New Jersey Ave
Somerset MA 02726

Call Sign: WA1MZS
Wayne G Cabral
168 New Jersey Ave
Somerset MA 02726

Call Sign: N1QYM
Sati P Mitra
7 Oak Lane
Somerset MA
027264018

Call Sign: KB1LJH
Megan L Desouza
217 Pleasant View Ave
Somerset MA 02724

Call Sign: N1GYE
Thomas Harrison
1166 Prospect St
Somerset MA 02726

Call Sign: WB1CMT
Bonas Perry
133 Purington St
Somerset MA
027264637

Call Sign: WA1MAA
Dennis N Robillard
27 Quental St
Somerset MA 02726

Call Sign: AA1KO
Denis R Gaudreau
5 Ranger Rd
Somerset MA 02726

Call Sign: W1BOJ
Frank S Benevides Jr
549 Read St
Somerset MA 02726

Call Sign: N1KBI
Jesse N Medeiros
905 Read St
Somerset MA 02726

Call Sign: KA1AIW
Thomas R Russell
1385 Read St
Somerset MA 02726

Call Sign: WA1HVD
Robert V Bernard

1545 Read St
Somerset MA 02726

Call Sign: KB1TUF
Dana T Copley
457 Regan Rd
Somerset MA 02726

Call Sign: N1AGE
Dana T Copley
457 Regan Rd
Somerset MA 02726

Call Sign: KA1OCF
Laurie A Pavao
70 Remington Dr
Somerset MA 02726

Call Sign: WA1LPM
John D Pavao
70 Remington Dr
Somerset MA
027265916

Call Sign: W1QKZ
Lloyd Durfee Jr
2156 Riverside Ave
Somerset MA 02726

Call Sign: WA1ZNC
Joseph Medeiros
3515 Riverside Ave
Somerset MA 02726

Call Sign: N1XQK
Peter C Seddon
50 School St
Somerset MA 02726

Call Sign: N1TSQ
Richard V Dionne
547 Shirley Ave
Somerset MA 02725

Call Sign: N1YOB
Michael T Gagne
537 South
Somerset MA 02726

Call Sign: N1EMQ
Peter Pelletier
13 Stoddard St
Somerset MA 02725

Call Sign: N1ZRC
Jeffrey P Sullivan
90 Taft Ave
Somerset MA 02726

Call Sign: N1MWB
George P Souza
2 Walnut St
Somerset MA
027264419

Call Sign: KB1TQG
John D Delong
237 Washington Ave
Somerset MA 02726

Call Sign: KB1TQH
Susan M Dubois
237 Washington Ave
Somerset MA 02726

Call Sign: N1RPW
Karen S Augustine
70 Windward Drive
Somerset MA 02726

Call Sign: W1BMQ
Paul E Augustine
70 Windward Drive
Somerset MA 02726

Call Sign: KB1PNJ
Dean G Chouinard
134 Yankee Peddler Dr
Somerset MA 02726

Call Sign: K1KJT
Edward J Peters
Somerset MA 02726

Call Sign: N1JWH
Brenda L Carr
Somerset MA 02726

Call Sign: N1UON
Kyle L Sousa
Somerset MA 02726

Call Sign: KB1CTJ
Jeffrey L Wasserman

15 A Pearson Ave
Somerville MA 02144

Call Sign: K1OUM
Joseph S Pirroni
15 A Porter St
Somerville MA 02143

Call Sign: KB1DMJ
Hans E Kieserman
28 Aberdeen Rd
Somerville MA 02144

Call Sign: N1TAX
Chris A Patti
33 Aberdeen Rd
Somerville MA 02144

Call Sign: WA1VXN
James R Mason
56 Albion St
Somerville MA 02143

Call Sign: KA1ZPR
Christopher W
Farnham
122 Albion St
Somerville MA 02144

Call Sign: KA1GKQ
Laura A Sosnoski
32 Belknap St 2
Somerville MA 02144

Call Sign: W1FYL
Robert A Holdt
36 Belmont St
Somerville MA 02143

Call Sign: KB1GXX
James H Mc Carthy
21 Berkeley St
Somerville MA
021431603

Call Sign: N1PHI
Robert A Brimer
22 Bowdoin St
Somerville MA 02143

Call Sign: N1LRW
Craig A Counterman
2 Brastow Ave
Somerville MA 02143

Call Sign: N2LXR
Niels E La White
438 Broadway
Somerville MA 02145

Call Sign: KB1HBN
Niels E La White
438 Broadway
Somerville MA 02145

Call Sign: KB1HVY
Peter D Hurd
735 Broadway
Somerville MA 02144

Call Sign: N1TPM
Angela K Suh
783 Broadway 3
Somerville MA 02144

Call Sign: W1STW
Robert P Healey
1374 Broadway Apt 80
Somerville MA 02144

Call Sign: N2KRV
Martin A Jaspan
81 Bromfield Rd
Somerville MA 02144

Call Sign: K1PML
Peter M Langevin
101 Bromfield Rd
Somerville MA 02144

Call Sign: KC1SY
Mario E Inchiosa
15 Burnside Ave
Somerville MA 02144

Call Sign: KE4CXF
Jonathan H Whitmore
21 Cedar St
Somerville MA 02143

Call Sign: KB1KVS
Keith R Baker
95 Cedar St Unit 1
Somerville MA 02143

Call Sign: KB1OHG
Craig I Hagan
46 Central St -2

Somerville MA 02143

Call Sign: N1MCZ
Steven M Spungin
19 Central St Apt 16
Somerville MA 02143

Call Sign: WA1BUJ
George A Brooks
8 Charles Ryan Rd
Somerville MA 02145

Call Sign: N1QLQ
Luis A Ortega
28 Charm Wood Rd
Somerville MA 02144

Call Sign: W1GTC
Theodore A Robertson
Cherry St
Somerville MA 02144

Call Sign: N1ZST
Jered J Floyd
36 Cherry St
Somerville MA 02144

Call Sign: W1ULB
Frank J Santangelo
6 Columbus Ave
Somerville MA 02143

Call Sign: N1OBJ
Christopher J Wysopal
27 Columbus Ave
Somerville MA 02143

Call Sign: N1VDU
Bonny D Zeh
50 Columbus Ave 4b
Somerville MA 02143

Call Sign: KB1FMS
Jelena Antonic
45 Concord Ave Apt
11
Somerville MA
021433939

Call Sign: KB1EHK
Leonard N Foner
28 Cottage Ave
Somerville MA 02144

Call Sign: N1SSQ
Timothy C Worsley
Craigie St
Somerville MA 02134

Call Sign: AB0YT
Andrew W Cowan
33 Crocker St
Somerville MA 02143

Call Sign: KB1HQM
Christopher Z Collier
23 Crocker St Apt 1
Somerville MA 02143

Call Sign: KA1YFG
Diego M Rubinowicz
56 Curtis St
Somerville MA 02144

Call Sign: N6QXA
Ted M Slater
38 Day St Apt 40
Somerville MA 02144

Call Sign: KB1JOZ
Richard J Ryan
33 Edgar Ave
Somerville MA 02145

Call Sign: KD7CTJ
Richard E Hansen
23 Elm St Apt 106
Somerville MA
021432200

Call Sign: KB1FEO
Cana L Williams
31 Elmwood St
Somerville MA 02144

Call Sign: KB1CXI
Nathan J Williams
31 Elmwood St
Somerville MA 02144

Call Sign: KB1OKB
Aaron M Dulles-
Coelho
61 Elmwood St 2
Somerville MA 02144

Call Sign: KB1NGY
Steven D Brennan

16 Fairfax St
Somerville MA 02144

Call Sign: KD4MBG
Lonnie W Cahoon Jr
230 Fellsway
Somerville MA 02145

Call Sign: K1EEA
Eric E Austin
21 Forster St Apt 2
Somerville MA
021452706

Call Sign: KB1WJE
Brett C Smith
22 Francesca Ave 1
Somerville MA 02144

Call Sign: KC2FTB
Daniel R Fairchild
20 Fremont St Apt 2
Somerville MA 02145

Call Sign: KB1VWV
Stephen Quaratiello
19 Gibbens St
Somerville MA 02143

Call Sign: KA1GHP
Michael J Tierney
15 Gilman Ter
Somerville MA 02145

Call Sign: N1ZOE
Susan M Leite
39 Gorham St
Somerville MA 02144

Call Sign: N1NLH
Sandro D Wallach
97 Gov Winthrop Rd
Somerville MA 02145

Call Sign: N1TPN
Harvard U Park
20 Grove St 21
Somerville MA 02144

Call Sign: N1TPT
William H Chung
20 Grove St 24
Somerville MA 02144

Call Sign: N1TPO
Cindy H Limb
20 Grove St 53
Somerville MA 02144

Call Sign: KC1B
Joseph A Clements
19 Hancock St
Somerville MA 02144

Call Sign: N1XQC
David M Dahlbacka
25 Hancock St
Somerville MA 02144

Call Sign: KD6FEC
Rex Y Landreth
26 Hancock St
Somerville MA 02144

Call Sign: KB1DEM
Christopher T
Lesniewski-Laas
112 Hancock St
Somerville MA 02144

Call Sign: KB1RMI
Jennifer Tu
112 Hancock St
Somerville MA 02144

Call Sign: KA1YYC
Alexandra C Strelka
51 Hancock St 3
Somerville MA 02144

Call Sign: N1KCM
Mark A Johnson
16 Harrison St
Somerville MA 02144

Call Sign: N1NSR
George Jacob
7 Hathorn St
Somerville MA 02145

Call Sign: KA1YPN
Vivian
Theodoracopoulos
8 High St
Somerville MA 02144

Call Sign: W1AUQ
Clarence E Hinchley

186 Highland Ave
Somerville MA 02143

Call Sign: KB9SDQ
Joshua W Phinney
324 Highland Ave #1
Somerville MA 02144

Call Sign: N2JLY
Thomas M Farrell
Highland Ave #1
Somerville MA 02144

Call Sign: KB1JGQ
Donald W Gadsby
105 Hillsdale Rd
Somerville MA 02144

Call Sign: W1DON
Donald W Gadsby
105 Hillsdale Rd
Somerville MA 02144

Call Sign: KC2IND
James J Wnorowski
98 Holland St
Somerville MA 02144

Call Sign: N1EPR
Marlena E Erdos
158 Holland St #3
Somerville MA 02144

Call Sign: KB1CXE
Erik L Nygren
60 Irving St
Somerville MA 02144

Call Sign: N1JDZ
Michael J Jones
5 Irving St 2
Somerville MA 02144

Call Sign: WA1WPS
Meredith J Porter
104 Josephine Ave
Somerville MA 02144

Call Sign: N1AJP
Joseph A Martin
26 Kidder Ave
Somerville MA 02144

Call Sign: N1NLB

James C Campbell Iii
18 Kingston St
Somerville MA 02144

Call Sign: KB1PBV
Edward R Poznysz
43 Kingston St
Somerville MA 02144

Call Sign: KA1WKH
Heather K Hagerty
7 Laurel Ave
Somerville MA 02143

Call Sign: W1XTC
Daniel J Jordan
10 Lee St #2
Somerville MA 02145

Call Sign: KB1EUO
Daniel J Jordan
10 Lee St 2
Somerville MA 02145

Call Sign: KD7GUR
Carl J Alexander
95 Liberty Ave
Somerville MA 02144

Call Sign: WA2CGU
Joseph B Bernstein
65 Lowden Ave 2
Somerville MA 02144

Call Sign: KB1WKG
Eric M Timmons
85 Lowden Ave Apt 2
Somerville MA 02144

Call Sign: N1MGS
Hung Hsien Chang
5 Lowell Cir Apt 3
Somerville MA 02143

Call Sign: N1NIH
Kevin M Antaya
92 Lowell St
Somerville MA 02143

Call Sign: N1NLJ
Joseph F Antaya Jr
92 Lowell St
Somerville MA 02143

Call Sign: AB1IF
Charles M Coldwell
36 Lowell St Fl 2
Somerville MA
021432407

Call Sign: N1LPM
Conrad C Nobili
10 Magnus Ave 3
Somerville MA 02143

Call Sign: KB1RCN
Charles Goumas
42 Mansfield St Apt 1
Somerville MA 02143

Call Sign: KB1RCO
Rosalie Hoffman
Goumas
42 Mansfield St Apt 1
Somerville MA 02143

Call Sign: KC2JWE
Matthew W Hirsch
18 Mansfield St Apt 2
Somerville MA 02143

Call Sign: N1OAU
Helen Greiner
46 Marion St Apt 2
Somerville MA 02143

Call Sign: WB1GYG
Gary B Coke
19 Mason St
Somerville MA 02144

Call Sign: KB1DEO
Lara M Karbiner
41 Mason St 1
Somerville MA 02144

Call Sign: N1ENZ
Vincent J Mattera
24 Morrison Ave
Somerville MA 02144

Call Sign: KB9MMZ
James P Goldenberg
185 Morrison Ave
Somerville MA
021442330

Call Sign: N1LDK

James W O Toole Jr
15 Munroe St
Somerville MA 02143

Call Sign: KC2MGA
Ferdinand Kuemmeth
115 Museum Str 3r
Somerville MA 02143

Call Sign: KA1GON
Charles A Di Cecca
501 Mystic Valley
Pkwy
Somerville MA 02144

Call Sign: N1UQD
David L Albert
7 N St 1a
Somerville MA 02144

Call Sign: KB1GXV
Paul E Nash
32 Nashua St
Somerville MA 02145

Call Sign: WA1OTE
Jeffrey F Warschauer
29 Newbury St
Somerville MA 02144

Call Sign: AB1GI
Charles C Able
72 Newbury St -2
Somerville MA 02144

Call Sign: N1SLO
Thomas S Yang
86 Newbury St 9
Somerville MA 02144

Call Sign: N1LBD
Mary B Dean
420 Norfolk St
Somerville MA 02143

Call Sign: KA1INE
Mark F Nelson
184 North St
Somerville MA 02144

Call Sign: AA1ZH
Brian N Shimkin
95 Orchard St #3
Somerville MA 02144

Call Sign: WA1PPN
Michael J Lanza
37 Ossipee Rd
Somerville MA 02144

Call Sign: N1RZJ
David M Shull
47 Paulina St
Somerville MA 02144

Call Sign: KA1DVE
Greg L Arnette
71 Pearson Rd
Somerville MA 02144

Call Sign: KB1TKA
Thomas W Kirby
7 Pembroke St Apt 1
Somerville MA 02145

Call Sign: KB1WYD
Nelson Hernandez
126 Pennsylvania Ave
Somerville MA 02145

Call Sign: KB1CAX
Jonathan P Backstrom
15 Pinckney St
Somerville MA 02145

Call Sign: K1LVI
Mariano Lameiras
129 Powderhouse Blvd
Somerville MA 02144

Call Sign: KB1TUH
Paul F Moran
27 Puritan Rd
Somerville MA 02145

Call Sign: KB1PFM
Paul F Moran
27 Puritan Rd
Somerville MA 02145

Call Sign: N1VUL
Theodric W Young
68 Puritan Rd
Somerville MA
021451014

Call Sign: KB0UFV
Mark J Donnelly

14 Putnam Rd
Somerville MA 02145

Call Sign: KB2TJT
Aaron M Applebaum
19 Putnam St
Somerville MA 02143

Call Sign: KB1ISS
Kathryn M Cerow
63 Putnam St Apt 1
Somerville MA 02143

Call Sign: KH7PL
Jessica Wong
29 Quincy St #1
Somerville MA
021431719

Call Sign: KG6EVH
Daniel S Mclaughlin
78 Rogers Ave
Somerville MA 02144

Call Sign: N1KFP
John D Desharnais
25 Rossmore St
Somerville MA 02143

Call Sign: W1WQQ
Leon D Gingras Jr
8 Rush St
Somerville MA
021453215

Call Sign: N2IKR
Richard C Kinne
17 Rush St Apt 2
Somerville MA 02145

Call Sign: KE1ML
Richard C Kinne
17 Rush St Apt 2
Somerville MA 02145

Call Sign: KB1PCB
Chris O Norman
30 Saint James Ave
Apt -1
Somerville MA 02144

Call Sign: KD8ARD
Jeremy E Lavergne
21 Sartwell Ave #1

Somerville MA
021443251

Call Sign: W1TGL
Albert D Moore
18 Sewall St
Somerville MA 02145

Call Sign: N1TLA
James A Kofalt
105 Shore Dr
Somerville MA 02145

Call Sign: AA1CK
Valassios Antoniou
47 Simpson Ave
Somerville MA 02144

Call Sign: N8IV
Marc D Tanner
7 Spencer Ave
Somerville MA 02144

Call Sign: KB1FVD
David C Todd
8 Spencer Ave 1
Somerville MA 02144

Call Sign: WB2JCT
Kenneth E Cohn
20 Spring St
Somerville MA 02143

Call Sign: K1SMQ
Frank J Griskus Sr
9 Sterling St
Somerville MA 02144

Call Sign: N1XQI
Agrimalda C
Brumbaugh
9 Sterling St
Somerville MA 02144

Call Sign: N1KXE
Regis M Donovan
24 Stickney Ave 2
Somerville MA 02145

Call Sign: KB1PTV
Carrick J Detweiler
4 Stickney Ave Unit 1
Somerville MA 02145

Call Sign: KA1WLQ
John F Carr
179 Summer St
Somerville MA 02143

Call Sign: KC0KWF
Kenneth M Silva
198 Summer St
Somerville MA 02143

Call Sign: N1HLQ
Lewis H Warren
254 Summer St
Somerville MA 02143

Call Sign: KA1RBK
Jeff Abrahamson
273 Summer St
Somerville MA 02144

Call Sign: N1XUO
Linda L Julien
206 Summer St #1
Somerville MA 02143

Call Sign: KB1GRS
Joel N Weber Ii
225 Summer St #3
Somerville MA 02143

Call Sign: KB1VGP
Patrik Jonsson
215 Summer St 1
Somerville MA 02143

Call Sign: KJ4QJX
Aaron E Engelhart
147 Summer St Apt 45
Somerville MA 02143

Call Sign: KB1KPP
Jared D Colburn
155 Summer St Apt B1
Somerville MA 02143

Call Sign: N1SNN
Eugene E Kelso
86 Sycamore St
Somerville MA 02145

Call Sign: KB1WNL
Micah Z Brodsky
73 Sycamore St 3
Somerville MA 02145

Call Sign: KB1VJB
George Kiwada
5 Tannery Brook Row
Unit 1
Somerville MA 02144

Call Sign: KB1NCQ
Laurence C Stone
6 Tower St
Somerville MA
021431427

Call Sign: N1YDD
Christopher W Blake
69 Victoria St
Somerville MA 02144

Call Sign: N1NQM
Carl L Haak
46 Vinal Ave
Somerville MA 02143

Call Sign: KA1TAO
Charles C Behrens
64 Vinal Ave 1
Somerville MA 02143

Call Sign: K1RHD
Sermonie Recinito
88 Wallace St
Somerville MA 02144

Call Sign: N1PAX
Pierre R Douyon
97 Wallace St
Somerville MA 02144

Call Sign: KB1QIG
Philip Weiss
102 Wallace St
Somerville MA 02144

Call Sign: KB1UUF
Bryca Song-Weiss
102 Wallace St
Somerville MA 02144

Call Sign: N2QMK
Elise A Carpenter
23 Walnut Rd
Somerville MA 02145

Call Sign: K1KJ

William F Desmond Jr
21 Walnut St
Somerville MA 02143

Call Sign: KB1WVX
Eric J Testen
118 Walnut St
Somerville MA 02145

Call Sign: KB1DJL
Brian D Caruso
Washington St Apt 2
Somerville MA 02143

Call Sign: KB1MOF
Victoria G Landgraf
7 West St Apt A
Somerville MA 02144

Call Sign: AB1FG
Victoria G Landgraf
7 West St Apt A
Somerville MA 02144

Call Sign: N1QLD
Andrew M Siegel
Westwood Rd
Somerville MA 02143

Call Sign: KB1DJG
Ana Marie White
22 White St Place 2
Somerville MA 02144

Call Sign: N1GDH
Robert A O Neil Jr
71 Winslow Ave
Somerville MA 02144

Call Sign: KF5EJV
Nick L Marcoux
15 Wyatt St Apt 2
Somerville MA 02143

Call Sign: N1FJY
Kent C Leonard
Somerville MA 02144

Call Sign: KB1WNT
Benjamin F Cleaves
Somerville MA 02144

Call Sign: KB1GFQ
Thomas C Gray

88 Beacon St 33
Sommerville MA
02143

Call Sign: N1QJZ
David G Leip
81 Lexington Ave
Sommerville MA
02144

Call Sign: KB1SVM
Adam W Fletcher
22 Sewall St 6
Sommerville MA
02145

Call Sign: KB1SVN
JESSICA T Mckellar
22 Sewall St 6
Sommerville MA
02145

FCC Amateur Radio Licenses in South Acton

Call Sign: WA1VDJ
Alfons W Krysieniel
13 Independence Rd
South Acton MA
01720

FCC Amateur Radio Licenses in South Ashburnham

Call Sign: W1GKI
Kenneth E Thomas
43 High St
South Ashburnham
MA 01466

FCC Amateur Radio Licenses in South Attleboro

Call Sign: W1EOJ
Anthony V Perilli
47 Bretton Rd
South Attleboro MA
02703

Call Sign: KB1HTL
Richard W Carr

73 Capt Courtios Dr
South Attleboro MA
02703

Call Sign: KC1HD
Michael P Marcoccio
94 Carrier Ave
South Attleboro MA
02703

Call Sign: N1FLO
John C Benson
101 Collins St
South Attleboro MA
02703

Call Sign: KA1UYJ
Georgette M Prew
2 Colvin St
South Attleboro MA
02703

Call Sign: NZ1P
Paul F Prew
2 Colvin St
South Attleboro MA
02703

Call Sign: WA1QKP
Albert R Hebert
25 Cumberland St
South Attleboro MA
027036805

Call Sign: N1EGQ
John G Panagou
31 Curtis Ave
South Attleboro MA
02703

Call Sign: KA1NAT
Joseph Koukell
45 E Bacon St
South Attleboro MA
02703

Call Sign: W1GOL
Horace Valente
33 Jessie Ave
South Attleboro MA
02703

Call Sign: N1RWW
Scott N Slater

23 Lord St
South Attleboro MA
02703

Call Sign: K1JHR
Leonard R Hathaway
48 Lynn Dr
South Attleboro MA
02703

Call Sign: N1RAH
David L Hathaway
43 Lynn Drive
South Attleboro MA
027037106

Call Sign: AE1X
Kenneth E Stringham
Jr
223 Mendon Rd
South Attleboro MA
02703

Call Sign: KA1JVQ
Brian L Foss
78 Middle St
South Attleboro MA
02703

Call Sign: K1KFE
Willard E Whipple
400 Newport Ave
South Attleboro MA
02703

Call Sign: KA2TNI
Michael A Van Hamel
532 Newport Ave
South Attleboro MA
02703

Call Sign: WA1QKJ
Thomas G Kozinski
824 Newport Ave
South Attleboro MA
02703

Call Sign: KB1OBA
David G Salvas
51 Norton St
South Attleboro MA
02703

Call Sign: N1HXV

Evelyn G Brogan
440 Robinson Ave
South Attleboro MA
02703

Call Sign: N1HXW
Raymond J Brogan
440 Robinson Ave
South Attleboro MA
02703

Call Sign: N1WVP
Charleen J Foley
South Attleboro MA
02703

FCC Amateur Radio Licenses in South Barre

Call Sign: N1YXZ
Thomas M Rondeau
27 Elm St
South Barre MA 01074

Call Sign: N1ZTB
Erik C Lowell
2 Primrose Lane
South Barre MA
010740083

FCC Amateur Radio Licenses in South Bellingham

Call Sign: K1BIR
Normand J Casavant
70 Mann St
South Bellingham MA
02019

FCC Amateur Radio Licenses in South Borough

Call Sign: N1ZWG
Jonathan H Isabelle
22 Presidential Dr
South Borough MA
01772

FCC Amateur Radio Licenses in South Boston

Call Sign: N1AJE
George A Fichtner
607 Dorchester Ave
South Boston MA
02127

Call Sign: WA1ZKH
William C Moynihan
Sr
Dorchester Ave
South Boston MA
02127

Call Sign: KB1GQL
Michael P Moynihan
Dorchester Ave
South Boston MA
02127

Call Sign: KB1OHB
Nora A Nagle
695 E 5th St Unit D
South Boston MA
02127

Call Sign: KA1WKO
Jean H Ennis
569 E 8th St
South Boston MA
02127

Call Sign: W1DMH
Frank J Galvin
665 E 8th St
South Boston MA
02127

Call Sign: K1KB
Kenneth S Bertino
514 E Fourth St
South Boston MA
021272916

Call Sign: W1MIT
John Scullion
696 East 5th St
South Boston MA
02127

Call Sign: KB1MCL

Matthew C Campbell
745 East 6th St - Apt 1
South Boston MA
02127

Call Sign: W1CCP
Harold N Bertino Sr
514 East Fourth St
South Boston MA
02127

Call Sign: W1IUQ
John C Zilinsky
629 East Sixth St
South Boston MA
02127

Call Sign: N1WVC
Joseph C Del Favero
8 Frederick St 75
South Boston MA
02127

Call Sign: N1YGO
Joseph R Leeman
2 Grimes St
South Boston MA
02127

Call Sign: W1DAK
Joseph J Elwood
149 H St
South Boston MA
02127

Call Sign: KA1UML
James E Henry
199 H St Apt 16
South Boston MA
02127

Call Sign: N1IWC
Paul M Gustowski
24 P St Apt B
South Boston MA
02127

Call Sign: KB1KTQ
Joseph S Mogan
41 W Second St
South Boston MA
02127

Call Sign: N1UQO

Yannick F Ferreira
19 Ward St
South Boston MA
021273528

Call Sign: KB1VEY
Markus Weber
171 West 4th St 2
South Boston MA
02127

Call Sign: KB1WFH
Karl J Hundhammer
171 West 4th St 2
South Boston MA
02127

Call Sign: AB1ON
Anke Rasmussen
171 West 4th St Unit 2
South Boston MA
02127

FCC Amateur Radio Licenses in South Braintree

Call Sign: AA1HT
Arthur F Porter Jr
42 Sagamore St
South Braintree MA
02184

FCC Amateur Radio Licenses in South Bridge

Call Sign: KA1BP
William H Ramsey Jr
8 Lapierre Ave
South Bridge MA
01550

Call Sign: NP3IV
Juan A Melendez
Sanchez
South Bridge MA
01550

FCC Amateur Radio Licenses in South Carver

Call Sign: KB1DPT

Kenneth L
Rosenberger
252 Tremont St
South Carver MA
023660676

Call Sign: N1OTC
John J Bowles
South Carver MA
02366

Call Sign: W1DTA
Jerome F Kelliher
South Carver MA
02366

Call Sign: KA1ZRF
Stephen G Howes
South Chatham MA
02659

Call Sign: N1SIR
David S Meservey
Box 128
South Chatham MA
02659

Call Sign: KA1WHT
Bill S Larned
137 Cockle Cove Rd
South Chatham MA
02659

Call Sign: KB1PDB
Zachary T Bennett
163 Holly Dr
South Chatham MA
02659

Call Sign: KB1UZZ
Frank A Messina
58 Island View Ln
South Chatham MA
02659

Call Sign: KB1VAI
Daniel S Gross
2337 Main St
South Chatham MA
02659

Call Sign: K1WF
William H Farris Jr
2620 Main St
South Chatham MA
02659

Call Sign: AA1KZ
Thomas R Howes
2621 Main St
South Chatham MA
02659

Call Sign: W2UC
Union College
Amateur Radio Society
21 Paulding Dr
South Chatham MA
026591354

Call Sign: N1UI
Barbara G Leiden
21 Paulding Drive
South Chatham MA
026591354

Call Sign: K1UI
Robert G Leiden
21 Paulding Drive
South Chatham MA
026591354

Call Sign: KB1SRK
Alfred W Doucette
79 Pleasant St
South Chatham MA
02659

Call Sign: KB1WPL
Joseph F Mador
93 Pleasant St
South Chatham MA
02659

Call Sign: K1MRO
Robert E Kessler
189 Pleasant St
South Chatham MA
02659

Call Sign: KB1VAD
Raymond Russ
South Chatham MA
02659

Call Sign: W8WJW
Frank J Pavlica Jr
89 Mason Ave
South Chelmsford MA
018243350

Call Sign: W1AWU
Gerald P Chandler
18 Proctor Rd
South Chelmsford MA
01824

Call Sign: KB1TE
Herbert D Marcus
4 Westview Ave
South Chelmsford MA
01824

Call Sign: AF1C
Dennis Hebert
42 Abner Potters Way
South Dartmouth MA
02748

Call Sign: W1POW
William L Vincent
26 Arch St
South Dartmouth MA
02748

Call Sign: WA1FXV
John S Monteiga Jr
6 Cherry St
South Dartmouth MA
02748

Call Sign: KA1YFV
Martin F Jordan
23 Clinton St
South Dartmouth MA
02748

Call Sign: KC1SH
Carol A Harrison
236 Cushman Ln

South Dartmouth MA
02748

Call Sign: N1BUD
Charles H Leach Jr
236 Cushman Ln
South Dartmouth MA
02748

Call Sign: WA1UPY
Eugene R Rheaume
530 Division Rd
South Dartmouth MA
02748

Call Sign: WB1AOK
Bradford S Gatenby
35 Dutra Ave
South Dartmouth MA
02748

Call Sign: N1JBE
Manuel C Arruda
22 Edgeworth St
South Dartmouth MA
02748

Call Sign: KB1SJX
Robert T Decampos
34 Edgeworth St
South Dartmouth MA
027483039

Call Sign: KA1WOG
Alexander Altschuller
21 Fremont St
South Dartmouth MA
02748

Call Sign: W1OBJ
James F Aguiar
29 George St
South Dartmouth MA
027482007

Call Sign: AF1Q
James F Aguiar Sr
29 George St
South Dartmouth MA
027482007

Call Sign: W1OBJ
James F Aguiar Sr
29 George St

South Dartmouth MA
027482007

Call Sign: AF1Q
James F Aguiar Sr
29 George St
South Dartmouth MA
027482007

Call Sign: W1OBJ
James F Aguiar Sr
29 George St
South Dartmouth MA
027482007

Call Sign: N1DXD
Ronald D Correia
10 Gorham St
South Dartmouth MA
02748

Call Sign: N1JVK
Manuel J Cabral
24 Greendale St
South Dartmouth MA
02748

Call Sign: KB1DPM
Stephen L Edwards
6 Holland St
South Dartmouth MA
02748

Call Sign: N1WXY
Eduino M Costa
195 Mc Cabe St
South Dartmouth MA
02748

Call Sign: N1MWH
Leonard Cabral
11 Meadowood Dr
South Dartmouth MA
02748

Call Sign: N1RFH
Richard J Cabral
24 Mishawum Dr
South Dartmouth MA
02748

Call Sign: N1RFI
Richard Cabral
24 Mishawum Dr

South Dartmouth MA
02748

Call Sign: KB1OJA
John L Pacine
12 Mohawk Drive
South Dartmouth MA
02748

Call Sign: KC2ILY
James D Phyfe
21 Nonquitt Ave
South Dartmouth MA
02748

Call Sign: K1TPH
J Malcolm Arsenault
15 Prospect St
South Dartmouth MA
02748

Call Sign: W1HLJ
Mildred M Arsenault
15 Prospect St
South Dartmouth MA
02748

Call Sign: KA1DSE
Rand O Torman
2 Rowley Ln
South Dartmouth MA
02748

Call Sign: N1YFJ
Tony Nazare
939 Russells Mills Rd
South Dartmouth MA
02748

Call Sign: WA1JFD
Charles A Days
30 Sagamore Dr
South Dartmouth MA
02748

Call Sign: N1DSN
Stephen J Spulock
119 Seabreez Dr
South Dartmouth MA
027483080

Call Sign: WA1FNM
Andrew J Reuter
11 Seth Davis Way

South Dartmouth MA
027481137

Call Sign: K1UPI
Peter H Smith
1 Shore Acres Rd
South Dartmouth MA
02748

Call Sign: KB1GPL
Peter W Ryder
600 Smith Neck Rd
South Dartmouth MA
027481502

Call Sign: WB1ATR
James J Ricci
830 Smith Neck Rd
South Dartmouth MA
02748

Call Sign: K1BBF
Phyllis M Hardy
840 Smith Neck Rd
South Dartmouth MA
02748

Call Sign: N1AVA
Kenneth J Howland
882 Smith Neck Rd
South Dartmouth MA
02748

Call Sign: WA1TNB
Leo J Jodoin
Sun & Sea Dr
South Dartmouth MA
02748

Call Sign: WA1UGK
Bruce I Cartwright
16 Utley St
South Dartmouth MA
02748

Call Sign: KC0AEO
Rasim Arikan
120 William St
South Dartmouth MA
027483725

Call Sign: N1QMV
Lawrence A Martin
88 Willis St

South Dartmouth MA
02748

Call Sign: NO1O
John L Whitehead Jr
South Dartmouth MA
027480031

**FCC Amateur Radio
Licenses in South
Deerfield**

Call Sign: N1PMA
Craig A Gagne
69 A Hillside Rd
South Deerfield MA
01373

Call Sign: KB1CZS
Robert J Dash
Adams Court
South Deerfield MA
01373

Call Sign: WB2PMT
Frank N Milewski
17 Captain Lathrop Dr
South Deerfield MA
01373

Call Sign: WA1TVS
Carter M Mac Donald
170 Christian Lane
South Deerfield MA
013737309

Call Sign: K1SF
Robert D
Archambeault
176 Conway Rd
South Deerfield MA
01373

Call Sign: N1FMV
William R Pichette
Conway Rd Rr 116
South Deerfield MA
01373

Call Sign: KB1RDF
Matthew P Baj Jr
16 Conway St
South Deerfield MA
01373

Call Sign: KA1YUK
Suzanne M Walton
Elm Cir
South Deerfield MA
01373

Call Sign: KA1YUL
Richard A Walton Sr
Elm Cir
South Deerfield MA
01373

Call Sign: KB1QWB
Katherine E Skipper
Hillside Rd
South Deerfield MA
01373

Call Sign: N1GLI
Glenn R Nichols
16 King Philip Ave
South Deerfield MA
01373

Call Sign: K1OME
Richard C Roth
29 Lee Rd
South Deerfield MA
01373

Call Sign: KB2WCA
Alyce S Battey
59 Mill Village Rd
South Deerfield MA
01373

Call Sign: KA1UUY
Dirk E Mahling
294 N Main
South Deerfield MA
01373

Call Sign: KB1WTR
Gary R Bunker
102 N Main St
South Deerfield MA
01373

Call Sign: WA2VNR
Thomas A Corso
171 State Rd
South Deerfield MA
01373

Call Sign: WA1NPL
Thora F Dumont
66 Sugarloaf St
South Deerfield MA
01373

**FCC Amateur Radio
Licenses in South
Dennis**

Call Sign: N1ZPO
Mark L Avery
77 Agnes Rd
South Dennis MA
02660

Call Sign: KB1TLU
Elizabeth M Avery
77 Agnes Rd
South Dennis MA
02660

Call Sign: KB1HIZ
Alan R Savage
102 Bay Ridge Rd
South Dennis MA
02660

Call Sign: KX1D
Alan R Savage
102 Bay Ridge Rd
South Dennis MA
02660

Call Sign: KB1CHT
Kenneth C Low
25 Beaver Dam Way
South Dennis MA
02660

Call Sign: N1DIV
Charles W Olson
25 Beaver Dam Way
South Dennis MA
02660

Call Sign: N1ECS
Sterling W Farrenkopf
167 Center St
South Dennis MA
02660

Call Sign: W1IYA

Joseph W Homan
19 Charing Cross Rd
Rr2
South Dennis MA
026602913

Call Sign: KB1UWQ
David E Moran
23 Coach House Ln
South Dennis MA
02660

Call Sign: W1BSG
David E Moran
23 Coach House Ln
South Dennis MA
02660

Call Sign: K1RVG
Helen L Robsham
9 Conifer Ln
South Dennis MA
02660

Call Sign: W1YBY
Richard E Robsham
9 Conifer Ln
South Dennis MA
026603628

Call Sign: WA1BPE
Stanley E Mc Grane
7 Debbie Ln
South Dennis MA
02660

Call Sign: WB1CUA
Benjamin L
Richardson
43 Eastover
South Dennis MA
02660

Call Sign: K1LUI
William T Brown Jr
29 Eastover Rd
South Dennis MA
02660

Call Sign: AA1I
Alan Crowell
73 Farm Ln Box 1479
South Dennis MA
026601479

Call Sign: W1QWZ
Cleophas D Boisvert
36 Fiord Dr
South Dennis MA
02660

Call Sign: KB5SQF
David A Brouillette
71 Hazelwood Rd
South Dennis MA
02660

Call Sign: KB1ROE
Gaynor R Foster
17 Hibiscus Way
South Dennis MA
02660

Call Sign: K1GRF
Gaynor R Foster
17 Hibiscus Way
South Dennis MA
02660

Call Sign: WA1OMG
Cora G Ford
36 Highland St
South Dennis MA
026603757

Call Sign: KB1WRW
John P New
85 King James Dr
South Dennis MA
02660

Call Sign: KA1GOL
Fred W Ramhorst
90 Kings Row Dr
South Dennis MA
02660

Call Sign: W3ZUE
Robert V Anderson
430 Main St
South Dennis MA
02660

Call Sign: KB1OFV
Geoffrey M Stevenson
14 Nautical Way
South Dennis MA
02660

Call Sign: KB1IMO
Ross Lloyd
227 Old Bass River Rd
South Dennis MA
02660

Call Sign: N1BPD
Ross Lloyd
227 Old Bass River Rd
South Dennis MA
02660

Call Sign: W6SRW
John J Donovan
343 Old Bass River Rd
South Dennis MA
02660

Call Sign: W6SRX
Dorothy Q Donovan
343 Old Bass River Rd
South Dennis MA
02660

Call Sign: WB1CBB
Samuel L D Angona
15 Peteroliver Rd
South Dennis MA
02660

Call Sign: N1DAD
Paul A Iwanski
17 Pinedale Rd
South Dennis MA
026603126

Call Sign: N1SGM
Wendy K Iwanski
17 Pinedale Rd
South Dennis MA
026603126

Call Sign: N1SNY
Alec K Iwanski
17 Pinedale Rd
South Dennis MA
026603126

Call Sign: W0ZEN
James D Whitehill
6 Willowford Rd
South Dennis MA
02660

Call Sign: W1ZRO
James D Whitehill
6 Willowford Rd
South Dennis MA
02660

Call Sign: N1QV
James D Whitehill
6 Willowford Rd
South Dennis MA
02660

Call Sign: N1VLG
Stephen P Boyson
15 Windmill Way
South Dennis MA
02660

Call Sign: N1WCQ
Karen W Boyson
15 Windmill Way
South Dennis MA
02660

Call Sign: KB1UOC
Benjamin M Coakley
6 Winslow Rd
South Dennis MA
02660

Call Sign: K1RCN
Benjamin M Coakley
6 Winslow Rd
South Dennis MA
02660

Call Sign: KC1UM
James M Campbell
South Dennis MA
02660

Call Sign: N1EYH
Charles H Mattson
South Dennis MA
02660

Call Sign: W1LCA
Richard M Dunham
South Dennis MA
02660

Call Sign: KB1SMR
Alex D Moorehead

South Dennis MA
02660

FCC Amateur Radio Licenses in South Easton

Call Sign: N1TDY
Jennifer S Hagy
12 Adam St - 6
South Easton MA
02375

Call Sign: KB1VPT
Nicholas D Palmieri
12 Adam St Unit 3
South Easton MA
02375

Call Sign: K1MIG
Thomas L Kane
282 Depot St
South Easton MA
02375

Call Sign: KA1BSY
Peter C Zatzos
16 Eisenhower Dr
South Easton MA
02375

Call Sign: WA1WEX
Joseph J Gustowski Jr
117 Highland St
South Easton MA
02375

Call Sign: N1ODC
Jeremy B Barber
138 Highland St
South Easton MA
02372035

Call Sign: K1BXN
James G Daley
50 Katherine Grant Rd
South Easton MA
02375

Call Sign: WC1N
Robert C Farquharson
6 Lyman Wheelock Rd
South Easton MA
02375

Call Sign: W1LHJ
Patrick W Crozier
52 Meadow Hill Ct
South Easton MA
02375

Call Sign: KB1ASI
Thomas L Burbridge
4 Meetinghouse Ln
South Easton MA
02375

Call Sign: KB1OHW
Walter M Newell Jr
198 Prospect St
South Easton MA
02375

Call Sign: K1WMN
Walter M Newell Jr
198 Prospect St
South Easton MA
02375

Call Sign: KB1ROA
Nicholas F Pickett
9 Short St
South Easton MA
02375

Call Sign: K1TLI
John C Hurley
5 Sweetmeadow Dr
South Easton MA
02375

Call Sign: N1SOO
James P Dumoulin
94 Turnpike St
South Easton MA
02375

Call Sign: N1LRL
Donald B Coe
109 Turnpike St
South Easton MA
02375

Call Sign: N1OCO
Nancy G Coe
109 Turnpike St
South Easton MA
02375

Call Sign: W1NJP
Richard C Anderson Sr
156 Turnpike St
South Easton MA
02375

Call Sign: KD1ND
James H Buccigross
4 Wilson Dr
South Easton MA
02375

Call Sign: KA1EWT
Shirley J Jerman
South Easton MA
02375

Call Sign: N1AE
John S Bohane Jr
South Easton MA
02375

**FCC Amateur Radio
Licenses in South
Egremont**

Call Sign: KB1AOB
George D Barberis
South Egremont MA
01258

**FCC Amateur Radio
Licenses in South
Grafton**

Call Sign: KB1UGY
Daniel E Barsum
35 Brookmeadow Lane
South Grafton MA
01560

Call Sign: KA1MOU
Dennis Plante
10 Harding St
South Grafton MA
01560

Call Sign: WB3EJA
Arthur A Hall Iii
107 Main St
South Grafton MA
01560

Call Sign: N1TDC
Beverly J Tavano
112 Main St
South Grafton MA
01560

Call Sign: WA1OAS
Anna Moreau
173 Main St
South Grafton MA
01560

Call Sign: K1WKL
Lucien S Morin
24 Orchard St
South Grafton MA
01560

Call Sign: KB1SAV
Robert F Morin Jr
26 Orchard St
South Grafton MA
01560

Call Sign: KB1SXJ
Joseph P Morin
26 Orchard St
South Grafton MA
01560

Call Sign: K1WKL
Joseph P Morin
26 Orchard St
South Grafton MA
01560

Call Sign: AB1OG
Robert F Morin Jr
26 Orchard St
South Grafton MA
01560

Call Sign: KQ1T
Robert F Morin Jr
26 Orchard St
South Grafton MA
01560

Call Sign: KA1RTP
Edward N Girouard
177 Pleasant St
South Grafton MA
01560

Call Sign: KA1HWP
Henry W Piel
10 Pratt St
South Grafton MA
01560

Call Sign: KQ1V
Henry W Piel
10 Pratt St
South Grafton MA
01560

Call Sign: KD4WNQ
Robert A Sosin
220 Providence Rd Apt
315
South Grafton MA
01560

Call Sign: WA1MLH
Samuel J Gillett
12 Veterans Cir
South Grafton MA
01560

**FCC Amateur Radio
Licenses in South
Hadley**

Call Sign: W1DDK
Fred Salloom
20 Bayon Dr Apt 106
South Hadley MA
01075

Call Sign: W1CY
Leonard A Webb
20 Bayon Dr Apt 106
South Hadley MA
010753332

Call Sign: WA1IDK
Arthur T Fieldsend
20 Bayon Dr Apt 124
South Hadley MA
01075

Call Sign: W1YPK
Carrol W Bailey
20 Bayon Dr Apt 227
South Hadley MA
01075

Call Sign: N1QKJ

Thora C Fieldsend
20 Bayon Drive Apt
124
South Hadley MA
01075

Call Sign: N1LQB
William J Judd
160 Brainerd St
South Hadley MA
01075

Call Sign: W1SHF
William J Judd
160 Brainerd St
South Hadley MA
010751306

Call Sign: KA1ZLK
Robert A Chartier
18 Broad St
South Hadley MA
01075

Call Sign: KB1IGM
Brian R Regan
11 Carol Ann Dr
South Hadley MA
01075

Call Sign: KA1UIV
Jeffrey R Barna
119 College St
South Hadley MA
01075

Call Sign: N1LZE
M Susan Barna
119 College St
South Hadley MA
01075

Call Sign: KA1ZWE
John J Kuczma
35 Fairlawn St
South Hadley MA
01075

Call Sign: KA1CRX
Robert Brough
57 Fairview St
South Hadley MA
01075

Call Sign: N1JOH
Scott R Brough
34 Ferry St
South Hadley MA
01075

Call Sign: KD1KU
Kenneth R Dion
10 Graves St
South Hadley MA
01075

Call Sign: N1MOJ
Cecile A Dion
10 Graves St
South Hadley MA
01075

Call Sign: K1ESN
Joseph J Syrek
48 Hadley St
South Hadley MA
01075

Call Sign: KB1DSY
James M Riley
Hadley Village Rd
South Hadley MA
01075

Call Sign: KB1JVL
Walter L Ziemba Jr
8 Helm St
South Hadley MA
01075

Call Sign: W1WLZ
Walter L Ziemba Jr
8 Helm St
South Hadley MA
01075

Call Sign: N1QFT
Irving E Gemme
24 High St
South Hadley MA
01075

Call Sign: KB1TRH
Donald Norwood
70 High St
South Hadley MA
01075

Call Sign: N1MOF
Robert J Labbee
19 Hillside Ave
South Hadley MA
01075

Call Sign: KB1FRF
Ovide Flannery
7 Hunter Terrace
South Hadley MA
010752367

Call Sign: WB1DKU
Joseph R Beauvais Sr
8 Hunter Terrace
South Hadley MA
01075

Call Sign: W1EZD
Roger J Farley
73 Judd Ave
South Hadley MA
01075

Call Sign: KE1DW
John M Kelley
22 Laurie Ave
South Hadley MA
01075

Call Sign: KB1IPG
Kevin Phillips
33 Lawn St
South Hadley MA
01075

Call Sign: N1EYT
James F Mello
71 Lincoln Ave
South Hadley MA
010752322

Call Sign: N1YRE
William R Forget
6 Linda St
South Hadley MA
01075

Call Sign: AA1NF
Bernard J Hudon
42 Ludlow Rd
South Hadley MA
01075

Call Sign: KA1TDL
Schley A Warren Iii
51 Ludlow Rd
South Hadley MA
01075

Call Sign: N1KQE
John J Hogan
1 Lynch Pl
South Hadley MA
01075

Call Sign: N1KXK
Stephen M Gonneville
19 Magnolia Terrace
South Hadley MA
01075

Call Sign: N1ZIO
Daniel C Martinez
12 Maria Dr
South Hadley MA
01075

Call Sign: KA1PDT
Richard C Gardella Jr
45 Noel St
South Hadley MA
01075

Call Sign: N1KHX
Daniel E Mendrala
4 Paul St
South Hadley MA
01075

Call Sign: N1KHY
Edwin J Mendrala
4 Paul St
South Hadley MA
01075

Call Sign: N1LIN
Kenneth A Beaudoin
175 Pine Grove Dr
South Hadley MA
01075

Call Sign: KB1WGZ
Pamela F Connors
30 Pine Hill Rd
South Hadley MA
01075

Call Sign: N1KXM
Ronald J Kolek
95 Richview Ave
South Hadley MA
01075

Call Sign: N1TBX
Peter A Dawson
43 Riverboat Village
Rd
South Hadley MA
01075

Call Sign: W1ZZG
Jules G Fredey Jr
26 Summit St
South Hadley MA
01075

Call Sign: WT3I
Eugene Schwartz
4 Sycamore Knolls
South Hadley MA
01075

Call Sign: WA1ICA
Robert C Piela
8 Valley View Drive
South Hadley MA
01075

Call Sign: W1OJA
Robert C Harvey
39 W Summit St
South Hadley MA
010752738

Call Sign: KX1X
John J Pise Jr
195 Willimansett St
South Hadley MA
01075

Call Sign: KB1FBK
Mount Tom Amateur
Repeater Assn
195 Willimansett St
South Hadley MA
01075

Call Sign: WM1FD
Mount Tom Amateur
Repeater Assn
195 Willimansett St

South Hadley MA
01075

Call Sign: KA1MPA
Robert E Barrett
92 Woodbridge St
South Hadley MA
01075

Call Sign: WF1O
Phillip W Davis
25 Woodlawn St
South Hadley MA
010752240

Call Sign: W1HOD
Leonard A Webb
4 Worthington Dr
South Hadley MA
01075

Call Sign: N1LZM
Alan H Rifkin
South Hadley MA
01075

Call Sign: N1TUS
Donald Norwood
South Hadley MA
01075

Call Sign: WB2YCH
Leonard M Rubin
462 Asbury St
South Hamilton MA
019821314

Call Sign: K1AID
Paul H Sedgwick
35 Bradford Rd
South Hamilton MA
01982

Call Sign: KB1NVI
Christopher A Conte
116 Bridge St
South Hamilton MA
019821404

Call Sign: WA1KZN

Peter Westland
44 Chestnut St
South Hamilton MA
01982

Call Sign: KB1PGF
Andrew D Kulhavy
246 Highland St
South Hamilton MA
01982

Call Sign: K1YJD
George G Preston
288 Highland St
South Hamilton MA
01982

Call Sign: KB1NRX
James P Gorman
62 Lake Shore Dr
South Hamilton MA
01982

Call Sign: KB1NSA
Nancy Gorman
62 Lake Shore Dr
South Hamilton MA
01982

Call Sign: KB1NRY
Liam W Gorman
62 Lakeshore Dr
South Hamilton MA
01982

Call Sign: KB1NRZ
William J Gorman
62 Lakeshore Dr
South Hamilton MA
01982

Call Sign: W1HLF
Harvey F Nichols Jr
63 Lincoln Ave
South Hamilton MA
01982

Call Sign: W1ENJ
Alvin P Whipple
4 Pleasant St
South Hamilton MA
01982

Call Sign: W1KVQ

Herbert G Ryan
18 Postgate Rd
South Hamilton MA
01982

Call Sign: KA1KMM
Ernest S Jones Sr
17 Western Ave
South Hamilton MA
019822023

Call Sign: N1JWD
Kevin M Signore
119 Woodbury St
South Hamilton MA
01982

Call Sign: K1DN
Donald C Nesmith
11 Red River Rd
South Harwich MA
026610156

Call Sign: WA1KYU
Dana S Henrique
129 Uncle Venie S Rd
South Harwich MA
02661

Call Sign: W1QMS
Werner M Maurer
51 Kelly Dr
South Lancaster MA
01561

Call Sign: W1JCV
Roy A Mc Coy
30 Parker Rd
South Lancaster MA
01561

Call Sign: KA1GHA
Stanley Y Roberts Jr
South Lancaster MA
01561

Call Sign: N4LTZ
Mark E Thompson
South Lancaster MA
01561

Call Sign: KB1GXA
Marilyn Fleming
South Lancaster MA
015610734

Call Sign: N1LLS
Thomas J Meunier
South Lee MA 01260

Call Sign: WA1UBT
Laurence H Lebowitz
13 Phillips Pond
South Natick MA
01760

Call Sign: K1CQF
Robert N Rehn
18 Pleasant St
South Natick MA
01760

Call Sign: K1TZT
Edith B Stevens
31 Water St
South Natick MA
01760

Call Sign: W1IKO
Myles P Byrne
7 Woodleigh Rd
South Natick MA
01760

Call Sign: W1AMB
Samuel Samour
30 Grannys Ln
South Orleans MA
02662

Call Sign: N1PIR
Harold F Rusch
81 Namequoit Rd Box
855
South Orleans MA
02662

Call Sign: W1AOL
William A Dickson
176 Quanset Rd
South Orleans MA
02662

Call Sign: W1ZSJ
Robert H Melcher
South Orleans MA
02662

Call Sign: K1ZM
Jeffrey T Briggs
South Orleans MA
02662

Call Sign: KA1SD
Emery Thompson Iii
South Orleans MA
02662

Call Sign: KA1TVC
Elisha M Sullivan
South Orleans MA
02662

Call Sign: W1BB
Stew Perry Memorial
Radio Club
South Orleans MA
02662

Call Sign: W2OLU
Neil A Johnson
South Orleans MA
02662

Call Sign: KB1NMR
Trinity College Alumni
Radio Club
South Orleans MA
026621073

Call Sign: KB1OQN
Trinity College Alumni
Radio Club

South Orleans MA
026621073

Call Sign: KB1ORV
Massachusetts
Wireless Society
South Orleans MA
026621073

Call Sign: WA1MA
Massachusetts
Wireless Society
South Orleans MA
026621073

Call Sign: NA1CC
Wesley M Baden
South Orleans MA
02662

FCC Amateur Radio Licenses in South Peabody

Call Sign: WA1SHY
Charles G Bellefeuille
4 Elaine Ave
South Peabody MA
019606530

FCC Amateur Radio Licenses in South Plymouth

Call Sign: KB1FVT
Robert J Simcik
18 Great Wind Dr
South Plymouth MA
02360

Call Sign: WX1MAN
Robert J Simcik
18 Great Wind Dr
South Plymouth MA
02360

FCC Amateur Radio Licenses in South Royalston

Call Sign: KB1IPC
Catherine Offutt
13 River Rd

South Royalston MA
013689525

Call Sign: KB1IPS
Robert J Laakkonen
13 River Rd
South Royalston MA
013689525

Call Sign: W2OWO
Catherine Offutt
13 River Rd
South Royalston MA
013689525

FCC Amateur Radio Licenses in South Walpole

Call Sign: WA1TGI
George E Doyle
29 Eldor Dr
South Walpole MA
02071

Call Sign: K1UHU
Mario J De Cristofaro
Route 1
South Walpole MA
02071

Call Sign: W1IXI
Wilfred J Sheehan Sr
111 Summer St
South Walpole MA
02071

Call Sign: WB1ETZ
Forrest E Preble
16 Water St
South Walpole MA
02071

Call Sign: KA1IQN
Edward A Preble
South Walpole MA
02071

FCC Amateur Radio Licenses in South Wellfleet

Call Sign: W1WXZ
James B Caton

75 Cottontail Rd
South Wellfleet MA
02663

Call Sign: N1DVG
Kenneth J Cole
55 Pleasant Pt Rd
South Wellfleet MA
02663

Call Sign: KA1YWL
Nicole Mari Maguire
South Wellfleet MA
02663

Call Sign: KA2LFU
Sarah K Multer
South Wellfleet MA
02663

Call Sign: KC2BDB
Robert Angelelli
South Wellfleet MA
02663

Call Sign: KB1IHX
Anthony T Tullio
South Wellfleet MA
02663

FCC Amateur Radio Licenses in South Weymouth

Call Sign: N1ICN
James J Clogher Jr
10 Abbott St
South Weymouth MA
021901302

Call Sign: K1CQI
Paul J Keough
20 Camelot Way Apt
3n
South Weymouth MA
02190

Call Sign: N1LRA
Andrew M Curran
36 Christine Ter
South Weymouth MA
02190

Call Sign: W1OSO

Robert H Johnson
370 Columbian St
South Weymouth MA
02190

Call Sign: KB1RNN
Richard N Dispirito
41 Elwood Dr
South Weymouth MA
02190

Call Sign: KB1UQA
South Shore Hospital
Amateur Radio Club
55 Fogg Rd - Mail
Stop 25
South Weymouth MA
02190

Call Sign: W1SSH
South Shore Hospital
Amateur Radio Club
55 Fogg Rd - Mail
Stop 25
South Weymouth MA
02190

Call Sign: W1ZSZ
Leigh B Trop
28 Georgia Rd
South Weymouth MA
02190

Call Sign: KB1FVQ
David C Hathaway
36 Green Tree Lane
Apt 28
South Weymouth MA
02190

Call Sign: KA1GLH
Ralph B Haddix
5 Mac Dougall Ct
South Weymouth MA
02190

Call Sign: KA1SFL
Eugene F Corridan Jr
650 Main St
South Weymouth MA
02190

Call Sign: K1ELA

Ernest W Mac
Lauchlan
666 Main St
South Weymouth MA
02190

Call Sign: KB1ESF
Ann M Maclauchlan
666 Main St
South Weymouth MA
02190

Call Sign: K1RFM
Ann M Maclauchlan
666 Main St
South Weymouth MA
02190

Call Sign: N1FXB
George E Ward
26 Massapoag St
South Weymouth MA
02190

Call Sign: K1CUR
Benjamin A Durgin
20 Merrymount Rd
South Weymouth MA
02190

Call Sign: KB1LKM
William H James
17 Michele Dr
South Weymouth MA
02190

Call Sign: KB1LRU
Sandra L James
17 Michelle Dr
South Weymouth MA
02190

Call Sign: W1KEL
John Mills
26 Oak St
South Weymouth MA
02190

Call Sign: WA1VPF
Esio J Grassi
156 Oak St
South Weymouth MA
02190

Call Sign: KA1KHJ
Dennis D Kelley
119 Park Ave West
South Weymouth MA
02190

Call Sign: WA1QPE
Benton B Levinson
449 Pine St
South Weymouth MA
02190

Call Sign: K1NFZ
Philip D Barber
446 Pleasant St
South Weymouth MA
021902637

Call Sign: KB1WKB
Geoffrey K Ayres
189 Pond St
South Weymouth MA
02190

Call Sign: WA1YOE
Russell C Deming
440 Thicket St
South Weymouth MA
02190

Call Sign: W1AK
Luther W Eldridge
55 Torrey St
South Weymouth MA
02190

Call Sign: KA1FJO
Herbert E Scott
84 Torrey St
South Weymouth MA
02190

Call Sign: KA1KID
Dorothea M Scott
84 Torrey St
South Weymouth MA
02190

Call Sign: WA1LVF
Roy A Colella
33 Union St
South Weymouth MA
02190

Call Sign: KB1TJH
Frank V Schiarizzi
216 Union St
South Weymouth MA
02190

Call Sign: KB1OEL
Paul R Casey
310 Union St
South Weymouth MA
02190

Call Sign: N1SAM
John R Parker
629 Union St
South Weymouth MA
02190

Call Sign: KA2GRE
Jonathan H Sternstein
65 Webster St Apt 103
South Weymouth MA
02190

Call Sign: KG4YRD
Richard B Anderson
50 Webster St Unit 213
South Weymouth MA
021900233

Call Sign: KB1KJF
Richard B Anderson
50 Webster St Unit 213
South Weymouth MA
021900233

Call Sign: W1KPX
Richard B Anderson
50 Webster St Unit 213
South Weymouth MA
021900233

Call Sign: K1QVU
Harold N Bertino Jr
150 White St
South Weymouth MA
02190

Call Sign: WA2KKR
Vito Pavia
South Waymouth MA
02190

Call Sign: KB1KCZ
Jesse A Sherman
75 Abbott Rd
South Yarmouth MA
02664

Call Sign: KB1VFB
Donald R Klimm
16 Antlers Rd
South Yarmouth MA
02664

Call Sign: KA1EMA
Thomas J Cawett
138 Bakers Path Apt
C55
South Yarmouth MA
026646208

Call Sign: N1YSR
Noal D Reid
156 Blue Rock Rd
South Yarmouth MA
02664

Call Sign: KC1DA
Edward J Vogel
2 Brae Burn Ln
South Yarmouth MA
02664

Call Sign: WA1USB
George W Gow
8 Browning Ave
South Yarmouth MA
026641804

Call Sign: K1WQO
Richard O Allen
15 Bryar Ln
South Yarmouth MA
02664

Call Sign: K1WQT
Nancie J Allen
15 Bryar Ln
South Yarmouth MA
02664

Call Sign: KB1MDW

Melissa S Bertrand
25 Captain Besse Rd
South Yarmouth MA
02664

Call Sign: KB1KKC
Brian M Connors
21 Captain Chase Rd
South Yarmouth MA
02664

Call Sign: KB1TAK
Dawn M Clarke
109 Captain Chase Rd
South Yarmouth MA
02664

Call Sign: K1IDA
Clarence M Bowley
47 Captain Daniel Rd
South Yarmouth MA
02664

Call Sign: WA2CGF
Daniel A Hubecky
105 Chipping Green
Circle
South Yarmouth MA
02664

Call Sign: KB1UUP
John P Troiano Jr
82 Clifford St
South Yarmouth MA
02664

Call Sign: K1VKY
Victor L Ballerini
80 Country Club Dr
Oaks 6
South Yarmouth MA
02664

Call Sign: WN4M
Victor L Ballerini
80 Country Club Dr
Oaks 6
South Yarmouth MA
026642073

Call Sign: N1CP
Lawrence C Black
12 Cypress Point Way

South Yarmouth MA
02664

Call Sign: K1BIE
John G Waters Jr
35 Deacon St
South Yarmouth MA
02664

Call Sign: N1MJY
Joseph W Callahan
3 Diane Ave
South Yarmouth MA
02664

Call Sign: KB1ROJ
Sally M Place
8 Diane Ave
South Yarmouth MA
02664

Call Sign: KM1K
John F Walker
136 Diane Ave
South Yarmouth MA
026641998

Call Sign: KA1PNN
William R Camire
55 Evergreen St
South Yarmouth MA
026645611

Call Sign: W1RSK
Arthur L Bauer Sr
5 General Lawrence
Rd
South Yarmouth MA
02664

Call Sign: WA1QBX
Kenneth L Blass
71 Grandview Dr
South Yarmouth MA
02664

Call Sign: KB1QCQ
Thomas L Wruk
32 Harbour Hill Run
South Yarmouth MA
02664

Call Sign: AA1NB
Roy A Nelson

65 Hatch Rd
South Yarmouth MA
02664

Call Sign: N1EDV
Patricia A Baker
2 High Grove Rd
South Yarmouth MA
02664

Call Sign: NQ1Q
Harry J Bichsel
7 High Grove Rd
South Yarmouth MA
02664

Call Sign: W1CDR
Edward B Krevis
31 Joyce St
South Yarmouth MA
02664

Call Sign: WB2SOC
Robert M Milne
32 Keel Cape Drive
South Yarmouth MA
02664

Call Sign: W1RMM
Robert M Milne
32 Keel Cape Drive
South Yarmouth MA
02664

Call Sign: KW3M
Thomas B Keller Jr
7 Legend Dr
South Yarmouth MA
026641315

Call Sign: N1VBH
Albert J Muldoon
28 Little Dipper Ln
South Yarmouth MA
02664

Call Sign: N1XWK
Albert J Muldoon Jr
28 Little Dipper Ln
South Yarmouth MA
02664

Call Sign: KA1QVB
Callum Watson

770 Main St
South Yarmouth MA
02664

Call Sign: W1RTD
Laurier L Collin
844 Main St 6a
South Yarmouth MA
02664

Call Sign: WA1HCD
Edward T Fogarty
88 Mattachee Rd
South Yarmouth MA
02664

Call Sign: N1IQJ
John F Olsen
36 May Flower Ter
South Yarmouth MA
02664

Call Sign: W1HQW
William E Bowman
15 Mistletoe Ln
South Yarmouth MA
02664

Call Sign: KB1OAA
Carl H Brackett
53 N Dennis Rd
South Yarmouth MA
02664

Call Sign: KB1OMW
Vanessa P Ford
53 N Dennis Rd
South Yarmouth MA
02664

Call Sign: N2FAA
Carl H Brackett
53 N Dennis Rd
South Yarmouth MA
02664

Call Sign: WA1RTD
Thomas R Yocom
26 Nautical Lane
South Yarmouth MA
02664

Call Sign: KB1PVQ
Christopher J Dean

4 Old Colony Way
South Yarmouth MA
02664

Call Sign: KB1PVR
Celeste Marie Dean
4 Old Colony Way
South Yarmouth MA
02664

Call Sign: W1CMD
Celeste Marie Dean
4 Old Colony Way
South Yarmouth MA
02664

Call Sign: KB1RPC
Olivia Marie Dean
4 Old Colony Way
South Yarmouth MA
02664

Call Sign: K1KEK
Christopher J Dean
4 Old Colony Way
South Yarmouth MA
02664

Call Sign: W1GDQ
David L Miller
75 Regional Ave
South Yarmouth MA
02664

Call Sign: KA1VNQ
Frank P Scanzillo
9 River St
South Yarmouth MA
02664

Call Sign: N1VBG
John A Cooke
40 Turtle Cove Rd
South Yarmouth MA
02664

Call Sign: KB1AWQ
Stuart T Brown
17 Wild Rose Ter
South Yarmouth MA
02664

Call Sign: KA1VNR
Ian S Baum

118 Witchwood Rd
South Yarmouth MA
02664

Call Sign: K1KEK
Bradford R Dean
Memorial Repeater
Assn
South Yarmouth MA
02664

Call Sign: N1SGL
Bradford M Erickson
South Yarmouth MA
02664

Call Sign: KB1RVS
Artie L Kuipers
South Yarmouth MA
02664

Call Sign: K1ALK
Artie L Kuipers
South Yarmouth MA
02664

**FCC Amateur Radio
Licenses in
Southampton**

Call Sign: KB1KQK
Andrew C Cawrse
6 Birchwood Dr
Southampton MA
01073

Call Sign: N1KXQ
Richard L Vrabel
38 Coleman Rd
Southampton MA
01073

Call Sign: WA1OXO
Walter W Forbush Jr
60 Coleman Rd
Southampton MA
01073

Call Sign: KA1AKR
David C Gustavson
102 College Hwy
Southampton MA
01073

Call Sign: WA4KRX
Nancy F Rice
231 College Hwy
Southampton MA
01073

Call Sign: N1LIR
David W Tilbe
128 College Hwy Apt
106
Southampton MA
01073

Call Sign: KB1OWD
Arthur C Lawrence
113 Crooked Ledge Rd
Southampton MA
01073

Call Sign: KA1KGW
Angela M Thomas
7 East St
Southampton MA
01073

Call Sign: AA1UE
Gary F Thomas
7 East St
Southampton MA
01073

Call Sign: WA1WRK
Richard I Hillenbrand
Jr
92 East St
Southampton MA
01073

Call Sign: N1WGX
William M Wilks
7 Edward Ave
Southampton MA
01073

Call Sign: WB1FXM
William C Walden Iii
21 Fomer Rd
Southampton MA
01073

Call Sign: KB1UYG
Douglas M Henrichon
7 Geryk Ct

Southampton MA
01073

Call Sign: WV1I
Barry Sussman
9 Golden Circle
Southampton MA
01073

Call Sign: N1DJP
Gerald W Carboneau
10 Hillside Meadows
Dr
Southampton MA
01073

Call Sign: K1CSB
Raymond J Feeley
92 Line St
Southampton MA
01073

Call Sign: N1SXW
David L Maynard
14 Lynn Dr
Southampton MA
01073

Call Sign: NQ1A
Robert T Rush
50 Pequot Rd
Southampton MA
010739587

Call Sign: KA1HUM
Kenneth R Boucher
95 Pequot Rd
Southampton MA
01073

Call Sign: KB4YJC
Joseph A Yaple
123 Russellville Rd
Southampton MA
01073

Call Sign: N1SFD
Gerald B West
125 Russellville Rd
Southampton MA
01073

Call Sign: WA1BDG
Arthur L Peters

103 Strong Rd
Southampton MA
01073

Call Sign: KB1GTE
Thomas E Neill
18 Thomas Circle
Southampton MA
01073

Call Sign: K1ANX
George H Rancourt
82 White Loaf Rd
Southampton MA
01073

Call Sign: WA1ZBL
Jody M Boucher
66 Whiteloaf Rd
Southampton MA
01073

FCC Amateur Radio
Licenses in Southboro

See also FCC
Amateur Radio
Licenses in
Southborough

Call Sign: N1JWC
Cola R Nelson Jr
59 Central·St Apt 1
Southboro MA 01772

Call Sign: KB1FFF
David C Aker
28 Flagg Rd
Southboro MA 01772

Call Sign: KB1LIW
John L Heyl
67 Main St
Southboro MA 01772

Call Sign: K1TXQ
Bernard L Phillips
9 Walker St
Southboro MA 01772

FCC Amateur Radio
Licenses in
Southborough

See also FCC
Amateur Radio
Licenses in Southboro

Call Sign: N1MGF
Lisa G Sussman
18 Atwood Rd
Southborough MA
01772

Call Sign: KB1CVZ
Robert H Titus
27 Atwood Rd
Southborough MA
017720392

Call Sign: KB1DAW
Robert H Titus Jr
27 Atwood Rd
Southborough MA
017720392

Call Sign: N1YUT
Ronald E Blight
8 B Newton St
Southborough MA
01772

Call Sign: N1MPK
Andrew L Duca
9 Birchwood Drive
Southborough MA
01772

Call Sign: N1DDI
Rita A Baker
34 Clifford Rd
Southborough MA
01772

Call Sign: N1HOJ
William H Baker Iii
34 Clifford Rd
Southborough MA
01772

Call Sign: WA1CNU
Warren N Stern
10 Cross St
Southborough MA
01772

Call Sign: WD1H
Daniel J Segarra

17 E Main St
Southborough MA
01772

Call Sign: N1GUZ
John L Cook Iii
11 Graystone Way
Southborough MA
01772

Call Sign: KB1WBU
Emma K Poellmitz
12 Joslin Lane
Southborough MA
01772

Call Sign: K1EMA
Emma K Poellmitz
12 Joslin Lane
Southborough MA
01772

Call Sign: K1MM
William C Poellmitz
12 Joslin Ln
Southborough MA
01772

Call Sign: KA1ESR
Karen A Poellmitz
12 Joslin Ln
Southborough MA
01772

Call Sign: KM1YL
Karen A Poellmitz
12 Joslin Ln
Southborough MA
01772

Call Sign: KB3JAD
Jaiwant N Mulik
25 Latisquama Rd
Southborough MA
01772

Call Sign: W1ZYB
Charles E Wood
144 Marlboro Rd
Southborough MA
01772

Call Sign: W1AQI
George E Palmer Jr

21 Meeting House Ln
Southborough MA
017721527

Call Sign: K1VXD
Douglas P Linden
60 Parkerville Rd
Southborough MA
01772

Call Sign: WB1FCW
Laurence F Heine
171 Parkerville Rd
Southborough MA
01772

Call Sign: WB1FCX
Madeline M Heine
171 Parkerville Rd
Southborough MA
01772

Call Sign: WB1GUQ
Anthony W Rea Ii
37 Pine Hill Rd
Southborough MA
01772

Call Sign: N1KE
William R Short
47 Pine Hill Rd
Southborough MA
017721313

Call Sign: WB1EUP
Lee S Perrin
3 Powder Mill Lane
Southborough MA
01772

Call Sign: N1ALG
Robert C Lagasse
10 Powdermill Ln
Southborough MA
017722047

Call Sign: W1RCL
Robert C Lagasse
10 Powdermill Ln
Southborough MA
017722047

Call Sign: WA1KQH
Michael T Keller

12 Prentiss St
Southborough MA
01772

Call Sign: W1BNC
Michael T Keller
12 Prentiss St
Southborough MA
01772

Call Sign: KA1QJC
Robert Somers
84 Sears Rd
Southborough MA
01772

Call Sign: KB1WJQ
Bashu K Kanal
5 Stub Toe Ln
Southborough MA
01772

Call Sign: WA2UVH
Michael A Form
47 Valley Rd
Southborough MA
01772

Call Sign: AB1IV
James J Cavan Jr
10 Vickery Hill Lane
Southborough MA
01772

Call Sign: KB1TQY
Julia A Cavan
10 Vickery Hill Lane
Southborough MA
01772

Call Sign: K1WIV
James J Noone Jr
5 Whistler Ln
Southborough MA
01772

Call Sign: KA1TIH
Kendell A Chilton
12 Wolfpen Lane
Southborough MA
017721129

Call Sign: KA1ZLO
Pamela A Chilton

12 Wolfpen Lane
Southborough MA
01772

Call Sign: KA1EMQ
Lindsay W Blake
Southborough MA
01772

Call Sign: W1SRG
Southboro Rod & Gun
Amateur Radio
Committee
Southborough MA
017720091

**FCC Amateur Radio
Licenses in
Southbridge**

Call Sign: N1YYG
Michael A Dineen
779 Alpine Drive
Southbridge MA
01550

Call Sign: W1QFJ
Robert J Lareau
15 Brook Rd
Southbridge MA
01550

Call Sign: KA1IET
Joseph E Chouinard
193 Chapin St
Southbridge MA
01550

Call Sign: KO0I
David E Chouinard
193 Chapin St Apt 2
Southbridge MA
01550

Call Sign: N1SCD
Gilberto Vazquez
211 Charlton St
Southbridge MA
01550

Call Sign: K1FOG
George E Syriac
518 Charlton St

Southbridge MA
01550

Call Sign: KB1RTC
Justin S Houle
141 Charlton St
Southbridge MA
01550

Call Sign: N1TEQ
Melissa A Peters
208 Clemence Hill
Southbridge MA
01550

Call Sign: WB1CNY
Phillip G Jacquart
44 Dennison Hill Rd
Southbridge MA
01550

Call Sign: K1RCA
Phillip G Jacquart
44 Dennison Hill Rd
Southbridge MA
01550

Call Sign: K1ICW
Mary B Mc Lam
89 Dennison Ln
Southbridge MA
01550

Call Sign: N1HTU
Fern J Phillips
264 Dennison Ln
Southbridge MA
01550

Call Sign: WA1RTX
Conrad G Corriveau
265 Dudley River Rd
Southbridge MA
01550

Call Sign: N1PWC
Kevin M Tremblay
103 Eastford Rd Apt 2
Southbridge MA
01550

Call Sign: W1EFC
Laurent R Mc Donald
95 Elm St 2

Southbridge MA
01550

Call Sign: N1HBS
Brent S Abrahamson
26 Franklin Ter
Southbridge MA
01550

Call Sign: K1LVO
Bernard W Walkowiak
167 Hamilton St
Southbridge MA
01550

Call Sign: N1NGJ
Robert C Cantara
480 Hamilton St
Southbridge MA
01550

Call Sign: W1NEP
Donald B Whitney
122 Litchfield Ave
Southbridge MA
01550

Call Sign: W1FBF
Richard Gobeille
10 Oak St
Southbridge MA
01550

Call Sign: K1CRK
J Lionel R Anger
182 Pleasant
Southbridge MA
01550

Call Sign: W1KAS
Kenneth A Stein
146 Pleasant St
Southbridge MA
01550

Call Sign: KA1PUL
Tellis T Nale
Rb 566
Southbridge MA
01550

Call Sign: N1TYT
Arthur F Martin
161 South St

Southbridge MA
015504009

Call Sign: KD1WO
Edgars A Andersons
444 South St
Southbridge MA
01550

Call Sign: KA1ZWR
David R Gagnon
210 South St Apt 3
Southbridge MA
01550

Call Sign: WP4JF
Jose A Figueroa
247 Torrey Rd
Southbridge MA
01550

Call Sign: WB1DZK
Eugene A Gregoire
31 Village Dr Apt 5
Southbridge MA
01550

Call Sign: KE1MK
Eugene A Gregoire
31 Village Dr Apt 5
Southbridge MA
01550

Call Sign: KB1WXC
Eric C Wilhelm
73 Vista Lane
Southbridge MA
01550

Call Sign: N1HKL
Ronald C Delage
115 Vista Ln
Southbridge MA
01550

Call Sign: WN1D
Gary R Bellinger
657 Worcester St Apt
607
Southbridge MA
01550

Call Sign: W1EVC
Herbert Cassell Jr

Southbridge MA
01550

Call Sign: N1SBL
John E Sypek
Southbridge MA
01550

Call Sign: W1IQU
George P Bentley
Southbridge MA
01550

FCC Amateur Radio Licenses in Southfield

Call Sign: KA1KNL
Jeralee Mornhinweg
1415 Canaan
Southfield Rd
Southfield MA 01259

Call Sign: KB1DIP
June R Stalker
1415 Canaan
Southfield Rd
Southfield MA 01259

Call Sign: WS1MA
Wilbur H Stalker
1415 Canaan
Southfield Rd
Southfield MA 01259

Call Sign: N1ZNH
Russell P Riva
Cross To Canaan Vly
Rd
Southfield MA 01259

Call Sign: N1HHM
Eric Nelson
Norfolk Rd
Southfield MA 01259

FCC Amateur Radio Licenses in Southwick

Call Sign: N1JTU
Leonard D Shaffer
32 Ahrend Circle
Southwick MA 01077

Call Sign: WB1Y

Nobuyuki Fujita
6 Amberleaf Way
Southwick MA 01077

Call Sign: WA1YCA
Tryon W Cote
4 Arcadia Lane
Southwick MA
010779717

Call Sign: WB1EFE
Keith G Roy
3 Brayton Drive
Southwick MA 01077

Call Sign: KA1QIT
Alice M Davey
22 Buckingham Dr
Southwick MA
010779541

Call Sign: KD1EK
Charles R Davey
22 Buckingham Dr
Southwick MA 01077

Call Sign: N1MFM
James J Mercey Jr
22 Buckingham Dr
Southwick MA 01077

Call Sign: NC1I
Francis M Potts
5 Charles Johnson Rd
Southwick MA 01077

Call Sign: KB1UNB
Emily E Potts
5 Charles Johnson Rd
Southwick MA 01077

Call Sign: K1EEP
Emily E Potts
5 Charles Johnson Rd
Southwick MA 01077

Call Sign: WB1FTX
Robert R Leavitt
19 College Hwy
Southwick MA 01077

Call Sign: N1PZJ
Bernard L Mickna
132 College Hwy

Southwick MA 01077

Call Sign: N1MOC
Keith N Stromgren
441 College Hwy
Southwick MA 01077

Call Sign: N1QBL
James E Shaw
441 College Hwy
Southwick MA 01077

Call Sign: AA1WN
Robert J Meneguzzo
3 Dairy Lane
Southwick MA 01077

Call Sign: K1YO
Robert J Meneguzzo
3 Dairy Lane
Southwick MA 01077

Call Sign: W1BXB
Harvey P Mensch
7 Echo Rd
Southwick MA 01077

Call Sign: N1QXR
Mary A Brown
2 Evergreen St
Southwick MA 01077

Call Sign: KB1VWQ
Daniel E Vierno
6 Evergreen Terrace
Southwick MA 01077

Call Sign: WB1DLG
Louis J Ottmann
49 Feeding Hills Rd
Southwick MA 01077

Call Sign: N1NEM
James A Brown Ii
51 Feeding Hills Rd
Southwick MA 01077

Call Sign: N1WHA
Bernard M Keefe
42 Fernwood Rd
Southwick MA 01077

Call Sign: KB1RQV
Dennis J Clark

75 Fred Jackson Rd
Southwick MA 01077

Call Sign: KA1PIW
Leo J Hamilton
1 Gargon Ter
Southwick MA 01077

Call Sign: KB1AXI
Matthew L Drenen
6 Gloria Dr
Southwick MA 01077

Call Sign: KA1QAL
Judith A Potts
154 Hillside Rd
Southwick MA
010779729

Call Sign: WA1ECR
Gary F Potts
154 Hillside Rd
Southwick MA
010779729

Call Sign: K1BE
Jeffrey J Duquette
26 Iroquois Dr
Southwick MA
010779632

Call Sign: N1JJD
Nicolas J Duquette
26 Iroquois Dr
Southwick MA
010779632

Call Sign: KB1GXI
Mary M Zeppa
13 Kimberly Dr
Southwick MA 01077

Call Sign: N1LKG
Eric J Zeppa
13 Kimberly Drive
Southwick MA 01077

Call Sign: N1OZH
Conrad L Chrystal
10 Lakemont St
Southwick MA 01077

Call Sign: N1XXL
Robert F Miller

60 Lakemont St
Southwick MA 01077

Call Sign: KA1SMF
Michael P Burrage Jr
59 Lakeview St
Southwick MA 01077

Call Sign: KA1MZS
William J Fisher Jr
1925 Long Yard Rd
Southwick MA 01077

Call Sign: KB1IAB
Christopher J
Grabowski
8 Maple St
Southwick MA 01077

Call Sign: KB1AXR
Ernest R Lempke Iii
141 Mortvining Rd
Southwick MA 01077

Call Sign: KB1NCL
Sarah A Houle
15 N Longyard Rd
Southwick MA 01077

Call Sign: N1SVO
Justin M Hamberg
31 N Longyard Rd
Southwick MA 01077

Call Sign: KB1NCK
David A Houle
15 North Longyard Rd
Southwick MA 01077

Call Sign: KB1TVY
John J Cashman
40 North Longyard Rd
Southwick MA 01077

Call Sign: K1BZM
William R Ferry
17 Pearl Brook Rd
Southwick MA 01077

Call Sign: KB1TLP
Edward G Faits
19 Pine Knoll
Southwick MA 01077

Call Sign: KB1CLY
Daniel E Lynch
16 Point Grove Rd
Southwick MA 01077

Call Sign: KA1EWX
Don J Lapenas
4 Rising Corner Rd
Southwick MA 01077

Call Sign: WA1DL
Don J Lapenas
4 Rising Corner Rd
Southwick MA 01077

Call Sign: KB1FRH
David F Cain
94 S Longyard Rd
Southwick MA 01077

Call Sign: AA1YW
David F Cain
94 S Longyard Rd
Southwick MA 01077

Call Sign: N1YFH
Tyler G Moore
126 S Loomis St
Southwick MA 01077

Call Sign: KB1VPI
Stephen M Baker
196 S Loomis St
Southwick MA 01077

Call Sign: N1SIS
Peter R Davis
217 Sheep Pasture Rd
Southwick MA 01077

Call Sign: WA1MUH
Ralph L Benedict
So Village East #4
Southwick MA 01077

Call Sign: KB1FTX
John F Cain
94 South Longyard Rd
Southwick MA 01077

Call Sign: K1II
Charles H Dunlap Jr
66 Vining Hill Rd
Southwick MA 01077

Call Sign: KB1CDL
Southwick Auxiliary
Police Association
66 Vining Hill Rd
Southwick MA 01077

Call Sign: N1EVE
Pauline I Dunlap
66 Vining Hill Rd
Southwick MA
010779406

Call Sign: N1FFZ
Jeffrey A Dunlap
66 Vining Hill Rd
Southwick MA 01077

Call Sign: N1FMT
Deborah J Dunlap
66 Vining Hill Rd
Southwick MA 01077

Call Sign: WC1SW
Southwick Auxiliary
Police Association
66 Vining Hill Rd
Southwick MA 01077

Call Sign: KA1HKJ
Charles F Darling
151 Vining Hill Rd
Southwick MA 01077

Call Sign: KA1TRF
Paul R Kokoszyna
162 Vining Hill Rd
Southwick MA 01077

Call Sign: WB1AEW
James C Morse
185 Vining Hill Rd
Southwick MA 01077

Call Sign: N1JBW
Alvin B See
Southwick MA 01077

Call Sign: W1ALL
George H Hughes
Southwick MA 01077

Call Sign: K1ZY
Alfred V Pooler

Southwick MA 01077

Call Sign: KA1TBS
Frederick J Gore
Southwick MA
010770396

Call Sign: N1HVM
Eric L Carroll
Southwick MA 01077

Call Sign: N1TET
Muriel E Pinard
Southwick MA 01077

Call Sign: NF1I
Robert A Pinard
Southwick MA 01077

Call Sign: KB1FWJ
Jonathan D Youens
Southwick MA 01077

Call Sign: WM1SAR
Jonathan D Youens
Southwick MA 01077

**FCC Amateur Radio
Licenses in Spencer**

Call Sign: N1WSF
Rob J Fecteau
101 Ash St
Spencer MA 01562

Call Sign: N1RFL
Edson P Gebo Sr
165 Ash St
Spencer MA 01562

Call Sign: W1ERC
Edson P Gebo
165 Ash St
Spencer MA 01562

Call Sign: N1OIA
Jeremy J Burque
183 Ash St
Spencer MA 01562

Call Sign: KB1EHQ
Dennis J Desplaines Jr
36 Ash St
Spencer MA 01562

Call Sign: N1IDX
Nathan D Youngs
58 Bacon Hill Rd
Spencer MA 01562

Call Sign: N1VOR
Paul C Wood
3 Bemis St
Spencer MA 01562

Call Sign: KB0ZYI
Scott E Dorsey
4 Bemis St
Spencer MA 01562

Call Sign: KB1BHC
Mathew A Herholz
11 Briarcliff Ln
Spencer MA 01562

Call Sign: KD1CW
Dana G Reed
70 Brooks Pond Rd
Spencer MA 01562

Call Sign: W1LC
Dana G Reed
70 Brooks Pond Rd
Spencer MA 01562

Call Sign: KB1EEH
Curtis J Bellemer
56 Browning Pond Rd
Spencer MA 01562

Call Sign: W1MOW
Mark A Corbin
12 Buteau Rd
Spencer MA 01562

Call Sign: KB1FFG
Jonathan A Corbin
12 Buteau Rd
Spencer MA 01562

Call Sign: WR1O
Mark A Corbin
12 Buteau Rd
Spencer MA 01562

Call Sign: KB1IJY
Spencer Emergency
Mngmt Agency

12 Buteau Rd
Spencer MA 01562

Call Sign: KB1INA
Lisa B Corbin
12 Buteau Rd
Spencer MA 01562

Call Sign: KB1EEI
Matt R Bulak
231 Charlton Rd
Spencer MA 01562

Call Sign: KB1CYS
Jane E Frigon
84 Cherry St
Spencer MA 01562

Call Sign: KB1ART
Karl W Holden
18 Cherry St Apt 1
Spencer MA 01562

Call Sign: KA1SAZ
Gerald Peter Murphy
34 Chickering Rd
Spencer MA 01562

Call Sign: KB1CEA
David W Hickamn
77 Chickering Rd
Spencer MA 01562

Call Sign: KB1CEB
Raymond F Chapin Jr
82 Chickering Rd
Spencer MA 01562

Call Sign: WA1UOP
Uno W Penttila
16 Clark Rd
Spencer MA 01562

Call Sign: KB1MFH
Nathan D Youngs
104 Clark Rd
Spencer MA 01562

Call Sign: KB1SLK
Diana M Richard
18 Condon Dr
Spencer MA 01562

Call Sign: KB1SLL

John D Richard
18 Condon Dr
Spencer MA 01562

Call Sign: KB1OJJ
Justin M Genest
4 Crestview Dr Apt 54
Spencer MA 01562

Call Sign: N1QYJ
Arthur A Benoit
27 Donnelly Rd
Spencer MA 01562

Call Sign: N1VFT
Richard G Hamelin
3 Duggan St
Spencer MA 01562

Call Sign: KB1GNC
Robert N Potvin
42 E Charlton Rd
Spencer MA 01562

Call Sign: N1XH
Robert N Potvin
42 E Charlton Rd
Spencer MA 01562

Call Sign: KB1AEY
Sean T Westcott
1 Early St
Spencer MA 01562

Call Sign: KB1ARU
Craig S Fontaine
15 Franklin St
Spencer MA 01562

Call Sign: KA1PNH
Richard L Kaiser Sr
14 Grove St
Spencer MA
015621706

Call Sign: N1ZKL
Brian R Thibeault
86 Hastings Rd
Spencer MA 01562

Call Sign: WA1QZI
Llewellyn R Pomeroy
25 High St
Spencer MA 01562

Call Sign: KB1AEW
Arthur F White Jr
28 High St
Spencer MA 01562

Call Sign: KB1FJW
Joseph E Gendron Jr
12 Howe Village Apt F
Spencer MA 01562

Call Sign: KA1FIH
Arthur A Snow Jr
5 Irving St
Spencer MA 01652

Call Sign: N1YQI
Paul W Cote
5 Irving St
Spencer MA 01562

Call Sign: N1VMD
James F Gebo
4 Jones St
Spencer MA 01562

Call Sign: KB1FQH
Martin W Sivula
10 Kittredge Rd
Spencer MA 01562

Call Sign: KB1GV
Daniel P Meloche
7 Lake Ave
Spencer MA 01562

Call Sign: W1DPM
Daniel P Meloche
7 Lake Ave Stiles
Spencer MA 01562

Call Sign: N1YQF
Nicholas A Guerin
66 Lake Shore Dr
Spencer MA 01562

Call Sign: KB1EEK
Jeff A Simakauskas
35 Lake St
Spencer MA 01562

Call Sign: KB1QXY
Steven H Evilia

25 Lake Whittemore
Drive
Spencer MA 01562

Call Sign: KA1UVK
Richard S Chabior
26 Lakeview Dr
Spencer MA 01562

Call Sign: KB1GQG
James F Sniffen
4 Langevin St
Spencer MA 01562

Call Sign: KB1IGP
Deborah L Sniffen
4 Langevin St 10
Spencer MA 01562

Call Sign: K1DLS
Deborah L Sniffen
4 Langevin St 10
Spencer MA 01562

Call Sign: N1WSE
Thomas P Flannery
17 Laurel Ln
Spencer MA 01562

Call Sign: N1ZKI
Richard J Hurley
22 Ledge Ave
Spencer MA 01562

Call Sign: K1POR
Fletcher C Baughn
106 Main St
Spencer MA 01562

Call Sign: KS1B
Lawrence F Rizzo
243 Main St
Spencer MA
015621832

Call Sign: W1BIM
Central Mass Amateur
Radio Assoc Inc
243 Main St
Spencer MA 01562

Call Sign: WA1HVI
Doris L Campbell
425 Main St

Spencer MA 01562

Call Sign: WA1HVJ
Colin F Campbell
425 Main St
Spencer MA 01562

Call Sign: N1YUM
Jeffrey W Knox
350 Main St Apt 25
Spencer MA 01562

Call Sign: WA1DRZ
John F Cote Sr
17 May St
Spencer MA
015622220

Call Sign: N1RFX
Joseph S Gebo Jr
5 N Brookfield Rd
Spencer MA 01562

Call Sign: KA1ERF
Julia A Czajkowski
71 N Brookfield Rd
Spencer MA 01562

Call Sign: N1TZ
Robert J Czajkowski
71 N Brookfield Rd
Spencer MA 01562

Call Sign: KB1ARY
Peter L Sargent
108 Northwest Rd
Spencer MA 01562

Call Sign: KB1ARW
Aaron Hilsinger
102 Old E Charlton Rd
Spencer MA 01562

Call Sign: KB1FJS
John P Gagne
36 Old Farm Rd
Spencer MA 01562

Call Sign: WB1COM
Susan Meloche
2 Paxton Rd
Spencer MA 01562

Call Sign: W1MKO

Roger B Ela
227 Paxton Rd
Spencer MA 01562

Call Sign: KB1EKU
Dennis J Des Plaines
Sr
9 Pearl St
Spencer MA 01562

Call Sign: WF1X
Dennis J Des Plaines
Sr
9 Pearl St
Spencer MA 01562

Call Sign: N1ZKH
Pamela J Mikos
32 Prospect St
Spencer MA
015622570

Call Sign: KB1EEL
John D Zanauskas
111 S Spencer Rd
Spencer MA 01562

Call Sign: W1ERC
Roger A Lacaire
1 Salem St
Spencer MA 01562

Call Sign: K1JYE
Walter R Thurlow
22 Smithville Rd
Spencer MA 01562

Call Sign: N1FUE
Joseph B Shea
130 Smithville Rd
Spencer MA 01562

Call Sign: K1DUH
Martin P Lewis
12 Sunset Ln
Spencer MA 01562

Call Sign: KB1ARX
Daniel G Boquist
47 Temple St
Spencer MA 01562

Call Sign: KB1SAU
Patrick R O'malley

35 Thompson Pond Rd
Spencer MA 01562

Call Sign: KB1FJV
Sandra J Fritze
6 Vernon St
Spencer MA 01562

Call Sign: WB1FBZ
Christoph D Cavigioli
6 Watson St
Spencer MA 01562

Call Sign: N1GAE
Douglas E Shogren
5 Wilson Ave
Spencer MA 01562

Call Sign: WA1ZUR
William C Locke
9 Wilson St
Spencer MA 01562

Call Sign: KB1AEX
Paul J Braney Jr
Spencer MA 01562

Call Sign: W1NYF
Leslie L Swindell Sr
Spencer MA 01562

Call Sign: W1ZWL
John H Sluckis
Spencer MA 01562

Call Sign: KB1FJP
Joanne M Rice
Spencer MA
015620047

Call Sign: KA1RKZ
Bernard R Tatro Jr
Springfield MA 01101

Call Sign: KA1RTR
Juan A Rodriguez
Springfield MA 01107

Call Sign: N1LYF
Paul P Benoit

61 Acushnet Ave
Springfield MA 01105

Call Sign: KB1TSC
Ray A Millstein
89 Alden St
Springfield MA 01109

Call Sign: KB1IVG
Robert J Hassett
30 Archie St
Springfield MA 01109

Call Sign: KA1DCV
Donald L Farley Ii
907 Armory St
Springfield MA
011071283

Call Sign: WA1SDY
Donald L Farley
907 Armory St
Springfield MA
011071283

Call Sign: KB1JOP
Richard C Ericksberg
155 Ashbrook St
Springfield MA 01118

Call Sign: KB1WPJ
Andrew R Lafleur
115 Atwater Rd
Springfield MA 01107

Call Sign: NQ1C
Robert D Lafleur
115 Atwater Rd
Springfield MA
011071281

Call Sign: KC1ZJ
James C Davis
59 Baird Trace
Springfield MA 01118

Call Sign: NJ1U
Joseph E Brown
118 Balboa Dr
Springfield MA 01119

Call Sign: NM1U
Elaine R Brown
118 Balboa Dr

Springfield MA 01119

Call Sign: N1AHW
Carl D Prairie
40 Ballard Ave
Springfield MA 01119

Call Sign: N1ERB
Barbara E Prairie
40 Ballard Ave
Springfield MA 01119

Call Sign: KB1JVG
Katie L Melbourne
1451 Bay St
Springfield MA 01109

Call Sign: KA1AHR
Robert A Bluteau
1455 Bay St
Springfield MA 01109

Call Sign: KA1LPS
Donald W Wilson
1455 Bay St
Springfield MA 01109

Call Sign: KB1LCB
Jason F Kosek
684 Beacon Cir
Springfield MA 01119

Call Sign: KA1WLJ
Uyen T Vu
18 Beaumont Ter
Springfield MA 01108

Call Sign: KB1HJT
Allen R Demers
81 Bellamy Rd
Springfield MA 01119

Call Sign: KB1HOR
Pierre P Girard
97 Bellevue Ave
Springfield MA
011081792

Call Sign: N1MOD
Timothy J Lynch
115 Bellevue Ave
Springfield MA 01108

Call Sign: N1NBF

James R Targonski
34 Berard Cir
Springfield MA 01128

Call Sign: KA1OXM
Mary A Campana
25 Berard Circle
Springfield MA 01128

Call Sign: ND1K
Peter Campana
25 Berard Circle
Springfield MA 01128

Call Sign: KA1HZD
George A Jolly Sr
252 Berkshire Ave
Springfield MA 01109

Call Sign: KB1TBZ
Justin R Dandurand
64 Bessemer St
Springfield MA 01119

Call Sign: W1NUD
Jeffrey M Akley
76 Biltmore St
Springfield MA 01108

Call Sign: N1EPE
Lawrence A Lemoine
131 Birchland Ave
Springfield MA 01119

Call Sign: N1JJO
Diane F Lemoine
131 Birchland Ave
Springfield MA 01119

Call Sign: KB1VTF
Michael J Leclair
100 Blueberry Hill
Springfield MA 01128

Call Sign: N1ZIN
Elizabeth J Simpson
80 Brookside Cir
Springfield MA 01129

Call Sign: KA1VCU
John J Minto Sr
2 Buchholz St
Springfield MA 01109

Call Sign: W1NQG
Wesley J Andrews
53 Burns Ave
Springfield MA 01119

Call Sign: KB1RGI
Nicholas M Hudson
56 Burton St
Springfield MA 01108

Call Sign: KA1PHI
Pasquale M Lamagna
5 Butternut Circle
Springfield MA 01128

Call Sign: N1QHO
David F Piela Sr
453 Carew St
Springfield MA
011042306

Call Sign: N1AFX
George C Houldson
1619 Carew St
Springfield MA
011041403

Call Sign: W1RVW
Rollin E Pedersen
37 Castle St
Springfield MA 01118

Call Sign: K1BBC
James M Kane
Castlegate Drive
Springfield MA 01129

Call Sign: KB1HUN
David S Chambers
22 Chalfonte Dr
Springfield MA
011181854

Call Sign: KB2BUL
Lydia M Coss
10 Chestnut St 3006
Springfield MA 01103

Call Sign: N1XVQ
Lilly Fontanez
10 Chestnut St Apt
1907
Springfield MA 01103

Call Sign: KB1WPH
Peter A Nelson
414 Chestnut St Apt
224
Springfield MA 01104

Call Sign: KB2QZX
Marcos Hernandez
10 Chestnut St Apt
2807
Springfield MA 01103

Call Sign: N2MRL
Angel Hernandez Sr
10 Chestnut St Apt
2807
Springfield MA 01103

Call Sign: KA1LB
Paul H Turcotte
414 Chestnut St Apt
807
Springfield MA 01104

Call Sign: WP4NKW
Marisol Torres
Laureano
85 Cleveland St
Springfield MA
011042401

Call Sign: KA1UAH
John M Tillotson
107 Connecticut Ave
Springfield MA 01104

Call Sign: KB1DUW
Jack G Mc Ghee
17 Crismer Pl
Springfield MA
011091608

Call Sign: KP4JC
Juan Cruz
53 Crystal Ave
Springfield MA 01108

Call Sign: WB1CWF
Theodore B Gordon
45 Crystal Brook Dr
Springfield MA 01118

Call Sign: KB1WAO
Andrew A Vezis

53 Daviston St
Springfield MA 01108

Call Sign: K1AAV
Andrew A Vezis
53 Daviston St
Springfield MA 01108

Call Sign: KB1BPA
Hispanic Amateur
Society
105 Dickinson St
Springfield MA
011081226

Call Sign: W1NX
Ricardo Ramirez Sr
105 Dickinson St
Springfield MA
011081226

Call Sign: W1HAS
Hispanic Amateur
Society
105 Dickinson St
Springfield MA
011081226

Call Sign: K1ZKH
Donald E Leinhauser
46 Doyle Ave
Springfield MA 01104

Call Sign: N1URE
Laurence J Steiner
62 Druid Hill Rd
Springfield MA 01129

Call Sign: KB1HXP
William A Ulasewich
25 East St
Springfield MA 01104

Call Sign: KB1NGG
Anthony L Fiorentino
264 East St
Springfield MA 01104

Call Sign: KP4RCD
Roberto Carrasquillo Jr
8 Eddy St
Springfield MA 01104

Call Sign: W1SRM

Kenneth F De Celle
146 Eddy St
Springfield MA
011042633

Call Sign: W1KJB
Armand R Gamache
83 Eddywood St
Springfield MA 01118

Call Sign: N1XKM
Timothy A Di Rocco
278 Edendale St
Springfield MA 01104

Call Sign: KB1MQX
Wallace J Wight
23 Ellsworth Ave
Springfield MA 01118

Call Sign: W1WJW
Wallace J Wight
23 Ellsworth Ave
Springfield MA 01118

Call Sign: WD4RFS
Robert A Smith
209 Ellsworth Ave
Springfield MA 01118

Call Sign: KB1LEY
Gerald J Ducharme Sr
38 Eloise St
Springfield MA 01118

Call Sign: N1RAL
Daniel J Mc Kay
44 Eloise St
Springfield MA 01118

Call Sign: N1MFK
Scott Sokolowski
29 Endicott St
Springfield MA 01118

Call Sign: KB1NGH
Scott A Fairbanks
6 Etna Court
Springfield MA 01119

Call Sign: WA1TPP
Herbert A Belin
1 Fair Oak Rd
Springfield MA 01128

Call Sign: W1TPP
Herbert A Belin
1 Fair Oak Rd
Springfield MA 01128

Call Sign: W1XU
Herbert A Belin
1 Fair Oak Rd
Springfield MA 01128

Call Sign: KA1TAZ
Joseph P Henefield
26 Fairfield St
Springfield MA 01108

Call Sign: N1RUV
Carmelita Rodrigues
23 Felicia St
Springfield MA 01104

Call Sign: WB1GAK
Julius A Mc Combs
120 Fenwick St
Springfield MA 01109

Call Sign: N1ZFW
Paul M Garde
63 Flint St
Springfield MA 01129

Call Sign: N1LKC
Hans Van Der Leeden
43 Florentine Gardens
Springfield MA 01108

Call Sign: KB1NTP
Ronald R Campagna
54 Forest St
Springfield MA 01108

Call Sign: N1MOH
Edwin A Fett Jr
381 Gifford St
Springfield MA 01118

Call Sign: KB1HGH
Timothy J Davies
476 Gifford St
Springfield MA 01118

Call Sign: WB1BQQ
Emil Carlson Iii
66 Gilbert Ave

Springfield MA 01119

Call Sign: N3DYE
Charles G Larsen Sr
64 Gilman St
Springfield MA 01118

Call Sign: KB1UZV
Hector L Diaz
95 Girard Ave
Springfield MA 01109

Call Sign: N1JBP
John A Robertson
22 Gowey St
Springfield MA 01108

Call Sign: WA1EDN
James P Bagge
110 Gralia Dr
Springfield MA 01128

Call Sign: WB1GLN
Robert G Vezeau
116 Granger St
Springfield MA 01119

Call Sign: K1JAO
Leo R Comeau
830 Grayson Dr
Springfield MA 01119

Call Sign: KB1OWE
Bruce J Charpentier
82 Grover St
Springfield MA 01105

Call Sign: WP4KYR
Roberto Cancel
103 Grover St
Springfield MA
011042401

Call Sign: KB1ENI
John E Ladue
67 Hamilton St
Springfield MA 01119

Call Sign: KB1HHR
Ricarda K Ladue
67 Hamilton St
Springfield MA 01119

Call Sign: AA1YZ

John E Ladue
67 Hamilton St
Springfield MA 01119

Call Sign: N1EWT
Jeffrey A Whittemore
73 Hanson Dr
Springfield MA 01128

Call Sign: N1LKD
Daniel L Whittemore
73 Hanson Dr
Springfield MA 01128

Call Sign: N1VOM
Robert M Perusse
106 Hartwick St
Springfield MA 01108

Call Sign: NC1W
George W Sweatt
96 Helberg Rd
Springfield MA 01128

Call Sign: KA1KBL
William D Clarke
115 Hood St
Springfield MA 01109

Call Sign: N1NPE
Dennis W Chausse
16 Hunt St
Springfield MA 01108

Call Sign: N1MAS
Peter J Mc Kenzie
37 Ina
Springfield MA 01109

Call Sign: N1VSD
Ramon F Torres Jr
135 Ingersoll Grove
Springfield MA 01109

Call Sign: WA1PNE
Donald E Foster
69 Intervale Rd
Springfield MA 01118

Call Sign: N1LKI
James F Brochu
326 Island Pond Rd
Springfield MA 01118

Call Sign: W1NLE
Robert A Adolphson
90 Jeffrey Rd
Springfield MA 01119

Call Sign: N1XFJ
Martinho J Francisco
189 K Essex St
Springfield MA 01151

Call Sign: KB1HRQ
Tim L Wells
25 Katie Way
Springfield MA 01128

Call Sign: WA1QWS
Robert A Vander Vliet
154 Keddy St
Springfield MA 01109

Call Sign: KB1MWI
Roger P Duquette
216 Keddy St
Springfield MA 01109

Call Sign: N1AY
Wilbert V Porter
83 Kimberly Ave
Springfield MA 01101

Call Sign: KB1ALQ
Malaquias Contorreal
25 King St
Springfield MA 01109

Call Sign: KB1JFR
Robert W Cormier
41 Kipling St
Springfield MA 01118

Call Sign: WP4AZJ
Dionisio Ruiz Mercado
78 Leyfield Terr
Springfield MA 01108

Call Sign: N1INO
Michael D Rivers
28 Leyfred Ter
Springfield MA 01108

Call Sign: WA1LES
Joseph P Chistolini
1086 Liberty St

Springfield MA
011041122

Call Sign: KB1BXL
Robert E Guyotte
167 Louis Rd
Springfield MA 01118

Call Sign: KB1VGA
Gerald H Russell Jr
18 Lumae St
Springfield MA 01119

Call Sign: KA1QCV
Steven C Piubeni
84 Lumae St
Springfield MA 01119

Call Sign: KA1TZG
Linda M Piubeni
84 Lumae St
Springfield MA 01119

Call Sign: KB1OPW
Blaine F Forbort
27 Lyman St Apt -104
Springfield MA 01103

Call Sign: KB1OPZ
Arthur E Von
Marschall
27 Lyman St- D104
Springfield MA 01103

Call Sign: KA1HME
Dennis J Dowling Jr
25 Lynebrook Rd
Springfield MA 01118

Call Sign: N1YQS
Kenneth S Robbins
50 Macomber Ave
Springfield MA 01119

Call Sign: KB6CBE
Chong T Lee Sr
1567 Main St
Springfield MA 01103

Call Sign: W1POM
Robert P Flanagan
48 Manchester Ter
Springfield MA 01108

Call Sign: KD1QJ
Randy G Spaulding
118 Manchester Ter
Springfield MA 01108

Call Sign: WM1P
Donald L Le May Sr
20 Manhattan St
Springfield MA 01109

Call Sign: NP3HK
Jose A Rodriguez
Rodriguez
303 Maple St Apt C-38
Springfield MA 01105

Call Sign: N1NEI
Michael W Porter
82 Mapledell St
Springfield MA 01109

Call Sign: KA1RAR
Chester D Palmer
8 Meredith St
Springfield MA 01108

Call Sign: NE1Q
Raymond W Mazza
14 Meredith St
Springfield MA 01108

Call Sign: N1VHB
Ginette M Veilleux
238 Merrimac Ave
Springfield MA 01104

Call Sign: KB1HOG
Nels E Huuskonen
52 Methuen St
Springfield MA 01119

Call Sign: WB1DKG
George L Hartmann Iii
141 Mill St
Springfield MA 01108

Call Sign: KB1KDF
Henrik Glockenberg
14 Milton St
Springfield MA 01151

Call Sign: KB1DMC
Robert S Powell Ii
34 Mohawk Dr

Springfield MA
011292040

Call Sign: KB1QWM
Michael H Thomes
101 Mulberry St
Springfield MA 01105

Call Sign: KB2UZY
Bryan F Torres
19 Mystic St
Springfield MA 01104

Call Sign: N1AV
Osman J Ladue
631 Newbury St
Springfield MA 01104

Call Sign: KF4PRL
Francis K Le
95 Newfield Rd
Springfield MA 01119

Call Sign: KB1RNG
Gary J Warner
34 Noel St
Springfield MA 01108

Call Sign: N1DPJ
Neil A Martelli
45 Nokomis St
Springfield MA 01109

Call Sign: KB1HEM
Dennis F Pimental
49 Northway Dr
Springfield MA 01119

Call Sign: NA1W
Alan A Carpin
184 Nottingham St
Springfield MA
011042617

Call Sign: KB1AZ
Frank J Piatek
814 Parker St
Springfield MA 01129

Call Sign: N1NYF
Angel A Diaz Jr
60 Partridge Drive
Springfield MA 01119

Call Sign: KB1NNR
Thomas A Tremblay
58 Patricia Circle
Springfield MA 01119

Call Sign: KX1F
Lawrence D Savoy
51 Pine Hill Rd
Springfield MA 01118

Call Sign: N1ZXJ
Robert H Isabelle
4 Pioneer Way
Springfield MA
011191720

Call Sign: KA1CAX
Francis J De Santis
1280 Plumtree Rd
Springfield MA 01119

Call Sign: KA1DNX
Leslie W Prentice
1472 Plumtree Rd
Springfield MA 01119

Call Sign: K1DNX
Leslie W Prentice
1472 Plumtree Rd
Springfield MA
011192965

Call Sign: KP4CMR
Carlos Mendez Ramos
97 Putnam Cir
Springfield MA 01104

Call Sign: AB1NR
Carlos Mendez Ramos
97 Putnam Cir
Springfield MA 01104

Call Sign: KQ1C
Carlos Mendez Ramos
97 Putnam Cir
Springfield MA 01104

Call Sign: KP4MHG
Maria R Hernandez
Gonzalez
97 Putnam Circle
Springfield MA 01104

Call Sign: KA1OTW

Frank T Chidsey Jr
46 Randolph St
Springfield MA 01108

Call Sign: N1WNF
James J Martin
55 Redlands St
Springfield MA 01104

Call Sign: KB1NOY
Joyce A Lane
243 Redlands St
Springfield MA
011042134

Call Sign: KB1MWH
Roy D Lane
243 Redlands St
Springfield MA
011042134

Call Sign: N1CCC
Michael R Dulac
41 Riverview St
Springfield MA
011081634

Call Sign: KB1ALV
Eugene J Miller
50 Rochford Cir
Springfield MA 01128

Call Sign: N1TGA
Nicholas J Cannata
460 Roosevelt Ave
Springfield MA 01118

Call Sign: KB1PQZ
Basil C Maurice
1475 Roosevelt Ave
Apt 510
Springfield MA 01109

Call Sign: N1ONU
Fred W Foss
79 Rosella St
Springfield MA 01118

Call Sign: WF1Z
Anthony M Renaud
27 Rutledge Ave
Springfield MA 01105

Call Sign: K1SUD

Robert J Mayo
323 S Branch Pkwy
Springfield MA
011181304

Call Sign: WA1SCW
Thomas J Wolos
1139 Saint James Ave
Springfield MA 01104

Call Sign: WA1WXS
Donald K Duval
68 Scarsdale Rd
Springfield MA 01129

Call Sign: KB1MKF
Donald L Stebbins
15 Shamrock St
Springfield MA 01108

Call Sign: N1WNX
Richard L Stebbins
83 Skyridge Drive
Springfield MA 01128

Call Sign: N1SIO
Hisham Guess
28 Southern Rd
Springfield MA 01129

Call Sign: WA1IKO
Ivan J Romashko
279 Springfield St
Springfield MA 01107

Call Sign: KP4EAZ
John A Davison
435 Springfield St
Springfield MA 01107

Call Sign: KB1AKV
Michelle L Joubert
722 St James Ave
Springfield MA 01104

Call Sign: KD1MP
Christopher J Joubert
722 St James Ave
Springfield MA 01104

Call Sign: KG1S
Ronald A Joubert
722 St James Ave

Springfield MA
011042803

Call Sign: N1RKX
Paul Morrissey Sr
54 Starling Rd
Springfield MA 01119

Call Sign: KB1WUH
Gene A Gamble
937 State St Apt 431
Springfield MA 01109

Call Sign: N1OIF
Elvis S Berrios Sr
44 Suffolk St
Springfield MA 01109

Call Sign: N1RHW
C Tom Sawyer
193 Sumner Ave
Springfield MA 01108

Call Sign: KA1NVC
Jules G Fredey Jr
659 Sumner Ave
Springfield MA 01108

Call Sign: W9RJL
Merle W Jacobson
36 Sunbrier Rd
Springfield MA 01129

Call Sign: N1CQT
Albert J Drake
114 Sunrise Ter
Springfield MA 01119

Call Sign: N1MOG
John F Kowinski
40 Swan Hill Dr
Springfield MA 01129

Call Sign: N1ARX
Dennis P Badger
207 Talmadge Dr
Springfield MA 01118

Call Sign: KA1WKR
Francis X Asselin
79 Tavistock St
Springfield MA 01119

Call Sign: KA1DAR

Raymond A Pauze
94 Thornfell St
Springfield MA
011041133

Call Sign: N1LFX
Frederick H D Amato
220 Tiffany St
Springfield MA 01108

Call Sign: KB1PKJ
Michael S Lavery
88 Tioga St
Springfield MA 01128

Call Sign: KB1UUN
Virginia J Lavery
88 Tioga St
Springfield MA 01128

Call Sign: N1VOB
James G Mc Grath
107 Tioga St
Springfield MA 01128

Call Sign: KB1DWU
Daniel L Blessington
159 Trafton Rd
Springfield MA 01108

Call Sign: N1PF
Norman P Forest
36 Valley Rd
Springfield MA 01119

Call Sign: N1NNE
Norbert R Davignon
26 W Canton Cir
Springfield MA 01104

Call Sign: AA1DM
Eugene V Albright Sr
74 Walnut St Apt 421
Springfield MA 01105

Call Sign: KB1FYT
Jesse L Rein
100 Walsh St
Springfield MA 01109

Call Sign: N1GEY
Paul R Campagna
118 Washington Rd
Springfield MA 01108

Call Sign: KB1DEW
Steven A Metivier
93 West Canton Circle
Springfield MA 01104

Call Sign: N1FVP
John A Krull
35 Westbrook Dr
Springfield MA
011292025

Call Sign: N1FYU
Robert E Chandler Sr
508 Wilbraham Rd
Springfield MA 01109

Call Sign: KF4ZLR
Richard D Mahaffey
1976 Wilbraham Rd
Springfield MA 01129

Call Sign: KB1MXM
Michael S Bullington
216 Wildwood Ave
Springfield MA 01118

Call Sign: N1FCQ
Susan M Rheaume
17 Willowbrook Dr
Springfield MA 01129

Call Sign: WZ1I
James P Kearney
119 Windemere St
Springfield MA 01104

Call Sign: KB1KYK
Daniel T Beaven
152 Windemere St
Springfield MA 01104

Call Sign: KB1TEU
Curtis E Gibson
108 Wollaston St
Springfield MA 01119

Call Sign: N1FOP
Sylvester Jamieson
5 Woodland Rd
Springfield MA 01129

Call Sign: K1PQR
Robert E Bohn

126 Woodlawn St
Springfield MA 01108

Call Sign: KB1TPW
Emmett Anderson Jr
86 Woodruff St
Springfield MA 01109

Call Sign: AB1LV
Emmett Anderson Jr
86 Woodruff St
Springfield MA 01109

Call Sign: WA1PLS
Edward M Goldberg
29 Woodside Ter
Springfield MA
011081624

Call Sign: W1TXS
Richard E Downing
16 Woodside Terr
Springfield MA
011081625

Call Sign: KA3KSX
Brenda L Klingensmith
43 Wrenwood St
Springfield MA 01119

Call Sign: N1PLX
Caren D Mc Kenzie
Springfield MA 01139

Call Sign: KA1RUV
Julio C Ramirez
Springfield MA
011011863

Call Sign: W1TOM
Mount Tom Amateur
Repeater Assn Inc
Springfield MA 01101

Call Sign: KB1ILM
South Mountain
Contest Club
Springfield MA 01101

Call Sign: WP4FCC
Magda E Bonilla
Springfield MA 01138

Call Sign: KB1VCT

Massachusetts
Hispanic Dx Club
Springfield MA 01138

Call Sign: NK1Y
Massachusetts
Hispanic Dx Club
Springfield MA 01138

Call Sign: KP4EC
Enrique (Carlos) Ruiz
Springfield MA 01138

Call Sign: KB1NL
Lincoln S Berkley
62 Bay St
Squantum MA 02171

Call Sign: N1JOU
Jay M Tarantino
781 East Squantum St
Apt 3
Squantum MA 02171

Call Sign: K1VKX
Walter J Wigmore
110 Standish Rd
Squantum MA 02171

Call Sign: W1HFN
Barry W Fox
101 Albright Rd
Sterling MA 01564

Call Sign: KD1LV
Reid A Squier
4 Beaman Rd
Sterling MA 01564

Call Sign: W1UEO
Francis W Kendall
4 Bird St
Sterling MA 01564

Call Sign: KD1DM
Peter H Johnson
32 Chace Hill Rd
Sterling MA 01564

Call Sign: K1PAL
Peter A Lothian
7 Gates Terrace
Sterling MA 01564

Call Sign: K1SCP
William F Quinn
6 James Patten Dr Box
354
Sterling MA 01564

Call Sign: KB1AGV
David M Vaughn
39 Jewett Rd
Sterling MA 01564

Call Sign: KA1WET
Yeasah G Pell
176 Justice Hill Cutoff
Sterling MA 01564

Call Sign: WA1ZYU
Alan F Rux
171 Justice Hill Cutoff
Rd
Sterling MA 01565

Call Sign: W1HQA
John J Goullis
20 N Cove Rd
Sterling MA 01564

Call Sign: KB1LOR
Mark L Kerrigan
86 Osgood Rd
Sterling MA 01564

Call Sign: KB1UXH
Mary A Larrousse
107 Osgood Rd
Sterling MA 01564

Call Sign: N2UEG
Joseph A Walker Iv
Po Box 183
Sterling MA 01564

Call Sign: WW6A
Byron E Brumbaugh
77 Redstone Hill Rd
Sterling MA 01564

Call Sign: W1TC

Thomas E Chase
65 S Nelson Rd
Sterling MA 01564

Call Sign: KB1GZG
Daniel W Patterson
31 Taft Rd
Sterling MA 01564

Call Sign: WB1FNI
Steven C Fuller
3 Tuttle Rd
Sterling MA 01564

Call Sign: KD1TO
Kenneth S Miller
177 Upper North Row
Rd
Sterling MA 01564

Call Sign: N1PJ
John P Howe Jr
10 Walnut Dr
Sterling MA 01564

Call Sign: WB2ISQ
Robert A Brown
Sterling MA 01564

Call Sign: KB1ISB
John Manning
Sterling MA 01564

Call Sign: KD5WBY
Robert M Doherty
Sterling MA 01564

Call Sign: KB1TSV
Joseph Fernandez
Sterling MA 01564

Call Sign: KB1TTY
Steven C Fuller
Sterling MA 01564

FCC Amateur Radio Licenses in Sterling Junction

Call Sign: KA1FXP
Sherman L Hill
13 Myrtle Ave
Sterling Junction MA
01565

Call Sign: K1QQI
Howard J Besnia
57 Swett Hill Rd
Sterling Junction MA
015641524

FCC Amateur Radio Licenses in Still River

Call Sign: W1SBC
Saint Benedict Center
Amateur Radio Club
265 Still River Rd
Still River MA 01467

Call Sign: KB1CFA
Anthony T Brackett
282 Still River Rd
Still River MA 01467

Call Sign: W1WO
George W Randig
Still River MA 01467

FCC Amateur Radio Licenses in Stockbridge

Call Sign: N1NDG
Ronald L Muir Jr
33 Church St Box 774
Stockbridge MA
012620774

Call Sign: WT2Q
Robert Tublitz
Stockbridge MA 01262

Call Sign: N1ETB
Robert A Andenmatten
Stockbridge MA 01262

Call Sign: N1TU
Berkshire Amateur
Radio Club
Stockbridge MA 01262

Call Sign: KB1HAB
Berkshire Amateur
Radio Club
Stockbridge MA 01262

Call Sign: N1TU

Berkshire Amateur
Radio Club
Stockbridge MA 01262

Call Sign: KB1TWQ
Franklin L Ripley
Stockbridge MA 01262

FCC Amateur Radio Licenses in Stoneham

Call Sign: W3PYF
Melvin A Snyder
10 Albion Ave
Stoneham MA 02180

Call Sign: KA1IN
Alexander H Janko
25 Beacon St
Stoneham MA 02180

Call Sign: N1YVN
Philip E Donovan
15 Bear Hill Rd
Stoneham MA 02180

Call Sign: K1HMV
Raymond L Sorenson
31 Bear Hill Rd
Stoneham MA 02180

Call Sign: W1FNO
Alfred Taddeo
20 Bonad Rd
Stoneham MA 02180

Call Sign: K1CNG
Raffaele J Pisaturo
5 Brook St
Stoneham MA 02176

Call Sign: N1MSF
Karen B Russell
50 Butler Ave
Stoneham MA 02180

Call Sign: WA1HUD
Stephen H Russell
50 Butler Ave
Stoneham MA 02180

Call Sign: KB1UNS

New England
Historical Radio
Society
50 Butler Ave
Stoneham MA 02180

Call Sign: W1WNE
New England
Historical Radio
Society
50 Butler Ave
Stoneham MA 02180

Call Sign: WW2DD
Uss Cassin Young
Amateur Radio Club
50 Butler Ave
Stoneham MA 02180

Call Sign: N1SBQ
David F Palermo
12 Cedar Ave
Stoneham MA 02180

Call Sign: WA1TQQ
Guy S Quartarone
14 Cedar Way
Stoneham MA 02180

Call Sign: W1OL
Guy S Quartarone
14 Cedar Way
Stoneham MA 02180

Call Sign: K1BIL
Violet M Graham
24 Cherry Ave
Stoneham MA 02180

Call Sign: N1KKF
Samuel L Krakow
12 Clearview Rd
Stoneham MA 02180

Call Sign: W1ZLG
John Moran
120 Collincote St
Stoneham MA 02180

Call Sign: KB1UYM
John Silvestro Jr
23 Dewitt Rd
Stoneham MA 02180

Call Sign: W1EYZ
George R Ringland
24 Drury Ln
Stoneham MA 02180

Call Sign: W1OQF
George M Rich
20 Duncklee Ave
Stoneham MA
021804500

Call Sign: NN1O
John M Foley
13 East St
Stoneham MA 02180

Call Sign: KB1IAF
Dennis A Stevens
17 Elmhurst Rd
Stoneham MA
021801247

Call Sign: W1TAN
Dennis A Stevens
17 Elmhurst Rd
Stoneham MA
021801247

Call Sign: KA1WXV
Richard A Morris Jr
1 Elwood Ave
Stoneham MA 02180

Call Sign: W1OPT
John A Prusak
16 Emerald Ct
Stoneham MA 02180

Call Sign: WA1CUQ
David R Adamson
9 Fatima Rd
Stoneham MA 02180

Call Sign: KA1EEQ
Robert L Harrington
15 Flint Ave
Stoneham MA 02180

Call Sign: KB1LCI
Brian A Gudzevich
83 Franklin St
Stoneham MA
021801847

Call Sign: WO1VES
Brian A Gudzevich
83 Franklin St
Stoneham MA
021801847

Call Sign: KA1RMF
Ronald H Crooker
116 Franklin St
Stoneham MA 02180

Call Sign: KB1FJM
Mark D De Lellis
7 Hall Rd
Stoneham MA 02180

Call Sign: K1DEL
Mark D De Lellis
7 Hall Rd
Stoneham MA 02180

Call Sign: KB1FJM
Mark D De Lellis
7 Hall Rd
Stoneham MA 02180

Call Sign: K1DIX
Richard L Watts
35 Hancock St
Stoneham MA 02180

Call Sign: K1PKX
Robert D Shediac Sr
48 High St
Stoneham MA 02180

Call Sign: KV1U
Ormsby L Court
101 High St
Stoneham MA 02180

Call Sign: KA1ASP
William R Allen Jr
5 Kirmes Rd
Stoneham MA 02180

Call Sign: KB1MVJ
Brenda T Barbour
7 Ledge St
Stoneham MA 02180

Call Sign: WA1PII
Lawrence V Keegan
46 Mac Arthur Rd

Stoneham MA 02180

Call Sign: KB1ALR
Dalton J Acosta
393 Main St
Stoneham MA 02180

Call Sign: W1AUO
Francis T Arena
601 Main St
Stoneham MA 02180

Call Sign: N1NXT
Phil Taylor
2 Main St Ate 320
Stoneham MA 02180

Call Sign: N1KLL
James D Cryan
44 Maple St
Stoneham MA 02180

Call Sign: N1KQN
Michael G Cryan
44 Maple St
Stoneham MA 02180

Call Sign: KB1HBM
James D Cryan
44 Maple St
Stoneham MA 02180

Call Sign: N1RWP
Salvatore V Calabro
91 Marble St
Stoneham MA 02180

Call Sign: AB1FV
Thomas M
Thorndycraft
109 Marble St   Apt 8
Stoneham MA 02180

Call Sign: KB1FEB
Thomas M
Thorndycraft
109 Marble St Apt 8
Stoneham MA 02180

Call Sign: AB1FU
Thomas M
Thorndycraft
109 Marble St Apt 8
Stoneham MA 02180

Call Sign: W1EW
John J Johnston
7 Marie Ave
Stoneham MA 02180

Call Sign: N1IRR
Ronald B
Dombrowsky
100 Mountain View Dr
412
Stoneham MA 02180

Call Sign: K1GVW
David L Thorley
67 Oak St
Stoneham MA 02180

Call Sign: KB1OSK
David A Medeiros
70 Park Ave
Stoneham MA 02180

Call Sign: AB1IB
David A Medeiros
70 Park Ave
Stoneham MA 02180

Call Sign: ND1G
David A Medeiros
70 Park Ave
Stoneham MA 02180

Call Sign: KB1PFQ
Prentesse G O'gorman
23 Park St - 1
Stoneham MA 02180

Call Sign: KA1TQT
David J Hartnett
14 Perkins St
Stoneham MA 02180

Call Sign: KB1FQA
Trudy C Sevier
4 Philips Rd
Stoneham MA
021804424

Call Sign: W1DKC
Fred E Sevier
4 Phillips Rd
Stoneham MA 02180

Call Sign: KW1P
Carl M Smith
24 Rowe Hill Rd
Stoneham MA 02180

Call Sign: WA1WSI
John R Pineau
16 Seward Rd
Stoneham MA 02180

Call Sign: KB1JKK
Jennifer B Black
5 Sheridan Rd
Stoneham MA 02180

Call Sign: N1LPZ
Andrew C Black
5 Sheridan Rd
Stoneham MA 02180

Call Sign: WB1APK
Dante V Consalvo
7 Stonehill Dr Apt 4f
Stoneham MA 02180

Call Sign: K1CQL
Charles R Lombardi Sr
23 Sunrise Ave
Stoneham MA
021803048

Call Sign: KB1UAC
Russell E Wilson
35 Tamarock Terrace
Stoneham MA 02180

Call Sign: W3PET
Patrick M Shields
41 Upland Rd
Stoneham MA 02180

Call Sign: W1TOD
John R Halchak
10 Victoria
Stoneham MA 02180

Call Sign: N1IRG
Jerome J Kaufman Ii
295 W Wyoming Ave
3c
Stoneham MA 02180

Call Sign: N1EGF
Mark A Eramo

51 Walsh Ave
Stoneham MA 02180

Call Sign: N1HID
Richard A Meuse
26 Washington Ave
Stoneham MA 02180

Call Sign: K1YPB
Daniel P Zdanowicz
28 Waverly St
Stoneham MA
021801615

Call Sign: KA2NJK
Carla M Zdanowicz
28 Waverly St
Stoneham MA
021801615

Call Sign: KA1OFD
Joseph B Boyd
5 Woodland Rd
Stoneham MA 02180

Call Sign: KB1QML
Jessica M Dipietro
10 Perkins St
Stonehem MA 02180

**FCC Amateur Radio
Licenses in Stoughton**

Call Sign: KB1KCO
Harold W Curtis Jr
108 Ash St
Stoughton MA 02072

Call Sign: W1AYW
Paul O Litchfield
72 Bassick Cir
Stoughton MA 02072

Call Sign: KB1BWM
Stoughton High School
Radio Club
806 Bay Rd
Stoughton MA 02072

Call Sign: KB1HLS
Thomas H Grimsley
1308 Bay Rd
Stoughton MA
020723959

Call Sign: N1JXS
Alan H Molin
85 Birch St
Stoughton MA 02072

Call Sign: N1LRI
Judith I Thompson
56 Blackstone St
Stoughton MA 02072

Call Sign: WX1I
George W Thompson
56 Blackstone St
Stoughton MA 02072

Call Sign: K1GRB
Arthur M Kullen
Box 575
Stoughton MA 02072

Call Sign: WA1DWU
Richard J Juskewicz
156 Brickel Rd
Stoughton MA 02072

Call Sign: KB1OMX
Steve A Mark
44 Brookdale Rd
Stoughton MA 02072

Call Sign: K1SMK
Steve A Mark
44 Brookdale Rd
Stoughton MA 02072

Call Sign: KC1H
Steve A Mark
44 Brookdale Rd
Stoughton MA 02072

Call Sign: N1GQ
Charles Costa Jr
184 Cedar St
Stoughton MA 02072

Call Sign: WB1GQO
Pamela J Costa
184 Cedar St
Stoughton MA 02072

Call Sign: KB1TML
Tracey J Oliver
8 Central St

Stoughton MA 02072

Call Sign: KB1HKI
David J Walsh
52 Central St
Stoughton MA 02072

Call Sign: KB1INM
Maryann L Walsh
52 Central St
Stoughton MA 02072

Call Sign: KA1ALS
Edward A Rudis
569 Central St
Stoughton MA 02072

Call Sign: N1HFA
Christopher D Giffin
1402 Central St
Stoughton MA 02072

Call Sign: N1BSJ
Edward S Starr
99 Charles Cir
Stoughton MA 02072

Call Sign: KB1WCL
Fred S Minsker
129 Chemung St
Stoughton MA 02072

Call Sign: N1VER
Harvey R Weisthal
30 Copperwood Dr
Stoughton MA 02072

Call Sign: KB1PFE
Andrey Kuklin
90 Cottonwood Dr
Stoughton MA 02072

Call Sign: N1JDH
Paul E Krueger
33 Darling Way
Stoughton MA 02072

Call Sign: KA1EKE
Raymond W
Kirchdorfer
24 Doty Dr
Stoughton MA 02072

Call Sign: N1KLV

Eileen M Kirchdorfer
24 Doty Dr
Stoughton MA 02072

Call Sign: KA1EU
Victor L Bernotas
104 E Vanston Rd
Stoughton MA 02072

Call Sign: WB1DEM
Walter J Mac Donald
Jr
41 Ellsworth Ave
Stoughton MA 02072

Call Sign: KB1KKD
Edward M Eidelman
394 Erin Rd
Stoughton MA 02072

Call Sign: N1UPY
Ronald J Dardano
11 Farnham Rd
Stoughton MA 02072

Call Sign: KA1PGU
Robert F Schillinger
29 Farrington St
Stoughton MA 02072

Call Sign: KA1DJB
De Wolf Merriam
24 Greg Rd
Stoughton MA 02072

Call Sign: N1PWI
John F Corbett
326 Highland St
Stoughton MA 02072

Call Sign: N1WII
Ricahrd J Bown
34 Howland Ter
Stoughton MA 02072

Call Sign: W1HVR
Max W Clere
6 Jessica Dr
Stoughton MA 02072

Call Sign: WA1ZZX
Leonard H Westbrook
24 Kelsey Dr
Stoughton MA 02072

Call Sign: KB1LND
Jared M Lindros
49 King St
Stoughton MA 02072

Call Sign: N1CAD
Roy E Rathbun
415 Lincoln St
Stoughton MA 02072

Call Sign: KA1QZJ
Daniels E Allan
159 Lowe Ave
Stoughton MA 02072

Call Sign: WA1YXR
Arthur Stepner
50 Mahoney Ave
Stoughton MA 02072

Call Sign: WA1EEC
Robert W Hanna
68 Marron Ave
Stoughton MA 02072

Call Sign: KA1G
David P Konigsberg
10 Mc Namara St
Stoughton MA 02072

Call Sign: KN1J
Koichi Nakase
450 Morton St
Stoughton MA 02072

Call Sign: KB1CVM
Raffaele Sellitto
553 Morton St
Stoughton MA 02072

Call Sign: K1CVM
Raffaele Sellitto
553 Morton St
Stoughton MA 02072

Call Sign: W1MQX
John Hanko
86 Packard Rd
Stoughton MA
020721817

Call Sign: N1OIT
Jeffrey B Wallace

449 Page St
Stoughton MA 02072

Call Sign: KB1JTS
Eamonn G Roddy
701 Park St
Stoughton MA 02072

Call Sign: KB1OXZ
Richard W Friberg Sr
941 Park St
Stoughton MA 02072

Call Sign: W1ASM
Richard W Friberg Sr
941 Park St
Stoughton MA 02072

Call Sign: K1JNQ
Sharon Amateur Radio
Assn
1219 Park St
Stoughton MA 02072

Call Sign: WA1WUV
Walter P Bjornson
1219 Park St
Stoughton MA 02072

Call Sign: WB1CFX
Joan C Bjornson
1219 Park St
Stoughton MA 02072

Call Sign: WA1AEU
Edward J Ross
10 Patricia Dr
Stoughton MA
020721223

Call Sign: N1CJZ
Dolores B Goldstone
29 Patricia Dr
Stoughton MA 02072

Call Sign: W1TEA
Stanley Goldstone
29 Patricia Dr
Stoughton MA 02072

Call Sign: KB1FHR
Jose M Dacosta
22 Pearl St
Stoughton MA 02072

Call Sign: N1HJU
Binney F Stone
215 Pearl St #9
Stoughton MA
020722342

Call Sign: N1VCF
Michael L Comella
215 Pearl St 7
Stoughton MA 02072

Call Sign: W1MMM
Robert W Sikes
32 Perry St
Stoughton MA 02072

Call Sign: WB1COJ
Michael C Swiderski
52 Pine St
Stoughton MA
020721825

Call Sign: KA1CJC
Frank Gola
342 Plain St
Stoughton MA 02072

Call Sign: KA1FJL
Robert G Cushing Sr
528 Plain St
Stoughton MA 02072

Call Sign: WB1ANM
Harry Burtman
52 Pond View Lane
Stoughton MA
020720387

Call Sign: N1LP
Lourenco R Pires
97 Poskus St
Stoughton MA 02072

Call Sign: N1OIR
Richard J Smith
75 Ralph Mann Dr
Stoughton MA 02072

Call Sign: N1BFP
Gary H Saffer
6 Roach Rd
Stoughton MA
020723334

Call Sign: N1YEG
Cindy C America
172 Rogers Dr
Stoughton MA 02072

Call Sign: K1VNU
Richard Carbone
10 Simpson St
Stoughton MA 02072

Call Sign: N1YGQ
Jon M Christopher
33 Springwood Ave
Stoughton MA 02072

Call Sign: KB1OAW
Gregory R Noyes
981 Sumner St
Stoughton MA 02072

Call Sign: KB1OAY
Daniel Noyes
981 Sumner St
Stoughton MA 02072

Call Sign: K1CPV
Richard P Freeman
105 Swanson Ter
Stoughton MA 02072

Call Sign: KB1OOH
Lawrence Pellegrini
210 Third St
Stoughton MA 02072

Call Sign: W1FRZ
Donald E Hinds
329 Walnut St
Stoughton MA 02072

Call Sign: WA1INY
Anthony N Petta
30 Wellesley Rd
Stoughton MA 02072

Call Sign: WA1LKG
Barbara A Petta
30 Wellesley Rd
Stoughton MA 02072

Call Sign: KD1PY
James E Lewis
362 West St

Stoughton MA 02072

Call Sign: KC2OJB
Eric D Stone
29 Wheeler Cir # 184
Stoughton MA 02072

Call Sign: AA1WO
Mark E Bronson
42 Wheeler Cir Apt 38
Stoughton MA 02072

Call Sign: N1YIB
Marc A Siciliano
56 Woodbine Rd
Stoughton MA 02072

Call Sign: N1ANS
Charles J Sheputa
82 Woodbine Rd
Stoughton MA
020721755

Call Sign: WA1VJR
Michael E Lynch
150 York St Rm 240
Stoughton MA 02072

FCC Amateur Radio Licenses in Stow

Call Sign: WB1GLD
Kurt P Schwan
29 Apple Blossom Ln
Stow MA 01775

Call Sign: K4EH
Oscar E Sanden
18 Arbor Glen Drive
Stow MA 01775

Call Sign: W1IMQ
Thomas M French
151 Barton Rd
Stow MA 01775

Call Sign: AB1JQ
Fabio Bonucci
151 Barton Rd
Stow MA 01775

Call Sign: K3QS
Fabio Bonucci
151 Barton Rd

Stow MA 01775

Call Sign: K0IXI
Fabio Bonucci
151 Barton Rd
Stow MA 01775

Call Sign: NB1V
Fabio Bonucci
151 Barton Rd
Stow MA 01775

Call Sign: KF1B
Fabio Bonucci
151 Barton Rd
Stow MA 01775

Call Sign: KB1HKN
Dirk H Hart
174 Barton Rd
Stow MA 01775

Call Sign: WG1V
Carl D Howe
27 Birch Hill Rd
Stow MA 01775

Call Sign: WA1IAI
Leonard F Halio
32 Birch Hill Rd
Stow MA 01775

Call Sign: W1IS
Robert M Glorioso
70 Birch Hill Rd
Stow MA 017751307

Call Sign: W1MGA
L Deanne Glorioso
70 Birch Hill Rd
Stow MA 017751307

Call Sign: K1QAR
Theodore N Robinson
Boxboro Rd
Stow MA 01775

Call Sign: KB1MBW
Richard S Sproul
12 Bradley Ln
Stow MA 01775

Call Sign: KB1PVI
Thomas J Coughlin Jr

9 Brookmill Rd
Stow MA 01775

Call Sign: KB1VC
Matthew H Reilly
7 Conant Dr
Stow MA 01775

Call Sign: N5CQU
John P Wendler Jr
22 Cross St
Stow MA 01775

Call Sign: KB1OUW
Rene F Doucette
2 Dawes Rd
Stow MA 01775

Call Sign: K1YT
William S Ewing
14 Dunster Dr
Stow MA 01775

Call Sign: WA1AOS
Joseph J Passafiume
29 Dunster Dr
Stow MA 01775

Call Sign: W1UAX
George R Cogswell Jr
33 Edgehill Rd
Stow MA 01775

Call Sign: W1AJW
George R Cogswell Jr
33 Edgehill Rd
Stow MA 017751407

Call Sign: N1JAH
John G Mc Carthy
80 Edgehill Rd
Stow MA 01775

Call Sign: N1JYK
John E Grundy
39 Edson St
Stow MA 017751228

Call Sign: WB1AKB
Peter M Barmakian
324 Gleasondale Rd
Stow MA 01775

Call Sign: W1SPP

Peter M Barmakian
324 Gleasondale Rd
Stow MA 01775

Call Sign: KB1MNQ
Duncan Amos
414 Gleasondale Rd
Stow MA 01775

Call Sign: KB1MNR
Barrett Amos
414 Gleasondale Rd
Stow MA 01775

Call Sign: KA1WZP
Lindol A French
350 Great Rd
Stow MA 01775

Call Sign: AI3E
Dwight Sipler
493 Great Rd
Stow MA 017751055

Call Sign: KB8INO
Rose A Persichetti
375 Harvard Rd
Stow MA 01775

Call Sign: N1MWE
Thomas C Vales
21 High St
Stow MA 01775

Call Sign: WA1QXJ
Maila E Clayton
210 Hudson Rd
Stow MA 01775

Call Sign: WA1QXK
William E Clayton
210 Hudson Rd
Stow MA 01775

Call Sign: KC6KJB
Lynne E Sauta
218 Hudson Rd
Stow MA 01775

Call Sign: KJ6EP
Gregory A Bassett
218 Hudson Rd
Stow MA 01775

Call Sign: N1OGW
James V Sauta
218 Hudson St
Stow MA 01775

Call Sign: KB1LWA
Brent R Midwood
32 Kirkland Dr
Stow MA 01775

Call Sign: KB1TGP
Sarah L Hart
174 Marton Rd
Stow MA 01775

Call Sign: W1HLQ
Robert C Mong
94 Old Bolton Rd
Stow MA 01775

Call Sign: WA9ANK
George E Peo Jr
111 Old Bolton Rd
Stow MA 01775

Call Sign: KJ1T
Milton E Stymiest
72 Packard Rd
Stow MA 01775

Call Sign: KC1RP
Michael P Jordan
166 Packard Rd
Stow MA 01775

Call Sign: N1JKH
Leslie A Miller
166 Packard Rd
Stow MA 01775

Call Sign: WA1CYB
Raymond A Roberge
73 Peabody Dr
Stow MA 01775

Call Sign: N3PYV
David M Gray
12 Pine Point Rd
Stow MA 01775

Call Sign: N3PYW
Neil A Gray
12 Pine Point Rd
Stow MA 01775

Call Sign: K1PAK
Peter A Kent
5 Robert Rd
Stow MA 01775

Call Sign: W1HK
Marshall W Cross
333 Sudbury Rd
Stow MA 01775

Call Sign: KB1OTU
Mark D Robinson
3 Taylor Rd
Stow MA 01775

Call Sign: KB1OUV
David F Lombardi
119 Taylor Rd
Stow MA 01775

Call Sign: W1CSP
Marvin Norman
324 Taylor Rd
Stow MA 01775

Call Sign: KB1FTA
Theodore A Johnson
352 Taylor Rd
Stow MA 01775

Call Sign: K1TAJ
Theodore A Johnson
352 Taylor Rd
Stow MA 01775

Call Sign: N1IUR
Edwin B Merrick
274 W Acton Rd
Stow MA 01775

Call Sign: WA1OQK
John Clayton Jr
15 Walnut Ridge Rd
Stow MA 01775

Call Sign: WA1QXI
Carol A Clayton
15 Walnut Ridge Rd
Stow MA 01775

Call Sign: KA1FNF
Michael R Pelletier
28 Wedgewood Rd

Stow MA 01775

Call Sign: K1GOI
Gerald A Horne
51 Wheeler Rd
Stow MA 01775

Call Sign: KA1LRC
Bradford E Horne
51 Wheeler Rd
Stow MA 01775

Call Sign: KB1FLQ
Gregor Trinkaus-
Randall
56 Wheeler Rd
Stow MA 017751232

Call Sign: K1JIU
Dean S Adler
126 Whitman St
Stow MA 01775

Call Sign: KB1DXK
Scott A Horvath
16 Wildwood Rd
Stow MA 01775

Call Sign: N1BE
Robert N Evans
22 Wildwood Rd
Stow MA 01775

Call Sign: N1MPF
Anne D Vantine
22 Wildwood Rd
Stow MA 01775

Call Sign: KB1KMT
Stow Ares Team
22 Wildwood Rd
Stow MA 017751503

Call Sign: W1STO
Stow Ares Team
22 Wildwood Rd
Stow MA 017751503

Call Sign: KN1O
Alan Amos Jr
Stow MA 01775

Call Sign: N1CPK

William J Chiarchiaro
Ii
Stow MA 01775

Call Sign: N1DAM
Gregory D Troxel
Stow MA 01775

Call Sign: N1FLR
Martha A Chiarchiaro
Stow MA 01775

Call Sign: N1MGT
Mary E Troxel
Stow MA 01775

Call Sign: K1YW
Gregory T Wasik
Stow MA 01775

Call Sign: KB1FHB
Laurie L King
Stow MA 01775

Call Sign: KB1GTA
Minuteman Repeater
Association
Stow MA 017750669

Call Sign: W1MRA
Minuteman Repeater
Association
Stow MA 017750669

**FCC Amateur Radio
Licenses in
Sturbridge**

Call Sign: KA1JRT
Robert F Lynch
51 Breakneck Rd
Sturbridge MA 01566

Call Sign: W1NMQ
Joseph A Boudreau Jr
48 Cedar St
Sturbridge MA 01566

Call Sign: KA1ZYC
Kahl C Nicholas
12 Country Hill Rd
Sturbridge MA 01566

Call Sign: W1SCG

Marino Di
Bonaventura
80 Fiske Hill Rd
Sturbridge MA 01566

Call Sign: AA1GC
Peter D Lucey
109 Fiske Hill Rd
Sturbridge MA 01566

Call Sign: N1PH
Peter D Lucey
109 Fiske Hill Rd
Sturbridge MA 01566

Call Sign: WG1D
Alfred H Watson Jr
110 Fiske Hill Rd
Sturbridge MA 01566

Call Sign: W1SAL
Mortimer D Williams
15 Forest Lane
Sturbridge MA 01566

Call Sign: KB1PWR
Alan R Jeskey
36 Hamilton Rd
Sturbridge MA 01566

Call Sign: KB1HEN
Kiran N Patel
358 Main St
Sturbridge MA 01566

Call Sign: W1FFV
Donald A Young
239 Park Cir
Sturbridge MA
015661443

Call Sign: W1DUH
Ronald W Smith
18 Podunk Rd
Sturbridge MA 01566

Call Sign: K1ISW
David G Boudreau
21 Podunk Rd
Sturbridge MA 01566

Call Sign: KB1IUY
Donald E Carlton Jr
146 Podunk Rd

Sturbridge MA 01566

Call Sign: KA2BEC
Howard L Ser
108 S Shore Rd
Sturbridge MA 01566

Call Sign: N1JWP
Mark A Pincince
59 South Shore Dr
Sturbridge MA 01566

Call Sign: K1RNH
Albert C Mach
24 Taft St Box 652
Sturbridge MA 01566

Call Sign: KB1IOQ
Matthew B Levesque
8 Tantasqua Shore
Drive
Sturbridge MA 01566

Call Sign: KB1JBI
Peter T Levesque
8 Tantasqua Shore
Drive
Sturbridge MA 01566

Call Sign: KA1OUK
Kristine M Wade
18 Whitemore Rd
Sturbridge MA 01566

Call Sign: N1HTB
Dimitris Paliyannis
Sturbridge MA 01566

**FCC Amateur Radio
Licenses in Sudbury**

Call Sign: N1JDD
Phylis K Sharko
12 Barbara Rd
Sudbury MA
017761903

Call Sign: KB1HVK
John R Sharko
12 Barbara Rd
Sudbury MA 01776

Call Sign: KD6HNZ
Alan S Louie

56 Barton Drive
Sudbury MA 01776

Call Sign: KE6DIB
Cheryl A Louie
56 Barton Drive
Sudbury MA 01776

Call Sign: N1KZP
Jacqueline K Reiner
68 Barton Drive
Sudbury MA 01776

Call Sign: KB1MCJ
John K Baranowsky
103 Belcher Dr
Sudbury MA 01776

Call Sign: KB1TEP
Christopher J Carter
123 Belcher Dr
Sudbury MA 01776

Call Sign: W1YD
John K Baranowsky
103 Belcher Drive
Sudbury MA 01776

Call Sign: W2KO
Donald P Orofino Ii
32 Bent Rd
Sudbury MA 01776

Call Sign: KB1UHJ
William Woyda
11 Birchwood Ave
Sudbury MA 01776

Call Sign: KB1TWO
Marie D Royea
42 Blacksmith Dr
Sudbury MA 01776

Call Sign: KB1TWP
Daniel D Rosen
42 Blacksmith Dr
Sudbury MA 01776

Call Sign: KA1GDW
Diane E Spottswood
41 Blueberry Hill Ln
Sudbury MA 01776

Call Sign: K1ZGR

Kenneth R Walker
61 Blueberry Hill Ln
Sudbury MA 01776

Call Sign: KA1TAU
Jeremy A Grossman
36 Bridle Path
Sudbury MA 01776

Call Sign: KA1YRP
Stephen E Grossman
36 Bridle Path
Sudbury MA 01776

Call Sign: W1HNZ
Bruce R Rusch
97 Brimstone Ln
Sudbury MA 01776

Call Sign: WA1NVY
John W Sullivan
7 Brookdale Ln
Sudbury MA
017763466

Call Sign: W1LHV
William T Frizzell
4 Butler Rd
Sudbury MA
017761514

Call Sign: KB1RHY
Pascal Cleve
3 Camperdown Lane
Sudbury MA 01776

Call Sign: K1LEZ
William P Reed
31 Candy Hill Ln
Sudbury MA 01776

Call Sign: KB1QAO
Gail L Close
78 Cedar Creek Rd
Sudbury MA 01776

Call Sign: KB1ELV
Christopher J Mccarthy
68 Churchill St
Sudbury MA
017762134

Call Sign: N1JBB
Nadine G Rutledge

444 Concord Rd
Sudbury MA 01776

Call Sign: KB1ONA
Kelsey J Byers
30 Coolidge Ln
Sudbury MA
017763439

Call Sign: K1MEM
James L Dionne
31 De Marco Rd
Sudbury MA 01776

Call Sign: KA1FYD
Jan E Holm
31 De Marco Rd
Sudbury MA 01776

Call Sign: KA1NOK
Giuseppe Solimano
31 De Marco Rd
Sudbury MA 01776

Call Sign: K1GNT
David A Waible
587 Dutton Rd
Sudbury MA 01776

Call Sign: KA1GZN
Amelia H Waible
587 Dutton Rd
Sudbury MA 01776

Call Sign: K1NS
Neil R Smith
37 Easy St
Sudbury MA 01776

Call Sign: NV1R
Thomas Schieb
37 Easy St
Sudbury MA 01776

Call Sign: W1DA
George E Hitz Jr
37 Easy St
Sudbury MA 01776

Call Sign: W1UMM
Robert G Mugford
11 Eddy St
Sudbury MA 01776

Call Sign: W1DCD
Frederick W
Cunningham
11 Elsbeth Rd
Sudbury MA 01776

Call Sign: KI2B
Terry S Mayer
61 Fairbank Rd
Sudbury MA 01776

Call Sign: K1HQ
Robert P Olsen
138 Ford Rd
Sudbury MA 01776

Call Sign: N1NWY
Daniel P Olsen
138 Ford Rd
Sudbury MA 01776

Call Sign: W1IBF
Robert G Ling
245 Goodman Hill Rd
Sudbury MA 01776

Call Sign: KB1NIS
Christopher J Cole
253 Goodmans Hill Rd
Sudbury MA 01776

Call Sign: K1CJC
Christopher J Cole
253 Goodmans Hill Rd
Sudbury MA 01776

Call Sign: K1KEB
Karen E Brothers
253 Goodman's Hill
Rd
Sudbury MA 01776

Call Sign: KE6DPL
Dennis F Brothers
253 Goodman's Hill
Rd
Sudbury MA 01776

Call Sign: N1DB
Dennis F Brothers
253 Goodman's Hill
Rd
Sudbury MA 01776

Call Sign: KB1RIB
Don R Lund
36 Great Lake Dr
Sudbury MA 01776

Call Sign: KB1WNQ
Paul H Alfille
81 Greystone Ln
Sudbury MA 01776

Call Sign: W1HKB
Louis E Arnold
11 Hadley Rd
Sudbury MA 01776

Call Sign: N1KO
Adam J M Kern
7 Hammond Cir
Sudbury MA 01776

Call Sign: N1ZPF
Donald C Kern
7 Hammond Cir
Sudbury MA
017762714

Call Sign: KD1LP
Neal B Dowling Jr
25 Harness Ln
Sudbury MA 01776

Call Sign: N1JQB
Thomas A Greenwood
126 Haynes Rd
Sudbury MA 01776

Call Sign: K1HT
David C Hoaglin
73 Hickory Rd
Sudbury MA 01776

Call Sign: N1DEV
Harrison G Ball Iii
14 Hillside Pl
Sudbury MA 01776

Call Sign: W1OKI
Lawrence F Smith Sr
178 Horse Pond Rd
Sudbury MA 01776

Call Sign: K3BUZ
Barrie L Brozenske
216 Hudson Rd

Sudbury MA 01776

Call Sign: N1HJW
Claire F Brozenske
216 Hudson Rd
Sudbury MA 01776

Call Sign: N1MMC
Matthew W Brozenske
216 Hudson Rd
Sudbury MA 01776

Call Sign: N1JWB
Spencer R Goldstein
40 Indian Ridge Rd
Sudbury MA 01776

Call Sign: W1LAV
Marvis M Fickett
90 Indian Ridge Rd
Sudbury MA 01776

Call Sign: KB1KNB
Kenneth S Hawes
38 King Philip Rd
Sudbury MA 01776

Call Sign: AK1Q
Kenneth S Hawes
38 King Philip Rd
Sudbury MA 01776

Call Sign: N1NEL
George H Kiesewetter
15 Lands End Ln
Sudbury MA 01776

Call Sign: KB1UMG
Daniel A Stutman
27 Lilian Ave
Sudbury MA 01776

Call Sign: K1DAS
Daniel A Stutman
27 Lilian Ave
Sudbury MA 01776

Call Sign: KL7JT
Peter S Stutman
27 Lillian Ave
Sudbury MA 01776

Call Sign: KB1MXN
Radial Ice Rc

27 Lillian Ave
Sudbury MA 01776

Call Sign: KR1AA
Radial Ice Rc
27 Lillian Ave
Sudbury MA 01776

Call Sign: KR1A
Radial Ice Rc
27 Lillian Ave
Sudbury MA 01776

Call Sign: KA1RVY
Sandra L Harmon
17 Lincoln Ln
Sudbury MA 01776

Call Sign: KA1BAY
Carol C Ballou
415 Lincoln Rd
Sudbury MA 01776

Call Sign: KB1CIY
Jeffrey W Weil
95 Longfellow Rd
Sudbury MA 01776

Call Sign: WB2UMF
Donald A Lewine
40 Maclean Dr
Sudbury MA 01776

Call Sign: KB1QAR
Arden L Steinbach
83 Maynard Farm Rd
Sudbury MA 01776

Call Sign: K1NFD
Mark Hubelbank
167 Maynard Rd
Sudbury MA 01776

Call Sign: KB1IZZ
David Hubelbank
167 Maynard Rd
Sudbury MA 01776

Call Sign: KB1LZZ
Chance W Parker
288 Maynard Rd
Sudbury MA 01776

Call Sign: K4JMD

Chance W Parker
288 Maynard Rd
Sudbury MA 01776

Call Sign: N1CTX
Robin D Robins
35 Meadow Dr
Sudbury MA 01776

Call Sign: N1NQB
Peter J Singer
16 Meadowbrook Cir
Sudbury MA 01776

Call Sign: W1QO
David R Kirshner
120 Moore Rd
Sudbury MA 01776

Call Sign: K1IR
James S Idelson
96 Morse Rd
Sudbury MA 01776

Call Sign: KB1MEJ
The Morse Contesters
96 Morse Rd
Sudbury MA 01776

Call Sign: NM1Z
The Morse Contesters
96 Morse Rd
Sudbury MA 01776

Call Sign: KB1TID
The Morse Contesters
96 Morse Rd
Sudbury MA 01776

Call Sign: NN1AA
The Morse Contesters
96 Morse Rd
Sudbury MA 01776

Call Sign: NN1ZZ
The Morse Contesters
96 Morse Rd
Sudbury MA 01776

Call Sign: KB1FPU
Sander L Idelson
96 Morse Rd
Sudbury MA 01776

Call Sign: N1AJK
Edward D Ostroff
154 Morse Rd
Sudbury MA 01776

Call Sign: KA1UJK
Arthur K Smith
5 Mossman Rd
Sudbury MA 01776

Call Sign: WA1LTH
Quintus C Wilson
109 Newbridge Rd
Sudbury MA 01776

Call Sign: KB1RIA
Arnold A Barnes Jr
223 Nobscot Rd
Sudbury MA 01776

Call Sign: WD1T
Theodore Bially
30 Nobscot Rd Unit 3
Sudbury MA 01776

Call Sign: K1JBC
Herbert L Hardy Sr
37 Normandy Dr
Sudbury MA 01776

Call Sign: KB1IOO
Sean D Mcenroe
436 North Rd
Sudbury MA 01776

Call Sign: KA1GJ
Jeffrey K Parker
19 Old Forge Ln
Sudbury MA 01776

Call Sign: W1GJ
Jeffrey K Parker
19 Old Forge Ln
Sudbury MA 01776

Call Sign: WA1RQB
Robert M Weiman
114 Old Lancaster Rd
Sudbury MA 01776

Call Sign: WA1VMW
Ernest G Crane Jr
334 Old Lancaster Rd
Sudbury MA 01776

Call Sign: K1VCO
Howard C Kelley
430 Peakham Rd
Sodbury MA 01776

Call Sign: NC1Q
Timothy W Anderson
25 Pennymeadow Rd
Sudbury MA 01776

Call Sign: N5PTY
Rebecca A Menke
21 Pinewood Ave
Sudbury MA 01776

Call Sign: KB1TWS
Charles G Guthy
24 Pinewood Ave
Sudbury MA 01776

Call Sign: KB1CGG
Charles G Guthy
24 Pinewood Ave
Sudbury MA 01776

Call Sign: WA1WUB
John D Mac Knight
51 Powers Rd
Sudbury MA 01776

Call Sign: KB1WHM
Armen S Kaleshian
191 Pratts Mill Rd
Sudbury MA 01776

Call Sign: W1XYZ
Robert J Crowley
64 Puritan Ln
Sudbury MA 01776

Call Sign: WB1PAT
Patricia L Crowley
64 Puritan Ln
Sudbury MA 01776

Call Sign: K1YIK
John H Newitt
123 Puritan Ln
Sudbury MA 02154

Call Sign: WA1OEJ
Donald S Sherman
42 Raynor Rd

Sudbury MA 01776

Call Sign: WB1CTM
Brian D Mulcahey
14 Read Rd
Sudbury MA
017763488

Call Sign: KC1RD
Lawrence S Sletzinger
4 Revere St
Sudbury MA 01776

Call Sign: W1WAI
David S Allen
22 Saxony Dr
Sudbury MA 01776

Call Sign: WB1CMI
Peter G Allen
22 Saxony Dr
Sudbury MA 01776

Call Sign: KA1SPR
Jason A Tracy
10 Scotts Wood Dr
Sudbury MA 01776

Call Sign: K1GXT
George F Maier
64 Shadow Oak Dr
Sudbury MA 01776

Call Sign: W1LSB
George F Maier
64 Shadow Oak Dr
Sudbury MA 01776

Call Sign: KB1KMR
Charles V Giambalvo
25 Skyview Ln
Sudbury MA 01776

Call Sign: WA1RRQ
Sheldon B Michaels
21 Stonebrook Rd
Sudbury MA 01776

Call Sign: K2MWB
Robert H Boughrum
24 Surrey Ln
Sudbury MA 01776

Call Sign: KB1ATR

Anthony P Russell
173 Union Ave
Sudbury MA 01776

Call Sign: KD1WP
Edmund O Russell
173 Union Ave
Sudbury MA 01776

Call Sign: KB1DEI
Fred R Huettig Iii
54 Wake Robin Rd
Sudbury MA 01776

Call Sign: KA1UXW
Wayne E Keseberg
67 Wake Robin Rd
Sudbury MA 01776

Call Sign: KB1KZK
William J Weddleton
34 Washington Dr
Sudbury MA 01776

Call Sign: KA4SSO
Christopher W Stubbs
14 Weir Hill Rd
Sudbury MA 01776

Call Sign: N2OEV
John A Trotter
41 Whispering Pine Rd
Sudbury MA 01776

Call Sign: WO1H
John H Derry Md
20 White Tail Lane
Sudbury MA 01776

Call Sign: KB1LIY
George D Thome
218 Wiilis Rd
Sudbury MA 01776

Call Sign: AB1DV
George D Thome
218 Wiilis Rd
Sudbury MA 01776

Call Sign: KK1F
William R Baker
77 Willard Grant Rd
Sudbury MA 01776

Call Sign: KK1G
Mary C Baker
77 Willard Grant Rd
Sudbury MA 01776

Call Sign: KB0TFB
Michael A Mc Larney
306 Willis Rd
Sudbury MA 01776

Call Sign: W1ZQK
Ernest J Wilkinson
382 Willis Rd
Sudbury MA 01776

Call Sign: KA1NLD
Lynne M Ausman
68 Willow Rd
Sudbury MA 01776

Call Sign: KT1X
David H Croll
68 Willow Rd
Sudbury MA 01776

Call Sign: N1JSM
Robert J Croll
68 Willow Rd
Sudbury MA 01776

Call Sign: KA1ZPE
Bruce Osterling
73 Winsor Rd
Sudbury MA 01776

Call Sign: KE1J
Lars O Mohlin
22 Wyman Dr
Sudbury MA 01776

Call Sign: KC1SO
Lawrence W Black
Sudbury MA 01776

Call Sign: KD1D
John F Stevens
Sudbury MA 01776

Call Sign: W1ZU
Richard J Maley
Sudbury MA 01776

Call Sign: N1VAM
Paul G King

Sudbury MA
017760000

Call Sign: N2EDC
Daniel B Reiner
Sudbury MA
017760795

Call Sign: WN1A
James S Congdon
Sudbury MA 01776

Call Sign: KB1OTP
Elizabeth A Black
Sudbury MA 01776

Call Sign: W1RJM
Richard J Maley
Sudbury MA 01776

FCC Amateur Radio Licenses in Sunderland

Call Sign: N1VMH
James S Bernotas
183 Bull Hill Rd
Sunderland MA 01375

Call Sign: N1XPI
Laurie J Bernotas
183 Bull Hill Rd
Sunderland MA 01375

Call Sign: W2GKS
Herbert J Sinofsky
62 Claybrook Rd
Sunderland MA
013759479

Call Sign: WA1KUZ
Robert A Shotwell
351 Montague Rd
Sunderland MA 01375

Call Sign: KB1WTS
Thomas D Fydenkevez
445 Montague Rd
Sunderland MA 01375

Call Sign: AB1AK
Jennifer L Wilkerson
117 N Plain Rd
Sunderland MA 01375

Call Sign: KB1EQW
Raymond Z
Barszewski
660 Old Amherst Rd
Sunderland MA 01375

Call Sign: KC1RH
Edward W Skutnik
58 Reservation Rd
Sunderland MA 01375

Call Sign: K1IDF
Donald E Scott
52 Reservoir Rd
Sunderland MA 01375

Call Sign: N1TOU
Andrew S Gelina
52 River Rd Apt 10
Sunderland MA 01375

Call Sign: N1IHL
Michael H Barnard
52 River Rd Apt 24
Sunderland MA 01375

Call Sign: N1BAA
Jose A Castillo
75 Russell St
Sunderland MA 01375

Call Sign: N4BAA
Jose A Castillo
75 Russell St
Sunderland MA 01375

Call Sign: N1MFT
Richard W Strycharz
Sr
22 Silver Ln
Sunderland MA
013759475

Call Sign: W1PUO
University Of Mass
Amateur Radio Club
22 Silver Ln
Sunderland MA 01375

Call Sign: KB1FWK
Joseph P Broussard
86 So Plain Rd
Sunderland MA 01375

Call Sign: KB1NNX
Marc F Tremblay
4 Valley View Lane
Sunderland MA 01375

Call Sign: KD1XP
Richard W Strycharz Jr
Sunderland MA
013750004

Call Sign: KB1NTK
Rail-Scan
Sunderland MA
013750004

Call Sign: AB1RS
Richard W Strycharz Jr
Sunderland MA
013750004

FCC Amateur Radio Licenses in Sutton

Call Sign: KB1TTB
Maura E Killeen
6 Apple Ridge Rd
Sutton MA 01590

Call Sign: KB1SFY
Brad J Courville
6 Attitash Ave
Sutton MA 01590

Call Sign: WA1WOB
Gerald A Henault
29 Blackstone
Sutton MA 01590

Call Sign: K1NVF
Robert E Smith
23 Blackstone St
Sutton MA 01590

Call Sign: N1KXX
Susan Z Robsky
328 Boston Rd
Sutton MA 01590

Call Sign: K1HEC
Heck Family Radio
Club
60 Burbank Rd
Sutton MA 01590

Call Sign: K1ZUU
Nancy Heck
60 Burbank Rd
Sutton MA 01527

Call Sign: W1JLA
Robert L Heck
60 Burbank Rd
Sutton MA 015902426

Call Sign: KB1HIN
Adam R Cox
18 Butternut Dr
Sutton MA 01590

Call Sign: KA1UUP
Elizabeth A Lindell
2 Cole Ave
Sutton MA 01590

Call Sign: KA1UXL
Daniel W Muller
2 Cole Ave
Sutton MA 01590

Call Sign: N1XXD
James J Geneva
89 Eight Lots Rd
Sutton MA 01590

Call Sign: KB1LYS
Gregory Cofsky
105 Eight Lots Rd
Sutton MA 01590

Call Sign: WA2PMA
William P Powers Jr
15 Mc Guire Rd
Sutton MA 01590

Call Sign: AA1NP
William P Powers Jr
15 Mc Guire Rd
Sutton MA 01590

Call Sign: KC1HF
Brenda L Yates
32 Mc Guire Rd
Sutton MA 01590

Call Sign: KB1JRU
Jonathan C Rocheleau
31 Mendon Rd

Sutton MA 01590

Call Sign: KB1UMF
Christopher R
Rocheleau
31 Mendon Rd
Sutton MA 01590

Call Sign: N1IEZ
John M Owens
114 Mendon Rd
Sutton MA 01590

Call Sign: N1KXW
Kathleen J Owens
114 Mendon Rd
Sutton MA 01590

Call Sign: W1GPT
Conrad P Berthold
501 Mendon Rd
Sutton MA 01590

Call Sign: KB1EVD
Paul S Sepuka
25 Merrill Rd
Sutton MA 015903883

Call Sign: W1GGL
Paul S Sepuka
25 Merrill Rd
Sutton MA 01590

Call Sign: N1IWD
Alan Capewell
51 Pierce Rd
Sutton MA 015901905

Call Sign: KB1PWC
Paul J Pepka Jr
52 Putnam Hill Rd
Sutton MA 01590

Call Sign: KA1OTA
Thomas R Gauvin
12 Stone School Rd
Sutton MA 01590

Call Sign: N1SBM
Theodore L Agos
85 Town Farm Rd
Sutton MA 01590

Call Sign: W1NJC

Nicholas J Cannata
222 W Sutton Rd
Sutton MA 01590

Call Sign: KB1GIC
Justin M Woodard
266 West Sutton Rd
Sutton MA 01590

Call Sign: KB1PVH
David M Webb
29 Wheelock Rd
Sutton MA 01590

Call Sign: N1LSM
Kris J Oliver
Sutton MA 01590

Call Sign: N1PVS
Arthur D Keown Iii
Sutton MA 01590

Call Sign: N1DIZ
Dennis E Ditto
Sutton MA 015900342

Call Sign: N1MGU
Karen B Ditto
Sutton MA 015900342

Call Sign: N1PVT
Jane K Oliver
Sutton MA 01590

**FCC Amateur Radio
Licenses in
Swampscott**

Call Sign: K1WGM
Robert L Ansell
1 Archer St
Swampscott MA
01907

Call Sign: N1CHK
John J Boyle
179 Aspen Rd
Swampscott MA
019072161

Call Sign: N1IBS
Steven J Ross
200 Atlantic Ave

Swampscott MA
01907

Call Sign: N1DKR
Bradley C Litman
228 Atlantic Ave
Swampscott MA
01907

Call Sign: WA1ZNH
Arthur H Bogus
75 Barnstable St
Swampscott MA
01907

Call Sign: KB1LHA
Gayle C Willman
61 Bates Rd
Swampscott MA
01907

Call Sign: KA1RCP
Eric E Austin
64 Bates Rd
Swampscott MA
019072659

Call Sign: N1GIE
Harold R Austin Jr
64 Bates Rd
Swampscott MA
019072659

Call Sign: K1HRA
Harold R Austin Jr
64 Bates Rd
Swampscott MA
019072659

Call Sign: WA1HUY
George A Allen
27 Bay View Ave
Swampscott MA
01907

Call Sign: WB1APQ
George F Rogers
252 Burrill St
Swampscott MA
019071754

Call Sign: WA1MWQ
Arthur R Messinger
17 Cherry St

Swampscott MA
01907

Swampscott MA
01907

Swampscott MA
01407

Swampscott MA
01907

Call Sign: N1QCA
Adam I Seligman
52 Crosmen Ave
Swampscott MA
01907

Call Sign: W1JUB
John Zorzy
5 Fuller Ter
Swampscott MA
019072507

Call Sign: KA1YRH
Lynne C Brustin
1 Loring Ave Ph2
Swampscott MA
01907

Call Sign: KB1QKU
Peter M Jahnes
98 Pine St Apt 1
Swampscott MA
01907

Call Sign: KB1LCL
Gabriele Mongiello
55 Eastman Ave
Swampscott MA
01907

Call Sign: N1BB
William G Bithell Jr
96 Greenwood Ave
Swampscott MA
01907

Call Sign: W1YZM
Philip B Shiff
39 Manton Rd
Swampscott MA
01907

Call Sign: N1HCF
James E Finlay
33 Plymouth Ave
Swampscott MA
019071159

Call Sign: N1VXE
Sergey I Andreyev
14 Elm Pl
Swampscott MA
01907

Call Sign: KB1GKI
Andrew K Withrow
27 Greenwood Ter
Swampscott MA
01907

Call Sign: KB1LJD
James M Fox
19 Maple Ave
Swampscott MA
01907

Call Sign: KA1OC
Max J Fuchs
11 Plymouth Ln
Swampscott MA
01907

Call Sign: K1SUJ
Angelo G Peluso
Elmwood Rd
Swampscott MA
019070386

Call Sign: KB1CHB
Buckley R Withrow
27 Greenwood Terr
Swampscott MA
019072126

Call Sign: W1ULR
Stanley Cokas
11 Merrymount Dr
Swampscott MA
01907

Call Sign: K1NJE
William G Bithell
55 Puritan Rd
Swampscott MA
01907

Call Sign: N1ZUP
Colin J Mcallister
10 Fairview Ave
Swampscott MA
01907

Call Sign: KB1EUN
Marysusan B Withrow
27 Greenwood Terr
Swampscott MA
01907

Call Sign: KA1USD
Roland Scott Robson
2 Millett Rd
Swampscott MA
01907

Call Sign: K1NST
Doris C Bithell
55 Puritan Rd
Swampscott MA
01907

Call Sign: KK1CQ
James E Murphy
22 Fairview Ave
Swampscott MA
01907

Call Sign: W1GSF
Kathleen H Reynolds
36 Hillside Ave
Swampscott MA
01907

Call Sign: N1IVW
Paul H Bilodeau
16 Muriel Rd
Swampscott MA
01907

Call Sign: N1PME
Mike J Murphy
524 Puritan Rd
Swampscott MA
01907

Call Sign: N1MVR
Richard J Brown
6 Fisher Ave
Swampscott MA
01907

Call Sign: W1GWL
Arthur H Reynolds
36 Hillside Ave
Swampscott MA
01907

Call Sign: N1HGD
Peter J Vasiliou
505 Paradise Rd #223
Swampscott MA
01907

Call Sign: N1JRA
Jonathan R Austin
150 Redington St
Swampscott MA
01907

Call Sign: WB1CNI
Arthur Saxe
363 Forest Ave
Swampscott MA
01907

Call Sign: N1PSR
Matthew D Jacobs
86 Kensington Ln
Swampscott MA
01907

Call Sign: KA1RQN
Frederick C Anderson
55 Pine St
Swampscott MA
01907

Call Sign: N1DS
Dennis M Scolamiero
182 Redington St
Swampscott MA
019072135

Call Sign: KA1MSV
David I Gustavsen
37 Franklin Ave

Call Sign: N1QBZ
Mike D Jacobs
86 Kersington Ln

Call Sign: KA1TQJ
Mary A Anderson
55 Pine St

Call Sign: KB1TRI
Paula A Ray
35 Salem St

Swampscott MA
01907

Call Sign: W1ETL
Domenic F Spinale
41 Spinale Rd
Swampscott MA
01907

Call Sign: KB1RYF
Christina M Catino
126 Stetson Ave
Swampscott MA
01907

Call Sign: N1BGC
Larry A Dunn
145 Stetson Ave
Swampscott MA
01907

Call Sign: K2AJY
Gary G Young
1 Sutton Pl
Swampscott MA
019072609

Call Sign: WA8BYL
Larry H Taitelbaum
10 Walnut Rd
Swampscott MA
01907

Call Sign: KA4LIE
Les M Nieman
Swampscott MA
01907

Call Sign: KA1OMD
Thomas J Baldwin
Swampscott MA
01907

Call Sign: KB1FDY
Brian M Gaff
Swampscott MA
019070266

Call Sign: N1SI
Brian M Gaff
Swampscott MA
019070266

Call Sign: KB1PBL

Cabot W Dodge
Swampscott MA
01907

**FCC Amateur Radio
Licenses in Swansea**

Call Sign: W1TBY
Bernard M Grabert
149 Alsada Rd
Swansea MA 02777

Call Sign: WA1PCD
Jeffrey E Smith
104 Baptist St
Swansea MA 02777

Call Sign: KB1LPF
James M Kern
8 Bark Circle
Swansea MA 02777

Call Sign: WA1PQT
Carl F Sawejko
447 Bark St
Swansea MA 02777

Call Sign: N1RGC
Paul T Hague
70 Bayside Ave
Swansea MA 02777

Call Sign: N1QQZ
Brian A La Fleur
66 Bayview Ave
Swansea MA 02777

Call Sign: N1KHL
Edwin T Scallon Esq
311 Bushee Rd
Swansea MA 02777

Call Sign: KB1RCJ
Kathleen P Scallon
311 Bushee Rd
Swansea MA 02777

Call Sign: KB1FIP
Timothy Jean
30 Carvalho Dr
Swansea MA 02777

Call Sign: KB1ZF
Alexander C Vezina

62 Cedar Cove Ln
Swansea MA 02777

Call Sign: W1QFN
Alexander C Vezina
62 Cedar Cove Ln
Swansea MA 02777

Call Sign: WB1GYW
Rene R Martel
5 Chace St
Swansea MA 02777

Call Sign: N1GYL
Robert L Barnwell
27 Crest Ct
Swansea MA
027774626

Call Sign: KA1CSL
Richard Philibert
95 Delmage Rd
Swansea MA 02777

Call Sign: KA1QGM
Bertrand R Boulay
222 Dillon Ln
Swansea MA
027773652

Call Sign: WA1ZCD
Clifford A Woollam Sr
35 Fourth St
Swansea MA 02777

Call Sign: KA1IHT
Robert S Custer
94 Gardners Neck Rd
Swansea MA 02777

Call Sign: KB1CGH
Robert M Paquette
994 Gardners Neck Rd
Swansea MA 02777

Call Sign: W1PEP
Philip E Przymierski
1065 Gardners Neck
Rd
Swansea MA 02777

Call Sign: KB1QOJ
Gary B Huntress

1357 Gardners Neck
Rd
Swansea MA 02777

Call Sign: KB1NYT
James T Hodkinson Jr
1364 Gardners Neck
Rd
Swansea MA 02777

Call Sign: WA1CKU
Laurence M Curtis Jr
130 Harbor Rd
Swansea MA
027771423

Call Sign: N1DVR
Paul M Clement
19 Hemlock Dr
Swansea MA 02777

Call Sign: N1LIX
William G Sefton
163 Hortonville Rd
Swansea MA 02777

Call Sign: KA1HRW
Robert J Hogarth
334 Hortonville Rd
Swansea MA 02777

Call Sign: KB1TCP
Ronald F Laverdiere
484 Hortonville Rd
Swansea MA 02777

Call Sign: KB1TCN
Ryan K Laverdiere
484 Hortonville Rd
Swansea MA 02777

Call Sign: W1IJC
Alva Viveiros
38 Houlton St
Swansea MA 02777

Call Sign: KB1FIL
Michael S Wilcox
50 Joanne Lane
Swansea MA 02777

Call Sign: N1NRL
Kenneth A Miller
23 Laurel Ave

Swansea MA 02777

Call Sign: KB1BPS
John J Biszko
61 Little Neck Ave
Swansea MA 02777

Call Sign: N1VZO
Rita M Biszko
61 Little Neck Ave
Swansea MA 02777

Call Sign: K1RFI
Southeastern
Massachusetts
Amateur Radio Group
66 Louis St
Swansea MA 02777

Call Sign: N1LDY
Antone Souza Iii
66 Louis St
Swansea MA 02777

Call Sign: NN1D
Antone Souza Iii
66 Louis St
Swansea MA 02777

Call Sign: N1IBC
Steven D Desmarais
216 Luther Ave
Swansea MA 02777

Call Sign: KA1UDB
Herman C Falcon Jr
26 Macomber Ave
Swansea MA 02777

Call Sign: W1DT
Barton G Albert
102 Maple Ave
Swansea MA 02777

Call Sign: AA1OT
Russell W Herritt
340 Market St
Swansea MA 02777

Call Sign: K1CH
Russell W Herritt
340 Market St
Swansea MA
027773916

Call Sign: N1VBD
Thomas A Paiva
98 O Bannon Pl
Swansea MA 02777

Call Sign: KB1IWC
Arthur E Irwin
45 O Bannon Place
Swansea MA 02777

Call Sign: W1TGA
Arthur E Irwin
45 O Bannon Place
Swansea MA 02777

Call Sign: W1AEI
Arthur E Irwin
45 O Bannon Place
Swansea MA 02777

Call Sign: N1LLW
Victor P Jorge
333 Oak St
Swansea MA 02777

Call Sign: N1SMR
Duane E Tew Jr
28 Ocean View Ave
Swansea MA 02777

Call Sign: N1HBM
Roger T Ouellette
163 Ocean View Ave
Swansea MA 02777

Call Sign: WA1PYY
Joseph Cabral Jr
455 Park St
Swansea MA 02777

Call Sign: KA1TNU
Peter P Du Biel
165 Puffer Ave
Swansea MA 02777

Call Sign: WA1ZCC
Joseph Berube
71 Randall Shea Dr
Swansea MA 02777

Call Sign: NY1W
Paul Machado
1147 Sharps Lot Rd

Swansea MA
027775024

Call Sign: KB1HWX
Mark Oribello
1790 Sharps Lot Rd
Swansea MA 02777

Call Sign: KD1HW
Richard A Beliveau
71 Shawmut Ave
Swansea MA 02777

Call Sign: KB1TUX
Charles R Bardsley
91 Smoke Rise Circle
Swansea MA 02777

Call Sign: WA1JUB
Peter J Mc Connell
715 Stevens Rd
Swansea MA 02777

Call Sign: KB1UAN
Robert J Levesque
500 Swansea Mall Dr
Apt 138c
Swansea MA 02777

Call Sign: N1RJL
Robert J Levesque
500 Swansea Mall Dr
Apt 138c
Swansea MA 02777

Call Sign: K1HRN
Robin G Congdon
4 Touissett Ave
Swansea MA 02777

Call Sign: KB1GEF
Kenneth K Perreault
124 Vinnicum Rd
Swansea MA 02777

Call Sign: N1KP
Kenneth K Perreault
124 Vinnicum Rd
Swansea MA 02777

Call Sign: KA1PCN
Fernando G Pacheco
1419 Wilbur Ave
Swansea MA 02777

Call Sign: W1IMA
Robert H Eddy
159 Wood St
Swansea MA 02777

Call Sign: K1EYJ
Albert A Desrosiers
Swansea MA 02777

Call Sign: K1EYK
Eileen Desrosiers
Swansea MA 02777

Call Sign: AB1JJ
Mel G Davey
Swansea MA 02777

**FCC Amateur Radio
Licenses in Taunton**

Call Sign: WA1WNS
Neil C Rasmussen
14 Anawan St
Taunton MA 02780

Call Sign: KB1NLX
Gregory D Glynn
112 Bay St
Taunton MA 02780

Call Sign: W1VFB
Gregory D Glynn
112 Bay St
Taunton MA 02780

Call Sign: KA1VVJ
Colby L Crossman
179 Bay St
Taunton MA 02780

Call Sign: W1GUJ
Harry F Holland
207 Bay St
Taunton MA 02780

Call Sign: KA1QPR
Robert J Dias
1841 Bay St
Taunton MA
027801006

Call Sign: KB1QIN
Antonio Pinheiro

46 Baylies Rd
Taunton MA 02780

Call Sign: WA1KFD
Charles F Rowe Iii
11 Birch Cir
Taunton MA 02780

Call Sign: KB1SUM
Keith Rowe
9 Birch Circle
Taunton MA 02780

Call Sign: KA1WPW
Elizabeth A Figlock
7 Bradford Pl
Taunton MA 02780

Call Sign: N1JOT
John L Perry
400 Broadway
Taunton MA 02780

Call Sign: KB1NMP
David F Souza
953 Burt St
Taunton MA
027802250

Call Sign: W1DFS
David F Souza
953 Burt St
Taunton MA
027802250

Call Sign: KB1LJ
Edward J Polgroszek
65 Cedar St
Taunton MA 02780

Call Sign: KA1CGD
John J Mc Mahon
19 Charles St
Taunton MA 02780

Call Sign: K1CCF
Joseph Furtado
1281 Cohannet St
Taunton MA 02780

Call Sign: KB1KZU
Joseph M Soares Jr
1316 Cohannet St
Taunton MA 02780

Call Sign: WA1VSY
Richard K Roth
476 Cohannet St
Taunton MA 02780

Call Sign: KA1LRB
Larry R Franklin
60 Coolidge St
Taunton MA 02780

Call Sign: WA1CPI
Julian J Niedziocha
35 Cottage St
Taunton MA 02780

Call Sign: WA1CPJ
Priscilla L Niedziocha
35 Cottage St
Taunton MA 02780

Call Sign: KA1JAI
Rosalie A Patrello
90 County St
Taunton MA 02780

Call Sign: N1BLG
Chester P Fortun
330 County St
Taunton MA 02780

Call Sign: KA1UDC
Rene R Charest
488 County St Apt 2
Taunton MA 02780

Call Sign: KA1OZX
Steven A Bird
819 County St Apt19a
Taunton MA 02780

Call Sign: N1NTA
John D Moots
18 Crocker St
Taunton MA 02780

Call Sign: N1UMJ
John E Miller
27 Cypress Rd
Taunton MA 02780

Call Sign: N1YOC
William A Fisher
30 D Davis St

Taunton MA 02780

Call Sign: W1YDW
Patrick J Romano
52 Daisy Ave
Taunton MA
027801162

Call Sign: K1NDD
Michael E Murray
144 Devon St
Taunton MA 02780

Call Sign: KA1NEA
Luis A Reis
89 Dighton Ave
Taunton MA 02780

Call Sign: K1JFL
Jason F Levenson
655 Dighton Ave
Taunton MA 02780

Call Sign: N1EZH
Barry S Kennedy
188 Dunbar St
Taunton MA 02780

Call Sign: N1JCK
Diane C Kennedy
188 Dunbar St
Taunton MA 02780

Call Sign: KB1LAB
Robert C Barbour
67 Fieldstone Rd
Taunton MA
027804377

Call Sign: K1BAR
Robert C Barbour
67 Fieldstone Rd
Taunton MA
027804377

Call Sign: KB1OHV
Winthrop H
Richardson
130 Fisher St
Taunton MA 02780

Call Sign: KB1KVD
Jason E Legrow
25 Floyd Ave

Taunton MA 02780

Call Sign: N1SKP
Tim Clish
81 Forest Hill Drive
Taunton MA 02780

Call Sign: KB1DKF
Rodger S Furey
81 Foxhill Dr
Taunton MA 02780

Call Sign: N1YKI
David B Leonard
98 Frazier Pasture Rd
Taunton MA 02780

Call Sign: KB1LXH
Donald E Burke
81 Fremont St
Taunton MA
027802324

Call Sign: KC1TAC
Taunton Area
Communications
Group
81 Fremont St
Taunton MA 02780

Call Sign: KA1GSL
Richard T La France
9 General Cobb St
Taunton MA 02780

Call Sign: KA1LEY
John D Beaulieu
15 Hamilton St Apt 5
Taunton MA 02780

Call Sign: WP4US
Carlos G Wharton Sr
53 Hart St
Taunton MA 02780

Call Sign: N8AO
Roger F Hathaway
170 Highland St Apt
223
Taunton MA 02780

Call Sign: K1VUJ
Malcolm A Staples
50 Highland St Lot 104

Taunton MA 02780

Call Sign: KB1KWF
Richard E Ferreira
170 Highland St Unit
114
Taunton MA
027804454

Call Sign: N1CYN
Joseph F De
Christopher
50 Highland St Unit
226
Taunton MA 02780

Call Sign: W1EM
Roger E Marrotte
17 Hopewell St
Taunton MA 02780

Call Sign: W1REM
Bristol County Contest
Club
17 Hopewell St
Taunton MA 02780

Call Sign: KB1LXI
Rudolf J Burer
Indian Meadow Dr
Taunton MA 02780

Call Sign: N1VST
Alexander Ortiz
109 Ingell St
Taunton MA 02780

Call Sign: KA1GSK
Roger Ouellette
50 Kendra Ln
Taunton MA 02780

Call Sign: NY1G
Francis J Pacheco
14 Kurts Pl
Taunton MA 02780

Call Sign: N1LNX
James R Armstrong Jr
59 Linden St Unit 1314
Taunton MA 02780

Call Sign: KB1LBF
Larry V Richards

363 Lothropt St
Taunton MA 02780

Call Sign: N2UVP
Michael J Coryer
37 Main St
Taunton MA 02780

Call Sign: N1MFY
Elizabeth M Valdes
19 Maple St
Taunton MA 02780

Call Sign: N1XVA
Tara A Staple
59 Maria La
Taunton MA 02780

Call Sign: N1JCE
Joseph L Fernandes Jr
42 Maria Ln
Taunton MA 02780

Call Sign: N1SZS
Arnold F Staple
59 Maria Ln
Taunton MA 02780

Call Sign: KB1LXG
Peter J Ferreira
5 Marvel St
Taunton MA 02780

Call Sign: KB1SZF
Everett Plant Jr
12 Monica St
Taunton MA 02780

Call Sign: WE9U
Everett Plant Jr
12 Monica St
Taunton MA 02780

Call Sign: WU1G
Everett Plant Jr
12 Monica St
Taunton MA 02780

Call Sign: KA1SPH
Rodger A Salley
41 Myrtle St
Taunton MA 02780

Call Sign: KB1UJE

Christine M Persechino
77 Nichols Dr
Taunton MA 02780

Call Sign: W1HHY
Christine M Persechino
77 Nichols Dr
Taunton MA 02780

Call Sign: KA1VWV
Angelo M Leite
53 North Pleasant St
Taunton MA 02780

Call Sign: KB1JZL
Michael T Nye
29 Paul Bunker Dr
Taunton MA 02780

Call Sign: KA1ALN
Ronald J Morris
100 Paul Revere
Terrace
Taunton MA 02780

Call Sign: KB1STN
Emily M Terra
100 Paul Revere
Terrace
Taunton MA 02780

Call Sign: KA1ZGS
Gary L Bornstein
35 Pilgrim Rd Unit
1502
Taunton MA 02780

Call Sign: KB1RFD
Sean M O'connor
99 Plain St Apt 1
Taunton MA 02780

Call Sign: W1BDB
Mims Memorial Radio
Club
189 Powderhorn Dr
Taunton MA 02780

Call Sign: WA1OEZ
Robert M Mims Sr
189 Powderhorn Dr
Taunton MA 02780

Call Sign: WA1UPE

Sandra L Mims
189 Powderhorn Dr
Taunton MA 02780

Call Sign: KB1HFX
Area Ii Mema Races
Club
189 Powderhorn Drive
Taunton MA 02780

Call Sign: WA1OOE
Robert J Bowen Iii
142 Prospect Hill St
Taunton MA 02780

Call Sign: KB1NPP
Matthew V Poltrino
426 Prospect Hill St
Taunton MA 02780

Call Sign: KA1QPM
Stephen L Rowell Jr
444 Prospect Hill St
Taunton MA 02780

Call Sign: W1OLA
John C Fulton
12 Rockland St
Taunton MA 02780

Call Sign: N1IND
Robert M Adams
6 Russell St
Taunton MA 02780

Call Sign: KB1NMI
Marc E Levesque
30 Russell St
Taunton MA 02780

Call Sign: K1AMH
Peter B Spencer
175 S Walker St
Taunton MA 02780

Call Sign: N1OTY
John E Frye
11 Sara Dr
Taunton MA 02780

Call Sign: KB8PGJ
Bryan S Klugh
46 Scadding St
Taunton MA 02780

Call Sign: KB1INN
Kenneth C Waine
80 School St
Taunton MA 02780

Call Sign: WA1KSM
Henry E Jacques
180 School St
Taunton MA 02780

Call Sign: N1MXH
Alan T Smallhoover
49 Shores St
Taunton MA 02780

Call Sign: N1ZJG
Eric L Chalifoux
66 Silversmith Way
Taunton MA 02780

Call Sign: KB1ASC
Dawn L Parmeggiani
159 Silverwood Dr
Taunton MA 02780

Call Sign: WA1JXG
Donald A Clay
647 Somerset Ave
Taunton MA 02780

Call Sign: KF2BY
Francis J Amaral
1643 Somerset Ave
Taunton MA
027805000

Call Sign: K1MRC
Joseph F Nates
54 Summer St
Taunton MA 02780

Call Sign: KA1HFL
Duarte S Pereira
41 Theresa St
Taunton MA
027801304

Call Sign: N1JJH
Bruce R Hickox
331 Thrasher St
Taunton MA
027801504

Call Sign: KB1NYY
Taunton Area
Communications
Group
101 Tremont St Apt -1
Taunton MA 02780

Call Sign: KA1DTA
David A Rezendes
16 Van Buren St
Taunton MA
027801428

Call Sign: KB1NAS
Carlos A Matos
26 Walkerr Ave
Taunton MA 02780

Call Sign: W1LOL
Henry A Sawinski
37 Warren St
Taunton MA 02780

Call Sign: N1PWK
Christopher R
Moulding
331 Washington St
Taunton MA 02780

Call Sign: N1XHE
Andrew Serriello
30 Washington St Apt
218
Taunton MA 02780

Call Sign: KB1NHI
James W Bowman
431 Washington St -7
Taunton MA 02780

Call Sign: KB1SZI
Charles G Brooks
234 Weir St
Taunton MA 02780

Call Sign: KB1TCM
Charles G Brooks
234 Weir St
Taunton MA 02780

Call Sign: N1CHB
Charles G Brooks
234 Weir St
Taunton MA 02780

Call Sign: K1JOE
Joseph P Machado
426 Weir St
Taunton MA 02780

Call Sign: KA1RTM
Louis M Botelho
32 White St
Taunton MA 02780

Call Sign: KB1KZY
Michael F Cote
480 Whittenton St
Taunton MA 02780

Call Sign: KB1KZW
Stephen R Foster
755 Whittenton St
Taunton MA
027807505

Call Sign: KB1KZX
Barbara A Foster
755 Whittenton St
Taunton MA 02780

Call Sign: KB1FD
William Silva
67 Winter St
Taunton MA 02780

Call Sign: KA1WPY
Mary Ellen E Figlock
236 Winthrop St
Taunton MA 02780

Call Sign: KA1YHN
Mary M Figlock
236 Winthrop St
Taunton MA 02780

Call Sign: W1HGY
Thaddeus A Figlock
236 Winthrop St
Taunton MA
027804429

Call Sign: KB1UVB
Saint Maximilian
Kolbe Radio Club
236 Winthrop St
Taunton MA 02780

Call Sign: KA1MDG
Saint Maximilian
Kolbe Radio Club
236 Winthrop St
Taunton MA 02780

Call Sign: KB1SRJ
Andreas Kalthoff
306 Winthrop St 12
Taunton MA 02780

Call Sign: AB1LH
Andreas Kalthoff
306 Winthrop St 12
Taunton MA 02780

Call Sign: W1RZH
John J Sikorski Sr
8 Woodwards Ln
Taunton MA 02780

Call Sign: KA1VNS
John R Damon
Taunton MA 02780

Call Sign: KB1JCH
Steven A Wieczorek
Taunton MA 02780

**FCC Amateur Radio
Licenses in Teaticket**

Call Sign: N1YRR
Scott A Mc Intyre
94 Falmouth Landing
Rd
Teaticket MA
025365115

Call Sign: N1LNE
Joanne W Reid
29 Hiawatha St
Teaticket MA
025367371

Call Sign: N1LNF
John H Reid
29 Hiawatha St
Teaticket MA 02536

Call Sign: KB1GSU
Barbara J Silva
36 Mattapan St
Teaticket MA 02536

Call Sign: KB1GSV
Paul K Silva
36 Mattapan St
Teaticket MA 02536

Call Sign: KA1PHM
Harold W Hammond
31 Oak Ridge Rd
Teaticket MA 02536

Call Sign: KB1QND
David T Vieira
221 Teaticket Hwy
Teaticket MA 02536

Call Sign: K1HNQ
Stewart S Mitchell
104 Teaticket Path
Teaticket MA 02536

Call Sign: WA1YXP
Jeffrey D Thomas
170 Teaticket Path
Teaticket MA 02536

Call Sign: K1JZ
John D Miller
7 Village Ln
Teaticket MA
025366543

Call Sign: KB5FNF
James J Pepin Jr
Teaticket MA 02536

Call Sign: KC8CEV
Ronald L Trainor
Teaticket MA 02536

FCC Amateur Radio Licenses in Templeton

Call Sign: N1HBN
Kevin R Kimball
Templeton MA 01468

Call Sign: N1EZD
Frederic F Donaldson
Jr
Baldwinville Rd
Templeton MA
014680104

Call Sign: K1NPA
Frank W Wells
Barre Rd
Templeton MA 01468

Call Sign: KA1SZY
James W Curtis
Gardner Rd
Templeton MA 01468

Call Sign: KB1LJK
John P Tenney
132 Gray Rd
Templeton MA 01468

Call Sign: KB1PZF
Timothy P Toth
141 Gray Rd
Templeton MA 01468

Call Sign: N1LOZ
Alan J Hutchinson
475 Hubbardston Rd
Templeton MA 01468

Call Sign: KB1DPB
Robert M Jacques
124 N Main St
Templeton MA
014681425

Call Sign: KB1OTT
Edward Niemczura
114 Otter River Rd
Templeton MA 01468

Call Sign: K1HEY
Lawrence G Stanley
207 Partridgeville Rd
Templeton MA 01468

Call Sign: KA1QGA
Richard W Curtis
Patriots Rd
Templeton MA
014680361

Call Sign: N1OPS
Robert T Buckley Jr
3 Peaceful Pines
Templeton MA 01468

Call Sign: KD1HS

Clifford A Violette
80 S Main St
Templeton MA 01468

Call Sign: KZ1F
Walter R Corey
308 South Rd
Templeton MA
014681238

Call Sign: N1HPZ
Robert E Murray Jr
27 Victoria Lane
Templeton MA 01468

Call Sign: KT1M
Wallace R Teto Jr
Templeton MA 01468

Call Sign: N1OYM
Robert E Merriam
Templeton MA 01468

Call Sign: KA1QGO
John P R Brooks
Templeton MA 01468

Call Sign: KA1QGP
John L Brooks
Templeton MA 01468

Call Sign: KB1WII
Patricia L Lisle
Templeton MA 01468

FCC Amateur Radio Licenses in Tewksbury

Call Sign: N1FTN
Wayne A Sterner
1205 Andover St
Tewksbury MA 01876

Call Sign: N1RHY
James W Boudreau Jr
1304 Andover St
Tewksbury MA 01876

Call Sign: WA1KWA
Colin W Brace
31 Anthony Rd
Tewksbury MA 01876

Call Sign: KB1GNS
Charlotte T Brace
31 Anthony Rd
Tewksbury MA 01876

Call Sign: KD1VP
David H Bagdigian
274 Apache Way
Tewksbury MA 01876

Call Sign: KB1SNH
Wing Hin Wong
2311 Archstone Ave
Tewksbury MA 01876

Call Sign: KB1OEA
Steve M Staffier
3305 Archstone Ave
Tewksbury MA 01876

Call Sign: K1SMS
Steve M Staffier
2306 Archstone Ave
Tewksbury MA 01876

Call Sign: KA1ZHA
Ronald E Ostiguy
6 Avon St
Tewksbury MA 01876

Call Sign: KB1OPQ
David R Feick
71 Babicz Rd
Tewksbury MA 01876

Call Sign: W8JVY
David R Feick
71 Babicz Rd
Tewksbury MA 01876

Call Sign: N1FLE
Elizabeth K Mulcahy
33 Barbara D Ln
Tewksbury MA 01876

Call Sign: WB1CPJ
Michael P Mulcahy
33 Barbara D Ln
Tewksbury MA 01876

Call Sign: WA1IMX
James D Covington Sr
15 Bay State Ave
Tewksbury MA 01876

Call Sign: WA1PMU
Elizabeth A Covington
15 Bay State Ave
Tewksbury MA
018763305

Call Sign: N1PDI
Scott F Thomas
17 Bell Rd
Tewksbury MA 01876

Call Sign: KB1JUM
Robert G Stewart Sr
131 Bligh St
Tewksbury MA 01876

Call Sign: KA1OJQ
Thomas E Gagnon
50 Bonnie Ln
Tewksbury MA 01876

Call Sign: KA1KSO
Thomas E Flynn
Box 275
Tewksbury MA 01876

Call Sign: WA1DGA
Joanne C May
Box 343
Tewksbury MA 01876

Call Sign: KA1UTN
Joseph W Kearns
21 Brian Ln
Tewksbury MA 01876

Call Sign: N1FRI
Edward J Kearns
21 Brian Ln
Tewksbury MA 01876

Call Sign: N1BDK
Alfred W Manninen
19 Brook St
Tewksbury MA 01876

Call Sign: KA1NMY
Thomas P Mc Guire
2 Catamount Rd
Tewksbury MA 01876

Call Sign: KA1JMF
John A Morley

157 Catamount Rd
Tewksbury MA 01876

Call Sign: N1HDY
Michael W Sitar Jr
568 Chandler St
Tewksbury MA 01876

Call Sign: W1VTK
Robert L Bonyman
70 Chestnut Rd
Tewksbury MA 01876

Call Sign: WA1OEB
Marianne L Bonyman
70 Chestnut Rd
Tewksbury MA 01876

Call Sign: W1FTY
Raymond M Pendleton
Sr
60 Dufresne Dr
Tewksbury MA 01876

Call Sign: W1PRJ
Patrick R Joy
101 Ferncroft Rd
Tewksbury MA 01876

Call Sign: K1MAV
Charles W Gerrard
44 Fiske St
Tewksbury MA 01876

Call Sign: N1CRH
Keith Stockton
117 Foster Rd
Tewksburg MA 01876

Call Sign: WA1CTS
Paul E May
75 Franklin St
Tewksbury MA 01876

Call Sign: WB8OGK
Bruce E Conner
25 Greenmeadow
Drive
Tewksbury MA 01876

Call Sign: KB1ETL
Timothy A Headle
48 Harrison Rd
Tewksbury MA 01876

Call Sign: N1NTI
Karyn P Curtis
127 Heath St
Tewksbury MA 01876

Call Sign: N1NTJ
David P Curtis
127 Heath St
Tewksbury MA 01876

Call Sign: AA1HF
Richard J Donahue
24 Henry J Dr
Tewksbury MA 01876

Call Sign: AA1KJ
Catherine F Donahue
24 Henry J Dr
Tewksbury MA 01876

Call Sign: W1SEP
Joseph G Lefebvre Sr
61 Highland Ave
Tewksbury MA 01876

Call Sign: KB1IJZ
Serafim Makris
40 Katie Way
Tewksbury MA 01876

Call Sign: KB1NJM
Jeffrey A D'amico
1 Kingfisher Rd
Tewksbury MA 01876

Call Sign: KA1LQV
Judith C Matfess
45 Kingston Rd
Tewksbury MA 01876

Call Sign: KE1Y
Rolf Dieter Seichter
80 Lancaster Dr
Tewksbury MA 01876

Call Sign: KF4KT
Christoph J Janker
80 Lancaster Dr
Tewksbury MA 01876

Call Sign: KD1EA
Albert R Kinnon Iii
113 Lancaster Dr

Tewksbury MA 01876

Call Sign: N1RQK
Louis H Beverly Jr
74 Leighton Ln
Tewksbury MA 01876

Call Sign: KB1FRY
Adam O Brenden
978 Livingston St
Tewksbury MA 01876

Call Sign: WA1FCU
George E Kelley Sr
9 Lloyd Rd
Tewksbury MA 01876

Call Sign: KA1QOY
Deborah S Carleen
521 Main St
Tewksbury MA 01876

Call Sign: AB1IC
Deborah S Carleen
521 Main St
Tewksbury MA 01876

Call Sign: K1STV
Regis A Mannion
2581 Main St
Tewksbury MA 01876

Call Sign: KB1ONZ
Michael R Holmes
225 Maple St
Tewksbury MA 01876

Call Sign: WB1CKD
George E Yost
7 Margaret Rd
Tewksbury MA 01876

Call Sign: KB1NMZ
Steven S Reid
10 Marion Dr
Tewksbury MA
018761264

Call Sign: W1YEI
Joseph A Sullivan
15 Miles Rd
Tewksbury MA 01876

Call Sign: KA1QFC

Jo Anne M Nelson
17 Miles Rd
Tewksbury MA 01876

Call Sign: WB2DDB
Richard B Smith
62 Mount Joy Dr
Tewksbury MA 01876

Call Sign: W1EZ
Richard B Smith
62 Mount Joy Dr
Tewksbury MA 01876

Call Sign: KC1PV
Mark A Bristol
251 N Billerica Rd
Tewksbury MA 01876

Call Sign: N1ITO
Nelson J Thompson
50 Navillus Rd
Tewksbury MA 01876

Call Sign: N1HQN
David N Jones
75 New Jersey Rd
Tewksbury MA 01876

Call Sign: WA1YMQ
John Lu
43 North St
Tewksbury MA 01876

Call Sign: KB1INS
Shane M Nevins
50 North St
Tewksbury MA 01876

Call Sign: KA1SPV
Dana O Burns
53 North St
Tewksbury MA 01876

Call Sign: WA1GOS
John C Sliva
254 North St
Tewksbury MA
018761910

Call Sign: WB1CAN
Robert W Hazard
51 Oak Rd
Tewksbury MA 01876

Call Sign: W1GMT
Robert C Mores
3 Old Boston Rd
Tewksbury MA 01876

Call Sign: N1JZL
Christopher A Augusta
844 Old Shawsheen St
Tewksbury MA 01876

Call Sign: KB1UGW
Daniel W Post
140 Patricia Dr
Tewksbury MA 01876

Call Sign: KA1QPX
Darrell E Sprague
8 Patriot Rd
Tewksbury MA 01876

Call Sign: KB1HMA
David M Casey
100 Pine St
Tewksbury MA 01876

Call Sign: W1KXL
Richard M Lena
32 Pinewold Ave
Tewksbury MA 01876

Call Sign: KB1DKG
George V Colburn
7 Pocahontas Rd
Tewksbury MA 01876

Call Sign: KB1FYX
William E Milne
110 Regina S Drive
Tewksbury MA 01876

Call Sign: W1LUS
Bruce C Anderson
16 Regis Rd
Tewksbury MA 01876

Call Sign: KB1RLV
Anton H Verhulst
320 Rogers St
Tewksbury MA 01876

Call Sign: W1DYS
Anton H Verhulst
320 Rogers St

Tewksbury MA 01876

Call Sign: KO1Q
Robert T Bucci
461 Rogers St
Tewksbury MA 01876

Call Sign: KA1ICF
Karl A Albrecht
696 Rogers St
Tewksbury MA 01876

Call Sign: KA1MHQ
Emmi Albrecht
696 Rogers St
Tewksbury MA 01876

Call Sign: N1DXP
Joerg W Walzenbach
696 Rogers St
Tewksbury MA 01876

Call Sign: KA1RDF
Donald E Payne
91 Ronald Dr
Tewksbury MA 01876

Call Sign: W1UCP
Salvatore F Cogliano
91 Ronald Dr
Tewksbury MA 01876

Call Sign: WB1DGU
Sean Cogliano
91 Ronald Dr
Tewksbury MA 01876

Call Sign: KB1IRS
Brian J Ristuccia
Sharon St
Tewksbury MA
018763233

Call Sign: N1GGB
Christopher G Krueger
1243 Shawsheen St
Tewksbury MA 01876

Call Sign: KB1WK
Lawrence M De Vito
250 South St
Tewksbury MA 01876

Call Sign: N1KFK

John G Caramanis
125 Starr Ave
Tewksbury MA 01876

Call Sign: N1HTS
James J Evans
90 Tenth St
Tewksbury MA 01876

Call Sign: W1GGB
Donald G Hicks
541 Trull Rd
Tewksbury MA 01876

Call Sign: KA2VBW
Christine Williams
85 Vale St
Tewksbury MA 01876

Call Sign: KA2VBX
Bryon L Williams
85 Vale St
Tewksbury MA 01876

Call Sign: NC1U
Peter P Bongiorno
16 Villa Roma Drive
Tewksbury MA 01876

Call Sign: WB1EYB
Richard F Plasse
735 Whipple Rd
Tewksbury MA 01876

Call Sign: K1HN
Richard F Plasse
735 Whipple Rd
Tewksbury MA 01876

Call Sign: W1TFJ
Edward G Daly Jr
20 Willow St
Tewksbury MA 01876

Call Sign: WA1GRC
Gary A Field
70 Worthen Pl
Tewksbury MA 01876

Call Sign: N1QEZ
Larry C Garneau Sr
Tewksbury MA 01876

Call Sign: N1QFA

Virginia A Garneau
Tewksbury MA 01876

Call Sign: N1QIG
Louis A Mascia
Tewksbury MA 01876

Call Sign: WA1LWI
David H Parisi
Tewksbury MA
018760006

Call Sign: KB1HRZ
Region One Radio
Club
Tewksbury MA
018760116

Call Sign: WC1MAA
Mema Region One
Radio Club
Tewksbury MA
018760116

Call Sign: KB1MVC
Paul R Nichols
Tewksbury MA 01876

Call Sign: KB1DGE
Gerald J Kukler
Tewsbury MA 01876

Call Sign: N1ZFX
Scott A Giard
4035 Church St
Thorndike MA 01079

Call Sign: WB1BPS
Kenneth N Pincince
Thorndike MA 01079

Call Sign: KB1GPG
Allan J Krantz
45 Bourne St
Three Rivers MA
01080

Call Sign: KB1VYZ
Nicholas A Maslon
81 Bourne St
Three Rivers MA
01080

Call Sign: K1MAZ
Nicholas A Maslon
81 Bourne St
Three Rivers MA
01080

Call Sign: KB1RAS
Ronald P Ciejka
2026 Cross St
Three Rivers MA
01080

Call Sign: KB1VKX
David J Uguccioni
75 Lariviere Ave
Three Rivers MA
01080

Call Sign: KB1WHC
David J Uguccioni
75 Lariviere Ave
Three Rivers MA
01080

Call Sign: KA1GYT
Roland J Chartier
2021 Overlook Dr
Three Rivers MA
010801028

Call Sign: WB1CND
Wayne A Nareau Sr
1 Overlook St
Three Rivers MA
01080

Call Sign: WA1YSS
Maurice E Dufresne
10 Sibley St
Three Rivers MA
01080

Call Sign: W0RBN
John W Clough

125 Main St
Tisbury MA 02568

Call Sign: W1SQZ
James A Warren
132 Brook Ln
Tolland MA 01034

Call Sign: KB1CEI
Joseph J Clark Iv
927 Burt Hill Rd
Tolland MA
010349565

Call Sign: K3OQ
Ian O Mcalister
103 Hartland R
Tolland MA 01034

Call Sign: KB1EVM
Ian O Mcalister
103 Hartland Rd
Tolland MA 01034

Call Sign: W1PZ
Pocahontas Radio Club
286 Boston St
Topsfield MA
019831919

Call Sign: N1HOW
Donald Y Wood
286 Boston St
Topsfield MA 01983

Call Sign: KB1MEI
Edmund D Berry
22 Canterbury Hill
Topsfield MA 01983

Call Sign: W1ZNY
John H Wilcox
197 Central St
Topsfield MA 01983

Call Sign: N1DJU
Ruth M Mott
40 Gail St

Topsfield MA 01983

Call Sign: W1FJ
Alfred C Rousseau
40 Gail St
Topsfield MA 01983

Call Sign: KB1SRS
Gregory A Tucker
1 Glen Rd
Topsfield MA 01983

Call Sign: KA1KQI
Donald E Nulk
87 Haverhill Rd
Topsfield MA 01983

Call Sign: N1RK
Roy L Knudsen
161 High St
Topsfield MA 01983

Call Sign: N1VUM
Raymond A Beaulieu
High St
Topsfield MA 01983

Call Sign: KA1DLD
Georgianna K Magner
84 Hill St
Topsfield MA 01983

Call Sign: N1OQZ
Mary L Penta
88 Hill St
Topsfield MA
019832404

Call Sign: W1ABC
Anthony J Penta
88 Hill St
Topsfield MA
019832404

Call Sign: N1AP
Anthony J Penta
88 Hill St
Topsfield MA
019832404

Call Sign: KA1MHO
Wayne L Miller
16 Normandy Row
Topsfield MA 01983

Call Sign: KB1HXN
Maria Haeussler
85 Parsonage Lane
Topsfield MA 01983

Call Sign: KB1HXQ
Klaus Haeussler
85 Parsonage Lane
Topsfield MA 01983

Call Sign: ND1B
Edwin R Bowerman
47 Parsonage Ln
Topsfield MA
019831314

Call Sign: KB1TRB
Allan F Edwards
68 Parsonage Ln
Topsfield MA 01983

Call Sign: AB1LT
Robert N Edwards
68 Parsonage Ln
Topsfield MA 01983

Call Sign: KB1LCM
Ricky S Webster
116 Perkins Row
Topsfield MA 01983

Call Sign: KB1DZL
Harry C Reifel
137 Perkins Row
Topsfield MA 01983

Call Sign: N1HSZ
William A Wood
14 Ross Rd
Topsfield MA 01983

Call Sign: N1VDA
Derek B Kolakowski
16 Rowley Rd
Topsfield MA 01983

Call Sign: WA1KAT
Roger K Kolakowski
16 Rowley Rd
Topsfield MA 01983

Call Sign: KA7EBP
Laurie J Butler

51 Rowley Rd
Topsfield MA
019831038

Call Sign: KS1O
James R Butler
51 Rowley Rd
Topsfield MA
019831038

Call Sign: N1NFF
David T Reifel
21 Summer St
Topsfield MA 01983

Call Sign: N1DCF
Thomas E Geary
32 Summer St
Topsfield MA 01983

Call Sign: KA1OMA
Gary A Bell
45 Washington St
Topsfield MA 01983

Call Sign: N1RTA
Stephen M Mackey
90 Washington St
Topsfield MA 01983

Call Sign: KA1VPA
Tamara L Harper
158 Washington St
Topsfield MA 01983

Call Sign: KA1VPC
David C Harper
158 Washington St
Topsfield MA 01983

Call Sign: N1ONS
Wayne L Killian
186 Washington St
Topsfield MA 01983

Call Sign: KD1AV
David M Scherman
69 Washington St 10b
Topsfield MA 01983

Call Sign: KA1JBJ
Dean L Harwood
69 Washington St Apt
10c

Topsfield MA
019831743

Call Sign: N0BMQ
Joel P Hariton
12 Willowdale Rd
Topsfield MA 01983

Call Sign: N1UPW
Alan S Finger
5 Woodbrier Rd
Topsfield MA 01983

Call Sign: N1HSY
Charles B Wood
6 Woodbrier Rd
Topsfield MA
019832225

Call Sign: W1GPU
Joseph F Sciora
30 Woodside Rd
Topsfield MA 01983

**FCC Amateur Radio
Licenses in Townsend**

Call Sign: KA1LDP
Erica R Davenport
33 Ash St
Townsend MA 01469

Call Sign: N1CSF
Drew A Davenport
33 Ash St
Townsend MA 01469

Call Sign: W1PCQ
Drew A Davenport
33 Ash St
Townsend MA 01469

Call Sign: AA1MT
Dwight E Fitch
72 Ash St
Townsend MA
014691410

Call Sign: KB1NTS
Edward C Mason
86 Bayberry Hill Rd
Townsend MA 01474

Call Sign: AE1Y

Edward C Mason
86 Bayberry Hill Rd
Townsend MA 01474

Call Sign: N1HMV
Richard L Coit
4 Blood Rd
Townsend MA 01469

Call Sign: WA1SMM
Susan A Amero
31 Blood Rd
Townsend MA 01469

Call Sign: KC4IOT
Randy J Karr
46 Blood Rd
Townsend MA 01469

Call Sign: W1OSS
Edwin S West
16 Boutelle Rd
Townsend MA 01469

Call Sign: KB1DSK
Sandy P Massalski
100 Brookline Rd
Townsend MA 01469

Call Sign: N8TJO
Timothy Chernosky
16 Brookline St
Townsend MA 01469

Call Sign: KD1YH
Paul H Upham
50 Brookline St
Townsend MA 01469

Call Sign: N1ZQM
Charles C Smith Jr
67 Brookline St
Townsend MA 01469

Call Sign: KB1KHM
Peter F Hill
12 Center St
Townsend MA 01469

Call Sign: N1VPT
John H Dickerson
2 Dix St
Townsend MA 01469

Call Sign: KB1RGT
Frederick J Darling Jr
20 Dudley Rd
Townsend MA 01469

Call Sign: WA1ETC
John J Martin
20 Edward Rd
Townsend MA 01469

Call Sign: N1VEU
Theodore Bjornson
50 Edward Rd
Townsend MA 01469

Call Sign: KB1VRA
Garrett Cavanaugh
10 Emory Rd
Townsend MA 01469

Call Sign: KA1ZJC
Robert J Lee
4 Fitchburg Rd 425
Townsend MA 01469

Call Sign: K1ABA
Henry J Conner
21 Haines Rd
Townsend MA 01469

Call Sign: KA1DZV
Leslie R Peters Iii
33 Haynes Rd
Townsend MA 01469

Call Sign: N1SV
Leslie R Peters Iii
33 Haynes Rd
Townsend MA 01469

Call Sign: K1LN
James W Hunt
16 Hickory Dr
Townsend MA 01469

Call Sign: N1VAL
Michael P
Shaughnessy
3 Howard St
Townsend MA 01469

Call Sign: K1PNB
Paul E F Morey
304 Main St

Townsend MA 01469

Call Sign: KB1ZK
David A Glow
14 Maple St
Townsend MA 01469

Call Sign: W1NZD
George R Martin
7 Oak St Box 149
Townsend MA 01469

Call Sign: N1TCC
Glenn J Sundberg
5 Pisces Ln
Townsend MA 01469

Call Sign: KB1BMJ
Brandon M Kilgore
9 Ponderosa Dr
Townsend MA 01469

Call Sign: N1XOU
Joseph J Burbage
11 Ponderosa Dr
Townsend MA 01469

Call Sign: KB1LRD
Lee L Duckett Iii
23 Ponderosa Dr
Townsend MA
014691320

Call Sign: KA1MVM
Walter Parfenuk
6 Ponderosa Drive
Townsend MA
014691321

Call Sign: KB1BSW
Nathanael C Anding
4 Redwood St
Townsend MA 01469

Call Sign: KB1LBV
James M Kinsella
91 S Harbor Rd
Townsend MA 01469

Call Sign: N1HZF
Christopher A
Struthers
25 South St
Townsend MA 01469

Call Sign: KB1UMI
Brendan Kelley
46 Spaulding St
Townsend MA 01469

Call Sign: KB1TCY
Frederick J Wheeler Iii
22 Sumac Dr
Townsend MA 01469

Call Sign: KA1HCU
Richard P Selfridge
83 Turner Rd
Townsend MA 01469

Call Sign: KA1KNY
Walter T Beese Jr
81 Turnpike Rd
Townsend MA 01469

Call Sign: K1YTS
Gary W Busler
92 Turnpike Rd
Townsend MA
014691054

Call Sign: KA1ZAQ
Robert E Kwiatkowski
5 Turnpike Rd - 123
Townsend MA 01469

Call Sign: KB1RLC
Joseph E Gordon
29 Tyler Rd
Townsend MA 01469

Call Sign: KB1PAQ
Michael F Cloutier
79 Tyler Rd
Townsend MA 01469

Call Sign: W1SLH
Michael Cloutier
79 Tyler Rd
Townsend MA 01469

Call Sign: AA1YA
Stephen R Cloutier
79 Tyler Rd
Townsend MA 01469

Call Sign: WA1QIX
Stephen R Cloutier

79 Tyler Rd
Townsend MA 01469

Call Sign: WW4EN
Eugene Novacek
144 Tyler Rd
Townsend MA 01469

Call Sign: KA1QL
Edmund J Walsh
3 Virgo Ln
Townsend MA 01469

Call Sign: K1MVN
Peter H Lukesh
85 Wallace Hill Rd
Townsend MA
014691159

Call Sign: WA1UMK
Jill R Lukesh
85 Wallace Hill Rd
Townsend MA 01469

Call Sign: KB1QZE
John E Santosuosso
23 Walnut St
Townsend MA 01469

Call Sign: WB1AMN
Edwin I Salmi Jr
2 Warner Rd
Townsend MA 01469

Call Sign: W1FDW
Donald P Girard
25 Warren Rd
Townsend MA 01469

Call Sign: KA1UQO
Daniel T Roche
26 Warren Rd
Townsend MA 01469

Call Sign: KA1ZEB
Michael A Coulter
4 Willow Dr
Townsend MA 01469

Call Sign: KA1IMP
David E Whiting
36 Worcester Rd
Townsend MA 01469

Call Sign: W1FEM
Daniel H Kaney Jr
Townsend MA 01469

Call Sign: N4ANG
Richard S Shuford
Townsend MA
014690886

Call Sign: KB1RVX
David A Sawyer
Townsend MA 01469

Call Sign: WA1VNQ
Jay T Thiel
78 Main St
Townsend Harbor MA
01469

Call Sign: W1LZV
Dennis Cole
Higgins Hollow Rd
Truro MA 02666

Call Sign: W1CQC
James J Mullins
Truro MA 02666

Call Sign: KB1JUJ
John Skoyles
Truro MA 02666

Call Sign: KB1MJR
Lon C Morris
Truro MA 02666

Call Sign: KB1TLV
Michael A Janoplis
Truro MA 02666

Call Sign: KB1GCV
David B Allen
41 Davis St

Turner Falls MA
01376

Call Sign: N1XWX
Kenneth D Jordan Jr
10 Park St
Turner Falls MA
01376

Call Sign: N1GAP
Carol L Mc Farland
119 Ave A
Turners Falls MA
01376

Call Sign: KA1WOL
Stuart B Carlisle
13 Carlisle Ave
Turners Falls MA
01376

Call Sign: KB1HBR
Chris G Wood
43 Central St Apt 3
Turners Falls MA
01376

Call Sign: N1HNK
Richard E Kovalsick
12 Crocker Ave
Turners Falls MA
01376

Call Sign: K1MGF
Martin E Glaser
4 Davis St
Turners Falls MA
01376

Call Sign: KB1STW
William E Markowski
8 Keith St
Turners Falls MA
01376

Call Sign: AB1LR
William E Markowski
8 Keith St
Turners Falls MA
01376

Call Sign: N1XPT
Chester Chin
65 Millers Falls Rd

Turners Falls MA
01376

Call Sign: KB1NQL
Edith M Chin
65 Millers Falls Rd
Turners Falls MA
01376

Call Sign: WA1YRV
Kyle J Scott
103 Millers Falls Rd
Turners Falls MA
01376

Call Sign: N1WQZ
Lucas G Cote
8 Morris Ave
Turners Falls MA
01376

Call Sign: KE1FB
Andrew G Humpel
25 N St
Turners Falls MA
01376

Call Sign: KB1BNG
Edward F Boutwell
5 Poplar St
Turners Falls MA
01376

Call Sign: KA1OQY
Roger W Boutwell
9 Turnpike Rd
Turners Falls MA
01376

Call Sign: N1OWB
Russell A Holt
94 Turnpike Rd
Turners Falls MA
013762601

Call Sign: AB1DY
Russell A Holt
94 Turnpike Rd
Turners Falls MA
013762601

Call Sign: N1XSP
Stanley M Wozniak

Turners Falls MA
01376

Call Sign: KA1YSK
Russell F Bent
171 Beech St
Tweksbury MA 02186

See also FCC Amateur Radio Licenses in Tyngborough

Call Sign: KA1HLK
Rita A Evicci
8 Trotting Park Rd
Tyngboro MA 01879

Call Sign: KB1IVV
Christopher M Whynot
3 Benoit Ln
Tyngsboro MA 01879

Call Sign: N1NCL
Allan S Douglas
12 Bridget Ave
Tyngsboro MA 01879

Call Sign: N1IWF
Terence A Koen
22 Cannongate Rd
Tyngsboro MA 01879

Call Sign: KA1SMH
Joseph A Costa
601 Cardinal Ln
Tyngsboro MA 01879

Call Sign: KB1FZM
Patricia A Crowley
92 Chestnut Rd
Tyngsboro MA 01879

Call Sign: KC1RS
Norman E Martell Sr
62 Constantine Dr
Tyngsboro MA 01879

Call Sign: KI6MF
Wallace M Brooks
49 Derby Lane
Tyngsboro MA 01879

Call Sign: KD6BLK
Lisa M Scheuplein
49 Derby Ln
Tyngsboro MA 01879

Call Sign: KD6IKM
Laura I Sousa
454 Dunstable Rd
Tyngsboro MA 01879

Call Sign: KD6IKO
Helio F Sousa
454 Dunstable Rd
Tyngsboro MA 01879

Call Sign: N1HDH
Thomas F Sheehy
50 Farwell Rd
Tyngsboro MA 01879

Call Sign: K1ASB
Raymond N Wear
185 Frost Rd
Tyngsboro MA 01879

Call Sign: N1YRD
John R Pelletier
186 Frost Rd Unit 11
Tyngsboro MA 01879

Call Sign: KE6ODX
Robert E Wilcox
14 Highland St
Tyngsboro MA
018791011

Call Sign: K1NPB
Ross K Whynot
76 Kendall Rd
Tyngsboro MA 01879

Call Sign: KB1SEI
Wesley W Russell
187 Kendall Rd
Tyngsboro MA 01879

Call Sign: K1TJV
Albert F Lescard

39 Maplewood Ave
Tyngsboro MA 01879

Call Sign: AA5JO
Howard E Miller
127 Massapoag Rd
Tyngsboro MA 01879

Call Sign: AB1CW
Howard E Miller
127 Massapoag Rd
Tyngsboro MA 01879

Call Sign: KA1TGL
James R Banyas Jr
36 Middlesex Rd
Tyngsboro MA 01879

Call Sign: KB1SXB
Corliss H Lambert
204 Middlesex Rd
Tyngsboro MA 01879

Call Sign: K6KAQ
John M Davis
342 Middlesex Rd
Tyngsboro MA 01879

Call Sign: KA1YLU
Bruce G Preston
52 Pawtucket Blvd
Unit 28
Tyngsboro MA 01879

Call Sign: KA1VNZ
Sadao Adachi
504 Pondview Village
Tyngsboro MA 01879

Call Sign: N1SFH
Nancy A Kelly
50 Scribner Rd
Tyngsboro MA 01879

Call Sign: WA1EFK
Edward F Kelly
50 Scribner Rd
Tyngsboro MA 01879

Call Sign: KA1HOX
Raymond J Evicci Sr
8 Trotting Pk Rd
Tyngsboro MA 01879

Call Sign: NW1U
Paul L Randazzo
12 Turnbuckle Ln
Tyngsboro MA 01879

Call Sign: N1CIF
Bernhard A Ziegner
7 Village Ln 14b
Tyngsboro MA 01879

Call Sign: WA1ISF
Eugene M Zenoni
291 Westford Rd
Tyngsboro MA 01879

Call Sign: N1KMH
Michael V Chandonnet
26 Wicasse Rd
Tyngsboro MA 01879

Call Sign: KA1WHL
Frederick S Reed
81 Willowdale Rd
Tyngsboro MA 01879

Call Sign: KB1DY
William F
Shaughnessy
82 Windemere Circle
Tyngsboro MA 01879

Call Sign: N1BMI
Michael J Witt
8 Wyoming Rd
Tyngsboro MA 01879

Call Sign: AA1RJ
Osamu Ishiguro
Tyngsboro MA
018790623

Call Sign: KJ4CDP
Heather M Urwiller
Tyngsboro MA 01879

**FCC Amateur Radio
Licenses in
Tyngsborough**

**See also FCC
Amateur Radio
Licenses in
Tyngsboro**

Call Sign: N1CXO
Ronald F Crowley
92 Chestnut Rd
Tyngsborough MA
01879

Call Sign: W1WBV
Ronald F Crowley
92 Chestnut Rd
Tyngsborough MA
01879

Call Sign: WB1FUA
William A Flaherty
10 Davis Rd
Tyngsborough MA
01879

Call Sign: W1WAF
William A Flaherty
10 Davis Rd
Tyngsborough MA
01879

Call Sign: N1PTU
Dennis M Darcy
14 Gail Ave
Tyngsborough MA
01879

Call Sign: KB1FEA
Richard E Raymond Jr
62 Lawndale Rd
Tyngsborough MA
01879

Call Sign: N1KMW
Frank A Bunker
134 Middlesex Rd
Tyngsborough MA
01879

Call Sign: N1NQX
David B Swanay
2 Paddock Rd
Tyngsborough MA
01879

Call Sign: KB1JLY
Michael S Kastanas
261 Pawtucket Blvd
Tyngsborough MA
01879

Call Sign: KE6JYB
David L Masters
114 Scribner Rd
Tyngsborough MA
01879

Call Sign: K1NKR
James W Youngberg
7 Turnbuckle Ln
Tyngsborough MA
01879

Call Sign: K1SZI
Leonard Martell
62 Constantine Dr
Tynsgboro MA 01879

Call Sign: K1NP
Main Rd Tyringham
Bandits Arc
Tyringham MA 01264

**FCC Amateur Radio
Licenses in Upton**

Call Sign: N1LIJ
Robert A Frascatore
32 Cider Mill Lane
Upton MA 01568

Call Sign: WA1OMW
Richard R Creed
4 Cristian Hill Rd
Upton MA 01568

Call Sign: N1KIN
Terry L Saunders Ii
18 Francis Drive
Upton MA 01568

Call Sign: N1APU
Scott M Ferguson
5 Glen Ave
Upton MA 01568

Call Sign: WB1Q
Chandler W Jones
79 Glen Ave
Upton MA 01568

Call Sign: W1JZ
Michael R Samarco
111 Glen Ave
Upton MA 01568

Call Sign: N1ZWH
Christopher C Mauro
149 Glenview St
Upton MA 01568

Call Sign: AG1C
Lawrence F Mccoskery
21 Hartford Ave S
Upton MA 01568

Call Sign: KA1SRF
Jean L Anderson
93 Mechanic St
Upton MA 01568

Call Sign: WA1MDS
Ernest R Hart
5 Mendon St
Upton MA 01568

Call Sign: KB1JQW
Michel E Lareau
343 Mendon St
Upton MA 01568

Call Sign: N1OQ
Robert S Trotte
32 North St
Upton MA 01568

Call Sign: KB1UAI
Christopher C Marsden
3 Pease Rd
Upton MA 01568

Call Sign: WA1LWC
Peter J Hart
11 Pleasant St
Upton MA 01568

Call Sign: W1VP
Gerald L Meiler
27 Pleasant St
Upton MA 015681429

Call Sign: N1YMY
Jeanne M Glagowski
147 Pleasant St
Upton MA 01568

Call Sign: N1PUB
Monika R Horsefield
19 Prospect St

Upton MA 01568

Call Sign: AA1JX
Charles J Schoumaker
43 South St
Upton MA 01568

Call Sign: W1ZJS
Edith J Shaughnessy
12 Stoddard St
Upton MA 01568

Call Sign: KV1I
Robert E Genoa
135 West River St
Upton MA 01568

Call Sign: N1VYA
Paul A W Baumgarner
5 Whitney Ln
Upton MA 01568

Call Sign: KA1LQF
Robert C Humes Jr
35 Williams St
Upton MA 01568

Call Sign: KB1MNV
James C Marsden
Upton MA 01568

Call Sign: KB1QWL
Amy K Coughlin
Upton MA 01568

**FCC Amateur Radio
Licenses in Uxbridge**

Call Sign: N1KDA
Robert J Wondolowski
163 Albee Rd
Uxbridge MA
015691981

Call Sign: N1SYS
Elizabeth M
Wondolowski
163 Albee Rd
Uxbridge MA 01569

Call Sign: N1ORR
Michael C Bretana
836 Aldrich St
Uxbridge MA 01569

Call Sign: K1UKX
Fred S Randall
490 Blackstone St
Uxbridge MA 01569

Call Sign: KA1KFD
John J Lawless
Box 2071 Apt 5
Uxbridge MA 01569

Call Sign: KB1FCE
John S Roe
37 Brookside Dr
Uxbridge MA 01569

Call Sign: K0END
John S Roe
37 Brookside Drive
Uxbridge MA 01569

Call Sign: KB1WNK
Luke A Macneil
50 Brown Ter
Uxbridge MA 01569

Call Sign: N1QFW
Abby R Williams
75 Carney St
Uxbridge MA 01569

Call Sign: WB2HSI
Kenneth A Williams
75 Carney St
Uxbridge MA 01569

Call Sign: N1AZL
William J Ross
382 Chestnut St
Uxbridge MA 01569

Call Sign: WB2PJE
Stephen J Suchanek
41 Conestoga Dr
Uxbridge MA 01569

Call Sign: N1QMK
George L Fitzpatrick
26 Crown Eagle Rd
Uxbridge MA 01569

Call Sign: N1CX
Scott R Bullock
36 Deanna Dr

Uxbridge MA 01569

Call Sign: K1CTY
Ralph V Borden
126 Douglas St
Uxbridge MA 01569

Call Sign: N8TVJ
Milan C Wright
55 Dunleavey Brook
Rd
Uxbridge MA 01569

Call Sign: KO1R
Milan C Wright
55 Dunleavey Brook
Rd
Uxbridge MA 01569

Call Sign: NR1U
Alan J Anderson
373 East St
Uxbridge MA
015691947

Call Sign: KB1JRX
Andrew D Garabedian
92 Elm St
Uxbridge MA 01569

Call Sign: KB1KCW
Linda J Garabedian
92 Elm St
Uxbridge MA 01569

Call Sign: WB1GVC
Stephen M Swift
46 Granite St Apt E
Uxbridge MA 01569

Call Sign: N1FJU
Paul A Milke
50 Harvest Rd
Uxbridge MA 01569

Call Sign: WA1IWI
Lance B Salmonsen
322 High St
Uxbridge MA 01569

Call Sign: K5ZD
Randall A Thompson
11 Hollis St
Uxbridge MA 01569

Call Sign: KB1KBM
Uxbridge Contest Club
11 Hollis St
Uxbridge MA 01569

Call Sign: AK1W
Uxbridge Contest Club
11 Hollis St
Uxbridge MA 01569

Call Sign: KB1NXJ
Andrew B Thompson
11 Hollis St
Uxbridge MA 01569

Call Sign: W1JAL
Regis E Breault
3 Loyalist Dr
Uxbridge MA 01569

Call Sign: KB1QYS
Paul K Nichols
30 Maple St
Uxbridge MA 01569

Call Sign: N1UFN
Adam P Bielski
141 Mendon St
Uxbridge MA 01569

Call Sign: N9NEO
Robert A La France
21 Moorland Drive
Uxbridge MA 01569

Call Sign: KB1MPD
James D Hoard
95 N Main St
Uxbridge MA
015691720

Call Sign: KB1PQJ
Edward R Tejeiro
36 Olde Canal Way
Uxbridge MA 01569

Call Sign: WA1KVU
Konrad L Schultz
216 Quaker Hwy
Uxbridge MA 01569

Call Sign: KA1QOX
Lorraine Towne

65 Richardson St
Uxbridge MA 01569

Call Sign: KB1AGN
Donald E Salome
440 River Rd
Uxbridge MA
015692247

Call Sign: KA1JK
Joseph F Actor
56 Rockmeadow Dr
Ext
Uxbridge MA 01569

Call Sign: K1AUI
John Santoian
36 Rockmeadow Rd
Uxbridge MA
015691416

Call Sign: N1KFR
Todd C Thompson
7 Rose Lane
Uxbridge MA 01569

Call Sign: WA1NLM
Gary D Gutowski
91 S Main St
Uxbridge MA 01569

Call Sign: KB1FI
Howard M Sears
38 Saratoga Dr
Uxbridge MA 01569

Call Sign: AB1HO
Spencer K Borden Jr
63 Spinning Wheel Dr
Uxbridge MA 01569

Call Sign: WB1AML
Frank J Lennox Jr
123 Sutton St
Uxbridge MA 01569

Call Sign: WA1YGW
Kendall W Jacquart
9 Taft St
Uxbridge MA 01569

Call Sign: KB1MH
John M Smoot
17 Teresa Dr

Uxbridge MA 01569

Call Sign: N1NBB
Diane M Smoot
17 Teresa Dr
Uxbridge MA 01569

Call Sign: KB1JUG
Teresa A
Vanfechtmann
156 W Hartford Ave
Uxbridge MA 01569

Call Sign: N1OCB
James M Lynch
262 W River Rd
Uxbridge MA 01569

Call Sign: KB1MJI
Peter Demers
4 Waucantuck Dr
Uxbridge MA 01569

Call Sign: W2KVP
Peter Demers
4 Waucantuck Dr
Uxbridge MA 01569

Call Sign: KB1EBZ
Nancy F O Sullivan
105 West Hartford Ave
Uxbridge MA 01569

Call Sign: N1PSE
Michael J Baril
Uxbridge MA
015690072

Call Sign: KB1HKK
Michael J Baril
Uxbridge MA
015690072

Call Sign: KB1IIE
Mema Regional Races
Club
Uxbridge MA
015690072

Call Sign: KB1IVI
Inc Canton Ma Public
Safety Assn
Uxbridge MA
015690072

Call Sign: W1PAX
Central Ma Public
Safety Assn Inc
Uxbridge MA
015690072

FCC Amateur Radio Licenses in Vineyard Haven

Call Sign: KA1UOF
John M Clarke
Box 1939
Vineyard Haven MA
02568

Call Sign: KA1SET
Philip D Fleischman
Box 1951
Vineyard Haven MA
02568

Call Sign: KB1IYV
Peter V Behr
Box 220e
Vineyard Haven MA
02568

Call Sign: N1BWA
Ronald H Tolin
Box 2k
Vineyard Haven MA
02568

Call Sign: WB1ESS
Irving Warner Jr
Box 607
Vineyard Haven MA
02568

Call Sign: K1LEP
Thomas A Norton
Daggett Ave
Vineyard Haven MA
02568

Call Sign: K1CK
Samuel B Issokson
31 Davis St
Vineyard Haven MA
02568

Call Sign: KA1YXB

Edward S Child
Lamberts Cove Rd
Vineyard Haven MA
025689777

Call Sign: N1PRM
Jeffrey S Baker
131 Midland Ave
Vineyard Haven MA
02568

Call Sign: KA1VFT
Jacqueline R Fitts
Rfd 336a
Vineyard Haven MA
02568

Call Sign: KA3GWI
Diana H Helfrich
Rfd Box 399
Vineyard Haven MA
02568

Call Sign: W2WCT
Harold S Stamm
Rfd Box 473
Vineyard Haven MA
02568

Call Sign: WA1CUH
David W Dunham
43 Skiff Ave
Vineyard Haven MA
02568

Call Sign: N1WRL
Harold F Croft
Tashmoo Ave
Vineyard Haven MA
02568

Call Sign: KB1IHV
Robert E Maciel Sr
70 Tiahs Cove Rd
Vineyard Haven MA
02568

Call Sign: N1KHI
Cedric Belain
Vineyard Haven MA
02568

Call Sign: K1ISJ
Bruce I Coggins

Vineyard Haven MA
025682047

Call Sign: WA1LZI
Ronald A Walsh
Vineyard Haven MA
025680547

Call Sign: KB1IHU
Charles J Cotnoir
Vineyard Haven MA
025681299

Call Sign: W1FML
Ronald A Walsh
Vineyard Haven MA
025680547

FCC Amateur Radio Licenses in Waban

Call Sign: WB1EWP
Sheldon Peck
1615 Beacon St
Waban MA 024681507

Call Sign: W1QUP
Francis D Kirchoff
585 Chestnut St
Waban MA 02168

Call Sign: WB1GOP
Alan E Geller
41 Collins Rd
Waban MA 02468

Call Sign: AA1FG
David H Hubel
98 Collins Rd
Waban MA 02168

Call Sign: K2EN
John P Costas
145 Collins Rd
Waban MA 021682211

Call Sign: KA1WZR
Carol L Bracken
14 Cotter Rd
Waban MA 02168

Call Sign: N1KAQ
Robert G Huntley
31 Cotter Rd

Waban MA 02468

Call Sign: KB1INO
Michael S
Leuchtenburg
40 Devonshire Rd
Waban MA 02468

Call Sign: N2NSG
Alex Klimov
202 Evelyn Rd
Waban MA 02468

Call Sign: W1IDG
Gerald D Rosen
20 Holly Rd
Waban MA 02168

Call Sign: KB1SSN
Alexander L Dills
37 Lawmarissa Rd
Waban MA 02468

Call Sign: KB1EFN
Gary S Chan
91 Mary Ellen Rd
Waban MA 024681026

Call Sign: KB1ULF
Nathan A Oasis
167 Nehoiden Rd
Waban MA 02468

Call Sign: W1NVW
Robert M Zakon
130 Oliver Rd
Waban MA 021680002

Call Sign: W1TSP
Richard M Finkel
70 Paulson Rd
Waban MA 024681028

Call Sign: W1AZG
Marvin C Grossman
21 Pilgrim Rd
Waban MA 021682124

Call Sign: K1QHQ
Joseph Ress
45 Pontiac Rd
Waban MA 02168

Call Sign: AJ1J

Joseph Ress
45 Pontiac Rd
Waban MA 02168

Call Sign: WA2ZBS
James A Rothendler
51 Upland Rd
Waban MA 02168

Call Sign: KB1SUI
Simon G Korn
41 Wamesit Rd
Waban MA 02468

Call Sign: W1LRS
Harvey Karp
32 Warren Rd
Waban MA 02168

Call Sign: W1LMU
Henry J Mc Dade
194 Winslow Rd
Waban MA 02168

Call Sign: WA1UDS
Mark E Costa
631 Woodward St
Waban MA 02468

**FCC Amateur Radio
Licenses in Wakefield**

Call Sign: N1TWD
Vincent F Carreiro
272 Albion St
Wakefield MA
018803160

Call Sign: W1WXJ
George C Mc Lemore
Jr
276 Albion St Apt 17
Wakefield MA 01880

Call Sign: KB1FYW
John J Frautten
35 Albion St Apt 5
Wakefield MA 01880

Call Sign: N1KYL
David B Johnson Jr
10 Appleton Rd
Wakefield MA 01880

Call Sign: KB1TST
John R Pozark
95 Audubon Rd Apt
606
Wakefield MA 01880

Call Sign: N1PMD
Stephen C Timmins
Bartley St
Wakefield MA
018803103

Call Sign: N1XKB
Roger B Cooper
52 Bay State Rd
Wakefield MA 01880

Call Sign: KA1MYG
Clifford E Leavitt
1 Border St
Wakefield MA 01880

Call Sign: KA1NCJ
Donna Lee E Leavitt
1 Border St
Wakefield MA 01880

Call Sign: KB1GRT
Daniel J Macmonagle
129 Broadway
Wakefield MA 01880

Call Sign: W2FQD
Barry Innerfield
159 Broadway
Wakefield MA 01880

Call Sign: W1JEF
Peter K Sweet
170 Broadway St
Wakefield MA 01880

Call Sign: KB1TRA
Peter D Dolan
58 Brook St
Wakefield MA 01880

Call Sign: KB1UAE
Richard V Tobey Jr
114 Butler Ave
Wakefield MA 01880

Call Sign: KA1CVF
J Eduardo M Lucas

6 Castle Clare Cir
Wakefield MA 01880

Call Sign: N1DGD
Laura C Lucas
6 Castle Clare Cir
Wakefield MA 01880

Call Sign: KA1BOP
John J Doucette
41 Cedar St
Wakefield MA 01880

Call Sign: N3ILJ
Roland M Roehrich
89 Cedar St
Wakefield MA 01880

Call Sign: WA1PLK
Albert M Nardone
98 Cedar St Unit 3
Wakefield MA 01880

Call Sign: W1PLK
Albert M Nardone
98 Cedar St Unit 3
Wakefield MA 01880

Call Sign: KB1PFR
Leonard F Hunzelman
Jr
27 Converse St
Wakefield MA 01880

Call Sign: K1MXH
Leonard F Hunzelman
Jr
27 Converse St
Wakefield MA 01880

Call Sign: K1NQV
S Peter Volpe
11 Coolidge Park
Wakefield MA 01880

Call Sign: K1ZUP
J Henry Sleeper
7 Cordis St
Wakefield MA 01880

Call Sign: W1UZZ
Henry I White
26 Crescent St
Wakefield MA 01880

Call Sign: W1TUM
Dexter R Wheeler
18 Crosby Rd
Wakefield MA 01880

Call Sign: WB1APW
Elmo J Turner
18 Curve St
Wakefield MA 01880

Call Sign: KB1EAF
Hector E French
9 Davidson Rd
Wakefield MA 01880

Call Sign: KA1GFA
Jon W Robertson
4 Eaton St
Wakefield MA 01880

Call Sign: WD4LUG
John C Apostle
540 Edgewater Dr
Wakefield MA 01880

Call Sign: KA1NB
Edwin F Burnett
31 Elm Crest Rd
Wakefield MA
018801536

Call Sign: KA1NKX
George R Borstell
22 Elm St
Wakefield MA 01880

Call Sign: K1RGR
William L Giglio
113 Farm St
Wakefield MA 01880

Call Sign: W1NXW
Joseph Basilesco
33 Fox Rd
Wakefield MA 01880

Call Sign: N1OMN
David C Airhart
10 Franklin St
Wakefield MA 01880

Call Sign: N1MHQ
Barry W Gehron

32 Gregory Rd
Wakefield MA 01880

Call Sign: K1COK
Michael Blaho
21 Griffen Dr
Wakefield MA 01880

Call Sign: K1SPI
Jonathan D Hannaford
27 Griffen Dr
Wakefield MA 01880

Call Sign: KA1HKW
Rita T Hannaford
27 Griffen Dr
Wakefield MA 01880

Call Sign: WA1SIW
Erasmo A Capobianco
28 Griffin Dr
Wakefield MA 01880

Call Sign: KB1UCB
Jason Meade
26 Hamilton Rd
Wakefield MA 01880

Call Sign: W1KYU
Melvin G Murley
11 Indian Hill Rd
Wakefield MA 01880

Call Sign: KB1SDX
Brian A Martins
13 Jennifer Rd
Wakefield MA 01880

Call Sign: K1PAW
James H Meuse
25 Karen Rd
Wakefield MA
018801442

Call Sign: KB1WOD
David S Colson
44 Keeling Rd
Wakefield MA 01880

Call Sign: KO1B
Richard M Connors
158 Main St
Wakefield MA 01880

Call Sign: KB1DWJ
Priscilla C Mitchell
743 Main St
Wakefield MA 01880

Call Sign: N1BTH
Talmadge J
Hattabaugh
1221 Main St
Wakefield MA
018804107

Call Sign: N1DFU
Joseph K Hattabaugh
1221 Main St
Wakefield MA 01880

Call Sign: K1XQ
David M Smith
1077 Main St #107
Wakefield MA 01880

Call Sign: KB1VZR
David B Mac Culloch
317 Main St 2
Wakefield MA 01880

Call Sign: W1KPB
Frank G Lopez
1053 Main St Apt 13
Wakefield MA 01880

Call Sign: KB1TQ
Deborah L Bongiorno
64 Montrose Ave
Wakefield MA 01880

Call Sign: K1UGM
James C Morris
9 Morningside Rd
Wakefield MA 01880

Call Sign: N1CSI
Rhoda U Morris
9 Morningside Rd
Wakefield MA
018801515

Call Sign: KA1WOD
Kyle C Nickerson
69 Nahant St
Wakefield MA 01880

Call Sign: NQ1Y

Paul A Chirone
132 New Salem St
Wakefield MA
018801957

Call Sign: W1EED
Joseph F Poges
67 Parker Rd
Wakefield MA
018801424

Call Sign: N1IQE
Steven G Fausett
103 Pleasant St
Wakefield MA 01880

Call Sign: WA1GII
Robert A Sanchez
40 Putnam Ave
Wakefield MA 01880

Call Sign: W1MXV
Michael A Cavalier
22 Richardson St
Wakefield MA 01880

Call Sign: W1HN
William G Watt
28 Robert St
Wakefield MA
018803630

Call Sign: KB1MST
Wolfram C Stiebler
314 Salem St
Wakefield MA 01880

Call Sign: KB1MPW
Barbara A Conwell
28 Salem St 2f
Wakefield MA 01880

Call Sign: KB1MPX
Paul D Conwell
28 Salem St 2f
Wakefield MA 01880

Call Sign: K1RVL
Robert A Cruickshank
2 Scott Ln
Wakefield MA
018803509

Call Sign: KA1IIB

Geraldine V
Cruickshank
2 Scott Ln
Wakefield MA
018803509

Call Sign: K1MX
Harry J Chekos
59 Shumway Cir
Wakefield MA 01880

Call Sign: KB2UIH
James Fang
12 Spaulding St #3
Wakefield MA 01880

Call Sign: N1HTJ
Kendrick R Bennett
12 Spaulding St Apt 5
Wakefield MA 01880

Call Sign: N1LJC
Herbert L Fletcher
50 Spring St
Wakefield MA 01880

Call Sign: N1WOK
William J Watt
59 Spring St
Wakefield MA 01880

Call Sign: KB1QII
Timothy B Bertrand
59 Spring St 3
Wakefield MA 01880

Call Sign: KA1TC
Charles B Bolkcom
31 Strathmore Rd
Wakefield MA 01880

Call Sign: KA1EDV
Barbara A Day
53 Tamworth Hill Ave
Wakefield MA 01880

Call Sign: KA1EDW
RONELLEN A
Gagnon
53 Tamworth Hill Ave
Wakefield MA
018804213

Call Sign: N1OJM

Eric D Gagnon
53 Tamworth Hill
Ave`
Wakefield MA
018804213

Call Sign: KB1WGD
Mark L Mccormack
Tuttle St
Wakefield MA 01880

Call Sign: W1DMA
Fred A Goddard Jr
21 Walton St
Wakefield MA 01880

Call Sign: KA1RLD
Eric R Jappe
427 Water St
Wakefield MA 01880

Call Sign: WA1AXU
Bartlett P Murphy
6 Webster Rd
Wakefield MA
018803848

Call Sign: KB1OZS
Jeanne M Boland
25 West Water St
Wakefield MA 01880

Call Sign: KB1OZU
Albert V Boland Jr
25 West Water St
Wakefield MA 01880

Call Sign: KB1OZW
Timothy R Boland
25 West Water St
Wakefield MA 01880

Call Sign: WB1DNS
John H Johnson
5 Wharton Pk
Wakefield MA 01880

Call Sign: W1KV
Stephen F Terry
26 Winn St
Wakefield MA 01880

Call Sign: WB1GNM
Donald E Hawes

7 Winnisimette Ave
Wakefield MA 01880

Call Sign: KB1QXA
Samuel J Bruce
21 Yale Ave
Wakefield MA 01880

Call Sign: KB1QXB
David M Bruce
21 Yale Ave
Wakefield MA 01880

Call Sign: KB1QZT
Myra J Bruce
21 Yale Ave
Wakefield MA 01880

Call Sign: KA1MTQ
Alan S Goldberg
Wakefield MA 01880

Call Sign: KA1RUM
Suzanne L Goldberg
Wakefield MA 01880

FCC Amateur Radio Licenses in Wales

Call Sign: KB1IPQ
Cecile A Housand
39 Main St
Wales MA 010810155

Call Sign: KB1WCV
Theodore W Siok
73 Main St
Wales MA 01081

Call Sign: N1DON
Noel J Lavallee
84 Monson Rd
Wales MA 01081

Call Sign: KC8BLC
Brian T Savage
15 Reed Hill Rd
Wales MA 01081

Call Sign: K7RQO
Michael Krasnoff
Wales MA 01081

Call Sign: N1WRG

Eric A Szoka
Wales MA 010810017

Call Sign: N1ZPH
Jon C Breed
Wales MA 010810006

Call Sign: KB1GQY
Robert C Housand
Wales MA 010810155

FCC Amateur Radio Licenses in Walpole

Call Sign: KB1NLW
Christopher I Reynolds
7 Alma Rd
Walpole MA 02081

Call Sign: KA1JSW
David W Clark
84 Alton St
Walpole MA 02081

Call Sign: AA1MR
Steven J Connors
24 Broad St
Walpole MA 02081

Call Sign: K1HJ
Steven J Connors
24 Broad St
Walpole MA 02081

Call Sign: WE1R
Kenneth F Coop
35 Carl Rd
Walpole MA 02081

Call Sign: W1PNH
Joseph S Lord
5 Chicatabut Dr
Walpole MA 02081

Call Sign: KB1TJI
Jeff C Marden
108 Common St
Walpole MA 02081

Call Sign: N1HGJ
Patricia L Kelly
280 Common St
Walpole MA
020813233

Call Sign: W1CHC
George W De Lisle
10 Countryside Ln
Walpole MA 02081

Call Sign: KB1PGM
Roy H Ghantous
17 Crosswoods Path
Walpole
Walpole MA 02081

Call Sign: AA1IV
Carolann B
Montgomery
19 Edgewood Ave
Walpole MA 02081

Call Sign: KB1BOI
Sarah M Montgomery
19 Edgewood Ave
Walpole MA 02081

Call Sign: N1UYN
William T Hamilton
45 Eldor Dr
Walpole MA 02071

Call Sign: KB1QWF
Kelvin R Mahoney
280 Elm St
Walpole MA 02081

Call Sign: K1WFD
Kelvin R Mahoney
280 Elm St
Walpole MA 02081

Call Sign: KB1OZP
Jay A Lewis
297 Fisher St
Walpole MA 02081

Call Sign: KB1OHS
John B Nemec
30 Forsythia Dr
Walpole MA 02081

Call Sign: KB1JWG
Eoin T O Corcora
183 High Plain St
Walpole MA 02081

Call Sign: KB1LPJ

Phillip P Russell
68 Highland St
Walpole MA 02081

Call Sign: W1CQN
Allyn H Fisher
55 Homeward Ln
Walpole MA
020812239

Call Sign: KB1HIO
Todd W Sandahl
55 Hoover Rd
Walpole MA 02081

Call Sign: KB1TEC
John L Lightbody
191 Kendall St
Walpole MA 02081

Call Sign: KB1LPI
Allan J Deblasio
3 Lamplighter Ln
Walpole MA
020812858

Call Sign: W1ADB
Allan J Deblasio
3 Lamplighter Ln
Walpole MA
020812858

Call Sign: K1HRV
David G Doe
75 Lincoln Rd
Walpole MA 02081

Call Sign: KB1DYM
Blue Hill Observatory
Science Center
75 Lincoln Rd
Walpole MA 02081

Call Sign: N1LMT
James A Buckley Jr
132 Lincoln Rd
Walpole MA 02081

Call Sign: N1KMM
Richard F Buckley
132 Lincoln Rd
Walpole MA 02081

Call Sign: KB1NSO

Saida E Buckley
132 Lincoln Rd
Walpole MA
020811621

Call Sign: KA1PYP
Raymond E Mosher
180 Lincoln Rd
Walpole MA 02081

Call Sign: WA2WFC
Arthur V Lynch
881 Main St
Walpole MA 02081

Call Sign: KB1JLR
Erskine L Metcalf
2114 Main St
Walpole MA 02081

Call Sign: KB1CDG
North Shore Radio
Association
2224 Main St
Walpole MA 02081

Call Sign: KB2SYM
Donna L Harris
2224 Main St
Walpole MA
020811015

Call Sign: N1UEC
Louis D Harris
2224 Main St
Walpole MA 02081

Call Sign: NS1RA
North Shore Radio
Association
2224 Main St
Walpole MA 02081

Call Sign: KB1LTL
New England
Spectrum Management
Council
2224 Main St
Walpole MA 02081

Call Sign: NS1MC
New England
Spectrum Management
Council

2224 Main St
Walpole MA 02081

Call Sign: K1DLH
Donna L Harris
2224 Main St
Walpole MA
020811015

Call Sign: W1JLI
Norwood Amateur
Radio Club Repeaters
2224 Main St
Walpole MA 02081

Call Sign: W1WTF
George C Rummell
180 Main St Apt 130
Walpole MA 02081

Call Sign: KB1NXF
Gerard F O'farrell
32 Marisa Lane
Walpole MA 02081

Call Sign: N1EST
William N Johnson
25 Mass Ave
Walpole MA 02081

Call Sign: KB1NXT
Peter O'farrell
15 Maude Terr
Walpole MA 02081

Call Sign: KB1LMX
Philip R Dubois
18 Mill Pond Rd
Walpole MA
020811915

Call Sign: KB1LMY
Philip S Dubois
18 Mill Pond Rd
Walpole MA
020811915

Call Sign: W1PAT
Patrick Fasanello
23 Neal St
Walpole MA 02081

Call Sign: KB1HXF
Gayle M Fasanello

23 Neal St
Walpole MA 02081

Call Sign: N1VCY
Walter I Barnes Jr
86 Norfolk St
Walpole MA 02081

Call Sign: KB1QWE
Joseph R Palermo
180 North St
Walpole MA 02081

Call Sign: KB1SMT
Gianna M Potito
177 North St 4
Walpole MA 02081

Call Sign: W1PHM
Philip H Macchi
15 Northwood Dr Box
381
Walpole MA 02081

Call Sign: N1NDR
Brian E Portanova
37 Page Ave
Walpole MA 02081

Call Sign: KS1D
Thomas M Trainor Sr
12 Pelican Dr
Walpole MA 02081

Call Sign: KA1NXY
Ann E Pellowe
83 Pemberton St
Walpole MA 02081

Call Sign: KA1NVG
Steven R Pellowe
83 Pemberton St
Walpole MA 02081

Call Sign: N1UDT
Richard F Donlan
70 Pocahontas St
Walpole MA 02081

Call Sign: WA5EDS
James R Shelton
238 School St
Walpole MA 02081

Call Sign: KB1KHI
Christopher J Phillips
1467 Washington St
Walpole MA 02081

Call Sign: KA1CRV
Clyde R Shappee
72 William St
Walpole MA 02081

Call Sign: N1MX
Michael E Amaral
3 Winthrop St
Walpole MA 02081

Call Sign: KB1BWI
Walpole Emergency
Communication
Association
Walpole MA
020810305

Call Sign: W1ZSA
Roger F Turner Jr
Walpole MA
020810305

FCC Amateur Radio
Licenses in Waltham

Call Sign: KB1NFY
Mark R Ciravolo
184 A Charles St
Waltham MA 02453

Call Sign: KA1FWU
Andrew J Long
22 Abbott Rd
Waltham MA 02154

Call Sign: W1ZTL
Lennart E Long
22 Abbott Rd
Waltham MA
021547840

Call Sign: KF0IM
Andrew D Oliver
192 Adams St #2
Waltham MA 02453

Call Sign: N1MLR
Brian E Mc Carthy
42 Agrillo Cir

Waltham MA 02154

Call Sign: N1HYX
Donald J O Shea
73 Albemarle Rd
Waltham MA 02154

Call Sign: KB1LNK
Denise R Cremin
146 Alder St
Waltham MA 02453

Call Sign: K1LMN
Denise R Cremin
146 Alder St
Waltham MA 02453

Call Sign: K1BEE
Daniel J Jordan
146 Alder St
Waltham MA 02453

Call Sign: W1XVT
Daniel J Jordan
146 Alder St
Waltham MA 02453

Call Sign: KB3EEE
Jordan Greenberg
7 Alder St Apt 2f
Waltham MA 02453

Call Sign: N1WKQ
Craig P Aucoin
28 Allen Rd
Waltham MA 02154

Call Sign: KB1SZU
Justin D Cheschi
55 Ash St
Waltham MA 02453

Call Sign: KA1BER
Justin D Cheschi
55 Ash St
Waltham MA 02453

Call Sign: N1IZN
Karen L Megerdichian
235 Ash St #2
Waltham MA 02453

Call Sign: KB1SFU
Aaron M Zschau

55 Ash St 24
Waltham MA 02453

Call Sign: KA1LEO
Aaron M Zschau
55 Ash St 24
Waltham MA 02453

Call Sign: KA6BUV
Alfred E Williams Jr
65 Augustus Rd
Waltham MA 02452

Call Sign: KB1FHA
George J Leblanc
33 Azalea Rd
Waltham MA 02452

Call Sign: KA1HS
Michael Yuen
30 Bancroft St
Waltham MA 02154

Call Sign: W1OER
Donald A Kadish
135 Barbara Rd
Waltham MA 02154

Call Sign: WA1MTH
Frank J Bottari
22 Beal Rd
Waltham MA 02453

Call Sign: K1TCY
Stanley Bloomenthal
635 Beaver St
Waltham MA
024524744

Call Sign: N1MWN
Jerry D Burchfiel
270 Bishops Forest Dr
Waltham MA 02452

Call Sign: N1HLC
Nathan A Weinsaft
109 Bishops Forest
Drive
Waltham MA 02452

Call Sign: W1YSW
David J Goldman
237 Bishops Forest
Drive

Waltham MA
024528804

Call Sign: WA8FRY
Reed R Prior
336 Bishops Forest
Drive
Waltham MA 02452

Call Sign: W1TF
Reed R Prior
336 Bishops Forest
Drive
Waltham MA 02452

Call Sign: AB1J
Kermit W Lehman
36 Blossom St
Waltham MA 02154

Call Sign: K1AEO
Arthur Pereira
94 Brewster Rd
Waltham MA 02154

Call Sign: K1IJ
William R Wade
12 Brigham Rd
Waltham MA
024536649

Call Sign: N1MLU
David W Wade
12 Brigham Rd
Waltham MA 02154

Call Sign: N1MLV
Rose M Wade
12 Brigham Rd
Waltham MA 02154

Call Sign: K1IOE
James R Regan
35 Brigham Rd
Waltham MA 02154

Call Sign: N1HIE
David M Segalini
109 Bright St
Waltham MA 02453

Call Sign: KB1JXS
Robert J Reynolds
242 Brown St

Waltham MA 02453

Call Sign: N1XNX
Stephen Hersey
67 Canterbury Rd
Waltham MA 02154

Call Sign: KB1JQX
Wayne H Gunnell Jr
31 Casey Circle
Waltham MA 02451

Call Sign: WA1HXQ
William Sidell
Charles River Rd
Waltham MA 02154

Call Sign: K1GB
Gordon T Bello
Charlesbank Way
Waltham MA
024532510

Call Sign: N1VYE
David M Lash
53 Cherry St 2
Waltham MA 02453

Call Sign: N1YWI
Friederike C Haeusgen
53 Cherry St 2
Waltham MA 02453

Call Sign: WA1IFE
John D Winslow
111 Chestnut St
Waltham MA 02154

Call Sign: KB1STS
Virginia A Meaney
172 College Farm Rd
Waltham MA 02451

Call Sign: KB1QMY
William P Meaney
172 College Farm Rd
Waltham MA 02451

Call Sign: KB1KTT
Alderice J Melanson
267 College Farm Rd
Waltham MA 02451

Call Sign: KC9GKW

Ramon Bannister
273 College Farm Rd
Waltham MA 02451

Call Sign: N1QOM
Jeffrey D Sullivan
101 Colonial Ave
Waltham MA 02154

Call Sign: N2UJW
Michael T Lanieri
32 Common St Unit 2-3
Waltham MA 02451

Call Sign: K1TWC
Stephen L Mc Quiston
179 Copeland St
Waltham MA 02451

Call Sign: W1YGC
Leonard R Hadley
82 Dale St
Waltham MA 02154

Call Sign: AA1JW
David W Greehan
46 Dale St Apt B6
Waltham MA 02451

Call Sign: N1NMF
Philip M Pagliazzo
42 Dobbins St
Waltham MA 02154

Call Sign: KB1VAO
Ian J Mcclymonds
27 Drury Ln
Waltham MA 02452

Call Sign: N2WIV
Brian T Sniffen
128 Ellison Park
Waltham MA 02452

Call Sign: KB1KRC
Gavin J Heneghan
26 Everett St
Waltham MA 02453

Call Sign: N1VQR
Robert E Martinson
96 F Lionel Ave

Waltham MA
024524829

Call Sign: K1REM
Robert E Martinson
96 F Lionel Ave
Waltham MA
024524829

Call Sign: N1MMZ
Stephen H Mont
97 Fiske Ave
Waltham MA 02453

Call Sign: K1IXM
Joseph P Welsch
88 Fiske St
Waltham MA 02154

Call Sign: KB1FAA
Charles Apollonio
370 Forest St
Waltham MA 02452

Call Sign: K1APO
Charles Apollonio
370 Forest St
Waltham MA 02452

Call Sign: KB1HAI
Miodrag Z Danilovic
52 Fuller St
Waltham MA
024535053

Call Sign: KB1HQL
Matthew Silverstein
38 Gordon St #3
Waltham MA 02453

Call Sign: KD2PI
Uri D Richter
24 Graymoore Rd
Waltham MA 02154

Call Sign: N1RTM
William A Mc Gean
10 Grosvenor Rd
Waltham MA 02154

Call Sign: N1RVP
Michael P Landry
31 Grosvenor Rd
Waltham MA 02154

Call Sign: N1SGB
Scott J Cassidy
31 Guinan St
Waltham MA 02451

Call Sign: WA2NKL
Gary M Madison
173 Hammond St
Waltham MA 02451

Call Sign: KA1HPL
Paul L Maillet
160 Hardy Pond Rd
Waltham MA 02154

Call Sign: W1TSN
Donald R Lester
25 Harland Rd
Waltham MA 02154

Call Sign: KB1MOW
John W Siemiatkoski
30 Harvard St Apt 2
Waltham MA 02453

Call Sign: KB1VCZ
Jeremy A Cote
25 Hastings Ave 3
Waltham MA 02453

Call Sign: W1JMK
Alfred J Zerega
73 Hatherly Rd
Waltham MA 02154

Call Sign: N1NHQ
Bailey B Bramer
20 Hiawatha Ave
Waltham MA
024513214

Call Sign: W1IIX
Ronald A Salamy
56 Hillcrest Rd
Waltham MA 02451

Call Sign: N1XFG
Jason M La Penta
72 Hillcrest St
Waltham MA 02451

Call Sign: AA1AJ
George A Darcy Iii

94 Hobbs Rd
Waltham MA 02154

Call Sign: KB1QQZ
JOSHUA L Mcginnis
Howard St
Waltham MA 02451

Call Sign: KB1UHH
Nicholas A Flanagan
9 Jaqueline Rd Unit C
Waltham MA 02452

Call Sign: K1AZU
Nicholas A Flanagan
9 Jaqueline Rd Unit C
Waltham MA 02452

Call Sign: KA1ZGA
Richard B Ryder
38 Judith Ln #11
Waltham MA 02452

Call Sign: W7MK
Mark R Kloongian
46 Juniper Hill Rd
Waltham MA 02154

Call Sign: WA1JAU
Winthrop E Stone Jr
57 Kendall Pk
Waltham MA 02154

Call Sign: W1PKX
Eckert M Baillio
99 Kingston Rd
Waltham MA 02154

Call Sign: W1HVC
Harry Solov
48 Knollwood Dr
Waltham MA
024532407

Call Sign: N1CQY
Silve J Iannetti
78 Lafayette St
Waltham MA 02154

Call Sign: KA1KFG
John C Lull
96 Lafayette St
Waltham MA
021546829

Call Sign: KA1KFH
Carolyn Lull
96 Lafayette St
Waltham MA 02154

Call Sign: N1EHM
William D Furbish
20 Lakeview Ave
Waltham MA 02154

Call Sign: KA1OID
William D Furbish
20 Lakeview Ave
Waltham MA 02154

Call Sign: N1MLS
Russell H Milligan Jr
Lakeview Ave
Waltham MA 02154

Call Sign: K1EJW
Paul Morabito
20 Leitha Dr
Waltham MA 02154

Call Sign: KB1MXJ
Thomas C Hebb
27 Leonard St
Waltham MA 02451

Call Sign: KB1MXK
Ralph M Hebb
27 Leonard St
Waltham MA 02451

Call Sign: K1WAV
Ralph M Hebb
27 Leonard St
Waltham MA 02451

Call Sign: KB1JIB
Pepin Torres
78 Lincoln St
Waltham MA 02451

Call Sign: KB1LRZ
Barry W Stearns
197 Linden St
Waltham MA 02452

Call Sign: W1SNN
Stirling M Olberg
19 Loretta Rd

Waltham MA 02154

Call Sign: WA1IKR
Florence V Olberg
19 Loretta Rd
Waltham MA 02154

Call Sign: K1OZN
Fred W Hamilton
262 Lowell St
Waltham MA 02154

Call Sign: W1FWH
Fred W Hamilton
262 Lowell St
Waltham MA 02154

Call Sign: KB1TPV
Kirk M Nahabedian
125 Lura Lane
Waltham MA 02451

Call Sign: KB1TUL
Travis H Robinson
125 Lura Lane
Waltham MA 02451

Call Sign: KN1Q
Kirk M Nahabedian
125 Lura Lane
Waltham MA 02451

Call Sign: K1THR
Travis H Robinson
125 Lura Lane
Waltham MA 02451

Call Sign: KB1GIU
Bruce A Lawson
10 Lyman St
Waltham MA
024525511

Call Sign: N1FKO
Walter G Horbert
738 Main St #130
Waltham MA
024510616

Call Sign: KB1VXQ
Christopher R Laprade
507 Main St Apt 1
Waltham MA 02452

Call Sign: WB1FTD
Romolo G A Fusco
69 Mallard Way
Waltham MA
021548115

Call Sign: N1RDW
William Kadzis
70 Marlborough Rd
Waltham MA 02154

Call Sign: KB1UI
Joseph Murphy
42 Melody Ln
Waltham MA 02154

Call Sign: W1LHP
Joseph E Rose
24 Middlesex Cir
Waltham MA 02154

Call Sign: K1YSN
Stephen G Mc Hugh
33 Middlesex Cir Apt
2
Waltham MA
024526239

Call Sign: KB1WHN
Meher V Nerkizian
32 Middlesex Circle
Apt 11
Waltham MA 02452

Call Sign: AB1OT
Paul J Rowe
30 Middlesex Rd #4
Waltham MA 02452

Call Sign: N1ZWJ
Ayres Hall
70 Mokema Ave
Waltham MA
024510840

Call Sign: KC1MG
Earl G Nangle
174 Moody St Apt 344
Waltham MA
024535344

Call Sign: K1PTO
Douglas L Swank
Nathan Rd

Waltham MA 02154

Call Sign: WA1TCV
Barbara M Mac
Donald
22 Palmer St
Waltham MA 02154

Call Sign: KB1LGQ
Stephen A Zerby
30 Park St
Waltham MA 02453

Call Sign: N8ZRY
Greg L Charvat
30 Park St
Waltham MA 02453

Call Sign: W1HLZ
Vahram Sookikian
26 Pelham Rd
Waltham MA
024536711

Call Sign: KB1UGR
Steven E Whalen
53 Pine Hill Circle
Waltham MA 02451

Call Sign: KA1SNE
Paul R Dube
11 Pond St Apt 34
Waltham MA 02154

Call Sign: KB1PUD
Laurie A Seymour
51 Prospect Hill Rd
Waltham MA 02451

Call Sign: KB1GQJ
Stephen M Kasparian
184 Prospect St
Waltham MA 02453

Call Sign: KF6NVT
Gunther Kern
71 Ravenswood Rd
Waltham MA 02453

Call Sign: W1JCI
Waldo H Clark
9 Riverview Ave
Waltham MA
021543817

Call Sign: KB1NSX
James M Van Donsel
32 Riverview Ave
Waltham MA 02453

Call Sign: KC7HTF
Joris Naiman
89 Riverview Ave
Waltham MA
024533819

Call Sign: KC7IKX
Lesya A Struz
89 Riverview Ave
Waltham MA
024533819

Call Sign: KC2IEN
Michael F Balma
212 Robbins St
Waltham MA 02453

Call Sign: KB1AVL
Peter P Lanoie
34 Robbins St # 2
Waltham MA 02453

Call Sign: KA1ZFM
Lawrence F Galligan
33 Sherbourne Pl
Waltham MA 02154

Call Sign: W1SXV
Raymond L Gagnon
93 Sherbourne Pl
Waltham MA 02451

Call Sign: WA1VDW
Joseph A Aucoin
11 Sheridan Rd
Waltham MA 02154

Call Sign: W1VDW
Joseph A Aucoin
11 Sheridan Rd
Waltham MA 02154

Call Sign: KS1E
Donald C Mabie
38 Shore Rd
Waltham MA 02154

Call Sign: N1MLQ

Eric G Mabie
38 Shore Rd
Waltham MA 02154

Call Sign: KB1CSA
Duane M Roth
414 Stearns Hill Rd
Waltham MA 02154

Call Sign: KB1LPB
Jon R Pellant
706 Stearns Hill Rd
Waltham MA 02451

Call Sign: AB1FF
Jon R Pellant
706 Stearns Hill Rd
Waltham MA 02451

Call Sign: KB1CLN
Manish K Sinha
128 Technology Dr
Parametric Tech
Waltham MA 02154

Call Sign: K1ETR
Thomas W Petrie
289 Temple Rd
Waltham MA 02154

Call Sign: KB1RAB
Fractal Radio Amateur
Club
130 Third Ave
Waltham MA 02451

Call Sign: W1FRX
Fractal Radio Amateur
Club
130 Third Ave
Waltham MA 02451

Call Sign: W1KF
Ralph H Vacca
45 Thornton Rd
Waltham MA 02154

Call Sign: KH2EH
Albert C Huegel Iii
46 Thornton Rd
Waltham MA
024531585

Call Sign: N1ZH

Albert C Huegel Iii
46 Thornton Rd
Waltham MA
024531585

Call Sign: N1WPI
Thomas J Poltrino
94 Trapelo Rd
Waltham MA 02452

Call Sign: W1DOV
Richard D Warren
550 Trapelo Rd
Waltham MA 02154

Call Sign: KB1LPC
Christopher P Higgins
1369 Trapelo Rd
Waltham MA 02451

Call Sign: KB1DOV
Kathleen M Fratto
1687 Trapelo Rd
Waltham MA
024517329

Call Sign: N1RLO
Joseph T Fratto
1687 Trapelo Rd
Waltham MA
024517329

Call Sign: KA1PLZ
John C Di Leo
1806 Trapelo Rd
Waltham MA 02154

Call Sign: AA1EP
John S Allen
7 University Park
Waltham MA 02154

Call Sign: N1TNM
Elisse Ghitelman
7 University Park
Waltham MA
021541523

Call Sign: KA1JXK
Robert J Dusza
Vernon St
Waltham MA 02453

Call Sign: N1FYT

Kenneth D Brady
47 Vernon St Apt 2
Waltham MA 02154

Call Sign: N1MJX
Johnson Muyukatita
Wadsworth Ave
Waltham MA 02154

Call Sign: KB1NJH
Philip M Clark
329 Warren St
Waltham MA 02453

Call Sign: W1TIY
Malcolm Kasparian Jr
113 Warwick Ave
Waltham MA
024527830

Call Sign: KA1QAB
Mark H Nolan
74 Wayne Ave
Waltham MA 02453

Call Sign: KB1FXJ
David Lafountain
292 Weston St
Waltham MA 02453

Call Sign: K1CEI
Angelo M Ruggelo
77 Wetherbee Rd
Waltham MA
024537624

Call Sign: KA1EDY
Edwin H Sternfelt
45 Woburn St
Waltham MA
024527919

Call Sign: KA1HDO
Hillyer Senning
Waltham MA 02454

**FCC Amateur Radio
Licenses in Waquoit**

Call Sign: K1DIW
Robert B Lamkin
155 Meadow Neck Rd
Waquoit MA 02536

Call Sign: WB1GPY
Carleton H Collins
4 Moonakis Rd
Waquoit MA 02536

Call Sign: K1AIR
Falmouth Amateur
Radio Assoc
15 Moonakis Rd
Waquoit MA 02536

Call Sign: W1SBD
Saul B Dinman
15 Moonakis Rd
Waquoit MA 02536

Call Sign: K1BI
Saul B Dinman
15 Moonakis Rd
Waquoit MA 02536

Call Sign: KB1ILZ
Falmouth Amateur
Radio Association
15 Moonakis Rd
Waquoit MA 02536

Call Sign: W1NOB
Falmouth Amateur
Radio Association
15 Moonakis Rd
Waquoit MA 02536

Call Sign: N1LNB
Eugene A Bradeen
24 Ostrom Rd
Waquoit MA
025367731

Call Sign: KX1C
Eugene A Bradeen
24 Ostrom Rd
Waquoit MA
025367731

Call Sign: AK1V
Herbert H Luther
92 Overlook Circle
Waquoit MA 02536

Call Sign: W1HQH
Falmouth Amateur
Radio Assoc
36 Quashnet Way

Waquoit MA 02536

Call Sign: W1OH
Geoffrey P Allsup
73 Tasina Drive
Waquoit MA 02536

Call Sign: N1HIK
Paul A Andrews
Waquoit MA 02536

Call Sign: N1SBR
Rosemary E Servis
Waquoit MA 02536

Call Sign: KB1GHN
Paul D Fucile
Waquoit MA 02356

Call Sign: KB1IGI
Leo P Ledwell
Waquoit MA 02536

Call Sign: KB1TBT
Dominic S Fucile
Waquoit MA 02536

Call Sign: N1SBP
Aaron B Servis
Waquoit MA 02636

**FCC Amateur Radio
Licenses in Ward Hill**

Call Sign: KA1URI
Northrup W Marr
1252 Boston Rd
Ward Hill MA
018358008

**FCC Amateur Radio
Licenses in Ware**

Call Sign: N1QFU
Henry A Brown Sr
17 Aspen St
Ware MA 010821008

Call Sign: N1QKN
Henry A Brown Jr
17 Aspen St
Ware MA 010821008

Call Sign: KB1DAD

Jayant D Singh
42 Aspen St
Ware MA 01082

Call Sign: KB1VXI
Michael S Meehan
65 Babcock Tavern Rd
Ware MA 01082

Call Sign: N1DQW
Linda M Martelli
48 Bacon Rd
Ware MA 01082

Call Sign: KB1OHP
Andrew F Champagne
6 Belair Dr
Ware MA 01082

Call Sign: KB1BYN
John E Motyka
375 Belchertown Rd
Ware MA 01082

Call Sign: W1TTC
David J Beaubien
84 Doane Rd
Ware MA 010829387

Call Sign: N1JZO
Robert P Chartier
57 Eagle St
Ware MA 01082

Call Sign: W1FYL
Joseph E Hoener
22 Elm St
Ware MA 01082

Call Sign: KB1HRO
Leo J Flamand
58 Gould Rd
Ware MA 01082

Call Sign: KB1WQE
J Scott Davidson
112 Greenwich Rd
Ware MA 01082

Call Sign: KB1LWK
Michael A Ciejka
2759 Greenwich Rd
Ware MA 01082

Call Sign: KB1ALX
Ronald S Haynes
221 North St Lot 22
Ware MA 01082

Call Sign: KB1VHS
Michael F Trombley Jr
143 Old Belchertown
Rd
Ware MA 01082

Call Sign: N1XON
John J Aliengena
401 Palmer Rd
Ware MA 01082

Call Sign: N1SIQ
Walter R Trzpit
2 Pinecrest Cir
Ware MA 01082

Call Sign: KB1CSY
John H Stanton Jr
40 Pleasant St
Ware MA 01082

Call Sign: W1USB
John H Stanton Jr
40 Pleasant St
Ware MA 010821268

Call Sign: N1EDZ
Gary M Reardon
8 Prospect St
Ware MA 010821116

Call Sign: N1NJ
Anthony Naglieri Jr
22 Sherwin St
Ware MA 010821020

Call Sign: N1PAD
Lorraine M Naglieri
22 Sherwin St
Ware MA 01082

Call Sign: N1YPN
Kimberly M La Croix
22 Sherwin St
Ware MA 01082

Call Sign: N1TOY
Mary R Elkins
24 Shoreline Dr

Ware MA 01082

Call Sign: KB1ME
Mary R Elkins
24 Shoreline Dr
Ware MA 01082

Call Sign: N1QKO
Eric W Tuller
83 Shoreline Dr
Ware MA 01082

Call Sign: K1KLY
William H St Cyr Jr
146 W Main St
Ware MA 01082

Call Sign: KB1AFZ
Thomas H Worden Jr
151 W Main St
Ware MA 01082

Call Sign: WA1CMD
Aaron Reifowitz
29 Walnut St
Ware MA 010821134

FCC Amateur Radio Licenses in Wareham

Call Sign: N1VQZ
Charlet E Sherman
8 Anchorage Dr
Wareham MA 02571

Call Sign: N1WWI
Christopher D Tilden
8 Anchorage Drive
Wareham MA 02571

Call Sign: KA1YZN
Marion C Hall
6 Arlington Rd
Wareham MA 02571

Call Sign: WA1YZX
Edward F Hall
6 Arlington Rd
Wareham MA 02571

Call Sign: N1BBT
Brian C Churchill
63 Bayview St
Wareham MA 02571

Call Sign: N1NXD
John W Bonell
3 Bodfish Ave
Wareham MA 02571

Call Sign: N1WCO
Eric V Pierce
8 Bodfish Ave
Wareham MA 02571

Call Sign: W1VFY
Leslie M Holmes
Box 304
Wareham MA 02571

Call Sign: KB1NDB
Lawrence M Marvill
61 C Minot Ave
Wareham MA 02571

Call Sign: W1STX
Harry E Adams
Cranberry Grove Way
Wareham MA 02571

Call Sign: KB1JQT
Paul C Nardella
12 Cromesett Point Rd
Wareham MA 02571

Call Sign: N1SGR
Nancy B Morse
10 Cromesett Rd
Wareham MA 02571

Call Sign: N1GLD
George V Roberts
8 D Angelo Rd
Wareham MA
025711823

Call Sign: KA1SMY
Noel P Texeira
12 E Terry Ln
Wareham MA 02571

Call Sign: KA1NXO
Jerome Field
12 Eleventh Ave
Wareham MA 02581

Call Sign: KA1YON
Bob Kish

11 Fir St
Wareham MA
025712348

Call Sign: KA1HFY
Bruce E Dickinson
4 Galavotti Ave
Wareham MA 02571

Call Sign: KA1WBW
Christopher H Foster
101 Great Neck Rd
Wareham MA 02571

Call Sign: N1NRE
Dorothy A Waff
102 Highland Shore Dr
Wareham MA 02571

Call Sign: KB1UJO
Robert A Richardson
498 Main St
Wareham MA 02571

Call Sign: KB1VKP
Wilfred L Provost
795 Main St
Wareham MA 02571

Call Sign: WA1ETS
Joseph D Rose
325 Marion Rd
Wareham MA
025711454

Call Sign: K1PZR
John D Bergeron
26 Maritime Dr
Wareham MA
025712630

Call Sign: W1MWC
Michael W Correia
28 Mc Gann Terrace
Wareham MA 02719

Call Sign: W1MO
John E Mc Master
30 Oak St Tempest
Knob Ter
Wareham MA 02571

Call Sign: KB1FHM
Carl E Bredberg

16 Swan Lane
Wareham MA 02571

Call Sign: K1KID
Carl E Bredberg
16 Swan Lane
Wareham MA 02571

Call Sign: KB1UJK
Peter D Hasenfuss
4 Taffrail Path
Wareham MA 02571

Call Sign: W1PDH
Peter D Hasenfuss
4 Taffrail Path
Wareham MA 02571

Call Sign: KA1BTI
Stephen A Clang
9 Tenth Ave
Wareham MA 02571

Call Sign: KA1KHI
George H Glidden
3 Weston Ave
Wareham MA 02571

Call Sign: KA1PGW
Barbara A Glidden
3 Weston Ave
Wareham MA 02571

Call Sign: KB1WHD
Sally Shuttle
18 Winslow Ln
Wareham MA 02571

Call Sign: KB1MLQ
Duarte M Bettencourt
7 Wren Terrace
Wareham MA 02571

Call Sign: KA1TXN
Robert Kent
Wareham MA 02571

Call Sign: KB1BSG
Wareham Amateur
Radio Club
Wareham MA
025713143

Call Sign: KB1FVR

Brian T Geagan
Wareham MA 02571

Call Sign: N1UZI
Thomas F Mc
Laughlin
Wareham MA 02571

Call Sign: KB1RUG
Robert A Mckernan
Wareham MA 02571

**FCC Amateur Radio
Licenses in Warren**

Call Sign: KC4IFA
Glenn A Slate
East Rd
Warren MA 01083

Call Sign: N1XOP
Mark A Sweet
24 Elm St
Warren MA 01083

Call Sign: KV1Z
Stephen F Garr
38 Elm St
Warren MA 01083

Call Sign: WJ1SG
Stephen F Garr
38 Elm St
Warren MA 01083

Call Sign: WA1SG
Stephen F Garr
38 Elm St
Warren MA 01083

Call Sign: KB1JID
Robert E Watson
59 Hines Ave
Warren MA 01083

Call Sign: K1JNT
Boleslaw Doktor
20 Liberty St
Warren MA 01083

Call Sign: K1UJU
John P Dunbar
2 Nelson St
Warren MA 01083

Call Sign: K1UJT
John Antonovitch
7 Quaboag St
Warren MA 01083

Call Sign: KB1BKK
Jerome B Stiles
51 Sarty Rd
Warren MA
010830649

Call Sign: KB1HGK
Radio Operators For
Missing Children
51 Sarty Rd
Warren MA
010850649

Call Sign: KB1RXE
Jason P Ferris
95 School St
Warren MA
010830498

Call Sign: N1GPL
Kenneth H Tatro
Warren MA 01083

Call Sign: N1JQE
Linda P Tatro
Warren MA 01083

Call Sign: N1VRL
Aleksander
Tenerowicz
Warren MA
010830592

Call Sign: WB1BPM
David E Rosati
Warren MA 01083

Call Sign: KB1ETM
Central Ma Public
Safety Assn Inc
Warren MA 01083

Call Sign: KB1HLZ
Sheree L Greenwood
Warren MA
010830649

Call Sign: KB1HRM

David A Gancorz
Warren MA 01083

Call Sign: KB1HXO
Ken M Rozzen
Warren MA 01083

Call Sign: N1PSE
Michael J Baril
Warren MA
010830542

Call Sign: K1SQ
Sheree L Greenwood
Warren MA
010830649

Call Sign: KB1LHM
Quaboag Valley
Amateur Radio Club
Warren MA 01083

Call Sign: K1QVR
Quaboag Valley
Amateur Radio Club
Warren MA 01083

Call Sign: KB1RWX
Rodney S Carlson
Warren MA
010831420

**FCC Amateur Radio
Licenses in Warwick**

Call Sign: WB1CWH
Edward W Lemon Jr
700 Old Winchester
Rd
Warwick MA 01378

Call Sign: KB1VPO
Lucinda R Seago
405 Richmond Rd
Warwick MA 01378

Call Sign: N1LXO
Stanley E Thompson
371 Wendell Rd
Warwick MA 01364

Call Sign: KB1DRD
Ingeborg Petschik
425 Winchester Rd

Warwick MA 01378

FCC Amateur Radio Licenses in Washington

Call Sign: K1CPG
Harvey E Fish Sr
Pittsfield Rd
Washington MA 01223

Call Sign: KB1JOA
Philip G Clark
169 Upper Valley Rd
Washington MA 01223

Call Sign: KB1BLQ
Harvey E Fish Jr
629 Washington Mtn Rd
Washington MA 01223

FCC Amateur Radio Licenses in Watertown

Call Sign: NO1W
Tatsuya Hirahara
30 Arden Rd
Watertown MA 02472

Call Sign: KB1SZS
William E Collins
105 B Irving St
Watertown MA 02472

Call Sign: W1LDE
William E Collins
105 B Irving St
Watertown MA 02472

Call Sign: W1PL
William E Collins
105 B Irving St
Watertown MA 02472

Call Sign: W1TCC
Timothy C Constable
109 Barnard Ave
Watertown MA 02472

Call Sign: KB1PMQ
Edward P Ambrogio
141 Bellevue Rd

Watertown MA 02472

Call Sign: KA3YXM
Sean H Breheny
700 Belmont St Apt 1
Watertown MA 02472

Call Sign: K1VPJ
Bruce A Dean
39 Bridge St
Watertown MA 021724813

Call Sign: KA1AGE
David H Kaufman
44 Brimmer St
Watertown MA 02172

Call Sign: N1FXZ
Carol C Millard
44 Brimmer St
Watertown MA 02172

Call Sign: WA2TXL
Gotham City Radio Association
103 Chuch St
Watertown MA 024724726

Call Sign: KB1UMA
Sumrit Panyasai
33 Church Ln Unit 1
Watertown MA 02472

Call Sign: WB2TXL
Lawrence D Rand
103 Church St
Watertown MA 024724726

Call Sign: KB1BWD
Satellife Amateur Radio Society
125 Coolidge Ave
Watertown MA 021722875

Call Sign: K9ERA
Barb A Cohen
125 Coolidge Ave 803
Watertown MA 02472

Call Sign: K9HI

Phillip E Temples
125 Coolidge Ave 803
Watertown MA 02472

Call Sign: W1GOH
Stephen A Ward
199 Coolidge Ave 803
Watertown MA 02172

Call Sign: AA1BW
Lajos Gergely
125 Coolidge Ave Ste 803
Watertown MA 02472

Call Sign: AA1R
Andrew B Sweet
46 Cottage St
Watertown MA 024721515

Call Sign: WX1G
David A Hunt
18 Cross St #1
Watertown MA 02472

Call Sign: KA1JHZ
William E Wyckoff Jr
43 Cross St Apt 1
Watertown MA 024722325

Call Sign: N1SWG
Charles J Myra
11 Falmouth Rd
Watertown MA 024722219

Call Sign: N1ONL
James P Mc Laughlin
20 Fayette St
Watertown MA 02172

Call Sign: KE1IK
Kenneth A Branco
54 Fayette St
Watertown MA 02472

Call Sign: K1XF
J Roger Cicchese
17 Gleason St
Watertown MA 02172

Call Sign: KB1DBY

Daniel P Kamalic
14 Hearn St
Watertown MA 02472

Call Sign: N2QQT
Drew T Housten
8 Hearn St Apt 1
Watertown MA 02472

Call Sign: N1XOD
Emily K Schulz
101 Highland Ave
Watertown MA 02172

Call Sign: N1NZT
Colin M Angle
28 Hillcrest Cir
Watertown MA 02172

Call Sign: N1NZW
Frank A Bronzo
21 Hudson St
Watertown MA 02472

Call Sign: KB1KLD
Debra D Martin
9 Kimball Rd
Watertown MA 02472

Call Sign: WD4NFQ
Daniel S Hunter
33 Kimball Rd
Watertown MA 02172

Call Sign: N1NSS
Mark R Ciravolo
56 Lexington St
Watertown MA 02172

Call Sign: W1GBH
Robert E Weeden
102 Lexington St
Watertown MA 02172

Call Sign: KA1JHT
Dorothy F Adamo
153 Lexington St
Watertown MA 02172

Call Sign: KB1OCO
John Kindzerske
326 Lexington St
Watertown MA 02472

Call Sign: KB1TRC
Robert J Jackson
354 Lexington St
Watertown MA 02472

Call Sign: N1KZC
Arthur K Minasian
26 Louise St
Watertown MA
024722745

Call Sign: N1ISU
Susan L Phillips
152 Lovell Rd
Watertown MA 02172

Call Sign: KA1RLJ
William C O Neil
537 Main St
Watertown MA 02172

Call Sign: K1ZMQ
Earl T Spicer
275 Main St #304
Watertown MA
021724344

Call Sign: KB1CPH
Christopher P Higgins
125 Morse St
Watertown MA 02472

Call Sign: KB1NSF
Gakuta Toba
260 Mount Auburn St
Apt 1f
Watertown MA 02472

Call Sign: KB1NSD
Aki Ejima
260 Mt Auburn St 1f
Watertown MA 02472

Call Sign: KC0BJK
Matthew A Stewart
222 N Beacon St Unit
2
Watertown MA 02472

Call Sign: WA1LS
Leonard M Shames
81 Nyack St
Watertown MA 02172

Call Sign: KA1WWD
Robert L Holcomb
28 Olcott St
Watertown MA 02172

Call Sign: W1HOL
Jason D Ash
28 Olcott St
Watertown MA 02472

Call Sign: WA1JAR
Dean G Di Gregorio
166 Palfrey St
Watertown MA 02172

Call Sign: N1OMK
Donato Alonzi
238 Palfrey St
Watertown MA 02472

Call Sign: KB1QLS
John M Steeves
60 Phillips St
Watertown MA 02472

Call Sign: W1JMS
John M Steeves
60 Phillips St
Watertown MA 02472

Call Sign: N1PHK
Glen S Kominik
469 Pleasant St
Watertown MA 02472

Call Sign: W1TOW
Glen S Kominik
469 Pleasant St
Watertown MA 02472

Call Sign: KB1MBN
Guy T Germana Iii
21 Prescott St
Watertown MA 02472

Call Sign: WA1BHD
Dominic E Bottaro
36 Quirk St
Watertown MA 02172

Call Sign: KB1QHV
Bill C Thompson
12 Riverside St
Watertown MA 02472

Call Sign: KC0HLL
Heather F Cougar
18 Royal St
Watertown MA 02472

Call Sign: AB7IO
Arne A Henden
20 Saint Mary's St
Watertown MA 02472

Call Sign: WB1BUS
Anthony D De Cicco
22 Sawin St
Watertown MA 02172

Call Sign: KA1DHR
Robert C Currie
18 School Ln
Watertown MA 02172

Call Sign: KB1WOE
Aleksey Akhonen
28 Springfield St
Watertown MA 02472

Call Sign: K1JLT
Herbert L Erikson
86 Stoneleigh Rd
Watertown MA
024721339

Call Sign: KC9CJH
David J Suther
48 Stuart St
Watertown MA 02472

Call Sign: N1BAN
J Barry Hawkes Jr
87 Summer St
Watertown MA 02172

Call Sign: K1TOF
Christophe J Gerard
61 Warren St
Watertown MA 02472

Call Sign: N1HEQ
Richard D Wade
215 Warren St
Watertown MA 02472

Call Sign: KB1JNP
Kwan Ho Derrick Lui

20 Watertown St 346
Watertown MA 02472

Call Sign: N3FGW
Ralph W Hyre Jr
20 Watertown St Unit
414
Watertown MA 02472

Call Sign: N1EHI
Louis J Marotta
55 Waverley Ave
Watertown MA 02472

Call Sign: N1XZI
Andrew J Cerier
234 Westminster Ave
Watertown MA 02172

Call Sign: N1ZPR
Paul C Morganthall
234 Westminster Ave
Watertown MA 02172

Call Sign: KA1JIP
George L Joubert
37 William St
Watertown MA 02172

Call Sign: N1MXX
Michael N Legere
Watertown MA 02272

Call Sign: WA1FBQ
Robert A Ebeling
Watertown MA 02272

Call Sign: KE1LU
Michael N Legere
Watertown MA
024710037

**FCC Amateur Radio
Licenses in Watham**

Call Sign: N1XNK
George H Phifer
28 Meade Rd
Watham MA
021543216

**FCC Amateur Radio
Licenses in Waverly**

Call Sign: N1ZLZ
Patricia Breen
Waverly MA 02179

**FCC Amateur Radio
Licenses in Wayland**

Call Sign: KA1RLP
Adele C Sobel
47 Barney Hill Rd
Wayland MA 01778

Call Sign: WB1FCT
Herbert S Sobel
47 Barney Hill Rd
Wayland MA 01778

Call Sign: N1PYD
Arthur I Moses
7 Cameron Rd
Wayland MA 01778

Call Sign: N1LAH
Ralph T Devlin
1 Caulfield Rd
Wayland MA 01778

Call Sign: N1IDZ
Dominique P Verly
82 Claypit Hill Rd
Wayland MA 01778

Call Sign: N1AOO
Steven D Rosenberg
59 Clubhouse Ln
Wayland MA 01778

Call Sign: W1JZX
Richard A Stanley
60 Cochituate Rd
Wayland MA
017782602

Call Sign: W1AFP
David C Paris
226 Cochituate Rd
Wayland MA 01778

Call Sign: N1GES
Jeffrey M Downing
197 Commonwealth
Rd
Wayland MA 01778

Call Sign: KA1GFQ
Edward A Leonard
15 Doran Rd
Wayland MA 01778

Call Sign: WA1IYN
Wilfred E Casavant
88 Dudley Rd
Wayland MA 01778

Call Sign: AF1J
Charles J Peters
98 Dudley Rd
Wayland MA 01778

Call Sign: W1KD
Charles J Peters
98 Dudley Rd
Wayland MA 01778

Call Sign: N1SNK
Kim Wyke
135 Dudley Rd
Wayland MA 01778

Call Sign: N1LLE
Kevin J Morin
50 E Plain St
Wayland MA 01778

Call Sign: WA1CEB
Edwin J Rudenauer
36 Edgewood Rd
Wayland MA 01778

Call Sign: K4EO
Lawrence C Stewart
7 Erwin Rd
Wayland MA 01778

Call Sign: N1QKA
Leroy W White Jr
5 Gage Rd
Wayland MA 01778

Call Sign: WB1FEG
Sheldon Viles
17 Glezen Ln
Wayland MA 01778

Call Sign: AA6YQ
David H Bernstein
25 Glezen Ln
Wayland MA 01778

Call Sign: K1NUN
Eric E Falkof
2 Hickory Hill Rd
Wayland MA
017781212

Call Sign: KB1OCP
Nancy L Falkof
2 Hickory Hill Rd
Wayland MA 01778

Call Sign: N1TEX
Benjamin J Zeskind
14 Hickory Hill Rd
Wayland MA 01778

Call Sign: WB1CVG
Gerald L Wilson
29 Highgate Rd
Wayland MA 01778

Call Sign: NB1B
Dennis G Egan
3 Keith Rd
Wayland MA
017784517

Call Sign: KA1ZMJ
Josephine A Hardesty
1 Lake Rd Ter
Wayland MA 01778

Call Sign: KB1IOU
Mike Gvili
18 Loblolly Ln
Wayland MA 01778

Call Sign: N1JMY
Kevin S Goodwin
18 Lodge Rd
Wayland MA 01778

Call Sign: KA1Y
Isidor Straus
8 Longfellow Rd
Wayland MA 01778

Call Sign: W1MEX
Kevin S Goodwin
106 Main St - Apt 310
Wayland MA
017784951

Call Sign: KA1DHO
Carol M Collins
10 Marshall Ter
Wayland MA 01778

Call Sign: W1GXT
Lewis D Collins
10 Marshall Terrace
Wayland MA 01778

Call Sign: KA1RBH
Robert H Flanagan
22 Millbrook Rd
Wayland MA 01778

Call Sign: KA1RVS
Robert W Dugas
56 Moore Rd
Wayland MA 01778

Call Sign: KA1OPT
Timothy P Largy
59 Moore Rd
Wayland MA 01778

Call Sign: KO5O
Elizabeth A Levy
16 Morrill Drive
Wayland MA
017784710

Call Sign: KB1OQA
Thomas J Turner
7 Nob Hill Rd
Wayland MA
017782216

Call Sign: W1UIU
Francis W Bartol
19 Old Connecticut
Path
Wayland MA 01778

Call Sign: KB1EB
John H Antes
11 Old Farm Cir
Wayland MA
017783115

Call Sign: W1SI
Hunter C Harris Jr
73 Old Sudbury Rd
Wayland MA 01778

Call Sign: W1CO
Arthur T Rieders
20 Old Weston Rd
Wayland MA 01778

Call Sign: N1AKY
Gerald A Isenberg
36 Old Weston Rd
Wayland MA 01778

Call Sign: KB1NYQ
Eilif H Mikkelsen
5 Oxbow Rd
Wayland MA 01778

Call Sign: KB1NXK
Carl M Mikkelsen
5 Oxbow Rd
Wayland MA 01778

Call Sign: K1UZK
Carl M Mikkelsen
5 Oxbow Rd
Wayland MA 01778

Call Sign: W1DC
Radio Club 1200
68 Plain Rd
Wayland MA
017782312

Call Sign: W1UB
Donald V Rider
68 Plain Rd
Wayland MA
017782312

Call Sign: K2ORS
Warren H Ziegler Jr
157 Plain Rd
Wayland MA 01778

Call Sign: KA1KVH
Barbara M Eagle
16 Reservoir Rd
Wayland MA 01778

Call Sign: N1CLA
Morton G Eagle
16 Reservoir Rd
Wayland MA 01778

Call Sign: N1NHI
David C Robbins

44 River Rd
Wayland MA 01778

Call Sign: KB1OSL
Thomas J Abdella
78 Riverview Cir
Wayland MA 01778

Call Sign: W1SHO
Thomas J Abdella
78 Riverview Cir
Wayland MA 01778

Call Sign: KA1SLN
Craig Harris
14 Rolling Ln
Wayland MA 01778

Call Sign: K1NYD
Richard W Giuliani
27 Sears Rd
Wayland MA 01778

Call Sign: N1WPO
Thomas P Sosnowski
58 Sears Rd
Wayland MA 01778

Call Sign: KB1LDN
Susan P Klein
52 Sedgemeadow Rd
Wayland MA 01778

Call Sign: KA1TZW
Nicholas C Manikas
13 Smokey Hill Rd
Wayland MA 01778

Call Sign: KB1WIP
Nick Brandaleone
7 Spencer Cir
Wayland MA 01778

Call Sign: W1EQX
Carmine M Iannace
15 Standish Rd
Wayland MA 01778

Call Sign: KA1SVX
Jeffrey A Swarz
61 Three Ponds Rd
Wayland MA 01778

Call Sign: W1MXX

Orville E Bean
15 Timber Ln
Wayland MA
017785118

Call Sign: W2PCR
Bruce C Levens
17 Timber Ln
Wayland MA 01778

Call Sign: W1HSM
Glenn E Whitham
9 Trinity Pl
Wayland MA 01778

Call Sign: KC5GYR
Zhiming Mai
174 West Plain St
Wayland MA 01778

Call Sign: W1TAK
Lawrence F Mc Court
3 Wheelock Rd
Wayland MA
017782309

Call Sign: W1QUT
Erich N Kather
22 Woodridge Rd
Wayland MA 01778

Call Sign: W1EYI
Allan D White
28 Woodridge Rd
Wayland MA 01778

Call Sign: KC1KG
William J Bowhers
85 Woodridge Rd
Wayland MA 01778

Call Sign: AG1D
Dale A Zeskind
Wayland MA 01778

Call Sign: KA1OXQ
Kenneth C Nelson
Wayland MA
017780060

Call Sign: KB1MNW
Robert R Dandekar
Wayland MA 01778

Call Sign: KB1TWN
Christopher A Strang
Wayland MA 01778

Call Sign: KB1TWR
Linda M Mcinnis
Wayland MA 01778

**FCC Amateur Radio
Licenses in Webster**

Call Sign: KA1CLM
Anthony S Surozenski
10 Bates Point Rd
Webster MA 01570

Call Sign: K1BEL
Russell S Pratt
91 Birch Island Rd
Webster MA 01570

Call Sign: KB1OJG
Gregory E Lynskey
29 Blueberry Hill
Webster MA 01570

Call Sign: W2GEL
Gregory E Lynskey
29 Blueberry Hill
Webster MA 01570

Call Sign: KA1CJP
Lawrence Bonnette
16 Brookside Ave
Webster MA 01570

Call Sign: W1UJ
Jason V Corriveau
16 Dragon Rd
Webster MA 01570

Call Sign: KB1PAN
Budlog Radio Group
16 Dragon Rd
Webster MA 01570

Call Sign: WA1BUD
Budlog Radio Group
16 Dragon Rd
Webster MA 01570

Call Sign: N1GKI
Jason V Corriveau
Dragon Rd

Webster MA 01570

Call Sign: K1JRY
Clarence W Gelineau
13 E Main St
Webster MA 01570

Call Sign: KB1FNQ
Harley L Smith Jr
55 East Main St Apt 21
Webster MA
015700172

Call Sign: KA1XQ
Ronald W Siegmund
4 First St
Webster MA 01570

Call Sign: KA1MPG
Jonathan J Fournier
12 Harris St
Webster MA 01570

Call Sign: KA1MPI
Ronald J Fournier Sr
12 Harris St
Webster MA 01570

Call Sign: N1NNP
Margaret A Fournier
12 Harris St
Webster MA 01570

Call Sign: KB2RLB
Timothy C Mc Fadden
17 Harvard St
Webster MA 01570

Call Sign: KB1QXM
Michael J Mariano
161 High St
Webster MA 01570

Call Sign: K1DBZ
Richard W Hinchliffe
41 Hillside Ave
Webster MA 01570

Call Sign: K1RGT
Marjorie C Hinchliffe
41 Hillside Ave
Webster MA 01570

Call Sign: K1SYI

Richard E Spahl
6 Lake Pky
Webster MA 01570

Call Sign: N1VXL
David M Baker
89 Lake St
Webster MA 01570

Call Sign: N1LKT
Steven L Raymond
22 Lakeside Ave
Webster MA
015703570

Call Sign: N1GRZ
Richard A Jakubowski
20 Lincoln St
Webster MA 01570

Call Sign: WA1AIT
Frank Para
188 Lower Gore Rd
Webster MA
015703416

Call Sign: N1YMB
Robert A Rainha
10 Market St
Webster MA
015702245

Call Sign: KB1MBH
Troy Coverstone
14 Market St
Webster MA 01570

Call Sign: N1FFS
George H Mc Govern
4 Mc Govern Ln
Webster MA 01570

Call Sign: K1JQU
Mary Ann
Ciabaszewski
13 Mc Govern Ln
Webster MA 01570

Call Sign: W1JCT
William R
Ciabaszewski
13 Mc Govern Ln
Webster MA 01570

Call Sign: N1LSL
Stephen P Jones
25 Myrtle Ave
Webster MA 01570

Call Sign: N1RRR
John P Lasell
2 Normandy Ave
Webster MA 01570

Call Sign: KB1HXU
Erika M Kitty
60 Pond Ct
Webster MA 01570

Call Sign: KB1EBV
George P Chabot
62 Pond Ct
Webster MA
015701404

Call Sign: KB1EBW
Mary L Chabot
62 Pond Ct
Webster MA
015701404

Call Sign: KA1EVE
Michelle A Mach
15 Prospect St
Webster MA 01570

Call Sign: K1HLE
Anthony G Placzek
30 Robinson St
Webster MA 01570

Call Sign: N1TRT
Barbara H Ciesla
714 School St
Webster MA 01570

Call Sign: N1TRU
Tom Ciesla
714 School St
Webster MA 01570

Call Sign: W1QEA
Peter P Popiak
924 School St
Webster MA
015703027

Call Sign: K1PSF

Joseph V Waskiewicz
Jr
929 School St
Webster MA 01570

Call Sign: K1GDH
Edward J Jarmolowicz
21 South Shore Rd
Webster MA
015702504

Call Sign: KB1QDD
Jonathan A Shaw
105 South Shore Rd
Webster MA 01570

Call Sign: W1JAS
Jonathan A Shaw
105 South Shore Rd
Webster MA 01570

Call Sign: N1PFC
Kurt A Ludwig
4 Summit St
Webster MA 01570

Call Sign: K1VSG
Dennis J Zonia
27 Tanner Rd
Webster MA 01570

Call Sign: KB1JFX
Webster Wireless Assn
27 Tanner Rd
Webster MA
015702124

Call Sign: KB1KSX
Webster Rgn 4c Races
Radio Club
27 Tanner Rd
Webster MA
015702124

Call Sign: K1RDD
Rene D Daniels Jr
405 Treasure Island Rd
Webster MA 01570

Call Sign: KA1RMW
Albert C Locke Iii
27 Valley St
Webster MA 01570

Call Sign: KB1COH
Joseph D Reed
18 Vecchia St
Webster MA 01570

Call Sign: KA1MLN
Joseph M Jolda
49 Wawela Rd
Webster MA 01570

Call Sign: K1YHN
Albert P Penkala
Webster MA 01570

FCC Amateur Radio Licenses in Wellesley

Call Sign: N2SXU
Nathaniel L Hodes
39 Abbott Rd
Wellesley MA 02181

Call Sign: KB1WDW
A Richard Palatino Jr
14 Abbott St Apt 3
Wellesley MA 02482

Call Sign: KB1WEP
Marcia L Steger
14 Abbott St Apt 3
Wellesley MA 02482

Call Sign: N1NDV
Anthony M Pallett
33 Allen Rd
Wellesley MA 02181

Call Sign: WB1CYD
Robert A Bower
27 Atwood St
Wellesley MA 02181

Call Sign: K7DWA
Edward D Folland
5 Belair Rd
Wellesley MA 02181

Call Sign: W1EOA
Roger P Smith
7 Berkeley Rd
Wellesley MA 02181

Call Sign: N1EHG
John S Waugh

20 Bernard Rd
Wellesley MA 02181

Call Sign: K1FB
Michael G Adlerstein
24 Bobolink Rd
Wellesley MA 02481

Call Sign: WB1CTZ
Evelyn M Adlerstein
24 Bobolink Rd
Wellesley MA 02481

Call Sign: N1UTU
Randolph W Drewrey
29 Boulder Rd
Wellesley MA 02181

Call Sign: N1UWK
Anthony C Donato
22 Brewster Rd
Wellesley MA 02181

Call Sign: KB1STP
David R Gasdia
12 Carver Rd
Wellesley MA 02481

Call Sign: KB1QXX
Forrest W Gasdia
12 Carver Rd
Wellesley MA 02481

Call Sign: AB1LG
Forrest W Gasdia
12 Carver Rd
Wellesley MA 02481

Call Sign: N1MXN
Steven R Taylor
21 Chestnut St
Wellesley MA 02181

Call Sign: KA1ZHY
Benjamin F Stonberg
12 Cottonwood Rd
Wellesley MA 02181

Call Sign: N3ER
Dennis A Yao
55 Crestwood Drive
Wellesley MA 02481

Call Sign: KB1LPK

David S Taiclet
5 Dearborn
Wellesley MA 02481

Call Sign: KB1SZT
Matthew W Ebel
74 Donizetti St
Wellesley MA 02482

Call Sign: KA1AWK
Matthew W Ebel
74 Donizetti St
Wellesley MA 02482

Call Sign: KB1TPD
Bradley W Bonn
74 Donizetti St
Wellesley MA 02482

Call Sign: N1JPS
Robert S Gould
21 Elmwood Rd
Wellesley MA 02181

Call Sign: WB3JHD
Paul F Nesdore
77 Elmwood Rd
Wellesley MA 02181

Call Sign: N1EUW
John F Drum
3 Falmouth Dr
Wellesley MA 02181

Call Sign: WB0GUA
Dwight T Jones
120 Forest St
Wellesley MA
024816829

Call Sign: K1FWB
Roger W Stern
11 Framar Rd
Wellesley MA 02481

Call Sign: KA1OJB
Robert Ferguson
54 Fuller Brook Rd
Wellesley MA 02181

Call Sign: KA1RAS
Gary F Egan
66 Fuller Brook Rd
Wellesley MA 02181

Call Sign: KB1TYR
Ryan M Speers
187 Grove St
Wellesley MA 02482

Call Sign: N1NIC
Daniel J Model
50 Grove St - Apt 5410
Wellesley MA 02482

Call Sign: KE1CK
John P Carter
1 Highland Rd
Wellesley MA 02482

Call Sign: N1ABZ
Alexander C Johnson
90 Hundreds Rd
Wellesley MA 02181

Call Sign: AK1I
Richard V Magnanti
80 Kingsbury St
Wellesley MA 02181

Call Sign: KB1THJ
Nicholas H Astley
52 Leighton Rd
Wellesley MA 02482

Call Sign: WB1FSE
Roland P Upham
15 Linden Sq
Wellesley MA 02482

Call Sign: N1PYK
Richard C Smith
76 Manor Ave
Wellesley MA 02181

Call Sign: W1HGS
Kenneth O Lind
15 Maugus Hill Rd
Wellesley MA
021817605

Call Sign: W1ZPI
Paul E Farris
16 Mayo Rd
Wellesley MA 02181

Call Sign: WA2EHV
Gregory P Livingston

27 Morses Pond Rd
Wellesley MA 02482

Call Sign: N1GSM
Charles M Spooner
42 Northgate Rd
Wellesley MA 02181

Call Sign: WB1ELO
Alfred B Downes
12 Old Farm Rd
Wellesley MA 02181

Call Sign: N1XXY
Sara W Costa
95 Overbrook Dr
Wellesley MA 02181

Call Sign: W1ZZZ
Peter T Costa
95 Overbrook Dr
Wellesley MA 02482

Call Sign: N1EDF
Donald C Eklund
114 Overbrook Dr
Wellesley MA 02482

Call Sign: WA3ITR
Charles Bures
7 Pilgrim Cir
Wellesley MA 02181

Call Sign: K1WVY
Bruce P Tis
18 Pine Plain Rd
Wellesley MA
021811124

Call Sign: K1LF
Ludwig G Fasolino
34 Pine Plain Rd
Wellesley MA 02181

Call Sign: N1CNK
Marie E Fasolino
34 Pine Plain Rd
Wellesley MA 02181

Call Sign: N1RYA
Marc S Taylor
57 Pine Plain Rd
Wellesley MA 02181

Call Sign: K1AUP
William D Byard
17 Pinewood Rd
Wellesley MA 02101

Call Sign: KB1MCX
Laurence B Lutvak
69 Pleasant St
Wellesley MA 02482

Call Sign: KB1TEO
Marianne M Brinker
25 Poplar Rd
Wellesley MA 02482

Call Sign: W1HRY
Donald W Scully
12 Priscilla Rd
Wellesley MA 02181

Call Sign: KB1VYK
Quinn M Collins
17 Rice St
Wellesley MA 02481

Call Sign: W1FFO
Theodore D Hale
42 Sheridan Rd
Wellesley MA
021815449

Call Sign: KA1SBG
Christopher J Hubbard
60 Sheridan Rd
Wellesley MA 02481

Call Sign: K1HU
Christopher J Hubbard
60 Sheridan Rd
Wellesley MA 02481

Call Sign: KB1KZH
Leroy B Fraser
4 Stearns Rd
Wellesley MA 02482

Call Sign: KD6NA
James T Shank
30 Sunset Rd
Wellesley MA 02482

Call Sign: NX1O
Claudia E Wulz
30 Sunset Rd

Wellesley MA 02481

Call Sign: KA2FEW
Kenneth A Minklei
20 Swarthmore Rd
Wellesley MA 02482

Call Sign: KB1NRL
Carl M Fleischer
314 Walnut St
Wellesley MA 02481

Call Sign: N1QJY
Aoonsak
Saengarsapaviriya
196 Washington St
Wellesley MA 02181

Call Sign: KA1SMG
Kevin A Epstein
8 Wedgewood Rd
Wellesley MA 02181

Call Sign: WA1WLX
Dennis E Vaccaro
280 Wellesley Ave
Wellesley MA 02181

Call Sign: WA1EVD
William H Emerson
115 Westgate Rd
Wellesley MA 02181

Call Sign: KE6QQK
Jeremy E Bento
237 Weston Rd
Wellesley MA 02482

Call Sign: WA2HQQ
Werner F Meyer
340 Weston Rd
Wellesley MA
024822310

Call Sign: WB2HWG
Madge M Meyer
340 Weston Rd
Wellesley MA
024822310

Call Sign: WB1BVB
George C Sline
395 Weston Rd
Wellesley MA 02181

Call Sign: KB1TZJ
Sam H Lapides
471 Weston Rd
Wellesley MA 02482

Call Sign: KX1H
Thomas M Burton
61 Whittier Rd
Wellesley MA
021815235

Call Sign: KA1ELU
William E Stanwood
35 Windemere Rd
Wellesley MA 02481

Call Sign: WA1RYY
Robert W Weinig
190 Winding River Rd
Wellesley MA 02181

Call Sign: KC1PO
Clifford J Robinson
33 Windsor Rd
Wellesley MA 02181

Call Sign: K1ILL
Harvey B Chess
3 Woodland Rd
Wellesley MA 02181

Call Sign: KB1BXQ
Robert J Mc Guane Jr
507 Worcester St
Wellesley MA
021814927

Call Sign: W1TKZ
Wellesley Amateur
Radio Society
Wellesley MA 02181

**FCC Amateur Radio
Licenses in Wellesley
Hills**

Call Sign: KO1T
Kevin W Donnelly
123 Abbott Rd
Wellesley Hills MA
02481

Call Sign: W3IKG

John H Sangster
9 Bellevue Rd
Wellesley Hills MA
02481

Call Sign: W1FHW
Stephen A A White
18 Chatham Cir
Wellesley Hills MA
02181

Call Sign: N1AGB
Charles F Lovejoy
128 Edmunds Rd
Wellesley Hills MA
024812740

Call Sign: KE4DK
William D Reed
1 Gilson Rd
Wellesley Hills MA
02481

Call Sign: W1EK
Joe Rich
396 Washington St
Wellesley Hills MA
02481

Call Sign: WA2YHV
John Bernardo
77 Whittier Rd
Wellesley Hills MA
02481

Call Sign: KA1UQK
Mitchel B Sayare
15 Woodcliff Rd
Wellesley Hills MA
02181

Call Sign: KA2RSF
John P Mccormick
1025 Chequessett Neck
Rd
Wellfleet MA 02667

Call Sign: K1ATT
Anthony T Tullio Mr
50 Homestead Lane
Wellfleet MA 02667

Call Sign: WA1YFV
Pilgrim Amateur Radio
Club
45 Howland Lane
Wellfleet MA 02667

Call Sign: KB1ULX
Pilgrim Amateur Radio
Club
45 Howland Lane
Wellfleet MA 02667

Call Sign: K1TCO
Pilgrim Amateur Radio
Club
45 Howland Lane
Wellfleet MA 02667

Call Sign: W1GCA
David W Rego
45 Howland Ln
Wellfleet MA 02667

Call Sign: KM1CC
Cape Cod National
Seashore 99 Marconi
Cape Cod Radio Club
Marco
Wellfleet MA 02667

Call Sign: W1GVV
Stanley C Macie
80 Marvenway Box
643
Wellfleet MA 02667

Call Sign: KB1OSX
Jamie Devlin
114 Pamet Point Rd
Wellfleet MA 02667

Call Sign: WA1ZEL
Jonathan D Grout
3053 Rt 6
Wellfleet MA
026670751

Call Sign: N1OA
David W Gardiner
40 Third Ave
Wellfleet MA 02663

Call Sign: KA1SEE

George R King
Wellfleet MA 02667

Call Sign: KA1VCQ
Edward W Tesson
Wellfleet MA 02667

Call Sign: N1XOR
Bruce L Mac Gibbon
Wellfleet MA 02667

Call Sign: N1ZOB
Katerine M Mac
Gibbon
Wellfleet MA 02667

Call Sign: W2LAR
Kenneth R Kimball Jr
Wellfleet MA 02667

Call Sign: WB2MQM
Henry L Boriskin
Wellfleet MA 02667

Call Sign: KB1JXK
Richard F Sheehan
Wellfleet MA
026670117

Call Sign: KB1VAK
Russell T Apgar
Wellfleet MA 02667

Call Sign: K1HLB
Henry L Boriskin
Wellfleet MA 02667

Call Sign: K1RTA
Russell T Apgar
Wellfleet MA 02667

Call Sign: KA1RKI
Rita E Jean
19 Morse Village Rd
Wendell MA
013799704

Call Sign: KA1RKJ
Roland L Jean Sr
19 Morse Village Rd

Wendell MA
013799704

Call Sign: N1WGQ
John M Davis
252 New Salem Rd
Wendell MA 01379

Call Sign: KB1EUI
James D Delaronde
39 Old Farley Rd
Wendell MA 01379

Call Sign: KB1NOC
Dawn M Josefski
74 West St
Wendell MA 01379

Call Sign: KB1OOK
Kathleen O'kane
Wendell MA 01379

Call Sign: WB1FEE
George E Andrews
1 Burnham Rd
Wenham MA 01984

Call Sign: W1JEP
Wendell H Campbell
66 Cedar
Wenham MA 01984

Call Sign: W1KXG
Robert A Barker
15 Conrad Cir
Wenham MA 01984

Call Sign: KB1RXX
Margaret V Whittaker
7 Enon Rd
Wenham MA 01984

Call Sign: N1XQO
Kevin C Van Brunt
255 Grapevine Rd
Wenham MA 01984

Call Sign: KA1UJM
Stefan P Foerster
255 Grapevine Rd
Wenham MA 01984

Call Sign: KB1BPN
Sandra Stolle
2 Great Pond Rd
Wenham MA 01984

Call Sign: KA1OMG
James G Perkins Jr
18 Great Pond Rd
Wenham MA 01984

Call Sign: K2OP
Andrew J Buckler
13 Larch Row
Wenham MA 01984

Call Sign: W1QNJ
Owen I Haszard
36 Maple St
Wenham MA 01984

Call Sign: W1RRF
Lucien J Paquette
401 Old Country Rd
Wenham MA 01984

Call Sign: WZ1Q
Melrose R Cole
809 Old Country Rd
Wenham MA 01984

Call Sign: KA1LCI
Ernie E Yeo
15 Pleasant St
Wenham MA 01984

FCC Amateur Radio Licenses in Wesport

Call Sign: N1NKA
John W O Brien Jr
22 O Dr
Wesport MA 02790

FCC Amateur Radio Licenses in West Acton

Call Sign: KC1ZK
C John Beanland
17 Deacon Hunt Dr
West Acton MA 01720

Call Sign: AA1YE

C John Beanland
17 Deacon Hunt Dr
West Acton MA 01720

Call Sign: W1MAY
Elis A Guditz
11 Mac Leod Ln
West Acton MA 01720

FCC Amateur Radio Licenses in West Barnstable

Call Sign: KB1VIE
Dean F Meece
93 Barnhill Rd
West Barnstable MA
02668

Call Sign: KA1PY
Robert B Wood
216 Church St
West Barnstable MA
026681412

Call Sign: KA1N
Max E Voegelin
164 Great Hill Dr
West Barnstable MA
02668

Call Sign: KB1QDG
Chrystal A Lapine
630 Parker Ln
West Barnstable MA
02668

Call Sign: W2CTX
Ronald A Pfeiffer
143 Saddler Lane
West Barnstable MA
02668

Call Sign: N1GVW
Robert W Russell
West Barnstable MA
02668

Call Sign: W1DER
John O Dellamorte Sr
West Barnstable MA
02668

Call Sign: W1NKT

Howard S Davis
West Barnstable MA
02668

Call Sign: KB1WLY
William D Plikaitis
West Barnstable MA
026680280

FCC Amateur Radio Licenses in West Boylston

Call Sign: N1AXA
Michael J Barnaby
2 Brooks Crossing
West Boylston MA
01583

Call Sign: N1ASV
Guy D Metcalf
58 Bunker Hill Pkwy
West Boylston MA
01583

Call Sign: N1PFS
Joseph Sugarman
47 Campground Rd
West Boylston MA
01583

Call Sign: W1LFI
John Klar
62 Central St
West Boylston MA
01583

Call Sign: KB1QHK
Louis E Drew
107 Central St
West Boylston MA
01583

Call Sign: W1AAJ
Louis E Drew
107 Central St
West Boylston MA
01583

Call Sign: N1SKM
Carolyn R Welch
332 Goodale St
West Boylston MA
01583

Call Sign: N1RRT
James J Frietsch
363 Goodale St
West Boylston MA
01583

Call Sign: KE2TC
John J Isbell
86 Hillside Village Dr
West Boylston MA
01583

Call Sign: KB1MBI
David I Galena
37 King Mtn Dr
West Boylston MA
01583

Call Sign: WA1HLW
Stanley T Johnson
49 Lawrence St
West Boylston MA
01583

Call Sign: AD1G
Richard L Gilley
124 Malden St
West Boylston MA
01583

Call Sign: K1RKO
James F Bonci Sr
59 Maple St
West Boylston MA
01583

Call Sign: K1RKP
Donald W Bonci
69 Maple St
West Boylston MA
015831808

Call Sign: W1AKC
Amy K Coughlin
152 Maple St
West Boylston MA
01583

Call Sign: KA1WII
Richard L Gilley
124 Molden St
West Boylston MA
01583

Call Sign: KA1NAV
Verne A Smith Jr
59 N Main St
West Boylston MA
01583

Call Sign: W1FGP
J Hamilton Givan
107 Pierce St
West Boylston MA
01583

Call Sign: N1KPJ
Marc S Frieden
8 Pinewood Drive
West Boylston MA
01583

Call Sign: KE1LQ
James K Ross
64 Prescott St
West Boylston MA
015831104

Call Sign: N1UTP
James F Ross
64 Prescott St
West Boylston MA
01583

Call Sign: K1EDD
Gordon P White
77 Prescott St
West Boylston MA
01583

Call Sign: K1TDN
Frank A Meanor
131 Prescott St
West Boylston MA
01583

Call Sign: KB1HSK
John P Howe Jr
158 Prospect St
West Boylston MA
01583

Call Sign: KA1WOC
Jason A Kunst
515 Prospect St
West Boylston MA
01583

Call Sign: N1IJQ
Jonathan T Filgate
322 Sterling St D6
West Boylston MA
01583

Call Sign: W1VPH
Lawrence J Caron
34 Waushacum St
West Boylston MA
01583

Call Sign: K1VNO
Richard H Fancy
23 Western Ave
West Boylston MA
01583

Call Sign: KB1CRC
Mark A Sawyer
10 Wood St
West Boylston MA
01583

Call Sign: N1CAJ
Francis E Siderski
256 Worcester St
West Boylston MA
01583

Call Sign: W1PA
William P Acito Jr
West Boylston MA
015830088

FCC Amateur Radio Licenses in West Bridgewater

Call Sign: W1NXX
Lionel Simon
12 Aldrich Rd
West Bridgewater MA
02379

Call Sign: K1WKO
Paul J Thoms
179 Ash St
West Bridgewater MA
02379

Call Sign: KB1BTC

Eastern Mass Eme
Society
82 Belmont St
West Bridgewater MA
02379

Call Sign: KB1BVM
Westbridge Repeater
Assn
82 Belmont St
West Bridgewater MA
02379

Call Sign: WA1OFR
Robert E Johnson
82 Belmont St
West Bridgewater MA
02379

Call Sign: K1VU
Robert E Johnson
82 Belmont St
West Bridgewater MA
02379

Call Sign: N1TWP
Albert C Yucicis
48 Clinton Rd
West Bridgewater MA
023791902

Call Sign: W1DGD
Harry Ketler
85 Columbus Ave
West Bridgewater MA
02379

Call Sign: WA1WFA
Stephen H Ketler
85 Columbus Ave
West Bridgewater MA
02379

Call Sign: W5VRD
James L Grandfield
66 Forest St
West Bridgewater MA
023791904

Call Sign: N1XJH
Robert E Lindgren
237 Forest St
West Bridgewater MA
02379

Call Sign: WA1YPD
Richard J Benecchi
7 Keenan St
West Bridgewater MA
02379

Call Sign: N1XCM
Linda M Fowles
332 Matfield St
West Bridgewater MA
02379

Call Sign: N1IFB
John S Loos
332 Matfield St
West Bridgewater MA
02379

Call Sign: W1KBM
James Eng
28 Mile Brook Rd
West Bridgewater MA
02379

Call Sign: KA1JHG
John De Costa Jr
447 N Main St
West Bridgewater MA
02379

Call Sign: K1MTM
Paul R Wipperman
17 Oliver St
West Bridgewater MA
02379

Call Sign: KB1BZB
North Atlantic Radio
Club
17 Oliver St
West Bridgewater MA
02379

Call Sign: W1ACB
North Atlantic Radio
Club
17 Oliver St
West Bridgewater MA
02379

Call Sign: KA1FAM
Robert E Beck Sr
18 Orchard Dr

West Bridgewater MA
02379

Call Sign: N1OTZ
Raymond E Wall Jr
45 S Main St
West Bridgewater MA
02379

Call Sign: KA1DRG
George E Kyller Sr
108 Scotland St
West Bridgewater MA
02379

Call Sign: N1UDW
Francis T Santry Sr
54 Tiffany Cir
West Bridgewater MA
02379

Call Sign: N1JFU
Stephen D Meuse
80 Walnut St
West Bridgewater MA
02379

Call Sign: N1PAO
Robert E White
27 Woodland Rd
West Bridgewater MA
02379

Call Sign: KA1WYW
Vincent T Hallisey
West Bridgewater MA
02379

Call Sign: W1CIX
Norman W Roscoe
West Bridgewater MA
023790402

FCC Amateur Radio Licenses in West Brookfield

Call Sign: K1KCQ
George E Burnham Jr
42 Birch Hill Rd
West Brookfield MA
01585

Call Sign: K1GYK

George G Richards
51 Cottage Box 185
West Brookfield MA
01585

Call Sign: KD1RW
Lindsey E Smith Jr
84 E Main
West Brookfield MA
01585

Call Sign: KB1PIQ
Eric R Engel
56 Front St
West Brookfield MA
01585

Call Sign: K1EX
Eric R Engel
56 Front St
West Brookfield MA
01585

Call Sign: KB1RFT
Catherine H Engel
56 Front St
West Brookfield MA
01585

Call Sign: K1VJD
James A Nardi
24 George Allen Rd
West Brookfield MA
01585

Call Sign: WA1CAW
Roughsedge W
Higginson
43 Kennedy Rd
West Brookfield MA
015852705

Call Sign: N1MIA
Robert J Hayes
New Brain Tree Rd
West Brookfield MA
01585

Call Sign: KB1FFH
Robert J Hayes
New Brain Tree Rd
West Brookfield MA
01585

Call Sign: N1MIA
Robert J Hayes
35 New Braintree Rd
West Brookfield MA
01585

Call Sign: KA1RKD
Reed E Ostiguy
187 Ragged Hill Rd
West Brookfield MA
01585

Call Sign: KA1AFX
Reed E Ostiguy
187 Ragged Hill Rd
West Brookfield MA
01585

Call Sign: K1HBW
Robert P Tamm
20 Shea Rd
West Brookfield MA
01585

Call Sign: WB1ABW
Jean E Tamm
20 Shea Rd
West Brookfield MA
01585

Call Sign: W1AAE
Ronald D Lucier
134 Tucker Rd
West Brookfield MA
01585

Call Sign: WA1FMT
Robert P Conlon Sr
12 W Main St
West Brookfield MA
01585

Call Sign: KB1CDE
Robert D Rutter
26 Ware St
West Brookfield MA
01585

Call Sign: N1AOX
Walter C Ambach
5 Wickaboag Valley
Rd
West Brookfield MA
01585

Call Sign: WA1UUN
John L Higgins
West Brookfield MA
01585

Call Sign: N1GDY
Dennis F King
West Brookfield MA
01585

Call Sign: KC1TL
Frank M Latwis
West Brookfield MA
01585

Call Sign: N1REM
Matthew A Koziol
West Brookfield MA
01585

FCC Amateur Radio Licenses in West Chatham

Call Sign: W2KPS
Andrew J Sifflard
36 Geranium Dr
West Chatham MA
02669

Call Sign: N1PID
John J Cullen Jr
West Chatham MA
02669

Call Sign: W1SCZ
J Samuel Slicer
West Chatham MA
02669

Call Sign: W1ARM
Alexander R
Mackenzie
West Chatham MA
02669

Call Sign: KB1TAU
Winifred M Lord-
Meservey
West Chatham MA
02669

Call Sign: KB1UHN

Kevin P Nicolai
West Chatham MA
02669

Call Sign: KB1UHO
Keith D Nicolai
West Chatham MA
02669

Call Sign: KB1UUO
Thomas A Olson
West Chatham MA
02669

Call Sign: KB1VAB
Robert W Redding
West Chatham MA
02669

FCC Amateur Radio Licenses in West Chelmsford

Call Sign: KA1JOP
Fred R Mark
3 School
West Chelmsford MA
01863

Call Sign: K1JHD
Leonard E Haberman
4 Susan Ave
West Chelmsford MA
01863

Call Sign: KB1JWY
Robert B Lovell
669 Main Rd
West Chesterfield MA
01084

FCC Amateur Radio Licenses in West Concord

Call Sign: KB1DTA
Michael E Gallagher
West Concord MA
01742

FCC Amateur Radio Licenses in West Dennis

Call Sign: K1SRR
Robert Close
8 Allain Way
West Dennis MA
026700681

Call Sign: KC4TXL
Marie A Ewing Mrs
50 Ferry St
West Dennis MA
02670

Call Sign: W1YXJ
Waldo W Guy
34 South Main St
West Dennis MA
02670

Call Sign: KB1ROH
Sandra E Finstein
17 South Village
Circle
West Dennis MA
02670

Call Sign: KB1ROC
Janet Radziewicz
337 Trotting Park Rd
West Dennis MA
02670

Call Sign: KB1ROD
Kevin D Morley
337 Trotting Park Rd
West Dennis MA
02670

Call Sign: KA1RLK
Eugene L Tougas
West Dennis MA
02670

Call Sign: W1YPT
Louise U Guy
West Dennis MA
02670

Call Sign: KB1PDV
Davis C Bruce
West Dennis MA
02670

FCC Amateur Radio Licenses in West Falmouth

Call Sign: K1IZB
Alden H Cook
100 Ambleside Dr Box
191
West Falmouth MA
02574

Call Sign: N1IVD
Louise A Stanwood
Box 173
West Falmouth MA
02574

Call Sign: N1KHE
Richard L Bedell
Box 533
West Falmouth MA
02574

Call Sign: KA1SGL
Mary Ellen Stephen
Box 567
West Falmouth MA
02574

Call Sign: WB1CRJ
Frederic A Stanwood
Jr
96 Chapoquott Rd Box
173
West Falmouth MA
02574

Call Sign: KA1IDY
Howard V Redgate
70 Colonial Way
West Falmouth MA
02574

Call Sign: K5MA
R Jan Carman
66 Fairway Ln
West Falmouth MA
02574

Call Sign: W1ISD
Barry M Martin
16 Fairway Ln Box
397

West Falmouth MA
02574

Call Sign: K1BGH
Arthur E Hawkes
9 Old Rd
West Falmouth MA
02574

Call Sign: K8VM
Vincent G Martlew
49 Westmoreland Dr
West Falmouth MA
025740520

Call Sign: KB1PVO
Aaron B Nighelli
West Falmouth MA
02574

Call Sign: KB1PVP
Jeston Nighelli
West Falmouth MA
02574

Call Sign: KA1IWI
Janet B Martin
West Falmouth MA
02574

Call Sign: KA1RMH
Barbara L Krance
West Falmouth MA
025740436

Call Sign: KB1QXT
Tim R Fallon
West Falmouth MA
02574

FCC Amateur Radio Licenses in West Groton

Call Sign: N1PIP
Allyn St C Richardson
81 Pepperell Rd
West Groton MA
01472

FCC Amateur Radio Licenses in West Harwich

Call Sign: W1JAW
John A Wyatt
6 Bayport Rd
West Harwich MA
02671

Call Sign: N1BQY
Dennis F Broderick
10 Damon Rd
West Harwich MA
02671

Call Sign: KB1HJH
Joseph Mcneil
119 Depot Rd W
West Harwich MA
02671

Call Sign: K1HFD
Joseph Mcneil
119 Depot Rd W
West Harwich MA
02671

Call Sign: K1POU
Leonard V Molan
124 Depot Rd W
West Harwich MA
02671

Call Sign: KB1ORE
Eric W Bush
6 Hall Ave
West Harwich MA
02671

Call Sign: K1EWB
Eric W Bush
6 Hall Ave
West Harwich MA
02671

Call Sign: KB1SMQ
Alex W Vargus
17 Harniss Rd
West Harwich MA
02671

FCC Amateur Radio Licenses in West Hatfield

Call Sign: KB1ISQ
Justin R Aquadro

38 Linseed Rd
West Hatfield MA
01088

Call Sign: WA1SMH
Alphonse J Jackowski
68 Linseed Rd
West Hatfield MA
010889505

Call Sign: KB1EEJ
Jared I Greenberg
186 Linseed Rd
West Hatfield MA
01088

Call Sign: N1CYT
Stephen M Curtis
205 Linseed Rd
West Hatfield MA
01088

FCC Amateur Radio Licenses in West Hyannisport

Call Sign: KB1SYS
Lillian J Seely
West Hyannisport MA
02672

FCC Amateur Radio Licenses in West Lynn

Call Sign: WA1ZOC
George E Timlin
86 Woodman St
West Lynn MA 01905

FCC Amateur Radio Licenses in West Medford

Call Sign: KC1BN
Laurie H Cote
36 Circuit St
West Medford MA
021553656

Call Sign: W1EEC
John A Connors
41 Franklin Ave

West Medford MA
02155

Call Sign: WA1HMX
Samuel A Reid
18 Mystic River Rd
West Medford MA
02155

FCC Amateur Radio Licenses in West Millbury

Call Sign: KA1AQP
Richard D Kenadek
Box 58
West Millbury MA
01586

FCC Amateur Radio Licenses in West Newbury

Call Sign: W1CRM
John J Andriotakis
8 Albion Ln
West Newbury MA
01985

Call Sign: K1DBB
David B Belsky
2 Barberry Ln
West Newbury MA
01985

Call Sign: WA1PPD
William Stasiuk
2 Carlsen Rd
West Newbury MA
01985

Call Sign: N1BCB
Christopher N
Anderson
4 Coffin St
West Newbury MA
01985

Call Sign: K1LU
James E Mc Cobb Jr
65 Coffin St
West Newbury MA
019851209

Call Sign: KB1WBQ
Guy A Navarra
8 Cortland Ln
West Newbury MA
01985

Call Sign: NK1V
Edward M Buckley
43 Garden St
West Newbury MA
01985

Call Sign: KB1EDA
John V Connolly Jr
29 Hilltop Cir
West Newbury MA
01985

Call Sign: N1SOD
Wayne G Maglione
56 Main St
West Newbury MA
01985

Call Sign: K1UMW
Charles P Susen
171 Main St
West Newbury MA
01985

Call Sign: KA1SKZ
Christopher C
Majauckas
18 Maple St
West Newbury MA
01985

Call Sign: KA1TDI
Susan L Anderson
29 Pleasant St
West Newbury MA
019851403

Call Sign: N1DQF
Joseph M Grifoni Jr
16 Spring Hill Rd
West Newbury MA
01985

Call Sign: N1OTQ
Carolyn P Grifoni
16 Spring Hill Rd
West Newbury MA
01985

Call Sign: N1KYU
Vincent J Attenasio Jr
17 Stewart St
West Newbury MA
01985

Call Sign: KB1EQR
Mark Hemingway
93 Stewart St
West Newbury MA
01985

FCC Amateur Radio
Licenses in West
Newton

Call Sign: W1GEC
Louis Sooho
220 Adams Ave
West Newton MA
02165

Call Sign: W1YWR
Matthew Jefferson
94 Adena Rd
West Newton MA
02165

Call Sign: KA1OKB
Dennis L Delicata
15 Bonita St
West Newton MA
02165

Call Sign: KA1MSM
Roger Wallace
182 Cherry St
West Newton MA
02165

Call Sign: N1PJC
Edward G Cappadona
Jr
247 Cherry St
West Newton MA
02165

Call Sign: KA1RSK
Peter C Saliba
1169 Commonwealth
Ave
West Newton MA
02165

Call Sign: KA1PLB
Martin Idelson
1603 Commonwealth
Ave
West Newton MA
02165

Call Sign: N1HYN
Paulette J Idelson
1603 Commonwealth
Ave
West Newton MA
021652800

Call Sign: N1RHC
Jamie Tan
73 Fordham Rd
West Newton MA
02165

Call Sign: N1RHQ
Hong Z Tan
73 Fordham Rd
West Newton MA
02165

Call Sign: W1IBK
Louis Nelson
54 Jerome Ave
West Newton MA
02165

Call Sign: KA1LQN
George J Goldin
14 Llewellyn Rd
West Newton MA
02165

Call Sign: KB1RT
Daniel C Halbert
74 Maynard St
West Newton MA
024651359

Call Sign: K1OQX
Perry R Lipson
51 Pratt Dr
West Newton MA
02165

Call Sign: WB1ADC
Cheryl J Carpenter
51 Pratt Drive

West Newton MA
02465

Call Sign: N1GDM
Douglas T Hall
103 Prince St
West Newton MA
02165

Call Sign: WA1GFA
Charles J Porfert
11 Rose Dr
West Newton MA
02465

Call Sign: KB1QYL
George W Sampson
123 Russell Rd
West Newton MA
02465

Call Sign: K1GWS
George W Sampson
123 Russell Rd
West Newton MA
02465

Call Sign: N1RHD
Gilbert V Boro
26 Sewall St
West Newton MA
02165

Call Sign: KB1GLH
Richard R Malone
49 Sheridan St
West Newton MA
024651037

Call Sign: W1RYP
Joseph A Castagnino
12 Taft Ave
West Newton MA
02165

Call Sign: KB1DAP
Matthew E Coarr
12 Upham St
West Newton MA
024651520

Call Sign: N1YDG
John F Donahue
1354 Washington St

West Newton MA
02165

Call Sign: KB1GI
Stephanie D Karger
38 Wauwinet Rd
West Newton MA
024652957

Call Sign: WA2WWV
Arieh M Karger
38 Wauwinet Rd
West Newton MA
024652957

Call Sign: K1PHI
Lawrence D Laven
35 Whitlowe Rd
West Newton MA
02165

Call Sign: W1TYY
Justin L Altshuler
12 Wimbledon Cir
West Newton MA
02165

FCC Amateur Radio
Licenses in West
Peabody

Call Sign: KA1PJD
Thomas Bayliss
3 Connors Rd
West Peabody MA
01960

Call Sign: WA1QWG
Edward P Gustat
21 Hamilton Rd
West Peabody MA
01960

Call Sign: NZ1AF
Christopher J Jasper
737 Lowell St
West Peabody MA
019603462

Call Sign: KA1NQP
Robert J Visco
11 Stockton Rd
West Peabody MA
019603450

Call Sign: W1OAL
Constantine Tingus
3 Wentworth Rd
West Peabody MA
019601045

Call Sign: N1GXY
Robert M Smith
34 Emerald St
West Quincy MA
02169

Call Sign: K1RAV
Richard A Veneziano
54 Unity St
West Quincy MA
02169

Call Sign: KA1MKC
John P Curtis
30 Addington Rd
West Roxbury MA
02132

Call Sign: K1MKC
John P Curtis
30 Addington Rd
West Roxbury MA
02132

Call Sign: N1ALJ
Otto T Gustin
155 Bellevue St
West Roxbury MA
02132

Call Sign: K1IPA
International Police
Association Radio
Club
18 Carrol St
West Roxbury MA
02132

Call Sign: WA1CFX

Howard L Mintz
18 Carroll St
West Roxbury MA
02132

Call Sign: W1HHW
Philip V Barden
2331 Centre St
West Roxbury MA
02132

Call Sign: W1KRU
James A Warakois
2626 Centre St
West Roxbury MA
02132

Call Sign: W1ATU
Paul R Kennedy
2221 Centre St
West Roxbury MA
02132

Call Sign: KB1KGU
Michael B Yaffe
1 Chesbrough Rd
West Roxbury MA
02132

Call Sign: KE1HR
Gregory P Charest
124 Church St
West Roxbury MA
02132

Call Sign: K9MVS
Mark Silveri
78 Clement Ave
West Roxbury MA
02132

Call Sign: KB1WNJ
William M Kaminsky
11 Furbush Rd
West Roxbury MA
02132

Call Sign: KB1TJQ
Phyllis I Meserlian
12 Hastings St
West Roxbury MA
02132

Call Sign: KA1INO

Richard C Simonson
15 High View Ave
West Roxbury MA
02132

Call Sign: N1LVC
Earl D Durst
35 Hillcrest
West Roxbury MA
02132

Call Sign: N1LVD
Mary T Durst
35 Hillcrest St
West Roxbury MA
02132

Call Sign: W1ZGW
George W Flint
12 Keane Rd
West Roxbury MA
021321620

Call Sign: W1MTM
John J Sexton Jr
6 Kershaw Rd
West Roxbury MA
021324513

Call Sign: KA1LN
Leo J Burke
4 Lantern Ln
West Roxbury MA
02132

Call Sign: W1ZKU
Paul A Lydon
12 Larkhill Rd
West Roxbury MA
02132

Call Sign: N1ZQI
Frederick L Smith
15 Latin Rd
West Roxbury MA
02132

Call Sign: N1FKC
Francis J Power
15 Libbey St
West Roxbury MA
02132

Call Sign: WA1VCT

Robert E Lockwood
72 Manthorne Rd
West Roxbury MA
02132

Call Sign: KE4WPZ
April M Trussell-Smith
147 Manthorne Rd Apt
1
West Roxbury MA
02132

Call Sign: KB1PTW
Stephen T Hazam
16 March Ave Apt 3
West Roxbury MA
021322604

Call Sign: K1QOQ
William L Roberts
29 Meredith St
West Roxbury MA
021322004

Call Sign: N1BNI
George L Beaupre Jr
35 Oakmere St
West Roxbury MA
02132

Call Sign: K1UVD
Joseph S Aversa
44 Oriole St
West Roxbury MA
021322619

Call Sign: N1QHI
Patrick J Leonard
41 Park St
West Roxbury MA
02132

Call Sign: KA1KMN
William J Kocen Jr
297 Park St
West Roxbury MA
02132

Call Sign: W1ZFQ
Robert F King
20 Pelton St
West Roxbury MA
02132

Call Sign: KB1HGJ
Maxim Eskin
64 Potomac St
West Roxbury MA
02132

Call Sign: N1QCX
Irving N Allen
40 Rockingham Ave
408
West Roxbury MA
02132

Call Sign: W1AYI
Walter H Boynton
32 Rockland St
West Roxbury MA
02132

Call Sign: N1VLJ
Theodore J Zaborski
19 Tobin Rd
West Roxbury MA
02132

Call Sign: N1KYV
Hristos Kotsiopoulos
4807 Washington St
West Roxbury MA
02132

Call Sign: WA1ROS
Frederick L Duntley
4881 Washington St
Suite 2
West Roxbury MA
02132

Call Sign: KB1EVZ
Thomas J Tuttle
88 Westover St
West Roxbury MA
021321342

Call Sign: AB1HU
Thomas J Tuttle
88 Westover St
West Roxbury MA
021321342

Call Sign: KB1TIC
John P Tuttle
88 Westover St

West Roxbury MA
02132

Call Sign: N1OZT
Jeffrey Z Wolf
236 Willow St
West Roxbury MA
02132

Call Sign: W1MIX
Joseph A Vinci
West Roxbury MA
02132

FCC Amateur Radio Licenses in West Somerville

Call Sign: W1OIH
Frank V Mancusi
764 Broadway
West Somerville MA
02144

Call Sign: KA1NEY
Gail E Abate
37 Lowden
West Somerville MA
02144

FCC Amateur Radio Licenses in West Springfield

Call Sign: N1QBA
William E Grabowski
70 Almon Ave
West Springfield MA
01089

Call Sign: KA1BKJ
Michael E Mathews
128 Almon Ave
West Springfield MA
010892908

Call Sign: KB1TOD
Benjamin R Quinn
75 Apple Ridge Rd
West Springfield MA
01089

Call Sign: KC1O

Thomas A D Andrea
Sr
373 Birnie Ave
West Springfield MA
01089

Call Sign: AA1OP
Jens Guenther
798 Birnie Ave
West Springfield MA
01089

Call Sign: KA1VIS
Thomas S Coard
72 Braintree Rd
West Springfield MA
01089

Call Sign: W1HYO
Thomas J Shea
111 Bridle Path Rd
West Springfield MA
01089

Call Sign: N1XGI
Jane S Smith
48 Cataumet Ln
West Springfield MA
01089

Call Sign: KA1WGD
Claude I Hollingshead
97 Chester St
West Springfield MA
01089

Call Sign: KB1QZZ
Charles R Ford
59 City View Ave
West Springfield MA
01089

Call Sign: W1CRF
Charles R Ford
59 City View Ave
West Springfield MA
01089

Call Sign: KB1CSK
Arthur C Brunell
14 Clayton Dr
West Springfield MA
01089

Call Sign: WB1EMB
Joseph H Dumais
39 Clayton Dr
West Springfield MA
01089

Call Sign: KA1RXI
Kristi L Demers
71 Craig Dr Apt H4
West Springfield MA
01089

Call Sign: KB1MDS
Mariusz R Zielinski
57 Deer Run Rd
West Springfield MA
01089

Call Sign: KA1WGR
Lisa M Schneider
145 Dewey St
West Springfield MA
01089

Call Sign: KB1OO
Bernard Michaels
514 Dewey St
West Springfield MA
010891608

Call Sign: W2LFV
Bernard Michaels
514 Dewey St
West Springfield MA
010891608

Call Sign: KB1MII
Stephen M Martone
48 Elm Cir
West Springfield MA
01089

Call Sign: WA1BXQ
William Beattie
569 Elm St
West Springfield MA
01089

Call Sign: N1JIO
John E Stark Jr
75 Elmwood Ave
West Springfield MA
01089

Call Sign: W1TAT
Thomas L Nutting
96 Ely Ave
West Springfield MA
010892214

Call Sign: WA1WKG
James D Larkin
179 Forest Glen
West Springfield MA
010891900

Call Sign: WA1YKY
William R Cass
235 Forest Glen
West Springfield MA
01089

Call Sign: KB2GPT
Paul A Weinberg
29 Garden St
West Springfield MA
01089

Call Sign: KB1TOE
Jacob W Page
49 Greenleaf Ave
West Springfield MA
01089

Call Sign: KA1JEC
James E Finnie
33 Hale St
West Springfield MA
01089

Call Sign: KC1CC
Chester S Szydlowski
41 Hale St
West Springfield MA
01089

Call Sign: KB1WQJ
Nicholas C Hansmann
67 Harwich Rd
West Springfield MA
01089

Call Sign: KA1ZLL
Scott M Rainville
111 Harwich Rd
West Springfield MA
01089

Call Sign: KA1QCN
Anthony J Barto
47 Hewitt St
West Springfield MA
01089

Call Sign: N1POH
Richard J Tallman
67 Hill St
West Springfield MA
01089

Call Sign: NL7FJ
Richard H Monroe
29 Humphrey Ln
West Springfield MA
01089

Call Sign: N1EOU
J Lawrence Spinks
27 Kent St
West Springfield MA
010891510

Call Sign: KB1QZY
Darren R Rovatti
540 Kings Highway 2fl
West Springfield MA
01089

Call Sign: N1TQQ
Marcia L Day
137 Kings Hwy
West Springfield MA
01089

Call Sign: N1TBW
Peter Moriarty
572 Kings Hwy
West Springfield MA
010892340

Call Sign: N1VPC
Ernest R Guyette
16 Labelle St
West Springfield MA
01089

Call Sign: KD1TV
Lawrence E Bergeron
137 Lancaster Ave
West Springfield MA
01089

Call Sign: KB1LVT
Dean M Graziano
190 Laurel Rd
West Springfield MA
01089

Call Sign: K1NJC
John J Sheehan
44 Main St
West Springfield MA
010893901

Call Sign: KA1JJM
Raymond R Weber
209 Main St
West Springfield MA
01089

Call Sign: KB1CNO
Michael A Skowron
109 Morton St
West Springfield MA
01089

Call Sign: W1HIF
Victor S Peterson
432 Morton St
West Springfield MA
01089

Call Sign: KB1DUY
Abimael Salas
140 Newbridge St
West Springfield MA
01089

Call Sign: N1LFW
Katherine P Hessink
185 Ohio Ave
West Springfield MA
01089

Call Sign: K1QIZ
Richard A Austin
32 Old Barn Rd
West Springfield MA
01089

Call Sign: KA1CPT
Mustafa I Adham
79 Orchard View St
West Springfield MA
01089

Call Sign: N1MIF
Dominic P Beggetta
22 Oxford Pl
West Springfield MA
01089

Call Sign: N1IJK
Barry M Mason
32 Park Ave Court 16
West Springfield MA
010893342

Call Sign: KB1LEZ
Elaine J Gedney
350 Park St Apt 219
West Springfield MA
01089

Call Sign: KA1ACE
Louis A Marino
182 Riverdale St
West Springfield MA
01089

Call Sign: KF5BRB
William B Ashley
Riverdale St
West Springfield MA
01089

Call Sign: KB1MKG
James S Dodge
1440 Riverdale St Apt
B-14
West Springfield MA
01089

Call Sign: WA1UZX
Lawrence R Kida
38 Robinson Rd
West Springfield MA
01089

Call Sign: KA1NBT
Frank J Mazza
14 Rochelle St
West Springfield MA
01089

Call Sign: W1MAZ
Frank J Mazza
14 Rochelle St
West Springfield MA
01089

Call Sign: W1MBT
Provin Mtn Amateur
Repeater Assn
616 Rogers Ave
West Springfield MA
01089

Call Sign: KD1YF
Roy R Sanden
25 Sagamore Rd
West Springfield MA
01089

Call Sign: W1EME
Philmore H Smith Jr
282 Sawmill Rd
West Springfield MA
01089

Call Sign: KB1BOB
Stephen J Stefanik
111 Upper Beverly
Hills
West Springfield MA
01289

Call Sign: N1WCC
Arol B Hill
17 Van Horn St
West Springfield MA
01089

Call Sign: KB1NCM
Andrew G Plourde
49 Verdugo St
West Springfield MA
010892248

Call Sign: N1MIJ
Kenneth L Mac
Donald
109 Warren St
West Springfield MA
010892730

Call Sign: N1UZB
Adam M Frechette
742 Westfield St
West Springfield MA
01089

Call Sign: K1CRJ
Jeffrey B Walters

2401 Westfield St
West Springfield MA
01089

Call Sign: KD1FU
Howard H Hanson
14 Windpath W
West Springfield MA
01089

Call Sign: KB1MZU
Patrick A O'brien
113 Woodmont St
West Springfield MA
01089

Call Sign: KA1PFX
Donald R Gardella
West Springfield MA
01090

Call Sign: K1ZCD
Francis R Antal
West Springfield MA
01090

Call Sign: KA1NLC
Donald N Senecal
West Springfield MA
01090

Call Sign: N1DJM
Ronald L Carroll Jr
West Springfield MA
01090

Call Sign: N1DOO
Lynda A Carroll
West Springfield MA
01090

Call Sign: N1QKR
Gail E Vogel
West Springfield MA
01090

Call Sign: WA1AHC
Jeffrey W Zimmerman
West Springfield MA
01090

Call Sign: N1BMX
Jeffrey E Bail

West Springfield MA
010900484

Call Sign: KB1MXU
Lyle S Tise
West Springfield MA
01090

Call Sign: NT1K
Jeffrey E Bail
West Springfield MA
010900484

Call Sign: WB1CSJ
John J Astore
Box 75
West Stockbridge MA
01266

Call Sign: KA1YD
Ormond A Gigli
Box 84
West Stockbridge MA
01266

Call Sign: KA1ZWQ
Matthew D Lopez
29 Iron Mine Rd
West Stockbridge MA
01266

Call Sign: WA1AZX
George E Allen Jr
3 Maple St
West Stockbridge MA
01266

Call Sign: KA2YCN
Scott H Herrick
West Stockbridge MA
012660285

Call Sign: N1VTB
Robert W Yapp
13 Otis Bassett Rd Box
579

West Tisbury MA
02575

Call Sign: KB1IHW
Norman L Perry
12 Pond Ln
West Tisbury MA
02575

Call Sign: N1QAM
Philip J Shea
59 Clement Rd
West Townsend MA
01474

Call Sign: N1YFK
Edward A Snapp
3 Jonathan Ln
West Townsend MA
01474

Call Sign: N1ZIY
Nicholas G Lockyer
16 Laurel Woods Dr
West Townsend MA
01474

Call Sign: N1MLM
Lawrence P Aulenback
90 Lunenburg Rd
West Townsend MA
01474

Call Sign: WA1HIR
Petter E Carlson
121 Lunenburg Rd
West Townsend MA
01474

Call Sign: N1MVP
Edward C Jackson Sr
4 Ryan Rd
West Townsend MA
01474

Call Sign: KA1IZC
Donald C Smith
41 Sauna Row Rd
West Townsend MA
01474

Call Sign: WA1SJS
Edwin B Haman Jr
11 Saunders Rd
West Townsend MA
014741133

Call Sign: N1MLI
Robert W Potter
19 West Meadow
Estates Drive
West Townsend MA
01474

FCC Amateur Radio Licenses in West Upton

Call Sign: KB1ASJ
Joseph P Flynn
15 Hartford Ave
West Upton MA 01587

FCC Amateur Radio Licenses in West Wareham

Call Sign: KB1HJD
David Ramos
117 Castle Dr
West Wareham MA
02576

Call Sign: KA1YPK
Lawrence A Trahan
32 Charlotte Furnace
Rd
West Wareham MA
025761124

Call Sign: N1YW
Lawrence A Trahan
32 Charlotte Furnace
Rd
West Wareham MA
025761124

Call Sign: K1KHT
Alonzo G Snell
106 Fearing Hill Rd
West Wareham MA
02576

Call Sign: KA1TJS

Rodolphe L Gendron
11 Gault Rd
West Wareham MA
02576

Call Sign: K1DGG
Richard L Leach
7 Gordon St
West Wareham MA
02576

Call Sign: KB1LJO
Christopher M Maxim
12 Helen St
West Wareham MA
02576

Call Sign: KB1TYI
Cary A Johnson
10 Island Brook Dr
West Wareham MA
02576

Call Sign: KB1LQQ
Ernest L Trox
20 Naushon Rd
West Wareham MA
02576

Call Sign: N1RVY
Brian L Ouellette
8 West St
West Wareham MA
02576

Call Sign: KA1EYN
Robert E Lawrence
26 Windswept Rd
West Wareham MA
02576

Call Sign: W4NWM
William J Madden Jr
150 Windswept Rd
West Wareham MA
02576

Call Sign: KB1THH
Joseph E Leggett
West Wareham MA
02576

Call Sign: KB1WGV
Lisa J Rizza

West Wareham MA
02576

FCC Amateur Radio Licenses in West Warrne

Call Sign: KB1FET
Ted Colgate
98 Highland St
West Warren MA
010920724

Call Sign: KA1RJN
Robert J Gancorz
1994 Main St
West Warren MA
01585

Call Sign: KB1WQH
Ricardo Bellavita
2375 Main St
West Warren MA
01092

FCC Amateur Radio Licenses in West Woburn

Call Sign: N1ELC
George Stringos
5 Robinson Rd
West Woburn MA
01801

FCC Amateur Radio Licenses in West Yarmough

Call Sign: W1RQZ
Francis J Egan
36 Beaver Brook Rd
West Yarmouth MA
02673

Call Sign: W1HWS
John E Fitzpatrick
70 Berry Ave
West Yarmouth MA
02673

Call Sign: KA1YQS
Corey L Viera
47 Beverly Rd

West Yarmouth MA
02673

Call Sign: W1QFO
Clifford A Wilkins
481 Buck Island Rd
15a
West Yarmouth MA
026733369

Call Sign: KB1CCR
Hugh R Gilbert
84 Camp St
West Yarmouth MA
02673

Call Sign: WA1EXA
Mark P Petruzzi
121 Camp St Unit 105
West Yarmouth MA
026733261

Call Sign: W1VTS
David E Plante
17 Canvasback Ln
West Yarmouth MA
02673

Call Sign: KB1HJP
Gary L Gordon
47 Clover Rd
West Yarmouth MA
02673

Call Sign: K1KCP
John L Bamforth
24 Coachman Ln
West Yarmouth MA
02673

Call Sign: KB1TLQ
Josh W Richards
12 Colburn Path
West Yarmouth MA
02763

Call Sign: KA1VDT
Michael O Wilder
21 Colburne Path
West Yarmouth MA
02673

Call Sign: N1IZI
David A Manzi

11 Connemara Way
West Yarmouth MA
02673

Call Sign: KA1VNP
Matthew W Knowland
25 Constance Ave
West Yarmouth MA
02673

Call Sign: KA1VNM
Alexander M
Pendleton
62 Constance Ave
West Yarmouth MA
02673

Call Sign: KB1VAG
Jonathan P Barker
92 Constance Ave
West Yarmouth MA
02673

Call Sign: KA1VUT
Wesley J Mc Cormick
9 Coolidge Rd
West Yarmouth MA
02673

Call Sign: K1GTX
Wesley J Mc Cormick
9 Coolidge Rd
West Yarmouth MA
02673

Call Sign: W1BKM
Delbert E Patton
73 Crowes Purchase
Rd
West Yarmouth MA
026735005

Call Sign: WA1NMX
Joseph W Dulkie
62 Danas Path
West Yarmouth MA
02673

Call Sign: W1CCL
Robert K Edwards
19 Dove Ln
West Yarmouth MA
02673

Call Sign: W1IRS
Waldo I Powell
8 Dunster Path
West Yarmouth MA
06273

Call Sign: KA1VNO
Michael T Muncey
57 Exeter Rd
West Yarmouth MA
02673

Call Sign: KB1FPE
David J Sullivan
15 Grouse Ln
West Yarmouth MA
02673

Call Sign: W1PLH
Charles H Winslow Jr
34 Harding Ln
West Yarmouth MA
02673

Call Sign: KB1QVU
Mark F Walters
18 Hastings Ave
West Yarmouth MA
02673

Call Sign: KB1TAV
Raymond J O'leary Jr
34 Meadowbrook Rd
West Yarmouth MA
02673

Call Sign: KB1VBW
Matthew J Zurowick
11 Monroe Ln
West Yarmouth MA
02673

Call Sign: N1PIE
Donald H Crocker
22 Rosemary Ln
West Yarmouth MA
02673

Call Sign: N1OWF
Reta W Russell
49 Sierra Way
West Yarmouth MA
02673

Call Sign: N1PGO
John H Russell
49 Sierra Way
West Yarmouth MA
02673

Call Sign: N1CAH
William F Lovejoy
33 Standish Way
West Yarmouth MA
02673

Call Sign: KA1FSB
Karl B Norton
92 Trowbridge Path
West Yarmouth MA
02673

Call Sign: KB5FNC
Catherine P Kowalski
27 Vernon St
West Yarmouth MA
02673

Call Sign: KB1ROI
Mary M Manwaring
39 Virginia St
West Yarmouth MA
02673

Call Sign: KA1VUV
Paul T Manwaring
39 Virginia St
West Yarmouth MA
02673

Call Sign: KA1YUN
Matthew P Martin
63 Williams Rd
West Yarmouth MA
02673

Call Sign: N1CBC
Gregory G Jigerjian
West Yarmouth MA
02673

Call Sign: KB1TAO
Joseph T Gibbs
West Yarmouth MA
02673

**FCC Amateur Radio
Licenses in Westboro**

**See also FCC
Amateur Radio
Licenses in
Westborough**

Call Sign: KA1AIY
Roger A Barnes
5 Canfield St
Westboro MA 01581

Call Sign: N1JGF
Robert J Buckland
9 Cortland Dr
Westboro MA 01581

Call Sign: KA1TLJ
Thomas M Olson
5 Deerslayer Rd
Westboro MA 01581

Call Sign: WX1K
Eric J Hawkesworth
177 E Main St
Westboro MA 01581

Call Sign: KB3IP
Ronald R Woodcock
7 Edmund Brigham
Way
Westboro MA 01581

Call Sign: N1PHC
Brian T Sullivan
59 Fisher St
Westboro MA 01581

Call Sign: W1HYC
Michael J Orlando
10 Green St
Westboro MA 01581

Call Sign: N1ICY
Paul N Hackett
31 Hundreds Rd
Westboro MA 01581

Call Sign: KA1ALU
Frank G Eastman
6 Kimball Rd
Westboro MA 01581

Call Sign: W1YPF
Paul J Wolf

2 Maynard St
Westboro MA 01581

Call Sign: WA1MDO
Thomas Porada
212 Milk St
Westboro MA 01581

Call Sign: WA1HYI
Bruce R Johnson
16 Phylmor Dr
Westboro MA 01581

Call Sign: WA1PVO
Ira J Cohen
7 Richardson Ct
Westboro MA 01581

Call Sign: KB1LOD
Charles F Butala
47 Treetop Park
Westboro MA 01581

Call Sign: KB1MFG
Willard A Mcconnell
110 Upton Rd
Westboro MA 01581

Call Sign: K1HOK
Robert F Milewski
23 Wheeler Rd
Westboro MA 01581

Call Sign: KB1HJW
Rene D Daniels Jr
1212 Windsor Ridge
Dr
Westboro MA 01581

Call Sign: KB1GFP
Frank W Gladu
Westboro MA 01581

**FCC Amateur Radio
Licenses in
Westborough**

**See also FCC
Amateur Radio
Licenses in Westboro**

Call Sign: KA1JKW
Thomas E Green
10 Baxter St

Westborough MA
01581

Call Sign: KA1PAL
Cheryl Y Dion
23 Blake St
Westborough MA
01581

Call Sign: KA1CEW
Richard B Lambert B
15 Bowman Lane
Westborough MA
01581

Call Sign: KB1MIV
Dale H Weaver
7 Capt Forbush Rd
Westborough MA
01581

Call Sign: K1PNQ
Kevin J Norby
125 Charlestown
Meadows Drive
Westborough MA
01581

Call Sign: K1BRX
Henry D Parker Jr
6 Chestnut St
Westborough MA
01581

Call Sign: KB1WMB
Steven M Bolduc
6 Chestnut St
Westborough MA
01581

Call Sign: KB1ODI
Christopher A Perry
16 Crownridge Rd
Westborough MA
01581

Call Sign: N2RFJ
Michael J Cassata
8 Deerfield Way
Westborough MA
015811198

Call Sign: W1ZBD
Francis D Ciannella

250 E Main St
Westborough MA
01581

Call Sign: K1UXD
Paul F Kelley
135 E Main St V8
Westborough MA
015812741

Call Sign: KA1BCJ
Robin E Wittmann
14 Endicott Dr
Westborough MA
01581

Call Sign: WB1DCH
Gary R Wittmann
14 Endicott Dr
Westborough MA
01581

Call Sign: N1KFV
Robert C Tripi
23 Endicott Dr
Westborough MA
015812613

Call Sign: KA1RFA
Dana M Pollard
Fisher St
Westborough MA
01581

Call Sign: KA1SBQ
Stanley F Mc Collum
Fisher St
Westborough MA
01581

Call Sign: KB1OZK
Paul M Kafig
36 Glen St
Westborough MA
01581

Call Sign: AB1HT
Paul M Kafig
36 Glen St
Westborough MA
01581

Call Sign: N1ADX
Peter M Bradley

5 Granger Rd
Westborough MA
015811716

Call Sign: W1NXP
Nathan W Talbot
4 Hancock Way
Westborough MA
015811151

Call Sign: KA1RV
Erik A Piip
4 Jacob Amsden Rd
Westborough MA
01581

Call Sign: N4BGJ
David L Innis
16 Kay St
Westborough MA
01581

Call Sign: N1GJI
Jonathan W Mechling
15 Kendall Dr
Westborough MA
01581

Call Sign: KA2AEI
Penelope B Thompson
31 Linda St
Westborough MA
015813711

Call Sign: N1KQP
Nancy J Ayers
9 Lyons St
Westborough MA
01581

Call Sign: N1EHL
Barbara J Potaski
2 Maple Cir
Westborough MA
01581

Call Sign: KB1TTC
Erik Macchi
15 Maple Cir
Westborough MA
01581

Call Sign: KB1TDP
Bradley A Miller

15 Maple Circle
Westborough MA
01581

Call Sign: KA1BY
Stephen J Tufts
28 Maynard St
Westborough MA
01581

Call Sign: W1TBT
Joseph P Orlando
5 Meadow Rd
Westborough MA
01581

Call Sign: WA2ZWB
Zigmund J Porada
212 Milk St
Westborough MA
01581

Call Sign: KH0AO
David L Morais
6 Mill Rd
Westborough MA
015812902

Call Sign: KB1LDT
Douglas K Brown
10 Morse St
Westborough MA
01581

Call Sign: WB1DWK
Peter J Markou
25 Mountain View Dr
Westborough MA
01581

Call Sign: W1OR
Peter J Markou
25 Mountain View Dr
Westborough MA
01581

Call Sign: KB1JMC
William L Glatfelter
41 Old Colony Dr
Westborough MA
01581

Call Sign: WA1SRI
Craig H Lippman

28 Old Nourse Rd
Westborough MA
01581

Call Sign: W1DZO
Dexter P Blois
2 Old Nourse St
Westborough MA
01581

Call Sign: KB1ON
Richard M Weiland
14 Olde Coach Rd
Westborough MA
01581

Call Sign: KC1JP
Michael J Karp
8 Olde Stonebridge
Path
Westborough MA
01581

Call Sign: KV1W
Richard B Plummer
56 Powder Hill Way
Westborough MA
01581

Call Sign: N2NJW
Andrew G Gilicinski
10 Reed Ave
Westborough MA
01581

Call Sign: WD4ASW
Barry A Baines
86 Ruggles St
Westborough MA
015812121

Call Sign: WD4ASX
Kathryn B Baines
86 Ruggles St
Westborough MA
015812121

Call Sign: KA1KA
Adam D Shapiro
21 South St
Westborough MA
01581

Call Sign: WA1AS

Adam D Shapiro
21 South St Suite 34
Westborough MA
01581

Call Sign: KB1DHH
Margaret V Mc Nulty
22 Spring Rd
Westborough MA
01581

Call Sign: N1KRC
Paul R Mc Nulty
22 Spring Rd
Westborough MA
01581

Call Sign: KB1JQU
Frank A Mcnulty
22 Spring Rd
Westborough MA
01589

Call Sign: KC2BI
William T Wolfe
28 Spring Rd
Westborough MA
01581

Call Sign: KB1DXP
Daniels Pavolis
6 Spring St
Westborough MA
015811514

Call Sign: W1KBA
Brian R Boda
25 Steven Rd
Westborough MA
01581

Call Sign: AB1GX
Thomas Slade
32 Thomas Newton Dr
Westborough MA
01581

Call Sign: N1TQF
Robert L Washburn
11 Thos Hooker Rd
Westborough MA
01581

Call Sign: KB1THW

Christopher A Apgar
21 Treetop Park
Westborough MA
01581

Call Sign: KB1WUJ
Brian P Keating
198 Turnpike Rd
Westborough MA
01581

Call Sign: KB1MAB
James W Ramsey
293 Turnpike Rd Apt
113
Westborough MA
01581

Call Sign: AB1LX
James W Ramsey
293 Turnpike Rd Apt
113
Westborough MA
01581

Call Sign: KA1VM
Harrison K Cook
8 West St
Westborough MA
01581

Call Sign: N1RBU
Robert G Lister Jr
10 West St
Westborough MA
01581

Call Sign: N1OUW
Ryan C Spring
21 Westminster Way
Westborough MA
01581

Call Sign: KB1QWJ
Brian R Boda
602 Windsor Ridge Dr
Westborough MA
01581

Call Sign: KB1WRQ
James Kristoff
705 Windsor Ridge Dr
Westborough MA
01581

Call Sign: N1UAX
Michael G Roberts
1201 Windsor Ridge
Dr
Westborough MA
01581

Call Sign: KC1OT
Ajai Thirumalai
2506 Windsor Ridge
Dr
Westborough MA
015812352

Call Sign: KA4KVC
Mike G Newman
1905 Windsor Ridge
Drive
Westborough MA
01581

Call Sign: KI6MEU
Joseph G Horrigan
2910 Windsor Ridge
Drive
Westborough MA
01581

Call Sign: KI6MEV
Patricia A Horrigan
2910 Windsor Ridge
Drive
Westborough MA
01581

Call Sign: N1ACJ
Kenneth G Deahl
Westborough MA
01581

Call Sign: N1JLS
John S Copeland
Westborough MA
01581

Call Sign: KB1DXM
Prashant B Dhoria
Westborough MA
01581

Call Sign: KE4GI
Gary A Rodgers

Westborough MA
01581

Call Sign: N1XYR
Lawrence F Mccoskery
Westborough MA
015810444

Call Sign: WC1MAD
Races Club Mema
Region 4
Westborough MA
01581

Call Sign: KB1OCJ
Kathleen Lynch
Westborough MA
01581

FCC Amateur Radio Licenses in Westfield

Call Sign: K1BUB
Robert E Gravel
74 Apple Orchard
Heights
Westfield MA 01085

Call Sign: KB1SHD
Richard J Surowy
85 Bevely Dr
Westfield MA 01085

Call Sign: KA1HAB
Richard L Puffer
1 Brentwood Dr
Westfield MA 01085

Call Sign: KB1GPE
Miles A Burns Iii
22 Briarwood Pl
Westfield MA 01085

Call Sign: KA1BPF
Ronald J Gamache
47 Briarwood Pl
Westfield MA
010854703

Call Sign: KA1DTR
Armand C Erickson
63 Brookline Ave
Westfield MA 01085

Call Sign: N1PLD
Thomas A Erickson
63 Brookline Ave
Westfield MA 01085

Call Sign: WB1ACE
Armand C Erickson
63 Brookline Ave
Westfield MA 01085

Call Sign: WB1DNT
William J Majka
267 Buck Pond Rd
Westfield MA 01085

Call Sign: N1PAB
Craig G Bates
16 Carroll Dr
Westfield MA 01085

Call Sign: WA1PVP
Gordon F Bates
16 Carroll Dr
Westfield MA 01085

Call Sign: W1NRK
Robert W Gardner
20 Chestnut St
Westfield MA 01085

Call Sign: KB1Y
James E Markvart
22 Church St
Westfield MA 01085

Call Sign: KA1PKD
Joan B Ackerman
96 Colony Dr
Westfield MA 01085

Call Sign: KA1MPS
Lillian D Beauchemin
25 Crescent Ridge Rd
Westfield MA
010854000

Call Sign: WB1ETS
Ronald Beauchemin
25 Crescent Ridge Rd
Westfield MA
010854000

Call Sign: N1LIO
James A Brown Sr

14 Cross St
Westfield MA 01085

Call Sign: K1ISS
Cynthia A Loiero
27 Deepwood Dr
Westfield MA 01085

Call Sign: N1FI
Paul J Loiero
27 Deepwood Dr
Westfield MA 01085

Call Sign: KB1OMJ
Joseph E Murphy
234 Dox Rd
Westfield MA 01085

Call Sign: WA1CTQ
Philip J Mac Donald
975 E Mountian Rd
Westfield MA 01085

Call Sign: N1MTG
Frederick J Mc Graw
86 E Silver St
Westfield MA 01085

Call Sign: KA1BAW
Neil G Newman
1527 East Mountain
Rd
Westfield MA 01085

Call Sign: KA1HAA
Barbara H Kress
216 Eastwood Dr
Westfield MA 01085

Call Sign: WA1ZKT
Paul J Kress
216 Eastwood Dr
Westfield MA 01085

Call Sign: KB1QOY
Peter A Cowles
18 Egleston Rd
Westfield MA 01085

Call Sign: KA1ILF
Terry W Carlson
327 Falley Dr
Westfield MA
010854913

Call Sign: KB1UNC
Adam J Strzempko
22 Feeding Hills Rd
Apt B 8
Westfield MA 01085

Call Sign: W1AJS
Adam J Strzempko
22 Feeding Hills Rd
Apt B 8
Westfield MA 01085

Call Sign: K1HTS
Frederick S Kirby
66 Furrowtown Rd
Westfield MA 01085

Call Sign: WA1PIW
Linda M Kirby
66 Furrowtown Rd
Westfield MA 01085

Call Sign: WB1DLH
George H Nelson
919 Granville Rd
Westfield MA 01085

Call Sign: WA1CYK
Edward C Stefanik
33 Green Pine Ln
Westfield MA 01085

Call Sign: KB1TIZ
Joseph J Zammuto
17 Hassler St
Westfield MA 01085

Call Sign: WJ1C
Craig A Kratovil
32 Hickory Ave
Westfield MA 01085

Call Sign: W1SPV
Stanley A Kusnierz
450 Holyoke Rd
Westfield MA 01085

Call Sign: KB1JVJ
Kathleen A Smith
Kasper Dr
Westfield MA 01085

Call Sign: KB1DEY

Melvin E Kring
19 King St
Westfield MA 01085

Call Sign: WA1CQF
Gent C Lam
19 Knollwood Cir
Westfield MA 01085

Call Sign: KB1FPI
Paul L Brunelle
16 Kristen Lane
Westfield MA
010851455

Call Sign: W1VMN
Kazimir Pulaski
125 Lindbergh Blvd
Westfield MA 01085

Call Sign: K1ZXY
Leonard R Bombardier
227 Loomis St
Westfield MA
010853919

Call Sign: KA1SIU
Anne D Pasquino
293 Loomis St
Westfield MA 01085

Call Sign: WA1MTZ
Michael P Koscak
605 Loomis St
Westfield MA 01085

Call Sign: KB1TAB
Frederick A Noble
7 Mainline Dr
Westfield MA 01085

Call Sign: N1IED
Joseph C Dunlap
31 Mather St
Westfield MA 01085

Call Sign: N1TSI
Carrie B Gorman
43 Mc Kinley Terrace
Westfield MA 01085

Call Sign: W1MTV
Francis H Black Jr
143 Meadow St

Westfield MA
010852339

Call Sign: KB1FST
Rebecca Q Miller
41 Mechanic St F
Westfield MA 01085

Call Sign: KA1TRJ
William M Tower Jr
125 Montgomery
Rooad
Westfield MA 01085

Call Sign: N1WNY
Nancy L Howard
120 Mullen Ave
Westfield MA
010851010

Call Sign: K1ZLE
Leroy W Devol
48 Murphy Circle
Westfield MA 01085

Call Sign: AB7VT
Andreas Nagel
6 Noble Ave
Westfield MA 01085

Call Sign: KA1VPI
Edward J Judd
60 Noble St
Westfield MA 01085

Call Sign: WA1FTR
Robert J Knapik
106 Noble St
Westfield MA 01085

Call Sign: KA2JYR
Roy W Thompson
108 North Rd
Westfield MA 01085

Call Sign: KB1MQY
Jeanne K Hampton
90 Northridge Rd
Westfield MA 01085

Call Sign: AB1FQ
Jeanne M Keller
90 Northridge Rd
Westfield MA 01085

Call Sign: KJ1E
Jeanne M Keller
90 Northridge Rd
Westfield MA 01085

Call Sign: K1MBM
Kenn E Sinclair
99 Northridge Rd
Westfield MA 01085

Call Sign: KB1FSS
Francis J Cain
9 Oak Ave
Westfield MA 01085

Call Sign: KB1WQI
Roger V Latvis
15 Oak Ave
Westfield MA 01085

Call Sign: N1WLC
Michael J Mc Mullan
104 Old County Rd
Westfield MA 01085

Call Sign: KA1TDQ
Jonathan B Rines
54 Orange St Apt 1
Westfield MA 01085

Call Sign: WA1ARZ
Richard E Curtis
328 Papermill Rd
Westfield MA 01020

Call Sign: KB1UEG
Edwin S Pemberton
130 Park Dr
Westfield MA 01085

Call Sign: KB1BEV
James A Gamache
65 Patriots Dr
Westfield MA 01085

Call Sign: WB1ARW
Philip R Le Febvre
63 Pine St
Westfield MA 01085

Call Sign: KB1EGC
Daniel T Shea
80 Pineridge Dr

Westfield MA 01085

Call Sign: KB1FFJ
Christopher M Shea
80 Pineridge Dr
Westfield MA 01085

Call Sign: N1OE
Daniel T Shea
80 Pineridge Dr
Westfield MA 01085

Call Sign: N1JBV
Martha M Sienkiewicz
760 Pochassic Rd
Westfield MA 01085

Call Sign: K1FUA
Frederick L La Valley
Pochassic Rd
Westfield MA 01085

Call Sign: KB1OWF
Robert O Moore
326 Prospect St Ext
Westfield MA 01085

Call Sign: WA1VAH
Robert M Tippett
4 Putnam Dr
Westfield MA 01085

Call Sign: KA1ZUK
Alfred A Decoteau
120 Roosevelt
Westfield MA 01085

Call Sign: N1VME
Mary Beth Berrien
106 Roosevelt Ave
Westfield MA 01085

Call Sign: N1VMJ
Kevin F Berrien
106 Roosevelt Ave
Westfield MA
010855700

Call Sign: N1SCE
Jason M Hayden
263 Russell Rd
Westfield MA 01085

Call Sign: N1PAC

Michael S Chaloux Jr
311 Russell Rd
Westfield MA 01085

Call Sign: KA1LXU
John J Murphy
544 Russellville Rd
Westfield MA 01085

Call Sign: N1PLZ
Lawrence G Blascak
33 Sackett Rd
Westfield MA 01085

Call Sign: K1HYI
Sheldon M Titcomb
262 Sackett Rd
Westfield MA 01085

Call Sign: KB1UJU
Vladimir Zhylkovski
14 Sackett St
Westfield MA 01085

Call Sign: K1FAB
104th Communications
Flight Mass Ang
Scm Barnes Ang Base
Westfield MA
010851482

Call Sign: N1FMB
Ralph T Lees
39 Shaker Rd
Westfield MA 01085

Call Sign: N1JTV
Deborah L Lees
39 Shaker Rd
Westfield MA 01085

Call Sign: N1LQC
William R Mc Manus
460 Shaker Rd
Westfield MA 01085

Call Sign: KB1FDD
Tiffany L Cashman
482 Shaker Rd
Westfield MA 01085

Call Sign: N1VAQ
Keith M Stevens
88 Shannon Ln

Westfield MA
010854818

Call Sign: N1MUW
John A De Nardo Jr
628 Southampton Rd
Westfield MA 01085

Call Sign: KA1ZPQ
Jeffrey W Elander
919 Southampton Rd
Westfield MA 01085

Call Sign: W1KUL
Robert E Gordon
919 Southampton Rd
Apt J2
Westfield MA
010855318

Call Sign: KB1VNH
Albert G Giguere Jr
34 Southgate Ave
Westfield MA 01085

Call Sign: KB1GMN
Robert P Ingalls
34 Squawfield Rd
Westfield MA 01085

Call Sign: KA1HIG
Timothy J Puffer Sr
20 State St
Westfield MA 01085

Call Sign: KA1ERS
William F Mc Carthy
91 Steiger Dr
Westfield MA 01085

Call Sign: K1TS
Marc A Camerlin
195 Susan Dr
Westfield MA 01085

Call Sign: KB1EGR
Southern New England
Amateur Radio Group
195 Susan Dr
Westfield MA 01085

Call Sign: K1TMA
Alvah C Buckmore Jr
18 Tannery Rd

Westfield MA
010854822

Call Sign: WA1PDJ
Joan L Fenton
25 Tannery Rd Unit #7
Westfield MA 01085

Call Sign: KB1PLT
Edward Mello
58 Vadnais St
Westfield MA
010854232

Call Sign: KB1UMZ
Greater Westfield
Medical Reserve Corps
58 Vadnais St
Westfield MA 01085

Call Sign: N1TBZ
Peter F O Malley
4 W School St
Westfield MA 01085

Call Sign: NA1V
Richard P Gagne
33 Walker Ave
Westfield MA
010861927

Call Sign: KA1WGS
Kyle E Gutowski
69 Western Ave
Westfield MA 01085

Call Sign: KA1WHH
Michaela B Votteler
69 Western Ave
Westfield MA 01085

Call Sign: N1PFA
William D Bennett
64 Whitaker Rd
Westfield MA 01085

Call Sign: N1PVX
Stephen M Kulewicz
67 Wilson Ave
Westfield MA
010854268

Call Sign: W1MBT

Southern New England
Amateur Radio Group
53 Woodcliff Dr
Westfield MA 01085

Call Sign: K1MZ
Marc A Camerlin
53 Woodcliff Dr
Westfield MA 01085

Call Sign: K1PES
Francis X Neylon
141 Wyben Rd
Westfield MA 01085

Call Sign: WB1BZV
Samuel T Scott
24 Yankee Cir
Westfield MA 01085

Call Sign: WB1BZX
Valorie L Scott
24 Yankee Cir
Westfield MA
010854034

Call Sign: KB2YHD
Theresa K Dengler
8 Zephyr Dr
Westfield MA 01085

Call Sign: N2XCX
Thomas P Dengler
8 Zephyr Drive
Westfield MA 01085

Call Sign: KA1FIY
Bill Pennington
Westfield MA 01086

Call Sign: KI1I
Peter M Beauregard
Westfield MA
010860091

Call Sign: N1PFB
Robert K Wilson
Westfield MA 01086

Call Sign: W1NT
Bradford L Denison
Westfield MA 01086

Call Sign: WA1NIC

Richard A Kominsky
Westfield MA
010861816

Call Sign: N1FU
Tbdbs Wireless
Association
Westfield MA 01086

Call Sign: NR1I
Tbdbs Wireless
Association
Westfield MA 01086

Call Sign: KB1PRC
Michael A Beauregard
Westfield MA 01086

FCC Amateur Radio Licenses in Westford

Call Sign: WB9PRU
Stephen R Mann
12 April Lane
Westford MA 01886

Call Sign: KB1ERK
Harold A English
5 Bates Lane
Westford MA 01886

Call Sign: KA1AKX
Joseph T Targ
24 Bayberry Rd
Westford MA 01886

Call Sign: KB1PBA
Peter S Mudgett
10 Beaver Brook Rd
Westford MA 01886

Call Sign: N1HZI
Deborah A Burns
58 Beaver Brook Rd
Westford MA 01886

Call Sign: N1HZJ
Bruce G Burns
58 Beaver Brook Rd
Westford MA 01886

Call Sign: N1YSN
Amy L Kazura
5 Beaver Dam Dr

Westford MA 01886

Call Sign: KD1GX
Amy L Kazura
5 Beaver Dam Dr
Westford MA 01886

Call Sign: WA1KBE
Stephen B Rimsa
5 Blueberry Lane
Westford MA 01886

Call Sign: KB2RSF
Hee S Jun
8 Bolger Ln
Westford MA 01886

Call Sign: KB1VCS
Andrew Olson
5 Boston Rd
Westford MA 01886

Call Sign: W2IPS
Joseph M Hudak
Box 680
Westford MA 01886

Call Sign: KB1AGO
Allen B Kelly
25 Bradford St
Westford MA 01886

Call Sign: NQ1X
Pavel Dudek
2 Bradford St Apt 6
Westford MA 01886

Call Sign: N1CZ
Pavel Dudek
2 Bradford St Apt 6
Westford MA 01886

Call Sign: K1VUX
Joseph J Rand
8 Bradley Ln
Westford MA 01886

Call Sign: N1ITS
Gary B Hayward
2 Buckboard Dr
Westford MA 01886

Call Sign: K1IPC
Gerald A Bourque

71 Buckboard Dr
Westford MA 01886

Call Sign: AE3E
Daniel E Kreithen
15 Butterfield Lane
Westford MA 01886

Call Sign: KB1ICE
Susan L Goldman-
Kreithen
15 Butterfield Ln
Westford MA 01886

Call Sign: K1MJV
Bette R Hook
125 Carlisle Rd
Westford MA 01886

Call Sign: N1JTT
Susan J Kent
138 Carlisle Rd
Westford MA 01886

Call Sign: WG1Y
James S Gozzo
6 Carolina Ln
Westford MA
018861446

Call Sign: K1BFA
Roy H Erickson
8 Carolina Ln
Westford MA 01886

Call Sign: KB1KRD
Tadmuck Swamp
Amateur Radio Society
16 Chippewa Rd
Westford MA 01886

Call Sign: W1UZ
Tadmuck Swamp
Amateur Radio Society
16 Chippewa Rd
Westford MA 01886

Call Sign: WA1HPI
Edward R Minott
21 Chippewa St
Westford MA
018862725

Call Sign: WA1QYM

Arthur B Budinger
11 Christophen Rd
Westford MA 01886

Call Sign: N1MXM
Philip W Servita
95 Cold Spring Rd
Westford MA 01886

Call Sign: N1QGE
Hugh C Maguire
127 Coldspring Rd
Westford MA 01886

Call Sign: KB1GZU
Sarah F Kay
5 Concord Rd
Westford MA 01886

Call Sign: KB1IGF
Nashoba Area Dx'ers
5 Concord Rd
Westford MA 01886

Call Sign: KD1DJ
Alan J Hicks
130 Concord Rd
Westford MA 01886

Call Sign: N1NSX
Andrew F Hicks
130 Concord Rd
Westford MA 01886

Call Sign: KD1D
Alan J Hicks
130 Concord Rd
Westford MA 01886

Call Sign: KB1FGN
John Stacy Technical
Amateur Radio Society
130 Concord Rd
Westford MA 01886

Call Sign: W1KIM
John Stacy Technical
Amateur Radio Society
130 Concord Rd
Westford MA 01886

Call Sign: WA1UYR
Joseph R Connell
Connell Dr

Westford MA
018862520

Call Sign: KA1WCM
Kristen E Welsh
36 Country Rd
Westford MA
018862823

Call Sign: WB1GOF
Police Ama Radio
Team Of Westford
36 Country Rd
Westford MA 01886

Call Sign: WI1R
David L Welsh
36 Country Rd
Westford MA 01886

Call Sign: KB1SBJ
Police Amateur Radio
Team Of Westford
36 Country Rd
Westford MA 01886

Call Sign: K1RZK
Frank P Karkota Jr
17 Cowdry Hill Rd
Westford MA 01886

Call Sign: WA1RZE
Mark P Himelfarb
14 Crest Dr
Westford MA 01886

Call Sign: AA4GR
George Rulffs Jr
14 Dana Dr
Westford MA 01886

Call Sign: W1HCJ
James D Hunter
85 Depot Rd
Westford MA
018861368

Call Sign: N1UAP
Kenneth P Haagenson
14 Dunstable Rd
Westford MA 01886

Call Sign: N1RKB
William E Carney

96 Dunstable Rd
Westford MA 01886

Call Sign: W1BXM
William E Carney
96 Dunstable Rd
Westford MA 01886

Call Sign: K1EGQ
James R Riel
1 Elm Rd
Westford MA 01886

Call Sign: KB1LNJ
Michael J Eisenhower
25 Endmoor Rd
Westford MA 01886

Call Sign: KB1KNH
Everett A Johnston
29 Endmoor Rd
Westford MA
018861450

Call Sign: W1RS
Robert J Snyder
6 Flagg Rd
Westford MA 01886

Call Sign: KB1DMP
Leonard D Waters
45 Flagg Rd
Westford MA 01886

Call Sign: N1FLJ
Stella F Snyder
6 Flagg Rd
Westford MA
018862614

Call Sign: NC1M
Hugh C Masterman
24 Fletcher Rd
Westford MA 01886

Call Sign: KB1GED
Anthony B Fisher
43 Flushing Pond Rd
Westford MA 01886

Call Sign: KC2CRB
Karl Paxton
32 Forge Village Rd

Westford MA
018862920

Call Sign: N1TRB
Dennis P Kane
81 Forge Village Rd
Westford MA 01886

Call Sign: N1XOI
Paolo Battezzato
38 Forrest Rd
Westford MA 01886

Call Sign: KB1FKR
Joseph S Whalley
11 Frances Hill Rd
Westford MA 01886

Call Sign: N1CV
Joseph S Whalley
11 Frances Hill Rd
Westford MA 01886

Call Sign: N1LKP
Eric E Humphrey
12 Gassett Rd
Westford MA 01886

Call Sign: N1FUU
Eric E Humphrey
12 Gassett Rd
Westford MA 01886

Call Sign: KB1NFC
Philip W Day
51 Graniteville Rd
Westford MA 01886

Call Sign: W1QEY
Walter H Brzezinski
60 Graniteville Rd
Westford MA 01886

Call Sign: K1OPE
Chauncey Chu
1 Green Needles Rd
Westford MA 01886

Call Sign: N1JRH
Barbara G Chu
1 Green Needles Rd
Westford MA 01886

Call Sign: KB1NEX

Raymond E Kaarsberg
4 Green Needles Rd
Westford MA 01886

Call Sign: WB1FWF
Doris R Karkota
46 Groton Rd
Westford MA
018861218

Call Sign: WA1EJW
James C De Rosa
404 Groton Rd
Westford MA 01886

Call Sign: N3SX
Jeffrey A Rosenberger
12 Grove St
Westford MA 01886

Call Sign: N2BJK
David C Carpenter
4 Haywagon Circle
Westford MA
018862755

Call Sign: KB1JSP
Buzz M Mc Mann
22 Hemlock Rd
Westford MA 01886

Call Sign: KB1IFG
Jeremy J Franklin
6 Heywood Rd
Westford MA 01886

Call Sign: KD1MG
Meyer P Franklin
6 Heywood Rd
Westford MA 01886

Call Sign: KA1OWH
William M Frost
44 Hildreth St
Westford MA
018863003

Call Sign: KB1FLO
Graham R Campbell
58 Hildreth St
Westford MA 01886

Call Sign: AA1YJ
Graham R Campbell

58 Hildreth St
Westford MA 01886

Call Sign: W1AOP
A Operators Club 1
88 Hildreth St
Westford MA 01886

Call Sign: KN1T
Nashoba Area Dx'ers
88 Hildreth St
Westford MA 01886

Call Sign: K1SFK
Sarah F Kay
88 Hildreth St
Westford MA 01886

Call Sign: KB1IMY
Janet C Kay
88 Hildreth St
Westford MA 01886

Call Sign: K1NU
Leonard E Kay
88 Hildreth St
Westford MA 01886

Call Sign: K1PD
Durfee B Hill
12 Hillside Ave Rfd 2
Westford MA 01886

Call Sign: W1ARB
Alan R Bugos
3 Jocelyn Lane
Westford MA
018864500

Call Sign: W1GXH
Alan L Chaffee
6 Kirsi Cir
Westford MA 01886

Call Sign: KB1WWL
Curt J Cunningham
28 Kirsi Circle
Westford MA 01886

Call Sign: KB1WXG
Curt J Cunningham
28 Kirsi Circle
Westford MA 01886

Call Sign: KB1CVG
Robert W Terrell
5 Landmark Rd
Westford MA
018864427

Call Sign: KA1LDA
Michael J Geser
6 Little Bear Hill Rd
Westford MA 01886

Call Sign: N1JRF
Beth Ann Cadigan
8 Longmeadow Rd
Westford MA 01886

Call Sign: N1RTF
Ralph N Shaver Ii
10 Longmeadow Rd
Westford MA 01886

Call Sign: N1HXH
John S Fridrich
11 Longmeadow Rd
Westford MA 01886

Call Sign: AB1DU
R Gary Cutbill
13 Main St
Westford MA 01886

Call Sign: WA1GMT
Lindsay W Armstrong
56 Main St
Westford MA 01886

Call Sign: W1EGY
Richard J Hoebeke
28 Maple Rd
Westford MA 01886

Call Sign: KA1ZLX
Christian F Greig
14 Maple St
Westford MA 01886

Call Sign: N1JRE
Seymour B Pizette
23 Meadow Ln
Westford MA 01886

Call Sign: KB1KJK
Alan H Martin
31 Meadow Ln

Westford MA
018861257

Call Sign: W1AHM
Alan H Martin
31 Meadow Ln
Westford MA
018861257

Call Sign: KB1NIQ
Michelle M Martin
31 Meadow Ln
Westford MA 01886

Call Sign: W1ZSG
David W Calkins
45 Monadnock Dr
Westford MA 01886

Call Sign: N1CKE
Robert E Norris
55 Monadnock Dr
Westford MA 01886

Call Sign: N1ZUW
Carl P Gerstle
62 Monadnock Dr
Westford MA
018863022

Call Sign: KB1UT
George S Beals
11 Myrtle Ave
Westford MA 01886

Call Sign: N1BLN
John P Ferrara
31 N Hill Rd
Westford MA 01886

Call Sign: AG1I
Thomas A Hughes Jr
13 N Main
Westford MA
018861203

Call Sign: W1BP
Brian P Mccaffrey
98 N Main St
Westford MA 01886

Call Sign: KA1MHJ
Nancy J Rayne
26 Newport Dr

Westford MA
018861430

Call Sign: N1HXK
Peter L Seymour
66 Newport Dr
Westford MA 01886

Call Sign: KB1VSG
John P Ferrara
31 North Hill Rd
Westford MA 01886

Call Sign: AB1PD
John P Ferrara
31 North Hill Rd
Westford MA 01886

Call Sign: KB1EKJ
Daniel S Wedge
2 North St
Westford MA 01886

Call Sign: W1LMT
Walker H Merritt Jr
22 Nutting Rd
Westford MA
018864895

Call Sign: KA5HWL
Steven H Garrett
26 Nutting Rd
Westford MA 01886

Call Sign: AA9DY
Wayne L Wagner Jr
14 Oak Rd
Westford MA 01886

Call Sign: KC9BLP
Michelle R Wagner
14 Oak Rd
Westford MA 01886

Call Sign: KA8SCP
Terry M Stader
Old Colony Dr
Westford MA 01886

Call Sign: K2HLR
Ramon A Cacossa
13 Old Homestead Rd
Westford MA 01886

Call Sign: WA1KYW
Earle C Hopkins Jr
58 Old Lowell Rd
Westford MA 01886

Call Sign: N1OSD
Adrien L
Laboissonniere
87 Old Lowell Rd
Westford MA 01886

Call Sign: N1AEW
Ernest W Bauer Jr
1 Overlook Cir
Westford MA 01886

Call Sign: N1JRG
Madaline J Bauer
1 Overlook Cir
Westford MA 01886

Call Sign: W1APS
Armando P Stettner
2 Pacific Lane
Westford MA
018863418

Call Sign: KB1GKR
David M Bernella
2 Pacific Ln
Westford MA
018863418

Call Sign: KB1GYT
Brenda M Bernella
2 Pacific Ln
Westford MA
018863418

Call Sign: AA1YQ
David M Bernella
2 Pacific Ln
Westford MA
018863418

Call Sign: N1ANH
John W Baranauskas
72 Parkhurst Drive
Westford MA 01886

Call Sign: W4ECD
Byron L Dennison
70 Patten Rd
Westford MA 01886

Call Sign: KA1LEQ
Debbie S Vardaro
79 Patten Rd
Westford MA 01886

Call Sign: WB1CUF
Anthony P Vardaro
79 Patten Rd
Westford MA 01886

Call Sign: KB1DNS
Esha Mathew
2 Phillips Dr
Westford MA 01886

Call Sign: KB1DNW
Abbie Mathew
2 Phillips Dr
Westford MA 01886

Call Sign: WA1PHR
David B O Keefe
17 Phillips Dr
Westford MA 01886

Call Sign: KB1IGS
John L Ryan
26 Phillips Dr Box
4030
Westford MA 01886

Call Sign: N1SPP
Alan B Miller
22 Phillips Drive
Westford MA 01886

Call Sign: KB1FFM
Kenneth D Rolt
27 Phillips Drive
Westford MA
018863404

Call Sign: KB1WSR
Raymond D Marchand
5 Pine Rd
Westford MA 01886

Call Sign: K4UFV
David H Amos
14 Pine Tree Trail
Westford MA 01886

Call Sign: N2RIU

Uri Blumenthal
14 Plain Rd
Westford MA
018861947

Call Sign: KA1TTX
Donald M Stevens
146 Plain Rd
Westford MA 01886

Call Sign: N1FGF
John G Shine
37 Plain Rd Box 311
Westford MA 01886

Call Sign: WA2QKC
Stephen S Weinrich
15 Polley Rd
Westford MA
018860156

Call Sign: K1LDX
Walter R Murphy
15 Pond Rd
Westford MA 01886

Call Sign: KA1WZL
Timothy M Martin
22 Preservation Way
Westford MA 01886

Call Sign: N1RIA
Elizabeth B Martin
22 Preservation Way
Westford MA 01886

Call Sign: N2OQT
Paul J Drongowski
3 Rebecca Ln
Westford MA 01886

Call Sign: W1FW
Merrimack Valley
Amateur Radio Club
1 Robbins Rd - Room
2
Westford MA 01886

Call Sign: N1JSI
Robert W Oliphant
3 Robinson Rd
Westford MA 01886

Call Sign: WB9AIA

Daniel G Swanson Jr
12 Rolling Meadow
Lane
Westford MA 01886

Call Sign: K3XL
J Bradford Cole
48 Russell S Way
Westford MA 01886

Call Sign: N1OGY
Albert J Daniele
17 Salem Rd
Westford MA 01886

Call Sign: KH6JU
Michael A Koerber
18 Sassafras Rd
Westford MA 01886

Call Sign: KA1YUY
Jonathan P Worthley
66 Sleigh Rd
Westford MA 01886

Call Sign: KB1JKF
Nicholas H Worthley
66 Sleigh Rd
Westford MA 01886

Call Sign: KB1RPT
Donald E Shreve
51 Stone Ridge Rd
Westford MA 01886

Call Sign: K9FJ
John A Facella
61 Stone Ridge Rd
Westford MA 01886

Call Sign: N1XZG
Jason C Sawyer
19 Story St
Westford MA 01886

Call Sign: N1XZK
Melissa S Sawyer
19 Story St
Westford MA 01886

Call Sign: KB1AXE
Richard J Bohne
1 Sunny Meadow Ln
Westford MA 01886

Call Sign: KA1WCJ
Edward H R Lyman
3 Tadmuck Ln
Westford MA 01886

Call Sign: KA1YYS
Scott S Lyman
3 Tadmuck Ln
Westford MA 01886

Call Sign: AB1A
Richard D Ferry
3 Tenney Rd
Westford MA 01886

Call Sign: N1GTJ
Susan M Ferry
3 Tenney Rd
Westford MA 01886

Call Sign: N1HIR
Christopher J Diamond
19 Tenney Rd
Westford MA 01886

Call Sign: N1HZG
James R David Jr
11 Texas Rd
Westford MA 01886

Call Sign: N1DQZ
Paul H Fassbender
14 Texas Rd
Westford MA 01886

Call Sign: KA1EQ
Suzanne E W Niles
19 Texas Rd
Westford MA 01886

Call Sign: KB1JXR
Thomas A Bielicki
70 Tyngsboro Rd
Westford MA 01886

Call Sign: KE8UW
Robert C Putala
6 Unicorn Dr
Westford MA 01886

Call Sign: KB1LSA
Randall T Boyd Iii
20 Vine Brook Rd

Westford MA 01886

Call Sign: K1RML
Randall T Boyd Iii
20 Vine Brook Rd
Westford MA 01886

Call Sign: WB1CMM
Joseph Castagno Iii
22 Vine Brook Rd
Westford MA 01886

Call Sign: K1CPD
Joseph Castagno Iii
22 Vine Brook Rd
Westford MA 01886

Call Sign: KB1LSH
Annette J Allison
157 Westview Dr
Westford MA 01886

Call Sign: K5IJ
George B Allison
157 Westview Drive
Westford MA 01886

Call Sign: K1IG
George B Allison
157 Westview Drive
Westford MA 01886

Call Sign: KB1WSL
Christopher A
Cotroneo
4 Wintergreen Ln
Westford MA 01886

Call Sign: WB1AEC
Gary K Montress
15 Woodridge Ln
Westford MA 01886

Call Sign: AA1HV
Zoel A Sawyer
Westford MA 01886

Call Sign: KA1UND
Mark W Lynch
Westford MA 01886

Call Sign: N1JLA
Thomas G Bryant
Westford MA 01886

Call Sign: AA1VL
Christopher J
Karpinsky
Westford MA 01886

Call Sign: AB1IN
Ralf Baechle
Westford MA 01886

FCC Amateur Radio Licenses in Westhampton

Call Sign: KB1EDZ
Gary P Dion
127 Edwards Rd
Westhampton MA
01027

Call Sign: N1LZN
Lorrie A Gougeon
95 Montague Rd
Westhampton MA
01027

FCC Amateur Radio Licenses in Westminister

Call Sign: KB1LZD
Richard J Doucette
225 Ashburn Ham
State Rd
Westminster MA
01473

Call Sign: K1FEE
Louis R De Felippi Jr
242 Bragg Hill Rd Rr 2
Westminster MA
01473

Call Sign: KA1YSC
William J Jamsa
71 Carter Rd
Westminster MA
01473

Call Sign: KA1QX
Albert L Hughes
24 Church St
Westminster MA
01473

Call Sign: AA1WC
Albert L Hughes
24 Church St
Westminster MA
01473

Call Sign: KX1Q
Albert L Hughes
24 Church St
Westminster MA
01473

Call Sign: WJ1E
Joseph P Ragusa
29 Church St
Westminster MA
01473

Call Sign: K1JFK
John F Keena Jr
36 Church St
Westminster MA
014731569

Call Sign: K8ATI
William J Metevia
66 Edro Isle Rd
Westminster MA
01473

Call Sign: KB1NQS
Brian G Stone
5 Elliott St
Westminster MA
01473

Call Sign: W1EON
William T Daring
31 Ellis Rd
Westminster MA
01473

Call Sign: WA1KPO
Donald L Bolden
223 Ellis Rd
Westminster MA
014731328

Call Sign: KC1FC
Dimitri S Bugnolo
16 Laurie Ln
Westminster MA
014731621

Call Sign: N1ZWA
Bruce J Dombrowik
106 Main St
Westminster MA
01473

Call Sign: KA1VV
Douglas C Sargent
142 Main St
Westminster MA
01473

Call Sign: K1VPN
Roland B Morin
67 Minott Rd
Westminster MA
01473

Call Sign: KB1FRM
John M Loiselle
220 Minott Rd
Westminster MA
01473

Call Sign: AA1BL
Gordon W Gormley
52 N Common Rd
Westminster MA
01473

Call Sign: N1VTU
Michael C
Hatzopoulos
189 North Common
Rd
Westminster MA
01473

Call Sign: KA1YOE
Tammy L Martin
85 Oakmont Ave
Westminster MA
014731020

Call Sign: N1MNY
Bruce W Martin
85 Oakmont Ave
Westminster MA
01473

Call Sign: W1GPM
Glenn P Martin Sr
85 Oakmont Ave

Westminster MA
01473

Call Sign: W1OOY
Le Roy H Ryder
4 Old County Rd
Westminster MA
01473

Call Sign: W1PII
George E Engman
21 Pierce Rd
Westminster MA
01473

Call Sign: N1WSB
Richard C Martin
17 Ridge St
Westminster MA
014731320

Call Sign: N1BUS
Stephen C Nickerson
142 State Rd W
Westminster MA
01473

Call Sign: N1PBJ
James T Giblin
10 Sunset Rd
Westminster MA
01473

Call Sign: N1ROQ
Herman C Vieweg
44 Turnpike Rd
Westminster MA
01473

Call Sign: N1AIF
Raymond E Chatigny
74 West Main St
Westminster MA
01473

Call Sign: N1TJA
David R Grennell
28 Willard Rd
Westminster MA
01473

Call Sign: KB1FCI
David T Grennell
28 Willard Rd

Westminster MA
014731201

Call Sign: KB3CUS
Seth M Gasper
Scavette
7 Wyman Rd
Westminster MA
01475

Call Sign: K1TAE
Helen F Van Der Mark
11 Wyman Rd
Westminster MA
01473

Call Sign: N1JUF
Glenn P Martin Sr
Westminster MA
01473

Call Sign: N1MNV
Peter G Trei
Westminster MA
01473

Call Sign: KB1DPC
Timothy D Locke
Westminster MA
01473

Call Sign: W1DF
James V Kane
Westminster MA
014730519

Call Sign: KB1FTR
Samantha S Kane
Westminster MA
01473

Call Sign: K1VHS
Samantha S Kane
Westminster MA
014730519

Call Sign: KB1GRB
Zachary G Root
Westminster MA
01473

**FCC Amateur Radio
Licenses in Weston**

Call Sign: WB1ENC
John D Galligan
30 Bakers Hill Rd
Weston MA 02193

Call Sign: WB1ELD
Alan H Jacobson
70 Beaver Rd
Weston MA 02193

Call Sign: N1RYM
Richard A Sacks
167 Beaver Rd
Weston MA 02193

Call Sign: KA1POL
Stephen C Mallett
21 Bemis St
Weston MA 02193

Call Sign: WA1BFA
David C Mallett
21 Bemis St
Weston MA 02193

Call Sign: KB1KJU
Michael J Pastrone
49 Bemis St
Weston MA 02493

Call Sign: W1MJP
Michael J Pastrone
49 Bemis St
Weston MA 02493

Call Sign: N1HKE
Charles A Whitney
527 Boston Post Rd
Weston MA 02193

Call Sign: N1PRE
David I Emery
646 Boston Post Rd
Weston MA
024931542

Call Sign: W1YAA
Joseph H Wolenski
661 Boston Post Rd
Weston MA 02493

Call Sign: KA1SFN
Arthur H Stutz
707 Boston Post Rd

Weston MA 02193

Call Sign: KB1FPL
William C Newell
9 Bradyll Rd
Weston MA 02493

Call Sign: KB1FPM
John O Newell Iv
9 Bradyll Rd
Weston MA 02493

Call Sign: KB1ITH
Alexander B Newell
9 Bradyll Rd
Weston MA 02493

Call Sign: N1WJN
Thomas J Hollyday
55 Chestnut St
Weston MA 02493

Call Sign: NK1S
David S Mc Lellan
77 Chestnut St
Weston MA 02193

Call Sign: KB1RJV
Andrew A Tamoney Jr
35 Cliff Rd
Weston MA 02493

Call Sign: N1ILU
Joseph P Mori
51 Colchester Rd
Weston MA 02493

Call Sign: KB1SZQ
Javed A Aslam
15 Columbine Rd
Weston MA 02493

Call Sign: KB1TNK
Isabella C Aslarus
15 Columbine Rd
Weston MA 02493

Call Sign: N1QFC
Justin S Stamen
6 Conant Rd
Weston MA 02193

Call Sign: KB1OTQ
Donald F Bumpus·

427 Conant Rd
Weston MA 02493

Call Sign: K1TTY
James P Mc Caffrey
319 Concord Rd
Weston MA 02193

Call Sign: N1ILN
David O Jones
82 Deer Path Ln
Weston MA 02193

Call Sign: W1PRI
Robert A Waters
23 Derby Ln
Weston MA 02193

Call Sign: WA1QQM
Eugenia B Waters
23 Derby Ln
Weston MA 02193

Call Sign: KB1FHK
Benjamin S Brody
4 Elliston Rd
Weston MA 02493

Call Sign: W1CT
George L Downs
85 Fairview Rd
Weston MA 02193

Call Sign: N1QZI
Eric M Elfman
19 Gypsy Trail
Weston MA 02493

Call Sign: N1XSV
Neil M Day Jr
50 Hobbard Rd
Weston MA 02193

Call Sign: K1EPH
Howard J Fine
50 Loring Rd
Weston MA 02193

Call Sign: W1VFJ
Arthur M Coates
30 Myles Standish Rd
Weston MA
024932124

Call Sign: KB1SVL
Nelson Elhage
153 North Ave
Weston MA 02493

Call Sign: K1NNM
Paul J Desorcy
520 North Ave
Weston MA 02193

Call Sign: W1MWM
Eli N Rostler
99 Norumbega Rd Apt
129
Weston MA 02193

Call Sign: N1EXL
Edward E Benson
147 Orchard Ave
Weston MA 02193

Call Sign: KB1KNO
David K Gifford
26 Pigeon Hill Rd
Weston MA 02493

Call Sign: KB1KNP
Heidi R Wyle
26 Pigeon Hill Rd
Weston MA 02493

Call Sign: AB4AT
David K Gifford
26 Pigeon Hill Rd
Weston MA 02493

Call Sign: K1PYB
Gary C Koger
26 Pond Brook Cir
Weston MA 02493

Call Sign: KA1FFW
Willard E Dotter
30 Radcliffe Rd
Weston MA 02193

Call Sign: WA1RVD
Robert A Gaughan Jr
72 River Rd
Weston MA 02193

Call Sign: W3EG
Henry Klapholz
25 Rockport Rd

Weston MA 02193

Call Sign: W1TCD
Carter P Pfaelzer
20 Rolling Ln
Weston MA 02193

Call Sign: KC1KQ
John W Stuart
137 Sherburn Cir
Weston MA 02193

Call Sign: N1AAG
Stephen M Lorusso
56 Silver Hill Rd
Weston MA 02493

Call Sign: KA1RHT
Mohiddin K Khwaja
5 Summer St
Weston MA 02193

Call Sign: KB1PBJ
Edward L Buckner
14 Summer St
Weston MA 02493

Call Sign: WN1FVQ
Douglas A Bowker
101 Westland Rd
Weston MA 02493

Call Sign: KD1BK
Edwin H Wolfe
36 Whitney Tavern Rd
Weston MA 02193

Call Sign: W1IHO
John Memishian
14 Wits End
Weston MA 02493

Call Sign: KB1RUY
Carl F Nelson
41 Young Rd
Weston MA 02493

Call Sign: W1TAT
Carl F Nelson
41 Young Rd
Weston MA 02493

Call Sign: WA1AJO
Steven Olasky

Weston MA 02493

Call Sign: AB1NB
Kent H Lundberg
Weston MA 02493

**FCC Amateur Radio
Licenses in Westport**

Call Sign: N1WVU
Matthew B Souza
244 Adamsville Rd
Westport MA 02790

Call Sign: N1BZQ
John B Walsh
281 Amer Leg Hwy
Westport MA 02790

Call Sign: WA1LSH
John B Walsh
281 American Legion
Hwy
Westport MA 02790

Call Sign: KA1MNU
George P Hancock Jr
287 American Legion
Hwy
Westport MA 02790

Call Sign: KB1IQT
Daniel Rioux
567 B Drift Rd
Westport MA 02790

Call Sign: N1VJM
Bruce C Belling
113 Brayton Point Rd
Westport MA 02790

Call Sign: N1BCB
Bruce C Belling
113 Brayton Point Rd
Westport MA 02790

Call Sign: N1ZCR
Jeannine E Lavigne
394 Briggs Rd
Westport MA 02790

Call Sign: N1BOU
Ernest J Chadwick
Cadmans Neck Rd

Westport MA 02790

Call Sign: W1HMD
Loreto J Stracqualursi
16 Crestview Drive
Westport MA 02790

Call Sign: N1JOY
Roland Daignault Jr
19 Davis Rd
Westport MA
027903433

Call Sign: W1ACT
Fall River Amateur
Radio Club
19 Davis Rd
Westport MA 02790

Call Sign: KB1TQB
Melanie A Daignault
19 Davis Rd
Westport MA 02790

Call Sign: KA1NZW
Jules J Perry
300 Davis Rd
Westport MA 02790

Call Sign: KB1RTF
Brian R Legendre
1118 Drift Rd
Westport MA 02790

Call Sign: KB1WFD
Brian R Legendre
1118 Drift Rd
Westport MA 02790

Call Sign: KB1WKC
Westport CERT
1118 Drift Rd
Westport MA 02790

Call Sign: KB1QYR
Gregory O Stone
1346 Drift Rd
Westport MA 02790

Call Sign: WA1MSB
Gregory O Stone
1346 Drift Rd
Westport MA 02790

Call Sign: N1PMW
Hamilton De Sousa
39 Faulkner St
Westport MA 02790

Call Sign: KB1ALA
Gabriel A Angelini Jr
36 First St
Westport MA 02790

Call Sign: WB1EOW
Robert M Hollins
Fisherville Ln
Westport MA 02790

Call Sign: WB1AVK
David J De Moss
41 Forsythia Lane
Westport MA 02790

Call Sign: N1OCY
Antone Pereira Jr
34 Frontage
Westport MA 02790

Call Sign: KB1QYP
William E Szurley
10 Greenfield Rd
Westport MA 02790

Call Sign: W1MWM
William E Szurley
10 Greenfield Rd
Westport MA 02790

Call Sign: KB1RTG
Bruce Martin Jr
390 Highland Ave
Westport MA 02790

Call Sign: KB1BKW
Richard J Brum
460 Highland Ave
Westport MA 02790

Call Sign: N1SGJ
Altino J Brum
460 Highland Ave
Westport MA 02790

Call Sign: KA1YDM
Thomas S Johnson
395 Hixbridge Rd
Westport MA 02790

Call Sign: KB1HUV
Richard C Brochu
15 Idola St
Westport MA 02790

Call Sign: KB1RTD
Brian A Beaulieu
23 Kirby Rd
Westport MA 02790

Call Sign: K1MYL
Leonard A Moniz
43 Kirby Rd
Westport MA 02790

Call Sign: N1DKV
Ruth M Moniz
43 Kirby Rd
Westport MA 02790

Call Sign: KB1WOO
John T Mitchell
6 Lincoln Ave
Westport MA 02790

Call Sign: WA1YDH
David J Rotondo
2 Longwood Drive
Westport MA 02790

Call Sign: KB1LVG
William W Allen
1058 Main Rd
Westport MA 02790

Call Sign: NY1U
Michael J O Dwyer
1247 Main Rd
Westport MA 02790

Call Sign: N1TSS
Craig M Gifford
1467 Main Rd
Westport MA 02790

Call Sign: K1ETH
Daniel P Alexander
14 Mary Lou Ave
Westport MA 02790

Call Sign: KB1VYE
James K Cordeiro
142 Meadow Brook Ln

Westport MA 02790

Call Sign: KB1WQO
Jean Pierre Chiron
149 Old Pine Hill Rd
Westport MA 02790

Call Sign: AG1Y
Jean Pierre Chiron
149 Old Pine Hill Rd
Westport MA 02790

Call Sign: N1XTU
Mark N Dumont
426 Pine Hill Rd
Westport MA 02790

Call Sign: N1DU
Mark N Dumont
426 Pine Hill Rd
Westport MA 02790

Call Sign: N8SOH
Sheilah Seebaugh
477 Pine Hill Rd
Westport MA 02790

Call Sign: KB1HJL
George G Kirkwood
4 Primrose Ln
Westport MA 02790

Call Sign: KB1JUW
Jessica A Kirkwood
4 Primrose Ln
Westport MA 02790

Call Sign: WA1HKJ
William E Gifford
42 Reed Rd
Westport MA 02790

Call Sign: WA1GCS
Thomas J Lapointe
223 Reed Rd Box
N567
Westport MA 02790

Call Sign: KI4IK
Oliver H Jones Jr
19 River Rd
Westport MA 02790

Call Sign: KB1MNP

Matthew S Weaver
266 Robert St
Westport MA 02790

Call Sign: W1ADC
Alfred D Croft
209 Sanford Rd
Westport MA 02790

Call Sign: KA1JNB
William Guay
868 Sanford Rd
Westport MA 02790

Call Sign: N1QKZ
Michael G Altshuler
103 Sodom Rd
Westport MA 02790

Call Sign: N1XFS
Donn L Robidoux
696 Sodom Rd
Westport MA 02790

Call Sign: N1XKE
Sean A Robidoux
696 Sodom Rd
Westport MA 02790

Call Sign: N1TTR
Victor Aguiar
722 Sodom Rd
Westport MA 02790

Call Sign: N1UOM
Gary L Priest
1009 Sodom Rd
Westport MA 02790

Call Sign: KB1UUK
Todd H Mackay
586 State Rd
Westport MA 02790

Call Sign: K1WJQ
J Duncan Albert
27 Steven Ave
Westport MA 02790

Call Sign: W2TSL
Thomas S Loebl
14 Strawberry Lane
Westport MA 02790

Call Sign: W1TSL
Thomas S Loebl
14 Strawberry Lane
Westport MA 02790

Call Sign: WA1BYM
Thomas P Riley
12 Tickle Rd
Westport MA 02790

Call Sign: N1TEO
Neill F Nugent
149 Tickle Rd
Westport MA 02790

Call Sign: N1QLB
John S Ferus Jr
3 Watuppa Rd
Westport MA 02790

Call Sign: K1DML
Alfred D Croft
Westport MA 02790

Call Sign: K1RL
Roger M Lavoie
Westport MA 02790

Call Sign: KA1RM
Karl G Daxland
Westport MA 02790

Call Sign: N1JYI
Joanne R Larrivee
Westport MA 02790

Call Sign: N1JYJ
Paul L Larrivee
Westport MA 02790

Call Sign: N1KYO
Ellen M Guenette
Westport MA 02790

Call Sign: W1MMQ
Stefan C Zalewski
Westport MA 02790

Call Sign: N1NMZ
Kathi M Ledoux
Westport MA 02790

Call Sign: WA1DPR
Paul R Ledoux

Westport MA 02790

Call Sign: KB1JBC
Robert B Manchester
Westport MA 02790

Call Sign: KB1VTX
Susan B Strong
Westport MA 02790

**FCC Amateur Radio
Licenses in Westwood**

Call Sign: W1RCY
Joseph R Palmeira
17 Alder Rd
Westwood MA 02090

Call Sign: K1NHD
Peter K Toli
35 Aran
Westwood MA 02090

Call Sign: WA0ZAW
James C Anderson
40 Aran Rd
Westwood MA 02090

Call Sign: KB1NUV
Judson A Boisvert
97 Blueberry Lane
Westwood MA 02090

Call Sign: N1AT
Clayton A Boisvert
97 Blueberry Ln
Westwood MA 02090

Call Sign: N1BK
Carol A Boisvert
97 Blueberry Ln
Westwood MA 02090

Call Sign: KB1PWT
Steven Z Fanara
27 Briar Ln
Westwood MA 02090

Call Sign: N1ENG
Gary M Kotler
47 Briar Ln
Westwood MA 02090

Call Sign: KA1SQ

George E Tawa
79 Brookfield Rd
Westwood MA 02090

Call Sign: KA1KVO
William C Small
151 Burgess Ave
Westwood MA 02090

Call Sign: KB1DDK
John H Gottschalk Jr
192 Canton St
Westwood MA
020902204

Call Sign: K4JHG
John H Gottschalk Jr
192 Canton St
Westwood MA
020902204

Call Sign: WA1NWF
Karen M Field
158 Carroll Ave
Westwood MA 02090

Call Sign: K1IAO
Hazen J Saltmarsh
164 Carroll Ave
Westwood MA 02090

Call Sign: N1ICQ
Barbara E Holdridge
107 Church St
Westwood MA 02090

Call Sign: N1PYM
Douglas W Holdridge
107 Church St
Westwood MA 02090

Call Sign: WA1WUU
Daniel A Gentile
77 Colburn St
Westwood MA 02090

Call Sign: KB1DIX
William L Curwen
140 Conant Rd
Westwood MA 02090

Call Sign: K1NZ
William L Curwen
140 Conant Rd

Westwood MA 02090

Call Sign: KD1XN
Daniel J Goodwin
99 Country Lane
Westwood MA 02090

Call Sign: N8AOI
David A Vogel
41 Delapa Circle
Westwood MA 02090

Call Sign: N1DIE
Olive N Gross
446 Dover Rd
Westwood MA 02090

Call Sign: K1GBH
Gail A Bean
422 Everett St
Westwood MA 02090

Call Sign: K1HC
Richard C Bean
422 Everett St
Westwood MA 02090

Call Sign: K1HX
Westwood Vhf Society
422 Everett St
Westwood MA
020902218

Call Sign: W1AGR
Norfolk County Radio
Association
422 Everett St
Westwood MA
020902218

Call Sign: KB1QYQ
Kevin Bean
422 Everett St
Westwood MA 02090

Call Sign: KB1EAN
Kevin Bean
422 Everett St
Westwood MA 02090

Call Sign: WB1GMA
Thomas L Qualtieri
56 Fisher St
Westwood MA 02090

Call Sign: KB1SAN
Michael L Raskin
137 Forbes Rd
Westwood MA 02090

Call Sign: KA1TWW
Michael J Cafarella
147 Forbes Rd
Westwood MA 02090

Call Sign: KB1QYG
Daniel A Lampie
281 Fox Hill St
Westwood MA 02090

Call Sign: K1CHY
Irwin C Stone
718 Gay St
Westwood MA 02090

Call Sign: KB1LCO
David W White-Lief
870 Gay St
Westwood MA 02090

Call Sign: K1DWL
David W White-Lief
870 Gay St
Westwood MA 02090

Call Sign: N1PXC
Erik A Nordstrom
40 Greenhill Rd
Westwood MA 02090

Call Sign: N1BHA
Dorothy H Hilbrunner
322 High St
Westwood MA
020901104

Call Sign: W1JDO
A Francis Hilbrunner
322 High St
Westwood MA
020901104

Call Sign: N1YSS
Eric I Dana
790 High St
Westwood MA
020902503

Call Sign: KB1SQQ
Frederick H Getman
1501 High St
Westwood MA
020903028

Call Sign: W1AX
Roger E Corey
10 Longwood Dr Apt
429
Westwood MA 02090

Call Sign: KA1TPW
John J Patterson
26 Magaletta Dr
Westwood MA 02090

Call Sign: KA1GC
James T Patten
67 Margery Ln
Westwood MA 02090

Call Sign: KB1UDI
Alberto Martini
4 Metcalf Rd
Westwood MA 02090

Call Sign: K1CEL
Marilyn C Stone
258 Oak St
Westwood MA 02090

Call Sign: N1YZT
David M Troiano
280 Oak St
Westwood MA
020903221

Call Sign: KB1PPR
Daniel E Glenn
281 Oak St
Westwood MA 02090

Call Sign: N1GIH
Randa Fawaz
592 Oak St
Westwood MA 02090

Call Sign: W1HSV
John H Ivers
17 Oxford Terrace
Westwood MA 02090

Call Sign: WB9WEO

Jon A Shipp
190 Partridge Drive
Westwood MA 02090

Call Sign: W1CCV
George S Kelemen
28 Pheasant Hill St
Westwood MA 02090

Call Sign: W2HMT
David K Lewis
51 Salisbury Dr
Westwood MA 02090

Call Sign: KA1GVY
Richard P Ahigian
102 Sexton Ave
Westwood MA 02090

Call Sign: N1MNA
Terrence W Earls
31 Sterling Rd
Westwood MA 02090

Call Sign: KA1JRN
Louise E Kraus
59 Strafford Rd
Westwood MA 02090

Call Sign: KA1ZWG
Thomas L Flaherty
24 Strasser Ave
Westwood MA 02090

Call Sign: K1VRC
Ronald E Bolser
233 Weatherbee Dr
Westwood MA 02090

Call Sign: W1UDN
Alex A Andrus
86 Westwood Glen Rd
Westwood MA 02090

Call Sign: WA1YKK
Gary J Oberstein
55 Whitney Ave
Westwood MA 02090

Call Sign: WA1WVV
David P Mc Cracken
Westwood MA 02090

Call Sign: K1EKO

Edith P Mc Cracken
Westwood MA 02090

**FCC Amateur Radio
Licenses in
Weymouth**

Call Sign: K1WSM
William F Neiland
11 Athens St
Weymouth MA 02191

Call Sign: KB1UTU
John R Mcelroy
5222 Avalon Dr
Weymouth MA 02188

Call Sign: N1HJE
Edwin B Short
2103 Avalon Drive
Weymouth MA 02188

Call Sign: K1BXR
Edwin B Short
2103 Avalon Drive
Weymouth MA 02188

Call Sign: K1CJI
Craig J Ingram
68 Bald Eagle Rd
Weymouth MA 02190

Call Sign: KB1GBR
Mark S Loveridge
60 Blackstone Rd
Weymouth MA 02191

Call Sign: KA1VQG
Scott J Fitzgerald
587 Bridge St Apt 36
Weymouth MA 02191

Call Sign: K1SEH
Steven E Hillson
231 Broad St
Weymouth MA
021882933

Call Sign: N1PTL
Ann R Mc Grath
316 Broad St
Weymouth MA 02188

Call Sign: KA3QEF

Paul V Smith
95 Broad St Apt 302
Weymouth MA 02188

Call Sign: KA1BNS
William B Quimby
95 Broad St Apt 905
Weymouth MA 02188

Call Sign: N1BGT
John J Mulveyhill Iii
160 Burkhall St 613
Weymouth MA 02190

Call Sign: KA1HQI
Joseph H Hayes
200 Burkhall St Unit
501
Weymouth MA 02190

Call Sign: W1VTH
Walter T Beard Sr
52 Calnan Cir Apt B
Weymouth MA 02188

Call Sign: WB1FSP
James A Mac Donald
10 Chapman St Unit
107
Weymouth MA 02189

Call Sign: N1NNA
Patrick H Greene
92 Circuit Rd
Weymouth MA
021902606

Call Sign: KA1OZS
Paul M Sodano
48 Danbury St
Weymouth MA 02190

Call Sign: WA1TPC
Robert B Sibbald
92 Doris Dr
Weymouth MA 02191

Call Sign: KB1UPO
Andrew W Luscombe
32 Dorothea Dr
Weymouth MA 02188

Call Sign: KA1AG
Thomas J Ward

14 Elva Rd
Weymouth MA 02191

Call Sign: N1XQX
Dennis M Girardi
143 Essex Heights Dr
Weymouth MA 02188

Call Sign: KB1CKI
Jason P Tedeschi
31 Essex St
Weymouth MA
021883501

Call Sign: KB1MJL
Elvin H Marshall
330 Essex St
Weymouth MA 02188

Call Sign: KU1B
Ronald F Mason
57 Federal St
Weymouth MA 02188

Call Sign: KD5ORF
Stephanie D Ratchford
9 Field Ave
Weymouth MA 02188

Call Sign: KB1IKY
Christopher C
Raymond
71 Fisher Rd
Weymouth MA 02190

Call Sign: WJ1G
Carl D Nelson
90 Front St
Weymouth MA 02188

Call Sign: N1KMX
Scott A Beers
81 Front St #1r
Weymouth MA 02188

Call Sign: N1NXJ
Philip E Johnson
22 Gaslight Dr 2
Weymouth MA 02190

Call Sign: KA1EKF
William E Tormey
7 Granite St

Weymouth MA
021882510

Call Sign: W1OBD
Raymond E King
108 Great Hill Dr
Weymouth MA 02191

Call Sign: W1OIZ
Jack W Burfitt
42 Heritage Ln
Weymouth MA 02189

Call Sign: WA1HDN
Stephen P Maher
20 Homestead Ave
Weymouth MA 02188

Call Sign: WA1MFG
Daniel M Carroll Sr
32 Karlyn Rd
Weymouth MA 02188

Call Sign: N1ENS
Robert X Cassell Sr
42 Lakehurst Ave
Weymouth MA
021891428

Call Sign: KA1HEJ
Jean F Chase
96 Lakehurst Ave
Weymouth MA 02189

Call Sign: KA1PJX
Donald W Keene
48 Lindale Ave
Weymouth MA
021911908

Call Sign: N1WAJ
George A Hickey
16 Longmeadow Rd
Weymouth MA
021902927

Call Sign: KB1DAU
Charles F Lynn
75 Longwood Rd
Weymouth MA
021884134

Call Sign: KB1NRJ
Robert E Perry

185 Mediterranean Dr
-64
Weymouth MA 02188

Call Sign: KB1QNI
Lars Ahlzen
844 Middle St
Weymouth MA 02188

Call Sign: WB1GSK
John A Barcellos
115 Mill St
Weymouth MA 02188

Call Sign: KB1QLM
Russell L Drysdale Iii
14 Mount Vernon Rd
West
Weymouth MA 02189

Call Sign: W1BFZ
Anthony J Shalna Jr
20 Mulligan Dr
Weymouth MA 02190

Call Sign: KB1JZM
Robert B Gage Jr
48 Oak St
Weymouth MA 02190

Call Sign: KB1MOA
Henry D Goldman
33 Old Country Way
Weymouth MA 02188

Call Sign: W1BJS
Henry D Goldman
33 Old Country Way
Weymouth MA 02188

Call Sign: N1UOV
James H Mc Knight
115 Old Country Way
Weymouth MA 02188

Call Sign: N1MYD
Patricia M Duffy
39 Perry St
Weymouth MA 02189

Call Sign: KB1VEB
Andrew M Farrell
27 Pierce Court
Weymouth MA 02191

Call Sign: KB1VEC
Robert M Farrell
27 Pierce Court
Weymouth MA 02191

Call Sign: WA1GHU
Richard B Drown
30 Pierce Rd
Weymouth MA 02188

Call Sign: KB1LHW
Robert E Settle
19 Pine Ridge Rd
Weymouth MA 02189

Call Sign: N1RES
Robert E Settle
19 Pine Ridge Rd
Weymouth MA 02189

Call Sign: N1VCD
Marianthe Isakson
2 Pleasant St
Weymouth MA 02189

Call Sign: K1LSV
Ernest T Taylor
692 Pleasant St
Weymouth MA 02189

Call Sign: N1PFQ
Russell F Landrigan Jr
703 Pleasant St
Weymouth MA 02189

Call Sign: N1DVI
Kevin R Cahill
1127 Pleasant St
Weymouth MA
021892600

Call Sign: KB1MOB
Kevin W Dyer
87 Prospect St
Weymouth MA 02188

Call Sign: K1KWD
Kevin W Dyer
87 Prospect St
Weymouth MA 02188

Call Sign: KB1QPQ
Ellen A Blackburn

55 Queen Anne Dr 31
Weymouth MA 02189

Call Sign: KB1IKZ
Patrick C Scanlon
80 Raymond St
Weymouth MA 02189

Call Sign: N1KBS
Kevin T Riley
36 Rosalind Rd N
Weymouth 36
Weymouth MA 02191

Call Sign: K1WTD
James T Sullivan
102 Rosemary Ln
Weymouth MA
021902640

Call Sign: N1ODF
Sarah A Comella
7 Saint Margaret St
Weymouth MA 02189

Call Sign: WB1ABM
Harold T Jones
48 Saning Rd
Weymouth MA 02191

Call Sign: W1ABM
Harold T Jones
48 Saning Rd
Weymouth MA 02191

Call Sign: KA1AD
Albert A Drollett Jr
299 Summer St
Weymouth MA 02188

Call Sign: N1XIT
Richard L Mc Culley
Jr
348 Summer St
Weymouth MA 02188

Call Sign: KA1ABG
David K Plahn
15 Sundin Rd
Weymouth MA 02188

Call Sign: KB1FXK
Shane M Gould

55 Tall Oaks Dr Unit
306
Weymouth MA 02190

Call Sign: N1OYI
Michael W Godwin
26 Tirrell St
Weymouth MA 02188

Call Sign: WB2EQO
Robert S Chasen
54 Union St
Weymouth MA 02190

Call Sign: KB1MYQ
David R Stevens
283 Union St
Weymouth MA 02190

Call Sign: N1DRS
David R Stevens
283 Union St
Weymouth MA 02190

Call Sign: N1POW
Richard E Driscoll
4 Valley Rd
Weymouth MA 02188

Call Sign: N1KAF
Paul L Colon
84 Walton St
Weymouth MA 02189

Call Sign: KB1UGZ
Matthew Crockett
576 Washington St
#401
Weymouth MA 02188

Call Sign: KA1ACJ
Pearl R Maloney
18 Webb St
Weymouth MA
021882523

Call Sign: KB1OXA
Arnold E Goldie
70 Welland Rd
Weymouth MA 02188

Call Sign: WB1USA
Arnold E Goldie
70 Welland Rd

Weymouth MA 02188

Call Sign: KB1ZJ
Roger L Cufaude
54 Wessagussett Rd
Weymouth MA
021911528

Call Sign: W1VRN
Forrest A Hill
12 Winter Ct
Weymouth MA 02188

Call Sign: N1RLD
Michael G Farris
215 Winter St Unit 1q
Weymouth MA 02188

FCC Amateur Radio Licenses in Weymouth Heights

Call Sign: K1CM
Paul M O Brien
7 Old Coach Dr
Weymouth Heights
MA 02189

FCC Amateur Radio Licenses in Whately

Call Sign: KB1GQZ
Theodore J Boyer
33 Webber Rd
Whately MA 01093

Call Sign: N1OWI
Wendy S Curtis
Whately MA 01093

Call Sign: KB1FVU
Mark B Boyer
Whately MA 01093

Call Sign: KB1IPR
Richard C Chedester
Whately MA 01093

FCC Amateur Radio Licenses in Wheelwright

Call Sign: N9SC
Stephen B Craven

2319 Barre Rd
Wheelwright MA
01094

Call Sign: KB1OOE
S K Amateur Radio
Club
2319 Barre Rd
Wheelwright MA
01094

Call Sign: AB1MA
S K Amateur Radio
Club
2319 Barre Rd
Wheelwright MA
01094

Call Sign: KB1QEZ
Hardwick Hams A R C
2319 Barre Rd
Wheelwright MA
01094

Call Sign: AB1VT
Hardwick Hams A R C
2319 Barre Rd
Wheelwright MA
01094

Call Sign: KB1RYH
Qof Amateur Radio
Club
2319 Barre Rd
Wheelwright MA
01094

Call Sign: KA1ICO
Starr S Klein
56 Pine St
Wheelwright MA
01094

Call Sign: N1PTN
Edwin Ward
133 Prouty Rd
Wheelwright MA
010940182

Call Sign: KB1OQF
Wireless Operators Of
Wheelwright
36 School St

Wheelwright MA
01094

Call Sign: N1KL
Kevin J Lynch
36 School St
Wheelright MA 01094

Call Sign: K3RI
Wireless Operators Of
Wheelwright
36 School St
Wheelwright MA
01094

Call Sign: KB1QEV
Bay State Amateur
Radio Club
36 School St
Wheelwright MA
01094

Call Sign: AC1CT
Bay State Amateur
Radio Club
36 School St
Wheelwright MA
01094

Call Sign: KB1RVR
Quinapoxit Amateur
Radio Club
36 School St
Wheelwright MA
01094

Call Sign: AB1ME
Quinapoxit Amateur
Radio Club
36 School St
Wheelwright MA
01094

Call Sign: W1CCM
Kenneth J Berlo Sr
32 Cary Rd
White Horse Beach
MA 02381

Call Sign: KA1CQD

Frederic C Sanford
White Horse Beach
MA 02381

Call Sign: WA1YIL
Kenneth J Berlo Sr
White Horse Beach
MA 02381

Call Sign: KB1QNB
Diane G Smith
White Horse Beach
MA 02381

Call Sign: N1XZA
Dean H Davis Jr
657 Benson Rd
Whitinsville MA
01588

Call Sign: KB1ONX
James K Brown
408 Church St
Whitinsville MA
01588

Call Sign: K1BAP
Michael J Friend
97 Cottage St
Whitinsville MA
01588

Call Sign: N1IQR
Raymond S Hewett Jr
445 Douglas Rd
Whitinsville MA
01588

Call Sign: WB1CSS
David C Lavallee
East St
Whitinsville MA
01588

Call Sign: N1BIS
Ralph M Gentry
33 Fairlawn St
Whitinsville MA
01588

Call Sign: N1RMG
Paul H Mulrenin
34 Forest St
Whitinsville MA
01588

Call Sign: K1BZI
W James Budzyna
49 Gill Ct
Whitinsville MA
01588

Call Sign: KB1RDO
Jack S Alexander
27 Heritage Dr
Whitinsville MA
01588

Call Sign: K1VIB
Jack S Alexander
27 Heritage Dr
Whitinsville MA
01588

Call Sign: W1ART
Arthur R Theroux Jr
106 Hickory Ln
Whitinsville MA
015881364

Call Sign: N1RLL
Charles P Hobart
50 Highland St
Whitinsville MA
01588

Call Sign: K1IAG
Adrien J Desillier Jr
896 Hill St
Whitinaville MA
01588

Call Sign: KB1PPY
Benjamin T Holmes
935 Hill St
Whitinsville MA
01588

Call Sign: AB1JE
Benjamin T Holmes
935 Hill St
Whitinsville MA
01588

Call Sign: AC1E
Louis C Lemire
994 Hill St
Whitinsville MA
015881045

Call Sign: KA1GUB
David W Mackeil
13 Hillside Drive
Whitinsville MA
01588

Call Sign: WA4IWL
Donald R Spencer
351 Linwood Ave
Whitinsville MA
015882313

Call Sign: KB1IXL
Francis D Bilodeau
413 Linwood Ave
Whitinsville MA
01588

Call Sign: WA1YYJ
Francis D Bilodeau
413 Linwood Ave
Whitinsville MA
01588

Call Sign: KB1HXT
Chris Henderson
64 Michael Ln
Whitinsville MA
01588

Call Sign: KB1SIL
Richard N Roberts
27 Prospect St
Whitinsville MA
01588

Call Sign: N1PFY
Michael J Brita
1567 Prividence Rd
Whitinsville MA
01588

Call Sign: N1USC
Eric H Lord
1024 Providence Rd
Whitinsville MA
01588

Call Sign: KB1IBB
Robert C Wicker
1361 Providence Rd
Whitinsville MA
015881540

Call Sign: KE6UMW
Roy F Deschene
31 Roy St
Whitinsville MA
01588

Call Sign: K1DNC
John R Sanderson
35 Sunset Dr
Whitinsville MA
01588

Call Sign: K1KDG
John T Giemza
87 Swift Rd
Whitinsville MA
01588

Call Sign: K1CWJ
Brian L Hazel
269 Union St
Whitinsville MA
015881972

Call Sign: N1DVJ
Michael J Yetsko
55 Walker St
Whitinsville MA
01588

Call Sign: AF3S
Edward W Hall
9 Willow St
Whitinsville MA
01588

Call Sign: KD1XB
David Z Clark
Whitinsville MA
015880087

Call Sign: N1SKS
Richard J May
980 Providence Rd
Whitinvilles MA
01757

FCC Amateur Radio Licenses in Whitman

Call Sign: K1BZD
Walter J Dolson
208 Auburn
Whitman MA 02382

Call Sign: KB1SGD
Jake W Hadfield
933 Bedford St
Whitman MA 02382

Call Sign: KB1ODT
Joshua J Macneil
646 Bedford St Unit
C3
Whitman MA 02382

Call Sign: KB1MTV
Erika A Laflamme
344 Beulah St
Whitman MA 02382

Call Sign: KA1OOC
Leroy Mc Carthy
111 Broad St
Whitman MA 02382

Call Sign: N1UJO
Micheal J O Shea
90 Burton Ave
Whitman MA 02382

Call Sign: KJ1X
Arnold G Seamans
32 Chestnut St
Whitman MA
023821302

Call Sign: KB1MTY
Robert H Schmitt
53 Chestnut St
Whitman MA 02382

Call Sign: KB1OAV
Gloria Chiaramonte
36 Church St
Whitman MA
023822424

Call Sign: KB1UDZ
Edwin M Monahan
42 Corthell Ave

Whitman MA 02382

Call Sign: N1SOL
Patrick J Whelan
40 Crescent St
Whitman MA 02382

Call Sign: KB1SVY
John J Duprey
69 Dewey Ave
Whitman MA 02382

Call Sign: N1HEU
Michael F Mc Cabe
37 Erin St
Whitman MA 02382

Call Sign: WB1CLZ
Martha E Avallon
524 Franklin St
Whitman MA 02382

Call Sign: KB1HYX
Marshfield Fair Radio
Club
27 George St - Apt 3
Whitman MA
023822510

Call Sign: K1RB
Robert F Burns
27 George St Apt 3
Whitman MA
023822510

Call Sign: N1BPG
Robert R Lelievre
27 Glen
Whitman MA 02382

Call Sign: KB1OEP
Michael T Supple
119 Green Acres
Whitman MA 02382

Call Sign: KB1CYX
Edward C Mcsweeney
214 Harvard Court
Whitman MA 02382

Call Sign: KB4HQX
Ryan D Merck
381 Harvard St
Whitman MA 02382

Call Sign: KB1SGC
Kevin P Odom
338 Homeland Dr
Whitman MA 02382

Call Sign: K1XRB
Peter Q George
48 Homeland Drive
Whitman MA 02382

Call Sign: K1SZG
Ronald M Bryant
16 Indian Trail
Whitman MA
023821654

Call Sign: KB1UTA
Laura S Valler
14 Jenkins Ave
Whitman MA 02382

Call Sign: KB1UBY
Carol J Lopilato
32 Joyce Terrace
Whitman MA 02382

Call Sign: KB1WLX
William A Robinson
39 Lazel St
Whitman MA 02382

Call Sign: W1FSW
David M Blakeman
16 Martin St
Whitman MA 02382

Call Sign: KB1MTZ
Mathias T O Malley
8 Perry Ave
Whitman MA
023822212

Call Sign: KB1OEK
Adam J Casey
173 Pine St
Whitman MA 02382

Call Sign: KB1OEU
Richard F Petersen
260 Raynor Ave
Whitman MA 02382

Call Sign: KB1OEQ

Ronald F Stundze
91 Regal St
Whitman MA 02382

Call Sign: KA1JIW
Vaughn H Schlieff
59 School St
Whitman MA 02382

Call Sign: N1LBV
Daniel P Mc Carthy
32 Simmons Ave
Whitman MA 02382

Call Sign: KB1IIU
William D Spear
260 South Ave
Whitman MA 02382

Call Sign: KB1JYQ
Sarah J Spear
260 South Ave
Whitman MA 02382

Call Sign: KB1MTW
Paul F Moss
59 Sportsmans Trail
Whitman MA
023821713

Call Sign: N1XZD
Bruce D Weir
12 Stetson Ter
Whitman MA 02382

Call Sign: KB1LKU
Whitman Emergency
Management Agency
Races Club
56 Temple St
Whitman MA
023820168

Call Sign: WC1WH
Whitman Emergency
Management Agency
Races Club
56 Temple St
Whitman MA
023820168

Call Sign: N1NJC
Vaughn H Nickerson
242 Temple St

Whitman MA 02382

Call Sign: KB1OEO
Ross A Hochstrasser
40 Walnut St
Whitman MA 02382

Call Sign: W1EKG
Ross A Hochstrasser
40 Walnut St
Whitman MA 02382

Call Sign: N1FRE
William F Hayden
118 Washington St
Whitman MA 02382

Call Sign: KA1YDL
Margaret A Smith
213 Washington St
Whitman MA 02382

Call Sign: KB1MTX
Catherine A Costello
49 Washington Terrace
Whitman MA 02382

Call Sign: WA1IMD
Frederick P Krause
155 Washington
Terrace
Whitman MA 02382

Call Sign: N1OGP
Francis E Hayes
Whitman MA 02382

Call Sign: W1PXO
Arthur M Allen
15 Bartlett Ct
Wilbraham MA 01095

Call Sign: N1RHV
John A Bennett
11 Belli Dr
Wilbraham MA 01095

**FCC Amateur Radio
Licenses in
Wilbraham**

Call Sign: K1JAB
John A Bennett
11 Belli Dr

Wilbraham MA 01095

Call Sign: K1GIU
James D Beaudry Sr
16 Bolles Rd
Wilbraham MA 01095

Call Sign: WB1GNQ
Kenneth E Parsons
2387 Boston Rd 108
Wilbraham MA 01095

Call Sign: NB1R
Edwin H Carpenter
2205 Boston Rd Q160
Wilbraham MA
010951175

Call Sign: KA1NVM
Gary J Moskal
2205 Boston Rd Unit
0-143
Wilbraham MA 01095

Call Sign: KB1RBY
William R Caruana
59 Brainard Rd
Wilbraham MA 01095

Call Sign: KB1QOC
Lauren Viscito
18 Briar City Dr
Wilbraham MA 01095

Call Sign: N1ZJW
Jeffrey B Snow
7 Broadview Rd
Wilbraham MA 01095

Call Sign: K1UE
Edwin N Putnam
100 Burleigh Rd
Wilbraham MA 01095

Call Sign: K1GEG
Terrence T Reidy
13 Cottage Ave
Wilbraham MA 01095

Call Sign: N1ZJU
Eric J Gill
7 Deer Run Dr
Wilbraham MA 01095

Call Sign: KB1MU
David W Isham
6 Devonshire Dr
Wilbraham MA 01095

Call Sign: KA1CDS
Peter Shapras
18 Devonshire Dr
Wilbraham MA 01095

Call Sign: KB1NPC
Donald R Bourcier
24 High Pine Circle
Wilbraham MA 01095

Call Sign: N1TCX
William W Schubach
3 Highmoor Dr
Wilbraham MA 01095

Call Sign: WB1BZH
Kenneth R Nickolls
2 Hilltop Dr
Wilbraham MA 01095

Call Sign: N1PAS
Donald L Hebert
9 Ladd Ln
Wilbraham MA 01095

Call Sign: KC1OR
Roy W Gero Sr
3 Longview Drive
Wilbraham MA 01095

Call Sign: KB1NKR
John D Mcbride
196 Main St
Wilbraham MA 01095

Call Sign: K1UQB
Rudolph Bayerle Jr
228 Manchonis Rd Ext
Wilbraham MA 01095

Call Sign: N1MUV
Thomas J Doyle
4 Maplewood Dr
Wilbraham MA 01095

Call Sign: WA1EYF
Steven K Nelson
5 Marilyn Dr
Wilbraham MA 01095

Call Sign: W3UQ
George W Walsh
Miles Morgan Ct
Wilbraham MA 01095

Call Sign: N1QFS
Thomas S Halgas
512 Mountian Rd
Wilbraham MA 01095

Call Sign: KB1QMK
Dennis R Lessard
7 Old Homestead Dr
Wilbraham MA 01095

Call Sign: KB1DWK
Victor B Scibelli
12 Old Orchard Rd
Wilbraham MA 01095

Call Sign: N1LQA
Paul J Krawczynski
14 Pease St
Wilbraham MA 01095

Call Sign: W5PTV
William G Sutton
1 Pidgeon Dr
Wilbraham MA 01095

Call Sign: W1KZJ
Richard B Phelps
12 Primrose Ln
Wilbraham MA 01095

Call Sign: N1ZLV
Paul J Lizak
13 Primrose Ln
Wilbraham MA 01095

Call Sign: N1DVL
Raymond J Cavallini
688 Ridge Rd
Wilbraham MA 01095

Call Sign: KA1HXH
Bernard A O Donnell
10 Rockford Dr
Wilbraham MA 01095

Call Sign: N1VMR
Philip C Provost
43 Shirley St

Wilbraham MA 01095

Call Sign: KA1AHW
R Gregory Gale
17 Southwood Rd
Wilbraham MA 01095

Call Sign: N1RJK
Reib B Savoie
647 Springfield St
Wilbraham MA 01095

Call Sign: KA5GWU
Charles J Marsman
1097 Stony Hill
Wilbraham MA 01095

Call Sign: KA1AKE
Leonard H Pauze Sr
344 Stony Hill Rd
Wilbraham MA 01095

Call Sign: N1VMT
Nathan A Merritt
1249 Stony Hill Rd
Wilbraham MA 01095

Call Sign: WB1GLX
Raymond D Burk
19 Sunset Rock Rd
Wilbraham MA 01095

Call Sign: KA1TGV
Robert J Bish
17 Tall Timber Dr
Wilbraham MA 01095

Call Sign: N1LKS
Robert G Paulhus Jr
60 W Colonial Rd
Wilbraham MA 01095

Call Sign: N1ZJV
Minoru Matsuura
5 Wildwood Ln
Wilbraham MA 01095

Call Sign: KB1WQF
Kevin P Brogle
Wilbraham MA 01095

Call Sign: N1RRV
Seann J Coughlin
12 Brentwood

Willbraham MA 01095

Call Sign: N1WNG
Patrick D Finn
443 Briar Hill Rd
Williamsburg MA
01096

Call Sign: KB1CTO
Ann Marie V Finn
443 Brier Hill Rd
Williamsburg MA
01096

Call Sign: N1WGR
Donald V Finn
Brier Hill Rd
Williamsburg MA
01096

Call Sign: KB1IGL
William N Arduser Jr
502 E Guinea Rd
Williamsburg MA
01096

Call Sign: W1MSW
Matthew S Wilhelm
P O Box 501
Williamsburg MA
01096

Call Sign: N1YY
Anthony Kord
Village Hill Rd
Williamsburg MA
01096

Call Sign: NK1U
David Favaro
1594 West Rd
Williamsburg MA
01096

Call Sign: NE1SJ
Sota Jerks
Williamsburg MA
01096

Call Sign: KC3VJ
Verda M Smith
61 Arnold St Apt 2
Williamstown MA
01267

Call Sign: N1PUN
Jeffrey O Brien
19 Belden St
Williamstown MA
01267

Call Sign: KA1VGN
Allan H Clark
46 Benlise Dr
Williamstown MA
01267

Call Sign: N1TSF
Allan B Neville
46 Benlise Dr
Williamstown MA
01267

Call Sign: N1XBI
Ramon J Couture
61 Bridges Rd
Williamstown MA
01267

Call Sign: N1PUM
Jonathan M Sussman
88 Forest Rd
Williamstown MA
01267

Call Sign: W1FYT
Reinhard A Wobus
20 Grandview Dr
Williamstown MA
01267

Call Sign: N1ITL
Kevin L Brazee Sr
2908 Hancock Rd
Williamstown MA
01267

Call Sign: KB1AIP
Connie M Rash

Hancock Rd
Williamstown MA
01267

Call Sign: W1QM
John F Marion
21 Harwood St
Williamstown MA
012672911

Call Sign: KB1AUY
Christopher M Weimer
45 Moorland St
Williamstown MA
01267

Call Sign: WB1EWL
Patricia P Benoit
857 N Hoosac Rd
Williamstown MA
01267

Call Sign: WB1GBM
Christine N Benoit
857 N Hoosac Rd
Williamstown MA
01267

Call Sign: N1JWO
Adrian W Sebborn
1190 N Hoosac Rd
Williamstown MA
01267

Call Sign: KB1BNF
Stacey L Ely
1231 N Hoosac Rd
Williamstown MA
01267

Call Sign: KB1AUX
Samuel A Tadros
35 Park St
Williamstown MA
01267

Call Sign: KB1AUZ
Christopher E
Langston
97 S Worth St
Williamstown MA
01267

Call Sign: KB1AKG

George F Sarrouf
213 Sand Springs Rd
Williamstown MA
01267

Call Sign: KB1TOC
Kevin M Hartmann
106 South Hemlock
Lane
Williamstown MA
01267

Call Sign: NK1X
Kevin M Hartmann
106 South Hemlock
Lane
Williamstown MA
01267

Call Sign: N1THF
Harvey A Silberstein
68 South St
Williamstown MA
01267

Call Sign: KB1VNJ
Corydon L Thurston
464 Stratton Rd
Williamstown MA
01267

Call Sign: WB1ELK
James S Wondoloski
10 White Oaks Rd
Williamstown MA
01267

Call Sign: N1MWJ
Ellis A Rud
55 White Rd New
Ashford Ma 01237
Williamstown MA
01267

Call Sign: NJ1D
Donald S Herr
13 Windflower Way
Williamstown MA
01267

Call Sign: KA1MUI
David J Childs
Williamstown MA
01267

Call Sign: KD1WF
Daniel I Becker
Williamstown MA
01267

FCC Amateur Radio Licenses in Wilmington

Call Sign: K1AHJ
John D Kavanaugh
48 Adam St
Wilmington MA 01887

Call Sign: KA1TTP
Jason P Gardner
47 Adams St
Wilmington MA 01887

Call Sign: WB1DGS
Russell F Gardner
47 Adams St
Wilmington MA 01887

Call Sign: N1DRU
John W La Bossiere
1 Adelman Rd
Wilmington MA 01887

Call Sign: KB1BMV
J T Hollis
123 Aldrich Rd
Wilmington MA
018872225

Call Sign: WB8OTX
Diane M Delap
37 Arlene Ave
Wilmington MA 01887

Call Sign: WB8TYZ
Janice K De Lap
37 Arlene Ave
Wilmington MA 01887

Call Sign: WI1K
Louis A Tetreault
11 Auburn Ave
Wilmington MA
018872620

Call Sign: AB1NV
Steven J Mullett

19 Auburn Ave
Wilmington MA 01887

Call Sign: KB1QHN
William Patriacca
5111 Avalon Dr
Wilmington MA 01887

Call Sign: KC8IUK
Johnny R West Jr
9124 Avalon Dr
Wilmington MA 01887

Call Sign: N1AEZ
Russell H Anderson
6 Barbara Ave
Wilmington MA 01887

Call Sign: KC5PCZ
Joseph A Laria
2 Birch Rd
Wilmington MA 01887

Call Sign: WA1BLG
Douglas A Chisholm
41 Birchwood Rd
Wilmington MA
018874017

Call Sign: KA1NJC
Walter J Sowyrda
160 Burlington Ave
Wilmington MA 01887

Call Sign: N1MYL
Thomas K Alberty
304 Burlington Ave
Wilmington MA 01887

Call Sign: W1LWY
Gilbert Masse
19 Carter Ln
Wilmington MA 01887

Call Sign: KA1BKX
Lyle M Stockbridge
3 Catherine Ave
Wilmington MA 01887

Call Sign: W1PIN
Robert E Tadgell
14 Chapman Ave
Wilmington MA 01887

Call Sign: N1KSS
Ban T Dinh
3 Chelsea St
Wilmington MA 01887

Call Sign: N1TAW
Richard J Macchi Jr
66 Chestnut St
Wilmington MA 01887

Call Sign: N1GII
Gerald S Swiniarski
5 Colonial Dr
Wilmington MA 01887

Call Sign: KB1DDC
Jonathan B Edwards
30 Columbia St
Wilmington MA 01887

Call Sign: N1FDP
Roland W Vidito
21 Crescent St
Wilmington MA 01887

Call Sign: KA1ZTN
John F Stira
2 Dell Dr
Wilmington MA 01887

Call Sign: W1THL
John Stira
2 Dell Dr
Wilmington MA 01887

Call Sign: KD1LX
Alan C Hunter
44 Dell Dr
Wilmington MA 01887

Call Sign: K1WET
Christian J Jensen
4 Dorothy Ave
Wilmington MA 01887

Call Sign: KB1PBB
Paul F Keating
35 Dunton Rd
Wilmington MA 01887

Call Sign: KB1LRK
Kevin P Medeiros
8 Earles Row
Wilmington MA 01887

Call Sign: KD1EO
Martin W Cox
11 Elizabeth Drive
Wilmington MA 01887

Call Sign: N1ADB
Franklin J D
Entremont
1 Emerson St
Wilmington MA 01887

Call Sign: KA1HEI
Russell E Wilson
14 Evans Dr
Wilmington MA 01887

Call Sign: KB1MQV
Brian Martiniello
31 Fay St
Wilmington MA 01887

Call Sign: KB1OSD
Brian C Healy
5 Fiorenza Dr
Wilmington MA 01887

Call Sign: KB1OSE
Martin W Healy
5 Fiorenza Dr
Wilmington MA 01887

Call Sign: KB1PZE
Brendan J Healy
5 Fiorenza Dr
Wilmington MA 01887

Call Sign: KB1DJN
Aleppo Temple
Amateur Radio
Association
99 Fordham Rd
Wilmington MA
018870578

Call Sign: N1QDY
John E Walsh
6 Forest St
Wilmington MA 01887

Call Sign: W1EQM
Earl A Ellsworth Jr
45 Forest St

Wilmington MA
018872824

Call Sign: W1NRO
Roger G Carignan
39 Glen Rd
Wilmington MA 01887

Call Sign: K1SHH
Richard E Gage
9 Gowing Rd
Wilmington MA 01887

Call Sign: K1VEL
Louis E Gage
9 Gowing Rd
Wilmington MA 01887

Call Sign: K1SKZ
Vincent C Caccamesi
44 Grace Dr
Wilmington MA 01887

Call Sign: N1KBW
Michael T Emmons
7 Grand St
Wilmington MA 01887

Call Sign: WB1FXW
John P Goggin
28 Indian Rd
Wilmington MA 01887

Call Sign: W1NF
John P Goggin
28 Indian Rd
Wilmington MA 01887

Call Sign: K1JTV
Harvey M Elfman
31 Jaquith Rd
Wilmington MA 01887

Call Sign: N1FDY
Robert J Higgins
5 Laurel Ave
Wilmington MA 01887

Call Sign: KB1HFP
James L Pemantell
24 Laurel Ave
Wilmington MA 01887

Call Sign: KB1TSL

Gary B Berg
12 Lawrence St
Wilmington MA 01887

Call Sign: NM1V
Joseph E Long Jr
67 Lawrence St
Wilmington MA 01887

Call Sign: KA1YBA
Nickerson L Gladys
13 Marie Dr
Wilmington MA 01887

Call Sign: NS1P
Herbert D Nickerson
13 Marie Dr
Wilmington MA
018871460

Call Sign: KB1WGK
John B Mellen
8 Mcgrane Rd
Wilmington MA 01887

Call Sign: KB1WGL
Scott P Mellen
8 Mcgrane Rd
Wilmington MA 01887

Call Sign: N1BNG
Arthur E Krugaluk
239 Middlesex Ave
Wilmington MA 01887

Call Sign: WA1CSH
Vincent B Narduzzo
26 Miller Rd
Wilmington MA 01887

Call Sign: WB1GCQ
John J O'shea
126 Nichols St
Wilmington MA 01887

Call Sign: WB1CUZ
George G Dahl
9 Pilling Rd
Wilmington MA 01887

Call Sign: WB1APL
Clinton F De Cecca
12 Pilling Rd
Wilmington MA 01887

Call Sign: KA1URA
Thomas S Bissett
12 Powderhouse Cir
Wilmington MA 01887

Call Sign: N1VUV
Eric S Worrall
5 Quincy St
Wilmington MA 01887

Call Sign: WA1KQZ
Walter F Allen
5 Ridge Rd
Wilmington MA
018873416

Call Sign: AE1Y
Carl L Noelcke
15 Roberts Rd
Wilmington MA 01887

Call Sign: K1OMT
Richard E Mac
Pherson
8 Roosevelt Rd
Wilmington MA
018872816

Call Sign: WB1W
Richard E Mac
Pherson
8 Roosevelt Rd
Wilmington MA
018872816

Call Sign: K1KZP
Edward E Thompson
59 Salem St
Wilmington MA 01887

Call Sign: N1WDA
Lawrence W Gordon
20 School St
Wilmington MA 01887

Call Sign: KA1QYT
Dexter H Atkinson
164 Shawsheen Ave
Wilmington MA 01887

Call Sign: W1MYH
Dexter H Atkinson
164 Shawsheen Ave

Wilmington MA 01887

Call Sign: K1BLV
Robert T Graham Jr
514 Shawsheen Ave
Wilmington MA 01887

Call Sign: N1EVG
William H
Gronemeyer
10 Shawsheer Ave
Wilmington MA 01887

Call Sign: N1MOO
Sumate Tumsaroch
23 Thurston Ave
Wilmington MA 01887

Call Sign: KB1ICC
Phyllis J Tumsaroch
23 Thurston Ave
Wilmington MA
018872431

Call Sign: KA1AFR
Clyde F Shufelt
2 Wedgewood Ave
Wilmington MA 01887

Call Sign: KB1OZV
Michael P Cloonan
25 West St
Wilmington MA 01887

Call Sign: KA1LOB
Justin C Cheverie
26 West St
Wilmington MA 01887

Call Sign: KF2VV
Andrew M Boardman
9 Winston Ave
Wilmington MA
018872856

Call Sign: N2ZJZ
Theresa A Berger
9 Winston Ave
Wilmington MA 01887

Call Sign: N1RQL
Dennis M Hudson
27 Woburn St
Wilmington MA 01887

Call Sign: WA1ZTF
Earl W Zimmerman Jr
Wilmington MA 01887

Call Sign: KD1CF
Stefano I D Aquino
Wilmington MA 01887

Call Sign: N1LHP
Douglas E Elfman
Wilmington MA 01887

Call Sign: W1FT
O Neal Isom
Wilmington MA 01887

**FCC Amateur Radio
Licenses in
Winchedon**

Call Sign: KA1WGP
Mark Anderson
41 Elmwood Rd
Winchedon MA 01475

Call Sign: K1SH
Kenneth J Shampine Jr
65 A Mill St
Winchendon MA
01475

Call Sign: KB1GDX
Mark A Kirsch
287 Alger St
Winchendon MA
01475

Call Sign: WB3JMM
Janine L Martin
254 Ash St
Winchendon MA
01475

Call Sign: W1GZ
Montachusett Amateur
Radio Assn Inc
163 Baldwinville State
Rd
Winchendon MA
01475

Call Sign: KT1I
Charles R Cayen

163 Baldwinville State
Rd
Winchendon MA
01475

Call Sign: KB1TYO
Brucy A Traudt
81 Benjamin St
Winchendon MA
01475

Call Sign: WA1ORP
Bruce A Traudt
81 Benjamin St
Winchendon MA
01475

Call Sign: KA1PNB
Audrey H La Brie
54 Brooks Rd
Winchendon MA
014751903

Call Sign: N1EGO
Richard N La Brie
54 Brooks Rd
Winchendon MA
014751903

Call Sign: K1LZN
Thomas F Smith
2 Brown Ave
Winchendon MA
01475

Call Sign: N1YXO
Donna M Bursey
295 Brown St
Winchendon MA
01475

Call Sign: N1ZMM
James P Bursey
295 Brown St
Winchendon MA
01475

Call Sign: N1BNH
Donald S Peters
11 Center Lane
Winchendon MA
01475

Call Sign: N1IFR

James E Underwood
197 Central St
Winchendon MA
01475

Call Sign: KB1SXI
David J Le Blanc
40 Cross St
Winchendon MA
01475

Call Sign: KB1KLQ
Brian E Mack
35 Eagle Rd
Winchendon MA
01475

Call Sign: N1IQP
Charles R Wilson
160 Glenallen St
Winchendon MA
01475

Call Sign: KB1DIJ
Arthur P Tyler
161 Glenallen St
Winchendon MA
01477

Call Sign: KD1AE
Peter J Laperriere
185 Goodrich St
Winchendon MA
01475

Call Sign: WC1P
Urvin P Laperriere
185 Goodrich St
Winchendon MA
01475

Call Sign: AA1JD
Matthew P Slomcheck
71 Hapgood Rd
Winchendon MA
01475

Call Sign: KA1TTW
Ann Marie Slomcheck
71 Hapgood Rd
Winchendon MA
014751686

Call Sign: N1ZOY

Frank Yatko
61 High St
Winchendon MA
01475

Call Sign: N1HRF
Frederick M Gibbs
Hyde Park Dr
Winchendon MA
01475

Call Sign: K1GRM
James E Richards
122 Ipswich Drive -
Apt A
Winchendon MA
01475

Call Sign: N1XWW
William E Pierce
49 Joslin Rd
Winchendon MA
01475

Call Sign: N1MGP
Joseph S Browning Jr
159 Mill Glen Rd
Winchendon MA
01475

Call Sign: N1JJP
Randall E La Brake
12 Mill St Apt 3
Winchendon MA
01475

Call Sign: KB1RRT
Matthew C Gwinn
701 North Central St
Winchendon MA
01475

Call Sign: N0HJS
Clifford F Wilder
8 Otter River Rd
Winchendon MA
014752040

Call Sign: N1WVD
Roderic J Mc Laren
14 Otter River Rd
Winchendon MA
01475

Call Sign: KB1TGQ
David C Susman
18 Pond St
Winchendon MA
01475

Call Sign: N1YXM
Marie E Ostrowski
40 Pond St
Winchendon MA
01475

Call Sign: N1ZCC
Pamela E Ostrowski
40 Pond St
Winchendon MA
01475

Call Sign: N1KWA
Michael E Ostrowski
44 Pond St
Winchendon MA
01475

Call Sign: N1YVL
Michael B Thurlow
44 Pond St
Winchendon MA
01475

Call Sign: N1GAI
Marcia Kostick
17 Poplar St
Winchendon MA
01475

Call Sign: WA1H
Glenn C Kostick
17 Poplar St
Winchendon MA
01475

Call Sign: N1QCH
Jason R Gibbs
170 Rice Rd
Winchendon MA
01475

Call Sign: KA1RED
Kenneth W Campbell
156 School St
Winchendon MA
01475

Call Sign: KB1QZF
Donna J Roberts
126 Second St
Winchendon MA
01475

Call Sign: N1NNY
Donna Roberts
126 Second St
Winchendon MA
01475

Call Sign: WA1MQB
Raymond G Sideleau
226 Spring St
Winchendon MA
014751754

Call Sign: N1YXT
Michael R Kenney
271 Teel Rd
Winchendon MA
01475

Call Sign: KB1NMS
Matthew Aliskevicz
96 Toy Town Ln
Winchendon MA
01475

Call Sign: N1REK
Shawn D Martin
160 West St
Winchendon MA
01475

Call Sign: KB1ICB
Amy B Hughes
12 Winter St
Winchendon MA
01475

Call Sign: KA1OT
Camille J Le Blanc Jr
40 Woodlawn St
Winchendon MA
01475

**FCC Amateur Radio
Licenses in
Winchendon Springs**

Call Sign: KB1DIL
Gail M Tyler

Winchendon Springs
MA 014770038

Call Sign: WA1OSN
John R O Neill
22 Albamont Rd
Winchester MA 01890

Call Sign: NJ1X
William F Kirk
17 Bellevue Ave
Winchester MA 01890

Call Sign: W3IEY
Alban Landry
22 Berkshire Dr
Winchester MA 01890

Call Sign: KC1LK
Paul J Pinella
12 Blossom Hill Rd
Winchester MA 01890

Call Sign: W1NHM
Andrew B Saviano Sr
28 Brookside Ave
Winchester MA 01890

Call Sign: NB1Y
Donald E Nelsen
97 Cambridge St
Winchester MA 01890

Call Sign: W1NWZ
John R Blakely
28 Canterbury Rd
Winchester MA 01890

Call Sign: AG1A
William A Schromm
120 Church St
Winchester MA 01890

Call Sign: N1IZJ
George J Roberts
8 Churchill Rd
Winchester MA 01890

Call Sign: N1VIC
Vincent L Moxley

303 Cross St
Winchester MA
018901143

Call Sign: KA1TKO
James G Cook
8 Edward Dr
Winchester MA 01890

Call Sign: KB1WRJ
William A Bicks
10 Everell
Winchester MA 01890

Call Sign: KB1WJF
Edward T Bicks
10 Everell Rd
Winchester MA 01890

Call Sign: K1ETB
Edward T Bicks
10 Everell Rd
Winchester MA 01890

Call Sign: W1GPP
Edwin A Dokus
7 Fairmount St
Winchester MA 01890

Call Sign: N1CIH
Robert C Thompson
28 Fells Rd
Winchester MA 01890

Call Sign: KA1UR
Fioravante A Bares
68 Fletcher St
Winchester MA 01890

Call Sign: N1RPB
David R Lerman
27 Forest Cir
Winchester MA 01890

Call Sign: N1JXO
Cheryl A Pike
16 George Rd
Winchester MA 01890

Call Sign: KB1JPV
Robert W Rucker
73 George Rd
Winchester MA 01890

Call Sign: N1HEL
Paul Grigorieff
14 Grove St
Winchester MA 01890

Call Sign: AB1E
Thomas W Stinson Iii
179 High St
Winchester MA 01890

Call Sign: KA1MDS
Peter J Heim
43 Holland St
Winchester MA 01890

Call Sign: N1DUC
John F Merk
17 Jefferson Rd
Winchester MA 01890

Call Sign: KB1JR
David P Gale
121 Johnson Rd
Winchester MA 01890

Call Sign: KB1LNO
Christopher Bellows
4 Lantern Ln
Winchester MA 01890

Call Sign: N2ANN
Michael D Sintchak
34 Lloyd St
Winchester MA 01890

Call Sign: KF2SF
Sampath Krishna
115 Main St
Winchester MA 01890

Call Sign: W1MZY
John N Harris
20 Mason St
Winchester MA 01890

Call Sign: KB1JLB
Andrew H Hildick-
Smith
29 Maxwell Rd
Winchester MA 01890

Call Sign: KB1JTV
Claire H Jacobus
29 Maxwell Rd

Winchester MA 01890

Call Sign: KB1KGD
Gordon J Hildick-
Smith
29 Maxwell Rd
Winchester MA 01890

Call Sign: KB1PKC
Seth J Hildick-Smith
29 Maxwell Rd
Winchester MA 01890

Call Sign: KB1QYV
Neil J Hildick-Smith
29 Maxwell Rd
Winchester MA 01890

Call Sign: N1CIU
John J Williams
18 Mystic Ave
Winchester MA
018902934

Call Sign: KA1IIG
Kevin P Ray
235 Mystic Valley
Pkw
Winchester MA 01890

Call Sign: W1EX
Thomas V Cefalo Jr
51 Oak St
Winchester MA 01890

Call Sign: WA1IQX
Walter A Finneran
3 Oneida Cir
Winchester MA 01890

Call Sign: W1GYD
John J Bubbers
6 Ox Pasture
Winchester MA 01890

Call Sign: AG1V
John J Bubbers
6 Ox Pasture
Winchester MA 01890

Call Sign: KB1USO
Kathleen E Murphy
25 Pierrepont Rd
Winchester MA 01890

Call Sign: K1MHC
John W Baldwin
7 Plymouth Rd
Winchester MA 01890

Call Sign: K1JP
James E Potter
19 Ravine Rd
Winchester MA 01890

Call Sign: N1NAZ
George A Moranian
3 Raymond Pl
Winchester MA 01890

Call Sign: KA1LEK
Albert D Russo
62 Ridge St
Winchester MA 01890

Call Sign: N1AEV
Patrick J Capobianco
Sr
131 Ridge St
Winchester MA 01890

Call Sign: KB1VEW
Tyler J Ruminski
10 River St
Winchester MA 01890

Call Sign: KA1HDH
Adelbert R Brink
33 Samoset Rd
Winchester MA 01890

Call Sign: W1BSV
Jeffry A Wisnia
20 Surrey Rd
Winchester MA 01890

Call Sign: N1QMO
J T Travers
37 Swanton St
Winchester MA 01890

Call Sign: K9WFD
JT Travers
37 Swanton St
Winchester MA 01890

Call Sign: WA1NKQ

Marita Mullan
Sandstrom
200 Swanton St L31
Winchester MA 01890

Call Sign: WY1Z
Scott R Ehrlich
171 Swanton St Unit
60
Winchester MA 01890

Call Sign: N0RCW
David S Andreasen
25 Thompson St
Winchester MA 01890

Call Sign: KA1CYC
Karen A Mowrey
246 Washington St
Winchester MA 01890

Call Sign: N1FR
Robert W Rucker
408 Washington St
Winchester MA 01890

Call Sign: KB1TBV
Vladislav Glina
48 Waterfield Rd
Winchester MA
018909998

Call Sign: KA1PVQ
Francis L Santosuosso
Sr
4 Webster St
Winchester MA 01890

Call Sign: KA1PVR
Frank Santosuosso Jr
4 Webster St
Winchester MA 01890

Call Sign: W1NNB
Raymond A Dillon
24 Wedgemere Ave
Winchester MA 01890

Call Sign: N1EPV
Louis N Arbeene
4 Wellington Rd
Winchester MA 01890

Call Sign: WA1PZK

Helmut H Pichler
33 Westley St
Winchester MA
018902130

Call Sign: N1ENW
Joseph M Grifoni Sr
10 Wickham Rd
Winchester MA 01890

FCC Amateur Radio Licenses in Windsor

Call Sign: W1TDS
Arthur R Needham
Box 116
Windsor MA 01270

Call Sign: KA1SLU
Peter J Pyskaty
604 E Windsor Rd
Windsor MA 01270

Call Sign: N1LYE
Stephen L Bird
113 Hinsdale Rd
Windsor MA 01270

Call Sign: N1PAG
Mark A Schaffrick
133 North St
Windsor MA 01270

Call Sign: KB1LWE
Joseph D Rufo
3623 Rte 9
Windsor MA 01270

Call Sign: W1IM
Blake E Edwards
1575 Savoy Rd
Windsor MA 01270

Call Sign: KA1YMR
Norman L Baker
Tirrell Hill Rd
Windsor MA 01270

Call Sign: N1SJU
Daniel A Peterson
Windsor MA 01270

Call Sign: KB1OEV
Blake E Edwards

Windsor MA 01270

Call Sign: KB1VNL
Justin Peterson
Windsor MA 01270

FCC Amateur Radio Licenses in Winthrop

Call Sign: N1EQK
Marguerite M Moran
41 Atlantic St
Winthrop MA
021523005

Call Sign: W1ND
James P Moran
41 Atlantic St
Winthrop MA 02152

Call Sign: W1NK
Robert E Coleman
19 Banks St
Winthrop MA 02152

Call Sign: N1LYR
Robert J Douglass
51 Birch Rd
Winthrop MA 02152

Call Sign: WB1FJH
Steven R Wright
74 Bowdoin St
Winthrop MA 02152

Call Sign: W1MQB
Le Roy P Everbeck
20 Chester Ave
Winthrop MA 02152

Call Sign: N1FOV
Wayne L Gilbert
38 Circuit Rd
Winthrop MA 02152

Call Sign: KB1FIW
Stephen J Dalton Jr
35 Cottage Park
Winthrop MA 02152

Call Sign: KB1CEH
Rachel M Dalton
35 Cottage Park Rd
Winthrop MA 02152

Call Sign: N1SOG
David E Huizenga
38 Forrest St Apt 3r
Winthrop MA 02152

Call Sign: W1ULN
Anthony J Pastore
620 Governors Drive
Winthrop MA 02152

Call Sign: N1YLY
Joan Tweed
160 Hermon St
Winthrop MA
021523027

Call Sign: KA1SJB
Claire E Sullivan
15 Hutchinson St
Winthrop MA 02152

Call Sign: N1FYE
Thomas K Sullivan
15 Hutchinson St
Winthrop MA 02152

Call Sign: KB1WXV
Dante J Villani Ii
39 Hutchinson St
Winthrop MA 02152

Call Sign: N1WHC
Douglas I Collignon
4 Kennedy Rd
Winthrop MA 02152

Call Sign: KB1FMR
Henry L Dane
5 Sagamore Ave
Winthrop MA 02152

Call Sign: WR1TER
Henry L Dane
5 Sagamore Ave
Winthrop MA 02152

Call Sign: KA1RYF
Joseph R Zarba
114 Sewall Ave
Winthrop MA 02152

Call Sign: N1NUN
Bradley A Ross

66 Shore Drive 2
Winthrop MA
021521265

Call Sign: W1BDU
Boardman H Chace
40 Thornton Pk
Winthrop MA 02152

Call Sign: KA1MHT
Anthony M
Marcinkowski
33 Townsend St
Winthrop MA 02152

Call Sign: KB2AME
Charles M Hannum Ii
137 Winthrop Shore
Dr
Winthrop MA 02152

Call Sign: WA1HDD
Joseph B Cohen
200 Woodside Ave
Winthrop MA 02152

**FCC Amateur Radio
Licenses in Woburn**

Call Sign: N1OBK
David L Frizzell
6 Arbor Lane
Woburn MA 01801

Call Sign: KA6RCL
Gary E Lamb
12 Auburn St Apt 2
Woburn MA 01801

Call Sign: N1ZQO
Noel A Ramos
163 Bedford Rd
Woburn MA 01801

Call Sign: N2UPE
Shanmugasun S
Bavanantham
200 Bedford Rd 26e
Woburn MA
018013941

Call Sign: KB1ISH
Paul T Tenney
6 Belmont St

Woburn MA 01801

Call Sign: KB1JYS
Andrew S Tenney
6 Belmont St
Woburn MA 01801

Call Sign: W1DYJ
Lawrence W Banks
33 Blueberry Hill Rd
Woburn MA
018015258

Call Sign: KA1KNC
Ralph R Poillucci
10 Burlington St
Woburn MA 01801

Call Sign: KB1MBY
Michael J Benenate
83 Burlington St
Woburn MA 01801

Call Sign: N1INS
Erik A Marks
8 Buttaro Rd
Woburn MA 01801

Call Sign: KA1OYT
Cheryl A Balian
36 Cambridge Rd -
Unit 35
Woburn MA 01801

Call Sign: KB1MHZ
David R Shrewsbury
10 Carmen Terr
Woburn MA 01801

Call Sign: N1OTX
Paul R Anderson
29 Carroll Rd
Woburn MA 01801

Call Sign: W1WXQ
Russell S Braese
30 Carroll Rd
Woburn MA 01801

Call Sign: KA1WCU
Roy A Fowler
5 Carter St
Woburn MA 01801

Call Sign: K1ROY
Roy A Fowler
5 Carter St
Woburn MA 01801

Call Sign: N1XAJ
David P Hunt
2 Central Ct
Woburn MA 01801

Call Sign: KA1TAM
Marc A Rousseau
12 Charles St
Woburn MA
018013023

Call Sign: N1PXE
Robert L Solari
4 Crawford Dr
Woburn MA 01801

Call Sign: N1KSR
Cynthia L Tyndall
23 Duren Ave
Woburn MA 01801

Call Sign: NJ1A
Richard L Tyndall
23 Duren Ave
Woburn MA 01801

Call Sign: KB1MPP
George H Stimpson
2 Eagle Rd
Woburn MA 01801

Call Sign: KA1KFK
Alfred P Mavilio
7 Eagle Rd
Woburn MA 01801

Call Sign: KN1A
Robert J Isenstein
12 Exeter Drive
Woburn MA 01801

Call Sign: WA1CIH
Roy H Johnson
71 Fletcher Rd
Woburn MA 01801

Call Sign: WA1GRH
Arthur J Camerlengo
4 Forest Glen Cir

Woburn MA 01801

Call Sign: KA1HFH
Daniel L Burgess
9 Frances Rd
Woburn MA
018012234

Call Sign: KG4QXK
Brian P O Hanlon
30 Franklin St #2
Woburn MA
018012939

Call Sign: KF1A
Paul C Hopper
7 Grape St
Woburn MA 01801

Call Sign: N1BF
Eric L Blomberg
61 Hammond Pl
Woburn MA 01801

Call Sign: N1NKI
Robert W Swain
2 Hammond Place
Woburn MA 01801

Call Sign: N1SWU
Marie A Swain
2 Hammond Place
Woburn MA 01801

Call Sign: KB1DMI
Jeffrey C Barrett
76 Hammond Place
Woburn MA 01801

Call Sign: N1QJA
Glenn M Tremblay
68 Harrison Ave
Woburn MA 01801

Call Sign: W1DSD
Francis J Strazzere
17 Hiawatha R
Woburn MA 01801

Call Sign: KD1WI
Lawrence Siegel
11 Highet Ave
Woburn MA 01801

Call Sign: WD3I
Mark J Siegel
11 Highet Ave
Woburn MA 01801

Call Sign: WB3ALA
Cindy L Ungerer
39 Highland St
Woburn MA 01801

Call Sign: N1QIP
James V Kerrigan
12 Independence Dr
Woburn MA 01801

Call Sign: KD5NPK
Eric B Shirley
2214 Inwood Dr
Woburn MA 01801

Call Sign: W1NGB
John F Daley
72 Kilby St
Woburn MA
018012841

Call Sign: KA9FPR
Steve J Gerberding
3 Kimball Ct - 603
Woburn MA 01801

Call Sign: KA1QZN
Steven M Bachner
5 Kimball Ct 607
Woburn MA
018016485

Call Sign: W1HWW
Steven M Bachner
5 Kimball Ct 607
Woburn MA
018016485

Call Sign: N1ZGY
Linda S Spinale
12 Kosciusko St
Woburn MA
018013863

Call Sign: WG1Z
Joseph J Spinale
12 Kosciusko St
Woburn MA
018013863

Call Sign: N1THD
John B Kneen
48 Lake Ave Apt 2t
Woburn MA
018016056

Call Sign: N1AFJ
Robert P Knudsen
Lawrence St
Woburn MA 01801

Call Sign: KB1NMU
Philip P Hardcastle Jr
70 Locust St
Woburn MA 01801

Call Sign: KA3RMX
Catherine M Cooper
111 Locust St #87
Woburn MA 01801

Call Sign: KB1FTM
Brian N Shimkin
111 Locust St 33b2
Woburn MA 01801

Call Sign: KB1FMQ
Ira L Cooper
111 Locust St 87
Woburn MA 01801

Call Sign: N1EDN
Charles J Douglas
5 Manomet Rd
Woburn MA 01801

Call Sign: KA1PGX
Kevin L Mayfield
5 Marion Ave
Woburn MA 01801

Call Sign: KA1PWN
Henry D Twombly
23 Maura Dr
Woburn MA
018015930

Call Sign: WB1FKF
Donald F Twombly
23 Maura Dr
Woburn MA 01801

Call Sign: W1FKF

Donald F Twombly
23 Maura Dr
Woburn MA 01801

Call Sign: N1ENI
Eugene B Foley Jr
18 Maura Drive
Woburn MA 01801

Call Sign: WA1YWJ
Constance M Mc Grath
81 Montvale Ave
Woburn MA 01801

Call Sign: N1NID
Michael E Mackley Sr
34 Montvale Rd
Woburn MA 01801

Call Sign: KB1UHL
James A Breath
6 Mt Pleasant St 10
Woburn MA 01801

Call Sign: KC1HU
Roy B Craft
2 Oak Knoll Dr
Woburn MA 01801

Call Sign: K1LIH
George O Emery
10 Orange St
Woburn MA 01801

Call Sign: N1XBP
Jason J White
29 Park St
Woburn MA 01801

Call Sign: W1EMB
Richard M Carbone
22 Parliament Ln
Woburn MA 01801

Call Sign: KB1KAO
Alwin P Gandanegara
25 Pearl St
Woburn MA 01801

Call Sign: WA1OLB
Stephen S Glikas
482 Place Ln
Woburn MA 01801

Call Sign: N1TBQ
George F Rooney
8 Poplar St
Woburn MA 01801

Call Sign: WB1FGR
John D Kula
43 Porter St
Woburn MA 01801

Call Sign: KB1NEP
Daniel T Walters
7 Prescott Way
Woburn MA 01801

Call Sign: AB1PL
Suebsakoun
Kuntawong
35 Prospect St Apt 104
Woburn MA 01801

Call Sign: KB1WAF
Thammakamon
Akkaratham
35 Prospect St Apt 104
Woburn MA 01801

Call Sign: NV3A
Suebsakoun
Kuntawong
35 Prospect St Apt 104
Woburn MA 01801

Call Sign: W1OL
Iver Paulsen
1 Radclyffe Way
Woburn MA 01801

Call Sign: KF6VIG
Jason C Gerry
163 Russell St
Woburn MA 01801

Call Sign: KB1JIV
Jason C Gerry
163 Russell St
Woburn MA 01801

Call Sign: N1AEP
Joel W Govostes
320 Salem St
Woburn MA 01801

Call Sign: W5SKH

Ronald F Saulnier
350 Salem St
Woburn MA 01801

Call Sign: N2YTY
Robert D Hanks
27 Salem St Apt 2b
Woburn MA 01801

Call Sign: AA1YU
Robert D Hanks
27 Salem St Apt 2b
Woburn MA 01801

Call Sign: N2DLU
Hope N Tillman
6 Saw Mill Brook Way
Woburn MA 01801

Call Sign: W1DHU
Robert J Smith
121 School St
Woburn MA 01801

Call Sign: KB1NEO
Robert J Reynolds
33 Scott St
Woburn MA 01801

Call Sign: W1JNP
Richard Paulsen
17 Sherman Pl
Woburn MA 01801

Call Sign: KA1OJR
Elizabeth A Goodland
20 Sherman Pl
Woburn MA 01801

Call Sign: KA1OJS
John L Goodland
20 Sherman Pl
Woburn MA 01801

Call Sign: W1SRX
John H Guiggey
4 Tanners Cir
Woburn MA
018015334

Call Sign: N1PJU
Donald Cordeiro
7 W Dexter Ave
Woburn MA 01801

Call Sign: KB1UTR
Ajit Kumar
Somasekharan Nair
2 Westgate Dr Apt 204
Woburn MA 01801

Call Sign: KB1UGP
Gregory J Zborowski
2 Westgate Dr Apt 205
Woburn MA 01801

Call Sign: W1LOK
John B Mc Gowan
8 Westview Ter
Woburn MA
018013019

Call Sign: KA1CUH
Dennis P Kenney
9 Westview Ter
Woburn MA 01801

Call Sign: N1FTQ
Brian S Smith
38 Winter St
Woburn MA 01801

Call Sign: KB1FDT
Jeffrey T O'gorman
14 Woodside Ter
Woburn MA
018011954

Call Sign: KA1RHN
Daniel S Crovo
34 Wright St
Woburn MA 01801

Call Sign: WA1JEV
William C Wigton
51 Wyman St
Woburn MA 01801

Call Sign: N1NGO
David H Miller
Woburn MA
018882062

Call Sign: N1PXD
Carol S Wilson
Woburn MA 01888

Call Sign: KB1FXE

Michael J Harmon
Woburn MA 01888

Call Sign: KB1FX
Michael J Harmon
Woburn MA 01888

Call Sign: KB1MRW
Dawn M Braswell
Woburn MA 01888

FCC Amateur Radio Licenses in Wollaston

Call Sign: WA1ITJ
Howard H Healey
35 Acton St
Wollaston MA 02170

Call Sign: N1WIJ
Ralph D Costello
323 Elmwood Ave
Wollaston MA 02170

Call Sign: W1JBY
Bernard V Matarazzo
163 Reservoir Rd
Wollaston MA
021703612

FCC Amateur Radio Licenses in Woods Hole

Call Sign: N1XIZ
Daniel Gomez-Ibanez
30 A Albatross St
Woods Hole MA
02543

Call Sign: KA1NWQ
Ruth Shephard
Box 44
Woods Hole MA
02543

Call Sign: KA1NBK
Ann Martin
10 Buzzards Bay Ave
Woods Hole MA
02543

Call Sign: WA1HDW
Lowell V Martin

10 Buzzards Bay Ave
Woods Hole MA
02543

Call Sign: KC0KTG
James P Avery
21 Challenger Dr
Woods Hole MA
02543

Call Sign: KC0OBP
Christopher S Avery
21 Challenger Drive
Woods Hole MA
02543

Call Sign: KC1YK
Alexandr Ivliev
11 Church St
Woods Hole MA
02543

Call Sign: KA1OKR
Samuel P Trumbull
17 Church St
Woods Hole MA
02543

Call Sign: N1WFL
Serge G Khrapenok
17 Church St
Woods Hole MA
02543

Call Sign: K1MLN
Robert B Bosler
6 Gansett Rd
Woods Hole MA
02543

Call Sign: N1LTX
Arlette B Swift
98 Gansett Rd Box 27
Woods Hole MA
02543

Call Sign: KD6EWV
Robert S Brown
117 Gardiner Rd
Woods Hole MA
025431102

Call Sign: KB1DDE
Paul J Denton

49 Glendon Rd
Woods Hole MA
02543

Call Sign: K1SWR
Barry M Fleet
7 Mbl St
Woods Hole MA
02543

Call Sign: KA1TSH
John H Thomson
12 Park St
Woods Hole MA
02543

Call Sign: KA1TSI
Lucia Nelson
12 Park St
Woods Hole MA
02543

Call Sign: KA1TTK
Socrates J Carelo
Smith
Woods Hole MA
02543

Call Sign: KA1YRF
Scott A Madin
Woods Hole MA
02543

Call Sign: AA2OP
Frederick N
Sonnichsen
Woods Hole MA
02543

Call Sign: AI1W
E Kent Swift Jr
Woods Hole MA
02543

Call Sign: KA1GNY
Helen E Gordon
Woods Hole MA
02543

Call Sign: KC1WY
Nathaniel S Trumbull
Woods Hole MA
02543

Call Sign: N1LNH
Charles A Ochs
Woods Hole MA
02543

Call Sign: N1QKQ
Matthew D Grund
Woods Hole MA
025430536

Call Sign: KB1HLV
Jason R Merry
Woods Hole MA
02543

FCC Amateur Radio Licenses in Woodville

Call Sign: N1US
Dale C Cook
8 Fruit St
Woodville MA 01784

Call Sign: W1EQW
James R Weckback
Woodville MA 01784

FCC Amateur Radio Licenses in Worcester

Call Sign: N1WBF
Kathryn M Ferrie
238 A Lincoln St 2nd
Floor
Worcester MA 01605

Call Sign: N1QYK
George H Kronberg
14 Alexander Rd
Worcester MA 01606

Call Sign: N1KMI
Patrick A Chambers
45 Alsada Dr
Worcester MA
016031601

Call Sign: WA1CMW
Walter C Giard
76 Alvarado Ave
Worcester MA 01604

Call Sign: N1RBI
John J La Plume

122 Alvarado Ave
Worcester MA 01604

Call Sign: WK0A
Robert G Lamoureux
103 Andrews Ave
Worcester MA 01605

Call Sign: AJ1X
John J Zimmatore Jr
11 Ardmore Rd
Worcester MA 01609

Call Sign: KB1HXW
Janet H Brunetta
4 Ashton St
Worcester MA 01605

Call Sign: N1PCG
Robert W Piltzecker
36 Atlanta St
Worcester MA 01604

Call Sign: N1BFN
Wayne E Lilyestrom
17 Baker St
Worcester MA 01603

Call Sign: WB1DX
Kenneth S Miller
18 Bancroft Tower Rd
Worcester MA 01609

Call Sign: WA1WZX
Thomas W Sanford
92 Barnard Rd
Worcester MA
016051312

Call Sign: W1SAN
Thomas W Sanford
92 Barnard Rd
Worcester MA
016051312

Call Sign: N1RTO
Gary M Vinokur
11 Barr St
Worcester MA 01602

Call Sign: N2OMT
Patricia A Cavallaro
51 Barrett Av

Worcester MA
016051104

Call Sign: K2UOR
Robert N Cavallaro
51 Barrett Ave
Worcester MA
016051104

Call Sign: AF1M
Jonathan J Kanter
21 Barrows Rd
Worcester MA 01609

Call Sign: K1JK
Jonathan J Kanter
21 Barrows Rd
Worcester MA 01609

Call Sign: AF1M
Jonathan J Kanter
21 Barrows Rd
Worcester MA 01609

Call Sign: N1WGB
Daniel Jaffe
15 Barry Rd
Worcester MA 01609

Call Sign: WA1FIH
Laurence S Jaffe
15 Barry Rd
Worcester MA
016091105

Call Sign: N1HZB
Philip J Adams
83 Bay State Rd
Worcester MA
016062152

Call Sign: KA1ZES
Scott E Demars
93 Bay State Rd
Worcester MA 01606

Call Sign: WA1TLX
John K Bryant
41 Beaver St
Worcester MA 01603

Call Sign: KA1CDK
Arthur A Beford
2 Belisle Ave

Worcester MA 01610

Call Sign: KB1VDO
David L Gendler
10 Bellevue St
Worcester MA 01609

Call Sign: N1UNM
Gray N Harrison
36 Bellingham Rd
Worcester MA 01606

Call Sign: K1QPA
Richard A Bonofiglio
9 Benedict Rd
Worcester MA 01604

Call Sign: KB1FJT
David A Gilbert
5 Benefit Terr
Worcester MA
016101509

Call Sign: K1IQH
Edward L Cote
9 Berkmans St
Worcester MA 01602

Call Sign: N1RXU
James E Trudell Jr
80 Birch St
Worcester MA 01603

Call Sign: KA1ZEW
Jeffrey T Haffty
16 Birmingham Rd
Worcester MA 01606

Call Sign: KA1DGU
Theresa Moy
23 Birmingham Rd
Worcester MA
016061508

Call Sign: W1SPG
Francis K Moy
23 Birmingham Rd
Worcester MA
016061508

Call Sign: KA1OQT
Johnston Glass
10 Bishop Ave

Worcester MA
016031825

Call Sign: KB1HKO
Laurence A Oberman
74 Bjorklund Ave
Worcester MA 01605

Call Sign: N1TDA
Donald N Bing
31 Blithewood Ave
704
Worcester MA 01604

Call Sign: N1LIG
James F Mc Isaac
77 Blue Bell Rd
Worcester MA
016061534

Call Sign: KB1STX
Sarai Nichols
Boardman St
Worcester MA 01606

Call Sign: NM1E
Jerald A Nichols Jr
Boardman St
Worcester MA 01606

Call Sign: KB1SIM
Kimon Symeonidis
32 Bowdoin St
Worcester MA 01609

Call Sign: WA1TZW
Alvin G Goldsmith
Box 1136
Worcester MA 01613

Call Sign: KB1EKW
Luke B Knowles
27 Boylston St
Worcester MA 01605

Call Sign: KA1RUQ
Allen F Stansky
38 Brantwood Rd
Worcester MA 01602

Call Sign: WA1RCQ
Arthur B Kass
27 Brewster Rd
Worcester MA 01602

Call Sign: K4GJB
Clark G Berry
16 Briarwood Cir
Worcester MA 01606

Call Sign: WN1T
Earle W Keddy
102 Briarwood Circle
Worcester MA 01606

Call Sign: KB1SUA
Michael C Mccarthy
107 Brookline St
Worcester MA 01603

Call Sign: W1AMY
Amalia Emco
37 Bullard Ave
Worcester MA
016051643

Call Sign: W1KT
Edward P Emco
37 Bullard Ave
Worcester MA
016051643

Call Sign: N1ONB
Stephen W Derosier Sr
42 Burghardt St
Worcester MA 01604

Call Sign: N1VOS
Ronald J Mc Govern
42 Burncoat St
Worcester MA 01605

Call Sign: KB1RWK
Andrew M Greenleaf
23 Burncoat Ter
Worcester MA
016051301

Call Sign: N1AMG
Andrew M Greenleaf
23 Burncoat Ter
Worcester MA
016051301

Call Sign: KB1TYS
Lisa M Greenleaf
23 Burncoat Ter
Worcester MA 01605

Call Sign: KB1GNR
Phillip Aschoff
72 Cambridge St
Worcester MA 01603

Call Sign: KA1AA
Edward A Hannon
59 Camelot Dr
Worcester MA 01602

Call Sign: KB1AOT
Hector R Garcia
86 Canterbury St
Worcester MA 01603

Call Sign: N1JJQ
Jose L Valentin
152 Canterbury St
Worcester MA 01603

Call Sign: N1ZVG
Oscar G Almendarez
47 Carter Rd
Worcester MA 01609

Call Sign: KB1PWZ
James E Trudell Iii
67 Catharine St
Worcester MA 01605

Call Sign: KA1RPR
Philip C Thompson
101 Chadwick St
Worcester MA 01605

Call Sign: KA1QYL
Cheri A Lange
24 Chester St
Worcester MA 01605

Call Sign: N1TQN
Arol E Ambler
21 Chilmark St
Worcester MA 01604

Call Sign: N7MCI
Judith A Jeon
Chapman
1 Christy Ct
Worcester MA 01606

Call Sign: KB1SIJ
Peter M Singley

21 Claridge Rd
Worcester MA 01606

Call Sign: W1UBA
Alphonse Balchunas
18 Clearview Ave
Worcester MA
016051318

Call Sign: WA1GAT
Rene H Beaulieu
11 Cleveland Ave
Worcester MA 01603

Call Sign: N1ZVF
Haydee Ortiz
20 Clifton St 1
Worcester MA 01610

Call Sign: N1ZLW
Nelson Ortiz
20 Clifton St 11
Worcester MA 01610

Call Sign: N1HHQ
Francis J Hanratty Iii
66 College St
Worcester MA 01610

Call Sign: KA1TN
William E Stempsey
1 College St
Worcester MA
016102395

Call Sign: KB1KSI
Athanasios C Parousis
10 Columbus St
Worcester MA 01603

Call Sign: N1ZVH
Carmen Acevedo
9 Conger Rd
Worcester MA 01602

Call Sign: N1KIH
James J Mercey Sr
132 Constitution
Worcester MA 01605

Call Sign: N1RQF
Richard S Mercey
132 Constitution Ave
Worcester MA 01605

Call Sign: K1CPD
Bennett Lubin
105 Coolidge Rd
Worcester MA 01602

Call Sign: KB1RRQ
John Brusa
31 Courtland St
Worcester MA 01602

Call Sign: K1PF
John Brusa
31 Courtland St
Worcester MA 01602

Call Sign: KB1DJS
Elias Romero
20 D Mt Vernon St
Worcester MA 01605

Call Sign: N1RUO
Robbie S Beausoleil
47 Dawson Rd
Worcester MA 01602

Call Sign: KB1LQZ
Patrick M Shields
12 Dean St Apt 1a
Worcester MA 01609

Call Sign: K1ACP
Abram I Meltzer
9 Dellwood Rd
Worcester MA 01602

Call Sign: KB1TTA
Steven W Kaneb
20 Dellwood Rd
Worcester MA 01602

Call Sign: KA1OGM
Jeffrey E Barnard
31 Delmont Ave
Worcester MA 01604

Call Sign: N1SZP
Edith Claros
190 Delmont Ave
Worcester MA 01604

Call Sign: KB1CQH
Philip L Belliveau
51 Denmark St

Worcester MA 01605

Call Sign: WA1OYN
Jeffrey G Hovhanesian
4 Dennis Drive
Worcester MA 01606

Call Sign: N1TYS
Leo R St Denis
15 Devens Rd Apt 1
Worcester MA 01606

Call Sign: N1YQM
Philipp Herget
59 Dover St Apt 3
Worcester MA
016092219

Call Sign: KB1UPA
William S Wall
5 Duncannon Ave Apt
5
Worcester MA 01604

Call Sign: WA1MFF
Michael P Bafaro
53 E Central St
Worcester MA 01605

Call Sign: N1ZVD
Mary C Aviles
63 E Central St 2
Worcester MA
016053036

Call Sign: W1DIC
Homer A Martin
49 E Mountain St
Worcester MA 01606

Call Sign: N1URY
Scott A Beaucage
76 E Mountain St
Worcester MA 01606

Call Sign: N1DEM
Gregory K Doerschler
5 Einhorn Rd
Worcester MA
016092207

Call Sign: AE1DG
David A Gilbert
26 Electric St

Worcester MA 01610

Call Sign: KB1KKQ
Cindy L Gilbert
26 Electric St
Worcester MA 01610

Call Sign: KB1WPB
Alexander Wyglinski
Elm St Apt 16
Worcester MA 01609

Call Sign: N1RUN
Faith L Linsky
64 Esther St
Worcester MA 01607

Call Sign: N2YHK
John J Ruggiero
127 Fairhaven Rd
Worcester MA 01606

Call Sign: W1WPI
W P I Engineers Radio
Club
127 Fairhaven Rd
Worcester MA 01606

Call Sign: W1YK
Worcester Polytechnic
Inst Wireless Assn
127 Fairhaven Rd
Worcester MA 01606

Call Sign: WA1SS
Worcester Amateur
Students Society
127 Fairhaven Rd
Worcester MA 01606

Call Sign: N1SOQ
Marion C Taylor
172 Fairhaven Rd
Worcester MA 01606

Call Sign: N1VXK
Barbara T Reynolds
172 Fairhaven Rd
Worcester MA 01606

Call Sign: KB1LZF
Timothy J Mongeau
88 Fairmont Ave
Worcester MA 01604

Call Sign: N1TQH
Christopher J Riccio
57 Fales St
Worcester MA 01606

Call Sign: WA1ZHQ
Daniel J Becker
6 Farnum Terrace
Worcester MA 01602

Call Sign: KA1WTI
Marlene M Sherburne
Federal Station
Worcester MA 01601

Call Sign: N1GOB
Thomas W Swedis
7 Fernside Rd
Worcester MA 01606

Call Sign: KB1HJX
Neal A Huynh-Richard
37 Fielding St
Worcester MA 01603

Call Sign: KB1TPO
Zachary A Thistle
13 Fiske St
Worcester MA 01602

Call Sign: N1TDB
Karen J Marzilli
9 Florida Ave
Worcester MA 01606

Call Sign: NG1R
James R Splaine
14 Florida Ave
Worcester MA 01606

Call Sign: KA1WOO
Peter J Furman
19 Florida Ave
Worcester MA 01606

Call Sign: K1WNN
Donald J Eastwood
56 Forsberg St
Worcester MA 01607

Call Sign: KA3RLZ
George P Gumbrell
4 Fox Hollow Rd

Worcester MA 01605

Call Sign: N1ZIA
Luis A Lopez
82 Fox St
Worcester MA 01604

Call Sign: N3OWV
Keith A Ward
63 Frank St 93
Worcester MA 01604

Call Sign: WA1HZN
Jeffrey S Steinmetz
24 Frank St Apt 1
Worcester MA 01604

Call Sign: KB1PSH
Tsuyoshi Omae
61 Frank St Apt 6
Worcester MA 01604

Call Sign: N1QF
Tsuyoshi Omae
61 Frank St Apt 6
Worcester MA 01604

Call Sign: KB1WMA
Donald P Mastrovito
706 Franklin St
Worcester MA 01604

Call Sign: N1ZSW
Ronald A Pfeiffer
784 Franklin St
Worcester MA
016041706

Call Sign: N1RTG
Donald W Benoit
37 Freeland St
Worcester MA 01603

Call Sign: KA1DAY
Levi J Desjardins
136 Fremont St
Worcester MA 01603

Call Sign: KB1WOX
Thomas L Collins Iii
160 Fremont St 408
Worcester MA 01603

Call Sign: N1AXP

Thomas L Collins Iii
160 Fremont St 408
Worcester MA 01603

Call Sign: KB1LGE
Robert S Trotte
160 Fremont St Unit
215
Worcester MA 01603

Call Sign: KB1OJH
Matthew T Brennan
66 Fruit St
Worcester MA 01609

Call Sign: KA1NMI
Joseph Mahassel
10 Gambier Ave
Worcester MA 01604

Call Sign: N1YUO
Donna M Lee
3 Garland St
Worcester MA 01603

Call Sign: N1KVV
Thomas J Pierce
27 Gates St
Worcester MA
016101606

Call Sign: K1WZA
George W Lea
34 Gates St
Worcester MA 01610

Call Sign: N1OHZ
Eduardo Montanez
3 Genessee St
Worcester MA 01603

Call Sign: N1VHY
Michael J Hale
516 Grafton St
Worcester MA 01604

Call Sign: N1ZVE
Jose Feliciano
45 Grand St Apt 214
Worcester MA
016101669

Call Sign: KA1SPY
John J Kenney

96 Granite St
Worcester MA 01604

Call Sign: N1ZVC
Juan A Pagan
28 Great Brook Valley
3
Worcester MA 01605

Call Sign: N1KMG
Brian Bisceglia
5 Greenfield St
Worcester MA 01604

Call Sign: KA1JFL
William B Miller
624 Grove St
Worcester MA 01605

Call Sign: N1VKF
Sara Y Locantore
441 Grove St Apt 2
Worcester MA
016051225

Call Sign: N1EOQ
Fred H Furhman
14 Hadwen Ln
Worcester MA 01602

Call Sign: KA1KMA
Louis D Sear
277 Hamilton St
Worcester MA 01604

Call Sign: N1OCE
Constance A Morrison
485 Hamilton St
Worcester MA 01604

Call Sign: N1SWM
Paul W Shapter Jr
485 Hamilton St
Worcester MA 01604

Call Sign: N1OPB
Jorge L Torres
17 Hampden St Apt 2
Worcester MA 01609

Call Sign: KA1RSB
Jacques R Millette
1 Harrington Way
Worcester MA 01604

Call Sign: WA1OXT
Gary S Adamowicz
3 Harwich
Worcester MA 01607

Call Sign: KA1JFM
Carl B Erickson
31 Havana Rd
Worcester MA 01603

Call Sign: KB1GZF
Paul J Fullen
263 Heard St
Worcester MA 01603

Call Sign: KB1GWB
Angel L Rivera
3 Henery Terr 2b
Worcester MA 01607

Call Sign: KB1CLR
Andrew Agyei
34 Henshaw St
Worcester MA 01603

Call Sign: N1FBB
Clifford J Audette
74 Highland St
Worcester MA 01609

Call Sign: KA1YCL
Victoria R Roman
5 Hilda St
Worcester MA 01606

Call Sign: KB1LYX
Rabbit Owners
Amateur Radio Club
45 Hilltop Cir
Worcester MA 01609

Call Sign: KA1ZEX
Ronald E Dupont
45 Hilltop Circle
Worcester MA 01609

Call Sign: N1JDT
Jonathan W Blais
30 Hitchcock Rd
Worcester MA 01603

Call Sign: KB1UZN
Eric W Lind

11 Hockanum Way
Worcester MA 01606

Call Sign: K1EWL
Eric W Lind
11 Hockanum Way
Worcester MA 01606

Call Sign: NY1Q
Herbert W Fairbanks Jr
143 Holden St
Worcester MA 01606

Call Sign: KA1CDL
John Baker
42 Hollywood St
Worcester MA 01610

Call Sign: N1TQI
Matthew E Kornn
22 Home St Apt 2
Worcester MA 01609

Call Sign: N1KJC
Timothy M Connor
94 Houghtonst
Worcester MA 01604

Call Sign: KA1YCM
Mark D Turocy
35 Housatonic St
Worcester MA 01606

Call Sign: N1WSC
Sean W Carroll
55 Humes Ave
Worcester MA
016051609

Call Sign: KB1TYQ
Peter M Dolan
16 Hyatt St
Worcester MA 01603

Call Sign: W1DLR
Peter M Dolan
16 Hyatt St
Worcester MA 01603

Call Sign: N1LMC
Luis M Castellanos
180 Ingleside Ave Apt
#2
Worcester MA 01604

Call Sign: KB1VUA
Robert H Peloquin Jr
1 Inman Ave
Worcester MA 01605

Call Sign: KB1UUI
Jason V Rosenman
100 Institute Dr Wpi
Mailbox 370
Worcester MA 01609

Call Sign: KB1WPA
Henrique Polido
36 Institute Rd
Worcester MA 01609

Call Sign: N1IPW
Jeffrey C Brockway
100 Institute Rd
Worcester MA 01609

Call Sign: KB1SII
Scott R Rockwell
100 Institute Rd
Worcester MA 01609

Call Sign: KB1QLG
Katherine C Levinson
100 Institute Rd
Worcester MA 01609

Call Sign: AB1JD
Katherine C Levinson
100 Institute Rd
Worcester MA 01609

Call Sign: KB1UBN
Joseph L Amato
100 Institute Rd
Worcester MA 01609

Call Sign: KB1WRO
Natasa Trkulja
100 Institute Rd
Worcester MA 01609

Call Sign: KG4AQJ
Joseph E Stuart
100 Institute Rd
Worcester MA 01609

Call Sign: KB1RGK
John N Schaeffer Iv

100 Institute Rd 2817
Worcester MA 01609

Call Sign: KB1QLF
Joseph M Schlesinger
100 Institute Rd 3377
Worcester MA 01608

Call Sign: KB1PPX
Matthew J Houstle
100 Institute Rd Box
1542
Worcester MA 01609

Call Sign: KB1PWW
Andrew T Wilkins
100 Institute Rd Box
1612
Worcester MA 01609

Call Sign: KB1OZL
Jack A Carrozzo
100 Institute Rd Box
2359
Worcester MA 01609

Call Sign: KB1JLW
Hisham M Al-Beik
Institute Rd Box 471
Worcester MA 01609

Call Sign: KI6RKZ
Michael E Fagan
100 Institute Rd Box
539
Worcester MA 01609

Call Sign: KB1SIH
Killian Nelson
100 Institute Rd Box
592
Worcester MA 01609

Call Sign: WA3ZUW
Peter L Levin
100 Institute Rd Ece
Worcester MA 01609

Call Sign: KB1KCN
Muhammad A Assad
Institute Rd Wpi Box
1206
Worcester MA 01609

Call Sign: KB1KHF
Scott E Longley
100 Institute Rd Wpi
Box 1607
Worcester MA 01609

Call Sign: KB1KKU
Paul P Kastner
100 Institute Rd Wpi
Box 332
Worcester MA 01609

Call Sign: N1ZVX
Lee S Keyser Allen
100 Institute Rd Wpi
Box1564
Worcester MA 01604

Call Sign: KB1LGT
Hemish K Parikh
100 Institute Rd Wpi
Ece
Worcester MA 01609

Call Sign: KB1SIE
Brian E Franklin
100 Institute Rd Wpi
Mailbox 2650
Worcester MA 01609

Call Sign: KB1WCD
Michael J Ruzzi
100 Institute Rd Wpi
Mailbox 427
Worcester MA 01609

Call Sign: KB1JPO
Patricia A Norris
15 Inverness Ave
Worcester MA 01604

Call Sign: KB1LAS
Daniel S Bell
5 Ives St - 3
Worcester MA 01603

Call Sign: KB1EJV
Bradford J Solomon Jr
40 June St Terrace
Worcester MA 01602

Call Sign: K1AAL
Bradford J Solomon Sr
40 June Terrace

Worcester MA 01602

Call Sign: KB1RWH
Eric Bokankowitz
11 Kinney Dr
Worcester MA 01602

Call Sign: KA1NE
Eric Bokankowitz
11 Kinney Dr
Worcester MA 01602

Call Sign: KB1AIL
Carin Litani
704 Kittering Way
Worcester MA 01604

Call Sign: KA1MIV
Paul Fairbanks
157 Lake Ave
Worcester MA
016041137

Call Sign: WA1HRF
James S Horgan
323 Lake Ave
Worcester MA 01604

Call Sign: KA1SFS
Kristoffer J Pearson
26 Lancaster St Apt 2
Worcester MA 01609

Call Sign: N1EFR
Albert G Hayeck
6 Lapierre St
Worcester MA
016042922

Call Sign: NE1O
Peter B Kallanian
17 Leslie Rd
Worcester MA 01605

Call Sign: WB1EOU
James W Plamondon
27 Longmeadow Ave
Worcester MA 01606

Call Sign: WA1ZUP
Donald V Rudge
8 Lyndale Rd
Worcester MA 01606

Call Sign: KB1NUL
Donald R Speth
701 Main St
Worcester MA 01608

Call Sign: KB1WPM
Donald R Speth
701 Main St
Worcester MA 01608

Call Sign: K1QOG
Kenneth M Anderson
809 Main St
Worcester MA 01610

Call Sign: N1YXQ
Jose M Fuentes
977 Main St 2
Worcester MA 01603

Call Sign: WA1BJT
James M Stevenson
102 Malden St
Worcester MA 01606

Call Sign: KB1EBX
Nancy E Kudzal
11 Marble St Apt 305
Worcester MA 01603

Call Sign: WA1VVT
Robert F Nichols
14 March St
Worcester MA
016042926

Call Sign: N1FUS
Francis H Welch Jr
35 Marland Rd
Worcester MA 01606

Call Sign: KB1PWS
Sean R Waithe
28 Marsh Ave
Worcester MA 01605

Call Sign: N1WAS
Charles S Lord
7 Marston Way
Worcester MA 01609

Call Sign: K1NMK
John J Dehais
35 Mary Ann Dr

Worcester MA
016062452

Call Sign: K1MHD
Austin P Davitt
10 Mary Scano Drive
Worcester MA 01605

Call Sign: KJ4GES
Luis M Castellanos
103 Massasoit Rd
Worcester MA 01604

Call Sign: N1TNA
Roger A Plante
506 Massasoit Rd
Worcester MA 01604

Call Sign: W1ZIQ
Frank J Murphy
122 May St
Worcester MA 01602

Call Sign: W1TEN
Peter J Sullivan
59 Midland St
Worcester MA 01602

Call Sign: W1ABC
Peter J Sullivan
59 Midland St
Worcester MA 01602

Call Sign: KA1UKH
Bradford J Solomon Jr
363 Mill St 2b
Worcester MA 01602

Call Sign: KA1ZI
Paul T Babin
7 Miscoe Rd
Worcester MA
016043532

Call Sign: WA1VIQ
Sandra L Babin
7 Miscoe Rd
Worcester MA
016043532

Call Sign: WA1NRH
Jeffrey J Hopkins
24 Mohave Rd
Worcester MA 01606

Call Sign: W1LC
Herman R Sanborn
91 Moreland
Worcester MA 01609

Call Sign: KA1FP
Harit Majmudar
282 Moreland St
Worcester MA 01609

Call Sign: W1EMS
George J Simko
80 Moreland St
Worcester MA 01609

Call Sign: K1JLH
Terry S Vasil
49 Mount Ave
Worcester MA 01606

Call Sign: KA1TJH
William J Marengo Sr
27 Mt Vernon St Apt
711
Worcester MA 01605

Call Sign: KB1RCA
Nancy L Brodeur
15 Nelson Park Dr
Worcester MA 01605

Call Sign: KB1RCB
Donald F Brodeur
15 Nelson Park Dr
Worcester MA 01605

Call Sign: W1DFB
Donald F Brodeur
15 Nelson Park Dr
Worcester MA 01605

Call Sign: KA1OFY
Benjamin F Zukowski
69 Nelson Pl
Worcester MA 01605

Call Sign: KF1X
George H Belanger
11 Newburn Rd
Worcester MA 01602

Call Sign: KA1XL
Alan J Freeman

83 Newton Ave N
Worcester MA 01602

Call Sign: KA1VAB
Jack Hernandez
4 Norman Ave
Worcester MA 01602

Call Sign: KA1PZH
Albert V Rano Jr
115 Northeast Cut Off
Worcester MA 01606

Call Sign: KA1PZG
Frederick D Reiersen
115 Northeast Cutoff
Worcester MA 01606

Call Sign: N1PK
Paul F Kelley
3 Oakwood Lane
Worcester MA 01604

Call Sign: KB1HIS
Hiroshi Yoshida
Oakwood Ln
Worcester MA 01604

Call Sign: N1TMY
Andrew S Katz
8 Old Brook Dr
Worcester MA
016091304

Call Sign: N1JYD
Norman J Brooks
172 Olean St
Worcester MA 01602

Call Sign: KA1PNM
Barbara H Roberts
269 Olean St
Worcester MA 01602

Call Sign: KB1COP
Arthur A Roberts
269 Olean St
Worcester MA 01602

Call Sign: WA1YTW
Scott W Porter
25 Oriol Dr
Worcester MA 01605

Call Sign: KB1RUV
Steven J Gardner
28 Orono St
Worcester MA 01606

Call Sign: N1WSD
Kevin T Lorusso
24 Orton St
Worcester MA 01604

Call Sign: N1XNH
Gilbert W Hayes
28 Paine St Apt 31
Worcester MA 01605

Call Sign: WP4CKX
Ismael Toledo Sr
Park Ave
Worcester MA 01610

Call Sign: WP4CML
Carmen R Santiago
Park Ave
Worcester MA 01610

Call Sign: NA1C
Jack Carrozzo
210 Park Ave Ste 240
Worcester MA 01609

Call Sign: KB1WEF
William A Tyning
65 Pasadena Pkwy
Worcester MA 01605

Call Sign: N1IHO
Derek J Wolosz
14 Peacedale Ave
Worcester MA 01607

Call Sign: N1QYH
David J Luhta
20 Pelican Ave
Worcester MA 01605

Call Sign: N1LST
Walter P Wondolowski
146 Perry Ave
Worcester MA 01610

Call Sign: KA3TRR
Andrew T Feld
204 Perry Ave 1
Worcester MA 01610

Call Sign: N1VMX
Javier Viruet
44 Piedmont St
Worcester MA 01610

Call Sign: KB1MBF
Rajesh Sathiamurthy
285 Plantation St - Apt
522
Worcester MA 01604

Call Sign: AB1HS
Srinivas Chivukula
285 Plantation St -827
Worcester MA 01604

Call Sign: W1MWL
Leo F Jones
555 Plantation St Apt
301
Worcester MA 01605

Call Sign: N1GFJ
Victor R Winklaar
285 Plantation St Apt
906
Worcester MA 01604

Call Sign: KA1UGK
Thomas J Donabedian
425 Pleasant St
Worcester MA 01609

Call Sign: KA1MWT
Stephen L Foskett
230 Pleasant St 3
Worcester MA 01609

Call Sign: K1UID
Richard E Whitney
49 Pleasant Valley Dr
Apt 909
Worcester MA 01605

Call Sign: N1QCO
James D Fogg
25 Pocasset Ave
Worcester MA 01606

Call Sign: N1OGT
Wayne N Hart
41 Pointe Rok Dr
Worcester MA 01604

Call Sign: N1OAD
Francis D Taylor
14 Poniken Rd
Worcester MA 01606

Call Sign: KA1YLS
Walter P Pinkham
67 Prospect St
Worcester MA 01605

Call Sign: W1MJN
Paul D Handfield
13 Queen St
Worcester MA 01610

Call Sign: KB1KKP
Marvin L Neilson
66 Quinapoxet Lane
Worcester MA 01606

Call Sign: WB1CTF
Francis E Blanchard Sr
Quinsig Villiage Sta
Worcester MA 01607

Call Sign: N1FAH
Joseph R Meditz
43 Richmond Ave
Worcester MA 01602

Call Sign: W1VLN
John N Engelsted
17 Rockdale St
Worcester MA 01606

Call Sign: N1UQA
Gareth W Hendrixson
Ii
108 Rodney St 2
Worcester MA 01605

Call Sign: KB1GNO
Wilfredo Silva
112 Rodney St
Worcester MA 01605

Call Sign: N1IDA
Alden T Roys
12 Roxbury St
Worcester MA
016092108

Call Sign: NM1B

Matthew T Brennan
45 Roxbury St
Worcester MA 01609

Call Sign: N1TQJ
Suzanne R Wheeler
81 Russell St
Worcester MA 01609

Call Sign: N1VKG
Michael R Borelli
148 Russell St Apt 1
Worcester MA
016091910

Call Sign: KB1JLZ
Trudy Epstein
16 S Flagg
Worcester MA
016021822

Call Sign: KB1FNB
Anthony C Salce
16 S Stowell St
Worcester MA 01604

Call Sign: KB1HYB
Michael H Nazlian
13 Sachem Ave
Worcester MA
016061825

Call Sign: N1KWK
Louise J Mc Kenna
425 Salisbury St
Worcester MA 01609

Call Sign: KB1LAQ
Michael R Anger
16 Samosey Rd - Apt
14
Worcester MA 01604

Call Sign: KB1SM
Roger W Bostock
33 Savoy St
Worcester MA 01607

Call Sign: W1ATS
Alexander T Syriac
5 Scenic Dr
Worcester MA 01602

Call Sign: K1QQC

Raymond F
Mierzejewski
12 Sherman St
Worcester MA 01610

Call Sign: KC2DPN
Manuel Vasquez
6 Shirley St
Worcester MA 01605

Call Sign: KB1JQH
Worcester Emergency
Communications Team
50 Skyline Dr
Worcester MA 01605

Call Sign: WE1CT
Worcester Emergency
Communications Team
50 Skyline Dr
Worcester MA 01605

Call Sign: KB1VDV
Jennifer M Hanley
42 Somerset St Apt 1
Worcester MA 01609

Call Sign: W1VYK
Marvin A Singer
61 South Flagg St
Worcester MA 01602

Call Sign: N1ONH
Angel L Garcia
89 Southgate St Apt 1
Worcester MA 01603

Call Sign: N1KFE
Andrew J Vrooman
63 Stanton St 3
Worcester MA 01605

Call Sign: N1OUV
Diane M Vrooman
63 Stanton St 3
Worcester MA 01605

Call Sign: N1NSZ
Jeremy B Bruce
19 Sun Valley Dr
Worcester MA 01609

Call Sign: N1TQG
Ali K Khalaf

378 Sunderland Rd
21b
Worcester MA 01604

Call Sign: W1AAP
Ali K Khalaf
378 Sunderland Rd
21b
Worcester MA 01604

Call Sign: KB1HOL
Jeffrey S Rogers
376 Sunderland Rd 21-
B
Worcester MA 01604

Call Sign: WA1CZC
John J Fenuccio
32 Superior Rd
Worcester MA 01604

Call Sign: KD2SN
Serafin G Menocal Jr
6 Surrey Lane
Worcester MA 01609

Call Sign: W1DSE
Leo T Stebbins
34 Tamar Ave
Worcester MA 01604

Call Sign: KA1RUR
Steven W Spokowski
Timrod Dr
Worcester MA 01603

Call Sign: KA1RFL
Francis J Parslow
60 Tory Fort Ln
Worcester MA 01602

Call Sign: KG6ESV
John J Homko
2 Trowbridge Rd
Worcester MA 01609

Call Sign: AA1YS
John J Homko
2 Trowbridge Rd
Worcester MA 01609

Call Sign: KB1KAQ
Irma E Servatus
15 Trowbridge Rd

Worcester MA
016092215

Call Sign: N1ZVB
Rafael R Pastrana
36 Upland Gardens Dr
2
Worcester MA 01607

Call Sign: N1UTD
Robert K Samia
8 Valley Hill Dr
Worcester MA 01609

Call Sign: KB1HOK
Mark S Rubin
89 Vassar St
Worcester MA
016021534

Call Sign: WB1ARZ
Mark S Rubin
89 Vassar St
Worcester MA
016021534

Call Sign: KB1ILP
Joel A Rubin
89 Vassar St
Worcester MA 01602

Call Sign: KB1KEE
Brenda L Rubin
89 Vassar St
Worcester MA 01602

Call Sign: KB1EDC
Laurie A Irwin
171 Vernon St
Worcester MA
016102035

Call Sign: K1LAI
Laurie A Irwin
171 Vernon St
Worcester MA
016102035

Call Sign: N1QYI
Stephen F Slaney
200 Vernon St Apt 530
Worcester MA 01607

Call Sign: N1UAC

Tamara E Giumentaro
9 Victoria Ave
Worcester MA 01607

Call Sign: KA1QDB
Robert A Hennigan
3 Vineyard St
Worcester MA 01603

Call Sign: KB1WOW
John A Belliveau
28 Volkmar Rd
Worcester MA 01606

Call Sign: KA1UNV
Jamie A Lantinen
161 W Mountain St
Apt 216b
Worcester MA 01606

Call Sign: N1YZI
Isaac J Waldron
63 Wachusett St
Worcester MA 06109

Call Sign: KB1HXY
James E Vautin
63 Wachusett St
Worcester MA 01609

Call Sign: KB1WCI
Marie F Russo
45 Wachusett St Apt 1
Worcester MA 01609

Call Sign: W1MFR
Marie F Russo
45 Wachusett St Apt 1
Worcester MA 01609

Call Sign: KB1ISA
Benjamin M Ponder
32 Wachusett St Apt 2
Worcester MA 01609

Call Sign: KA1NYM
Richard A Spencer
6 Wachusett St H5
Worcester MA 01609

Call Sign: N1VMZ
Walberto Aponte
53 Walworth St
Worcester MA 01602

Call Sign: N1USB
Jose G Figueroa
159 Water St Apt 3
Worcester MA 01604

Call Sign: KB1PXA
Joseph M Tortorelli
137 West Boylston St
Worcester MA 01606

Call Sign: KB1GLQ
Virginia A Wholley
West Side Station
Worcester MA 01602

Call Sign: KA1ZLP
Shane A Emco
82 West St
Worcester MA 01609

Call Sign: KB1QLD
Daniel P Cianfrocco
142 West St Apartment
2
Worcester MA 01609

Call Sign: N1KJG
Aseem Bansal
78 West St Apt 1
Worcester MA 01609

Call Sign: KB1PWX
Elizabeth N Clardy
142 West St Apt -2
Worcester MA 01609

Call Sign: WA1MOJ
John R Wood
9 Westview Rd
Worcester MA 01602

Call Sign: KA1CIC
Wayne D Bushnoe
18 Whipple St
Worcester MA 01607

Call Sign: N1OGF
John M Primeau
315 Wildwood Ave
Worcester MA 01603

Call Sign: WA1ISO
Everett Mangsen Sr

30 Wilkinson St
Worcester MA
016062329

Call Sign: KB1WRP
Ryan J Linton
32 William St 3
Worcester MA 01609

Call Sign: KB1GXY
Luis M Quezada
15 Windham St
Worcester MA 01610

Call Sign: KB1QEQ
John E Gonyea
30 Woodford St
Worcester MA 01604

Call Sign: WA1JEG
John E Gonyea
30 Woodford St
Worcester MA 01604

Call Sign: W1JAT
John E Gonyea
30 Woodford St
Worcester MA 01604

Call Sign: N1XXG
Pierre R Telemaque
29 Wrentham Rd
Worcester MA 01602

Call Sign: KB1FND
Ronald B Jabara
Worcester MA 01602

Call Sign: W1OPQ
Leo F Di Monopoli
Worcester MA 01613

Call Sign: KE1HF
James P Hicks
Worcester MA 01602

Call Sign: N1XXJ
Debra A Kelley
Worcester MA 01601

Call Sign: N1VR
Ronald B Jabara
Worcester MA 01602

Call Sign: KB1JSV
William Driscoll
Worcester MA 01613

Call Sign: KB1QZD
Clovis Padilha Jr
Worcester MA 01606

FCC Amateur Radio Licenses in Worthington

Call Sign: WA8WHN
Charles S Rose
193 Huntington Rd
Worthington MA
01098

Call Sign: WB2BOE
Ginny Monteleone
Old North Rd
Worthington MA
010980011

Call Sign: WB2BTG
Sam Monteleone
Old North Rd
Worthington MA
01098

Call Sign: N1LYI
Linda S Cunningham
54 Starkweather Rd
Worthington MA
01098

FCC Amateur Radio Licenses in Wrentham

Call Sign: K1LBG
Joseph T Heck
35 Arrowhead Rd
Wrentham MA
020931663

Call Sign: KB1SMU
Scott A Langlands
280 Cowell Rd
Wrentham MA 02093

Call Sign: W1BI
William W Rollins
145 Creek St

Wrentham MA 02093

Call Sign: W1WL
William W Rollins
145 Creek St
Wrentham MA 02093

Call Sign: KB1S
Robert A D Amelio
65 Eastside Rd
Wrentham MA 02093

Call Sign: WA1ZCG
Robert A D Amelio
65 Eastside Rd
Wrentham MA 02093

Call Sign: WB1DTF
Camille A Legley Jr
308 Forest Grove Ave
Wrentham MA 02093

Call Sign: K1ABD
Edward O Haire
374 Forest Grove Ave
Wrentham MA 02093

Call Sign: WA1QCB
Robert A Beaver
17 Geordan Ave
Wrentham MA 02093

Call Sign: W3EVE
Stephen C Schwarm
30 Hayden Woods
Wrentham MA 02093

Call Sign: KD1TW
Robert A Penchuk
60 Hayden Woods
Wrentham MA 02093

Call Sign: W2ZYU
Robert C Campbell
46 John Druce Lane
Wrentham MA
020931390

Call Sign: K1BSM
Robert L Desimone
129 Lakeside Ave
Wrentham MA 02093

Call Sign: KB1NLG

Steven M Isner
376 Madison St
Wrentham MA 02093

Call Sign: WA1AR
Alan A Richard
20 Melanie Ln
Wrentham MA 02093

Call Sign: KA1YW
Gregory T Sutherland
30 Metacomet St
Wrentham MA
020931256

Call Sign: W1WM
Gregory T Sutherland
30 Metacomet St
Wrentham MA
020931256

Call Sign: KB1NWP
Thomas H Morse
65 Otis St
Wrentham MA 02093

Call Sign: N1PZF
Peter C Dubendris
60 Oxbow Dr
Wrentham MA 02093

Call Sign: KB1GSR
Robert Y Pellet
48 Pendelton Rd
Wrentham MA 02093

Call Sign: KB1JRW
Pamela A Pellet
48 Pendleton Rd
Wrentham MA 02093

Call Sign: KB1OUY
Walter Mahla
23 Rhodes Dr
Wrentham MA 02093

Call Sign: W1VQN
Joseph A Riley Jr
190 South
Wrentham MA 02093

Call Sign: WA1ISA
Peter E Dehman
325 Spring St

Wrentham MA 02093

Call Sign: KB1HTU
Richard L Dowall
75 Summer St
Wrentham MA 02093

Call Sign: N1SGS
David E Ziemba
65 Sumner Perry Dr
Wrentham MA 02093

Call Sign: W1YOP
John L Wojciechowski
169 Taunton
Wrentham MA 02093

Call Sign: W1SRR
Richard E Mc
Cullough
69 Taunton St
Wrentham MA 02093

Call Sign: K1ZFR
Martin L Kaufman
411 Taunton St
Wrentham MA 02093

Call Sign: KA1KR
Glen K Goodman
1488 W St
Wrentham MA 02093

Call Sign: KB1SCH
Jody M Najarian
1771 West St
Wrentham MA 02093

Call Sign: KB1RUW
Richard W Gagnon
2035 West St
Wrentham MA 02093

Call Sign: K1TMV
Richard W Gagnon
2035 West St
Wrentham MA 02093

Call Sign: KG1Y
Richard W Gagnon
2035 West St
Wrentham MA 02093

Call Sign: WA1IDZ

Leon J Berman
Wrentham MA 02093

Call Sign: WA1MJJ
Helene L Berman
Wrentham MA 02093

Call Sign: W1IDZ
Leon J Berman
Wrentham MA 02093

FCC Amateur Radio Licenses in Yarmouth

Call Sign: W0PAS
Bernard J Covner
42 Miriah Dr
Yarmouth MA 02675

Call Sign: WA1UKI
Kirby H Mc Clain
351 North Dennis Rd
Yarmouth MA 02675

FCC Amateur Radio Licenses in Yarmouthport

Call Sign: N1ZOC
Bernard M Tuohy
17 Avon Rd
Yarmouthport MA 02675

Call Sign: N1PIV
Trenor F Goodell
31 Belle Of The West Rd
Yarmouth Port MA 02675

Call Sign: K1ZTF
Paul R Corriveau
37 Canterbury Rd
Yarmouth Port MA 02675

Call Sign: W6SJI
M Frances Remington
61 Collingwood Drive
Yarmouthport MA 02675

Call Sign: W6SJK

Raymond C
Remington
61 Collingwood Drive
Yarmouthport MA 02675

Call Sign: K1VKP
John J Feeney
36 Debs Hill Rd
Yarmouthport MA 02675

Call Sign: W1KWS
Veikko A Oby
7 Deveau Ln
Yarmouth Port MA 02675

Call Sign: W1RA
Steven B Wilson
14 Elishas Pond Dr
Yarmouthport MA 02675

Call Sign: K2DCL
George J Goering
36 Follins Pond Rd
Yarmouthport MA 02675

Call Sign: KA1ONU
Werner H Schmidt
23 Forest Gate
Yarmouth Port MA 02675

Call Sign: KB1TAP
David A Howard
104 Freeman Rd
Yarmouth Port MA 02675

Call Sign: KD1B
George E Makris
11 Gunrock Rd
Yarmouth Port MA 02675

Call Sign: KB1AEP
Marshall K Lovelette
11 Homestead Ln
Yarmouthport MA 02675

Call Sign: W1OUC
Keith Handsaker
37 Kate S Path
Yarmouth Port MA 026751472

Call Sign: WA1GEM
Richard J Merrow
24 Kates Path
Yarmouth Port MA 02675

Call Sign: N1PIX
Peter V Tremblay
206 Kates Path
Yarmouth Port MA 02675

Call Sign: KB1QZB
Geoffrey S Newton
168 Main St
Yarmouth Port MA 02675

Call Sign: KA1YQT
Geoffrey A Deemer
152 Main St 6a
Yarmouth Port MA 02675

Call Sign: KC5ZSX
Daniel C Burbank
364 Main St
Yarmouthport MA 02675

Call Sign: N1CAI
Donald C Mac Keen
274 N Dennis Rd
Yarmouth Port MA 026750300

Call Sign: WA2MTE
Winston G Rockefeller
292 N Dennis Rd
Yarmouth Port MA 02675

Call Sign: WA1FSC
Mario B Mere
10 Old Church St
Yarmouth Port MA 02675

Call Sign: W8ES
Frank R L Daley Jr
24 Pine St
Yarmouth Port MA
026750282

Call Sign: KB1HJA
Louis J Sarkas
177 Pine St
Yarmouth Port MA
02675

Call Sign: KB1HJB
Louis H Sarkas
177 Pine St
Yarmouth Port MA
02675

Call Sign: N1GOD
Louis H Sarkas
177 Pine St
Yarmouth Port MA
02675

Call Sign: K1CQX
Maurice L Hatch Jr
20 Richard Rd
Yarmouth Port MA
02675

Call Sign: KJ7RL
Robert M Topolski
36 Ridgewood Dr
Yarmouth Port MA
02675

Call Sign: KE1MO
Robert M Topolski
36 Ridgewood Dr
Yarmouth Port MA
02675

Call Sign: KB1PBH
Evyn S Newton
168 Rt 6a
Yarmouth Port MA
02675

Call Sign: KA1VNN
Kelly E Wheeler
281 Setucket Rd
Yarmouth Port MA
02675

Call Sign: KB1TAX
Kai A Raiskio
33 Union St
Yarmouth Port MA
02675

Call Sign: KB1PDD
Nicholas M Borowski
73 Weir Rd
Yarmouth Port MA
02675

Call Sign: N1MJZ
William N Tedesco
96 Winter St
Yarmouth Port MA
02675

Call Sign: KA1URU
Dennis J Solomon
Yarmouth Port MA
02675

Call Sign: KA1YQR
John E Gilligan
281 Setucket Rd
Yarmouthport MA
02675

Call Sign: AA1YM
Bruce H Brundage
17 Uncle Jimmys Lane
Yarmouthport MA
02675

Call Sign: KB1BTU
Harry C Walker
8 Village Ln
Yarmouthport MA
02675

Call Sign: W1HJW
William A Haskins
806 W Yarmouth Rd
Yarmouthport MA
02675

Call Sign: K1JHT
David T Sanderson
8 Wildflower Lane
Yarmouthport MA
02675